D0947882

IRB WORLD RUGBY YEARBOOK 2014

IRB WORLD RUGBY YEARBOOK 2014

EDITED BY
KAREN BOND, JOHN MURRAY AND JOHN GRIFFITHS

Vision Sports Publishing
19-23 High Street
Kingston upon Thames
Surrey, KT1 1LL

www.visionsp.co.uk

Published by Vision Sports Publishing in 2013

Copyright © International Rugby Board 2013

ISBN 13: 978-1-909534-11-7

The right of the IRB and VSP to be identified as author of this work has been asserted by them in accordance with the Copyright, Designs and Patents Act, 1988.

All rights reserved. No part of this publication may be reproduced, stored in a retrieval system, or transmitted in any form or by any means, electronic, mechanical, photocopying, recording or otherwise, without the prior permission of the publishers.

This book is sold subject to the condition that it shall not, by way of trade or otherwise, be lent, re-sold, hired out, or otherwise circulated without the publishers' prior consent in any form of binding or cover other than that in which it is published and without a similar condition including this condition being imposed on the subsequent purchaser.

All pictures by Getty Images unless otherwise stated.
Cover image of Marie-Alice Yahé courtesy of I. Picarel/FFR.

Typeset by Palimpsest Book Production Limited, Falkirk, Stirlingshire

Printed and bound in the UK by Ashford Colour Press Ltd

The IRB World Rugby Yearbook is an independent publication supported by the International Rugby Board but the views throughout, expressed by the different authors, do not necessarily reflect the policies and opinions of the IRB.

International Rugby Board
Huguenot House
35-38 St Stephen's Green
Dublin 2, Ireland

t +353-1-240-9200
f +353-1-240-9201

www.irb.com

Contents

INTERNATIONAL SEVENS TOURNAMENTS

WOMEN'S RUGBY

INTERNATIONAL RECORDS AND STATISTICS

THE COUNTRIES

THE COMBINED TEAMS

ELITE COMPETITIONS

REFEREES

THE BACK ROW

Exciting times lie ahead for rugby

A message from Bernard Lapasset, Chairman of the International Rugby Board

Welcome to the eighth edition of the IRB World Rugby Yearbook. It has been another stellar year for rugby with global participation at an all-time high, Rugby World Cup 2015 on track to exceed all expectations and the road to Rio 2016 gathering momentum.

In less than two years, the world's top players, passionately supported by more than 400,000 fans, will gather in England for what promises to be the biggest and best Rugby World Cup to date.

Our pinnacle competition continues to go from strength to strength and while Australia 2003 was the first truly modern Rugby World Cup, France 2007 the global box office hit and New Zealand 2011 the event that invigorated a nation, I have no doubt that England 2015 will blend the best of each and add a new dimension to raise the bar once again.

England 2015 will be an event of opportunity for the host nation and for rugby worldwide. Preparation is on track to ensure a tournament that will be great for rugby and the host nation, providing the opportunity to engage new fans the length and breadth of a sports and major event-loving nation and beyond.

What I am particularly excited about is a balanced match schedule that optimises preparation time for our Tier Two unions and will provide the stage for these unions to maximise their talent and potential following considerable IRB support and assistance between Rugby World Cups. England 2015 should be the most competitive tournament to date.

The teams and travelling fans can also look forward to exceptional venues that celebrate rugby's heritage while embracing some of the most iconic theatres in world sport, from the London 2012 Olympic Stadium to the City of Manchester Stadium and Wembley.

Add to the mix, truly world-class training facilities and enthusiastic host cities and the scene is set for an exciting and nationwide festival that will celebrate the host nation, its culture, heritage and love of rugby. It will provide the UK with a 44-day trade and tourism shop window to a global audience of around four billion.

We also anticipate England 2015 will be the most engaging Rugby World Cup to date with a whole raft of exciting innovations that will inspire from the stadium to the armchair, capturing the imagination.

None of this is possible without teamwork, one of rugby's predominant values, and I am delighted to say that the partnership between the IRB, tournament organisers England Rugby 2015 and the RFU has been built on a shared vision of making the tournament accessible and welcoming to the world.

Of course, Rugby World Cup is much more than a global stage to showcase for our sport. It is also the financial engine that drives the global development of rugby in existing and emerging nations.

The commercial success of previous Rugby World Cups enabled the IRB to invest £150 million in rugby between 2009 and 2012 and will bankroll a further injection of £180 million between 2013 and 2016. All so more men, women and children can participate in rugby and enjoy its character-building values, while creating a more competitive, sustainable and attractive game at international level.

If 2012 and 2013 are anything to go by then we are on track. An unprecedented competition schedule for Tier Two nations, involving a blend of IRB World Ranking matches against similar opposition and opportunities against the world's top nations and the strengthening of IRB-funded competitions, has been compelling.

Samoa recorded wins over Wales, Scotland and Italy, while Tonga defeated Scotland and Japan recorded a first-ever win against Wales. It is a solid start and our unions are telling us that that the new structure is not just good for visibility with a greater number of inbound Tests against great opposition, but that it is hitting performance targets on the road to RWC 2015.

It was also another record-breaking year for Rugby Sevens. We are now well into the Rio 2016 Olympic Games cycle and Rugby World Cup Sevens 2013 continued to demonstrate that the shortened version of the game is flourishing and even more competitive than ever, reaching out to new fans, broadcasters and commercial partners along the way.

We are in good shape as we head towards Rio. The inaugural IRB Women's

Sevens World Series demonstrated the depth and competitiveness of women's rugby, one of the fastest-growing team sports in the world. The HSBC Sevens World Series was no less compelling.

Our unions are telling us that the benefits of Olympic inclusion are broad and significant and with three years to go until Rugby Sevens makes its debut on the world's greatest sporting stage, I have no doubt that our men's and women's tournaments will be compelling, competitive and ultimately a success.

Off the field, the IRB continues to invest heavily in making tomorrow sustainable today through comprehensive training and education programmes such as Rugby Ready and the Get Into Rugby mass participation programme which is being introduced to 40 countries to ensure that children have the opportunity to 'Try, Play and Stay' in rugby.

The programme is also a key element of the IRB's IMPACT Beyond initiative aimed at ensuring our unions are able to benefit fully from our marquee events being hosted in their region, such as Rugby World Cup, Women's Rugby World Cup and the IRB Junior World Championship.

Player welfare continues to be our priority at all levels of the game and I'm pleased to say that, driven by the IRB Medical Commission, rugby is implementing leading medical, player welfare and research strategies to protect and support our players. Concussion education, protocols and research are top of the agenda and the IRB has taken a common-sense and protective approach to ensure that we mitigate the risk. A combination of pitch-side care, return to play protocols and robust education will ensure that players at all levels are given the highest-possible standard of support.

Our message to the whole community is 'recognise and remove'. We all have a duty of care to players at all levels and coaches, medics, parents and players themselves need to recognise the symptoms of suspected concussion and remove the player from the field of play for the rest of the match or training.

Staying on the player welfare subject, the 'crouch, bind, set' global scrum trial made its debut in 2013 to enhance player welfare in this important area of the game. The trial has demonstrated a 25 per cent reduction of forces on engagement, which is great for long-term player welfare.

It is important to note that while addressing collapses and resets that blight the elite game, the new process has also demonstrated positive benefits for scrum stability. We are in the trial's infancy and time will tell as to its success, but the game must give this a go and buy-in must come from coaches and players to referees. We must be positive as only through working together will we effect positive player welfare and scrum management benefits.

So, as we look ahead to 2014 and a mouth-watering Women's Rugby World Cup in France, an expanded IRB Women's Sevens World Series, continuing Rugby World Cup preparations and continued participation growth, I am confident that the building blocks have been laid to ensure that we are well on our way to ensuring our mission of making rugby a truly global sport is realised.

The Front Row

2 Rugby World Cup 2015 set to engage a nation

You would be forgiven for believing that following what is widely regarded as the most successful Olympic Games would be a daunting task for the Rugby World Cup 2015 organisers, but England 2015 is on track to be something special for teams, fans and the people of the United Kingdom.

A truly nationwide festival of rugby, culture and sport will ensure that Rugby World Cup 2015 does not just follow the Olympic Games, but will engage a nation from the north-east to the south-west, deliver new participants in England and Europe, ensure the most competitive tournament to date and cement the event as a must-see experience and one of the world's largest and commercially attractive major sports events.

Planning is well underway and, at the time of writing, the building blocks for a successful event are well and truly embedded. In May 2013, after much anticipation and a detailed process, the 13 match venues and schedule were unveiled to the world in a truly nationwide package that would ensure England 2015 would be the most accessible tournament to date.

It was good reading. Not only would the tournament feature some of the most iconic venues in sport in the shape of the City of Manchester Stadium, Wembley and the Olympic Stadium, but rugby would remain at the heart of the event with mouth-watering fixtures pencilled in for Exeter and Gloucester, heartlands of rugby in the south-west.

More than 75 per cent of the population will live within 30 minutes' drive of a RWC 2015 venue, while the largest capacity venues and public ticketing starting at just £7 mean that the public will have great access to rugby's showcase event.

The ticketing announcement is due to take place by the end of 2013 and organisers project that there will be more than two million opportunities to be a part of a Rugby World Cup event. With more than 400,000 overseas visitors anticipated to visit the British Isles during the seven-week festival, plans are well and truly in place to ensure that the world is made very welcome indeed.

On the field, there was an exciting development too. Amid all the discussions regarding venues and reach, perhaps the most significant announcement was that the schedule for the eighth Rugby World Cup would be the best ever and fairest for the 'smaller' rugby nations.

True to its word at RWC 2015, the International Rugby Board has ensured that the likes of Canada, Samoa and the qualified teams will have equal preparation time in comparison with their opponents for the big matches against the tournament favourites, springing hope of yet more upsets and perhaps the likes of Samoa, Japan or Canada reaching the quarter-finals.

AFP/Getty Images

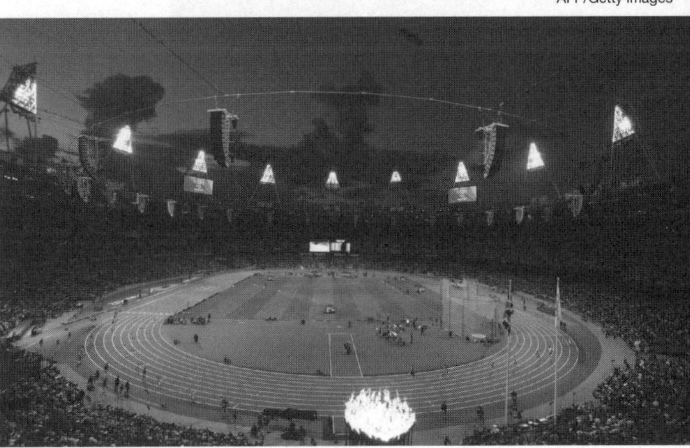

The Olympic Stadium will host four pool matches and the Bronze Final at Rugby World Cup 2015.

Indeed, Rugby World Cup 2011 delivered the most competitive tournament to date, with average winning margins for the pool stages between Tier One and Tier Two and Three teams the smallest ever at 28 points, while the volume of 'blowouts' also dropped. However, with tighter turnaround time and less strength in depth across their squads, Tier Two and Three team performances dropped off, prompting the IRB to act.

Supporting the schedule will be an impressive selection of team base camps to ensure that no stone is left unturned when it comes to providing the 600 players with England and Wales' best facilities. In total, 80 venues, authorities and schools have bid to host the 20 teams throughout their stay, and while the final selection is to be made, the record interest will further ensure a nationwide feel to the event.

Of course, the schedule alone will not deliver quarter-final glory and that is why the IRB continues to invest heavily in Test programmes, high performance programmes and tournaments to ensure that the Pacific Island nations, Georgia, Romania et al can perform to their peak and demonstrate the true depth, competitiveness and global spread of rugby.

With Rugby World Cup continuing to provide the financial engine to grow the sport around the world, the IRB announced in 2013 an unprecedented global funding programme of more than £180 million between 2013 and 2016 in high performance, competitions, education, training, player welfare and anti-doping to ensure that these unions have the platform to springboard onto the 2015 stage and beyond in 2019.

The signs, of course, are good. Samoa continues to record impressive results on the world stage with wins against Wales, Scotland and Italy in the past year, while Japan recorded a first-ever win against Tier One opposition when they beat Wales in front of a capacity Tokyo crowd in June, which bodes well for RWC 2019 in Japan on and off the field.

Getty Images

Traditional rivals England and Wales will go head to head at Twickenham.

RWC 2015 is on track to be the most commercially successful tournament to date, which is good news for the continued growth of the sport. Heineken, Société Générale, LandRover and DHL have all put pen to paper to renew as tournament Worldwide Partners and with interest high, the commercial programme looks set to be locked down in record time and with significant financial uplift.

Innovation will also be at the heart of the broadcast and digital experience, meaning that from the stadium to the armchair, fans new and old will be able to engage, participate and enjoy all that the tournament has to offer on and off the field.

While the Olympics showcased London as a host city and the British love of sport, RWC 2015 will engage the nation, spreading rugby's character-building values throughout new audiences within the British Isles and beyond.

The tournament's IMPACT Beyond programme, launched with two years to go, will ensure that Rugby World Cup 2015 will not just leave a lasting legacy of interest and participation, but will deliver the building blocks to ensure that participation can be sustained and retained.

The work is already advanced and the RFU Posts in the Parks programme and twinning of counties with emerging European rugby nations will boost participation. Underpinning it all will be the IRB's Get Into Rugby mass participation programme that will see more than one million children across 40 European nations engaged in tag rugby programmes.

So, with less than two years to go, RWC 2015 is on track to be an exceptional sporting tournament that will be good for rugby and good for England with superb facilities, a wonderful experience for teams and fans and will further rugby as a major global sport with a must-see pinnacle event.

To receive RWC 2015 news and updates, visit ***www.rugbyworldcup.com*** and Join the Front Row or follow ***@rugbyworldcup***.

Rugby World Cup 2015 fixtures

POOL A

18/09/2015	England v Oceania 1	Twickenham
20/09/2015	Wales v Play-Off Winner	Millennium Stadium
23/09/2015	Australia v Oceania 1	Millennium Stadium
26/09/2015	England v Wales	Twickenham
27/09/2015	Australia v Play-Off Winner	Villa Park
01/10/2015	Wales v Oceania 1	Millennium Stadium
03/10/2015	England v Australia	Twickenham
06/10/2015	Oceania 1 v Play-Off Winner	Stadiummk
10/10/2015	Australia v Wales	Twickenham
10/10/2015	England v Play-Off Winner	Manchester City Stadium

POOL B

19/09/2015	South Africa v Asia 1	Brighton Community Stadium
20/09/2015	Samoa v Americas 2	Brighton Community Stadium
23/09/2015	Scotland v Asia 1	Kingsholm
26/09/2015	South Africa v Samoa	Villa Park
27/09/2015	Scotland v Americas 2	Elland Road
03/10/2015	Samoa v Asia 1	Stadiummk
03/10/2015	South Africa v Scotland	St James Park
07/10/2015	South Africa v Americas 2	Olympic Stadium
10/10/2015	Samoa v Scotland	St James Park
11/10/2015	Americas 2 v Asia 1	Kingsholm

POOL C

19/09/2015	Tonga v Europe 1	Kingsholm
20/09/2015	New Zealand v Argentina	Wembley Stadium
24/09/2015	New Zealand v Africa 1	Olympic Stadium
25/09/2015	Argentina v Europe 1	Kingsholm
29/09/2015	Tonga v Africa 1	Sandy Park
02/10/2015	New Zealand v Europe 1	Millennium Stadium
04/10/2015	Argentina v Tonga	Leicester City Stadium
07/10/2015	Africa 1 v Europe 1	Sandy Park
09/10/2015	New Zealand v Tonga	St James Park
11/10/2015	Argentina v Africa 1	Leicester City Stadium

POOL D

19/09/2015	France v Italy	Twickenham
19/09/2015	Ireland v Canada	Millennium Stadium
23/09/2015	France v Europe 2	Olympic Stadium
26/09/2015	Italy v Canada	Elland Road
27/09/2015	Ireland v Europe 2	Wembley Stadium
01/10/2015	France v Canada	Stadiummk
04/10/2015	Ireland v Italy	Olympic Stadium
06/10/2015	Canada v Europe 2	Leicester City Stadium
11/10/2015	France v Ireland	Millennium Stadium
11/10/2015	Italy v Europe 2	Sandy Park

QUARTER-FINALS

17/10/2015	Winner Pool C v Runner-up Pool D	Millennium Stadium
17/10/2015	Winner Pool B v Runner-up Pool A	Twickenham
18/10/2015	Winner Pool D v Runner-up Pool C	Millennium Stadium
18/10/2015	Winner Pool A v Runner-up Pool B	Twickenham

SEMI-FINALS

24/10/2015	Winner QF1 v Winner QF2	Twickenham
25/10/2015	Winner QF3 v Winner QF4	Twickenham

BRONZE FINAL

30/10/2015	Loser SF1 v Loser SF2	Olympic Stadium

FINAL

31/10/2015	Winner SF1 v Winner SF2	Twickenham

Putting players first: Rugby's proactive player welfare approach

Rugby is experiencing unprecedented global growth and by the end of 2013 there will be twice as many men, women and children playing rugby as there were in 2007.

Boosted by the Olympic opportunity, a successful HSBC Sevens World Series, a flourishing IRB Women's Sevens World Series and a first Rugby World Cup in Asia in 2019, rugby is taking root in exciting new markets such as China, India, Mexico and Russia.

Such opportunities are fantastic for a sport with ambitions to be truly global, but this would not be achievable without the platform to ensure that members have access to the best possible coaching and education to ensure a safe and sustainable environment to enjoy rugby and its character-building values.

It is for this reason that the IRB has funded and driven forward a raft of player welfare programmes and initiatives, as Chairman Bernard Lapasset explains. "The welfare of players at all levels of the game is of paramount importance to the IRB and its Member Unions and the establishment of the IRB Medical Commission Conference in 2009 and an extensive ***www.irbplayerwelfare.com*** represents the IRB's commitment to 'putting players first' to ensure the continued dissemination of best possible practice for playing, coaching and officiating rugby."

Injury rates in elite rugby have returned to levels comparable before the game went professional in 1995 and while its work is largely unseen, the conference has been the driving force behind a suite of key medical and player

Getty Images

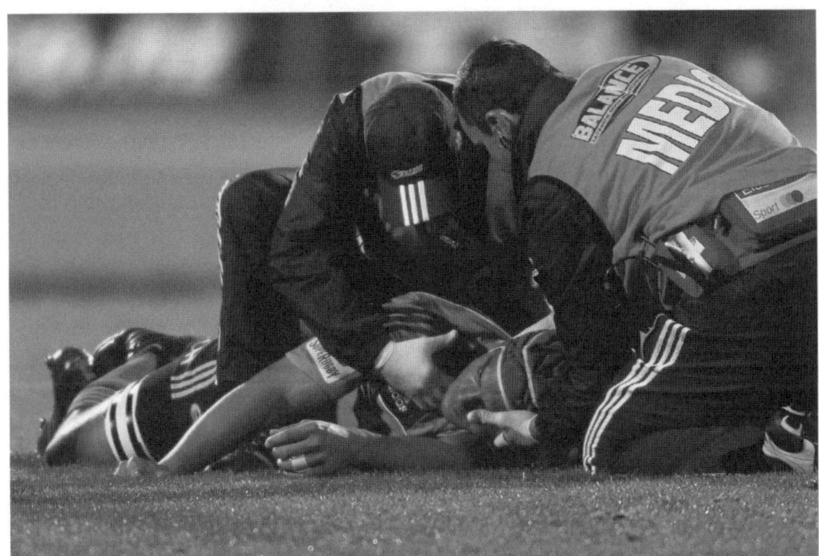

The IRB Medical Commission is driving the development of concussion management.

welfare policies that are already benefitting the game, including: catastrophic injury reporting – standardised worldwide register for catastrophic injuries; gender policy developed in line with IOC recommendations; dedicated player welfare website; best-practice game preparation techniques; standardised match-day doctor role criteria; pre-participation cardiac screening policy; game-wide injury prevention strategies; implementation of courses that improve care for all players with doctors at elite level, team doctors and sports first aid and concussion guidelines and education.

It is understood that nearly 50 per cent of injuries are potentially controllable with training injuries and non-contact match injuries contributing factors. Education is key and that is why the IRB's Rugby Ready and ***www.irbplayerwelfare.com*** online and practical resources are at the forefront of educating players, coaches, match officials and administrators on how best to prepare for rugby.

Concussion education and management is at the heart of player welfare. Concussion is a complex and emotive topic and one that is right at the top of the IRB's agenda. There has been much debate in the media as to rugby's approach but the IRB, along with leading independent neurologists and the International Rugby Players' Association, believes that programmes developed within the last three years are providing players at all levels with a strong level of protection, education and support.

While the risk of concussion in rugby can never be totally eradicated in a contact sport, as with any aspect of life, the IRB's approach to mitigate risk of concussion and concussion-related issues is based on a three-step approach:

1) educating the rugby community at all levels to recognise symptoms and remove players, 2) developing and implementing protocols in line with international best practice and 3) driving and supporting research that will benefit the game.

The IRB's approach, driven by the Medical Commission, is based entirely on the standard-bearing 2012 Zurich Consensus Statement on Concussion in Sport. It is a collaboration between sports federations and leading experts to deliver best-practice guidelines in this critical area.

The 2012 Statement determines that athletes should not be allowed to return to play after a diagnosed concussion and should not return to play or train on the same day. It also outlines an approach to help physicians determine when an athlete might be safe to return to sport.

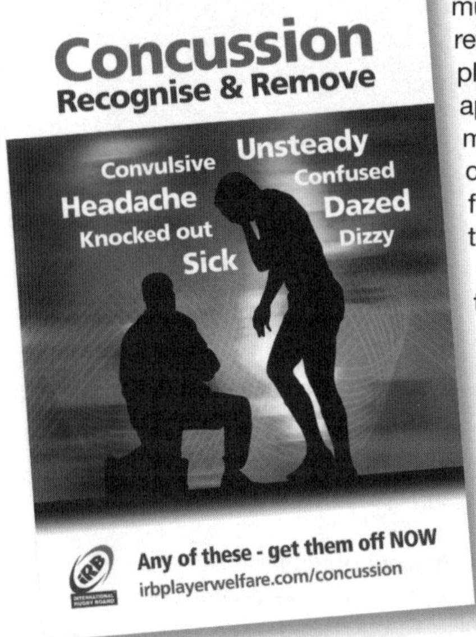

Concussion
Recognise & Remove
Unsteady
Convulsive
Confused
Headache
Dazed
Knocked out
Dizzy
Sick
Any of these - get them off NOW
irbplayerwelfare.com/concussion

All players with a diagnosed concussion must be removed from the field of play and not return to play or train on the same day. All players with a suspected concussion where no appropriately trained personnel are present must be assumed to have a diagnosed concussion and must be removed from the field of play and not return to play or train on the same day.

Players with a suspected concussion at the elite level must be removed from play and assessed by an experienced doctor assisted by an appropriate tool. At the elite level any player displaying clear concussion symptoms should be removed immediately and not return.

IRB Chief Medical Officer Dr Martin Raftery explains: "Concussion management is at the very heart of our player welfare strategy. The IRB Medical Commission has driven the development of concussion management and return-to-play protocol guidelines and importantly education best practice for elite and community rugby, all designed to further protect players at every level. Our message to players, coaches and officials at all levels is very clear: recognise the symptoms and remove the player. Symptoms should not be ignored.

"An additional layer of protection for elite athletes is the Pitch-side Suspected Concussion Assessment (PSCA) which is a triage tool designed to standardise the assessment of players in an elite match environment and support team medics to assess suspected concussion in a situation where otherwise a player may have been left on the field. PSCA is not a tool to clear a player, nor a tool to diagnose concussion."

The IRB believes that the PSCA is an important advancement for the care of elite players as it gives medics five minutes to assess players following a head knock and remove those with suspected concussion, rather than trying to assess on the field and on the run. Results from the first year of the PSCA trial show that the number of players left on the field and later determined to have confirmed concussion has halved, which is great news for the game.

A further layer of protection at the elite level is the implementation of a standardised accreditation programme for team medics and a full post-match assessment for any player who has been through the PSCA process, whether suspected concussion was determined or not.

Education at all levels is paramount and the IRB and its Unions continue to provide support to the community level of the game, reiterating the importance for players, coaches, match officials and parents to recognise the symptoms of concussion and remove the player.

Dr Raftery points to six simple steps that should be followed. Within the IRB's protocols any player at any level with suspected concussion must leave the field immediately and not return.

Recognise – Learn the signs and symptoms of a concussion so you understand when a player might have a suspected concussion

Remove – If a player has a concussion or even a suspected concussion he or she must be removed from play immediately

Refer – Once removed, the player should be referred immediately to a qualified healthcare professional that is trained in evaluating and treating concussions

Rest – Players must rest from exercise until symptom-free and then start a graduated return to play (GRTP). The IRB recommends minimum rest periods for different ages (Under 6 to Under 15 – two weeks' minimum rest, Under 16 to Under 19 – one week minimum rest, and adults – 24 hours' minimum rest)

Recover – Full recovery from the concussion is required before return to play is authorised. This includes being symptom-free. Rest and specific treatment options are critical for the health of the injured participant

Return – In order for safe return to play in rugby, the player must be symptom-free and cleared in writing by a qualified healthcare professional who is trained in evaluating and treating concussions. The player completes the GRTP protocol.

"Understanding the importance of taking concussion seriously is important for everyone involved in our sport and if there is any doubt, a player must understand that they should leave the field permanently as per IRB Regulations. It is vital players understand and listen to their bodies. Players continuing to play while concussed are at risk," added Dr Raftery.

For more information on the IRB's player welfare initiatives, visit ***www.irbplayerwelfare.com***.

A once-in-a-lifetime occasion

By France captain Marie-Alice Yahé

Getty Images

With just over a year to go until France hosts Women's Rugby World Cup 2014 we can already feel the excitement in the squad. Selections will become increasingly more difficult and the desire to take part is building because this is a once-in-a-lifetime event and rare in a career, but there is also some caution as we tell ourselves that there is still time and some work to do in order to get there as well-prepared as possible because these tournaments are not to be missed. They are too important not to get there 300 per cent ready.

To play in a World Cup in France is the dream for any player in our squad, to have the opportunity to play in front of her family and friends. That means more pressure on the shoulders of the players with the hopes and expectations put on us to do well and to show our sport in the best possible way. Playing at home also means the ideal preparation for us as players and it will give us enormous pride. To defend our country and our colours abroad is already fantastic, but to play in our own country is something even stronger and a great recognition for our Union. This in turn, I hope, will result in more visibility for our sport and will contribute to the development of women's rugby.

AFP/Getty Images

France will carry the hopes and expectations of a nation at WRWC 2014.

To play in front of your friends and family is like having a 16th player on the pitch. In fact, looking at the familiar faces will make it possible for a player to rise to the big occasion, to get up quicker from a tackle and to never give up. It brings feelings and emotions multiplied by 10 on the pitch and in the individual performances.

This World Cup will inevitably be different from the tournament four years ago in England because our countries and our cultures are different. The 2014 tournament will be played largely at Marcoussis, an unique training venue and one of a kind in the world of rugby, and I hope that by being in Paris, our capital city, it will allow this event to attract big crowds with easy accessibility for our fans and also those from overseas.

There will also be matches like the semi-finals and final played in the brand new and mythical arena that is the Stade Jean-Bouin. Playing in these venues represents a milestone in a career and brings a higher profile to our event.

France, and the Fédération Française de Rugby, has a strong desire to organise a splendid Women's Rugby World Cup 2014 and to showcase the women's game in the best possible way. I think this World Cup, with Marcoussis and a splendid arena like Jean-Bouin, will put France 2014 at the same level as previous editions, and will, I hope, do better or at least match the last tournament in England.

AFP/ Getty Images

New Zealand will be aiming to retain their world crown in August 2014.

It will, of course, be important for France as hosts to perform well, not only to put our country as high as possible in the hierarchy of women's rugby, but for the pride of our country, the Union and to get more recognition for our sport and the players. This makes it possible to make more and more girls aware of our game and also to break certain taboos that are still present in the image of the women's game.

The World Cup is a great showcase for our sport. We represent 10,000 registered female players who do not wear the French national jersey but play our sport and we must represent them as well as we can.

France have never reached a Women's Rugby World Cup final but, having been lucky enough to play in a World Cup, I know that to reach the final is simply about being at your best for each match, to never fail and to be truly ready physically. This is what we learned from our last World Cup; it is this lack of physicality which was complicated for French players to understand four years ago.

Since then, we have decided with our coaching staff and our fitness adviser to focus on this, to make up for this deficit which meant that even when we competed technically or rugby-wise, we still somehow lost matches sometimes. It was a wake-up call – the way the game has evolved and is played at the highest level. We needed to be the best. The players work hard and all the rugby work we put in will, I hope and believe, allow us to play in our first final in Paris.

In my eyes this French team certainly has huge potential. It has a mix of young players who are dynamic, fast and skilful having played from an early age, but also older players who give the group some experience, better game management and make it an extraordinary adventure off the pitch, without which a rugby team would not succeed.

The principal challenge for us at the World Cup will be to start well, to aim for the top three and then, playing good rugby and with a bit of luck, win the title. That is our challenge and our dream.

Will there be a surprise team at the World Cup? I don't know, but in events like the Six Nations or the World Cup each match is unique and each match counts so anything is possible, no team is invincible over one match. It is necessary to be wary of all 12 nations and to expect that each country will want to be that famous surprise package.

Some teams are more fancied than others because of their track record, but things can change with just one match. Look at 2013 when Ireland won the Six Nations when everyone still saw England or France winning it, but given how well they played Ireland deserved their title without any doubt. Other nations are an unknown quantity, like Spain. Their game will be a surprise because we don't play them regularly, but we will be wary of all nations.

The France squad numbers around 40 now but the matches in November against Canada and England will make it possible for the coaches to see all the players and reduce the squad before the World Cup. We then have the Six Nations and our desire and objective is to win it, win every match and the competition ... but we will also have the desire to keep working because the ultimate objective for us remains the World Cup.

What more can I say, a World Cup is a once-in-a-lifetime opportunity for a country in any sport and we need our fans to support us and we also need to showcase our sport and our passion. Sporting events are always moments of joy and happiness and if we win the title, we know how to thank the supporters!

For more information on Women's Rugby World Cup 2014, which takes place from 1–17 August, visit the official website ***www.rwcwomens.com*** or follow ***@irbwomens***.

Get Into Rugby

By Morgan Buckley, IRB General Manager for Development

Rugby is growing at unprecedented levels with statistics showing that the number of players has more than doubled between 2007 and 2012. But the International Rugby Board is keen to see even more men, women and children playing the sport as we count down to the 2016 Olympic Games when Rugby Sevens will make its debut in Rio de Janeiro.

The groundbreaking Get Into Rugby programme is at the heart of the IRB's strategy to grow the global game in partnership with its Member Unions and Regional Associations. The aim of the programme is not just to increase player numbers but also to attract new coaches and referees through its 'Try, Play and Stay' philosophy.

To explain simply, the philosophy is first to encourage children to try rugby in clubs, schools and local communities through tag or flag rugby and then to play the game in a safe and fun environment. The final element is to support players so they stay in the game, be it as a player, coach, referee, administrator, volunteer or simply a fan.

Get Into Rugby was launched in 2012 with Brazil, Colombia, Mexico, Trinidad & Tobago, Zimbabwe and Tunisia among the first countries to benefit from the programme, but by the end of 2013 it will be up and running in 46 Unions around the world. A new regional participation programme with the IRB's six Regional Associations is in the process of being finalised and this will expand Get Into Rugby into 66 countries.

It is estimated that 50,000 have already participated in the Get Into Rugby programme across 870 registered locations, 20,000 of them females with women's rugby currently one of the fastest growing team sports.

While Get Into Rugby continues to evolve and take the game into new and existing markets, there have already been a number of highlights and positive feedback continues to flow back to the IRB.

Mexico Rugby, for example, are planning to roll the programme out across more than 240 locations in the country and see Get Into Rugby as a major boost to grow the game there. They are working on an exciting project in Mexico City involving 1,200 children in six locations with 200 children and three coaches at each venue.

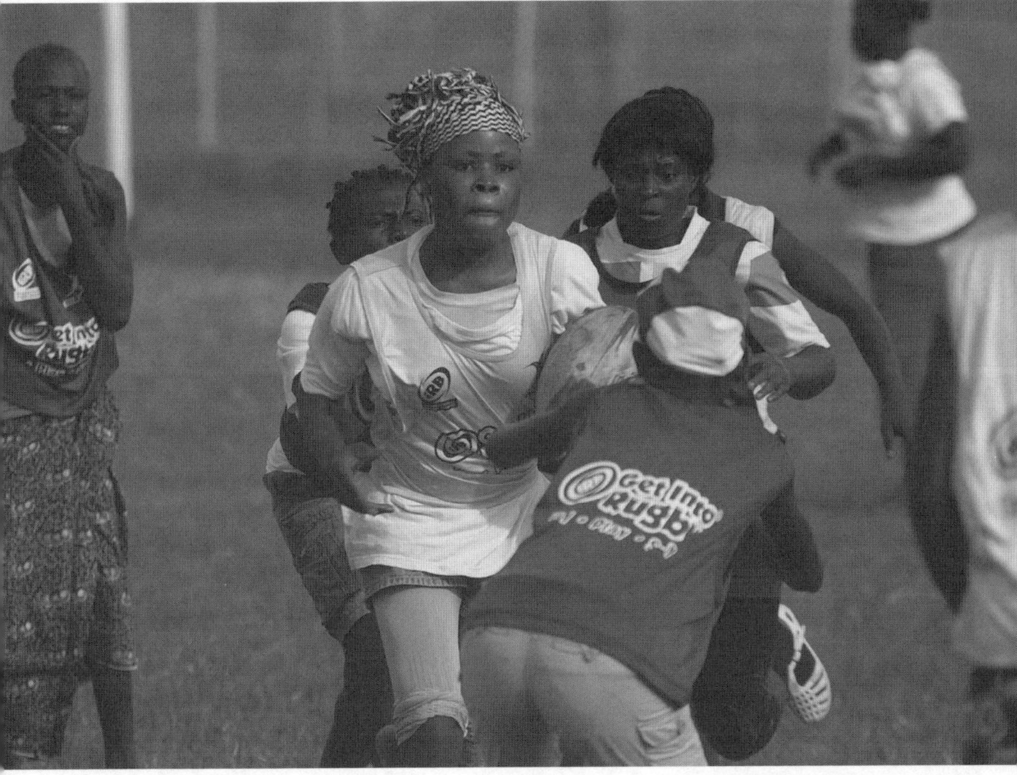

Yves Jamoneau, Peace and Sport

Youngsters take part in the Get Into Rugby programme in Daloa, Ivory Coast.

Elsewhere in the North America and Caribbean region, Curacao are delivering the programme in two locations and Trinidad & Tobago have more than 300 participants taking part in schools and clubs.

In South America, the Get Into Rugby programme was part of the IRB Junior World Rugby Trophy 2013 in Chile and also the recent World Games in the Colombian city of Cali. The programme is currently delivered in five main areas of Colombia and continues to flourish.

Meanwhile in Brazil, training has been provided for each of the provincial unions and the Confederação Brasileira de Rugby are keen to ramp up the delivery of the programme across the country and will use Get Into Rugby as a key element of their plan to grow rugby in Rio in the years leading up to the 2016 Games.

Staying on the Olympic theme, the programme is also being implemented in Nanjing, Guangzhou and Zengcheng in China. Nanjing will host the Youth Olympic Games from 16–28 August 2014 – when Rugby Sevens will make its debut – and Get Into Rugby was introduced in the city when it hosted the Asian Youth Games earlier this year.

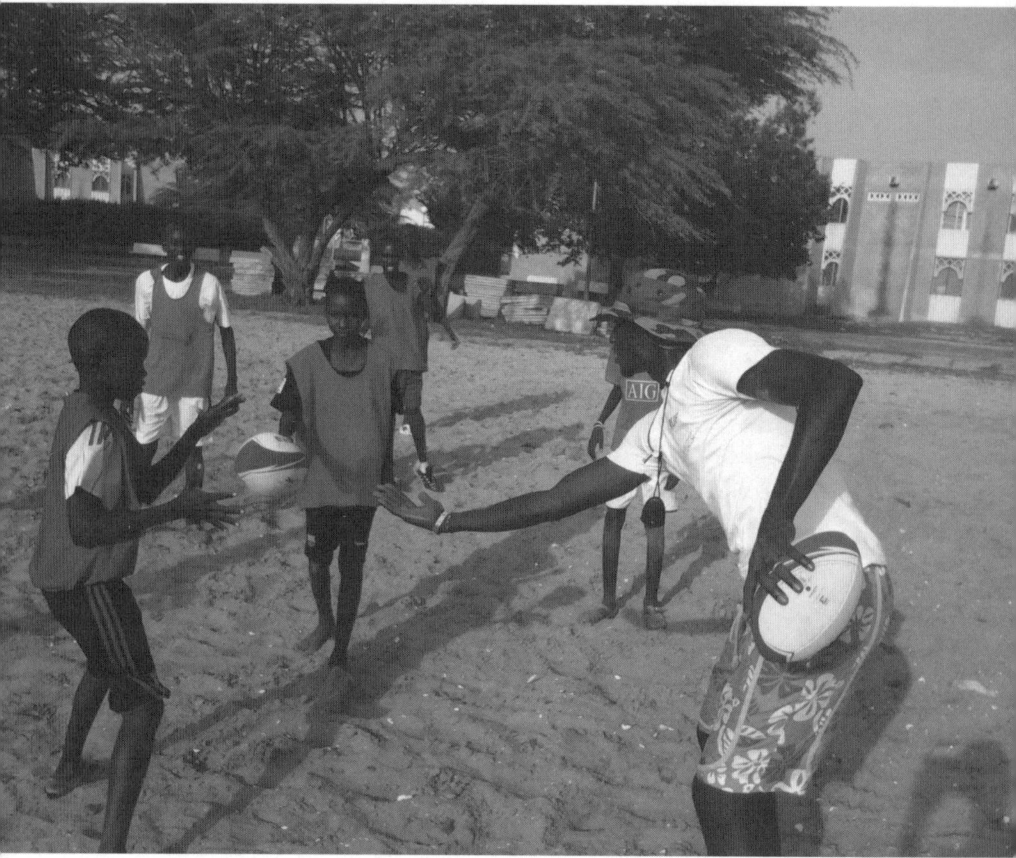

Senegal
Union

Senegal is one of many nations around the world to embrace Get Into Rugby.

Get Into Rugby is also spreading across India with the programme already introduced in Pune, Chennai, Bhubabesgwar, Srinagar, Kolkata, Delhi and Mumbai. India captain Nasser Hussain was the lead trainer at the Get Into Rugby launch in Srinagar in August, giving back to a sport that is growing quickly across the country.

The United Arab Emirates have also embraced Get Into Rugby with training held in Dubai for locals and representatives from India, Pakistan and Sri Lanka. In Dubai, 28 female teachers participated in the training and are now delivering the programme in Arabic and Emirati schools in the UAE.

In Oceania, the Get Into Rugby programme is now being included in the PE curriculum in Tonga and will be delivered in every primary school in the island nation. Their fellow islanders Fiji are looking to attract 50,000 new players as part of their programme to grow rugby over the next two years.

In Africa, the programme is up and running in 11 nations, including

Zimbabwe where the national Sevens team ran a legacy programme in the six months building up to Rugby World Cup Sevens 2013 in Moscow. Representatives from eight African nations also received training at Stellenbosch and since June more than 1,900 participants have been involved in a new initiative in South Africa's Western Cape.

The most recent country to launch Get Into Rugby was Georgia in early October, Lelos captain Irakli Machkhaneli among the national team players helping to introduce rugby at three schools in and around the capital Tbilisi. The Georgian Rugby Union has set the goal of increasing the number of registered players by 20 per cent by 2015 and for the number of women's players to account for 10 per cent of this rugby-playing population by 2016.

IRB

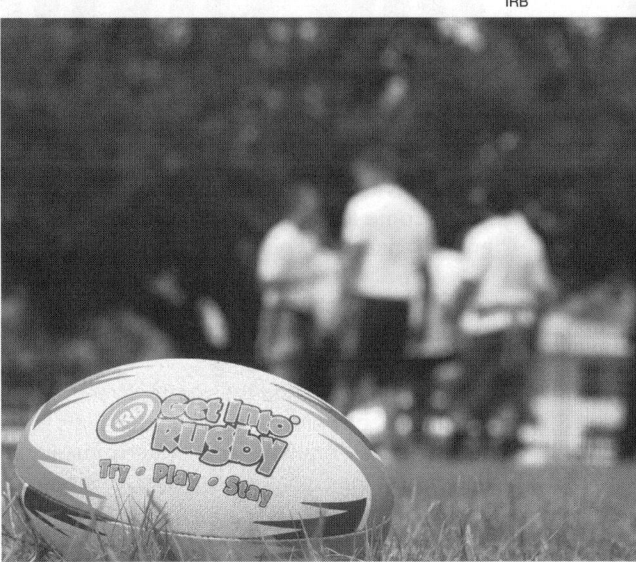

By the end of 2013 Get Into Rugby will be up and running in 46 Unions.

Elsewhere in Europe, the interest generated by the Get Into Rugby programme is continuing to blossom. In Germany, more than 12,000 participants have been recorded in the first three months of the programme, while in Belgium Get Into Rugby is being used as part of the Union's mass participation programme to grow the game in the country. To date, 1,300 repeat participants have been involved and that figure is expected to rise. Denmark, Norway and Sweden have joined forces to launch Get Into Rugby Scandinavia and demonstrated the programme at the FIRA-AER General Assembly in Stockholm.

With thousands having already experienced the Try and Play elements of Get Into Rugby, work is now progressing on the Stay phase to design Get Into Rugby for Sevens, Tens, 12s, Fifteens and Beach Rugby. This will enable Unions to progress from introducing the game to providing competitions, leagues and events to ensure these new players stay in the sport.

This is, in essence, the holy grail for any programme, providing a long-term and sustainable pathway for players and countries around the world.

For more information on Get Into Rugby visit ***www.irbgetintorugby.com*** – the official website which is available in English, Spanish, French, Portuguese, Mandarin and currently being translated into Arabic, Indonesian (Bahasa) and Laotian languages – or on Facebook at ***www.facebook.com/getintorugby***.

18

Rugby and the Olympics

By John Murray

The Olympic Games are a breeding ground for heroes. Athletes become idols, teams become legends, individual feats become immortalised. Every four years new heroes are born.

In this respect, the 1924 Games in Paris were no different from any other. 'Flying Finns' Paavo Nurmi and Ville Ritola enhanced their country's reputation as long-distance specialists, British duo Harold Abrahams and Eric Liddell dominated the shorter events, while Tarzan himself, Johnny Weismuller, powered to three gold medals in the pool.

Yet before Abrahams and Liddell's inspirational feats which were later depicted in the Oscar-winning film, *Chariots of Fire*, another piece of history took place at the Stade Colombes. On 4 May, the day of the opening ceremony, host nation France and Romania kicked off the Games with a 15-a-side rugby union match. Just 14 days and three matches after that grand opening, the rugby competition was over and the sport has not been played at the Games since.

Now, 90 years on, following the odd appearance as an exhibition sport and the IRB's successful campaign for reinstatement, rugby is preparing for its long-awaited return to the Olympic fold. Rio 2016 will host a men's and women's rugby competition – in Sevens format – after the International Olympic Committee (IOC) overwhelmingly voted in 2009 to reintroduce the sport.

Despite its absence, rugby boasts a strong Olympic history and represents the traditions and values which define the Olympic Movement. It was Baron Pierre de Coubertin, the founder of the modern Olympics, who championed the cause of the sport's initial inclusion in the Games after developing an interest on a visit to Rugby School.

Rugby was introduced at the second Olympic Games in 1900, also held in Paris. In a round robin tournament for three teams using a scoring system reportedly devised by De Coubertin, a mixed side, Union des Societes Francais de Sports Athletiques, won gold while Great Britain (Moseley Wanderers) and Germany (Frankfurt Club) shared silver.

Its popularity was immediately obvious, with a crowd of 6,000 – the biggest attendance of the whole Games – at one match. The competition was

Popperfoto/Getty Images

France launch an attack against Romania in the 1924 Olympic Games.

also notable for the participation of the first known black Olympic athlete, Constantin Henriquez de Zubiera.

The American organisers chose not to include it at St Louis 1904, but rugby returned at London 1908, where Australasia outscored Great Britain by six tries to one to win gold, and also featured at Antwerp 1920, the United States beating France 8–0 in the only match.

Those two nations returned, together with Romania, for the 1924 competition which has the highest profile of rugby's four Olympic appearances to date. France opened their home Games in stunning style, running in 13 tries in a 61–3 defeat of the Romanians. The scoreline was only slightly less emphatic a week later as the USA crushed Romania 39–0. For their vanquished opponents, there was the consolation of a bronze medal, the country's first ever at the Olympics.

That result effectively set up a final between the 1920 gold and silver medallists, watched by a staggering crowd of 50,000 at the Stade Colombes hoping to cheer France to gold. At times, the partisan atmosphere threatened to boil over, particularly after French player Adolphe Jauréguy was stretchered off following a strong tackle. The home fans ultimately left disappointed, though, as the USA – who required a police escort from the field at the final whistle – scored five tries in a shock 17–3 win, with points coming from six different players.

Despite its popularity, rugby was dropped from the Olympic programme for Amsterdam 1928 after De Coubertin stood down as IOC president. However, the impact of the 1924 competion was not to be forgotten. The story of the groundbreaking American side was told in the documentary *A Giant Awakens: the Rise of American Rugby*, while the USA teams of 1920 and 1924, along with their Romanian opponents in 1924, were inducted into the IRB Hall of Fame in 2012.

Rugby may have been absent from the Games for the best part of a century, but its Olympic legacy lives on.

IRB World Rankings

By Karen Bond

There may have been numerous changes in the IRB World Rankings over the past 12 months, but one thing has remained constant and that is New Zealand occupying the number one position. The world champions have now occupied top spot for more than 200 weeks since they replaced South Africa on 16 November 2009 and for more than 82 per cent of the time since the rankings were introduced in October 2003.

New Zealand's cushion at the top, though, is smaller than it was when they lifted The Rugby Championship trophy for the first time in 2012, albeit still healthy at 5.19 rating points – down from 7.43. However, it could have been far worse for the All Blacks: if South Africa had won an enthralling Rugby Championship title decider at Ellis Park on 5 October – rather than lost it 38–27 – then the sides could have been separated by as little as 0.16 rating points.

With a record of 12 wins, one draw and one loss – against England at Twickenham – since Richie McCaw's side were crowned the inaugural Rugby Championship winners, New Zealand are the only nation to remain stationary over this period. Thirteen other nations, though, have returned to the position they occupied 12 months ago after movement up or down. They are France (5), Wales (6), Scotland (9), Russia (19), Spain (20), Uruguay (21), Thailand (59), Venezuela (63), Botswana (77), Pakistan (78), Cameroon (79), St Vincent & The Grenadines (84) and Vanuatu (94).

Scotland managed to return to ninth but they did drop to 12th during the course of the season – their lowest-ever ranking. Ireland also hit a new low of ninth after losing to a lower-ranked Scotland and Italy during a Six Nations campaign which proved to be coach Declan Kidney's last at the helm. While the two Celtic nations hit their unwanted positions, the opposite was true for Samoa who climbed to a new high of seventh after victories over Wales, Scotland and Italy in the last year. This is the highest position any of the Pacific Island nations have ever occupied in the rankings. The victory over Wales at the Millennium Stadium came at a crucial time for Samoa as it ensured that they were among the second band of seeds for the Rugby World Cup 2015 Pool Allocation Draw on 3 December 2012.

Getty Images

A memorable win over Wales helped Samoa climb to seventh in the IRB World Rankings.

While Samoa were the biggest climbers in the top 20 after improving their rating by more than four points with these victories, the biggest losers were Australia and Argentina who both fell two places to fourth and 10th respectively. Australia were in danger of slipping to their lowest-ever position of sixth had they not finished The Rugby Championship with an emphatic 54–17 victory over Argentina in Rosario to give Ewen McKenzie his second win in six outings since he succeeded Robbie Deans as Wallabies coach.

In total, 40 nations improved their ranking over the last 12 months, while 44 ended this period lower than they began it. Four nations were also introduced to the IRB World Rankings in November in American Samoa, Greece, Mauritius and the United Arab Emirates, who all entered with a rating of 30.00, putting them equal 96th and causing Finland to fall to 100th. Mauritius and Greece slipped from that entry position, the latter beginning October 2013 at the foot of the rankings after losing 35–20 to Finland in a European Nations Cup Division 2D encounter.

Five other nations – Chile (26), Croatia (53), Tahiti (90), Austria (93) and Norway (95) – currently occupy their lowest position in the history of the rankings, but in contrast five countries, including Samoa, are enjoying their best-ever position. The other quartet are Kenya (31), the Cook Islands (46), Israel (48) and Bosnia & Herzegovina (86). Bulgaria fitted into this category too until they were humbled 67–5 by Hungary at home in Division 2C of the European Nations Cup on 5 October, a result which saw them drop 10 places to 85th. That victory lifted Hungary 10 places to 70th and meant they sit in a group of nations to enjoy the biggest climbs of the past 12 months.

Getty Im

New Zealand remained in top spot after retaining their Rugby Championship title.

The honour of being the biggest climber, though, goes to the Netherlands who rose 12 places to 35th after going through the European Nations Cup Division 2A season unbeaten. The victories over Lithuania, Switzerland, Malta and Croatia meant that the Netherlands remain in the hunt for RWC 2015 qualification. They were scheduled to face Israel in round three of the European play-off process on 26 October.

Other significant climbers in the rankings were the Cook Islands, Israel, Nigeria, Singapore, Sri Lanka and Switzerland. Singapore had fallen 17 places in the previous 12 months, but victories over Malaysia and India in winning the HSBC Asian 5 Nations Division II title and then Chinese Taipei in the Asian Tri Nations have lifted them 10 places to 56th.

Nigeria's 11-place climb to 80th came on the back of emphatic victories over Mauritius and Zambia in the Africa Cup Division 1C in June. Hungary and Switzerland also rose 11 places, the latter to 41st after winning three of their four European Nations Cup Division 2A matches. Sri Lanka, meanwhile, made the most of home advantage to beat Chinese Taipei, Thailand and Kazakhstan convincingly in April to win the Asian 5 Nations Division I title and earn promotion to the Top 5 in 2014 to keep them in the hunt for the region's place at RWC 2015.

The Cook Islands also rose on the back of success on the road to RWC

2015, a victory over their hosts Papua New Guinea in the Oceania Cup 2013 decider lifting them eight places to 46th and earning them a play-off against Fiji to determine the Oceania 1 qualifier who will join hosts England, Australia, Wales and the Repechage winner in Pool A. Israel also climbed eight places after going unbeaten through Division 2B of the European Nations Cup, but could have gained another place had they beaten Luxembourg by a slightly bigger margin than 26–12 in their European round two play-off at the start of October.

While these nations had plenty to smile about in the 2012/13 season, the same cannot be said for the Czech Republic, who suffered the biggest fall in this period, plummeting 12 places to 52nd after failing to win a match in the European Nations Cup Division 1B. They lost all five of their matches against Poland, Sweden, Ukraine, Germany and Moldova – four of them by a margin of more than 15 points which hit their ranking hard.

Uganda were the only other nation with a fall in double figures after losing three of their four matches in 2013, once to Kenya in the annual Elgon Cup battle between the two countries and then again to Kenya and hosts Madagascar in the Africa Cup Division 1A in July. With the last two defeats being by more than 15 points, Uganda dropped 10 places to 51st over the course of the last 12 months.

Another African side to slide down the rankings was Zambia, who fell seven places to 83rd after failing to win a match in the Africa Cup Division 1C, one of them against the lower-ranked Nigeria.

Two other sides to suffer significant falls over the last 12 months were Lithuania and Austria. Lithuania won only one of their European Nations Cup Division 2A matches in 2012/13 – against Croatia – and as a result have fallen nine places to 45th. Austria lost all of their matches in Division 2C and the cost was an eight-place drop to 93rd.

There is, though, still plenty of scope for movements throughout the length of the IRB World Rankings before we bid farewell to 2013 with some 30 nations involved in the traditional November internationals across Europe as well as the Americas, Africa and Asia, while the European Nations Cup 2014 continues with matches across five of its seven divisions.

The IRB World Rankings are published every Monday on ***www.irb.com***. They are calculated using a points exchange system in which teams take points off each other based on the match result. Whatever one team gains, the other team loses. The exchanges are determined by the match result, the relative strength of the team and the margin of victory. There is also an allowance for home advantage.

One hundred of the IRB's Member Unions have a rating, typically between 0 and 100 with the top side in the world usually having a rating above 90 – New Zealand's was 93.05 at the time of writing. Any match that is not a full international between two countries or a Test against the British & Irish Lions does not count towards the rankings. Likewise neither does a match against a country that is not an IRB Full Member Union. For more details, visit ***www.irb.com***.

IRB WORLD RANKINGS 08/10/12 – 07/10/13

POSITION	MEMBER UNION	RATING	MOVEMENT	HIGHEST EVER	LOWEST EVER
1	New Zealand	93.05		1	2
2	South Africa	87.86	Up 1	1	6
3	England	85.76	Up 1	1	8
4	Australia	84.25	Down 2	2	5
5	France	81.59		2	8
6	Wales	81.36		4	10
7	Samoa	80.42	Up 3	7	13
8	Ireland	79.58	Down 1	3	9
9	Scotland	76.95		6	12
10	Argentina	75.50	Down 2	3	9
11	Tonga	74.77	Up 1	9	20
12	Italy	74.17	Down 1	8	13
13	Fiji	73.56	Up 1	9	16
14	Canada	72.68	Down 1	11	16
15	Japan	71.98	Up 1	12	20
16	Georgia	67.66	Down 1	13	23
17	Romania	66.18	Up 1	13	19
18	USA	64.91	Down 1	14	20
19	Russia	61.99		16	26
20	Spain	60.44		18	32
21	Uruguay	59.87		14	23
22	Portugal	58.82	Up 4	16	27
23	Namibia	58.70	Down 1	19	29
24	Korea	58.10	Up 1	20	33
25	Belgium	57.52	Down 2	21	55
26	Chile	56.85	Down 2	23	26
27	Germany	55.96	Up 4	25	37
28	Poland	55.64	Down 1	25	42
29	Hong Kong	54.56	Down 1	26	39
30	Moldova	53.77	Up 4	27	53
31	Kenya	52.78	Up 8	31	53
32	Zimbabwe	52.63	Down 3	29	35
33	Sweden	51.87	Up 5	32	58
34	Brazil	51.86	Down 1	27	37
35	Netherlands	51.53	Up 12	30	48
36	Morocco	51.18	Down 4	19	36
37	Ukraine	50.97	Down 7	24	40
38	Paraguay	50.06	Down 1	29	42
39	Sri Lanka	49.88	Up 9	38	64
40	Ivory Coast	49.13	Up 6	38	48
41	Switzerland	48.80	Up 11	34	67
42	Tunisia	48.25	Up 1	27	44
43	Kazakhstan	48.11	Down 8	25	50
44	Madagascar	48.04	Down 2	41	56
45	Lithuania	47.47	Down 9	35	73
46	Cook Islands	47.11	Up 8	46	59
47	Senegal	46.89	Up 2	46	83
48	Israel	46.84	Up 8	48	94
49	Malta	46.63	Down 4	39	67
50	Trinidad & Tobago	46.38	Up 3	42	60
51	Uganda	46.36	Down 10	31	69
52	Czech Republic	46.11	Down 12	24	53

IRB WORLD RANKINGS 08/10/12 – 07/10/13

POSITION	MEMBER UNION	RATING	MOVEMENT	HIGHEST EVER	LOWEST EVER
53	Croatia	46.04	Down 9	34	53
54	Bermuda	45.53	Down 4	47	68
55	Papua New Guinea	45.27	Down 4	46	63
56	Singapore	44.54	Up 10	42	67
57	Philippines	44.09	Down 2	55	72
58	Chinese Taipei	43.41	Up 2	32	61
59	Thailand	43.37		52	74
60	Colombia	43.33	Down 3	53	86
61	Guyana	43.19	Down 3	56	79
62	Cayman Islands	42.52	Up 3	57	74
63	Venezuela	41.67		42	71
64	Denmark	41.56	Down 3	36	73
65	Latvia	41.31	Up 7	35	75
66	China	40.73	Up 3	38	70
67	Andorra	40.64	Down 5	52	74
68	Niue Islands	40.45	Up 3	60	72
69	Solomon Islands	40.35	Up 1	67	77
70	Hungary	40.24	Up 11	61	89
71	Malaysia	40.20	Down 7	56	83
72	Peru	40.13	Up 2	51	79
73	Barbados	39.68	Down 6	59	81
74	Mexico	39.38	Up 1	70	76
75	India	39.36	Down 7	65	93
76	Serbia	38.69	Down 3	56	77
77	Botswana	38.58		74	89
78	Pakistan	38.38		71	79
79	Cameroon	38.33		76	85
80	Nigeria	37.54	Up 11	73	92
81	Jamaica	37.08	Up 2	76	90
82	Slovenia	37.03	Down 2	42	83
83	Zambia	36.87	Down 7	60	84
84	St Vincent & The Grenadines	36.84		71	85
85	Bulgaria	36.81	Down 3	75	94
86	Bosnia & Herzegovina	35.89	Up 1	86	95
87	Guam	35.70	Up 1	70	90
88	Bahamas	35.68	Up 1	84	93
89	Swaziland	35.63	Up 1	80	90
90	Tahiti	35.37	Down 4	85	90
91	Monaco	35.17	Up 1	76	93
92	Luxembourg	34.93	Up 3	67	95
93	Austria	34.55	Down 8	63	93
94	Vanuatu	33.45		89	95
95	Norway	33.03	Down 2	78	95
96=	American Samoa	30.00	*	96	96
96=	UAE	30.00	*	96	96
98	Mauritius	29.29	*Down 2	96	98
99	Finland	28.80	Down 4	93	100
100	Greece	28.49	*Down 2	96	100

* UAE, Greece, Mauritius and American Samoa entered the IRB World Rankings at 30.00 in November so climb is based on entry ranking of joint 96th.

The Numbers Game

250

The number of players to graduate from the Junior World Championship to the Test arena by the conclusion of The Rugby Championship

40

The points Canada scored on aggregate against USA to become the first direct qualifier for RWC 2015

37

Tries scored in the Six Nations (15 matches)

1

First titles won in 2013 by New Zealand (IRB Women's Sevens World Series and Women's Rugby World Cup Sevens), Ireland (Women's Six Nations), England (IRB Junior World Championship), Fiji (IRB Pacific Nations Cup) and SA President's XV (IRB Tbilisi Cup)

646

Tries scored across the inaugural IRB Women's Sevens World Series

2,082

Tries scored across the HSBC Sevens World Series 2012/13

66

Tries scored in The Rugby Championship (12 matches)

11 **Sevens World Series won by New Zealand men's team**

562,486

Record attendance for HSBC Sevens World Series in 2012/13

12

Tries scored by Portia Woodman as New Zealand women were crowned RWC Sevens champions in Moscow

28 **Nations represented by the 24 men's and 16 women's teams at RWC Sevens 2013**

1,514

Number of days since New Zealand returned to the IRB World Rankings top spot (up to end of The Rugby Championship)

13

Number of venues to host RWC 2015 matches

400,000

The number of international fans expected to visit England for RWC 2015

IRB Awards

The November internationals will provide the climax in the race to succeed New Zealand fly half Dan Carter as IRB Player of the Year, just one of a number of IRB Awards still to be presented in 2013. The Player, Coach, Team and Women's Player of the Year awards will bring the curtain down on another busy year of international rugby.

At the Rugby World Cup 2015 Pool Allocation Draw in London on 3 December 2012, Carter was named IRB Player of the Year for the second time, becoming the only player other than his captain Richie McCaw to win the prestigious award more than once. McCaw was in contention to receive the accolade for a fourth time with England fly half Owen Farrell and Frédéric Michalak of France the other nominees after one of the most competitive years of voting.

McCaw did collect the IRB Team of the Year award for the third year in succession on behalf of New Zealand, while Steve Hansen celebrated his first year as All Blacks head coach with the Coach of the Year award.

The winners were selected by the Awards' independent panel of judges, chaired by Rugby World Cup winner John Eales and made up of former internationals with more than 500 caps between them. The panel of Will Greenwood, Gavin Hastings, Raphaël Ibanez, Francois Pienaar, Agustín Pichot, Scott Quinnell, Tana Umaga, Paul Wallace and Eales deliberated on every major Test match played.

While nine of the IRB Awards for 2013 are still to be presented at the time of writing, a number of players have already seen their achievements recognised, including New Zealand Sevens duo Kayla McAlister and Tim Mikkelson and Wales Under 20 fly half Sam Davies.

McAlister was named the first IRB Women's Sevens Player of the Year after helping New Zealand win the inaugural IRB Women's Sevens World Series and Rugby World Cup Sevens double. Mikkelson was outstanding as the All Blacks Sevens won an 11th HSBC Sevens World Series crown and a first RWC Sevens since 2001 and as such was a popular recipient of the IRB Sevens Player of the Year in association with HSBC accolade.

A week before this New Zealand double in Moscow, Davies had been an integral part of the first Welsh side to reach the IRB Junior World Championship final in France, a match they lost 23–15 to England. While disappointed at losing a second title decider with England in 2013, Davies could take some comfort from being named IRB Junior Player of the Year and following in the footsteps of 2012 winner and now Springbok centre Jan Serfontein.

The IRB Referee Award for Distinguished Service was also presented during the Junior World Championship to Frenchman Michel Lamoulie, while the IRB Special Development, IRB Development, Spirit of Rugby and the Vernon Pugh Award for Distinguished Service will all be presented at the IRB World Rugby Conference and Exhibition in Dublin in November.

A number of inductions to the IRB Hall of Fame also took place in 2012 and 2013 under the theme 'Rugby – a global game', including New Zealand Sevens coach Gordon Tietjens, Fijian Sevens maestro Waisale Serevi, Japanese legend Yoshihiro Sakata and Vladimir Ilyushin, a key figure in the development of rugby in both the Soviet Union and then Russia.

IRB AWARD WINNERS 2013

IRB Sevens Player of the Year in association with HSBC: Tim Mikkelson (New Zealand)
IRB Women's Sevens Player of the Year: Kayla McAlister (New Zealand)
IRB Junior Player of the Year: Sam Davies (Wales)
IRB Referee Award for Distinguished Service: Michel Lamoulie (France)

IRB AWARD WINNERS 2012

IRB Player of the Year: Dan Carter (New Zealand)
IRB Team of the Year: New Zealand
IRB Coach of the Year: Steve Hansen (New Zealand)
IRB Women's Player of the Year: Michaela Staniford (England)
IRB Sevens Player of the Year in association with HSBC: Tomasi Cama (New Zealand)
IRB Junior Player of the Year: Jan Serfontein (South Africa)
IRB Referee Award for Distinguished Service: Paul Dobson (South Africa)
Vernon Pugh Award for Distinguished Service: Viorel Morariu (Romania)
IRB Development Award: South African Rugby Union's Capital Works Project
Spirit of Rugby Award: Lindsay Hilton (Canada)
IRPA Try of the Year: Bryan Habana (South Africa v New Zealand)

IRB Hall of Fame inductees: Gordon Tietjens, Ian and Donald Campbell, Yoshihiro Sakata, 1924 Romanian Olympic team, 1920 and 1924 USA Olympic teams, Richard and Kennedy Tsimba, Alfred St George Hamersley, Vladimir Ilyushin and Waisale Serevi

For more information on the IRB Awards and IRB Hall of Fame, visit ***www.irb.com/history*.**

RBS Six Nations: Wales

The Rugby Championship: New Zealand

RBS Women's Six Nations: Ireland

IRB Pacific Nations Cup: Fiji

IRB Nations Cup: Romania

IRB Tbilisi Cup: SA President's XV

IRB Pacific Rugby Cup: Fiji Warriors

IRB Americas Rugby Championship: Argentina Jaguars

IRB Junior World Championship: England

IRB Junior World Rugby Trophy: Italy

HSBC Sevens World Series: New Zealand

IRB Women's Sevens World Series: New Zealand

Rugby World Cup Sevens: New Zealand

Women's Rugby World Cup Sevens: New Zealand

Aviva Premiership: Leicester Tigers

Top 14: Castres Olympique

RaboDirect PRO12: Leinster

Heineken Cup: Toulon

Amlin Challenge Cup: Leinster

Super Rugby: Chiefs

International Tournaments

THE ROAD TO RUGBY WORLD CUP 2015

By Karen Bond

Canada became the first nation to emerge from the global qualification process to book their place at Rugby World Cup 2015 by beating neighbours USA 40–20 on aggregate over two legs in August. The Canucks, as the Americas 1 qualifier, will join RWC 2011 runners-up France, Ireland, Italy and the Europe 2 qualifier in Pool D for England 2015.

It was fitting that North America provided the first direct qualifier as 17 months earlier the road to RWC 2015 had kicked off in the region when Mexico hosted Jamaica in the NACRA Caribbean Championship. Eighty other nations had since entered the process and nearly 150 matches been played before Canada took the honour as the first qualifier.

Canada had enjoyed the perfect start in their first match against the Eagles after Phil Mack touched down inside 30 seconds and the 27–9 victory in Charleston ensured they went into the second leg on home soil in the driving seat with an 18-point advantage. Seven days later in Toronto, the Eagles spent much of the early exchanges camped in the Canadian 22 but were unable to turn pressure into points and ultimately lost 13–11.

"It is an amazing feeling to know that we will be there proudly representing Canada at Rugby World Cup 2015," admitted captain Aaron Carpenter. "It caps an incredible year with more Test matches and Pacific Nations Cup inclusion and I am sure it will boost rugby interest here. I am really proud of the guys."

The RWC dream is not over for USA as they now face a home and away play-off against Uruguay in 2014 to determine the Americas 2 qualifier, who will slot into Pool B with South Africa, Samoa, Scotland and the Asia 1 qualifier. The Eagles took this route to New Zealand 2011 with Uruguay going into the Répechage and ultimately falling at the final hurdle to Romania.

The next qualifiers to emerge will be Europe 1 and 2 in March 2014 after the culmination of the top tier of the European Nations Cup 2014 involving Georgia, Romania, Russia, Portugal, Spain and Belgium. See the whole process unfold at *www.rugbyworldcup.com*.

AFRICA (CAR)

(One direct place – Africa 1 – and one Répechage place)

Namibia kept alive hopes of a fifth successive Rugby World Cup appearance by beating Tunisia 45–13 in the Africa Cup Division 1B final at the Stade Iba Mar Diop in Dakar, securing promotion to the top tier for 2014 when the Africa 1 qualifier will be decider.

Standing between the Welwitschias and a place alongside defending champions New Zealand, Argentina, Tonga and the Europe 1 qualifier in Pool C at England 2015 are now African champions Kenya, Zimbabwe – who graced the RWC stage in 1991 – and Madagascar, the side that beat them 57–54 in the 2012 Division 1B final.

Forty–thousand people again packed into Mahamasina Stadium in Antananarivo in July to cheer Madagascar to a 48–32 win over Uganda which guaranteed their Division 1A status for a second year. In the final, Kenya came from behind with tries in the last 25 minutes from Edwin Otieno and Nick Barasa to beat tournament favourites Zimbabwe 29–17. "It will be a thrilling competition and I can't wait to see who books their place at Rugby World Cup 2015 to fly the flag for Africa alongside South Africa," admitted Confédération Africaine de Rugby chairman Abdelaziz Bougja.

The RWC dream will not end for the Africa Cup runner-up in 2014 as they will enter the Répechage and face the European representative.

AMERICAS (NACRA/CONSUR)

(Two direct places – Americas 1 and 2 – and one Répechage place)

Chile and Uruguay took their first steps on the road to England when they faced Brazil and the already qualified Argentina in the South American Championship in 2013. The crucial match in the round robin was always expected to be the final-day showdown between hosts Uruguay and Chile in Montevideo and so it proved after both beat Brazil and lost to Argentina.

A vociferous 5,000 strong crowd packed into Charrúa Stadium, the new home of Uruguayan rugby, to cheer on Los Teros against their traditional rivals on 4 May, but with so much at stake it proved an error-strewn affair with both teams too nervous to be adventurous. Uruguay's strength in the scrum ultimately proved decisive and they scored the only tries, through Alberto Román and captain Nicolás Klappenbach, in the 23–9 win that kept their RWC 2015 dreams alive. Uruguay last qualified for a Rugby World Cup in 2003 under the coaching of Diego Ormaechea and his two sons – Juan and Agustín – played their part in Los Teros' victory over Chile with the latter kicking 13 points.

Uruguay had to wait a couple of months to learn who their opponents would be in the play-off for the Americas 2 spot, but now find the Eagles standing in their way again after suffering back-to-back losses to neighbours Canada in the penultimate stage of qualifying in the region.

Four years ago, the Eagles had won the first leg of their series with Canada before being blown away in the second leg. This time around at the same Blackbaud Stadium, tries from Mack, Harry Jones and DTH van der Merwe, together with the boot of James Pritchard, ensured Canada had the first-leg advantage. There was to be no way back from an 18-point deficit and tries from Pritchard and Jason Marshall cancelled out Takudzwa Ngwenya's score for the Eagles to ensure it was the Canadians celebrating come the final whistle.

ASIA (ARFU)

(One direct place – Asia 1 – and one Répechage place)

RWC 2019 hosts Japan will be favourites to claim the Asia 1 berth and remain the continent's only side to play on the Rugby World Cup stage by winning what would be a seventh successive HSBC Asian 5 Nations title in 2014. The Brave Blossoms have won all 24 matches they have played in the Top 5 with a bonus point and in 2013 scored 316 points and conceded just eight, so few would bet against Japan joining South Africa, Samoa, Scotland and the Americas 2 qualifier in Pool B at England 2015.

Japan had begun their title defence in ruthless fashion against Top 5 debutants the Philippines in rain-hit Fukuoka in late April with 13 players scoring their 18 tries. There was no let-up by Eddie Jones's men with victories following over Hong Kong (38–0), Korea (64–5) and UAE (93–3).

Korea would finish runners-up after beating Hong Kong 43–22, fly half Youn Hyung Oh crossing for a hat-trick in Ansan. A repeat of this placing in 2014 will see Korea enter the Répechage and face either USA or Uruguay in the initial round.

Hong Kong, the Philippines and Division I winners Sri Lanka will join Japan and Korea in the Top 5 competition in 2014. Sri Lanka had impressively earned promotion back to Asia's top tier in early April with victories over Chinese Taipei (39–8), Thailand (45–7) and top seeds Kazakhstan (49–18) in front of their rugby-loving president Mahinda Rajapaksa – who was watching his two sons play for the national team – in Colombo.

EUROPE (FIRA-AER)

(Two direct places – Europe 1 and 2 – and one Répechage place)

Thirty-one nations have been involved in the European qualifying process, although only those in Division 1A – Georgia, Romania, Russia, Portugal, Spain and Belgium – of the European Nations Cup 2014 are in the mix for the Europe 1 and 2 direct places. Defending champions Georgia and Romania currently sit in those positions after going through the first half of the competition spanning two years unbeaten, their encounter in Bucharest in March ending in a 9–9 stalemate.

Russia are only five points adrift in third – if the Bears still occupy that position come the end of the competition in March 2014 then they will find themselves in a play-off with another European side for the right to progress to the Répechage. That side will be known after four play-off matches involving sides from the lower divisions of the European Nations Cup.

The first saw Luxembourg, the Division 2C winners in 2012/13, make the most of home advantage to overcome Division 2D representatives Slovenia 22–10 in May. They then welcomed Division 2B winners Israel to the Stade Josy Barthel but lost 26–12 in October, earning the Israelis a meeting with Division 2A winners the Netherlands a few weeks later. Whoever emerges victorious from this play-off will have to wait until April to discover the identity of their next opponent, the Division 1B winner. The matches in Division 1B, along with the top tier, will continue to double as RWC 2015 qualifiers in 2013/14 with Germany currently occupying top spot, although Poland, Moldova, Sweden and Ukraine are still in contention to earn that play-off opportunity.

OCEANIA (FORU)

(One direct place – Oceania 1)

Papua New Guinea was the venue as the last regional qualification process kicked off in July 2013 with the hosts taking on Cook Islands, Solomon Islands and Tahiti in the 2013 Oceania Cup. The winner would face Fiji in a one-off match in 2014 to determine the Oceania 1 qualifier, who will join hosts England, Australia, Wales and the Répechage winner in Pool A at RWC 2015.

The title decider was between Papua New Guinea and the Cook Islands on the final day, the latter winning a thrilling match 37–31 before a crowd of more than 7,000 in Port Moresby. The Cook Islands fought back from 12–3 down to build a 17-point lead but four tries in the last quarter by their hosts ensured a nervous finale. *@rugbyworldcup*

RUGBY WORLD CUP RECORDS 1987–2011

(FINAL STAGES ONLY)

OVERALL RECORDS

MOST MATCHES WON IN FINAL STAGES

37	New Zealand
33	Australia
30	France
29	England

MOST OVERALL PENALTIES IN FINAL STAGES

58	JP Wilkinson	England	1999–2011
36	AG Hastings	Scotland	1987–95
35	G Quesada	Argentina	1999–2003
33	MP Lynagh	Australia	1987–95
33	AP Mehrtens	New Zealand	1995–99

MOST OVERALL POINTS IN FINAL STAGES

277	JP Wilkinson	England	1999–2011
227	AG Hastings	Scotland	1987–95
195	MP Lynagh	Australia	1987–95
170	GJ Fox	New Zealand	1987–91
163	AP Mehrtens	New Zealand	1995–99

MOST OVERALL DROP GOALS IN FINAL STAGES

14	JP Wilkinson	England	1999–2011
6	JH de Beer	South Africa	1999
5	CR Andrew	England	1987–95
5	GL Rees	Canada	1987–99
4	JM Hernández	Argentina	2003–07

MOST OVERALL TRIES IN FINAL STAGES

15	JT Lomu	New Zealand	1995–99
13	DC Howlett	New Zealand	2003–07
11	R Underwood	England	1987–95
11	JT Rokocoko	New Zealand	2003–07
11	CE Latham	Australia	1999–2007
11	V Clerc	France	2007–11

MOST MATCH APPEARANCES IN FINAL STAGES

22	J Leonard	England	1991–2003
20	GM Gregan	Australia	1995–2007
19	MJ Catt	England	1995–2007
19	JP Wilkinson	England	1999–2011
18	MO Johnson	England	1995–2003
18	BP Lima	Samoa	1991–2007
18	R Ibañez	France	1999–2007
18	ME Ledesma	Argentina	1999–2011
18	LW Moody	England	2003–11

MOST OVERALL CONVERSIONS IN FINAL STAGES

39	AG Hastings	Scotland	1987–95
37	GJ Fox	New Zealand	1987–91
36	MP Lynagh	Australia	1987–95
35	DW Carter	New Zealand	2003–11
28	JP Wilkinson	England	1999–2011
27	PJ Grayson	England	1999–2003
27	SM Jones	Wales	1999–2011

LEADING SCORERS

MOST POINTS IN ONE COMPETITION

126	GJ Fox	New Zealand	1987
113	JP Wilkinson	England	2003
112	T Lacroix	France	1995
105	PC Montgomery	South Africa	2007
104	AG Hastings	Scotland	1995
103	F Michalak	France	2003
102	G Quesada	Argentina	1999
101	M Burke	Australia	1999

MOST TRIES IN ONE COMPETITION

8	JT Lomu	New Zealand	1999
8	BG Habana	South Africa	2007
7	MCG Ellis	New Zealand	1995
7	JT Lomu	New Zealand	1995
7	DC Howlett	New Zealand	2003
7	JM Muliaina	New Zealand	2003
7	DA Mitchell	Australia	2007

MOST CONVERSIONS IN ONE COMPETITION

30	GJ Fox	New Zealand	1987
22	PC Montgomery	South Africa	2007
20	SD Culhane	New Zealand	1995
20	MP Lynagh	Australia	1987
20	LR MacDonald	New Zealand	2003
20	NJ Evans	New Zealand	2007

MOST PENALTY GOALS IN ONE COMPETITION

31	G Quesada	Argentina	1999
26	T Lacroix	France	1995
23	JP Wilkinson	England	2003
21	GJ Fox	New Zealand	1987
21	EJ Flatley	Australia	2003
20	CR Andrew	England	1995

MOST DROP GOALS IN ONE COMPETITION

8	JP Wilkinson	England	2003
6	JH de Beer	South Africa	1999
5	JP Wilkinson	England	2007
4	JM Hernández	Argentina	2007

MOST POINTS IN A MATCH

BY A TEAM

145	New Zealand v Japan	1995
142	Australia v Namibia	2003
111	England v Uruguay	2003
108	New Zealand v Portugal	2007
101	New Zealand v Italy	1999
101	England v Tonga	1999

BY A PLAYER

45	SD Culhane	New Zealand v Japan	1995
44	AG Hastings	Scotland v Ivory Coast	1995
42	MS Rogers	Australia v Namibia	2003
36	TE Brown	New Zealand v Italy	1999
36	PJ Grayson	England v Tonga	1999
34	JH de Beer	South Africa v England	1999
33	NJ Evans	New Zealand v Portugal	2007
32	JP Wilkinson	England v Italy	1999

MOST CONVERSIONS IN A MATCH

BY A TEAM

20	New Zealand v Japan	1995
16	Australia v Namibia	2003
14	New Zealand v Portugal	2007
13	New Zealand v Tonga	2003
13	England v Uruguay	2003

BY A PLAYER

20	SD Culhane	New Zealand v Japan	1995
16	MS Rogers	Australia v Namibia	2003
14	NJ Evans	New Zealand v Portugal	2007
12	PJ Grayson	England v Tonga	1999
12	LR MacDonald	New Zealand v Tonga	2003

MOST TRIES IN A MATCH

BY A TEAM

22	Australia v Namibia	2003
21	New Zealand v Japan	1995
17	England v Uruguay	2003
16	New Zealand v Portugal	2007
14	New Zealand v Italy	1999

BY A PLAYER

6	MCG Ellis	New Zealand v Japan	1995
5	CE Latham	Australia v Namibia	2003
5	OJ Lewsey	England v Uruguay	2003
4	IC Evans	Wales v Canada	1987
4	CI Green	New Zealand v Fiji	1987
4	JA Gallagher	New Zealand v Fiji	1987
4	BF Robinson	Ireland v Zimbabwe	1991
4	AG Hastings	Scotland v Ivory Coast	1995
4	CM Williams	South Africa v Western Samoa	1995
4	JT Lomu	New Zealand v England	1995
4	KGM Wood	Ireland v United States	1999
4	JM Muliaina	New Zealand v Canada	2003
4	BG Habana	South Africa v Samoa	2007
4	V Goneva	Fiji v Namibia	2011
4	ZR Guildford	New Zealand v Canada	2011

MOST PENALTY GOALS IN A MATCH

BY A TEAM

8	Australia v South Africa	1999
8	Argentina v Samoa	1999
8	Scotland v Tonga	1995
8	France v Ireland	1995

BY A PLAYER

8	M Burke	Australia v South Africa	1999
8	G Quesada	Argentina v Samoa	1999
8	AG Hastings	Scotland v Tonga	1995
8	T Lacroix	France v Ireland	1995

MOST DROP GOALS IN A MATCH

BY A TEAM

5	South Africa v England	1999
3	Fiji v Romania	1991
3	England v France	2003
3	Argentina v Ireland	2007
3	Namibia v Fiji	2011

BY A PLAYER

5	JH de Beer	South Africa v England	1999
3	JP Wilkinson	England v France	2003
3	JM Hernández	Argentina v Ireland	2007
3	TAW Kotze	Namibia v Fiji	2011

Argentina's Gonzalo Quesada kicks one of eight penalty goals against Samoa at RWC 1999.

Hulton Archive/Getty Images

FIRST TOURNAMENT: 1987 IN AUSTRALIA & NEW ZEALAND

POOL 1

Australia	19	England	6
USA	21	Japan	18
England	60	Japan	7
Australia	47	USA	12
England	34	USA	6
Australia	42	Japan	23

	P	W	D	L	F	A	Pts
Australia	3	3	0	0	108	41	6
England	3	2	0	1	100	32	4
USA	3	1	0	2	39	99	2
Japan	3	0	0	3	48	123	0

POOL 3

New Zealand	70	Italy	6
Fiji	28	Argentina	9
New Zealand	74	Fiji	13
Argentina	25	Italy	16
Italy	18	Fiji	15
New Zealand	46	Argentina	15

	P	W	D	L	F	A	Pts
New Zealand	3	3	0	0	190	34	6
Fiji	3	1	0	2	56	101	2
Argentina	3	1	0	2	49	90	2
Italy	3	1	0	2	40	110	2

POOL 2

Canada	37	Tonga	4
Wales	13	Ireland	6
Wales	29	Tonga	16
Ireland	46	Canada	19
Wales	40	Canada	9
Ireland	32	Tonga	9

	P	W	D	L	F	A	Pts
Wales	3	3	0	0	82	31	6
Ireland	3	2	0	1	84	41	4
Canada	3	1	0	2	65	90	2
Tonga	3	0	0	3	29	98	0

POOL 4

Romania	21	Zimbabwe	20
France	20	Scotland	20
France	55	Romania	12
Scotland	60	Zimbabwe	21
France	70	Zimbabwe	12
Scotland	55	Romania	28

	P	W	D	L	F	A	Pts
France	3	2	1	0	145	44	5
Scotland	3	2	1	0	135	69	5
Romania	3	1	0	2	61	130	2
Zimbabwe	3	0	0	3	53	151	0

QUARTER-FINALS

New Zealand	30	Scotland	3
France	31	Fiji	16
Australia	33	Ireland	15
Wales	16	England	3

SEMI-FINALS

France	30	Australia	24
New Zealand	49	Wales	6

THIRD PLACE MATCH

Wales	22	Australia	21

First Rugby World Cup Final, Eden Park, Auckland, 20 June 1987

NEW ZEALAND 29 (1G 2T 4PG 1DG)
FRANCE 9 (1G 1PG)

NEW ZEALAND: JA Gallagher; JJ Kirwan, JT Stanley, WT Taylor, CI Green; GJ Fox, DE Kirk (*captain*); SC McDowell, SBT Fitzpatrick, JA Drake, MJ Pierce, GW Whetton, AJ Whetton, MN Jones, WT Shelford **SCORERS:** *Tries:* Jones, Kirk, Kirwan *Conversion:* Fox *Penalty Goals:* Fox (4) *Drop Goal:* Fox

FRANCE: S Blanco; D Camberabero, P Sella, D Charvet, P Lagisquet; F Mesnel, P Berbizier; P Ondarts, D Dubroca (*captain*), J-P Garuet, A Lorieux, J Condom, E Champ, D Erbani, L Rodriguez

SCORERS: *Try:* Berbizier *Conversion:* Camberabero *Penalty Goal:* Camberabero

REFEREE: KVJ Fitzgerald (Australia)

SECOND TOURNAMENT: 1991 IN BRITAIN, IRELAND & FRANCE

POOL 1

New Zealand	18	**England**	12
Italy	30	**USA**	9
New Zealand	46	**USA**	6
England	36	**Italy**	6
England	37	**USA**	9
New Zealand	31	**Italy**	21

	P	W	D	L	F	A	Pts
New Zealand	3	3	0	0	95	39	9
England	3	2	0	1	85	33	7
Italy	3	1	0	2	57	76	5
USA	3	0	0	3	24	113	3

POOL 2

Scotland	47	**Japan**	9
Ireland	55	**Zimbabwe**	11
Ireland	32	**Japan**	16
Scotland	51	**Zimbabwe**	12
Scotland	24	**Ireland**	15
Japan	52	**Zimbabwe**	8

	P	W	D	L	F	A	Pts
Scotland	3	3	0	0	122	36	9
Ireland	3	2	0	1	102	51	7
Japan	3	1	0	2	77	87	5
Zimbabwe	3	0	0	3	31	158	3

POOL 3

Australia	32	**Argentina**	19
Western Samoa	16	**Wales**	13
Australia	9	**Western Samoa**	3
Wales	16	**Argentina**	7
Australia	38	**Wales**	3
Western Samoa	35	**Argentina**	12

	P	W	D	L	F	A	Pts
Australia	3	3	0	0	79	25	9
Western Samoa	3	2	0	1	54	34	7
Wales	3	1	0	2	32	61	5
Argentina	3	0	0	3	38	83	3

POOL 4

France	30	**Romania**	3
Canada	13	**Fiji**	3
France	33	**Fiji**	9
Canada	19	**Romania**	11
Romania	17	**Fiji**	15
France	19	**Canada**	13

	P	W	D	L	F	A	Pts
France	3	3	0	0	82	25	9
Canada	3	2	0	1	45	33	7
Romania	3	1	0	2	31	64	5
Fiji	3	0	0	3	27	63	3

QUARTER-FINALS

England	19	**France**	10
Scotland	28	**Western Samoa**	6
Australia	19	**Ireland**	18
New Zealand	29	**Canada**	13

SEMI-FINALS

England	9	**Scotland**	6
Australia	16	**New Zealand**	6

THIRD PLACE MATCH

New Zealand	13	**Scotland**	6

Second Rugby World Cup Final, Twickenham, London, 2 November 1991

AUSTRALIA 12 (1G 2PG) ENGLAND 6 (2PG)

AUSTRALIA: MC Roebuck; DI Campese, JS Little, TJ Horan, RH Egerton; MP Lynagh, NC Farr-Jones (*captain*); AJ Daly, PN Kearns, EJA McKenzie, RJ McCall, JA Eales, SP Poidevin, V Ofahengaue, T Coker

SCORERS *Try:* Daly *Conversion:* Lynagh *Penalty Goals:* Lynagh (2)

ENGLAND: JM Webb; SJ Halliday, WDC Carling (*captain*), JC Guscott, R Underwood; CR Andrew, RJ Hill; J Leonard, BC Moore, JA Probyn, PJ Ackford, WA Dooley, MG Skinner, PJ Winterbottom, MC Teague

SCORER: *Penalty Goals:* Webb (2)

REFEREE: WD Bevan (Wales)

THIRD TOURNAMENT: 1995 IN SOUTH AFRICA

POOL A

South Africa	27	Australia	18
Canada	34	Romania	3
South Africa	21	Romania	8
Australia	27	Canada	11
Australia	42	Romania	3
South Africa	20	Canada	0

	P	W	D	L	F	A	Pts
South Africa	3	3	0	0	68	26	9
Australia	3	2	0	1	87	41	7
Canada	3	1	0	2	45	50	5
Romania	3	0	0	3	14	97	3

POOL B

Western Samoa	42	Italy	18
England	24	Argentina	18
Western Samoa	32	Argentina	26
England	27	Italy	20
Italy	31	Argentina	25
England	44	Western Samoa	22

	P	W	D	L	F	A	Pts
England	3	3	0	0	95	60	9
Western Samoa	3	2	0	1	96	88	7
Italy	3	1	0	2	69	94	5
Argentina	3	0	0	3	69	87	3

POOL C

Wales	57	Japan	10
New Zealand	43	Ireland	19
Ireland	50	Japan	28
New Zealand	34	Wales	9
New Zealand	145	Japan	17
Ireland	24	Wales	23

	P	W	D	L	F	A	Pts
New Zealand	3	3	0	0	222	45	9
Ireland	3	2	0	1	93	94	7
Wales	3	1	0	2	89	68	5
Japan	3	0	0	3	55	252	3

POOL D

Scotland	89	Ivory Coast	0
France	38	Tonga	10
France	54	Ivory Coast	18
Scotland	41	Tonga	5
Tonga	29	Ivory Coast	11
France	22	Scotland	19

	P	W	D	L	F	A	Pts
France	3	3	0	0	114	47	9
Scotland	3	2	0	1	149	27	7
Tonga	3	1	0	2	44	90	5
Ivory Coast	3	0	0	3	29	172	3

QUARTER-FINALS

France	36	Ireland	12
South Africa	42	Western Samoa	14
England	25	Australia	22
New Zealand	48	Scotland	30

SEMI-FINALS

South Africa	19	France	15
New Zealand	45	England	29

THIRD PLACE MATCH

France	19	England	9

Third Rugby World Cup Final, Ellis Park, Johannesburg, 24 June 1995

SOUTH AFRICA 15 (3PG 2DG)
NEW ZEALAND 12 (3PG 1DG) *

SOUTH AFRICA: AJ Joubert; JT Small, JC Mulder, HP Le Roux, CM Williams; JT Stransky, JH van der Westhuizen; JP du Randt, CLC Rossouw, IS Swart, JJ Wiese, JJ Strydom, JF Pienaar (*captain*), RJ Kruger, MG Andrews

SUBSTITUTIONS: GL Pagel for Swart (68 mins); RAW Straeuli for Andrews (90 mins); B Venter for Small (97 mins)

SCORER: *Penalty Goals:* Stransky (3) *Drop Goals:* Stransky (2)

NEW ZEALAND: GM Osborne; JW Wilson, FE Bunce, WK Little, JT Lomu; AP Mehrtens, GTM Bachop; CW Dowd, SBT Fitzpatrick (*captain*), OM Brown, ID Jones, RM Brooke, MR Brewer, JA Kronfeld, ZV Brooke

SUBSTITUTIONS: JW Joseph for Brewer (40 mins); MCG Ellis for Wilson (55 mins); RW Loe for Dowd (83 mins); AD Strachan for Bachop (temp 66 to 71 mins)

SCORER: *Penalty Goals:* Mehrtens (3) *Drop Goal:* Mehrtens

REFEREE: EF Morrison (England)

* *after extra time: 9–9 after normal time*

Hulton Archive/Getty Images

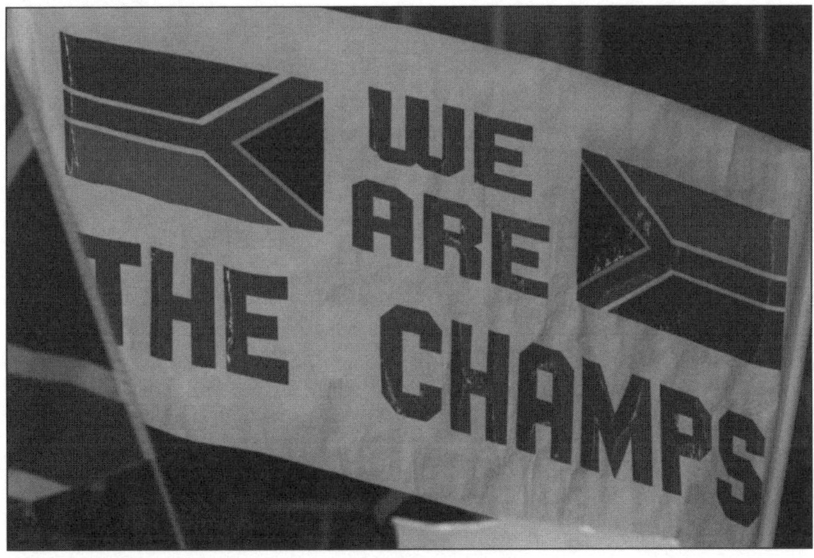

A South African flag sums up the feelings of a nation after the win over New Zealand.

FOURTH TOURNAMENT: 1999 IN BRITAIN, IRELAND & FRANCE

POOL A

Spain	15	**Uruguay**	27
South Africa	46	**Scotland**	29
Scotland	43	**Uruguay**	12
South Africa	47	**Spain**	3
South Africa	39	**Uruguay**	3
Scotland	48	**Spain**	0

	P	W	D	L	F	A	Pts
South Africa	3	3	0	0	132	35	9
Scotland	3	2	0	1	120	58	7
Uruguay	3	1	0	2	42	97	5
Spain	3	0	0	3	18	122	3

POOL B

England	67	**Italy**	7
New Zealand	45	**Tonga**	9
England	16	**New Zealand**	30
Italy	25	**Tonga**	28
New Zealand	101	**Italy**	3
England	101	**Tonga**	10

	P	W	D	L	F	A	Pts
New Zealand	3	3	0	0	176	28	9
England	3	2	0	1	184	47	7
Tonga	3	1	0	2	47	171	5
Italy	3	0	0	3	35	196	3

POOL C

Fiji	67	**Namibia**	18
France	33	**Canada**	20
France	47	**Namibia**	13
Fiji	38	**Canada**	22
Canada	72	**Namibia**	11
France	28	**Fiji**	19

	P	W	D	L	F	A	Pts
France	3	3	0	0	108	52	9
Fiji	3	2	0	1	124	68	7
Canada	3	1	0	2	114	82	5
Namibia	3	0	0	3	42	186	3

POOL D

Wales	23	**Argentina**	18
Samoa	43	**Japan**	9
Wales	64	**Japan**	15
Argentina	32	**Samoa**	16
Wales	31	**Samoa**	38
Argentina	33	**Japan**	12

	P	W	D	L	F	A	Pts
Wales	3	2	0	1	118	71	7
Samoa	3	2	0	1	97	72	7
Argentina	3	2	0	1	83	51	7
Japan	3	0	0	3	36	140	3

POOL E

Ireland	53	**United States**	8
Australia	57	**Romania**	9
United States	25	**Romania**	27
Ireland	3	**Australia**	23
Australia	55	**United States**	19
Ireland	44	**Romania**	14

	P	W	D	L	F	A	Pts
Australia	3	3	0	0	135	31	9
Ireland	3	2	0	1	100	45	7
Romania	3	1	0	2	50	126	5
United States	3	0	0	3	52	135	3

PLAY-OFFS FOR QUARTER-FINAL PLACES

England	45	**Fiji**	24
Scotland	35	**Samoa**	20
Ireland	24	**Argentina**	28

QUARTER-FINALS

Wales	9	**Australia**	24
South Africa	44	**England**	21
France	47	**Argentina**	26
Scotland	18	**New Zealand**	30

SEMI-FINALS

South Africa	21	**Australia**	27
New Zealand	31	**France**	43

THIRD PLACE MATCH

South Africa	22	**New Zealand**	18

Fourth Rugby World Cup Final, Millennium Stadium, Cardiff, 6 November 1999

AUSTRALIA 35 (2G 7PG) FRANCE 12 (4PG)

AUSTRALIA: M Burke; BN Tune, DJ Herbert, TJ Horan, JW Roff; SJ Larkham, GM Gregan; RLL Harry, MA Foley, AT Blades, DT Giffin, JA Eales (*captain*), MJ Cockbain, DJ Wilson, RST Kefu

SUBSTITUTIONS: JS Little for Herbert (46 mins); ODA Finegan for Cockbain (52 mins); MR Connors for Wilson (73 mins); DJ Crowley for Harry (75 mins); JA Paul for Foley (85 mins); CJ Whitaker for Gregan (86 mins); NP Grey for Horan (86 mins)

SCORERS: *Tries:* Tune, Finegan *Conversions:* Burke (2) *Penalty Goals:* Burke (7)

FRANCE: X Garbajosa; P Bernat Salles, R Dourthe, E Ntamack, C Dominici; C Lamaison, F Galthié; C Soulette, R Ibañez (*captain*), F Tournaire, A Benazzi, F Pelous, M Lièvremont, O Magne, C Juillet

SUBSTITUTIONS: O Brouzet for Juillet (HT); P de Villiers for Soulette (47 mins); A Costes for Magne (temp 19 to 22 mins) and for Lièvremont (67 mins); U Mola for Garbajosa (67 mins); S Glas for Dourthe (temp 49 to 55 mins and from 74 mins); S Castaignède for Galthié (76 mins); M Dal Maso for Ibañez (79 mins)

SCORER: *Penalty Goals:* Lamaison (4)

REFEREE: AJ Watson (South Africa)

AFP/Getty Images

Australia captain John Eales and his team-mates celebrate Ben Tune's try in the final against France.

FIFTH TOURNAMENT: 2003 IN AUSTRALIA

POOL A

Australia	24	Argentina	8
Ireland	45	Romania	17
Argentina	67	Namibia	14
Australia	90	Romania	8
Ireland	64	Namibia	7
Argentina	50	Romania	3
Australia	142	Namibia	0
Ireland	16	Argentina	15
Romania	37	Namibia	7
Australia	17	Ireland	16

	P	W	D	L	F	A	Pts
Australia	4	4	0	0	273	32	18
Ireland	4	3	0	1	141	56	15
Argentina	4	2	0	2	140	57	11
Romania	4	1	0	3	65	192	5
Namibia	4	0	0	4	28	310	0

POOL C

South Africa	72	Uruguay	6
England	84	Georgia	6
Samoa	60	Uruguay	13
England	25	South Africa	6
Samoa	46	Georgia	9
South Africa	46	Georgia	19
England	35	Samoa	22
Uruguay	24	Georgia	12
South Africa	60	Samoa	10
England	111	Uruguay	13

	P	W	D	L	F	A	Pts
England	4	4	0	0	255	47	19
South Africa	4	3	0	1	184	60	15
Samoa	4	2	0	2	138	117	10
Uruguay	4	1	0	3	56	255	4
Georgia	4	0	0	4	46	200	0

POOL B

France	61	Fiji	18
Scotland	32	Japan	11
Fiji	19	United States	18
France	51	Japan	29
Scotland	39	United States	15
Fiji	41	Japan	13
France	51	Scotland	9
United States	39	Japan	26
France	41	United States	14
Scotland	22	Fiji	20

	P	W	D	L	F	A	Pts
France	4	4	0	0	204	70	20
Scotland	4	3	0	1	102	97	14
Fiji	4	2	0	2	98	114	10
United States	4	1	0	3	86	125	6
Japan	4	0	0	4	79	163	0

POOL D

New Zealand	70	Italy	7
Wales	41	Canada	10
Italy	36	Tonga	12
New Zealand	68	Canada	6
Wales	27	Tonga	20
Italy	19	Canada	14
New Zealand	91	Tonga	7
Wales	27	Italy	15
Canada	24	Tonga	7
New Zealand	53	Wales	37

	P	W	D	L	F	A	Pts
New Zealand	4	4	0	0	282	57	20
Wales	4	3	0	1	132	98	14
Italy	4	2	0	2	77	123	8
Canada	4	1	0	3	54	135	5
Tonga	4	0	0	4	46	178	1

QUARTER-FINALS

New Zealand	29	South Africa	9
Australia	33	Scotland	16
France	43	Ireland	21
England	28	Wales	17

SEMI-FINALS

Australia	22	New Zealand	10
England	24	France	7

THIRD PLACE MATCH

New Zealand	40	France	13

Fifth Rugby World Cup Final, Telstra Stadium, Sydney, 22 November 2003

ENGLAND 20 (1T 4PG 1DG)
AUSTRALIA 17 (1T 4PG) *

ENGLAND: JT Robinson; OJ Lewsey, WJH Greenwood, MJ Tindall, BC Cohen; JP Wilkinson, MJS Dawson; TJ Woodman, SG Thompson, PJ Vickery, MO Johnson (*captain*), BJ Kay, RA Hill, NA Back, LBN Dallaglio

SUBSTITUTIONS: MJ Catt for Tindall (78 mins); J Leonard for Vickery (80 mins); IR Balshaw for Lewsey (85 mins); LW Moody for Hill (93 mins)

SCORERS: *Try:* Robinson *Penalty Goals:* Wilkinson (4) *Drop Goal:* Wilkinson

AUSTRALIA: MS Rogers; WJ Sailor, SA Mortlock, EJ Flatley, L Tuqiri; SJ Larkham, GM Gregan (*captain*); WK Young, BJ Cannon, AKE Baxter, JB Harrison, NC Sharpe, GB Smith, DJ Lyons, PR Waugh

SUBSTITUTIONS: DT Giffin for Sharpe (48 mins); JA Paul for Cannon (56 mins); MJ Cockbain for Lyons (56 mins); JW Roff for Sailor (70 mins); MJ Dunning for Young (92 mins); MJ Giteau for Larkham (temp 18 to 30 mins; 55 to 63 mins; 85 to 93 mins)

SCORERS: *Try*: Tuqiri *Penalty Goals*: Flatley (4)

REFEREE: AJ Watson (South Africa)

* *after extra time: 14–14 after normal time*

Getty Images

Ben Cohen celebrates as Jason Robinson dives over in the corner to score England's only try of the final.

SIXTH TOURNAMENT: 2007 IN FRANCE, WALES & SCOTLAND

POOL A

England	28	**USA**	10
South Africa	59	**Samoa**	7
USA	15	**Tonga**	25
England	0	**South Africa**	36
Samoa	15	**Tonga**	19
South Africa	30	**Tonga**	25
England	44	**Samoa**	22
Samoa	25	**USA**	21
England	36	**Tonga**	20
South Africa	64	**USA**	15

	P	W	D	L	F	A	Pts
South Africa	4	4	0	0	189	47	19
England	4	3	0	1	108	88	14
Tonga	4	2	0	2	89	96	9
Samoa	4	1	0	3	69	143	5
USA	4	0	0	4	61	142	1

POOL C

New Zealand	76	**Italy**	14
Scotland	56	**Portugal**	10
Italy	24	**Romania**	18
New Zealand	108	**Portugal**	13
Scotland	42	**Romania**	0
Italy	31	**Portugal**	5
Scotland	0	**New Zealand**	40
Romania	14	**Portugal**	10
New Zealand	85	**Romania**	8
Scotland	18	**Italy**	16

	P	W	D	L	F	A	Pts
New Zealand	4	4	0	0	309	35	20
Scotland	4	3	0	1	116	66	14
Italy	4	2	0	2	85	117	9
Romania	4	1	0	3	40	161	5
Portugal	4	0	0	4	38	209	1

POOL B

Australia	91	**Japan**	3
Wales	42	**Canada**	17
Japan	31	**Fiji**	35
Wales	20	**Australia**	32
Fiji	29	**Canada**	16
Wales	72	**Japan**	18
Australia	55	**Fiji**	12
Canada	12	**Japan**	12
Australia	37	**Canada**	6
Wales	34	**Fiji**	38

	P	W	D	L	F	A	Pts
Australia	4	4	0	0	215	41	20
Fiji	4	3	0	1	114	136	15
Wales	4	2	0	2	168	105	12
Japan	4	0	1	3	64	210	3
Canada	4	0	1	3	51	120	2

POOL D

France	12	**Argentina**	17
Ireland	32	**Namibia**	17
Argentina	33	**Georgia**	3
Ireland	14	**Georgia**	10
France	87	**Namibia**	10
France	25	**Ireland**	3
Argentina	63	**Namibia**	3
Georgia	30	**Namibia**	0
France	64	**Georgia**	7
Ireland	15	**Argentina**	30

	P	W	D	L	F	A	Pts
Argentina	4	4	0	0	143	33	18
France	4	3	0	1	188	37	15
Ireland	4	2	0	2	64	82	9
Georgia	4	1	0	3	50	111	5
Namibia	4	0	0	4	30	212	0

QUARTER-FINALS

Australia	10	**England**	12
New Zealand	18	**France**	20
South Africa	37	**Fiji**	20
Argentina	19	**Scotland**	13

SEMI-FINALS

France	9	**England**	14
South Africa	37	**Argentina**	13

BRONZE FINAL

France	10	**Argentina**	34

Sixth Rugby World Cup Final, Stade de France, Paris, 20 October 2007

SOUTH AFRICA 15 (5PG) ENGLAND 6 (2PG)

SOUTH AFRICA: PC Montgomery; J-PR Pietersen, J Fourie, FPL Steyn, BG Habana; AD James, PF du Preez; JP du Randt, JW Smit (*captain*), CJ van der Linde, JP Botha, V Matfield, JH Smith, SWP Burger, DJ Rossouw

SUBSTITUTIONS: JL van Heerden for Rossouw (72 mins); BW du Plessis for Smit (temp 71 to 76 mins)

SCORERS: *Penalty Goals*: Montgomery (4), Steyn

ENGLAND: JT Robinson; PH Sackey, MJM Tait, MJ Catt, MJ Cueto; JP Wilkinson, ACT Gomarsall; AJ Sheridan, MP Regan, PJ Vickery (*captain*), SD Shaw, BJ Kay, ME Corry, LW Moody, NJ Easter

SUBSTITUTIONS: MJH Stevens for Vickery (40 mins); DJ Hipkiss for Robinson (46 mins); TGAL Flood for Catt (50 mins); GS Chuter for Regan (62 mins); JPR Worsley for Moody (62 mins); LBN Dallaglio for Easter (64 mins); PC Richards for Worsley (70 mins)

SCORER: *Penalty Goals*: Wilkinson (2)

REFEREE: AC Rolland (Ireland)

Getty Images

South Africa President Thabo Mbeki is hoisted into the air by the victorious Springboks team.

SEVENTH TOURNAMENT: 2011 IN NEW ZEALAND

POOL A

New Zealand	41	Tonga	10
France	47	Japan	21
Tonga	20	Canada	25
New Zealand	83	Japan	7
France	46	Canada	19
Tonga	31	Japan	18
New Zealand	37	France	17
Canada	23	Japan	23
France	14	Tonga	19
New Zealand	79	Canada	15

	P	W	D	L	F	A	Pts
New Zealand	4	4	0	0	240	49	20
France	4	2	0	2	124	96	11
Tonga	4	2	0	2	80	98	9
Canada	4	1	1	2	82	168	6
Japan	4	0	1	3	69	184	1

POOL C

Australia	32	Italy	6
Ireland	22	USA	10
Russia	6	USA	13
Australia	6	Ireland	15
Italy	53	Russia	17
Australia	67	USA	5
Ireland	62	Russia	12
Italy	27	USA	10
Australia	68	Russia	22
Ireland	36	Italy	6

	P	W	D	L	F	A	Pts
Ireland	4	4	0	0	135	34	17
Australia	4	3	0	1	173	48	15
Italy	4	2	0	2	92	95	10
USA	4	1	0	3	38	122	4
Russia	4	0	0	4	57	196	1

POOL B

Scotland	34	Romania	24
Argentina	9	England	13
Scotland	15	Georgia	6
Argentina	43	Romania	8
England	41	Georgia	10
England	67	Romania	3
Argentina	13	Scotland	12
Georgia	25	Romania	9
England	16	Scotland	12
Argentina	25	Georgia	7

	P	W	D	L	F	A	Pts
England	4	4	0	0	137	34	18
Argentina	4	3	0	1	90	40	14
Scotland	4	2	0	2	73	59	11
Georgia	4	1	0	3	48	90	4
Romania	4	0	0	4	44	169	0

POOL D

Fiji	49	Namibia	25
South Africa	17	Wales	16
Samoa	49	Namibia	12
South Africa	49	Fiji	3
Wales	17	Samoa	10
South Africa	87	Namibia	0
Fiji	7	Samoa	27
Wales	81	Namibia	7
South Africa	13	Samoa	5
Wales	66	Fiji	0

	P	W	D	L	F	A	Pts
South Africa	4	4	0	0	166	24	18
Wales	4	3	0	1	180	34	15
Samoa	4	2	0	2	91	49	10
Fiji	4	1	0	3	59	167	5
Namibia	4	0	0	4	44	266	0

QUARTER-FINALS

Ireland	10	Wales	22
England	12	France	19
South Africa	9	Australia	11
New Zealand	33	Argentina	10

SEMI-FINALS

Wales	8	France	9
Australia	6	New Zealand	20

BRONZE FINAL

Australia	21	Wales	18

Seventh Rugby World Cup Final, Eden Park, Auckland, 23 October 2011

NEW ZEALAND 8 (1T 1PG) FRANCE 7 (1G)

NEW ZEALAND: IJA Dagg; CS Jane, CG Smith, MA Nonu, RD Kahui; AW Cruden, PAT Weepu; TD Woodcock, KF Mealamu, OT Franks, BC Thorn, SL Whitelock, J Kaino, RH McCaw (*captain*), KJ Read

SUBSTITUTIONS: SR Donald for Cruden (33 mins); AJ Williams for Whitelock (48 mins); AK Hore for Mealamu (48 mins); AM Ellis for Weepu (49 mins); S Williams for Nonu (75 mins)

SCORERS: *Try*: Woodcock *Penalty Goal*: Donald

FRANCE: M Médard; V Clerc, A Rougerie, M Mermoz, A Palisson; M Parra, D Yachvili; J-B Poux, W Servat, N Mas, P Papé, L Nallet, T Dusautoir (*captain*), J Bonnaire, I Harinordoquy,

SUBSTITUTIONS: F Trinh-Duc for Parra (temp 11 to 17 mins and 22 mins); D Traille for Clerc (45 mins); D Szarzewski for Servat (64 mins); F Barcella for Poux (64 mins); J Pierre for Papé (69 mins); J-M Doussain for Yachvili (75 mins)

SCORERS: *Try*: Dusautoir *Conversion:* Trinh-Duc

REFEREE: C Joubert (South Africa)

Getty Images

Twenty-four years after their first RWC success, the All Blacks treat their fans to one final haka.

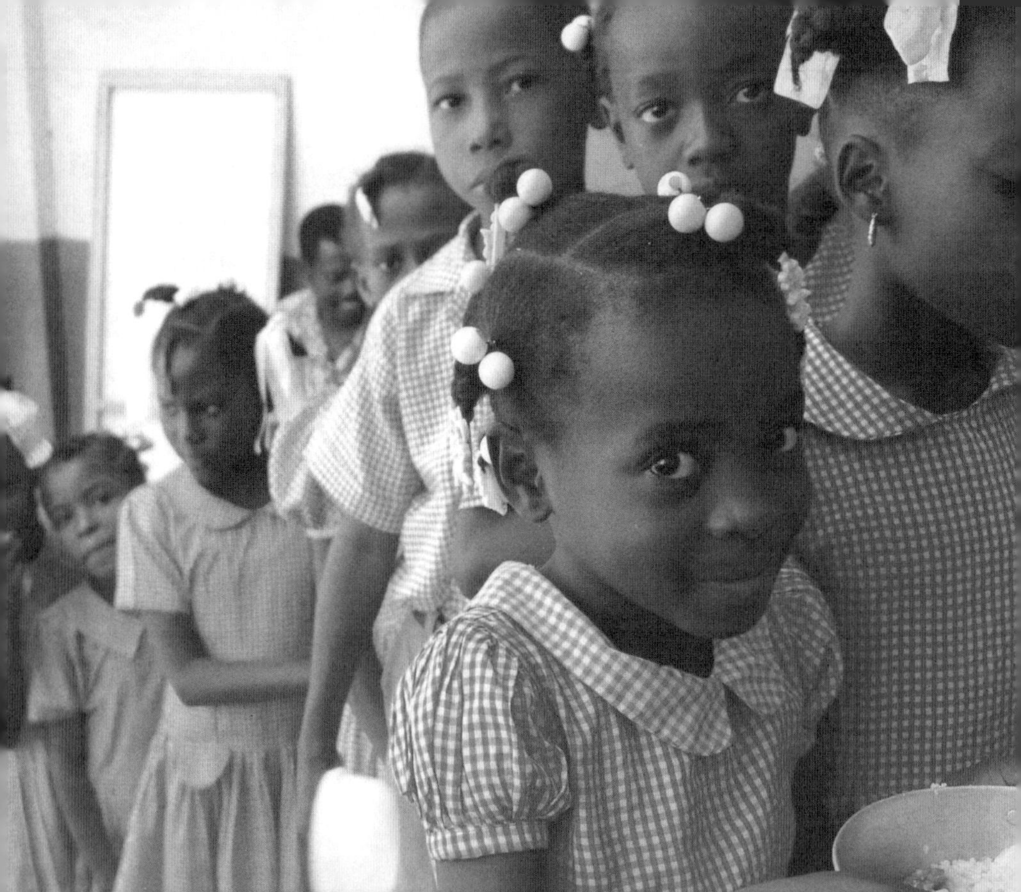

Their future is in your hands.

Your donation can make all the difference to these children.

Every year, the United Nations World Food Programme provides meals to millions of children around the world.

Together with partners like the International Rugby Board, WFP can change young lives forever.

Help us to tackle hunger: wfp.org/donate/tacklehunger

TACKLE HUNGER

The United Nations World Food Programme is the humanitarian partner of the IRB

TRANSFORMED WALES DEFEND SIX NATIONS CROWN

By Iain Spragg

Getty Images

Alex Cuthbert and Jonathan Davies celebrate after Wales retained the RBS Six Nations title.

Wales may have embarked on their RBS Six Nations campaign in disarray but they finished the 119th instalment of the tournament in spectacular style, crushing England in Cardiff in a dazzling denouement that saw them retain their crown and deny Stuart Lancaster's side the coveted Grand Slam.

A record-breaking 30–3 romp inside a vociferous Millennium Stadium secured Wales a third title in six seasons, their first back-to-back triumphs since 1979 and, after a miserable November series, redemption was at hand.

The omens at the beginning of the competition were far from encouraging. Decimated by injury and with head coach Warren Gatland on sabbatical with the British & Irish Lions, Wales lost seven successive Tests ahead of the Six Nations and in November they reached a demoralising nadir in the shape of a 26–19 defeat to Samoa in Cardiff. Just four months later they were champions of the northern hemisphere for a second time in 12 months.

"We kept on sending the message that good teams don't become bad teams overnight," said interim head coach Rob Howley after his side's stunning victory in Cardiff. "We were consistent with that message and the players have gone out and delivered.

"This is better than the Grand Slam last year. The players have shown great fortitude and they outclassed England and it's probably the best day of my coaching career to be honest. I'm just really proud to be a Welshman this evening."

The opening weekend of the Six Nations in February provided few clues to the impending Welsh renaissance. A 30–22 defeat to Ireland at the Millennium Stadium was certainly chastening but, having trailed 30–3 early in the second half, the defeat could have been significantly heavier.

In contrast, England began the Championship in explosive form with a 38–18 victory over Scotland at Twickenham, scoring four tries in a performance brimming with confidence and attacking ambition. France's shock 23–18 loss to Italy in Rome the following day completed the opening exchanges and, as early as it was in the tournament, England were promptly installed as favourites.

Wales' prospects of ending their eight-game losing streak a week later against France in Paris seemed remote. Captain Sam Warburton was ruled out with a shoulder injury and, stung by criticism of their performance against the Azzurri, many expected a brutal backlash from Les Bleus.

The reality was Howley's stubborn side were always in contention in the Stade de France and with the two sides locked at 6–6 in the 71st minute, it was wing George North who supplied the coup de grace when he collected Dan Biggar's chip to crash over for the only try of the match. Wales emerged 16–6 winners and finally had their first Test win since beating the French in Cardiff 11 months earlier.

"It was by no means a flawless display," admitted stand-in captain Ryan Jones. "There were a lot of errors there but the character and die-hard spirit was something special. Hopefully we'll kick on from here because winning is a habit and we've got the monkey off our back now."

On the same weekend, Italy were brought unceremoniously back down to earth with a 34–10 defeat against Scotland at Murrayfield while England maintained their momentum, if not their expansive style, with an attritional 12–6 win against Ireland at the Aviva Stadium, the side's first success in Dublin for a decade.

A fortnight's hiatus gave the six protagonists time to reflect and regroup and when battle recommenced it was England and Wales who both laid down convincing markers for the remainder of the tournament.

England entertained France at Twickenham and, despite a sublime solo try from Wesley Fofana for the visitors, the home side proved too strong. The reliable boot of Owen Farrell and an opportunistic second-half score from Manu Tuilagi completed a 23–13 victory and the third leg of a possible Grand Slam.

"It was a proper Test match," Lancaster said after the game. "That wasn't the France team that played a couple of weeks ago. That was a really strong, well-motivated French team who caused us a lot of problems in all sorts of areas.

"We're young in terms of age. There's a lot of 22 to 24-year-olds out there and I thought the players showed a lot of maturity. Our substitutes made a big difference when they came on and that closed the game out."

Wales headed to Italy to face Jacques Brunel's side at the Stadio Olimpico with Howley retaining the same starting XV that had despatched the French, and his faith was handsomely rewarded with a 26–9 win in Rome courtesy of converted tries from Jonathan Davies and Alex Cuthbert.

A day later Scotland beat Ireland 12–8 in Edinburgh but, with three games gone, the fight for the silverware was looking increasingly like a two-horse race.

That perception was significantly strengthened in March when Wales travelled to Murrayfield. It was a scrappy contest in the Scottish capital in which a world-record 18 penalties were attempted, and it was Leigh Halfpenny who proved the more prolific of the kickers with seven penalties and the conversion of Richard Hibbard's try to eclipse Greig Laidlaw's six penalties as Wales claimed a 28–18 success.

England preserved their unbeaten record with a stuttering and disjointed 18–11 win against Italy in London courtesy of six Toby Flood penalties, while France finally opened their Six Nations account, albeit with a solitary point, after their 13–13 draw with Ireland at the Aviva Stadium when Louis Picamoles bulldozed over with six minutes left to level the scores.

The stage was set for the climax of the campaign but before the main course of Wales and England in Cardiff, the Championship offered up the hors d'oeuvre of Italy and Ireland in Rome. The Azzurri had never previously toppled Ireland in a Six Nations meeting but made history in front of their own support with a 22–15 victory built on Giovanbattista Venditti's second-half try and 14 points from Luciano Orquera.

The result saw Italy match their best Six Nations finish of fourth from 2007, but the loss was ultimately to end Declan Kidney's five-year reign as Ireland coach when, two weeks later, the IRFU confirmed it would not renew his contract and subsequently appointed Joe Schmidt as his successor.

"We're a squad that's improving," said Italy captain Sergio Parisse. "We play France and Ireland in the group stage of the 2015 World Cup and we have sent a strong message to them.

"There were a lot of positives in this game from a psychological point of view because there was a good balance between our backs and forwards. In this Six Nations we have managed to put a lot of teams under pressure. We played against some great players like Brian O'Driscoll but have nothing to be envious of."

All eyes now turned to the Millennium Stadium but pre-match predictions of a tight, tense contest ultimately proved inaccurate as Wales comprehensively dismantled the England side.

Getty Images

Nigel Owens blows the final whistle as Italy record a famous win over France at the Stadio Olimpico.

Three first-half penalties from Halfpenny, who was subsequently voted the Player of the Tournament, to a single effort from Farrell saw the home side establish a 9–3 advantage at the break, but the second 40 minutes was one-way traffic as Wales ran riot.

A try from Cuthbert on 56 minutes all but extinguished English dreams of the Grand Slam. A Biggar drop goal stretched the lead and, when Cuthbert dived over again in the corner 15 minutes from time, parties throughout the Principality were already in full swing.

"We said from the start that we had a bit of blip [against Ireland] but we didn't want to let go of that trophy as easy as we could," Cuthbert said after Wales' record victory over England. "We wanted it back and we are so glad that we have. It is indescribable, to be fair. The last few years have been with such a great group of guys and we fully deserve this. We have worked hard in the last few weeks, it has all worked out and we couldn't ask for anything better."

Scotland's visit to Paris on Saturday evening was the Championship's only remaining business and the visitors edged the early exchanges with two Laidlaw penalties before Frédéric Michalak eased Les Bleus into a 9–6 lead early in the second half.

The game remained tantalisingly poised until the 65th minute when Fofana danced over as France began to go through the gears. Maxime Médard added a second try five minutes later and, although Tim Visser scored for the Scots late on, Philippe Saint-André's beleaguered side completed a 23–16 victory.

The win, though, was not enough to spare France the embarrassment of the Wooden Spoon while there was solace in defeat for Scotland with third place in the final table and their best finish in the Championship since 2006.

"I asked the guys at the start of the tournament not to send me out to defend the indefensible but that never happened," said interim head coach Scott Johnson. "They never put me in that position but we have got to get rid of this tag that near enough is good enough.

"There's been progress but it doesn't always improve as quickly as you like. We've got to take our opportunities to put teams to bed. I was really, really proud of our defence tonight. That was superb and I thought we were great in our resolve."

The Six Nations, however, belonged to Wales and their remarkable transformation from the side that seemed to have forgotten how to win a Test into the team that simply refused to lose.

RBS SIX NATIONS 2013 FINAL TABLE

	P	W	D	L	For	Against	Pts
Wales	5	4	0	1	122	66	8
England	5	4	0	1	94	78	8
Scotland	5	2	0	3	98	107	4
Italy	5	2	0	3	75	111	4
Ireland	5	1	1	3	72	81	3
France	5	1	1	3	73	91	3

Points: Win 2; Draw 1; Defeat 0. Champions determined on superior points difference.

There were 534 points scored at an average of 35.6 a match. The Championship record (803 points at an average of 53.5 a match) was set in 2000. Leigh Halfpenny was the leading individual points scorer with 74, 15 points shy of the Championship record Jonny Wilkinson set in 2001. Alex Cuthbert was the Championship's leading try-scorer with four, four short of the all-time record shared between England's Cyril Lowe (1914) and Scotland's Ian Smith (1925).

Getty Images

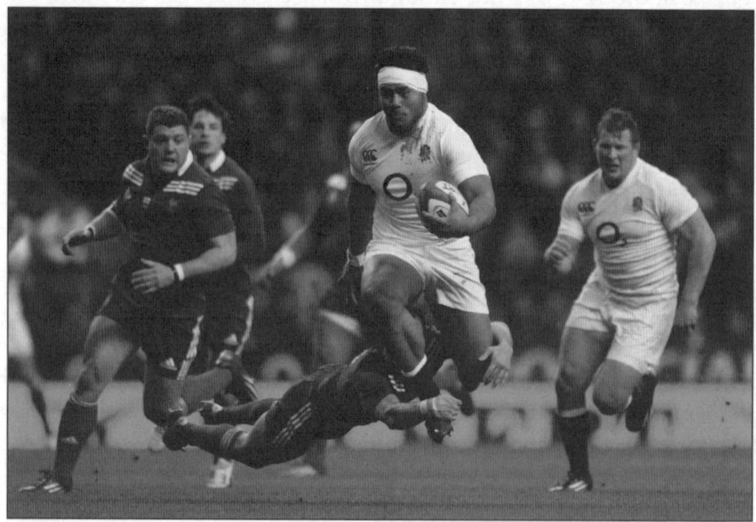

Manu Tuilagi bursts through the French defence to score a try for England at Twickenham.

2 February, Millennium Stadium, Cardiff

WALES 22 (2G 1T 1PG) IRELAND 30 (3G 3PG)

WALES: SL Halfpenny; ACG Cuthbert, JJV Davies, JH Roberts, GP North; DR Biggar, WM Phillips; GD Jenkins, M Rees, AR Jones, AJ Coombs, IR Evans, AC Shingler, S Warburton (captain), TT Faletau

SUBSTITUTIONS: JC Tipuric for Shingler (44 mins); KJ Owens for Rees (temp 13 to 21 mins and 51 mins); LD Williams for Phillips (63 mins); P James for Jenkins (temp 38 to 40 mins and 66 mins); C Mitchell for Jones (73 mins); OS Kohn for Evans (73 mins); JW Hook for Biggar (73 mins)

SCORERS: *Tries:* Cuthbert, Halfpenny, Mitchell *Conversions:* Halfpenny (2) *Penalty Goal:* Halfpenny

IRELAND: RDJ Kearney; CJH Gilroy, BG O'Driscoll, GW D'Arcy, SR Zebo; JJ Sexton, C Murray; CE Healy, RD Best, MR Ross, MP McCarthy, DC Ryan, P O'Mahony, SK O'Brien, JPR Heaslip (captain)

SUBSTITUTIONS: KG Earls for D'Arcy (44 mins); CG Henry for O'Mahony (51 mins); DJ Fitzpatrick for Ross (68 mins); DP O'Callaghan for McCarthy (73 mins); D Kilcoyne for Healy (73 mins); EG Reddan for Zebo (79 mins)

SCORERS: *Tries:* Zebo, Healy, O'Driscoll *Conversions:* Sexton (3) *Penalty Goals:* Sexton (3)

YELLOW CARDS: Best (57 mins); Murray (69 mins)

REFEREE: R Poite (France)

2 February, Twickenham, London

ENGLAND 38 (3G 1T 4PG) SCOTLAND 18 (1G 1T 2PG)

ENGLAND: DAV Goode; CJ Ashton, BM Barritt, WWF Twelvetrees, MN Brown; OA Farrell, BR Youngs; JWG Marler, TN Youngs, DR Cole, JO Launchbury, GMW Parling, TA Wood, CDC Robshaw (captain), BJ Morgan

SUBSTITUTIONS: JAW Haskell for Morgan (45 mins); DM Hartley for Youngs (53 mins); DS Care for Youngs (57 mins); MWIN Vunipola for Marler (57 mins); CL Lawes for Launchbury (64 mins); TGAL Flood for Twelvetrees (67 mins); D Strettle for Goode (67 mins); DG Wilson for Cole (73 mins)

SCORERS: *Tries:* Ashton, Twelvetrees, Parling, Care *Conversions:* Farrell (3) *Penalty Goals:* Farrell (4)

SCOTLAND: SW Hogg; SD Maitland, SF Lamont, MCM Scott, TJW Visser; RJH Jackson, GD Laidlaw; R Grant, DWH Hall, EA Murray, RJ Gray, JL Hamilton, AK Strokosch, KDR Brown (captain), JW Beattie

SUBSTITUTIONS: DK Denton for Strokosch (14 mins); RW Ford for Hall (47 mins); AD Kellock for Hamilton (55 mins); HB Pyrgos for Laidlaw (73 mins); MB Evans for Hogg (78 mins)

SCORERS: *Tries:* Maitland, Hogg *Conversion:* Laidlaw *Penalty Goals:* Laidlaw (2)

REFEREE: AC Rolland (Ireland)

3 February, Stadio Olimpico, Rome

ITALY 23 (2G 1PG 2DG) FRANCE 18 (1G 1T 2PG)

ITALY: A Masi; G Venditti, T Benvenuti, A Sgarbi, L McLean; L Orquera, T Botes; A Lo Cicero, L Ghiraldini, M-L Castrogiovanni, Q Geldenhuys, F Minto, A Zanni, S Favaro, S Parisse (captain)

SUBSTITUTIONS: D Giazzon for Ghiraldini (55 mins); A de Marchi for Lo Cicero (55 mins); E Gori for Botes (55 mins); L Cittadini for Castrogiovanni (62 mins); P Derbyshire for Favaro (63 mins); K Burton for Orquera (63 mins); A Pavanello for Geldenhuys (71 mins); G-J Canale for Benvenuti (71 mins); L Ghiraldini back for Burton (79 mins)

SCORERS: *Tries:* Parisse, Castrogiovanni *Conversions:* Orquera (2) *Penalty Goal:* Orquera *Drop Goals:* Orquera, Burton

YELLOW CARD: D Giazzon (79 mins)

FRANCE: Y Huget; W Fofana, M Mermoz, F Fritz, B Fall; F Michalak, M Machenaud; Y Forestier, D Szarzewski, N Mas, P Papé (captain), Y Maestri, T Dusautoir, F Ouedraogo, L Picamoles

SUBSTITUTIONS: B Kayser for Szarzewski (52 mins); V Debaty for Forestier (52 mins); R Taofifenua for Papé (58 mins); M Parra for Machenaud (62 mins); M Bastareaud for Fritz (62 mins); L Ducalcon for Mas (66 mins); D Chouly for Picamoles (68 mins); F Trinh-Duc for Huget (71 mins)

SCORERS: *Tries:* Picamoles, Fall *Conversion:* Michalak *Penalty Goals:* Michalak (2)

REFEREE: N Owens (Wales)

9 February, Murrayfield, Edinburgh

SCOTLAND 34 (4G 2PG) ITALY 10 (1G 1PG)

SCOTLAND: SW Hogg; SD Maitland, SF Lamont, MCM Scott, TJW Visser; RJH Jackson, GD Laidlaw; R Grant, RW Ford, EA Murray, RJ Gray, JL Hamilton, RJ Harley, KDR Brown (captain), JW Beattie

SUBSTITUTIONS: MJ Low for Grant (59 mins); AD Kellock for Hamilton (66 mins); GDS Cross for Murray (70 mins); DK Denton for Brown (70 mins); MB Evans for Hogg (72 mins); HB Pyrgos for Laidlaw (75 mins)

SCORERS: *Tries:* Visser, Scott, Hogg, Lamont *Conversions:* Laidlaw (4) *Penalty Goals:* Laidlaw (2)

YELLOW CARD: Cross (80 mins)

ITALY: A Masi; G Venditti, T Benvenuti, G-J Canale, L McLean; L Orquera, T Botes; A Lo Cicero, L Ghiraldini, M-L Castrogiovanni, Q Geldenhuys, F Minto, S Favaro, A Zanni, S Parisse (captain)

SUBSTITUTIONS: K Burton for Orquera (48 mins); E Gori for Botes (48 mins); D Giazzon for Ghiraldini (55 mins); A de Marchi for Lo Cicero (59 mins); A Pavanello for Geldenhuys (59 mins); L Cittadini for Castrogiovanni (63 mins); P Derbyshire for Favaro (67 mins)

SCORERS: *Try:* Zanni *Conversion:* Burton *Penalty Goal:* Orquera

REFEREE: J Peyper (South Africa)

9 February, Stade de France, Paris

FRANCE 6 (2PG) WALES 16 (1G 3PG)

FRANCE: Y Huget; W Fofana, M Mermoz, M Bastareaud, B Fall; F Michalak, M Machenaud; Y Forestier, D Szarzewski, N Mas, J Suta, Y Maestri, T Dusautoir (captain), F Ouedraogo, L Picamoles

SUBSTITUTIONS: F Trinh-Duc for Fall (40 mins); B Kayser for Szarzewski (50 mins); V Debaty for Forestier (50 mins); D Chouly for Ouedraogo (51 mins); M Parra for Machenaud (55 mins); L Ducalcon for Mas (55 mins); R Taofifenua for Suta (65 mins); F Fritz for Mermoz (75 mins)

SCORER: *Penalty Goals:* Michalak (2)

WALES: SL Halfpenny; ACG Cuthbert, JJV Davies, JH Roberts, GP North; DR Biggar, WM Phillips; GD Jenkins, RM Hibbard, AR Jones, AJ Coombs, IR Evans, RP Jones (*captain*), JC Tipuric, TT Faletau

SUBSTITUTIONS: KJ Owens for Hibbard (55 mins); P James for Jenkins (temp 38 to 40 mins and 58 mins); LD Williams for Phillips (70 mins); AC Shingler for RP Jones (78 mins); C Mitchell for AR Jones (78 mins); L Reed for Evans (78 mins); MS Williams for Roberts (78 mins)

SCORERS: *Try:* North *Conversion:* Halfpenny *Penalty Goals:* Halfpenny (3)

REFEREE: GJ Clancy (Ireland)

10 February, Aviva Stadium, Dublin

IRELAND 6 (2PG) ENGLAND 12 (4PG)

IRELAND: RDJ Kearney; CJH Gilroy, BG O'Driscoll, GW D'Arcy, SR Zebo; JJ Sexton, C Murray; CE Healy, RD Best, MR Ross, MP McCarthy, DC Ryan, P O'Mahony, SK O'Brien, JPR Heaslip (captain)

SUBSTITUTIONS: KG Earls for Zebo (10 mins); RJR O'Gara for Sexton (31 mins); DP O'Callaghan for Ryan (65 mins); CG Henry for O'Brien (65 mins); SM Cronin for Best (74 mins); D Kilcoyne for Healy (74mins); DJ Fitzpatrick for Ross (78 mins)

SCORERS: *Penalty Goals:* O'Gara (2)

ENGLAND: DAV Goode; CJ Ashton, BM Barritt, WWF Twelvetrees, MN Brown; OA Farrell, BR Youngs; JWG Marler, TN Youngs, DR Cole, JO Launchbury, GMW Parling, JAW Haskell, CDC Robshaw (captain), TA Wood

SUBSTITUTIONS: CL Lawes for Launchbury (47 mins); EM Tuilagi for Twelvetrees (47 mins); DM Hartley for TN Youngs (50 mins); MWIN Vunipola for Marler (58 mins); TR Waldrom for Lawes (70 mins); DG Wilson for Cole (76 mins)

SCORER: *Penalty Goals:* Farrell (4)

YELLOW CARD: Haskell (56 mins)

REFEREE: J Garces (France)

23 February, Stadio Olimpico, Rome

ITALY 9 (3PG) WALES 26 (2G 4PG)

ITALY: A Masi; G Venditti, T Benvenuti, G-J Canale, L McLean; K Burton, E Gori; A Lo Cicero, L Ghiraldini, M-L Castrogiovanni (captain), A Pavanello, F Minto, A Zanni, S Favaro, M Vosawai

SUBSTITUTIONS: D Giazzon for Ghiraldini (54 mins); A de Marchi for Lo Cicero (54 mins); Q Geldenhuys for Minto (54 mins); G Garcia for Canale (63 mins); T Botes for Gori (65 mins); P Derbyshire for Favaro (69 mins); L Cittadini for Vosawai (temp 65 to 68 mins) and for Castrogiovanni (70 mins)

SCORER: *Penalty Goals:* Burton (3)

YELLOW CARD: M-L Castrogiovanni (58 mins)

WALES: SL Halfpenny; ACG Cuthbert, JJV Davies, JH Roberts, GP North; DR Biggar, WM Phillips; GD Jenkins, RM Hibbard, AR Jones, AJ Coombs, IR Evans, RP Jones (captain), JC Tipuric, TT Faletau

SUBSTITUTIONS: P James for Jenkins (45 mins); KJ Owens for Hibbard (51 mins); AW Jones for Coombs (51 mins); LD Williams for Phillips (63 mins); JW Hook for Biggar (68 mins); S Warburton for RP Jones (68 mins); MS Williams for Roberts (70 mins); C Mitchell for AR Jones (73 mins)

SCORERS: *Tries:* Davies, Cuthbert *Conversions:* Halfpenny (2) *Penalty Goals:* Halfpenny (4)

REFEREE: R Poite (France)

23 February, Twickenham, London

ENGLAND 23 (1T 6PG) FRANCE 13 (1G 2PG)

ENGLAND: DAV Goode; CJ Ashton, EM Tuilagi, BM Barritt, MN Brown; OA Farrell, BR Youngs; JW G Marler, DM Hartley, DR Cole, JO Launchbury, GMW Parling, CL Lawes, CDC Robshaw (captain), TA Wood

SUBSTITUTIONS: MWIN Vunipola for Marler (51 mins); JAW Haskell for Lawes (51 mins); TN Youngs for Hartley (51 mins); DS Care for BR Youngs (58 mins); TGAL Flood for Farrell (61 mins)

SCORERS: *Try:* Tuilagi *Penalty Goals:* Farrell (4), Flood (2)

YELLOW CARD: Cole (79 mins)

FRANCE: Y Huget; V Clerc, W Fofana, M Bastareaud, B Fall; F Trinh-Duc, M Parra; T Domingo, B Kayser, N Mas, C Samson, Y Maestri, T Dusautoir (captain), Y Nyanga, L Picamoles

SUBSTITUTIONS: F Michalak for Trinh-Duc (52 mins); V Debaty for Domingo (55 mins); D Szarzewski for Kayser (55 mins); L Ducalcon for Mas (64 mins); J Suta for Samson (64 mins); M Machenaud for Parra (66 mins); A D Claassen for Nyanga (68 mins); F Fritz for Bastareaud (73 mins)

SCORERS: *Try:* Fofana *Conversion:* Parra *Penalty Goals:* Parra, Michalak

REFEREE: C Joubert (South Africa)

24 February, Murrayfield, Edinburgh

SCOTLAND 12 (4PG) IRELAND 8 (1T 1PG)

SCOTLAND: SW Hogg; SD Maitland, SF Lamont, MCM Scott, TJW Visser; RJH Jackson, GD Laidlaw; R Grant, RW Ford, GDS Cross, RJ Gray, JL Hamilton, RJ Harley, KDR Brown (captain), JW Beattie

SUBSTITUTIONS: DWH Hall for Ford (45 mins); D Weir for Jackson (59 mins); AD Kellock for Hamilton (71 mins); DK Denton for Brown (temp 45 to 50 mins) and for Beattie (71 mins); MJ Low for Harley (temp 18 to 25 mins) and for Cross (75 mins)

SCORER: *Penalty Goals:* Laidlaw (4)

YELLOW CARD: Grant (15 mins)

IRELAND: RDJ Kearney; CJH Gilroy, BG O'Driscoll, LD Marshall, KG Earls; DP Jackson, C Murray; TG Court, RD Best, MR Ross, DP O'Callaghan, DC Ryan, P O'Mahony, SK O'Brien, JPR Heaslip (captain)

SUBSTITUTIONS: D Kilcoyne for Court (55 mins); LM Fitzgerald for Gilroy (59 mins); RJR O'Gara for Jackson (64 mins); EG Reddan for Murray (69 mins); D Toner for O'Callaghan (71 mins); WI Henderson for O'Mahony (71 mins)

SCORERS: *Try:* Gilroy *Penalty Goal:* Jackson

REFEREE: W Barnes (England)

9 March, Murrayfield, Edinburgh

SCOTLAND 18 (6PG) WALES 28 (1G 7PG)

SCOTLAND: SW Hogg; SD Maitland, SF Lamont, MCM Scott, TJW Visser; D Weir, GD Laidlaw; R Grant, RW Ford, EA Murray, RJ Gray, JL Hamilton, RJ Harley, KDR Brown (captain), JW Beattie

SUBSTITUTIONS: AD Kellock for Gray (29 mins); R Wilson for Beattie (67 mins); GDS Cross for Murray (75 mins); RJH Jackson for Weir (78 mins)

SCORER: *Penalty Goals:* Laidlaw (6)

WALES: SL Halfpenny; ACG Cuthbert, JJV Davies, JH Roberts, GP North; DR Biggar, WM Phillips; P James, RM Hibbard, AR Jones, AW Jones, IR Evans, RP Jones (captain), S Warburton, TT Faletau

SUBSTITUTIONS: JC Tipuric for RP Jones (48 mins); KJ Owens for Hibbard (60 mins); LD Williams for Phillips (72 mins); MS Williams for Roberts (72 mins); RJ Bevington for Faletau (80 mins)

SCORERS: *Try:* Hibbard *Conversion:* Halfpenny *Penalty Goals:* Halfpenny (7)

YELLOW CARD: James (77 mins)

REFEREE: C Joubert (South Africa)

9 March, Aviva Stadium, Dublin

IRELAND 13 (1G 2PG) FRANCE 13 (1G 2PG)

IRELAND: RDJ Kearney; FL McFadden, BG O'Driscoll, LD Marshall, KG Earls; DP Jackson, C Murray; CE Healy, RD Best, MR Ross, MP McCarthy, DC Ryan, P O'Mahony, SK O'Brien, JPR Heaslip (captain)

SUBSTITUTIONS: LM Fitzgerald for McFadden (62 mins); EG Reddan for Murray (62 mins); DP O'Callaghan for Ryan (67 mins); I Madigan for Marshall (71 mins); WI Henderson for O'Mahony (76 mins); SM Cronin for Reddan (80 mins); Murray back for O'Driscoll (temp 71 to 75 mins)

SCORERS: *Try:* Heaslip *Conversion:* Jackson *Penalty Goals:* Jackson (2)

FRANCE: Y Huget; V Clerc, W Fofana, F Fritz, M Médard; F Michalak, M Parra; T Domingo, B Kayser, N Mas, C Samson, Y Maestri, T Dusautoir (captain), Y Nyanga, L Picamoles

SUBSTITUTIONS: S Vahaamahina for Maestri (50 mins); V Debaty for Domingo (65 mins); AD Claassen for Nyanga (65 mins); G Guirado for Kayser (67 mins); M Bastareaud for Fritz (temp 51 to 57 mins and 67 mins)

SCORERS: *Try:* Picamoles *Conversion:* Michalak *Penalty Goals:* Michalak, Parra

REFEREE: SR Walsh (Australia)

10 March, Twickenham, London

ENGLAND 18 (6PG) ITALY 11 (1T 2PG)

ENGLAND: DAV Goode; CJ Ashton, EM Tuilagi, BM Barritt, MN Brown; TGAL Flood, DS Care; MWIN Vunipola, TN Youngs, DR Cole, JO Launchbury, GMW Parling, JAW Haskell, CDC Robshaw (captain), TA Wood

SUBSTITUTIONS: CL Lawes for Parling (45 mins); TR Croft for Haskell (50 mins); JWG Marler for Vunipola (57 mins); BR Youngs for Care (57 mins); WWF Twelvetrees for Barritt (66 mins); DM Hartley for TN Youngs (71 mins); DG Wilson for Cole (75 mins)

SCORERS: *Penalty Goals:* Flood (6)

ITALY: A Masi; G Venditti, G-J Canale, G Garcia, L McLean; L Orquera, E Gori; A de Marchi, L Ghiraldini, M-L Castrogiovanni, Q Geldenhuys, J Furno, A Zanni, R Barbieri, S Parisse (captain)

SUBSTITUTIONS: L Cittadini for Castrogiovanni (28 mins); T Botes for Masi (temp 35 to 40 mins) and for Gori (57 mins); D Giazzon for Ghiraldini (58 mins); A Pavanello for Geldenhuys (62 mins); F Minto for Furno (62 mins); S Favaro for Barbieri (62 mins); T Benvenuti for McLean (71 mins); A Lo Cicero for De Marchi (75 mins)

SCORERS: *Try:* McLean *Penalty Goals:* Orquera (2)

YELLOW CARD: Gori (30 mins)

REFEREE: GJ Clancy (Ireland)

16 March, Stadio Olimpico, Rome

ITALY 22 (1G 5PG) IRELAND 15 (5PG)

ITALY: A Masi; G Venditti, G-J Canale, G Garcia, L McLean; L Orquera, E Gori; A Lo Cicero, L Ghiraldini, L Cittadini, Q Geldenhuys, J Furno, A Zanni, S Favaro, S Parisse (captain)

SUBSTITUTIONS: F Minto for Furno (57 mins); P Derbyshire for Favaro (57 mins); M Rizzo for Lo Cicero (64 mins); A Pavanello for Geldenhuys (64 mins); T Benvenuti for Masi (65 mins); D Giazzon for Ghiraldini (74 mins); A de Marchi for Cittadini (74 mins); T Botes for Gori (74 mins)

SCORERS: *Try:* Venditti *Conversion:* Orquera *Penalty Goals:* Orquera (4), Garcia

YELLOW CARD: S Parisse (51 mins)

IRELAND: RDJ Kearney; CJG Gilroy, BG O'Driscoll, LD Marshall, KG Earls; DP Jackson, C Murray; CE Healy, RD Best, MR Ross, MP McCarthy, DC Ryan, P O'Mahony, SK O'Brien, JPR Heaslip (captain)

SUBSTITUTIONS: LM Fitzgerald for Earls (24 mins); I Madigan for Marshall (27 mins); WI Henderson for Fitzgerald (36 mins); D Toner for McCarthy (64 mins); S Archer for Ross (66 mins); SM Cronin for Best (69 mins); D Kilcoyne for Healy (69 mins); P Marshall for Ryan (79 mins)

SCORER: *Penalty Goals:* Jackson (5)

YELLOW CARDS: O'Driscoll (29 mins); Ryan (69 mins); Murray (79 mins)

REFEREE: W Barnes (England)

16 March, Millennium Stadium, Cardiff

WALES 30 (1G 1T 5PG 1DG) ENGLAND 3 (1PG)

WALES: SL Halfpenny; ACG Cuthbert, JJV Davies, JH Roberts, GP North; DR Biggar, WM Phillips; GD Jenkins (captain), RM Hibbard, AR Jones, AW Jones, IR Evans, S Warburton, JC Tipuric, TT Faletau

SUBSTITUTIONS: KJ Owens for Hibbard (52 mins); P James for Jenkins (61 mins); AJ Coombs for Evans (70 mins); SA Andrews for Jones (73 mins); AC Shingler for Warburton (75 mins); LD Williams for Phillips (75 mins); JW Hook for Biggar (75 mins); MS Williams for Roberts (75 mins)

SCORERS: *Tries:* Cuthbert (2) *Conversion:* Biggar *Penalty Goals:* Halfpenny (4), Biggar *Drop Goal:* Biggar

ENGLAND: DAV Goode; CJ Ashton, EM Tuilagi, BM Barritt, MN Brown; OA Farrell, BR Youngs; JWG Marler, TN Youngs, DR Cole, JO Launchbury, GMW Parling, TR Croft, CDC Robshaw (captain), TA Wood

SUBSTITUTIONS: MWIN Vunipola for Marler (44 mins); DM Hartley for TN Youngs (52 mins); CL Lawes for Launchbury (52 mins); DS Care for BR Youngs (64 mins); WWF Twelvetrees for Goode (64 mins); TGAL Flood for Farrell (67 mins); JAW Haskell for Wood (67 mins); DG Wilson for Cole (72 mins)

SCORER: *Penalty Goal:* Farrell

REFEREE: SR Walsh (Australia)

16 March, Stade de France, Paris

FRANCE 23 (2G 3PG) SCOTLAND 16 (1G 3PG)

FRANCE: Y Huget; V Clerc, W Fofana, M Bastareaud, M Médard; F Michalak, M Parra; T Domingo, B Kayser, N Mas, S Vahaamahina, Y Maestri, T Dusautoir (captain), AD Claassen, L Picamoles

SUBSTITUTIONS: M Machenaud for Parra (HT); V Debaty for Domingo (54 mins); G Guirado for Kayser (54 mins); L Ducalcon for Mas (63 mins); Y Nyanga for Dusautoir (temp 63 to 67 mins) and for Claassen (67 mins); F Trinh-Duc for Michalak (70 mins); C Samson for Vahaamahina (70 mins); G Fickou for Bastareaud (74 mins)

SCORER: *Tries:* Fofana, Médard *Conversions:* Michalak, Machenaud *Penalty Goals:* Michalak (3)

SCOTLAND: SW Hogg; SD Maitland, SF Lamont, MCM Scott, TJW Visser; D Weir, GD Laidlaw; R Grant, RW Ford, EA Murray, GS Gilchrist, JL Hamilton, AK Strokosch, KDR Brown (captain), JW Beattie

SUBSTITUTIONS: MB Evans for Maitland (30 mins); AD Kellock for Gilchrist (53 mins); MJ Low for Grant (63 mins); GDS Cross for Murray (64 mins); RJH Jackson for Weir (67 mins); R Wilson for Beattie (70 mins); DWH Hall for Ford (74 mins); HB Pyrgos for Laidlaw (74 mins)

SCORERS: *Try:* Visser *Conversion:* Jackson *Penalty Goals:* Laidlaw (3)

REFEREE: N Owens (Wales)

Getty Images

A desperate tap tackle from Mike Brown stops Wales' George North in full flight at the Millennium Stadium.

INTERNATIONAL CHAMPIONSHIP RECORDS 1883–2013

PREVIOUS WINNERS:

1883 England; 1884 England; 1885 Not completed;
1886 England & Scotland; 1887 Scotland; 1888 Not completed;
1889 Not completed; 1890 England & Scotland; 1891 Scotland;
1892 England; 1893 Wales; 1894 Ireland;
1895 Scotland; 1896 Ireland; 1897 Not completed;
1898 Not completed; 1899 Ireland; 1900 Wales;
1901 Scotland; 1902 Wales; 1903 Scotland;
1904 Scotland; 1905 Wales; 1906 Ireland & Wales;
1907 Scotland; 1908 Wales; 1909 Wales;
1910 England; 1911 Wales; 1912 England & Ireland;
1913 England; 1914 England; 1920 England & Scotland & Wales;
1921 England; 1922 Wales; 1923 England;
1924 England; 1925 Scotland; 1926 Scotland & Ireland;
1927 Scotland & Ireland; 1928 England; 1929 Scotland;
1930 England; 1931 Wales; 1932 England & Ireland & Wales;
1933 Scotland; 1934 England; 1935 Ireland;
1936 Wales; 1937 England; 1938 Scotland;
1939 England & Ireland & Wales; 1947 England & Wales; 1948 Ireland;
1949 Ireland; 1950 Wales; 1951 Ireland;
1952 Wales; 1953 England; 1954 England & Wales & France;
1955 Wales & France; 1956 Wales; 1957 England;
1958 England; 1959 France; 1960 England & France;
1961 France; 1962 France; 1963 England;
1964 Scotland & Wales; 1965 Wales; 1966 Wales;
1967 France; 1968 France; 1969 Wales;
1970 Wales & France; 1971 Wales; 1972 Not completed;
1973 Five Nations tie; 1974 Ireland; 1975 Wales;
1976 Wales; 1977 France; 1978 Wales;
1979 Wales; 1980 England; 1981 France;
1982 Ireland; 1983 Ireland & France; 1984 Scotland;
1985 Ireland; 1986 Scotland & France; 1987 France;
1988 Wales & France; 1989 France; 1990 Scotland;
1991 England; 1992 England; 1993 France;
1994 Wales; 1995 England; 1996 England;
1997 France; 1998 France; 1999 Scotland;
2000 England; 2001 England; 2002 France;
2003 England; 2004 France; 2005 Wales;
2006 France; 2007 France; 2008 Wales;
2009 Ireland; 2010 France; 2011 England;
2012 Wales; 2013 Wales

England and Wales have both won the title outright 26 times; France 17; Scotland 14; Ireland 11; Italy 0.

TRIPLE CROWN WINNERS:

England (23 times) 1883, 1884, 1892, 1913, 1914, 1921, 1923, 1924, 1928, 1934, 1937, 1954, 1957, 1960, 1980, 1991, 1992, 1995, 1996, 1997, 1998, 2002, 2003

Wales (20 times) 1893, 1900, 1902, 1905, 1908, 1909, 1911, 1950, 1952, 1965, 1969, 1971, 1976, 1977, 1978, 1979, 1988, 2005, 2008, 2012

Scotland (10 times) 1891, 1895, 1901, 1903, 1907, 1925, 1933, 1938, 1984, 1990

Ireland (10 times) 1894, 1899, 1948, 1949, 1982, 1985, 2004, 2006, 2007, 2009

GRAND SLAM WINNERS:

England (12 times) 1913, 1914, 1921, 1923, 1924, 1928, 1957, 1980, 1991, 1992, 1995, 2003

Wales (11 times) 1908, 1909, 1911, 1950, 1952, 1971, 1976, 1978, 2005, 2008, 2012

France (Nine times) 1968, 1977, 1981, 1987, 1997, 1998, 2002, 2004, 2010

Scotland (Three times) 1925, 1984, 1990

Ireland (Twice) 1948, 2009

THE SIX NATIONS CHAMPIONSHIP 2000–2013:

COMPOSITE TABLE

	P	W	D	L	Pts
France	70	47	2	21	**96**
England	70	47	1	22	**95**
Ireland	70	45	2	23	**92**
Wales	70	37	2	31	**76**
Scotland	70	18	2	50	**38**
Italy	70	11	1	58	**23**

INTERNATIONAL CHAMPIONSHIP RECORDS

RECORD	DETAIL		SET
Most team points in season	229 by England	in five matches	2001
Most team tries in season	29 by England	in five matches	2001
Highest team score	80 by England	80–23 v Italy	2001
Biggest team win	57 by England	80–23 v Italy	2001
Most team tries in match	12 by Scotland	v Wales	1887
Most appearances	63 for Ireland	RJR O'Gara	2000–2013
Most points in matches	557 for Ireland	RJR O'Gara	2000–2013
Most points in season	89 for England	JP Wilkinson	2001
Most points in match	35 for England	JP Wilkinson	v Italy, 2001
Most tries in matches	26 for Ireland	BG O'Driscoll	2000–2013
Most tries in season	8 for England	CN Lowe	1914
	8 for Scotland	IS Smith	1925
Most tries in match	5 for Scotland	GC Lindsay	v Wales, 1887
Most cons in matches	89 for England	JP Wilkinson	1998–2011
Most cons in season	24 for England	JP Wilkinson	2001
Most cons in match	9 for England	JP Wilkinson	v Italy, 2001
Most pens in matches	109 for Ireland	RJR O'Gara	2000–2013
Most pens in season	19 for Wales	SL Halfpenny	2013
Most pens in match	7 for England	SD Hodgkinson	v Wales, 1991
	7 for England	CR Andrew	v Scotland, 1995
	7 for England	JP Wilkinson	v France, 1999
	7 for Wales	NR Jenkins	v Italy, 2000
	7 for France	G Merceron	v Italy, 2002
	7 for Scotland	CD Paterson	v Wales, 2007
	7 for Wales	SL Halfpenny	v Scotland, 2013
Most drops in matches	11 for England	JP Wilkinson	1998–2011
Most drops in season	5 for France	G Camberabero	1967
	5 for Italy	D Dominguez	2000
	5 for Wales	NR Jenkins	2001
	5 for England	JP Wilkinson	2003
	5 for Scotland	DA Parks	2010
Most drops in match	3 for France	P Albaladejo	v Ireland, 1960
	3 for France	J-P Lescarboura	v England, 1985
	3 for Italy	D Dominguez	v Scotland 2000
	3 for Wales	NR Jenkins	v Scotland 2001

INTERNATIONAL RUGBY BOARD

Around the world in 30 minutes

The IRB's weekly
television and
radio programmes
broadcast to over
150 countries

ALL BLACKS REIGN SUPREME TO DEFEND TITLE

By Greg Thomas

Getty Images

New Zealand retained The Rugby Championship after a thrilling victory over South Africa at Ellis Park in the final round.

New Zealand defended their Rugby Championship title in style by remaining unbeaten to confirm their status as the world's top team. Six victories, four with try bonus points, saw them win the Championship by nine points from South Africa to increase their cushion at the top of the IRB World Rankings.

What was impressive about the title defence was the emergence of a number of new players who stepped up to fill the shoes of some established stars. Dan Carter missed half of the Championship through injury but Aaron Cruden, Tom Taylor and Beauden Barrett all saw field time and impressed. Sam Cane proved to be a more than capable replacement for captain Richie McCaw on two occasions, while Steven Luatua was another to impress when he filled in for Liam Messam.

The seamless introduction of such talent must be of concern to the rest of the world's top nations as it signals the All Blacks still have incredible depth and are blooding new talent two years out from Rugby World Cup 2015 in England. It is a powerful squad already and in number 8 Kieran Read the All Blacks have a mighty presence in the back row. Wing Ben Smith is now among the best going around and scored a record eight tries in the Championship, while Conrad Smith was as majestic as ever in the centres.

South Africa had their chance in the Championship but ultimately they failed because they could not beat the All Blacks. That said their form was a step up from the previous year and in the end they could have sneaked it as the Championship came down to the very last match. If the Springboks could beat New Zealand at Ellis Park with a bonus point it was mathematically possible they could win the title on point difference, provided the All Blacks didn't manage a bonus point.

The Springboks flew into their visitors from the first whistle in a match of such pace, skill and intensity that it should be used by every coach as a benchmark for Test rugby. The first half saw five tries scored, three to the All Blacks, including one on the hooter, and two to Springbok wing Bryan Habana. The hosts would have been severely disappointed to head into the break 21–15 down but responded in remarkable fashion after the interval by scoring two further tries to take a 27–24 lead. And at the hour mark they looked on track to cause the upset.

With just 20 minutes to play the Springboks were leading and had a bonus point for four tries. Could they hold on to the lead and stop the All Blacks securing a bonus point themselves? Sadly the answer for the excitable crowd was no. The pace of the match was clearly starting to have an effect on the players. The visitors just kept on coming and, in their trademark, relentless way, scored two tries through replacement fly half Barrett and man-of-the-match Read to secure a 38–27 victory and the Championship.

The win was the All Blacks' 50th over their great rivals and just their fourth in 12 Tests at Ellis Park. It was also achieved despite being down to 14 men for a quarter of the game with Messam and prop Ben Franks both receiving yellow cards.

"We had to dig deep," McCaw declared after the match. "Both teams came here willing to play. We also had 20 minutes with 14 men and add into that a bit of travel, it was a very satisfying win. Going behind we could easily have got flustered, but the guys hung in there.

"We took our chances really well and there were times when we were under a lot of pressure and then got a critical turnover. The try on half-time was critical, I'm sure it changed their half-time talk. But credit to the Boks, they came out in the second half and scored again quickly."

Tactically New Zealand coach Steve Hansen said the All Blacks executed their game plan to perfection, and that the match was something a lot of people could be proud of. "In modern rugby you must have a lot of ball carriers and we had that today. Our scrum held up well, our lineouts were good, and we defended brilliantly. Coming to Johannesburg after all the travel and giving a performance like this can only make you proud to be a New Zealander."

For South Africa it was a disappointing result at a venue where they have had a good record against New Zealand. However, four wins was a better return than the two the previous year and improvement was the order of the day. In centre JJ Engelbrecht, wing Willie le Roux, number 8 Duane Vermeulen, flanker Siya Kolisi and second row Eben Etzebeth they have some new talent on the rise.

"There's not really too much you can say. We felt we let ourselves down. Full credit to the coaching staff, particularly Heyneke Meyer, for making us believe it was possible. But our defensive effort let us down. We just didn't play to our standard. Last year our defence was good, this year our attack was good and our defence wasn't always great. I am looking forward to seeing what happens if one day we get both right at the same time," admitted evergreen captain and centre Jean de Villiers after the match

Meyer was philosophical on the Championship. "I thought we played some great rugby, and today is one of the best games of rugby I've probably been involved in, but saying that you want to win and you want to win in style. I thought tonight, even though we went for four tries, they didn't score off our mistakes like usual, it was just bad defence. We are closing the gap, they are a quality side and we have no excuses."

For Australia The Rugby Championship was a disaster for a team that prides itself in always being highly competitive at the highest level, with just two wins over Argentina and losses home and away to the All Blacks and Springboks. Defensively they were frail, conceding far too many points to the two best teams in the world and the set piece was inconsistent and at times very ordinary.

For new coach Ewen McKenzie it was a baptism of fire, as it appeared the Wallabies had no answer to the size and strength of the All Black and Springbok forward packs. It was clear that translating his successful

Queensland Reds game plan to the Test arena was not the answer for the Wallabies. Far too much kicking also meant the Wallabies continually squandered too much possession.

That said, following the series loss to the British & Irish Lions, a new look squad and rebuilding was the order of the day. However, several experienced players, including Will Genia, captain James Horwill and Adam Ashley-Cooper, underperformed which clearly affected team confidence. McKenzie also had to do without overseas-bound Digby Ioane, the injured trio of hooker Tatafu Polota-Nau, flanker David Pocock and full back Kurtley Beale, and James O'Connor whose off-field behaviour saw his ARU contract terminated during the Championship.

One highlight was the continued emergence of rugby league/AFL convert Israel Folau. With a move to full back in the absence of Beale he slowly began to show huge promise that culminated in a hat-trick of tries against the Pumas in Rosario during their record 54–17 last match victory. It was a much-needed and, to many, surprising win that McKenzie must hope gives confidence to the evolving squad and new players such as backs Matt Toomua, Christian Leali'ifano and Joe Tomane and forwards Scott Fardy and Scott Sio.

For the Pumas it was again a case of huge endeavour, bloody determination but ultimately disappointment as they still search for their first Rugby Championship win. A five-point loss at home to the Springboks and a heart-wrenching one-point defeat by the Wallabies in Perth was as close as they came. The Pumas really fancied their chance of upsetting the Wallabies at home in Rosario but were never in the match and conceded four tries in the first half.

The addition of the Pumas to The Rugby Championship has injected new life into what was the Tri Nations. Fans are starting to enjoy the thrill of trips to Mendoza, Rosario and Buenos Aires, and local support is strong and vocal.

Hopefully it will not be long before the Pumas break their duck but first coach Santiago Phelan has the task, like McKenzie, of introducing new blood and rebuilding. Many of the stalwarts who took Argentina to giddy heights at the last two Rugby World Cups are now retiring or have done so already. An example is 36-year-old Felipe Contepomi who played his 87th and final Test against Australia in Rosario.

Phelan will be buoyed by the fact that he has talent at scrum half in Tomás Cubelli and Martín Landajo, the making of another robust front row in Matías Díaz, Juan Figallo, Eusebio Guiñazu and Nahuel Lobo, while flanker Pablo Matera looks hugely promising and is in the mould of his hard-working and tenacious captain Juan Martín Fernández Lobbe.

However, Argentina's successful future lies in a more expansive game rather than one based on forward dominance as in the past. Success in modern Test rugby demands such an approach and they started to show signs of a better all-round game in the 2013 Championship. The continued development of three-quarters such as Lucas González Amorosino, Marcelo Bosch, Gonzalo Camacho, Horacio Agulla, JJ Imhoff and Nicolás Sanchez, many of whom play for European clubs, is essential in this.

So too could be the involvement of more Argentina players in high-level tournaments such as Super Rugby. SANZAR is investigating an expansion of the competition that could see the introduction of teams from the Americas. If this was the case Argentina would more than likely be first in the queue.

AFP/Getty Images

Fans show their support for Argentina against Australia in Perth but ultimately left disappointed after a 14–13 loss.

THE RUGBY CHAMPIONSHIP 2013 FINAL STANDINGS

	P	W	D	L	F	A	BP	PTS
New Zealand	6	6	0	0	202	115	4	28
South Africa	6	4	0	2	203	117	3	19
Australia	6	2	0	4	133	170	1	9
Argentina	6	0	0	6	88	224	2	2

Points: win 4; draw 2; four or more tries, or defeat by seven or fewer points 1

Getty Images

Bryan Habana scored one of South Africa's nine tries in their record 73–13 win over Argentina.

17 August 2013, ANZ Stadium, Sydney

AUSTRALIA 29 (2G 5PG) NEW ZEALAND 47 (4G 2T 3PG)

AUSTRALIA: J Mogg; I Folau, A Ashley-Cooper, C Leali'ifano, J O'Connor; M Toomua, W Genia; J Slipper, S Moore, B Alexander, R Simmons, J Horwill (captain), H McMeniman, M Hooper, B Mowen

SUBSTITUTIONS: T Kuridrani for Mogg (52 mins); L Gill for McMeniman (52 mins); S Kepu for Alexander (57 mins); Q Cooper for Toomua (61 mins); S Fardy for Hooper (temp 61-66 mins); S Faingaa for Moore (70 mins); S Sio for Slipper (70 mins); N White for Genia (78 mins); Fardy for Mowen (78 mins)

SCORERS: *Tries*: Genia, O'Connor *Conversions*: Leali'ifano (2) *Penalty Goals*: Leali'ifano (5)

NEW ZEALAND: I Dagg; B Smith, C Smith, M Nonu, J Savea; A Cruden, A Smith; T Woodcock, A Hore, O Franks, L Romano, S Whitelock, S Luatua, R McCaw (captain), K Read

SUBSTITUTIONS: B Retallick for Romano (17 mins); K Mealamu for Hore (48 mins); B Franks for Woodcock (61 mins); C Faumuina for O Franks (61 mins); R Crotty for Nonu (63 mins); T Kerr-Barlow for A Smith (69 mins); B Barrett for Cruden (70 mins); S Cane for McCaw (73 mins)

SCORERS: *Tries:* B Smith (3), Cruden, McCaw, C Smith *Conversions:* Cruden (3), Barrett *Penalty Goals:* Cruden (3)

YELLOW CARD: Whitelock (80 mins)

REFEREE: C Joubert (South Africa)

17 August 2013, FNB Stadium, Soweto

SOUTH AFRICA 73 (8G 1T 4PG) ARGENTINA 13 (1G 2PG)

SOUTH AFRICA: W le Roux; B Basson, JJ Englebrecht, J de Villiers (captain), B Habana; M Steyn, R Pienaar; T Mtawarira, A Strauss, J du Plessis, E Etzebeth, J Kruger, F Louw, W Alberts, D Vermeulen

SUBSTITUTIONS: F du Preez for Pienaar (54 mins); B du Plessis for Strauss (54 mins); C Oosthuizen for J du Plessis (56 mins); G Steenkamp for Mtawarira (57 mins); Flip van der Merwe for Kurger (58 mins); P Lambie for Le Roux (58 mins); S Kolisi for Alberts (64 mins); J Serfontein for De Villiers (67 mins)

SCORERS: *Tries*: Penalty, Englebrecht, Strauss, Alberts, De Villiers, Du Preez, Habana, Vermeulen, B du Plessis *Conversions*: Steyn (8) *Penalty Goals*: Steyn (4)

ARGENTINA: JM Hernández; G Camacho, M Bosch, F Contepomi (captain), JJ Imhoff; N Sanchez, M Landajo; J Figallo, E Guiñazu, M Díaz, M Carizza, P Albacete, P Matera, JM Leguizamón, L Senatore

SUBSTITUTIONS: JF Cabello for Albacete (13 mins); H Agulla for Hernández (30 mins); A Creevy for JJ Imhoff (temp 34-41 mins); N Lobo for Díaz (41 mins); Creevy for Guiñazu (54 mins); T Cubelli for Landajo (58 mins); M Galarza for Carizza (59 mins); JP Orlandi for Figallo (60 mins)

SCORERS: *Try:* Contepomi *Conversion:* Contepomi *Penalty Goals:* Contepomi (2)

YELLOW CARDS: Guiñazu (31 mins); Senatore (50 mins)

REFEREE: C Pollock (New Zealand)

24 August 2013, Westpac Stadium, Wellington

NEW ZEALAND 27 (1G 1T 5PG) AUSTRALIA 16 (1G 3PG)

NEW ZEALAND: I Dagg; B Smith, C Smith, M Nonu, J Savea; T Taylor, A Smith; T Woodcock, A Hore, O Franks, B Retallick, S Whitelock, S Luatua, R McCaw (captain), K Read

SUBSTITUTIONS: D Coles for Hore (48 mins); W Crockett for Woodcock (62 mins); C Faumuina for Franks (66 mins); C Piutau for B Smith (70 mins); T Kerr-Barlow for A Smith (71 mins); C Slade for Nonu (77 mins); B Smith for Taylor (79 mins)

SCORERS: *Tries*: B Smith (2) *Conversion:* Taylor *Penalty Goals*: Taylor (4), Dagg

AUSTRALIA: J Mogg; I Folau, A Ashley-Cooper, C Leali'ifano, J O'Connor; M Toomua, W Genia; J Slipper, S Moore, B Alexander, R Simmons, J Horwill (captain), S Fardy, M Hooper, B Mowen

SUBSTITUTIONS: S Sio for Slipper (36 mins); S Kepu for Alexander (55 mins); Q Cooper for Toomua (58 mins); T Kuridrani for Ashley-Cooper (63 mins); L Gill for Mowen (65 mins); Douglas for Simmons (71 mins); S Faingaa for Moore (37 mins); N White for Genia (79 mins)

SCORERS: *Try:* Folau *Conversion:* Leali'ifano *Penalty Goals:* Leali'ifano (3)

REFEREE: J Peyper (South Africa)

24 August 2013, Estadio Malvinas Argentinas, Mendoza

ARGENTINA 17 (2G 1PG) SOUTH AFRICA 22 (1G 5PG)

ARGENTINA: L González Amorosino; G Camacho, M Bosch, F Contepomi (captain), H Agulla; N Sanchez, M Landajo; M Ayerza, E Guiñazu, J Figallo, J Farias Cabello, M Galarza, P Matera, JM Leguizamón, L Senatore

SUBSTITUTIONS: S Fernández for Contepomi (46 mins); T Cubelli for Landajo (57 mins); B Macome for Senatore (60 mins); A Creevy for Guiñazu (67 mins); T Lavanini for Galarza (75 mins)

SCORERS: *Tries*: Leguizamón, Bosch *Conversions*: Contepomi (2) *Penalty Goal*: Contepomi

SOUTH AFRICA: W le Roux; B Basson, JJ Englebrecht, J de Villiers (captain), B Habana; M Steyn, R Pienaar; T Mtawarira, A Strauss, J du Plessis, E Etzebeth, J Kruger, F Louw, W Alberts, D Vermeulen

SUBSTITUTIONS: B du Plessis for Strauss (52 mins); Flip van der Merwe for Kruger (56 mins); G Steenkamp for Mtawarira (58 mins); P Lambie for Basson (63 mins); S Kolisi for Alberts (68 mins); C Oosthuizen for J du Plessis (68 mins); J Serfontein for JJ Engelbrecht

SCORERS: *Try:* Basson *Conversion:* Steyn *Penalty Goals:* Steyn (5)

REFEREE: S Walsh (Australia)

7 September 2013, Waikato Stadium, Hamilton

NEW ZEALAND 28 (2G 1T 3PG) ARGENTINA 13 (1G 2PG)

NEW ZEALAND: I Dagg; B Smith, C Smith, F Saili, J Savea; D Carter, A Smith; T Woodcock, A Hore, C Faumuina, B Retallick, S Whitelock, S Luatua, R McCaw (captain), K Read

SUBSTITUTIONS: W Crockett for Woodcock (41 mins); D Coles for Hore (46 mins); B Barrett for Carter (55 mins); S Cane for McCaw (60 mins); B Franks for Faumuina (70 mins); C Piutau for Dagg (70 mins); J Thrush for Whitelock (75 mins); T Kerr-Barlow for A Smith (75 mins); C Faumuina for Crockett (79 mins)

SCORERS: *Tries:* A Smith (2), Savea *Conversion:* Carter (2) *Penalty Goals:* Carter (2), Barrett

ARGENTINA: JM Hernández; G Camacho, M Bosch, S Fernández, H Agulla; N Sanchez, M Landajo; M Ayerza, E Guiñazu, J Figallo, M Carizza, J Farias Cabello, JM Fernández Lobbe (captain), P Matera, JM Leguizamón

SUBSTITUTIONS: L González Amorosino for Camacho (45 mins); A Creevy for Guiñazu (50 mins); M Galarza for Farias Cabello (55 mins); JP Orlandi for Figallo (63 mins); T Cubelli for Landajo (66 mins); N Lobo for Ayerza (70 mins); F Contepomi for Fernández (70 mins); B Macome for Matera (75 mins)

SCORERS: *Try*: Leguizamón *Conversion*: Sanchez *Penalty Goals*: Sanchez (2)

YELLOW CARD: Guiñazu (23 mins)

REFEREE: J Garces (France)

7 September 2013, Suncorp Stadium, Brisbane

AUSTRALIA 12 (4PG) SOUTH AFRICA 38 (3G 1T 4PG)

AUSTRALIA: I Folau; J O'Connor, A Ashley-Cooper, C Leali'ifano, N Cummins; Q Cooper, W Genia (captain); J Slipper, S Moore, S Kepu, R Simmons, K Douglas, S Fardy, M Hooper, B Mowen

SUBSTITUTIONS: B McCalman for Simmons (temp 30-41 mins); B Alexander for Kepu (45 mins); S Sio for Slipper (64 mins); S Faingaa for Moore (66 mins); L Gill for Hooper (69 mins); N White for Genia (70 mins); B McCalman for Mowen (70 mins); M Toomua for Leali'ifano (72 mins)

SCORERS: *Penalty Goals*: Leali'ifano (4)

YELLOW CARD: M Hooper (50 mins)

SOUTH AFRICA: Z Kirchner; W le Roux, JJ Engelbrecht, J de Villiers (captain), B Habana; M Steyn, R Pienaar; T Mtawarira, B du Plessis, J du Plessis, E Etzebeth, Flip van der Merwe, F Louw, W Alberts, D Vermeulen

SUBSTITUTIONS: C Oosthuizen for J du Plessis (temp 4-13 mins); A Strauss for B du Plessis (57 mins); J Kruger for F van der Merwe (57 mins); G Steenkamp for Mtawarira (57 mins); C Oosthuizen for J du Plessis (57 mins); J Serfontein for De Villiers (70 mins); P Lambie for Steyn (71 mins); S Kolisi for Louw (71 mins); J Vermaak for Pienaar (76 mins)

SCORERS: *Tries:* Oosthuizen, De Villiers, Kirchner, Le Roux *Conversions:* Steyn (3) *Penalty Goals:* Steyn (4)

YELLOW CARD: Alberts (8 mins)

REFEREE: G Clancy (Ireland)

14 September 2013, Eden Park

NEW ZEALAND 29 (3G 1T 1PG) SOUTH AFRICA 15 (1G 1T 1PG)

NEW ZEALAND: I Dagg; B Smith, C Smith, M Nonu, J Savea; D Carter, A Smith; T Woodcock, D Coles, O Franks, B Retallick, S Whitelock, L Messam, S Cane, K Read (captain)

SUBSTITUTIONS: B Barrett for Carter (16 mins); M Todd for Cane (temp 31-41 mins); C Piutau for Dagg (41 mins); K Mealamu for Coles (52 mins); S Luatua for Messam (62 mins); C Faumuina for Franks (65 mins); W Crockett for Woodcock (70 mins); M Todd for Cane (temp 71-76 mins); T Kerr-Barlow for Savea (76 mins)

SCORERS: *Tries*: Read (2), Retallick, Cane *Conversions*: Carter, Barrett (2) *Penalty Goal*: Barrett

YELLOW CARDS: Read (72 mins), Nonu (74 mins)

SOUTH AFRICA: Z Kirchner; W le Roux, JJ Engelbrecht, J de Villiers (captain), B Habana; M Steyn, R Pienaar; T Mtawarira, B du Plessis, J du Plessis, E Etzebeth, Flip van der Merwe, F Louw, W Alberts, D Vermeulen

SUBSTITUTIONS: A Strauss for Alberts (temp 20-27 mins); J Kruger for van der Merwe (41 mins); A Strauss for Alberts (44 mins); C Oosthuizen for J du Plessis (56 mins); G Steenkamp for Mtawarira (56 mins); J Serfontein for le Roux (70 mins); J Vermaak for Pienaar (70 mins); Mtawarira for Steenkamp (70 mins); W le Roux for Engelbrecht (75 mins) S Kolisi for Louw (75 mins); P Lambie for Habana (75 mins)

SCORERS: *Tries:* B du Plessis, Lambie *Conversion:* Steyn *Penalty Goal:* Steyn

YELLOW CARD: B du Plessis (16 mins)

RED CARD: B du Plessis (42 mins)

REFEREE: R Poite (France)

14 September 2013, Patersons Stadium, Perth

AUSTRALIA 14 (1T 3PG) ARGENTINA 13 (1G 2PG)

AUSTRALIA: I Folau; J O'Connor, A Ashley-Cooper, C Leali'ifano, N Cummins; Q Cooper, N White; J Slipper, S Moore, B Alexander, R Simmons, K Douglas, S Fardy, M Hooper, B Mowen (captain)

SUBSTITUTIONS: S Sio for Slipper (46 mins); S Timani for Douglas (52 mins); S Kepu for Alexander (60 mins); M Toomua for Cooper (67 mins); S Faingaa for Moore (67 mins); B McCalman for Fardy (73 mins)

SCORERS: *Try*: Folau *Penalty Goals*: Leali'ifano (3)

ARGENTINA: JM Hernández; H Agulla, G Tiesi, F Contepomi, JJ Imhoff; N Sanchez, T Cubelli; M Ayerza, A Creevy, J Figallo, M Carizza, J Farias Cabello, JM Fernández Lobbe (captain), P Matera, JM Leguizamón

SUBSTITUTIONS: L González Amorosino for Agulla (52 mins); E Guiñazu for Creevy (52 mins); M Galarza for Farias Cabello (57 mins); M Landajo for Cubelli (62 mins); S Fernández for Tiesi (73 mins); N Lobo for Ayerza (75 mins);

SCORERS: *Try:* Leguizamón *Conversion:* Sanchez *Penalty Goals:* Sanchez (2)

REFEREE: N Owens (Wales)

28 September 2013, Newlands Stadium, Cape Town

SOUTH AFRICA 28 (2G 1T 3PG) AUSTRALIA 8 (1T 1PG)

SOUTH AFRICA: Z Kirchner; W le Roux, JJ Engelbrecht, J de Villiers (captain), B Habana; M Steyn, F du Preez; T Mtawarira, A Strauss, J du Plessis, E Etzebeth, Flip van der Merwe, F Louw, W Alberts, D Vermuelen

SUBSTITUTIONS: B du Plessis for Strauss (50 mins); G Steenkamp for Mtawarira (53 mins); J Serfontein for Engelbrecht (57 mins); S Kolisi for Alberts (59 mins); J Kruger for F van der Merwe (60 mins); C Oosthuizen for J du Plessis (66 mins); P Lambie for Kirchner (77 mins)

SCORERS: *Tries*: Strauss, Kirchner, le Roux *Conversions*: Steyn (2) *Penalty Goals*: Steyn (3)

YELLOW CARDS: van der Merwe (40 mins); Vermeulen (66 mins)

AUSTRALIA: I Folau; A Ashley-Cooper, T Kuridrani, C Leali'ifano, J Tomane; Q Cooper, N White; J Slipper, S Moore, B Alexander, R Simmons, J Horwill (captain), S Fardy, M Hooper, B Mowen

SUBSTITUTIONS: W Genia for White (41 mins); B Robinson for Slipper (50 mins); S Kepu for Alexander (54 mins); B McCalman for Fardy (57 mins); C Feauai-Sautia for Tomane (57 mins); S Faingaa for Moore (66 mins); S Timani for Simmons (66 mins); M Toomua for Leali'ifano (72 mins)

SCORERS: *Try:* Feauai-Sautia *Penalty Goal:* Leali'ifano

YELLOW CARDS: Hooper (27 mins); Timani (74 mins)

REFEREE: J Garces (France)

28 September 2013, Estadio Ciudad de la Plata, La Plata

ARGENTINA 15 (5PG) NEW ZEALAND 33 (2G 2T 3PG)

ARGENTINA: JM Hernández; L González Amorosino, M Bosch, S Fernández, JJ Imhoff; N Sanchez, M Landajo; M Ayerza, E Guiñazu, J Figallo, J Farias Cabello, P Albacete, JM Fernández Lobbe (captain), P Matera, JM Leguizamón

SUBSTITUTIONS: M Galarza for Farias Cabello (60 mins); F Contepomi for Fernández (61 mins); H Agulla for González Amorosino (61 mins); A Creevy for Guiñazu (64 mins); JP Orlandi for Figallo (64 mins); N Lobo for Ayerza (70 mins); B Macome for Leguizamón (72 mins);

SCORERS: *Penalty Goals*: Sanchez (4), Bosch

NEW ZEALAND: I Dagg, B Smith, C Smith, M Nonu, J Savea; A Cruden, A Smith; T Woodcock, A Hore, O Franks, B Retallick, S Whitelock, L Messam, S Cane, K Read (captain)

SUBSTITUTIONS: C Faumuina for Franks (41 mins); K Mealamu for Hore (56 mins); S Luatua for Messam (65 mins); T Kerr-Barlow for A Smith (68 mins); W Crockett for T Woodcock (70 mins); C Piutau for Nonu (71 mins); B Barrett for Cruden (73 mins); J Thrush for Retallick (76 mins)l

SCORERS: *Tries:* Savea, Cane, B Smith (2) *Conversions:* Cruden, Barrett *Penalty Goals:* Cruden (3)

REFEREE: J Peyper (South Africa)

5 October 2013, Ellis Park, Johannesburg

SOUTH AFRICA 27 (2G 2T 1PG) NEW ZEALAND 38 (5G 1PG)

SOUTH AFRICA: Z Kirchner; W le Roux, JJ Engelbrecht, J de Villiers (captain), B Habana; M Steyn, F du Preez; T Mtawarira, B du Plessis, J du Plessis, E Etzebeth, J Kruger, F Louw, W Alberts, D Vermeulen

SUBSTITUTIONS: J Serfontein for Habana (22 mins); S Kolisi for Alberts (39 mins); A Strauss for B du Plessis (51 mins); C Oosthuizen for J du Plessis (51 mins); G Steenkamp for Mtawarira (54 mins); Franco van der Merwe for Kruger (61 mins); P Lambie for Kirchner (72 mins); R Pienaar for du Preez (72 mins); S Cane for Retallick (73 mins)

SCORERS: *Tries*: Habana (2), le Roux, de Villiers *Conversions*: Steyn (2) *Penalty Goal*: Steyn

NEW ZEALAND: I Dagg; B Smith, C Smith, M Nonu, J Savea; A Cruden, A Smith; T Woodcock, A Hore, C Faumuina, B Retallick, S Whitelock, L Messam, R McCaw (captain), K Read

SUBSTITUTIONS: D Coles for Hore (43 mins); B Barrett for Cruden (48 mins); B Franks for Faumuina (51 mins); W Crockett for Woodcock (54 mins); S Luatua for Messam (64 mins); C Faumuina for Retallick (temp 68-73 mins); T Kerr-Barlow for A Smith (70 mins); C Piutau for Savea (70 mins);

SCORERS: *Tries:* B Smith, Messam (2), Barrett, Read *Conversions:* Cruden (3), Barrett (2) *Penalty Goal:* Barrett

YELLOW CARDS: Messam (46 mins); Franks (63 mins)

REFEREE: N Owens (Wales)

5 October 2013, Estadio Gigante de Arroyito, Rosario

ARGENTINA 17 (2G 1PG) AUSTRALIA 54 (5G 2T 3PG)

ARGENTINA: JM Hernández; H Agulla, M Bosch, F Contepomi, JJ Imhoff; N Sanchez, M Landajo; M Ayerza, E Guiñazu, JP Orlandi, J Farias Cabello, P Albacete, JM Fernández Lobbe (captain), P Matera, JM Leguizamón

SUBSTITUTIONS: M Díaz for Orlandi (45 mins); A Creevy for Guiñazu (48 mins); M Carizza for Farias Cabello (52 mins); S Fernández for Contepomi (67 mins); L González Amorosino for Imhoff (68 mins); N Lobo for Ayerza (73 mins); T Cubelli for Landajo (73 mins); B Macome for Leguizamón (77 mins)

SCORERS: *Tries*: Bosch, Landajo *Conversions*: Sanchez (2) *Penalty Goal*: Sanchez

YELLOW CARD: P Matera (31 mins)

AUSTRALIA: I Folau, A Ashley-Cooper, T Kuridrani, C Leali'ifano, J Tomane; Q Cooper, W Genia; J Slipper, S Moore, B Alexander, R Simmons, J Horwill (captain), S Fardy, M Hooper, B Mowen

SUBSTITUTIONS: B Robinson for Fardy (temp 16-25 mins); M Toomua for Leali'ifano (41 mins); S Kepu for Alexander (48 mins); S Faingaa for Moore (48 mins); S Timani for Horwill (61 mins); B Robinson for Slipper (61 mins); B Foley for Cooper (66 mins); B McCalman for Fardy (69 mins); N White for Genia (76 mins)

SCORERS: *Tries:* Folau (3), Ashley-Cooper, Tomane, Robinson, Foley *Conversions:* Leali'ifano (2), Cooper, Foley (2) *Penalty Goals:* Leali'ifano (2), Cooper

YELLOW CARDS: J Slipper (15 mins); R Simmons (51 mins)

REFEREE: W Barnes (England)

RUGBY CHAMPIONSHIP (FORMERLY TRI-NATIONS) RECORDS 1996–2013

PREVIOUS WINNERS

1996 New Zealand	1997 New Zealand	1998 South Africa	1999 New Zealand
2000 Australia	2001 Australia	2002 New Zealand	2003 New Zealand
2004 South Africa	2005 New Zealand	2006 New Zealand	2007 New Zealand
2008 New Zealand	2009 South Africa	2010 New Zealand	2011 Australia
2012 New Zealand	2013 New Zealand		

GRAND SLAM WINNERS

New Zealand (Six times) 1996, 1997, 2003, 2010, 2012 and 2013
South Africa (Once) 1998

TEAM RECORD	DETAIL		SET
Most team points in season	203 by S Africa	in six matches	2013
Most team tries in season	24 by N Zealand	in six matches	2013
Highest team score	73 by S Africa	73–13 v Argentina (h)	2013
Biggest team win	60 by S Africa	73–13 v Argentina (h)	2013
Most team tries in match	9 by S Africa	v Argentina (h)	2013

INDIVIDUAL RECORD	DETAIL		SET
Most appearances	49 for N Zealand	RH McCaw	2002 to 2013
Most points in matches	531 for N Zealand	DW Carter	2003 to 2013
Most points in season	99 for N Zealand	DW Carter	2006
Most points in match	31 for S Africa	M Steyn	v N Zealand (h) 2009
Most tries in matches	17 for S Africa	BG Habana	2005 to 2013
Most tries in season	8 for N Zealand	BR Smith	2013
Most tries in match	4 for S Africa	JL Nokwe	v Australia (h) 2008
Most cons in matches	72 for N Zealand	DW Carter	2003 to 2013
Most cons in season	17 for S Africa	M Steyn	2013
Most cons in match	8 for S Africa	M Steyn	v Argentina (h) 2013
Most pens in matches	115 for N Zealand	DW Carter	2003 to 2013
Most pens in season	23 for S Africa	M Steyn	2009
Most pens in match	9 for N Zealand	AP Mehrtens	v Australia (h) 1999
Most drops in matches	4 for S Africa	AS Pretorius	2002 to 2006
	4 for S Africa	M Steyn	2009 to 2013
	4 for N Zealand	DW Carter	2003 to 2013
Most drops in season	3 for S Africa	M Steyn	2009
Most drops in match	2 for S Africa	JH de Beer	v N Zealand (h) 1997
	2 for S Africa	FPL Steyn	v Australia (h) 2007

From 1996 to 2005 inclusive, each nation played four matches in a season. The nations have played six matches since, except in 2007 and 2011 (Rugby World Cup years) when they reverted to four.

FIJI MARK CENTENARY WITH MAIDEN TITLE

By Karen Bond

Kenji Demura (RJP)

Fiji's victory ensured the PNC trophy returned to the Pacific Islands for the third time in four years.

A **new name** was written on the IRB Pacific Nations Cup in 2013 after Fiji claimed the title for the first time following a 34–21 victory over Tonga on the final day, a fitting way to celebrate the Fiji Rugby Union's centenary year and "a touching achievement" in the words of captain Akapusi Qera.

The Fijians were one of three teams that went into the final day of the new-look competition with a chance of lifting the silverware, safe in the knowledge that victory – or a draw with a bonus point for scoring four tries – would see them succeed Samoa as champions. A loss and Tonga would claim the title, while a low-scoring draw would have been enough for Canada to be crowned champions.

It was an exciting climax to a tournament which had been expanded to include USA and Canada for the first time, underscoring the International Rugby Board's long-term commitment to boosting the Tier Two competition schedule and competitiveness of the game. Matches were played in four countries – Canada, Fiji, USA and Japan – with Japan coach Eddie Jones confident that "the physical nature of Canada and USA plus the Pacific flair of Fiji and Tonga will make for a compelling tournament".

Samoa took a sabbatical from the Pacific Nations Cup in 2013 to take part in a quadrangular tournament in South Africa in June alongside the Springboks, Scotland and Italy after earning their spot as the highest-ranked Tier Two nation in 2012, which left Japan as the only other winner in the competition's history to be involved.

The Brave Blossoms had the honour of hosting the first match in Yokohama on 25 May, the first ever Test match in the city where rugby was first played in Japan. However, their hopes of setting a new record of seven consecutive Test victories were ended by Tonga, who ran in four tries at the Nippatsu Mitsuzawa Stadium to win 27–17.

The increased physicality of Tonga, in comparison to the sides the Brave Blossoms had faced in retaining the HSBC Asian 5 Nations title a few weeks earlier, had Japan on the back foot from the start with Jones admitting afterwards that his side had "played in the first half like we had a hangover; we were still playing like we were playing Asian rugby".

Later that same day, nearly 5,000 miles away, Canada and USA made their PNC debut at a wet and windy Ellerslie Rugby Park in Edmonton, each eager to strike a psychological blow ahead of their back-to-back Rugby World Cup 2015 qualifiers in August that would determine the Americas 1 qualifier. The conditions were not conducive to attacking rugby, but it was Canada who emerged the 16–9 winners, John Moonlight scoring the only try in the match.

Japan then travelled to Lautoka to face Fiji in a match which saw wing Hirotoki Onozawa win his 80th cap to become his country's most capped player. The occasion was not marked by a victory, though, as Fiji ran out 22–8 winners in extremely wet conditions at Churchill Park, with wing Sireli Bobo taking just 33 seconds to announce his return to the international stage after a three-year absence to score the opening try.

While Japan returned home to prepare for a two-Test series with Six Nations champions Wales, Fiji headed straight to North America to face Canada four days later. Canada took the match to the visitors from the outset and were rewarded when captain Aaron Carpenter scored their first try, breaking Al Charron's national record for the most Test tries by a forward. Fiji's powerful runners found it difficult to find a way through the resolute Canadian defence and, despite Qera's try making for a nerve-racking end to the match, it was the hosts who ran out 20–18 winners to remain unbeaten after two matches.

Canada barely had time to celebrate a first win over Fiji since 1995 as just three days later they were back in action against Tonga in Kingston. Full back James Pritchard contributed 23 points to the Canadian cause in the 36–27 victory as Tonga paid the price for ill-discipline with prop Edmund Aholelei sent off and two other players yellow-carded. Tonga, though, did give Canada a scare, scoring three tries in the last 15 minutes as their hosts tired.

"It was closer than I would have liked it to be and my heart stopped a couple of times watching on the sideline," admitted Carpenter. "They started to play really well and scored a few times late in the game when we maybe ran out of gas a little bit, but we gutted it out and in the end it was a great win."

Canada took a breather with a six-point lead at the top of the standings as Tonga headed to California to tackle USA. The Ikale Tahi returned to winning ways with a dominant and clinical display, Sione Piukala scoring a brace of tries in the 18–9 win as the hosts paid the price for too many unforced errors.

The teams then headed to Japan for the climax of the competition with double-headers taking place in Nagoya and Tokyo. Fiji did all they could do to keep their title hopes alive with a bonus-point, 35–10 victory over the winless USA in the driving rain, but knew that a Canadian win over hosts Japan in match two at the Municipal Mizuho Park Rugby Ground would see the Canucks crowned champions.

Canada led 3–0 at half-time, using the conditions to slow the ball down at the breakdown and prevent Japan from playing their fast-paced game. The Japanese, who came into the match on a high after beating Wales to claim a first scalp over a top 10 nation, battled back and snatched a 16–13 win courtesy of Ayumu Goromaru's penalty eight minutes from time.

Japan's win meant Canada had a nervous wait to see if they had done enough to lift the title. Fiji recovered from an early 11–0 deficit against Tonga to match Canada's record of three wins and one defeat in the competition. The fact that Fiji had secured four bonus points – three of them for scoring four tries or more – to Canada's one meant that the trophy would return to the Pacific Islands for the third time in four years.

With the champions crowned, the final match saw Japan finish on a high with a 38–20 victory over USA at the Prince Chichibu Memorial Stadium, ensuring that the Eagles would not mark captain Todd Clever's 50th Test with their first Pacific Nations Cup victory. It was a tough baptism for the Eagles, but they will be better for the experience and eager to find the winning formula in 2014.

IRB PACIFIC NATIONS CUP 2013 RESULTS

25/05/2013	Japan 17–27 Tonga	Nippatsu Mitsuzawa Stadium, Yokohama
25/05/2013	Canada 16–9 USA	Ellerslie Rugby Park, Edmonton
01/06/2013	Fiji 22–8 Japan	Churchill Park, Lautoka
05/06/2013	Canada 20–18 Fiji	Twin Elms Rugby Park, Nepean
08/06/2013	Canada 36–27 Tonga	Richardson Stadium, Kingston
14/06/2013	USA 9–18 Tonga	Home Depot Center, Carson, California
19/06/2013	Fiji 35–10 USA	Nagoya Municipal Mizuho Park Rugby Ground, Nagoya
19/06/2013	Japan 16–13 Canada	Nagoya Municipal Mizuho Park Rugby Ground, Nagoya
23/06/2013	Tonga 21–34 Fiji	Prince Chichibu Memorial Stadium, Tokyo
23/06/2013	Japan 38–20 USA	Prince Chichibu Memorial Stadium, Tokyo

FINAL STANDINGS

	P	W	D	L	F	A	BP	PTS
Fiji	4	3	0	1	109	59	4	**16**
Canada	4	3	0	1	85	70	1	**13**
Tonga	4	2	0	2	93	96	2	**10**
Japan	4	2	0	2	79	82	1	**9**
USA	4	0	0	4	48	107	1	**1**

FIVE IN A ROW FOR WARRIORS

Joe Allison/Allison Images

Fiji Warriors drew 37–37 with the Highlanders Development XV on their way to a fifth Pacific Rugby Cup title.

Fijian rugby celebrated its centenary in 2013 and it was perhaps fitting that the Fiji Warriors were crowned IRB Pacific Rugby Cup champions for the fifth year in succession, albeit not in such a convincing fashion as their 2012 success when they won seven of their eight matches to finish 18 points clear at the top of the final standings.

This time the margin was just four points from Samoa A at the conclusion of the Australian and New Zealand series and the Warriors were confirmed as champions in late August when the traditional climax involving the core teams was cancelled by the International Rugby Board to enable the Unions to maximise preparations for their November Test programmes.

"This decision has been taken in the best interests of the Unions following a detailed high performance review and recognises their desire to concentrate on ensuring that preparations for the delivery of the Test programme are optimised," explained William Glenwright, the IRB Regional General Manager for Oceania.

"The IRB Pacific Rugby Cup 2013 has already achieved its strategic purpose of providing that competitive environment against Australian and New Zealand Super Rugby franchise opposition in the first two legs. We collectively believe that IRB funding would be better directed at optimising preparations for the November tour, which is often a financial challenge for these Unions."

The 2013 edition had seen Junior Japan join the Fiji Warriors, Samoa A and Tonga A as a core team and, while the mix of university students, Top League players and high school students making up the team found their debut season difficult, there were clear positives for national coach Eddie Jones.

Not only did the competition pit the young Japanese players against the best up-and-coming talent in Super Rugby, but it also unearthed players ready to step up to the national team. A perfect example was wing Kenki Fukuoka, who caught the eye throughout the Pacific Rugby Cup and was rewarded with his Test debut in the HSBC Asian 5 Nations opener against the Philippines in late April.

Junior Japan entered the fray a fortnight after the other core teams kicked off the 2013 edition in Australia – a series which for the first time featured all five of the country's Super Rugby development teams and the Australian Rugby Union's academies based in Sydney and Brisbane – at the beginning of March.

The defending champions were the only core team to get anything out of round one and only then because their match with the HSBC Waratah A team was postponed due to inclement weather in Sydney and declared a 0–0 draw. An ACT XV outfit containing 16 players contracted to the Brumbies ran out 58–19 winners over Samoa A at Viking Park in Canberra, while the Reds College XV beat Tonga A 24–3 at Ballymore in Brisbane.

Round two brought better news for the Pacific island nations with Samoa A and Fiji Warriors recording wins over the ARU's Sydney- and Brisbane-based academies respectively. There was to be no hat-trick of wins, though, as Tonga A fell to a 62–12 defeat against the ACT XV in the Australian capital. Despite the heavy loss, Tonga A and national team coach Mana 'Otai was still able to draw positives from the match. "I'm glad the boys have been exposed to the width and pace of the Brumbies style of play and they will have learnt a lot from today. This is exactly the standard of rugby we need to expose our local players to."

The Warriors remained unbeaten in round three with a tight 27–22 victory over the Rebel Rising in Melbourne, but they were the only core team to taste success with Emirates Western Force A beating Samoa A 34–11, the Brisbane Academy handing Junior Japan a 76–26 debut loss and the Sydney Academy beating Tonga A 32–18.

While the Pacific islands trio moved on to New Zealand to begin the next series, Junior Japan stayed on in Australia to complete their fixtures, losing 59–14 to Reds College XV and 47–28 to the Sydney Academy. They had established a 21–5 lead by end of the first quarter against the latter, but were unable to build on that and secure a first Pacific Rugby Cup win before heading across the Tasman.

The Warriors had accumulated 11 points in the Australian series, but didn't enjoy the same good fortune on New Zealand soil, their best result being the opening 37–37 draw with the Highlanders Development XV at the Forsyth Barr Stadium in Dunedin, Lima Sopoaga converting his own try in the dying seconds to deny the defending champions the win. Their next match, against a clinical Blues Development XV, resulted in a 41–10 defeat which brought to an end their 10-match unbeaten run in the Pacific Rugby Cup.

Samoa A fared better, winning their first match in the New Zealand series 19–17 against the Blues Development XV before losing another tight one 30–27 to the Crusaders Knights and then 35–25 to the Chiefs Development XV. This helped them close to within four points of the Warriors in the standings, but the cancellation of the final series denied them the opportunity to claim the Pacific Rugby Cup title for the first time.

It proved another difficult series for the Tongans with three more heavy defeats against the Hurricanes Development XV (68–3), the Chiefs Development XV (50–18) and the Crusaders Knights (70–19), and they ended the New Zealand series in late March bottom of the standings and without a point to their names.

Junior Japan, like Tonga A, would suffer six defeats from six in the competition, but they avoided bottom spot by virtue of the three try-scoring bonus points earned. Their matches were certainly high-scoring affairs, none more so than their final outing against the Hurricanes Development XV at the Community Trust Domain which finished with a 73–43 score line.

The match was an exciting conclusion to the series with the crowd treated to an 18–try fest, although at times it resembled a training run rather than a competitive match with loose defence and soft turnovers a common theme. Fukuoka was again the star for Junior Japan, the electric wing helping himself to a hat-trick in the defeat, including the try of the match in the first half when he accelerated into the backline after a scrum near halfway and put the afterburners on to score under the posts.

IRB PACIFIC RUGBY CUP 2013 RESULTS

AUSTRALIA SERIES

01/03/2013	HSBC Waratah A 0–0 Fiji Warriors	Allianz Stadium*
01/03/2013	ACT XV 58–19 Samoa A	Viking Park
02/03/2013	Reds College XV 24–3 Tonga A	Ballymore
07/03/2013	Sydney Academy 24–33 Samoa A	TG Milner Oval
07/03/2013	ACT XV 62–12 Tonga A	Viking Park
07/03/2013	Brisbane Academy 17–24 Fiji Warriors	Ballymore
12/03/2013	Emirates Western Force A 34–11 Samoa A	Ballymore
12/03/2013	Sydney Academy 32–18 Tonga A	TG Milner Oval
12/03/2013	Brisbane Academy 76–26 Junior Japan	Ballymore
12/03/2013	Rebel Rising 22–27 Fiji Warriors	Harlequins RC
18/03/2013	Reds College XV 59–14 Junior Japan	Ballymore
23/03/2013	Sydney Academy 47–28 Junior Japan	Griffith Oval

* match postponed due to weather – result declared a 0–0 draw

NEW ZEALAND SERIES

18/03/2013	Highlanders Development XV 37–37 Fiji Warriors	Forsyth Barr Stadium
18/03/2013	Hurricanes Development XV 68–3 Tonga A	Hutt Recreation Ground
18/03/2013	Blues Development XV 17–19 Samoa A	Waitemata Park
23/03/2013	Crusaders Knights 30–27 Samoa A	Christchurch Stadium
23/03/2013	Blues Development XV 41–10 Fiji Warriors	Waitemata Park
23/03/2013	Chiefs Development XV 50–18 Tonga A	Rugby Park
28/03/2013	Hurricanes Development XV 38–20 Fiji Warriors	Spriggens Park
28/03/2013	Crusaders Knights 70–19 Tonga A	Linfield Park
28/03/2013	Chiefs Development XV 35–25 Samoa A	Albert Park
28/03/2013	Blues Development XV 43–19 Junior Japan	Bell Park
02/04/2013	Highlanders Development XV 63–10 Junior Japan	Forsyth Barr Stadium
07/04/2013	Hurricanes Development XV 73–43 Junior Japan	Community Trust Domain

FINAL STANDINGS (CORE TEAMS)

	P	W	D	L	F	A	BP	PTS
Fiji Warriors	6	2	2	2	118	155	2	**14**
Samoa A	6	2	0	4	134	198	2	**10**
Junior Japan	6	0	0	6	140	361	3	**3**
Tonga A	6	0	0	6	73	306	0	**0**

SIX IN A ROW FOR JAPAN

ARFU

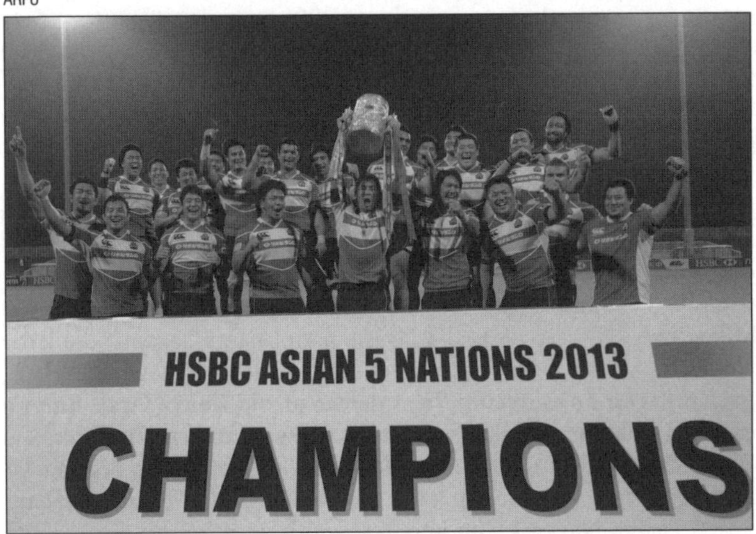

The Brave Blossoms were too strong once again for their HSBC Asian 5 Nations rivals in 2013.

Japan may have continued their dominance of the HSBC Asian 5 Nations in 2013 by claiming a sixth title but there was also cause for the Philippines and Sri Lanka to celebrate after ensuring they will be involved in the region's final stage of qualifying for Rugby World Cup 2015.

The Brave Blossoms scored 316 points and conceded just eight in their four matches to take their record to 24 from a possible 24 bonus point victories in the competition's history, and will be favourites to be crowned champions again in 2014 and claim the Asia 1 place alongside South Africa, Samoa, Scotland and the Americas 2 qualifier in Pool B at England 2015.

Korea, Hong Kong, the Philippines and Sri Lanka will hope to end Japan's record as the only Asian nation to grace the Rugby World Cup stage, but with the Brave Blossoms going on to record a first ever victory over a top 10 nation a few weeks after the Top 5 concluded – albeit a Welsh side missing 15 of its first-choice players with the British & Irish Lions in Australia – the size of the task they face is evident.

Japan had begun the competition in ruthless fashion in late April, defying the cold and wet conditions in Fukuoka to hand the Philippines a debut among Asia's elite they are unlikely to forget – a 121–0 defeat. Thirteen players crossed for Japan's 18 tries – including all four debutants – as their power and speed proved too much for the Volcanoes to handle.

It was the highest score recorded in the Asian 5 Nations and a tough baptism for a side that as recently as 2008 was in the bottom tier of the pyramid but, as coach Jarred Hodges put it, "Japan are the benchmark in Asian Rugby and showed us what it takes to be at that level." It was an experience that captain Michael Letts insisted his side would learn from as he promised, "We will be a completely different side for our next three games."

By the time the Philippines returned to action after sitting out round two, Japan had all but wrapped up the title after battling past a determined Hong Kong outfit 38–0 – their hosts making 124 tackles to the Brave Blossoms' 39 – and then Korea 64–5 in Tokyo with coach Eddie Jones labelling himself "very pleased with the performance" against the latter.

Jones was just as happy a week later when his Japanese charges signed off with an emphatic 93–3 defeat of the United Arab Emirates, wing Yuta Imamura scoring four of his side's 15 tries at 7he Sevens and captain Takashi Kikutani three. However, he knew that beating UAE was "a quantum leap" away from the challenge that awaited Japan in the IRB Pacific Nations Cup and Test series with Wales.

The Philippines' second outing was a 59–20 loss to Hong Kong, who scored seven second-half tries to leave their coach Leigh Jones admitting that the final score flattered them and their hosts hadn't deserved that margin of defeat. This was followed by a 62–19 defeat away to Korea which meant the Volcanoes returned home in the knowledge that victory over UAE on the final weekend would ensure their Top 5 adventure wasn't a brief one.

The encounter drew a record crowd for a rugby match in the Philippines of 5,700 and they did not leave Rizal Stadium disappointed as tries from Christopher Hitch, Gareth Holgate, Graeme Hagan and Matt Saunders secured the 24–8 victory and the Volcanoes' place among the elite nations for another year with UAE relegated to Division I.

"The atmosphere was electric tonight and that really helped us lift our game," admitted Hodges afterwards. "We are thrilled to be staying up in the top flight but most importantly we now know what it takes to compete at this level. We understand that we have a lot to work on in the coming 12 months to see how we can move one win in the campaign to two or three next year."

On the same weekend Korea beat Hong Kong 43–22 to finish as runners-up to Japan for the second year in a row. If they replicate this feat in 2014 then they will represent Asia in the Répechage for the 20th and final place available at England 2015.

Sri Lanka will replace UAE in the Top 5 in 2014 after they impressively beat Chinese Taipei (39–8), Thailand (45–7) and Kazakhstan (49–18) to win Division I on home soil in Colombo in April. With the country's rugby-loving president Mahinda Rajapaksa in attendance and proudly supporting his two sons – captain and flanker Yoshitha and prop Namal – the Sri Lankans scored 16 tries across the three matches to return to the Top 5 for the first time since 2011.

Kazakhstan had been the pre-tournament favourites to secure an immediate return to the Top 5, but they were stunned 33–10 by Division I newcomers Thailand on day one and, despite beating Chinese Taipei, simply had no answer to the potency of the Sri Lankan backline on the final day.

Eight teams converged on the Malaysian capital of Kuala Lumpur in early June for the Division II and III competitions at the Petaling Jaya Stadium. Singapore claimed the Division II title after edging hosts Malaysia 20–17 in the final – albeit only courtesy of scrum half Suhaimi Amran's penalty in the dying seconds – and will replace Thailand in the second tier of the Asian 5 Nations in 2014.

Qatar, meanwhile, continued their climb up the Asian 5 Nations pyramid by beating Guam 13–7 to win the Division III title in their first year, having won the Division IV title the two previous years. Captain Gavin Piek admitted the success was "going to do heaps for rugby in Qatar" and that they had "made everyone aware that Qatar is a nation that can play rugby".

A month earlier Lebanon had also tasted success by claiming the Division IV honours after defeating Pakistan in 45–12 in the final at 7he Sevens in a match which acted as the curtain-raiser to the Top 5 encounter between Japan and UAE.

The final chapter of the 2013 season, which involved 30 matches across eight countries over a 12-week period, saw Cambodia beat Brunei twice in the space of three days to claim their first piece of Asian 5 Nations silverware. Cambodia won the first Division V encounter 38–0 in Phnom Penh and were equally impressive in match two, winning 28–0.

HSBC ASIAN 5 NATIONS 2013 RESULTS

TOP 5

Japan 121–0 **Philippines**, **Hong Kong** 53–7 **UAE**, **UAE** 10–75 **Korea**, **Hong Kong** 0–38 **Japan**, **Japan** 64–5 **Korea**, **Philippines** 20–59 **Hong Kong**, **UAE** 3–93 **Japan**, **Korea** 62–19 **Philippines**, **Korea** 43–22 **Hong Kong**, **Philippines** 24–8 **UAE**

DIVISION I

Kazakhstan 10–33 **Thailand**, **Sri Lanka** 39–8 **Chinese Taipei**, **Kazakhstan** 42–10 **Chinese Taipei**, **Sri Lanka** 45–7 **Thailand**, **Chinese Taipei** 52–23 **Thailand**, **Sri Lanka** 49–8 **Kazakhstan**

DIVISION II

Singapore 67–8 **India**, **Malaysia** 48–10 **Iran**, **India** 13–30 **Iran**, **Singapore** 20–17 **Malaysia**

DIVISION III

Guam 33–15 **Indonesia**, **China** 0–76 **Qatar**, **Indonesia** 37–13 **China**, **Guam** 7–13 **Qatar**

DIVISION IV

Lebanon 35–25 **Uzbekistan**, **Pakistan** 31–25 **Laos**, **Uzbekistan** 18–15 **Laos**, **Lebanon** 45–12 **Pakistan**

DIVISION V

Cambodia 38–0 **Brunei**, **Brunei** 0–28 **Cambodia**

TOP 5 STANDINGS

Team	P	W	D	L	F	A	BP	PTS
Japan	4	4	0	0	316	8	4	24
Korea	4	3	0	1	185	115	3	18
Hong Kong	4	2	0	2	134	108	2	12
Philippines	4	1	0	3	63	250	1	6
UAE	4	0	0	4	28	245	0	0

ROMANIAN DELIGHT AT TITLE DEFENCE

By Jon Newcombe

With the great and the good of Romanian sport watching on at a packed Stadionul National Arcul de Triumf, the Oaks successfully defended the IRB Nations Cup title they won 12 months earlier when they beat Emerging Italy on a balmy June evening in Bucharest. In doing so, they became only the second side in the eight-year history of the competition to retain the trophy.

To the delight of a 6,000-strong capacity crowd that included the likes of gymnastics legend Nadia Comaneci, former tennis star Ion Tiriac, chairman of the National Olympic Committee Octavian Morariu and the Minister for Sport and Youth Nicolae Banicioiu, Romania overcame a slow start to eventually dominate their opponents and win 26–13, thus completing a hat-trick of victories following earlier successes over Russia (30–20) and an experienced Argentina Jaguars outfit (30–8).

Romania had to come from 14–3 behind to make it five Tests without defeat against Russia, while their victory over Argentina's second string provided the perfect 26th birthday present for try-scoring second row Valentin Poparlan.

Emerging Italy, like Romania, had won both their opening matches to set up a winner-takes-all finale against the hosts and defending champions, the exact scenario they had found themselves in last year.

Two tries from flanker Edoardo Ruffolo and 16 points from the boot of fly half James Ambrosini helped them to a 26–6 victory over the Jaguars in round one. Despite the concession of two yellow cards and an enforced stoppage due to an overhead thunderstorm, they followed that up with a 27–19 victory against Russia, for whom utility back Yury Kushnarev was influential.

In the decisive final match the Nations Cup title was definitely within the Italians' grasp after they twice took the lead during a tension-fuelled first half. But a try from Romania full back Catalin Fercu and eight points from the reliable boot of centre Florin Vlaicu pegged them back and the sides entered the break locked at 13–13.

The Fercu/Vlaicu double act accounted for all the points in the second half as Vlaicu punished Italian ill-discipline with his third and fourth penalties of the match. The show-stealing moment, though, was reserved for Fercu, who sent the crowd into raptures when he broke away from a driving maul to score a second opportunist try a couple of minutes from time.

While seeing Romania lift the trophy for a second successive year was a proud moment for head coach Lynn Howells, the former Wales coach took just as much pleasure in seeing new players come to the fore during the tournament. As many as six players were handed their international debuts at the Nations Cup, providing further evidence of its value as a vehicle for expanding the player pool available for selection at senior Test level. The most remarkable rise was undoubtedly that of rookie wing Stephen Hihetah, a lower league player based in England who was included in the Romania starting line-up for the Emerging Italy match just a month after being discovered at the Bournemouth Sevens.

"Our objective is to discover more talented players capable of playing at international level and so far this year we have been fairly successful," commented Howells, who is fast acquiring cult status among the Romanian rugby public through his easy-going nature and ability to deliver silverware.

IRB NATIONS CUP 2013 RESULTS

08/06/2013	Romania 30–20 Russia	Stadionul National Arcul de Triumf
08/06/2013	Argentina Jaguars 6–26 Emerging Italy	Stadionul National Arcul de Triumf
12/06/2013	Romania 30–8 Argentina Jaguars	Stadionul National Arcul de Triumf
12/06/2013	Russia 19–27 Emerging Italy	Stadionul National Arcul de Triumf
16/06/2013	Argentina Jaguars 30–17 Russia	Stadionul National Arcul de Triumf
16/06/2013	Romania 26–13 Emerging Italy	Stadionul National Arcul de Triumf

FINAL STANDINGS

	P	W	D	L	F	A	BP	PTS
Romania	3	3	0	0	86	41	0	**12**
Emerging Italy	3	2	0	1	66	51	0	**8**
Argentina Jaguars	3	1	0	2	44	73	0	**4**
Russia	3	0	0	3	56	87	0	**0**

SOUTH AFRICANS CLAIM INAUGURAL TITLE

By Jon Newcombe

Watched throughout by capacity crowds at the Achvala Stadium, the inaugural IRB Tbilisi Cup in the Georgian capital proved to be a popular and hugely competitive addition to the international rugby calendar.

Introduced as part of the IRB's ongoing strategy of increasing the competition schedule for Tier Two and Three nations as well as giving young players from higher-ranked nations the chance to shine on the global stage, the four-team tournament featured hosts Georgia, fellow Rugby World Cup 2015 hopefuls Uruguay, Emerging Ireland and the eventual winners, a South Africa President's XV.

Comprising players drawn mainly from the domestic Vodacom Cup competition and coached by Jimmy Stonehouse, the President's XV won all three of their matches in Georgia. Their path to glory was anything but straightforward, though, having had to come from behind to beat Uruguay on day one before prevailing in tight battles against Emerging Ireland and then Georgia in what was effectively a winner-takes-all finale.

Prior to his side's curtain-raiser against Uruguay coach Stonehouse spoke of the need for a fast start to the tournament. However, it was Los Teros who came out firing, scoring six points in as many minutes from the first whistle. The South Africans rallied and eventually emerged comfortable 37–9 winners.

Torrential rain made handling difficult in their next match against Emerging Ireland, the boot of fly half Carl Bezuidenhout proving crucial to a 19–8 success that put them on nine points – four ahead of Georgia with Emerging Ireland a point further back – going into the final day.

Cheered on by a partisan home crowd Georgia produced a hugely physical first-half performance, but 11 points from Bezuidenhout and a try from Rosko Specman handed the South Africans a 16–13 interval lead.

The scores were tied shortly after the restart when wing Beka Tsiklauri struck a third penalty for the Lelos, but the President's XV were not about to let the title slip from their grasp and they sealed a well-deserved 21–16 victory when Eduan van der Walt scored their second try.

"We are delighted to get the victory and win the tournament overall," said Stonehouse afterwards. "The tournament has been an excellent developmental tool for our players and will be fantastic for their progression as players."

Emerging Ireland leapfrogged Georgia into second place in the standings after signing off with a 42–33 bonus-point win over Uruguay who, in scoring five tries, recorded their first point of the tournament.

Fly half Ian Keatley was the Irish hero, converting all six of his side's tries which included two of his own as Emerging Ireland produced a blistering first-half display before the humid conditions took their toll, allowing Uruguay to stage a late comeback.

"The match was played in 36-degree heat and the boys were dying at the end, which probably explains why we went from being 42–14 in front after about an hour of play to only winning by nine points," explained wing Niall Morris, who also got on the scoresheet twice. Keatley finished the tournament as top points scorer with 40 points to his name having earlier kicked six penalties in Emerging Ireland's first two fixtures.

IRB TBILISI CUP 2013 RESULTS

07/06/2013	Uruguay 9–37 SA President's XV	Avchala Stadium, Tbilisi
07/06/2013	Georgia 15–20 Emerging Ireland	Avchala Stadium, Tbilisi
11/06/2013	Emerging Ireland 8–19 SA President's XV	Avchala Stadium, Tbilisi
11/06/2013	Georgia 27–3 Uruguay	Avchala Stadium, Tbilisi
16/06/2013	Uruguay 33–42 Emerging Ireland	Avchala Stadium, Tbilisi
16/06/2013	Georgia 16–21 SA President's XV	Avchala Stadium, Tbilisi

FINAL STANDINGS

	P	W	D	L	F	A	BP	PTS
SA President's XV	3	3	0	0	77	33	1	13
Emerging Ireland	3	2	0	1	70	67	1	9
Georgia	3	1	0	2	58	44	2	6
Uruguay	3	0	0	3	45	106	1	1

ENGLAND CELEBRATE FIRST TITLE AFTER HISTORIC FINAL

By Karen Bond

Getty Images

Jack Clifford holds aloft the trophy as England celebrate becoming the first northern hemisphere champions.

The 2013 edition of the IRB Junior World Championship had a lot to live up to after its predecessor in South Africa, but as records fell in north-west France a new champion was crowned after England came from behind to beat Wales 23–15 in the first all-northern hemisphere final and finally get their hands on the trophy after three previous appearances had ended in losses to New Zealand between 2008 and 2011.

The final was the proverbial game of two halves; the first belonged to Wales with their fly half Sam Davies producing some touches of brilliance, including a cross-field kick that fell into the arms of wing Ashley Evans for the opening try. The wing intercepted for his second try and, at half-time, Wales led 15–3 and seemed on track to avenge their loss to England in the Under 20 Six Nations title decider three months earlier that denied them a Grand Slam.

Wales had a man advantage for the opening 10 minutes of the second half with Dominic Barrow in the sin-bin but they failed to make it count and full back Jack Nowell began the England revival just before the hour mark with a try. The momentum had swung England's way and it seemed just a matter of when, rather than if, they would hit the front, Sam Hill's try and the boot of fly half Henry Slade ensuring it was their side celebrating at the final whistle in Vannes.

"I have never felt anything like it before, it's an awesome feeling and very humbling," England captain Jack Clifford admitted afterwards. "The support we had and the way the guys played was just fantastic. We had to pull together and it was all about heart and putting in 150 per cent. There was no point where I thought we had it definitely. All credit to Wales – they are a great team and they really took it to us."

For his counterpart Ellis Jenkins, it was another opportunity that had got away. "It's tough, that's the second time this season that we have come unstuck against England, but I'm extremely proud of the boys and what we have achieved in this tournament. We have come a long way as players, as a team and as friends. We have made history being the first Welsh side to get to the final but I suppose that makes it a lot harder to take. The smallest margins make the biggest difference so to get to the final and not make the most of it is tough to take."

There was some consolation for Wales with fly half Davies named the IRB Junior Player of the Year 2013 after the final, having beaten Clifford and New Zealand captain Ardie Savea to the prestigious honour after impressing throughout the tournament.

Davies had been pivotal in Wales reaching their first ever final as it was another perfectly weighted kick that allowed Evans to gather and touch down with a minute left on the clock of their semi-final against South Africa. The fly half then held his nerve to slot the touchline conversion and snatch the win 18–17, thereby ending South Africa's hopes of back-to-back titles.

The other semi-final was equally entertaining with England creating their own piece of history by beating New Zealand for the first time at age grade level, largely thanks to their impressive start which saw them lead 23–8 before the Baby Blacks came roaring back at them. Tom Smallbone's try ensured there would be no comeback victory as New

Zealand failed to reach the final for the first time in Junior World Championship history with the 33–21 loss.

New Zealand would ultimately finish fourth after losing an enthralling 11-try fest with South Africa 41–34. The Baby Blacks had raced into a 21–0 lead after the first quarter of the third place play-off and threatened to run away with it, but South Africa came racing back to tie things up. New Zealand edged ahead again but once more the outgoing champions responded, capitalising on two yellow cards for the Baby Blacks to hit the front just before the hour mark and ensure they finished on a positive note.

There were also wins on the final day for France, Australia and Samoa over Argentina, Ireland and Scotland respectively. Hosts France did it the hard way against Los Pumitas in La Roche-sur-Yon, trailing by 22 points at half-time before battling back to win 37–34 and finish fifth overall. Australia's 28–17 win avenged their loss to Ireland on the opening day and gave them a one-place better finish than 2012, while Samoa beat Scotland 33–24 in Nantes to claim ninth place.

USA found life extremely difficult on their return to the elite tier for the first time since the inaugural tournament in 2008 and had scored just six points going into the 11th place play-off against Fiji, who for the second year in a row faced a must-win finale to remain in the Championship. Fiji, as expected, proved too strong and ran out 46–12 winners, but at least the Americans crossed for two tries in defeat. They will now travel to Hong Kong next year, hoping to win the IRB Junior World Rugby Trophy for a second time in three years to secure a return.

The Junior All-Americans, as the team are known back home, knew they were in for a tough journey in France but, after conceding 16 tries in a 97–0 loss to South Africa on day one, they then slipped to a 45–3 defeat to their hosts. Worse was to come, though, as England ran riot on day three, setting a number of JWC records including the most tries (17), highest score (109) and the biggest winning margin (109).

Despite the emphatic defeats, captain Tom Bliss was able to find positives from the experience. "I think one of the positives that has come from this is the guys know what a professional environment is, they have come up against professional players and they know what they have to do to make that step up so it has been a good learning curve."

There had been plenty of excitement going into the sixth edition of the Junior World Championship in France with many mouth-watering matches on the cards in the pool stages after the 2012 results had shaken up the seedings. Defending champions South Africa had to face England and hosts France in Pool A, while New Zealand played trans-Tasman rivals Australia in Pool B and two of the previous year's semi-finalists met in Pool C in Wales and Argentina.

South Africa, with Sevens stars Seabelo Senatla and Cheslin Kolbe tormenting defences, topped Pool A after battling past both England and France, a converted try the difference at the final whistle in both matches. England joined the Junior Springboks in the semi-finals as the best runner-up, their record score against USA meaning they edged Ireland and Argentina on points differential.

For the second year in a row Ireland had come close to a maiden semi-final, this time claiming the scalp of Australia on day one and then giving four-time champions New Zealand an almighty scare, fighting back from 20 points down to ultimately lose 31–26. Savea, the heartbeat of the New Zealand side, admitted his Baby Blacks side were "lucky to get away with that win" against an Irish side that would have knocked England out of semi-final contention if they had scored another try.

The Wales-Argentina encounter that was part of a triple-header at La Roche-sur-Yon on 13 June was always expected to be the Pool C decider and a battle between two standout fly halves in Davies and Patricio Fernández, one of a number of players to have made their Test debut for Los Pumas a month earlier. Wales were in no mood to miss out on the semi-finals and Argentina barely created an opportunity in the first half to trail 16–0. They did rally but Wales were not to be denied and emerged the 25–20 winners. *@irbjuniors*

IRB JUNIOR WORLD CHAMPIONSHIP 2013 RESULTS

POOL A

Round One: **France** 6–30 **England**, **South Africa** 97–0 **USA**. Round Two: **South Africa** 31–24 **England**, **France** 45–3 **USA**. Round Three: **England** 109–0 **USA**, **France** 19–26 **South Africa**

POOL B

Round One: **Ireland** 19–15 **Australia**, **New Zealand** 59–6 **Fiji**. Round Two: **Ireland** 46–3 **Fiji**, **New Zealand** 14–10 **Australia**. Round Three: **New Zealand** 31–26 **Ireland**, **Australia** 46–12 **Fiji**

POOL C

Round One: **Wales** 42–3 **Samoa**, **Argentina** 44–13 **Scotland**. Round Two: **Argentina** 28–16 **Samoa**, **Wales** 26–21 **Scotland**. Round Three: **Wales** 25–20 **Argentina**, **Scotland** 36–33 **Samoa**

POOL TABLES

POOL A

	P	W	D	L	F	A	BP	PTS
South Africa	3	3	0	0	154	43	1	13
England	3	2	0	1	163	37	2	10
France	3	1	0	2	70	59	2	6
USA	3	0	0	3	3	251	0	0

POOL B

	P	W	D	L	F	A	BP	PTS
New Zealand	3	3	0	0	104	42	2	14
Ireland	3	2	0	1	91	49	2	10
Australia	3	1	0	2	71	45	3	7
Fiji	3	0	0	3	21	151	0	0

POOL C

	P	W	D	L	F	A	BP	PTS
Wales	3	3	0	0	93	44	1	13
Argentina	3	2	0	1	92	54	2	10
Scotland	3	1	0	2	70	103	2	6
Samoa	3	0	0	3	52	106	2	2

PLAY-OFFS FIRST PHASE

Ninth Place Semi-Finals	**Samoa** 19–18 **Fiji**
	Scotland 39–3 **USA**
Fifth Place Semi-Finals	**Argentina** 22–15 **Australia**
	Ireland 8–9 **France**
Semi-Finals	**South Africa** 17–18 **Wales**
	New Zealand 21–33 **England**

PLAY-OFFS SECOND PHASE

11th Place Play–off	**Fiji** 46–12 **USA**
Ninth Place Play-off	**Samoa** 33–24 **Scotland**
Seventh Place Play-off	**Australia** 28–17 **Ireland**
Fifth Place Play-off	**Argentina** 34–37 **France**

THIRD PLACE PLAY-OFF

23 June 2013, Stade de la Rabine, Vannes

SOUTH AFRICA 41 (4G 2T 1PG) NEW ZEALAND 34 (3G 2T 1PG)

SOUTH AFRICA: C Kolbe; L Obi, J Kriel, RJ van Rensburg, S Senatla; H Pollard, S Ungerer; S Sithole, M Willemse, L de Bruin, I Herbst, D Visser, R Steenkamp (captain), J du Plessis, A Davis

SUBSTITUTIONS: J du Toit for Willemse (25 mins); K Smith for Davis (46 mins); R du Preez for van Rensburg (54 mins); M Coetzee for Sithole (62 mins)

SCORERS: *Tries*: Obi, de Bruin, Senatla, Steenkamp, Smith, Ungerer *Conversions*: Pollard (4) *Penalty Goal*: Pollard

NEW ZEALAND: J Webber; P Latu, M Collins, T Walden, L Visinia; S Hickey, S Rangihuna; D Brighouse, N Grogan, S Mafileo, S Barrett, P Tuipulotu, J Manihera, A Savea (captain), J Edwards

SUBSTITUTIONS: T Adams for Rangihuna (41 mins); D Lienert-Brown for Brighouse (54 mins); J Te Rure for Hickey (58 mins); K Pongi for Grogan (62 mins); C Vui for Tuipulotu (68 mins); S Scrafton for Savea (70 mins); L Van Dam for Walden (71 mins); B Wiggins for Mafileo (75 mins)

SCORERS: *Tries*: Visinia (2), Edwards, Webber, Manihera *Conversions*: Hickey (3) Penalty *Goal*: Hickey

YELLOW CARDS: Manihera (52 mins); Pongi (62 mins)

REFEREE: D Phillips (Wales)

FINAL

23 June 2013, Stade de la Rabine, Vannes

WALES 15 (1G 1T 1PG) ENGLAND 23 (2G 3PG)

WALES: J Williams; A Evans, S Hughes, J Dixon, H Amos; S Davies, R Williams; G Thomas, E Dee, N Thomas, C Jones, R Hughes, J Jones, E Jenkins (captain), I Jones

SUBSTITUTIONS: J Benjamin for I Jones (60 mins); T Davies for G Thomas (64 mins); D Thomas for C Jones (64 mins); T Pascoe for S Hughes (68 mins); J Davies for R Williams (69 mins); O Jenkins for Amos (72 mins); D Suter for N Thomas (74 mins)

SCORERS: *Tries*: A Evans (2) *Conversion*: Davies *Penalty Goal:* Davies

ENGLAND: J Nowell; A Watson, H Sloan, S Hill, B Howard; H Slade, A Day; A Hepburn, L Cowan-Dickie, S Wilson, T Price, D Barrow, R Moriarty, M Hankin, J Clifford (captain)

SUBSTITUTIONS: D Sisi for Moriarty (48 mins); C Braley for Day (53 mins); D Hobbs-Awoyemi for Hepburn (55 mins); O Devoto for Howard (56 mins); H Purdy for Sloan (67 mins); S Spurling for Hankin (69 mins); H Wells for Price (69 mins)

SCORERS: *Tries*: Nowell, Hill *Conversions*: Slade (2) *Penalty Goals:* Slade (3)

YELLOW CARD: Barrow (40 mins)

REFEREE: M Fraser (New Zealand)

FINAL STANDINGS

1 England	**2 Wales**
3 South Africa	**4 New Zealand**
5 France	**6 Argentina**
7 Ireland	**8 Australia**
9 Samoa	**10 Scotland**
11 Fiji	**12 USA**

TOP POINTS SCORERS

Name	Pts
Patricio Fernández (Argentina)	**82**
Sam Davies (Wales)	**61**
Henry Slade (England)	**55**
Tommy Allan (Scotland)	**39**
Emori Waqa (Fiji)	**39**
Seabelo Senatla (South Africa)	**35**
Handrè Pollard (South Africa)	**34**
Simon Hickey (New Zealand)	**32**
Vincent Mallet (France)	**32**
Luke Burton (Australia)	**31**

TOP TRY SCORERS

Name	Tries
Seabelo Senatla (South Africa)	**7**
Luther Obi (South Africa)	**4**
Rory Scholes (Ireland)	**4**
Lolagi Visinia (New Zealand)	**4**
Emori Waqa (Fiji)	**4**
Mark Bennett (Scotland)	**3**
Alex Day (England)	**3**
Ashley Evans (Wales)	**3**
Epalahame Faiva (New Zealand)	**3**
Patricio Fernández (Argentina)	**3**
Pablo Matera (Argentina)	**3**
Ross Moriarty (England)	**3**
Melani Nanai (Samoa)	**3**
Alex Northam (Australia)	**3**
Henry Purdy (England)	**3**

2013 / 2014

#Sevens

www.irbsevens.com

get the World Series App from the iStore

ITALY INSPIRED BY INCREDIBLE SUPPORT

By Tom Chick

Italy secured an immediate return to the IRB Junior World Championship after overcoming Canada 45–23 in the final of the IRB Junior World Rugby Trophy 2013 in the Chilean city of Temuco in early June. The Azzurrini, who were relegated to the second tier after losing 19–17 to Fiji in the relegation play-off at JWC 2012, won all four of their matches in Chile to ensure their place among the world's elite Under 20 teams in New Zealand in 2014.

Having safely negotiated their way through the pool stages, Italy made their intentions clear from the start of the final at the Estadio Germán Becker with Marcello Violi crossing in the opening minute.

But, despite leading only 10–6 at half-time, Italy took advantage when Canada had two players sin-binned in the second half, scoring five tries, including a second by Violi, to run out impressive winners.

"I have no words to describe this moment," admitted delighted captain Angelo Espósito. "We are overjoyed that we have taken Italy back to the JWC. The way the public supported this tournament was incredible and it certainly pushed us to play our best rugby."

Gianluca Guidi's side had got off to a comfortable start, beating Namibia 33–7 at the Estadio Municipal Freire on 28 May.

Victories followed for the tournament favourites over hosts Chile (50–6) and Portugal (59–13) to confirm their place in the final as Pool A winners, while Canada defeated Tonga (24–6), Japan (39–15) and Uruguay (36–15) in the other pool.

The Italian defeat may have been hard to swallow for Canada, but it was a significant improvement on their sixth-place finish 12 months earlier. Canada coach Mike Shelley admitted that Temuco "had been the best" of his three tournaments.

Chile were perhaps the surprise package of the tournament, however, finishing an impressive third, two places higher than in 2012. Having beaten newcomers Portugal 18–6 on the opening day, they bounced back from their defeat to Italy to edge Namibia 23–21.

That set up a third place play-off with Japan, which was equally entertaining in front of 10,500 spectators ahead of the final.

The lead changed hands no less than nine times in the match, and once again it was Chile who struck late on to snatch the win against Japan, who had reached the three previous finals.

With the defence containing wing Kai Ishii, who had earlier scored five tries in Japan's 40–20 victory against Uruguay and a total of eight in the pool stages, Francisco Urroz was the hero again. Japan took the lead through Joji Sato with a minute remaining, before the Chile full back collected the ball in midfield and placed a perfectly weighted kick into the corner where wing Jan Hasenlechner jumped to take the ball and score a much celebrated try, fittingly converted by Urroz.

Despite Temuco stepping in to host the tournament just a month before when Antofagasta pulled out, the 2013 edition was a huge success with more than 35,000 spectators turning out – the most in the tournament's fledgling history. "It was a privilege for us and the region to host such a great tournament. Having eight nations in Temuco was not only good fun but great exposure for a region that has everything: mountains and sea, farmland and great people," said Araucanía Region Governor Andrés Molina. *@irbjuniors*

IRB JUNIOR WORLD RUGBY TROPHY 2013 RESULTS

POOL A

Round One: **Italy** 33–7 **Namibia**, **Chile** 18–6 **Portugal**. Round Two: **Portugal** 26–17 **Namibia**, **Chile** 6–50 **Italy**. Round Three: **Italy** 59–13 **Portugal**, **Chile** 23–21 **Namibia**

POOL B

Round One: **Japan** 40–20 **Uruguay**, **Tonga** 6–24 **Canada**. Round Two: **Japan** 15–39 **Canada**, **Tonga** 35–20 **Uruguay**. Round Three: **Japan** 43–22 **Tonga**, **Canada** 36–15 **Uruguay**

PLAY-OFFS

Seventh place play-off	**Namibia** 29–40 **Uruguay**
Fifth place play-off	**Portugal** 7–27 **Tonga**
Third place play-off	**Chile** 38–35 **Japan**
Final	**Italy** 45–23 **Canada**

FINAL STANDINGS

1 Italy	**2 Canada**
3 Chile	**4 Japan**
5 Tonga	**6 Portugal**
7 Uruguay	**8 Namibia**

JAGUARS RETAIN ARC TITLE

Argentina Jaguars continued their dominance of the IRB Americas Rugby Championship in 2013 by claiming the title for a fourth time with an unbeaten record after beating hosts Canada A, USA Select and Uruguay in October.

A young Jaguars side had the title in the bag after round two with USA Select's 30–10 victory over Canada A ensuring that the defending champions couldn't be caught in the standings, having themselves beaten the American side 27–9 and Uruguay 34–0 to record the maximum 10 points.

Argentina Jaguars arrived in Langford, British Columbia, with a squad containing three players who had featured in their second Rugby Championship campaign with one of them, full back Joaquín Tuculet, named captain.

The Jaguars scored two tries in each half as they beat USA Select in round one, dominating the first half and producing some good attacking rugby and remaining solid in defence on the few occasions their line was threatened. Coach Daniel Hourcade proclaimed himself "happy" after the win was secured with tries from flanker Martin Chiappesoni, Matías Orlando, Javier Rojas and Facundo Barrea.

The other match on day one was much tighter and only decided in the final seconds when centre Mike Scholz squeezed over to secure a 17–10 win for Canada A against Uruguay to the delight of the home fans. The Canadians had led 10–0 before Los Teros fought back to level and had their own chances to win with Joaquín Prada missing two penalty attempts.

"They did not make it easy, challenging every breakdown and making our life difficult," admitted Canada A captain Aaron Carpenter. "It was clear from today that the standard of rugby is growing and that has to be very good."

Day two of the tournament which is designed to develop locally-based players in the Americas into the next tier of international players saw two derby matches – one all-South American affair and one all-North American encounter.

The Jaguars proved too strong for Uruguay, although the score perhaps flattered them. Los Teros will take some comfort for shutting out the Jaguars for nearly an hour, but two tries from Ramiro Moyano had the win all wrapped up after 25 minutes.

USA Select then stunned their hosts, recording the first victory by an American national fifteens side over their neighbours since 2009. The Americans controlled the game throughout and were rewarded with tries from Daniel Barrett and Tim Maupin (2).

The Jaguars may have wrapped up the title but the final day still had plenty at stake with the other three teams all battling to finish second in the standings. In the end the USA Select team claimed that honour with a 20–8 victory over Uruguay, the key spell for the victors being the 15 minutes after half-time with tries from Chris Chapman, Barrett and Toby L'Estrange.

That left Canada A playing only for pride against the champions and they took the game to them, dominating in the set piece. However, the Jaguars showed a more clinical touch and seized on a Canadian yellow card to score tries through Rojas and Ignacio Sáenz Lancuba to lead 17–7 at half-time. Canada, urged on by their passionate supporters, scored once through Conor Trainor but two penalties from young fly half Patricio Fernández made certain of victory for the Jaguars.

IRB AMERICAS RUGBY CHAMPIONSHIP 2013 RESULTS		
11/10/2013	USA Select 9–27 Argentina Jaguars	Westhills Stadium
11/10/2013	Canada A 17–10 Uruguay	Westhills Stadium
15/10/2013	Uruguay 0–34 Argentina Jaguars	Westhills Stadium
15/10/2013	Canada A 10–30 USA Select	Westhills Stadium
19/10/2013	Uruguay 8–20 USA Select	Westhills Stadium
19/10/2013	Canada A 14–23 Argentina Jaguars	Westhills Stadium

International Sevens Tournaments

HISTORIC DOUBLE FOR NEW ZEALAND

By Keith Quinn

AFP/Getty Images

The New Zealand men's and women's Sevens teams kick off the victory celebrations in Moscow.

The eagerly awaited sixth Rugby World Cup Sevens held in the Russian capital Moscow on 28–30 June was justifiably deemed a significant success.

Both on and off the field the tournament, played in the city's vast Luzhniki Stadium, took rugby to a whole new fan base in one of the world's Olympic powerhouse nations, and certainly won't be quickly forgotten.

In the week leading up to the event Russian news channels were announcing the hottest temperatures in the country for 100 years, and the 24 men's and 16 women's teams from 28 countries were presented with scorching conditions in which to train and then play on the first two days of the competition.

The tournament looked to be set fair in this magnificent arena which, initially as the Central Lenin Stadium, had been built to offer 100,000 towering seats as the main venue for the 1980 Olympic Games. Thirty-three years later, against such a dramatic backdrop – now with a capacity just under 80,000 after redevelopment – Rugby World Cup Sevens 2013 was an inspiration for the young rugby players of today to perform just three years out from Rio 2016.

This they did with relish, and some of the play witnessed was as exciting, if not better, than previous World Cups. But there was to be a savage twist in the tale of this story and late on day three Mother Nature changed her tune and conspired against proceedings.

As the tournament was building brilliantly towards its two climactic finals, the early blazing sunshine gave way to an hour-long electrical storm which was so severe that the first of the men's Cup semi-finals between Fiji and New Zealand had to stop, the players forced to leave the field for reasons of safety. While the players went inside and regrouped, the centre-field turf took on a month's rainfall and became sodden in the extreme.

And so it was that the finals of both the men's and women's events became a totally different rugby 'test' – an exercise in slithering and sliding and dealing with treacherous conditions underfoot. Maybe that did not offer the best chance for all the players to showcase their Sevens talents but, truth be told, it was New Zealand who did not complain.

The Melrose Cup was won by the team whose name has now been officially changed to give the players 'All Black Sevens' status. The New Zealanders, under captain DJ Forbes and coach, the newly knighted Sir Gordon Tietjens, seemed to rise best to the challenge of all that the heavens – and the rugby gods – threw at them and beat England convincingly in the final, 33–0.

Only minutes earlier their 'Sis-taahss' from New Zealand had also triumphed, captain Huriana Manuel leading Sean Horan's side to a 29–12 win against a fine Canadian side, going one better than the runners-up spot they'd managed in 2009, when Australia had won the first ever women's title.

Would those two results have been the same had the finals been played in hard and fast conditions devoid of any rainstorms? We will never know, of course, but it is certainly fair to say that both New

Zealand teams presented brilliant players who were among the very best from any nation in any year of RWC Sevens history.

After the two finals Tietjens did offer one of several typically droll observations: "When our women's team was playing their final as the second-to-last game, my guys were to be on last against England," he said. "But it was our girls and not England who were the first to give our boys a hell of a fright. The girls were playing their final and were leading 17–5 in the wet when my team jogged out to warm up. The boys looked up and saw how well the sisters were going. I heard several of them say, 'Wow, we'd better do something better than what they're doing!'"

In keeping with the general feeling of competitiveness which has grown up in the last two seasons on the men's HSBC Sevens World Series, where any one of six or seven teams might win each event, the main contenders for the men's title in Moscow made for a long and impressive list. Beforehand any pundit could make a case for Fiji, South Africa, Wales, England, Kenya, Australia or New Zealand to win. Indeed, among the assembled news media there was little or no consensus.

It was true that New Zealand had only recently, and comfortably, won an 11th World Series in 14 seasons, reaching seven of the nine finals, but they had also lost five of those deciders. Of the other nations, England had shown signs of improvement and commitment from their players; the South Africans had high expectations with Kyle Brown returning from injury, but had lost their recent captain Frankie Horne to injury; Fiji presented the usual brilliant mix of new players and baffling return selections; Australia recalled three Super Rugby men who'd lined up against the British & Irish Lions – Luke Morahan, Bernard Foley and Matt Lucas – to bolster the wide-eyed and highly promising remainder of their squad; Wales presented their best team and to some looked to have a real chance of retaining their 2009 title, while Kenya, under their ebullient coach Mike Friday, brought along their usual bristling standards and confident crowd of supporters, reflecting their high hopes.

The only real surprises beforehand were Samoa, who seemed to have dropped away in performance over the season, and the 2009 runners-up Argentina, who also did not look to be a true challenger this time around.

Day one of the men's event was completed with all the victories going as per the seedings but the second day's programme was much more severe and testing for the players. With temperatures soaring to the hottest Moscow had seen in a century – up over 35 degrees – each men's team played two games over the 11 hours. Would upsets be more likely in the heat?

First there was a slow-starting New Zealand team against USA. After a lively opening period of play the men in black were knocked off their momentum and USA led 19–5, a position from which you might say a good team never ought to lose. But the Kiwis kept their heads and squeaked a last-second try to win 26–19.

Another team then took its chances in the soaring temperatures, Wales playing a stirring match against Fiji and one they desperately needed to win to qualify for the Cup quarter-finals. When Alex Webber scuttled away past the flailing hands of the Fijians a major upset was on the cards. If any teams are comfortable in extreme heat surely it is the Pacific nations, and yet Wales toppled Fiji 19–14, a massive shock after all the pre-tournament chat.

One other result on day two which would have been particularly pleasing to the IRB came when Hong Kong beat Portugal, one of the 2013/14 World Series core teams, showing that competitive edge at every level of the competition.

Finals day dawned fine and warm again but, by early afternoon, ominous clouds had started to gather over the top of the circular grandstands at the Luzhniki Stadium. Their gloomy sight was a reminder too that the dark and brutal disappointments of knock-out play awaited any team who didn't perform from now on.

RWC Sevens 2009 in Dubai had thrown up all manner of upsets in the quarter-finals, and the 2013 tournament's games were equally keenly anticipated. But this time most of the favoured teams came through.

In the very tight draw South Africa were the first of the highly fancied teams to crash out. They met the Fijians who, despite their loss to Wales the day before, remained in contention. Fiji played a high-speed game and kept the willing but ill-fated South Africans back on their heels for a 12–10 winning score.

New Zealand finally found some form to beat Wales 26–10, England stormed ahead against the very keen Australians and then held on frantically to win 21–17 and the Kenyans were as stylish as ever in beating France 24–19.

Then came the semis – and the rain! The draw first pitted New Zealand against their fiercest rivals Fiji and a fine game looked in prospect. It was too – that is until Fiji conceded two early tries to fall behind 12–0, followed by the deluge.

Seasoned reporters could not ever recall having seen a 'rain stopped play' sign at a significant rugby match. Under instruction, the two teams hurried from the field as flashes of lightning and claps of thunder resonated and the downpour made it impossible to continue.

The New Zealanders were obviously more relaxed and when play resumed after an hour there were whispers that the Fijian team did not have long studs for their boots in their playing kit while the New Zealanders did. Hence New Zealand restarted looking more secure and went on to win 17–0.

Then England came out to play Kenya in the other semi-final. This was a thriller all the way and England, looking slightly more comfortable in the rain, prevailed 12–5.

That left New Zealand to play England in the final but still the rain continued to tumble down.

Surprisingly, when the final kicked off, with South Africa's brilliant referee Rasta Rasivhenge in charge, there was only one team in it. You might say that the New Zealanders adapted better to the perilous conditions, but the 33–0 winning margin perhaps says it better. The game became a masterstroke for the crafty Tietjens.

In a plan presumably saved for such a day he had two of his team, Gillies Kaka and Tomasi Cama, go to a new tactic of kicking for position to the dark corners of the shifty surface. The England players, led by captain Rob Vickerman and coached by Ben Ryan, scrambled back, while the rest of the New Zealand team charged forward to disrupt in a solid attacking line. England became rattled and could only flail at hurried clearances. In the slippery conditions their hopes soon collapsed.

Nevertheless the wide winning margin was a surprise; no one could have picked such a result. For Tietjens it was the ultimate satisfaction, coming 12 years after he had won the same event in Mar del Plata, Argentina, in 2001. In another of his quirky asides Tietjens showed himself very much the modern coach. "Hey," he told several reporters, "I got a lot of my inside information for this tournament from the many tweets I followed from inside my opponents' camps. I never tweeted once but they told me a lot!"

Within the New Zealand ranks were the superbly elusive Tim Mikkelson, later to be named IRB Sevens Player of the Year, and Kurt Baker, the smiling assassin. Along with Cama and Lote Raikabula they marshalled the troops in excellent fashion and allowed younger men like Kaka (named Player of the Tournament), Bryce Heem and Pita Ahki to shine as well. The winning margin said it all. This was a great New Zealand performance.

Let us not forget, or underestimate, the importance and excitement too of the women's event, which ran alongside the men's in Moscow. There were 16 teams taking part and they showed a marked improvement and consistency in standards from those which had been so boldly set in the first Women's Rugby World Cup Sevens in Dubai in 2009.

Australia started as the defending champions in Moscow, while

Canada, USA, England and New Zealand also had high hopes of winning. The IRB's initiative in starting a Sevens World Series in 2012/13 had already helped women's rugby no end and there were many games in Moscow of an extremely high standard.

Once again it soon emerged that New Zealand were the team to beat. This was somewhat surprising given that Sevens rugby in New Zealand had had such modest exposure at home and very little top-class tournaments. But their new coach Sean Horan, like Tietjens, seemed to know how to hit the spot.

Horan used the four tournaments on the inaugural IRB Women's Sevens World Series to introduce and scrutinise a number of young contenders before making his final Moscow choice. Twenty-five young women played across the tournaments in Dubai, Houston, Guangzhou and Amsterdam and it was amazing that a number of them were brand new to the game.

Two of the new kids were Portia Woodman and Kayla McAlister, who had come from semi-professional netball. Yet as the tournaments unfolded over the season, including in Moscow, the two became almost unstoppable in their ability to manage the oval ball skilfully and run away from opponents to score. McAlister became the first IRB Women's Sevens Player of the Year, while Woodman was the Player of the Tournament in Moscow after scoring 12 tries.

The two-day women's tournament had also been given the best possible start, and promotion, and one result in particular thrilled local fans when host nation Russia finished the day by stunning the highly fancied English 12–5 with every move cheered to the echo. The Russians would narrowly lose their quarter-final against Canada, but that and a 7–5 loss to Australia in the Plate semi-finals spoke volumes about their potential.

The rest of the top contenders came through day one unbeaten, one result later confirmed as a portent of the Cup final when New Zealand beat Canada 20–5.

In the final a day later, played in vastly different weather conditions, once again it was McAlister and Woodman on song as the New Zealanders rose to the occasion to score a 29–12 win against captain Jennifer Kish and her fine Canadians.

Clearly the two wins for New Zealand will go down in the history books for RWC Sevens 2013 – uniting as they did for the first time the Sevens and Fifteens Rugby World Cups – and it was a great sight for all Kiwis to see not one but two hakas performed in celebration, yet so much more than that will live long in the memory.

For the players from all 28 countries, the fans and the media, one key and abiding memory will simply be playing, reporting and watching rugby in a country to which the sport had probably never taken them before.

Moscow was a fun place to visit, which might have surprised some who had notions of an austere place beforehand, and while the spirit of the 'friendly' Sevens still prevailed in the players' hotel the fierceness of rivalry between all the teams on the field was a further hint that by the time the Olympic Sevens competition is played in Rio in 2016 no one country will feel assured of medal status. *@irbsevens*

RUGBY WORLD CUP SEVENS 2013 RESULTS

MEN

CUP

QUARTER-FINALS	
South Africa 10–12 Fiji	England 21–17 Australia
New Zealand 26–10 Wales	Kenya 24–19 France (AET)

SEMI-FINALS	
Fiji 0–17 New Zealand	England 12–5 Kenya

THIRD PLACE
Fiji 29–5 Kenya

FINAL
New Zealand 33–0 England

PLATE

QUARTER-FINALS

Samoa 26–17 Zimbabwe
Argentina 28–5 USA
Scotland 17–0 Portugal
Canada 26–0 Tonga

SEMI-FINALS

Samoa 21–14 Argentina
Scotland 7–21 Canada

FINAL

Samoa 12–19 Canada

BOWL

QUARTER-FINALS

Tunisia 7–12 Uruguay
Russia 17–7 Spain
Hong Kong 10–31 Georgia
Japan 50–0 Philippines

SEMI-FINALS

Uruguay 0–38 Russia
Georgia 21–24 Japan

FINAL

Russia 29–5 Japan

WOMEN

CUP

QUARTER-FINALS

New Zealand 24–7 England
USA 14–5 Ireland
Russia 12–15 Canada
Australia 10–14 Spain

SEMI-FINALS

New Zealand 19–10 USA
Canada 10–0 Spain

THIRD PLACE

USA 10–5 Spain (AET)

FINAL

New Zealand 29–12 Canada

PLATE

SEMI-FINALS

England 22–0 Ireland
Russia 5–7 Australia

FINAL

England 5–14 Australia

BOWL

QUARTER-FINALS

Netherlands 19–14 Japan
Brazil 5–10 China
France 40–7 Tunisia
South Africa 5–22 Fiji

SEMI-FINALS

Netherlands 17–12 China
France 10–12 Fiji

FINAL

Netherlands 10–12 Fiji

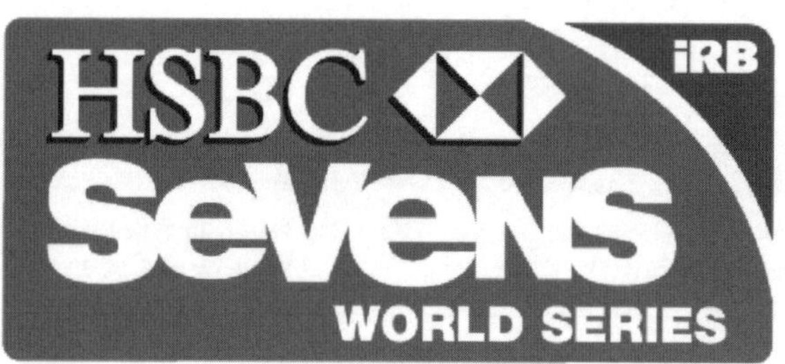

CONSISTENCY THE KEY FOR NEW ZEALAND

By Nigel Starmer-Smith

Getty Images

Victory at the London Sevens was a fitting end to the HSBC Sevens World Series for champions New Zealand.

This was a different, fascinating and nerve-racking season. Pressure was a constant for the players and even more so given selection for Rugby World Cup Sevens in Moscow was looming. Added to that, the 2012/13 HSBC Sevens World Series again cranked up a notch in its competitive edge with not 12 but 15 core teams playing in all nine rounds. Canada, Spain and Portugal arrived hoping they were duly equipped to rival the best, and so it proved.

Once again the Series began on Australia's Gold Coast in October and immediately the new core teams made their mark, Portugal coming within a try of France and Wales, Spain within three points of England in the pool and beating them in the Bowl final, and Canada beaten by only one try by the Series overall champions New Zealand.

There were new arrivals across all the teams, notably the two finalists, Fiji, who introduced seven new players, and New Zealand, who had six. Fiji impressed early with wins over Samoa and South Africa and produced a remarkable display to run riot in the final, winning 32–14 – almost New Zealand's biggest defeat. It seemed a perfect start for Fiji with Joji Raqamate magnificent and a new recruit, Alipate Raitini, scoring a hat-trick.

Six weeks later the teams arrived at 7he Sevens, the superb stadium of the famous Emirates Airline Dubai Sevens, and Fiji coach Alifereti Dere made nine more changes! Seven debutants joined recalled veteran Setefano Cakau and, unsurprisingly, the consequences were dramatic with the Fijians bowled out in the Cup semi-finals by France.

There were more surprises too. Portugal beat South Africa and England to make the Cup quarter-finals alongside Canada, who comfortably beat France and USA and drew with Australia. Meanwhile New Zealand, with six changes but still with their experienced quartet of Tim Mikkelson, DJ Forbes, Tomasi Cama and Lote Raikabula, moved impressively through to the final against Samoa.

Kurt Baker, Sherwin Stowers and Ben Lam brought a new edge to the New Zealand squad, but Samoa were outstanding with new captain Afa Aiono and Reupena Levasa impressing, while Paul Perez proved the match-winner with two tries in a rampaging 26–15 final victory.

After the drama of Dubai it was straight on to South Africa and the Nelson Mandela Bay Stadium in Port Elizabeth. South Africa has been the most successful venue for New Zealand in the history of the Series, and so it proved for a ninth time as they became the first country to win four successive Cup titles at a single event. After two runners-up finishes to start the season, their consistency gained its reward, even though en route to the final they fell to Fiji and just scraped past Scotland 14–7 on day one.

In the final Gordon Tietjens' men beat surprise package France, who had got the better of Portugal and Argentina, both by a 10–7 scoreline, to get there, the latter only with an extra-time penalty drop goal at the end of a match which sapped their energy so much that they were really up against it in the final. France lost 47–12, with Tietjens receiving the perfect birthday present.

As 2013 arrived, England were yet to make an impact on the Series and still had not reached a single Cup quarter-final. Injuries had hit them hard, but they arrived in Wellington with key men like John Brake, Mat Turner and Christian Lewis-Pratt recovered and fit. Somehow coach Ben Ryan managed to restore confidence in his squad and, crucially, they gained a pool win over the hosts New Zealand, who had their injury troubles too and gave debuts to Rocky Khan – the first ever Indo-Fijian to play for New Zealand – and Gillies Kaka, who was to make a big impact later in the Series.

Another side on the up was Kenya, already impressive under Mike Friday but here even more so with a brilliant win in the semi-finals against the hosts. England also won a nail-biter against Samoa and so it was Ryan against Friday in the final. Kenya's new captain Andrew Amonde and the outstanding Willy Ambaka put in tour de force performances as the final went to extra-time, but in the end it was England's young Sam Edgerley who sniped in for the winning try, and a reprieve for Ryan.

South Africa had so far blown hot and cold. Not helped by captain Kyle Brown's broken ankle in Dubai, the recurring knee troubles of Cecil Afrika and Branco du Preez's hamstring, instead it was giant Frankie Horne who emerged as a beacon of defiance, recording the most consecutive tournaments ever by a player with 44 events in a row, in Port Elizabeth. His consistent and immense power was supported by Chris Dry and the exceptional Paul Delport and Cornal Hendricks, and finally their reward came in Las Vegas. Exciting teenagers Seabelo Senatla and Cheslin Kolbe refreshed the team and, conceding just three tries in five games against Canada, Kenya, Uruguay, Wales and Samoa, they stormed to the final against New Zealand.

Certainly injuries had hit the All Blacks Sevens in Wellington with Forbes, Raikabula and Baker ruled out. There was still real potential in the outstanding Mikkelson and Cama, but the Cup final was a South African blitz, 35–0 at one stage before three converted tries put a degree of respectability on the final score of 40–21 for South Africa – the fifth different Cup champions of the season.

A month later 28 nations headed to Hong Kong for the three-day tournament, the normal 16 for the World Series event and 12 in the pre-qualifier for teams hoping to secure core team status in 2013/14.

In the main Cup, there was yet another story, another team rising to the occasion. Despite having lifted the Melrose Cup in 2009, Wales had never made a final in their 82 Series tournaments, but in Hong Kong in 2013 that drought ended. At half-time in the Cup final it must have seemed like a dream as they led Fiji 19–0 with two tries by 20-year-old

Cory Allen and one from Alex Webber. But somehow the Fijians rose to the challenge and super-sub Osea Kolinisau, who had last played on the Gold Coast, cut through the Welsh defence twice for two tries in quick succession, followed by another from Samisoni Viriviri. With two conversions the score was tied at 19–19, and inevitably Kolinisau's third broke the hearts of the valiant Welsh.

Meanwhile in the Series pre-qualifier it was Russia, Zimbabwe, Tonga and Georgia who rose to the occasion and the crowd to book their places with Asian champions Hong Kong at the season finale in London.

By their high standards, Australia had been muted until they returned to the Prince Chichibu Memorial Stadium where they had celebrated a thrilling Cup title last season. The return of experienced campaigner James Stannard also lifted the Australians and, with Lewis Holland, Pama Fou and Cameron Clark playing well beyond their years, they scored early wins over England and Argentina and a significant quarter-final success over Fiji. Ultimately they came undone against the powerful New Zealanders in the semi-finals, and so the final was a repeat of the Vegas decider against South Africa, now with Afrika back.

New Zealand led 12–0 at half-time, a try apiece for Kaka and Mikkelson, but strong words from coach Paul Treu must have worked as the Boks transformed the game with a run of 24 points through tries from Senatla, Afrika and finally the star of the final, Hendricks. The game was effectively over by the time Lam scored the final try and South Africa were right back on their game.

When the teams arrived at the penultimate round in Glasgow, the Series crown was as good as settled. Although New Zealand had only won one event their consistency – with four runners-up and two third-place finishes – put them 32 points clear of their closest rival. But the real tension was down the standings, where the bottom three core teams after Glasgow would need to try and win back core team status at Twickenham the following weekend.

Spain, the lowest ranked of the teams, accepted their fate and rested their best players. Portugal, too, were almost doomed, but Scotland and USA were level on points in 13th place. Portugal and Scotland both suffered in the same pool, losing to New Zealand and England, but the USA guaranteed their survival by reaching the Cup quarter-finals after beating Russia, losing by a single score to Wales and claiming a decisive win over France in a thrilling contest.

South Africa, meanwhile, were riding high, full of confidence after their win in Tokyo and, despite the absence again of Afrika and du Preez, Treu motivated his squad with the carrot of World Cup selection. Delport was back, Hendricks was still on top form and with Horne,

Dry and Senatla on song they reached another final with a clinical 24–17 semi-final win against England, who were themselves back near their best. The All Blacks Sevens continued their remarkable consistency, led again by Mikkelson in Forbes' absence, and with the return of Baker, Curry and Cama.

On day two they dismissed Argentina and Wales to set up the third Cup final in four events against South Africa, the only side to have beaten them since Kenya had surprised them back in Wellington. Once again it was a classic match, the two swapping tries until Hendricks gave South Africa a lead of 14 points with less than two minutes to go. So victory for the Blitzbokke in Glasgow, but even they were powerless to prevent New Zealand from claiming an 11th overall Series title.

For the final acts of the HSBC Sevens World Series, close to 70,000 descended on Twickenham for day one of the Marriott London Sevens, which for the first time featured two competitions: the top 12 core teams competed for final Series points, while the bottom three joined Hong Kong, Georgia, Russia, Zimbabwe and Tonga in a bid to win one of three core team places for 2013/14.

Series winners or not, there was no chance that New Zealand would rest on their laurels, especially knowing that they had not won the London Sevens for six years. It was no surprise, therefore, that the All Blacks Sevens raced out of the blocks on day one, ravaging Canada, Kenya and Wales by scoring 100 points and conceding just 29. England lifted their game in front of their tremendous Twickenham support with devastating wins over Fiji, Samoa and South Africa, Dan Norton back to his brilliant best alongside Marcus Watson, Brake and Turner, but once again Australia thwarted them, this time in the Cup semi-final. The young Australians had improved as the World Cup neared, led by the return of captain Ed Jenkins, Con Foley, Stannard, and Holland.

New Zealand brushed Argentina aside in the Cup quarter-finals, before Kenya so nearly upset the form guide in the semi-finals with the outstanding presence of Ambaka and the returning legend Humphrey Kayange, losing just 7–0. In truth it was a well-deserved final for the team that had finished no lower than third in any round. They had won just one title, but there was no doubt this time around. Yet again Mikkelson, who would later be named IRB Sevens Player of the Year, set the standard, scoring the first try within 30 seconds, and six more followed in a 47–12 trans-Tasman win. They may have only won two titles, but in truth they dominated almost from start to finish and were worthy Series champions.

The pressure continued for the eight teams playing for their lives in the dreaded qualifier. There was tension from the start as Tonga beat Spain, Hong Kong upset Scotland, Scotland edged Zimbabwe and Portugal beat Tonga. But in the end the core teams of this season emerged winners in knock-out play to retain their status, Scotland, Spain and Portugal confirming their place on the Gold Coast in 2013.

What a season! Never have there been so many close encounters and so many upsets! But that is what creates the excitement of this thrilling HSBC Sevens World Series. *@irbsevens*

HSBC SEVENS WORLD SERIES 2012/13 RESULTS

AUSTRALIA: 13–14 OCTOBER

Fiji (22), **New Zealand** (19), **South Africa** (17), **Kenya** (15), **Argentina** (13), **France** (12), **Samoa** (10), **Australia** (10), **Spain** (8), **England** (7), **Wales** (5), **Canada** (5), **Scotland** (3), **USA** (2), **Portugal** (1), **Tonga** (1)

DUBAI: 30 NOVEMBER–1 DECEMBER

Samoa (22), **New Zealand** (19), **Kenya** (17), **France** (15), **Wales** (13), **Canada** (12), **Fiji** (10), **Portugal** (10), **Argentina** (8), **South Africa** (7), **USA** (5), **Scotland** (5), **England** (3), **Spain** (2), **Russia** (1), **Australia** (1)

SOUTH AFRICA: 8–9 DECEMBER

New Zealand (22), **France** (19), **South Africa** (17), **Argentina** (15), **Wales** (13), **Fiji** (12), **Portugal** (10), **USA** (10), **Australia** (8), **Samoa** (7), **England** (5), **Kenya** (5), **Spain** (3), **Zimbabwe** (2), **Scotland** (1), **Canada** (1)

NEW ZEALAND: 1–2 FEBUARY

England (22), **Kenya** (19), **New Zealand** (17), **Samoa** (15), **Australia** (13), **Scotland** (12), **South Africa** (10), **Argentina** (10), **Canada** (8), **Fiji** (7), **Spain** (5), **France** (5), **Wales** (3), **Tonga** (2), **Portugal** (1), **USA** (1)

USA: 8–10 FEBUARY

South Africa (22), **New Zealand** (19), **Samoa** (17), **Fiji** (15), **Canada** (13), **Scotland** (12), **USA** (10), **Wales** (10), **France** (8), **Argentina** (7), **Spain** (5), **England** (5), **Australia** (3), **Uruguay** (2), **Portugal** (1), **Kenya** (1)

HONG KONG: 22–24 MARCH

Fiji (22), **Wales** (19), **New Zealand** (17), **Kenya** (15), **Samoa** (13), **Canada** (12), **Australia** (10), **Portugal** (10), **England** (8), **Hong Kong** (7), **South Africa** (5), **USA** (5), **France** (3), **Argentina** (2), **Spain** (1), **Scotland** (1)

JAPAN: 30–31 MARCH

South Africa (22), **New Zealand** (19), **Australia** (17), **France** (15), **USA** (13), **Scotland** (12), **Fiji** (10), **Samoa** (10), **England** (8), **Argentina** (7), **Wales** (5), **Kenya** (5), **Canada** (3), **Japan** (2), **Portugal** (1), **Spain** (1)

SCOTLAND: 4–5 MAY

South Africa (22), **New Zealand** (19), **England** (17), **Wales** (15), **USA** (13), **Argentina** (12), **Fiji** (10), **Canada** (10), **Australia** (8), **Kenya** (7), **Scotland** (5), **Samoa** (5), **France** (3), **Russia** (2), **Portugal** (1), **Spain** (1)

ENGLAND: 11–12 MAY

New Zealand (22), **Australia** (19), **England** (17), **Kenya** (15), **Fiji** (13), **USA** (12), **South Africa** (10), **Argentina** (10), **Wales** (8), **France** (7), **Canada** (5), **Samoa** (5)

FINAL STANDINGS

New Zealand – 173	Canada – 69
South Africa – 132	Scotland – 51
Fiji – 121	Portugal – 35
Samoa – 104	Spain – 26
Kenya – 99	Hong Kong – 7
England – 92	Russia – 3
Wales – 91	Tonga – 3
Australia – 89	Japan – 2
France – 87	Uruguay – 2
Argentina – 84	Zimbabwe – 2
USA – 71	

PREVIOUS WINNERS

1999/2000 – New Zealand	2006/2007 – New Zealand
2000/2001 – New Zealand	2007/2008 – New Zealand
2001/2002 – New Zealand	2008/2009 – South Africa
2002/2003 – New Zealand	2009/2010 – Samoa
2003/2004 – New Zealand	2010/2011 – New Zealand
2004/2005 – New Zealand	2011/2012 – New Zealand
2005/2006 – Fiji	2012/2013 – New Zealand

AFP/Getty Images

Fiji and South Africa both tasted success in the 2012/13 HSBC Sevens World Series.

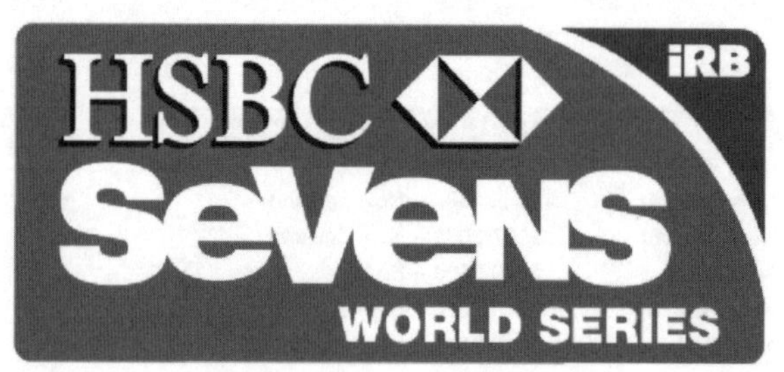

THE SEASON IN QUOTES

ROUND 1 – AUSTRALIA

On the sun-kissed Gold Coast Fiji, with seven Series debutants, successfully defended their title, beating New Zealand 32–14.

"I thank the Lord for everything he has done for us, especially the new boys," said the player of the tournament, Joji Raqamate. "They pulled up their socks and came to this level of rugby and I am thankful for that. This is the first time for us to go back-to-back and retain the title again. It was a hard effort and I take my hat off to the boys."

ROUND 2 – DUBAI

In Dubai New Zealand again reached the final, but were hit by another Pacific Island roadblock, this time in the shape of Samoa, who triumphed 26–15.

"It was touch and go," admitted captain Afa Aiono. "New Zealand are a pretty good team but our boys stepped up and played their hearts out. We are really proud of what the boys did today. They did a really good job and achieved what we were aiming for and won their first ever Cup in Dubai."

ROUND 3 – SOUTH AFRICA

It was third time lucky on Gordon Tietjens' birthday as his New Zealand side beat surprise finalists France 47–12 to claim a fourth straight title on South African soil.

"It was an awesome birthday present," Tietjens said. "My five core experienced players of Cama, Forbes, Mikkelson, Raikabula and Baker were just outstanding and for the younger players to learn and those guys will kick on when the others are not around. It was important. We were beaten by a good Samoa last time, beaten by Fiji in Australia. We had to win this one."

ROUND 4 – NEW ZEALAND

After misfiring badly in the first three rounds, England hit form in Wellington and stunned the hosts in pool play. Kenya also played well, memorably beating New Zealand in the semi-finals, but they came up just short of their first ever Series win in the final, Sam Edgerley diving over in sudden death extra-time to rescue England's season.

"It is just fantastic, I am overwhelmed to be honest," an emotional Edgerley admitted. "It is my first tournament win for England and I am the proudest man in the world. We didn't have the best start to the season so we made a promise to ourselves to get out of it, and we did."

ROUND 5 – USA

Round five would bring another different winner as the Blitzbokke, simply unstoppable, beat Series leaders New Zealand 40–21 to kick-start what would be an impressive second half of the season for them.

"There are no words. It was just tremendous fight from the boys," said outstanding playmaker Paul Delport. "We set such high standards for ourselves and this is huge for us. We put in so much effort back home, there are just no words, it is testament to the guys."

ROUND 6 – HONG KONG

Hong Kong took on double significance by also hosting the pre-qualifier for core team status in 2013/14. Russia, Zimbabwe, Tonga and Georgia all kept alive their hopes, but in the main event Wales were the talk of the town, leading 19–0 in the final before succumbing to super-sub Osea Kolinisau's second-half hat-trick as Fiji won 26–19.

"We just said that we needed hope and we needed to keep the faith, to keep on working because 10 minutes is a lot of time in Sevens. It is a really good feeling to go back-to-back here and especially to be the first team to win two Cups this season," said Kolinisau, perhaps inspired by the watching Waisale Serevi, who was inducted into the IRB Hall of Fame in Hong Kong.

ROUND 7 – JAPAN

If Fiji had clawed back some of New Zealand's lead in Hong Kong, the Kiwis did their Series aspirations no harm a week later by reaching another final in biting conditions. They led 12–0 at half-time, but again South Africa had their number and ran out 24–19 winners.

"It is unbelievable. For us we have been so unlucky throughout the year, and to come back again after a disappointing tournament in Hong Kong, to bounce back and give a performance like that, it is not every day you beat New Zealand twice in the final," said coach Paul Treu.

ROUND 8 – SCOTLAND

In Glasgow, much of the focus was on the bottom of the table, where hosts Scotland and USA faced an almighty tussle to avoid the relegation play-offs in London. With the Eagles lifting a second successive Plate Scotland were left in the mire, while in the Cup England and Wales both performed well to reach the semis. But once again it was green versus black in the final and for a third time the Blitzbokke responded with a heart-stopping 28–21 win.

"I'm so proud of the boys," insisted Delport. "Everyone stepped up this weekend. Our preparation wasn't great with lots of injuries and it means a lot to beat New Zealand. Once you get to the top teams it used to be three or four, but now it is like eight and to come out on top of that is just extra special."

ROUND 9 – ENGLAND

The All Blacks Sevens arrived in London looking to rubber-stamp an 11th Series success, which they did emphatically, beating Australia 47–12 in the final.

"We just took it one game at a time. Kenya was very hard, even Australia we knew was going to be a tough one. We work really hard and you get a lot when you work hard. We have got a great team here and a lot of young players. Tim Mikkelson was simply outstanding," said coach Tietjens.

In the nerve-jangling core team qualifier, Spain, Portugal and Scotland all re-booked that same status for 2013/14 – a giant relief for all three.

"We are delighted, we normally talk about enjoying our rugby but today that's not been possible," admitted Scotland captain Colin Gregor. "But we rose to the occasion and we are back on the Series. It is horrendous being down here so we need to make sure we start the season properly."

NEW ZEALAND SHINE ON INAUGURAL SERIES

By Ali Donnelly

Getty Images

Huriana Manuel holds up the trophy as New Zealand are crowned IRB Women's Sevens World Series champions.

The launch of the first IRB Women's Sevens World Series heralded a landmark moment in the history of the women's game, and the inaugural season certainly did not disappoint.

While New Zealand's ladies outdid even their male counterparts in winning three-quarters of the rounds en route to being crowned the first ever champions, there were plenty of twists and turns along the way, and some superb performances over the course of the season.

Indeed, it was a fitting testament to the breadth and depth of talent already surfacing all over the world that, by the end of the season, when the nominations were made for the first IRB Women's Sevens Player of the Year Award, the list of five included players from four different countries – Canada, the Netherlands, England and New Zealand – while others from Russia, Spain, USA, Australia and South Africa could count themselves unlucky to miss out.

The four venues chosen to host all of this excitement were the United Arab Emirates (Dubai), USA (Houston), China (Guangzhou) and the Netherlands (Amsterdam). At each tournament 12 teams competed, including a core group of six who played at each event – Australia, Canada, England, the Netherlands, New Zealand and USA – plus six invited teams who had booked their place through regional competition or by impressing over the previous couple of seasons.

Across the season South Africa, Brazil, Spain, Russia, China, France, Trinidad & Tobago, Argentina, Japan, Tunisia, Ireland and Fiji all contributed royally. Such was the overall standard that the decision was made to expand the number of core teams for 2013/14 to eight, with Russia, Spain and Ireland booking their places based on World Cup performances, and the Netherlands losing their core status but already steeled to win it back for 2014/15.

And so all eyes were trained on Dubai at the end of November 2012 for the opening round, which was held alongside the men's HSBC Sevens World Series event at 7he Sevens, purpose-built for Rugby World Cup Sevens 2009. Spain, Russia, South Africa, France, China and Brazil took their places in history alongside the six ever-presents and the first ever Series kicked off with Australia beating the Netherlands 24–12.

Having been absent from the international Sevens scene all of the previous year, ominously building a squad behind closed doors through their Olympic 'Go4Gold' campaign, New Zealand immediately announced themselves as the team to beat with a 31–0 win against China. But it was Russia who arguably made the biggest splash on day one, toppling one of the pre-tournament favourites Canada in the pool stages.

With the formidable Khamidova sisters, Baizat and Navrat, in full flow, the Russians set the tone in that opening game and then scored a fine 12–12 draw with the New Zealanders. Indeed Russia would go on to become one of the teams of the season, inspired by their passionate coach, Pavel Baranovsky.

Australia, winners of the first Women's Rugby World Cup Sevens in Dubai back in 2009, also started well with Emilee Cherry starring, but on day two it was all about the team in black as New Zealand mixed their power game with the raw talent of newcomers Kayla McAlister and Portia Woodman to stroll to the title.

South Africa were another surprise package, beating the Netherlands and Spain to reach the final, but New Zealand were simply too strong for them there, sweeping to an impressive 41–0 win in front of a record television audience for women's rugby.

The next stop was Houston, Texas, at the start of February 2013, where Japan, Argentina and Trinidad & Tobago all made their maiden appearances of the Series.

Hosts USA were clearly inspired by their familiar surroundings and home support and, with Nathalie Marchino and captain Vanesha McGee particularly impressive, they led the charge and made it all the way to the final with a strong win against Australia.

Elsewhere, a strengthened England narrowly beat New Zealand 7–5 in their pool. Barry Maddocks's side continued its strong form into day two, with Jo Watmore playing a starring role in a second win over the Series leaders. In the final Heather Fisher plundered the hosts in indomitable fashion, her powerful running and hard tackling a hallmark of the effort as the English won 29–12.

New Zealand and England may have claimed the first two titles, but a number of the invited sides had also shown that women's Sevens was well on its way with the likes of Brazil, Spain and Russia in particular continuing to showcase their immense potential.

China hosted round three at the end of March with Guangzhou, the country's third largest city, staging an historic weekend for the women's game. One year out from the sport's debut at the Youth Olympic Games in Nanjing, the action and the welcoming nature of the crowd further highlighted the growing appetite for rugby in non-traditional markets, especially in Asia.

Ireland, Fiji and Tunisia played in their first Series event, but it was the weather that made the news with constant rain and storms causing a delay in play at the Guangzhou University Town Stadium.

When the action resumed there was plenty to be impressed by. Ireland, featuring many players who had recently won an historic first Six Nations Grand Slam, reached the quarter-finals, while Brazil also made the last eight for the first time to join New Zealand, Canada, England, Australia, USA and the Netherlands. Hosts China were unlucky not to make the knock-outs, edged out by Ireland on points difference.

Day two brought better weather but a similar story as New Zealand swept all before them and took the title courtesy of a 19–5 win over England in the final – a victory that also extended their lead in the Series to eight points with just one event remaining.

Ireland would go on to lift the Plate, while Canada continued their steady uplift in form with a win over arch-rivals USA to finish third. China came close to lifting some silverware on home soil, but eventually succumbed to rivals Japan in the Bowl final.

Just under seven weeks later the teams converged on the Dutch capital Amsterdam where large crowds generated a fittingly jovial atmosphere for the fourth and final round of the Series.

With the first overall title there for the taking, leaders New Zealand were unstoppable on day one as they cruised to three easy wins and left themselves needing to beat Spain in the quarter-finals to guarantee the Series.

Russia once again proved their growing status with some sterling performances on day one, while USA also impressed with wins over Spain, Australia and Brazil, as did England. For their part France showed genuine improvement closer to home with a shock defeat of Canada.

In front of an appreciative crowd, the final day proved full of excitement. Early on New Zealand overcame a stubborn Spanish effort 14–5 in their quarter-final to ensure they would become the first winners of the IRB Women's Sevens World Series. Top scorer Woodman showed sublime form as they then defeated Russia 24–10 to reach the final against Canada, 12–7 victors over England.

The 136th and final match of the Series certainly did not disappoint, with many commentators labelling it the finest exhibition of the season. The lead swung back and forth with Canada never giving up, a spirit personified by their talisman and captain Jen Kish. However, with Woodman heavily involved, it was New Zealand who prevailed 33–24.

"It is pretty special, that (the Series title) was never a focus of ours when we go back to Dubai, it was just about building," insisted coach Sean Horan, who would also lead his players to the Rugby World Cup Sevens title later in the season. "We have some special girls and we've just come to learn. We are getting better and better and that is the ideal. We are proud of the girls, a good bunch and we're just enjoying the experiences."

At the end of the Series the top six read New Zealand, England, Canada, USA, Australia and Russia, who finished as the highest non-core team, but across the board the inaugural Series had proved a massive success. In allowing women's rugby players to compete in a global season-long competition for the first time ever, it paved the way for guaranteed development in the years to come and along the way also attracted new fans and introduced the game to new territories.

The Series generated significant TV interest with a large number of broadcasters showing matches in territories right around the world. The final round in Amsterdam was aired in 107 countries to a broadcast reach of over 250 million homes, while thousands of fans also tuned into the official website *wsws.irb.com*, where the matches were streamed live.

"The first ever IRB Women's Sevens World Series was an extraordinary success, and provided these elite athletes with a platform to display and improve their skills," said IRB Head of Competitions and Performance, Mark Egan. "The quality of rugby on display throughout the Series was magnificent and culminated in a spectacular cup final between Canada and New Zealand at the Amsterdam tournament."

In this Olympic era expansion and growth seem inevitable for the shorter format of the game, and nowhere is rugby and its playing numbers growing faster than among women and girls. *@irbwomens*

IRB WOMEN'S SEVENS WORLD SERIES 2012/13 RESULTS

DUBAI: 30 NOVEMBER–1 DECEMBER

New Zealand (20), **South Africa** (18), **Spain** (16), **Australia** (14), **Russia** (12), **Canada** (10), **England** (8), **Netherlands** (6), **USA** (4), **France** (3), **China** (2), **Brazil** (1)

USA: 1–2 FEBRUARY

England (20), **USA** (18), **Australia** (16), **New Zealand** (14), **Russia** (12), **Netherlands** (10), **Canada** (8), **South Africa** (6), **Brazil** (4), **Japan** (3), **Argentina** (2), **Trinidad & Tobago** (1)

CHINA: 30–31 MARCH

New Zealand (20), **England** (18), **Canada** (16), **USA** (14), **Ireland** (12), **Netherlands** (10), **Australia** (8), **Brazil** (6), **Japan** (4), **China** (3), **Fiji** (2), **Tunisia** (1)

NETHERLANDS: 17–18 MAY

New Zealand (20), **Canada** (18), **Russia** (16), **England** (14), **USA** (12), **Spain** (10), **Australia** (8), **France** (6), **Netherlands** (4), **South Africa** (3), **China** (2), **Brazil** (1)

FINAL STANDINGS

New Zealand – 74	**Brazil – 12**
England – 60	**Ireland – 12**
Canada – 52	**France – 9**
USA – 48	**China – 7**
Australia – 46	**Japan – 7**
Russia – 40	**Argentina – 2**
Netherlands – 30	**Fiji – 2**
South Africa – 27	**Trinidad & Tobago – 1**
	Tunisia – 1

SEVENS AROUND THE WORLD

By Seb Lauzier

AFRICA (CAR)

With the region's powerhouse South Africa not competing in the annual CAR Sevens, it was Kenya that underlined its growing authority in the African men's scene. The country's second string fed off the support and energy of a generous home Mombasa crowd to be crowned 2013 champions.

Kenya edged defending champions Zimbabwe 24–17 in the final after Tunisia had beaten Madagascar 26–10 to finish third.

The CAR Women's Sevens took place in Tunisia in April and it was South Africa who took the spoils. Denver Wannies's side beat fellow Rugby World Cup Sevens qualifiers Tunisia 29–5 in the final, while Uganda beat Kenya to third place.

NORTH AMERICA & CARRIBEAN (NACRA)

A record number of teams will compete in the men's and women's NACRA Sevens at the Truman Bodden National Stadium in the Cayman Islands on 9–10 November. In the men's event, the hosts will be joined by the USA, Canada, Mexico, Bermuda, Bahamas, Jamaica, Turks & Caicos, British Virgin Islands, St Lucia, St Vincent & The Grenadines, Barbados, Guyana, Trinidad & Tobago and Curacao. Eleven of these nations will also be represented in the women's event with Canada and USA the favourites in both tournaments.

The NACRA Sevens will also double as a qualifier for the 2014 Central American and Caribbean Sports Organization Games in Veracruz, Mexico. The top four Caribbean men's teams and top three women's teams will join Mexico in those Games. A further incentive is that the top men's Commonwealth team at the NACRA Sevens is likely to be invited to participate in the 2014 Commonwealth Games alongside Canada.

SOUTH AMERICA (CONSUR)

After an enthralling CONSUR Sevens in Rio de Janeiro in February, Argentina regained the men's crown they had lost for the first time to Uruguay the previous year. There was consolation for Uruguay as they secured a place at RWC Sevens and for Brazil who earned a place at the Hong Kong Sevens by finishing third.

Argentina were deserving champions. After beating Colombia 27–0, they opened the round robin against Brazil with a 31–12 win and then had to fight hard against Chile (14–0) and Uruguay (19–5). While Chile finished a heart-breaking fourth, Colombia beat Peru 19–14 for fifth and Guatemala overcame Ecuador 19–17 for seventh.

Brazil's women won a ninth consecutive CONSUR Sevens title, but this time were pushed hard by Argentina – coached by Sevens legend Santiago Gómez Cora – in the final with the 27–14 victory sparking celebrations every bit as loud as after their first title back in 2004. The added bonus for Brazil was a place at RWC Sevens. Uruguay beat Venezuela to third, Colombia overcame Chile for fifth and Peru won the battle for seventh against Paraguay.

ASIA (ARFU)

Arguably the biggest Asian Sevens story in 2012/13 was the Philippines qualifying for RWC Sevens. By beating Korea 22–19 to finish third at the final round of the 2012 HSBC Asian Sevens Series in Singapore the Volcanos became the country's first team to compete in a major championship event.

While Hong Kong finished the Series as champions for the first time, it was Japan who won that final round to ensure that competition between the two would reach fever pitch in 2013. And so it proved. In the first two Asian Series events Japan edged their rivals by a single score, first with a tense 14–10 victory in the Malaysia final and then in Thailand, where new star Lomano Lemeki scored in sudden death extra–time for a 17–12 win. The tables were turned, though, at round three in Mumbai in October with Hong Kong beating Japan 24–14 in the final to leave the rivals separated by one point going into the final round in Singapore on 9–10 November.

Japan's women, meanwhile, lost 14–10 to China in the Thailand final, Hong Kong beat Kazakhstan to third while Sri Lanka and Thailand won the Plate and Bowl respectively. The last event on the Asian Women's Sevens Series takes place in India in November.

EUROPE (FIRA-AER)

England's men won a second successive European title after beating France 31–7 in the FIRA European Sevens Grand Prix Series finale in

Bucharest in September. Under new coach Simon Amor, England's win added to their Lyon Sevens crown where they had beaten hosts France 21–7 and then Russia 33–5 in the final.

Russia also finished the Series strongly, beating the other Cup semi-finalists Italy 31–7 to finish third. Two months earlier, many of the same Russian side had also competed at the FISU World University Games, capturing a gold medal – just like their women's team – on home soil in Kazan.

Russia's women enjoyed even more success when they captured a first European title by winning the second FIRA Grand Prix Series event in Marbella. England had started the second round in top spot after winning in Brive, but crucially lost two pool games to open the door and Pavel Baronovsky's side hit form to win five of their pool games against Spain, Italy, Wales, Netherlands and Ukraine. They went on to beat Ireland and France to claim the Cup and clinch the overall European title on aggregate points. England rallied to win the Marbella Plate to ensure they finished second overall ahead of France, Spain, Ireland and Italy.

OCEANIA (FORU)

With New Zealand, Australia, Samoa and Fiji all comfortably in the upper echelons of men's world Sevens, it is often left to Tonga, Papua New Guinea, Niue and the Cook Islands to battle for qualifying spots on the World Series and at World Cups, and in 2012/13 it was Tonga who held sway.

As the highest-ranked non-World Series core team at the 2012 Oceania Sevens, Tonga lined up at the 2013 Gold Coast Sevens. They also booked their place at the 2014 Wellington Sevens, round five of the HSBC Sevens World Series, by finishing third at the ninth Pacific Mini Games in Wallis & Futuna. While Samoa retained their title with victory over Fiji, Tonga beat PNG to third. The door was opened to the region's other teams, however, when Tonga announced they wouldn't compete at the 2013 Oceania Sevens and the Cook Islands and American Samoa took advantage to qualify for the 2014 Hong Kong Sevens. Samoa beat hosts Fiji 31–17 to win the Oceania Sevens men's title, while Australia claimed the women's title, defeating surprise finalists Fiji 22–10 in Noosa.

Women's Rugby

IRELAND COME OF AGE

By Ali Donnelly

AFP/Getty Images

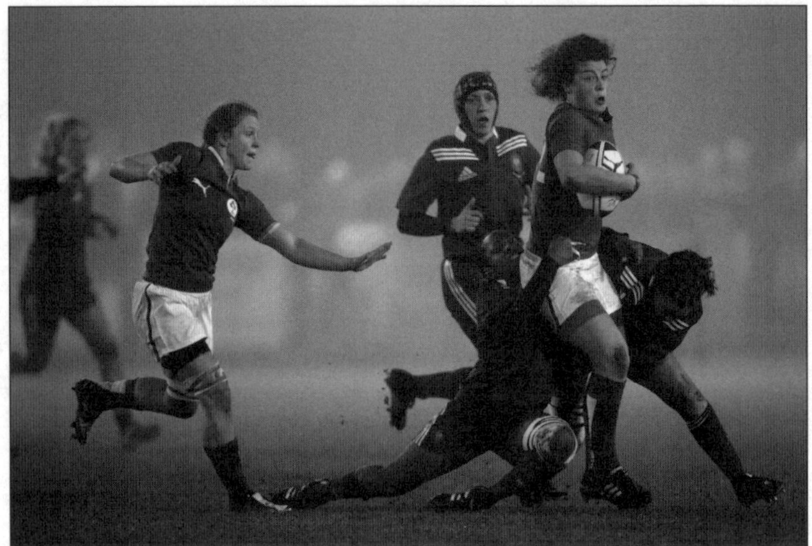

Jenny Murphy bursts forward for Ireland, who beat France on their way to winning a first Six Nations title.

The 2012/13 season will be remembered in the women's game as the year of the Irish breakthrough. Led by veteran Fiona Coghlan, Ireland finally made good on their promise and won the RBS Women's Six Nations for the first time, with a Grand Slam to boot. It had certainly been a long time coming and, for at least one member of the squad, the achievement may once have seemed an impossible dream.

In 2002, Ireland were crushed 79–0 by England. In the side that day was centre Lynne Cantwell, who 11 years later would see over a decade of progress come to fruition. Ireland's most capped player is still pinching herself months later.

"Every single game was difficult this year and thankfully we got there in the end," recalled Cantwell. "It is still really hard to put into words what it means and what a fantastic bunch of girls did it together. In 25 years' time we will see each other and we won't even have to speak. Winning the Six Nations is a memory we will share forever.

"Playing in that game against England in Worcester all those years ago, I still remember it quite well. We were chasing shadows and I was really new to rugby and just remember being wowed by how physical and quick England were. We've come an incredibly long way since then and I am just really proud to have been a part of it."

If Ireland were the main attraction in the Six Nations, there were also plenty of sideshows. Seven-time defending champions England had decided to prioritise Sevens in 2013 and sat out 17 of their leading players for much of the competition but, with much celebrated depth and an almost full-strength pack, Gary Street's side were still expected to be among the title contenders.

They started with a 76–0 rout of Scotland, but then faced Ireland who, playing at their favourite ground in Ashbourne, were far too strong, recording a first ever win (25–0) over England. France ended England's perfect record at Twickenham in late February and, with the visitors having previously suffered a shock defeat in Italy, the title was Ireland's to lose.

The final match, played on a mud bath in Italy, was an intense and nervous affair with not only a Grand Slam at stake but also a place at Women's Rugby World Cup 2014. Ireland had already qualified, but Italy needed a win to deny Wales the second spot available across the 2012 and 2013 Six Nations. It wasn't pretty, but St Patrick's Day 2013 will live long in the memories of Coghlan and her all-conquering team-mates following the 6–3 win.

All eyes will be on the girls in green in the season ahead as they try and retain their title to break into the top four at a Women's Rugby World Cup for the first time. "We know it's going to be a very tough year and we have to balance our Sevens commitments too with a fairly small group of players, but nothing will ever take away the achievements of 2013," admitted Cantwell.

While the Six Nations was the early focal point in the women's game, World Cup qualification continued at pace over the rest of the year, New Zealand completed a series whitewash of England and Canada enjoyed double success at senior and Under 20 level in the Women's Nations Cup.

With Ireland and Wales qualifying for WRWC 2014 through the Six Nations route, six teams – hosts Spain, Italy, Scotland, the Netherlands, Sweden and Samoa – came together in Madrid in late April hoping to join them at the showpiece event in France.

Spain finished on top of the standings after three wins from three, having conceded just one try in seeing off the challenge of Sweden (55–0), the Netherlands (78–0) and Italy (38–7). Samoa, coached by RWC 1991 captain Peter Fatialofa, were an unknown quantity and bounced back from a 65–22 opening loss to Italy to beat Sweden (29–0) and the Dutch (33–14) to secure the other qualification spot available.

"This is our reward for our hard work over the past year. This is our reward for the work by the Spanish Union. We have a lot more hard work in front of us but it is really exciting," enthused Spain coach Ines Etxegibel afterwards.

Fatialofa was equally delighted. "We came here to do our best and to qualify. We've achieved that and I'm delighted for the girls. We have to go back now and focus on the tough work ahead because we're going to be playing some incredible teams in France."

A busy June saw France travel to America for a three-Test series against a strong USA squad, which included 19 players who had suffered back-to-back defeats against the same opposition the previous year. Without any players who were preparing for Rugby World Cup Sevens at the end of the month, the series offered a great opportunity to try out some new combinations, and it was the hosts who won the opening Test 13–10, having trailed 10–0 at one point.

There was little between the sides in the second Test, with the French this time shading it 27–25, fly half Aurélie Bailon proving the difference with her excellent kicking and all-round attacking play. France took the series with an 18–12 win in the third Test in California in front of a big crowd as part of a double-header with the USA men playing Tonga afterwards.

Meanwhile, in Africa, the 2013 Elgon Cup – the annual two-legged series between Kenya and Uganda – took on extra significance with the winners going on to play South Africa in the region's WRWC 2014 qualifier later in the year. Kenya won the opening game 18–17 to set up a thrilling return leg in Kampala, which the home side won 13–8 to lift the trophy.

Attention then turned to the much-anticipated three-Test series between hosts New Zealand and England in July. England hadn't beaten the world champions in New Zealand since 2001, but the two sides had met six times since the WRWC 2010 final with the Black Ferns failing to win a single game. This series, on New Zealand soil, therefore was always going to be fascinating viewing.

The first encounter at Eden Park was an historic occasion, being the 1,000th women's Test match, and the world champions were not about to let the landmark pass them by, recording a perhaps flattering 29–10 win. The star of New Zealand's success at RWC Sevens, Portia Woodman excited on the wing on her Test debut for the Black Ferns while, for England, back row Marlie Packer was a standout performer.

The second Test was a more cagey affair and it took a last-ditch try for New Zealand to secure a 14–9 win at Waikato Stadium. Katy McLean had kicked England into a 6–0 lead with her side dominating the opening half, particularly up front, but New Zealand's bravery paid off with a try from Woodman and a last-second score from Selica Winiata to clinch the series win.

The clean sweep was theirs with a comfortable 29–8 win in the final Test, an outcome which ensured that Street's team returned home with much to think about a year out from the World Cup.

There were two exciting competitions to follow with the Under 20s Nations Cup taking place in England with the hosts joined by USA, Canada and South Africa and followed by the senior version in America with the same quartet of countries.

Canada were the team to beat in the Under 20s edition with young fly half Jess Neilson leading the way as one of the stars of the future. The Canadians dominated with four wins from four, confirming them as the current leaders of this age group.

It was then over to their older compatriots to impress at the senior edition in Colorado and they did just that. Under new head coach François Ratier, Canada started strongly with a 29–25 victory over a young-looking England side. It was an end-to-end thrilling game where Canada were rewarded for high-risk rugby and deadly finishing, with a last-minute try from Sevens star Magali Harvey sealing the win. Hosts USA beat South Africa in another exciting game on day one.

England bounced back with an 18–17 win over South Africa and then the Women's Eagles made the competition even more exciting with a 29–17 victory over the highly-rated Canadians. In the final round of pool matches, Canada and England emerged victorious to set up the title decider. England, steered well by Ceri Large at fly half, fought hard in the final, but the Canadians were too strong and, helped by a brace of tries from Bianca Farella, won 27–13.

South Africa lost the third place play-off 61–5 to USA but undoubtedly benefited from facing three of the world's top six sides, which was perfect preparation for their WRWC 2014 qualifier with Uganda on 7 September. The Springbok Women were too strong for their visitors, running out 63–3 winners in East London to claim the last place at France 2014. Earlier in the day, Kazakhstan had held on for a 25–23 win over Japan in Almaty to claim Asia's place, although only after the Japanese missed a late conversion attempt.

There were also outings for some less experienced nations in the women's game in 2013 with a good example being the Czech Republic playing their first ever Test match. They took on, and lost to, Switzerland, in an historic occasion in Prague, while Belgium also participated in a Test programme in 2013.

With the World Cup on the horizon, the next 12 months promise to be just as exciting. *@irbwomens*

2012/13 WOMEN'S INTERNATIONAL RESULTS

03/11/2012	**England** 23–13 **France**	Molesey Road, Hersham
18/11/2012	**Italy** 20–34 **USA**	Centro Sportivo Giulio Onesti, Rome
21/11/2012	**France** 13–0 **USA**	Stade Marcel Garcin, Orléans
23/11/2012	**England** 16–13 **New Zealand**	Molesey Road, Hersham
24/11/2012	**France** 27–3 **USA**	Stade de France, Paris
27/11/2012	**England** 17–8 **New Zealand**	Military Stadium, Aldershot
01/12/2012	**England** 32–23 **New Zealand**	Twickenham
09/12/2012	**Italy** 29–12 **Spain**	Centro Sportivo Giulio Onesti, Rome
12/12/2012	**Singapore** 21–45 **Hong Kong**	Yio Chu Kang Stadium, Singapore
15/12/2012	**Singapore** 17–44 **Hong Kong**	Yio Chu Kang Stadium, Singapore
02/02/2013	**Italy** 13–12 **France**	Stadio Giulio e Silvio Pagani, Rovato
02/02/2013	**England** 76–0 **Scotland**	Molesey Road, Hersham
03/02/2013	**Wales** 10–12 **Ireland**	Talbot Athletic Ground, Port Talbot
08/02/2013	**France** 32–0 **Wales**	Stade Marcel Levindrey, Laon
09/02/2013	**Ireland** 25–0 **England**	Ashbourne RFC, Ashbourne
10/02/2013	**Scotland** 0–8 **Italy**	Mayfield, Dundee
23/02/2013	**Scotland** 3–30 **Ireland**	Hawthornden, Bonnyrigg
23/02/2013	**England** 20–30 **France**	Twickenham
24/02/2013	**Italy** 15–16 **Wales**	Stadio Pacevecchia, Benevento
08/03/2013	**Ireland** 15–10 **France**	Ashbourne RFC, Ashbourne
09/03/2013	**England** 34–0 **Italy**	Molesey Road, Hersham
10/03/2013	**Scotland** 0–13 **Wales**	Scotstoun Stadium, Glasgow
15/03/2013	**France** 76–0 **Scotland**	Stade Bourillot, Dijon
17/03/2013	**Wales** 16–20 **England**	Talbot Athletic Ground, Port Talbot
17/03/2013	**Italy** 3–6 **Ireland**	Stadio Rino Venegoni, Parabiago
13/04/2013	**Switzerland** 5–25 **Belgium**	Stade de Colovray, Nyon
20/04/2013	**Italy** 65–22 **Samoa**	Estadio de la Universidad Complutense, Madrid
20/04/2013	**Netherlands** 7–29 **Scotland**	Estadio de la Universidad Complutense, Madrid
20/04/2013	**Sweden** 0–55 **Spain**	Estadio de la Universidad Complutense, Madrid
23/04/2013	**Italy** 27–3 **Scotland**	Estadio de la Universidad Complutense, Madrid
23/04/2013	**Sweden** 0–29 **Samoa**	Estadio de la Universidad Complutense, Madrid
23/04/2013	**Netherlands** 0–78 **Spain**	Estadio de la Universidad Complutense, Madrid
27/04/2013	**Hong Kong** 29–0 **Singapore**	Hong Kong Football Club, Hong Kong
27/04/2013	**Sweden** 8–63 **Scotland**	Estadio de la Universidad Complutense, Madrid
27/04/2013	**Netherlands** 14–33 **Samoa**	Estadio de la Universidad Complutense, Madrid
27/04/2013	**Italy** 7–38 **Spain**	Estadio de la Universidad Complutense, Madrid
07/06/2013	**USA** 13–10 **France**	Oxnard College, California, USA
11/06/2013	**USA** 25–27 **France**	Oxnard College, California, USA
14/06/2013	**USA** 12–18 **France**	StubHub Center, California, USA
15/06/2013	**Kenya** 18–17 **Uganda**	Moi International Sports Centre
22/06/2013	**Uganda** 13–8 **Kenya**	Kampala
29/06/2013	**Czech Republic** 15–27 **Switzerland**	Tatra Smichov Stadium Prague
13/07/2013	**New Zealand** 29–10 **England**	Eden Park, Auckland
16/07/2013	**New Zealand** 14–9 **England**	Waikato Stadium, Hamilton
20/07/2013	**New Zealand** 29–8 **England**	ECOLight Stadium, Pukekohe
30/07/2013	**USA** 32–22 **South Africa**	University of Northern Colorado, USA
30/07/2013	**Canada** 29–25 **England**	University of Northern Colorado, USA
04/08/2013	**England** 18–17 **South Africa**	University of Northern Colorado, USA
04/08/2013	**USA** 29–17 **Canada**	University of Northern Colorado, USA
07/08/2013	**USA** 21–36 **England**	University of Northern Colorado, USA
07/08/2013	**Canada** 53–17 **South Africa**	University of Northern Colorado, USA
10/08/2013	**Canada** 27–13 **England**	Infinity Park, Glendale, USA
10/08/2013	**USA** 61–5 **South Africa**	Infinity Park, Glendale, USA
04/09/2013	**Japan** 82–0 **Hong Kong**	Almaty Central Stadium, Kazakhstan
04/09/2013	**Kazakhstan** 91–7 **Singapore**	Almaty Central Stadium, Kazakhstan
07/09/2013	**Kazakhstan** 25–23 **Japan**	Almaty Central Stadium, Kazakhstan
07/09/2013	**Hong Kong** 15–17 **Singapore**	Almaty Central Stadium, Kazakhstan
07/09/2013	**South Africa** 63–3 **Uganda**	Buffalo City Stadium, East London

International Records and Statistics

INTERNATIONAL RECORDS

RESULTS OF INTERNATIONAL MATCHES

UP TO 10 OCTOBER 2013

Cap matches involving senior executive council member unions only. Years for International Championship matches are for the second half of the season: eg 1972 means season 1971–72. Years for matches against touring teams from the southern hemisphere refer to the actual year of the match.
Points-scoring was first introduced in 1886, when an International Board was formed by Scotland, Ireland and Wales. Points values varied among the countries until 1890, when England agreed to join the Board, and uniform values were adopted.

Northern hemisphere seasons	Try	Conversion	Penalty goal	Drop goal	Goal from mark
1890–91	1	2	2	3	3
1891–92 to 1892–93	2	3	3	4	4
1893–94 to 1904–05	3	2	3	4	4
1905–06 to 1947–48	3	2	3	4	3
1948–49 to 1970–71	3	2	3	3	3
1971–72 to 1991–92	4	2	3	3	3*
1992–93 onwards	5	2	3	3	–

*The goal from mark ceased to exist when the free-kick clause was introduced, 1977–78.

WC indicates a fixture played during a Rugby World Cup. LC indicates a fixture played in the Latin Cup. TN indicates a fixture played in the Tri Nations. RC indicates a fixture played in The Rugby Championship. QT indicates a fixture in the Quadrangular Tournament.

ENGLAND v SCOTLAND

Played 131 England won 71, Scotland won 42, Drawn 18
Highest scores England 43–3 in 2001 and 43–22 in 2005, Scotland 33–6 in 1986
Biggest wins England 43–3 in 2001, Scotland 33–6 in 1986

1871 Raeburn Place (Edinburgh) **Scotland** 1G 1T to 1T
1872 The Oval (London) **England** 1G 1DG 2T to 1DG
1873 Glasgow **Drawn** no score
1874 The Oval **England** 1DG to 1T
1875 Raeburn Place **Drawn** no score
1876 The Oval **England** 1G 1T to 0
1877 Raeburn Place **Scotland** 1 DG to 0
1878 The Oval **Drawn** no score
1879 Raeburn Place **Drawn** Scotland 1DG England 1G
1880 Manchester **England** 2G 3T to 1G
1881 Raeburn Place **Drawn** Scotland 1G 1T England 1DG 1T
1882 Manchester **Scotland** 2T to 0
1883 Raeburn Place **England** 2T to 1T
1884 Blackheath (London) **England** 1G to 1T
1885 No Match
1886 Raeburn Place **Drawn** no score
1887 Manchester **Drawn** 1T each
1888 No Match
1889 No Match
1890 Raeburn Place **England** 1G 1T to 0
1891 Richmond (London) **Scotland** 9–3
1892 Raeburn Place **England** 5–0
1893 Leeds **Scotland** 8–0
1894 Raeburn Place **Scotland** 6–0
1895 Richmond **Scotland** 6–3
1896 Glasgow **Scotland** 11–0
1897 Manchester **England** 12–3
1898 Powderhall (Edinburgh) **Drawn** 3–3
1899 Blackheath **Scotland** 5–0
1900 Inverleith (Edinburgh) **Drawn** 0–0
1901 Blackheath **Scotland** 18–3
1902 Inverleith **England** 6–3
1903 Richmond **Scotland** 10–6
1904 Inverleith **Scotland** 6–3
1905 Richmond **Scotland** 8–0
1906 Inverleith **England** 9–3
1907 Blackheath **Scotland** 8–3
1908 Inverleith **Scotland** 16–10
1909 Richmond **Scotland** 18–8
1910 Inverleith **England** 14–5
1911 Twickenham **England** 13–8
1912 Inverleith **Scotland** 8–3
1913 Twickenham **England** 3–0
1914 Inverleith **England** 16–15
1920 Twickenham **England** 13–4
1921 Inverleith **England** 18–0
1922 Twickenham **England** 11–5
1923 Inverleith **England** 8–6
1924 Twickenham **England** 19–0
1925 Murrayfield **Scotland** 14–11
1926 Twickenham **Scotland** 17–9
1927 Murrayfield **Scotland** 21–13
1928 Twickenham **England** 6–0
1929 Murrayfield **Scotland** 12–6
1930 Twickenham **Drawn** 0–0
1931 Murrayfield **Scotland** 28–19
1932 Twickenham **England** 16–3
1933 Murrayfield **Scotland** 3–0
1934 Twickenham **England** 6–3
1935 Murrayfield **Scotland** 10–7
1936 Twickenham **England** 9–8
1937 Murrayfield **England** 6–3
1938 Twickenham **Scotland** 21–16
1939 Murrayfield **England** 9–6
1947 Twickenham **England** 24–5
1948 Murrayfield **Scotland** 6–3
1949 Twickenham **England** 19–3
1950 Murrayfield **Scotland** 13–11
1951 Twickenham **England** 5–3
1952 Murrayfield **England** 19–3
1953 Twickenham **England** 26–8
1954 Murrayfield **England** 13–3
1955 Twickenham **England** 9–6
1956 Murrayfield **England** 11–6
1957 Twickenham **England** 16–3
1958 Murrayfield **Drawn** 3–3
1959 Twickenham **Drawn** 3–3
1960 Murrayfield **England** 21–12
1961 Twickenham **England** 6–0
1962 Murrayfield **Drawn** 3–3
1963 Twickenham **England** 10–8
1964 Murrayfield **Scotland** 15–6
1965 Twickenham **Drawn** 3–3
1966 Murrayfield **Scotland** 6–3

1967 Twickenham **England** 27–14
1968 Murrayfield **England** 8–6
1969 Twickenham **England** 8–3
1970 Murrayfield **Scotland** 14–5
1971 Twickenham **Scotland** 16–15
1971 Murrayfield **Scotland** 26–6 Special centenary match – non-championship
1972 Murrayfield **Scotland** 23–9
1973 Twickenham **England** 20–13
1974 Murrayfield **Scotland** 16–14
1975 Twickenham **England** 7–6
1976 Murrayfield **Scotland** 22–12
1977 Twickenham **England** 26–6
1978 Murrayfield **England** 15–0
1979 Twickenham **Drawn** 7–7
1980 Murrayfield **England** 30–18
1981 Twickenham **England** 23–17
1982 Murrayfield **Drawn** 9–9
1983 Twickenham **Scotland** 22–12
1984 Murrayfield **Scotland** 18–6
1985 Twickenham **England** 10–7
1986 Murrayfield **Scotland** 33–6
1987 Twickenham **England** 21–12
1988 Murrayfield **England** 9–6
1989 Twickenham **Drawn** 12–12
1990 Murrayfield **Scotland** 13–7
1991 Twickenham **England** 21–12
1991 Murrayfield WC **England** 9–6
1992 Murrayfield **England** 25–7
1993 Twickenham **England** 26–12
1994 Murrayfield **England** 15–14
1995 Twickenham **England** 24–12
1996 Murrayfield **England** 18–9
1997 Twickenham **England** 41–13
1998 Murrayfield **England** 34–20
1999 Twickenham **England** 24–21
2000 Murrayfield **Scotland** 19–13
2001 Twickenham **England** 43–3
2002 Murrayfield **England** 29–3
2003 Twickenham **England** 40–9
2004 Murrayfield **England** 35–13
2005 Twickenham **England** 43–22
2006 Murrayfield **Scotland** 18–12
2007 Twickenham **England** 42–20
2008 Murrayfield **Scotland** 15–9
2009 Twickenham **England** 26–12
2010 Murrayfield **Drawn** 15–15
2011 Twickenham **England** 22–16
2011 Auckland WC **England** 16–12
2012 Murrayfield **England** 13–6
2013 Twickenham **England** 38–18

ENGLAND v IRELAND

Played 127 England won 73, Ireland won 46, Drawn 8
Highest scores England 50–18 in 2000, Ireland 43–13 in 2007
Biggest wins England 46–6 in 1997, Ireland 43–13 in 2007

1875 The Oval (London) **England** 1G 1DG 1T to 0
1876 Dublin **England** 1G 1T to 0
1877 The Oval **England** 2G 2T to 0
1878 Dublin **England** 2G 1T to 0
1879 The Oval **England** 2G 1DG 2T to 0
1880 Dublin **England** 1G 1T to 1T
1881 Manchester **England** 2G 2T to 0
1882 Dublin **Drawn** 2T each
1883 Manchester **England** 1G 3T to 1T
1884 Dublin **England** 1G to 0
1885 Manchester **England** 2T to 1T
1886 Dublin **England** 1T to 0
1887 Dublin **Ireland** 2G to 0
1888 No Match
1889 No Match
1890 Blackheath (London) **England** 3T to 0
1891 Dublin **England** 9–0
1892 Manchester **England** 7–0
1893 Dublin **England** 4–0
1894 Blackheath **Ireland** 7–5
1895 Dublin **England** 6–3
1896 Leeds **Ireland** 10–4
1897 Dublin **Ireland** 13–9
1898 Richmond (London) **Ireland** 9–6
1899 Dublin **Ireland** 6–0
1900 Richmond **England** 15–4
1901 Dublin **Ireland** 10–6
1902 Leicester **England** 6–3
1903 Dublin **Ireland** 6–0
1904 Blackheath **England** 19–0
1905 Cork **Ireland** 17–3

1906 Leicester **Ireland** 16–6
1907 Dublin **Ireland** 17–9
1908 Richmond **England** 13–3
1909 Dublin **England** 11–5
1910 Twickenham **Drawn** 0–0
1911 Dublin **Ireland** 3–0
1912 Twickenham **England** 15–0
1913 Dublin **England** 15–4
1914 Twickenham **England** 17–12
1920 Dublin **England** 14–11
1921 Twickenham **England** 15–0
1922 Dublin **England** 12–3
1923 Leicester **England** 23–5
1924 Belfast **England** 14–3
1925 Twickenham **Drawn** 6–6
1926 Dublin **Ireland** 19–15
1927 Twickenham **England** 8–6
1928 Dublin **England** 7–6
1929 Twickenham **Ireland** 6–5
1930 Dublin **Ireland** 4–3
1931 Twickenham **Ireland** 6–5
1932 Dublin **England** 11–8
1933 Twickenham **England** 17–6
1934 Dublin **England** 13–3
1935 Twickenham **England** 14–3
1936 Dublin **Ireland** 6–3
1937 Twickenham **England** 9–8
1938 Dublin **England** 36–14
1939 Twickenham **Ireland** 5–0
1947 Dublin **Ireland** 22–0
1948 Twickenham **Ireland** 11–10
1949 Dublin **Ireland** 14–5
1950 Twickenham **England** 3–0
1951 Dublin **Ireland** 3–0
1952 Twickenham **England** 3–0
1953 Dublin **Drawn** 9–9
1954 Twickenham **England** 14–3
1955 Dublin **Drawn** 6–6
1956 Twickenham **England** 20–0
1957 Dublin **England** 6–0
1958 Twickenham **England** 6–0
1959 Dublin **England** 3–0
1960 Twickenham **England** 8–5
1961 Dublin **Ireland** 11–8
1962 Twickenham **England** 16–0
1963 Dublin **Drawn** 0–0
1964 Twickenham **Ireland** 18–5
1965 Dublin **Ireland** 5–0
1966 Twickenham **Drawn** 6–6
1967 Dublin **England** 8–3
1968 Twickenham **Drawn** 9–9
1969 Dublin **Ireland** 17–15
1970 Twickenham **England** 9–3
1971 Dublin **England** 9–6
1972 Twickenham **Ireland** 16–12
1973 Dublin **Ireland** 18–9
1974 Twickenham **Ireland** 26–21
1975 Dublin **Ireland** 12–9
1976 Twickenham **Ireland** 13–12
1977 Dublin **England** 4–0
1978 Twickenham **England** 15–9
1979 Dublin **Ireland** 12–7
1980 Twickenham **England** 24–9
1981 Dublin **England** 10–6
1982 Twickenham **Ireland** 16–15
1983 Dublin **Ireland** 25–15
1984 Twickenham **England** 12–9
1985 Dublin **Ireland** 13–10
1986 Twickenham **England** 25–20
1987 Dublin **Ireland** 17–0
1988 Twickenham **England** 35–3
1988 Dublin **England** 21–10
Non-championship match
1989 Dublin **England** 16–3
1990 Twickenham **England** 23–0
1991 Dublin **England** 16–7
1992 Twickenham **England** 38–9
1993 Dublin **Ireland** 17–3
1994 Twickenham **Ireland** 13–12
1995 Dublin **England** 20–8
1996 Twickenham **England** 28–15
1997 Dublin **England** 46–6
1998 Twickenham **England** 35–17
1999 Dublin **England** 27–15
2000 Twickenham **England** 50–18
2001 Dublin **Ireland** 20–14
2002 Twickenham **England** 45–11
2003 Dublin **England** 42–6
2004 Twickenham **Ireland** 19–13
2005 Dublin **Ireland** 19–13
2006 Twickenham **Ireland** 28–24
2007 Dublin **Ireland** 43–13
2008 Twickenham **England** 33–10
2009 Dublin **Ireland** 14–13
2010 Twickenham **Ireland** 20–16
2011 Dublin **Ireland** 24–8
2011 Dublin **England** 20–9
Non-championship match
2012 Twickenham **England** 30–9
2013 Dublin **England** 12–6

ENGLAND v WALES

Played 124 England won 56 Wales won 56, Drawn 12
Highest scores England 62–5 in 2007, Wales 34–21 in 1967
Biggest wins England 62–5 in 2007, Wales 30–3 in 2013

1881 Blackheath (London) **England** 7G 1DG 6T to 0
1882 No Match
1883 Swansea **England** 2G 4T to 0
1884 Leeds **England** 1G 2T to 1G
1885 Swansea **England** 1G 4T to 1G 1T
1886 Blackheath **England** 1GM 2T to 1G
1887 Llanelli **Drawn** no score
1888 No Match
1889 No Match
1890 Dewsbury **Wales** 1T to 0
1891 Newport **England** 7–3
1892 Blackheath **England** 17–0
1893 Cardiff **Wales** 12–11
1894 Birkenhead **England** 24–3
1895 Swansea **England** 14–6
1896 Blackheath **England** 25–0
1897 Newport **Wales** 11–0
1898 Blackheath **England** 14–7
1899 Swansea **Wales** 26–3
1900 Gloucester **Wales** 13–3
1901 Cardiff **Wales** 13–0
1902 Blackheath **Wales** 9–8
1903 Swansea **Wales** 21–5
1904 Leicester **Drawn** 14–14
1905 Cardiff **Wales** 25–0
1906 Richmond (London) **Wales** 16–3
1907 Swansea **Wales** 22–0
1908 Bristol **Wales** 28–18
1909 Cardiff **Wales** 8–0
1910 Twickenham **England** 11–6
1911 Swansea **Wales** 15–11
1912 Twickenham **England** 8–0
1913 Cardiff **England** 12–0
1914 Twickenham **England** 10–9
1920 Swansea **Wales** 19–5
1921 Twickenham **England** 18–3
1922 Cardiff **Wales** 28–6
1923 Twickenham **England** 7–3
1924 Swansea **England** 17–9
1925 Twickenham **England** 12–6
1926 Cardiff **Drawn** 3–3
1927 Twickenham **England** 11–9
1928 Swansea **England** 10–8
1929 Twickenham **England** 8–3
1930 Cardiff **England** 11–3
1931 Twickenham **Drawn** 11–11
1932 Swansea **Wales** 12–5
1933 Twickenham **Wales** 7–3
1934 Cardiff **England** 9–0
1935 Twickenham **Drawn** 3–3
1936 Swansea **Drawn** 0–0
1937 Twickenham **England** 4–3
1938 Cardiff **Wales** 14–8
1939 Twickenham **England** 3–0
1947 Cardiff **England** 9–6
1948 Twickenham **Drawn** 3–3
1949 Cardiff **Wales** 9–3
1950 Twickenham **Wales** 11–5
1951 Swansea **Wales** 23–5
1952 Twickenham **Wales** 8–6
1953 Cardiff **England** 8–3
1954 Twickenham **England** 9–6
1955 Cardiff **Wales** 3–0
1956 Twickenham **Wales** 8–3
1957 Cardiff **England** 3–0
1958 Twickenham **Drawn** 3–3
1959 Cardiff **Wales** 5–0
1960 Twickenham **England** 14–6
1961 Cardiff **Wales** 6–3
1962 Twickenham **Drawn** 0–0
1963 Cardiff **England** 13–6
1964 Twickenham **Drawn** 6–6
1965 Cardiff **Wales** 14–3
1966 Twickenham **Wales** 11–6
1967 Cardiff **Wales** 34–21
1968 Twickenham **Drawn** 11–11
1969 Cardiff **Wales** 30–9
1970 Twickenham **Wales** 17–13
1971 Cardiff **Wales** 22–6
1972 Twickenham **Wales** 12–3
1973 Cardiff **Wales** 25–9
1974 Twickenham **England** 16–12
1975 Cardiff **Wales** 20–4
1976 Twickenham **Wales** 21–9
1977 Cardiff **Wales** 14–9
1978 Twickenham **Wales** 9–6
1979 Cardiff **Wales** 27–3

1980 Twickenham **England** 9–8
1981 Cardiff **Wales** 21–19
1982 Twickenham **England** 17–7
1983 Cardiff **Drawn** 13–13
1984 Twickenham **Wales** 24–15
1985 Cardiff **Wales** 24–15
1986 Twickenham **England** 21–18
1987 Cardiff **Wales** 19–12
1987 Brisbane WC **Wales** 16–3
1988 Twickenham **Wales** 11–3
1989 Cardiff **Wales** 12–9
1990 Twickenham **England** 34–6
1991 Cardiff **England** 25–6
1992 Twickenham **England** 24–0
1993 Cardiff **Wales** 10–9
1994 Twickenham **England** 15–8
1995 Cardiff **England** 23–9
1996 Twickenham **England** 21–15
1997 Cardiff **England** 34–13
1998 Twickenham **England** 60–26
1999 Wembley **Wales** 32–31
2000 Twickenham **England** 46–12
2001 Cardiff **England** 44–15
2002 Twickenham **England** 50–10
2003 Cardiff **England** 26–9
2003 Cardiff **England** 43–9
Non-championship match
2003 Brisbane WC **England** 28–17
2004 Twickenham **England** 31–21
2005 Cardiff **Wales** 11–9
2006 Twickenham **England** 47–13
2007 Cardiff **Wales** 27–18
2007 Twickenham **England** 62–5
Non-championship match
2008 Twickenham **Wales** 26–19
2009 Cardiff **Wales** 23–15
2010 Twickenham **England** 30–17
2011 Cardiff **England** 26–19
2011 Twickenham **England** 23–19
Non-championship match
2011 Cardiff **Wales** 19–9
Non-championship match
2012 Twickenham **Wales** 19–12
2013 Cardiff **Wales** 30–3

ENGLAND v FRANCE

Played 97 England won 53, France won 37, Drawn 7
Highest scores England 48–19 in 2001, France 37–12 in 1972
Biggest wins England 37–0 in 1911, France 37–12 in 1972 and 31–6 in 2006

1906 Paris **England** 35–8
1907 Richmond (London) **England** 41–13
1908 Paris **England** 19–0
1909 Leicester **England** 22–0
1910 Paris **England** 11–3
1911 Twickenham **England** 37–0
1912 Paris **England** 18–8
1913 Twickenham **England** 20–0
1914 Paris **England** 39–13
1920 Twickenham **England** 8–3
1921 Paris **England** 10–6
1922 Twickenham **Drawn** 11–11
1923 Paris **England** 12–3
1924 Twickenham **England** 19–7
1925 Paris **England** 13–11
1926 Twickenham **England** 11–0
1927 Paris **France** 3–0
1928 Twickenham **England** 18–8
1929 Paris **England** 16–6
1930 Twickenham **England** 11–5
1931 Paris **France** 14–13
1947 Twickenham **England** 6–3
1948 Paris **France** 15–0
1949 Twickenham **England** 8–3
1950 Paris **France** 6–3
1951 Twickenham **France** 11–3
1952 Paris **England** 6–3
1953 Twickenham **England** 11–0
1954 Paris **France** 11–3
1955 Twickenham **France** 16–9
1956 Paris **France** 14–9
1957 Twickenham **England** 9–5
1958 Paris **England** 14–0
1959 Twickenham **Drawn** 3–3
1960 Paris **Drawn** 3–3
1961 Twickenham **Drawn** 5–5
1962 Paris **France** 13–0
1963 Twickenham **England** 6–5
1964 Paris **England** 6–3
1965 Twickenham **England** 9–6

1966 Paris **France** 13–0
1967 Twickenham **France** 16–12
1968 Paris **France** 14–9
1969 Twickenham **England** 22–8
1970 Paris **France** 35–13
1971 Twickenham **Drawn** 14–14
1972 Paris **France** 37–12
1973 Twickenham **England** 14–6
1974 Paris **Drawn** 12–12
1975 Twickenham **France** 27–20
1976 Paris **France** 30–9
1977 Twickenham **France** 4–3
1978 Paris **France** 15–6
1979 Twickenham **England** 7–6
1980 Paris **England** 17–13
1981 Twickenham **France** 16–12
1982 Paris **England** 27–15
1983 Twickenham **France** 19–15
1984 Paris **France** 32–18
1985 Twickenham **Drawn** 9–9
1986 Paris **France** 29–10
1987 Twickenham **France** 19–15
1988 Paris **France** 10–9
1989 Twickenham **England** 11–0
1990 Paris **England** 26–7
1991 Twickenham **England** 21–19
1991 Paris WC **England** 19–10
1992 Paris **England** 31–13
1993 Twickenham **England** 16–15
1994 Paris **England** 18–14
1995 Twickenham **England** 31–10
1995 Pretoria WC **France 19–9**
1996 Paris **France** 15–12
1997 Twickenham **France** 23–20
1998 Paris **France** 24–17
1999 Twickenham **England** 21–10
2000 Paris **England** 15–9
2001 Twickenham **England** 48–19
2002 Paris **France** 20–15
2003 Twickenham **England** 25–17
2003 Marseilles **France** 17–16
Non-championship match
2003 Twickenham **England** 45–14
Non-championship match
2003 Sydney WC **England** 24–7
2004 Paris **France** 24–21
2005 Twickenham **France** 18–17
2006 Paris **France** 31–6
2007 Twickenham **England** 26–18
2007 Twickenham **France** 21–15
Non-championship match
2007 Marseilles **France** 22–9
Non-championship match
2007 Paris WC **England** 14–9
2008 Paris **England** 24–13
2009 Twickenham **England** 34–10
2010 Paris **France** 12–10
2011 Twickenham **England** 17–9
2011 Auckland WC **France** 19–12
2012 Paris **England** 24–22
2013 Twickenham **England** 23–13

ENGLAND v SOUTH AFRICA

Played 36 England won 12, South Africa won 22, Drawn 2
Highest scores England 53–3 in 2002, South Africa 58–10 in 2007
Biggest wins England 53–3 in 2002, South Africa 58–10 in 2007

1906 Crystal Palace (London) **Drawn** 3–3
1913 Twickenham **South Africa** 9–3
1932 Twickenham **South Africa** 7–0
1952 Twickenham **South Africa** 8–3
1961 Twickenham **South Africa** 5–0
1969 Twickenham **England** 11–8
1972 Johannesburg **England** 18–9
1984 1 Port Elizabeth **South Africa** 33–15
2 Johannesburg **South Africa** 35–9
South Africa won series 2–0
1992 Twickenham **England** 33–16
1994 1 Pretoria **England** 32–15
2 Cape Town **South Africa** 27–9
Series drawn 1–1
1995 Twickenham **South Africa** 24–14
1997 Twickenham **South Africa** 29–11
1998 Cape Town **South Africa** 18–0
1998 Twickenham **England** 13–7
1999 Paris WC **South Africa** 44–21
2000 1 Pretoria **South Africa** 18–13
2 Bloemfontein **England** 27–22
Series drawn 1–1

2000 Twickenham **England** 25–17
2001 Twickenham **England** 29–9
2002 Twickenham **England** 53–3
2003 Perth WC **England** 25–6
2004 Twickenham **England** 32–16
2006 1 Twickenham **England** 23–21
2 Twickenham **South Africa** 25–14
Series drawn 1–1
2007 1 Bloemfontein **South Africa** 58–10
2 Pretoria **South Africa** 55–22
South Africa won series 2–0
2007 Paris WC **South Africa** 36–0
2007 Paris WC **South Africa** 15–6
2008 Twickenham **South Africa** 42–6
2010 Twickenham **South Africa** 21–11
2012 1 Durban **South Africa** 22–17
2 Johannesburg **South Africa** 36–27
3 Port Elizabeth **Drawn** 14–14
South Africa won series 2–0, with 1 draw
2012 Twickenham **South Africa** 16–15

ENGLAND v NEW ZEALAND

Played 35 England won 7, New Zealand won 27, Drawn 1
Highest scores England 38–21 in 2012, New Zealand 64–22 in 1998
Biggest wins England 38–21 in 2012, New Zealand 64–22 in 1998

1905 Crystal Palace (London) **New Zealand** 15–0
1925 Twickenham **New Zealand** 17–11
1936 Twickenham **England** 13–0
1954 Twickenham **New Zealand** 5–0
1963 1 Auckland **New Zealand** 21–11
2 Christchurch **New Zealand** 9–6
New Zealand won series 2–0
1964 Twickenham **New Zealand** 14–0
1967 Twickenham **New Zealand** 23–11
1973 Twickenham **New Zealand** 9–0
1973 Auckland **England** 16–10
1978 Twickenham **New Zealand** 16–6
1979 Twickenham **New Zealand** 10–9
1983 Twickenham **England** 15–9
1985 1 Christchurch **New Zealand** 18–13
2 Wellington **New Zealand** 42–15
New Zealand won series 2–0
1991 Twickenham WC **New Zealand** 18–12
1993 Twickenham **England** 15–9
1995 Cape Town WC **New Zealand 45–29**
1997 1 Manchester **New Zealand** 25–8
2 Twickenham **Drawn** 26–26
New Zealand won series 1–0, with 1 draw
1998 1 Dunedin **New Zealand** 64–22
2 Auckland **New Zealand** 40–10
New Zealand won series 2–0
1999 Twickenham WC **New Zealand** 30–16
2002 Twickenham **England** 31–28
2003 Wellington **England** 15–13
2004 1 Dunedin **New Zealand** 36–3
2 Auckland **New Zealand** 36–12
New Zealand won series 2–0
2005 Twickenham **New Zealand** 23–19
2006 Twickenham **New Zealand** 41–20
2008 1 Auckland **New Zealand** 37–20
2 Christchurch **New Zealand** 44–12
New Zealand won series 2–0
2008 Twickenham **New Zealand** 32–6
2009 Twickenham **New Zealand** 19–6
2010 Twickenham **New Zealand** 26–16
2012 Twickenham **England** 38–21

ENGLAND v AUSTRALIA

Played 41 England won 16, Australia won 24, Drawn 1
Highest scores England 35–18 in 2010, Australia 76–0 in 1998
Biggest wins England 20–3 in 1973, 23–6 in 1976 and 35–18 in 2010, Australia 76–0 in 1998

1909	Blackheath (London) **Australia** 9–3	1998	Brisbane **Australia** 76–0
1928	Twickenham **England** 18–11	1998	Twickenham **Australia** 12–11
1948	Twickenham **Australia** 11–0	1999	Sydney **Australia** 22–15
1958	Twickenham **England** 9–6	2000	Twickenham **England** 22–19
1963	Sydney **Australia** 18–9	2001	Twickenham **England** 21–15
1967	Twickenham **Australia** 23–11	2002	Twickenham **England** 32–31
1973	Twickenham **England** 20–3	2003	Melbourne **England** 25–14
1975	1 Sydney **Australia** 16–9	2003	Sydney WC **England** 20–17 (aet)
	2 Brisbane **Australia** 30–21	2004	Brisbane **Australia** 51–15
	Australia won series 2–0	2004	Twickenham **Australia** 21–19
1976	Twickenham **England** 23–6	2005	Twickenham **England** 26–16
1982	Twickenham **England** 15–11	2006	1 Sydney **Australia** 34–3
1984	Twickenham **Australia** 19–3		2 Melbourne **Australia** 43–18
1987	Sydney WC **Australia** 19–6		Australia won series 2–0
1988	1 Brisbane **Australia** 22–16	2007	Marseilles WC **England** 12–10
	2 Sydney **Australia** 28–8	2008	Twickenham **Australia** 28–14
	Australia won series 2–0	2009	Twickenham **Australia** 18–9
1988	Twickenham **England** 28–19	2010	1 Perth **Australia** 27–17
1991	Sydney **Australia** 40–15		2 Sydney **England** 21–20
1991	Twickenham WC **Australia** 12–6		Series drawn 1–1
1995	Cape Town WC **England** 25–22	2010	Twickenham **England** 35–18
1997	Sydney **Australia** 25–6	2012	Twickenham **Australia** 20–14
1997	Twickenham **Drawn** 15–15		

ENGLAND v NEW ZEALAND NATIVES

Played 1 England won 1
Highest score England 7–0 in 1889, NZ Natives 0–7 in 1889
Biggest win England 7–0 in 1889, NZ Natives no win

1889	Blackheath **England** 1G 4T to 0

ENGLAND v RFU PRESIDENT'S XV

Played 1 President's XV won 1
Highest score England 11–28 in 1971, RFU President's XV 28–11 in 1971
Biggest win RFU President's XV 28–11 in 1971

1971	Twickenham **President's XV** 28–11

ENGLAND v ARGENTINA

Played 18 England won 13, Argentina won 4, Drawn 1
Highest scores England 51–0 in 1990 and 51–26 in 2013, Argentina 33–13 in 1997
Biggest wins England 51–0 in 1990, Argentina 33–13 in 1997

1981	1 Buenos Aires **Drawn** 19–19
	2 Buenos Aires **England** 12–6
	England won series 1–0, with 1 draw
1990	1 Buenos Aires **England** 25–12
	2 Buenos Aires **Argentina** 15–13
	Series drawn 1–1
1990	Twickenham **England** 51–0
1995	Durban WC **England** 24–18
1996	Twickenham **England** 20–18
1997	1 Buenos Aires **England** 46–20
	2 Buenos Aires **Argentina** 33–13
	Series drawn 1–1
2000	Twickenham **England** 19–0
2002	Buenos Aires **England** 26–18
2006	Twickenham **Argentina** 25–18
2009	1 Manchester **England** 37–15
	2 Salta **Argentina** 24–22
	Series drawn 1–1
2009	Twickenham **England** 16–9
2011	Dunedin WC **England** 13–9
2013	1 Salta **England** 32–3
	2 Buenos Aires **England** 51–26
	England won series 2–0

ENGLAND v ROMANIA

Played 5 England won 5
Highest scores England 134–0 in 2001, Romania 15–22 in 1985
Biggest win England 134–0 in 2001, Romania no win

1985	Twickenham **England** 22–15
1989	Bucharest **England** 58–3
1994	Twickenham **England** 54–3
2001	Twickenham **England** 134–0
2011	Dunedin WC **England** 67–3

ENGLAND v JAPAN

Played 1 England won 1
Highest score England 60–7 in 1987, Japan 7–60 in 1987
Biggest win England 60–7 in 1987, Japan no win

1987	Sydney WC **England** 60–7

ENGLAND v UNITED STATES

Played 5 England won 5
Highest scores England 106–8 in 1999, United States 19–48 in 2001
Biggest win England 106–8 in 1999, United States no win

1987	Sydney WC **England** 34–6
1991	Twickenham WC **England** 37–9
1999	Twickenham **England** 106–8
2001	San Francisco **England** 48–19
2007	Lens WC **England** 28–10

ENGLAND v FIJI

Played 5 England won 5
Highest scores England 58–23 in 1989, Fiji 24–45 in 1999
Biggest win England 54–12 in 2012, Fiji no win

1988 Suva **England** 25–12	1999 Twickenham WC **England** 45–24
1989 Twickenham **England** 58–23	2012 Twickenham **England** 54–12
1991 Suva **England** 28–12	

ENGLAND v ITALY

Played 19 England won 19
Highest scores England 80–23 in 2001, Italy 23–80 in 2001
Biggest win England 67–7 in 1999, Italy no win

1991 Twickenham WC **England** 36–6	2005 Twickenham **England** 39–7
1995 Durban WC **England 27–20**	2006 Rome **England** 31–16
1996 Twickenham **England** 54–21	2007 Twickenham **England** 20–7
1998 Huddersfield **England** 23–15	2008 Rome **England** 23–19
1999 Twickenham WC **England** 67–7	2009 Twickenham **England** 36–11
2000 Rome **England** 59–12	2010 Rome **England** 17–12
2001 Twickenham **England** 80–23	2011 Twickenham **England** 59–13
2002 Rome **England** 45–9	2012 Rome **England** 19–15
2003 Twickenham **England** 40–5	2013 Twickenham **England** 18–11
2004 Rome **England** 50–9	

ENGLAND v CANADA

Played 6 England won 6
Highest scores England 70–0 in 2004, Canada 20–59 in 2001
Biggest win England 70–0 in 2004, Canada no win

1992 Wembley **England** 26–13	2 Burnaby **England** 59–20
1994 Twickenham **England** 60–19	England won series 2–0
1999 Twickenham **England** 36–11	2004 Twickenham **England** 70–0
2001 1 Markham **England** 22–10	

ENGLAND v SAMOA

Played 6 England won 6
Highest scores England 44–22 in 1995 and 44–22 in 2007, Samoa 22–44 in 1995, 22–35 in 2003 and 22–44 in 2007
Biggest win England 40–3 in 2005, Samoa no win

1995 Durban WC **England** 44–22	2005 Twickenham **England** 40–3
1995 Twickenham **England** 27–9	2007 Nantes WC **England** 44–22
2003 Melbourne WC **England** 35–22	2010 Twickenham **England** 26–13

ENGLAND v THE NETHERLANDS

Played 1 England won 1
Highest scores England 110–0 in 1998, The Netherlands 0–110 in 1998
Biggest win England 110–0 in 1998, The Netherlands no win

1998 Huddersfield **England** 110–0

ENGLAND v TONGA

Played 2 England won 2
Highest scores England 101–10 in 1999, Tonga 20–36 in 2007
Biggest win England 101–10 in 1999, Tonga no win

1999 Twickenham WC **England** 101–10	2007 Paris WC **England** 36–20

ENGLAND v GEORGIA

Played 2 England won 2
Highest scores England 84–6 in 2003, Georgia 10–41 in 2011
Biggest win England 84–6 in 2003, Georgia no win

2003 Perth WC **England** 84–6	2011 Dunedin WC **England** 41–10

ENGLAND v URUGUAY

Played 1 England won 1
Highest scores England 111–13 in 2003, Uruguay 13–111 in 2003
Biggest win England 111–13 in 2003, Uruguay no win

2003 Brisbane WC **England** 111–13

ENGLAND v PACIFIC ISLANDS

Played 1 England won 1
Highest scores England 39–13 in 2008, Pacific Islands 13–39 in 2008
Biggest win England 39–13 in 2008, Pacific Islands no win

2008 Twickenham **England** 39–13

SCOTLAND v IRELAND

Played 128 Scotland won 65, Ireland won 57, Drawn 5, Abandoned 1
Highest scores Scotland 38–10 in 1997, Ireland 44–22 in 2000
Biggest wins Scotland 38–10 in 1997, Ireland 36–6 in 2003

1877 Belfast **Scotland** 4G 2DG 2T to 0
1878 No Match
1879 Belfast **Scotland** 1G 1DG 1T to 0
1880 Glasgow **Scotland** 1G 2DG 2T to 0
1881 Belfast **Ireland** 1DG to 1T
1882 Glasgow **Scotland** 2T to 0
1883 Belfast **Scotland** 1G 1T to 0
1884 Raeburn Place (Edinburgh) **Scotland** 2G 2T to 1T
1885 Belfast **Abandoned** Ireland 0 Scotland 1T
1885 Raeburn Place **Scotland** 1G 2T to 0
1886 Raeburn Place **Scotland** 3G 1DG 2T to 0
1887 Belfast **Scotland** 1G 1GM 2T to 0
1888 Raeburn Place **Scotland** 1G to 0
1889 Belfast **Scotland** 1DG to 0
1890 Raeburn Place **Scotland** 1DG 1T to 0
1891 Belfast **Scotland** 14–0
1892 Raeburn Place **Scotland** 2–0
1893 Belfast **Drawn** 0–0
1894 Dublin **Ireland** 5–0
1895 Raeburn Place **Scotland** 6–0
1896 Dublin **Drawn** 0–0
1897 Powderhall (Edinburgh) **Scotland** 8–3
1898 Belfast **Scotland** 8–0
1899 Inverleith (Edinburgh) **Ireland** 9–3
1900 Dublin **Drawn** 0–0
1901 Inverleith **Scotland** 9–5
1902 Belfast **Ireland** 5–0
1903 Inverleith **Scotland** 3–0
1904 Dublin **Scotland** 19–3
1905 Inverleith **Ireland** 11–5
1906 Dublin **Scotland** 13–6
1907 Inverleith **Scotland** 15–3
1908 Dublin **Ireland** 16–11
1909 Inverleith **Scotland** 9–3
1910 Belfast **Scotland** 14–0
1911 Inverleith **Ireland** 16–10
1912 Dublin **Ireland** 10–8
1913 Inverleith **Scotland** 29–14
1914 Dublin **Ireland** 6–0
1920 Inverleith **Scotland** 19–0
1921 Dublin **Ireland** 9–8
1922 Inverleith **Scotland** 6–3
1923 Dublin **Scotland** 13–3
1924 Inverleith **Scotland** 13–8
1925 Dublin **Scotland** 14–8
1926 Murrayfield **Ireland** 3–0
1927 Dublin **Ireland** 6–0
1928 Murrayfield **Ireland** 13–5
1929 Dublin **Scotland** 16–7
1930 Murrayfield **Ireland** 14–11
1931 Dublin **Ireland** 8–5
1932 Murrayfield **Ireland** 20–8
1933 Dublin **Scotland** 8–6
1934 Murrayfield **Scotland** 16–9
1935 Dublin **Ireland** 12–5
1936 Murrayfield **Ireland** 10–4
1937 Dublin **Ireland** 11–4
1938 Murrayfield **Scotland** 23–14
1939 Dublin **Ireland** 12–3
1947 Murrayfield **Ireland** 3–0
1948 Dublin **Ireland** 6–0
1949 Murrayfield **Ireland** 13–3
1950 Dublin **Ireland** 21–0
1951 Murrayfield **Ireland** 6–5
1952 Dublin **Ireland** 12–8
1953 Murrayfield **Ireland** 26–8
1954 Belfast **Ireland** 6–0
1955 Murrayfield **Scotland** 12–3
1956 Dublin **Ireland** 14–10
1957 Murrayfield **Ireland** 5–3
1958 Dublin **Ireland** 12–6
1959 Murrayfield **Ireland** 8–3
1960 Dublin **Scotland** 6–5
1961 Murrayfield **Scotland** 16–8
1962 Dublin **Scotland** 20–6
1963 Murrayfield **Scotland** 3–0
1964 Dublin **Scotland** 6–3
1965 Murrayfield **Ireland** 16–6
1966 Dublin **Scotland** 11–3
1967 Murrayfield **Ireland** 5–3
1968 Dublin **Ireland** 14–6
1969 Murrayfield **Ireland** 16–0
1970 Dublin **Ireland** 16–11
1971 Murrayfield **Ireland** 17–5
1972 No Match

1973 Murrayfield **Scotland** 19–14
1974 Dublin **Ireland** 9–6
1975 Murrayfield **Scotland** 20–13
1976 Dublin **Scotland** 15–6
1977 Murrayfield **Scotland** 21–18
1978 Dublin **Ireland** 12–9
1979 Murrayfield **Drawn** 11–11
1980 Dublin **Ireland** 22–15
1981 Murrayfield **Scotland** 10–9
1982 Dublin **Ireland** 21–12
1983 Murrayfield **Ireland** 15–13
1984 Dublin **Scotland** 32–9
1985 Murrayfield **Ireland** 18–15
1986 Dublin **Scotland** 10–9
1987 Murrayfield **Scotland** 16–12
1988 Dublin **Ireland** 22–18
1989 Murrayfield **Scotland** 37–21
1990 Dublin **Scotland** 13–10
1991 Murrayfield **Scotland** 28–25
1991 Murrayfield WC **Scotland** 24–15
1992 Dublin **Scotland** 18–10
1993 Murrayfield **Scotland** 15–3
1994 Dublin **Drawn** 6–6
1995 Murrayfield **Scotland** 26–13
1996 Dublin **Scotland** 16–10
1997 Murrayfield **Scotland** 38–10
1998 Dublin **Scotland** 17–16
1999 Murrayfield **Scotland** 30–13
2000 Dublin **Ireland** 44–22
2001 Murrayfield **Scotland** 32–10
2002 Dublin **Ireland** 43–22
2003 Murrayfield **Ireland** 36–6
2003 Murrayfield **Ireland** 29–10
Non-championship match
2004 Dublin **Ireland** 37–16
2005 Murrayfield **Ireland** 40–13
2006 Dublin **Ireland** 15–9
2007 Murrayfield **Ireland** 19–18
2007 Murrayfield **Scotland** 31–21
Non-championship match
2008 Dublin **Ireland** 34–13
2009 Murrayfield **Ireland** 22–15
2010 Dublin **Scotland** 23–20
2011 Murrayfield **Ireland** 21–18
2011 Murrayfield **Scotland** 10–6
Non-championship match
2012 Dublin **Ireland** 32–14
2013 Murrayfield **Scotland** 12–8

SCOTLAND v WALES

Played 118 Scotland won 48, Wales won 67, Drawn 3
Highest scores Scotland 35–10 in 1924, Wales 46–22 in 2005
Biggest wins Scotland 35–10 in 1924, Wales 46–22 in 2005

1883 Raeburn Place (Edinburgh) **Scotland** 3G to 1G
1884 Newport **Scotland** 1DG 1T to 0
1885 Glasgow **Drawn** no score
1886 Cardiff **Scotland** 2G 1T to 0
1887 Raeburn Place **Scotland** 4G 8T to 0
1888 Newport **Wales** 1T to 0
1889 Raeburn Place **Scotland** 2T to 0
1890 Cardiff **Scotland** 1G 2T to 1T
1891 Raeburn Place **Scotland** 15–0
1892 Swansea **Scotland** 7–2
1893 Raeburn Place **Wales** 9–0
1894 Newport **Wales** 7–0
1895 Raeburn Place **Scotland** 5–4
1896 Cardiff **Wales** 6–0
1897 No Match
1898 No Match
1899 Inverleith (Edinburgh) **Scotland** 21–10
1900 Swansea **Wales** 12–3
1901 Inverleith **Scotland** 18–8
1902 Cardiff **Wales** 14–5
1903 Inverleith **Scotland** 6–0
1904 Swansea **Wales** 21–3
1905 Inverleith **Wales** 6–3
1906 Cardiff **Wales** 9–3
1907 Inverleith **Scotland** 6–3
1908 Swansea **Wales** 6–5
1909 Inverleith **Wales** 5–3
1910 Cardiff **Wales** 14–0
1911 Inverleith **Wales** 32–10
1912 Swansea **Wales** 21–6
1913 Inverleith **Wales** 8–0
1914 Cardiff **Wales** 24–5
1920 Inverleith **Scotland** 9–5

1921 Swansea **Scotland** 14–8
1922 Inverleith **Drawn** 9–9
1923 Cardiff **Scotland** 11–8
1924 Inverleith **Scotland** 35–10
1925 Swansea **Scotland** 24–14
1926 Murrayfield **Scotland** 8–5
1927 Cardiff **Scotland** 5–0
1928 Murrayfield **Wales** 13–0
1929 Swansea **Wales** 14–7
1930 Murrayfield **Scotland** 12–9
1931 Cardiff **Wales** 13–8
1932 Murrayfield **Wales** 6–0
1933 Swansea **Scotland** 11–3
1934 Murrayfield **Wales** 13–6
1935 Cardiff **Wales** 10–6
1936 Murrayfield **Wales** 13–3
1937 Swansea **Scotland** 13–6
1938 Murrayfield **Scotland** 8–6
1939 Cardiff **Wales** 11–3
1947 Murrayfield **Wales** 22–8
1948 Cardiff **Wales** 14–0
1949 Murrayfield **Scotland** 6–5
1950 Swansea **Wales** 12–0
1951 Murrayfield **Scotland** 19–0
1952 Cardiff **Wales** 11–0
1953 Murrayfield **Wales** 12–0
1954 Swansea **Wales** 15–3
1955 Murrayfield **Scotland** 14–8
1956 Cardiff **Wales** 9–3
1957 Murrayfield **Scotland** 9–6
1958 Cardiff **Wales** 8–3
1959 Murrayfield **Scotland** 6–5
1960 Cardiff **Wales** 8–0
1961 Murrayfield **Scotland** 3–0
1962 Cardiff **Scotland** 8–3
1963 Murrayfield **Wales** 6–0
1964 Cardiff **Wales** 11–3
1965 Murrayfield **Wales** 14–12
1966 Cardiff **Wales** 8–3
1967 Murrayfield **Scotland** 11–5
1968 Cardiff **Wales** 5–0
1969 Murrayfield **Wales** 17–3
1970 Cardiff **Wales** 18–9
1971 Murrayfield **Wales** 19–18
1972 Cardiff **Wales** 35–12
1973 Murrayfield **Scotland** 10–9
1974 Cardiff **Wales** 6–0
1975 Murrayfield **Scotland** 12–10
1976 Cardiff **Wales** 28–6
1977 Murrayfield **Wales** 18–9
1978 Cardiff **Wales** 22–14
1979 Murrayfield **Wales** 19–13
1980 Cardiff **Wales** 17–6
1981 Murrayfield **Scotland** 15–6
1982 Cardiff **Scotland** 34–18
1983 Murrayfield **Wales** 19–15
1984 Cardiff **Scotland** 15–9
1985 Murrayfield **Wales** 25–21
1986 Cardiff **Wales** 22–15
1987 Murrayfield **Scotland** 21–15
1988 Cardiff **Wales** 25–20
1989 Murrayfield **Scotland** 23–7
1990 Cardiff **Scotland** 13–9
1991 Murrayfield **Scotland** 32–12
1992 Cardiff **Wales** 15–12
1993 Murrayfield **Scotland** 20–0
1994 Cardiff **Wales** 29–6
1995 Murrayfield **Scotland** 26–13
1996 Cardiff **Scotland** 16–14
1997 Murrayfield **Wales** 34–19
1998 Wembley **Wales** 19–13
1999 Murrayfield **Scotland** 33–20
2000 Cardiff **Wales** 26–18
2001 Murrayfield **Drawn** 28–28
2002 Cardiff **Scotland** 27–22
2003 Murrayfield **Scotland** 30–22
2003 Cardiff **Wales** 23–9
Non-championship match
2004 Cardiff **Wales** 23–10
2005 Murrayfield **Wales** 46–22
2006 Cardiff **Wales** 28–18
2007 Murrayfield **Scotland** 21–9
2008 Cardiff **Wales** 30–15
2009 Murrayfield **Wales** 26–13
2010 Cardiff **Wales** 31–24
2011 Murrayfield **Wales** 24–6
2012 Cardiff **Wales** 27–13
2013 Murrayfield **Wales** 28–18

SCOTLAND v FRANCE

Played 86 Scotland won 34, France won 49, Drawn 3
Highest scores Scotland 36–22 in 1999, France 51–16 in 1998 and 51–9 in 2003
Biggest wins Scotland 31–3 in 1912, France 51–9 in 2003

1910 Inverleith (Edinburgh) **Scotland** 27–0
1911 Paris **France** 16–15
1912 Inverleith **Scotland** 31–3
1913 Paris **Scotland** 21–3
1914 No Match
1920 Paris **Scotland** 5–0
1921 Inverleith **France** 3–0
1922 Paris **Drawn** 3–3
1923 Inverleith **Scotland** 16–3
1924 Paris **France** 12–10
1925 Inverleith **Scotland** 25–4
1926 Paris **Scotland** 20–6
1927 Murrayfield **Scotland** 23–6
1928 Paris **Scotland** 15–6
1929 Murrayfield **Scotland** 6–3
1930 Paris **France** 7–3
1931 Murrayfield **Scotland** 6–4
1947 Paris **France** 8–3
1948 Murrayfield **Scotland** 9–8
1949 Paris **Scotland** 8–0
1950 Murrayfield **Scotland** 8–5
1951 Paris **France** 14–12
1952 Murrayfield **France** 13–11
1953 Paris **France** 11–5
1954 Murrayfield **France** 3–0
1955 Paris **France** 15–0
1956 Murrayfield **Scotland** 12–0
1957 Paris **Scotland** 6–0
1958 Murrayfield **Scotland** 11–9
1959 Paris **France** 9–0
1960 Murrayfield **France** 13–11
1961 Paris **France** 11–0
1962 Murrayfield **France** 11–3
1963 Paris **Scotland** 11–6
1964 Murrayfield **Scotland** 10–0
1965 Paris **France** 16–8
1966 Murrayfield **Drawn** 3–3
1967 Paris **Scotland** 9–8
1968 Murrayfield **France** 8–6
1969 Paris **Scotland** 6–3
1970 Murrayfield **France** 11–9
1971 Paris **France** 13–8
1972 Murrayfield **Scotland** 20–9
1973 Paris **France** 16–13
1974 Murrayfield **Scotland** 19–6
1975 Paris **France** 10–9
1976 Murrayfield **France** 13–6
1977 Paris **France** 23–3
1978 Murrayfield **France** 19–16
1979 Paris **France** 21–17
1980 Murrayfield **Scotland** 22–14
1981 Paris **France** 16–9
1982 Murrayfield **Scotland** 16–7
1983 Paris **France** 19–15
1984 Murrayfield **Scotland** 21–12
1985 Paris **France** 11–3
1986 Murrayfield **Scotland** 18–17
1987 Paris **France** 28–22
1987 Christchurch WC **Drawn** 20–20
1988 Murrayfield **Scotland** 23–12
1989 Paris **France** 19–3
1990 Murrayfield **Scotland** 21–0
1991 Paris **France** 15–9
1992 Murrayfield **Scotland** 10–6
1993 Paris **France** 11–3
1994 Murrayfield **France** 20–12
1995 Paris **Scotland** 23–21
1995 Pretoria WC **France** 22–19
1996 Murrayfield **Scotland** 19–14
1997 Paris **France** 47–20
1998 Murrayfield **France** 51–16
1999 Paris **Scotland** 36–22
2000 Murrayfield **France** 28–16
2001 Paris **France** 16–6
2002 Murrayfield **France** 22–10
2003 Paris **France** 38–3
2003 Sydney WC **France** 51–9
2004 Murrayfield **France** 31–0
2005 Paris **France** 16–9
2006 Murrayfield **Scotland** 20–16
2007 Paris **France** 46–19
2008 Murrayfield **France** 27–6
2009 Paris **France** 22–13
2010 Murrayfield **France** 18–9
2011 Paris **France** 34–21
2012 Murrayfield **France** 23–17
2013 Paris **France** 23–16

SCOTLAND v SOUTH AFRICA

Played 23 Scotland won 5, South Africa won 18, Drawn 0
Highest scores Scotland 29–46 in 1999, South Africa 68–10 in 1997
Biggest wins Scotland 21–6 in 2002, South Africa 68–10 in 1997

1906	Glasgow **Scotland** 6–0
1912	Inverleith **South Africa** 16–0
1932	Murrayfield **South Africa** 6–3
1951	Murrayfield **South Africa** 44–0
1960	Port Elizabeth **South Africa** 18–10
1961	Murrayfield **South Africa** 12–5
1965	Murrayfield **Scotland** 8–5
1969	Murrayfield **Scotland** 6–3
1994	Murrayfield **South Africa** 34–10
1997	Murrayfield **South Africa** 68–10
1998	Murrayfield **South Africa** 35–10
1999	Murrayfield WC **South Africa** 46–29
2002	Murrayfield **Scotland** 21–6
2003	1 Durban **South Africa** 29–25
	2 Johannesburg **South Africa** 28–19
	South Africa won series 2–0
2004	Murrayfield **South Africa** 45–10
2006	1 Durban **South Africa** 36–16
	2 Port Elizabeth **South Africa** 29–15
	South Africa won series 2–0
2007	Murrayfield **South Africa** 27–3
2008	Murrayfield **South Africa** 14–10
2010	Murrayfield **Scotland** 21–17
2012	Murrayfield **South Africa** 21–10
2013	Nelspruit QT **South Africa** 30–17

SCOTLAND v NEW ZEALAND

Played 29 Scotland won 0, New Zealand won 27, Drawn 2
Highest scores Scotland 31–62 in 1996, New Zealand 69–20 in 2000
Biggest wins Scotland no win, New Zealand 69–20 in 2000

1905	Inverleith (Edinburgh) **New Zealand** 12–7
1935	Murrayfield **New Zealand** 18–8
1954	Murrayfield **New Zealand** 3–0
1964	Murrayfield **Drawn** 0–0
1967	Murrayfield **New Zealand** 14–3
1972	Murrayfield **New Zealand** 14–9
1975	Auckland **New Zealand** 24–0
1978	Murrayfield **New Zealand** 18–9
1979	Murrayfield **New Zealand** 20–6
1981	1 Dunedin **New Zealand** 11–4
	2 Auckland **New Zealand** 40–15
	New Zealand won series 2–0
1983	Murrayfield **Drawn** 25–25
1987	Christchurch WC **New Zealand** 30–3
1990	1 Dunedin **New Zealand** 31–16
	2 Auckland **New Zealand** 21–18
	New Zealand won series 2–0
1991	Cardiff WC **New Zealand** 13–6
1993	Murrayfield **New Zealand** 51–15
1995	Pretoria WC **New Zealand** 48–30
1996	1 Dunedin **New Zealand** 62–31
	2 Auckland **New Zealand** 36–12
	New Zealand won series 2–0
1999	Murrayfield WC **New Zealand** 30–18
2000	1 Dunedin **New Zealand** 69–20
	2 Auckland **New Zealand** 48–14
	New Zealand won series 2–0
2001	Murrayfield **New Zealand** 37–6
2005	Murrayfield **New Zealand** 29–10
2007	Murrayfield WC **New Zealand** 40–0
2008	Murrayfield **New Zealand** 32–6
2010	Murrayfield **New Zealand** 49–3
2012	Murrayfield **New Zealand** 51–22

SCOTLAND v AUSTRALIA

Played 27 Scotland won 9, Australia won 18, Drawn 0
Highest scores Scotland 24–15 in 1981, Australia 45–3 in 1998
Biggest wins Scotland 24–15 in 1981, Australia 45–3 in 1998

1927 Murrayfield **Scotland** 10–8
1947 Murrayfield **Australia** 16–7
1958 Murrayfield **Scotland** 12–8
1966 Murrayfield **Scotland** 11–5
1968 Murrayfield **Scotland** 9–3
1970 Sydney **Australia** 23–3
1975 Murrayfield **Scotland** 10–3
1981 Murrayfield **Scotland** 24–15
1982 1 Brisbane **Scotland** 12–7
2 Sydney **Australia** 33–9
Series drawn 1–1
1984 Murrayfield **Australia** 37–12
1988 Murrayfield **Australia** 32–13
1992 1 Sydney **Australia** 27–12
2 Brisbane **Australia** 37–13
Australia won series 2–0
1996 Murrayfield **Australia** 29–19
1997 Murrayfield **Australia** 37–8
1998 1 Sydney **Australia** 45–3
2 Brisbane **Australia** 33–11
Australia won series 2–0
2000 Murrayfield **Australia** 30–9
2003 Brisbane WC **Australia** 33–16
2004 1 Melbourne **Australia** 35–15
2 Sydney **Australia** 34–13
Australia won series 2–0
2004 1 Murrayfield **Australia** 31–14
2 Glasgow **Australia** 31–17
Australia won series 2–0
2006 Murrayfield **Australia** 44–15
2009 Murrayfield **Scotland** 9–8
2012 Newcastle (Aus) **Scotland** 9–6

SCOTLAND v SRU PRESIDENT'S XV

Played 1 Scotland won 1
Highest scores Scotland 27–16 in 1972, SRU President's XV 16–27 in 1973
Biggest win Scotland 27–16 in 1973, SRU President's XV no win

1973 Murrayfield **Scotland** 27–16

SCOTLAND v ROMANIA

Played 13 Scotland won 11 Romania won 2, Drawn 0
Highest scores Scotland 60–19 in 1999, Romania 28–55 in 1987 and 28–22 in 1984
Biggest wins Scotland 48–6 in 2006 and 42–0 in 2007, Romania 28–22 in 1984 and 18–12 in 1991

1981 Murrayfield **Scotland** 12–6
1984 Bucharest **Romania** 28–22
1986 Bucharest **Scotland** 33–18
1987 Dunedin WC **Scotland** 55–28
1989 Murrayfield **Scotland** 32–0
1991 Bucharest **Romania** 18–12
1995 Murrayfield **Scotland** 49–16
1999 Glasgow **Scotland** 60–19
2002 Murrayfield **Scotland** 37–10
2005 Bucharest **Scotland** 39–19
2006 Murrayfield **Scotland** 48–6
2007 Murrayfield WC **Scotland** 42–0
2011 Invercargill WC **Scotland** 34–24

SCOTLAND v ZIMBABWE

Played 2 Scotland won 2
Highest scores Scotland 60–21 in 1987, Zimbabwe 21–60 in 1987
Biggest win Scotland 60–21 in 1987 and 51–12 in 1991, Zimbabwe no win

1987	Wellington WC **Scotland** 60–21	1991	Murrayfield WC **Scotland** 51–12

SCOTLAND v FIJI

Played 6 Scotland won 5, Fiji won 1
Highest scores Scotland 38–17 in 1989, Fiji 51–26 in 1998
Biggest win Scotland 38–17 in 1989, Fiji 51–26 in 1998

1989	Murrayfield **Scotland** 38–17	2003	Sydney WC **Scotland** 22–20
1998	Suva **Fiji** 51–26	2009	Murrayfield **Scotland** 23–10
2002	Murrayfield **Scotland** 36–22	2012	Lautoka **Scotland** 37–25

SCOTLAND v ARGENTINA

Played 13 Scotland won 4, Argentina won 9, Drawn 0
Highest scores Scotland 49–3 in 1990, Argentina 31–22 in 1999
Biggest wins Scotland 49–3 in 1990, Argentina 31–22 in 1999 and 25–16 in 2001

1990	Murrayfield **Scotland** 49–3	2008	1 Rosario **Argentina** 21–15
1994	1 Buenos Aires **Argentina** 16–15		2 Buenos Aires **Scotland** 26–14
	2 Buenos Aires **Argentina** 19–17		Series drawn 1–1
	Argentina won series 2–0	2009	Murrayfield **Argentina** 9–6
1999	Murrayfield **Argentina** 31–22	2010	1 Tucumán **Scotland** 24–16
2001	Murrayfield **Argentina** 25–16		2 Mar del Plata **Scotland** 13–9
2005	Murrayfield **Argentina** 23–19		Scotland won series 2–0
2007	Paris WC **Argentina** 19–13	2011	Wellington WC **Argentina** 13–12

SCOTLAND v JAPAN

Played 3 Scotland won 3
Highest scores Scotland 100–8 in 2004, Japan 11–32 in 2003
Biggest win Scotland 100–8 in 2004, Japan no win

1991	Murrayfield WC **Scotland** 47–9	2004	Perth **Scotland** 100–8
2003	Townsville WC **Scotland** 32–11		

SCOTLAND v SAMOA

Played 9 Scotland won 7, Samoa won 1, Drawn 1
Highest scores Scotland 38–3 in 2004, Samoa 27–17 in 2013
Biggest win Scotland 38–3 in 2004, Samoa 27–17 in 2013

1991	Murrayfield WC **Scotland** 28–6	2005	Murrayfield **Scotland** 18–11
1995	Murrayfield **Drawn** 15–15	2010	Aberdeen **Scotland** 19–16
1999	Murrayfield WC **Scotland** 35–20	2012	Apia **Scotland** 17–16
2000	Murrayfield **Scotland** 31–8	2013	Durban QT **Samoa** 27–17
2004	Wellington (NZ) **Scotland** 38–3		

SCOTLAND v CANADA

Played 3 Scotland won 2, Canada won 1
Highest scores Scotland 41–0 in 2008, Canada 26–23 in 2002
Biggest win Scotland 41–0 in 2008, Canada 26–23 in 2002

1995	Murrayfield **Scotland** 22–6	2008	Aberdeen **Scotland** 41–0
2002	Vancouver **Canada** 26–23		

SCOTLAND v IVORY COAST

Played 1 Scotland won 1
Highest scores Scotland 89–0 in 1995, Ivory Coast 0–89 in 1995
Biggest win Scotland 89–0 in 1995, Ivory Coast no win

1995	Rustenburg WC **Scotland** 89–0

SCOTLAND v TONGA

Played 3 Scotland won 2, Tonga won 1
Highest scores Scotland 43–20 in 2001, Tonga 21–15 in 2012
Biggest win Scotland 41–5 in 1995, Tonga 21–15 in 2012

1995	Pretoria WC **Scotland** 41–5	2012	Aberdeen **Tonga** 21–15
2001	Murrayfield **Scotland** 43–20		

SCOTLAND v ITALY

Played 21 Scotland won 14, Italy won 7
Highest scores Scotland 47–15 in 2003, Italy 37–17 in 2007
Biggest wins Scotland 47–15 in 2003, Italy 37–17 in 2007

1996	Murrayfield **Scotland** 29–22	2002	Rome **Scotland** 29–12
1998	Treviso **Italy** 25–21	2003	Murrayfield **Scotland** 33–25
1999	Murrayfield **Scotland** 30–12	2003	Murrayfield **Scotland** 47–15
2000	Rome **Italy** 34–20		Non-championship match
2001	Murrayfield **Scotland** 23–19	2004	Rome **Italy** 20–14

2005	Murrayfield **Scotland** 18–10	2011	Murrayfield **Scotland** 21–8
2006	Rome **Scotland** 13–10	2011	Murrayfield **Scotland** 23–12 Non-championship match
2007	Murrayfield **Italy** 37–17	2012	Rome **Italy** 13–6
2007	Saint Etienne WC **Scotland** 18–16	2013	Murrayfield **Scotland** 34–10
2008	Rome **Italy** 23–20	2013	Pretoria QT **Scotland** 30–29
2009	Murrayfield **Scotland** 26–6		
2010	Rome **Italy** 16–12		

SCOTLAND v URUGUAY

Played 1 Scotland won 1
Highest scores Scotland 43–12 in 1999, Uruguay 12–43 in 1999
Biggest win Scotland 43–12 in 1999, Uruguay no win

1999 Murrayfield WC **Scotland** 43–12

SCOTLAND v SPAIN

Played 1 Scotland won 1
Highest scores Scotland 48–0 in 1999, Spain 0–48 in 1999
Biggest win Scotland 48–0 in 1999, Spain no win

1999 Murrayfield WC **Scotland** 48–0

SCOTLAND v UNITED STATES

Played 3 Scotland won 3
Highest scores Scotland 65–23 in 2002, United States 23–65 in 2002
Biggest win Scotland 53–6 in 2000, United States no win

2000 Murrayfield **Scotland** 53–6
2002 San Francisco **Scotland** 65–23
2003 Brisbane WC **Scotland** 39–15

SCOTLAND v PACIFIC ISLANDS

Played 1 Scotland won 1
Highest scores Scotland 34–22 in 2006, Pacific Islands 22–34 in 2006
Biggest win Scotland 34–22 in 2006, Pacific Islands no win

2006 Murrayfield **Scotland** 34–22

SCOTLAND v PORTUGAL

Played 1 Scotland won 1
Highest scores Scotland 56–10 in 2007, Portugal 10–56 in 2007
Biggest win Scotland 56–10 in 2007, Portugal no win

2007 Saint Etienne WC **Scotland** 56–10

SCOTLAND v GEORGIA

Played 1 Scotland won 1
Highest scores Scotland 15–6 in 2011, Georgia 6–15 in 2011
Biggest win Scotland 15–6 in 2011, Georgia no win

2011	Invercargill WC **Scotland** 15–6

IRELAND v WALES

Played 119 Ireland won 48, Wales won 65, Drawn 6
Highest scores Ireland 54–10 in 2002, Wales 34–9 in 1976
Biggest wins Ireland 54–10 in 2002, Wales 29–0 in 1907

1882	Dublin **Wales** 2G 2T to 0
1883	No Match
1884	Cardiff **Wales** 1DG 2T to 0
1885	No Match
1886	No Match
1887	Birkenhead **Wales** 1DG 1T to 3T
1888	Dublin **Ireland** 1G 1DG 1T to 0
1889	Swansea **Ireland** 2T to 0
1890	Dublin **Drawn** 1G each
1891	Llanelli **Wales** 6–4
1892	Dublin **Ireland** 9–0
1893	Llanelli **Wales** 2–0
1894	Belfast **Ireland** 3–0
1895	Cardiff **Wales** 5–3
1896	Dublin **Ireland** 8–4
1897	No Match
1898	Limerick **Wales** 11–3
1899	Cardiff **Ireland** 3–0
1900	Belfast **Wales** 3–0
1901	Swansea **Wales** 10–9
1902	Dublin **Wales** 15–0
1903	Cardiff **Wales** 18–0
1904	Belfast **Ireland** 14–12
1905	Swansea **Wales** 10–3
1906	Belfast **Ireland** 11–6
1907	Cardiff **Wales** 29–0
1908	Belfast **Wales** 11–5
1909	Swansea **Wales** 18–5
1910	Dublin **Wales** 19–3
1911	Cardiff **Wales** 16–0
1912	Belfast **Ireland** 12–5
1913	Swansea **Wales** 16–13
1914	Belfast **Wales** 11–3
1920	Cardiff **Wales** 28–4
1921	Belfast **Wales** 6–0
1922	Swansea **Wales** 11–5
1923	Dublin **Ireland** 5–4
1924	Cardiff **Ireland** 13–10
1925	Belfast **Ireland** 19–3
1926	Swansea **Wales** 11–8
1927	Dublin **Ireland** 19–9
1928	Cardiff **Ireland** 13–10
1929	Belfast **Drawn** 5–5
1930	Swansea **Wales** 12–7
1931	Belfast **Wales** 15–3
1932	Cardiff **Ireland** 12–10
1933	Belfast **Ireland** 10–5
1934	Swansea **Wales** 13–0
1935	Belfast **Ireland** 9–3
1936	Cardiff **Wales** 3–0
1937	Belfast **Ireland** 5–3
1938	Swansea **Wales** 11–5
1939	Belfast **Wales** 7–0
1947	Swansea **Wales** 6–0
1948	Belfast **Ireland** 6–3
1949	Swansea **Ireland** 5–0
1950	Belfast **Wales** 6–3
1951	Cardiff **Drawn** 3–3
1952	Dublin **Wales** 14–3
1953	Swansea **Wales** 5–3
1954	Dublin **Wales** 12–9
1955	Cardiff **Wales** 21–3
1956	Dublin **Ireland** 11–3
1957	Cardiff **Wales** 6–5
1958	Dublin **Wales** 9–6
1959	Cardiff **Wales** 8–6
1960	Dublin **Wales** 10–9
1961	Cardiff **Wales** 9–0
1962	Dublin **Drawn** 3–3
1963	Cardiff **Ireland** 14–6

1964 Dublin **Wales** 15–6
1965 Cardiff **Wales** 14–8
1966 Dublin **Ireland** 9–6
1967 Cardiff **Ireland** 3–0
1968 Dublin **Ireland** 9–6
1969 Cardiff **Wales** 24–11
1970 Dublin **Ireland** 14–0
1971 Cardiff **Wales** 23–9
1972 No Match
1973 Cardiff **Wales** 16–12
1974 Dublin **Drawn** 9–9
1975 Cardiff **Wales** 32–4
1976 Dublin **Wales** 34–9
1977 Cardiff **Wales** 25–9
1978 Dublin **Wales** 20–16
1979 Cardiff **Wales** 24–21
1980 Dublin **Ireland** 21–7
1981 Cardiff **Wales** 9–8
1982 Dublin **Ireland** 20–12
1983 Cardiff **Wales** 23–9
1984 Dublin **Wales** 18–9
1985 Cardiff **Ireland** 21–9
1986 Dublin **Wales** 19–12
1987 Cardiff **Ireland** 15–11
1987 Wellington WC **Wales** 13–6
1988 Dublin **Wales** 12–9
1989 Cardiff **Ireland** 19–13
1990 Dublin **Ireland** 14–8
1991 Cardiff **Drawn** 21–21
1992 Dublin **Wales** 16–15
1993 Cardiff **Ireland** 19–14
1994 Dublin **Wales** 17–15
1995 Cardiff **Ireland** 16–12
1995 Johannesburg WC **Ireland** 24–23
1996 Dublin **Ireland** 30–17
1997 Cardiff **Ireland** 26–25
1998 Dublin **Wales** 30–21
1999 Wembley **Ireland** 29–23
2000 Dublin **Wales** 23–19
2001 Cardiff **Ireland** 36–6
2002 Dublin **Ireland** 54–10
2003 Cardiff **Ireland** 25–24
2003 Dublin **Ireland** 35–12
2004 Dublin **Ireland** 36–15
2005 Cardiff **Wales** 32–20
2006 Dublin **Ireland** 31–5
2007 Cardiff **Ireland** 19–9
2008 Dublin **Wales** 16–12
2009 Cardiff **Ireland** 17–15
2010 Dublin **Ireland** 27–12
2011 Cardiff **Wales** 19–13
2011 Wellington WC **Wales** 22–10
2012 Dublin **Wales** 23–21
2013 Cardiff **Ireland** 30–22

IRELAND v FRANCE

Played 91 Ireland won 29, France won 55, Drawn 7
Highest scores Ireland 31–43 in 2006, France 45–10 in 1996
Biggest wins Ireland 24–0 in 1913, France 44–5 in 2002

1909 Dublin **Ireland** 19–8
1910 Paris **Ireland** 8–3
1911 Cork **Ireland** 25–5
1912 Paris **Ireland** 11–6
1913 Cork **Ireland** 24–0
1914 Paris **Ireland** 8–6
1920 Dublin **France** 15–7
1921 Paris **France** 20–10
1922 Dublin **Ireland** 8–3
1923 Paris **France** 14–8
1924 Dublin **Ireland** 6–0
1925 Paris **Ireland** 9–3
1926 Belfast **Ireland** 11–0
1927 Paris **Ireland** 8–3
1928 Belfast **Ireland** 12–8
1929 Paris **Ireland** 6–0
1930 Belfast **France** 5–0
1931 Paris **France** 3–0
1947 Dublin **France** 12–8
1948 Paris **Ireland** 13–6
1949 Dublin **France** 16–9
1950 Paris **Drawn** 3–3
1951 Dublin **Ireland** 9–8
1952 Paris **Ireland** 11–8
1953 Belfast **Ireland** 16–3
1954 Paris **France** 8–0
1955 Dublin **France** 5–3
1956 Paris **France** 14–8
1957 Dublin **Ireland** 11–6
1958 Paris **France** 11–6
1959 Dublin **Ireland** 9–5
1960 Paris **France** 23–6

1961 Dublin **France** 15–3
1962 Paris **France** 11–0
1963 Dublin **France** 24–5
1964 Paris **France** 27–6
1965 Dublin **Drawn** 3–3
1966 Paris **France** 11–6
1967 Dublin **France** 11–6
1968 Paris **France** 16–6
1969 Dublin **Ireland** 17–9
1970 Paris **France** 8–0
1971 Dublin **Drawn** 9–9
1972 Paris **Ireland** 14–9
1972 Dublin **Ireland** 24–14
Non-championship match
1973 Dublin **Ireland** 6–4
1974 Paris **France** 9–6
1975 Dublin **Ireland** 25–6
1976 Paris **France** 26–3
1977 Dublin **France** 15–6
1978 Paris **France** 10–9
1979 Dublin **Drawn** 9–9
1980 Paris **France** 19–18
1981 Dublin **France** 19–13
1982 Paris **France** 22–9
1983 Dublin **Ireland** 22–16
1984 Paris **France** 25–12
1985 Dublin **Drawn** 15–15
1986 Paris **France** 29–9
1987 Dublin **France** 19–13
1988 Paris **France** 25–6
1989 Dublin **France** 26–21
1990 Paris **France** 31–12
1991 Dublin **France** 21–13
1992 Paris **France** 44–12
1993 Dublin **France** 21–6
1994 Paris **France** 35–15
1995 Dublin **France** 25–7
1995 Durban WC **France** 36–12
1996 Paris **France** 45–10
1997 Dublin **France** 32–15
1998 Paris **France** 18–16
1999 Dublin **France** 10–9
2000 Paris **Ireland** 27–25
2001 Dublin **Ireland** 22–15
2002 Paris **France** 44–5
2003 Dublin **Ireland** 15–12
2003 Melbourne WC **France** 43–21
2004 Paris **France** 35–17
2005 Dublin **France** 26–19
2006 Paris **France** 43–31
2007 Dublin **France** 20–17
2007 Paris WC **France** 25–3
2008 Paris **France** 26–21
2009 Dublin **Ireland** 30–21
2010 Paris **France** 33–10
2011 Dublin **France** 25–22
2011 Bordeaux **France** 19–12
Non-championship match
2011 Dublin **France** 26–22
Non-championship match
2012 Paris **Drawn** 17–17
2013 Dublin **Drawn** 13–13

IRELAND v SOUTH AFRICA

Played 21 Ireland won 4, South Africa won 16, Drawn 1
Highest scores Ireland 32–15 in 2006, South Africa 38–0 in 1912
Biggest wins Ireland 32–15 in 2006, South Africa 38–0 in 1912

1906 Belfast **South Africa** 15–12
1912 Dublin **South Africa** 38–0
1931 Dublin **South Africa** 8–3
1951 Dublin **South Africa** 17–5
1960 Dublin **South Africa** 8–3
1961 Cape Town **South Africa** 24–8
1965 Dublin **Ireland** 9–6
1970 Dublin **Drawn** 8–8
1981 1 Cape Town **South Africa** 23–15
2 Durban **South Africa** 12–10
South Africa won series 2–0
1998 1 Bloemfontein **South Africa** 37–13
2 Pretoria **South Africa** 33–0
South Africa won series 2–0
1998 Dublin **South Africa** 27–13
2000 Dublin **South Africa** 28–18
2004 1 Bloemfontein **South Africa** 31–17
2 Cape Town **South Africa** 26–17
South Africa won series 2–0
2004 Dublin **Ireland** 17–12
2006 Dublin **Ireland** 32–15
2009 Dublin **Ireland** 15–10
2010 Dublin **South Africa** 23–21
2012 Dublin **South Africa** 16–12

IRELAND v NEW ZEALAND

Played 27 Ireland won 0, New Zealand won 26, Drawn 1
Highest scores Ireland 29–40 in 2001, New Zealand 66–28 in 2010
Biggest win Ireland no win, New Zealand 60–0 in 2012

1905	Dublin **New Zealand** 15–0
1924	Dublin **New Zealand** 6–0
1935	Dublin **New Zealand** 17–9
1954	Dublin **New Zealand** 14–3
1963	Dublin **New Zealand** 6–5
1973	Dublin **Drawn** 10–10
1974	Dublin **New Zealand** 15–6
1976	Wellington **New Zealand** 11–3
1978	Dublin **New Zealand** 10–6
1989	Dublin **New Zealand** 23–6
1992	1 Dunedin **New Zealand** 24–21
	2 Wellington **New Zealand** 59–6
	New Zealand won series 2–0
1995	Johannesburg WC **New Zealand** 43–19
1997	Dublin **New Zealand** 63–15
2001	Dublin **New Zealand** 40–29
2002	1 Dunedin **New Zealand** 15–6
	2 Auckland **New Zealand** 40–8
	New Zealand won series 2–0
2005	Dublin **New Zealand** 45–7
2006	1 Hamilton **New Zealand** 34–23
	2 Auckland **New Zealand** 27–17
	New Zealand won series 2–0
2008	Wellington **New Zealand** 21–11
2008	Dublin **New Zealand** 22–3
2010	New Plymouth **New Zealand** 66–28
2010	Dublin **New Zealand** 38–18
2012	1 Auckland **New Zealand** 42–10
	2 Christchurch **New Zealand** 22–19
	3 Hamilton **New Zealand** 60–0
	New Zealand won series 3–0

IRELAND v AUSTRALIA

Played 30 Ireland won 9, Australia won 20, Drawn 1
Highest scores Ireland 27–12 in 1979, Australia 46–10 in 1999
Biggest wins Ireland 27–12 in 1979 and 21–6 in 2006, Australia 46–10 in 1999

1927	Dublin **Australia** 5–3
1947	Dublin **Australia** 16–3
1958	Dublin **Ireland** 9–6
1967	Dublin **Ireland** 15–8
1967	Sydney **Ireland** 11–5
1968	Dublin **Ireland** 10–3
1976	Dublin **Australia** 20–10
1979	1 Brisbane **Ireland** 27–12
	2 Sydney **Ireland** 9–3
	Ireland won series 2–0
1981	Dublin **Australia** 16–12
1984	Dublin **Australia** 16–9
1987	Sydney WC **Australia** 33–15
1991	Dublin WC **Australia** 19–18
1992	Dublin **Australia** 42–17
1994	1 Brisbane **Australia** 33–13
	2 Sydney **Australia** 32–18
	Australia won series 2–0
1996	Dublin **Australia** 22–12
1999	1 Brisbane **Australia** 46–10
	2 Perth **Australia** 32–26
	Australia won series 2–0
1999	Dublin WC **Australia** 23–3
2002	Dublin **Ireland** 18–9
2003	Perth **Australia** 45–16
2003	Melbourne WC **Australia** 17–16
2005	Dublin **Australia** 30–14
2006	Perth **Australia** 37–15
2006	Dublin **Ireland** 21–6
2008	Melbourne **Australia** 18–12
2009	Dublin **Drawn** 20–20
2010	Brisbane **Australia** 22–15
2011	Auckland WC **Ireland** 15–6

IRELAND v NEW ZEALAND NATIVES

Played 1 New Zealand Natives won 1
Highest scores Ireland 4–13 in 1888, Zew Zealand Natives 13–4 in 1888
Biggest win Ireland no win, New Zealand Natives 13–4 in 1888

1888	Dublin **New Zealand Natives** 4G 1T to 1G 1T

IRELAND v IRU PRESIDENT'S XV

Played 1 Drawn 1
Highest scores Ireland 18–18 in 1974, IRFU President's XV 18–18 in 1974

1974	Dublin **Drawn** 18–18

IRELAND v ROMANIA

Played 8 Ireland won 8
Highest scores Ireland 60–0 in 1986, Romania 35–53 in 1998
Biggest win Ireland 60–0 in 1986, Romania no win

1986	Dublin **Ireland** 60–0	2001	Bucharest **Ireland** 37–3
1993	Dublin **Ireland** 25–3	2002	Limerick **Ireland** 39–8
1998	Dublin **Ireland** 53–35	2003	Gosford WC **Ireland** 45–17
1999	Dublin WC **Ireland** 44–14	2005	Dublin **Ireland** 43–12

IRELAND v CANADA

Played 6 Ireland won 5 Drawn 1
Highest scores Ireland 55–0 in 2008, Canada 27–27 in 2000
Biggest win Ireland 55–0 in 2008, Canada no win

1987	Dunedin WC **Ireland** 46–19	2008	Limerick **Ireland** 55–0
1997	Dublin **Ireland** 33–11	2009	Vancouver **Ireland** 25–6
2000	Markham **Drawn** 27–27	2013	Toronto **Ireland** 40–14

IRELAND v TONGA

Played 2 Ireland won 2
Highest scores Ireland 40–19 in 2003, Tonga 19–40 in 2003
Biggest win Ireland 32–9 in 1987, Tonga no win

1987	Brisbane WC **Ireland** 32–9	2003	Nuku'alofa **Ireland** 40–19

IRELAND v SAMOA

Played 5 Ireland won 4, Samoa won 1, Drawn 0
Highest scores Ireland 49–22 in 1988, Samoa 40–25 in 1996
Biggest wins Ireland 49–22 in 1988 and 35–8 in 2001, Samoa 40–25 in 1996

1988	Dublin **Ireland** 49–22	2003	Apia **Ireland** 40–14
1996	Dublin **Samoa** 40–25	2010	Dublin **Ireland** 20–10
2001	Dublin **Ireland** 35–8		

IRELAND v ITALY

Played 22 Ireland won 18, Italy won 4, Drawn 0
Highest scores Ireland 61–6 in 2003, Italy 37–29 in 1997 and 37–22 in 1997
Biggest wins Ireland 61–6 in 2003, Italy 37–22 in 1997

1988	Dublin **Ireland** 31–15	2005	Rome **Ireland** 28–17
1995	Treviso **Italy** 22–12	2006	Dublin **Ireland** 26–16
1997	Dublin **Italy** 37–29	2007	Rome **Ireland** 51–24
1997	Bologna **Italy** 37–22	2007	Belfast **Ireland** 23–20
1999	Dublin **Ireland** 39–30		Non-championship match
2000	Dublin **Ireland** 60–13	2008	Dublin **Ireland** 16–11
2001	Rome **Ireland** 41–22	2009	Rome **Ireland** 38–9
2002	Dublin **Ireland** 32–17	2010	Dublin **Ireland** 29–11
2003	Rome **Ireland** 37–13	2011	Rome **Ireland** 13–11
2003	Limerick **Ireland** 61–6	2011	Dunedin WC **Ireland** 36–6
	Non-championship match	2012	Dublin **Ireland** 42–10
2004	Dublin **Ireland** 19–3	2013	Rome **Italy** 22–15

IRELAND v ARGENTINA

Played 13 Ireland won 8 Argentina won 5
Highest scores Ireland 46–24 in 2012, Argentina 34–23 in 2000
Biggest win Ireland 46–24 in 2012, Argentina 16–0 in 2007

1990	Dublin **Ireland** 20–18	2007	1 Santa Fé **Argentina** 22–20
1999	Dublin **Ireland** 32–24		2 Buenos Aires **Argentina** 16–0
1999	Lens WC **Argentina** 28–24		Argentina won series 2–0
2000	Buenos Aires **Argentina** 34–23	2007	Paris WC **Argentina** 30–15
2002	Dublin **Ireland** 16–7	2008	Dublin **Ireland** 17–3
2003	Adelaide WC **Ireland** 16–15	2010	Dublin **Ireland** 29–9
2004	Dublin **Ireland** 21–19	2012	Dublin **Ireland** 46–24

IRELAND v NAMIBIA

Played 4 Ireland won 2, Namibia won 2
Highest scores Ireland 64–7 in 2003, Namibia 26–15 in 1991
Biggest win Ireland 64–7 in 2003, Namibia 26–15 in 1991

1991	1 Windhoek **Namibia** 15–6	2003	Sydney WC **Ireland** 64–7
	2 Windhoek **Namibia** 26–15	2007	Bordeaux WC **Ireland** 32–17
	Namibia won series 2–0		

IRELAND v ZIMBABWE

Played 1 Ireland won 1
Highest scores Ireland 55–11 in 1991, Zimbabwe 11–55 in 1991
Biggest win Ireland 55–11 in 1991, Zimbabwe no win

1991	Dublin WC **Ireland** 55–11

IRELAND v JAPAN

Played 5 Ireland won 5
Highest scores Ireland 78–9 in 2000, Japan 28–50 in 1995
Biggest win Ireland 78–9 in 2000, Japan no win

1991	Dublin WC **Ireland** 32–16	2005	1 Osaka **Ireland** 44–12
1995	Bloemfontein WC **Ireland 50–28**		2 Tokyo **Ireland** 47–18
2000	Dublin **Ireland** 78–9		Ireland won series 2–0

IRELAND v UNITED STATES

Played 8 Ireland won 8
Highest scores Ireland 83–3 in 2000, United States 18–25 in 1996
Biggest win Ireland 83–3 in 2000, United States no win

1994	Dublin **Ireland** 26–15	2004	Dublin **Ireland** 55–6
1996	Atlanta **Ireland** 25–18	2009	Santa Clara **Ireland** 27–10
1999	Dublin WC **Ireland** 53–8	2011	New Plymouth WC **Ireland** 22–10
2000	Manchester (NH) **Ireland** 83–3	2013	Houston **Ireland** 15–12

IRELAND v FIJI

Played 3 Ireland won 3
Highest scores Ireland 64–17 in 2002, Fiji 17–64 in 2002
Biggest win Ireland 64–17 in 2002, Fiji no win

1995	Dublin **Ireland** 44–8	2009	Dublin **Ireland** 41–6
2002	Dublin **Ireland** 64–17		

IRELAND v GEORGIA

Played 3 Ireland won 3
Highest scores Ireland 70–0 in 1998, Georgia 14–63 in 2002
Biggest win Ireland 70–0 in 1998, Georgia no win

1998	Dublin **Ireland** 70–0	2007	Bordeaux WC **Ireland** 14–10
2002	Dublin **Ireland** 63–14		

IRELAND v RUSSIA

Played 2 Ireland won 2
Highest scores Ireland 62–12 in 2011, Russia 12–62 in 2011
Biggest win Ireland 62–12 in 2011, Russia no win

2002	Krasnoyarsk **Ireland** 35–3	2011	Rotorua WC **Ireland** 62–12

IRELAND v PACIFIC ISLANDS

Played 1 Ireland won 1
Highest scores Ireland 61–17 in 2006, Pacific Islands 17–61 in 2006
Biggest win Ireland 61–17 in 2006, Pacific Islands no win

2006	Dublin **Ireland** 61–17

WALES v FRANCE

Played 91 Wales won 45, France won 43, Drawn 3
Highest scores Wales 49–14 in 1910, France 51–0 in 1998
Biggest wins Wales 47–5 in 1909, France 51–0 in 1998

1908	Cardiff **Wales** 36–4
1909	Paris **Wales** 47–5
1910	Swansea **Wales** 49–14
1911	Paris **Wales** 15–0
1912	Newport **Wales** 14–8
1913	Paris **Wales** 11–8
1914	Swansea **Wales** 31–0
1920	Paris **Wales** 6–5
1921	Cardiff **Wales** 12–4
1922	Paris **Wales** 11–3
1923	Swansea **Wales** 16–8
1924	Paris **Wales** 10–6
1925	Cardiff **Wales** 11–5
1926	Paris **Wales** 7–5
1927	Swansea **Wales** 25–7
1928	Paris **France** 8–3
1929	Cardiff **Wales** 8–3
1930	Paris **Wales** 11–0
1931	Swansea **Wales** 35–3
1947	Paris **Wales** 3–0
1948	Swansea **France** 11–3
1949	Paris **France** 5–3
1950	Cardiff **Wales** 21–0
1951	Paris **France** 8–3
1952	Swansea **Wales** 9–5
1953	Paris **Wales** 6–3
1954	Cardiff **Wales** 19–13
1955	Paris **Wales** 16–11
1956	Cardiff **Wales** 5–3
1957	Paris **Wales** 19–13
1958	Cardiff **France** 16–6
1959	Paris **France** 11–3
1960	Cardiff **France** 16–8
1961	Paris **France** 8–6
1962	Cardiff **Wales** 3–0
1963	Paris **France** 5–3

1964 Cardiff **Drawn** 11–11
1965 Paris **France** 22–13
1966 Cardiff **Wales** 9–8
1967 Paris **France** 20–14
1968 Cardiff **France** 14–9
1969 Paris **Drawn** 8–8
1970 Cardiff **Wales** 11–6
1971 Paris **Wales** 9–5
1972 Cardiff **Wales** 20–6
1973 Paris **France** 12–3
1974 Cardiff **Drawn** 16–16
1975 Paris **Wales** 25–10
1976 Cardiff **Wales** 19–13
1977 Paris **France** 16–9
1978 Cardiff **Wales** 16–7
1979 Paris **France** 14–13
1980 Cardiff **Wales** 18–9
1981 Paris **France** 19–15
1982 Cardiff **Wales** 22–12
1983 Paris **France** 16–9
1984 Cardiff **France** 21–16
1985 Paris **France** 14–3
1986 Cardiff **France** 23–15
1987 Paris **France** 16–9
1988 Cardiff **France** 10–9
1989 Paris **France** 31–12
1990 Cardiff **France** 29–19
1991 Paris **France** 36–3
1991 Cardiff **France** 22–9
Non-championship match
1992 Cardiff **France** 12–9
1993 Paris **France** 26–10
1994 Cardiff **Wales** 24–15
1995 Paris **France** 21–9
1996 Cardiff **Wales** 16–15
1996 Cardiff **France** 40–33
Non-championship match
1997 Paris **France 27–22**
1998 Wembley **France** 51–0
1999 Paris **Wales** 34–33
1999 Cardiff **Wales** 34–23
Non-championship match
2000 Cardiff **France** 36–3
2001 Paris **Wales** 43–35
2002 Cardiff **France** 37–33
2003 Paris **France** 33–5
2004 Cardiff **France** 29–22
2005 Paris **Wales** 24–18
2006 Cardiff **France** 21–16
2007 Paris **France** 32–21
2007 Cardiff **France** 34–7
Non-championship match
2008 Cardiff **Wales** 29–12
2009 Paris **France** 21–16
2010 Cardiff **France** 26–20
2011 Paris **France** 28–9
2011 Auckland WC **France** 9–8
2012 Cardiff **Wales** 16–9
2013 Paris **Wales** 16–6

WALES v SOUTH AFRICA

Played 26 Wales won 1, South Africa won 24, Drawn 1
Highest scores Wales 36–38 in 2004, South Africa 96–13 in 1998
Biggest win Wales 29–19 in 1999, South Africa 96–13 in 1998

1906 Swansea **South Africa** 11–0
1912 Cardiff **South Africa** 3–0
1931 Swansea **South Africa** 8–3
1951 Cardiff **South Africa** 6–3
1960 Cardiff **South Africa** 3–0
1964 Durban **South Africa** 24–3
1970 Cardiff **Drawn** 6–6
1994 Cardiff **South Africa** 20–12
1995 Johannesburg **South Africa** 40–11
1996 Cardiff **South Africa** 37–20
1998 Pretoria **South Africa** 96–13
1998 Wembley **South Africa** 28–20
1999 Cardiff **Wales** 29–19
2000 Cardiff **South Africa** 23–13
2002 1 Bloemfontein **South Africa** 34–19
2 Cape Town **South Africa** 19–8
South Africa won series 2–0
2004 Pretoria **South Africa** 53–18
2004 Cardiff **South Africa** 38–36
2005 Cardiff **South Africa** 33–16
2007 Cardiff **South Africa** 34–12
2008 1 Bloemfontein **South Africa** 43–17
2 Pretoria **South Africa** 37–21
South Africa won series 2–0
2008 Cardiff **South Africa** 20–15
2010 Cardiff **South Africa** 34–31
2010 Cardiff **South Africa** 29–25
2011 Wellington WC **South Africa** 17–16

WALES v NEW ZEALAND

Played 29 Wales won 3, New Zealand won 26, Drawn 0
Highest scores Wales 37–53 in 2003, New Zealand 55–3 in 2003
Biggest wins Wales 13–8 in 1953, New Zealand 55–3 in 2003

1905	Cardiff **Wales** 3–0
1924	Swansea **New Zealand** 19–0
1935	Cardiff **Wales** 13–12
1953	Cardiff **Wales** 13–8
1963	Cardiff **New Zealand** 6–0
1967	Cardiff **New Zealand** 13–6
1969	1 Christchurch **New Zealand** 19–0
	2 Auckland **New Zealand** 33–12
	New Zealand won series 2–0
1972	Cardiff **New Zealand** 19–16
1978	Cardiff **New Zealand** 13–12
1980	Cardiff **New Zealand** 23–3
1987	Brisbane WC **New Zealand** 49–6
1988	1 Christchurch **New Zealand** 52–3
	2 Auckland **New Zealand** 54–9
	New Zealand won series 2–0
1989	Cardiff **New Zealand** 34–9
1995	Johannesburg WC **New Zealand 34–9**
1997	Wembley **New Zealand** 42–7
2002	Cardiff **New Zealand** 43–17
2003	Hamilton **New Zealand** 55–3
2003	Sydney WC **New Zealand** 53–37
2004	Cardiff **New Zealand** 26–25
2005	Cardiff **New Zealand** 41–3
2006	Cardiff **New Zealand** 45–10
2008	Cardiff **New Zealand** 29–9
2009	Cardiff **New Zealand** 19–12
2010	1 Dunedin **New Zealand** 42–9
	2 Hamilton **New Zealand** 29–10
	New Zealand won series 2–0
2010	Cardiff **New Zealand** 37–25
2012	Cardiff **New Zealand** 33–10

WALES v AUSTRALIA

Played 36 Wales won 10, Australia won 25, Drawn 1
Highest scores Wales 29–29 in 2006, Australia 63–6 in 1991
Biggest wins Wales 28–3 in 1975, Australia 63–6 in 1991

1908	Cardiff **Wales** 9–6
1927	Cardiff **Australia** 18–8
1947	Cardiff **Wales** 6–0
1958	Cardiff **Wales** 9–3
1966	Cardiff **Australia** 14–11
1969	Sydney **Wales** 19–16
1973	Cardiff **Wales** 24–0
1975	Cardiff **Wales** 28–3
1978	1 Brisbane **Australia** 18–8
	2 Sydney **Australia** 19–17
	Australia won series 2–0
1981	Cardiff **Wales** 18–13
1984	Cardiff **Australia** 28–9
1987	Rotorua WC **Wales** 22–21
1991	Brisbane **Australia** 63–6
1991	Cardiff WC **Australia** 38–3
1992	Cardiff **Australia** 23–6
1996	1 Brisbane **Australia** 56–25
	2 Sydney **Australia** 42–3
	Australia won series 2–0
1996	Cardiff **Australia** 28–19
1999	Cardiff WC **Australia** 24–9
2001	Cardiff **Australia** 21–13
2003	Sydney **Australia** 30–10
2005	Cardiff **Wales** 24–22
2006	Cardiff **Drawn** 29–29
2007	1 Sydney **Australia** 29–23
	2 Brisbane **Australia** 31–0
	Australia won series 2–0
2007	Cardiff WC **Australia** 32–20
2008	Cardiff **Wales** 21–18
2009	Cardiff **Australia** 33–12
2010	Cardiff **Australia** 25–16
2011	Auckland WC **Australia** 21–18
2011	Cardiff **Australia** 24–18
2012	1 Brisbane **Australia** 27–19
	2 Melbourne **Australia** 25–23
	3 Sydney **Australia** 20–19
	Australia won series 3–0
2012	Cardiff **Australia** 14–12

WALES v NEW ZEALAND NATIVES

Played 1 Wales won 1
Highest scores Wales 5–0 in 1888, New Zealand Natives 0–5 in 1888
Biggest win Wales 5–0 in 1888, New Zealand Natives no win

1888	Swansea **Wales** 1G 2T to 0	

WALES v NEW ZEALAND ARMY

Played 1 New Zealand Army won 1
Highest scores Wales 3–6 in 1919, New Zealand Army 6–3 in 1919
Biggest win Wales no win, New Zealand Army 6–3 in 1919

1919	Swansea **New Zealand Army** 6–3

WALES v ROMANIA

Played 8 Wales won 6, Romania won 2
Highest scores Wales 81–9 in 2001, Romania 24–6 in 1983
Biggest wins Wales 81–9 in 2001, Romania 24–6 in 1983

1983	Bucharest **Romania** 24–6	2001	Cardiff **Wales** 81–9
1988	Cardiff **Romania** 15–9	2002	Wrexham **Wales** 40–3
1994	Bucharest **Wales** 16–9	2003	Wrexham **Wales** 54–8
1997	Wrexham **Wales** 70–21	2004	Cardiff **Wales** 66–7

WALES v FIJI

Played 9 Wales won 7, Fiji won 1, Drawn 1
Highest scores Wales 66–0 in 2011, Fiji 38–34 in 2007
Biggest win Wales 66–0 in 2011, Fiji 38–34 in 2007

1985	Cardiff **Wales** 40–3	2005	Cardiff **Wales** 11–10
1986	Suva **Wales** 22–15	2007	Nantes WC **Fiji** 38–34
1994	Suva **Wales** 23–8	2010	Cardiff **Drawn** 16–16
1995	Cardiff **Wales** 19–15	2011	Hamilton WC **Wales** 66–0
2002	Cardiff **Wales** 58–14		

WALES v TONGA

Played 6 Wales won 6
Highest scores Wales 51–7 in 2001, Tonga 20–27 in 2003
Biggest win Wales 51–7 in 2001, Tonga no win

1986	Nuku'Alofa **Wales** 15–7	1997	Swansea **Wales** 46–12
1987	Palmerston North WC **Wales** 29–16	2001	Cardiff **Wales** 51–7
1994	Nuku'Alofa **Wales** 18–9	2003	Canberra WC **Wales** 27–20

WALES v SAMOA

Played 9 Wales won 5, Samoa won 4, Drawn 0
Highest scores Wales 50–6 in 2000, Samoa 38–31 in 1999
Biggest wins Wales 50–6 in 2000, Samoa 34–9 in 1994

1986	Apia **Wales** 32–14	2000	Cardiff **Wales** 50–6
1988	Cardiff **Wales** 28–6	2009	Cardiff **Wales** 17–13
1991	Cardiff WC **Samoa** 16–13	2011	Hamilton WC **Wales** 17–10
1994	Moamoa **Samoa** 34–9	2012	Cardiff **Samoa** 26–19
1999	Cardiff WC **Samoa** 38–31		

WALES v CANADA

Played 12 Wales won 11, Canada won 1, Drawn 0
Highest scores Wales 61–26 in 2006, Canada 26–24 in 1993 and 26–61 in 2006
Biggest wins Wales 60–3 in 2005, Canada 26–24 in 1993

1987	Invercargill WC **Wales** 40–9	2003	Melbourne WC **Wales** 41–10
1993	Cardiff **Canada** 26–24	2005	Toronto **Wales** 60–3
1994	Toronto **Wales** 33–15	2006	Cardiff **Wales** 61–26
1997	Toronto **Wales** 28–25	2007	Nantes WC **Wales** 42–17
1999	Cardiff **Wales** 33–19	2008	Cardiff **Wales** 34–13
2002	Cardiff **Wales** 32–21	2009	Toronto **Wales** 32–23

WALES v UNITED STATES

Played 7 Wales won 7
Highest scores Wales 77–3 in 2005, United States 23–28 in 1997
Biggest win Wales 77–3 in 2005, United States no win

1987	Cardiff **Wales** 46–0		Wales won series 2–0
1997	Cardiff **Wales** 34–14	2000	Cardiff **Wales** 42–11
1997	1 Wilmington **Wales** 30–20	2005	Hartford **Wales** 77–3
	2 San Francisco **Wales** 28–23	2009	Chicago **Wales** 48–15

WALES v NAMIBIA

Played 4 Wales won 4
Highest scores Wales 81–7 in 2011, Namibia 30–34 in 1990
Biggest win Wales 81–7 in 2011, Namibia no win

1990	1 Windhoek **Wales** 18–9	1993	Windhoek **Wales** 38–23
	2 Windhoek **Wales** 34–30	2011	New Plymouth WC **Wales** 81–7
	Wales won series 2–0		

WALES v BARBARIANS

Played 4 Wales won 2, Barbarians won 2
Highest scores Wales 31–10 in 1996, Barbarians 31–24 in 1990 and 31–28 in 2011
Biggest wins Wales 31–10 in 1996, Barbarians 31–24 in 1990

1990 Cardiff **Barbarians** 31–24
1996 Cardiff **Wales** 31–10
2011 Cardiff **Barbarians** 31–28
2012 Cardiff **Wales** 30–21

WALES v ARGENTINA

Played 14 Wales won 9, Argentina won 5
Highest scores Wales 44–50 in 2004, Argentina 50–44 in 2004
Biggest win Wales 33–16 in 2009, Argentina 45–27 in 2006

1991 Cardiff WC **Wales** 16–7
1998 Llanelli **Wales** 43–30
1999 1 Buenos Aires **Wales** 36–26
2 Buenos Aires **Wales** 23–16
Wales won series 2–0
1999 Cardiff WC **Wales** 23–18
2001 Cardiff **Argentina** 30–16
2004 1 Tucumán **Argentina** 50–44
2 Buenos Aires **Wales** 35–20
Series drawn 1–1
2006 1 Puerto Madryn **Argentina** 27–25
2 Buenos Aires **Argentina** 45–27
Argentina won series 2–0
2007 Cardiff **Wales** 27–20
2009 Cardiff **Wales** 33–16
2011 Cardiff **Wales** 28–13
2012 Cardiff **Argentina** 26–12

WALES v ZIMBABWE

Played 3 Wales won 3
Highest scores Wales 49–11 in 1998, Zimbabwe 14–35 in 1993
Biggest win Wales 49–11 in 1998, Zimbabwe no win

1993 1 Bulawayo **Wales** 35–14
2 Harare **Wales** 42–13
Wales won series 2–0
1998 Harare **Wales** 49–11

WALES v JAPAN

Played 9 Wales won 8, Japan won 1
Highest scores Wales 98–0 in 2004, Japan 30–53 in 2001
Biggest win Wales 98–0 in 2004, Japan 23–8 in 2013

1993 Cardiff **Wales** 55–5
1995 Bloemfontein WC **Wales 57–10**
1999 Cardiff WC **Wales** 64–15
2001 1 Osaka **Wales** 64–10
2 Tokyo **Wales** 53–30
Wales won series 2–0
2004 Cardiff **Wales** 98–0
2007 Cardiff WC **Wales** 72–18
2013 1 Osaka **Wales** 22–18
2 Tokyo **Japan** 23–8
Series drawn 1–1

WALES v PORTUGAL

Played 1 Wales won 1
Highest scores Wales 102–11 in 1994, Portugal 11–102 in 1994
Biggest win Wales 102–11 in 1994, Portugal no win

1994	Lisbon **Wales** 102–11

WALES v SPAIN

Played 1 Wales won 1
Highest scores Wales 54–0 in 1994, Spain 0–54 in 1994
Bigegst win Wales 54–0 in 1994, Spain no win

1994	Madrid **Wales** 54–0

WALES v ITALY

Played 20 Wales won 17, Italy won 2, Drawn 1
Highest scores Wales 60–21 in 1999, Italy 30–22 in 2003
Biggest win Wales 60–21 in 1999 and 47–8 in 2008, Italy 30–22 in 2003

1994	Cardiff **Wales** 29–19
1996	Cardiff **Wales** 31–26
1996	Rome **Wales** 31–22
1998	Llanelli **Wales** 23–20
1999	Treviso **Wales** 60–21
2000	Cardiff **Wales** 47–16
2001	Rome **Wales** 33–23
2002	Cardiff **Wales** 44–20
2003	Rome **Italy** 30–22
2003	Canberra WC **Wales** 27–15
2004	Cardiff **Wales** 44–10
2005	Rome **Wales** 38–8
2006	Cardiff **Drawn** 18–18
2007	Rome **Italy** 23–20
2008	Cardiff **Wales** 47–8
2009	Rome **Wales** 20–15
2010	Cardiff **Wales** 33–10
2011	Rome **Wales** 24–16
2012	Cardiff **Wales** 24–3
2013	Rome **Wales** 26–9

WALES v PACIFIC ISLANDS

Played 1 Wales won 1
Highest scores Wales 38–20 in 2006, Pacific Islands 20–38 in 2006
Biggest win Wales 38–20 in 2006, Pacific Islands no win

2006	Cardiff **Wales** 38–20

BRITISH/IRISH ISLES v SOUTH AFRICA

Played 46 British/Irish won 17, South Africa won 23, Drawn 6
Highest scores: British/Irish 28–9 in 1974 and 2009, South Africa 35–16 in 1997
Biggest wins: British/Irish 28–9 in 1974 and 2009, South Africa 34–14 in 1962

1891 1 Port Elizabeth **British/Irish** 4–0
2 Kimberley **British/Irish** 3–0
3 Cape Town **British/Irish** 4–0
British/Irish won series 3–0

1896 1 Port Elizabeth **British/Irish** 8–0
2 Johannesburg **British/Irish** 17–8
3 Kimberley **British/Irish** 9–3
4 Cape Town **South Africa** 5–0
British/Irish won series 3–1

1903 1 Johannesburg **Drawn** 10–10
2 Kimberley **Drawn** 0–0
3 Cape Town **South Africa** 8–0
South Africa won series 1–0 with two drawn

1910 1 Johannesburg **South Africa** 14–10
2 Port Elizabeth **British/Irish** 8–3
3 Cape Town **South Africa** 21–5
South Africa won series 2–1

1924 1 Durban **South Africa** 7–3
2 Johannesburg **South Africa** 17–0
3 Port Elizabeth **Drawn** 3–3
4 Cape Town **South Africa** 16–9
South Africa won series 3–0, with 1 draw

1938 1 Johannesburg **South Africa** 26–12
2 Port Elizabeth **South Africa** 19–3
3 Cape Town **British/Irish** 21–16
South Africa won series 2–1

1955 1 Johannesburg **British/Irish** 23–22
2 Cape Town **South Africa** 25–9
3 Pretoria **British/Irish** 9–6
4 Port Elizabeth **South Africa** 22–8
Series drawn 2–2

1962 1 Johannesburg **Drawn** 3–3
2 Durban **South Africa** 3–0
3 Cape Town **South Africa** 8–3
4 Bloemfontein **South Africa** 34–14
South Africa won series 3–0, with 1 draw

1968 1 Pretoria **South Africa** 25–20
2 Port Elizabeth **Drawn** 6–6
3 Cape Town **South Africa** 11–6
4 Johannesburg **South Africa** 19–6
South Africa won series 3–0, with 1 draw

1974 1 Cape Town **British/Irish** 12–3
2 Pretoria **British/Irish** 28–9
3 Port Elizabeth **British/Irish** 26–9
4 Johannesburg **Drawn** 13–13
British/Irish won series 3–0, with 1 draw

1980 1 Cape Town **South Africa** 26–22
2 Bloemfontein **South Africa** 26–19
3 Port Elizabeth **South Africa** 12–10
4 Pretoria **British/Irish** 17–13
South Africa won series 3–1

1997 1 Cape Town **British/Irish** 25–16
2 Durban **British/Irish** 18–15
3 Johannesburg **South Africa** 35–16
British/Irish won series 2–1

2009 1 Durban **South Africa** 26–21
2 Pretoria **South Africa** 28–25
3 Johannesburg **British/Irish** 28–9
South Africa won series 2–1

BRITISH/IRISH ISLES v NEW ZEALAND

Played 35 British/Irish won 6, New Zealand won 27, Drawn 2
Highest scores: British/Irish 20–7 in 1993, New Zealand 48–18 in 2005
Biggest wins: British/Irish 20–7 in 1993, New Zealand 38–6 in 1983

1904 Wellington **New Zealand** 9–3

1930 1 Dunedin **British/Irish** 6–3
2 Christchurch **New Zealand** 13–10
3 Auckland **New Zealand** 15–10
4 Wellington **New Zealand** 22–8
New Zealand won series 3–1

1950 1 Dunedin **Drawn** 9–9
2 Christchurch **New Zealand** 8–0

	3 Wellington **New Zealand** 6–3
	4 Auckland **New Zealand** 11–8
	New Zealand won series 3–0, with 1 draw
1959	1 Dunedin **New Zealand** 18–17
	2 Wellington **New Zealand** 11–8
	3 Christchurch **New Zealand** 22–8
	4 Auckland **British/Irish** 9–6
	New Zealand won series 3–1
1966	1 Dunedin **New Zealand** 20–3
	2 Wellington **New Zealand** 16–12
	3 Christchurch **New Zealand** 19–6
	4 Auckland **New Zealand** 24–11
	New Zealand won series 4–0
1971	1 Dunedin **British/Irish** 9–3
	2 Christchurch **New Zealand** 22–12
	3 Wellington **British/Irish** 13–3
	4 Auckland **Drawn** 14–14
	British/Irish won series 2–1, with 1 draw
1977	1 Wellington **New Zealand** 16–12
	2 Christchurch **British/Irish** 13–9
	3 Dunedin **New Zealand** 19–7
	4 Auckland **New Zealand** 10–9
	New Zealand won series 3–1
1983	1 Christchurch **New Zealand** 16–12
	2 Wellington **New Zealand** 9–0
	3 Dunedin **New Zealand** 15–8
	4 Auckland **New Zealand** 38–6
	New Zealand won series 4–0
1993	1 Christchurch **New Zealand** 20–18
	2 Wellington **British/Irish** 20–7
	3 Auckland **New Zealand** 30–13
	New Zealand won series 2–1
2005	1 Christchurch **New Zealand** 21–3
	2 Wellington **New Zealand** 48–18
	3 Auckland **New Zealand** 38–19
	New Zealand won series 3–0

ANGLO–WELSH v NEW ZEALAND

Played 3 New Zealand won 2, Drawn 1
Highest scores Anglo Welsh 5–32 in 1908, New Zealand 32–5 in 1908
Biggest win Anglo Welsh no win, New Zealand 29–0 in 1908

1908	1 Dunedin **New Zealand** 32–5
	2 Wellington **Drawn** 3–3
	3 Auckland **New Zealand** 29–0
	New Zealand won series 2–0, with 1 draw

BRITISH/IRISH ISLES v AUSTRALIA

Played 23 British/Irish won 17, Australia won 6, Drawn 0
Highest scores: British/Irish 41–16 in 2013, Australia 35–14 in 2001
Biggest wins: British/Irish 31–0 in 1966, Australia 35–14 in 2001

1899	1 Sydney **Australia** 13–3
	2 Brisbane **British/Irish** 11–0
	3 Sydney **British/Irish** 11–10
	4 Sydney **British/Irish** 13–0
	British/Irish won series 3–1
1904	1 Sydney **British/Irish** 17–0
	2 Brisbane **British/Irish** 17–3
	3 Sydney **British/Irish** 16–0
	British/Irish won series 3–0
1930	Sydney **Australia** 6–5
1950	1 Brisbane **British/Irish** 19–6
	2 Sydney **British/Irish** 24–3
	British/Irish won series 2–0
1959	1 Brisbane **British/Irish** 17–6
	2 Sydney **British/Irish** 24–3
	British/Irish won series 2–0
1966	1 Sydney **British/Irish** 11–8
	2 Brisbane **British/Irish** 31–0
	British/Irish won series 2–0
1989	1 Sydney **Australia** 30–12
	2 Brisbane **British/Irish** 19–12
	3 Sydney **British/Irish** 19–18

	British/Irish won series 2–1
2001	1 Brisbane **British/Irish** 29–13
	2 Melbourne **Australia** 35–14
	3 Sydney **Australia** 29–23
	Australia won series 2–1
2013	1 Brisbane **British/Irish** 23–21
	2 Melbourne **Australia** 16–15
	3 Sydney **British/Irish** 41–16
	British/Irish won series 2–1

BRITISH/IRISH ISLES v ARGENTINA

Played 1 British/Irish won 0, Argentina won 0, Drawn 1
Highest scores: British/Irish 25–25 in 2005, Argentina 25–25 in 2005
Biggest wins: British/Irish no win to date, Argentina no win to date

2005	Cardiff **Drawn** 25–25

FRANCE v SOUTH AFRICA

Played 38 France won 11, South Africa won 21, Drawn 6
Highest scores France 36–26 in 2006, South Africa 52–10 in 1997
Biggest wins France 30–10 in 2002, South Africa 52–10 in 1997

1913	Bordeaux **South Africa** 38–5
1952	Paris **South Africa** 25–3
1958	1 Cape Town **Drawn** 3–3
	2 Johannesburg **France** 9–5
	France won series 1–0, with 1 draw
1961	Paris **Drawn** 0–0
1964	Springs (SA) **France** 8–6
1967	1 Durban **South Africa** 26–3
	2 Bloemfontein **South Africa** 16–3
	3 Johannesburg **France** 19–14
	4 Cape Town **Drawn** 6–6
	South Africa won series 2–1, with 1 draw
1968	1 Bordeaux **South Africa** 12–9
	2 Paris **South Africa** 16–11
	South Africa won series 2–0
1971	1 Bloemfontein **South Africa** 22–9
	2 Durban **Drawn** 8–8
	South Africa won series 1–0, with 1 draw
1974	1 Toulouse **South Africa** 13–4
	2 Paris **South Africa** 10–8
	South Africa won series 2–0
1975	1 Bloemfontein **South Africa** 38–25
	2 Pretoria **South Africa** 33–18
	South Africa won series 2–0
1980	Pretoria **South Africa** 37–15
1992	1 Lyons **South Africa** 20–15
	2 Paris **France** 29–16
	Series drawn 1–1
1993	1 Durban **Drawn** 20–20
	2 Johannesburg **France** 18–17
	France won series 1–0, with 1 draw
1995	Durban WC **South Africa 19–15**
1996	1 Bordeaux **South Africa** 22–12
	2 Paris **South Africa** 13–12
	South Africa won series 2–0
1997	1 Lyons **South Africa** 36–32
	2 Paris **South Africa** 52–10
	South Africa won series 2–0
2001	1 Johannesburg **France** 32–23
	2 Durban **South Africa** 20–15
	Series drawn 1–1
2001	Paris **France** 20–10
2002	Marseilles **France** 30–10
2005	1 Durban **Drawn** 30–30
	2 Port Elizabeth **South Africa** 27–13
	South Africa won series 1–0, with 1 draw
2005	Paris **France** 26–20
2006	Cape Town **France** 36–26
2009	Toulouse **France** 20–13
2010	Cape Town **South Africa** 42–17

FRANCE v NEW ZEALAND

Played 54 France won 12, New Zealand won 41, Drawn 1
Highest scores France 43–31 in 1999, New Zealand 61–10 in 2007
Biggest wins France 22–8 in 1994, New Zealand 61–10 in 2007

1906	Paris **New Zealand** 38–8
1925	Toulouse **New Zealand** 30–6
1954	Paris **France** 3–0
1961	1 Auckland **New Zealand** 13–6
	2 Wellington **New Zealand** 5–3
	3 Christchurch **New Zealand** 32–3
	New Zealand won series 3–0
1964	Paris **New Zealand** 12–3
1967	Paris **New Zealand** 21–15
1968	1 Christchurch **New Zealand** 12–9
	2 Wellington **New Zealand** 9–3
	3 Auckland **New Zealand** 19–12
	New Zealand won series 3–0
1973	Paris **France** 13–6
1977	1 Toulouse **France** 18–13
	2 Paris **New Zealand** 15–3
	Series drawn 1–1
1979	1 Christchurch **New Zealand** 23–9
	2 Auckland **France** 24–19
	Series drawn 1–1
1981	1 Toulouse **New Zealand** 13–9
	2 Paris **New Zealand** 18–6
	New Zealand won series 2–0
1984	1 Christchurch **New Zealand** 10–9
	2 Auckland **New Zealand** 31–18
	New Zealand won series 2–0
1986	Christchurch **New Zealand** 18–9
1986	1 Toulouse **New Zealand** 19–7
	2 Nantes **France** 16–3
	Series drawn 1–1
1987	Auckland WC **New Zealand** 29–9
1989	1 Christchurch **New Zealand** 25–17
	2 Auckland **New Zealand** 34–20
	New Zealand won series 2–0
1990	1 Nantes **New Zealand** 24–3
	2 Paris **New Zealand** 30–12
	New Zealand won series 2–0
1994	1 Christchurch **France** 22–8
	2 Auckland **France** 23–20
	France won series 2–0
1995	1 Toulouse **France** 22–15
	2 Paris **New Zealand** 37–12
	Series drawn 1–1
1999	Wellington **New Zealand** 54–7
1999	Twickenham WC **France** 43–31
2000	1 Paris **New Zealand** 39–26
	2 Marseilles **France** 42–33
	Series drawn 1–1
2001	Wellington **New Zealand** 37–12
2002	Paris **Drawn** 20–20
2003	Christchurch **New Zealand** 31–23
2003	Sydney WC **New Zealand** 40–13
2004	Paris **New Zealand** 45–6
2006	1 Lyons **New Zealand** 47–3
	2 Paris **New Zealand** 23–11
	New Zealand won series 2–0
2007	1 Auckland **New Zealand** 42–11
	2 Wellington **New Zealand** 61–10
	New Zealand won series 2–0
2007	Cardiff WC **France** 20–18
2009	1 Dunedin **France** 27–22
	2 Wellington **New Zealand** 14–10
	Series drawn 1–1
2009	Marseilles **New Zealand** 39–12
2011	Auckland WC **New Zealand** 37–17
2011	Auckland WC **New Zealand** 8–7
2013	1 Auckland **New Zealand** 23–13
	2 Christchurch **New Zealand** 30–0
	3 New Plymouth **New Zealand** 24–9
	New Zealand won series 3–0

FRANCE v AUSTRALIA

Played 42 France won 17, Australia won 23, Drawn 2
Highest scores France 34–6 in 1976, Australia 59–16 in 2010
Biggest wins France 34–6 in 1976, Australia 59–16 in 2010

1928	Paris **Australia** 11–8
1948	Paris **France** 13–6
1958	Paris **France** 19–0
1961	Sydney **France** 15–8
1967	Paris **France** 20–14
1968	Sydney **Australia** 11–10
1971	1 Toulouse **Australia** 13–11
	2 Paris **France** 18–9
	Series drawn 1–1
1972	1 Sydney **Drawn** 14–14
	2 Brisbane **France** 16–15
	France won series 1–0, with 1 draw
1976	1 Bordeaux **France** 18–15
	2 Paris **France** 34–6
	France won series 2–0
1981	1 Brisbane **Australia** 17–15
	2 Sydney **Australia** 24–14
	Australia won series 2–0
1983	1 Clermont-Ferrand **Drawn** 15–15
	2 Paris **France** 15–6
	France won series 1–0, with 1 draw
1986	Sydney **Australia** 27–14
1987	Sydney WC **France** 30–24
1989	1 Strasbourg **Australia** 32–15
	2 Lille **France** 25–19
	Series drawn 1–1
1990	1 Sydney **Australia** 21–9
	2 Brisbane **Australia** 48–31
	3 Sydney **France** 28–19
	Australia won series 2–1
1993	1 Bordeaux **France** 16–13
	2 Paris **Australia** 24–3
	Series drawn 1–1
1997	1 Sydney **Australia** 29–15
	2 Brisbane **Australia** 26–19
	Australia won series 2–0
1998	Paris **Australia** 32–21
1999	Cardiff WC **Australia** 35–12
2000	Paris **Australia** 18–13
2001	Marseilles **France** 14–13
2002	1 Melbourne **Australia** 29–17
	2 Sydney **Australia** 31–25
	Australia won series 2–0
2004	Paris **France** 27–14
2005	Brisbane **Australia** 37–31
2005	Marseilles **France** 26–16
2008	1 Sydney **Australia** 34–13
	2 Brisbane **Australia** 40–10
	Australia won series 2–0
2008	Paris **Australia** 18–13
2009	Sydney **Australia** 22–6
2010	Paris **Australia** 59–16
2012	Paris **France** 33–6

FRANCE v UNITED STATES

Played 7 France won 6, United States won 1, Drawn 0
Highest scores France 41–9 in 1991 and 41–14 in 2003, United States 31–39 in 2004
Biggest wins France 41–9 in 1991, United States 17–3 in 1924

1920	Paris **France** 14–5
1924	Paris **United States** 17–3
1976	Chicago **France** 33–14
1991	1 Denver **France** 41–9
	2 Colorado Springs **France** 10–3*
	*Abandoned after 43 mins
	France won series 2–0
2003	Wollongong WC **France** 41–14
2004	Hartford **France** 39–31

FRANCE v ROMANIA

Played 49 France won 39, Romania won 8, Drawn 2
Highest scores France 67–20 in 2000, Romania 21–33 in 1991
Biggest wins France 59–3 in 1924, Romania 15–0 in 1980

1924 Paris **France** 59–3
1938 Bucharest **France** 11–8
1957 Bucharest **France** 18–15
1957 Bordeaux **France** 39–0
1960 Bucharest **Romania** 11–5
1961 Bayonne **Drawn** 5–5
1962 Bucharest **Romania** 3–0
1963 Toulouse **Drawn** 6–6
1964 Bucharest **France** 9–6
1965 Lyons **France** 8–3
1966 Bucharest **France** 9–3
1967 Nantes **France** 11–3
1968 Bucharest **Romania** 15–14
1969 Tarbes **France** 14–9
1970 Bucharest **France** 14–3
1971 Béziers **France** 31–12
1972 Constanza **France** 15–6
1973 Valence **France** 7–6
1974 Bucharest **Romania** 15–10
1975 Bordeaux **France** 36–12
1976 Bucharest **Romania** 15–12
1977 Clermont-Ferrand **France** 9–6
1978 Bucharest **France** 9–6
1979 Montauban **France** 30–12
1980 Bucharest **Romania** 15–0
1981 Narbonne **France** 17–9
1982 Bucharest **Romania** 13–9
1983 Toulouse **France** 26–15
1984 Bucharest **France** 18–3
1986 Lille **France** 25–13
1986 Bucharest **France** 20–3
1987 Wellington WC **France** 55–12
1987 Agen **France** 49–3
1988 Bucharest **France** 16–12
1990 Auch **Romania** 12–6
1991 Bucharest **France** 33–21
1991 Béziers WC **France** 30–3
1992 Le Havre **France** 25–6
1993 Bucharest **France** 37–20
1993 Brive **France** 51–0
1995 Bucharest **France** 24–15
1995 Tucumán LC **France 52–8**
1996 Aurillac **France** 64–12
1997 Bucharest **France** 51–20
1997 Lourdes LC **France 39–3**
1999 Castres **France** 62–8
2000 Bucharest **France** 67–20
2003 Lens **France** 56–8
2006 Bucharest **France** 62–14

FRANCE v NEW ZEALAND MAORI

Played 1 New Zealand Maori won 1
Highest scores France 3–12 in 1926, New Zealand Maori 12–3 in 1926
Biggest win France no win, New Zealand Maori 12–3 in 1926

1926 Paris **New Zealand Maori** 12–3

FRANCE v GERMANY

Played 15 France won 13, Germany won 2, Drawn 0
Highest scores France 38–17 in 1933, Germany 17–16 in 1927 and 17–38 in 1933
Biggest wins France 34–0 in 1931, Germany 3–0 in 1938

1927 Paris **France** 30–5
1927 Frankfurt **Germany** 17–16
1928 Hanover **France** 14–3
1929 Paris **France** 24–0
1930 Berlin **France** 31–0
1931 Paris **France** 34–0
1932 Frankfurt **France** 20–4
1933 Paris **France** 38–17
1934 Hanover **France** 13–9
1935 Paris **France** 18–3
1936 1 Berlin **France** 19–14
2 Hanover **France** 6–3
France won series 2–0
1937 Paris **France** 27–6
1938 Frankfurt **Germany** 3–0
1938 Bucharest **France** 8–5

FRANCE v ITALY

Played 34 France won 31, Italy won 3, Drawn 0
Highest scores France 60–13 in 1967, Italy 40–32 in 1997
Biggest wins France 60–13 in 1967, Italy 40–32 in 1997

1937 Paris **France** 43–5
1952 Milan **France** 17–8
1953 Lyons **France** 22–8
1954 Rome **France** 39–12
1955 Grenoble **France** 24–0
1956 Padua **France** 16–3
1957 Agen **France** 38–6
1958 Naples **France** 11–3
1959 Nantes **France** 22–0
1960 Treviso **France** 26–0
1961 Chambéry **France** 17–0
1962 Brescia **France** 6–3
1963 Grenoble **France** 14–12
1964 Parma **France** 12–3
1965 Pau **France** 21–0
1966 Naples **France** 21–0
1967 Toulon **France** 60–13
1995 Buenos Aires LC **France 34–22**
1997 Grenoble **Italy** 40–32
1997 Auch LC **France 30–19**
2000 Paris **France** 42–31
2001 Rome **France** 30–19
2002 Paris **France** 33–12
2003 Rome **France** 53–27
2004 Paris **France** 25–0
2005 Rome **France** 56–13
2006 Paris **France** 37–12
2007 Rome **France** 39–3
2008 Paris **France** 25–13
2009 Rome **France** 50–8
2010 Paris **France** 46–20
2011 Rome **Italy** 22–21
2012 Paris **France** 30–12
2013 Rome **Italy** 23–18

FRANCE v BRITISH XVs

Played 5 France won 2, British XVs won 3, Drawn 0
Highest scores France 27–29 in 1989, British XV 36–3 in 1940
Biggest wins France 21–9 in 1945, British XV 36–3 in 1940

1940 Paris **British XV** 36–3
1945 Paris **France** 21–9
1945 Richmond **British XV** 27–6
1946 Paris **France** 10–0
1989 Paris **British XV** 29–27

FRANCE v WALES XVs

Played 2 France won 1, Wales XV won 1
Highest scores France 12–0 in 1946, Wales XV 8–0 in 1945
Biggest win France 12–0 in 1946, Wales XV 8–0 in 1945

1945 Swansea **Wales XV** 8–0
1946 Paris **France** 12–0

FRANCE v IRELAND XVs

Played 1 France won 1
Highest scores France 4–3 in 1946, Ireland XV 3–4 in 1946
Biggest win France 4–3 in 1946, Ireland XV no win

1946 Dublin **France** 4–3

FRANCE v NEW ZEALAND ARMY

Played 1 New Zealand Army won 1
Highest scores France 9–14 in 1946, New Zealand Army 14–9 in 1946
Biggest win France no win, New Zealand Army 14–9 in 1946

1946 Paris **New Zealand Army** 14–9

FRANCE v ARGENTINA

Played 47 France won 34, Argentina won 12, Drawn 1
Highest scores France 49–10 in 2012, Argentina 41–13 in 2010
Biggest wins France 49–10 in 2012, Argentina 41–13 in 2010

1949 1 Buenos Aires **France** 5–0
2 Buenos Aires **France** 12–3
France won series 2–0
1954 1 Buenos Aires **France** 22–8
2 Buenos Aires **France** 30–3
France won series 2–0
1960 1 Buenos Aires **France** 37–3
2 Buenos Aires **France** 12–3
3 Buenos Aires **France** 29–6
France won series 3–0
1974 1 Buenos Aires **France** 20–15
2 Buenos Aires **France** 31–27
France won series 2–0
1975 1 Lyons **France** 29–6
2 Paris **France** 36–21
France won series 2–0
1977 1 Buenos Aires **France** 26–3
2 Buenos Aires **Drawn** 18–18
France won series 1–0, with 1 draw
1982 1 Toulouse **France** 25–12
2 Paris **France** 13–6
France won series 2–0
1985 1 Buenos Aires **Argentina** 24–16
2 Buenos Aires **France** 23–15
Series drawn 1–1
1986 1 Buenos Aires **Argentina** 15–13
2 Buenos Aires **France** 22–9
Series drawn 1–1
1988 1 Buenos Aires **France** 18–15
2 Buenos Aires **Argentina** 18–6
Series drawn 1–1
1988 1 Nantes **France** 29–9
2 Lille **France** 28–18
France won series 2–0
1992 1 Buenos Aires **France** 27–12
2 Buenos Aires **France** 33–9

	France won series 2–0
1992	Nantes **Argentina** 24–20
1995	Buenos Aires LC **France** 47–12
1996	1 Buenos Aires **France** 34–27
	2 Buenos Aires **France** 34–15
	France won series 2–0
1997	Tarbes LC **France** 32–27
1998	1 Buenos Aires **France** 35–18
	2 Buenos Aires **France** 37–12
	France won series 2–0
1998	Nantes **France** 34–14
1999	Dublin WC **France** 47–26
2002	Buenos Aires **Argentina** 28–27
2003	1 Buenos Aires **Argentina** 10–6
	2 Buenos Aires **Argentina** 33–32
	Argentina won series 2–0
2004	Marseilles **Argentina** 24–14
2006	Paris **France** 27–26
2007	Paris WC **Argentina** 17–12
2007	Paris WC **Argentina** 34–10
2008	Marseilles **France** 12–6
2010	Buenos Aires **Argentina** 41–13
2010	Montpellier **France** 15–9
2012	1 Cordoba **Argentina** 23–20
	2 Tucuman **France** 49–10
	Series drawn 1–1
2012	Lille **France** 39–22

FRANCE v CZECHOSLOVAKIA

Played 2 France won 2
Highest scores France 28–3 in 1956, Czechoslovakia 6–19 in 1968
Biggest win France 28–3 in 1956, Czechoslovakia no win

1956	Toulouse **France** 28–3
1968	Prague **France** 19–6

FRANCE v FIJI

Played 8 France won 8
Highest scores France 77–10 in 2001, Fiji 19–28 in 1999
Biggest win France 77–10 in 2001, Fiji no win

1964	Paris **France** 21–3
1987	Auckland WC **France** 31–16
1991	Grenoble WC **France** 33–9
1998	Suva **France** 34–9
1999	Toulouse WC **France** 28–19
2001	Saint Etienne **France** 77–10
2003	Brisbane WC **France** 61–18
2010	Nantes **France** 34–12

FRANCE v JAPAN

Played 3 France won 3
Highest scores France 51–29 in 2003, Japan 29–51 in 2003
Biggest win France 51–29 in 2003, Japan no win

1973	Bordeaux **France** 30–18
2003	Townsville WC **France** 51–29
2011	Albany WC **France** 47–21

FRANCE v ZIMBABWE

Played 1 France won 1
Highest scores France 70–12 in 1987, Zimbabwe 12–70 in 1987
Biggest win France 70–12 in 1987, Zimbabwe no win

1987 Auckland WC **France** 70–12

FRANCE v CANADA

Played 8 France won 7, Canada won 1, Drawn 0
Highest scores France 50–6 in 2005, Canada 20–33 in 1999
Biggest wins France 50–6 in 2005, Canada 18–16 in 1994

1991 Agen WC **France** 19–13
1994 Nepean **Canada** 18–16
1994 Besançon **France** 28–9
1999 Béziers WC **France** 33–20
2002 Paris **France** 35–3
2004 Toronto **France** 47–13
2005 Nantes **France** 50–6
2011 Napier WC **France** 46–19

FRANCE v TONGA

Played 4 France won 2, Tonga won 2
Highest scores France 43–8 in 2005, Tonga 20–16 in 1999
Biggest win France 43–8 in 2005, Tonga 19–14 in 2011

1995 Pretoria WC **France** 38–10
1999 Nuku'alofa **Tonga** 20–16
2005 Toulouse **France** 43–8
2011 Wellington WC **Tonga** 19–14

FRANCE v IVORY COAST

Played 1 France won 1
Highest scores France 54–18 in 1995, Ivory Coast 18–54 in 1995
Biggest win France 54–18 in 1995, Ivory Coast no win

1995 Rustenburg WC **France** 54–18

FRANCE v SAMOA

Played 3 France won 3
Highest scores France 43–5 in 2009, Samoa 22–39 in 1999
Biggest win France 43–5 in 2009, Samoa no win

1999 Apia **France** 39–22
2009 Paris **France** 43–5
2012 Paris **France** 22–14

FRANCE v NAMIBIA

Played 2 France won 2
Highest scores France 87–10 in 2007, Namibia 13–47 in 1999
Biggest win France 87–10 in 2007, Namibia no win

1999 Bordeaux WC **France** 47–13
2007 Toulouse WC **France** 87–10

FRANCE v GEORGIA

Played 1 France won 1
Highest scores France 64–7 in 2007, Georgia 7–64 in 2007
Biggest win France 64–7 in 2007, Georgia no win

2007 Marseilles WC **France** 64–7

FRANCE v PACIFIC ISLANDS

Played 1 Wales won 1
Highest scores France 42–17 in 2008, Pacific Islands 17–42 in 2008
Biggest win France 42–17 in 2008, Pacific Islands no win

2008 Sochaux **France** 42–17

SOUTH AFRICA v NEW ZEALAND

Played 87 New Zealand won 50, South Africa won 34, Drawn 3
Highest scores New Zealand 55–35 in 1997, South Africa 46–40 in 2000
Biggest wins New Zealand 52–16 in 2003, South Africa 17–0 in 1928

1921 1 Dunedin **New Zealand** 13–5
2 Auckland **South Africa** 9–5
3 Wellington **Drawn** 0–0
Series drawn 1–1, with 1 draw
1928 1 Durban **South Africa** 17–0
2 Johannesburg **New Zealand** 7–6
3 Port Elizabeth **South Africa** 11–6
4 Cape Town **New Zealand** 13–5
Series drawn 2–2
1937 1 Wellington **New Zealand** 13–7
2 Christchurch **South Africa** 13–6
3 Auckland **South Africa** 17–6
South Africa won series 2–1
1949 1 Cape Town **South Africa** 15–11
2 Johannesburg **South Africa** 12–6
3 Durban **South Africa** 9–3
4 Port Elizabeth **South Africa** 11–8
South Africa won series 4–0
1956 1 Dunedin **New Zealand** 10–6
2 Wellington **South Africa** 8–3
3 Christchurch **New Zealand** 17–10
4 Auckland **New Zealand** 11–5
New Zealand won series 3–1
1960 1 Johannesburg **South Africa** 13–0
2 Cape Town **New Zealand** 11–3
3 Bloemfontein **Drawn** 11–11
4 Port Elizabeth **South Africa** 8–3
South Africa won series 2–1, with 1 draw
1965 1 Wellington **New Zealand** 6–3
2 Dunedin **New Zealand** 13–0
3 Christchurch **South Africa** 19–16
4 Auckland **New Zealand** 20–3
New Zealand won series 3–1

1970 1 Pretoria **South Africa** 17–6
2 Cape Town **New Zealand** 9–8
3 Port Elizabeth **South Africa** 14–3
4 Johannesburg **South Africa** 20–17
South Africa won series 3–1
1976 1 Durban **South Africa** 16–7
2 Bloemfontein **New Zealand** 15–9
3 Cape Town **South Africa** 15–10
4 Johannesburg **South Africa** 15–14
South Africa won series 3–1
1981 1 Christchurch **New Zealand** 14–9
2 Wellington **South Africa** 24–12
3 Auckland **New Zealand** 25–22
New Zealand won series 2–1
1992 Johannesburg **New Zealand** 27–24
1994 1 Dunedin **New Zealand** 22–14
2 Wellington **New Zealand** 13–9
3 Auckland **Drawn** 18–18
New Zealand won series 2–0, with 1 draw
1995 Johannesburg WC **South Africa** 15–12 (aet)
1996 Christchurch TN **New Zealand** 15–11
1996 Cape Town TN **New Zealand** 29–18
1996 1 Durban **New Zealand** 23–19
2 Pretoria **New Zealand** 33–26
3 Johannesburg **South Africa** 32–22
New Zealand won series 2–1
1997 Johannesburg TN **New Zealand** 35–32
1997 Auckland TN **New Zealand** 55–35
1998 Wellington TN **South Africa** 13–3
1998 Durban TN **South Africa** 24–23
1999 Dunedin TN **New Zealand** 28–0
1999 Pretoria TN **New Zealand** 34–18
1999 Cardiff WC **South Africa** 22–18
2000 Christchurch TN **New Zealand** 25–12
2000 Johannesburg TN **South Africa** 46–40
2001 Cape Town TN **New Zealand** 12–3
2001 Auckland TN **New Zealand** 26–15
2002 Wellington TN **New Zealand** 41–20
2002 Durban TN **New Zealand** 30–23
2003 Pretoria TN **New Zealand** 52–16
2003 Dunedin TN **New Zealand** 19–11
2003 Melbourne WC **New Zealand** 29–9
2004 Christchurch TN **New Zealand** 23–21
2004 Johannesburg TN **South Africa** 40–26
2005 Cape Town TN **South Africa** 22–16
2005 Dunedin TN **New Zealand** 31–27
2006 Wellington TN **New Zealand** 35–17
2006 Pretoria TN **New Zealand** 45–26
2006 Rustenburg TN **South Africa** 21–20
2007 Durban TN **New Zealand** 26–21
2007 Christchurch TN **New Zealand** 33–6
2008 Wellington TN **New Zealand** 19–8
2008 Dunedin TN **South Africa** 30–28
2008 Cape Town TN **New Zealand** 19–0
2009 Bloemfontein TN **South Africa** 28–19
2009 Durban TN **South Africa** 31–19
2009 Hamilton TN **South Africa** 32–29
2010 Auckland TN **New Zealand** 32–12
2010 Wellington TN **New Zealand** 31–17
2010 Soweto TN **New Zealand** 29–22
2011 Wellington TN **New Zealand** 40–7
2011 Port Elizabeth TN **South Africa** 18–5
2012 Dunedin RC **New Zealand** 21–11
2012 Soweto RC **New Zealand** 32–16
2013 Auckland RC **New Zealand** 29–13
2013 Johannesburg RC **New Zealand** 38–27

SOUTH AFRICA v AUSTRALIA

Played 78 South Africa won 44, Australia won 33, Drawn 1
Highest scores South Africa 61–22 in 1997, Australia 49–0 in 2006
Biggest wins South Africa 53–8 in 2008, Australia 49–0 in 2006

1933 1 Cape Town **South Africa** 17–3
2 Durban **Australia** 21–6
3 Johannesburg **South Africa** 12–3
4 Port Elizabeth **South Africa** 11–0
5 Bloemfontein **Australia** 15–4
South Africa won series 3–2
1937 1 Sydney **South Africa** 9–5
2 Sydney **South Africa** 26–17
South Africa won series 2–0
1953 1 Johannesburg **South Africa** 25–3
2 Cape Town **Australia** 18–14
3 Durban **South Africa** 18–8
4 Port Elizabeth **South Africa** 22–9
South Africa won series 3–1
1956 1 Sydney **South Africa** 9–0
2 Brisbane **South Africa** 9–0

	South Africa won series 2–0
1961	1 Johannesburg **South Africa** 28–3
	2 Port Elizabeth **South Africa** 23–11
	South Africa won series 2–0
1963	1 Pretoria **South Africa** 14–3
	2 Cape Town **Australia** 9–5
	3 Johannesburg **Australia** 11–9
	4 Port Elizabeth **South Africa** 22–6
	Series drawn 2–2
1965	1 Sydney **Australia** 18–11
	2 Brisbane **Australia** 12–8
	Australia won series 2–0
1969	1 Johannesburg **South Africa** 30–11
	2 Durban **South Africa** 16–9
	3 Cape Town **South Africa** 11–3
	4 Bloemfontein **South Africa** 19–8
	South Africa won series 4–0
1971	1 Sydney **South Africa** 19–11
	2 Brisbane **South Africa** 14–6
	3 Sydney **South Africa** 18–6
	South Africa won series 3–0
1992	Cape Town **Australia** 26–3
1993	1 Sydney **South Africa** 19–12
	2 Brisbane **Australia** 28–20
	3 Sydney **Australia** 19–12
	Australia won series 2–1
1995	Cape Town WC **South Africa** 27–18
1996	Sydney TN **Australia** 21–16
1996	Bloemfontein TN **South Africa** 25–19
1997	Brisbane TN **Australia** 32–20
1997	Pretoria TN **South Africa** 61–22
1998	Perth TN **South Africa** 14–13
1998	Johannesburg TN **South Africa** 29–15
1999	Brisbane TN **Australia** 32–6
1999	Cape Town TN **South Africa** 10–9
1999	Twickenham WC **Australia** 27–21
2000	Melbourne **Australia** 44–23
2000	Sydney TN **Australia** 26–6
2000	Durban TN **Australia** 19–18
2001	Pretoria TN **South Africa** 20–15
2001	Perth TN **Drawn** 14–14
2002	Brisbane TN **Australia** 38–27
2002	Johannesburg TN **South Africa** 33–31
2003	Cape Town TN **South Africa** 26–22
2003	Brisbane TN **Australia** 29–9
2004	Perth TN **Australia** 30–26
2004	Durban TN **South Africa** 23–19
2005	Sydney **Australia** 30–12
2005	Johannesburg **South Africa** 33–20
2005	Pretoria TN **South Africa** 22–16
2005	Perth TN **South Africa** 22–19
2006	Brisbane TN **Australia** 49–0
2006	Sydney TN **Australia** 20–18
2006	Johannesburg TN **South Africa** 24–16
2007	Cape Town TN **South Africa** 22–19
2007	Sydney TN **Australia** 25–17
2008	Perth TN **Australia** 16–9
2008	Durban TN **Australia** 27–15
2008	Johannesburg TN **South Africa** 53–8
2009	Cape Town TN **South Africa** 29–17
2009	Perth TN **South Africa** 32–25
2009	Brisbane TN **Australia** 21–6
2010	Brisbane TN **Australia** 30–13
2010	Pretoria TN **South Africa** 44–31
2010	Bloemfontein TN **Australia** 41–39
2011	Sydney TN **Australia** 39–20
2011	Durban TN **Australia** 14–9
2011	Wellington WC **Australia** 11–9
2012	Perth RC **Australia** 26–19
2012	Pretoria RC **South Africa** 31–8
2013	Brisbane RC **South Africa** 38–12
2013	Cape Town RC **South Africa** 28–8

SOUTH AFRICA v WORLD XVs

Played 3 South Africa won 3
Highest scores South Africa 45–24 in 1977, World XV 24–45 in 1977
Biggest win South Africa 45–24 in 1977, World XV no win

1977	Pretoria **South Africa** 45–24
1989	1 Cape Town **South Africa** 20–19
	2 Johannesburg **South Africa** 22–16
	South Africa won series 2–0

SOUTH AFRICA v SOUTH AMERICA

Played 8 South Africa won 7, South America won 1, Drawn 0
Highest scores South Africa 50–18 in 1982, South America 21–12 in 1982
Biggest wins South Africa 50–18 in 1982, South America 21–12 in 1982

1980	1 Johannesburg **South Africa** 24–9	1982	1 Pretoria **South Africa** 50–18
	2 Durban **South Africa** 18–9		2 Bloemfontein **South America** 21–12
	South Africa won series 2–0		Series drawn 1–1
1980	1 Montevideo **South Africa** 22–13	1984	1 Pretoria **South Africa** 32–15
	2 Santiago **South Africa** 30–16		2 Cape Town **South Africa** 22–13
	South Africa won series 2–0		South Africa won series 2–0

SOUTH AFRICA v UNITED STATES

Played 3 South Africa won 3
Highest scores South Africa 64–10 in 2007, United States 20–43 in 2001
Biggest win South Africa 64–10 in 2007, United States no win

1981	Glenville **South Africa** 38–7	2007	Montpellier WC **South Africa** 64–10
2001	Houston **South Africa** 43–20		

SOUTH AFRICA v NEW ZEALAND CAVALIERS

Played 4 South Africa won 3, New Zealand Cavaliers won 1, Drawn 0
Highest scores South Africa 33–18 in 1986, New Zealand Cavaliers 19–18 in 1986
Biggest wins South Africa 33–18 in 1986, New Zealand Cavaliers 19–18 in 1986

1986	1 Cape Town **South Africa** 21–15		3 Pretoria **South Africa** 33–18
	2 Durban **New Zealand Cavaliers** 19–18		4 Johannesburg **South Africa** 24–10
			South Africa won series 3–1

SOUTH AFRICA v ARGENTINA

Played 17 South Africa won 16, Drawn 1
Highest scores South Africa 73–13 in 2013, Argentina 33–37 in 2000
Biggest wins South Africa 73–13 in 2013, Argentina no win

1993	1 Buenos Aires **South Africa** 29–26	2002	Springs **South Africa** 49–29
	2 Buenos Aires **South Africa** 52–23	2003	Port Elizabeth **South Africa** 26–25
	South Africa won series 2–0	2004	Buenos Aires **South Africa** 39–7
1994	1 Port Elizabeth **South Africa** 42–22	2005	Buenos Aires **South Africa** 34–23
	2 Johannesburg **South Africa** 46–26	2007	Paris WC **South Africa** 37–13
	South Africa won series 2–0	2008	Johannesburg **South Africa** 63–9
1996	1 Buenos Aires **South Africa** 46–15	2012	Cape Town RC **South Africa** 27–6
	2 Buenos Aires **South Africa** 44–21	2012	Mendoza RC **Drawn** 16–16
	South Africa win series 2–0	2013	Soweto RC **South Africa** 73–13
2000	Buenos Aires **South Africa** 37–33	2013	Mendoza RC **South Africa** 22–17

SOUTH AFRICA v SAMOA

Played 8 South Africa won 8
Highest scores South Africa 60–8 in 1995, 60–18 in 2002 and 60–10 in 2003, Samoa 23–56 in 2013
Biggest win South Africa 60–8 in 1995 and 59–7 in 2007, Samoa no win

1995	Johannesburg **South Africa** 60–8	2007	Johannesburg **South Africa** 35–8
1995	Johannesburg WC **South Africa** 42–14	2007	Paris WC **South Africa** 59–7
2002	Pretoria **South Africa** 60–18	2011	Albany WC **South Africa** 13–5
2003	Brisbane WC **South Africa** 60–10	2013	Pretoria QT **South Africa** 56–23

SOUTH AFRICA v ROMANIA

Played 1 South Africa won 1
Highest score South Africa 21–8 in 1995, Romania 8–21 in 1995
Biggest win South Africa 21–8 in 1995, Romania no win

1995	Cape Town WC **South Africa** 21–8

SOUTH AFRICA v CANADA

Played 2 South Africa won 2
Highest scores South Africa 51–18 in 2000, Canada 18–51 in 2000
Biggest win South Africa 51–18 in 2000, Canada no win

1995	Port Elizabeth WC **South Africa** 20–0	2000	East London **South Africa** 51–18

SOUTH AFRICA v ITALY

Played 11 South Africa won 11
Highest scores South Africa 101–0 in 1999, Italy 31–62 in 1997
Biggest win South Africa 101–0 in 1999, Italy no win

1995	Rome **South Africa** 40–21	2008	Cape Town **South Africa** 26–0
1997	Bologna **South Africa** 62–31	2009	Udine **South Africa** 32–10
1999	1 Port Elizabeth **South Africa** 74–3	2010	1 Witbank **South Africa** 29–13
	2 Durban **South Africa** 101–0		2 East London **South Africa** 55–11
	South Africa won series 2–0		South Africa won series 2–0
2001	Port Elizabeth **South Africa** 60–14	2013	Durban QT **South Africa** 44–10
2001	Genoa **South Africa** 54–26		

SOUTH AFRICA v FIJI

Played 3 South Africa won 3
Highest scores South Africa 49–3 in 2011, Fiji 20–37 in 2007
Biggest win South Africa 49–3 in 2011, Fiji no win

1996 Pretoria **South Africa** 43–18
2007 Marseilles WC **South Africa** 37–20
2011 Wellington WC **South Africa** 49–3

SOUTH AFRICA v TONGA

Played 2 South Africa won 2
Higest scores South Africa 74–10 in 1997, Tonga 25–30 in 2007
Biggest win South Africa 74–10 in 1997, Tonga no win

1997 Cape Town **South Africa** 74–10
2007 Lens WC **South Africa** 30–25

SOUTH AFRICA v SPAIN

Played 1 South Africa won 1
Highest scores South Africa 47–3 in 1999, Spain 3–47 in 1999
Biggest win South Africa 47–3 in 1999, Spain no win

1999 Murrayfield WC **South Africa** 47–3

SOUTH AFRICA v URUGUAY

Played 3 South Africa won 3
Highest scores South Africa 134–3 in 2005, Uruguay 6–72 in 2003
Biggest win South Africa 134–3 in 2005, Uruguay no win

1999 Glasgow WC **South Africa** 39–3
2003 Glasgow WC **South Africa** 39–3
Perth WC **South Africa** 72–6
2005 East London **South Africa** 134–3

SOUTH AFRICA v GEORGIA

Played 1 South Africa won 1
Highest scores South Africa 46–19 in 2003, Georgia 19–46 in 2003
Biggest win South Africa 46–19 in 2003, Georgia no win

2003 Sydney WC **South Africa** 46–19

SOUTH AFRICA v PACIFIC ISLANDS

Played 1 South Africa won 1
Highest scores South Africa 38–24 in 2004, Pacific Islands 24–38 in 2004
Biggest win South Africa 38–24 in 2004, Pacific Islands no win

2004 Gosford (Aus) **South Africa** 38–24

SOUTH AFRICA v NAMIBIA

Played 2 South Africa won 2
Highest scores South Africa 105–13 in 2007, Namibia 13–105 in 2007
Biggest win South Africa 105–13 in 2007, Namibia no win

2007 Cape Town **South Africa** 105–13
2011 Albany WC **South Africa** 87–0

NEW ZEALAND v AUSTRALIA

Played 148 New Zealand won 101, Australia won 41, Drawn 6
Highest scores New Zealand 50–21 in 2003, Australia 35–39 in 2000
Biggest wins New Zealand 43–6 in 1996, Australia 28–7 in 1999

1903 Sydney **New Zealand** 22–3
1905 Dunedin **New Zealand** 14–3
1907 1 Sydney **New Zealand** 26–6
2 Brisbane **New Zealand** 14–5
3 Sydney **Drawn** 5–5
New Zealand won series 2–0, with 1 draw
1910 1 Sydney **New Zealand** 6–0
2 Sydney **Australia** 11–0
3 Sydney **New Zealand** 28–13
New Zealand won series 2–1
1913 1 Wellington **New Zealand** 30–5
2 Dunedin **New Zealand** 25–13
3 Christchurch **Australia** 16–5
New Zealand won series 2–1
1914 1 Sydney **New Zealand** 5–0
2 Brisbane **New Zealand** 17–0
3 Sydney **New Zealand** 22–7
New Zealand won series 3–0
1929 1 Sydney **Australia** 9–8
2 Brisbane **Australia** 17–9
3 Sydney **Australia** 15–13
Australia won series 3–0
1931 Auckland **New Zealand** 20–13
1932 1 Sydney **Australia** 22–17
2 Brisbane **New Zealand** 21–3
3 Sydney **New Zealand** 21–13
New Zealand won series 2–1
1934 1 Sydney **Australia** 25–11
2 Sydney **Drawn** 3–3
Australia won series 1–0, with 1 draw
1936 1 Wellington **New Zealand** 11–6
2 Dunedin **New Zealand** 38–13
New Zealand won series 2–0
1938 1 Sydney **New Zealand** 24–9
2 Brisbane **New Zealand** 20–14
3 Sydney **New Zealand** 14–6
New Zealand won series 3–0
1946 1 Dunedin **New Zealand** 31–8
2 Auckland **New Zealand** 14–10
New Zealand won series 2–0
1947 1 Brisbane **New Zealand** 13–5
2 Sydney **New Zealand** 27–14
New Zealand won series 2–0
1949 1 Wellington **Australia** 11–6
2 Auckland **Australia** 16–9
Australia won series 2–0
1951 1 Sydney **New Zealand** 8–0
2 Sydney **New Zealand** 17–11
3 Brisbane **New Zealand** 16–6
New Zealand won series 3–0

1952 1 Christchurch **Australia** 14–9
2 Wellington **New Zealand** 15–8
Series drawn 1–1
1955 1 Wellington **New Zealand** 16–8
2 Dunedin **New Zealand** 8–0
3 Auckland **Australia** 8–3
New Zealand won series 2–1
1957 1 Sydney **New Zealand** 25–11
2 Brisbane **New Zealand** 22–9
New Zealand won series 2–0
1958 1 Wellington **New Zealand** 25–3
2 Christchurch **Australia** 6–3
3 Auckland **New Zealand** 17–8
New Zealand won series 2–1
1962 1 Brisbane **New Zealand** 20–6
2 Sydney **New Zealand** 14–5
New Zealand won series 2–0
1962 1 Wellington **Drawn** 9–9
2 Dunedin **New Zealand** 3–0
3 Auckland **New Zealand** 16–8
New Zealand won series 2–0, with 1 draw
1964 1 Dunedin **New Zealand** 14–9
2 Christchurch **New Zealand** 18–3
3 Wellington **Australia** 20–5
New Zealand won series 2–1
1967 Wellington **New Zealand** 29–9
1968 1 Sydney **New Zealand** 27–11
2 Brisbane **New Zealand** 19–18
New Zealand won series 2–0
1972 1 Wellington **New Zealand** 29–6
2 Christchurch **New Zealand** 30–17
3 Auckland **New Zealand** 38–3
New Zealand won series 3–0
1974 1 Sydney **New Zealand** 11–6
2 Brisbane **Drawn** 16–16
3 Sydney **New Zealand** 16–6
New Zealand won series 2–0, with 1 draw
1978 1 Wellington **New Zealand** 13–12
2 Christchurch **New Zealand** 22–6
3 Auckland **Australia** 30–16
New Zealand won series 2–1
1979 Sydney **Australia** 12–6
1980 1 Sydney **Australia** 13–9
2 Brisbane **New Zealand** 12–9
3 Sydney **Australia** 26–10
Australia won series 2–1
1982 1 Christchurch **New Zealand** 23–16
2 Wellington **Australia** 19–16
3 Auckland **New Zealand** 33–18
New Zealand won series 2–1
1983 Sydney **New Zealand** 18–8
1984 1 Sydney **Australia** 16–9
2 Brisbane **New Zealand** 19–15
3 Sydney **New Zealand** 25–24
New Zealand won series 2–1
1985 Auckland **New Zealand** 10–9
1986 1 Wellington **Australia** 13–12
2 Dunedin **New Zealand** 13–12
3 Auckland **Australia** 22–9
Australia won series 2–1
1987 Sydney **New Zealand** 30–16
1988 1 Sydney **New Zealand** 32–7
2 Brisbane **Drawn** 19–19
3 Sydney **New Zealand** 30–9
New Zealand won series 2–0, with 1 draw
1989 Auckland **New Zealand** 24–12
1990 1 Christchurch **New Zealand** 21–6
2 Auckland **New Zealand** 27–17
3 Wellington **Australia** 21–9
New Zealand won series 2–1
1991 1 Sydney **Australia** 21–12
2 Auckland **New Zealand** 6–3
1991 Dublin WC **Australia** 16–6
1992 1 Sydney **Australia** 16–15
2 Brisbane **Australia** 19–17
3 Sydney **New Zealand** 26–23
Australia won series 2–1
1993 Dunedin **New Zealand** 25–10
1994 Sydney **Australia** 20–16
1995 Auckland **New Zealand** 28–16
1995 Sydney **New Zealand** 34–23
1996 Wellington TN **New Zealand** 43–6
1996 Brisbane TN **New Zealand** 32–25
New Zealand won series 2–0
1997 Christchurch **New Zealand** 30–13
1997 Melbourne TN **New Zealand** 33–18
1997 Dunedin TN **New Zealand** 36–24
New Zealand won series 3–0
1998 Melbourne TN **Australia** 24–16
1998 Christchurch TN **Australia** 27–23
1998 Sydney Australia 19–14
Australia won series 3–0
1999 Auckland TN **New Zealand** 34–15
1999 Sydney TN **Australia** 28–7
Series drawn 1–1
2000 Sydney TN **New Zealand** 39–35
2000 Wellington TN **Australia** 24–23

Series drawn 1–1
2001 Dunedin TN **Australia** 23–15
2001 Sydney TN **Australia** 29–26
Australia won series 2–0
2002 Christchurch TN **New Zealand** 12–6
2002 Sydney TN **Australia** 16–14
Series drawn 1–1
2003 Sydney TN **New Zealand** 50–21
2003 Auckland TN **New Zealand** 21–17
New Zealand won series 2–0
2003 Sydney WC **Australia** 22–10
2004 Wellington TN **New Zealand** 16–7
2004 Sydney TN **Australia** 23–18
Series drawn 1–1
2005 Sydney TN **New Zealand** 30–13
2005 Auckland TN **New Zealand** 34–24
New Zealand won series 2–0
2006 Christchurch TN **New Zealand** 32–12
2006 Brisbane TN **New Zealand** 13–9
2006 Auckland TN **New Zealand** 34–27
New Zealand won series 3–0
2007 Melbourne TN **Australia** 20–15
2007 Auckland TN **New Zealand** 26–12
Series drawn 1–1
2008 Sydney TN **Australia** 34–19
2008 Auckland TN **New Zealand** 39–10
2008 Brisbane TN **New Zealand** 28–24
2008 Hong Kong **New Zealand** 19–14
New Zealand won series 3–1
2009 Auckland TN **New Zealand** 22–16
2009 Sydney TN **New Zealand** 19–18
2009 Wellington TN **New Zealand** 33–6
2009 Tokyo **New Zealand** 32–19
New Zealand won series 4–0
2010 Melbourne TN **New Zealand** 49–28
2010 Christchurch TN **New Zealand** 20–10
2010 Sydney TN **New Zealand** 23–22
2010 Hong Kong **Australia** 26–24
New Zealand won series 3–1
2011 Auckland TN **New Zealand** 30–14
2011 Brisbane TN **Australia** 25–20
2011 Auckland WC **New Zealand** 20–6
2012 Sydney RC **New Zealand** 27–19
2012 Auckland RC **New Zealand** 22–0
2012 Brisbane **Drawn** 18–18
New Zealand won series 2–0, with 1 draw
2013 Sydney RC **New Zealand** 47–29
2013 Wellington RC **New Zealand** 27–16

NEW ZEALAND v UNITED STATES

Played 2 New Zealand won 2
Highest scores New Zealand 51–3 in 1913, United States 6–46 in 1991
Biggest win New Zealand 51–3 in 1913, United States no win

1913 Berkeley **New Zealand** 51–3
1991 Gloucester WC **New Zealand** 46–6

NEW ZEALAND v ROMANIA

Played 2 New Zealand won 2
Highest score New Zealand 85–8 in 2007, Romania 8–85 in 2007
Biggest win New Zealand 85–8 in 2007, Romania no win

1981 Bucharest **New Zealand** 14–6
2007 Toulouse WC **New Zealand** 85–8

NEW ZEALAND v ARGENTINA

Played 18 New Zealand won 17, Drawn 1
Highest scores New Zealand 93–8 in 1997, Argentina 21–21 in 1985
Biggest win New Zealand 93–8 in 1997, Argentina no win

1985	1 Buenos Aires **New Zealand** 33–20
	2 Buenos Aires **Drawn** 21–21
	New Zealand won series 1–0, with 1 draw
1987	Wellington WC **New Zealand** 46–15
1989	1 Dunedin **New Zealand** 60–9
	2 Wellington **New Zealand** 49–12
	New Zealand won series 2–0
1991	1 Buenos Aires **New Zealand** 28–14
	2 Buenos Aires **New Zealand** 36–6
	New Zealand won series 2–0
1997	1 Wellington **New Zealand** 93–8
	2 Hamilton **New Zealand** 62–10
	New Zealand won series 2–0
2001	Christchurch **New Zealand** 67–19
2001	Buenos Aires **New Zealand** 24–20
2004	Hamilton **New Zealand** 41–7
2006	Buenos Aires **New Zealand** 25–19
2011	Auckland WC **New Zealand** 33–10
2012	Wellington RC **New Zealand** 21–5
2012	La Plata RC **New Zealand** 54–15
2013	Hamilton RC **New Zealand** 28–13
2013	La Plata RC **New Zealand** 33–15

NEW ZEALAND v ITALY

Played 12 New Zealand won 12
Highest scores New Zealand 101–3 in 1999, Italy 21–31 in 1991
Biggest win New Zealand 101–3 in 1999, Italy no win

1987	Auckland WC **New Zealand** 70–6
1991	Leicester WC **New Zealand** 31–21
1995	Bologna **New Zealand** 70–6
1999	Huddersfield WC **New Zealand** 101–3
2000	Genoa **New Zealand** 56–19
2002	Hamilton **New Zealand** 64–10
2003	Melbourne WC **New Zealand** 70–7
2004	Rome **New Zealand** 59–10
2007	Marseilles WC **New Zealand** 76–14
2009	Christchurch **New Zealand** 27–6
2009	Milan **New Zealand** 20–6
2012	Rome **New Zealand** 42–10

NEW ZEALAND v FIJI

Played 5 New Zealand won 5
Highest scores New Zealand 91–0 in 2005, Fiji 18–68 in 2002
Biggest win New Zealand 91–0 in 2005, Fiji no win

1987	Christchurch WC **New Zealand** 74–13
1997	Albany **New Zealand** 71–5
2002	Wellington **New Zealand** 68–18
2005	Albany **New Zealand** 91–0
2011	Dunedin **New Zealand** 60–14

NEW ZEALAND v CANADA

Played 5 New Zealand won 5
Highest scores New Zealand 79–15 in 2011, Canada 15–79 in 2011
Biggest win New Zealand 73–7 in 1995, Canada no win

1991	Lille WC **New Zealand** 29–13
1995	Auckland **New Zealand** 73–7
2003	Melbourne WC **New Zealand** 68–6
2007	Hamilton **New Zealand** 64–13
2011	Wellington WC **New Zealand** 79–15

NEW ZEALAND v WORLD XVs

Played 3 New Zealand won 2, World XV won 1, Drawn 0
Highest scores New Zealand 54–26 in 1992, World XV 28–14 in 1992
Biggest wins New Zealand 54–26 in 1992, World XV 28–14 in 1992

1992	1 Christchurch **World XV** 28–14	3 Auckland **New Zealand** 26–15
	2 Wellington **New Zealand** 54–26	New Zealand won series 2–1

NEW ZEALAND v SAMOA

Played 5 New Zealand won 5
Highest scores New Zealand 101–14 in 2008, Samoa 14–101 in 2008
Biggest win New Zealand 101–14 in 2008, Samoa no win

1993	Auckland **New Zealand** 35–13	2001	Albany **New Zealand** 50–6
1996	Napier **New Zealand** 51–10	2008	New Plymouth **New Zealand** 101–14
1999	Albany **New Zealand** 71–13		

NEW ZEALAND v JAPAN

Played 2 New Zealand won 2
Highest scores New Zealand 145–17 in 1995, Japan 17–145 in 1995
Biggest win New Zealand 145–17 in 1995, Japan no win

1995	Bloemfontein WC **New Zealand** 145–17	2011	Hamilton WC **New Zealand** 83–7

NEW ZEALAND v TONGA

Played 4 New Zealand won 4
Highest scores New Zealand 102–0 in 2000, Tonga 10–41 in 2011
Biggest win New Zealand 102–0 in 2000, Tonga no win

1999	Bristol WC **New Zealand** 45–9	2003	Brisbane WC **New Zealand** 91–7
2000	Albany **New Zealand** 102–0	2011	Auckland WC **New Zealand** 41–10

NEW ZEALAND v PACIFIC ISLANDS

Played 1 New Zealand won 1
Highest scores New Zealand 41–26 in 2004, Pacific Islands 26–41 in 2004
Biggest win New Zealand 41–26 in 2004, Pacific Islands no win

2004	Albany **New Zealand 41–26**

NEW ZEALAND v PORTUGAL

Played 1 New Zealand won 1
Highest scores New Zealand 108–13 in 2007, Portugal 13–108 in 2007
Biggest win New Zealand 108–13 in 2007, Portugal no win

2007 Lyons WC **New Zealand** 108–13

AUSTRALIA v UNITED STATES

Played 7 Australia won 7
Highest scores Australia 67–9 in 1990 and 67–5 in 2011, United States 19–55 in 1999
Biggest win Australia 67–5 in 2011, United States no win

1912 Berkeley **Australia** 12–8
1976 Los Angeles **Australia** 24–12
1983 Sydney **Australia** 49–3
1987 Brisbane WC **Australia** 47–12
1990 Brisbane **Australia** 67–9
1999 Limerick WC **Australia** 55–19
2011 Wellington WC **Australia** 67–5

AUSTRALIA v NEW ZEALAND XVs

Played 24 Australia won 6, New Zealand XVs won 18, Drawn 0
Highest scores Australia 26–20 in 1926, New Zealand XV 38–11 in 1923 and 38–8 in 1924
Biggest win Australia 17–0 in 1921, New Zealand XV 38–8 in 1924

1920 1 Sydney **New Zealand XV** 26–15
2 Sydney **New Zealand XV** 14–6
3 Sydney **New Zealand XV** 24–13
New Zealand XV won series 3–0
1921 Christchurch **Australia** 17–0
1922 1 Sydney **New Zealand XV** 26–19
2 Sydney **Australia** 14–8
3 Sydney **Australia** 8–6
Australia won series 2–1
1923 1 Dunedin **New Zealand XV** 19–9
2 Christchurch **New Zealand XV** 34–6
3 Wellington **New Zealand XV** 38–11
New Zealand XV won series 3–0
1924 1 Sydney **Australia** 20–16
2 Sydney **New Zealand XV** 21–5
3 Sydney **New Zealand XV** 38–8
New Zealand XV won series 2–1
1925 1 Sydney **New Zealand XV** 26–3
2 Sydney **New Zealand XV** 4–0
3 Sydney **New Zealand XV** 11–3
New Zealand XV won series 3–0
1925 Auckland **New Zealand XV** 36–10
1926 1 Sydney **Australia** 26–20
2 Sydney **New Zealand XV** 11–6
3 Sydney **New Zealand XV** 14–0
4 Sydney **New Zealand XV** 28–21
New Zealand XV won series 3–1
1928 1 Wellington **New Zealand XV** 15–12
2 Dunedin **New Zealand XV** 16–14
3 Christchurch **Australia** 11–8
New Zealand XV won series 2–1

AUSTRALIA v SOUTH AFRICA XVs

Played 3 South Africa XVs won 3
Highest scores Australia 11–16 in 1921, South Africa XV 28–9 in 1921
Biggest win Australia no win, South Africa XV 28–9 in 1921

1921 1 Sydney **South Africa XV** 25–10
2 Sydney **South Africa XV** 16–11
3 Sydney **South Africa XV** 28–9
South Africa XV won series 3–0

AUSTRALIA v NEW ZEALAND MAORIS

Played 16 Australia won 8, New Zealand Maoris won 6, Drawn 2
Highest scores Australia 31–6 in 1936, New Zealand Maoris 25–22 in 1922
Biggest wins Australia 31–6 in 1936, New Zealand Maoris 20–0 in 1946

1922 1 Sydney **New Zealand Maoris** 25–22
2 Sydney **Australia** 28–13
3 Sydney **New Zealand Maoris** 23–22
New Zealand Maoris won series 2–1
1923 1 Sydney **Australia** 27–23
2 Sydney **Australia** 21–16
3 Sydney **Australia** 14–12
Australia won series 3–0
1928 Wellington **New Zealand Maoris** 9–8
1931 Palmerston North **Australia** 14–3
1936 Palmerston North **Australia** 31–6
1946 Hamilton **New Zealand Maoris** 20–0
1949 1 Sydney **New Zealand Maoris** 12–3
2 Brisbane **Drawn** 8–8
3 Sydney **Australia** 18–3
Series drawn 1–1, with 1 draw
1958 1 Brisbane **Australia** 15–14
2 Sydney **Drawn** 3–3
3 Melbourne **New Zealand Maoris** 13–6
Series drawn 1–1, with 1 draw

AUSTRALIA v FIJI

Played 19 Australia won 16, Fiji won 2, Drawn 1
Highest scores Australia 66–20 in 1998, Fiji 28–52 in 1985
Biggest wins Australia 49–0 in 2007, Fiji 17–15 in 1952 and 18–16 in 1954

1952 1 Sydney **Australia** 15–9
2 Sydney **Fiji** 17–15
Series drawn 1–1
1954 1 Brisbane **Australia** 22–19
2 Sydney **Fiji** 18–16
Series drawn 1–1
1961 1 Brisbane **Australia** 24–6
2 Sydney **Australia** 20–14
3 Melbourne **Drawn** 3–3
Australia won series 2–0, with 1 draw
1972 Suva **Australia** 21–19
1976 1 Sydney **Australia** 22–6
2 Brisbane **Australia** 21–9
3 Sydney **Australia** 27–17
Australia won series 3–0
1980 Suva **Australia** 22–9
1984 Suva **Australia** 16–3
1985 1 Brisbane **Australia** 52–28
2 Sydney **Australia** 31–9
Australia won series 2–0
1998 Sydney **Australia** 66–20
2007 Perth **Australia** 49–0
2007 Montpellier WC **Australia** 55–12
2010 Canberra **Australia** 49–3

AUSTRALIA v TONGA

Played 4 Australia won 3, Tonga won 1, Drawn 0
Highest scores Australia 74–0 in 1998, Tonga 16–11 in 1973
Biggest wins Australia 74–0 in 1998, Tonga 16–11 in 1973

1973	1 Sydney **Australia** 30–12	1993	Brisbane **Australia** 52–14
	2 Brisbane **Tonga** 16–11	1998	Canberra **Australia** 74–0
	Series drawn 1–1		

AUSTRALIA v JAPAN

Played 4 Australia won 4
Highest scores Australia 91–3 in 2007, Japan 25–50 in 1973
Biggest win Australia 91–3 in 2007, Japan no win

1975	1 Sydney **Australia** 37–7	1987	Sydney WC **Australia** 42–23
	2 Brisbane **Australia** 50–25	2007	Lyons WC **Australia** 91–3
	Australia won series 2–0		

AUSTRALIA v ARGENTINA

Played 21 Australia won 16, Argentina won 4, Drawn 1
Highest scores Australia 54–17 in 2013, Argentina 27–19 in 1987
Biggest wins Australia 53–6 in 2000, Argentina 18–3 in 1983

1979	1 Buenos Aires **Argentina** 24–13
	2 Buenos Aires **Australia** 17–12
	Series drawn 1–1
1983	1 Brisbane **Argentina** 18–3
	2 Sydney **Australia** 29–13
	Series drawn 1–1
1986	1 Brisbane **Australia** 39–19
	2 Sydney **Australia** 26–0
	Australia won series 2–0
1987	1 Buenos Aires **Drawn** 19–19
	2 Buenos Aires **Argentina** 27–19
	Argentina won series 1–0, with 1 draw
1991	Llanelli WC **Australia** 32–19
1995	1 Brisbane **Australia** 53–7
	2 Sydney **Australia** 30–13
	Australia won series 2–0
1997	1 Buenos Aires **Australia** 23–15
	2 Buenos Aires **Argentina** 18–16
	Series drawn 1–1
2000	1 Brisbane **Australia** 53–6
	2 Canberra **Australia** 32–25
	Australia won series 2–0
2002	Buenos Aires **Australia** 17–6
2003	Sydney WC **Australia** 24–8
2012	Robina RC **Australia** 23–19
2012	Rosario RC **Australia** 25–19
2013	Perth RC **Australia** 14–13
2013	Rosario RC **Australia** 54–17

AUSTRALIA v SAMOA

Played 5 Australia won 4, Samoa won 1
Highest scores Australia 74–7 in 2005, Samoa 32–23 in 2011
Biggest win Australia 73–3 in 1994, Samoa 32–23 in 2011

1991	Pontypool WC **Australia** 9–3	2005	Sydney **Australia** 74–7
1994	Sydney **Australia** 73–3	2011	Sydney **Samoa** 32–23
1998	Brisbane **Australia** 25–13		

AUSTRALIA v ITALY

Played 15 Australia won 15
Highest scores Australia 69–21 in 2005, Italy 21–69 in 2005
Biggest win Australia 55–6 in 1988, Italy no win

1983	Rovigo **Australia** 29–7	2006	Rome **Australia** 25–18
1986	Brisbane **Australia** 39–18	2008	Padua **Australia** 30–20
1988	Rome **Australia** 55–6	2009	1 Canberra **Australia** 31–8
1994	1 Brisbane **Australia** 23–20		2 Melbourne **Australia** 34–12
	2 Melbourne **Australia** 20–7		Australia won series 2–0
	Australia won series 2–0	2010	Florence **Australia** 32–14
1996	Padua **Australia** 40–18	2011	Albany WC **Australia** 32–6
2002	Genoa **Australia** 34–3	2012	Florence **Australia** 22–19
2005	Melbourne **Australia** 69–21		

AUSTRALIA v CANADA

Played 6 Australia won 6
Highest scores Australia 74–9 in 1996, Canada 16–43 in 1993
Biggest win Australia 74–9 in 1996, Canada no win

1985	1 Sydney **Australia** 59–3	1995	Port Elizabeth WC **Australia** 27–11
	2 Brisbane **Australia** 43–15	1996	Brisbane **Australia** 74–9
	Australia won series 2–0	2007	Bordeaux WC **Australia** 37–6
1993	Calgary **Australia** 43–16		

AUSTRALIA v KOREA

Played 1 Australia won 1
Highest scores Australia 65–18 in 1987, Korea 18–65 in 1987
Biggest win Australia 65–18 in 1987, Korea no win

1987	Brisbane **Australia** 65–18

AUSTRALIA v ROMANIA

Played 3 Australia won 3
Highest scores Australia 90–8 in 2003, Romania 9–57 in 1999
Biggest win Australia 90–8 in 2003, Romania no win

1995	Stellenbosch WC **Australia** 42–3	2003	Brisbane WC **Australia** 90–8
1999	Belfast WC **Australia** 57–9		

AUSTRALIA v SPAIN

Played 1 Australia won 1
Highest scores Australia 92–10 in 2001, Spain 10–92 in 2001
Biggest win Australia 92–10 in 2001, Spain no win

2001 Madrid **Australia** 92–10

AUSTRALIA v NAMIBIA

Played 1 Australia won 1
Highest scores Australia 142–0 in 2003, Namibia 0–142 in 2003
Biggest win Australia 142–0 in 2003, Namibia no win

2003 Adelaide WC **Australia** 142–0

AUSTRALIA v PACIFIC ISLANDS

Played 1 Australia won 1
Highest scores Australia 29–14 in 2004, Pacific Islands 14–29 in 2004
Biggest win Australia 29–14 in 2004, Pacific Islands no win

2004 Adelaide **Australia** 29–14

AUSTRALIA v RUSSIA

Played 1 Australia won 1
Highest scores Australia 68–22 in 2011, Russia 22–68 in 2011
Biggest win Australia 68–22 in 2011, Russia no win

2011 Nelson WC **Australia** 68–22

In partnership with

Sam Warburton, Wales
IRB Anti-Doping Ambassador

Tackle Doping.
Join us in the fight
against doping –

KEEP RUGBY CLEAN
IRB ANTI-DOPING

WORLD RECORDS

The match and career records cover official Test matches played up to 10 October 2013.

MATCH RECORDS

MOST CONSECUTIVE TEST WINS

18 by Lithuania	2006 Hun, Nor, Bul 2007 Aus, Hun, Bul 2008 Lat, Aus, Hun, Nor, And, Swi 2009 Ser, Arm, Isr, Hol, And 2010 Ser
17 by N Zealand	1965 SA 4, 1966 BI 1,2,3,4, 1967 A, E, W, F, S, 1968 A 1,2, F 1,2,3, 1969 W 1,2
17 by S Africa	1997 A 2, It, F 1,2, E, S, 1998 I 1,2, W 1, E 1, A 1, NZ 1,2, A 2, W 2, S, I 3

*Cyprus have won 19 consecutive Tests since 2008 but are not an IRB Member Union

MOST CONSECUTIVE TESTS WITHOUT DEFEAT

Matches	Wins	Draws	Period
23 by N Zealand	22	1	1987 to 1990
20 by N Zealand	19	1	2011 to 2012
18 by Lithuania	18	0	2006 to 2010
17 by N Zealand	15	2	1961 to 1964
17 by N Zealand	17	0	1965 to 1969
17 by S Africa	17	0	1997 to 1998

MOST POINTS IN A MATCH

BY A TEAM

Pts	Opponents	Venue	Year
164 by Hong Kong	Singapore	Kuala Lumpur	1994
155 by Japan	Chinese Taipei	Tokyo	2002
152 by Argentina	Paraguay	Mendoza	2002
147 by Argentina	Venezuela	Santiago	2004
145 by N Zealand	Japan	Bloemfontein	1995
144 by Argentina	Paraguay	Montevideo	2003
142 by Australia	Namibia	Adelaide	2003
135 by Korea	Malaysia	Hong Kong	1992
134 by Japan	Chinese Taipei	Singapore	1998
134 by England	Romania	Twickenham	2001
134 by S Africa	Uruguay	East London	2005

BY A PLAYER

Pts	Player	Opponents	Venue	Year
60 for Japan	T Kurihara	Chinese Taipei	Tainan	2002
50 for Argentina	E Morgan	Paraguay	San Pablo	1973
50 for H Kong	A Billington	Singapore	Kuala Lumpur	1994
45 for N Zealand	SD Culhane	Japan	Bloemfontein	1995
45 for Argentina	J-M Nuñez-Piossek	Paraguay	Montevideo	2003
44 for Scotland	AG Hastings	Ivory Coast	Rustenburg	1995
44 for England	CC Hodgson	Romania	Twickenham	2001
42 for Australia	MS Rogers	Namibia	Adelaide	2003
41 for Sweden	J Hagstrom	Luxembourg	Cessange	2001
40 for Argentina	GM Jorge	Brazil	Sao Paulo	1993
40 for Japan	D Ohata	Chinese Taipei	Tokyo	2002
40 for Scotland	CD Paterson	Japan	Perth	2004

MOST TRIES IN A MATCH

BY THE TEAM

Tries	Opponents	Venue	Year
26 by Hong Kong	Singapore	Kuala Lumpur	1994
25 by Fiji	Solomon Is	Port Moresby	1969
24 by Argentina	Paraguay	Mendoza	2002
24 by Argentina	Paraguay	Montevideo	2003
23 by Japan	Chinese Taipei	Tokyo	2002
23 by Argentina	Venezuela	Santiago	2004
22 by Australia	Namibia	Adelaide	2003
21 by Fiji	Niue Island	Apia	1983
21 by N Zealand	Japan	Bloemfontein	1995
21 by S Africa	Uruguay	East London	2005

BY A PLAYER

Tries	Player	Opponents	Venue	Year
11 for Argentina	U O'Farrell	Brazil	Buenos Aires	1951
10 for H Kong	A Billington	Singapore	Kuala Lumpur	1994
9 for Argentina	J-M Nuñez-Piossek	Paraguay	Montevideo	2003
8 for Argentina	GM Jorge	Brazil	Sao Paulo	1993
8 for Japan	D Ohata	Chinese Taipei	Tokyo	2002
6 for Argentina	E Morgan	Paraguay	San Pablo	1973
6 for Fiji	T Makutu	Papua New Guinea	Suva	1979
6 for Argentina	GM Jorge	Brazil	Montevideo	1989
6 for Namibia	G Mans	Portugal	Windhoek	1990
6 for N Zealand	MCG Ellis	Japan	Bloemfontein	1995
6 for Japan	T Kurihara	Chinese Taipei	Tainan	2002
6 for S Africa	T Chavhanga	Uruguay	East London	2005
6 for Japan	D Ohata	Hong Kong	Tokyo	2005
6 for Japan	Y Fujita	UAE	Fukuoka	2012
6 for Argentina	F Barrea	Brazil	Santiago	2012

MOST CONVERSIONS IN A MATCH

BY THE TEAM

Cons	Opponents	Venue	Year
20 by N Zealand	Japan	Bloemfontein	1995
20 by Japan	Chinese Taipei	Tokyo	2002
19 by Fiji	Solomon Islands	Port Moresby	1969
18 by Fiji	Niue Island	Apia	1983
17 by Hong Kong	Singapore	Kuala Lumpur	1994
17 by Japan	Chinese Taipei	Singapore	1998
17 by Tonga	Korea	Nuku'alofa	2003
16 by Argentina	Paraguay	Mendoza	2002
16 by Australia	Namibia	Adelaide	2003
16 by Argentina	Venezuela	Santiago	2004

BY A PLAYER

Cons	Player	Opponents	Venue	Year
20 for New Zealand	SD Culhane	Japan	Bloemfontein	1995
18 for Fiji	S Koroduadua	Niue Island	Apia	1983
17 for Hong Kong	J McKee	Singapore	Kuala Lumpur	1994
17 for Tonga	P Hola	Korea	Nuku'alofa	2003
16 for Argentina	J-L Cilley	Paraguay	Mendoza	2002
16 for Australia	MS Rogers	Namibia	Adelaide	2003
15 for England	PJ Grayson	Netherlands	Huddersfield	1998
15 for Japan	T Kurihara	Chinese Taipei	Tainan	2002
14 for England	CC Hodgson	Romania	Twickenham	2001
14 for Wales	GL Henson	Japan	Cardiff	2004
14 for New Zealand	NJ Evans	Portugal	Lyon	2007
14 for Japan	A Goromaru	Philippines	Fukuoka	2013

MOST PENALTIES IN A MATCH

BY THE TEAM

Penalties	Opponents	Venue	Year
9 by Japan	Tonga	Tokyo	1999
9 by N Zealand	Australia	Auckland	1999
9 by Wales	France	Cardiff	1999
9 by Portugal	Georgia	Lisbon	2000
9 by N Zealand	France	Paris	2000
8 by many countries			

BY A PLAYER

Penalties	Player	Opponents	Venue	Year
9 for Japan	K Hirose	Tonga	Tokyo	1999
9 for N Zealand	AP Mehrtens	Australia	Auckland	1999
9 for Wales	NR Jenkins	France	Cardiff	1999
9 for Portugal	T Teixeira	Georgia	Lisbon	2000
9 for N Zealand	AP Mehrtens	France	Paris	2000
8 by many players				

MOST DROP GOALS IN A MATCH

BY THE TEAM

Drops	Opponents	Venue	Year
5 by South Africa	England	Paris	1999
4 by Romania	W Germany	Bucharest	1967
4 by Uruguay	Chile	Montevideo	2002
4 by South Africa	England	Twickenham	2006
3 by several nations			

BY A PLAYER

Drops	Player	Opponents	Venue	Year
5 for S Africa	JH de Beer	England	Paris	1999
4 for Uruguay	J Menchaca	Chile	Montevideo	2002
4 for S Africa	AS Pretorius	England	Twickenham	2006
3 for several nations				

CAREER RECORDS

MOST TEST APPEARANCES

Tests	Player	Career Span
139	GM Gregan (Australia)	1994 to 2007
133 (8)	BG O'Driscoll (Ireland/Lions)	1999 to 2013
130 (2)	RJR O'Gara (Ireland/Lions)	2000 to 2013
120	RH McCaw (N Zealand)	2001 to 2013
119 (5)	J Leonard (England/Lions)	1990 to 2004
118	F Pelous (France)	1995 to 2007
116	NC Sharpe (Australia)	2002 to 2012
111	P Sella (France)	1982 to 1995
111	JW Smit (S Africa)	2000 to 2011
111	GB Smith (Australia)	2000 to 2013
110	V Matfield (S Africa)	2001 to 2011
110 (6)	SM Jones (Wales/Lions)	1998 to 2011
109	CD Paterson (Scotland)	1999 to 2011
107 (2)	JJ Hayes (Ireland/Lions)	2000 to 2011
107	KF Mealamu (N Zealand)	2002 to 2013
104 (4)	ME Williams (Wales/Lions)	1996 to 2012
104	TD Woodcock (N Zealand)	2002 to 2013
103 (3)	Gareth Thomas (Wales/Lions)	1995 to 2007
103 (5)	GD Jenkins (Wales/Lions)	2002 to 2013
103	A Lo Cicero (Italy)	2000 to 2013
102	SJ Larkham (Australia)	1996 to 2007
102	PC Montgomery (S Africa)	1997 to 2008
101	DI Campese (Australia)	1982 to 1996
101	A Troncon (Italy)	1994 to 2007
100	JM Muliaina (N Zealand)	2003 to 2011

The figures include Test appearances for the British & Irish Lions which are shown in brackets. Thus 133 (8) for Brian O'Driscoll (Ireland/Lions) indicates 125 caps for Ireland and eight Tests for the Lions.

MOST CONSECUTIVE TESTS

Tests	Player	Career Span
63	SBT Fitzpatrick (N Zealand)	1986 to 1995
62	JWC Roff (Australia)	1996 to 2001
53	GO Edwards (Wales)	1967 to 1978
52	WJ McBride (Ireland)	1964 to 1975
51	CM Cullen (N Zealand)	1996 to 2000

MOST TESTS AS CAPTAIN

Tests	Captain	Span as captain
84 (1)	BG O'Driscoll (Ireland/Lions)	2002 to 2012
83	JW Smit (S Africa)	2003 to 2011
83*	RH McCaw (N Zealand)	2004 to 2013
59	WDC Carling (England)	1988 to 1996
59	GM Gregan (Australia)	2001 to 2007
55	JA Eales (Australia)	1996 to 2001*

** McCaw's figure includes the world record of 73 Test wins as captain.*
The figures include Test captaincies of the British & Irish Lions which are shown in brackets. Thus 84 (1) for Brian O'Driscoll (Ireland/Lions) indicates 83 captaincies for Ireland and one in Tests for the Lions.

Getty Images

Ronan O'Gara played 130 Tests for Ireland and the British & Irish Lions before retiring in 2013.

MOST POINTS IN TESTS

Points	Player	Tests	Career Span
1411	DW Carter (N Zealand)	97	2003 to 2013
1246 (67)	JP Wilkinson (England/Lions)	97 (6)	1998 to 2011
1090 (41)	NR Jenkins (Wales/Lions))	91 (4)	1991 to 2002
1083 (0)	RJR O'Gara (Ireland/Lions)	130 (2)	2000 to 2013
1010 (27)	D Dominguez (Italy/Argentina)	76 (2)	1989 to 2003
970 (53)	SM Jones (Wales/Lions)	110 (6)	1998 to 2011
967	AP Mehrtens (N Zealand)	70	1995 to 2004
911	MP Lynagh (Australia)	72	1984 to 1995
893	PC Montgomery (S Africa)	102	1997 to 2008
878	MC Burke (Australia)	81	1993 to 2004
809	CD Paterson (Scotland)	109	1999 to 2011
733 (66)	AG Hastings (Scotland/Lions)	67 (6)	1986 to 1995
684	MJ Giteau (Australia)	92	2002 to 2011
670	NJ Little (Fiji)	71	1996 to 2011

The figures include Test appearances for the British & Irish Lions or a second nation which are shown in brackets. Thus 1,246 (67) for Jonny Wilkinson (England/Lions) indicates 1179 points for England and 67 in Tests for the Lions.

MOST TRIES IN TESTS

Tries	Player	Tests	Career Span
69	D Ohata (Japan)	58	1996 to 2006
64	DI Campese (Australia)	101	1982 to 1996
60 (2)	SM Williams (Wales/Lions)	91 (4)	2000 to 2011
55	H Onozawa (Japan)	81	2001 to 2013
53	BG Habana (South Africa)	92	2004 to 2013
50 (1)	R Underwood (England/Lions)	91 (6)	1984 to 1996
49	DC Howlett (N Zealand)	62	2000 to 2007
47 (1)	BG O'Driscoll (Ireland/Lions)	133 (8)	1999 to 2013
46	CM Cullen (N Zealand)	58	1996 to 2002
46	JT Rokocoko (N Zealand)	68	2003 to 2010
44	JW Wilson (N Zealand)	60	1993 to 2001
41 (1)	Gareth Thomas (Wales/Lions)	103 (3)	1995 to 2007
40	CE Latham (Australia)	78	1998 to 2007

The figures include Test appearances for the British & Irish Lions which are shown in brackets. Thus 60 (2) for Shane Williams (Wales/Lions) indicates 58 tries for Wales and two in Tests for the Lions.

AFP/Getty Images

Daisuke Ohata scored a record 69 tries for Japan between 1996 and 2006.

MOST CONVERSIONS IN TESTS

Cons	Player	Tests	Career Span
249	DW Carter (N Zealand)	97	2003 to 2013
176 (0)	RJR O'Gara (Ireland/Lions)	130 (2)	2000 to 2013
169	AP Mehrtens (N Zealand)	70	1995 to 2004
169 (7)	JP Wilkinson (England/Lions)	97 (6)	1998 to 2011
160 (7)	SM Jones (Wales/Lions)	110 (6)	1998 to 2011
153	PC Montgomery (S Africa)	102	1997 to 2008
140	MP Lynagh (Australia)	72	1984 to 1995
133 (6)	D Dominguez (Italy/Argentina)	76 (2)	1989 to 2003
131 (1)	NR Jenkins (Wales/Lions)	91 (4)	1991 to 2002
118	GJ Fox (N Zealand)	46	1985 to 1993

The figures include Test appearances for the British & Irish Lions or a second nation which are shown in brackets. Thus 169 (7) for Jonny Wilkinson (England/Lions) indicates 162 conversions for England and seven in Tests for the Lions.

MOST DROP GOALS IN TESTS

Drops	Player	Tests	Career Span
36 (0)	JP Wilkinson (England/Lions)	97 (6)	1998 to 2011
28 (2)	H Porta (Argentina/Jaguars)	68 (8)	1971 to 1999
23 (2)	CR Andrew (England/Lions)	76 (5)	1985 to 1997
19 (0)	D Dominguez (Italy/Argentina)	76 (2)	1989 to 2003
18	HE Botha (S Africa)	28	1980 to 1992
17	S Bettarello (Italy)	55	1979 to 1988
17	DA Parks (Scotland)	67	2004 to 2012
15	J-P Lescarboura (France)	28	1982 to 1990
15 (0)	RJR O'Gara (Ireland/Lions)	130 (2)	2000 to 2013

The figures include Test appearances for the British & Irish Lions, South American Jaguars or a second nation shown in brackets. Thus 28 (2) for Hugo Porta (Argentina/Jaguars) indicates 26 drop goals for Argentina and two in Tests (against South Africa in the 1980s) for the South American Jaguars.

MOST PENALTY GOALS IN TESTS

Penalties	Player	Tests	Career Span
255 (16)	JP Wilkinson (England/Lions)	97 (6)	1998 to 2011
250	DW Carter (N Zealand)	97	2003 to 2013
248 (13)	NR Jenkins (Wales/Lions)	91 (4)	1991 to 2002
214 (5)	D Dominguez (Italy/Argentina)	76 (2)	1989 to 2003
202 (0)	RJR O'Gara (Ireland/Lions)	130 (2)	2000 to 2013
198 (12)	SM Jones (Wales/Lions)	110 (6)	1998 to 2011
188	AP Mehrtens (N Zealand)	70	1995 to 2004
177	MP Lynagh (Australia)	72	1984 to 1995
174	MC Burke (Australia)	81	1993 to 2004
170	CD Paterson (Scotland)	109	1999 to 2011
160 (20)	AG Hastings (Scotland/Lions)	67 (6)	1986 to 1995

The figures include Test appearances for the British & Irish Lions or a second nation which are shown in brackets. Thus 255 (16) for Jonny Wilkinson (England/Lions) indicates 239 penalties for England and 16 in Tests for the Lions.

RUGBY'S VALUES

integrity

Integrity is central to the fabric of the Game and is generated through honesty and fair play

respect

Respect for team mates, opponents, match officials and those involved in the Game is paramount

solidarity

Rugby provides a unifying spirit that leads to life long friendships, camaraderie, teamwork and loyalty which transcends cultural, geographic, political and religious differences

passion

Rugby people have a passionate enthusiasm for the Game. Rugby generates excitement, emotional attachment and a sense of belonging to the global Rugby Family

discipline

Discipline is an integral part of the Game both on and off the field and is reflected through adherence to the Laws, the Regulations and Rugby's core values

www.**irb.com**

The Countries

Juan Martín Fernández Lobbe soars to the skies to win a lineout against Ireland at the Aviva Stadium.

AFP/Getty Images

ARGENTINA

ARGENTINA'S 2012–13 TEST RECORD

OPPONENTS	DATE	VENUE	RESULT
Wales	10 Nov	A	Won 26–12
France	17 Nov	A	Lost 39–22
Ireland	24 Nov	A	Lost 46–24
Uruguay	27 Apr	A	Won 29–18
Chile	1 May	N	Won 85–10
Brazil	4 May	N	Won 83–0
England	8 Jun	H	Lost 3–32
England	15 Jun	H	Lost 26–51
Georgia	22 Jun	H	Won 29–18
South Africa	17 Aug	A	Lost 73–13
South Africa	24 Aug	H	Lost 17–22
New Zealand	7 Sep	A	Lost 28–13
Australia	14 Sep	A	Lost 14–13
New Zealand	28 Sep	H	Lost 15–33
Australia	5 Oct	H	Lost 17–54

YOUNGSTERS HOLD THE KEY FOR FUTURE SUCCESS

By Frankie Deges

AFP/Getty Images

Felipe Contepomi played his 87th and last Test for Argentina against Australia in The Rugby Championship.

Twenty-year old Pablo Matera was thrown, many thought, into the deep end when chosen to start the opening match of The Rugby Championship against South Africa.

Argentina had worked hard on and off the field to receive an invitation to join an annual international competition and a key one among the many boxes that had to be ticked before gaining inclusion was that it had to set up a solid development structure for players still at home.

In February 2009, with the assistance of the International Rugby Board, the Unión Argentina de Rugby High Performance Academies were born in five key rugby centres in the country. These provided opportunities for local players seeking a professional standard of rugby, as well as age grade players with ambitions, as in the centres they could be developed and prepared to cope with the demands of rugby at its highest level.

Soon after, the Pampas XV was born to play rugby in South Africa's Vodacom Cup. Again, a higher standard of rugby to what could be found at home was given as part of that promotion of Argentine players. Many from that team, mostly in the opening two seasons – the second of which saw them win the title – found their way into the national side and overseas contracts.

Matera was only 17 when first spotted playing for Alumni, his Buenos Aires club. Big and strong, he was a diamond in the rough. He was to shine at Under 19 level before playing the first of two IRB Junior World Championships, helping Los Pumitas to a first ever semi-final in 2012 with wins over Scotland, France and Australia. In 2013, Argentina beat Scotland, Samoa and Australia and this team will produce a core of players for the future as seven of them have already made their Test debuts.

What had started as five national academies in 2009 has evolved and by 2014 another nine will be operational, some jointly run by the national and local provincial unions. In all, more than 300 players, including age grade, seniors, Sevens and women's, are working in these centres with the numbers expected to grow by next year.

The future seems to be well catered for, and by Rugby World Cup 2015 Matera could be joined by a handful of his former Pumitas team-mates. The national team that has dropped to 10th in the IRB World Rankings might get a big youth push soon. The form of Matera, probably the most consistent of Pumas, having started each of The Rugby Championship games, bodes very well for the future.

"We knew he was ready as he had gone through our system and we had clear indications that he was up to the challenge," said National High Performance Director Francisco Rubio. "He is a special player and, fortunately for us, there are many more like him that are waiting for an opportunity."

Matera grabbed his chance with both hands, even if it was in another winless campaign and as soon as the Championship was over, he signed a contract with the English champions Leicester Tigers, confirming his real value.

The lack of celebration drinks is something that was hard to swallow as after an inaugural season in which important strides were made, many expected those elusive victories to arrive finally.

"This season will be about getting the first win," said Pumas captain Juan Martín Fernández Lobbe before the Championship. Preparation was again of the highest standard, including a fitness camp in the USA with all the players selected by coach Santiago Phelan. Again, clubs in Europe released their players beyond the international window and that goodwill must be applauded.

Travelling to Soweto for the opening game was emotionally charged as South African rugby joined forces with SA Soccer for what was a huge homage to Nelson Mandela, in the aptly named Mandela Sports Day. Los Pumas failed to perform and were heavily beaten 73–13 by Jean de Villiers's side. Scoring the only try was Felipe Contepomi who, at 36, made his Rugby Championship debut, having missed last year's tournament through injury. He was to retire at the end of the Championship as the most capped and highest points scoring Puma and with legend status in Argentina.

The return match a week later in Mendoza saw a different Argentina, albeit with most of the same players, cut the deficit from 60 points to five. Playing with flair and commitment that was natural to the Pumas of yesteryear, they picked up a first point in losing 22–17 to the baffled Springboks.

For a second consecutive year under the mentorship of five-time IRB Coach of the Year Sir Graham Henry, they took the All Blacks head on in the rain in Hamilton a fortnight later. A two-try spell while Argentina had a man in the sin-bin put the game beyond reach, but that was certainly the best performance of the year with fly half Nicolás Sánchez tackling like a man possessed. Wing Gonzalo Camacho, one of the most consistent players in a Pumas jersey, had to be replaced and later have an operation on his right shoulder, which was to be a big loss for the squad.

Much was expected from the next match against Australia in Perth and again the rain was an issue. With the new scrum engagement trial law playing to the benefit of Los Pumas, the Wallabies' pack was pushed all around the park. Number eight Juan Manuel Leguizamón scored a try for the third match in a row, becoming only the second Puma to score tries against the three southern hemisphere giants. It finished 14–13 and could have well been a win had Los Pumas not dropped their fitness towards the end.

"They are not accustomed to playing at this level and their fitness is good enough for an hour," said Henry when trying to explain their fifth loss two weeks later against the All Blacks in La Plata. Using a solid scrum platform, they put the All Blacks under pressure yet were never in a real try-scoring situation. New Zealand only managed the relieving try-scoring bonus point with the last move to triumph 33–15.

Much was expected of the last match at home against an under-performing Australia. With Contepomi playing his 87th and final Test, the Wallabies recaptured their magic as Los Pumas lost their touch. It was a seven tries to two, 54–17 loss that surprised many. It was the end of a hard Rugby Championship in which the team had been cold and hot but finished cold again.

Looking back at the 2012/13 season as a whole, it was far from auspicious as a team. In November 2012, on the back of their inaugural Rugby Championship, they were impressive in beating Wales 26–12 at the Millennium Stadium – probably their best match under coach Santiago Phelan.

With high hopes, they travelled to Nantes where a good start soon turned into another below-par performance and a 39–22 defeat to France. The year's last match was a total mismatch, with Argentina unrecognisable against an Ireland team that dominated throughout, winning 46–24.

In 2013 there was another South African jaunt with the Pampas XV in which younger players were given important experience. Some of them were then involved in the South American Championship, which once again was won with no real challenge, even without Argentina's top players.

With some of Argentina's best players being rested for The Rugby Championship, as per agreement with European clubs, an England team shorn of their British & Irish Lions played three matches in South America. Two were against Los Pumas, who had in Contepomi, Gonzalo Tiesi and Julio Farías Cabello experienced hands. However, the team failed to compete against a young team that were too good in the series. Back-to-back losses – 32–3 and 51–26 – were hard to swallow, with June bringing a solitary win, 29–18 against Georgia.

June was very busy for the country's national teams with the Under 20s finishing sixth at the IRB Junior World Championship in France, the Argentina Jaguars – who at the end of 2012 had won a third IRB Americas Rugby Championship – only managed one win in three games in Bucharest at the IRB Nations Cup, and at Rugby World Cup Sevens 2013 in Moscow the team failed to reach the Cup quarter-finals but had overall enjoyed a positive season on the HSBC Sevens World Series. The Sevens team will, in the 2013/14 World Series, be coached by the legendary Santiago Gómez Cora, which augurs well for the future as the road to Rio 2016 intensifies.

The women's game also continues to grow as players benefit from being in the high performance centres. Argentina made their debut in the IRB Women's Sevens World Series in Houston in early February and benefited from the exposure of playing South Africa, Canada, USA, Brazil and Trinidad & Tobago, beating the latter 25–5 to finish 11th of the 12 teams. A few weeks later they halved the deficit to the region's dominant side Brazil in the CONSUR Sevens final and they have set high targets for the future.

As Rugby World Cup 2015 fast approaches, Los Pumas are starting to experiment with young players and Matera is proof that the production line continues to come up with stars for the future. They will do so, though, under a new coach after Phelan resigned on the eve of the European tour.

ARGENTINA INTERNATIONAL STATISTICS

MATCH RECORDS UP TO 10 OCTOBER 2013

WINNING MARGIN

Date	Opponent	Result	Winning Margin
01/05/2002	Paraguay	152–0	**152**
27/04/2003	Paraguay	144–0	**144**
01/05/2004	Venezuela	147–7	**140**
02/10/1993	Brazil	114–3	**111**
23/05/2012	Brazil	111–0	**111**

MOST POINTS IN A MATCH

BY THE TEAM

Date	Opponent	Result	Points
01/05/2002	Paraguay	152–0	**152**
01/05/2004	Venezuela	147–7	**147**
27/04/2003	Paraguay	144–0	**144**
02/10/1993	Brazil	114–3	**114**
23/05/2012	Brazil	111–0	**111**

BY A PLAYER

Date	Player	Opponent	Points
14/10/1973	Eduardo Morgan	Paraguay	**50**
27/04/2003	José María Nuñez Piossek	Paraguay	**45**
02/10/1993	Gustavo Jorge	Brazil	**40**
24/10/1977	Martin Sansot	Brazil	**36**
13/09/1951	Uriel O'Farrell	Brazil	**33**

MOST DROP GOALS IN A MATCH

BY THE TEAM

Date	Opponent	Result	DGs
27/10/1979	Australia	24–13	**3**
02/11/1985	New Zealand	21–21	**3**
26/05/2001	Canada	20–6	**3**
21/09/1975	Uruguay	30–15	**3**
07/08/1971	SA Gazelles	12–0	**3**
30/09/2007	Ireland	30–15	**3**

BY A PLAYER

Date	Player	Opponent	DGs
27/10/1979	Hugo Porta	Australia	**3**
02/11/1985	Hugo Porta	New Zealand	**3**
07/08/1971	Tomas Harris-Smith	SA Gazelles	**3**
26/05/2001	Juan Fernández Miranda	Canada	**3**
30/09/2007	Juan Martín Hernández	Ireland	**3**

MOST CONVERSIONS IN A MATCH

BY THE TEAM

Date	Opponent	Result	Cons
01/05/2002	Paraguay	152–0	**16**
01/05/2004	Venezuela	147–7	**16**
09/10/1979	Brazil	109–3	**15**
21/09/1985	Paraguay	102–3	**13**
14/10/1973	Paraguay	98–3	**13**
23/05/2012	Brazil	111–0	**13**

BY A PLAYER

Date	Player	Opponent	Cons
01/05/2002	Jose Cilley	Paraguay	**16**
21/09/1985	Hugo Porta	Paraguay	**13**
14/10/1973	Eduardo Morgan	Paraguay	**13**
25/09/1975	Eduardo de Forteza	Paraguay	**11**

MOST PENALTIES IN A MATCH

BY THE TEAM

Date	Opponent	Result	Pens
10/10/1999	Samoa	32–16	**8**
10/03/1995	Canada	29–26	**8**
17/06/2006	Wales	45–27	**8**
22/06/2013	Georgia	29–18	**8**

BY A PLAYER

Date	Player	Opponent	Pens
10/10/1999	Gonzalo Quesada	Samoa	**8**
10/03/1995	Santiago Meson	Canada	**8**
17/06/2006	Federico Todeschini	Wales	**8**
22/06/2013	Martin Bustos Moyano	Georgia	**8**

MOST TRIES IN A MATCH

BY THE TEAM

Date	Opponent	Result	Tries
01/05/2002	Paraguay	152–0	**24**
27/04/2003	Paraguay	144–0	**24**
01/05/2004	Venezuela	147–7	**23**
08/10/1989	Brazil	103–0	**20**

BY A PLAYER

Date	Player	Opponent	Tries
13/09/1951	Uriel O'Farrell	Brazil	**11**
27/04/2003	José María Nuñez Piossek	Paraguay	**9**
02/10/1993	Gustavo Jorge	Brazil	**8**
08/10/1989	Gustavo Jorge	Brazil	**6**
14/10/1973	Eduardo Morgan	Paraguay	**6**

MOST CAPPED PLAYERS

Name	Caps
Felipe Contepomi	87
Lisandro Arbizu	86
Rolando Martin	86
Mario Ledesma	84
Pedro Sporleder	78

LEADING PENALTY SCORERS

Name	Penalties
Felipe Contepomi	139
Gonzalo Quesada	103
Hugo Porta	101
Santiago Meson	63
Federico Todeschini	54

LEADING TRY SCORERS

Name	Tries
José María Nuñez Piossek	29
Diego Cuesta Silva	28
Gustavo Jorge	24
Facundo Soler	18
Rolando Martin	18

LEADING DROP GOAL SCORERS

Name	DGs
Hugo Porta	26
Lisandro Arbizu	11
Gonzalo Quesada	7
Tomas Harris-Smith	6
Juan Martín Hernández	6

LEADING CONVERSION SCORERS

Name	Conversions
Hugo Porta	84
Felipe Contepomi	74
Gonzalo Quesada	68
Santiago Meson	68
Juan Fernández Miranda	41

LEADING POINT SCORERS

Name	Points
Felipe Contepomi	651
Hugo Porta	590
Gonzalo Quesada	486
Santiago Meson	370
Federico Todeschini	256

ARGENTINA INTERNATIONAL PLAYERS

UP TO 10 OCTOBER 2013

A Abadie 2007 *CHL*, 2009 *E*, *W*, *S*
A Abella 1969 *Ur*, *CHL*
C Abud 1975 *Par*, *Bra*, *CHL*
H Achaval 1948 *OCC*
J Aguilar 1983 *CHL*, *Ur*
A Aguirre 1997 *Par*, *CHL*
ME Aguirre 1990 *E*, *S*, 1991 *Sa*
B Agulla 2010 *Ur*, *CHL*, 2011 *CHL*, *Ur*, 2012 *It*, *F*, 2013 *E*, *E*, *Geo*
H Agulla 2005 *Sa*, 2006 *Ur*, *E*, *It*, 2007 *It*, *F*, *Nm*, *I*, *S*, *SA*, *F*, 2008 *S*, *It*, *SA*, *F*, *It*, *I*, 2009 *E*, *E*, *E*, *W*, *S*, 2010 *Ur*, *CHL*, *S*, *S*, *F*, *I*, 2011 *W*, *E*, *R*, *S*, *Geo*, *NZ*, 2012 *SA*, *SA*, *NZ*, *A*, *NZ*, *A*, *W*, *F*, 2013 *SA*, *SA*, *NZ*, *A*, *NZ*, *A*
L Ahaulli De Chazal 2012 *Ur*, *CHL*
P Albacete 2003 *Par*, *Ur*, *F*, *SA*, *Ur*, *C*, *A*, *R*, 2004 *W*, *W*, *NZ*, *F*, *I*, 2005 *It*, *It*, 2006 *E*, *It*, *F*, 2007 *W*, *F*, *Geo*, *Nm*, *I*, *S*, *SA*, *F*, 2008 *SA*, *F*, *It*, *I*, 2009 *E*, *E*, *E*, *W*, *S*, 2010 *S*, *S*, *F*, *F*, *I*, 2011 *W*, *E*, *R*, *S*, *Geo*, *NZ*, 2012 *SA*, *SA*, *NZ*, *A*, *NZ*, *A*, 2013 *SA*, *NZ*, *A*
DL Albanese 1995 *Ur*, *C*, *E*, *F*, 1996 *Ur*, *F*, *SA*, *E*, 1997 *NZ*, *Ur*, *R*, *It*, *F*, *A*, *A*, 1998 *F*, *F*, *R*, *US*, *C*, *It*, *F*, *W*, 1999 *W*, *W*, *S*, *I*, *W*, *Sa*, *J*, *I*, *F*, 2000 *I*, *A*, *A*, *SA*, 2001 *NZ*, *It*, *W*, *S*, *NZ*, 2002 *F*, *E*, *SA*, *A*, *It*, *I*, 2003 *F*, *F*, *SA*, *US*, *C*, *A*, *Nm*, *I*
F Albarracin 2007 *CHL*
M Albina 2001 *Ur*, *US*, 2003 *Par*, *Ur*, *Fj*, 2004 *CHL*, *Ven*, *W*, *W*, 2005 *J*
C Aldao 1961 *CHL*, *Bra*, *Ur*
P Alexenicer 1997 *Par*, *CHL*
H Alfonso 1936 *BI*, *CHL*
G Allen 1977 *Par*
JG Allen 1981 *C*, 1985 *F*, *F*, *Ur*, *NZ*, *NZ*, 1986 *F*, *F*, *A*, *A*, 1987 *Ur*, *Fj*, *It*, *NZ*, *Sp*, *A*, *A*, 1988 *F*, *F*, *F*, *F*, 1989 *Bra*, *CHL*, *Par*, *Ur*, *US*
L Allen 1951 *Ur*, *Bra*, *CHL*
M Allen 1990 *C*, *E*, *S*, 1991 *NZ*, *CHL*
F Allogio 2011 *CHL*, *Ur*
A Allub 1997 *Par*, *Ur*, *It*, *F*, *A*, *A*, 1998 *F*, *F*, *US*, *C*, *J*, *It*, *F*, *W*, 1999 *W*, *W*, *S*, *I*, *W*, *Sa*, *J*, *I*, *F*, 2000 *I*, *A*, *A*, *SA*, *E*, 2001 *NZ*
M Alonso 1973 *R*, *R*, *S*, 1977 *F*, *F*
A Altberg 1972 *SAG*, *SAG*, 1973 *R*, *R*, *Par*
J Altube 1998 *Par*, *CHL*, *Ur*
C Alvarez 1958 *Ur*, *Per*, *CHL*, 1959 *JSB*, *JSB*, 1960 *F*
GM Alvarez 1975 *Ur*, *Par*, *Bra*, *CHL*, 1976 *NZ*, 1977 *Bra*, *Ur*, *Par*, *CHL*
S Alvarez 2013 *Ur*, *CHL*, *Bra*
R Álvarez Kairelis 1998 *Par*, *CHL*, *Ur*, 2001 *Ur*, *US*, *C*, *W*, *S*, *NZ*, 2002 *F*, *E*, *SA*, *A*, *It*, *I*, 2003 *F*, *SA*, *Fj*, *Ur*, *C*, *Nm*, *I*, 2004 *F*, *I*, 2006 *W*, *W*, *NZ*, *CHL*, *Ur*, 2007 *I*, *It*, *W*, *F*, *Geo*, *Nm*, *I*, *S*, *SA*, *F*, 2008 *SA*, *F*, *It*, *I*, 2009 *E*
S Ambrosio 2012 *Ur*, *Bra*
F Amelong 2007 *CHL*

A Amuchastegui 2002 *Ur, Par, CHL*
GP Angaut 1987 *NZ, Ur, CHL*, 1990 *S*, 1991 *NZ, Sa*
JJ Angelillo 1987 *Ur, CHL, A*, 1988 *F, F, F*, 1989 *It, Bra, CHL, Par, Ur, US*, 1990 *C, US, E, E*, 1994 *US, S, S, US*, 1995 *Par, CHL, R, F*
W Aniz 1960 *F*
R Annichini 1983 *CHL, Ur*, 1985 *F, CHL, Par*
A Anthony 1965 *OCC, CHL*, 1967 *Ur, CHL*, 1968 *W, W*, 1969 *S, S, Ur, CHL*, 1970 *I, I*, 1971 *SAG, SAG, OCC*, 1972 *SAG, SAG*, 1974 *F, F*
F Aranguren 2007 *CHL*, 2011 *CHL, Ur*
G Araoz 2012 *Bra, CHL*
L Arbizu 1990 *I, S*, 1991 *NZ, NZ, CHL, A, W, Sa*, 1992 *F, F, Sp, Sp, R, F*, 1993 *J, J, Bra, CHL, Par, Ur, SA, SA*, 1995 *Ur, A, A, E, Sa, It, Par, CHL, Ur, R, It, F*, 1996 *Ur, US, Ur, C, SA, SA, E*, 1997 *E, E, NZ, NZ, R, It, F, A, A*, 1998 *F, F, R, US, C, It, F, W*, 1999 *W, W, S, I, W, Sa, J, I, F*, 2000 *A, A, SA, E*, 2001 *NZ, It, W, S, NZ*, 2002 *F, A, It, I*, 2003 *F, F, US, C*, 2005 *It, It*
F Argerich 1979 *Ur*
G Aristide 1997 *E*
J Arocena Messones 2005 *Sa*
E Arriaga 1936 *CHL, CHL*
S Artese 2004 *SA*
G Ascarate 2007 *CHL*, 2010 *CHL*, 2012 *It, F*, 2013 *E, E, Geo*
M Avellaneda 1948 *OCC, OCC*, 1951 *Bra, CHL*
M Avramovic 2005 *J, Sa*, 2006 *CHL, Ur, E, It*, 2007 *I*, 2008 *It, SA, I*, 2009 *E*
M Ayerra 1927 *GBR*
MI Ayerza 2004 *SA*, 2005 *J, It, Sa*, 2006 *W, W, CHL, Ur, E, It, F*, 2007 *I, I, Geo, F*, 2008 *S, S, SA, F, It, I*, 2009 *E, E, E, W, S*, 2010 *S, S, F, It, F, I*, 2011 *Geo, NZ*, 2012 *SA, SA, NZ, W, F, I*, 2013 *SA, NZ, A, NZ, A*
N Azorin 2012 *Ur, Bra*
M Azpiroz 1956 *OCC*, 1958 *Ur, Per, CHL*, 1959 *JSB, JSB*

J Bach 1975 *Par, Bra, CHL*
A Badano 1977 *Bra, Ur, Par, CHL*
J Baeck 1983 *Par*
M Baeck 1985 *Ur, CHL, Par*, 1990 *US, E, E*
DR Baetti Sabah 1980 *WXV, Fj, Fj*, 1981 *E, E, C*, 1983 *WXV*, 1987 *Ur, Par, CHL*, 1988 *F, F*, 1989 *It, NZ, NZ*
R Baez 2010 *CHL*, 2011 *CHL, Ur*, 2012 *F, F*, 2013 *E, Geo*
L Balfour 1977 *Bra, Ur, Par, CHL*
T Baravalle 2011 *Ur*
C Barrea 1996 *Ur, C, SA*
F Barrea 2012 *Ur, Bra, CHL, F*
O Bartolucci 1996 *US, C, SA*, 1998 *CHL, Ur*, 1999 *W, W, S, I, W, Sa*, 2000 *I, A, A, SA, E*, 2001 *US, C*, 2003 *Par, Ur*
E Basile 1983 *CHL, Ur*
JL Basile 2011 *CHL, Ur*
L Bavio 1954 *F*
R Bazan 1951 *Ur, Bra, CHL*, 1956 *OCC*
D Beccar Varela 1975 *F, F*, 1976 *W, NZ*, 1977 *F, F*
M Beccar Varela 1965 *Rho, OCC, OCC*
G Begino 2007 *CHL*
J Benzi 1965 *Rho*, 1969 *S, Ur, CHL*
E Bergamaschi 2001 *US*
O Bernacchi 1954 *F*, 1956 *OCC, OCC*, 1958 *Ur, Per, CHL*
G Bernardi 1997 *CHL*
O Bernat 1932 *JSB*
MM Berro 1964 *Ur, Bra, CHL*
MJS Bertranou 1989 *It, NZ, NZ, CHL, Par*, 1990 *C, US, C, E, E, I, E, S*, 1993 *SA*
E Bianchetti 1959 *JSB, JSB*
G Blacksley 1971 *SAG*
T Blades 1938 *CHL*
G Bocca 1998 *J, Par*
C Bofelli 1997 *Ur*, 1998 *Par*, 2004 *CHL, Ur, Ven*
A Bordoy 2012 *F, F*
L Borges 2003 *Par, CHL, Ur*, 2004 *CHL, Ur, Ven, W, W, NZ, F, I, SA*, 2005 *SA, S*, 2006 *W, W, CHL, Ur*, 2007 *W, F, Geo, I, S, SA*, 2008 *S, It*, 2009 *E, W, S*, 2010 *Ur, S, I*
T Borghi 2013 *Ur, CHL, Bra*
C Bori 1975 *F*
F Bosch 2004 *CHL, SA*, 2005 *J, Sa*
MT Bosch 2007 *It*, 2008 *It*, 2010 *F, I*, 2011 *W, E, R, S, Geo, NZ*, 2012 *SA, SA, NZ, A, NZ, A, F, I*, 2013 *SA, SA, NZ, NZ, A*
MA Bosch 1991 *A, Sa*, 1992 *F, F*
N Bossicovich 1995 *Ur, C*
CA Bottarini 1973 *Par, Ur, Bra, I*, 1974 *F*, 1975 *F, F*, 1979 *Ur, CHL, Bra*, 1983 *CHL, Par, Ur*
R Botting 1927 *GBR, GBR, GBR*
S Bottini 2011 *CHL, Ur*
L Bouza 1992 *Sp*
M Bouza 1966 *SAG, SAG*, 1967 *Ur, CHL*
P Bouza 1996 *Ur, F, F, E*, 1997 *E, NZ, NZ, Ur, R*, 1998 *Ur*, 2002 *Ur, Par, CHL*, 2003 *Par, CHL, Ur, US, Ur, Nm, R*, 2004 *CHL, Ur, Ven, W, NZ, SA*, 2005 *J, It, It, SA, S, It*, 2006 *CHL, Ur*, 2007 *I, I*
A Bovet 1910 *GBR*
N Bozzo 1975 *Bra*
JG Braceras 1971 *Bra, Par*, 1976 *W, NZ*, 1977 *F*
W Braddon 1927 *GBR*
EN Branca 1976 *W, NZ, NZ*, 1977 *F, F*, 1980 *Fj*, 1981 *E, E, C*, 1983 *WXV, A, A*, 1985 *F, F, Ur, CHL, Par, NZ, NZ*, 1986 *F, F, A, A*, 1987 *Ur, Fj, It, NZ, Sp, A, A*, 1988 *F, F, F, F*, 1989 *Bra, Par, Ur*, 1990 *E, E*
M Brandi 1997 *Par, CHL*, 1998 *Par, CHL, Ur*
J Bridger 1932 *JSB*
J Brolese 1998 *CHL, Ur*
E Brouchou 1975 *Ur, Par, Bra, CHL*
R Bruno 2010 *Ur, CHL*, 2012 *Bra, CHL, F*
F Buabse 1991 *Ur, Par, Bra*, 1992 *Sp*
PM Buabse 1989 *NZ, US*, 1991 *Sa*, 1993 *Bra*, 1995 *Ur, C, A*
E Buckley 1938 *CHL*
R Bullrich 1991 *Ur, Bra*, 1992 *R*, 1993 *Bra, CHL, SA*, 1994 *SA, SA*
S Bunader 1989 *US*, 1990 *C*
K Bush 1938 *CHL*
E Bustamante 1927 *GBR, GBR, GBR, GBR*
F Bustillo 1977 *F, F, Bra, Ur, Par, CHL*
G Bustos 2003 *Par, Ur*, 2004 *CHL, Ven*
MA Bustos 2012 *I*, 2013 *E, E, Geo*
MJ Bustos Moyano 2013 *E, E, Geo*

CJ Cáceres 2010 *Ur, CHL*
E Caffarone 1949 *F, F*, 1951 *Bra, CHL*, 1952 *I, I*, 1954 *F, F*
M Caldwell 1956 *OCC*
GO Camacho 2009 *E, E*, 2010 *It, F*, 2011 *W, E, R, S, NZ*, 2012 *SA, SA, NZ, A, NZ, A, W, F, I*, 2013 *SA, SA, NZ*
GF Camardon 1990 *E*, 1991 *NZ, CHL, A, W, Sa*, 1992 *F, F, Sp, R, F*, 1993 *J, Par, Ur, SA, SA*, 1995 *A*, 1996 *Ur, US, Ur, C, SA, E*, 1999 *W, W, Sa, J, I, F*, 2001 *US, C, NZ, It, W, S, NZ*, 2002 *F, E, SA, It, I*
PJ Camerlinckx 1989 *Bra, Par, Ur*, 1990 *C, US*, 1994 *S*, 1995 *CHL*, 1996 *Ur, F, F, US, Ur, C, SA, SA, E*, 1997 *E, E, NZ, NZ, Ur, R, It, F, A, A*, 1998 *R, US, C, F, W*, 1999 *W*
A Cameron 1936 *BI, CHL, CHL*, 1938 *CHL*
R Cameron 1927 *GBR, GBR*
J Caminotti 1987 *Ur, Par, CHL*
M Campo 1978 *E, It*, 1979 *NZ, NZ, A, A*, 1980 *WXV, Fj*, 1981 *E, E, C*, 1982 *F, F, Sp*, 1983 *WXV, A, A*, 1987 *Ur, Fj, NZ*
AT Campos 2007 *CHL*, 2008 *S, It, F, It*, 2009 *E, W, S*, 2010 *Ur, S, F*, 2011 *W, E, R, NZ*
A Canalda 1999 *S, I, F*, 2000 *A*, 2001 *Ur, US, C*
R Cano 1997 *Par*
J Capalbo 1975 *Bra*, 1977 *Bra, Ur, CHL*
AE Capelletti 1977 *F, F*, 1978 *E, It*, 1979 *NZ, NZ, A, A*, 1980 *WXV, Fj, Fj*, 1981 *E, E*
J Cappiello 2013 *Ur, CHL, Bra*
R Carballo 2006 *W, CHL, Ur*, 2008 *SA, It, I*, 2010 *S, F*
N Carbone 1969 *Ur, CHL*, 1971 *SAG*, 1973 *I, S*
PF Cardinali 2001 *US*, 2002 *Ur, Par*, 2004 *W*, 2007 *I*
M Carizza 2004 *SA*, 2005 *J, SA, S, It*, 2006 *W, CHL, Ur*, 2007 *It*, 2008 *It*, 2009 *E, E, W, S*, 2010 *S, S, F, It*, 2011 *W, E, R, S, NZ*, 2012 *SA, SA, NZ, A, NZ, A, W, F, I*, 2013 *SA, NZ, A, A*
J Carlos Galvalisi 1983 *Par, Ur*
MA Carluccio 1973 *R, R, Ur, Bra, I*, 1975 *F, F*, 1976 *NZ*, 1977 *F, F*
M Carmona 1997 *Par, CHL*
SC Carossio 1985 *NZ*, 1987 *It, NZ*

J Carracedo 1971 *CHL, Bra, Par,* 1972 *SAG, SAG,* 1973 *R, R, Par, Ur, Bra, CHL, I, S,* 1975 *F,* 1976 *W, NZ, NZ,* 1977 *F*
M Carreras 1987 *Par,* 1991 *NZ, NZ, CHL, A, W, Sa,* 1992 *F*
T Carrio 2013 *Ur, CHL, Bra, Geo*
M Carrique 1983 *Par, Ur*
J Casanegra 1959 *JSB, JSB,* 1960 *F, F*
GF Casas 1971 *OCC,* 1973 *Par, CHL, I,* 1975 *F, F*
DM Cash 1985 *F, F, Ur, CHL, NZ, NZ,* 1986 *F, F, A, A,* 1987 *Ur, Fj, It, NZ, Sp, A, A,* 1988 *F, F, F, F,* 1989 *It, NZ, NZ, US,* 1990 *C, US, C, E, I, E, S,* 1991 *NZ, NZ, CHL, A, Sa,* 1992 *F, F*
R Castagna 1977 *F*
A Castellina 2004 *CHL, Ur, Ven*
R Castro 1971 *CHL, Bra, Par*
J Cato 1975 *Ur, Par*
R Cazenave 1965 *Rho, JSB, OCC, CHL,* 1966 *SAG, SAG*
N Centurion 2011 *CHL, Ur*
A Cerioni 1975 *F,* 1978 *E, It,* 1979 *CHL, Bra*
G Cernegoy 1938 *CHL*
H Cespedes 1997 *Ur, CHL*
M Chesta 1966 *SAG, SAG,* 1967 *Ur, CHL,* 1968 *W, W*
ML Chiappesoni 2013 *Ur, CHL, Bra*
W Chiswell 1949 *F*
V Christianson 1954 *F, F,* 1956 *OCC*
E Cilley 1932 *JSB, JSB*
J Cilley 1936 *BI, CHL, CHL,* 1938 *CHL*
JL Cilley 1994 *SA,* 1995 *Sa, It, Par, CHL,* 1996 *Ur, F, F, SA, SA,* 1999 *W,* 2000 *A,* 2002 *Par*
J Clement 1987 *Par,* 1989 *Bra*
R Cobelo 1987 *Ur, Par, CHL*
I Comas 1951 *Bra, CHL,* 1958 *Per, CHL,* 1960 *F*
MA Comuzzi 2009 *E, W,* 2011 *CHL, Ur*
A Conen 1951 *CHL,* 1952 *I, I*
J Conrard 1927 *GBR, GBR*
CA Contepomi 1964 *Bra, CHL*
F Contepomi 1998 *CHL, Ur, F, W,* 1999 *W, S, I, J, I, F,* 2000 *I, A, A, SA, E,* 2001 *Ur, US, C, NZ, It, W, S, NZ,* 2002 *F, E, SA, A, It, I,* 2003 *F, F, SA, US, C, A, Nm, I,* 2004 *W, W, F, I,* 2005 *It, It, SA, S, It,* 2006 *W, NZ, E, F,* 2007 *I, W, F, Geo, Nm, I, S, SA, F,* 2008 *S, S, SA, F, It,* 2010 *S, S, F, It, F, I,* 2011 *W, E, S, Geo, NZ,* 2012 *It, F, F, W,* 2013 *E, E, SA, SA, NZ, A, NZ, A*
M Contepomi 1998 *US, C, It, F, W,* 1999 *S, I, W, Sa, F,* 2003 *Ur, F, Fj, Ur, A, R,* 2004 *CHL, Ur, Ven, W, W, NZ, F, I, SA,* 2005 *SA, S,* 2006 *It, F,* 2007 *I, It, W, F, Nm, I, S, SA, F*
F Conti 1988 *F*
GEF Cooke 1927 *GBR*
KAM Cookson 1932 *JSB*
N Cooper 1936 *BI, CHL, CHL*
R Cooper 1927 *GBR, GBR, GBR, GBR*
J Copello 1975 *Ur, Bra*
C Cordeiro 1983 *Par*
J Coria 1987 *Ur, Par, CHL,* 1989 *Bra*
I Corleto 1998 *J, F, W,* 1999 *I, J, I, F,* 2000 *I, A, SA, E,* 2001 *W, S, NZ,* 2002 *F, E, SA, A, It, I,* 2003 *F, Fj, US, Ur, C, A, I,* 2006 *It, F,* 2007 *W, F, Geo, Nm, I, S, SA, F*
ME Corral 1993 *J, Bra, Par, Ur, SA, SA,* 1994 *US, S, SA, SA,* 1995 *Ur, C, A, A, E, Sa, It*
RG Cortes 2011 *CHL, Ur,* 2012 *Ur, CHL*
M Cortese 2005 *Sa,* 2010 *Ur, CHL*
F Cortopasso 2003 *CHL, Ur*
A Costa Repetto 2005 *Sa*
JD Costante 1971 *OCC, OCC, CHL, Bra, Par, Ur,* 1976 *W, NZ,* 1977 *F*
AF Courreges 1979 *Ur, Par, Bra,* 1982 *F, F, Sp,* 1983 *WXV, A, A,* 1987 *Sp, A, A,* 1988 *F*
PH Cox 1938 *CHL*
S Craig 2012 *Bra, CHL*
A Creevy 2005 *J, Sa,* 2006 *Ur,* 2009 *S,* 2010 *S, S, F, It, F, I,* 2011 *W, E, R, S, Geo, NZ,* 2012 *A, NZ, A, W, F, I,* 2013 *SA, SA, NZ, A, NZ, A*
P Cremaschi 1993 *J, J,* 1995 *Par, CHL, Ur, It*
RH Crexell 1990 *I, S,* 1991 *Par,* 1992 *Sp,* 1993 *J,* 1995 *Ur, C, A, E, Sa, It, Par, CHL, Ur*
L Criscuolo 1992 *F, F,* 1993 *Bra, SA,* 1996 *Ur, F, F*
V Cruz 2012 *Ur, Bra, CHL*
J Cruz Legora 2002 *Par, CHL*
J Cruz Meabe 1997 *Par*
AG Cubelli 1977 *Bra, Ur, CHL,* 1978 *E, It,* 1979 *A, A,* 1980 *WXV, Fj,* 1983 *Par,* 1985 *F, F, Ur, Par, NZ, NZ,* 1990 *S*
TM Cubelli 2010 *Ur, CHL,* 2011 *CHL, Ur,* 2012 *Ur, Bra, CHL, It, F, F, F,* 2013 *E, Geo, SA, SA, NZ, A, A*
D Cuesta Silva 1983 *CHL, Ur,* 1985 *F, F, Ur, CHL, NZ, NZ,* 1986 *F, F, A, A,* 1987 *Ur, Fj, It, Sp, A, A,* 1988 *F, F, F, F,* 1989 *It, NZ, NZ,* 1990 *C, E, E, I, E, S,* 1991 *NZ, NZ, CHL, A, W, Sa,* 1992 *F, F, Sp, R, F,* 1993 *J, J, Bra, Par, Ur, SA, SA,* 1994 *US, S, S, US, SA,* 1995 *Ur, C, E, Sa, It, Par, R, It, F*
J Cuesta Silva 1927 *GBR, GBR, GBR, GBR*
B Cuezzo 2007 *CHL*
M Cutler 1969 *Ur,* 1971 *CHL, Bra, Par, Ur*

A Da Milano 1964 *Bra, CHL*
F D'Agnillo 1975 *Ur, Bra,* 1977 *Bra, Ur, Par, CHL*
JL Damioli 1991 *Ur, Par, Bra*
H Dande 2001 *Ur, C,* 2004 *CHL, Ven*
J Dartiguelongue 1964 *Bra, CHL,* 1968 *W, W*
S Dassen 1983 *CHL, Par, Ur*
R de Abelleyra 1932 *JSB, JSB*
M De Achaval 2010 *It, F*
L de Chazal 2001 *Ur, C,* 2004 *SA*
E de Forteza 1975 *Ur, Par, Bra, CHL*
R de la Arena 1992 *F, Sp*
T De La Vega 2011 *CHL, Ur,* 2012 *It, F, F, F,* 2013 *E, E, Geo*
JC De Pablo 1948 *OCC*
G De Robertis 2005 *Sa,* 2006 *CHL, Ur,* 2011 *CHL*
R de Vedia 1982 *F, Sp*
T de Vedia 2007 *I, I,* 2008 *S*
R del Busto 2007 *CHL*
F del Castillo 1994 *US, SA,* 1995 *Ur, C, A,* 1996 *Ur, F,* 1997 *Par, Ur,* 1998 *Ur*
GJ del Castillo 1991 *NZ, NZ, CHL, A, W,* 1993 *J,* 1994 *S, S, US, SA,* 1995 *C, A*
L del Chazal 1983 *CHL, Par, Ur*
R Dell'Acqua 1956 *OCC*
S Dengra 1982 *F, Sp,* 1983 *WXV, A, A,* 1986 *A,* 1987 *It, NZ, Sp, A, A,* 1988 *F, F, F, F,* 1989 *It, NZ, NZ*
C Derkheim 1927 *GBR*
M Devoto 1975 *Par, Bra,* 1977 *Par*
PM Devoto 1982 *F, F, Sp,* 1983 *WXV*
R Devoto 1960 *F*
M Diaz 1997 *Par, CHL,* 1998 *J, Par, CHL*
MD Diaz 2013 *Ur, CHL, Bra, SA, A*
F Diaz Alberdi 1997 *Ur,* 1999 *S, I,* 2000 *A, A*
J Diez 1956 *OCC*
R Dillon 1956 *OCC*
P Dinisio 1989 *NZ,* 1990 *C, US*
M Dip 1979 *Par, Bra*
D Dominguez 1989 *CHL, Par*
E Dominguez 1949 *F, F,* 1952 *I, I,* 1954 *F, F*
A Donnelly 1910 *GBR*
L Dorado 1949 *F*
J Dumas 1973 *R, R, Ur, Bra, S*
M Dumas 1966 *SAG, SAG*
MA Durand 1997 *CHL,* 1998 *Par, CHL, Ur, It, F, W,* 2000 *SA,* 2001 *Ur, US, C, It, NZ,* 2002 *F, SA, A, It, I,* 2003 *CHL, Ur, Fj, US, Ur, C, A, Nm, R,* 2004 *CHL, Ur, Ven, W, W, NZ, F, I, SA,* 2005 *SA, S, It,* 2006 *W, NZ, CHL, Ur, It, F,* 2007 *I, I, It, W, F, Geo, I, F,* 2008 *S, S, It, SA, F, It, I*

C Echeverria 1932 *JSB*
G Ehrman 1948 *OCC,* 1949 *F, F,* 1951 *Ur, Bra, CHL,* 1952 *I, I,* 1954 *F, F*
O Elia 1954 *F*
R Elliot 1936 *BI,* 1938 *CHL*
J Escalante 1975 *Ur, Par, CHL,* 1978 *It,* 1979 *Ur, CHL, Par, Bra*
N Escary 1927 *GBR, GBR,* 1932 *JSB, JSB*
R Espagnol 1971 *SAG*
AM Etchegaray 1964 *Ur, Bra, CHL,* 1965 *Rho, JSB, CHL,* 1967 *Ur, CHL,* 1968 *W, W,* 1969 *S, S,* 1971 *SAG, OCC, OCC,* 1972 *SAG, SAG,* 1973 *Par, Bra, I,* 1974 *F, F,* 1976 *W, NZ, NZ*
R Etchegoyen 1991 *Ur, Par, Bra*
C Ezcurra 1958 *Ur, Per, CHL*
E Ezcurra 1990 *I, E, S*

JA Farias Cabello 2010 *F, I,* 2011 *W, E, S, Geo, NZ,* 2012 *It, F, F, SA, SA, NZ, A, NZ, A, W, F, I,* 2013 *E, E, SA, SA, NZ, A, NZ, A*
R Fariello 1973 *Par, Ur, CHL, S*
M Farina 1968 *W, W,* 1969 *S, S*
D Farrell 1951 *Ur*
P Felisari 1956 *OCC*
JJ Fernandez 1971 *SAG, CHL, Bra, Par, Ur,* 1972 *SAG, SAG,* 1973 *R, R, Par, Ur, CHL, I, S,* 1974 *F, F,* 1975 *F,* 1976 *W, NZ, NZ,* 1977 *F, F*
S Fernández 2008 *It, I,* 2009 *E, E, E, W, S,* 2010 *S, S, F, It, F,* 2011 *W, E, R, S, Geo, NZ,* 2012 *SA, SA, NZ, A, NZ, A, I,* 2013 *SA, NZ, A, NZ, A*
Pablo Fernandez Bravo 1993 *SA, SA*
E Fernandez del Casal 1951 *Ur, Bra, CHL,* 1952 *I, I,* 1956 *OCC, OCC*
PF Fernandez 2013 *CHL, Bra*
CI Fernandez Lobbe 1996 *US,* 1997 *E, E,* 1998 *F, F, R, US, Ur, C, J, It, F,* 1999 *W, W, S, I, W, Sa, J, I, F,* 2000 *I, A, A, SA, E,* 2001 *NZ, It, W, S, NZ,* 2002 *F, E, SA, A, It, I,* 2003 *F, F, SA, US, C, A, Nm, I,* 2004 *W, W, NZ,* 2005 *SA, S, It,* 2006 *W, W, NZ, E, F,* 2007 *It, W, F, Nm, I, S, SA,* 2008 *S, S*
JM Fernandez Lobbe 2004 *Ur, Ven,* 2005 *S, It, Sa,* 2006 *W, W, NZ, E, It, F,* 2007 *I, I, It, W, F, Geo, Nm, I, S, SA, F,* 2008 *S, S, SA, F, It, I,* 2009 *E, E, E, W, S,* 2010 *S, S, F, It, F, I,* 2011 *W, E, R, S,* 2012 *SA, SA, NZ, A, NZ, A, W, F, I,* 2013 *NZ, A, NZ, A*
JC Fernández Miranda 1997 *Ur, R, It,* 1998 *Ur, It,* 2000 *I,* 2001 *US, C,* 2002 *Ur, Par, CHL, It, I,* 2003 *Par, CHL, Ur, Fj, US, Nm, R,* 2004 *W, NZ, SA,* 2005 *J, Sa,* 2006 *CHL, Ur,* 2007 *It*
N Fernandez Miranda 1994 *US, S, S, US,* 1995 *CHL, Ur,* 1996 *F, SA, SA, E,* 1997 *E, E, NZ, NZ, Ur, R,* 1998 *R, US, C, It,* 1999 *I, F,* 2002 *Ur, CHL, It,* 2003 *CHL, Ur, F, F, SA, US, Ur, Nm, R,* 2004 *W, NZ,* 2005 *J, It, It,* 2006 *W, It,* 2007 *It, Geo, Nm, F*
N Ferrari 1992 *Sp, Sp*
G Fessia 2007 *I,* 2009 *E,* 2010 *S, S, F, It, F, I,* 2011 *R, S, Geo,* 2012 *It*
JG Figallo 2010 *F, It, I,* 2011 *W, E, R, S, Geo, NZ,* 2012 *SA, SA, NZ, A, NZ, A, W, F,* 2013 *SA, SA, NZ, A, NZ*
A Figuerola 2008 *It, I,* 2009 *E, W, S,* 2010 *S, S*
R Follett 1948 *OCC, OCC,* 1952 *I, I,* 1954 *F*
G Foster 1971 *CHL, Bra, Par, Ur*
R Foster 1965 *Rho, JSB, OCC, OCC, CHL,* 1966 *SAG, SAG,* 1970 *I, I,* 1971 *SAG, SAG, OCC,* 1972 *SAG, SAG*
P Franchi 1987 *Ur, Par, CHL*
JL Francombe 1932 *JSB, JSB,* 1936 *BI*
J Freixas 2003 *CHL, Ur*
R Frigerio 1948 *OCC, OCC,* 1954 *F*
J Frigoli 1936 *BI, CHL, CHL*
C Fruttero 2012 *Ur, Bra, CHL,* 2013 *Ur, CHL, Bra*
P Fuselli 1998 *J, Par*

E Gahan 1954 *F, F*
M Gaitán 1998 *Ur,* 2002 *Par, CHL,* 2003 *Fj, US, Nm, R,* 2004 *W,* 2007 *It, W*
MT Galarza 2010 *S, F, It, F, I,* 2011 *W, E, R, Geo,* 2013 *E, E, Geo, SA, SA, NZ, A, NZ*
AM Galindo 2004 *Ur, Ven,* 2008 *S, It, SA, F, It,* 2009 *E,* 2010 *Ur, It, F,* 2012 *SA, SA*
R Gallo 1964 *Bra*
P Gambarini 2006 *W, CHL, Ur,* 2007 *I, It, CHL,* 2008 *S*
E Garbarino 1992 *Sp, Sp*
FL Garcia 1994 *SA,* 1995 *A, A, Par, CHL,* 1996 *Ur, F, F,* 1997 *NZ,* 1998 *R, Ur, J*
J Garcia 1998 *Par, Ur,* 2000 *A*
PT Garcia 1948 *OCC*
SE Garcia Botta 2013 *CHL, Bra*
E Garcia Hamilton 1993 *Bra*
P Garcia Hamilton 1998 *CHL*
HM Garcia Simon 1990 *I,* 1992 *F*
M Garcia Veiga 2012 *Ur, Bra, CHL,* 2013 *E, E, Geo*
G Garcia-Orsetti 1992 *R, F*
PA Garreton 1987 *Sp, Ur, CHL, A, A,* 1988 *F, F, F, F,* 1989 *It, NZ, Bra, CHL, Ur, US,* 1990 *C, E, E, I, E, S,* 1991 *NZ, NZ, CHL, A, W, Sa,* 1992 *F, F,* 1993 *J, J*
P Garzon 1990 *C,* 1991 *Par, Bra*
G Gasso 1983 *CHL, Par*
JM Gauweloose 1975 *F, F,* 1976 *W, NZ, NZ,* 1977 *F, F,* 1981 *C*
E Gavina 1956 *OCC, OCC,* 1958 *Ur, Per, CHL,* 1959 *JSB, JSB,* 1960 *F, F,* 1961 *CHL, Bra, Ur*
OST Gebbie 1910 *GBR*
FA Genoud 2004 *CHL, Ur, Ven,* 2005 *J, It*
J Genoud 1952 *I, I,* 1956 *OCC, OCC*
M Gerosa 1987 *Ur, CHL*
D Giannantonio 1996 *Ur,* 1997 *Par, Ur, It, A, A,* 1998 *F, F,* 2000 *A,* 2002 *E*
MC Giargia 1973 *Par, Ur, Bra,* 1975 *Par, CHL*
T Gilardon 2013 *Ur, CHL, Bra*
R Giles 1948 *OCC,* 1949 *F, F,* 1951 *Ur,* 1952 *I, I*
C Giuliano 1959 *JSB, JSB,* 1960 *F*
L Glastra 1948 *OCC, OCC,* 1952 *I, I*
M Glastra 1979 *Ur, CHL,* 1981 *C*
FE Gomez 1985 *Ur,* 1987 *Ur, Fj, It, NZ,* 1989 *NZ,* 1990 *C, E, E*
JF Gomez 2006 *It,* 2008 *S, S, It,* 2012 *W*
N Gomez 1997 *Par, CHL*
PM Gomez Cora 2004 *NZ, SA,* 2005 *Sa,* 2006 *E*
F Gómez Kodela 2011 *CHL, Ur,* 2012 *It, F, F, I,* 2013 *E, E, Geo*
D Gonzalez 1987 *Par,* 1988 *F, F*
T Gonzalez 1975 *Ur, CHL*
LP Gonzalez Amorosino 2007 *CHL,* 2009 *E, E,* 2010 *S, S, F, It, F, I,* 2011 *R, S, Geo, NZ,* 2012 *SA, SA, NZ, A, NZ, A, F,* 2013 *SA, NZ, A, NZ, A*
S Gonzalez Bonorino 2001 *Ur, US, C,* 2002 *Par, CHL,* 2003 *F, SA,* 2007 *I, I, It, W, F, Geo,* 2008 *S, S*
E Gonzalez del Solar 1960 *F,* 1961 *CHL, Bra, Ur*
N Gonzalez del Solar 1964 *Ur, Bra, CHL,* 1965 *Rho, JSB, OCC, OCC, CHL*
S Gonzalez Iglesias 2011 *CHL*
AO Gosio 2011 *Geo,* 2012 *It, F*
H Goti 1961 *CHL, Bra, Ur,* 1964 *Ur, Bra, CHL,* 1965 *Rho,* 1966 *SAG*
LM Gradin 1965 *OCC, OCC, CHL,* 1966 *SAG, SAG,* 1969 *CHL,* 1970 *I, I,* 1973 *R, R, Par, Ur, CHL, S*
P Grande 1998 *Par, CHL, Ur*
RD Grau 1993 *J, Bra, CHL,* 1995 *Par, CHL,* 1996 *F, F, US, Ur, C, SA, SA, E,* 1997 *E, E, NZ, NZ, A, A,* 1998 *F, It, F,* 1999 *W, W, S, I, W, F,* 2000 *A, SA, E,* 2001 *NZ, W, S, NZ,* 2002 *F, E, SA, A, It,* 2003 *F, SA, US, Ur, C, A, I*
L Gravano 1997 *CHL,* 1998 *CHL, Ur*
LH Gribell 1910 *GBR*
B Grigolon 1948 *OCC,* 1954 *F, F*
V Grimoldi 1927 *GBR, GBR*
J Grondona 1990 *C*
R Grosse 1952 *I, I,* 1954 *F, F*
P Guarrochena 1977 *Par*
A Guastella 1956 *OCC,* 1959 *JSB, JSB,* 1960 *F*
J Guidi 1958 *Ur, Per, CHL,* 1959 *JSB,* 1960 *F,* 1961 *CHL, Bra, Ur*
MR Guidone 2011 *CHL, Ur,* 2013 *Ur, Bra, E, E, Geo*
E Guiñazu 2003 *Par, CHL, Ur,* 2004 *CHL, Ur, Ven, W, W, SA,* 2005 *J, It,* 2007 *I, It, F,* 2009 *E,* 2012 *It, F, F, SA, SA, NZ, A, NZ, A, W, F, I,* 2013 *SA, SA, NZ, A, NZ, A*
JA Guzman 2007 *CHL,* 2010 *Ur, CHL*
SN Guzmán 2010 *S, I,* 2012 *Ur, Bra, CHL, It*

D Halle 1989 *Bra, CHL, Ur, US,* 1990 *US*
R Handley 1966 *SAG, SAG,* 1968 *W, W,* 1969 *S, S, Ur, CHL,* 1970 *I, I,* 1971 *SAG, SAG,* 1972 *SAG, SAG*
G Hardie 1948 *OCC*
TA Harris-Smith 1969 *S, S,* 1971 *SAG, OCC, OCC,* 1973 *Par, Ur*
O Hasan Jalil 1995 *Ur,* 1996 *Ur, C, SA, SA,* 1997 *E, E, NZ, R, It, F, A,* 1998 *F, F, R, US, C, It, F, W,* 1999 *W, W, S, W, Sa, J, I,* 2000 *SA, E,* 2001 *NZ, It, W, S, NZ,* 2002 *F, E, SA, A, It, I,* 2003 *US, C, A, R,* 2004 *W, W, NZ, F, I,* 2005 *It, It, SA, S, It,* 2006 *NZ, E, F,* 2007 *It, Geo, Nm, I, S, SA, F*
WM Hayman 1910 *GBR*
BH Heatlie 1910 *GBR*
P Henn 2004 *CHL, Ur, Ven,* 2005 *J, It,* 2007 *It,* 2012 *F,* 2013 *E, E*
F Henrys 1910 *GBR*
F Heriot 1910 *GBR*
JM Hernández 2003 *Par, Ur, F, F, SA, C, A, Nm, R,* 2004 *F, I, SA,* 2005 *SA, S, It,* 2006 *W, W, NZ, E, It, F,* 2007 *F, Geo,*

THE COUNTRIES

I, S, SA, F, 2008 *It, F, It,* 2009 *E, E,* 2012 *SA, NZ, A, NZ, A, W, I,* 2013 *SA, NZ, A, NZ, A*
M Hernandez 1927 *GBR, GBR, GBR*
L Herrera 1991 *Ur, Par*
FA Higgs 2004 *Ur, Ven,* 2005 *J*
D Hine 1938 *CHL*
C Hirsch 1960 *F*
C Hirsch 1960 *F*
E Hirsch 1954 *F,* 1956 *OCC*
R Hogg 1958 *Ur, Per, CHL,* 1959 *JSB, JSB,* 1961 *CHL, Bra, Ur*
S Hogg 1956 *OCC, OCC,* 1958 *Ur, Per, CHL,* 1959 *JSB, JSB*
E Holmberg 1948 *OCC*
B Holmes 1949 *F, F*
E Holmgren 1958 *Ur, Per, CHL,* 1959 *JSB, JSB,* 1960 *F, F*
G Holmgren 1985 *NZ, NZ*
E Horan 1956 *OCC*
L Hughes 1936 *CHL*
M Hughes 1954 *F, F*
M Hughes 1949 *F, F*
CA Huntley Robertson 1932 *JSB, JSB*

A Iachetti 1977 *Bra,* 1987 *CHL*
A Iachetti 1975 *Ur, Par,* 1977 *Ur, Par, CHL,* 1978 *E, It,* 1979 *NZ, NZ, A, A,* 1980 *WXV, Fj, Fj,* 1981 *E, E,* 1982 *F, F, Sp,* 1987 *Ur, Par, A, A,* 1988 *F, F, F, F,* 1989 *It, NZ,* 1990 *C, E, E*
ME Iachetti 1979 *NZ, NZ, A, A*
M Iglesias 1973 *R,* 1974 *F, F*
S Iglesias 2013 *Ur, CHL*
G Illia 1965 *Rho*
JL Imhoff 1967 *Ur, CHL*
JJ Imhoff 2010 *CHL,* 2011 *W, E, R, Geo, NZ,* 2012 *A, NZ, A, W, F, I,* 2013 *SA, A, NZ, A*
P Imhoff 2013 *Ur, CHL, Bra*
V Inchausti 1936 *BI, CHL, CHL*
F Insua 1971 *CHL, Bra, Par, Ur,* 1972 *SAG, SAG,* 1973 *R, R, Bra, CHL, I, S,* 1974 *F, F,* 1976 *W, NZ, NZ,* 1977 *F, F*
R Iraneta 1974 *F,* 1976 *W, NZ*
FJ Irarrazabal 1991 *Sa,* 1992 *Sp, Sp*
S Irazoqui 1993 *J, CHL, Par, Ur,* 1995 *E, Sa, Par*
A Irigoyen 1997 *Par*
DJ Isaack 2013 *Ur, CHL*

C Jacobi 1979 *CHL, Par*
AG Jacobs 1927 *GBR, GBR*
AGW Jones 1948 *OCC*
GM Jorge 1989 *Bra, CHL, Par, Ur,* 1990 *I, E,* 1992 *F, F, Sp, Sp, R, F,* 1993 *J, J, Bra, CHL, Ur, SA, SA,* 1994 *US, S, S, US*
E Jurado 1995 *A, A, E, Sa, It, Par, CHL, Ur, R, It, F,* 1996 *SA, E,* 1997 *E, E, NZ, NZ, Ur, R, It, F, A, A,* 1998 *F, Ur, C, It,* 1999 *W*

E Karplus 1959 *JSB, JSB,* 1960 *F, F, F*
A Ker 1936 *CHL,* 1938 *CHL*
E Kossler 1960 *F, F, F*

EH Laborde 1991 *A, W, Sa*
G Laborde 1979 *CHL, Bra*
J Lacarra 1989 *Par, Ur*
R Lagarde 1956 *OCC*
A Lalanne 2008 *SA,* 2009 *E, E, W, S,* 2010 *S, I,* 2011 *R, Geo, NZ*
M Lamas 1998 *Par, CHL*
F Lamy 2013 *Ur, CHL, Bra*
M Landajo 2010 *Ur, CHL,* 2012 *Ur, Bra, CHL, It, F, SA, SA, NZ, A, NZ, A, W, F, I,* 2013 *E, SA, SA, NZ, A, NZ, A*
TR Landajo 1977 *F, Bra, Ur, CHL,* 1978 *E,* 1979 *A, A,* 1980 *WXV, Fj, Fj,* 1981 *E, E*
M Lanfranco 1991 *Ur, Par, Bra*
AR Lanusse 1932 *JSB*
M Lanusse 1951 *Ur, Bra, CHL*
J Lanza 1985 *F, Ur, Par, NZ, NZ,* 1986 *F, F, A, A,* 1987 *Ur, Fj, It, NZ*
P Lanza 1983 *CHL, Par, Ur,* 1985 *F, F, Ur, CHL, Par, NZ, NZ,* 1986 *F, F, A, A,* 1987 *It, NZ*
J Lasalle 1964 *Ur*
TE Lavanini 2013 *Ur, Bra, SA*
J Lavayen 1961 *CHL, Bra, Ur*
CG Lazcano Miranda 1998 *CHL,* 2004 *CHL, Ur, Ven,* 2005 *J*

RA le Fort 1990 *I, E,* 1991 *NZ, NZ, CHL, A, W,* 1992 *R, F,* 1993 *J, SA, SA,* 1995 *Ur, It*
F Lecot 2003 *Par, Ur,* 2005 *J,* 2007 *CHL*
P Ledesma 2008 *It, SA*
ME Ledesma Arocena 1996 *Ur, C,* 1997 *NZ, NZ, Ur, R, It, F, A, A,* 1998 *F, F, Ur, C, J, Ur, F, W,* 1999 *W, W, Sa, J, I, F,* 2000 *SA,* 2001 *It, W, NZ,* 2002 *F, E, SA, A, It, I,* 2003 *F, SA, Fj, US, C, A, Nm, R,* 2004 *W, NZ, F, I,* 2005 *It, It, SA, S, It,* 2006 *W, W, NZ, CHL, Ur, E, It, F,* 2007 *W, F, Geo, I, S, SA,* 2008 *SA, F, It, I,* 2009 *E, E, W,* 2010 *S, S, F, It, F, I,* 2011 *W, E, R, S, Geo, NZ*
J Legora 1996 *F, F, US, Ur,* 1997 *CHL,* 1998 *Par*
JM Leguizamón 2005 *J, It, It, SA, S, It,* 2006 *W, NZ, CHL, Ur, E, It, F,* 2007 *I, I, It, W, F, Geo, Nm, S, SA, F,* 2008 *S, S, It, SA, I,* 2009 *E, E,* 2010 *S, S, F,* 2011 *W, E, R, S, Geo, NZ,* 2012 *NZ, A, NZ, A, W, F, I,* 2013 *SA, SA, NZ, A, NZ, A*
GP Leiros 1973 *Bra, I*
C Lennon 1958 *Ur, Per*
TC Leonardi 2009 *E, W, S,* 2012 *It, F, F, SA, SA, NZ, A, NZ, A, W, I,* 2013 *E, E, Geo*
FJ Leonelli Morey 2001 *Ur,* 2004 *Ur, Ven,* 2005 *J, It, SA, S, It,* 2006 *W, W,* 2007 *I, I, It,* 2008 *F, I,* 2009 *E*
M Lerga 1995 *Par, CHL, Ur*
Lesianado 1948 *OCC*
I Lewis 1932 *JSB*
GA Llanes 1990 *I, E, S,* 1991 *NZ, NZ, CHL, A, W,* 1992 *F, F, Sp, R, F,* 1993 *Bra, CHL, SA, SA,* 1994 *US, S, S, SA, SA,* 1995 *A, A, E, Sa, It, R, It, F,* 1996 *SA, SA, E,* 1997 *E, E, NZ, NZ, R, It, F,* 1998 *F,* 2000 *A*
MA Lobato 2010 *Ur, CHL*
N Lobo 2012 *F, I,* 2013 *SA, NZ, A, NZ, A*
L Lobrauco 1996 *US,* 1997 *CHL,* 1998 *J, CHL, Ur*
MH Loffreda 1978 *E,* 1979 *NZ, NZ, A, A,* 1980 *WXV, Fj, Fj,* 1981 *E, E, C,* 1982 *F, F, Sp,* 1983 *WXV, A, A,* 1985 *Ur, CHL, Par,* 1987 *Ur, Par, CHL, A, A,* 1988 *F, F, F, F,* 1989 *It, NZ, Bra, CHL, Par, Ur, US,* 1990 *C, US, E, E,* 1994 *US, S, S, US, SA, SA*
G Logan 1936 *BI*
GM Longo Elía 1999 *W, W, S, I, W, Sa, I, F,* 2000 *I, A, A, SA, E,* 2001 *US, NZ, It, W, S, NZ,* 2002 *F, E, SA, A, It, I,* 2003 *F, F, SA, Fj, C, A, I,* 2004 *W, W, NZ, F, I,* 2005 *It, It, SA,* 2006 *W, W, NZ, E, It, F,* 2007 *W, Nm, I, S, SA, F*
L Lopez Fleming 2004 *Ur, Ven, W,* 2005 *Sa*
A Lopresti 1997 *Par, CHL*
J Loures 1954 *F*
R Loyola 1964 *Ur, CHL,* 1965 *Rho, JSB, OCC, OCC, CHL,* 1966 *SAG, SAG,* 1968 *W, W,* 1969 *S, S,* 1970 *I, I,* 1971 *CHL, Bra, Par, Ur*
E Lozada 2006 *E, It,* 2007 *I, I, Geo, F,* 2008 *S, S, It, SA, F, It, I,* 2009 *E, E, E,* 2010 *It,* 2012 *F, F,* 2013 *E, E, Geo*
F Lucioni 1927 *GBR*
R Lucke 1975 *Ur, Par, Bra, CHL,* 1981 *C*
FD Luna 2011 *Ur*
J Luna 1995 *Par, CHL, Ur, R, It, F,* 1997 *Par, CHL*

P Macadam 1949 *F, F*
AM Macome 1990 *I, E,* 1995 *Ur, C*
B Macome 2012 *Ur, Bra, CHL, It, F, F,* 2013 *E, E, Geo, SA, NZ, NZ, A*
B Madero 2011 *CHL, Ur,* 2013 *E, Geo*
RM Madero 1978 *E, It,* 1979 *NZ, NZ, A, A,* 1980 *WXV, Fj, Fj,* 1981 *E, E, C,* 1982 *F, F, Sp,* 1983 *WXV, A, A,* 1985 *F, NZ,* 1986 *A, A,* 1987 *Ur, It, NZ, Sp, Ur, Par, CHL, A, A,* 1988 *F, F, F,* 1989 *It, NZ, NZ,* 1990 *E, E*
M Maineri 2011 *CHL, Ur*
L Makin 1927 *GBR*
A Mamanna 1991 *Par,* 1997 *Par*
G Manso 2013 *CHL, Bra*
J Manuel Belgrano 1956 *OCC*
A Marguery 1991 *Ur, Bra,* 1993 *CHL, Par*
R Martin 1938 *CHL*
RA Martin 1994 *US, S, S, US, SA, SA,* 1995 *Ur, C, A, A, E, Sa, It, CHL, Ur, R, It, F,* 1996 *Ur, F, F, Ur, C, SA, SA, E,* 1997 *E, E, NZ, NZ, It, F, A, A,* 1998 *F, F, R, US, Ur, J, Par, CHL, Ur, It, W,* 1999 *W, W, S, I, W, Sa, J, I, F,* 2000 *I, A, A, SA, E,* 2001 *Ur, US, C, NZ, It, W, S, NZ,* 2002 *Ur, Par, CHL, F, E, SA, A, It, I,* 2003 *Par, CHL, Ur, F, SA, Ur, C, A, R, I*

F Martin Aramburu 2004 *CHL, Ven, W, NZ, F, I*, 2005 *It, SA, S, It*, 2006 *NZ*, 2007 *Geo, F*, 2008 *S, SA, F, It, I*, 2009 *E, S*
J Martin Copella 1989 *CHL, Par*
C Martinez 1969 *Ur, CHL*, 1970 *I, I*
E Martinez 1971 *CHL, Bra, Ur*
O Martinez Basante 1954 *F*
M Martinez Mosquera 1971 *CHL*
RC Mastai 1975 *F*, 1976 *W, NZ, NZ*, 1977 *F, F, Bra, Ur, Par, CHL*, 1980 *WXV*
R Matarazzo 1971 *SAG, SAG, Par, Ur*, 1972 *SAG, SAG*, 1973 *R, R, Par, Ur, CHL, I, S*, 1974 *F, F*
PN Matera 2013 *CHL, Bra, SA, SA, NZ, A, NZ, A*
H Maurer 1932 *JSB, JSB*
L Maurette 1948 *OCC, OCC*
C Mazzini 1977 *F, F*
CJ McCarthy 1910 *GBR*
G McCormick 1964 *Bra, CHL*, 1965 *Rho, OCC, OCC, CHL*, 1966 *SAG, SAG*
M McCormick 1927 *GBR*
A Memoli 1979 *Ur, Par, Bra*
FJ Mendez 1991 *Ur, Par, Bra*, 1992 *Sp, Sp*
FE Méndez 1990 *I, E*, 1991 *NZ, NZ, CHL, A, W*, 1992 *F, F, Sp, Sp, R, F*, 1994 *S, US, SA, SA*, 1995 *Ur, C, A, A, E, Sa, It, Par, CHL, Ur, R, It, F*, 1996 *SA, SA*, 1997 *E*, 1998 *F, F, R, US, Ur, C, It, F, W*, 1999 *W, W*, 2000 *I, A, A, SA, E*, 2001 *NZ, It, W, S, NZ*, 2002 *Ur, CHL, F, E, SA, A*, 2003 *F, F, SA, Fj, Ur, Nm, I*, 2004 *CHL, Ur, W, W, NZ, SA*
H Mendez 1967 *Ur, CHL*
L Mendez 1958 *Ur, Per, CHL*, 1959 *JSB*
S Mendez 2013 *Ur, CHL, Bra*
CI Mendy 1987 *Ur, Par, CHL, A, A*, 1988 *F, F, F, F*, 1989 *It, NZ, NZ, US*, 1990 *C*, 1991 *Ur, Bra*
FJ Merello 2007 *CHL*, 2010 *Ur, CHL*
I Merlo 1993 *Bra, CHL*
P Merlo 1985 *CHL, Par*
SE Meson 1987 *Par*, 1989 *Bra, Par, Ur, US*, 1990 *US, C, S*, 1991 *NZ, NZ, CHL, Sa*, 1992 *F, F, Sp, R, F*, 1993 *J, Bra, Par, Ur, SA, SA*, 1994 *US, S, S, US*, 1995 *Ur, C, A, A*, 1996 *US, C*, 1997 *CHL*
I Mieres 2007 *CHL*, 2010 *Ur, CHL*, 2012 *It, F*
BH Miguens 1983 *WXV, A, A*, 1985 *F, F, NZ, NZ*, 1986 *F, F, A, A*, 1987 *Sp*
E Miguens 1975 *Ur, Par, CHL*
H Miguens 1969 *S, S, Ur, CHL*, 1970 *I, I*, 1971 *OCC*, 1972 *SAG, SAG*, 1973 *R, R, Par, Ur, Bra, CHL, I, S*, 1975 *F*
J Miguens 1982 *F*, 1985 *F, F*, 1986 *F, F, A, A*
GE Milano 1982 *F, F, Sp*, 1983 *WXV, A, A*, 1985 *F, F, Ur, CHL, Par, NZ, NZ*, 1986 *F, F, A, A*, 1987 *Ur, Fj, Sp, Ur, CHL, A, A*, 1988 *F, F, F*, 1989 *It, NZ, NZ*
A Mimesi 1998 *J, Par, CHL*
B Minguez 1975 *Par, Bra, CHL*, 1979 *Ur, CHL, Par*, 1983 *WXV, A, A*, 1985 *Ur, CHL*
R Miralles 2011 *CHL*, 2012 *CHL, F*
B Mitchelstein 1936 *BI*
E Mitchelstein 1956 *OCC*, 1960 *F, F*
C Mold 1910 *GBR*
LE Molina 1985 *CHL*, 1987 *Ur, Fj, It, NZ*, 1989 *NZ, NZ, Bra, CHL, Par*, 1990 *C, E*, 1991 *W*
M Molina 1998 *Par, CHL, Ur*
M Montero 2012 *Ur, Bra, CHL, It, F, F, I*, 2013 *E, E*
G Montes de Oca 1961 *CHL, Bra, Ur*
E Montpelat 1948 *OCC, OCC*
G Morales Oliver 2001 *Ur, US, C*
C Morea 1951 *Ur, Bra, CHL*
FR Morel 1979 *A, A*, 1980 *WXV, Fj, Fj*, 1981 *E, E, C*, 1982 *F*, 1985 *F, F, Ur, Par, NZ, NZ*, 1986 *F, F, A*, 1987 *Ur, Fj*
A Moreno 1998 *Par, CHL, Ur*
D Morgan 1967 *CHL*, 1970 *I, I*, 1971 *SAG, SAG, OCC, OCC*, 1972 *SAG, SAG*
E Morgan 1969 *S, S*, 1972 *SAG, SAG*, 1973 *R, R, Par, Ur, Bra, CHL, I, S*, 1975 *F, F*
G Morgan 1977 *Bra, Ur, Par, CHL*, 1979 *Ur, Par, Bra*
M Morgan 1971 *SAG, OCC, OCC*
JS Morganti 1951 *Ur, Bra, CHL*
J Mostany 1987 *Ur, Fj, NZ*
R Moyano 2011 *CHL, Ur*, 2012 *Ur, Bra*
E Muliero 1997 *CHL*
S Muller 1927 *GBR*
R Muniz 1975 *Par, Bra, CHL*

M Nannini 2002 *Ur, Par, CHL*, 2003 *Par, CHL*
A Navajas 1932 *JSB, JSB*
E Naveyra 1998 *CHL*
G Nazassi 1997 *CHL*
ML Negri 1979 *CHL, Bra*
E Neri 1960 *F, F*, 1961 *CHL, Bra, Ur*, 1964 *Ur, Bra, CHL*, 1965 *Rho, JSB, OCC*, 1966 *SAG, SAG*
CM Neyra 1975 *F, F*, 1976 *W, NZ, NZ*, 1983 *WXV*
A Nicholson 1979 *Ur, Par, Bra*
HM Nicola 1971 *SAG, OCC, OCC, CHL, Bra, Par, Ur*, 1975 *F, F*, 1978 *E, It*, 1979 *NZ, NZ*
EP Noriega 1991 *Par*, 1992 *Sp, Sp, R, F*, 1993 *J, J, CHL, Par, Ur, SA, SA*, 1994 *US, S, S, US, SA, SA*, 1995 *Ur, C, A, A, E, Sa, It*
JM Nuñez Piossek 2001 *Ur, NZ*, 2002 *Ur, Par, CHL, A*, 2003 *Par, Ur, F, SA, Ur, C, A, R, I*, 2004 *CHL, Ur, W, W*, 2005 *It, It*, 2006 *W, W, NZ, E, F*, 2008 *S, SA*

R Ochoa 1956 *OCC*
M Odriozola 1961 *CHL, Ur*
J O'Farrell 1948 *OCC*, 1951 *Ur, Bra*, 1956 *OCC*
U O'Farrell 1951 *Ur, Bra, CHL*
C Ohanian 1998 *Par, Ur*
C Olivera 1958 *Ur, Per, CHL*, 1959 *JSB, JSB*
R Olivieri 1960 *F, F, F*, 1961 *CHL, Bra, Ur*
J Orengo 1996 *Ur*, 1997 *Ur, R, It*, 1998 *F, F, R, US, C, F, W*, 1999 *W*, 2000 *A, SA, E*, 2001 *Ur, US, C, NZ, W, S, NZ*, 2002 *F, E, SA, A, It, I*, 2003 *F, SA, Ur, C, A, I*, 2004 *W, W*
JP Orlandi 2008 *F, It, I*, 2009 *E, E*, 2012 *SA, NZ, A, NZ, A*, 2013 *SA, NZ, NZ, A*
M Orlando 2012 *Ur, Bra, CHL*, 2013 *E, E, Geo*
J Ortega 2012 *Ur, Bra, CHL*
C Orti 1949 *F, F*
L Ortiz 2003 *Par, CHL, Ur*
A Orzabal 1974 *F, F*
L Ostiglia 1999 *W, W, S, I, W, J, F*, 2001 *NZ, It, W, S*, 2002 *E, SA*, 2003 *Par, CHL, Ur, F, F, SA, Nm, I*, 2004 *W, W, NZ, F, I, SA*, 2007 *F, Nm, I, S, SA*
B Otaño 1960 *F, F, F*, 1961 *CHL, Bra, Ur*, 1964 *Ur, Bra, CHL*, 1965 *Rho, JSB, OCC, OCC, CHL*, 1966 *SAG, SAG*, 1968 *W, W*, 1969 *S, S, Ur, CHL*, 1970 *I, I*, 1971 *SAG, OCC, OCC*
J Otaola 1970 *I*, 1971 *CHL, Bra, Par, Ur*, 1974 *F, F*

M Pacheco 1938 *CHL*
RL Pacheco 2010 *Ur, CHL*
A Palma 1949 *F, F*, 1952 *I, I*, 1954 *F, F*
D Palma 2012 *Ur, CHL*
JMC Palma 1982 *F, Sp*, 1983 *WXV, A, A*
R Palma 1985 *CHL, Par*
M Palou 1996 *US, Ur*
F Panessi 2013 *Ur, CHL*
M Parra 1975 *Ur, Bra, CHL*
A Pasalagua 1927 *GBR, GBR*
M Pascual 1965 *Rho, JSB, OCC, OCC, CHL*, 1966 *SAG, SAG*, 1967 *Ur, CHL*, 1968 *W, W*, 1969 *S, S, Ur, CHL*, 1970 *I, I*, 1971 *SAG, SAG, OCC, OCC*
HR Pascuali 1936 *BI*
H Pasman 1936 *CHL*
R Passaglia 1977 *Bra, Ur, CHL*, 1978 *E, It*
G Paz 1979 *Ur, CHL, Par, Bra*, 1983 *CHL, Par, Ur*
J Paz 2013 *Ur, CHL, Bra*
JJ Paz 1991 *Ur, Bra*
S Peretti 1993 *Bra, Par, SA*
L Pereyra 2010 *Ur, CHL*
N Perez 1968 *W*
RN Perez 1992 *F, F, Sp, R, F*, 1993 *Bra, Par, Ur, SA*, 1995 *Ur, R, It, F*, 1996 *US, Ur, C, SA, SA*, 1998 *Ur*, 1999 *I*
J Perez Cobo 1979 *NZ, NZ*, 1980 *Fj*, 1981 *E, E, C*
M Peri Brusa 1998 *CHL*
R Pesce 1958 *Ur, Per, CHL*
TA Petersen 1978 *E, It*, 1979 *NZ, NZ, A, A*, 1980 *Fj, Fj*, 1981 *E, E, C*, 1982 *F*, 1983 *WXV, A, A*, 1985 *F, F, Ur, CHL, Par, NZ, NZ*, 1986 *F, F, A*
AD Petrilli 2004 *SA*, 2005 *J*

J Petrone 1949 *F, F*
R Petti 1995 *Par, CHL*
M Pfister 1994 *SA, SA,* 1996 *F,* 1998 *R, Ur, J*
S Phelan 1997 *Ur, CHL, R, It,* 1998 *F, F, R, US, C, It,* 1999 *S, I, W, Sa, J, I, F,* 2000 *I, A, A, SA, E,* 2001 *NZ, It, W, S, NZ,* 2002 *Ur, Par, CHL, F, E, SA, A, It, I,* 2003 *CHL, Ur, F, SA, Fj, C, A, R*
A Phillips 1948 *OCC,* 1949 *F, F*
JP Piccardo 1981 *E,* 1983 *CHL, Par, Ur*
A Pichot 1995 *A, R, It, F,* 1996 *Ur, F, F,* 1997 *It, F, A, A,* 1998 *F, F, R, It, F, W,* 1999 *W, W, S, I, W, Sa, J, I, F,* 2000 *I, A, A, SA, E,* 2001 *Ur, US, C, NZ, It, W, S, NZ,* 2002 *F, E, SA, A, It, I,* 2003 *Ur, C, A, R, I,* 2004 *F, I, SA,* 2005 *It, SA, S, It,* 2006 *W, W, NZ, CHL, Ur, E, F,* 2007 *W, F, Nm, I, S, SA, F*
G Pimentel 1971 *Bra*
R Pineo 1954 *F*
E Pittinari 1991 *Ur, Par, Bra*
SA Poet 2013 *Ur, CHL, Bra*
E Poggi 1965 *JSB, OCC, OCC, CHL,* 1966 *SAG,* 1967 *Ur,* 1969 *Ur*
C Pollano 1927 *GBR*
S Ponce 2007 *CHL*
R Pont Lezica 1951 *Ur, Bra, CHL*
H Porta 1971 *CHL, Bra, Par, Ur,* 1972 *SAG, SAG,* 1973 *R, R, Ur, Bra, CHL, I, S,* 1974 *F, F,* 1975 *F, F,* 1976 *W, NZ, NZ,* 1977 *F, F,* 1978 *E, It,* 1979 *NZ, NZ, A, A,* 1980 *WXV, Fj, Fj,* 1981 *E, E, C,* 1982 *F, F, Sp,* 1983 *A, A,* 1985 *F, F, Ur, CHL, Par, NZ, NZ,* 1986 *F, F, A,* 1987 *Fj, It, NZ, Sp, A, A,* 1990 *I, E, S*
O Portillo 1995 *Par, CHL,* 1997 *Par, CHL*
J Posse 1977 *Par*
S Posse 1991 *Par,* 1993 *Bra, CHL, Ur*
B Postiglioni 2012 *Ur, Bra, CHL, It, F, F, W,* 2013 *Geo*
C Promanzio 1995 *C,* 1996 *Ur, F, F, E,* 1997 *E, E, NZ, Ur,* 1998 *R, J*
U Propato 1956 *OCC*
L Proto 2010 *Ur, CHL*
A Puccio 1979 *CHL, Par, Bra*
M Puigdeval 1964 *Ur, Bra*
J Pulido 1960 *F*

JC Queirolo 1964 *Ur, Bra, CHL*
G Quesada 1996 *US, Ur, C, SA, E,* 1997 *E, E, NZ, NZ,* 1998 *F, R, US, C, It,* 1999 *W, S, I, W, Sa, J, I, F,* 2000 *I, SA, E,* 2001 *NZ, It, NZ,* 2002 *F, E, SA,* 2003 *F, SA, Ur, C, Nm, R, I*
E Quetglas 1965 *CHL*
G Quinones 2004 *Ur, Ven*

R Raimundez 1959 *JSB, JSB*
C Ramallo 1979 *Ur, CHL, Par*
S Ratcliff 1936 *CHL*
F Rave 1997 *Par*
M Reggiardo 1996 *Ur, F, F, E,* 1997 *E, E, NZ, NZ, R, F, A, A,* 1998 *F, F, R, US, Ur, C, It, W,* 1999 *W, W, S, I, W, Sa, J, I, F,* 2000 *I, SA,* 2001 *NZ, It, W, S, NZ,* 2002 *F, E, SA, A, It, I,* 2003 *F, SA, Fj, US, Ur, A, Nm, I*
A Reid 1910 *GBR*
C Reyes 1927 *GBR, GBR, GBR*
M Ricci 1987 *Sp*
A Riganti 1927 *GBR, GBR, GBR*
MA Righentini 1989 *NZ*
J Rios 1960 *F, F*
G Rivero 1996 *Ur, US, Ur*
G Roan 2010 *Ur, CHL,* 2013 *E, E, Geo*
T Roan 2007 *CHL*
F Robson 1927 *GBR*
M Roby 1992 *Sp,* 1993 *J*
A Rocca 1989 *US,* 1990 *C, US, C, E,* 1991 *Ur, Bra*
S Rocchia 2013 *Ur, CHL, Bra*
O Rocha 1974 *F, F*
D Rodriguez 1998 *J, Par, CHL, Ur*
D Rodriguez 2002 *Ur, Par, CHL*
EE Rodriguez 1979 *NZ, NZ, A, A,* 1980 *WXV, Fj, Fj,* 1981 *E, E, C,* 1983 *WXV, A, A*
F Rodriguez 2007 *CHL*
M Rodriguez 2009 *E, W, S,* 2010 *S, S, F, It, F, I,* 2011 *W, E, R, S, Geo, NZ,* 2012 *SA, SA, NZ, NZ*
A Rodriguez Jurado 1965 *JSB, OCC, OCC, CHL,* 1966 *SAG, SAG,* 1968 *W, W,* 1969 *S, CHL,* 1970 *I,* 1971 *SAG,* 1973 *R, Par, Bra, CHL, I, S,* 1974 *F, F,* 1975 *F, F*
A Rodriguez Jurado 1927 *GBR, GBR, GBR, GBR,* 1932 *JSB, JSB,* 1936 *CHL, CHL*
M Rodriguez Jurado 1971 *SAG, OCC, CHL, Bra, Par, Ur*
J Rojas 2012 *Ur, Bra, CHL*
L Roldan 2001 *Ur, C*
AS Romagnoli 2004 *CHL, Ur, Ven*
R Roncero 1998 *J,* 2002 *Ur, Par, CHL,* 2003 *Fj, US, Nm, R,* 2004 *W, W, NZ, F, I,* 2005 *It, SA, S, It,* 2006 *W, W, NZ,* 2007 *W, F, Nm, I, S, SA, F,* 2008 *It, SA, F, It, I,* 2009 *E, E, E, W, S,* 2010 *S, S, F, It, F, I,* 2011 *W, E, R, S, NZ,* 2012 *It, SA, SA, NZ, A, NZ, A*
S Rondinelli 2005 *Sa*
T Rosati 2011 *CHL, Ur*
S Rosatti 1977 *Par, CHL*
M Rospide 2003 *Par, CHL, Ur*
F Rossi 1991 *Ur, Par, Bra,* 1998 *F*
D Rotondo 1997 *Par, CHL*
MA Ruiz 1997 *NZ, CHL, R, It, F, A, A,* 1998 *F, F, R, US, Ur, C, J, It, F, W,* 1999 *W, Sa, J, F,* 2002 *Ur, Par, CHL*

I Saenz Lancuba 2012 *Ur, Bra,* 2013 *Ur, CHL, Bra*
JE Saffery 1910 *GBR*
CMS Sainz Trapaga 1979 *Ur, Par, Bra*
A Salinas 1954 *F,* 1956 *OCC,* 1958 *Ur, CHL,* 1960 *F, F*
S Salvat 1987 *Ur, Fj, It,* 1988 *F,* 1989 *It, NZ,* 1990 *C, US, C, E, E,* 1991 *Ur, Par, Bra,* 1992 *Sp, F,* 1993 *Bra, CHL, Par, Ur, SA, SA,* 1994 *SA, SA,* 1995 *Ur, C, A, A, E, Sa, It, Par, CHL, Ur, R, It, F*
T Salzman 1936 *BI, CHL, CHL*
M Sambucetti 2001 *Ur, US, C,* 2002 *Ur, CHL,* 2003 *Par, CHL, Fj,* 2005 *It, Sa,* 2009 *W*
HA San Martin 2009 *W, S*
FN Sanchez 2010 *Ur, CHL,* 2011 *R,* 2012 *SA, A, W, F, I,* 2013 *SA, SA, NZ, A, NZ, A*
T Sanderson 1932 *JSB*
D Sanes 1985 *CHL, Par,* 1986 *F, F,* 1987 *Ur, Par, CHL,* 1989 *Bra, CHL, Ur*
EJ Sanguinetti 1975 *Ur, Par, CHL,* 1978 *It,* 1979 *A,* 1982 *F, F, Sp*
G Sanguinetti 1979 *Ur, CHL, Par, Bra*
J Sansot 1948 *OCC*
M Sansot 1975 *F, F,* 1976 *W, NZ, NZ,* 1977 *Bra, CHL,* 1978 *E, It,* 1979 *NZ, NZ, A, A,* 1980 *WXV, Fj,* 1983 *WXV*
Jm Santamarina 1991 *NZ, NZ, CHL, A, W, Sa,* 1992 *F, Sp, R, F,* 1993 *J, J,* 1994 *US, S, US,* 1995 *A, A, E, Sa, It, Ur, R, It, F*
J Santiago 1948 *OCC,* 1952 *I, I*
JR Sanz 1973 *Par, Ur, Bra, CHL,* 1974 *F, F,* 1977 *F, F*
S Sanz 2003 *US,* 2004 *CHL, Ven,* 2005 *It, Sa,* 2007 *CHL*
M Sarandon 1948 *OCC, OCC,* 1949 *F, F,* 1951 *Ur, Bra, CHL,* 1952 *I, I,* 1954 *F*
J Sartori 1979 *CHL, Par, Bra*
R Sauze 1983 *Par*
FW Saywer 1910 *GBR*
MA Scelzo 1996 *US, SA,* 1997 *R, It, F, A,* 1998 *F, US, Ur, C, CHL, F,* 1999 *I, Sa, I, F,* 2000 *I, A, A,* 2003 *F, F, Fj, Ur, C, Nm, R, I,* 2005 *SA, S, It,* 2006 *W, W, NZ, CHL, Ur, E, It, F,* 2007 *W, F, Nm, I, S, SA,* 2009 *E, W, S,* 2010 *S, S, F, It, F, I,* 2011 *W, E, R, S, Geo, NZ*
F Schacht 1989 *Bra, CHL, Par, Ur, US,* 1990 *C*
E Scharemberg 1961 *CHL, Bra, Ur,* 1964 *Ur, Bra,* 1965 *Rho, JSB, OCC, OCC,* 1967 *Ur, CHL*
AM Schiavio 1983 *CHL, Ur,* 1986 *A,* 1987 *Fj, It, NZ*
E Schiavio 1936 *BI, CHL, CHL*
H Schierano 2011 *CHL, Ur*
R Schmidt 1960 *F, F, F,* 1961 *Bra,* 1964 *Ur,* 1965 *JSB*
G Schmitt 1964 *Ur, CHL*
G Schulz 2013 *Ur, Bra*
M Schusterman 2003 *Par, Fj,* 2004 *W, W, NZ, F,* 2005 *It, It, SA, S,* 2006 *W, CHL, Ur, E,* 2007 *I, It, Geo*
AA Scolni 1983 *CHL, Par, Ur,* 1985 *F,* 1987 *Sp, A,* 1988 *F, F, F, F,* 1989 *NZ, US,* 1990 *C, US, E, E, I, E, S*
J Seaton 1968 *W, W,* 1969 *Ur, CHL*
R Seaton 1967 *Ur, CHL*
LV Senatore 2011 *Geo, NZ,* 2012 *Ur, Bra, CHL, It, F, SA, SA, NZ, A, A, W, F, I,* 2013 *SA, SA*

H Senillosa 2002 *Ur, Par, CHL*, 2003 *Par, CHL, Ur, F, SA, Fj, US, Nm, R*, 2004 *CHL, Ur, Ven, W, W, NZ, F, I*, 2005 *It, It*, 2006 *CHL, It, F*, 2007 *I, I, F, Geo, Nm, I, S, F*, 2008 *It*
R Serra 1927 *GBR, GBR, GBR*
F Serra Miras 2003 *CHL*, 2005 *J*, 2006 *W, CHL, Ur*, 2007 *I, It, W, Nm*, 2008 *S*
C Serrano 1978 *It*, 1980 *Fj*, 1983 *CHL, Par, Ur*
R Sharpe 1948 *OCC*
HL Silva 1965 *JSB, OCC*, 1967 *Ur, CHL*, 1968 *W, W*, 1969 *S, S, Ur, CHL*, 1970 *I, I*, 1971 *SAG, SAG, OCC, OCC, Ur*, 1978 *E*, 1979 *NZ, NZ, A, A*, 1980 *WXV*
R Silva 1998 *J*
F Silvestre 1988 *F*, 1989 *Bra, Par, Ur, US*, 1990 *C, US*
D Silvetti 1993 *J*
J Simes 1989 *Bra, CHL*, 1990 *C, US*, 1993 *J, J*, 1996 *Ur, F, F, US, C*
HG Simon 1991 *NZ, NZ, A, W, Sa*
E Simone 1996 *US, SA, SA, E*, 1997 *E, E, NZ, NZ, R, F, A, A*, 1998 *F, F, US, Ur, C, J, It, F, W*, 1999 *W, S, I, W, Sa, J, I, F*, 2000 *I, SA*, 2001 *Ur, US, It*, 2002 *Ur, CHL*
A Smidt 2010 *Ur, CHL*
A Soares-Gache 1978 *It*, 1979 *NZ, NZ*, 1981 *C*, 1982 *F, Sp*, 1983 *WXV, A, A*, 1987 *Sp, A, A*, 1988 *F*
T Solari 1996 *Ur, C, SA*, 1997 *E, E, NZ, NZ*
F Soler 1996 *Ur, F, F, SA, SA*, 1997 *E, E, NZ, NZ, Ur, R, It, F*, 1998 *F, F, R, US, C, It, W*, 2001 *Ur, US*, 2002 *Ur, Par, CHL*
JS Soler Valls 1989 *It, Bra, Par, Ur*
H Solveira 1951 *Ur*
J Sommer 1927 *GBR*
E Sorhaburu 1958 *Ur, Per*, 1960 *F*, 1961 *CHL, Ur*
E Spain 1965 *JSB, OCC, OCC, CHL*, 1967 *Ur, CHL*
PL Sporleder 1990 *I, E, S*, 1991 *NZ, NZ, CHL, A, W, Sa*, 1992 *F, F, Sp, Sp, R, F*, 1993 *J, J, Bra, CHL, Par, Ur, SA, SA*, 1994 *US, S, S, US, SA, SA*, 1995 *A, A, E, Sa, It*, 1996 *Ur, F, F, Ur, C, SA, SA, E*, 1997 *E, E, NZ, NZ, Par, Ur, R, It, F, A, A*, 1998 *F, R, US, Ur, C, Ur, It, F, W*, 1999 *W, W, J*, 2002 *Ur, Par, CHL, It, I*, 2003 *Par, CHL, Ur, F, Fj, US, Nm, R*
J Stanfield 1932 *JSB*
J Stewart 1932 *JSB, JSB*
BM Stortoni 1998 *J, Par*, 2001 *Ur, US, C, NZ, It, NZ*, 2002 *Ur, Par, CHL*, 2003 *F, Fj, US*, 2005 *It, It, S, It*, 2007 *I*, 2008 *S, S, It, SA, F, It, I*
J Stuart 2007 *CHL*, 2008 *S, It*
M Sugasti 1995 *Par, CHL*
W Sutton 1936 *CHL*
C Swain 1948 *OCC*, 1949 *F, F*, 1951 *Ur, Bra, CHL*, 1952 *I, I*

J Tagliabue 1936 *CHL, CHL*
L Tahier 1964 *Ur, CHL*
HF Talbot 1910 *GBR*
H Talbot 1936 *BI, CHL, CHL*, 1938 *CHL*
F Talbot 1936 *BI*, 1938 *CHL*
A Tejeda 2008 *S, S, It*
RE Tejerizo 2011 *CHL, Ur*, 2012 *Ur, Bra, CHL*
EG Teran 1977 *Bra, Ur, Par, CHL*, 1979 *CHL, Par, Bra*
G Teran 1988 *F*
MJ Teran 1991 *NZ, NZ, CHL, A, W, Sa*, 1992 *F, Sp, R, F*, 1993 *J, J, Ur, SA, SA*, 1994 *US, S, S, US, SA, SA*, 1995 *A, A, E, Sa, It, Ur, R, It, F*
FN Tetaz Chaparro 2010 *CHL*, 2012 *It, F*
GP Tiesi 2004 *SA*, 2005 *J, It, Sa*, 2006 *W, W, NZ, CHL, Ur, E*, 2007 *Geo, Nm, SA*, 2008 *S, S, F, It*, 2009 *E, E, E, W, S*, 2010 *S, S, F, It, F, I*, 2011 *E*, 2012 *W, F, I*, 2013 *E, E, Geo, A*
FJ Todeschini 1998 *R, Ur*, 2005 *J, It, It, S*, 2006 *W, W, NZ, CHL, Ur, E, It, F*, 2007 *I, W, Geo, Nm*, 2008 *S, S*
A Tolomei 1991 *Par, Bra*, 1993 *Bra, CHL, Par*
N Tompkins 1948 *OCC*, 1949 *F, F*, 1952 *I, I*
JA Topping 1938 *CHL*
E Torello 1983 *Par*, 1989 *CHL*
F Torino 1927 *GBR, GBR*
NC Tozer 1932 *JSB, JSB*
AA Travaglini 1967 *Ur, CHL*, 1968 *W*, 1969 *S, S*, 1970 *I, I*, 1971 *SAG, SAG, OCC, OCC*, 1972 *SAG, SAG*, 1973 *R, Par, Ur, Bra, CHL, I, S*, 1974 *F, F*, 1975 *F, F*, 1976 *W, NZ, NZ*
G Travaglini 1978 *E, It*, 1979 *NZ, NZ, A, A*, 1980 *WXV, Fj, Fj*, 1981 *E, E*, 1982 *F, F, Sp*, 1983 *WXV, A*, 1987 *Ur, Fj, It, NZ*
R Travaglini 1996 *US, Ur, C*, 1997 *NZ, R, F*, 1998 *Ur, C*
J Trucco 1977 *Bra, Ur, Par, CHL*
J Tuculet 2012 *It, F, F, W, F*
A Turner 1932 *JSB, JSB*
FA Turnes 1985 *F, F, Ur, NZ, NZ*, 1986 *F, F, A, A*, 1987 *Ur, Fj, NZ, Sp, A, A*, 1988 *F, F, F, F*, 1989 *It, NZ, NZ*, 1997 *Ur, F, A, A*

G Ugartemendia 1991 *Ur*, 1993 *J, CHL, Par, Ur, SA, SA*, 1994 *US, SA, SA*, 1997 *Ur*, 1998 *Par*, 2000 *E*
M Urbano 1991 *Ur, Bra*, 1995 *Par, CHL, R, It, F*
B Urdapilleta 2007 *CHL*, 2008 *SA*, 2009 *W*, 2010 *Ur*, 2012 *F, F*, 2013 *E, Geo*
EM Ure 1980 *WXV, Fj, Fj*, 1981 *E, E*, 1982 *F, F, Sp*, 1983 *A*, 1985 *F, F, NZ, NZ*, 1986 *F, F, A*
J Uriarte 1986 *A*, 1987 *Par*

E Valesani 1986 *A, A*
MR Valesani 1989 *It, NZ, NZ, CHL, Par, Ur, US*, 1990 *C, US, C*
T Vallejos 2011 *Geo*, 2012 *NZ, W, F, I*, 2013 *E, Geo*
GB Varela 1976 *W, NZ, NZ*, 1977 *F, F*, 1979 *Ur, CHL*
L Varela 1961 *CHL, Bra, Ur*
F Varella 1960 *F*
GM Varone 1982 *F*
C Vazquez 1927 *GBR, GBR, GBR*
A Velazquez 1971 *CHL, Par*
R Ventura 1975 *Ur, Bra, CHL*, 1977 *Bra, Ur*, 1978 *It*, 1979 *Ur, CHL, Par*, 1983 *CHL, Par, Ur*
E Verardo 1958 *CHL*, 1959 *JSB, JSB*, 1964 *Ur, Bra, CHL*, 1967 *Ur, CHL*
N Vergallo 2005 *Sa*, 2006 *CHL, Ur*, 2007 *I, I, CHL*, 2008 *S, S, It, SA, F, It, I*, 2009 *E*, 2010 *F, It, F, I*, 2011 *W, E, R, S, Geo, NZ*, 2012 *SA, SA, NZ, A, NZ, W, I*, 2013 *E, E*
AV Vernet Basualdo 2004 *SA*, 2005 *J*, 2006 *It*, 2007 *I, Geo, Nm, I, F*, 2008 *SA, It*, 2009 *E, E, S*
G Veron 1997 *Par*
M Viazzo 2010 *Ur, CHL*
J Vibart 1960 *F*
H Vidou 1987 *Par*, 1990 *C, US, E, E*, 1991 *NZ*
H Vidou 1960 *F*, 1961 *Bra*
C Viel Temperley 1993 *Bra, CHL, Par, Ur*, 1994 *US, S, S, US, SA, SA*, 1995 *Ur, C, A, A, E, Sa, It, Par, Ur, R, It, F*, 1996 *SA*, 1997 *E, NZ*
E Vila 1975 *Ur, Par, CHL*
M Villaluenga 2013 *CHL, Bra*
JJ Villar 2001 *Ur, US, C*, 2002 *Par, CHL*
D Villen 1998 *J, Par*
M Viola 1993 *Bra*
J Virasoro 1973 *R, R, Ur, Bra, CHL, S*
JL Visca 1985 *Par*

J Walther 1971 *OCC*
M Walther 1967 *Ur, CHL*, 1968 *W, W*, 1969 *S, S, Ur, CHL*, 1970 *I, I*, 1971 *SAG, OCC, OCC*, 1973 *Bra, CHL*, 1974 *F, F*
WA Watson 1910 *GBR*
W Weiss 2011 *Ur*
F Werner 1996 *US*, 1997 *Ur*
Wessek 1960 *F*
R Wilkins 1936 *CHL, CHL*
J Wittman 1971 *SAG, SAG, OCC, OCC, Ur*, 1972 *SAG, SAG*, 1973 *R*

L Yanez 1965 *Rho, JSB, OCC, OCC, CHL*, 1966 *SAG, SAG*, 1968 *W, W*, 1969 *S, S, Ur, CHL*, 1970 *I, I*, 1971 *SAG, OCC, OCC, Ur*
EP Yanguela 1956 *OCC*
M Yanguela 1987 *It*
B Yustini 1954 *F*, 1956 *OCC*

R Zanero 1990 *C*
E Zapiola 1998 *Par*
A Zappa 1927 *GBR*

AUSTRALIA

AUSTRALIA'S 2012–13 TEST RECORD

OPPONENTS	DATE	VENUE	RESULT
New Zealand	20 Oct	H	Drew 18–18
France	10 Nov	A	Lost 33–6
England	17 Nov	A	Won 20–14
Italy	24 Nov	A	Won 22–19
Wales	1 Dec	A	Won 14–12
B&I Lions	22 Jun	H	Lost 21–23
B&I Lions	29 Jun	H	Won 16–15
B&I Lions	6 Jul	H	Lost 16–41
New Zealand	17 Aug	H	Lost 29–47
New Zealand	24 Aug	A	Lost 27–16
South Africa	7 Sep	H	Lost 12–38
Argentina	14 Sep	H	Won 14–13
South Africa	28 Sep	A	Lost 28–8
Argentina	5 Oct	A	Won 54–17

CONSISTENCY AND PRECISION LACKING WHEN IT COUNTED

By Matt Burke

Getty Images

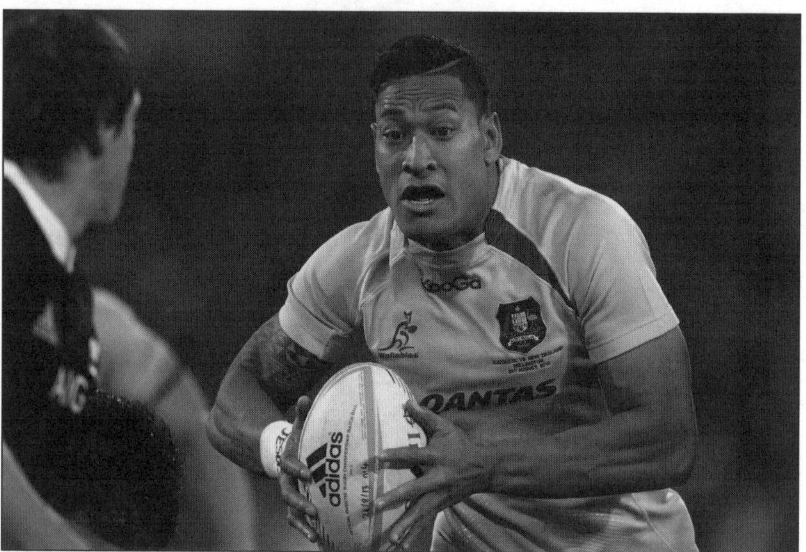

Israel Folau was a revelation for Australia in 2013 against the British & Irish Lions and in The Rugby Championship.

It has been a challenging year for the Wallabies, with a lack of consistency, precision and ability to cope under pressure contributing to mixed results.

The thrill of hosting the British & Irish Lions and their many cheerful and vocal supporters was met with a crushing defeat in the third and deciding Test, while the optimism associated with the appointment of a new coach was followed by a won two, lost four record in The Rugby Championship.

Injuries played their part in the team's performance in 2012/13, but they also provided opportunities for new talent to emerge. One of the highlights was the arrival of utility back Israel Folau, who impressively combines size, speed and power in only his first season of domestic and international rugby following a successful career in Rugby League and Australian Rules Football.

To start the season, a clean sweep was on the menu for the Wallabies'

European tour in November 2012. But a lethargic performance against France meant they were unable to match the precision of Frédéric Michalak's boot or the physicality of Les Bleus.

The English fortress of Twickenham was next and the Wallabies claimed a gutsy 20–14 victory, with Nick Phipps and Nick Cummins combining with impressive passing and running to score an exciting sideline try. The win reclaimed the Cook Cup for the first time in more than three years and gave the team a psychological edge ahead of the Lions tour.

It proved to be a pressure-cooker second half in Florence as Italy came within three points at the 50-minute mark and had the opportunity to tie the match in the final minute with a penalty goal. Luciano Orquera's kick couldn't find the uprights, keeping spirits high in the Australian squad and giving the Wallabies a chance to release a huge sigh of relief.

As a traditional powerhouse of world rugby some people are surprised the Wallabies experience such tight encounters, but teams like Italy and Argentina are physical and gaining confidence, while Australia are unfortunately in a rebuilding phase with plenty of young players who are still adjusting to the pressure of stepping up to the international Test match arena.

Australia had already beaten Wales three times in 2012 during the home Test series and, when the teams met again in December in Cardiff, the Welsh were seeking revenge and had plenty to prove after disappointing results against Argentina, Samoa and New Zealand. The Wallabies, though, were intent on ending stalwart Nathan Sharpe's career on a high.

Down 12–9 with less than a minute to play, and staring at defeat, the Wallabies launched an attacking raid from deep in their own half, with Dave Dennis providing the last pass for Kurtley Beale to secure a dramatic 14–12 victory. This was the ultimate 'get out of jail free card', which saw the Wallabies dig deep and piece together a courageous win.

Next up was the Lions tour, which was monumental with the tourists playing three Tests against the Wallabies, five matches against Australian Super Rugby sides and one against a combined New South Wales-Queensland Country team.

The Lions had plenty to prove following their defeat on Australian soil 12 long years ago. For the Lions, this tour had the incentive of writing the wrongs of that 2001 trip.

With plenty of action on the field, it was that support for the Lions and the incredible spirit of their supporters that made the tour so memorable for everyone involved with cities across Australia awash with red and pubs doing a terrific trade!

From the first Test, the Wallabies' decision not to have any lead-up matches seemed to be ill-advised. The Lions had adjusted to the southern hemisphere with six warm-up matches across the country, and looked fit and ready from the opening whistle in Brisbane.

Two tries from Israel Folau on debut electrified the Aussies in the crowd, but it was the final kick of the match that proved to be crucial. With the Lions leading 23–21, the Wallabies had an opportunity to snatch the win with a penalty in the 79th minute. A slip by Beale as he ran in to kick the penalty had a mixed reaction – with Lions fans overjoyed and Australians wondering what might have been.

The Melbourne fixture a week later became a must-win for Australia and, after being knocked out on debut in the first minute of the opening Test, Christian Leali'ifano showed incredible composure in front of goal and Adam Ashley-Cooper brought life to the series with a 75th-minute try to give the Wallabies a one-point lead which they held onto for the remainder of the game.

The tables were turned from the first Test, with Leigh Halfpenny given an opportunity to kick a penalty in the dying seconds of the match to claim victory and the Tom Richards Cup for the Lions. A tough assignment at halfway and 10 metres infield, the kick was short and presented the Wallabies with a chance to claim the series in Sydney the following week.

Lions coach Warren Gatland's brave decision to replace revered veteran Brian O'Driscoll with Jamie Roberts was a talking point for the third and deciding Test in Sydney. As history now shows, it was an inspired move to ensure the best players took to the field, while Wallabies coach Robbie Deans controversially persevered with the selection of James O'Connor at fly half.

A knock-on from the kick-off by Will Genia meant the Australians were shell-shocked and on the defensive from the first moments of the match, a position they never really recovered from to go down 41–16, much to the delight of the visitors, including Daniel Craig on a special mission to show his support for the Lions.

Put simply, the Wallabies were out-played and out-muscled.

The Lions tour was followed by a swift coaching transition from Robbie Deans after five years at the helm to former Wallaby Ewen McKenzie.

Full of optimism and with plenty to prove for those on and off the field, the Wallabies dared to dream of claiming first blood in the battle for the Bledisloe Cup – for the first time since 2002. But, as is often the case with the All Blacks, Australian dreams of victory were just that – dreams. The Wallabies were out-classed and the defence was soft, letting in six tries to the visitors.

It was a similar situation a week later in Wellington, with the world champions too strong for a Wallabies team with much promise, but little 'big game' experience.

In a theme that reflects the Wallabies' performance throughout the 2012/13 season they showed plenty of energy and effort in Brisbane against the powerful Springboks, but lacked consistency and precision in crucial moments to match their opponents. The 38–12 loss reminded Australia where the Wallabies are placed against the world's best on the rugby ladder.

The match against Argentina in Perth a week later was full of tension with a coach wanting to post his first victory, members of the team keen to cement their positions and a new captain Ben Mowen looking to impress having replaced the injured James Horwill. But it was the pressure of the scrum and driving rain that proved to be the biggest challenges for the Wallabies. However, a brave and strong defensive performance saw the Wallabies maintain a one-point lead and clinch their first victory of The Rugby Championship.

With confidence restored, the Wallabies travelled to Cape Town in late September in an attempt to reverse their recent result against South Africa. Despite showing great resolve and intensity in the opening 10–15 minutes, the Springboks were too powerful, reminding the recently-capped players among the Wallabies what Test-level rugby is all about by recording a 28–8 victory.

The Wallabies travelled to Rosario to face Argentina in the final game of The Rugby Championship. It was the last match for the Los Pumas veteran Felipe Contepomi and emotions were running high for the home side with great expectations to get their first win of the tournament.

With pressure mounting on the Wallaby coaches and players, they produced their best performance of the season. An emphatic seven-try haul ensured the Wallabies finished in third position on The Rugby Championship ladder. It was the first time in this tournament that the Wallabies played with some kind of poise. They executed their attack with width that gave space for the outside backs to relish in attacking rugby. The final score was 54–17 with three tries by Folau.

It's been a year of mixed results for the Wallabies, but there are plenty of reasons for optimism in the year ahead. The players have a terrific opportunity to prove the doubters wrong when they travel for a Grand Slam tour against England, Italy, Ireland, Scotland and Wales in November.

The experiences of the past year will contribute to the team finding greater consistency and precision in key pressure moments on the field in 2013/14. Ensuring there is a balanced team environment off the field will also play a key role to ensure the potential of this new group of Wallabies is fulfilled.

AUSTRALIA INTERNATIONAL STATISTICS

MATCH RECORDS UP TO 10 OCTOBER 2013

MOST CONSECUTIVE TEST WINS

10 1991 *Arg, WS, W, I, NZ, E,* 1992 *S* 1,2, *NZ* 1,2
10 1998 *NZ* 3, *Fj, Tg, Sm, F, E* 2, 1999 *I* 1,2, *E, SA* 1
10 1999 *NZ* 2, *R, I* 3, *US, W, SA* 3, *F,* 2000 *Arg* 1,2, *SA* 1

MOST CONSECUTIVE TESTS WITHOUT DEFEAT

Matches	Wins	Draws	Period
10	10	0	1991 to 1992
10	10	0	1998 to 1999
10	10	0	1999 to 2000

MOST POINTS IN A MATCH BY THE TEAM

Pts	Opponents	Venue	Year
142	Namibia	Adelaide	2003
92	Spain	Madrid	2001
91	Japan	Lyons	2007
90	Romania	Brisbane	2003
76	England	Brisbane	1998
74	Canada	Brisbane	1996
74	Tonga	Canberra	1998
74	Samoa	Sydney	2005
73	W Samoa	Sydney	1994
69	Italy	Melbourne	2005
68	Russia	Nelson	2011
67	United States	Brisbane	1990
67	United States	Wellington	2011

MOST POINTS IN A MATCH BY A PLAYER

Pts	Player	Opponents	Venue	Year
42	MS Rogers	Namibia	Adelaide	2003
39	MC Burke	Canada	Brisbane	1996
30	EJ Flatley	Romania	Brisbane	2003
29	SA Mortlock	South Africa	Melbourne	2000
29	JD O'Connor	France	Paris	2010
28	MP Lynagh	Argentina	Brisbane	1995
27	MJ Giteau	Fiji	Montpellier	2007
25	MC Burke	Scotland	Sydney	1998
25	MC Burke	France	Cardiff	1999
25	MC Burke	British/Irish Lions	Melbourne	2001
25	EJ Flatley*	Ireland	Perth	2003
25	CE Latham	Namibia	Adelaide	2003
24	MP Lynagh	United States	Brisbane	1990
24	MP Lynagh	France	Brisbane	1990
24	MC Burke	New Zealand	Melbourne	1998
24	MC Burke	South Africa	Twickenham	1999

* *includes a penalty try*

MOST TRIES IN A MATCH BY THE TEAM

Tries	Opponents	Venue	Year
22	Namibia	Adelaide	2003
13	South Korea	Brisbane	1987
13	Spain	Madrid	2001
13	Romania	Brisbane	2003
13	Japan	Lyons	2007
12	United States	Brisbane	1990
12	Wales	Brisbane	1991
12	Tonga	Canberra	1998
12	Samoa	Sydney	2005
11	Western Samoa	Sydney	1994
11	England	Brisbane	1998
11	Italy	Melbourne	2005
11	United States	Wellington	2011

BY A PLAYER

Tries	Player	Opponents	Venue	Year
5	CE Latham	Namibia	Adelaide	2003
4	G Cornelsen	New Zealand	Auckland	1978
4	DI Campese	United States	Sydney	1983
4	JS Little	Tonga	Canberra	1998
4	CE Latham	Argentina	Brisbane	2000
4	LD Tuqiri	Italy	Melbourne	2005

MOST CONVERSIONS IN A MATCH

BY THE TEAM

Cons	Opponents	Venue	Year
16	Namibia	Adelaide	2003
12	Spain	Madrid	2001
11	Romania	Brisbane	2003
10	Japan	Lyons	2007
9	Canada	Brisbane	1996
9	Fiji	Parramatta	1998
9	Russia	Nelson	2011
8	Italy	Rome	1988
8	United States	Brisbane	1990
7	Canada	Sydney	1985
7	Tonga	Canberra	1998
7	Samoa	Sydney	2005
7	Italy	Melbourne	2005
7	Fiji	Canberra	2010

BY A PLAYER

Cons	Player	Opponents	Venue	Year
16	MS Rogers	Namibia	Adelaide	2003
11	EJ Flatley	Romania	Brisbane	2003
10	MC Burke	Spain	Madrid	2001
9	MC Burke	Canada	Brisbane	1996
9	JA Eales	Fiji	Parramatta	1998
9	JD O'Connor	Russia	Nelson	2011
8	MP Lynagh	Italy	Rome	1988
8	MP Lynagh	United States	Brisbane	1990
7	MP Lynagh	Canada	Sydney	1985
7	SA Mortlock	Japan	Lyons	2007

MOST DROP GOALS IN A MATCH

BY THE TEAM

Drops	Opponents	Venue	Year
3	England	Twickenham	1967
3	Ireland	Dublin	1984
3	Fiji	Brisbane	1985

BY A PLAYER

Drops	Player	Opponents	Venue	Year
3	PF Hawthorne	England	Twickenham	1967
2	MG Ella	Ireland	Dublin	1984
2	DJ Knox	Fiji	Brisbane	1985

MOST PENALTIES IN A MATCH

BY THE TEAM

Penalties	Opponents	Venue	Year
8	South Africa	Twickenham	1999
7	New Zealand	Sydney	1999
7	France	Cardiff	1999
7	Wales	Cardiff	2001
7	England	Twickenham	2008
6	New Zealand	Sydney	1984
6	France	Sydney	1986
6	England	Brisbane	1988
6	Argentina	Buenos Aires	1997
6	Ireland	Perth	1999
6	France	Paris	2000
6	British/Irish Lions	Melbourne	2001
6	New Zealand	Sydney	2004
6	Italy	Padua	2008
6	New Zealand	Sydney	2009
6	South Africa	Brisbane	2010
6	Italy	Florence	2010
6	Wales	Melbourne	2012
6	Argentina	Rosario	2012
6	New Zealand	Brisbane	2012

BY A PLAYER

Pens	Player	Opponents	Venue	Year
8	MC Burke	South Africa	Twickenham	1999
7	MC Burke	New Zealand	Sydney	1999
7	MC Burke	France	Cardiff	1999
7	MC Burke	Wales	Cardiff	2001
6	MP Lynagh	France	Sydney	1986
6	MP Lynagh	England	Brisbane	1988
6	DJ Knox	Argentina	Buenos Aires	1997
6	MC Burke	France	Paris	2000
6	MC Burke	British/Irish Lions	Melbourne	2001
6	MJ Giteau	England	Twickenham	2008
6	MJ Giteau	New Zealand	Sydney	2009
6	BS Barnes	Italy	Florence	2010
6	MJ Harris	Argentina	Rosario	2012

CAREER RECORDS

MOST CAPPED PLAYERS

Caps	Player	Career Span
139	GM Gregan	1994 to 2007
116	NC Sharpe	2002 to 2012
111	GB Smith	2000 to 2013
102	SJ Larkham	1996 to 2007
101	DI Campese	1982 to 1996
92	MJ Giteau	2002 to 2011
86	JA Eales	1991 to 2001
86	JWC Roff	1995 to 2004
86	AP Ashley-Cooper	2005 to 2013
85	ST Moore	2005 to 2013
81	MC Burke	1993 to 2004
80	TJ Horan	1989 to 2000
80	SA Mortlock	2000 to 2009
79	DJ Wilson	1992 to 2000
79	PR Waugh	2000 to 2009
78	CE Latham	1998 to 2007
75	JS Little	1989 to 2000
75	RD Elsom	2005 to 2011
72	MP Lynagh	1984 to 1995
72	JA Paul	1998 to 2006
69	AKE Baxter	2003 to 2009
67	PN Kearns	1989 to 1999
67	DJ Herbert	1994 to 2002
67	LD Tuqiri	2003 to 2008
63	NC Farr-Jones	1984 to 1993
63	MJ Cockbain	1997 to 2003
63	DJ Vickerman	2002 to 2011
63	DA Mitchell	2005 to 2012
61	BA Robinson	2006 to 2013

MOST CONSECUTIVE TESTS

Tests	Player	Span
62	JWC Roff	1996 to 2001
46	PN Kearns	1989 to 1995
44	GB Smith	2003 to 2006
42	DI Campese	1990 to 1995
37	PG Johnson	1959 to 1968

MOST TESTS AS CAPTAIN

Tests	Captain	Span
59	GM Gregan	2001 to 2007
55	JA Eales	1996 to 2001
36	NC Farr-Jones	1988 to 1992
29	SA Mortlock	2006 to 2009
24	RD Elsom	2009 to 2011
19	AG Slack	1984 to 1987
16	JE Thornett	1962 to 1967
16	GV Davis	1969 to 1972

MOST POINTS IN TESTS

Points	Player	Tests	Career
911	MP Lynagh	72	1984 to 1995
878	MC Burke	81	1993 to 2004
684	MJ Giteau	92	2002 to 2011
489	SA Mortlock	80	2000 to 2009
315	DI Campese	101	1982 to 1996
260	PE McLean	30	1974 to 1982
249*	JW Roff	86	1995 to 2004
223	JD O'Connor	44	2008 to 2013
200	CE Latham	78	1998 to 2007
200	BS Barnes	51	2007 to 2013
187*	EJ Flatley	38	1997 to 2005
173	JA Eales	86	1991 to 2001

** Roff and Flatley's totals include a penalty try*

MOST TRIES IN TESTS

Tries	Player	Tests	Career
64	DI Campese	101	1982 to 1996
40	CE Latham	78	1998 to 2007
31*	JW Roff	86	1995 to 2004
30	TJ Horan	80	1989 to 2000
30	LD Tuqiri	67	2003 to 2008
30	DA Mitchell	63	2005 to 2012
29	MC Burke	81	1993 to 2004
29	SA Mortlock	80	2000 to 2009
29	MJ Giteau	92	2002 to 2011
25	SJ Larkham	102	1996 to 2007
24	BN Tune	47	1996 to 2006
24	AP Ashley-Cooper	86	2005 to 2013
21	JS Little	75	1989 to 2000

** Roff's total includes a penalty try*

MOST CONVERSIONS IN TESTS

Cons	Player	Tests	Career
140	MP Lynagh	72	1984 to 1995
104	MC Burke	81	1993 to 2004
103	MJ Giteau	92	2002 to 2011
61	SA Mortlock	80	2000 to 2009
39	JD O'Connor	44	2008 to 2013
31	JA Eales	86	1991 to 2001
30	EJ Flatley	38	1997 to 2005
27	PE McLean	30	1974 to 1982
27	MS Rogers	45	2002 to 2006
20	JW Roff	86	1995 to 2004
19	DJ Knox	13	1985 to 1997

MOST PENALTY GOALS IN TESTS

Penalties	Player	Tests	Career
177	MP Lynagh	72	1984 to 1995
174	MC Burke	81	1993 to 2004
107	MJ Giteau	92	2002 to 2011
74	SA Mortlock	80	2000 to 2009
62	PE McLean	30	1974 to 1982
34	JA Eales	86	1991 to 2001
34	EJ Flatley	38	1997 to 2005
34	BS Barnes	51	2007 to 2013
25	JD O'Connor	44	2008 to 2013
24	CP Leali'ifano	9	2013 to 2013
23	MC Roebuck	23	1991 to 1993

MOST DROP GOALS IN TESTS

Drops	Player	Tests	Career
9	PF Hawthorne	21	1962 to 1967
9	MP Lynagh	72	1984 to 1995
8	MG Ella	25	1980 to 1984
8	BS Barnes	51	2007 to 2013
4	PE McLean	30	1974 to 1982
4	MJ Giteau	92	2002 to 2011

RUGBY CHAMPIONSHIP (FORMERLY TRI-NATIONS) RECORDS

RECORD	DETAIL	HOLDER	SET
Most points in season	162	in six matches	2010
Most tries in season	17	in six matches	2010
Highest score	54	54–17 v Argentina (a)	2013
Biggest win	49	49–0 v S Africa (h)	2006
Highest score conceded	61	22–61 v S Africa (a)	1997
Biggest defeat	45	8–53 v S Africa (a)	2008
Most appearances	48	GM Gregan	1996 to 2007
Most points in matches	271	MC Burke	1996 to 2004
Most points in season	72	MJ Giteau	2009
Most points in match	24	MC Burke	v N Zealand (h) 1998
Most tries in matches	9	JWC Roff	1996 to 2003
	9	SA Mortlock	2000 to 2009
	9	LD Tuqiri	2003 to 2008
	9	AP Ashley-Cooper	2005 to 2013
Most tries in season	5	I Folau	2013
Most tries in match	3	I Folau	v Argentina (a) 2013
Most cons in matches	36	MJ Giteau	2003 to 2010
Most cons in season	12	SA Mortlock	2006
Most cons in match	5	SA Mortlock	v S Africa (h) 2006
Most pens in matches	65	MC Burke	1996 to 2004
Most pens in season	18	CP Leali'ifano	2013
Most pens in match	7	MC Burke	v N Zealand (h) 1999

MISCELLANEOUS RECORDS

RECORD	HOLDER	DETAIL
Longest Test career	GM Cooke	1932–1948
Youngest Test cap	BW Ford	18 yrs 90 days in 1957
Oldest Test cap	AR Miller	38 yrs 113 days in 1967

CAREER RECORDS OF AUSTRALIAN INTERNATIONAL PLAYERS

UP TO 10 OCTOBER 2013

PLAYER BACKS:	DEBUT	CAPS	T	C	P	D	PTS
AP Ashley-Cooper	2005 v SA	86	24	0	0	0	120
BS Barnes	2007 v J	51	8	17	34	8	200
KJ Beale	2009 v W	39	10	0	12	0	86
QS Cooper	2008 v It	44	6	8	8	1	73
NM Cummins	2012 v Arg	8	2	0	0	0	10
AS Faingaa	2010 v NZ	23	2	0	0	0	10
C Feauai-Sautia	2013 v SA	1	1	0	0	0	5
I Folau	2013 v BI	9	7	0	0	0	35
BT Foley	2013 v Arg	1	1	2	0	0	9
SW Genia	2009 v NZ	49	8	0	0	0	40
MJ Harris	2012 v S	8	1	1	16	0	55
RG Horne	2010 v Fj	15	3	0	0	0	15
DAN Ioane	2007 v W	35	11	0	0	0	55
RTRN Kuridrani	2013 v NZ	4	0	0	0	0	0
CP Leali'ifano	2013 v BI	9	0	7	24	0	86
PJ McCabe	2010 v It	20	4	0	0	0	20
DA Mitchell	2005 v SA	63	30	0	0	0	150
JD Mogg	2013 v BI	3	0	0	0	0	0
LJ Morahan	2012 v S	1	0	0	0	0	0
JD O'Connor	2008 v It	44	14	39	25	0	223
NJ Phipps	2011 v Sm	14	0	0	0	0	0
BR Sheehan	2006 v SA	7	0	0	0	0	0
DP Shipperley	2012 v SA	3	0	0	0	0	0
BNL Tapuai	2011 v W	7	0	0	0	0	0
JM Tomane	2012 v S	5	1	0	0	0	5
MP Toomua	2013 v NZ	6	0	0	0	0	0
NW White	2013 v NZ	6	0	0	0	0	0

FORWARDS:							
BE Alexander	2008 v F	57	4	0	0	0	20
DA Dennis	2012 v S	15	0	0	0	0	0
KP Douglas	2012 v Arg	12	0	0	0	0	0
SM Faingaa	2010 v Fj	25	0	0	0	0	0
SM Fardy	2013 v NZ	6	0	0	0	0	0
LB Gill	2012 v NZ	13	0	0	0	0	0
JE Hanson	2012 v NZ	1	0	0	0	0	0
S Higginbotham	2010 v F	23	2	0	0	0	10
MK Hooper	2012 v S	22	0	0	0	0	0
JE Horwill	2007 v Fj	42	6	0	0	0	30
SM Kepu	2008 v It	32	0	0	0	0	0
BJ McCalman	2010 v SA	26	2	0	0	0	10
HJ McMeniman	2005 v Sm	22	0	0	0	0	0
ST Moore	2005 v Sm	85	5	0	0	0	25
BSC Mowen	2013 v BI	9	0	0	0	0	0
DP Palmer	2012 v S	1	0	0	0	0	0
WL Palu	2006 v E	49	1	0	0	0	5
DW Pocock	2008 v NZ	46	4	0	0	0	20
SUT Polota-Nau	2005 v E	44	2	0	0	0	10
BA Robinson	2006 v SA	61	3	0	0	0	15
PJ Ryan	2012 v F	1	0	0	0	0	0
UR Samo	2004 v S	23	2	0	0	0	10
NC Sharpe	2002 v F	116	8	0	0	0	40
RA Simmons	2010 v SA	32	0	0	0	0	0
ST Sio	2013 v NZ	4	0	0	0	0	0
JA Slipper	2010 v E	43	0	0	0	0	0
GB Smith	2000 v F	111	9	0	0	0	45
S Timani	2011 v Sm	13	0	0	0	0	0

AUSTRALIAN INTERNATIONAL PLAYERS

UP TO 10 OCTOBER 2013

Entries in square brackets denote matches played in RWC Finals.

Abrahams, A M F (NSW) 1967 NZ, 1968 NZ 1, 1969 W
Adams, N J (NSW) 1955 NZ 1
Adamson, R W (NSW) 1912 US
Alexander, B E (ACT) 2008 F1(R), 2(R), It, F3, 2009 It1(R), 2, F(R), NZ1(R), SA1(R), NZ2(t&R), SA2, 3, NZ3, 4, E, I, S, W, 2010 Fj, NZ4, W, E3, It, F, 2011 Sm, SA1, NZ1, SA2, NZ2, [It, I, US, SA, NZ, W(R)], W(R), 2012 S(R), W1(R), 2(R), 3(R), NZ2, SA1, Arg1, SA2, Arg2, E, It, W4, 2013 BI 1, 2, 3, NZ1, 2, SA1(R), Arg1, SA2, Arg2
Allan, T (NSW) 1946 NZ 1, M, NZ 2, 1947 NZ 2, S, I, W, 1948 E, F, 1949 M 1, 2, 3, NZ 1,2
Anderson, R P (NSW) 1925 NZ 1
Anlezark, E A (NSW) 1905 NZ
Armstrong, A R (NSW) 1923 NZ 1,2
Ashley-Cooper, A P (ACT, NSW) 2005 SA4(R), 2007 W1, 2, Fj, SA1(R), NZ1, SA2, NZ2, [J, Fj, C, E], 2008 F1(R), 2, SA1, NZ1, 2, SA3, NZ3, 4, It, E, F3, 2009It1(R), 2(t&R), F, NZ1, SA1, NZ2, SA2, 3, NZ3, 4, E, I, S, W, 2010 Fj, E2(R), I, SA1, NZ1, 2, SA2, 3, NZ3, 4, W, E3, It, F, 2011 Sm, SA1, NZ1, SA2, NZ2, [It, I, US, Ru, SA, NZ, W], W, 2012 W1, 2, 3, NZ1, 2, SA1, Arg1, SA2, NZ3, F, E, It, W4, 2013 BI 1, 2, 3, NZ1, 2, SA1, Arg1, SA2, Arg2
Austin, L R (NSW) 1963 E

Baker, R L (NSW) 1904 BI 1,2
Baker, W H (NSW) 1914 NZ 1,2,3
Ballesty, J P (NSW) 1968 NZ 1,2, F, I, S, 1969 W, SA 2,3,4,
Bannon, D P (NSW) 1946 M
Bardsley, E J (NSW) 1928 NZ 1,3, M (R)
Barker, H S (NSW) 1952 Fj 1,2, NZ 1,2, 1953 SA 4, 1954 Fj 1,2

Barnes, B S (Q, NSW) 2007 [J(R), W, Fj, E], 2008 I, F1, 2, SA1, NZ1, 2, SA2, NZ4(R), It, 2009 It1, 2, F, NZ1, SA1, NZ2, SA3, NZ3, 2010 E1, SA1(R), NZ1, SA3(R), NZ3(t&R), 4(R), W(R), E3(R), It, F, 2011 [US(R), Ru, SA(R), NZ(t&R), W], W, 2012 S, W1, 2, 3, NZ1, 2, SA1, Arg1, SA2, F(R), E, It, W4, 2013 BI 1
Barnett, J T (NSW) 1907 NZ 1,2,3, 1908 W, 1909 E
Barry, M J (Q) 1971 SA 3
Bartholomeusz, M A (ACT) 2002 It (R)
Barton, R F D (NSW) 1899 BI 3
Batch, P G (Q) 1975 S, W, 1976 E, Fj 1,2,3, F 1,2, 1978 W 1,2, NZ 1,2,3, 1979 Arg 2
Batterham, R P (NSW) 1967 NZ, 1970 S
Battishall, B R (NSW) 1973 E
Baxter, A J (NSW) 1949 M 1,2,3, NZ 1,2, 1951 NZ 1,2, 1952 NZ 1,2
Baxter, A K E (NSW) 2003 NZ 2(R), [Arg, R, I(R), S(R), NZ(R), E], 2004 S1, 2, E1, PI, NZ1, SA1, NZ2, SA2, S3, F, S4, E2, 2005 It, F1, SA1, 2, 3(R), NZ1, SA4, NZ2, F2, E, I(R), W(R), 2006 E1(R), 2(R), I1(R), NZ1(R), SA1(R), NZ3(R), SA3(R), W, It, I2, S(R), 2007 Fj, SA1(R), NZ1(R), SA2(R), NZ2(R), [J, W(R), C, E(R)], 2008 I(R), F1, 2, SA1, NZ1, 2, SA2(R), 3(R), NZ3, 4, E, F3, W, 2009 It1, F, NZ1, SA1, NZ2
Baxter, T J (Q) 1958 NZ 3
Beale, K J (NSW, MR) 2009 W(R), 2010 Fj, E1(R), I(R), NZ1(R), 2, SA2, 3, NZ3, 4, W, E3, It, F, 2011 Sm(R), SA1, NZ1, SA2, NZ2, [It, I, US, SA, W], 2012 W3, NZ1, 2(R), SA1, Arg1(t&R), SA2, Arg2, NZ3, F, E, It, W4, 2013 BI 1(R), 2, 3
Beith, B McN (NSW) 1914 NZ 3, 1920 NZ 1, 2, 3
Bell, K R (Q) 1968 S
Bell, M D NSW) 1996 C
Bennett, W G (Q) 1931 M, 1933 SA 1,2,3,
Bermingham, J V (Q) 1934 NZ 1, 2, 1937 SA 1
Berne, J E (NSW) 1975 S
Besomo, K S (NSW) 1979 I 2
Betts, T N (Q) 1951 NZ 2, 3, 1954 Fj 2
Biilmann, R R (NSW) 1933 SA 1,2,3,4
Birt, R S W (Q) 1914 NZ 2
Black, J W (NSW) 1985 C 1,2, NZ, Fj 1
Blackwood, J G (NSW) 1922 M 1, NZ 1, 2, 3, 1923 M 1, NZ 1, 2, 3, 1924 NZ 1,2,3, 1925 NZ 1, 4, 1926 NZ 1, 2, 3, 1927 I, W, S, 1928 E, F
Blades, A T (NSW) 1996 S, I, W 3, 1997 NZ 1(R), E 1(R), SA 1(R), NZ 3, SA 2, Arg 1,2, E 2, S, 1998 E 1, S 1,2, NZ 1, SA 1, NZ 2, SA 2, NZ 3, Fj, WS, F, E 2, 1999 I 1(R), SA 2, NZ 2, [R, I 3, W, SA 3, F]
Blades, C D (NSW) 1997 E 1
Blake, R C (Q) 2006 E1,2, NZ2,SA2,NZ3,SA3,W
Blair, M R (NSW) 1928 F, 1931 M, NZ
Bland, G V (NSW) 1928 NZ 3, M, 1932 NZ 1,2,3, 1933 SA 1,2,4,5
Blomley, J (NSW) 1949 M 1,2,3, NZ 1,2, 1950 BI 1,2
Boland, S B (Q) 1899 BI 3,4, 1903 NZ
Bond, G S G (ACT) 2001 SA 2(R), Sp (R), E (R), F, W
Bond, J H (NSW) 1920 NZ 1,2,3, 1921 NZ
Bondfield, C (NSW) 1925 NZ 2
Bonis, E T (Q) 1929 NZ 1, 2, 3, 1930 BI, 1931 M, NZ, 1932 NZ 1,2,3, 1933 SA 1, 2, 3, 4, 5, 1934 NZ 1, 2, 1936 NZ 1, 2, M, 1937 SA 1, 1938 NZ 1
Bonner, J E (NSW) 1922 NZ 1,2,3, 1923 M 1,2,3, 1924 NZ 1,2
Bosler, J M (NSW) 1953 SA 1
Bouffler, R G (NSW) 1899 BI 3
Bourke, T K (Q) 1947 NZ 2
Bowden, R (NSW) 1926 NZ 4
Bowen, S (NSW) 1993 SA 1, 2, 3, 1995 [R], NZ 1, 2, 1996 C, NZ 1, SA 2
Bowers, A J A (NSW) 1923 M 2(R),3, NZ, 3, 1925 NZ 1,4, 1926 NZ 1, 1927 I
Bowman, T M (NSW) 1998 E 1, S 1,2, NZ 1, SA 1, NZ 2, SA 2, NZ 3, Fj, WS, F, E 2, 1999 I 1,2, SA 2, [US]
Boyce, E S (NSW) 1962 NZ 1,2, 1964 NZ 1,2,3, 1965 SA 1,2, 1966 W, S, 1967 E, I 1, F, I 2
Boyce, J S (NSW) 1962 NZ 3,4,5, 1963 E, SA 1,2,3,4, 1964 NZ 1,3, 1965 SA 1,2
Boyd, A (NSW) 1899 BI 3
Boyd, A F McC (Q) 1958 M 1
Brass, J E (NSW) 1966 BI 2, W, S, 1967 E, I 1, F, I 2, NZ, 1968 NZ 1, F, I, S
Breckenridge, J W (NSW) 1925 NZ 2(R),3, 1927 I, W, S, 1928 E, F, 1929 NZ 1,2,3, 1930 BI
Brial, M C (NSW) 1993 F 1(R), 2, 1996 W 1(R), 2, C, NZ 1, SA 1, NZ 2, SA 2, It, I, W 3, 1997 NZ 2
Bridle, O L (V) 1931 M, 1932 NZ 1,2,3, 1933 SA 3,4,5, 1934 NZ 1,2, 1936 NZ 1,2, M
Broad, E G (Q) 1949 M 1
Brockhoff, J D (NSW) 1949 M 2,3, NZ 1,2, 1950 BI 1,2, 1951 NZ 2,3
Brown, B R (Q) 1972 NZ 1,3
Brown, J V (NSW) 1956 SA 1,2, 1957 NZ 1,2, 1958 W, I, E, S, F
Brown, R C (NSW) 1975 E 1,2
Brown, R N (WF) 2008 NZ3(R), 4, It, E, W, 2009 It1, F, NZ1, SA1, NZ2, SA2, S(R), 2010 Fj, E1, 2, I, SA1, NZ1, 2, SA2, 3(R), NZ3(R), E3(R)
Brown, S W (NSW) 1953 SA 2,3,4
Bryant, H (NSW) 1925 NZ 1,3,4
Buchan, A J (NSW) 1946 NZ 1,2, 1947 NZ 1,2, S, I, W, 1948 E, F, 1949 M 3
Buchanan, P N (NSW) 1923 M 2(R),3
Bull, D (NSW) 1928 M
Buntine, H (NSW) 1923 NZ 1(R), 1924 NZ 2
Burdon, A (NSW) 1903 NZ, 1904 BI 1,2, 1905 NZ
Burge, A B (NSW) 1907 NZ 3, 1908 W
Burge, P H (NSW) 1907 NZ 1,2,3
Burge, R (NSW) 1928 NZ 1,2,3(R), M (R)
Burgess, L (NSW) 2008 I, F1, 2, SA1, NZ1, 2, 4, It, E, F3, W, 2009 It1, 2, F, NZ1, SA1, NZ2, SA2, NZ3(R), S(R), W(R), 2010 Fj, E1, I, NZ1(R), SA3(R), NZ3(R), 4(R), W(R), E3(R), It, F(R), 2011 NZ2(R), [It(R), US(R), Ru, W(R)]
Burke, B T (NSW) 1988 S (R)
Burke, C T (NSW) 1946 NZ 2, 1947 NZ 1,2, S, I, W, 1948 E, F, 1949 M 2,3, NZ 1,2, 1950 BI 1,2, 1951 NZ 1, 2, 3, 1953 SA 2, 3, 4, 1954 Fj 1, 1955 NZ 1, 2, 3, 1956 SA 1, 2,
Burke, M C (NSW) 1993 SA 3(R), F 1, 1994 I 1,2, It 1,2, 1995 [C, R, E], NZ 1,2, 1996 W 1,2, C, NZ 1, SA 1, NZ 2, SA 2, It, S, I, W 3, 1997 E 1, NZ 2 , 1998 E 1, S 1,2, NZ 1, SA 1, NZ 2, SA 2, NZ 3, 1999 I 2(R), E (R), SA 1, NZ 1, SA 2, NZ 2, [R, I 3, US, W, SA 3, F], 2000 F, S, E, 2001 BI 1(R),2,3, SA 1, NZ 1, SA 2, NZ 2, Sp, E, F, W, 2002 F 1,2, NZ 1, SA 1, NZ 2, SA 2, Arg, I, E, It, 2003 SA 1, NZ 1, SA 2(R), NZ 2(R), [Arg,R, Nm(R), I], 2004 S1(R), PI(R), SA1(R), NZ2(t&R), SA2(R)
Burke, M P (NSW) 1984 E (R), I, 1985 C 1,2, NZ, Fj 1,2, 1986 It (R), F, Arg 1, 2, NZ 1, 2, 3, 1987 SK, [US, J, I, F, W], NZ, Arg 1, 2
Burnet, D R (NSW) 1972 F 1,2, NZ 1,2,3, Fj
Butler, O F (NSW) 1969 SA 1,2, 1970 S, 1971 SA 2,3, F 1,2

Calcraft, W J (NSW) 1985 C 1, 1986 It, Arg 2
Caldwell, B C (NSW) 1928 NZ 3
Cameron, A S (NSW) 1951 NZ 1, 2, 3, 1952 Fj 1, 2, NZ 1, 2, 1953 SA 1, 2, 3, 4, 1954 Fj 1, 2, 1955 NZ 1,2,3, 1956 SA 1, 2, 1957 NZ 1, 1958 I
Campbell, A M (ACT) 2005 F1(R), 2006 It(R),I2(R),S
Campbell, J D (NSW) 1910 NZ 1,2,3
Campbell, W A (Q) 1984 Fj, 1986 It, F, Arg 1,2, NZ 1,2,3, 1987 SK, [E, US, J (R), I, F], NZ, 1988 E, 1989 BI 1,2,3, NZ, 1990 NZ 2,3
Campese, D I (ACT, NSW) 1982 NZ 1,2,3, 1983 US, Arg 1,2, NZ, It, F 1,2, 1984 Fj, NZ 1,2,3, E, I, W, S, 1985 Fj 1,2, 1986 It, F, Arg 1,2, NZ 1,2,3, 1987 [E, US, J, I, F, W], NZ, 1988 E 1,2, NZ 1,2,3, E, S, It, 1989 BI 1,2,3, NZ, F 1,2, 1990 F 2,3, US, NZ 1,2,3, 1991 W, E, NZ 1,2, [Arg, WS, W, I, NZ, E], 1992 S 1,2, NZ 1,2,3, SA, I, W, 1993 Tg, NZ, SA 1,2,3, C, F 1,2, 1994 I 1,2, It 1,2, WS, NZ, 1995 Arg 1,2, [SA, C, E], NZ 2(R), 1996 W 1,2, C, NZ 1, SA 1, NZ 2, SA 2, It, W3
Canniffe, W D (Q) 1907 NZ 2
Cannon, B J (NSW, WF) 2001 BI 2(R), NZ 1(R), Sp (R), F (R), W (R), 2002 F 1(R), 2, SA 1(t), 2(R), I (t), It (R), 2003 I (R), W (R), E (R), SA 1, NZ 1, SA 2, NZ 2, [Arg, R, I, S, NZ, E], 2004 S1, 2, E1, PI, NZ1, 2, SA2, S3(R), 4(R), 2005 NZ1(R), SA4, NZ2, F2, E, I, W, 2006 W(R), It
Caputo, M E (ACT) 1996 W 1,2, 1997 F 1,2, NZ 1
Carberry, C M (NSW, Q) 1973 Tg 2, E, 1976 I, US, Fj 1,2,3, 1981 F 1,2, I, W, S, 1982 E
Cardy, A M (NSW) 1966 BI 1,2, W, S, 1967 E, I 1, F, 1968 NZ 1,2
Carew, P J (Q) 1899 BI 1,2,3,4
Carmichael, P (Q) 1904 BI 2, 1907 NZ 1, 1908 W, 1909 E
Carozza, P V (Q) 1990 F 1,2,3, NZ 2,3, 1992 S 1,2, NZ 1,2,3, SA, I, W, 1993 Tg, NZ
Carpenter, M G (V) 1938 NZ 1,2,
Carr, E T A (NSW) 1913 NZ 1,2,3, 1914 NZ 1,2,3
Carr, E W (NSW) 1921 SA 1,2,3, NZ (R)
Carroll, D B (NSW) 1908 W, 1912 US

Carroll, J C (NSW) 1953 SA 1
Carroll, J H (NSW) 1958 M 2,3, NZ 1,2,3, 1959 BI 1,2
Carson, J (NSW) 1899 BI 1
Carson, P J (NSW) 1979 NZ, 1980 NZ 3
Carter, D G (NSW) 1988 E 1,2, NZ 1, 1989 F 1,2
Casey, T V (NSW) 1963 SA 2,3,4, 1964 NZ 1,2,3
Catchpole, K W (NSW) 1961 Fj 1,2,3, SA 1,2, F, 1962 NZ 1,2,4, 1963 SA 2,3,4, 1964 NZ 1,2,3, 1965 SA 1,2, 1966 BI 1,2, W, S, 1967 E, I 1, F, I 2, NZ, 1968 NZ 1
Cawsey, R M (NSW) 1949 M 1, NZ 1,2
Cerutti, W H (NSW) 1928 NZ 1,2,3, M, 1929 NZ 1,2,3, 1930 BI, 1931 M, NZ, 1932 NZ 1,2,3, 1933 SA 1,2,3,4,5, 1936 M, 1937 SA 1,2
Challoner, R L (NSW) 1899 BI 2
Chambers, R (NSW) 1920 NZ 1,3
Chapman, G A (NSW) 1962 NZ 3,4,5
Chisholm, M D (ACT) 2004 S3(R), 2005 Sm, It, F1, SA1, 2, 3(R), NZ1(R), 2, F2, E(t&R), I(R), W(R), 2006 E1(R), 2, I1, NZ1, SA1(R), NZ2(R), SA2(R), NZ3(t&R), SA3(R), W(R), It, I2, S(t&R), 2007 W1, 2(R), Fj, SA1(R), NZ1(R), 2(R), [W(R), Fj, C], 2008 NZ4, It, E, F3(R), W, 2009 SA2, 3, NZ3, 4, E, I, S, W(R), 2010 E1(R),2(R), I, SA3, NZ3, 4, W, E3, It(R), F(R)
Clark, J G (Q) 1931 M, NZ, 1932 NZ 1, 2, 1933 SA 1
Clarken, J C (NSW) 1905 NZ, 1910 NZ 1, 2, 3
Cleary, M A (NSW) 1961 Fj 1, 2, 3, SA 1,2, F
Clements, P (NSW) 1982 NZ 3
Clifford, M (NSW) 1938 NZ 3
Cobb, W G (NSW) 1899 BI 3,4
Cockbain, M J (Q) 1997 F 2(R), NZ 1, SA 1,2, 1998 E 1, S 1,2, NZ 1, SA 1, NZ 2, SA 2, NZ 3, Fj, Tg (R), WS, F, E 2, 1999 I 1,2, E, SA 1, NZ 1, SA 2, NZ 2, [US (t&R), W, SA 3, F], 2000 Arg 1,2, SA 2(t&R),3(t&R), F, S, E (R), 2001 BI 1(R),2(R),3(R), SA 1(R), NZ 1(R), SA 2(R), NZ 2(R), Sp (R), E (R), F (t+R), W, 2002 F 1(R),2(R), NZ 1(R), SA 1(R), NZ 2(R), SA 2(R), Arg, I, E, It, 2003 [Arg(R), R(R), Nm(R), I(R), S(R), NZ(R), E(R)]
Cocks, M R (NSW, Q) 1972 F 1,2, NZ 2,3, Fj, 1973 Tg 1,2, W, E, 1975 J 1
Codey, D (NSW Country, Q) 1983 Arg 1, 1984 E, W, S, 1985 C 2, NZ, 1986 F, Arg 1, 1987 [US, J, F (R), W], NZ
Cody, E W (NSW) 1913 NZ 1,2,3
Coker, T (Q, ACT) 1987 [E, US, F, W], 1991 NZ 2, [Arg, WS, NZ, E], 1992 NZ 1,2,3, W (R), 1993 Tg, NZ, 1995 Arg 2, NZ 1(R), 1997 F 1(R), 2, NZ 1, E 1, NZ 2(R), SA 1(R), NZ 3, SA 2, Arg 1,2
Colbert, R (NSW) 1952 Fj 2, NZ 1,2, 1953 SA 2,3,4
Cole, J W (NSW) 1968 NZ 1,2, F, I, S, 1969 W, SA 1,2,3,4, 1970 S, 1971 SA 1,2,3, F 1,2, 1972 NZ 1,2,3, 1973 Tg 1,2, 1974 NZ 1,2,3
Collins, P K (NSW) 1937 SA 2, 1938 NZ 2,3
Colton, A J (Q) 1899 BI 1,3
Colton, T (Q) 1904 BI 1,2
Comrie-Thomson, I R (NSW) 1926 NZ 4, 1928 NZ 1,2,3 M
Connor, D M (Q) 1958 W, I, E, S, F, M 2,3, NZ 1,2,3, 1959 BI 1,2
Connors, M R (Q) 1999 SA 1(R), NZ 1(R), SA 2(R), NZ 2, [R (R), I 3, US, W (R), SA 3(R), F(R)], 2000 Arg 1(R),2(R), SA 1, NZ 1, SA 2, NZ 2(t&R), SA 3, F (R), S (R), E (R)
Constable, R (Q) 1994 I 2(t & R)
Cook, M T (Q) 1986 F, 1987 SK, [J], 1988 E 1,2, NZ 1,2,3, E, S, It
Cooke, B P (Q) 1979 I 1
Cooke, G M (Q) 1932 NZ 1,2,3, 1933 SA 1,2,3, 1946 NZ 2, 1947 NZ 2, S, I, W, 1948 E, F
Coolican, J E (NSW) 1982 NZ 1, 1983 It, F 1,2
Cooney, R C (NSW) 1922 M 2
Cooper, Q S (Q) 2008 It(R), F3(R), W(R), 2009 It1(R), 2, SA2(R), 3(R), E, I, S, W, 2010 Fj, E1, 2, I, SA1, 2, 3, NZ3, 4, W, E3, It, F, 2011 SA1, NZ1, SA2, NZ2, [It, I, US, Ru, SA, NZ, W], 2012 NZ2, SA1, Arg1, 2013 NZ1(R), 2(R), SA1, Arg1, SA2, Arg2
Cordingley, S J (Q, Grenoble) 2000 Arg 1(R), SA 1(R), F, S, E, 2006 E2, I1(R), NZ1(R), SA1(R), NZ2(R), SA2(R), 2007 Fj(R), [Fj(R), C], 2008 I(R), F1(R), 2(t&R), SA1(R), 2, 3, NZ3, F3(R)
Corfe, A C (Q) 1899 BI 2
Cornelsen, G (NSW) 1974 NZ 2,3, 1975 J 2, S, W, 1976 E, F 1,2, 1978 W 1,2, NZ 1,2,3, 1979 I 1,2, NZ, Arg 1,2, 1980 NZ 1,2,3, 1981 I, W, S, 1982 E
Cornes, J R (Q) 1972 Fj
Cornforth, R G W (NSW) 1947 NZ 1, 1950 BI 2
Cornish, P (ACT) 1990 F 2,3, NZ 1
Costello, P P S (Q) 1950 BI 2
Cottrell, N V (Q) 1949 M 1,2,3, NZ 1,2, 1950 BI 1,2, 1951 NZ 1,2,3, 1952 Fj 1,2, NZ 1,2
Cowan, P J M (WF) 2009 It2,SA3(R),NZ3(R), 2010 Fj(R), 2011 SA1(R)
Cowper, D L (V) 1931 NZ, 1932 NZ 1,2,3, 1933 SA 1,2,3,4,5
Cox, B P (NSW) 1952 Fj 1,2, NZ 1,2, 1954 Fj 2, 1955 NZ 1, 1956 SA 2, 1957 NZ 1,2
Cox, M H (NSW) 1981 W, S
Cox, P A (NSW) 1979 Arg 1,2, 1980 Fj, NZ 1,2, 1981 W (R), S, 1982 S 1,2, NZ 1,2,3, 1984 Fj, NZ 1,2,3
Craig, R R (NSW) 1908 W
Crakanthorp, J S (NSW) 1923 NZ 3
Cremin, J F (NSW) 1946 NZ 1,2, 1947 NZ 1
Crittle, C P (NSW) 1962 NZ 4,5, 1963 SA 2,3,4, 1964 NZ 1,2,3, 1965 SA 1,2, 1966 BI 1,2, S, 1967 E, I
Croft, B H D (NSW) 1928 M
Croft, D N (Q) 2002 Arg (t&R), I (R), E (t&R), It (R), 2003 [Nm]
Cross, J R (NSW) 1955 NZ 1,2,3
Cross, K A (NSW) 1949 M 1, NZ 1,2, 1950 BI 1,2, 1951 NZ 2,3, 1952 NZ 1, 1953 SA 1,2,3,4, 1954 Fj 1,2, 1955 NZ 3, 1956 SA 1,2, 1957 NZ 1,2
Cross, R P (WF) 2008 F1(R), 2(R), SA1(R), NZ1, 2(R), SA2(R), 3(R), NZ3, 4, E, W, 2009 It2, F(R), NZ2(R), SA2, NZ4, E(R), S
Crossman, O C (NSW) 1923 M 1(R),2,3, 1924, NZ 1,2,3, 1925 NZ 1,3,4, 1926 NZ 1,2,3,4, 1929 NZ 2, 1930 BI
Crowe, P J (NSW) 1976 F 2, 1978 W 1,2, 1979 I 2, NZ, Arg 1
Crowley, D J (Q) 1989 BI 1,2,3, 1991 [WS], 1992 I, W, 1993 C (R), 1995 Arg 1,2, [SA, E], NZ 1, 1996 W 2(R), C, NZ 1, SA 1,2, I, W 3, 1998 E 1(R), S 1(R),2(R), NZ 1(R), SA 1, NZ 2, SA 2, NZ 3, Tg, WS, 1999 I 1,2(R), E (R), SA 1, NZ 1(R), [R (R), I 3(t&R), US, F(R)]
Cummins, N M (WF) 2012 Arg2,NZ3,F,E,It,W4, 2013 SA1,Arg1
Curley, T G P (NSW) 1957 NZ 1,2, 1958 W, I, E, S, F, M 1, NZ 1,2,3
Curran, D J (NSW) 1980 NZ 3, 1981 F 1,2, W, 1983 Arg 1
Currie, E W (Q) 1899 BI 2
Cutler, S A G (NSW) 1982 NZ 2(R), 1984 NZ 1, 2, 3, E, I, W, S, 1985 C 1, 2, NZ, Fj 1, 2, 1986 It, F, NZ 1, 2, 3, 1987 SK, [E, J, I, F, W], NZ, Arg 1, 2, 1988 E 1, 2, NZ 1, 2, 3, E, S, It, 1989 BI 1, 2, 3, NZ, 1991 [WS]

Daley, B P (Q) 2010 E1,2,I
Daly, A J (NSW) 1989 NZ, F 1,2, 1990 F 1,2,3, US, NZ 1,2,3, 1991 W, E, NZ 1,2, [Arg, W, I, NZ, E], 1992 S 1,2, NZ 1,2,3, SA, 1993 Tg, NZ, SA 1,2,3, C, F 1,2, 1994 I 1,2, It 1,2, WS, NZ, 1995 [C, R]
D'Arcy, A M (Q) 1980 Fj, NZ 3, 1981 F 1,2, I, W, S, 1982 E, S 1,2
Darveniza, P (NSW) 1969 W, SA 2,3,4
Darwin, B J (ACT) 2001 BI 1(R), SA 1(R), NZ 1(R), SA 2(R), NZ 2(t&R), Sp, E, F, W, 2002 NZ 1(R), SA 1(R), NZ 2(R), SA 2, Arg (R), I (R), E (R), It (R), 2003 I (R), W (t&R), E (R), SA 1(R), NZ 1(R), [Arg(R), R(R), Nm, I, S, NZ]
Davidson, R A L (NSW) 1952 Fj 1,2, NZ 1,2, 1953 SA 1, 1957 NZ 1,2, 1958 W, I, E, S, F, M 1
Davies, R W (Q) 2011 Sm
Davis, C C (NSW) 1949 NZ 1, 1951 NZ 1,2,3
Davis, E H (V) 1947 S, W, 1949 M 1,2
Davis, G V (NSW) 1963 E, SA 1,2,3,4, 1964 NZ 1,2,3, 1965 SA 1, 1966 BI 1,2, W, S, 1967 E, I 1, F, I 2, NZ, 1968 NZ 1,2, F, I, S, 1969 W, SA 1,2,3,4, 1970 S, 1971 SA 1,2,3, F 1,2, 1972 F 1,2, NZ 1,2,3
Davis, G W G (NSW) 1955 NZ 2,3
Davis, R A (NSW) 1974 NZ 1,2,3
Davis, T S R (NSW) 1920 NZ 1,2,3, 1921 SA 1,2,3, NZ, 1922 M 1,2,3, NZ 1,2,3, 1923 M 3, NZ 1,2,3, 1924 NZ 1,2, 1925 NZ 1
Davis, W (NSW) 1899 BI 1,3,4
Dawson, W L (NSW) 1946 NZ 1,2
Dennis, D A (NSW) 2012 S, W1(R), 2(R), 3(R), NZ1, 2, SA1, Arg1, SA2, Arg2(R), NZ3(R), F, E, It(R), W4(R)
Diett, L J (NSW) 1959 BI 1,2
Dix, W (NSW) 1907 NZ 1,2,3, 1909 E
Dixon, E J (Q) 1904 BI 3
Donald, K J (Q) 1957 NZ 1, 1958 W, I, E, S, M 2, 3, 1959 BI 1,2
Dore, E (Q) 1904 BI 1
Dore, M J (Q) 1905 NZ
Dorr, R W (V) 1936 M, 1937 SA 1
Douglas, J A (V) 1962 NZ 3,4,5
Douglas, K P (NSW) 2012 Arg1, SA2, Arg2, NZ3(R), F, W4, 2013 BI 1, 2, 3, NZ2(R), SA1, Arg1

Douglas, W A (NSW) 1922 NZ 3(R)
Dowse, J H (NSW) 1961 Fj 1,2, SA 1,2
Dunbar, A R (NSW) 1910 NZ 1,2,3, 1912 US
Duncan, J L (NSW) 1926 NZ 4
Dunlop, E E (V) 1932 NZ 3, 1934 NZ 1
Dunn, P K (NSW) 1958 NZ 1,2,3, 1959 BI 1,2
Dunn, V A (NSW) 1920 NZ 1,2,3, 1921 SA 1,2,3, NZ
Dunning, M J (NSW, WF) 2003 [Nm,E(R)], 2004 S1(R), 2(R), E1(R), NZ1(R), SA1(R), NZ2(t&R), SA2(R), S3(R), F(R), S4(R), E2(R), 2005 Sm, It(R), F1(t&R), SA1(R), 2(R), 3, NZ1(t&R), SA4(t&R), NZ2(R), F2, E, W, 2007 W1, 2(R), Fj, SA1, NZ1, SA2, NZ2, [J, W, Fj, E], 2008 I, SA1(R), NZ1(R), SA2, 3, NZ4(R), It, 2009 E(R), W(R)
Dunworth, D A (Q) 1971 F 1,2, 1972 F 1,2, 1976 Fj 2
Dwyer, L J (NSW) 1910 NZ 1, 2, 3, 1912 US, 1913 NZ 3, 1914 NZ 1, 2, 3
Dyson, F J (Q) 2000 Arg 1, 2, SA 1, NZ 1, SA 2, NZ 2, SA 3, F, S, E

Eales, J A (Q) 1991 W, E, NZ 1,2, [Arg, WS, W, I, NZ, E], 1992 S 1,2, NZ 1,2,3, SA, I, 1994 I 1,2, It 1,2, WS, NZ, 1995 Arg 1,2, [SA, C, R, E], NZ 1,2, 1996 W 1,2, C, NZ 1, SA 1, NZ 2, SA 2, It, S, I, 1997 F 1,2, NZ 1, E 1, NZ 2, SA 1, Arg 1,2, E 2, S, 1998 E 1, S 1,2, NZ 1, SA 1, NZ 2, SA 2, NZ 3, Fj, Tg, WS, F, E 2, 1999 [R, I 3, W, SA 3, F], 2000 Arg 1,2, SA 1, NZ 1, SA 2, NZ 2, SA 3, F, S, E, 2001 BI 1,2,3, SA 1, NZ 1, SA 2, NZ 2
Eastes, C C (NSW) 1946 NZ 1,2, 1947 NZ 1,2, 1949 M 1,2
Edmonds, H (ACT) 2010 Fj,E1(R),2(R),W(R)
Edmonds, M H M (NSW) 1998 Tg, 2001 SA 1(R)
Egerton, R H (NSW) 1991 W, E, NZ 1,2, [Arg, W, I, NZ, E]
Ella, G A (NSW) 1982 NZ 1,2, 1983 F 1,2, 1988 E 2, NZ 1
Ella, G J (NSW) 1982 S 1, 1983 It, 1985 C 2(R), Fj 2
Ella, M G (NSW) 1980 NZ 1,2,3, 1981 F 2, S, 1982 E, S 1, NZ 1,2,3, 1983 US, Arg 1,2, NZ, It, F 1,2, 1984 Fj, NZ 1,2,3, E, I, W, S
Ellem, M A (NSW) 1976 Fj 3(R)
Elliott, F M (NSW) 1957 NZ 1
Elliott, R E (NSW) 1920 NZ 1, 1921 NZ, 1922 M 1,2, NZ 1(R),2,3, 1923 M 1,2,3, NZ 1,2,3
Ellis, C S (NSW) 1899 BI 1,2,3,4
Ellis, K J (NSW) 1958 NZ 1,2,3, 1959 BI 1,2
Ellwood, B J (NSW) 1958 NZ 1,2,3, 1961 Fj 2,3, SA 1, F, 1962 NZ 1,2,3,4,5, 1963 SA 1,2,3,4, 1964 NZ 3, 1965 SA 1,2, 1966 BI 1
Elsom, R D (NSW, ACT) 2005 Sm, It, F1, SA1, 2, 3(R), 4, NZ2, F2, 2006 E1, 2, I1, NZ1, SA1, NZ2, SA2, NZ3, SA3, W, It, I2, S, 2007 W1, 2, SA1, NZ1, SA2, NZ2, [J, W, Fj, E], 2008 I, F1, 2, SA1, NZ1, SA2, 3, NZ3, 2009 NZ2, SA2, 3, NZ3, 4, E, I, S, W, 2010 Fj, E1, 2,I, SA1, NZ1, 2, SA2, 3, NZ3, 4, W, E3, It, F, 2011 Sm, SA1, NZ1, SA2, NZ2, [It, I, US, Ru(R), SA, NZ]
Emanuel, D M (NSW) 1957 NZ 2, 1958 W, I, E, S, F, M 1,2,3
Emery, N A (NSW) 1947 NZ 2, S, I, W, 1948 E, F, 1949 M 2,3, NZ 1,2
Erasmus, D J (NSW) 1923 NZ 1,2
Erby, A B (NSW) 1923 M 1,2, NZ 2,3, 1925 NZ 2
Evans, L J (Q) 1903 NZ, 1904 BI 1,3
Evans, W T (Q) 1899 BI 1,2

Fahey, E J (NSW) 1912 US, 1913 NZ 1,2, 1914 NZ 3
Faingaa, A S (Q) 2010 NZ1(R), 2, SA3(R), NZ3(R), 2011 SA1(R), 2(R), NZ2, [It, I, US, SA(R), NZ, W(R)], W, 2012 S, W1(t&R), 2(R), 3(R), NZ1, 2(R), SA1(R), Arg1(R), SA2(t&R)
Faingaa, S M (Q) 2010 Fj(R), E1, 2, I, SA1, NZ1(R), 2, SA2, 3(R), NZ4(R), W, 2011 SA1(R), NZ1(R), 2(R), [Ru(R), W(R)], 2012 NZ2(R), SA1(R), 2013 BI 3(t&R), NZ1(R), 2(R), SA1(R), Arg1(R), SA2(R), Arg2(R)
Fairfax, R L (NSW) 1971 F 1, 2, 1972 F 1, 2, NZ 1, Fj, 1973 W, E
Fardy, S M (ACT) 2013 NZ1(t&R), 2, SA1, Arg1, SA2, Arg2
Farmer, E H (Q) 1910 NZ 1
Farquhar, C R (NSW) 1920 NZ 2
Farr-Jones, N C (NSW) 1984 E, I, W, S, 1985 C 1,2, NZ, Fj 1, 2, 1986 It, F, Arg 1, 2, NZ 1, 2, 3, 1987 SK, [E, I, F, W (R)], NZ, Arg 2, 1988 E 1,2, NZ 1,2,3, E, S, It, 1989 BI 1,2,3, NZ, F 1,2, 1990 F 1,2,3, US, NZ 1,2,3, 1991 W, E, NZ 1,2, [Arg, WS, I, NZ, E], 1992 S 1,2, NZ 1,2,3, SA, 1993 NZ, SA 1,2,3
Fava, S G (ACT, WF) 2005 E(R),I(R), 2006 NZ1(R),SA1,NZ2
Fay, G (NSW) 1971 SA 2, 1972 NZ 1,2,3, 1973 Tg 1,2, W, E, 1974 NZ 1,2,3, 1975 E 1,2, J 1, S, W, 1976 I, US, 1978 W 1,2, NZ 1,2,3, 1979 I 1
Feauai-Sautia, C (Q) 2013 SA2(R)
Fenwicke, P T (NSW) 1957 NZ 1, 1958 W, I, E, 1959 BI 1,2
Ferguson, R T (NSW) 1922 M 3, NZ 1, 1923 M 3, NZ 3
Fihelly, J A (Q) 1907 NZ 2
Finau, S F (NSW) 1997 NZ 3
Finegan, O D A (ACT) 1996 W 1,2, C, NZ 1, SA 1(t), S, W 3, 1997 SA 1, NZ 3, SA 2, Arg 1,2, E 2, S, 1998 E 1(R), S 1(t + R),2(t + R), NZ 1(R), SA 1(t),2(R), NZ 3(R), Fj (R), Tg, WS (t + R), F (R), E 2(R), 1999 NZ 2(R), [R, I 3(R), US, W (R), SA 3(R), F (R)], 2001 BI 1,2,3, SA 1, NZ 1, SA 2, NZ 2, Sp, E, F, W, 2002 F 1,2, NZ 1, SA 1, NZ 2, SA 2, I, 2003 SA 1(t&R), NZ 1(R), SA 2(R), NZ 2(R)
Finlay, A N (NSW) 1926 NZ 1,2,3, 1927 I, W, S, 1928 E, F, 1929 NZ 1,2,3, 1930 BI
Finley, F G (NSW) 1904 BI 3
Finnane, S C (NSW) 1975 E 1, J 1,2, 1976 E, 1978 W 1,2
Fitter, D E S (ACT) 2005 I,W
FitzSimons, P (NSW) 1989 F 1,2, 1990 F 1,2,3, US, NZ 1
Flanagan, P (Q) 1907 NZ 1,2
Flatley, E J (Q) 1997 E 2, S, 2000 S (R), 2001 BI 1(R), 2(R), 3, SA 1, NZ 1(R), 2(R), Sp (R), F (R), W, 2002 F 1(R), 2(R), NZ 1(t+R), SA 1(R), NZ 2(t), Arg (R), I (R), E, It, 2003 I, W, SA 1, NZ 1, SA 2, NZ 2, [Arg, R, I, S, NZ, E], 2004 S3(R), F(R), S4(R), E2, 2005 NZ1(R)
Flett, J A (NSW) 1990 US, NZ 2,3, 1991 [WS]
Flynn, J P (Q) 1914 NZ 1,2
Fogarty, J R (Q) 1949 M 2,3
Folau, I (NSW) 2013 BI 1, 2, 3, NZ1, 2, SA1, Arg1, SA2, Arg2
Foley, B T (NSW) 2013 Arg2(R)
Foley, M A (Q) 1995 [C (R), R], 1996 W 2(R), NZ 1, SA 1, NZ 2, SA 2, It, S, I, W 3, 1997 NZ 1(R), E 1, NZ 2, SA 1, NZ 3, SA 2, Arg 1,2, E 2, S, 1998 Tg (R), F (R), E 2(R), 1999 NZ 2(R), [US, W, SA 3, F], 2000 Arg 1,2, SA 1, NZ 1, SA 2, NZ 2, SA 3, F, S, E, 2001 BI 1(R),2,3, SA 1, NZ 1, SA 2, NZ 2, Sp, E, F, W
Foote, R H (NSW) 1924 NZ 2,3, 1926 NZ 2
Forbes, C F (Q) 1953 SA 2,3,4, 1954 Fj 1, 1956 SA 1,2
Ford, B (Q) 1957 NZ 2
Ford, E E (NSW) 1927 I, W, S, 1928 E, F, 1929 NZ 1,3
Ford, J A (NSW) 1925 NZ 4, 1926 NZ 1,2, 1927 I, W, S, 1928 E, 1929 NZ 1,2,3, 1930 BI
Forman, T R (NSW) 1968 I, S, 1969 W, SA 1,2,3,4
Fowles, D G (NSW) 1921 SA 1,2,3, 1922 M 2,3, 1923 M 2,3
Fox, C L (NSW) 1920 NZ 1,2,3, 1921 SA 1, NZ, 1922 M 1,2, NZ 1, 1924 NZ 1,2,3, 1925 NZ 1,2,3, 1926 NZ 1,3, 1928 F
Fox, O G (NSW) 1958 F
Francis, E (Q) 1914 NZ 1,2
Frawley, D (Q, NSW) 1986 Arg 2(R), 1987 Arg 1,2, 1988 E 1,2, NZ 1,2,3, S, It
Freedman, J E (NSW) 1962 NZ 3,4,5, 1963 SA 1
Freeman, E (NSW) 1946 NZ 1(R), M
Freier, A L (NSW) 2002 Arg (R), I, E (R), It, 2003 SA 1(R), NZ 1(t), 2005 NZ2(R), 2006 E2, 2007 W1(R), 2(R), Fj, SA1(R), NZ1(R), SA2, NZ2(R), [J(R), W(R), Fj(R), C, E(R)], 2008 I(R), F1(R), 2(R), NZ3(R), W(t&R)
Freney, M E (Q) 1972 NZ 1, 2, 3, 1973 Tg 1, W, E (R)
Friend, W S (NSW) 1920 NZ 3, 1921 SA 1,2,3, 1922 NZ 1,2,3, 1923 M 1,2,3
Furness, D C (NSW) 1946 M
Futter, F C (NSW) 1904 BI 3

Gardner, J M (Q) 1987 Arg 2, 1988 E 1, NZ 1, E
Gardner, W C (NSW) 1950 BI 1
Garner, R L (NSW) 1949 NZ 1,2
Gavin, K A (NSW) 1909 E
Gavin, T B (NSW) 1988 NZ 2,3, S, It (R), 1989 NZ (R), F 1,2, 1990 F 1,2,3, US, NZ 1,2,3, 1991 W, E, NZ 1, 1992 S 1,2, SA, I, W, 1993 Tg, NZ, SA 1,2,3, C, F 1,2, 1994 I 1,2, It 1,2, WS, NZ, 1995 Arg 1,2, [SA, C, R, E], NZ 1,2, 1996 NZ 2(R), SA 2, W 3
Gelling, A M (NSW) 1972 NZ 1, Fj
Genia, S W (Q) 2009 NZ1(R), SA1(R), NZ2(R), SA2(R), 3, NZ3, 4, E, I, S, W, 2010 E2, SA1, NZ1, 2, SA2, 3, NZ3, 4, W, E3, F, 2011 Sm(R), SA1, NZ1, SA2, NZ2, [It, I, US, SA, NZ, W], W, 2012 S, W1, 2, 3, NZ1, 2, SA1, 2013 BI 1, 2, 3, NZ1, 2, SA1, 2(R), Arg2
George, H W (NSW) 1910 NZ 1, 2, 3, 1912 US, 1913 NZ 1, 3, 1914 NZ 1, 3
George, W G (NSW) 1923 M 1,3, NZ 1,2, 1924 NZ 3, 1925 NZ 2,3, 1926 NZ 4, 1928 NZ 1,2,3, M

Gerrard, M A (ACT,MR) 2005 It(R), SA1(R), NZ1, 2, E, I, W, 2006 E1, 2, I1, NZ1, SA1, NZ2, SA2, NZ3(t), SA3(R), I2, S, 2007 W1, 2(R), SA2, NZ2, [J(R)], 2011 Sm
Gibbons, E de C (NSW) 1936 NZ 1,2, M
Gibbs, P R (V) 1966 S
Giffin, D T (ACT) 1996 W 3, 1997 F 1,2, 1999 I 1,2, E, SA 1, NZ 1, SA 2, NZ 2, [R, I 3, US (R), W, SA 3, F], 2000 Arg 1,2, SA 1, NZ 1, SA 2, NZ 2, SA 3, F, S, E, 2001 BI 1,2, SA 1, NZ 2, Sp, E, F, W, 2002 Arg (R), I, E (R), It (R), 2003 I, W, E, SA 1, NZ 1, SA 2, NZ 2, [Arg,Nm(R),I,NZ(t&R),E(R)]
Gilbert, H (NSW) 1910 NZ 1,2,3
Gill, L B (Q) 2012 NZ2(R), SA1(R), Arg1(R), SA2(R), Arg2(R), NZ3(R), F(R), E(t&R), 2013 BI 1(R), 2(R), NZ1(R), 2(R), SA1(R)
Girvan, B (ACT) 1988 E
Giteau, M J (ACT, WF) 2002 E (R), It (R), 2003 SA 2(R), NZ 2(R), [Arg(R), R(R), Nm, I(R), S(R), E(t)], 2004 S1, E1, PI, NZ1, SA1, NZ2, SA2, S3, F, S4, E2, 2005 Sm, It, F1, SA1, 2, 3, NZ1, SA4, F2, E(t&R), 2006 NZ1(R), SA1, NZ2, SA2, NZ3, SA3, W, It, I2, S, 2007 W1, 2, SA1, NZ1, SA2, NZ2, [J, W, Fj, E], 2008 I, F1, 2, SA1, NZ1, 2, SA2, 3, NZ3, 4, It(R), E, F3, W, 2009 It1, F, NZ1, SA1, NZ2, SA2, 3, NZ3, 4, E, I, S, W, 2010 Fj, E2, I, SA1, NZ1, 2, SA2, 3, NZ3, 4, W, E3, F(R), 2011 Sm
Gordon, G C (NSW) 1929 NZ 1
Gordon, K M (NSW) 1950 BI 1,2
Gould, R G (Q) 1980 NZ 1,2,3, 1981 I, W, S, 1982 S 2, NZ 1,2,3, 1983 US, Arg 1, F 1,2, 1984 NZ 1,2,3, E, I, W, S, 1985 NZ, 1986 It, 1987 SK, [E]
Gourley, S R (NSW) 1988 S, It, 1989 BI 1,2,3
Graham, C S (Q) 1899 BI 2
Graham, R (NSW) 1973 Tg 1,2, W, E, 1974 NZ 2,3, 1975 E 2, J 1,2, S, W, 1976 I, US, Fj 1,2,3, F 1,2
Gralton, A S I (Q) 1899 BI 1,4, 1903 NZ
Grant, J C (NSW) 1988 E 1, NZ 2,3, E
Graves, R H (NSW) 1907 NZ 1(R)
Greatorex, E N (NSW) 1923 M 3, NZ 3, 1924 NZ 1,2,3, 1925 NZ 1, 1928 E, F
Gregan, G M (ACT) 1994 It 1,2, WS, NZ, 1995 Arg 1,2, [SA, C (R), R, E], 1996 W 1, C (t), SA 1, NZ 2, SA 2, It, I, W 3, 1997 F 1,2, NZ 1, E 1, NZ 2, SA 1, NZ 3, SA 2, Arg 1,2, E 2, S, 1998 E 1, S 1,2, NZ 1, SA 1, NZ 2, SA 2, NZ 3, Fj, WS, F, E 2, 1999 I 1,2, E, SA 1, NZ 1, SA 2, NZ 2, [R, I 3, W, SA 3, F], 2000 Arg 1,2, SA 1, NZ 1, SA 2, NZ 2, SA 3, 2001 BI 1,2,3, SA 1, NZ 1, SA 2, NZ 2, Sp, E, F, W, 2002 F 1,2, NZ 1, SA 1, NZ 2, SA 2, Arg, I, E, It, 2003 I, W, E, SA 1, NZ 1, SA 2, NZ 2, [Arg, R, I, S, NZ, E], 2004 S1, 2, E1, PI, SA1, NZ2, SA2, S3, F, S4, E2, 2005 It, F1, SA1, 2, 3, NZ1, SA4, NZ2, F2, E, I, W, 2006 E1, 2(R), I1, NZ1, SA1, NZ2, SA2, NZ3, SA3, 2007 W1(R), 2(R), Fj, SA1, NZ1, SA2, NZ2, [J, W, Fj, C(R), E]
Gregory, S C (Q) 1968 NZ 3, F, I, S, 1969 SA 1,3, 1971 SA 1,3, F 1,2, 1972 F 1,2, 1973 Tg 1,2, W, E
Grey, G O (NSW) 1972 F 2(R), NZ 1,2,3, Fj (R)
Grey, N P (NSW) 1998 S 2(R), SA 2(R), Fj (R), Tg (R), F, E 2, 1999 I 1(R),2(R), E, SA 1, NZ 1, SA 2, NZ 2(t&R), [R (R), I 3(R), US, SA 3(R), F (R)], 2000 S (R), E (R), 2001 BI 1,2,3, SA 1, NZ 1, SA 2, NZ 2, Sp, E, F, 2003 I (R), W (R), E, [Nm,NZ(t)]
Griffin, T S (NSW) 1907 NZ 1,3, 1908 W, 1910 NZ 1,2, 1912 US
Grigg, P C (Q) 1980 NZ 3, 1982 S 2, NZ 1,2,3, 1983 Arg 2, NZ, 1984 Fj, W, S, 1985 C 1,2, NZ, Fj 1,2, 1986 Arg 1,2, NZ 1,2, 1987 SK, [E, J, I, F, W]
Grimmond, D N (NSW) 1964 NZ 2
Gudsell, K E (NSW) 1951 NZ 1,2,3
Guerassimoff, J (Q) 1963 SA 2,3,4, 1964 NZ 1,2,3, 1965 SA 2, 1966 BI 1,2, 1967 E, I, F
Gunther, W J (NSW) 1957 NZ 2

Hall, D (Q) 1980 Fj, NZ 1,2,3, 1981 F 1,2, 1982 S 1,2, NZ 1,2, 1983 US, Arg 1,2, NZ, It
Hamalainen, H A (Q) 1929 NZ 1,2,3
Hamilton, B G (NSW) 1946 M
Hammand, C A (NSW) 1908 W, 1909 E
Hammon, J D C (V) 1937 SA 2
Handy, C B (Q) 1978 NZ 3, 1979 NZ, Arg 1,2, 1980 NZ 1,2
Hanley, R G (Q) 1983 US (R), It (R), 1985 Fj 2(R)
Hanson, J E (Q) 2012 NZ3(R)
Hardcastle, P A (NSW) 1946 NZ 1, M, NZ 2, 1947 NZ 1, 1949 M 3
Hardcastle, W R (NSW) 1899 BI 4, 1903 NZ
Harding, M A (NSW) 1983 It
Hardman, S P (Q) 2002 F 2(R), 2006 SA1(R), 2007 SA2(t&R), [C(R)]
Hardy, M D (ACT) 1997 F 1(t), 2(R), NZ 1(R), 3(R), Arg 1(R), 2(R), 1998 Tg, WS
Harris, M J (Q) 2012 S, W2(R), SA1(R), 2(R), Arg2, NZ3, F, W4(R)
Harrison, J B (ACT, NSW) 2001 BI 3, NZ 1, SA 2, Sp, E, F, W (R), 2002 F 1,2, NZ 1, SA 1, NZ 2, SA 2, Arg, I (R), E, It, 2003 [R(R), Nm, S, NZ, E], 2004 S1, 2, E1, PI, NZ1, SA1, NZ2, SA2, S3, F, S4, E2
Harry, R L L (NSW) 1996 W 1,2, NZ 1, SA 1(t), NZ 2, It, S, 1997 F 1,2, NZ 1,2, SA 1, NZ 3, SA 2, Arg 1,2, E 2, S, 1998 E 1, S 1,2, NZ 1, Fj, 1999 SA 2, NZ 2, [R, I 3, W, SA 3, F], 2000 Arg 1,2, SA 1, NZ 1, SA 2, NZ 2, SA 3
Hartill, M N (NSW) 1986 NZ 1,2,3, 1987 SK, [J], Arg 1, 1988 NZ 1,2, E, It, 1989 BI 1(R), 2,3, F 1,2, 1995 Arg 1(R), 2(R), [C], NZ 1,2
Harvey, P B (Q) 1949 M 1,2
Harvey, R M (NSW) 1958 F, M 3
Hatherell, W I (Q) 1952 Fj 1,2
Hauser, R G (Q) 1975 J 1(R), 2, W (R), 1976 E, I, US, Fj 1,2,3, F 1,2, 1978 W 1,2, 1979 I 1,2
Hawker, M J (NSW) 1980 Fj, NZ 1,2,3, 1981 F 1,2, I, W, 1982 E, S 1,2, NZ 1,2,3, 1983 US, Arg 1,2, NZ, It, F 1,2, 1984 NZ 1,2,3, 1987 NZ
Hawthorne, P F (NSW) 1962 NZ 3,4,5, 1963 E, SA 1,2,3,4, 1964 NZ 1,2,3, 1965 SA 1,2, 1966 BI 1,2, W, 1967 E, I 1, F, I 2, NZ
Hayes, E S (Q) 1934 NZ 1,2, 1938 NZ 1,2,3
Heath, A (NSW) 1996 C, SA 1, NZ 2, SA 2, It, 1997 NZ 2, SA 1, E 2(R)
Heenan, D P (Q, ACT) 2003 W, 2006 E1
Heinrich, E L (NSW) 1961 Fj 1,2,3, SA 2, F, 1962 NZ 1,2,3, 1963 E, SA 1
Heinrich, V W (NSW) 1954 Fj 1,2
Heming, R J (NSW) 1961 Fj 2,3, SA 1,2, F, 1962 NZ 2,3,4,5, 1963 SA 2,3,4, 1964 NZ 1,2,3, 1965 SA 1,2, 1966 BI 1,2, W, 1967 F
Hemingway, W H (NSW) 1928 NZ 2,3, 1931 M, NZ, 1932 NZ 3
Henderson, N J (ACT) 2004 PI(R), 2005 Sm(R), 2006 It(R)
Henjak, M T (ACT) 2004 E1(R),NZ1(R), 2005 Sm(R),I(R)
Henry, A R (Q) 1899 BI 2
Herbert, A G (Q) 1987 SK (R), [F (R)], 1990 F 1(R), US, NZ 2,3, 1991 [WS], 1992 NZ 3(R), 1993 NZ (R), SA 2(R)
Herbert, D J (Q) 1994 I 2, It 1,2, WS (R), 1995 Arg 1,2, [SA, R], 1996 C, SA 2, It, S, I, 1997 NZ 1, 1998 E 1, S 1,2, NZ 1, SA 1, NZ 2, SA 2, Fj, Tg, WS, F, E 2, 1999 I 1,2, E, SA 1, NZ 1, SA 2, NZ 2, [R, I 3, W, SA 3, F], 2000 Arg 1,2, SA 1, NZ 1, SA 2, NZ 2, SA 3, F, S, E, 2001 BI 1,2,3, SA 1, NZ 1, SA 2, NZ 2, Sp, E, 2002 F 1,2, NZ 1, SA 1, NZ 2, SA 2, Arg, I, E, It
Herd, H V (NSW) 1931 M
Hickey, J (NSW) 1908 W, 1909 E
Higginbotham, S (Q, MR) 2010 F(R), 2011 Sm(R), SA1(R), NZ1(R), SA2, NZ2(R), [It(R), I(R), Ru, W], W, 2012 S, W1, 2, 3, NZ1, 2, SA1(R), Arg1(R), 2(R), NZ3, It, W4
Hill, J (NSW) 1925 NZ 1
Hillhouse, D W (Q) 1975 S, 1976 E, Fj 1,2,3, F 1,2, 1978 W 1,2, 1983 US, Arg 1,2, NZ, It, F 1,2
Hills, E F (V) 1950 BI 1,2
Hindmarsh, J A (Q) 1904 BI 1
Hindmarsh, J C (NSW) 1975 J 2, S, W, 1976 US, Fj 1,2,3, F 1,2
Hipwell, J N B (NSW) 1968 NZ 1(R), 2, F, I, S, 1969 W, SA 1,2,3,4, 1970 S, 1971 SA 1,2, F 1,2, 1972 F 1,2, 1973 Tg 1, W, E, 1974 NZ 1,2,3, 1975 E 1,2, J 1, S, W, 1978 NZ 1,2,3, 1981 F 1,2, I, W, 1982 E
Hirschberg, W A (NSW) 1905 NZ
Hodgins, C H (NSW) 1910 NZ 1,2,3
Hodgson, A J (NSW) 1933 SA 2,3,4, 1934 NZ 1, 1936 NZ 1,2, M, 1937 SA 2, 1938 NZ 1,2,3
Hodgson, M J (WF) 2010 Fj(R), E1(R), NZ2(R), It(R), 2011 Sm, SA1(R)
Hoiles, S A (NSW, ACT) 2004 S4(R),E2(R), 2006 W(R), 2007 W1(R), 2(R), Fj(R), SA1(R), NZ1(R), SA2, NZ2, [J(R), W(R), Fj(R), C(R), E(R)] 2006 W(R), 2007 W1(R), 2(R), Fj(R), SA1(R), NZ1(R), SA2, NZ2, [J(R), W(R), Fj(R), C(R), E(R)], 2008 F2
Holbeck, J C (ACT) 1997 NZ 1(R), E 1, NZ 2, SA 1, NZ 3, SA 2, 2001 BI 3(R)
Holdsworth, J W (NSW) 1921 SA 1,2,3, 1922 M 2,3, NZ 1(R)
Holmes, G S (Q) 2005 F2(R), E(t&R), I, 2006 E1, 2, I1, NZ1, SA1, NZ2, SA2, NZ3, 2007 [Fj(R), C]
Holt, N C (Q) 1984 Fj
Honan, B D (Q) 1968 NZ 1(R), 2, F, I, S, 1969 SA 1,2,3,4
Honan, R E (Q) 1964 NZ 1,2
Hooper, M K (ACT, NSW) 2012 S(R), W1(R), 2(R), NZ2, SA1, Arg1, SA2, Arg2, NZ3, F, E, It, W4(R), 2013 BI 1, 2, 3(t&R), NZ1, 2, SA1, Arg1, SA2, Arg2

Horan, T J (Q) 1989 NZ, F 1,2, 1990 F 1, NZ 1,2,3, 1991 W, E, NZ 1,2, [Arg, WS, W, I, NZ, E], 1992 S 1,2, NZ 1,2,3, SA, I, W, 1993 Tg, NZ, SA 1,2,3, C, F 1,2, 1995 [C, R, E], NZ 1,2, 1996 W 1,2, C, NZ 1, SA 1, It, S, I, W 3, 1997 F 1,2, NZ 1, E 1, NZ 2, Arg 1,2, E 2, S, 1998 E 1, S 1,2, NZ 1, SA 1, NZ 2, SA 2, NZ 3, Fj, Tg, WS, 1999 I 1,2, E, SA 1, NZ 1, SA 2, NZ 2, [R, I 3, W, SA 3, F], 2000 Arg 1

Horne, R G (NSW) 2010 Fj, E1, 2, I, SA1, NZ1, 2011 [US, NZ(R), W(R)], 2012 W1, 2, 3, NZ1, 2, 2013 BI 2(R)

Horodam, D J (Q) 1913 NZ 2

Horsley, G R (Q) 1954 Fj 2

Horton, P A (NSW) 1974 NZ 1,2,3, 1975 E 1,2, J 1,2, S, W, 1976 E, F 1,2, 1978 W 1,2, NZ 1,2,3, 1979 NZ, Arg 1

Horwill, J E (Q) 2007 Fj, 2008 I, F1, 2, SA1, NZ1, 2, SA2, 3, NZ3, 2009 It1, 2, F, NZ1, SA1, NZ2, SA2, 3, NZ3, 4, E, I, S, W, 2011 SA1, NZ1, SA2, NZ2, [It, I, Ru, SA, NZ, W], W, 2013 BI 1, 2, 3, NZ1, 2, SA2, Arg2

Hoskins, J E (NSW) 1924 NZ 1,2,3

How, R A (NSW) 1967 I 2

Howard, J (Q) 1938 NZ 1,2

Howard, J L (NSW) 1970 S, 1971 SA 1, 1972 F 1(R), NZ 2, 1973 Tg 1,2, W

Howard, P W (Q, ACT) 1993 NZ, 1994 WS, NZ, 1995 NZ 1(R), 2(t), 1996 W 1,2, SA 1, NZ 2, SA 2, It, S, W 3, 1997 F 1,2, NZ 1, Arg 1,2, E 2, S

Howell, M L (NSW) 1946 NZ 1(R), 1947 NZ 1, S, I, W

Hughes, B D (NSW) 1913 NZ 2,3

Hughes, J C (NSW) 1907 NZ 1,3

Hughes, N McL (NSW) 1953 SA 1,2,3,4, 1955 NZ 1,2,3, 1956 SA 1,2, 1958 W, I, E, S, F

Humphreys, O W (NSW) 1920 NZ 3, 1921 NZ, 1922 M 1,2,3, 1925 NZ 1

Hutchinson, E E (NSW) 1937 SA 1,2

Hutchinson, F E (NSW) 1936 NZ 1,2, 1938 NZ 1,3

Huxley, J L (ACT) 2007 W1,2,Fj,SA1,NZ1,SA2, [W(R),Fj(R),C]

Hynes, P J (Q) 2008 I, F1, 2, SA1, NZ1, 2, SA2, 3, NZ3, 4, E, F3, W, 2009 It2, NZ2(R), SA2, 3(R), NZ4, E, I, S, W

Ide, W P J (Q) 1938 NZ 2,3

Ioane, D A N (WF, Q) 2007 W2, 2008 It, F3, W, 2009 NZ4, E, I, W, 2010 Fj, E1, 2, 2011 Sm, SA1, NZ1, SA2, NZ2, [It, SA, NZ, W], W, 2012 S, W1, 2, 3, NZ1, 2, SA1, Arg1, SA2, Arg2, E, It(R), W4(R), 2013 BI 1

Ives, W N (NSW) 1926 NZ 1,2,3,4, 1929 NZ 3

James, P M (Q) 1958 M 2,3

James, S L (NSW) 1987 SK (R), [E (R)], NZ, Arg 1,2, 1988 NZ 2(R)

Jamieson, A E (NSW) 1925 NZ 3(R)

Jaques, T (ACT) 2000 SA 1(R), NZ 1(R)

Jessep, E M (V) 1934 NZ 1,2

Johansson, L D T (Q) 2005 NZ2(R),F2(R),E(R)

Johnson, A P (NSW) 1946 NZ 1, M

Johnson, B B (NSW) 1952 Fj 1,2, NZ 1,2, 1953 SA 2,3,4, 1955 NZ 1,2

Johnson, P G (NSW) 1959 BI 1,2, 1961 Fj 1,2,3, SA 1,2, F, 1962 NZ 1,2,3,4,5, 1963 E, SA 1,2,3,4, 1964 NZ 1,2,3, 1965 SA 1,2, 1966 BI 1,2, W, S, 1967 E, I 1, F, I 2, NZ, 1968 NZ 1,2, F, I, S, 1970 S, 1971 SA 1,2, F 1,2

Johnstone, B (Q) 1993 Tg (R)

Jones, G G (Q) 1952 Fj 1,2, 1953 SA 1,2,3,4, 1954 Fj 1,2, 1955 NZ 1,2,3, 1956 SA 1

Jones, H (NSW) 1913 NZ 1,2,3

Jones, P A (NSW) 1963 E, SA 1

Jorgensen, P (NSW) 1992 S 1(R), 2(R)

Joyce, J E (NSW) 1903 NZ

Judd, H A (NSW) 1903 NZ, 1904 BI 1,2,3, 1905 NZ

Judd, P B (NSW) 1925 NZ 4, 1926 NZ 1,2,3,4, 1927 I, W, S, 1928 E, 1931 M, NZ

Junee, D K (NSW) 1989 F 1(R), 2(R), 1994 WS (R), NZ (R)

Kafer, R B (ACT) 1999 NZ 2, [R, US (R)], 2000 Arg 1(R),2, SA 1, NZ 1(t&R), SA 2(R),3(R), F, S, E

Kahl, P R (Q) 1992 W

Kanaar, A (NSW) 2005 NZ2(R)

Kassulke, N (Q) 1985 C 1,2

Kay, A R (V) 1958 NZ 2, 1959 BI 2

Kay, P (NSW) 1988 E 2

Kearney, K H (NSW) 1947 NZ 1,2, S, I, W, 1948 E, F

Kearns, P N (NSW) 1989 NZ, F 1,2, 1990 F 1,2,3, US, NZ 1,2,3, 1991 W, E, NZ 1,2, [Arg, WS, W, I, NZ, E], 1992 S 1,2, NZ 1,2,3, SA, I, W, 1993 Tg, NZ, SA 1,2,3, C, F 1,2, 1994 I 1,2, It 1,2, WS, NZ, 1995 Arg 1,2, [SA, C, E], NZ 1,2, 1998 E 1, S 1,2, NZ 1, SA 1, NZ 2, SA 2, NZ 3, Fj, WS, F, E 2, 1999 I 2(R), SA 1(R),2, NZ 2, [R, I 3]

Kefu, R S T (Q) 1997 SA 2(R), 1998 E 1, S 1,2, NZ 1, SA 1, NZ 2, SA 2, NZ 3, Fj (R), Tg, WS (R), F, E 2, 1999 I 1,2, E, SA 1, NZ 1(R), SA 2, NZ 2, [R, I 3, SA 3, F], 2000 SA 1(t&R), NZ 1(R), SA 2(R), NZ 2, SA 3(R), F, S, E, 2001 BI 1,2,3, SA 1, NZ 1, SA 2, NZ 2, Sp, E, F, W, 2002 F 1, NZ 1, SA 1, NZ 2, SA 2, Arg, I, E, It, 2003 I, W, E, SA 1, NZ 1, SA 2, NZ 2

Kefu, S (Q) 2001 W (R), 2003 I, W, E, SA 1, NZ 1(R)

Kelaher, J D (NSW) 1933 SA 1,2,3,4,5, 1934 NZ 1,2, 1936 NZ 1,2, M, 1937 SA 1,2, 1938 NZ 3

Kelaher, T P (NSW) 1992 NZ 1, I (R), 1993 NZ

Kelleher, R J (Q) 1969 SA 2,3

Keller, D H (NSW) 1947 NZ 1, S, I, W, 1948 E, F

Kelly, A J (NSW) 1899 BI 1

Kelly, R L F (NSW) 1936 NZ 1,2, M, 1937 SA 1,2, 1938 NZ 1,2

Kent, A (Q) 1912 US

Kepu, S M (NSW) 2008 It(R), F3(R), 2009 S(R), 2011 Sm, SA1, NZ1, SA2, NZ2, [It, I, US(R), Ru, SA, NZ], 2012 W1, 2, 3, NZ1, 3(R), F, E(R), It(R), W4(R), 2013 BI 1(R), 2(R), 3(t&R), NZ1(R),2(R), SA1, Arg1(R), SA2(R), Arg2(R)

Kerr, F R (V) 1938 NZ 1

Kimlin, P J (ACT) 2009 It1(R),2

King, S C (NSW) 1926 NZ 1,2,3,4(R), 1927 W, S, 1928 E, F, 1929 NZ 1,2,3, 1930 BI, 1932 NZ 1,2

Knight, M (NSW) 1978 W 1,2, NZ 1

Knight, S O (NSW) 1969 SA 2,4, 1970 S, 1971 SA 1,2,3

Knox, D J (NSW, ACT) 1985 Fj 1,2, 1990 US (R), 1994 WS, NZ, 1996 It, S, I, 1997 SA 1, NZ 3, SA 2, Arg 1,2

Kraefft, D F (NSW) 1947 NZ 2, S, I, W, 1948 E, F

Kreutzer, S D (Q) 1914 NZ 2

Kuridrani, R T R N (ACT) 2013 NZ1(R), 2(R), SA2, Arg2

Lamb, J S (NSW) 1928 NZ 1,2, M

Lambie, J K (NSW) 1974 NZ 1,2,3, 1975 W

Lane, R E (NSW) 1921 SA 1

Lane, T A (Q) 1985 C 1,2, NZ

Lang, C W P (V) 1938 NZ 2,3

Langford, J F (ACT) 1997 NZ 3, SA 2, E 2, S

Larkham, S J (ACT) 1996 W 2(R), 1997 F 1,2, NZ 1,2(R), SA 1, NZ 3, SA 2, Arg 1,2, E 2, S, 1998 E 1, S 1,2, NZ 1, SA 1, NZ 2, SA 2, NZ 3, Fj, Tg (t), WS, F, E 2, 1999 [I 3, US, W, SA 3, F], 2000 Arg 1,2, SA 1, NZ 1, SA 2, NZ 2, SA 3, 2001 BI 1,2, NZ 1, SA 2, NZ 2, Sp, E, F, W, 2002 F 1,2, NZ 1, SA 1, NZ 2, SA 2, Arg, I, E, 2003 SA 1(R), NZ 1, SA 2, NZ 2, [Arg, R, I, S, NZ, E], 2004S1, 2, E1, PI, NZ1, SA1, NZ2, SA2, S3, F, S4, 2005 Sm(R), It, F1, SA1, 2, 3, 2006 E1, 2, I1, NZ1, SA1, NZ2, SA2, NZ3, SA3, W, It, I2, S, 2007 W2, Fj, SA1, NZ1, SA2, NZ2, [J]

Larkin, E R (NSW) 1903 NZ

Larkin, K K (Q) 1958 M 2,3

Latham, C E (Q) 1998 F, E 2, 1999 I 1,2, E, [US], 2000 Arg 1,2, SA 1, NZ 1, SA 2, NZ 2, SA 3, F, S, E, 2001 BI 1,2(R), SA 1(R), NZ 1(R), SA 2, NZ 2, Sp, E, F, W (R), 2002 F 1,2, NZ 1, SA 1, NZ 2, SA 2, 2003 I, W, E, NZ 1(R), SA 2, NZ 2,[Nm], 2004 S1(R), 2(R), E1(R), PI(t&R), NZ1, SA1, NZ2, SA2, S3, F, S4, E2, 2005 Sm, F1, SA2, 3, F2, E, I, W, 2006 E1, 2, I1, NZ1,SA1, NZ2, SA2, NZ3, SA3, W, It, I2, S, 2007 NZ2(R), [J, W, Fj, C, E]

Latimer, N B (NSW) 1957 NZ 2

Lawton, R (Q) 1988 E 1, NZ 2(R), 3, S

Lawton, T (NSW, Q) 1920 NZ 1, 2, 1925 NZ 4, 1927 I, W, S, 1928 E, F, 1929 NZ 1, 2, 3, 1930 BI, 1932 NZ 1, 2

Lawton, T A (Q) 1983 F 1(R), 2, 1984 Fj, NZ 1, 2, 3, E, I, W, S, 1985 C 1, 2, NZ, Fj 1, 1986 It, F, Arg 1,2, NZ 1, 2, 3, 1987 SK, [E, US, I, F, W], NZ, Arg 1,2, 1988 E 1,2, NZ 1,2,3, E, S, It, 1989 BI 1,2,3

Laycock, W M B (NSW) 1925 NZ 2,3,4, 1926 NZ 2

Leali'ifano, C P (ACT) 2013 BI 1,2,3,NZ1,2,SA1,Arg1,SA2,Arg2

Leeds, A J (NSW) 1986 NZ 3, 1987 [US, W], NZ, Arg 1,2, 1988 E 1,2, NZ 1,2,3, E, S, It

Lenehan, J K (NSW) 1958 W, E, S, F, M 1,2,3, 1959 BI 1,2, 1961 SA 1,2, F, 1962 NZ 2,3,4,5, 1965 SA 1,2, 1966 W, S, 1967 E, I 1, F, I 2

L'Estrange, R D (Q) 1971 F 1,2, 1972 NZ 1,2,3, 1973 Tg 1,2, W, E, 1974 NZ 1,2,3, 1975 S, W, 1976 I, US

Lewis, L S (Q) 1934 NZ 1,2, 1936 NZ 2, 1938 NZ 1

Lidbury, S (NSW) 1987 Arg 1, 1988 E 2
Lillicrap, C P (Q) 1985 Fj 2, 1987 [US, I, F, W], 1989 BI 1, 1991 [WS]
Lindsay, R T G (Q) 1932 NZ 3
Lisle, R J (NSW) 1961 Fj 1,2,3, SA 1
Little, J S (Q, NSW) 1989 F 1,2, 1990 F 1,2,3, US, 1991 W, E, NZ 1,2, [Arg, W, I, NZ, E], 1992 NZ 1,2,3, SA, I, W, 1993 Tg, NZ, SA 1,2,3, C, F 1,2, 1994 WS, NZ, 1995 Arg 1,2, [SA, C, E], NZ 1,2, 1996 It (R), I, W 3, 1997 F 1,2, E 1, NZ 2, SA 1, NZ 3, SA 2, 1998 E 1(R), S 2(R), NZ 2, SA 2(R), NZ 3, Fj, Tg, WS, F, E 2, 1999 I 1(R),2, SA 2(R), NZ 2, [R, I 3(t&R), US, W (R), SA 3(t&R), F (R)], 2000 Arg 1(R),2(R), SA 1(R), NZ 1, SA 2, NZ 2, SA 3
Livermore, A E (Q) 1946 NZ 1, M
Loane, M E (Q) 1973 Tg 1,2, 1974 NZ 1, 1975 E 1,2, J 1, 1976 E, I, Fj 1,2,3, F 1,2, 1978 W 1,2, 1979 I 1,2, NZ, Arg 1,2, 1981 F 1,2, I, W, S, 1982 E, S 1,2
Logan, D L (NSW) 1958 M 1
Loudon, D B (NSW) 1921 NZ, 1922 M 1,2,3
Loudon, R B (NSW) 1923 NZ 1(R), 2,3, 1928 NZ 1,2,3, M, 1929 NZ 2, 1933 SA 2,3,4,5, 1934 NZ 2
Love, E W (NSW) 1932 NZ 1,2,3
Lowth, D R (NSW) 1958 NZ 1
Lucas, B C (Q) 1905 NZ
Lucas, P W (NSW) 1982 NZ 1,2,3
Lutge, D (NSW) 1903 NZ, 1904 BI 1,2,3
Lynagh, M P (Q) 1984 Fj, E, I, W, S, 1985 C 1,2, NZ, 1986 It, F, Arg 1,2, NZ 1,2,3, 1987 [E, US, J, I, F, W], Arg 1,2, 1988 E 1,2, NZ 1,3(R), E, S, It, 1989 BI 1,2,3, NZ, F 1,2, 1990 F 1,2,3, US, NZ 1,2,3, 1991 W, E, NZ 1,2, [Arg, WS, W, I, NZ, E], 1992 S 1,2, NZ 1,2,3, SA, I, 1993 Tg, C, F 1,2, 1994 I 1,2, It 1, 1995 Arg 1,2, [SA, C, E]
Lyons, D J (NSW) 2000 Arg 1(t&R),2(R), 2001 BI 1(R), SA 1(R), 2002 F 1(R),2, NZ 1(R), SA 1(R), NZ 2(R), SA 2(t+R), 2003 I, W, E, SA 1, [Arg,R,Nm,I,S,NZ,E], 2004 S1,2,E1,PI,NZ1,SA1, NZ2,SA2,S3(R),F(R),S4,E2, 2005 Sm,It,F1,SA1,2,NZ1,SA4, 2006 S, 2007 Fj,SA2(R), [C]

McArthur, M (NSW) 1909 E
McBain, M I (Q) 1983 It, F 1, 1985 Fj 2, 1986 It (R), 1987 [J], 1988 E 2(R), 1989 BI 1(R)
MacBride, J W T (NSW) 1946 NZ 1, M, NZ 2, 1947 NZ 1,2, S, I, W, 1948 E, F
McCabe, A J M (NSW) 1909 E
McCabe, P J (ACT) 2010 It(R), 2011 Sm,SA1,NZ1,SA2,NZ2,[It,I,US(R),SA,NZ], 2012 W1,2,3,Arg1,SA2,Arg2,NZ3,F, 2013 BI 1(R)
McCall, R J (Q) 1989 F 1,2, 1990 F 1,2,3, US, NZ 1,2,3, 1991 W, E, NZ 1,2, [Arg, W, I, NZ, E], 1992 S 1,2, NZ 1,2,3, SA, I, W, 1993 Tg, NZ, SA 1,2,3, C, F 1,2, 1994 It 2, 1995 Arg 1,2, [SA, R, E]
McCalman, B J (WF) 2010 SA1(R), 2(R), 3, NZ3, 4, W, E3, It, F, 2011 Sm, SA1, NZ1, 2(R), [It(R), I, US, Ru, SA(R), NZ(R), W], W, 2013 BI 3(R), SA1(t&R), Arg1(R), SA2(R), Arg2(R)
McCarthy, F J C (Q) 1950 BI 1
McCowan, R H (Q) 1899 BI 1,2,4
McCue, P A (NSW) 1907 NZ 1,3, 1908 W, 1909 E
McDermott, L C (Q) 1962 NZ 1,2
McDonald, B S (NSW) 1969 SA 4, 1970 S
McDonald, J C (Q) 1938 NZ 2,3
Macdougall, D G (NSW) 1961 Fj 1, SA 1
Macdougall, S G (NSW, ACT) 1971 SA 3, 1973 E, 1974 NZ 1,2,3, 1975 E 1,2, 1976 E
McGhie, G H (Q) 1929 NZ 2,3, 1930 BI
McGill, A N (NSW) 1968 NZ 1,2, F, 1969 W, SA 1,2,3,4, 1970 S, 1971 SA 1,2,3, F 1,2, 1972 F 1,2, NZ 1,2,3, 1973 Tg 1,2
McIntyre, A J (Q) 1982 NZ 1,2,3, 1983 F 1,2, 1984 Fj, NZ 1,2,3, E, I, W, S, 1985 C 1,2, NZ, Fj 1,2, 1986 It, F, Arg 1,2, 1987 [E, US, I, F, W], NZ, Arg 2, 1988 E 1,2, NZ 1,2,3, E, S, It, 1989 NZ
McIsaac, T P (WF) 2006 E1,I1,NZ1,2(R),SA2,3(R),W,I2
McKay, G R (NSW) 1920 NZ 2, 1921 SA 2,3, 1922 M 1,2,3
MacKay, L J (NSW) 2005 NZ2(R)
McKenzie, E J A (NSW, ACT) 1990 F 1,2,3, US, NZ 1,2,3, 1991 W, E, NZ 1,2, [Arg, W, I, NZ, E], 1992 S 1,2, NZ 1,2,3, SA, I, W, 1993 Tg, NZ, SA 1,2,3, C, F 1,2, 1994 I 1,2, It 1,2, WS, NZ, 1995 Arg 1,2, [SA, C (R), R, E], NZ 2, 1996 W 1,2, 1997 F 1,2, NZ 1, E 1
McKid, W A (NSW) 1976 E, Fj 1, 1978 NZ 2,3, 1979 I 1,2
McKinnon, A (Q) 1904 BI 2
McKivat, C H (NSW) 1907 NZ 1,3, 1908 W, 1909 E

McLaren, S D (NSW) 1926 NZ 4
McLaughlin, R E M (NSW) 1936 NZ 1,2
McLean, A D (Q) 1933 SA 1,2,3,4,5, 1934 NZ 1,2, 1936 NZ 1,2, M
McLean, J D (Q) 1904 BI 2,3, 1905 NZ
McLean, J J (Q) 1971 SA 2,3, F 1,2, 1972 F 1,2, NZ 1,2,3, Fj, 1973 W, E, 1974 NZ 1
McLean, P E (Q) 1974 NZ 1,2,3, 1975 J 1,2, S, W, 1976 E, I, Fj 1,2,3, F 1,2, 1978 W 1,2, NZ 2, 1979 I 1,2, NZ, Arg 1,2, 1980 Fj, 1981 F 1,2, I, W, S, 1982 E, S 2
McLean, P W (Q) 1978 NZ 1,2,3, 1979 I 1,2, NZ, Arg 1,2, 1980 Fj (R), NZ 3, 1981 I, W, S, 1982 E, S 1,2
McLean, R A (NSW) 1971 SA 1,2,3, F 1,2
McLean, W M (Q) 1946 NZ 1, M, NZ 2, 1947 NZ 1,2
McMahon, M J (Q) 1913 NZ 1
McMaster, R E (Q) 1946 NZ 1, M, NZ 2, 1947 NZ 1,2, I, W
McMeniman, H J (Q, WF) 2005 Sm(R), It(R), F2(R), E, I, W, 2007 SA2(R), NZ2(R), [J(R), Fj(R), C, E(t&R)], 2008 F2(R), SA1(t&R), NZ2(R), SA3, NZ3(R), It, E, F3, W, 2013 NZ1
MacMillan, D I (Q) 1950 BI 1,2
McMullen, K V (NSW) 1962 NZ 3,5, 1963 E, SA 1
McShane, J M S (NSW) 1937 SA 1,2
Ma'afu, R S L (ACT, WF) 2010 Fj, E1, 2, I, SA1, NZ1, 2, SA2, 3, NZ3, 2011 NZ2(R), [Ru(R), W], W
Mackay, G (NSW) 1926 NZ 4
Mackney, W A R (NSW) 1933 SA 1,5, 1934 NZ 1,2
Magrath, E (NSW) 1961 Fj 1, SA 2, F
Maguire, D J (Q) 1989 BI 1,2,3
Malcolm, S J (NSW) 1927 S, 1928 E, F, NZ 1,2, M, 1929 NZ 1,2,3, 1930 BI, 1931 NZ, 1932 NZ 1,2,3, 1933 SA 4,5, 1934 NZ 1,2
Malone, J H (NSW) 1936 NZ 1,2, M, 1937 SA 2
Malouf, B P (NSW) 1982 NZ 1
Mandible, E F (NSW) 1907 NZ 2,3, 1908 W
Manning, J (NSW) 1904 BI 2
Manning, R C S (Q) 1967 NZ
Mansfield, B W (NSW) 1975 J 2
Manu, D T (NSW) 1995 [R (t)], NZ 1,2, 1996 W 1,2(R), SA 1, NZ 2, It, S, I, 1997 F 1, NZ 1(t), E 1, NZ 2, SA 1
Marks, H (NSW) 1899 BI 1,2
Marks, R J P (Q) 1962 NZ 4,5, 1963 E, SA 2,3,4, 1964 NZ 1,2,3, 1965 SA 1,2, 1966 W, S, 1967 E, I 1, F, I 2
Marrott, R (NSW) 1920 NZ 1,3
Marrott, W J (NSW) 1922 NZ 2,3, 1923 M 1,2,3, NZ 1,2
Marshall, J S (NSW) 1949 M 1
Martin, G J (Q) 1989 BI 1,2,3, NZ, F 1,2, 1990 F 1,3(R), NZ 1
Martin, M C (NSW) 1980 Fj, NZ 1,2, 1981 F 1,2, W (R)
Massey-Westropp, M (NSW) 1914 NZ 3
Mathers, M J (NSW) 1980 Fj, NZ 2(R)
Maund, J W (NSW) 1903 NZ
Mayne, A V (NSW) 1920 NZ 1,2,3, 1922 M 1
Meadows, J E C (V, Q) 1974 NZ 1, 1975 S, W, 1976 I, US, Fj 1,3, F 1,2, 1978 NZ 1,2,3, 1979 I 1,2, 1981 I, S, 1982 E, NZ 2,3, 1983 US, Arg 2, NZ
Meadows, R W (NSW) 1958 M 1,2,3, NZ 1,2,3
Meagher, F W (NSW) 1923 NZ 3, 1924 NZ 3, 1925 NZ 4, 1926 NZ 1,2,3, 1927 I, W
Meibusch, J H (Q) 1904 BI 3
Meibusch, L S (Q) 1912 US
Melrose, T C (NSW) 1978 NZ 3, 1979 I 1,2, NZ, Arg 1,2
Merrick, S (NSW) 1995 NZ 1,2
Messenger, H H (NSW) 1907 NZ 2,3
Middleton, S A (NSW) 1909 E, 1910 NZ 1,2,3
Miller, A R (NSW) 1952 Fj 1,2, NZ 1,2, 1953 SA 1,2,3,4, 1954 Fj 1,2, 1955 NZ 1,2,3, 1956 SA 1,2, 1957 NZ 1,2, 1958 W, E, S, F, M 1,2,3, 1959 BI 1,2, 1961 Fj 1,2,3, SA 2, F, 1962 NZ 1,2, 1966 BI 1,2, W, S, 1967 I 1, F, I 2, NZ
Miller, J M (NSW) 1962 NZ 1, 1963 E, SA 1, 1966 W, S, 1967 E
Miller, J S (Q) 1986 NZ 2,3, 1987 SK, [US, I, F], NZ, Arg 1,2, 1988 E 1,2, NZ 2,3, E, S, It, 1989 BI 1,2,3, NZ, 1990 F 1,3, 1991 W, [WS, W, I]
Miller, S W J (NSW) 1899 BI 3
Mingey, N (NSW) 1920 NZ 3, 1921 SA 1,2,3, 1923 M 1, NZ 1,2
Mitchell, D A (Q, WF, NSW) 2005 SA1(R), 2(R), 3(R), NZ1, SA4, NZ2, F2(R), E, I, W, 2007 W1, 2, Fj, SA1, 2(R), NZ2, [J(R), W, Fj, C, E(R)], 2008 SA1(R), NZ2(R), SA2, 3(R), NZ4, E, F3, W, 2009 It1, F, NZ1, SA1, NZ2, SA2(R), 3, NZ3, E, I, S, W, 2010 Fj(t&R), E1, 2, I, SA1, NZ1, 2, SA2, 3, NZ4, W, E3, It, F, 2011 [I(R), US, Ru], 2012 NZ2, 3(R), E(R), It, W4
Mogg, J D (ACT) 2013 BI 3(R),NZ1,2

Monaghan, L E (NSW) 1973 E, 1974 NZ 1,2,3, 1975 E 1,2, S, W, 1976 E, I, US, F 1, 1978 W 1,2, NZ 1, 1979 I 1,2
Monti, C I A (Q) 1938 NZ 2
Moon, B J (Q) 1978 NZ 2,3, 1979 I 1,2, NZ, Arg 1,2, 1980 Fj, NZ 1,2,3, 1981 F 1,2, I, W, S, 1982 E, S 1,2, 1983 US, Arg 1,2, NZ, It, F 1,2, 1984 Fj, NZ 1,2,3, E, 1986 It, F, Arg 1,2
Mooney, T P (Q) 1954 Fj 1,2
Moore, R C (ACT, NSW) 1999 [US], 2001 BI 2,3, SA 1, NZ 1, SA 2, NZ 2, Sp (R), E (R), F (R), W (R), 2002 F 1(R),2(R), SA 2(R)
Moore, S T (Q, ACT) 2005 Sm(R), It(R), F1(R), SA2(R), 3(R), F2(t&R), 2006 It(t), I2(R), S, 2007 W1, 2, Fj(R), SA1, NZ1, 2, [J, W, Fj, E], 2008 I, F1, 2, SA1, NZ1, 2, SA2, 3(R), NZ3, 4, It, E, F3, W, 2009 It1, F, NZ1, SA1, NZ2, SA2, 3(R), NZ3(R), 4, E, I, S, W, 2010 SA1(R), NZ1, SA2(t), 3, NZ3, 4, E3, It, F, 2011 Sm, SA1, NZ1, SA2, NZ2, [It, US(R), Ru, SA, NZ], W(R), 2012 S, W1(R), 2(R), 3(R), NZ1(R), 2, F(R), E(R), It, W4(R), 2013 BI 1, 2, 3, NZ1, 2, SA1, Arg1, SA2, Arg2
Morahan, L J (Q) 2012 S
Moran, H M (NSW) 1908 W
Morgan, G (Q) 1992 NZ 1(R), 3(R), W, 1993 Tg, NZ, SA 1,2,3, C, F 1,2, 1994 I 1,2, It 1, WS, NZ, 1996 W 1,2, C, NZ 1, SA 1, NZ 2, 1997 E 1, NZ 2
Morrissey, C V (NSW) 1925 NZ 2,3,4, 1926 NZ 2,3
Morrissey, W (Q) 1914 NZ 2
Mortlock, S A (ACT) 2000 Arg 1, 2, SA 1, NZ 1, SA 2, NZ 2, SA 3, F, S, E, 2002 F 1,2, NZ 1, SA 1, NZ 2, SA 2, Arg, I, E, It, 2003 [R(R), Nm, S, NZ, E], 2004 S2, E1, PI, NZ1, SA1, NZ2, SA2, S3, F, S4, 2005 Sm, It, F1, SA2, 3(R), NZ1, 2006 E1, 2, I1, NZ1, SA1, NZ2, SA2, NZ3, SA3, It, I2, S, 2007 W1, 2, Fj(R), SA1, NZ1, SA2, NZ2, [J, W, E], 2008 I, F1, 2, SA1, NZ2, SA2, 3, NZ3, 4, It, E, F3, W, 2009 It1, F, NZ1, SA1
Morton, A R (NSW) 1957 NZ 1,2, 1958 F, M 1,2,3, NZ 1,2,3, 1959 BI 1,2
Mossop, R P (NSW) 1949 NZ 1, 2, 1950 BI 1, 2, 1951 NZ 1
Moutray, I E (NSW) 1963 SA 2
Mowen, B S C (ACT) 2013 BI 1,2,3,NZ1,2,SA1,Arg1,SA2,Arg2
Mulligan, P J (NSW) 1925 NZ 1(R)
Mumm, D W (NSW) 2008 I(t&R), F1(R), 2, SA2(R), 3(R), NZ4, It, E(R), F3, W(R), 2009 It1, 2, F, NZ1(t), SA1(R), NZ2(R), 4(R), E(R), S(R), W, 2010 Fj, E1, 2, I, SA1, NZ1, 2, SA2, 3(R), NZ3(R), 4(R), W(R), E3(R)
Munsie, A (NSW) 1928 NZ 2
Murdoch, A R (NSW) 1993 F 1, 1996 W 1
Murphy, P J (Q) 1910 NZ 1, 2, 3, 1913 NZ 1, 2, 3, 1914 NZ 1, 2, 3
Murphy, W (Q) 1912 US

Nasser, B P (Q) 1989 F 1,2, 1990 F 1,2,3, US, NZ 2, 1991 [WS]
Newman, E W (NSW) 1922 NZ 1
Nicholson, F C (Q) 1904 BI 3
Nicholson, F V (Q) 1903 NZ, 1904 BI 1
Niuqila, A S (NSW) 1988 S, It, 1989 BI 1
Noriega, E P (ACT, NSW) 1998 F, E 2, 1999 I 1,2, E, SA 1, NZ 1, SA 2(R), NZ 2(R), 2002 F 1,2, NZ 1, SA 1, NZ 2, Arg, I, E, It, 2003 I, W, E, SA 1, NZ 1, SA 2
Norton-Knight, S H (NSW) 2007 W1,Fj(R)
Nothling, O E (NSW) 1921 SA 1,2,3, NZ, 1922 M 1,2,3, NZ 1,2,3, 1923 M 1,2,3, NZ 1,2,3, 1924 NZ 1,2,3
Nucifora, D V (Q) 1991 [Arg (R)], 1993 C (R)

O'Brien, F W H (NSW) 1937 SA 2, 1938 NZ 3
O'Connor, J A (NSW) 1928 NZ 1,2,3, M
O'Connor, J D (WF, MR) 2008 It(R), 2009 It1, 2, F(R), NZ1(R), SA1(R), NZ2, SA2, 3, NZ3, 4, I(R), S(R), W(R), 2010 E1, 2, I, SA1, NZ1, 2, SA2, 3, NZ3, 4, W, E3, F, 2011 SA1, NZ1, SA2, [It(R), I, Ru, SA, NZ, W], W, 2013 BI 1, 2, 3, NZ1, 2, SA1, Arg1
O'Connor, M (ACT) 1994 I 1
O'Connor, M D (ACT, Q) 1979 Arg 1,2, 1980 Fj, NZ 1,2,3, 1981 F 1,2, I, 1982 E, S 1,2
O'Donnell, C (NSW) 1913 NZ 1,2
O'Donnell, I C (NSW) 1899 BI 3,4
O'Donnell, J B (NSW) 1928 NZ 1,3, M
O'Donnell, J M (NSW) 1899 BI 4
O'Gorman, J F (NSW) 1961 Fj 1, SA 1,2, F, 1962 NZ 2, 1963 E, SA 1,2,3,4, 1965 SA 1,2, 1966 W, S, 1967 E, I 1, F, I 2
O'Neill, D J (Q) 1964 NZ 1,2
O'Neill, J M (Q) 1952 NZ 1,2, 1956 SA 1,2
Ofahengaue, V (NSW) 1990 NZ 1,2,3, 1991 W, E, NZ 1,2, [Arg, W, I, NZ, E], 1992 S 1,2, SA, I, W, 1994 WS, NZ, 1995 Arg 1,2(R), [SA, C, E], NZ 1,2, 1997 Arg 1(t + R), 2(R), E 2, S, 1998 E 1(R), S 1(R),2(R), NZ 1(R), SA 1(R), NZ 2(R), SA 2(R), NZ 3(R), Fj, WS, F (R)
Ormiston, I W L (NSW) 1920 NZ 1,2,3
Osborne, D H (V) 1975 E 1,2, J 1
Outterside, R (NSW) 1959 BI 1,2
Oxenham, A McE (Q) 1904 BI 2, 1907 NZ 2
Oxlade, A M (Q) 1904 BI 2,3, 1905 NZ, 1907 NZ 2
Oxlade, B D (Q) 1938 NZ 1,2,3

Palfreyman, J R L (NSW) 1929 NZ 1, 1930 BI, 1931 NZ, 1932 NZ 3
Palmer, D P (ACT) 2012 S
Palu, W L (NSW) 2006 E2(t&R), I1(R), SA2, NZ3, SA3, W, It, I2, S(R), 2007 W1, 2, SA1, NZ1, [J, W, Fj, E], 2008 I, F1, SA1, NZ1, 2, SA2, 3, NZ3, It(R), E(R), F3, 2009 NZ1, SA1, NZ3(t&R), 4, E, I, S, W, 2011 [I(R), US], 2012 W1, 2, 3, NZ3, F, E, It, W4, 2013 BI 1, 2, 3
Panoho, G M (Q) 1998 SA 2(R), NZ 3(R), Fj (R), Tg, WS (R), 1999 I 2, E, SA 1(R), NZ 1, 2000 Arg 1(R),2(R), SA 1(R), NZ 1(R), SA 2(R),3(R), F (R), S (R), E (R), 2001 BI 1, 2003 SA 2(R), NZ 2
Papworth, B (NSW) 1985 Fj 1,2, 1986 It, Arg 1,2, NZ 1,2,3, 1987 [E, US, J (R), I, F], NZ, Arg 1,2
Parker, A J (Q) 1983 Arg 1(R), 2, NZ
Parkinson, C E (Q) 1907 NZ 2
Pashley, J J (NSW) 1954 Fj 1,2, 1958 M 1,2,3
Paul, J A (ACT) 1998 S 1(R), NZ 1(R), SA 1(t), Fj (R), Tg, 1999 I 1,2, E, SA 1, NZ 1, [R (R), I 3(R), W (t), F (R)], 2000 Arg 1(R),2(R), SA 1(R), NZ 1(R), SA 2(R), NZ 2(R), SA 3(R), F (R), S (R), E (R), 2001 BI 1, 2002 F 1, NZ 1, SA 1, NZ 2, SA 2, Arg, E, 2003 I, W, E, SA 2(t&R), NZ2(R), [Arg(R), R(R), Nm, I(R), S(R), NZ(R), E(R)], 2004 S1(R), 2(R), E1(R), PI(R), NZ1(t&R), SA1, NZ2(R), SA2(R), S3, F, S4, E2, 2005 Sm, It, F1, SA1, 2, 3, NZ1, 2006 E1(R), 2(R), I1(R) NZ1(R), SA1, NZ2, SA2(R), NZ3, SA3
Pauling, T P (NSW) 1936 NZ 1, 1937 SA 1
Payne, S J (NSW) 1996 W 2, C, NZ 1, S, 1997 F 1(t), NZ 2(R), Arg 2(t)
Pearse, G K (NSW) 1975 W (R), 1976 I, US, Fj 1,2,3, 1978 NZ 1,2,3
Penman, A P (NSW) 1905 NZ
Perrin, P D (Q) 1962 NZ 1
Perrin, T D (NSW) 1931 M, NZ
Phelps, R (NSW) 1955 NZ 2,3, 1956 SA 1,2, 1957 NZ 1,2, 1958 W, I, E, S, F, M 1, NZ 1,2,3, 1961 Fj 1,2,3, SA 1,2, F, 1962 NZ 1,2
Phipps, J A (NSW) 1953 SA 1,2,3,4, 1954 Fj 1,2, 1955 NZ 1,2,3, 1956 SA 1,2
Phipps, N J (MR) 2011 Sm, SA1(R), [Ru(R)], 2012 SA1(R), Arg1, SA2, Arg2, NZ3, F, E, It(R), W4, 2013 BI 1(R), 3(R)
Phipps, W J (NSW) 1928 NZ 2
Piggott, H R (NSW) 1922 M 3(R)
Pilecki, S J (Q) 1978 W 1,2, NZ 1,2, 1979 I 1,2, NZ, Arg 1,2, 1980 Fj, NZ 1,2, 1982 S 1,2, 1983 US, Arg 1,2, NZ
Pini, M (Q) 1994 I 1, It 2, WS, NZ, 1995 Arg 1,2, [SA, R (t)]
Piper, B J C (NSW) 1946 NZ 1, M, NZ 2, 1947 NZ 1, S, I, W, 1948 E, F, 1949 M, 1,2,3
Pocock, D W (WF, ACT) 2008 NZ4(R), It(R), 2009 It1(R), 2, F(R), NZ1(R), SA1(R), NZ2(R), SA2(R), 3, NZ3, 4, E(R), I, W, 2010 Fj, E1, 2, I, SA1, NZ1, 2, SA2, 3, NZ3, 4, W, E3, It, F, 2011 SA1, NZ1, SA2, NZ2, [It, Ru, SA, NZ, W], W, 2012 S, W1, 2, 3, NZ1, W4
Poidevin, S P (NSW) 1980 Fj, NZ 1,2,3, 1981 F 1,2, I, W, S, 1982 E, NZ 1,2,3, 1983 US, Arg 1,2, NZ, It, F 1,2, 1984 Fj, NZ 1,2,3, E, I, W, S, 1985 C 1,2, NZ, Fj 1,2, 1986 It, F, Arg 1,2, NZ 1,2,3, 1987 SK, [E, J, I, F, W], Arg 1, 1988 NZ 1,2,3, 1989 NZ, 1991 E, NZ 1,2, [Arg, W, I, NZ, E]
Polota-Nau, S U T (NSW) 2005 E(R), I(R), 2006 S(R), 2008 SA1(R), NZ1(R), 2(R), SA2(R), 3, It(R), E(R), 2009 It1(R), 2, F(R), SA1(R), NZ2(t&R), SA2(R), 3, NZ3, 4(R), E(R), I(R), S(R), W(R), 2010 It(R), F(R), 2011 [It(R), I, US, SA(R), NZ(R), W], W, 2012 W1, 2, 3, NZ1, SA1, Arg1, SA2, Arg2, NZ3, F, E, W4
Pope, A M (Q) 1968 NZ 2(R)
Potter, R T (Q) 1961 Fj 2
Potts, J M (NSW) 1957 NZ 1,2, 1958 W, I, 1959 BI 1
Prentice, C W (NSW) 1914 NZ 3
Prentice, W S (NSW) 1908 W, 1909 E, 1910 NZ 1,2,3, 1912 US
Price, R A (NSW) 1974 NZ 1,2,3, 1975 E 1,2, J 1,2, 1976 US

Primmer, C J (Q) 1951 NZ 1,3
Proctor, I J (NSW)) 1967 NZ
Prosser, R B (NSW) 1967 E, I 1, 2, NZ, 1968 NZ 1, 2, F, I, S, 1969 W, SA 1, 2, 3, 4, 1971 SA 1, 2, 3, F 1, 2, 1972 F 1, 2, NZ 1, 2, 3, Fj
Pugh, G H (NSW) 1912 US
Purcell, M P (Q) 1966 W, S, 1967 I 2
Purkis, E M (NSW) 1958 S, M 1
Pym, J E (NSW) 1923 M 1

Rainbow, A E (NSW) 1925 NZ 1
Ramalli, C (NSW) 1938 NZ 2,3
Ramsay, K M (NSW) 1936 M, 1937 SA 1, 1938 NZ 1,3
Rankin, R (NSW) 1936 NZ 1,2, M, 1937 SA 1,2, 1938 NZ 1,2
Rathbone, C (ACT) 2004 S1, 2(R), E1, PI, NZ1, SA1, NZ2, SA2, S3, F, S4, 2005 Sm, NZ1(R), SA4, NZ2, 2006E1(R), 2(R), I1(R), SA1(R), NZ2(R), SA2(R), NZ3, SA3, W, It, I2
Rathie, D S (Q) 1972 F 1,2
Raymond, R L (NSW) 1920 NZ 1, 2, 1921 SA 2, 3, NZ, 1922 M 1, 2, 3, NZ 1, 2, 3, 1923 M 1, 2
Redwood, C (Q) 1903 NZ, 1904 BI 1, 2, 3
Reid, E J (NSW) 1925 NZ 2,3,4
Reid, T W (NSW) 1961 Fj 1,2,3, SA 1, 1962 NZ 1
Reilly, N P (Q) 1968 NZ 1,2, F, I, S, 1969 W, SA 1,2,3,4
Reynolds, L J (NSW) 1910 NZ 2(R), 3
Reynolds, R J (NSW) 1984 Fj, NZ 1, 2, 3, 1985 Fj 1, 2, 1986 Arg 1, 2, NZ 1, 1987 [J]
Richards, E W (Q) 1904 BI 1,3, 1905 NZ, 1907 NZ 1(R), 2
Richards, G (NSW) 1978 NZ 2(R), 3, 1981 F 1
Richards, T J (Q) 1908 W, 1909 E, 1912 US
Richards, V S (NSW) 1936 NZ 1,2(R), M, 1937 SA 1, 1938 NZ 1
Richardson, G C (Q) 1971 SA 1,2,3, 1972 NZ 2,3, Fj, 1973 Tg 1,2, W
Rigney, W A (NSW) 1925 NZ 2,4, 1926 NZ 4
Riley, S A (NSW) 1903 NZ
Ritchie, E V (NSW) 1924 NZ 1,3, 1925 NZ 2,3
Roberts, B T (NSW) 1956 SA 2
Roberts, H F (Q) 1961 Fj 1,3, SA 2, F
Robertson, I J (NSW) 1975 J 1,2
Robinson, B A (NSW) 2006 SA3, I2(R), S, 2007 W1(R), 2, Fj(R), 2008 I, F1, 2, SA1, NZ1, 2, SA2, 3, NZ3, 4, E, W, 2009 It1, F, NZ1, SA1, NZ2, SA2, 3, NZ3, 4, E, I, S, W, 2010 SA1, NZ1, 2, SA2, 3, NZ3, 4, W, E3, It(R), F(t&R), 2012 W1, 2, 3, NZ1, 2, SA1, Arg1, SA2, Arg2(R), NZ3, F, E, It, W4, 2013 BI 1, 2, 3, SA2(R), Arg2(t&R)
Robinson, B J (ACT) 1996 It (R), S (R), I (R), 1997 F 1,2, NZ 1, E 1, NZ 2, SA 1(R), NZ 3(R), SA 2(R), Arg 1,2, E 2, S, 1998 Tg
Robinson, B S (Q) 2011 Sm(R)
Roche, C (Q) 1982 S 1,2, NZ 1,2,3, 1983 US, Arg 1,2, NZ, It, F 1,2, 1984 Fj, NZ 1,2,3, I
Rodriguez, E E (NSW) 1984 Fj, NZ 1,2,3, E, I, W, S, 1985 C 1,2, NZ, Fj 1, 1986 It, F, Arg 1,2, NZ 1,2,3, 1987 SK, [E, J, W (R)], NZ, Arg 1,2
Roe, J A (Q) 2003 [Nm(R)], 2004 E1(R), SA1(R), NZ2(R), SA2(t&R), S3, F, 2005 Sm(R), It(R), F1(R), SA1(R), 3, NZ1, SA4(t&R), NZ2(R), F2(R), E, I, W
Roebuck, M C (NSW) 1991 W, E, NZ 1,2, [Arg, WS, W, I, NZ, E], 1992 S 1,2, NZ 2,3, SA, I, W, 1993 Tg, SA 1,2,3, C, F 2
Roff, J W (ACT) 1995 [C, R], NZ 1,2, 1996 W 1,2, NZ 1, SA 1, NZ 2, SA 2(R), S, I, W 3, 1997 F 1,2, NZ 1, E 1, NZ 2, SA 1, NZ 3, SA 2, Arg 1,2, E 2, S, 1998 E 1, S 1,2, NZ 1, SA 1, NZ 2, SA 2, NZ 3, Fj, Tg, WS, F, E 2, 1999 I 1,2, E, SA 1, NZ 1, SA 2, NZ 2(R), [R (R), I 3, US (R), W, SA 3, F], 2000 Arg 1,2, SA 1, NZ 1, SA 2, NZ 2, SA 3, F, S, E, 2001 BI 1,2,3, SA 1, NZ 1, SA 2, NZ 2, Sp, E, F, W, 2003 I, W, E, SA 1, [Arg, R, I, S(R), NZ(t&R), E(R)], 2004 S1, 2, E1, PI
Rogers, M S (NSW) 2002 F 1(R),2(R), NZ 1(R), SA 1(R), NZ 2(R), SA 2(t&R), Arg, 2003 E (R), SA 1, NZ 1, SA 2, NZ 2, [Arg,R,Nm, I, S, NZ, E], 2004S3(R), F(R), S4(R), E2(R), 2005 Sm(R), It, F1(R), SA1, 4, NZ2, F2, E, I, W, 2006 E1, 2, I1, NZ1, SA1(R), NZ2(R), SA2(R), NZ3(R), W, It, I2(R), S(R)
Rose, H A (NSW), 1967 I 2, NZ, 1968 NZ 1, 2, F, I, S, 1969 W, SA 1, 2, 3, 4, 1970 S
Rosenblum, M E (NSW) 1928 NZ 1, 2, 3, M
Rosenblum, R G (NSW) 1969 SA 1, 3, 1970 S
Rosewell, J S H (NSW) 1907 NZ 1,3
Ross, A W (NSW) 1925 NZ 1, 2, 3, 1926 NZ 1, 2, 3, 1927 I, W, S, 1928 E, F, 1929 NZ 1, 1930 BI, 1931 M, NZ, 1932 NZ 2, 3, 1933 SA 5, 1934 NZ 1,2
Ross, W S (Q) 1979 I 1, 2, Arg 2, 1980 Fj, NZ 1, 2, 3, 1982 S 1, 2, 1983 US, Arg 1, 2, NZ
Rothwell, P R (NSW) 1951 NZ 1, 2, 3, 1952 Fj 1
Row, F L (NSW) 1899 BI 1, 3, 4
Row, N E (NSW) 1907 NZ 1,3, 1909 E, 1910 NZ 1,2,3
Rowles, P G (NSW) 1972 Fj, 1973 E
Roxburgh, J R (NSW) 1968 NZ 1, 2, F, 1969 W, SA 1, 2, 3, 4, 1970 S
Ruebner, G (NSW) 1966 BI 1,2
Russell, C J (NSW) 1907 NZ 1,2,3, 1908 W, 1909 E
Ryan, J R (NSW) 1975 J 2, 1976 I, US, Fj 1,2,3
Ryan, K J (Q) 1958 E, M 1, NZ 1,2,3
Ryan, P F (NSW) 1963 E, SA 1, 1966 BI 1,2
Ryan, P J (NSW) 2012 F(R)
Rylance, M H (NSW) 1926 NZ 4(R)

Sailor, W J (Q) 2002 F 1, 2, Arg (R), I, E, It, 2003 I, W, E, SA 1, NZ 1, SA 2, NZ 2, [Arg, R, I, S, NZ, E], 2004 S1, 2, NZ1(R), 2(R), SA2(R), S3(R), F(R), S4(R), E2, 2005 Sm, It, F1, SA1, 2, 3, F2, I(R), W(R)
Samo, U R (ACT,Q) 2004 S1, 2, E1, PI, NZ1, S4(R), 2011 SA2(R), NZ2, [It, I, US(R), Ru, SA, NZ, W(t&R)], W(R), 2012 NZ1(R), 2(R), SA1, Arg1, SA2, Arg2, F(R)
Sampson, J H (NSW) 1899 BI 4
Sayle, J L (NSW) 1967 NZ
Schulte, B G (Q) 1946 NZ 1, M
Scott, P R I (NSW) 1962 NZ 1,2
Scott-Young, S J (Q) 1990 F 2,3(R), US, NZ 3, 1992 NZ 1,2,3
Shambrook, G G (Q) 1976 Fj 2,3
Sharpe, N C (Q, WF) 2002 F 1,2, NZ 1, SA 1, NZ 2, SA 2, 2003 I, W, E, SA 1(R), NZ 1(R), SA 2(R), NZ 2(R), [Arg, R, Nm, I, S, NZ, E], 2004 S1, 2, E1, PI, NZ1, SA1, NZ2, SA2, 2005 Sm,It, F1, SA1, 2, 3, NZ1, SA4, NZ2, F2, E, I, W, 2006 E1, 2, I1, NZ1, SA1, NZ2, SA2, NZ3, SA3, W, It, I2, S, 2007 W1, 2, SA1, NZ1, SA2, NZ2, [J, W, C, E], 2008 I, F1, SA1, NZ1, 2, 3, 4, E, F3, W, 2009 It1, F, NZ1, SA1, NZ2, 2010 Fj, E1, 2, SA1, NZ1, 2, SA2, 3, NZ3, 4, W, E3, It, F, 2011 Sm, SA1(R), 2, [US, Ru, SA(R), W], W(R), 2012 S, W1, 2, 3, NZ1, 2, SA1, Arg1, SA2, Arg2, NZ3, F, E, It, W4
Shaw, A A (Q) 1973 W, E, 1975 E 1,2, J 2, S, W, 1976 E, I, US, Fj 1,2,3, F 1,2, 1978 W 1,2, NZ 1,2,3, 1979 I 1,2, NZ, Arg 1,2, 1980 Fj, NZ 1,2,3, 1981 F 1,2, I, W, S, 1982 S 1,2
Shaw, C (NSW) 1925 NZ 2,3,4(R)
Shaw, G A (NSW, Q) 1969 W, SA 1(R), 1970 S, 1971 SA 1,2,3, F 1,2, 1973 W, E, 1974 NZ 1, 2, 3, 1975 E 1,2, J 1, 2, W, 1976 E, I, US, Fj 1, 2, 3, F 1,2, 1979 NZ
Sheehan, B R (ACT, WF) 2006 SA3(R), 2008 SA2(R), 3(R), 2012 SA2(R), Arg2(R), NZ3(R), It
Sheehan, W B J (NSW) 1921 SA 1,2,3, 1922 NZ 1, 2, 3, 1923 M 1, 2, NZ 1, 2, 3, 1924 NZ 1, 2, 1926 NZ 1, 2, 3, 1927 W, S
Shehadie, N M (NSW) 1947 NZ 2, 1948 E, F, 1949 M 1, 2, 3, NZ 1, 2, 1950 BI 1, 2, 1951 NZ 1, 2, 3, 1952 Fj 1, 2, NZ 2, 1953 SA 1, 2, 3, 4, 1954 Fj 1, 2, 1955 NZ 1, 2, 3, 1956 SA 1, 2, 1957 NZ 2, 1958 W, I
Sheil, A G R (Q) 1956 SA 1
Shepherd, C B (WF) 2006 E1(R), 2(R), I1(R), SA3, W, 2007 [C], 2008 I, F1, 2(R)
Shepherd, D J (V) 1964 NZ 3, 1965 SA 1,2, 1966 BI 1,2
Shepherdson, G T (ACT) 2006 I1, NZ1, SA1, NZ2(R), SA2(R), It, I2, S, 2007 W1, 2, SA1, NZ1, SA2, NZ2, [J(R), W, Fj, E]
Shipperley, D P (Q) 2012 SA1,Arg1,SA2
Shute, J L (NSW) 1920 NZ 3, 1922 M 2,3
Simmons, R A (Q) 2010 SA1(R), NZ1(R), 2(R), SA2(R), It, F, 2011 SA1, NZ1, 2(R), [It(R), I(R), US, Ru(R), NZ(t&R), W(R)], W, 2012 S(R), W1, 2, 3(R), NZ1(t), SA2(R), F(R), 2013 BI 1(R), 2(R), 3(R), NZ1, 2, SA1, Arg1, SA2, Arg2
Simpson, R J (NSW) 1913 NZ 2
Sio, S T (ACT) 2013 NZ1(R), 2(R), SA1(R), Arg1(R)
Skinner, A J (NSW) 1969 W, SA 4, 1970 S
Slack, A G (Q) 1978 W 1,2, NZ 1,2, 1979 NZ, Arg 1,2, 1980 Fj, 1981 I, W, S, 1982 E, S 1, NZ 3, 1983 US, Arg 1,2 NZ, It, 1984 Fj, NZ 1,2,3, E, I, W, S, 1986 It, F, NZ 1,2,3, 1987 SK, [E, US, J, I, F, W]
Slater, S H (NSW) 1910 NZ 3
Slattery, P J (Q) 1990 US (R), 1991 W (R), E (R), [WS (R), W, I (R)], 1992 I, W, 1993 Tg, C, F 1,2, 1994 I 1,2, It 1(R), 1995 [C, R (R)]
Slipper, J A (Q) 2010 E1(R), 2(R), I(R), SA1(R), NZ1(R), 2(R), SA2(R), 3(R), NZ3(R), 4(R), W(R), E3(R), It, F, 2011 [It(R), I(R), US, Ru, SA(R), NZ(R), W], W, 2012 S, NZ1(R), 2(R), SA1(R), Arg1(R),

SA2(R), Arg2, NZ3, F(t&R), E(R), It(R), W4(R), 2013 BI 1(R), 2(R), 3(R), NZ1, 2, SA1, Arg1, SA2, Arg2
Smairl, A M (NSW) 1928 NZ 1, 2, 3
Smith, B A (Q) 1987 SK, [US, J, I (R), W], Arg 1
Smith, D P (Q) 1993 SA 1,2,3, C, F 2, 1994 I 1,2, It 1,2, WS, NZ, 1995 Arg 1,2, [SA, R, E], NZ 1,2, 1998 SA 1(R), NZ 3(R), Fj
Smith, F B (NSW) 1905 NZ, 1907 NZ 1,2,3
Smith, G B (ACT) 2000 F, S, E, 2001 BI 1, 2, 3, SA 1, NZ 1, SA 2, NZ 2, Sp, E, F (R), W (R), 2002 F 1,2, NZ 1, SA 1, NZ 2, SA 2, Arg, I, E, It, 2003 I, NZ 1, SA 2, NZ 2, [Arg, R, Nm, I, S, NZ, E], 2004 S1, 2(R), E1(t&R), PI(R), NZ1(R), SA1, NZ2, SA2, S3, F, S4, E2, 2005 Sm, It, F1, SA1, 2, 3, NZ1, SA4(R), NZ2, F2, E, I, W, 2006 E1, 2, I1, NZ1, SA1, NZ2, SA2, NZ3(t), SA3(R), It, I2(R), S, 2007 W1(R), 2, Fj(R), SA1, NZ1, SA2, NZ2, [J, W, C, E], 2008 I, F1, 2(R), SA1, NZ1, 2, SA2, 3(R), NZ3, 4, E, F3, W(R), 2009 It1, 2, F, NZ1, SA1, NZ2, SA2, 3, NZ3, 4(R), E, I(t), S, W(R), 2013 BI 3
Smith, L M (NSW) 1905 NZ
Smith, N C (NSW) 1922 NZ 2,3, 1923 NZ 1, 1924 NZ 1,3(R), 1925 NZ 2,3
Smith, P V (NSW) 1967 NZ, 1968 NZ 1,2, F, I, S, 1969 W, SA 1
Smith, R A (NSW) 1971 SA 1,2, 1972 F 1,2, NZ 1,2(R), 3, Fj, 1975 E 1,2, J 1,2, S, W, 1976 E, I, US, Fj 1,2,3, F 1,2
Smith, T S (NSW) 1921 SA 1,2,3, NZ, 1922 M 2,3, NZ 1,2,3, 1925 NZ 1,3,4
Snell, H W (NSW) 1925 NZ 2,3, 1928 NZ 3
Solomon, H J (NSW) 1949 M 3, NZ 2, 1950 BI 1,2, 1951 NZ 1,2, 1952 Fj 1,2, NZ 1,2, 1953 SA 1,2,3, 1955 NZ 1
Spooner, N R (Q) 1999 I 1,2
Spragg, S A (NSW) 1899 BI 1,2,3,4
Staniforth, S N G (NSW,WF) 1999 [US], 2002 I, It, 2006 SA3(R), I2(R), S, 2007 Fj, NZ1(R), SA2(R), NZ2(R), [W(R), Fj(R)]
Stanley, R G (NSW) 1921 NZ, 1922 M 1,2,3, NZ 1,2,3, 1923 M 2,3, NZ 1,2,3, 1924 NZ 1,3
Stapleton, E T (NSW) 1951 NZ 1,2,3, 1952 Fj 1,2, NZ 1,2, 1953 SA 1,2,3,4, 1954 Fj 1, 1955 NZ 1,2,3, 1958 NZ 1
Steggall, J C (Q) 1931 M, NZ, 1932 NZ 1,2,3, 1933 SA 1,2,3,4,5
Stegman, T R (NSW) 1973 Tg 1,2
Stephens, O G (NSW) 1973 Tg 1,2, W, 1974 NZ 2,3
Stewart, A A (NSW) 1979 NZ, Arg 1,2
Stiles, N B (Q) 2001 BI 1,2,3, SA 1, NZ 1, SA 2, NZ 2, Sp, E, F, W, 2002 I
Stone, A H (NSW) 1937 SA 2, 1938 NZ 2,3
Stone, C G (NSW) 1938 NZ 1
Stone, J M (NSW) 1946 M, NZ 2
Storey, G P (NSW) 1926 NZ 4, 1927 I, W, S, 1928 E, F, 1929 NZ 3(R), 1930 BI
Storey, K P (NSW) 1936 NZ 2
Storey, N J D (NSW) 1962 NZ 1
Strachan, D J (NSW) 1955 NZ 2,3
Strauss, C P (NSW) 1999 I 1(R),2(R), E (R), SA 1(R), NZ 1, SA 2(R), NZ 2(R), [R (R), I 3(R), US, W]
Street, N O (NSW) 1899 BI 2
Streeter, S F (NSW) 1978 NZ 1
Stuart, R (NSW) 1910 NZ 2,3
Stumbles, B D (NSW) 1972 NZ 1(R), 2,3, Fj
Sturtridge, G S (V) 1929 NZ 2, 1932 NZ 1, 2, 3, 1933 SA 1, 2, 3, 4, 5
Sullivan, P D (NSW) 1971 SA 1,2,3, F 1,2, 1972 F 1,2, NZ 1,2, Fj, 1973 Tg 1,2, W
Summons, A J (NSW) 1958 W, I, E, S, M 2, NZ 1,2,3, 1959 BI 1,2
Suttor, D C (NSW) 1913 NZ 1,2,3
Swannell, B I (NSW) 1905 NZ
Sweeney, T L (Q) 1953 SA 1

Taafe, B S (NSW) 1969 SA 1, 1972 F 1,2
Tabua, I (Q) 1993 SA 2,3, C, F 1, 1994 I 1,2, It 1,2, 1995 [C, R]
Tahu, P J A (NSW) 2008 NZ1(R), SA2(R), 3, It
Tancred, A J (NSW) 1927 I, W, S
Tancred, H E (NSW) 1923 M 1,2
Tancred, J L (NSW) 1926 NZ 3,4, 1928 F
Tanner, W H (Q) 1899 BI 1,2
Tapuai, B N L (Q) 2011 W(R), 2012 Arg2, NZ3, F, E, It, W4
Tarleton, K (NSW) 1925 NZ 2,3
Tasker, W G (NSW) 1913 NZ 1,2,3, 1914 NZ 1,2,3
Tate, M J (NSW) 1951 NZ 3, 1952 Fj 1,2, NZ 1,2, 1953 SA 1, 1954 Fj 1,2
Taylor, D A (Q) 1968 NZ 1,2, F, I, S
Taylor, H C (NSW) 1923 NZ 1,2,3, 1924 NZ 4
Taylor, J I (NSW) 1971 SA 1, 1972 F 1,2, Fj
Taylor, J M (NSW) 1922 M 1,2
Teitzel, R G (Q) 1966 W, S, 1967 E, I 1, F, I 2, NZ
Telford, D G (NSW) 1926 NZ 3(R)
Thompson, C E (NSW) 1922 M 1, 1923 M 1,2, NZ 1, 1924 NZ 2,3
Thompson, E G (Q) 1929 NZ 1,2,3, 1930 BI
Thompson, F (NSW) 1913 NZ 1,2,3, 1914 NZ 1,3
Thompson, J (Q) 1914 NZ 1, 2
Thompson, P D (Q) 1950 BI 1
Thompson, R J (WA) 1971 SA 3, F 2(R), 1972 Fj
Thorn, A M (NSW) 1921 SA 1,2,3, NZ, 1922 M 1,3
Thorn, E J (NSW) 1922 NZ 1,2,3, 1923 NZ 1,2,3, 1924 NZ 1,2,3, 1925 NZ 1,2, 1926 NZ 1,2,3,4
Thornett, J E (NSW) 1955 NZ 1,2,3, 1956 SA 1,2, 1958 W, I, S, F, M 2,3, NZ 2,3, 1959 BI 1,2, 1961 Fj 2,3, SA 1,2, F, 1962 NZ 2,3,4,5, 1963 E, SA 1,2,3,4, 1964 NZ 1,2,3, 1965 SA 1,2, 1966 BI 1,2, 1967 F
Thornett, R N (NSW) 1961 Fj 1,2,3, SA 1,2, F, 1962 NZ 1,2,3,4,5
Thorpe, A C (NSW) 1929 NZ 1(R)
Timani, S (NSW) 2011 Sm, 2012 S, W3, NZ1, 2, SA1, Arg2, NZ3, E, It, 2013 Arg1(R), SA2(R), Arg2(R)
Timbury, F R V (Q) 1910 NZ 1,2,
Tindall, E N (NSW) 1973 Tg 2
Toby, A E (NSW) 1925 NZ 1,4
Tolhurst, H A (NSW) 1931 M, NZ
Tomane, J M (ACT) 2012 S, 2013 BI 2,3,SA2,Arg2
Tombs, R C (NSW) 1992 S 1,2, 1994 I 2, It 1, 1996 NZ 2
Tonkin, A E J (NSW) 1947 S, I, W, 1948 E, F, 1950 BI 2
Toomua, M P (ACT) 2013 NZ1,2,SA1(R),Arg1(R),SA2(R),Arg2(R)
Tooth, R M (NSW) 1951 NZ 1,2,3, 1954 Fj 1,2, 1955 NZ 1,2,3, 1957 NZ 1,2
Towers, C H T (NSW) 1926 NZ 1,3(R),4, 1927 I, 1928 E, F, NZ 1,2,3, M, 1929 NZ 1,3, 1930 BI, 1931 M, NZ, 1934 NZ 1,2, 1937 SA 1,2
Trivett, R K (Q) 1966 BI 1,2
Tune, B N (Q) 1996 W 2, C, NZ 1, SA 1, NZ 2, SA 2, 1997 F 1,2, NZ 1, E 1, NZ 2, SA 1, NZ 3, SA 2, Arg, 1,2, E 2, S, 1998 E 1, S 1,2, NZ 1, SA 1,2, NZ 3, 1999 I 1, E, SA 1, NZ 1, SA 2, NZ 2, [R, I 3, W, SA 3, F], 2000 SA 2(R), NZ 2(t&R), SA 3(R), 2001 F (R), W, 2002 NZ 1, SA 1, NZ 2, SA 2, Arg, 2006 NZ1(R)
Tuqiri, L D (NSW) 2003 I (R), W (R), E (R), SA 1(R), NZ 1, SA 2, NZ 2, [Arg(R), R(R), Nm, I(R), S, NZ, E], 2004 S1, 2, E1, PI, NZ1, SA1, NZ2, SA2, S3, F, S4, E2, 2005 It, F1, SA1, 2, 3, NZ1, SA4, NZ2, F2, E, I, W, 2006 E1, 2, I1, NZ1, SA1, NZ2, SA2, NZ3, W, It, I2, S, 2007 Fj, SA1, NZ1, [J, W, Fj, C, E], 2008 I, F1, SA1, NZ1, 2, SA2, 3, NZ3, W(R)
Turinui, M P (NSW) 2003 I, W, E, 2003 [Nm(R)], 2004 S1(R), 2, E2, 2005 Sm, It(R), F1(R), SA1, 2(t&R), 3, NZ1, SA4, NZ2, F2, E, I, W
Turnbull, A (V) 1961 Fj 3
Turnbull, R V (NSW) 1968 I
Turner, L D (NSW) 2008 F2, It, 2009 It1, 2, F, NZ1, SA1, NZ2, SA2, 3, NZ3, 2010 NZ3, It, F(R), 2011 W
Tuynman, S N (NSW) 1983 F 1,2, 1984 E, I, W, S, 1985 C 1,2, NZ, Fj 1,2, 1986 It, F, Arg 1,2, NZ 1,2,3, 1987 SK, [E, US, J, I, W], NZ, Arg 1(R), 2, 1988 E, It, 1989 BI 1,2,3, NZ, 1990 NZ 1
Tweedale, E (NSW) 1946 NZ 1,2, 1947 NZ 2, S, I, 1948 E, F, 1949 M 1,2,3

Valentine, J J (Q, WF) 2006 E1(R), W(R), I2(R), S(R), 2009 It2(R), F(R)
Vaughan, D (NSW) 1983 US, Arg 1, It, F 1,2
Vaughan, G N (V) 1958 E, S, F, M 1,2,3
Verge, A (NSW) 1904 BI 1,2
Vickerman, D J (ACT, NSW) 2002 F 2(R), Arg, E, It, 2003 I (R), W (R), E (R), SA 1, NZ 1, SA 2, NZ 2, [Arg(R), R, I(R), S(R)], 2004 S1(t&R), 2(R), E1(R), PI(R), NZ1(R), SA1(R), NZ2(R), SA2(R), S3, F, S4, E2, 2005 SA2(R), 3, NZ1, SA4, 2006 E1, 2, I1, NZ1, SA1, NZ2, SA2, NZ3, SA3, W, 2007 W1(R), 2, Fj, SA1, NZ1, SA2, NZ2, [J, W, Fj, E], 2008 NZ1(R), 2(t&R), SA2, 2011 Sm(R), NZ1(R), 2, [It, I, US(R), SA, NZ]
Vuna, K C (MR) 2012 W1,2

Walden, R J (NSW) 1934 NZ 2, 1936 NZ 1,2, M
Walker, A K (NSW) 1947 NZ 1, 1948 E, F, 1950 BI 1,2
Walker, A M (ACT) 2000 NZ 1(R), 2001 BI 1,2,3, SA 1, NZ 1,2(R)
Walker, A S B (NSW) 1912 US, 1920 NZ 1,2, 1921 SA 1,2,3, NZ, 1922 M 1,3, NZ 1,2,3, 1923 M 2,3, 1924 NZ 1,2
Walker, L F (NSW) 1988 NZ 2,3, S, It, 1989 BI 1,2,3, NZ

Walker, L R (NSW) 1982 NZ 2,3
Wallace, A C (NSW) 1921 NZ, 1926 NZ 3,4, 1927 I, W, S, 1928 E, F
Wallace, T M (NSW) 1994 It 1(R), 2
Wallach, C (NSW) 1913 NZ 1,3, 1914 NZ 1,2,3
Walsh, J J (NSW) 1953 SA 1,2,3,4
Walsh, P B (NSW) 1904 BI 1,2,3
Walsham, K P (NSW) 1962 NZ 3, 1963 E
Ward, P G (NSW) 1899 BI 1,2,3,4
Ward, T (Q) 1899 BI 2
Watson, G W (Q) 1907 NZ 1
Watson, W T (NSW) 1912 US, 1913 NZ 1,2,3, 1914 NZ 1, 1920 NZ 1,2,3
Waugh, P R (NSW) 2000 E (R), 2001 NZ 1(R), SA 2(R), NZ 2(R), Sp (R), E (R), F, W, 2003 I (R), W, E, SA 1, NZ 1, SA 2, NZ2, [Arg, R, I, S, NZ, E], 2004 S1(R), 2, E1, PI, NZ1, SA1, NZ2, SA2, S3, F, S4, E2, 2005 SA1(R), 2(R), 3, NZ1(R), SA4, NZ2, F2, E, I, W, 2006 E1(R), 2(R), I1(R), NZ1(R), SA1(R), NZ2(R), SA2(R), NZ3, SA3, W, I2, S(R), 2007 W1, 2(R), Fj, SA1(R), NZ1(R), SA2(R), NZ2(R), [W(R), Fj, C(R), E(R)], 2008 I(R), F1(R), 2, SA1(R), NZ1(R), 2, SA2(t&R), 3, NZ4(R), It, W, 2009 It2(R), F(R)
Waugh, W W (NSW, ACT) 1993 SA 1, 1995 [C], NZ 1,2, 1996 S, I, 1997 Arg 1,2
Weatherstone, L J (ACT) 1975 E 1,2, J 1,2, S (R), 1976 E, I
Webb, W (NSW) 1899 BI 3,4
Welborn J P (NSW) 1996 SA 2, It, 1998 Tg, 1999 E, SA 1, NZ 1
Wells, B G (NSW) 1958 M 1
Westfield, R E (NSW) 1928 NZ 1,2,3, M, 1929 NZ 2,3
Whitaker, C J (NSW) 1998 SA 2(R), Fj (R), Tg, 1999 NZ 2(R), [R (R), US, F (R)], 2000 S (R), 2001 Sp (R), W (R), 2002 Arg (R), It (R), 2003 I (R), W (R), SA 2(R),[Arg(R),Nm,S(R)], 2004 PI(R),NZ1, 2005 Sm, It(R), F1(R), SA1(R), 2(R), NZ1(t&R), SA4(R), NZ2(R), F2(R), E(R), W(R)
White, C J B (NSW) 1899 BI 1, 1903 NZ, 1904 BI 1
White, J M (NSW) 1904 BI 3
White, J P L (NSW) 1958 NZ 1,2,3, 1961 Fj 1,2,3, SA 1,2, F, 1962 NZ 1,2,3,4,5, 1963 E, SA 1,2,3,4, 1964 NZ 1,2,3, 1965 SA 1,2
White, M C (Q) 1931 M, NZ 1932 NZ 1,2, 1933 SA 1,2,3,4,5
White, N W (ACT) 2013 NZ1(R),2(R),SA1(R),Arg1,SA2,Arg2(R)
White, S W (NSW) 1956 SA 1,2, 1958 I, E, S, M 2,3
White, W G S (Q) 1933 SA 1,2,3,4,5, 1934 NZ 1,2, 1936 NZ 1,2, M
White, W J (NSW) 1928 NZ 1, M, 1932 NZ 1
Wickham, S M (NSW) 1903 NZ, 1904 BI 1,2,3, 1905 NZ
Williams, D (Q) 1913 NZ 3, 1914 NZ 1,2,3
Williams, I M (NSW) 1987 Arg 1,2, 1988 E 1,2, NZ 1,2,3, 1989 BI 2,3, NZ, F 1,2, 1990 F 1,2,3, US, NZ 1
Williams, J L (NSW) 1963 SA 1,3,4
Williams, R W (ACT) 1999 I 1(t&R),2(t&R), E (R), [US], 2000 Arg 1,2, SA 1, NZ 1, SA 2, NZ 2, SA 3, F (R), S (R), E
Williams, S A (NSW) 1980 Fj, NZ 1,2, 1981 F 1,2, 1982 E, NZ 1,2,3, 1983 US, Arg 1(R), 2, NZ, It, F 1,2, 1984 NZ 1,2,3, E, I, W, S, 1985 C 1,2, NZ, Fj 1,2
Wilson, B J (NSW) 1949 NZ 1,2
Wilson, C R (Q) 1957 NZ 1, 1958 NZ 1,2,3
Wilson, D J (Q) 1992 S 1,2, NZ 1,2,3, SA, I, W, 1993 Tg, NZ, SA 1,2,3, C, F 1,2, 1994 I 1,2, It 1,2, WS, NZ, 1995 Arg 1,2, [SA, R, E], 1996 W 1,2, C, NZ 1, SA 1, NZ 2, SA 2, It, S, I, W 3, 1997 F 1,2, NZ 1, E 1(t + R), NZ 2(R), SA 1, NZ 3, SA 2, E 2(R), S (R), 1998 E 1, S 1,2, NZ 1, SA 1, NZ 2, SA 2, NZ 3, Fj, WS, F, E 2, 1999 I 1,2, E, SA 1, NZ 1, SA 2, NZ 2, [R, I 3, W, SA 3, F], 2000 Arg 1,2, SA 1, NZ 1, SA 2, NZ 2, SA 3
Wilson, V W (Q) 1937 SA 1,2, 1938 NZ 1,2,3
Windon, C J (NSW) 1946 NZ 1,2, 1947 NZ 1, S, I, W, 1948 E, F, 1949 M 1,2,3, NZ 1,2, 1951 NZ 1,2,3, 1952 Fj 1,2, NZ 1,2
Windon, K S (NSW) 1937 SA 1,2, 1946 M
Windsor, J C (Q) 1947 NZ 2
Winning, K C (Q) 1951 NZ 1
Wogan, L W (NSW) 1913 NZ 1,2,3, 1914 NZ 1,2,3, 1920 NZ 1,2,3, 1921 SA 1,2,3, NZ, 1922 M 3, NZ 1,2,3, 1923 M 1,2, 1924 NZ 1,2,3
Wood, F (NSW) 1907 NZ 1,2,3, 1910 NZ 1,2,3, 1913 NZ 1,2,3, 1914 NZ 1,2,3
Wood, R N (Q) 1972 Fj
Woods, H F (NSW) 1925 NZ 4, 1926 NZ 1,2,3, 1927 I, W, S, 1928 E
Wright, K J (NSW) 1975 E 1,2, J 1, 1976 US, F 1,2, 1978 NZ 1,2,3
Wyld, G (NSW) 1920 NZ 2

Yanz, K (NSW) 1958 F
Young, W K (ACT, NSW) 2000 F, S, E, 2002 F 1,2, NZ 1, SA 1, NZ 2, SA 2, Arg, E, It, 2003 I, W, E, SA 1, NZ 1, SA 2, NZ 2, [Arg, R, I, S, NZ, E], 2004 S1, 2, E1, PI, NZ1, SA1, NZ2, SA2, S3, F, S4, E2, 2005 Sm, It, F1, SA1, 2, 3, NZ1, SA4, NZ2

Canada players celebrate beating Fiji in the Bowl final of the Wellington Sevens.

AFP/Getty Images

CANADA

CANADA'S 2012–13 TEST RECORD

OPPONENTS	DATE	VENUE	RESULT
Samoa	9 Nov	N	Lost 42–12
Russia	17 Nov	N	Won 35–3
USA	25 May	H	Won 16–9
Fiji	5 Jun	H	Won 20–18
Tonga	8 Jun	H	Won 36–27
Ireland	15 Jun	H	Lost 14–40
Japan	19 Jun	A	Lost 16–13
USA	17 Aug	A	Won 27–9
USA	24 Aug	H	Won 13–11

MISSION ACCOMPLISHED FOR CANADA

By Ian Gilbert

Caity McCulloch

Canada's victory over the USA in August ensured they would maintain their ever-present record at the Rugby World Cup.

The undoubted high point of Canada's season was securing their place at Rugby World Cup 2015 thanks to a two-match series win over traditional rivals USA. The achievement continues the Canucks' run of appearing at every Rugby World Cup since the inaugural tournament in 1987 when participation was by invitation rather than qualification.

The North American rivals faced off home and away in August to decide who would proceed to England 2015 as the Americas 1 qualifier. With the overall winners being decided by aggregate score, Canada put themselves in a commanding position in the first leg with a convincing 27–9 victory in Charleston, South Carolina. The scorers included the prolific DTH van der Merwe, who became the record try-scorer for his Glasgow Warriors side during the year.

In the return fixture, which was played a week later in Toronto, Canada made home advantage count to secure their World Cup spot with a 13–11 victory, making the aggregate score 40–20.

Eight of the points in the deciding match came from James Pritchard, who became Canada's all-time leading scorer during 2013 by overtaking Gareth Rees's national record. The full back summed up the players' sentiments after a dour victory, saying, "Today we got a win, we did our job, we qualified for the World Cup, but it was anything but pretty."

Coach Kieran Crowley didn't mince his words either: "It was ugly, but it was a win."

Canada have contributed several notable landmarks in RWC history, such as when Rees and Al Charron joined the exclusive group of players to appear in four World Cups. The Canadians reached the quarter-finals in 1991, when they went down to the All Blacks, and gave France a fright in their pool match eight years later before Les Bleus pulled away to win.

The Canadians will again be grouped with France, in Pool D, alongside Ireland, Italy and the Europe 2 qualifier. They haven't met the Irish in a World Cup since the 1987 tournament but the sides met as recently as June when, even without their British & Irish Lions contingent, Ireland were too strong for their hosts and posted a 40–14 win in Toronto.

Until then, Canada had registered three wins from three in 2013, leaving them well-placed in their debut season in the IRB Pacific Nations Cup. Canada beat USA (16–9), eventual champions Fiji (20–18) and Tonga (36–27), but defeat by Japan in their final match of the tournament consigned them to the runners-up spot. The 16–13 reverse in Nagoya may have been a disappointment for Canada but defeat was no disgrace against a Japanese side that had posted their first-ever win over Wales the week before.

The season had begun with Canada taking part in the inaugural IRB International Rugby Series in Colwyn Bay, north Wales, where they lost 42–12 to Samoa but beat Russia 35–3.

Regular international competition is the key to Canada's continued progress on the world stage, and in October 2013 the country again hosted the IRB Americas Rugby Championship, featuring USA Select, Uruguay and Argentina Jaguars. The Championship also gave Canada some solid preparation for their November tour to Georgia, Romania and Portugal.

While Canada may lack a professional league, the national side is bolstered by the number of key players who are battle-hardened from playing in some of the top club competitions around the world. The latest member of the foreign legion is scrum half Phil Mack, who was signed as short-term cover by the Ospreys, completing a trio of Canadians at the Welsh side with Tyler Ardron and Jeff Hassler.

Still plying his trade in the French Top 14 is Canadian veteran Jamie Cudmore, who is in his ninth season with Clermont Auvergne. The second row, who featured in Clermont's Heineken Cup final loss to Toulon, turned 35 in September but has already said he hopes to make RWC 2015.

France also figures prominently in the future of the Canadian women's team, who enjoyed a stellar 2013. With Women's Rugby World Cup 2014 to be held in France, the squad has been steadfastly building for the tournament.

The Canadian women are a force to be reckoned with on the world stage, as demonstrated by their success in the Nations Cup, held in Colorado, in August. They beat England 27–13 in the final of an event that also included USA and South Africa.

"Every win over a team like England is an enormous accomplishment, and this is a victory that should live long in the memory for Canada fans," insisted new head coach François Ratier, who was determined his team did not rest on their laurels. "Our victory at the Nations Cup was a good performance, but now we need to look forward. This tour in Europe (in November) is another step in our preparation and selection process for the World Cup. We will have the opportunity to play France and England on their home grounds and that will be a great challenge as they both have a better ranking."

The Canada Under 20 team had also claimed their Nations Cup title, defeating neighbours USA 27–3 in London to become the first side other than England to lift the silverware. Their male counterparts, meanwhile, came up just short at the IRB Junior World Rugby Trophy 2013 in Chile, losing 45–23 to Italy in the final to miss out on a return to the IRB Junior World Championship in 2014.

The women's Sevens team also gave a strong showing during the season, finishing third in the inaugural IRB Women's Sevens World Series behind champions New Zealand and England, the highlight undoubtedly their passage to the final in Amsterdam where they lost an enthralling encounter with New Zealand. They were also runners-up at Rugby World Cup Sevens 2013 in Moscow, losing the final 29–12 to the impressive New Zealanders.

The women's Sevens set-up is an area of strength for Canada, and the country also scooped bronze at the World University Games in Russia. The year also heralded the announcement of the creation of a new full-time centralised squad and a fully-funded training base.

The men's Sevens team finished mid-table in the HSBC Sevens World Series, enjoying their best showing at the USA round in Las Vegas where they beat Scotland in the Plate final.

On the domestic front, the Ontario Blues were crowned Canadian Rugby Championship winners in September by defeating British Columbia Bears 50–27 in Lindsay, Ontario. The Blues wrapped up their third consecutive MacTier Cup with one round remaining in the round robin.

In the National Women's League, Quebec were crowned champions for the first time in more than a decade after the round robin format for the provincial teams.

CANADA INTERNATIONAL STATISTICS

MATCH RECORDS UP TO 10 OCTOBER 2013

WINNING MARGIN

Date	Opponent	Result	Winning Margin
24/06/2006	Barbados	69–3	66
14/10/1999	Namibia	72–11	61
12/08/2006	USA	56–7	49
06/07/1996	Hong Kong	57–9	48

MOST POINTS IN A MATCH

BY THE TEAM

Date	Opponent	Result	Points
14/10/1999	Namibia	72–11	72
24/06/2006	Barbados	69–3	69
15/07/2000	Japan	62–18	62
13/11/2010	Spain	60–22	60
06/07/1996	Hong Kong	57–9	57

BY A PLAYER

Date	Player	Opponent	Points
12/08/2006	James Pritchard	USA	36
24/06/2006	James Pritchard	Barbados	29
14/10/1999	Gareth Rees	Namibia	27
13/07/1996	Bobby Ross	Japan	26
25/05/1991	Mark Wyatt	Scotland	24

MOST TRIES IN A MATCH

BY THE TEAM

Date	Opponent	Result	Tries
24/06/2006	Barbados	69–3	11
14/10/1999	Namibia	72–11	9
11/05/1991	Japan	49–26	8
15/07/2000	Japan	62–18	8
13/11/2010	Spain	60 – 22	8

BY A PLAYER

Date	Player	Opponent	Tries
15/07/2000	Kyle Nichols	Japan	4
24/06/2006	James Pritchard	Barbados	3
12/08/2006	James Pritchard	USA	3
10/05/1987	Steve Gray	USA	3

MOST CONVERSIONS IN A MATCH

BY THE TEAM

Date	Opponent	Result	Cons
14/10/1999	Namibia	72–11	9
15/07/2000	Japan	62–18	8

BY A PLAYER

Date	Player	Opponent	Cons
14/10/1999	Gareth Rees	Namibia	9
15/07/2000	Jared Barker	Japan	8

MOST PENALTIES IN A MATCH

BY THE TEAM

Date	Opponent	Result	Pens
25/05/1991	Scotland	24–19	8
22/08/1998	Argentina	28–54	7

BY A PLAYER

Date	Player	Opponent	Pens
25/05/1991	Mark Wyatt	Scotland	8
22/08/1998	Gareth Rees	Argentina	7

MOST DROP GOALS IN A MATCH

BY THE TEAM

Date	Opponent	Result	DGs
08/11/1986	USA	27–16	2
04/07/2001	Fiji	23–52	2
08/06/1980	USA	16–0	2
24/05/1997	Hong Kong	35–27	2
18/09/2011	France	19–46	2

BY A PLAYER

Date	Player	Opponent	DGs
04/07/2001	Bobby Ross	Fiji	2
24/05/1997	Bobby Ross	Hong Kong	2
18/09/2011	Ander Monro	France	2

MOST CAPPED PLAYERS

Name	Caps
Al Charron	76
Winston Stanley	66
Scott Stewart	64
Rod Snow	62

LEADING PENALTY SCORERS

Name	Penalties
Gareth Rees	110
James Pritchard	89
Bobby Ross	84
Mark Wyatt	64
Jared Barker	55

LEADING TRY SCORERS

Name	Tries
Winston Stanley	24
James Pritchard	15
DTH van der Merwe	14
Morgan Williams	13

LEADING DROP GOAL SCORERS

Name	DGs
Bobby Ross	10
Gareth Rees	9
Mark Wyatt	5

LEADING CONVERSION SCORERS

Name	Conversions
James Pritchard	90
Bobby Ross	52
Gareth Rees	51
Jared Barker	24
Mark Wyatt	24

LEADING POINT SCORERS

Name	Points
James Pritchard	522
Gareth Rees	491
Bobby Ross	421
Mark Wyatt	263
Jared Barker	226

CANADA INTERNATIONAL PLAYERS

UP TO 10 OCTOBER 2013

AD Abrams 2003 *US, NZ, Tg*, 2004 *US, J, EngA, US, F, It, E*, 2005 *US, J, W, EngA, US, Ar, F, R*, 2006 *S, E, US, It*
MJ Alder 1976 *Bb*
P Aldous 1971 *W*
TJ Ardron 2012 *US, It, Geo, Sa, Rus*, 2013 *US, Fj, Tg, I, J, US*
AS Arthurs 1988 *US*
M Ashton 1971 *W*
F Asselin 1999 *Fj*, 2000 *Tg, US, SA*, 2001 *Ur, Ar, Fj*, 2002 *S, US, US, Ur, Ur, CHL, W, F*
O Atkinson 2005 *J, Ar*, 2006 *E, US, It*
S Ault 2006 *W, It*, 2008 *US, Pt*, 2009 *Geo, US, US*

JC Bain 1932 *J*
RG Banks 1999 *J, Fj, Sa, US, Tg, W, E, F, Nm*, 2000 *US, SA, I, J, It*, 2001 *US, Ur, Ar, E, Fj, J*, 2002 *S, US, US, Ur, CHL, Ur, CHL, W, F*, 2003 *EngA, US, M, M, Ur, NZ, It*
S Barber 1973 *W*, 1976 *Bb*
M Barbieri 2006 *E, US*
B Barker 1966 *BI*, 1971 *W*
J Barker 2000 *Tg, J, It*, 2002 *S, US, US, Ur, CHL, Ur, CHL, W*, 2003 *US, NZ, It*, 2004 *US, J, F, It*
R Barkwill 2012 *Sa, Rus*, 2013 *US, Fj, Tg, I, J, US, US*
T Bauer 1977 *US, E*, 1978 *US, F*, 1979 *US*
DR Baugh 1998 *J, HK, US, HK, J, Ur, Ar*, 1999 *J, Fj, Sa, US, Tg, W, E, F, Fj, Nm*, 2000 *US, SA, I, It*, 2001 *E, E*, 2002 *S, US, Ur, CHL*
BG Beukeboom 2012 *US, Geo, Sa*, 2013 *US, Tg, J*
A Bianco 1966 *BI*
AJ Bibby 1979 *US, F*, 1980 *W, US, NZ*, 1981 *US, Ar*
R Bice 1996 *US, A*, 1997 *US, J, HK, US, W, I*, 1998 *US, US, HK, J, Ur, US, Ar*, 1999 *J, Fj, Sa, US, Tg, W, F*
P Bickerton 2004 *US, J*
D Biddle 2006 *S, E, Bar*, 2007 *W, Fj, A*
JM Billingsley 1974 *Tg*, 1977 *US*, 1978 *F*, 1979 *US*, 1980 *W*, 1983 *US, It, It*, 1984 *US*
WG Bjarneson 1962 *Bb*
TJH Blackwell 1973 *W*
N Blevins 2009 *J, J*, 2010 *Bel, Sp, Geo, Pt*, 2012 *Sa, Rus*, 2013 *US, Fj, Tg, J, US, US*
B Bonenberg 1983 *US, It, It*
J Boone 1932 *J, J*
T Bourne 1967 *E*
CJ Braid 2010 *Bel, Geo*, 2012 *Sa, Rus*, 2013 *US, Fj, I, J*
R Breen 1986 *US*, 1987 *W*, 1990 *US*, 1991 *J, S, US, R*, 1993 *E, US*
R Breen 1983 *E*, 1987 *US*
R Brewer 1967 *E*
STT Brown 1989 *I, US*
N Browne 1973 *W*, 1974 *Tg*
S Bryan 1996 *Ur, US, Ar*, 1997 *HK, J, US, W*, 1998 *HK, J, US, Ar*, 1999 *Fj, Sa, US, Tg, W, E, F, Fj, Nm*
M Burak 2004 *US, J, EngA, US, F, It, E*, 2005 *EngA, US, Ar, F, R*, 2006 *US, Bar, W*, 2007 *NZ, Pt, W, Fj, J, A*, 2008 *I, W, S*, 2009 *I, W, Geo, US, US*
C Burford 1970 *Fj*
D Burgess 1962 *Bb, W23*
D Burleigh 2001 *Ur, Ar, E, E*

JB Burnham 1966 *Bl*, 1967 *E*, 1970 *Fj*, 1971 *W*
HAW Buydens 2006 *E*, *Bar*, 2008 *US*, 2011 *Rus*, *US*, *US*, *Tg*, *F*, *J*, *NZ*, 2012 *US*, *It*, *Sa*, *Rus*, 2013 *US*, *Fj*, *Tg*, *I*, *J*

GE Cameron 1932 *J*
JWD Cannon 2001 *US*, *Ar*, *E*, *E*, *Fj*, *J*, 2002 *S*, *US*, *Ur*, *CHL*, *Ur*, *CHL*, *W*, *F*, 2003 *EngA*, *US*, *M*, *M*, *Ur*, *US*, *Ar*, *NZ*, *It*, 2004 *US*, *F*, *It*, *E*, 2005 *W*, *EngA*, *US*, *F*
R Card 1996 *US*, *A*, *Ur*, *US*, *Ar*, 1997 *US*, *J*, *HK*
ME Cardinal 1986 *US*, 1987 *US*, *Tg*, *I*, *US*, 1991 *S*, 1993 *A*, 1994 *US*, *F*, *E*, *F*, 1995 *S*, *Fj*, *NZ*, *R*, *SA*, 1996 *US*, *US*, *HK*, *J*, *A*, *HK*, *J*, 1997 *US*, *US*, *W*, *I*, 1998 *US*, *HK*, 1999 *Fj*, *US*, *W*, *E*, *Fj*, *Nm*
LAG Carlson 2002 *Ur*, *W*, 2003 *EngA*
A Carpenter 2005 *US*, *J*, *EngA*, *US*, *Ar*, *F*, *R*, 2006 *S*, *E*, *US*, *W*, *It*, 2007 *US*, *NZ*, *Pt*, *W*, *Fj*, *J*, *A*, 2008 *US*, *Pt*, *I*, *W*, *S*, 2009 *I*, *W*, *Geo*, *US*, *J*, *J*, *Rus*, 2010 *Ur*, *Sp*, *Geo*, *Pt*, 2011 *Rus*, *US*, *US*, *Tg*, *F*, *J*, *NZ*, 2012 *US*, *It*, *Geo*, *Sa*, *Rus*, 2013 *US*, *Fj*, *Tg*, *I*, *J*, *US*, *US*
NS Carr 1985 *A*, *A*
SFB Carson 1977 *E*
DJ Carson 1980 *W*, *US*, *NZ*, 1981 *US*, *Ar*, 1982 *J*, *E*, *US*, 1983 *It*, *It*
MP Chambers 1962 *Bb*, *W23*, 1966 *Bl*
AJ Charron 1990 *Ar*, *US*, *Ar*, 1991 *J*, *S*, *Fj*, *F*, *NZ*, 1992 *US*, 1993 *E*, *E*, *US*, *A*, *W*, 1994 *US*, *F*, *W*, 1995 *Fj*, *NZ*, *R*, *A*, *SA*, *US*, 1996 *US*, *US*, *A*, *HK*, *J*, *Ur*, *US*, *Ar*, 1997 *US*, *J*, *HK*, *HK*, *J*, *US*, *W*, *I*, 1998 *US*, *HK*, *J*, *Ur*, *US*, *Ar*, 1999 *Fj*, *Sa*, *US*, *Tg*, *W*, *E*, *F*, *Fj*, *Nm*, 2000 *Tg*, *US*, *SA*, *Sa*, *Fj*, *J*, *It*, 2001 *Ur*, *Ar*, *E*, *E*, 2002 *S*, *US*, *US*, *Ur*, *CHL*, *Ur*, *CHL*, *F*, 2003 *W*, *It*, *Tg*
L Chung 1978 *F*
N Clapinson 1995 *US*, 1996 *US*
RM Clark 1962 *Bb*
D Clarke 1996 *A*
ME Clarkin 1985 *A*, *A*
W Collins 1977 *US*, *E*
B Collins 2004 *US*, *J*
GG Cooke 2000 *Tg*, *US*, 2001 *Fj*, *J*, 2003 *EngA*, *US*, *M*, *M*, *Ur*, *US*, *Ar*, *W*, *NZ*, *Tg*, 2004 *EngA*, *US*, *It*, *E*, 2005 *US*, *J*, *W*, *Ar*, *F*, *R*, 2006 *US*
I Cooper 1993 *W*
JA Cordle 1998 *HK*, *J*, 1999 *J*, *Fj*, *Sa*, 2001 *J*
GER Cox 1932 *J*
S Creagh 1988 *US*
JN Cudmore 2002 *US*, *CHL*, *W*, *F*, 2003 *EngA*, *US*, *W*, *NZ*, *It*, *Tg*, 2004 *US*, *F*, *It*, *E*, 2005 *W*, *F*, 2006 *US*, 2007 *Pt*, *W*, *Fj*, 2011 *Rus*, *US*, *US*, *Tg*, *F*, *J*, *NZ*, 2013 *US*
L Cudmore 2008 *US*
C Culpan 2006 *E*, 2007 *US*, *NZ*, *Pt*, *W*, *Fj*, *J*
TJ Cummings 1966 *Bl*, 1973 *W*
Z Cvitak 1983 *E*

N Dala 2007 *US*, 2008 *US*, 2009 *I*, *W*, *Geo*, *US*, *US*, *J*, *J*, 2010 *Ur*, 2011 *Rus*, *Tg*, *F*, *NZ*, 2012 *US*, *It*, *Geo*, *Rus*, 2013 *US*, *Fj*, *Tg*, *I*, *J*, *US*, *US*
MJW Dandy 1977 *E*, *E*
M Danskin 2001 *J*, 2004 *EngA*, *F*
D Daypuck 2004 *EngA*, *F*, *It*, *E*, 2005 *US*, *J*, *W*, *EngA*, *Ar*, *F*, *R*, 2006 *S*, *US*, *US*, *W*, *It*, 2007 *A*
H de Goede 1974 *Tg*, 1976 *Bb*, 1977 *US*, *E*, *E*, 1978 *US*, 1979 *US*, *F*, 1980 *W*, *US*, *NZ*, 1981 *US*, 1982 *J*, *J*, *E*, *US*, 1984 *US*, 1985 *US*, 1986 *J*, *US*, 1987 *US*, *Tg*, *I*, *W*
F Deacy 1973 *W*
J Delaney 1983 *E*
P Densmore 2005 *EngA*
JD Devlin 1985 *US*, 1986 *US*
M di Girolamo 2001 *Ur*, *Ar*, 2002 *US*, *Ur*, *CHL*, *Ur*, *W*, *F*, 2003 *US*, *M*, *M*, *Ur*, *W*, *NZ*, *It*, *Tg*, 2004 *EngA*, *US*, *F*, *It*, *E*
GA Dixon 2000 *US*, *SA*, *I*, *Sa*, *Fj*, *J*, *It*, 2001 *US*, *Ar*, *E*, *E*
D Docherty 1973 *W*
TJ Dolezel 2009 *Rus*, 2010 *Ur*, *Bel*, *Sp*, *Geo*, *Pt*, 2011 *Rus*, 2012 *US*, *It*, *Geo*, 2013 *Tg*, *J*, *US*, *US*
WJ Donaldson 1978 *F*, 1979 *US*, *F*, 1980 *W*, *US*, *NZ*, 1981 *US*, 1982 *E*, *US*, 1983 *US*, *It*, *It*, 1984 *US*
A Douglas 1974 *Tg*
JT Douglas 2003 *M*, *M*, *Ur*, *US*, *Ar*, *NZ*, *It*, 2004 *US*, *F*
A du Temple 1932 *J*, *J*
SR Duke 2008 *S*, 2009 *W*, *Geo*, *J*, *J*, *Rus*, 2010 *Bel*, 2012 *US*, *Geo*, 2013 *Tg*
G Dukelow 1980 *W*, *US*, *NZ*, 1981 *US*, 1982 *J*, *J*, *E*, *US*, 1983 *US*, *It*, *It*, *E*, 1984 *US*, 1990 *US*
PJ Dunkley 1998 *J*, *HK*, *US*, *HK*, *J*, *US*, *Ar*, 1999 *J*, *Fj*, *Sa*, *US*, *Tg*, *E*, *F*, *Fj*, *Nm*, 2000 *Tg*, *SA*, *I*, *Sa*, *Fj*, 2001 *US*, *Ar*, *E*, *Fj*, *J*, 2002 *S*, *US*, *US*, *Ur*, *CHL*, *W*, *F*, 2003 *M*, *M*, *Ur*, *Ar*, 2005 *W*
C Dunning 2005 *EngA*, *US*, *Ar*, *F*, *R*

B Ebl 1995 *NZ*, 1998 *J*, *HK*
DC Eburne 1977 *US*, *E*, *E*
MA Eckardt 1974 *Tg*, 1977 *US*, *E*, *E*, 1978 *US*
IJ Edwards 1967 *E*
G Ellwand 1973 *W*
GD Ennis 1986 *J*, *US*, 1987 *US*, *Tg*, *I*, *W*, 1988 *US*, 1989 *I*, *US*, 1990 *Ar*, *US*, *Ar*, 1991 *J*, *S*, *US*, *Fj*, *R*, *F*, *NZ*, 1993 *E*, *E*, 1994 *US*, *W*, 1995 *Fj*, *NZ*, *R*, *A*, *SA*, 1998 *J*, *HK*, *US*, *US*
BW Erichsen 2009 *Rus*, 2010 *Ur*, *Bel*, 2011 *US*, *US*
EA Evans 1986 *US*, 1987 *US*, *Tg*, *I*, *US*, 1989 *I*, *US*, 1990 *Ar*, *Ar*, 1991 *J*, *S*, *US*, *Fj*, *R*, *F*, *NZ*, 1992 *US*, *E*, 1993 *E*, *E*, 1994 *US*, *F*, *W*, *E*, *F*, 1995 *S*, *Ur*, *Ar*, *Fj*, *NZ*, *R*, *A*, *SA*, 1996 *J*, *HK*, *J*, 1997 *US*, *J*, *HK*, *J*, *US*, *W*, *I*, 1998 *J*, *HK*, *US*, *US*, *US*, *Ar*
MC Evans 2008 *I*, *W*, *S*, 2009 *W*, *Geo*, *US*, *US*, *J*, *Rus*, 2010 *Ur*, 2011 *Rus*, *US*, *J*, *NZ*, 2012 *US*, *It*, *Geo*, *Sa*, 2013 *Fj*, *Tg*, *US*, *US*
I Exner 2005 *EngA*, *US*

A Fagan 2008 *Pt*
EG Fairhurst 2001 *US*, *Ar*, 2002 *US*, *Ur*, *CHL*, *Ur*, *CHL*, *W*, *F*, 2003 *EngA*, *M*, *M*, *US*, *NZ*, *Tg*, 2004 *US*, *J*, *EngA*, *US*, *F*, *It*, *E*, 2005 *US*, *W*, *EngA*, *US*, *F*, 2006 *S*, *E*, *US*, *Bar*, *US*, *W*, *It*, 2007 *US*, *NZ*, *Pt*, *W*, *A*, 2008 *US*, *I*, *W*, *S*, 2009 *I*, *W*, *Geo*, *US*, *US*, 2010 *Ur*, 2011 *Rus*, *US*, *Tg*, *F*, *J*, *NZ*, 2012 *It*, *Geo*
SC Fauth 2000 *Tg*, *US*, *SA*, *I*, *Sa*, *Fj*, *J*, *It*, 2001 *US*, *Ar*, *E*, *E*, *Fj*, *J*, 2002 *S*, *US*, *US*, *Ur*, *CHL*, *CHL*, *W*, *F*, 2003 *US*, *M*, *Ur*, *US*, *Ar*, *NZ*, *Tg*
M Felix 1985 *A*, *A*, 1996 *Ur*, *US*
A Flagg 2013 *J*
P Fleck 2004 *US*, *J*, *It*, *E*, 2005 *US*, *W*, 2008 *US*
I Fleming 1976 *Bb*
AC Forbes 1932 *J*, *J*
F Forster 1983 *US*, *It*, *It*
AE Foster 1970 *Fj*, 1976 *Bb*, 1977 *US*, *E*, *E*
C Fowler 1988 *US*, 1990 *US*
TE Fraine 1967 *E*
RP Frame 1986 *J*, 1987 *US*, *Tg*, *I*, *W*, *US*
S Franklin 2007 *US*, *NZ*, *J*, 2008 *US*, *S*, 2009 *I*, 2011 *Rus*, *US*, *Tg*, *F*, *J*, *NZ*
G Fraser 1983 *E*
P Frize 1962 *Bb*, *W23*
MS Fuailefau 2013 *J*
GW Fumano 1967 *E*, 1970 *Fj*
QA Fyffe 2003 *EngA*, *US*, *NZ*, *It*, *Tg*, 2004 *US*, *J*, *EngA*, *US*, *F*, *It*, 2005 *US*, *J*, *W*, *Ar*

F Gainer 2004 *US*, *J*, *EngA*, *US*, *F*, *It*, *E*, 2005 *US*, *J*, *W*, *EngA*, *US*, *F*, *R*, 2006 *W*, *It*
A Godziek 1982 *J*, *E*, *US*, 1983 *US*, *It*, *It*, *E*, 1984 *US*
GG Gonis 1977 *US*, *E*, *E*, 1978 *US*
K Goodland 2005 *US*
I Gordon 1991 *S*, 1992 *US*, *E*, 1993 *US*, *A*, *W*, 1994 *F*, *W*, *E*, *F*, 1995 *S*, *R*, *SA*, *US*, 1996 *US*, *HK*, *J*, *A*, *HK*, 1997 *US*, *J*, *HK*, 1998 *J*, *HK*, *US*, *J*, *US*, *Ar*
JD Graf 1989 *I*, *US*, 1990 *Ar*, 1991 *S*, *R*, 1992 *US*, *E*, 1993 *E*, *E*, *US*, *A*, 1994 *US*, *F*, *W*, *E*, *F*, 1995 *S*, *Ur*, *Ar*, *Fj*, *NZ*, *R*, *A*, *SA*, *US*, 1996 *US*, *HK*, *J*, *A*, *HK*, *J*, 1997 *US*, *J*, *HK*, *HK*, *US*, *W*, *I*, 1998 *J*, *HK*, *US*, *US*, *HK*, *J*, *Ur*, *US*, *Ar*, 1999 *J*, *Fj*, *Sa*, *US*, *Tg*, *F*, *Nm*
W Granleese 1962 *W23*
G Grant 1977 *E*, *E*, 1978 *US*, 1979 *US*, *F*, 1980 *W*
I Grant 1983 *US*, *It*, *It*, *E*

PR Grantham 1962 *Bb, W23*, 1966 *BI*
SD Gray 1984 *US*, 1987 *US, W, US*, 1989 *I*, 1990 *Ar, US, Ar*, 1991 *J, S, Fj, F, NZ*, 1992 *US, E*, 1993 *E, E, US, A, W*, 1994 *US, F, W, E, F*, 1995 *S, Ar, Fj, NZ, R, A, SA, US*, 1996 *US, US, HK, J, A, HK, J, US, Ar*, 1997 *US, J, HK, J, US*
GR Greig 1973 *W*
JR Grieg 1977 *US, E*, 1978 *US*, 1979 *US, F*, 1980 *W, US, NZ*, 1981 *Ar*
J Grout 1995 *Ur*
MR Gudgeon 2010 *Bel*, 2011 *Rus*
G Gudmundseth 1973 *W*

N Hadley 1987 *US*, 1989 *I, US*, 1990 *Ar*, 1991 *S, US, Fj, R, F, NZ*, 1992 *US, E*, 1993 *E*, 1994 *E, F*
J Haley 1996 *Ur*
J Hall 1996 *US, US*, 1997 *HK*, 1998 *J, HK, J, US, Ar*
GRO Hamilton 2010 *Ur*, 2011 *Rus, US, US, Tg, F, J, NZ*, 2012 *US, Sa, Rus*, 2013 *US, Fj, Tg, I, J, US*
WT Handson 1985 *A, A, US*, 1986 *J, US*, 1987 *US, Tg, I, W*
J Hassler 2012 *US, Geo, Sa, Rus*
JP Hawthorn 1982 *J, J, E*, 1983 *US, It, It*
A Healy 1996 *HK, J, HK, J, Ur, US, Ar*, 1997 *US, HK, HK, I*, 1998 *HK, J, Ur*, 1999 *J*
AR Heaman 1988 *US*
C Hearn 2008 *I, W, S*, 2009 *I, W, Geo, US, US, J, J*, 2010 *Ur, Bel, Sp, Geo, Pt*, 2011 *US, US, Tg, F*, 2012 *US, It, Geo, Sa, Rus*, 2013 *US, Fj, Tg, I, J, US, US*
B Henderson 2005 *J, F, R*
S Hendry 1996 *Ur, US, Ar*
G Henrikson 1971 *W*
L Hillier 1973 *W*
RE Hindson 1973 *W*, 1974 *Tg*, 1976 *Bb*, 1977 *US, E, E*, 1978 *US, F*, 1979 *US, F*, 1980 *W, US, NZ*, 1981 *US, Ar*, 1982 *J, J, E, US*, 1983 *US, It, It*, 1984 *US*, 1985 *A, A, US*, 1986 *J*, 1987 *US, I, W*, 1990 *Ar*
G Hirayama 1977 *E, E*, 1978 *US*, 1979 *US, F*, 1980 *W, US, NZ*, 1981 *US*, 1982 *J, E, US*
NS Hirayama 2008 *Pt, S*, 2009 *J, J, Rus*, 2010 *Bel*, 2011 *US, F, NZ*, 2013 *Tg, I, US, US*
M Holmes 1987 *US*
TN Hotson 2008 *US, Pt, I, W, S*, 2009 *I, W, Geo, US, US, J, J, Rus*, 2010 *Ur, Sp, Geo, Pt*, 2011 *Rus, US, US, Tg, F, J, NZ*, 2012 *US, It, Geo, Sa, Rus*, 2013 *US, Fj, Tg, I, US, US*
P Howlett 1974 *Tg*
BM Hunnings 1932 *J, J*
E Hunt 1966 *BI*, 1967 *E*
S Hunter 2005 *R*
J Hutchinson 1993 *E, A, W*, 1995 *S, Ar, Fj, A, SA, US*, 1996 *US, US, HK, J, A, HK, J, Ur, US, Ar*, 1997 *US, J, HK, HK, J, US, W, I*, 1998 *J, HK, US, US, HK, J, Ur, US, Ar*, 1999 *J, Fj, Sa, US, Tg, W, E, F, Fj, Nm*, 2000 *US, Sa, Fj, J*
I Hyde-Lay 1986 *J*, 1987 *US*, 1988 *US*

M Irvine 2000 *Tg, SA, I, Sa, Fj, J*, 2001 *US, Ar*

DC Jackart 1991 *J, S, US, Fj, R, F*, 1992 *US, E*, 1993 *E, E, US, A, W*, 1994 *US, F, W, E, F*, 1995 *S, Ar, Fj*
RO Jackson 1970 *Fj*, 1971 *W*
J Jackson 2003 *Ur, US, Ar, W, It, Tg*, 2004 *EngA, US, It, E*, 2005 *W, US, Ar, R*, 2006 *S*, 2007 *US, NZ, J*, 2008 *I, W, S*, 2009 *J*, 2010 *Sp, Geo*
MB James 1994 *US, F, W, E, F*, 1995 *S, Ur, Ar, Fj, NZ, R, A, US*, 1996 *US, US, HK, J, A, HK, J*, 1997 *J, US, W, I*, 1998 *US, US, Ur, US, Ar*, 1999 *Sa, W, E, F, Fj, Nm*, 2000 *It*, 2002 *S, US, US, Ur, CHL, W, F*, 2003 *M, M, Ur, US, Ar, W, Tg*, 2005 *F*, 2006 *US*, 2007 *Pt, W, Fj, J, A*
G Jennings 1981 *Ar*, 1983 *US, It, It, E*
O Johnson 1970 *Fj*
G Johnston 1978 *F*
RR Johnstone 2001 *Ur, Fj, J*, 2002 *CHL, Ur, CHL*, 2003 *EngA*
CWB Jones 1987 *US*
C Jones 1983 *E*
EL Jones 1982 *J*, 1983 *US*
H Jones 2012 *Rus*, 2013 *US, Fj, I, US, US*

TK Kariya 1967 *E*, 1970 *Fj*, 1971 *W*
A Kennedy 1985 *A, A*
I Kennedy 1993 *A, W*
ED Kettleson 1985 *US*
B Keys 2008 *US, Pt, I, W, S*, 2009 *Geo, US, J*
MMG King 2002 *US, Ur*, 2003 *M, US, Ar, NZ*, 2005 *US, J, W, EngA, US, Ar*
A Kingham 1974 *Tg*
A Kleeberger 2005 *F, R*, 2006 *S, E, US, Bar, It*, 2007 *US, NZ, Pt, J*, 2008 *US, Pt, I, W, S*, 2009 *I, W, Geo, US, US, J, J, Rus*, 2010 *Ur, Bel, Sp, Geo, Pt*, 2011 *US, US, Tg, F, J, NZ*
ERP Knaggs 2000 *Tg, US, SA, I, Sa, Fj, J*, 2001 *US, Ur, Ar, E, E, Fj, J*, 2002 *S*, 2003 *EngA, Ur, Ar, NZ*
JD Knauer 1992 *E*, 1993 *E, E, US, W*
MJ Kokan 1984 *US*, 1985 *US*
P Kyle 1984 *US*
JA Kyne 2010 *Bel*, 2011 *J*

A La Carte 2004 *US, J*
M Langley 2004 *EngA*, 2005 *Ar*
MJ Lawson 2002 *US, Ur, CHL, Ur, CHL, F*, 2003 *EngA, US, M, M, Ur, US, Ar, W, It, Tg*, 2004 *F, It, E*, 2005 *US, J, F, R*, 2006 *Bar, US, W*
P le Blanc 1994 *F*, 1995 *Ur, Fj, NZ*
CE le Fevre 1976 *Bb*
J Lecky 1962 *Bb, W23*
JL Lecky 1982 *J, US*, 1983 *US, It, It*, 1984 *US*, 1985 *A, US*, 1986 *J, US*, 1987 *I, W, US*, 1991 *J, S, Fj, R*
GB Legh 1973 *W*, 1974 *Tg*, 1976 *Bb*
LSF Leroy 1932 *J*
J Lorenz 1966 *BI*, 1970 *Fj*, 1971 *W*
DC Lougheed 1990 *Ar*, 1991 *J, US*, 1992 *US, E*, 1993 *E, E, US*, 1994 *F, W, E, F*, 1995 *Fj, NZ, R, A, SA*, 1996 *A, HK*, 1997 *J, W, I*, 1998 *US, Ar*, 1999 *US, Tg, W, E, F, Fj, Nm*, 2003 *W, It*
J Loveday 1993 *E, E, US, A*, 1996 *HK, J*, 1998 *J, Ur*, 1999 *Sa, US*
B Luke 2004 *US, J*
M Luke 1974 *Tg*, 1976 *Bb*, 1977 *US, E, E*, 1978 *US, F*, 1979 *US, F*, 1980 *W, US, NZ*, 1981 *US*, 1982 *J, US*
S Lytton 1995 *Ur, Ar, US*, 1996 *US, HK, J, J, US, Ar*

GDT MacDonald 1998 *HK*
G MacDonald 1970 *Fj*
P Mack 2009 *I, W, Geo, US, US, J, J, Rus*, 2012 *Rus*, 2013 *US, Fj, Tg, I, US, US*
I MacKay 1993 *A, W*
JL Mackenzie 2010 *Bel, Sp*, 2011 *US*
PW Mackenzie 2008 *Pt, I*, 2010 *Ur, Sp, Geo, Pt*, 2011 *Rus, US, US, Tg, F, J, NZ*, 2012 *US, It, Geo, Sa*, 2013 *US, US*
GI MacKinnon 1985 *US*, 1986 *J*, 1988 *US*, 1989 *I, US*, 1990 *Ar, Ar*, 1991 *J, S, Fj, R, F, NZ*, 1992 *US, E*, 1993 *E*, 1994 *US, F, W, E, F*, 1995 *S, Ur, Ar, Fj, NZ, A, SA*
S MacKinnon 1992 *US*, 1995 *Ur, Ar, Fj*
C MacLachlan 1981 *Ar*, 1982 *J, E*
P Maclean 1983 *US, It, It, E*
I Macmillan 1981 *Ar*, 1982 *J, J, E, US*
M MacSween 2009 *Rus*
B Major 2001 *Fj, J*
D Major 1999 *E, Fj, Nm*, 2000 *Tg, US, SA, I, Fj*, 2001 *Ur, E, E*
A Marshall 1997 *J*, 1998 *Ur*
JA Marshall 2008 *S*, 2010 *Ur, Bel, Sp, Geo, Pt*, 2011 *US, US, Tg, F, J, NZ*, 2012 *US, It, Geo, Sa, Rus*, 2013 *US, Fj, Tg, I, J, US, US*
P Mason 1974 *Tg*
B McCarthy 1996 *US, Ar*, 1998 *J, HK, J*
J McDonald 1974 *Tg*
RN McDonald 1966 *BI*, 1967 *E*, 1970 *Fj*
AG McGann 1985 *A, A*
R McGeein 1973 *W*
RI McInnes 1979 *F*, 1980 *NZ*, 1981 *US, Ar*, 1982 *J, J, E, US*, 1983 *US, It, It*, 1984 *US*, 1985 *US*
B McKee 1962 *Bb, W23*
B Mckee 1966 *BI*, 1970 *Fj*
SS McKeen 2004 *US, J, EngA, US, F, It, E*, 2005 *US, J, W, EngA, F, R*, 2006 *S, US, US, W, It*, 2007 *US, NZ*
JR McKellar 1985 *A, A*, 1986 *J*, 1987 *W*

JH McKenna 1967 *E*
C McKenzie 1992 *US, E*, 1993 *E, US, A, W*, 1994 *US, F, W, E, F*, 1995 *S, Ur, Ar, Fj, NZ, R, SA*, 1996 *US, HK, J, J*, 1997 *J, HK, I*
SG McTavish 1970 *Fj*, 1971 *W*, 1976 *Bb*, 1977 *US, E, E*, 1978 *US, F*, 1979 *US, F*, 1980 *W, US*, 1981 *US, Ar*, 1982 *J, J, E, US*, 1985 *US*, 1987 *US, Tg, I*
R McWhinney 2005 *F, R*
J Mensah-Coker 2006 *S, E, US, Bar, US, W, It*, 2007 *US, NZ, Pt, J, A*, 2008 *US, I, W, S*, 2009 *US, US, J, J, Rus*, 2010 *Ur, Sp, Geo, Pt*, 2011 *Rus*
C Michaluk 1995 *SA*, 1996 *US, J*, 1997 *US, HK*
N Milau 2000 *US, J*
DRW Milne 1966 *BI*, 1967 *E*
AB Mitchell 1932 *J, J*
P Monaghan 1982 *J*
AHB Monro 2006 *E, US, Bar, US, W, It*, 2007 *W, A*, 2008 *US, Pt, I, W*, 2009 *I, W, Geo, US, US, J, J, Rus*, 2010 *Ur, Bel, Pt*, 2011 *Rus, US, US, Tg, F, J, NZ*
D Moonlight 2003 *EngA*, 2004 *EngA, E*, 2005 *US*
JI Moonlight 2009 *Geo*, 2012 *Sa, Rus*, 2013 *US, Fj, Tg, I, US, US*
DL Moore 1962 *Bb, W23*
K Morgan 1997 *HK, HK, J, W*
VJP Moroney 1962 *Bb*
B Mosychuk 1996 *Ur*, 1997 *J*
J Moyes 1981 *Ar*, 1982 *J, J, E, US*
PT Murphy 2000 *Tg, US, SA, I, Sa, Fj, J*, 2001 *Fj, J*, 2002 *S, US, US, Ur, CHL, W, F*, 2003 *US, M, M*, 2004 *F*
WA Murray 1932 *J*
K Myhre 1970 *Fj*

J Newton 1962 *W23*
GN Niblo 1932 *J, J*
K Nichols 1996 *Ur*, 1998 *J, HK, US, US, Ur*, 1999 *J, Fj, Sa, US, Tg, Fj, Nm*, 2000 *Tg, US, SA, I, Sa, Fj, J, It*, 2001 *Ur, E, Fj, J*, 2002 *S*
D Nikas 1995 *Ur, Ar*

S O'Leary 2004 *US, J, EngA, E*, 2005 *US, J*
C O'Toole 2009 *I, US, J, J, Rus*, 2010 *Ur, Bel, Sp, Geo, Pt*, 2011 *Rus, US, US, Tg, F, J, NZ*, 2012 *US, It, Sa, Rus*

S Pacey 2005 *W*
C Pack 2006 *S, US*
J Pagano 1997 *I*, 1998 *J, HK, US, HK, J, US*, 1999 *J, Fj, Nm*
DV Pahl 1971 *W*
P Palmer 1983 *E*, 1984 *US*, 1985 *A*, 1986 *J, US*, 1987 *Tg, I, W*, 1988 *US*, 1990 *Ar, US*, 1991 *J, US, Fj, R, F*, 1992 *US*
K Parfrey 2005 *J*
PB Parfrey 2013 *US, Tg, I, J*
TF Paris 2010 *Bel, Sp, Pt*, 2012 *Sa, Rus*, 2013 *US, Fj, I, J*
A Pasutto 2004 *US, J*
K Peace 1978 *F*, 1979 *US, F*, 1980 *W, US*
J Penaluna 1996 *Ur*
DN Penney 1995 *US*, 1996 *US, A, US, Ar*, 1997 *HK*, 1999 *E*
JM Phelan 1980 *NZ*, 1981 *Ar*, 1982 *J, J*, 1985 *A, A*
J Phelan 2010 *Bel, Sp, Pt*, 2012 *It, Geo, Sa, Rus*, 2013 *US, Fj, I, J, US*
M Phinney 2006 *S, E*
CD Pierce 2013 *J*
EC Pinkham 1932 *J*
C Plater 2003 *EngA*
D Pletch 2004 *US, J, EngA, It, E*, 2005 *US, J, W, EngA*, 2006 *S, E, US, Bar, US, W, It*, 2007 *US, NZ, Pt, W, Fj, J, A*, 2009 *US, US, J, J, Rus*, 2010 *Bel, Sp, Pt*
MT Pletch 2005 *Ar*, 2006 *S, E, US, Bar, W, It*, 2007 *US, NZ, Pt, W, J, A*, 2008 *US, Pt, I, W, S*, 2009 *W, Geo, US, US, J, Rus*, 2012 *It, Geo*
JG Pritchard 2003 *M, M, Ur, US, Ar, W, Tg*, 2006 *S, US, Bar, US, W*, 2007 *US, NZ, Pt, W, Fj, J, A*, 2008 *US, Pt, I, W, S*, 2009 *I, W, Geo, US, US, J, J, Rus*, 2010 *Ur, Sp, Geo, Pt*, 2011 *Rus, US, US, Tg, F, J*, 2012 *US, It, Geo, Sa, Rus*, 2013 *Tg, I, J, US, US*
G Puil 1962 *Bb, W23*
M Pyke 2004 *US, J, US, It*, 2005 *US, F, R*, 2006 *S, E, US, Bar, US, W, It*, 2007 *US, NZ, Pt, W, Fj, J, A*, 2008 *US*

DLJ Quigley 1976 *Bb*, 1979 *F*

RE Radu 1985 *A*, 1986 *US*, 1987 *US, Tg, I, US*, 1988 *US*, 1989 *I, US*, 1990 *Ar, Ar*, 1991 *US*
D Ramsey 2005 *US*
GL Rees 1986 *US*, 1987 *US, Tg, I, W, US*, 1989 *I, US*, 1990 *Ar, Ar*, 1991 *J, S, US, Fj, R, F, NZ*, 1992 *US, E*, 1993 *E, E, US, W*, 1994 *US, F, W, E, F*, 1995 *S, Fj, NZ, R, A, SA*, 1996 *HK, J*, 1997 *US, J, HK, J, US, W, I*, 1998 *US, US, Ur, US, Ar*, 1999 *Sa, Tg, W, E, F, Fj, Nm*
J Reid 2003 *M, US, Ar, NZ, Tg*
G Relph 1974 *Tg*
S Richmond 2004 *EngA, US, F, It, E*, 2005 *US, W, EngA, US*
PD Riordan 2003 *EngA*, 2004 *US, J, EngA, US*, 2006 *S, E, US, Bar, US, W, It*, 2007 *US, NZ, Pt, W, Fj, J, A*, 2008 *US, Pt, I, W*, 2009 *I, W, Geo, US, US, J, J, Rus*, 2010 *Ur, Bel, Sp, Geo, Pt*, 2011 *Rus, US, US, Tg, F, J, NZ*
JR Robertsen 1985 *A, A, US*, 1986 *US*, 1987 *US*, 1989 *I, US*, 1990 *Ar, US, Ar*, 1991 *Fj, F*
C Robertson 1997 *HK*, 1998 *US, US, HK, J, Ur*, 2001 *Ur*
AK Robinson 1998 *HK*
G Robinson 1966 *BI*
R Robson 1998 *HK, US*, 1999 *J, Tg*
S Rodgers 2005 *US*
RP Ross 1989 *I, US*, 1990 *US*, 1995 *Ar, NZ*, 1996 *US, US, HK, J, A, HK, J, Ur, US, Ar*, 1997 *US, J, HK, HK, J, US, W*, 1998 *J, HK, US, US, HK, J, Ur, US*, 1999 *J, Fj, Sa, US, W, E, F, Nm*, 2001 *Ur, E, E, Fj, J*, 2002 *US, US, Ur, CHL, Ur, CHL, F*, 2003 *EngA, US, M, Ur, Ar, W, Tg*
JG Rowland 1932 *J, J*
G Rowlands 1995 *Ar, NZ, A, US*, 1996 *US, US*
RJ Russell 1979 *US*, 1983 *E*, 1985 *A, A*
JB Ryan 1966 *BI*, 1967 *E*

IH Saundry 1932 *J, J*
MD Schiefler 1980 *US, NZ*, 1981 *US, Ar*, 1982 *J, E, US*, 1983 *US*, 1984 *US*
M Schmid 1996 *Ur, US, Ar*, 1997 *US, J, US, W, I*, 1998 *US, HK, J, Ur, Ar*, 1999 *Sa, US, W, E, F, Fj, Nm*, 2001 *US, Ur, E, E*
MA Scholz 2009 *Rus*, 2011 *Rus, US, US*, 2012 *US, It*
T Scott 1976 *Bb*
S Selkirk 1932 *J*
JD Shaw 1978 *F*
CJ Shergold 1980 *US, NZ*, 1981 *US*
DM Shick 1970 *Fj*, 1971 *W*
JL Sinclair 2008 *Pt, I, W, S*, 2009 *I, US, US, J, J, Rus*, 2010 *Bel, Sp, Geo, Pt*, 2011 *Rus, US, US, Tg, F, J, NZ*, 2012 *US, It, Geo, Rus*, 2013 *Fj, Tg, I, US, US*
DC Sinnott 1979 *F*, 1981 *US, Ar*
FG Skillings 1932 *J, J*
DM Slater 1971 *W*
C Smith 1995 *Ur, US*, 1996 *HK, J, Ur, US, Ar*, 1997 *US*, 1998 *J, HK, US, HK, Ur*, 1999 *J, Fj, Sa, US, Tg, W, E, F*
RJ Smith 2003 *EngA, M, M, Ur, US, Ar, W, NZ, Tg*, 2004 *US, J, EngA, US, F, It, E*, 2005 *US, J, W, EngA, US, Ar, F, R*, 2006 *S, Bar, US, W, It*, 2007 *US, NZ, Pt, W, Fj, J*, 2008 *US, Pt, I, W, S*, 2009 *I, W, US, US*, 2010 *Bel*, 2011 *US, US, Tg, F, J, NZ*
C Smythe 1997 *J, HK*
RGA Snow 1995 *Ar, NZ, R, A, SA, US*, 1996 *HK, J, A, HK, J*, 1997 *US, HK, J, W, I*, 1998 *US, US, US, Ar*, 1999 *J, Fj, Sa, US, W, E, F, Fj, Nm*, 2000 *I, J, It*, 2001 *US, Ar, E, E, Fj, J*, 2002 *S, US, US, Ur, CHL, Ur, CHL, W, F*, 2003 *Ur, US, Ar, W, NZ, It, Tg*, 2006 *US, Bar, US*, 2007 *Pt, W, Fj, J, A*
D Spicer 2004 *E*, 2005 *R*, 2006 *S, E, US, Bar, US, W*, 2007 *US, NZ, Pt, W, Fj, J*, 2008 *US*, 2009 *I, W*
DA Speirs 1988 *US*, 1989 *I, US*, 1991 *Fj, NZ*
WE Spofford 1981 *Ar*
W Stanley 1994 *US, F*, 1995 *S, Ur, Ar, R, A, SA, US*, 1996 *US, US, A, HK, J*, 1997 *US, J, HK, HK, US, W, I*, 1998 *US, US, HK, Ur, US, Ar*, 1999 *J, Fj, Sa, US, Tg, W, E, F,*

Fj, Nm, 2000 *Tg, US, SA, I, Sa, Fj, J, It*, 2001 *E, E*, 2002 *S, US, US, Ur, CHL, Ur, CHL, W, F*, 2003 *EngA, US, M, M, Ur, US, Ar, W, It, Tg*
Al Stanton 1971 *W*, 1973 *W*, 1974 *Tg*
E Stapleton 1978 *US, F*
D Steen 1966 *BI*
SM Stephen 2005 *EngA, US*, 2006 *S, E, US, Bar, US, W*, 2007 *US, NZ, Pt, W, Fj, A*, 2008 *I, W, S*, 2009 *I, W*, 2010 *Sp, Geo, Pt*
C Stewart 1991 *S, US, Fj, R, F, NZ*, 1994 *E, F*, 1995 *S, Fj, NZ, R, A, SA*
R Stewart 2005 *R*
DS Stewart 1989 *US*, 1990 *Ar*, 1991 *US, Fj, R, F, NZ*, 1992 *E*, 1993 *E, E, US, A, W*, 1994 *US, F, W, E, F*, 1995 *S, Fj, NZ, R, A, SA, US*, 1996 *US, US, A, HK, J, Ur, US, Ar*, 1997 *US, J, HK, HK, J, US, W, I*, 1998 *US, J, Ur, Ar*, 1999 *Sa, US, Tg, W, E, F, Fj, Nm*, 2000 *US, SA, I, Sa, Fj, It*, 2001 *US, Ur, Ar, E, E*
B Stoikos 2001 *Ur*
G Stover 1962 *Bb*
R Strang 1983 *E*
C Strubin 2004 *EngA, E*
IC Stuart 1984 *US*, 1985 *A, A*, 1986 *J*, 1987 *US, Tg, I, W, US*, 1988 *US*, 1989 *US*, 1990 *Ar, US, Ar*, 1992 *E*, 1993 *A, W*, 1994 *US, F, W, E*
JD Stubbs 1962 *Bb, W23*
FJ Sturrock 1971 *W*
CW Suter 1932 *J*
KF Svoboda 1985 *A, A, US*, 1986 *J, US*, 1987 *W*, 1990 *Ar, US, Ar*, 1991 *J, US, R, F*, 1992 *US, E*, 1993 *E, E, US*, 1994 *F, W, F*, 1995 *Fj, A, US*
P Szabo 1989 *I, US*, 1990 *Ar, US, Ar*, 1991 *NZ*, 1993 *US, A, W*

JN Tait 1997 *US, J, HK, HK, J, US, W, I*, 1998 *US, Ur, Ar*, 1999 *J, Fj, Sa, US, Tg, W, E, F, Fj, Nm*, 2000 *Tg, US, SA, I, Sa, Fj, J, It*, 2001 *US, Ur, Ar, E, E*, 2002 *US, W, F*
L Tait 2005 *US, J, W, EngA*, 2006 *S, E, US, Bar, US, W, It*, 2007 *US, NZ, Pt, W, Fj, A*, 2009 *I, W*, 2010 *Ur*
WG Taylor 1978 *F*, 1979 *US, F*, 1980 *W, US, NZ*, 1981 *US, Ar*, 1983 *US, It*
J Thiel 1998 *HK, J, Ur*, 1999 *J, Fj, Sa, US, Tg, W, E, F, Fj, Nm*, 2000 *SA, I, Sa, Fj, J*, 2001 *US, Ar, E, E*, 2002 *S, US, US, Ur, CHL, Ur, W, F*, 2003 *Ur, US, Ar, W, It*, 2004 *F*, 2007 *Pt, W, Fj, J, A*, 2008 *I, W*
S Thompson 2001 *Fj, J*, 2004 *US*
W Thomson 1970 *Fj*
AA Tiedemann 2009 *W, Geo, US, US*, 2010 *Ur, Bel, Geo, Pt*, 2011 *Rus, US, NZ*, 2012 *US, It, Geo, Sa, Rus*, 2013 *US, Fj, I, J, US, US*
K Tkachuk 2000 *Tg, US, SA, Sa, Fj, It*, 2001 *Fj, J*, 2002 *CHL, Ur, CHL, W, F*, 2003 *EngA, US, M, M, Ur, US, Ar, W, NZ, It, Tg*, 2004 *EngA, US, F, It, E*, 2005 *US, J, W, Ar, F, R*, 2006 *US, W, It*, 2007 *US, NZ*, 2008 *US, Pt, I, W, S*, 2009 *I, W, Geo, US, US, J, J, Rus*, 2010 *Sp, Geo*
H Toews 1998 *J, HK, HK, Ur*, 1999 *Tg*, 2000 *US, Sa, J, It*, 2001 *Fj, J*
R Toews 1993 *W*, 1994 *US, F, W, E*, 1995 *S, Ur, Ar, Fj*, 1996 *US, HK, J, A*, 1997 *HK, US, I*
J Tomlinson 1996 *A*, 2001 *Ur*
CA Trainor 2011 *Rus, Tg, F, J, NZ*, 2012 *It, Geo*
N Trenkel 2007 *A*
DM Tucker 1985 *A, A, US*, 1986 *US*, 1987 *US, W*
A Tyler 2005 *Ar*
A Tynan 1995 *Ur, Ar, NZ, US*, 1997 *J*
CJ Tynan 1987 *US*, 1988 *US*, 1990 *Ar, US, Ar*, 1991 *J, US, Fj, F, NZ*, 1992 *US*, 1993 *E, E, US, W*, 1996 *US, J*, 1997 *HK, J*, 1998 *US*

LD Underwood 2013 *US, Fj, Tg, I, J*
DN Ure 1962 *Bb, W23*

PC Vaesen 1985 *US*, 1986 *J*, 1987 *US, Tg, US*
D van Camp 2005 *J, R*, 2006 *It*, 2007 *US, NZ*, 2008 *Pt, W*, 2009 *I, Geo*
R van den Brink 1986 *US*, 1987 *Tg*, 1988 *US*, 1991 *J, US, R, F, NZ*
DTH van Der Merwe 2006 *Bar, It*, 2007 *Pt, W, Fj, J, A*, 2009 *I, W, Geo, US, US*, 2010 *Ur, Sp, Geo*, 2011 *US, US, Tg, F, J, NZ*, 2012 *US, It, Geo*, 2013 *US, US*
D van Eeuwen 1978 *F*, 1979 *US*
A van Staveren 2000 *Tg, Sa, Fj*, 2002 *US, US, Ur, CHL, Ur, CHL, W, F*, 2003 *EngA, US, M, M, Ur, US, W, NZ, Tg*
J Verstraten 2000 *US, SA, Fj, J*
J Vivian 1983 *E*, 1984 *US*

FG Walsh 2008 *I, W, S*, 2009 *US*
KC Walt 1976 *Bb*, 1977 *US, E, E*, 1978 *US, F*
JM Ward 1962 *W23*
M Webb 2004 *US, J, US, F, It*, 2005 *US, J, W, EngA, US, Ar, F*, 2006 *US, W, It*, 2007 *J, A*, 2008 *US*
M Weingart 2004 *J*, 2005 *J, EngA, US, F, R*, 2007 *Pt*
GJM Wessels 1962 *W23*
WR Wharton 1932 *J, J*
ST White 2009 *J, J, Rus*, 2010 *Ur, Bel, Sp, Geo, Pt*, 2011 *Rus, US, F, J, NZ*, 2012 *US, It, Geo, Sa*, 2013 *US, Fj, Tg, I, J, US, US*
K Whitley 1995 *S*
C Whittaker 1993 *US, A*, 1995 *Ur*, 1996 *A*, 1997 *J*, 1998 *J, HK, US, US, HK, J, US, Ar*, 1999 *J, Fj, US*
LW Whitty 1967 *E*
DW Whyte 1974 *Tg*, 1977 *US, E, E*
RR Wickland 1966 *BI*, 1967 *E*
JP Wiley 1977 *US, E, E*, 1978 *US, F*, 1979 *US*, 1980 *W, US, NZ*, 1981 *US*
K Wilke 1971 *W*, 1973 *W*, 1976 *Bb*, 1978 *US*
K Wilkinson 1976 *Bb*, 1978 *F*, 1979 *F*
BN Williams 1962 *W23*
J Williams 2001 *US, Ur, Ar, Fj, J*
M Williams 1992 *E*, 1993 *A, W*
MH Williams 1978 *US, F*, 1980 *US*, 1982 *J*
M Williams 1999 *Tg, W, E, F, Fj, Nm*, 2000 *Tg, SA, I, Sa, Fj, J, It*, 2001 *E, E, Fj, J*, 2002 *S, US, US, Ur, CHL, W, F*, 2003 *EngA, US, M, M, Ur, US, Ar, W, It, Tg*, 2004 *EngA, US, F*, 2005 *W, Ar, F, R*, 2006 *E, US, Bar, US, W, It*, 2007 *US, NZ, W, Fj, J, A*, 2008 *Pt, W, S*
A Wilson 2008 *US*
EA Wilson 2012 *Sa, Rus*
PG Wilson 1932 *J, J*
RS Wilson 1962 *Bb*
K Wirachowski 1992 *E*, 1993 *US*, 1996 *US, HK, Ur, US, Ar*, 1997 *US, HK*, 2000 *It*, 2001 *Ur, E, Fj, J*, 2002 *S, CHL*, 2003 *EngA, US, M*
T Wish 2004 *US, J*
K Witkowski 2005 *EngA, Ar*, 2006 *E*
N Witkowski 1998 *US, J*, 2000 *Tg, US, SA, I, Sa, Fj, J, It*, 2001 *US, E, E*, 2002 *S, US, US, Ur, CHL, Ur, CHL, W, F*, 2003 *EngA, US, M, M, Ur, Ar, W, NZ, Tg*, 2005 *EngA, US*, 2006 *E*
AH Woller 1967 *E*
S Wood 1977 *E*
TA Woods 1984 *US*, 1986 *J, US*, 1987 *US, Tg, I, W*, 1988 *US*, 1989 *I, US*, 1990 *Ar, US*, 1991 *S, F, NZ*, 1996 *US, US*, 1997 *US, J*
DP Wooldridge 2009 *I, Geo, J, J, Rus*, 2010 *Ur*, 2012 *Geo, Sa, Rus*, 2013 *Tg, I, US, US*
MA Wyatt 1982 *J, J, E, US*, 1983 *US, It, It, E*, 1985 *A, A, US*, 1986 *J, US*, 1987 *Tg, I, W, US*, 1988 *US*, 1989 *I, US*, 1990 *Ar, US, Ar*, 1991 *J, S, US, R, F, NZ*
H Wyndham 1973 *W*

JJ Yeganegi 1996 *US*, 1998 *J*
C Yukes 2001 *Ur, Fj, J*, 2002 *S, US, Ur, Ur*, 2003 *EngA, US, M, M, US, Ar, W, NZ, It, Tg*, 2004 *US, J, EngA, US, F, It, E*, 2005 *W, EngA, US*, 2006 *Bar, US*, 2007 *US, NZ, Pt, W, Fj, J, A*

ENGLAND

ENGLAND'S 2012–13 TEST RECORD

OPPONENTS	DATE	VENUE	RESULT
Fiji	10 Nov	H	Won 54–12
Australia	17 Nov	H	Lost 14–20
South Africa	24 Nov	H	Lost 15–16
New Zealand	1 Dec	H	Won 38–21
Scotland	2 Feb	H	Won 38–18
Ireland	10 Feb	A	Won 12–6
France	23 Feb	H	Won 23–13
Italy	10 Mar	H	Won 18–11
Wales	16 Mar	A	Lost 30–3
Argentina	8 Jun	A	Won 32–3
Argentina	15 Jun	A	Won 51–26

A SEASON OF HIGHS AND LOWS

By Will Greenwood

Getty Images

Manu Tuilagi was one of three England try-scorers in the famous win over New Zealand at Twickenham.

I wrote in my England piece in the *IRB World Rugby Yearbook 2013* that I believed Stuart Lancaster's young side were on the cusp of achieving something special and, although they suffered some painful setbacks in the 2012/13 season, I have not changed my view. England undoubtedly remain a work in progress but, in my opinion, they will mature into a force to be reckoned with at Rugby World Cup 2015.

The headline result of their campaign was the 38–21 demolition of the All Blacks at Twickenham in December. It was a breathtaking performance, New Zealand's first defeat in 20 Tests, and any side capable of inflicting that kind of damage on the reigning world champions cannot be dismissed.

The euphoria of that superb victory against the All Blacks dispelled the disappointment of failing to beat both Australia and South Africa at Twickenham on the preceding weekends when both teams seemed to be there for the taking, but in turn it was easy to forget what England had achieved after they were comprehensively taken apart in Cardiff by Wales in March as the Grand Slam slipped through their fingers.

A season of peaks and troughs but, with another year of Test rugby under their belts, England's relatively inexperienced players will be far stronger for it. In doing this Stuart underlined his disregard for selecting on reputation, which has been one of the hallmarks of his regime so far.

The season began with confirmation of the reappointment of Chris Robshaw as captain in late October. No one seriously expected Stuart to hand the armband to anybody else but he kept him waiting and I thought it was astute man-management, ensuring Chris had to earn it on the merits of his performances for Harlequins.

England kicked off the autumn with what was a straightforward win over Fiji (54–12) before the back-to-back losses against the Wallabies and the Springboks. They were narrow defeats but there was no disguising the sense of lost opportunity in both Tests.

Chris's captaincy was criticised after both games. In the 20–14 loss against Australia he was knocked for turning down second-half penalty opportunities in pursuit of tries while conversely his decision to go for a late penalty rather than a lineout and drive against South Africa was blamed for the 16–15 defeat.

It's easy to be critical with the benefit of hindsight. I would particularly defend him in terms of the Springboks game because I think the only mistake he made was the time it took to make the decision. The decision itself was sound because the number of times a team successfully catches, drives and scores from those situations is miniscule and he wanted to set England up for a winning drop goal or another penalty.

The defeat meant England were not one of the top four seeds for the RWC 2015 draw and, as a result, they will now face Australia and Wales in the pool stages. The pessimists will argue they've made life unnecessarily difficult for themselves but I remain an optimist when it comes to the national side and I believe they will get out of the group. If they do, they will be in great shape and battle-hardened for the latter stages of the tournament.

I really cannot claim I saw the performance against the All Blacks coming. I was watching the match in the Sky studio with Sean Fitzpatrick and I have never seen him look so stunned or in such a state of utter disbelief. England tore New Zealand to shreds.

It was England's biggest ever win against the Kiwis but what really impressed me was the way the team responded early in the second half when the All Blacks scored through Kieran Read and the lead was cut to a single point. Everyone at Twickenham held their breath as they waited for the New Zealand fightback but it never materialised. England looked them straight in the eye and pulled away convincingly with three tries in a magical 10 minutes of rugby.

I was part of the England side that beat the All Blacks at Twickenham in 2002 but the comparison ends there. We eventually ran out 31–28 winners but were clinging on for dear life at the end whereas Stuart's side were much more comfortable. It was a result that proved beyond any doubt that England have the personnel to hurt any team. It was also hugely significant because this group of players now has no reason to fear the famous black shirt, an important psychological factor as they look ahead to three Tests in New Zealand in the summer of 2014.

The Six Nations promised much initially for England but ended ignominiously in the Millennium Stadium with the 30–3 mauling at the hands of Wales. It was a bitter reality check and, while the tournament did expose some issues about the team's consistency, there were still positives to take from it.

England were not particularly stretched in their opener against a decent Scotland side at Twickenham, scoring four tries in a 38–18 victory, while my personal highlight of the Championship came a week later when the team battled the wind and the rain at the Aviva Stadium to beat Ireland 12–6.

It was a display at the time which convinced me that England had turned the corner. It was an ugly win in horrendous conditions but any team with aspirations to become world champions has to learn to get over the line in those sticky situations and England went to Dublin and bullied the Irish in their own backyard. From an aesthetic perspective, it's not a match that will live long in the memory but it was a hell of a performance.

Unfortunately the side struggled to find its rhythm after that, getting past France 23–13 and then Italy 18–11 without convincing in either match. Creativity was the issue (more of which later) and England ultimately had to fall back on their collective stubbornness and forward power to keep the Grand Slam dream alive.

And so it was to Cardiff. It was never going to be a fixture for the fainthearted and England simply could not cope with Wales' ferocity.

What I hoped they learned from what was a chastening 80 minutes is that you have to take your chances in Test rugby. England had a couple of chances in the first half which they did not take and they were made to pay. Their profligacy meant they were always playing catch-up rugby and, as Wales fed on the support of the home crowd in the second half, there was no way back.

Shorn of their Lions players, England headed to Argentina in the summer for two Tests with a young squad. Stuart decided to rest the captain and senior players like Toby Flood, Danny Care, Brad Barritt and Chris Ashton, and I'd have to agree with his decision.

He must have been tempted to take some of his big hitters because

Argentina is a tough place to tour but players desperately need a break. I was rested for the tour of Argentina back in 2002 and I honestly don't think my body would have held together for the Rugby World Cup in Australia the following year if Clive Woodward hadn't given me that summer off.

England came home with a 32–3 win in the first Test in Salta and a high-scoring 51–26 victory in Buenos Aires. It was England's first clean sweep against the Pumas away from home and, considering the number of new caps and young players on show, Stuart will have been delighted.

He cannot, however, have been blind to the fact it was a de facto Argentina second string. Felipe Contepomi was the only survivor of the side that played in Buenos Aires who also featured in The Rugby Championship opener against the Springboks two months later, so it's important to put both results into context.

Stuart must on balance be pleased with the squad's progress. The emergence of Mako Vunipola and Joe Launchbury, the quality performances of Geoff Parling, the battle between Tom Youngs and Dylan Hartley for the hooker berth and the good form of David Wilson at tighthead prop mean he can rely on a combative front five where there is plenty of competition for places.

His big challenge now is the issue of creativity out wide. After their opener against Scotland, England scored just one try in their next four Six Nations games and if the team want to move to the next level, they have to address that.

The good news is Stuart has options. Kyle Eastmond, Marland Yarde, Billy Twelvetrees and Christian Wade all proved in Argentina that they can provide that cutting edge, and Stuart now has to balance the solidity and dependability which the likes of Barritt epitomise with the need to give the side an extra dimension in the backline. It's a dilemma but he has options in terms of personnel.

The other question is consistency. England cannot have anticipated being as good as they were against New Zealand but neither can they have imagined they would be so bad in the second half against Wales. They've got to iron out that discrepancy in their levels of performance.

But I remain upbeat. They have another chance to despatch Australia in the November series, which would be another box ticked, and with home games against Wales and Ireland in the Six Nations, you could reasonably argue that a win in Paris would give them a superb chance to win the Championship. The main priority, however, with the Rugby World Cup looming is to ensure Twickenham becomes a real fortress where other sides fear to tread.

ENGLAND INTERNATIONAL STATISTICS

MATCH RECORDS UP TO 10 OCTOBER 2013

MOST CONSECUTIVE TEST WINS

14 2002 W, It, Arg, NZ, A, SA, 2003 F1, W1, It, S, I, NZ, A, W2
11 2000 SA2, A, Arg, SA3, 2001 W, It, S, F, C1,2, US
10 1882 W, 1883 I, S, 1884 W, I, S, 1885 W, I, 1886 W, I
10 1994 R, C, 1995 I, F, W, S, Arg, It, WS, A
10 2003 F, Gg, SA, Sm, U, W, F, A, 2004 It, S

MOST CONSECUTIVE TESTS WITHOUT DEFEAT

Matches	Wins	Draws	Period
14	14	0	2002 to 2003
12	10	2	1882 to 1887
11	10	1	1922 to 1924
11	11	0	2000 to 2001

MOST POINTS IN A MATCH

BY THE TEAM

Pts	Opponents	Venue	Year
134	Romania	Twickenham	2001
111	Uruguay	Brisbane	2003
110	Netherlands	Huddersfield	1998
106	USA	Twickenham	1999
101	Tonga	Twickenham	1999
84	Georgia	Perth	2003
80	Italy	Twickenham	2001

BY A PLAYER

Pts	Player	Opponents	Venue	Year
44	CC Hodgson	Romania	Twickenham	2001
36	PJ Grayson	Tonga	Twickenham	1999
35	JP Wilkinson	Italy	Twickenham	2001
32	JP Wilkinson	Italy	Twickenham	1999
30	CR Andrew	Canada	Twickenham	1994
30	PJ Grayson	Netherlands	Huddersfield	1998
30	JP Wilkinson	Wales	Twickenham	2002
29	DJH Walder	Canada	Burnaby	2001
27	CR Andrew	South Africa	Pretoria	1994
27	JP Wilkinson	South Africa	Bloemfontein	2000
27	CC Hodgson	South Africa	Twickenham	2004
27	JP Wilkinson	Scotland	Twickenham	2007
26	JP Wilkinson	United States	Twickenham	1999

MOST TRIES IN A MATCH

BY THE TEAM

Tries	Opponents	Venue	Year
20	Romania	Twickenham	2001
17	Uruguay	Brisbane	2003
16	Netherlands	Huddersfield	1998
16	United States	Twickenham	1999
13	Wales	Blackheath	1881
13	Tonga	Twickenham	1999
12	Georgia	Perth	2003
12	Canada	Twickenham	2004
10	Japan	Sydney	1987
10	Fiji	Twickenham	1989
10	Italy	Twickenham	2001
10	Romania	Dunedin	2011

BY A PLAYER

Tries	Player	Opponents	Venue	Year
5	D Lambert	France	Richmond	1907
5	R Underwood	Fiji	Twickenham	1989
5	OJ Lewsey	Uruguay	Brisbane	2003
4	GW Burton	Wales	Blackheath	1881
4	A Hudson	France	Paris	1906
4	RW Poulton	France	Paris	1914
4	C Oti	Romania	Bucharest	1989
4	JC Guscott	Netherlands	Huddersfield	1998
4	NA Back	Netherlands	Huddersfield	1998
4	JC Guscott	United States	Twickenham	1999
4	J Robinson	Romania	Twickenham	2001
4	N Easter	Wales	Twickenham	2007
4	CJ Ashton	Italy	Twickenham	2011

MOST CONVERSIONS IN A MATCH

BY THE TEAM

Cons	Opponents	Venue	Year
15	Netherlands	Huddersfield	1998
14	Romania	Twickenham	2001
13	United States	Twickenham	1999
13	Uruguay	Brisbane	2003
12	Tonga	Twickenham	1999
9	Italy	Twickenham	2001
9	Georgia	Perth	2003
8	Romania	Bucharest	1989
8	Italy	Twickenham	2011
7	Wales	Blackheath	1881
7	Japan	Sydney	1987
7	Argentina	Twickenham	1990
7	Wales	Twickenham	1998
7	Wales	Twickenham	2007
7	Romania	Dunedin	2011

BY A PLAYER

Cons	Player	Opponents	Venue	Year
15	PJ Grayson	Netherlands	Huddersfield	1998
14	CC Hodgson	Romania	Twickenham	2001
13	JP Wilkinson	United States	Twickenham	1999
12	PJ Grayson	Tonga	Twickenham	1999
11	PJ Grayson	Uruguay	Brisbane	2003
9	JP Wilkinson	Italy	Twickenham	2001
8	SD Hodgkinson	Romania	Bucharest	1989
7	JM Webb	Japan	Sydney	1987
7	SD Hodgkinson	Argentina	Twickenham	1990
7	PJ Grayson	Wales	Twickenham	1998
7	JP Wilkinson	Wales	Twickenham	2007

MOST PENALTIES IN A MATCH

BY THE TEAM

Penalties	Opponents	Venue	Year
8	South Africa	Bloemfontein	2000
7	Wales	Cardiff	1991
7	Scotland	Twickenham	1995
7	France	Twickenham	1999
7	Fiji	Twickenham	1999
7	South Africa	Paris	1999
7	South Africa	Twickenham	2001
7	Australia	Twickenham	2010
6	Wales	Twickenham	1986
6	Canada	Twickenham	1994
6	Argentina	Durban	1995
6	Scotland	Murrayfield	1996
6	Ireland	Twickenham	1996
6	South Africa	Twickenham	2000
6	Australia	Twickenham	2002
6	Wales	Brisbane	2003
6	Ireland	Twickenham	2012
6	New Zealand	Twickenham	2012
6	France	Twickenham	2013
6	Italy	Twickenham	2013

BY A PLAYER

Penalties	Player	Opponents	Venue	Year
8	JP Wilkinson	South Africa	Bloemfontein	2000
7	SD Hodgkinson	Wales	Cardiff	1991
7	CR Andrew	Scotland	Twickenham	1995
7	JP Wilkinson	France	Twickenham	1999
7	JP Wilkinson	Fiji	Twickenham	1999
7	JP Wilkinson	South Africa	Twickenham	2001
7	TGAL Flood	Australia	Twickenham	2010
6	CR Andrew	Wales	Twickenham	1986
6	CR Andrew	Canada	Twickenham	1994
6	CR Andrew	Argentina	Durban	1995
6	PJ Grayson	Scotland	Murrayfield	1996
6	PJ Grayson	Ireland	Twickenham	1996
6	PJ Grayson	South Africa	Paris	1999
6	JP Wilkinson	South Africa	Twickenham	2000
6	JP Wilkinson	Australia	Twickenham	2002
6	JP Wilkinson	Wales	Brisbane	2003
6	OA Farrell	Ireland	Twickenham	2012
6	OA Farrell	Italy	Twickenham	2013

MOST DROP GOALS IN A MATCH

BY THE TEAM

Drops	Opponents	Venue	Year
3	France	Sydney	2003
2	Ireland	Twickenham	1970
2	France	Paris	1978
2	France	Paris	1980
2	Romania	Twickenham	1985
2	Fiji	Suva	1991
2	Argentina	Durban	1995
2	France	Paris	1996
2	Australia	Twickenham	2001
2	Wales	Cardiff	2003
2	Ireland	Dublin	2003
2	South Africa	Perth	2003
2	Samoa	Nantes	2007
2	Tonga	Paris	2007
2	Wales	Twickenham	2011
2	Argentina	Manchester	2009

BY A PLAYER

Drops	Player	Opponents	Venue	Year
3	JP Wilkinson	France	Sydney	2003
2	R Hiller	Ireland	Twickenham	1970
2	AGB Old	France	Paris	1978
2	JP Horton	France	Paris	1980
2	CR Andrew	Romania	Twickenham	1985
2	CR Andrew	Fiji	Suva	1991
2	CR Andrew	Argentina	Durban	1995
2	PJ Grayson	France	Paris	1996
2	JP Wilkinson	Australia	Twickenham	2001
2	JP Wilkinson	Wales	Cardiff	2003
2	JP Wilkinson	Ireland	Dublin	2003
2	JP Wilkinson	South Africa	Perth	2003
2	JP Wilkinson	Samoa	Nantes	2007
2	JP Wilkinson	Tonga	Paris	2007
2	AJ Goode	Argentina	Manchester	2009
2	JP Wilkinson	Wales	Twickenham	2011

CAREER RECORDS

MOST CAPPED PLAYERS

Caps	Player	Career Span
114	J Leonard	1990 to 2004
91	JP Wilkinson	1998 to 2011
85	R Underwood	1984 to 1996
85	LBN Dallaglio	1995 to 2007
84	MO Johnson	1993 to 2003
78	JPR Worsley	1999 to 2011
77	MJS Dawson	1995 to 2006
75	MJ Catt	1994 to 2007
75	MJ Tindall	2000 to 2011
73	PJ Vickery	1998 to 2009
73	SG Thompson	2002 to 2011
72	WDC Carling	1988 to 1997
71	CR Andrew	1985 to 1997
71	RA Hill	1997 to 2004
71	LW Moody	2001 to 2011
71	SD Shaw	1996 to 2011
69	DJ Grewcock	1997 to 2007
66	NA Back	1994 to 2003
65	JC Guscott	1989 to 1999
64	BC Moore	1987 to 1995
64	ME Corry	1997 to 2007
62	BJ Kay	2001 to 2009
58	PJ Winterbottom	1982 to 1993
57	BC Cohen	2000 to 2006
57	SW Borthwick	2001 to 2010
57	TGAL Flood	2006 to 2013
55	WA Dooley	1985 to 1993
55	WJH Greenwood	1997 to 2004
55	OJ Lewsey	1998 to 2007
55	MJ Cueto	2004 to 2011
54	GC Rowntree	1995 to 2006

MOST CONSECUTIVE TESTS

Tests	Player	Span
44	WDC Carling	1989 to 1995
40	J Leonard	1990 to 1995
36	JV Pullin	1968 to 1975
33	WB Beaumont	1975 to 1982
30	R Underwood	1992 to 1996

MOST TESTS AS CAPTAIN

Tests	Captain	Span
59	WDC Carling	1988 to 1996
39	MO Johnson	1998 to 2003
22	LBN Dallaglio	1997 to 2004
21	WB Beaumont	1978 to 1982
21	SW Borthwick	2008 to 2010
17	ME Corry	2005 to 2007
16	CDC Robshaw	2012 to 2013
15	PJ Vickery	2002 to 2008
13	WW Wakefield	1924 to 1926
13	NM Hall	1949 to 1955
13	E Evans	1956 to 1958
13	REG Jeeps	1960 to 1962
13	JV Pullin	1972 to 1975

MOST POINTS IN TESTS

Points	Player	Tests	Career
1179	JP Wilkinson	91	1998 to 2011
400	PJ Grayson	32	1995 to 2004
396	CR Andrew	71	1985 to 1997
299	TGAL Flood	57	2006 to 2013
296	JM Webb	33	1987 to 1993
269	CC Hodgson	38	2001 to 2012
240	WH Hare	25	1974 to 1984
210	R Underwood	85	1984 to 1996

MOST TRIES IN TESTS

Tries	Player	Tests	Career
49	R Underwood	85	1984 to 1996
31	WJH Greenwood	55	1997 to 2004
31	BC Cohen	57	2000 to 2006
30	JC Guscott	65	1989 to 1999
28	JT Robinson	51	2001 to 2007
24	DD Luger	38	1998 to 2003
22	OJ Lewsey	55	1998 to 2007
20	MJ Cueto	55	2004 to 2011
18	CN Lowe	25	1913 to 1923
17	LBN Dallaglio	85	1995 to 2007
17	CJ Ashton	34	2010 to 2013
16	NA Back	66	1994 to 2003
16	MJS Dawson	77	1995 to 2006
15	AS Healey	51	1997 to 2003

MOST CONVERSIONS IN TESTS

Cons	Player	Tests	Career
162	JP Wilkinson	91	1998 to 2011
78	PJ Grayson	32	1995 to 2004
44	CC Hodgson	38	2001 to 2012
41	JM Webb	33	1987 to 1993
39	TGAL Flood	57	2006 to 2013
35	SD Hodgkinson	14	1989 to 1991
33	CR Andrew	71	1985 to 1997
17	L Stokes	12	1875 to 1881

MOST PENALTY GOALS IN TESTS

Penalties	Player	Tests	Career
239	JP Wilkinson	91	1998 to 2011
86	CR Andrew	71	1985 to 1997
72	PJ Grayson	32	1995 to 2004
67	WH Hare	25	1974 to 1984
66	JM Webb	33	1987 to 1993
66	TGAL Flood	57	2006 to 2013
44	CC Hodgson	38	2001 to 2012
43	SD Hodgkinson	14	1989 to 1991
43	OA Farrell	16	2012 to 2013

MOST DROP GOALS IN TESTS

Drops	Player	Tests	Career
36	JP Wilkinson	91	1998 to 2011
21	CR Andrew	71	1985 to 1997
6	PJ Grayson	32	1995 to 2004
4	JP Horton	13	1978 to 1984
4	L Cusworth	12	1979 to 1988
4	AJ Goode	17	2005 to 2009

INTERNATIONAL CHAMPIONSHIP RECORDS

RECORD	DETAIL	HOLDER	SET
Most points in season	229	in five matches	2001
Most tries in season	29	in five matches	2001
Highest score	80	80–23 v Italy	2001
Biggest win	57	80–23 v Italy	2001
Highest score conceded	43	13–43 v Ireland	2007
Biggest defeat	30	13–43 v Ireland	2007
Most appearances	54	J Leonard	1991–2004
Most points in matches	546	JP Wilkinson	1998–2011
Most points in season	89	JP Wilkinson	2001
Most points in match	35	JP Wilkinson	v Italy, 2001
Most tries in matches	18	CN Lowe	1913–1923
	18	R Underwood	1984–1996
Most tries in season	8	CN Lowe	1914
Most tries in match	4	RW Poulton	v France, 1914
	4	CJ Ashton	v Italy, 2011
Most cons in matches	89	JP Wilkinson	1998–2011
Most cons in season	24	JP Wilkinson	2001
Most cons in match	9	JP Wilkinson	v Italy, 2001
Most pens in matches	105	JP Wilkinson	1998–2011
Most pens in season	18	SD Hodgkinson	1991
	18	JP Wilkinson	2000
Most pens in match	7	SD Hodgkinson	v Wales, 1991
	7	CR Andrew	v Scotland, 1995
	7	JP Wilkinson	v France, 1999
Most drops in matches	11	JP Wilkinson	1998–2011
Most drops in season	5	JP Wilkinson	2003
Most drops in match	2	R Hiller	v Ireland, 1970
	2	AGB Old	v France, 1978
	2	JP Horton	v France, 1980
	2	PJ Grayson	v France, 1996
	2	JP Wilkinson	v Wales, 2003
	2	JP Wilkinson	v Ireland, 2003

MISCELLANEOUS RECORDS

RECORD	HOLDER	DETAIL
Longest Test career	SD Shaw	1996 to 2011
Youngest Test cap	HCC Laird	18 yrs 134 days in 1927
Oldest Test cap	F Gilbert	38 yrs 362 days in 1923

CAREER RECORDS OF ENGLAND INTERNATIONAL PLAYERS

UP TO 10 OCTOBER 2013

PLAYER BACKS:	DEBUT	CAPS	T	C	P	D	PTS
DA Armitage	2008 v PI	26	7	0	2	1	44
CJ Ashton	2010 v F	34	17	0	0	0	85
BM Barritt	2012 v S	16	1	0	0	0	5
MN Brown	2007 v SA	18	0	0	0	0	0
FS Burns	2012 v NZ	3	1	7	6	0	37
DS Care	2008 v NZ	41	5	0	0	1	28
LAW Dickson	2012 v S	9	0	0	0	0	0
KO Eastmond	2013 v Arg	2	1	0	0	0	5
OA Farrell	2012 v S	16	0	11	43	1	154
TGAL Flood	2006 v Arg	57	4	39	66	1	299
BJ Foden	2009 v It	32	7	0	0	0	35
DAV Goode	2012 v SA	11	0	0	0	0	0
JBA Joseph	2012 v SA	6	0	0	0	0	0
JJ May	2013 v Arg	1	0	0	0	0	0
YCC Monye	2008 v PI	14	2	0	0	0	10
SJ Myler	2013 v Arg	1	0	1	0	0	2
CDJ Sharples	2011 v W	4	2	0	0	0	10
D Strettle	2007 v I	14	2	0	0	0	10
EM Tuilagi	2011 v W	21	10	0	0	0	50
WWF Twelvetrees	2013 v S	5	2	0	0	0	10
C Wade	2013 v Arg	1	0	0	0	0	0
REP Wigglesworth	2008 v It	14	1	0	0	0	5
MD Yarde	2013 v Arg	1	2	0	0	0	10
BR Youngs	2010 v S	33	6	0	0	0	30

FORWARDS:							
DMJ Attwood	2010 v NZ	4	0	0	0	0	0
MJ Botha	2011 v W	10	0	0	0	0	0
DR Cole	2010 v W	40	1	0	0	0	5
AR Corbisiero	2011 v It	18	0	0	0	0	0
TR Croft	2008 v F	38	4	0	0	0	20
PPL Doran-Jones	2009 v Arg	6	0	0	0	0	0
DM Hartley	2008 v PI	47	1	0	0	0	5
JAW Haskell	2007 v W	50	4	0	0	0	20
TA Johnson	2012 v SA	5	1	0	0	0	5
MB Kvesic	2013 v Arg	2	0	0	0	0	0
JO Launchbury	2012 v Fj	11	0	0	0	0	0
CL Lawes	2009 v A	22	0	0	0	0	0
JWG Marler	2012 v SA	12	0	0	0	0	0
BJ Morgan	2012 v S	12	1	0	0	0	5
DJ Paice	2008 v NZ	8	0	0	0	0	0
TP Palmer	2001 v US	42	0	0	0	0	0
GMW Parling	2012 v S	17	1	0	0	0	5
CDC Robshaw	2009 v Arg	17	0	0	0	0	0
HM Thomas	2013 v Arg	2	0	0	0	0	0
MWIN Vunipola	2012 v Fj	9	0	0	0	0	0
VML Vunipola	2013 v Arg	2	1	0	0	0	5
TR Waldrom	2012 v SA	5	0	0	0	0	0
RW Webber	2012 v It	5	1	0	0	0	5
DG Wilson	2009 v Arg	28	0	0	0	0	0
TA Wood	2011 v W	20	0	0	0	0	0
TN Youngs	2012 v Fj	9	0	0	0	0	0

ENGLAND INTERNATIONAL PLAYERS

UP TO 10 OCTOBER 2013

Note: Years given for International Championship matches are for second half of season; e.g. 1972 means season 1971–72. Years for all other matches refer to the actual year of the match. Entries in square brackets denote matches played in RWC Finals.

Aarvold, C D (Cambridge U, W Hartlepool, Headingley, Blackheath) 1928 A, W, I, F, S, 1929 W, I, F, 1931 W, S, F, 1932 SA, W, I, S, 1933 W

Abbott, S R (Wasps, Harlequins) 2003 W2, F3, [Sm, U, W(R)], 2004 NZ1(t&R), 2, 2006 I, A2(R)

Abendanon, N A (Bath) 2007 SA2(R), F2

Ackford, P J (Harlequins) 1988 A, 1989 S, I, F, W, R, Fj, 1990 I, F, W, S, Arg 3, 1991 W, S, I, F, A, [NZ, It, F, S, A]

Adams, A A (London Hospital) 1910 F

Adams, F R (Richmond) 1875 I, S, 1876 S, 1877 I, 1878 S, 1879 S, I

Adebayo, A A (Bath) 1996, It, 1997 Arg 1, 2, A 2, NZ 1, 1998 S

Adey, G J (Leicester) 1976 I, F

Adkins, S J (Coventry) 1950 I, F, S, 1953 W, I, F, S

Agar, A E (Harlequins) 1952 SA, W, S, I, F, 1953 W, I

Alcock, A (Guy's Hospital) 1906 SA

Alderson, F H R (Hartlepool R) 1891 W, I, S, 1892 W, S, 1893 W

Alexander, H (Richmond) 1900 I, S, 1901 W, I, S, 1902 W, I

Alexander, W (Northern) 1927 F

Allen, A O (Gloucester) 2006 NZ, Arg

Allison, D F (Coventry) 1956 W, I, S, F, 1957 W, 1958 W, S

Allport, A (Blackheath) 1892 W, 1893 I, 1894 W, I, S

Anderson, S (Rockcliff) 1899 I

Anderson, W F (Orrell) 1973 NZ 1

Anderton, C (Manchester FW) 1889 M

Andrew, C R (Cambridge U, Nottingham, Wasps, Toulouse, Newcastle) 1985 R, F, S, I, W, 1986 W, S, I, F, 1987 I, F, W, [J (R), US], 1988 S, I 1, 2, A 1, 2, Fj, A, 1989 S, I, F, W, R, Fj, 1990

I, F, W, S, Arg 3, 1991 W, S, I, F, Fj, A, [NZ, It, US, F, S, A], 1992 S, I, F, W, C, SA, 1993 F, W, NZ, 1994 S, I, F, W, SA 1, 2, R, C, 1995 I, F, W, S, [Arg, It, A, NZ, F], 1997 W (R)
Appleford, G N (London Irish) 2002 Arg
Archer, G S (Bristol, Army, Newcastle) 1996 S, I, 1997 A 2, NZ 1, SA, NZ 2, 1998 F, W, S, I, A 1, NZ 1, H, It, 1999 Tg, Fj, 2000 I, F, W, It, S
Archer, H (Bridgwater A) 1909 W, F, I
Armitage, D A (London Irish) 2008 PI, A, SA, NZ3, 2009 It, W, I, F, S, Arg 1, 2, 2010 W, It, I, S, A2(R), NZ(R), A3(R), Sm(R), 2011 W2, 3(t&R), I2(R), [Arg, Gg, R(R), S]
Armitage, S E (London Irish) 2009 It, Arg 1, 2, 2010 W(R), It(R)
Armstrong, R (Northern) 1925 W
Arthur, T G (Wasps) 1966 W, I
Ashby, R C (Wasps) 1966 I, F, 1967 A
Ashcroft, A (Waterloo) 1956 W, I, S, F, 1957 W, I, F, S, 1958 W, A, I, F, S, 1959 I, F, S
Ashcroft, A H (Birkenhead Park) 1909 A
Ashford, W (Richmond) 1897 W, I, 1898 S, W
Ashton, C J (Northampton, Saracens) 2010 F, A1, 2, NZ, A3, Sm, SA, 2011 W1, It, F, S, I1, 2, [Arg, Gg, R, S, F], 2012 S, It, W, F, I, SA 1, 2, 3, A, SA4, NZ, 2013 S, I, F, It, W
Ashworth, A (Oldham) 1892 I
Askew, J G (Cambridge U) 1930 W, I, F
Aslett, A R (Richmond) 1926 W, I, F, S, 1929 S, F
Assinder, E W (O Edwardians) 1909 A, W
Aston, R L (Blackheath) 1890 S, I
Attwood, D M J (Gloucester, Bath) 2010 NZ(R), Sm(R), 2013 Arg1, 2
Auty, J R (Headingley) 1935 S

Back, N A (Leicester) 1994 S, I, 1995 [Arg (t), It, WS], 1997 NZ 1(R), SA, NZ 2, 1998 F, W, S, I, H, It, A 2, SA 2, 1999 S, I, F, W, A, US, C, [It, NZ, Fj, SA], 2000 I, F, W, It, S, SA 1, 2, A, Arg, SA 3, 2001 W, It, S, F, I, A, R, SA, 2002 S, I, F, W, It, NZ (t + R), A, SA, 2003 F 1, W 1, S, I, NZ, A, F 3, [Gg, SA, Sm, W, F, A]
Bailey, M D (Cambridge U, Wasps) 1984 SA 1, 2, 1987 [US], 1989 Fj, 1990 I, F, S (R)
Bainbridge, S (Gosforth, Fylde) 1982 F, W, 1983 F, W, S, I, NZ, 1984 S, I, F, W, 1985 NZ 1, 2, 1987 F, W, S, [J, US]
Baker, D G S (OMTs) 1955 W, I, F, S
Baker, E M (Moseley) 1895 W, I, S, 1896 W, I, S, 1897 W
Baker, H C (Clifton) 1887 W
Balshaw, I R (Bath, Leeds, Gloucester) 2000 I (R), F (R), It (R), S (R), A (R), Arg, SA 3(R), 2001 W, It, S, F, I, 2002 S (R), I (R), 2003 F2, 3, [Sm, U, A(R)], 2004 It, S, I, 2005 It, S, 2006 A1, 2, NZ, Arg, 2007 It, SA1, 2008 W, It, F, S, I
Banahan, M A (Bath) 2009 Arg 1, 2, A, Arg 3, NZ, 2010 Sm, SA(R), 2011 It(R), F(R), S(R), I1, W2, 3, [Gg(R), S(R), F(R)]
Bance, J F (Bedford) 1954 S
Barkley, O J (Bath) 2001 US (R), 2004 It(R), I(t), W, F, NZ2(R), A1(R), 2005 W(R), F, I, It, S, A(R), Sm(R), 2006 A1, 2(R), 2007 F2, 3(R), [US, Sm, Tg], 2008 NZ1, 2(R)
Barley, B (Wakefield) 1984 I, F, W, A, 1988 A 1, 2, Fj
Barnes, S (Bristol, Bath) 1984 A, 1985 R (R), NZ 1, 2, 1986 S (R), F (R), 1987 I (R), 1988 Fj, 1993 S, I
Barr, R J (Leicester) 1932 SA, W, I
Barrett, E I M (Lennox) 1903 S
Barrington, T J M (Bristol) 1931 W, I
Barrington-Ward, L E (Edinburgh U) 1910 W, I, F, S
Barritt, B M (Saracens) 2012 S, It, W, F, I, SA 1, 3(t&R), Fj, A, SA4, NZ, 2013 S, I, F, It, W
Barron, J H (Bingley) 1896 S, 1897 W, I
Bartlett, J T (Waterloo) 1951 W
Bartlett, R M (Harlequins) 1957 W, I, F, S, 1958 I, F, S
Barton, J (Coventry) 1967 I, F, W, 1972 F
Batchelor, T B (Oxford U) 1907 F
Bates, S M (Wasps) 1989 R
Bateson, A H (Otley) 1930 W, I, F, S
Bateson, H D (Liverpool) 1879 I
Batson, T (Blackheath) 1872 S, 1874 S, 1875 I
Batten, J M (Cambridge U) 1874 S
Baume, J L (Northern) 1950 S
Baxendell, J J N (Sale) 1998 NZ 2, SA 1
Baxter, J (Birkenhead Park) 1900 W, I, S
Bayfield, M C (Northampton) 1991 Fj, A, 1992 S, I, F, W, C, SA, 1993 F, W, S, I, 1994 S, I, SA 1, 2, R, C, 1995 I, F, W, S, [Arg, It, A, NZ, F], SA, WS, 1996 F, W
Bazley, R C (Waterloo) 1952 I, F, 1953 W, I, F, S, 1955 W, I, F, S
Beal, N D (Northampton) 1996 Arg, 1997 A 1, 1998 NZ 1, 2, SA 1, H (R), SA 2, 1999 S, F (R), A (t), C (R), [It (R), Tg (R), Fj, SA]
Beaumont, W B (Fylde) 1975 I, A 1(R), 2, 1976 A, W, S, I, F, 1977 S, I, F, W, 1978 F, W, S, I, NZ, 1979 S, I, F, W, NZ, 1980 I, F, W, S, 1981 W, S, I, F, Arg 1, 2, 1982 A, S
Bedford, H (Morley) 1889 M, 1890 S, I
Bedford, L L (Headingley) 1931 W, I
Beer, I D S (Harlequins) 1955 F, S
Beese, M C (Liverpool) 1972 W, I, F
Beim, T D (Sale) 1998 NZ 1(R), 2
Bell, D S C (Bath) 2005 It(R), S, 2009 A(R), Arg 3, NZ
Bell, F J (Northern) 1900 W
Bell, H (New Brighton) 1884 I
Bell, J L (Darlington) 1878 I
Bell, P J (Blackheath) 1968 W, I, F, S
Bell, R W (Northern) 1900 W, I, S
Bendon, G J (Wasps) 1959 W, I, F, S
Bennett, N O (St Mary's Hospital, Waterloo) 1947 W, S, F, 1948 A, W, I, S
Bennett, W N (Bedford, London Welsh) 1975 S, A1, 1976 S (R), 1979 S, I, F, W
Bennetts, B B (Penzance) 1909 A, W
Bentley, J (Sale, Newcastle) 1988 I 2, A 1, 1997 A 1, SA
Bentley, J E (Gipsies) 1871 S, 1872 S
Benton, S (Gloucester) 1998 A 1
Berridge, M J (Northampton) 1949 W, I
Berry, H (Gloucester) 1910 W, I, F, S
Berry, J (Tyldesley) 1891 W, I, S
Berry, J T W (Leicester) 1939 W, I, S
Beswick, E (Swinton) 1882 I, S
Biggs, J M (UCH) 1878 S, 1879 I
Birkett, J G G (Harlequins) 1906 S, F, SA, 1907 F, W, S, 1908 F, W, I , S, 1910 W, I, S, 1911 W, F, I , S, 1912 W, I , S, F
Birkett L (Clapham R) 1875 S, 1877 I, S
Birkett, R H (Clapham R) 1871 S, 1875 S, 1876 S, 1877 I
Bishop, C C (Blackheath) 1927 F
Black, B H (Blackheath) 1930 W, I, F, S, 1931 W, I, S, F, 1932 S, 1933 W
Blacklock, J H (Aspatria) 1898 I, 1899 I
Blakeway, P J (Gloucester) 1980 I, F, W, S, 1981 W, S, I, F, 1982 I, F, W, 1984 I, F, W, SA 1, 1985 R, F, S, I
Blakiston, A F (Northampton) 1920 S, 1921 W, I, S, F, 1922 W, 1923 S, F, 1924 W, I, F, S, 1925 NZ, W, I, S, F
Blatherwick, T (Manchester) 1878 I
Body, J A (Gipsies) 1872 S, 1873 S
Bolton, C A (United Services) 1909 F
Bolton, R (Harlequins) 1933 W, 1936 S, 1937 S, 1938 W, I
Bolton, W N (Blackheath) 1882 I, S, 1883 W, I, S, 1884 W, I, S, 1885 I, 1887 I, S
Bonaventura, M S (Blackheath) 1931 W
Bond, A M (Sale) 1978 NZ, 1979 S, I, NZ, 1980 I, 1982 I
Bonham-Carter, E (Oxford U) 1891 S
Bonsor, F (Bradford) 1886 W, I, S, 1887 W, S, 1889 M
Boobbyer, B (Rosslyn Park) 1950 W, I, F, S, 1951 W, F, 1952 S, I, F
Booth, L A (Headingley) 1933 W, I, S, 1934 S, 1935 W, I, S
Borthwick, S W (Bath, Saracens) 2001 F, C 1, 2(R), US, R, 2003 A(t), W 2(t), F 2, 2004 I, F(R), NZ1(R), 2, A1, C, SA, A2, 2005 W(R), It(R), S(R), A, NZ, Sm, 2006 W, It, S, F, I, 2007 W2, F3, [SA1(t&R), Sm(R), Tg], 2008 W, It, F, S, I, NZ1, 2, PI, A, SA, NZ3, 2009 It, W, I, F, S, Arg 1, 2, A, Arg 3, NZ, 2010 W, It, I, S
Botha, M J (Saracens) 2011 W2(R), 2012 S, It, W, F, I, SA 1, 2, 3(R), 4(R)
Botting, I J (Oxford U) 1950 W, I
Boughton, H J (Gloucester) 1935 W, I, S
Boyle, C W (Oxford U) 1873 S
Boyle, S B (Gloucester) 1983 W, S, I
Boylen, F (Hartlepool R) 1908 F, W, I, S
Bracken, K P P (Bristol, Saracens) 1993 NZ, 1994 S, I, C, 1995 I, F, W, S, [It, WS (t)], SA, 1996 It (R), 1997 Arg 1, 2, A 2, NZ 1, 2, 1998 F, W, 1999 S(R), I, F, A, 2000 SA 1, 2, A, 2001 It (R), S (R), F (R), C 1, 2, US, I (R), A, R (R), SA, 2002 S, I, F, W, It, 2003 W 1, It(R), I(t), NZ, A, F3, [SA, U(R), W(R), F(t&R)]
Bradby, M S (United Services) 1922 I, F
Bradley, R (W Hartlepool) 1903 W
Bradshaw, H (Bramley) 1892 S, 1893 W, I, S, 1894 W, I, S
Brain, S E (Coventry) 1984 SA 2, A (R), 1985 R, F, S, I, W, NZ 1, 2, 1986 W, S, I, F
Braithwaite, J (Leicester) 1905 NZ
Braithwaite-Exley, B (Headingley) 1949 W
Brettargh, A T (Liverpool OB) 1900 W, 1903 I, S, 1904 W, I, S, 1905 I, S
Brewer, J (Gipsies) 1876 I
Briggs, A (Bradford) 1892 W, I, S
Brinn, A (Gloucester) 1972 W, I, S
Broadley, T (Bingley) 1893 W, S, 1894 W, I, S, 1896 S

Bromet, W E (Richmond) 1891 W, I, 1892 W, I, S, 1893 W, I, S, 1895 W, I, S, 1896 I
Brook, P W P (Harlequins) 1930 S, 1931 F, 1936 S
Brooke, T J (Richmond) 1968 F, S
Brooks, F G (Bedford) 1906 SA
Brooks, M J (Oxford U) 1874 S
Brophy, T J (Liverpool) 1964 I, F, S, 1965 W, I, 1966 W, I, F
Brough, J W (Silloth) 1925 NZ, W
Brougham, H (Harlequins) 1912 W, I, S, F
Brown, A A (Exeter) 1938 S
Brown A T (Gloucester) 2006 A1, 2007 SA1, 2
Brown, L G (Oxford U, Blackheath) 1911 W, F, I, S, 1913 SA, W, F, I, S, 1914 W, I, S, F, 1921 W, I, S, F, 1922 W
Brown, M N (Harlequins) 2007 SA1, 2, 2008 NZ1, 2012 S(R), W(R), I(R), SA 1, Fj(R), A(R), SA4, NZ, 2013 S, I, F, It, W, Arg1, 2
Brown S P (Richmond) 1998 A 1, SA 1
Brown, T W (Bristol) 1928 S, 1929 W, I, S, F, 1932 S, 1933 W, I, S
Brunton, J (N Durham) 1914 W, I, S
Brutton, E B (Cambridge U) 1886 S
Bryden, C C (Clapham R) 1876 I, 1877 S
Bryden, H A (Clapham R) 1874 S
Buckingham, R A (Leicester) 1927 F
Bucknall, A L (Richmond) 1969 SA, 1970 I, W, S, F, 1971 W, I, F, S (2[1C])
Buckton, J R D (Saracens) 1988 A (R), 1990 Arg 1, 2
Budd, A J (Blackheath) 1878 I, 1879 S, I, 1881 W, S
Budworth, R T D (Blackheath) 1890 W, 1891 W, S
Bull, A G (Northampton) 1914 W
Bullough, E (Wigan) 1892 W, I, S
Bulpitt, M P (Blackheath) 1970 S
Bulteel, A J (Manchester) 1876 I
Bunting, W L (Moseley) 1897 I, S, 1898 I, S, W, 1899 S, 1900 S, 1901 I, S
Burland, D W (Bristol) 1931 W, I, F, 1932 I, S, 1933 W, I, S
Burns, B H (Blackheath) 1871 S
Burns, F S (Gloucester) 2012 NZ(R), 2013 Arg1, 2
Burton, G W (Blackheath) 1879 S, I, 1880 S, 1881 I, W, S
Burton, H C (Richmond) 1926 W
Burton, M A (Gloucester) 1972 W, I, F, S, SA, 1974 F, W, 1975 S, A 1, 2, 1976 A, W, S, I, F, 1978 F, W
Bush, J A (Clifton) 1872 S, 1873 S, 1875 S, 1876 I, S
Butcher, C J S (Harlequins) 1984 SA 1, 2, A
Butcher, W V (Streatham) 1903 S, 1904 W, I, S, 1905 W, I, S
Butler, A G (Harlequins) 1937 W, I
Butler, P E (Gloucester) 1975 A 1, 1976 F
Butterfield, J (Northampton) 1953 F, S, 1954 W, NZ, I, S, F, 1955 W, I, F, S, 1956 W, I, S, F, 1957 W, I, F, S, 1958 W, A, I, F, S, 1959 W, I, F, S
Byrne, F A (Moseley) 1897 W
Byrne, J F (Moseley) 1894 W, I, S, 1895 I, S, 1896 I, 1897 W, I, S, 1898 I, S, W, 1899 I

Cain, J J (Waterloo) 1950 W
Cairns, M I (Saracens) 2007 SA1(R)
Callard, J E B (Bath) 1993 NZ, 1994 S, I, 1995 [WS], SA
Campbell, D A (Cambridge U) 1937 W, I
Candler, P L (St Bart's Hospital) 1935 W, 1936 NZ, W, I, S, 1937 W, I, S, 1938 W, S
Cannell, L B (Oxford U, St Mary's Hospital) 1948 F, 1949 W, I, F, S, 1950 W, I, F, S, 1952 SA, W, 1953 W, I, F, 1956 I, S, F, 1957 W, I
Caplan, D W N (Headingley) 1978 S, I
Cardus, R M (Roundhay) 1979 F, W
Care, D S (Harlequins) 2008 NZ1(R), 2, Pl, A, SA, NZ3, 2009 I(R), F(R), S(R), Arg 1, 2, A, Arg 3(R), NZ(R), 2010 W, It, I, S, F, A1, 2(R), NZ(R), A3(R), Sm(R), SA(R), 2011 W1(R), It(R), F(R), S(R), I1(R), W2, 3(R), 2012 SA 3, Fj, A, SA4(R), NZ(R), 2013 S(R), F(R), It, W(R)
Carey, G M (Blackheath) 1895 W, I, S, 1896 W, I
Carleton, J (Orrell) 1979 NZ, 1980 I, F, W, S, 1981 W, S, I, F, Arg 1, 2, 1982 A, S, I, F, W, 1983 F, W, S, I, NZ, 1984 S, I, F, W, A
Carling, W D C (Durham U, Harlequins) 1988 F, W, S, I 1, 2, A2, Fj, A, 1989 S, I, F, W, Fj, 1990 I, F, W, S, Arg 1, 2, 3, 1991 W, S, I, F, Fj, A, [NZ, It, US, F, S, A], 1992 S, I, F, W, C, SA, 1993 F, W, S, I, NZ, 1994 S, I, F, W, SA 1, 2, R, C, 1995 I, F, W, S, [Arg, WS, A, NZ, F], SA, WS, 1996 F, W, S, I, It, Arg, 1997 S, I, F, W
Carpenter, A D (Gloucester) 1932 SA
Carr, R S L (Manchester) 1939 W, I, S
Cartwright, V H (Nottingham) 1903 W, I, S, 1904 W, S, 1905 W, I, S, NZ, 1906 W, I, S, F, SA
Catcheside, H C (Percy Park) 1924 W, I, F, S, 1926 W, I, 1927 I, S

Catt, M J (Bath, London Irish) 1994 W (R), C (R), 1995 I, F, W, S, [Arg, It, WS, A, NZ, F], SA, WS, 1996 F, W, S, I, It, Arg, 1997 W, Arg 1, A 1, 2, NZ 1, SA, 1998 F, W (R), I, A 2(R), SA 2, 1999 S, F, W, A, C (R), [Tg (R), Fj, SA (R)], 2000 I, F, W, It, S, SA 1, 2, A, Arg, 2001 W, It, S, F, I, A, R (R), SA, 2003 [Sm(R), U, W(R), F, A(R)], 2004 W(R), F(R), NZ1, A1, 2006 A1, 2, 2007 F1, W1, F2, [US, SA1, A, F, SA2]
Cattell, R H B (Blackheath) 1895 W, I, S, 1896 W, I, S, 1900 W
Cave, J W (Richmond) 1889 M
Cave, W T C (Blackheath) 1905 W
Challis, R (Bristol) 1957 I, F, S
Chambers, E L (Bedford) 1908 F, 1910 W, I
Chantrill, B S (Bristol) 1924 W, I, F, S
Chapman, C E (Cambridge U) 1884 W
Chapman D E (Richmond) 1998 A 1(R)
Chapman, F E (Hartlepool) 1910 W, I, F, S, 1912 W, 1914 W, I
Cheesman, W I (OMTs) 1913 SA, W, F, I
Cheston, E C (Richmond) 1873 S, 1874 S, 1875 I, S, 1876 S
Chilcott, G J (Bath) 1984 A, 1986 I, F, 1987 F (R), W, [J, US, W (R)], 1988 I 2(R), Fj, 1989 I (R), F, W, R
Christophers, P D (Bristol) 2002 Arg, SA, 2003 W 1 (R)
Christopherson, P (Blackheath) 1891 W, S
Chuter, G S (Leicester) 2006 A1(R), 2, NZ, Arg, SA1, 2(R), 2007 S, It, I, F1, W1, 2(R), [US(R), SA1(R), Sm, Tg, A(R), F(R), SA2(R)], 2008 S(R), I(R), 2009 Arg 2(R), 2010 A1(R), 2(R)
Cipriani, D J (Wasps) 2008 W(R), It(R), I, Pl, A, SA, NZ3(R)
Clark, C W H (Liverpool) 1876 I
Clarke, A J (Coventry) 1935 W, I, S, 1936 NZ, W, I
Clarke, B B (Bath, Richmond) 1992 SA, 1993 F, W, S, I, NZ, 1994 S, F, W, SA 1, 2, R, C, 1995 I, F, W, S, [Arg, It, A, NZ, F], SA, WS, 1996 F, W, S, I, Arg (R), 1997 W, Arg 1, 2, A 1(R), 1998 A 1(t), NZ 1, 2, SA 1, H, It, 1999 A (R)
Clarke, S J S (Cambridge U, Blackheath) 1963 W, I, F, S, NZ 1, 2, A, 1964 NZ, W, I, 1965 I, F, S
Clayton, J H (Liverpool) 1871 S
Clements, J W (O Cranleighans) 1959 I, F, S
Cleveland, C R (Blackheath) 1887 W, S
Clibborn, W G (Richmond) 1886 W, I, S, 1887 W, I, S
Clough, F J (Cambridge U, Orrell) 1986 I, F, 1987 [J (R), US]
Coates, C H (Yorkshire W) 1880 S, 1881 S, 1882 S
Coates, V H M (Bath) 1913 SA, W, F, I, S
Cobby, W (Hull) 1900 W
Cockerham, A (Bradford Olicana) 1900 W
Cockerill, R (Leicester) 1997 Arg 1(R), 2, A 2(t+R), NZ 1, SA, NZ 2, 1998 W, S, I, A 1, NZ 1, 2, SA 1, H, It, A 2, SA 2, 1999 S, I, F, W, A, C (R), [It, NZ, Tg (R), Fj (R)]
Codling, A J (Harlequins) 2002 Arg
Cohen, B C (Northampton) 2000 I, F, W, It, S, SA 2, Arg, SA 3, 2001 W, It, S, F, R, 2002 S, I, F, W, It, NZ, A, SA, 2003 F 1, W 1, S, I, NZ, A, F2, 3, [Gg, SA, Sm, W, F, A], 2004 It, S, I, W, F, NZ1, 2, A1, C(R), A2(R), 2005 F(R), A, NZ, 2006 W, It, S, F, I, NZ, Arg, SA1, 2
Colclough, M J (Angoulême, Wasps, Swansea) 1978 S, I, 1979 NZ, 1980 F, W, S, 1981 W, S, I, F, 1982 A, S, I, F, W, 1983 F, NZ, 1984 S, I, F, W, 1986 W, S, I, F
Cole, D R (Leicester) 2010 W(R), It, I, S, F, A1, 2, NZ, A3, Sm(R), SA, 2011 W1, It, F, S, I1, W3, I2, [Arg, Gg, R, S, F], 2012 S, It, W, F, I, SA 1, 2, 3, Fj, A, SA4, NZ, 2013 S, I, F, It, W
Coley, E (Northampton) 1929 F, 1932 W
Collins, P J (Camborne) 1952 S, I, F
Collins, W E (O Cheltonians) 1874 S, 1875 I, S, 1876 I, S
Considine, S G U (Bath) 1925 F
Conway, G S (Cambridge U, Rugby, Manchester) 1920 F, I, S, 1921 F, 1922 W, I, F, S, 1923 W, I, S, F, 1924 W, I, F, S, 1925 NZ, 1927 W
Cook, J G (Bedford) 1937 S
Cook, P W (Richmond) 1965 I, F
Cooke, D A (Harlequins) 1976 W, S, I, F
Cooke, D H (Harlequins) 1981 W, S, I, F, 1984 I, 1985 R, F, S, I, W, NZ 1, 2
Cooke, P (Richmond) 1939 W, I
Coop, T (Leigh) 1892 S
Cooper, J G (Moseley) 1909 A, W
Cooper, M J (Moseley) 1973 F, S, NZ 2(R), 1975 F, W, 1976 A, W, 1977 S, I, F, W
Coopper, S F (Blackheath) 1900 W, 1902 W, I, 1905 W, I, S, 1907 W
Corbett, L J (Bristol) 1921 F, 1923 W, I, 1924 W, I, F, S, 1925 NZ, W, I, S, F, 1927 W, I, S, F
Corbisiero, A R (London Irish) 2011 It, F(R), S, I1, W2, 3, [Gg(R), R, S(R), F(R)], 2012 S, It, W, F, I, SA 2(t&R), 4, NZ
Corless, B J (Coventry, Moseley) 1976 A, I (R), 1977 S, I, F, W, 1978 F, W, S, I

Corry, M E (Bristol, Leicester) 1997 Arg 1, 2, 1998 H, It, SA 2(t), 1999 F(R), A, C (t), [It (R), NZ (t+R), SA (R)], 2000 I (R), F (R), W (R), It (R), S (R), Arg (R), SA 3(t), 2001 W (R), It (R), F (t), C 1, I, 2002 F (t+R), W (t), 2003 W 2, F 2, 3, [U], 2004 A1(R), C, SA, A2, 2005 F, I, It, S, A, NZ, Sm, 2006 W, It, S, F, I, NZ, Arg, SA1, 2, 2007 S, It, I, F1, W1, 2, F2(R), 3, [US(R), SA1, Sm, Tg, A, F, SA2]
Cotton, F E (Loughborough Colls, Coventry, Sale) 1971 S (2[1C]), P, 1973 W, I, F, S, NZ 2, A, 1974 S, I, 1975 I, F, W, 1976 A, W, S, I, F, 1977 S, I, F, W, 1978 S, I, 1979 NZ, 1980 I, F, W, S, 1981 W
Coulman, M J (Moseley) 1967 A, I, F, S, W, 1968 W, I, F, S
Coulson, T J (Coventry) 1927 W, 1928 A, W
Court, E D (Blackheath) 1885 W
Coverdale, H (Blackheath) 1910 F, 1912 I, F, 1920 W
Cove-Smith, R (OMTs) 1921 S, F, 1922 I, F, S, 1923 W, I, S, F, 1924 W, I, S, F, 1925 NZ, W, I, S, F, 1927 W, I, S, F, 1928 A, W, I, F, S, 1929 W, I
Cowling, R J (Leicester) 1977 S, I, F, W, 1978 F, NZ, 1979 S, I
Cowman, A R (Loughborough Colls, Coventry) 1971 S (2[1C]), P, 1973 W, I
Cox, N S (Sunderland) 1901 S
Crane, J S (Leicester) 2008 SA(R), 2009 Arg 1(R), A
Cranmer, P (Richmond, Moseley) 1934 W, I, S, 1935 W, I, S, 1936 NZ, W, I, S, 1937 W, I, S, 1938 W, I, S
Creed, R N (Coventry) 1971 P
Cridlan, A G (Blackheath) 1935 W, I, S
Croft, T R (Leicester) 2008 F(R), S, I, NZ2(R), PI, A, SA(R), NZ3(R), 2009 It(R), W(R), I(R), F, S, A, Arg 3, NZ(R), 2010 A1, 2, NZ, A3, Sm(R), SA, 2011 S(R), I1(R), W2, I2, [Arg, Gg(R), R, S, F], 2012 S, It, W, F, I, 2013 It(R), W
Crompton, C A (Blackheath) 1871 S
Crompton, D E (Bristol) 2007 SA1(R)
Crosse, C W (Oxford U) 1874 S, 1875 I
Cueto, M J (Sale) 2004 C, SA, A2, 2005 W, F, I, It, S, A, NZ, Sm, 2006 W, It, S, F, I, SA1, 2, 2007 W1, F3, [US, Sm, Tg, SA2], 2009 It, W, I, F, S, Arg 1, 2, A, Arg 3, NZ, 2010 W, It, I, S, F, A1, 2, NZ, A3, Sm, SA, 2011 W1, It, F, S, I1, W2, 3, I2, [R, F]
Cumberlege, B S (Blackheath) 1920 W, I, S, 1921 W, I, S, F, 1922 W
Cumming, D C (Blackheath) 1925 S, F
Cunliffe, F L (RMA) 1874 S
Currey, F I (Marlborough N) 1872 S
Currie, J D (Oxford U, Harlequins, Bristol) 1956 W, I, S, F, 1957 W, I, F, S, 1958 W, A, I, F, S, 1959 W, I, F, S, 1960 W, I, F, S, 1961 SA, 1962 W, I, F
Cusani, D A (Orrell) 1987 I
Cusworth, L (Leicester) 1979 NZ, 1982 F, W, 1983 F, W, NZ, 1984 S, I, F, W, 1988 F, W

D'Aguilar, F B G (Royal Engineers) 1872 S
Dallaglio, L B N (Wasps) 1995 SA (R), WS, 1996 F, W, S, I, It, Arg, 1997 S, I, F, A 1, 2, NZ 1, SA, NZ 2, 1998 F, W, S, I, A 2, SA 2, 1999 S, I, F, W, US, C, [It, NZ, Tg, Fj, SA], 2000 I, F, W, It, S, SA 1, 2, A, Arg, SA 3, 2001 W, It, S, F, 2002 It (R), NZ, A (t), SA(R), 2003 F 1 (R), W 1, It, S, I, NZ, A, [Gg, SA, Sm, U, W, F, A], 2004 It, S, I, W, F, NZ1, 2, A1, 2006 W(t&R), It(R), S(R), F(R), 2007 W2(R), F2, 3(R), [US, Tg(R), A(R), F(R), SA2(R)]
Dalton, T J (Coventry) 1969 S(R)
Danby, T (Harlequins) 1949 W
Daniell, J (Richmond) 1899 W, 1900 I, S, 1902 I, S, 1904 I, S
Darby, A J L (Birkenhead Park) 1899 I
Davenport, A (Ravenscourt Park) 1871 S
Davey, J (Redruth) 1908 S, 1909 W
Davey, R F (Teignmouth) 1931 W
Davidson, Jas (Aspatria) 1897 S, 1898 S, W, 1899 I, S
Davidson, Jos (Aspatria) 1899 W, S
Davies, G H (Cambridge U, Coventry, Wasps) 1981 S, I, F, Arg 1, 2, 1982 A, S, I, 1983 F, W, S, 1984 S, SA 1, 2, 1985 R (R), NZ 1, 2, 1986 W, S, I, F
Davies, P H (Sale) 1927 I
Davies, V G (Harlequins) 1922 W, 1925 NZ
Davies, W J A (United Services, RN) 1913 SA, W, F, I, S, 1914 I, S, F, 1920 F, I, S, 1921 W, I, S, F, 1922 I, F, S, 1923 W, I, S, F
Davies, W P C (Harlequins) 1953 S, 1954 NZ, I, 1955 W, I, F, S, 1956 W, 1957 F, S, 1958 W
Davis, A M (Torquay Ath, Harlequins) 1963 W, I, S, NZ 1, 2, 1964 NZ, W, I, F, S, 1966 W, 1967 A, 1969 SA, 1970 I, W, S
Dawe, R G R (Bath) 1987 I, F, W, [US], 1995 [WS]
Dawson, E F (RIEC) 1878 I
Dawson, M J S (Northampton, Wasps) 1995 WS, 1996 F, W, S, I, 1997 A 1, SA, NZ 2(R), 1998 W (R), S, I, NZ 1, 2, SA 1, H, It, A 2, SA 2, 1999 S, F(R), W, A(R), US, C, [It, NZ, Tg, Fj (R), SA], 2000 I, F, W, It, S, A (R), Arg, SA 3, 2001 W, It, S, F, I, 2002 W (R), It (R), NZ, A, SA, 2003 It, S, I, A(R), F3(R), [Gg, Sm, W, F, A], 2004It(R), S(R), I, W, F, NZ1, 2(R), A1(R), 2005 W, F(R), I(R), It(R), S(R), A, NZ, 2006 W(R), It(R), S(t&R), F, I(R)
Day, H L V (Leicester) 1920 W, 1922 W, F, 1926 S
Deacon, L P (Leicester) 2005 Sm, 2006 A1, 2(R), 2007 S, It, I, F1(R), W1(R), 2009 Arg 1, 2, A, Arg 3, NZ(R), 2010 W(R), It(R), I(R), S, F, 2011 W1, It, F, S, I1, W3, I2, [Arg, R, S, F]
Dean, G J (Harlequins) 1931 I
Dee, J M (Hartlepool R) 1962 S, 1963 NZ 1
Devitt, Sir T G (Blackheath) 1926 I, F, 1928 A, W
Dewhurst, J H (Richmond) 1887 W, I, S, 1890 W
De Glanville, P R (Bath) 1992 SA (R), 1993 W (R), NZ, 1994 S, I, F, W, SA 1, 2, C (R), 1995 [Arg (R), It, WS], SA (R), 1996 W (R), I (R), It, 1997 S, I, F, W, Arg 1, 2, A 1, 2, NZ 1, 2, 1998 W (R), S (R), I (R), A 2, SA 2, 1999 A (R), US, [It, NZ, Fj (R), SA]
De Winton, R F C (Marlborough N) 1893 W
Dibble, R (Bridgwater A) 1906 S, F, SA, 1908 F, W, I, S, 1909 A, W, F, I, S, 1910 S, 1911 W, F, S, 1912 W, I, S
Dicks, J (Northampton) 1934 W, I, S, 1935 W, I, S, 1936 S, 1937 I
Dickson, L A W (Northampton) 2012 S(R), It(R), W, F, I, SA 1(R), 2(R), 2013 Arg1, 2
Dillon, E W (Blackheath) 1904 W, I, S, 1905 W
Dingle, A J (Hartlepool R) 1913 I, 1914 S, F
Diprose, A J (Saracens) 1997 Arg 1, 2, A 2, NZ 1, 1998 W (R), S (R), I, A 1, NZ 2, SA 1
Dixon, P J (Harlequins, Gosforth) 1971 P, 1972 W, I, F, S, 1973 I, F, S, 1974 S, I, F, W, 1975 I, 1976 F, 1977 S, I, F, W, 1978 F, S, I, NZ
Dobbs, G E B (Plymouth Albion) 1906 W, I
Doble, S A (Moseley) 1972 SA, 1973 NZ 1, W
Dobson, D D (Newton Abbot) 1902 W, I, S, 1903 W, I, S
Dobson, T H (Bradford) 1895 S
Dodge, P W (Leicester) 1978 W, S, I, NZ, 1979 S, I, F, W, 1980 W, S, 1981 W, S, I, F, Arg 1, 2, 1982 A, S, F, W, 1983 F, W, S, I, NZ, 1985 R, F, S, I, W, NZ 1, 2
Donnelly, M P (Oxford U) 1947 I
Dooley, W A (Preston Grasshoppers, Fylde) 1985 R, F, S, I, W, NZ 2(R), 1986 W, S, I, F, 1987 F, W, [A, US, W], 1988 F, W, S, I 1, 2, A 1, 2, Fj, A, 1989 S, I, F, W, R, Fj, 1990 I, F, W, S, Arg 1, 2, 3, 1991 W, S, I, F, [NZ, US, F, S, A], 1992 S, I, F, W, C, SA, 1993 W, S, I
Doran-Jones, P P L (Gloucester, Northampton) 2009 Arg 3(R), 2011 S(R), I1(R), 2012 SA 1(R), 2013 Arg1(R), 2(R)
Dovey, B A (Rosslyn Park) 1963 W, I
Down, P J (Bristol) 1909 A
Dowson, A O (Moseley) 1899 S
Dowson, P D A (Northampton) 2012 S, It, W(R), F(R), I(R), SA 1(R), 3(R)
Drake-Lee, N J (Cambridge U, Leicester) 1963 W, I, F, S, 1964 NZ, W, I, 1965 W
Duckett, H (Bradford) 1893 I, S
Duckham, D J (Coventry) 1969 I, F, S, W, SA, 1970 I, W, S, F, 1971 W, I, F, S (2[1C]), P, 1972 W, I, F, S, 1973 NZ 1, W, I, F, S, NZ 2, A, 1974 S, I, F, W, 1975 I, F, W, 1976 A, W, S
Dudgeon, H W (Richmond) 1897 S, 1898 I, S, W, 1899 W, I, S
Dugdale, J M (Ravenscourt Park) 1871 S
Dun, A F (Wasps) 1984 W
Duncan, R F H (Guy's Hospital) 1922 I, F, S
Duncombe, N S (Harlequins) 2002 S (R), I (R)
Dunkley, P E (Harlequins) 1931 I, S, 1936 NZ, W, I, S
Duthie, J (W Hartlepool) 1903 W
Dyson, J W (Huddersfield) 1890 S, 1892 S, 1893 I, S

Easter, N J (Harlequins) 2007 It, F1, SA1, 2, W2, F3, [SA1, Sm, Tg, A, F, SA2], 2008 It, F, S, I, PI, A, SA, NZ3, 2009 It, W, I, F, S, Arg 1, 2, 2010 W, It, I, S, F, A1, 2, NZ, A3, Sm, SA, 2011 W1, It, F, S, I1, W3, [Arg, S(t&R), F]
Eastmond, K O (Bath) 2013 Arg1(R), 2
Ebdon, P J (Wellington) 1897 W, I
Eddison, J H (Headingley) 1912 W, I, S, F
Edgar, C S (Birkenhead Park) 1901 S
Edwards, R (Newport) 1921 W, I, S, F, 1922 W, F, 1923 W, 1924 W, F, S, 1925 NZ
Egerton, D W (Bath) 1988 I 2, A 1, Fj (R), A, 1989 Fj, 1990 I, Arg 2(R)
Elliot, C H (Sunderland) 1886 W
Elliot, E W (Sunderland) 1901 W, I, S, 1904 W
Elliot, W (United Services, RN) 1932 I, S, 1933 W, I, S, 1934 W, I
Elliott, A E (St Thomas's Hospital) 1894 S
Ellis, H A (Leicester) 2004 SA(R), A2(R), 2005 W(R), F, I, It, S, Sm, 2006 W, It, S, F(R), I, 2007 S, It, I, F1, W1, 2008 PI(R), A(R), SA(R), NZ3(R), 2009 It, W, I, F, S

Ellis, J (Wakefield) 1939 S
Ellis, S S (Queen's House) 1880 I
Emmott, C (Bradford) 1892 W
Enthoven, H J (Richmond) 1878 I
Erinle, A O (Biarritz) 2009 A(R), NZ
Estcourt, N S D (Blackheath) 1955 S
Evans, B J (Leicester) 1988 A 2, Fj
Evans, E (Sale) 1948 A, 1950 W, 1951 I, F, S, 1952 SA, W, S, I, F, 1953 I, F, S, 1954 W, NZ, I, F, 1956 W, I, S, F, 1957 W, I, F, S, 1958 W, A, I, F, S
Evans, G W (Coventry) 1972 S, 1973 W (R), F, S, NZ 2, 1974 S, I, F, W
Evans, N L (RNEC) 1932 W, I, S, 1933 W, I
Evanson, A M (Richmond) 1883 W, I, S, 1884 S
Evanson, W A D (Richmond) 1875 S, 1877 S, 1878 S, 1879 S, I
Evershed, F (Blackheath) 1889 M, 1890 W, S, I, 1892 W, I, S, 1893 W, I, S
Eyres, W C T (Richmond) 1927 I

Fagan, A R St L (Richmond) 1887 I
Fairbrother, K E (Coventry) 1969 I, F, S, W, SA, 1970 I, W, S, F, 1971 W, I, F
Faithfull, C K T (Harlequins) 1924 I, 1926 F, S
Fallas, H (Wakefield T) 1884 I
Farrell, A D (Saracens) 2007 S, It, I, W2, F3, [US(R), SA1, Tg(R)]
Farrell, O A (Saracens) 2012 S, It, W, F, I, SA 1, 2(R), 3(R), Fj(R), A(R), SA4(t&R), NZ, 2013 S, I, F, W
Fegan, J H C (Blackheath) 1895 W, I, S
Fernandes, C W L (Leeds) 1881 I, W, S
Fidler, J H (Gloucester) 1981 Arg 1, 2, 1984 SA 1, 2
Fidler, R J (Gloucester) 1998 NZ 2, SA 1
Field, E (Middlesex W) 1893 W, I
Fielding, K J (Moseley, Loughborough Colls) 1969 I, F, S, SA, 1970 I, F, 1972 W, I, F, S
Finch, R T (Cambridge U) 1880 S
Finlan, J F (Moseley) 1967 I, F, S, W, NZ, 1968 W, I, 1969 I, F, S, W, 1970 F, 1973 NZ 1
Finlinson, H W (Blackheath) 1895 W, I, S
Finney, S (RIE Coll) 1872 S, 1873 S
Firth, F (Halifax) 1894 W, I, S
Flatman, D L (Saracens) 2000 SA 1(t), 2(t+R), A (t), Arg (t+R), 2001 F (t), C 2(t+R), US (t+R), 2002 Arg
Fletcher, N C (OMTs) 1901 W, I, S, 1903 S
Fletcher, T (Seaton) 1897 W
Fletcher, W R B (Marlborough N) 1873 S, 1875 S
Flood, T G A L (Newcastle, Leicester) 2006 Arg(R), SA2(R), 2007 S(R), It(R), F1, W1, SA1, 2, W2(t), [A(R), F(R), SA2(R)], 2008 W, It, F, S, I, NZ2, PI(R), A(R), SA(R), NZ3, 2009 W(R), I, F, S, 2010 W, S(R), F, A1, 2, NZ, A3, Sm, SA, 2011 W1, It, F, S, I1, W3, I2(R), [Gg, R(R), S(R), F], 2012 W(R), SA 1(R), 2, 3, Fj, A, SA4, 2013 S(R), F(R), It, W(R)
Flutey, R J (Wasps, Brive) 2008 PI, A, SA, NZ3, 2009 It, W, I, F, S, 2010 It, I, S, F, 2011 W2
Foden, B J (Northampton) 2009 It(R), 2010 I(R), S(R), F, A1, 2, NZ, A3, Sm, SA, 2011 W1, It, F, S, I1, W3, I2, [Arg, Gg, R, S, F], 2012 S, It, W, F, I, SA 1, 2, 3, 2013 Arg1(R), 2(R)
Fookes, E F (Sowerby Bridge) 1896 W, I, S, 1897 W, I, S, 1898 I, W, 1899 I, S
Ford, P J (Gloucester) 1964 W, I, F, S
Forrest, J W (United Services, RN) 1930 W, I, F, S, 1931 W, I, S, F, 1934 I, S
Forrest, R (Wellington) 1899 W, 1900 S, 1902 I, S, 1903 I, S
Forrester, J (Gloucester) 2005 W(t), Sm(t&R)
Foulds, R T (Waterloo) 1929 W, I
Fourie, C H (Leeds, Sale) 2010 NZ(R), A3(R), Sm, SA(R), 2011 It(R), F(R), W3, I2
Fowler, F D (Manchester) 1878 S, 1879 S
Fowler, H (Oxford U) 1878 S, 1881 W, S
Fowler, R H (Leeds) 1877 I
Fox, F H (Wellington) 1890 W, S
Francis, T E S (Cambridge U) 1926 W, I, F, S
Frankcom, G P (Cambridge U, Bedford) 1965 W, I, F, S
Fraser, E C (Blackheath) 1875 I
Fraser, G (Richmond) 1902 W, I, S, 1903 W, I
Freakes, H D (Oxford U) 1938 W, 1939 W, I
Freeman, H (Marlborough N) 1872 S, 1873 S, 1874 S
French, R J (St Helens) 1961 W, I, F, S
Freshwater, P T (Perpignan) 2005 v Sm(R), 2006 S(t&R), I(R), Arg, 2007 S, It, I, F3, [SA1(R), Sm(R)]
Fry, H A (Liverpool) 1934 W, I, S
Fry, T W (Queen's House) 1880 I, S, 1881 W
Fuller, H G (Cambridge U) 1882 I, S, 1883 W, I, S, 1884 W

Gadney, B C (Leicester, Headingley) 1932 I, S, 1933 I, S, 1934 W, I, S, 1935 S, 1936 NZ, W, I, S, 1937 S, 1938 W
Gamlin, H T (Blackheath) 1899 W, S, 1900 W, I, S, 1901 S, 1902 W, I, S, 1903 W, I, S, 1904 W, I, S
Gardner, E R (Devonport Services) 1921 W, I, S, 1922 W, I, F, 1923 W, I, S, F
Gardner, H P (Richmond) 1878 I
Garforth, D J (Leicester) 1997 W (R), Arg 1, 2, A 1, NZ 1, SA, NZ 2, 1998 F, W (R), S, I, H, It, A 2, SA 2, 1999 S, I, F, W, A, C (R), [It (R), NZ (R), Fj], 2000 It
Garnett, H W T (Bradford) 1877 S
Gavins, M N (Leicester) 1961 W
Gay, D J (Bath) 1968 W, I, F, S
Gent, D R (Gloucester) 1905 NZ, 1906 W, I, 1910 W, I
Genth, J S M (Manchester) 1874 S, 1875 S
George, J T (Falmouth) 1947 S, F, 1949 I
Geraghty, S J J (London Irish, Northampton) 2007 F1(R), W1(R), 2009 It(R), A, Arg 3, NZ(R)
Gerrard, R A (Bath) 1932 SA, W, I, S, 1933 W, I, S, 1934 W, I, S, 1936 NZ, W, I, S
Gibbs, G A (Bristol) 1947 F, 1948 I
Gibbs, J C (Harlequins) 1925 NZ, W, 1926 F, 1927 W, I, S, F
Gibbs, N (Harlequins) 1954 S, F
Giblin, L F (Blackheath) 1896 W, I, 1897 S
Gibson, A S (Manchester) 1871 S
Gibson, C O P (Northern) 1901 W
Gibson, G R (Northern) 1899 W, 1901 S
Gibson, T A (Northern) 1905 W, S
Gilbert, F G (Devonport Services) 1923 W, I
Gilbert, R (Devonport A) 1908 W, I, S
Giles, J L (Coventry) 1935 W, I, 1937 W, I, 1938 I, S
Gittings, W J (Coventry) 1967 NZ
Glover, P B (Bath) 1967 A, 1971 F, P
Godfray, R E (Richmond) 1905 NZ
Godwin, H O (Coventry) 1959 F, S, 1963 S, NZ 1, 2, A, 1964 NZ, I, F, S, 1967 NZ
Gomarsall, A C T (Wasps, Bedford, Gloucester, Harlequins) 1996 It, Arg, 1997 S, I, F, Arg 2(R) 2000 It (R), 2002 Arg, SA(R), 2003 F 1, W 1(R), 2, F2(R), [Gg(R), U], 2004 It, S, NZ1(R), 2, A1, C, SA, A2, 2007 SA1, 2, F2(R), 3(R), [SA1(R), Sm, Tg, A, F, SA2], 2008 W, It
Goode, A J (Leicester, Brive) 2005 It(R), S(R), 2006 W(R), F(R), I, A1(R), 2, SA1(R), 2, 2009 It, W, I(R), F(R), S(R), Arg1, 2, 3(R)
Goode, D A V (Saracens) 2012 SA2(R), 3, Fj, A, SA4, NZ, 2013 S, I, F, It, W
Gordon-Smith, G W (Blackheath) 1900 W, I, S
Gotley, A L H (Oxford U) 1910 F, S, 1911 W, F, I, S
Graham, D (Aspatria) 1901 W
Graham, H J (Wimbledon H) 1875 I, S, 1876 I, S
Graham, J D G (Wimbledon H) 1876 I
Gray, A (Otley) 1947 W, I, S
Grayson, P J (Northampton) 1995 WS, 1996 F, W, S, I, 1997 S, I, F, A 2(t), SA (R), NZ 2, 1998 F, W, S, I, H, It, A 2, 1999 I, [NZ (R), Tg, Fj (R), SA], 2003 S(R), I(t), F2, 3(R), [Gg(R), U], 2004 It, S, I
Green, J (Skipton) 1905 I, 1906 S, F, SA, 1907 F, W, I, S
Green, J F (West Kent) 1871 S
Green, W R (Wasps) 1997 A 2, 1998 NZ 1(t+R), 1999 US (R), 2003 W 2(R)
Greening, P B T (Gloucester, Wasps) 1996 It (R), 1997 W (R), Arg 1 1998 NZ 1(R), 2(R), 1999 A (R), US, C, [It (R), NZ (R), Tg, Fj, SA], 2000 I, F, W, It, S, SA 1, 2, A, SA 3, 2001 F, I
Greenstock, N J J (Wasps) 1997 Arg 1, 2, A 1, SA
Greenwell, J H (Rockcliff) 1893 W, I
Greenwood, J E (Cambridge U, Leicester) 1912 F, 1913 SA, W, F, I, S, 1914 W, S, F, 1920 W, F, I, S
Greenwood, J R H (Waterloo) 1966 I, F, S, 1967 A, 1969 I
Greenwood, W J H (Leicester, Harlequins) 1997 A 2, NZ 1, SA, NZ 2, 1998 F, W, S, I, H, It, 1999 C, [It, Tg, Fj, SA], 2000 Arg (R), SA 3, 2001 W, It, S, F, I, A, R, SA, 2002 S, I, F, W, It, NZ, A, SA, 2003 F 1, W 1, It, S, I, NZ, A, F3, [Gg, SA, U(R), W, F, A], 2004 It, S, I, W, F, C(R), SA(R), A2(R)
Greg, W (Manchester) 1876 I, S
Gregory, G G (Bristol) 1931 I, S, F, 1932 SA, W, I, S, 1933 W, I, S, 1934 W, I, S
Gregory, J A (Blackheath) 1949 W
Grewcock, D J (Coventry, Saracens, Bath) 1997 Arg 2, SA, 1998 W (R), S (R), I (R), A 1, NZ 1, SA 2(R), 1999 S (R), A (R), US, C, [It, NZ, Tg (R), SA], 2000 SA 1, 2, A, Arg, SA 3, 2001 W, It, S, I, A, R (R), SA, 2002 S (R), I (R), F (R), W, It, NZ, SA (R), 2003 F 1 (R), W 1 (R), It, S (R), I (t), W 2, F 2, [U], 2004 It, S, W, F, NZ1, 2(R), C, SA, A2, 2005 W, F, I, It, S, A, NZ, 2006 W, It, S, F, I(R), NZ, Arg, 2007 S, It, I

THE COUNTRIES

Grylls, W M (Redruth) 1905 I
Guest, R H (Waterloo) 1939 W, I, S, 1947 W, I, S, F, 1948 A, W, I, S, 1949 F, S
Guillemard, A G (West Kent) 1871 S, 1872 S
Gummer, C H A (Plymouth A) 1929 F
Gunner, C R (Marlborough N) 1876 I
Gurdon, C (Richmond) 1880 I, S, 1881 I, W, S, 1882 I, S, 1883 S, 1884 W, S, 1885 I, 1886 W, I, S
Gurdon, E T (Richmond) 1878 S, 1879 I, 1880 S, 1881 I, W, S, 1882 S, 1883 W, I, S, 1884 W, I, S, 1885 W, I, 1886 S
Guscott, J C (Bath) 1989 R, Fj, 1990 I, F, W, S, Arg 3, 1991 W, S, I, F, Fj, A, [NZ, It, F, S, A], 1992 S, I, F, W, C, SA, 1993 F, W, S, I, 1994 R, C, 1995 I, F, W, S, [Arg, It, A, NZ, F], SA, WS, 1996 F, W, S, I, Arg, 1997 I (R), W (R), 1998 F, W, S, I, H, It, A 2, SA 2, 1999 S, I, F, A, US, C, [It (R), NZ, Tg]

Haag, M (Bath) 1997 Arg 1, 2
Haigh, L (Manchester) 1910 W, I, S, 1911 W, F, I, S
Hale, P M (Moseley) 1969 SA, 1970 I, W
Hall, C (Gloucester) 1901 I, S
Hall, J (N Durham) 1894 W, I, S
Hall, J P (Bath) 1984 S (R), I, F, SA 1, 2, A, 1985 R, F, S, I, W, NZ 1, 2, 1986 W, S, 1987 I, F, W, S, 1990 Arg 3, 1994 S
Hall, N M (Richmond) 1947 W, I, S, F, 1949 W, I, 1952 SA, W, S, I, F, 1953 W, I, F, S, 1955 W, I
Halliday, S J (Bath, Harlequins) 1986 W, S, 1987 S, 1988 S, I 1, 2, A 1, A, 1989 S, I, F, W, R, Fj (R), 1990 W, S, 1991 [US, S, A], 1992 S, I, F, W
Hamersley, A St G (Marlborough N) 1871 S, 1872 S, 1873 S, 1874 S
Hamilton-Hill, E A (Harlequins) 1936 NZ, W, I
Hamilton-Wickes, R H (Cambridge U) 1924 I, 1925 NZ, W, I, S, F, 1926 W, I, S, 1927 W
Hammett, E D G (Newport) 1920 W, F, S, 1921 W, I, S, F, 1922 W
Hammond, C E L (Harlequins) 1905 S, NZ, 1906 W, I, S, F, 1908 W, I
Hancock, A W (Northampton) 1965 F, S, 1966 F
Hancock, G E (Birkenhead Park) 1939 W, I, S
Hancock, J H (Newport) 1955 W, I
Hancock, P F (Blackheath) 1886 W, I, 1890 W
Hancock, P S (Richmond) 1904 W, I, S
Handford, F G (Manchester) 1909 W, F, I, S
Hands, R H M (Blackheath) 1910 F, S
Hanley, J (Plymouth A) 1927 W, S, F, 1928 W, I, F, S
Hanley, S M (Sale) 1999 W
Hannaford, R C (Bristol) 1971 W, I, F
Hanvey, R J (Aspatria) 1926 W, I, F, S
Hape, S E (Bath, London Irish) 2010 A1, 2, NZ, A3, Sm, SA, 2011 W1, It, F, S, I1, W3, [Gg]
Harding, E H (Devonport Services) 1931 I
Harding, R M (Bristol) 1985 R, F, S, 1987 S, [A, J, W], 1988 I 1(R), 2, A 1, 2, Fj
Harding, V S J (Saracens) 1961 F, S, 1962 W, I, F, S
Hardwick, P F (Percy Park) 1902 I, S, 1903 W, I, S, 1904 W, I, S
Hardwick, R J K (Coventry) 1996 It (R)
Hardy, E M P (Blackheath) 1951 I, F, S
Hare, W H (Nottingham, Leicester) 1974 W, 1978 F, NZ, 1979 NZ, 1980 I, F, W, S, 1981 W, S, Arg 1, 2, 1982 F, W, 1983 F, W, S, I, NZ, 1984 S, I, F, W, SA 1, 2
Harper, C H (Exeter) 1899 W
Harriman, A T (Harlequins) 1988 A
Harris, S W (Blackheath) 1920 I, S
Harris, T W (Northampton) 1929 S, 1932 I
Harrison, A C (Hartlepool R) 1931 I, S
Harrison, A L (United Services, RN) 1914 I, F
Harrison, G (Hull) 1877 I, S, 1879 S, I, 1880 S, 1885 W, I
Harrison, H C (United Services, RN) 1909 S, 1914 I, S, F
Harrison, M E (Wakefield) 1985 NZ 1, 2, 1986 S, I, F, 1987 I, F, W, S, [A, J, US, W], 1988 F, W
Hartley, B C (Blackheath) 1901 S, 1902 S
Hartley, D M (Northampton) 2008 PI(R), A(R), SA(R), NZ3(R), 2009 It(R), W(R), I(R), F(R), S(R), Arg 1, 2, A(R), Arg 3, NZ, 2010 W, It, I, S, F, NZ(R), A3, Sm, SA, 2011 W1, It, F, S, I1, W2, I2(R), [Arg(R), Gg, S(R), F(R)], 2012 S, It, W, F, I, SA 1, 2, 3, 2013 S(R), I(R), F, It(R), W(R)
Haskell, J A W (Wasps, Stade Français, Ricoh Black Rams, Otago Highlanders) 2007 W1, F2, 2008 W, It, F, I(R), NZ1, 2, PI(t&R), A(R), SA, NZ3, 2009 It, W, I, F(R), S(R), Arg 1, 2(R), A(R), Arg 3, NZ, 2010 W, It, I, S, F(R), A1(R), Sm, 2011 W1, It, F, S, I1, W2, 3(R), I2, [Arg, Gg, R, S, F(R)], 2012 SA 3, 4(R), NZ(R), 2013 S(R), I, F(R), It, W(R)
Haslett, L W (Birkenhead Park) 1926 I, F
Hastings, G W D (Gloucester) 1955 W, I, F, S, 1957 W, I, F, S, 1958 W, A, I, F, S
Havelock, H (Hartlepool R) 1908 F, W, I
Hawcridge, J J (Bradford) 1885 W, I
Hayward, L W (Cheltenham) 1910 I
Hazell, A R (Gloucester) 2004 C, SA(t&R), 2005 W, F(t), It(R), S(R), 2007 SA1
Hazell, D St G (Leicester) 1955 W, I, F, S
Healey, A S (Leicester) 1997 I (R), W, A 1(R), 2(R), NZ 1(R), SA (R), NZ 2, 1998 F, W, S, I, A 1, NZ 1, 2, H, It, A 2, SA 2(R), 1999 US, C, [It, NZ, Tg, Fj, SA (R)], 2000 I, F, W, It, S, SA 1, 2, A, SA 3(R), 2001 W (R), It, S, F, I (R), A, R, SA, 2002 S, I, F, W, It (R), NZ (R), A (R), SA(R), 2003 F2
Hearn, R D (Bedford) 1966 F, S, 1967 I, F, S, W
Heath, A H (Oxford U) 1876 S
Heaton, J (Waterloo) 1935 W, I, S, 1939 W, I, S, 1947 I, S, F
Henderson, A P (Edinburgh Wands) 1947 W, I, S, F, 1948 I, S, F, 1949 W, I
Henderson, R S F (Blackheath) 1883 W, S, 1884 W, S, 1885 W
Heppell, W G (Devonport A) 1903 I
Herbert, A J (Wasps) 1958 F, S, 1959 W, I, F, S
Hesford, R (Bristol) 1981 S (R), 1982 A, S, F (R), 1983 F (R), 1985 R, F, S, I, W
Heslop, N J (Orrell) 1990 Arg 1, 2, 3, 1991 W, S, I, F, [US, F], 1992 W (R)
Hetherington, J G G (Northampton) 1958 A, I, 1959 W, I, F, S
Hewitt, E N (Coventry) 1951 W, I, F
Hewitt, W W (Queen's House) 1881 I, W, S, 1882 I
Hickson, J L (Bradford) 1887 W, I, S, 1890 W, S, I
Higgins, R (Liverpool) 1954 W, NZ, I, S, 1955 W, I, F, S, 1957 W, I, F, S, 1959 W
Hignell, A J (Cambridge U, Bristol) 1975 A 2, 1976 A, W, S, I, 1977 S, I, F, W, 1978 W, 1979 S, I, F, W
Hill, B A (Blackheath) 1903 I, S, 1904 W, I, 1905 W, NZ, 1906 SA, 1907 F, W
Hill, R A (Saracens) 1997 S, I, F, W, A 1, 2, NZ 1, SA, NZ 2, 1998 F, W, H (R), It (R), A 2, SA 2, 1999 S, I, F, W, A, US, C, [It, NZ, Tg, Fj (R), SA], 2000 I, F, W, It, S, SA 1, 2, A, Arg, SA 3, 2001 W, It, S, F, I, A, SA, 2002 S, I, F, W, It, NZ, A, SA, 2003 F 1, W 1, It, S, I, NZ, A, F 3, [Gg, F, A], 2004 It, S, I, W, F, NZ1, 2, A1
Hill, R J (Bath) 1984 SA 1, 2, 1985 I (R), NZ 2(R), 1986 F (R), 1987 I, F, W, [US], 1989 Fj, 1990 I, F, W, S, Arg 1, 2, 3, 1991 W, S, I, F, Fj, A, [NZ, It, US, F, S, A]
Hillard, R J (Oxford U) 1925 NZ
Hiller, R (Harlequins) 1968 W, I, F, S, 1969 I, F, S, W, SA, 1970 I, W, S, 1971 I, F, S (2[1C]), P, 1972 W, I
Hind, A E (Leicester) 1905 NZ, 1906 W
Hind, G R (Blackheath) 1910 S, 1911 I
Hipkiss, D J (Leicester) 2007 W2, F3, [Sm(R), Tg(R), F(R), SA2(R)], 2008 NZ3(R), 2009 Arg 1, 2, A, Arg 3, NZ, 2010 W(R)
Hobbs, R F A (Blackheath) 1899 S, 1903 W
Hobbs, R G S (Richmond) 1932 SA, W, I, S
Hobson, J D (Bristol) 2008 NZ2(R)
Hodges, H A (Nottingham) 1906 W, I
Hodgkinson, S D (Nottingham) 1989 R, Fj, 1990 I, F, W, S, Arg 1, 2, 3, 1991 W, S, I, F, [US]
Hodgson, C C (Sale, Saracens) 2001 R, 2002 S (R), I (R), It (R), Arg, 2003 F 1, W 1, It (R), 2004 NZ1, 2, A1, C, SA, A2, 2005 W, F, I, It, S, A, NZ, Sm, 2006 W, It, S, F, NZ, Arg, SA1, 2008 S(R), NZ1, 2010 A3(R), Sm(R), SA(R), 2011 W2(R), 3(R), 2012 S, It
Hodgson, J McD (Northern) 1932 SA, W, I, S, 1934 W, I, 1936 I
Hodgson, P K (London Irish) 2008 I(R), 2009 Arg 1(R), 2(R), A(R), Arg 3, NZ, 2010 W(R), It(R), I(R)
Hodgson, S A M (Durham City) 1960 W, I, F, S, 1961 SA, W, 1962 W, I, F, S, 1964 W
Hofmeyr, M B (Oxford U) 1950 W, F, S
Hogarth, T B (Hartlepool R) 1906 F
Holford, G (Gloucester) 1920 W, F
Holland, D (Devonport A) 1912 W, I, S
Holliday, T E (Aspatria) 1923 S, F, 1925 I, S, F, 1926 F, S
Holmes, C B (Manchester) 1947 S, 1948 I, F
Holmes, E (Manningham) 1890 S, I
Holmes, W A (Nuneaton) 1950 W, I, F, S, 1951 W, I, F, S, 1952 SA, S, I, F, 1953 W, I, F, S
Holmes, W B (Cambridge U) 1949 W, I, F, S
Hook, W G (Gloucester) 1951 S, 1952 SA, W
Hooper, C A (Middlesex W) 1894 W, I, S
Hopley, D P (Wasps) 1995 [WS (R)], SA, WS
Hopley, F J V (Blackheath) 1907 F, W, 1908 I
Horak, M J (London Irish) 2002 Arg
Hordern, P C (Gloucester) 1931 I, S, F, 1934 W
Horley, C H (Swinton) 1885 I
Hornby, A N (Manchester) 1877 I, S, 1878 S, I, 1880 I, 1881 I, S, 1882 I, S
Horrocks-Taylor, J P (Cambridge U, Leicester, Middlesbrough) 1958 W, A, 1961 S, 1962 S, 1963 NZ 1, 2, A, 1964 NZ, W

Horsfall, E L (Harlequins) 1949 W
Horton, A L (Blackheath) 1965 W, I, F, S, 1966 F, S, 1967 NZ
Horton, J P (Bath) 1978 W, S, I, NZ, 1980 I, F, W, S, 1981 W, 1983 S, I, 1984 SA 1, 2
Horton, N E (Moseley, Toulouse) 1969 I, F, S, W, 1971 I, F, S, 1974 S, 1975 W, 1977 S, I, F, W, 1978 F, W, 1979 S, I, F, W, 1980 I
Hosen, R W (Bristol, Northampton) 1963 NZ 1, 2, A, 1964 F, S, 1967 A, I, F, S, W
Hosking, G R d'A (Devonport Services) 1949 W, I, F, S, 1950 W
Houghton, S (Runcorn) 1892 I, 1896 W
Howard, P D (O Millhillians) 1930 W, I, F, S, 1931 W, I, S, F
Hubbard, G C (Blackheath) 1892 W, I
Hubbard, J C (Harlequins) 1930 S
Hudson, A (Gloucester) 1906 W, I, F, 1908 F, W, I, S, 1910 F
Hughes, G E (Barrow) 1896 S
Hull, P A (Bristol, RAF) 1994 SA 1, 2, R, C
Hulme, F C (Birkenhead Park) 1903 W, I, 1905 W, I
Hunt, J T (Manchester) 1882 I, S, 1884 W
Hunt, R (Manchester) 1880 I, 1881 W, S, 1882 I
Hunt, W H (Manchester) 1876 S, 1877 I, S, 1878 I
Hunter, I (Northampton) 1992 C, 1993 F, W, 1994 F, W, 1995 [WS, F]
Huntsman, R P (Headingley) 1985 NZ 1, 2
Hurst, A C B (Wasps) 1962 S
Huskisson, T F (OMTs) 1937 W, I, S, 1938 W, I, 1939 W, I, S
Hutchinson, F (Headingley) 1909 F, I, S
Hutchinson, J E (Durham City) 1906 I
Hutchinson, W C (RIE Coll) 1876 S, 1877 I
Hutchinson, W H H (Hull) 1875 I, 1876 I
Huth, H (Huddersfield) 1879 S
Hyde, J P (Northampton) 1950 F, S
Hynes, W B (United Services, RN) 1912 F

Ibbitson, E D (Headingley) 1909 W, F, I, S
Imrie, H M (Durham City) 1906 NZ, 1907 I
Inglis, R E (Blackheath) 1886 W, I, S
Irvin, S H (Devonport A) 1905 W
Isherwood, F W (Ravenscourt Park) 1872 S

Jackett, E J (Leicester, Falmouth) 1905 NZ, 1906 W, I, S, F, SA, 1907 W, I, S, 1909 W, F, I, S
Jackson, A H (Blackheath) 1878 I, 1880 I
Jackson, B S (Broughton Park) 1970 S (R), F
Jackson, P B (Coventry) 1956 W, I, F, 1957 W, I, F, S, 1958 W, A, F, S, 1959 W, I, F, S, 1961 S, 1963 W, I, F, S
Jackson, W J (Halifax) 1894 S
Jacob, F (Cambridge U) 1897 W, I, S, 1898 I, S, W, 1899 W, I
Jacob, H P (Blackheath) 1924 W, I, F, S, 1930 F
Jacob, P G (Blackheath) 1898 I
Jacobs, C R (Northampton) 1956 W, I, S, F, 1957 W, I, F, S, 1958 W, A, I, F, S, 1960 W, I, F, S, 1961 SA, W, I, F, S, 1963 NZ 1, 2, A, 1964 W, I, F, S
Jago, R A (Devonport A) 1906 W, I, SA, 1907 W, I
Janion, J P A G (Bedford) 1971 W, I, F, S (2[1C]), P, 1972 W, S, SA, 1973 A, 1975 A 1, 2
Jarman, J W (Bristol) 1900 W
Jeavons, N C (Moseley) 1981 S, I, F, Arg 1, 2, 1982 A, S, I, F, W, 1983 F, W, S, I
Jeeps, R E G (Northampton) 1956 W, 1957 W, I, F, S, 1958 W, A, I, F, S, 1959 I, 1960 W, I, F, S, 1961 SA, W, I, F, S, 1962 W, I, F, S
Jeffery, G L (Blackheath) 1886 W, I, S, 1887 W, I, S
Jennins, C R (Waterloo) 1967 A, I, F
Jewitt, J (Hartlepool R) 1902 W
Johns, W A (Gloucester) 1909 W, F, I, S, 1910 W, I, F
Johnson, M O (Leicester) 1993 F, NZ, 1994 S, I, F, W, R, C, 1995 I, F, W, S, [Arg, It, WS, A, NZ, F], SA, WS, 1996 F, W, S, I, It, Arg, 1997 S, I, F, W, A 2, NZ 1, 2, 1998 F, W, S, I, H, It, A 2, SA 2, 1999 S, I, F, W, A, US, C, [It, NZ, Tg, Fj, SA], 2000 SA 1, 2, A, Arg, SA 3, 2001 W, It, S, F, SA, 2002 S, I, F, It (t+R), NZ, A, SA, 2003 F 1, W 1, S, I, NZ, A, F 3, [Gg, SA, Sm, U(R), W, F, A]
Johnson, T A (Exeter) 2012 SA 1, 2, 3, Fj, A
Johnston, J B (Saracens) 2002 Arg, NZ (R)
Johnston, W R (Bristol) 1910 W, I, S, 1912 W, I, S, F, 1913 SA, W, F, I, S, 1914 W, I, S, F
Jones, C M (Sale) 2004 It(R), S, I(R), W, NZ1, 2005 W, 2006 A1(R), 2, SA1(R), 2, 2007 SA1, 2(R)
Jones, F P (New Brighton) 1893 S
Jones, H A (Barnstaple) 1950 W, I, F
Jorden, A M (Cambridge U, Blackheath, Bedford) 1970 F, 1973 I, F, S, 1974 F, 1975 W, S
Joseph, J B A (London Irish) 2012 SA 1(R), 2, 3, NZ(R), 2013 Arg1, 2
Jowett, D (Heckmondwike) 1889 M, 1890 S, I, 1891 W, I, S
Judd, P E (Coventry) 1962 W, I, F, S, 1963 S, NZ 1, 2, A, 1964 NZ, 1965 I, F, S, 1966 W, I, F, S, 1967 A, I, F, S, W, NZ

Kay, B J (Leicester) 2001 C 1, 2, A, R, SA (t+R), 2002 S, I, F, W, It, Arg, NZ (R), A, SA, 2003 F 1, W 1, It, S, I, NZ, A, F 3, [Gg, SA, Sm, W, F, A], 2004 It, S, I, W, F, C(R), SA(R), 2005 W, F, I, It, S, 2006 A2, NZ, Arg, SA1, 2(R), 2007 F2, [US, SA1, Sm, Tg, A, F, SA2], 2008 W(R), It(R), F(R), S(R), I(R), NZ1(R), 2(R), 2009 Arg 1(R), 2(t&R)
Kayll, H E (Sunderland) 1878 S
Keeling, J H (Guy's Hospital) 1948 A, W
Keen, B W (Newcastle U) 1968 W, I, F, S
Keeton, G H (Leicester) 1904 W, I, S
Kelly, G A (Bedford) 1947 W, I, S, 1948 W
Kelly, T S (London Devonians) 1906 W, I, S, F, SA, 1907 F, W, I, S, 1908 F, I, S
Kemble, A T (Liverpool) 1885 W, I, 1887 I
Kemp, D T (Blackheath) 1935 W
Kemp, T A (Richmond) 1937 W, I, 1939 S, 1948 A, W
Kendall, P D (Birkenhead Park) 1901 S, 1902 W, 1903 S
Kendall-Carpenter, J MacG K (Oxford U, Bath) 1949 I, F, S, 1950 W, I, F, S, 1951 I, F, S, 1952 SA, W, S, I, F, 1953 W, I, F, S, 1954 W, NZ, I, F
Kendrew, D A (Leicester) 1930 W, I, 1933 I, S, 1934 S, 1935 W, I, 1936 NZ, W, I
Kennedy, N J (London Irish) 2008 PI, NZ3, 2009 It, W, I, F(R), S(R)
Kennedy, R D (Camborne S of M) 1949 I, F, S
Kent, C P (Rosslyn Park) 1977 S, I, F, W, 1978 F (R)
Kent, T (Salford) 1891 W, I, S, 1892 W, I, S
Kershaw, C A (United Services, RN) 1920 W, F, I, S, 1921 W, I, S, F, 1922 W, I, F, S, 1923 W, I, S, F
Kewley, E (Liverpool) 1874 S, 1875 S, 1876 I, S, 1877 I, S, 1878 S
Kewney, A L (Leicester) 1906 W, I, S, F, 1909 A, W, F, I, S, 1911 W, F, I, S, 1912 I, S, 1913 SA
Key, A (O Cranleighans) 1930 I, 1933 W
Keyworth, M (Swansea) 1976 A, W, S, I
Kilner, B (Wakefield T) 1880 I
Kindersley, R S (Exeter) 1883 W, 1884 S, 1885 W
King, A D (Wasps) 1997 Arg 2(R), 1998 SA 2(R), 2000 It (R), 2001 C 2(R), 2003 W2
King, I (Harrogate) 1954 W, NZ, I
King, J A (Headingley) 1911 W, F, I, S, 1912 W, I, S, 1913 SA, W, F, I, S
King, Q E M A (Army) 1921 S
Kingston, P (Gloucester) 1975 A 1, 2, 1979 I, F, W
Kitching, A E (Blackheath) 1913 I
Kittermaster, H J (Harlequins) 1925 NZ, W, I, 1926 W, I, F, S
Knight, F (Plymouth) 1909 A
Knight, P M (Bristol) 1972 F, S, SA
Knowles, E (Millom) 1896 S, 1897 S
Knowles, T C (Birkenhead Park) 1931 S
Krige, J A (Guy's Hospital) 1920 W
Kvesic, M B (Worcester) 2013 Arg 1, 2

Labuschagne, N A (Harlequins, Guy's Hospital) 1953 W, 1955 W, I, F, S
Lagden, R O (Richmond) 1911 S
Laird, H C C (Harlequins) 1927 W, I, S, 1928 A, W, I, F, S, 1929 W, I
Lambert, D (Harlequins) 1907 F, 1908 F, W, S, 1911 W, F, I
Lampkowski, M S (Headingley) 1976 A, W, S, I
Lapage, W N (United Services, RN) 1908 F, W, I, S
Larter, P J (Northampton, RAF) 1967 A, NZ, 1968 W, I, F, S, 1969 I, F, S, W, SA, 1970 I, W, F, S, 1971 W, I, F, S (2[1C]), P, 1972 SA, 1973 NZ 1, W
Launchbury, J O (Wasps) 2012 Fj(R), A(R), SA4, NZ, 2013 S, I, F, It, W, Arg1, 2
Law, A F (Richmond) 1877 S
Law, D E (Birkenhead Park) 1927 I
Lawes, C L (Northampton) 2009 A(R), 2010 S(R), A1(R), 2, NZ, A3, Sm, SA, 2011 W3, I2, [Arg, S, F(R)], 2012 W(R), NZ(R), 2013 S(R), I(R), F, It(R), W(R), Arg1(R), 2(R)
Lawrence, Hon H A (Richmond) 1873 S, 1874 S, 1875 I, S
Lawrie, P W (Leicester) 1910 S, 1911 S
Lawson, R G (Workington) 1925 I
Lawson, T M (Workington) 1928 A, W
Leadbetter, M M (Broughton Park) 1970 F
Leadbetter, V H (Edinburgh Wands) 1954 S, F
Leake, W R M (Harlequins) 1891 W, I, S
Leather, G (Liverpool) 1907 I
Lee, F H (Marlborough N) 1876 S, 1877 I

Lee, H (Blackheath) 1907 F
Le Fleming, J (Blackheath) 1887 W
Leonard, J (Saracens, Harlequins) 1990 Arg 1, 2, 3, 1991 W, S, I, F, Fj, A, [NZ, It, US, F, S, A], 1992 S, I, F, W, C, SA, 1993 F, W, S, I, NZ, 1994 S, I, F, W, SA 1, 2, R, C, 1995 I, F, W, S, [Arg, It, A, NZ, F], SA, WS, 1996 F, W, S, I, It, Arg, 1997 S, I, F, W, A 2, NZ 1, SA, NZ 2, 1998 F, W, S, I, H, It, A 2 SA 2, 1999 S, I, F, W, A, C (R), [It, NZ, Fj, SA], 2000 I, F, W, It, S, SA 1, 2, A, Arg, SA 3, 2001 W, It, S, F, I, R, 2002 S (R), I (R), F (R), It (R), A, SA, 2003 F 1, S, I, NZ, W 2, F 2(t+R), 3(R), [Gg(t&R), SA(R), Sm, U, W, F(t&R), A(R)], 2004 It(R)
Leslie-Jones, F A (Richmond) 1895 W, I
Lewis, A O (Bath) 1952 SA, W, S, I, F, 1953 W, I, F, S, 1954 F
Lewsey, O J (Wasps) 1998 NZ 1, 2, SA 1, 2001 C 1, 2, US, 2003 It, S, I, NZ, A, F2, 3(t+R), [Gg, SA, U, F, A], 2004 It, S, I, W, F, NZ1, 2, A1, C, SA, A2, 2005 W, F, I, It, S, A, NZ, Sm, 2006 W, S, F, Arg(R), SA1, 2, 2007 S, It, I, F1, 2, 3, [US, SA1, Sm, Tg, A, F]
Leyland, R (Waterloo) 1935 W, I, S
Linnett, M S (Moseley) 1989 Fj
Lipman, M R (Bath) 2004 NZ2(R), A1(R), 2006 A2, 2008 It, F, S, I, PI(R), A(R), NZ3
Livesay, R O'H (Blackheath) 1898 W, 1899 W
Lloyd, L D (Leicester) 2000 SA 1(R), 2(R), 2001 C 1, 2, US
Lloyd, R H (Harlequins) 1967 NZ, 1968 W, I, F, S
Locke, H M (Birkenhead Park) 1923 S, F, 1924 W, F, S, 1925 W, I, S, F, 1927 W, I, S
Lockwood, R E (Heckmondwike) 1887 W, I, S, 1889 M, 1891 W, I, S, 1892 W, I, S, 1893 W, I, 1894 W, I
Login, S H M (RN Coll) 1876 I
Lohden, F C (Blackheath) 1893 W
Long, A E (Bath) 1997 A 2, 2001 US (R)
Longland, R J (Northampton) 1932 S, 1933 W, S, 1934 W, I, S, 1935 W, I, S, 1936 NZ, W, I, S, 1937 W, I, S, 1938 W, I, S
Lowe, C N (Cambridge U, Blackheath) 1913 SA, W, F, I, S, 1914 W, I, S, F, 1920 W, F, I, S, 1921 W, I, S, F, 1922 W, I, F, S, 1923 W, I, S, F
Lowrie, F W (Wakefield T) 1889 M, 1890 W
Lowry, W M (Birkenhead Park) 1920 F
Lozowski, R A P (Wasps) 1984 A
Luddington, W G E (Devonport Services) 1923 W, I, S, F, 1924 W, I, F, S, 1925 W, I, S, F, 1926 W
Luger, D D (Harlequins, Saracens) 1998 H, It, SA 2, 1999 S, I, F, W, A, US, C, [It, NZ, Tg, Fj, SA], 2000 SA 1, A, Arg, SA 3, 2001 W, I, A, R, SA, 2002 F (R), W, It, 2003 F 1, W 1, It, S (R), I (R), NZ(R), W 2, [Gg(R), SA(R), U, W]
Lund, M B (Sale) 2006 A1, 2(R), NZ(R), Arg(t&R), 2007 S, It, I, F1(R), W1(R), SA2
Luscombe, F (Gipsies) 1872 S, 1873 S, 1875 I, S, 1876 I, S
Luscombe, J H (Gipsies) 1871 S
Luxmoore, A F C C (Richmond) 1900 S, 1901 W
Luya, H F (Waterloo, Headingley) 1948 W, I, S, F, 1949 W
Lyon, A (Liverpool) 1871 S
Lyon, G H d'O (United Services, RN) 1908 S, 1909 A

McCanlis, M A (Gloucester) 1931 W, I
McCarthy, N (Gloucester) 1999 I (t), US (R), 2000 It (R)
McFadyean, C W (Moseley) 1966 I, F, S, 1967 A, I, F, S, W, NZ, 1968 W, I
MacIlwaine, A H (United Services, Hull & E Riding) 1912 W, I, S, F, 1920 I
Mackie, O G (Wakefield T, Cambridge U) 1897 S, 1898 I
Mackinlay, J E H (St George's Hospital) 1872 S, 1873 S, 1875 I
MacLaren, W (Manchester) 1871 S
MacLennan, R R F (OMTs) 1925 I, S, F
McLeod, N F (RIE Coll) 1879 S, I
Madge, R J P (Exeter) 1948 A, W, I, S
Malir, F W S (Otley) 1930 W, I, S
Mallett, J A (Bath) 1995 [WS (R)]
Mallinder, J (Sale) 1997 Arg 1, 2
Mangles, R H (Richmond) 1897 W, I
Manley, D C (Exeter) 1963 W, I, F, S
Mann, W E (United Services, Army) 1911 W, F, I
Mantell, N D (Rosslyn Park) 1975 A 1
Mapletoft, M S (Gloucester) 1997 Arg 2
Markendale, E T (Manchester R) 1880 I
Marler, J W G (Harlequins) 2012 SA 1, 2, 3, Fj, A, 2013 S, I, F, It(R), W, Arg1, 2
Marques, R W D (Cambridge U, Harlequins) 1956 W, I, S, F, 1957 W, I, F, S, 1958 W, A, I, F, S, 1959 W, I, F, S, 1960 W, I, F, S, 1961 SA, W
Marquis, J C (Birkenhead Park) 1900 I, S
Marriott, C J B (Blackheath) 1884 W, I, S, 1886 W, I, S, 1887 I
Marriott, E E (Manchester) 1876 I
Marriott, V R (Harlequins) 1963 NZ 1, 2, A, 1964 NZ
Marsden, G H (Morley) 1900 W, I, S
Marsh, H (RIE Coll) 1873 S
Marsh, J (Swinton) 1892 I
Marshall, H (Blackheath) 1893 W
Marshall, M W (Blackheath) 1873 S, 1874 S, 1875 I, S, 1876 I, S, 1877 I, S, 1878 S, I
Marshall, R M (Oxford U) 1938 I, S, 1939 W, I, S
Martin, C R (Bath) 1985 F, S, I, W
Martin, N O (Harlequins) 1972 F (R)
Martindale, S A (Kendal) 1929 F
Massey, E J (Leicester) 1925 W, I, S
Mather, B-J (Sale) 1999 W
Mathias, J L (Bristol) 1905 W, I, S, NZ
Matters, J C (RNE Coll) 1899 S
Matthews, J R C (Harlequins) 1949 F, S, 1950 I, F, S, 1952 SA, W, S, I, F
Maud, P (Blackheath) 1893 W, I
Maxwell, A W (New Brighton, Headingley) 1975 A 1, 1976 A, W, S, I, F, 1978 F
Maxwell-Hyslop, J E (Oxford U) 1922 I, F, S
May, J J (Gloucester) 2013 Arg 2
May, T A (Newcastle) 2009 Arg 1, 2
Maynard, A F (Cambridge U) 1914 W, I, S
Mears, L A (Bath) 2005 Sm(R), 2006 W(R), It(R), F(R), I, A1, 2(R), NZ(R), Arg(R), SA1(R), 2, 2007 S(R), It(R), I(R), W1(R), F2(R), 3(R), [Tg(R)], 2008 W(R), It(R), F(R), S, I, NZ1, 2, PI, A, SA, NZ3, 2009 It, W, I, F, S, 2010 I(R), 2011 W2(R), 3(R), [R(R)], 2012 I(R), SA 1(R), 2(R), 3(t)
Meikle, G W C (Waterloo) 1934 W, I, S
Meikle, S S C (Waterloo) 1929 S
Mellish, F W (Blackheath) 1920 W, F, I, S, 1921 W, I
Melville, N D (Wasps) 1984 A, 1985 I, W, NZ 1, 2, 1986 W, S, I, F, 1988 F, W, S, I 1
Merriam, L P B (Blackheath) 1920 W, F
Michell, A T (Oxford U) 1875 I, S, 1876 I
Middleton, B B (Birkenhead Park) 1882 I, 1883 I
Middleton, J A (Richmond) 1922 S
Miles, J H (Leicester) 1903 W
Millett, H (Richmond) 1920 F
Mills, F W (Marlborough N) 1872 S, 1873 S
Mills, S G F (Gloucester) 1981 Arg 1, 2, 1983 W, 1984 SA 1, A
Mills, W A (Devonport A) 1906 W, I, S, F, SA, 1907 F, W, I, S, 1908 F, W
Milman, D L K (Bedford) 1937 W, 1938 W, I, S
Milton, C H (Camborne S of M) 1906 I
Milton, J G (Camborne S of M) 1904 W, I, S, 1905 S, 1907 I
Milton, W H (Marlborough N) 1874 S, 1875 I
Mitchell, F (Blackheath) 1895 W, I, S, 1896 W, I, S
Mitchell, W G (Richmond) 1890 W, S, I, 1891 W, I, S, 1893 S
Mobbs, E R (Northampton) 1909 A, W, F, I, S, 1910 I, F
Moberley, W O (Ravenscourt Park) 1872 S
Monye, Y C C (Harlequins) 2008 PI, A, SA, NZ3, 2009 F, S, A, Arg 3, NZ, 2010 W, It, I, S, 2012 Fj
Moody, L W (Leicester, Bath) 2001 C 1, 2, US, I (R), R, SA (R), 2002 I (R), W, It, Arg, NZ, A, SA, 2003 F 1, W 2, F 2, 3(R), [Gg(R), SA, Sm(R), U, W, F(R), A(R)], 2004 C, SA, A2, 2005 F, I, It, S, A, NZ, Sm, 2006 W, It, S, F, I, A1, NZ, Arg, SA1(R), 2(R), W2(R), 2007 [US(R), SA1(R), Sm(R), Tg, A, F, SA2], 2008 W, 2009 A, Arg 3, NZ, 2010 W, It, I, S(R), F, A1, 2, NZ, A3, SA, 2011 W2, [Gg, R, S, F]
Moore, B C (Nottingham, Harlequins) 1987 S, [A, J, W], 1988 F, W, S, I 1, 2, A 1, 2, Fj, A, 1989 S, I, F, W, R, Fj, 1990 I, F, W, S, Arg 1, 2, 1991 W, S, I, F, Fj, A, [NZ, It, F, S, A], 1992 S, I, F, W, SA, 1993 F, W, S, I, NZ, 1994 S, I, F, W, SA 1, 2, R, C, 1995 I, F, W, S, [Arg, It, WS (R), A, NZ, F]
Moore, E J (Blackheath) 1883 I, S
Moore, N J N H (Bristol) 1904 W, I, S
Moore, P B C (Blackheath) 1951 W
Moore, W K T (Leicester) 1947 W, I, 1949 F, S, 1950 I, F, S
Mordell, R J (Rosslyn Park) 1978 W
Morfitt, S (W Hartlepool) 1894 W, I, S, 1896 W, I, S
Morgan, B J (Scarlets, Gloucester) 2012 S(R), It(R), W, F, I, SA 1, 2, 4, NZ, 2013 S, Arg1, 2
Morgan, J R (Hawick) 1920 W
Morgan, O C (Gloucester) 2007 S, I
Morgan, W G D (Medicals, Newcastle) 1960 W, I, F, S, 1961 SA, W, I, F, S
Morley, A J (Bristol) 1972 SA, 1973 NZ 1, W, I, 1975 S, A 1, 2
Morris, A D W (United Services, RN) 1909 A, W, F
Morris, C D (Liverpool St Helens, Orrell) 1988 A, 1989 S, I, F, W, 1992 S, I, F, W, C, SA, 1993 F, W, S, I, 1994 F, W, SA 1, 2, R, 1995 S (t), [Arg, WS, A, NZ, F]

Morris, R (Northampton) 2003 W 1, It
Morrison, P H (Cambridge U) 1890 W, S, I, 1891 I
Morse, S (Marlborough N) 1873 S, 1874 S, 1875 S
Mortimer, W (Marlborough N) 1899 W
Morton, H J S (Blackheath) 1909 I, S, 1910 W, I
Moss, F (Broughton) 1885 W, I, 1886 W
Mullan, M J (Worcester) 2010 It(R)
Mullins, A R (Harlequins) 1989 Fj
Mycock, J (Sale) 1947 W, I, S, F, 1948 A
Myers, E (Bradford) 1920 I, S, 1921 W, I, 1922 W, I, F, S, 1923 W, I, S, F, 1924 W, I, F, S, 1925 S, F
Myers, H (Keighley) 1898 I
Myler, S J (Northampton) 2013 Arg 2(R)

Nanson, W M B (Carlisle) 1907 F, W
Narraway, L J W (Gloucester) 2008 W, It(R), S(R), NZ1, 2, 2009 W(R), I(R)
Nash, E H (Richmond) 1875 I
Neale, B A (Rosslyn Park) 1951 I, F, S
Neale, M E (Blackheath) 1912 F
Neame, S (O Cheltonians) 1879 S, I, 1880 I, S
Neary, A (Broughton Park) 1971 W, I, F, S (2[1C]), P, 1972 W, I, F, S, SA, 1973 NZ 1, W, I, F, S, NZ 2, A, 1974 S, I, F, W, 1975 I, F, W, S, A 1, 1976 A, W, S, I, F, 1977 I, 1978 F (R), 1979 S, I, F, W, NZ, 1980 I, F, W, S
Nelmes, B G (Cardiff) 1975 A 1, 2, 1978 W, S, I, NZ
Newbold, C J (Blackheath) 1904 W, I, S, 1905 W, I, S
Newman, S C (Oxford U) 1947 F, 1948 A, W
Newton, A W (Blackheath) 1907 S
Newton, P A (Blackheath) 1882 S
Newton-Thompson, J O (Oxford U) 1947 S, F
Nichol, W (Brighouse R) 1892 W, S
Nicholas, P L (Exeter) 1902 W
Nicholson, B E (Harlequins) 1938 W, I
Nicholson, E S (Leicester) 1935 W, I, S, 1936 NZ, W
Nicholson, E T (Birkenhead Park) 1900 W, I
Nicholson, T (Rockcliff) 1893 I
Ninnes, B F (Coventry) 1971 W
Noon, J D (Newcastle) 2001 C 1, 2, US, 2003 W 2, F 2(t+R), 2005 W, F, I, It, S, A, NZ, 2006 W, It, S, F, I, 2006 A1(R), 2, NZ, Arg, SA1, 2, 2007 SA2, F2, [US, SA1], 2008 It, F, S, I, NZ1(R), 2, PI, A, SA, NZ3, 2009 It
Norman, D J (Leicester) 1932 SA, W
North, E H G (Blackheath) 1891 W, I, S
Northmore, S (Millom) 1897 I
Novak, M J (Harlequins) 1970 W, S, F
Novis, A L (Blackheath) 1929 S, F, 1930 W, I, F, 1933 I, S

Oakeley, F E (United Services, RN) 1913 S, 1914 I, S, F
Oakes, R F (Hartlepool R) 1897 W, I, S, 1898 I, S, W, 1899 W, S
Oakley, L F L (Bedford) 1951 W
Obolensky, A (Oxford U) 1936 NZ, W, I, S
Ojo, T O (London Irish) 2008 NZ1, 2
Ojomoh, S O (Bath, Gloucester) 1994 I, F, SA 1(R), 2, R, 1995 S (R), [Arg, WS, A (t), F], 1996 F, 1998 NZ 1
Old, A G B (Middlesbrough, Leicester, Sheffield) 1972 W, I, F, S, SA, 1973 NZ 2, A, 1974 S, I, F, W, 1975 I, A 2, 1976 S, I, 1978 F
Oldham, W L (Coventry) 1908 S, 1909 A
Olver, C J (Northampton) 1990 Arg 3, 1991 [US], 1992 C
O'Neill, A (Teignmouth, Torquay A) 1901 W, I, S
Openshaw, W E (Manchester) 1879 I
Orwin, J (Gloucester, RAF, Bedford) 1985 R, F, S, I, W, NZ 1, 2, 1988 F, W, S, I 1, 2, A 1, 2
Osborne, R R (Manchester) 1871 S
Osborne, S H (Oxford U) 1905 S
Oti, C (Cambridge U, Nottingham, Wasps) 1988 S, I 1, 1989 S, I, F, W, R, 1990 Arg 1, 2, 1991 Fj, A, [NZ, It]
Oughtred, B (Hartlepool R) 1901 S, 1902 W, I, S, 1903 W, I
Owen, J E (Coventry) 1963 W, I, F, S, A, 1964 NZ, 1965 W, I, F, S, 1966 I, F, S, 1967 NZ
Owen-Smith, H G O (St Mary's Hospital) 1934 W, I, S, 1936 NZ, W, I, S, 1937 W, I, S

Page, J J (Bedford, Northampton) 1971 W, I, F, S, 1975 S
Paice, D J (London Irish) 2008 NZ1(R), 2(R), 2012 Fj(R), A(R), SA4(R), NZ(R), 2013 Arg1(R), 2(R)
Pallant, J N (Notts) 1967 I, F, S
Palmer, A C (London Hospital) 1909 I, S
Palmer, F H (Richmond) 1905 W
Palmer, G V (Richmond) 1928 I, F, S
Palmer, J A (Bath) 1984 SA 1, 2, 1986 I (R)
Palmer, T P (Leeds, Wasps, Stade Français) 2001 US (R), 2006 Arg(R), SA1, 2, 2007 It(R), I(R), F1, W1, 2008 NZ1, 2, PI(R), A, SA, 2010 F(R), A1, 2, NZ, A3, Sm, SA, 2011 W1, It, F, S, I1, W2, 3(R), I2(R), [Arg(R), Gg, R, S(R), F], 2012 S, It, F(R), I(R), SA 1(R), 2(R), 3, Fj, A
Pargetter, T A (Coventry) 1962 S, 1963 F, NZ 1
Parker, G W (Gloucester) 1938 I, S
Parker, Hon S (Liverpool) 1874 S, 1875 S
Parling, G M W (Leicester) 2012 S(R), It(R), W, F, I, SA 1, 2, 3, Fj, A, SA4, NZ, 2013 S, I, F, It, W
Parsons, E I (RAF) 1939 S
Parsons, M J (Northampton) 1968 W, I, F, S
Patterson, W M (Sale) 1961 SA, S
Pattisson, R M (Blackheath) 1883 I, S
Paul, H R (Gloucester) 2002 F(R), 2004 It(t&R), S(R), C, SA, A2
Paul, J E (RIE Coll) 1875 S
Payne, A T (Bristol) 1935 I, S
Payne, C M (Harlequins) 1964 I, F, S, 1965 I, F, S, 1966 W, I, F, S
Payne, J H (Broughton) 1882 S, 1883 W, I, S, 1884 I, 1885 W, I
Payne, T A N (Wasps) 2004 A1, 2006 A1(R), 2(R), 2007 F1, W1, 2008 It, NZ1(R), 2, SA, NZ3, 2009 Arg 1, 2, A, Arg 3, NZ, 2010 W, It, I, S, F, A1, 2
Pearce, G S (Northampton) 1979 S, I, F, W, 1981 Arg 1, 2, 1982 A, S, 1983 F, W, S, I, NZ, 1984 S, SA 2, A, 1985 R, F, S, I, W, NZ 1, 2, 1986 W, S, I, F, 1987 I, F, W, S, [A, US, W], 1988 Fj, 1991 [US]
Pears, D (Harlequins) 1990 Arg 1, 2, 1992 F (R), 1994 F
Pearson, A W (Blackheath) 1875 I, S, 1876 I, S, 1877 S, 1878 S, I
Peart, T G A H (Hartlepool R) 1964 F, S
Pease, F E (Hartlepool R) 1887 I
Penny, S H (Leicester) 1909 A
Penny, W J (United Hospitals) 1878 I, 1879 S, I
Percival, L J (Rugby) 1891 I, 1892 I, 1893 S
Periton, H G (Waterloo) 1925 W, 1926 W, I, F, S, 1927 W, I, S, F, 1928 A, I, F, S, 1929 W, I, S, F, 1930 W, I, F, S
Perrott, E S (O Cheltonians) 1875 I
Perry, D G (Bedford) 1963 F, S, NZ 1, 2, A 1964 NZ, W, I, 1965 W, I, F, S, 1966 W, I, F
Perry, M B (Bath) 1997 A 2, NZ 1, SA, NZ 2, 1998 W, S, I, A 1, NZ 1, 2, SA 1, H, It, A 2, 1999 I, F, W, A US, C, [It, NZ, Tg, Fj, SA], 2000 I, F, W, It, S, SA 1, 2, A, SA 3, 2001 W (R), F (R)
Perry, S A (Bristol) 2006 NZ, Arg, SA1(R), 2(R), 2007 I(R), F1(R), W1(R), SA1(R), 2(R), W2, F2, 3, [US, SA1]
Perry, S V (Cambridge U, Waterloo) 1947 W, I, 1948 A, W, I, S, F
Peters, J (Plymouth) 1906 S, F, 1907 I, S, 1908 W
Phillips, C (Birkenhead Park) 1880 S, 1881 I, S
Phillips, M S (Fylde) 1958 A, I, F, S, 1959 W, I, F, S, 1960 W, I, F, S, 1961 W, 1963 W, I, F, S, NZ 1, 2, A, 1964 NZ, W, I, F, S
Pickering, A S (Harrogate) 1907 I
Pickering, R D A (Bradford) 1967 I, F, S, W, 1968 F, S
Pickles, R C W (Bristol) 1922 I, F
Pierce, R (Liverpool) 1898 I, 1903 S
Pilkington, W N (Cambridge U) 1898 S
Pillman, C H (Blackheath) 1910 W, I, F, S, 1911 W, F, I, S, 1912 W, F, 1913 SA, W, F, I, S, 1914 W, I, S
Pillman, R L (Blackheath) 1914 F
Pinch, J (Lancaster) 1896 W, I, 1897 S
Pinching, W W (Guy's Hospital) 1872 S
Pitman, I J (Oxford U) 1922 S
Plummer, K C (Bristol) 1969 W, 1976 S, I, F
Pool-Jones, R J (Stade Francais) 1998 A 1
Poole, F O (Oxford U) 1895 W, I, S
Poole, R W (Hartlepool R) 1896 S
Pope, E B (Blackheath) 1931 W, S, F
Portus, G V (Blackheath) 1908 F, I
Potter, S (Leicester) 1998 A 1(t)
Poulton, R W (later Poulton Palmer) (Oxford U, Harlequins, Liverpool) 1909 F, I, S, 1910 W, 1911 S, 1912 W, I, S, 1913 SA, W, F, I, S, 1914 W, I, S, F
Powell, D L (Northampton) 1966 W, I, 1969 I, F, S, W, 1971 W, I, F, S (2[1C])
Pratten, W E (Blackheath) 1927 S, F
Preece, I (Coventry) 1948 I, S, F, 1949 F, S, 1950 W, I, F, S, 1951 W, I, F
Preece, P S (Coventry) 1972 SA, 1973 NZ 1, W, I, F, S, NZ 2, 1975 I, F, W, A 2, 1976 W (R)
Preedy, M (Gloucester) 1984 SA 1
Prentice, F D (Leicester) 1928 I, F, S
Prescott, R E (Harlequins) 1937 W, I, 1938 I, 1939 W, I, S
Preston, N J (Richmond) 1979 NZ, 1980 I, F
Price, H L (Harlequins) 1922 I, S, 1923 W, I
Price, J (Coventry) 1961 I
Price, P L A (RIE Coll) 1877 I, S, 1878 S

Price, T W (Cheltenham) 1948 S, F, 1949 W, I, F, S
Probyn, J A (Wasps, Askeans) 1988 F, W, S, I 1, 2, A 1, 2, A, 1989 S, I, R (R), 1990 I, F, W, S, Arg 1, 2, 3, 1991 W, S, I, F, Fj, A, [NZ, It, F, S, A], 1992 S, I, F, W, 1993 F, W, S, I
Prout, D H (Northampton) 1968 W, I
Pullin, J V (Bristol) 1966 W, 1968 W, I, F, S, 1969 I, F, S, W, SA, 1970 I, W, S, F, 1971 W, I, F, S (2[1C]), P, 1972 W, I, F, S, SA, 1973 NZ 1, W, I, F, S, NZ 2, A, 1974 S, I, F, W, 1975 I, W (R), S, A 1, 2, 1976 F
Purdy, S J (Rugby) 1962 S
Pyke, J (St Helens Recreation) 1892 W
Pym, J A (Blackheath) 1912 W, I, S, F

Quinn, J P (New Brighton) 1954 W, NZ, I, S, F

Rafter, M (Bristol) 1977 S, F, W, 1978 F, W, S, I, NZ, 1979 S, I, F, W, NZ, 1980 W(R), 1981 W, Arg 1, 2
Ralston, C W (Richmond) 1971 S (C), P, 1972 W, I, F, S, SA, 1973 NZ 1, W, I, F, S, NZ 2, A, 1974 S, I, F, W, 1975 I, F, W, S
Ramsden, H E (Bingley) 1898 S, W
Ranson, J M (Rosslyn Park) 1963 NZ 1, 2, A, 1964 W, I, F, S
Raphael, J E (OMTs) 1902 W, I, S, 1905 W, S, NZ, 1906 W, S, F
Ravenscroft, J (Birkenhead Park) 1881 I
Ravenscroft, S C W (Saracens) 1998 A 1, NZ 2(R)
Rawlinson, W C W (Blackheath) 1876 S
Redfern, S P (Leicester) 1984 I (R)
Redman, N C (Bath) 1984 A, 1986 S (R), 1987 I, S, [A, J, W], 1988 Fj, 1990 Arg 1, 2, 1991 Fj, [It, US], 1993 NZ, 1994 F, W, SA 1, 2, 1997 Arg 1, A 1
Redmond, G F (Cambridge U) 1970 F
Redwood, B W (Bristol) 1968 W, I
Rees, D L (Sale) 1997 A 2, NZ 1, SA, NZ 2, 1998 F, W, SA 2(R), 1999 S, I, F, A
Rees, G W (Nottingham) 1984 SA 2(R), A, 1986 I, F, 1987 F, W, S, [A, J, US, W], 1988 S (R), I 1, 2, A 1, 2, Fj, 1989 W (R), R (R), Fj (R), 1990 Arg 3(R), 1991 Fj, [US]
Rees, T (Wasps) 2007 S(R), It(R), I(R), F1, W1, F3, [US, SA1], 2008 W(R), NZ1, 2, PI, A, SA, NZ3(R)
Reeve, J S R (Harlequins) 1929 F, 1930 W, I, F, S, 1931 W, I, S
Regan, M (Liverpool) 1953 W, I, F, S, 1954 W, NZ, I, S, F, 1956 I, S, F
Regan, M P (Bristol, Bath, Leeds) 1995 SA, WS, 1996 F, W, S, I, It, Arg, 1997 S, I, F, W, A 1, NZ 2(R), 1998 F, 2000 SA 1(t), A(R), Arg, SA 3(t), 2001 It(R), S(R), C 2(R), R, 2003 F 1(t), It(R), W 2, [Gg(R), Sm], 2004 It(R), I(R), NZ1(R), 2, A1, 2007 SA1, 2, W2, F2, 3, [US, SA1, A, F, SA2], 2008 W, It, F
Rendall, P A G (Wasps, Askeans) 1984 W, SA 2, 1986 W, S, 1987 I, F, S, [A, J, W], 1988 F, W, S, I 1, 2, A 1, 2, A, 1989 S, I, F, W, R, 1990 I, F, W, S, 1991 [It (R)]
Rew, H (Blackheath) 1929 S, F, 1930 F, S, 1931 W, S, F, 1934 W, I, S
Reynolds, F J (O Cranleighans) 1937 S, 1938 I, S
Reynolds, S (Richmond) 1900 W, I, S, 1901 I
Rhodes, J (Castleford) 1896 W, I, S
Richards, D (Leicester) 1986 I, F, 1987 S, [A, J, US, W], 1988 F, W, S, I 1, A 1, 2, Fj, A, 1989 S, I, F, W, R, 1990 Arg 3, 1991 W, S, I, F, Fj, A, [NZ, It, US], 1992 S (R), F, W, C, 1993 NZ, 1994 W, SA 1, C, 1995 I, F, W, S, [WS, A, NZ], 1996 F (t), S, I
Richards, E E (Plymouth A) 1929 S, F
Richards, J (Bradford) 1891 W, I, S
Richards, P C (Gloucester, London Irish) 2006 A1, 2, NZ(R), Arg(R), SA1, 2, 2007 [US(R), SA1(R), Tg(R), A(t), F(R), SA2(R)], 2008 NZ2(R)
Richards, S B (Richmond) 1965 W, I, F, S, 1967 A, I, F, S, W
Richardson, J V (Birkenhead Park) 1928 A, W, I, F, S
Richardson, W R (Manchester) 1881 I
Rickards, C H (Gipsies) 1873 S
Rimmer, G (Waterloo) 1949 W, I, 1950 W, 1951 W, I, F, 1952 SA, W, 1954 W, NZ, I, S
Rimmer, L I (Bath) 1961 SA, W, I, F, S
Ripley, A G (Rosslyn Park) 1972 W, I, F, S, SA, 1973 NZ 1, W, I, F, S, NZ 2, A, 1974 S, I, F, W, 1975 I, F, S, A 1, 2, 1976 A, W, S
Risman, A B W (Loughborough Coll) 1959 W, I, F, S, 1961 SA, W, I, F
Ritson, J A S (Northern) 1910 F, S, 1912 F, 1913 SA, W, F, I, S
Rittson-Thomas, G C (Oxford U) 1951 W, I, F
Robbins, G L (Coventry) 1986 W, S
Robbins, P G D (Oxford U, Moseley, Coventry) 1956 W, I, S, F, 1957 W, I, F, S, 1958 W, A, I, S, 1960 W, I, F, S, 1961 SA, W, 1962 S
Roberts, A D (Northern) 1911 W, F, I, S, 1912 I, S, F, 1914 I
Roberts, E W (RNE Coll) 1901 W, I, 1905 NZ, 1906 W, I, 1907 S
Roberts, G D (Harlequins) 1907 S, 1908 F, W
Roberts, J (Sale) 1960 W, I, F, S, 1961 SA, W, I, F, S, 1962 W, I, F, S, 1963 W, I, F, S, 1964 NZ
Roberts, R S (Coventry) 1932 I
Roberts, S (Swinton) 1887 W, I
Roberts, V G (Penryn, Harlequins) 1947 F, 1949 W, I, F, S, 1950 I, F, S, 1951 W, I, F, S, 1956 W, I, S, F
Robertshaw, A R (Bradford) 1886 W, I, S, 1887 W, S
Robinson, A (Blackheath) 1889 M, 1890 W, S, I
Robinson, E T (Coventry) 1954 S, 1961 I, F, S
Robinson, G C (Percy Park) 1897 I, S, 1898 I, 1899 W, 1900 I, S, 1901 I, S
Robinson, J T (Sale) 2001 It (R), S (R), F (R), I, A, R, SA, 2002 S, I, F, It, NZ, A, SA, 2003 F 1, W 1, S, I, NZ, A, F 3, [Gg, SA, Sm, U(R), W, F, A], 2004 It, S, I, W, F, C, SA, A2, 2005 W, F, I, 2007 S, It, F1, W1, SA1, W2, F3, [US, SA1, A, F, SA2]
Robinson, J J (Headingley) 1893 S, 1902 W, I, S
Robinson, R A (Bath) 1988 A 2, Fj, A, 1989 S, I, F, W, 1995 SA
Robshaw, C D C (Harlequins) 2009 Arg 2, 2012 S, It, W, F, I, SA 1, 2, Fj, A, SA4, NZ, 2013 S, I, F, It, W
Robson, A (Northern) 1924 W, I, F, S, 1926 W
Robson, M (Oxford U) 1930 W, I, F, S
Rodber, T A K (Army, Northampton) 1992 S, I, 1993 NZ, 1994 I, F, W, SA 1, 2, R, C, 1995 I, F, W, S, [Arg, It, WS (R), A, NZ, F], SA, WS, 1996 W, S (R), I (t), It, Arg, 1997 S, I, F, W, A 1, 1998 H (R), It (R), A 2, SA 2, 1999 S, I, F, W, A, US (R), [NZ (R), Fj (R)]
Rogers, D P (Bedford) 1961 I, F, S, 1962 W, I, F, 1963 W, I, F, S, NZ 1, 2, A, 1964 NZ, W, I, F, S, 1965 W, I, F, S, 1966 W, I, F, S, 1967 A, S, W, NZ, 1969 I, F, S, W
Rogers, J H (Moseley) 1890 W, S, I, 1891 S
Rogers, W L Y (Blackheath) 1905 W, I
Rollitt, D M (Bristol) 1967 I, F, S, W, 1969 I, F, S, W, 1975 S, A 1, 2
Roncoroni, A D S (West Herts, Richmond) 1933 W, I, S
Rose, W M H (Cambridge U, Coventry, Harlequins) 1981 I, F, 1982 A, S, I, 1987 I, F, W, S, [A]
Rossborough, P A (Coventry) 1971 W, 1973 NZ 2, A, 1974 S, I, 1975 I, F
Rosser, D W A (Wasps) 1965 W, I, F, S, 1966 W
Rotherham, Alan (Richmond) 1883 W, S, 1884 W, S, 1885 W, I, 1886 W, I, S, 1887 W, I, S
Rotherham, Arthur (Richmond) 1898 S, W, 1899 W, I, S
Roughley, D (Liverpool) 1973 A, 1974 S, I
Rowell, R E (Leicester) 1964 W, 1965 W
Rowley, A J (Coventry) 1932 SA
Rowley, H C (Manchester) 1879 S, I, 1880 I, S, 1881 I, W, S, 1882 I, S
Rowntree, G C (Leicester) 1995 S (t), [It, WS], WS, 1996 F, W, S, I, It, Arg, 1997 S, I, F, W, A 1, 1998 A 1, NZ 1, 2, SA 1, H (R), It (R), 1999 US, C, [It (R), Tg, Fj (R)], 2001 C 1, 2, US, I(R), A, R, SA, 2002 S, I, F, W, It, 2003 F 1(R), W 1, It, S, I, NZ, F 2, 2004 C, SA, A2, 2005 W, F, I, It, 2006 A1, 2
Royds, P M R (Blackheath) 1898 S, W, 1899 W
Royle, A V (Broughton R) 1889 M
Rudd, E L (Liverpool) 1965 W, I, S, 1966 W, I, S
Russell, R F (Leicester) 1905 NZ
Rutherford, D (Percy Park, Gloucester) 1960 W, I, F, S, 1961 SA, 1965 W, I, F, S, 1966 W, I, F, S, 1967 NZ
Ryalls, H J (New Brighton) 1885 W, I
Ryan, D (Wasps, Newcastle) 1990 Arg 1, 2, 1992 C, 1998 S
Ryan, P H (Richmond) 1955 W, I

Sackey, P H (Wasps) 2006 NZ, Arg, 2007 F2, 3(R), [SA1, Sm, Tg, A, F, SA2], 2008 W, It, F, S, I, PI, A, SA, NZ3, 2009 It, W, I
Sadler, E H (Army) 1933 I, S
Sagar, J W (Cambridge U) 1901 W, I
Salmon, J L B (Harlequins) 1985 NZ 1, 2, 1986 W, S, 1987 I, F, W, S, [A, J, US, W]
Sample, C H (Cambridge U) 1884 I, 1885 I, 1886 S
Sampson, P C (Wasps) 1998 SA 1, 2001 C 1, 2
Sanders, D L (Harlequins) 1954 W, NZ, I, S, F, 1956 W, I, S, F
Sanders, F W (Plymouth A) 1923 I, S, F
Sanderson, A (Sale) 2001 R (R), 2002 Arg, 2003 It(t + R), W 2(R), F 2
Sanderson, P H (Sale, Harlequins, Worcester) 1998 NZ 1, 2, SA 1, 2001 C 1(R), 2(R), US(t+R), 2005 A, NZ, Sm, 2006 A1, 2, NZ, Arg, SA1, 2, 2007 SA1(R)
Sandford, J R P (Marlborough N) 1906 I
Sangwin, R D (Hull and E Riding) 1964 NZ, W
Sargent, G A F (Gloucester) 1981 I (R)
Savage, K F (Northampton) 1966 W, I, F, S, 1967 A, I, F, S, W, NZ, 1968 W, F, S
Sawyer, C M (Broughton) 1880 S, 1881 I

Saxby, L E (Gloucester) 1932 SA, W
Scarbrough, D G R (Leeds, Saracens) 2003 W 2, 2007 SA2
Schofield, D F (Sale) 2007 SA1, 2(R)
Schofield, J W (Manchester) 1880 I
Scholfield, J A (Preston Grasshoppers) 1911 W
Schwarz, R O (Richmond) 1899 S, 1901 W, I
Scorfield, E S (Percy Park) 1910 F
Scott, C T (Blackheath) 1900 W, I, 1901 W, I
Scott, E K (St Mary's Hospital, Redruth) 1947 W, 1948 A, W, I, S
Scott, F S (Bristol) 1907 W
Scott, H (Manchester) 1955 F
Scott, J P (Rosslyn Park, Cardiff) 1978 F, W, S, I, NZ, 1979 S (R), I, F, W, NZ, 1980 I, F, W, S, 1981 W, S, I, F, Arg 1, 2, 1982 I, F, W, 1983 F, W, S, I, NZ, 1984 S, I, F, W, SA 1, 2
Scott, J S M (Oxford U) 1958 F
Scott, M T (Cambridge U) 1887 I, 1890 S, I
Scott, W M (Cambridge U) 1889 M
Seddon, R L (Broughton R) 1887 W, I, S
Sellar, K A (United Services, RN) 1927 W, I, S, 1928 A, W, I, F
Sever, H S (Sale) 1936 NZ, W, I, S, 1937 W, I, S, 1938 W, I, S
Shackleton, I R (Cambridge U) 1969 SA, 1970 I, W, S
Sharp, R A W (Oxford U, Wasps, Redruth) 1960 W, I, F, S, 1961 I, F, 1962 W, I, F, 1963 W, I, F, S, 1967 A
Sharples, C D J (Gloucester) 2011 W2(R), 2012 F, Fj, A
Shaw, C H (Moseley) 1906 S, SA, 1907 F, W, I, S
Shaw, F (Cleckheaton) 1898 I
Shaw, J F (RNE Coll) 1898 S, W
Shaw, S D (Bristol, Wasps) 1996 It, Arg, 1997 S, I, F, W, A 1, SA (R), 2000 I, F, W, It, S, SA 1(R), 2(R), 2001 C 1(R), 2, US, I, 2003 It (R), W 2, F 2(R), 3(R), 2004 It(t&R), S(R), NZ1, 2, A1, 2005 Sm(R), 2006 W(R), It(R), S(R), F(R), I, 2007 W2, F2, 3, [US, SA1, Sm, A, F, SA2], 2008 W, It, F, S, I, A(R), SA(R), 2009 F, S, NZ, 2010 W, It, I, F, A1, 2(R), 3(R), SA(R), 2011 W1(R), It(R), F(R), S(R), I1(R), W2, I2(R), [Gg, R(R), F(R)]
Sheasby, C M A (Wasps) 1996 It, Arg, 1997 W (R), Arg 1(R), 2(R), SA (R), NZ 2(t)
Sheppard, A (Bristol) 1981 W (R), 1985 W
Sheridan, A J (Sale) 2004 C(R), 2005 A, NZ, Sm, 2006 W, It, S, F(R), I, NZ, SA1, 2007 W2, F2, [US, SA1, Sm, Tg, A, F, SA2], 2008 W, F, S, I, NZ1, PI, A, 2009 It, W, I, F, S, 2010 NZ, A3, Sm, SA, 2011 W1, F, I2, [Arg]
Sherrard, C W (Blackheath) 1871 S, 1872 S
Sherriff, G A (Saracens) 1966 S, 1967 A, NZ
Shewring, H E (Bristol) 1905 I, NZ, 1906 W, S, F, SA, 1907 F, W, I, S
Shooter, J H (Morley) 1899 I, S, 1900 I, S
Shuttleworth, D W (Headingley) 1951 S, 1953 S
Sibree, H J H (Harlequins) 1908 F, 1909 I, S
Silk, N (Harlequins) 1965 W, I, F, S
Simms, K G (Cambridge U, Liverpool, Wasps) 1985 R, F, S, I, W, 1986 I, F, 1987 I, F, W, [A, J, W], 1988 F, W
Simpson, C P (Harlequins) 1965 W
Simpson, J P M (Wasps) 2011 [Gg(R)]
Simpson, P D (Bath) 1983 NZ, 1984 S, 1987 I
Simpson, T (Rockcliff) 1902 S, 1903 W, I, S, 1904 I, S, 1905 I, S, 1906 S, SA, 1909 F
Simpson-Daniel, J D (Gloucester) 2002 NZ, A, 2003 W 1(t + R), It, W 2, 2004 I(R), NZ1, 2005 Sm, 2006 It(R), 2007 SA1(R)
Sims, D (Gloucester) 1998 NZ 1(R), 2, SA 1
Skinner, M G (Harlequins) 1988 F, W, S, I 1, 2, 1989 Fj, 1990 I, F, W, S, Arg 1, 2, 1991 Fj (R), [US, F, S, A], 1992 S, I, F, W
Skirving, B D (Saracens) 2007 SA2
Sladen, G M (United Services, RN) 1929 W, I, S
Sleightholme, J M (Bath) 1996 F, W, S, I, It, Arg, 1997 S, I, F, W, Arg 1, 2
Slemen, M A C (Liverpool) 1976 I, F, 1977 S, I, F, W, 1978 F, W, S, I, NZ, 1979 S, I, F, W, NZ, 1980 I, F, W, S, 1981 W, S, I, F, 1982 A, S, I, F, W, 1983 NZ, 1984 S
Slocock, L A N (Liverpool) 1907 F, W, I, S, 1908 F, W, I, S
Slow, C F (Leicester) 1934 S
Small, H D (Oxford U) 1950 W, I, F, S
Smallwood, A M (Leicester) 1920 F, I, 1921 W, I, S, F, 1922 I, S, 1923 W, I, S, F, 1925 I, S
Smart, C E (Newport) 1979 F, W, NZ, 1981 S, I, F, Arg 1, 2, 1982 A, S, I, F, W, 1983 F, W, S, I
Smart, S E J (Gloucester) 1913 SA, W, F, I, S, 1914 W, I, S, F, 1920 W, I, S
Smeddle, R W (Cambridge U) 1929 W, I, S, 1931 F
Smith, C C (Gloucester) 1901 W
Smith, D F (Richmond) 1910 W, I
Smith, J V (Cambridge U, Rosslyn Park) 1950 W, I, F, S
Smith, K (Roundhay) 1974 F, W, 1975 W, S
Smith, M J K (Oxford U) 1956 W
Smith, O J (Leicester) 2003 It (R), W 2(R), F 2, 2005 It(R), S(R)
Smith, S J (Sale) 1973 I, F, S, A, 1974 I, F, 1975 W (R), 1976 F, 1977 F (R), 1979 NZ, 1980 I, F, W, S, 1981 W, S, I, F, Arg 1, 2, 1982 A, S, I, F, W, 1983 F, W, S
Smith, S R (Richmond) 1959 W, F, S, 1964 F, S
Smith, S T (Wasps) 1985 R, F, S, I, W, NZ 1, 2, 1986 W, S
Smith, T H (Northampton) 1951 W
Soane, F (Bath) 1893 S, 1894 W, I, S
Sobey, W H (O Millhillians) 1930 W, F, S, 1932 SA, W
Solomon, B (Redruth) 1910 W
Sparks, R H W (Plymouth A) 1928 I, F, S, 1929 W, I, S, 1931 I, S, F
Speed, H (Castleford) 1894 W, I, S, 1896 S
Spence, F W (Birkenhead Park) 1890 I
Spencer, J (Harlequins) 1966 W
Spencer, J S (Cambridge U, Headingley) 1969 I, F, S, W, SA, 1970 I, W, S, F, 1971 W, I, S (2[1C]), P
Spong, R S (O Millhillians) 1929 F, 1930 W, I, F, S, 1931 F, 1932 SA, W
Spooner, R H (Liverpool) 1903 W
Springman, H H (Liverpool) 1879 S, 1887 S
Spurling, A (Blackheath) 1882 I
Spurling, N (Blackheath) 1886 I, S, 1887 W
Squires, P J (Harrogate) 1973 F, S, NZ 2, A, 1974 S, I, F, W, 1975 I, F, W, S, A 1, 2, 1976 A, W, 1977 S, I, F, W, 1978 F, W, S, I, NZ, 1979 S, I, F, W
Stafford R C (Bedford) 1912 W, I, S, F
Stafford, W F H (RE) 1874 S
Stanbury, E (Plymouth A) 1926 W, I, S, 1927 W, I, S, F, 1928 A, W, I, F, S, 1929 W, I, S, F
Standing, G (Blackheath) 1883 W, I
Stanger-Leathes, C F (Northern) 1905 I
Stark, K J (O Alleynians) 1927 W, I, S, F, 1928 A, W, I, F, S
Starks, A (Castleford) 1896 W, I
Starmer-Smith, N C (Harlequins) 1969 SA, 1970 I, W, S, F, 1971 S (C), P
Start, S P (United Services, RN) 1907 S
Steeds, J H (Saracens) 1949 F, S, 1950 I, F, S
Steele-Bodger, M R (Cambridge U) 1947 W, I, S, F, 1948 A, W, I, S, F
Steinthal, F E (Ilkley) 1913 W, F
Stephenson, M (Newcastle) 2001 C 1, 2, US
Stevens, C B (Penzance-Newlyn, Harlequins) 1969 SA, 1970 I, W, S, 1971 P, 1972 W, I, F, S, SA, 1973 NZ 1, W, I, F, S, NZ 2, A, 1974 S, I, F, W, 1975 I, F, W, S
Stevens, M J H (Bath, Saracens) 2004 NZ1(R), 2(t), 2005 I, It, S, NZ(R), Sm, 2006 W, It, F, 2007 SA2, W2(R), F2, 3(R), [US(R), SA1, Sm, Tg, A(R), F(R), SA2(R)], 2008 W(R), It, F(R), S(R), I(R), NZ1, 2, PI, A(t&R), SA(R), NZ3(R), 2011 W2, 3(R), I2(R), [Arg(R), Gg, S, F], 2012 S(R), It(R), W(R), F(R), I(R)
Still, E R (Oxford U, Ravenscourt P) 1873 S
Stimpson, T R G (Newcastle, Leicester) 1996 It, 1997 S, I, F, W, A 1, NZ 2(t+R), 1998 A 1, NZ 1, 2(R), SA 1(R), 1999 US (R), C (R), 2000 SA 1, 2001 C 1(t), 2(R), 2002 W (R), Arg, SA (R)
Stirling, R V (Leicester, RAF, Wasps) 1951 W, I, F, S, 1952 SA, W, S, I, F, 1953 W, I, F, S, 1954 W, NZ, I, S, F
Stoddart, A E (Blackheath) 1885 W, I, 1886 W, I, S, 1889 M, 1890 W, I, 1893 W, S
Stoddart, W B (Liverpool) 1897 W, I, S
Stokes, F (Blackheath) 1871 S, 1872 S, 1873 S
Stokes, L (Blackheath) 1875 I, 1876 S, 1877 I, S, 1878 S, 1879 S, I, 1880 I, S, 1881 I, W, S
Stone, F le S (Blackheath) 1914 F
Stoop, A D (Harlequins) 1905 S, 1906 S, F, SA, 1907 F, W, 1910 W, I, S, 1911 W, F, I, S, 1912 W, S
Stoop, F M (Harlequins) 1910 S, 1911 F, I, 1913 SA
Stout, F M (Richmond) 1897 W, I, 1898 I, S, W, 1899 I, S, 1903 S, 1904 W, I, S, 1905 W, I, S
Stout, P W (Richmond) 1898 S, W, 1899 W, I, S
Strettle, D (Harlequins, Saracens) 2007 I, F1, W1, 2, 2008 W, NZ1, 2011 I1(R), 2012 S, It, W, I, SA2, 2013 S(R), Arg1
Stringer, N C (Wasps) 1982 A (R), 1983 NZ (R), 1984 SA 1(R), A, 1985 R
Strong, E L (Oxford U) 1884 W, I, S
Sturnham B (Saracens) 1998 A 1, NZ 1(t), 2(t)
Summerscales, G E (Durham City) 1905 NZ
Sutcliffe, J W (Heckmondwike) 1889 M
Swarbrick, D W (Oxford U) 1947 W, I, F, 1948 A, W, 1949 I
Swayne, D H (Oxford U) 1931 W
Swayne, J W R (Bridgwater) 1929 W
Swift, A H (Swansea) 1981 Arg 1, 2, 1983 F, W, S, 1984 SA 2
Syddall, J P (Waterloo) 1982 I, 1984 A
Sykes, A R V (Blackheath) 1914 F
Sykes, F D (Northampton) 1955 F, S, 1963 NZ 2, A

Sykes, P W (Wasps) 1948 F, 1952 S, I, F, 1953 W, I, F
Syrett, R E (Wasps) 1958 W, A, I, F, 1960 W, I, F, S, 1962 W, I, F

Tait, M J M (Newcastle, Sale) 2005 W, 2006 A1, 2, SA1, 2, 2007 It(R), I(R), F1(R), W1, SA1, 2, W2, [US(R), SA1(R), Sm, Tg, A, F, SA2], 2008 It(t), F(R), S(R), I(t&R), NZ2, 2009 It(R), W(R), I(R), F(R), S(R), Arg 1(R), 2(R), NZ(R), 2010 W, It, I, S, F(R), A1(R)
Tallent, J A (Cambridge U, Blackheath) 1931 S, F, 1932 SA, W, 1935 I
Tanner, C C (Cambridge U, Gloucester) 1930 S, 1932 SA, W, I, S
Tarr, F N (Leicester) 1909 A, W, F, 1913 S
Tatham, W M (Oxford U) 1882 S, 1883 W, I, S, 1884 W, I, S
Taylor, A S (Blackheath) 1883 W, I, 1886 W, I
Taylor, E W (Rockcliff) 1892 I, 1893 I, 1894 W, I, S, 1895 W, I, S, 1896 W, I, 1897 W, I, S, 1899 I
Taylor, F (Leicester) 1920 F, I
Taylor, F M (Leicester) 1914 W
Taylor, H H (Blackheath) 1879 S, 1880 S, 1881 I, W, 1882 S
Taylor, J T (W Hartlepool) 1897 I, 1899 I, 1900 I, 1901 W, I, 1902 W, I, S, 1903 W, I, 1905 S
Taylor, P J (Northampton) 1955 W, I, 1962 W, I, F, S
Taylor, R B (Northampton) 1966 W, 1967 I, F, S, W, NZ, 1969 F, S, W, SA, 1970 I, W, S, F, 1971 S (2[1C])
Taylor, W J (Blackheath) 1928 A, W, I, F, S
Teague, M C (Gloucester, Moseley) 1985 F (R), NZ 1, 2, 1989 S, I, F, W, R, 1990 F, W, S, 1991 W, S, I, F, Fj, A, [NZ, It, F, S, A], 1992 SA, 1993 F, W, S, I
Teden, D E (Richmond) 1939 W, I, S
Teggin, A (Broughton R) 1884 I, 1885 W, 1886 I, S, 1887 I, S
Tetley, T S (Bradford) 1876 S
Thomas, C (Barnstaple) 1895 W, I, S, 1899 I
Thomas, H M (Sale) 2013 Arg 1(R), 2(R)
Thompson, P H (Headingley, Waterloo) 1956 W, I, S, F, 1957 W, I, F, S, 1958 W, A, I, F, S, 1959 W, I, F, S
Thompson, S G (Northampton, Brive, Leeds, Wasps) 2002 S, I, F, W, It, Arg, NZ, A, SA, 2003 F 1, W 1, It, S, I, NZ, A, F 2(R), 3, [Gg, SA, Sm(R), W, F, A], 2004 It, S, I, W, F, NZ1, A1(R), C, SA, A2, 2005 W, F, I, It, S, A, NZ, Sm, 2006 W, It, S, F, I(R), 2009 Arg 1(R), A, Arg 3(R), NZ(R), 2010 W(R), It(R), S(R), F(R), A1, 2, NZ, A3(R), Sm(R), SA(R), 2011 W1(R), It(R), F(R), S(R), I1(R), W3, I2, [Arg, Gg(t&R), R, S, F]
Thomson, G T (Halifax) 1878 S, 1882 I, S, 1883 W, I, S, 1884 I, S, 1885 I
Thomson, W B (Blackheath) 1892 W, 1895 W, I, S
Thorne, J D (Bristol) 1963 W, I, F
Tindall, M J (Bath, Gloucester) 2000 I, F, W, It, S, SA 1, 2, A, Arg, SA 3, 2001 W (R), R, SA (R), 2002 S, I, F, W, It, NZ, A, SA, 2003 It, S, I, NZ, A, F 2, [Gg, SA, Sm, W, F(R), A], 2004 W, F, NZ1, 2, A1, C, SA, A2, 2005 A, NZ, Sm, 2006 W, It, S, F, I(t&R), 2007 S, It, I, F1, 2008 W, NZ1, 2, 2009 W, I, F, S, 2010 F, A1, 2, NZ, A3, SA, 2011 W1, It, F, S, W3, I2, [Arg, R, S]
Tindall, V R (Liverpool U) 1951 W, I, F, S
Titterrell, A J (Sale) 2004 NZ2(R), C(R), 2005 It(R), S(R), 2007 SA2(R)
Tobin, F (Liverpool) 1871 S
Todd, A F (Blackheath) 1900 I, S
Todd, R (Manchester) 1877 S
Toft, H B (Waterloo) 1936 S, 1937 W, I, S, 1938 W, I, S, 1939 W, I, S
Toothill, J T (Bradford) 1890 S, I, 1891 W, I, 1892 W, I, S, 1893 W, I, S, 1894 W, I
Tosswill, L R (Exeter) 1902 W, I, S
Touzel, C J C (Liverpool) 1877 I, S
Towell, A C (Bedford) 1948 F, 1951 S
Travers, B H (Harlequins) 1947 W, I, 1948 A, W, 1949 F, S
Treadwell, W T (Wasps) 1966 I, F, S
Trick, D M (Bath) 1983 I, 1984 SA 1
Tristram, H B (Oxford U) 1883 S, 1884 W, S, 1885 W, 1887 S
Troop, C L (Aldershot S) 1933 I, S
Tucker, J S (Bristol) 1922 W, 1925 NZ, W, I, S, F, 1926 W, I, F, S, 1927 W, I, S, F, 1928 A, W, I, F, S, 1929 W, I, F, 1930 W, I, F, S, 1931 W
Tucker, W E (Blackheath) 1894 W, I, 1895 W, I, S
Tucker, W E (Blackheath) 1926 I, 1930 W, I
Tuilagi, E M (Leicester) 2011 W2, I2, [Arg, Gg, R, S, F], 2012 W, F, I, SA 1, 2, 3, Fj, A, SA4, NZ, 2013 I(R), F, It, W
Turner, D P (Richmond) 1871 S, 1872 S, 1873 S, 1874 S, 1875 I, S
Turner, E B (St George's Hospital) 1876 I, 1877 I, 1878 I
Turner, G R (St George's Hospital) 1876 S
Turner, H J C (Manchester) 1871 S
Turner, M F (Blackheath) 1948 S, F
Turner, S C (Sale) 2007 W1(R), SA1, 2(R)
Turner-Hall, J (Harlequins) 2012 S(R), It(R)
Turquand-Young, D (Richmond) 1928 A, W, 1929 I, S, F
Twelvetrees, W W F (Gloucester) 2013 S, I, It(R), W(R), Arg1
Twynam, H T (Richmond) 1879 I, 1880 I, 1881 W, 1882 I, 1883 I, 1884 W, I, S

Ubogu, V E (Bath) 1992 C, SA, 1993 NZ, 1994 S, I, F, W, SA 1, 2, R, C, 1995 I, F, W, S, [Arg, WS, A, NZ, F], SA, 1999 F (R), W (R), A (R)
Underwood, A M (Exeter) 1962 W, I, F, S, 1964 I
Underwood, R (Leicester, RAF) 1984 I, F, W, A, 1985 R, F, S, I, W, 1986 W, I, F, 1987 I, F, W, S, [A, J, W], 1988 F, W, S, I 1, 2, A 1, 2, Fj, A, 1989 S, I, F, W, R, Fj, 1990 I, F, W, S, Arg 3, 1991 W, S, I, F, Fj, A, [NZ, It, US, F, S, A], 1992 S, I, F, W, SA, 1993 F, W, S, I, NZ, 1994 S, I, F, W, SA 1, 2, R, C, 1995 I, F, W, S, [Arg, It, WS, A, NZ, F], SA, WS, 1996 F, W, S, I
Underwood, T (Leicester, Newcastle) 1992 C, SA, 1993 S, I, NZ, 1994 S, I, W, SA 1, 2, R, C, 1995 I, F, W, S, [Arg, It, A, NZ], 1996 Arg, 1997 S, I, F, W, 1998 A 2, SA 2
Unwin, E J (Rosslyn Park, Army) 1937 S, 1938 W, I, S
Unwin, G T (Blackheath) 1898 S
Uren, R (Waterloo) 1948 I, S, F, 1950 I
Uttley, R M (Gosforth) 1973 I, F, S, NZ 2, A, 1974 I, F, W, 1975 F, W, S, A 1, 2, 1977 S, I, F, W, 1978 NZ 1979 S, 1980 I, F, W, S

Vainikolo, L P I (Gloucester) 2008 W(R), It, F, S, I
Valentine J (Swinton) 1890 W, 1896 W, I, S
Vanderspar, C H R (Richmond) 1873 S
Van Gisbergen, M C (Wasps) 2005 A(t)
Van Ryneveld, C B (Oxford U) 1949 W, I, F, S
Varley, H (Liversedge) 1892 S
Varndell, T W (Leicester) 2005 Sm(R), 2006 A1, 2, 2008 NZ2
Vassall, H (Blackheath) 1881 W, S, 1882 I, S, 1883 W
Vassall, H H (Blackheath) 1908 I
Vaughan, D B (Headingley) 1948 A, W, I, S, 1949 I, F, S, 1950 W
Vaughan-Jones, A (Army) 1932 I, S, 1933 W
Verelst, C L (Liverpool) 1876 I, 1878 I
Vernon, G F (Blackheath) 1878 S, I, 1880 I, S, 1881 I
Vesty, S B (Leicester) 2009 Arg 1(R), 2(R)
Vickery, G (Aberavon) 1905 I
Vickery, P J (Gloucester, Wasps) 1998 W, A 1, NZ 1, 2, SA 1, 1999 US, C, [It, NZ, Tg, SA], 2000 I, F, W, S, A, Arg (R), SA 3(R), 2001 W, It, S, A, SA, 2002 I, F, Arg, NZ, A, SA, 2003 NZ(R), A, [Gg, SA, Sm(R), U, W, F, A], 2004 It, S, I, W, F, 2005 W(R), F, A, NZ, 2006 SA1(R), 2, 2007 S, It, I, W2, F2(R), 3, [US, Tg(R), A, F, SA2], 2008 W, F, S, I, Pl(R), A, SA, NZ3, 2009 It, W, I, F, S
Vivyan, E J (Devonport A) 1901 W, 1904 W, I, S
Voyce, A T (Gloucester) 1920 I, S, 1921 W, I, S, F, 1922 W, I, F, S, 1923 W, I, S, F, 1924 W, I, F, S, 1925 NZ, W, I, S, F, 1926 W, I, F, S
Voyce, T M D (Bath, Wasps) 2001 US (R), 2004 NZ2, A1, 2005 Sm, 2006 W(R), It, F(R), I, A1
Vunipola, M W I N (Saracens) 2012 Fj(R), A(R), SA4(R), NZ(R), 2013 S(R), I(R), F(R), It, W(R)
Vunipola, V M L (Wasps) 2013 Arg1(R), 2(R)
Vyvyan, H D (Saracens) 2004 C(R)

Wackett, J A S (Rosslyn Park) 1959 W, I
Wade, C (Wasps) 2013 Arg 1
Wade, C G (Richmond) 1883 W, I, S, 1884 W, S, 1885 W, 1886 W, I
Wade, M R (Cambridge U) 1962 W, I, F
Wakefield, W W (Harlequins) 1920 W, F, I, S, 1921 W, I, S, F, 1922 W, I, F, S, 1923 W, I, S, F, 1924 W, I, F, S, 1925 NZ, W, I, S, F, 1926 W, I, F, S, 1927 S, F
Walder, D J H (Newcastle) 2001 C 1, 2, US, 2003 W 2(R)
Waldrom, T R (Leicester) 2012 SA 2(R), 3, Fj, A, 2013 I(R)
Walker, G A (Blackheath) 1939 W, I
Walker, H W (Coventry) 1947 W, I, S, F, 1948 A, W, I, S, F
Walker, R (Manchester) 1874 S, 1875 I, 1876 S, 1879 S, 1880 S
Wallens, J N S (Waterloo) 1927 F
Walshe, N P J (Bath) 2006 A1(R), 2(R)
Walton, E J (Castleford) 1901 W, I, 1902 I, S
Walton, W (Castleford) 1894 S
Ward, G (Leicester) 1913 W, F, S, 1914 W, I, S
Ward, H (Bradford) 1895 W
Ward, J I (Richmond) 1881 I, 1882 I
Ward, J W (Castleford) 1896 W, I, S
Wardlow, C S (Northampton) 1969 SA (R), 1971 W, I, F, S (2[1C])
Warfield, P J (Rosslyn Park, Durham U) 1973 NZ 1, W, I, 1975 I, F, S
Warr, A L (Oxford U) 1934 W, I
Waters, F H H (Wasps) 2001 US, 2004 NZ2(R), A1(R)
Watkins, J A (Gloucester) 1972 SA, 1973 NZ 1, W, NZ 2, A, 1975 F, W
Watkins, J K (United Services, RN) 1939 W, I, S

Watson, F B (United Services, RN) 1908 S, 1909 S
Watson, J H D (Blackheath) 1914 W, S, F
Watt, D E J (Bristol) 1967 I, F, S, W
Webb, C S H (Devonport Services, RN) 1932 SA, W, I, S, 1933 W, I, S, 1935 S, 1936 NZ, W, I, S
Webb, J M (Bristol, Bath) 1987 [A (R), J, US, W], 1988 F, W, S, I 1, 2, A 1, 2, A, 1989 S, I, F, W, 1991 Fj, A, [NZ, It, F, S, A], 1992 S, I, F, W, C, SA, 1993 F, W, S, I
Webb, J W G (Northampton) 1926 F, S, 1929 S
Webb, R E (Coventry) 1967 S, W, NZ, 1968 I, F, S, 1969 I, F, S, W, 1972 I, F
Webb, St L H (Bedford) 1959 W, I, F, S
Webber, R W (Wasps, Bath) 2012 It(R), W(R), F(R), 2013 Arg1, 2
Webster, J G (Moseley) 1972 W, I, SA, 1973 NZ 1, W, NZ 2, 1974 S, W, 1975 I, F, W
Wedge, T G (St Ives) 1907 F, 1909 W
Weighill, R H G (RAF, Harlequins) 1947 S, F, 1948 S, F
Wells, C M (Cambridge U, Harlequins) 1893 S, 1894 W, S, 1896 S, 1897 W, S
West, B R (Loughborough Colls, Northampton) 1968 W, I, F, S, 1969 SA, 1970 I, W, S
West, D E (Leicester) 1998 F (R), S (R), 2000 Arg (R), 2001 W, It, S, F (t), C 1, 2, US, I (R), A, SA, 2002 F (R), W (R), It (R), 2003 W 2(R), F 2, 3(t+R), [U, F(R)]
West, R (Gloucester) 1995 [WS]
Weston, H T F (Northampton) 1901 S
Weston, L E (W of Scotland) 1972 F, S
Weston, M P (Richmond, Durham City) 1960 W, I, F, S, 1961 SA, W, I, F, S, 1962 W, I, F, 1963 W, I, F, S, NZ 1, 2, A, 1964 NZ, W, I, F, S, 1965 F, S, 1966 S, 1968 F, S
Weston, W H (Northampton) 1933 I, S, 1934 I, S, 1935 W, I, S, 1936 NZ, W, S, 1937 W, I, S, 1938 W, I, S
Wheatley, A A (Coventry) 1937 W, I, S, 1938 W, S
Wheatley, H F (Coventry) 1936 I, 1937 S, 1938 W, S, 1939 W, I, S
Wheeler, P J (Leicester) 1975 F, W, 1976 A, W, S, I, 1977 S, I, F, W, 1978 F, W, S, I, NZ, 1979 S, I, F, W, NZ, 1980 I, F, W, S, 1981 W, S, I, F, 1982 A, S, I, F, W, 1983 F, S, I, NZ, 1984 S, I, F, W
White, C (Gosforth) 1983 NZ, 1984 S, I, F
White, D F (Northampton) 1947 W, I, S, 1948 I, F, 1951 S, 1952 SA, W, S, I, F, 1953 W, I, S
White, J M (Saracens, Bristol, Leicester) 2000 SA 1, 2, Arg, SA 3, 2001 F, C 1, 2, US, I, R (R), 2002 S, W, It, 2003 F 1(R), W 2, F 2, 3, [Sm, U(R)], 2004 W(R), F(R), NZ1, 2, A1, C, SA, A2, 2005 W, 2006 W(R), It(R), S, F, I, A1, 2, NZ, Arg, SA1, 2, 2007 S(R), It(R), I(R), F1, W1, 2009 It(R), W(R), I(t&R), F(t&R), S(R), Arg 1(R), 2
White-Cooper, W R S (Harlequins) 2001 C 2, US
Whiteley, E C P (O Alleynians) 1931 S, F
Whiteley, W (Bramley) 1896 W
Whitely, H (Northern) 1929 W
Wightman, B J (Moseley, Coventry) 1959 W, 1963 W, I, NZ 2, A
Wigglesworth, H J (Thornes) 1884 I
Wigglesworth, R E P (Sale, Saracens) 2008 It(R), F, S, I, NZ1, 2011 W2(R), 3, I2, [Arg, R(R), S(R), F(R)], 2013 Arg1(R), 2(R)
Wilkins, D T (United Services, RN, Roundhay) 1951 W, I, F, S, 1952 SA, W, S, I, F, 1953 W, I, F, S
Wilkinson, E (Bradford) 1886 W, I, S, 1887 W, S
Wilkinson, H (Halifax) 1929 W, I, S, 1930 F
Wilkinson, H J (Halifax) 1889 M
Wilkinson, J P (Newcastle, Toulon) 1998 I (R), A 1, NZ 1, 1999 S, I, F, W, A, US, C, [It, NZ, Fj, SA (R)], 2000 I, F, W, It, S, SA 2, A, Arg, SA 3, 2001 W, It, S, F, I, A, SA, 2002 S, I, F, W, It, NZ, A, SA, 2003 F 1, W 1, It, S, I, NZ, A, F 3, [Gg, SA, Sm, W, F, A], 2007 S, It, I, SA1, 2, W2, F2(R), F3, [Sm, Tg, A, F, SA2], 2008 W, It, F, S, I(R), 2009 A, Arg 3, NZ, 2010 W, It, I, S, F(R), A1(R), 2(R), 2011 W1(R), It(R), F(R), S(R), I1(R), W2, I2, [Arg, R, S, F]
Wilkinson, P (Law Club) 1872 S
Wilkinson, R M (Bedford) 1975 A 2, 1976 A, W, S, I, F
Willcocks, T J (Plymouth) 1902 W
Willcox, J G (Oxford U, Harlequins) 1961 I, F, S, 1962 W, I, F, S, 1963 W, I, F, S, 1964 NZ, W, I, F, S
William-Powlett, P B R W (United Services, RN) 1922 S
Williams, C G (Gloucester, RAF) 1976 F
Williams, C S (Manchester) 1910 F
Williams, J E (O Millhillians, Sale) 1954 F, 1955 W, I, F, S, 1956 I, S, F, 1965 W
Williams, J M (Penzance-Newlyn) 1951 I, S
Williams, P N (Orrell) 1987 S, [A, J, W]
Williams, S G (Devonport A) 1902 W, I, S, 1903 I, S, 1907 I, S
Williams, S H (Newport) 1911 W, F, I, S
Williamson, R H (Oxford U) 1908 W, I, S, 1909 A, F
Wilson, A J (Camborne S of M) 1909 I
Wilson, C E (Blackheath) 1898 I
Wilson, C P (Cambridge U, Marlborough N) 1881 W
Wilson, D G (Newcastle, Bath) 2009 Arg 1, 2(R), A, NZ(R), 2010 W, It(R), I(R), S(R), F(R), A1(R), 2(t&R), NZ(R), A3(R), Sm, SA(R), 2011 W1(R), It(R), W2(R), [R(R)], 2012 Fj(R), SA4(R), NZ(R), 2013 S(R), I(R), It(R), W(R), Arg1, 2
Wilson, D S (Met Police, Harlequins) 1953 F, 1954 W, NZ, I, S, F, 1955 F, S
Wilson, G S (Tyldesley) 1929 W, I
Wilson, K J (Gloucester) 1963 F
Wilson, R P (Liverpool OB) 1891 W, I, S
Wilson, W C (Richmond) 1907 I, S
Winn, C E (Rosslyn Park) 1952 SA, W, S, I, F, 1954 W, S, F
Winterbottom, P J (Headingley, Harlequins) 1982 A, S, I, F, W, 1983 F, W, S, I, NZ, 1984 S, F, W, SA 1, 2, 1986 W, S, I, F, 1987 I, F, W, [A, J, US, W], 1988 F, W, S, 1989 R, Fj, 1990 I, F, W, S, Arg 1, 2, 3, 1991 W, S, I, F, A, [NZ, It, F, S, A], 1992 S, I, F, W, C, SA, 1993 F, W, S, I
Winters, R A (Bristol) 2007 SA1(R), 2
Wintle, T C (Northampton) 1966 S, 1969 I, F, S, W
Wodehouse, N A (United Services, RN) 1910 F, 1911 W, F, I, S, 1912 W, I, S, F, 1913 SA, W, F, I, S
Wood, A (Halifax) 1884 I
Wood, A E (Gloucester, Cheltenham) 1908 F, W, I
Wood, G W (Leicester) 1914 W
Wood, M B (Wasps) 2001 C 2(R), US (R)
Wood, R (Liversedge) 1894 I
Wood, R D (Liverpool OB) 1901 I, 1903 W, I
Wood, T A (Northampton) 2011 W1, It, F, S, I1, W2(R), 3, [Gg, R(R)], 2012 Fj(R), A(R), SA4, NZ, 2013 S, I, F, It, W, Arg1, 2
Woodgate, E E (Paignton) 1952 W
Woodhead, E (Huddersfield) 1880 I
Woodman, T J (Gloucester) 1999 US (R), 2000 I (R), It (R), 2001 W (R), It (R), 2002 NZ, 2003 S (R), I(t + R), A, F 3, [Gg, SA, W(R), F, A], 2004 It, S, I, W, F, NZ1, 2
Woodruff, C G (Harlequins) 1951 W, I, F, S
Woods, S M J (Cambridge U, Wellington) 1890 W, S, I, 1891 W, I, S, 1892 I, S, 1893 W, I, 1895 W, I, S
Woods, T (Bridgwater) 1908 S
Woods, T (United Services, RN, Pontypool) 1920 S, 1921 W, I, S, F
Woodward, C R (Leicester) 1980 I (R), F, W, S, 1981 W, S, I, F, Arg 1, 2, 1982 A, S, I, F, W, 1983 I, NZ, 1984 S, I, F, W
Woodward, J E (Wasps) 1952 SA, W, S, 1953 W, I, F, S, 1954 W, NZ, I, S, F, 1955 W, I, 1956 S
Wooldridge, C S (Oxford U, Blackheath) 1883 W, I, S, 1884 W, I, S, 1885 I
Wordsworth, A J (Cambridge U) 1975 A 1(R)
Worsley, J P R (Wasps) 1999 [Tg, Fj], 2000 It (R), S (R), SA 1(R), 2(R), 2001 It (R), S (R), F (R), C 1, 2, US, A, R, SA, 2002 S, I, F, W (t+R), Arg, 2003 W 1(R), It, S(R), I(t), NZ(R), A(R), W 2, [SA(t), Sm, U], 2004 It, I, W(R), F, NZ1(R), 2, A1, SA, A2, 2005 W, F, I, It, S, 2006 W, It, S, F, I, A1(R), 2, SA1, 2, 2007 S, I, F1, W1, 2, F2, 3(R), [US, Sm, A(R), F(R), SA2(R)], 2008 NZ1(R), 2(R), 2009 It(R), W, I, F, S, Arg 3(R), NZ, 2010 I(R), S, F, 2011 W1(R)
Worsley, M A (London Irish, Harlequins) 2003 It(R), 2004 A1(R), 2005 S(R)
Worton, J R B (Harlequins, Army) 1926 W, 1927 W
Wrench, D F B (Harlequins) 1964 F, S
Wright, C C G (Cambridge U, Blackheath) 1909 I, S
Wright, F T (Edinburgh Acady, Manchester) 1881 S
Wright, I D (Northampton) 1971 W, I, F, S (R)
Wright. J C (Met Police) 1934 W
Wright, J F (Bradford) 1890 W
Wright, T P (Blackheath) 1960 W, I, F, S, 1961 SA, W, I, F, S, 1962 W, I, F, S
Wright, W H G (Plymouth) 1920 W, F
Wyatt, D M (Bedford) 1976 S (R)

Yarde, M D (London Irish) 2013 Arg 2
Yarranton, P G (RAF, Wasps) 1954 W, NZ, I, 1955 F, S
Yates, K P (Bath, Saracens) 1997 Arg 1, 2, 2007 SA1, 2
Yiend, W (Hartlepool R, Gloucester) 1889 M, 1892 W, I, S, 1893 I, S
Young, A T (Cambridge U, Blackheath, Army) 1924 W, I, F, S, 1925 NZ, F, 1926 I, F, S, 1927 I, S, F, 1928 A, W, I, F, S, 1929 I
Young, J R C (Oxford U, Harlequins) 1958 I, 1960 W, I, F, S, 1961 SA, W, I, F
Young, M (Gosforth) 1977 S, I, F, W, 1978 F, W, S, I, NZ, 1979 S
Young, P D (Dublin Wands) 1954 W, NZ, I, S, F, 1955 W, I, F, S
Youngs, N G (Leicester) 1983 I, NZ, 1984 S, I, F, W
Youngs, B R (Leicester) 2010 S(R), A1(R), 2, NZ, A3, Sm, SA, 2011 W1, It, F, S, I1, [Arg(R), Gg, R, S, F], 2012 S, It, W(R), F(R), I(R), SA 1, 2, Fj(R), A(R), SA4, NZ, 2013 S, I, F, It(R), W
Youngs, T N (Leicester) 2012 Fj, A, SA4, NZ, 2013 S, I, F(R), It, W

FIJI

FIJI'S 2012–13 TEST RECORD

OPPONENTS	DATE	VENUE	RESULT
England	10 Nov	A	Lost 54–12
Georgia	24 Nov	A	Won 24–19
Japan	1 Jun	H	Won 22–8
Canada	5 Jun	A	Lost 20–18
USA	19 Jun	N	Won 35–10
Tonga	23 Jun	N	Won 34–21

FIJI CELEBRATE CENTENARY YEAR WITH SILVERWARE

Kenji Demura (RJP)

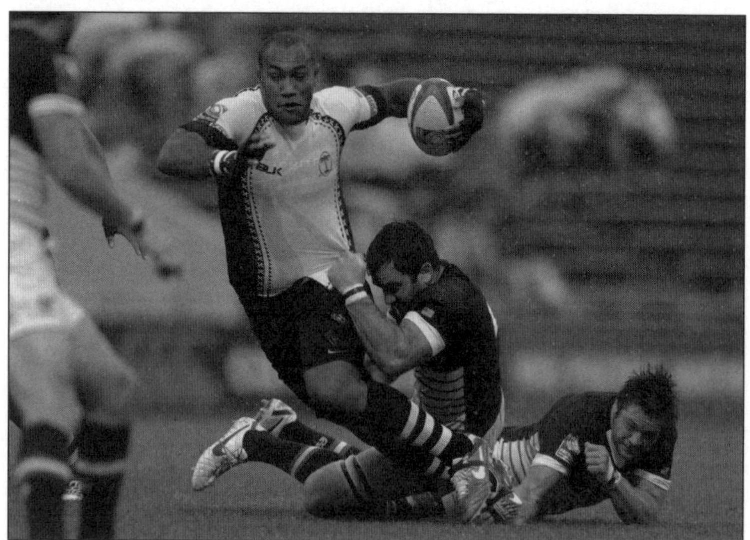

Fiji crushed the USA 35–10 on their way to winning their first IRB Pacific Nations Cup crown.

A disappointing northern hemisphere tour sparked something of a revival for the Flying Fijians in 2013, the year in which the Pacific Island nation marked 100 years of rugby with a maiden IRB Pacific Nations Cup title and a fifth successive IRB Pacific Rugby Cup crown.

This success was a far cry from the disappointment experienced in November 2012 when Fiji kicked off their European tour with a 54–12 loss to England in front of 82,000 people at Twickenham. Worse was to follow with a 53–0 defeat by an Ireland XV at Thomond Park. The tour then concluded with an historic first visit to Georgia. Fiji didn't have it all their own way, needing two second-half penalties to secure a 24–19 victory in Tbilisi.

Fiji then learned the pool that potentially awaited them at Rugby World Cup 2015 with the Oceania 1 qualifier drawn alongside hosts England, Australia, Wales and the Répechage winner in Pool A. Three mouth-watering matches that will undoubtedly mobilise the Fijians, who must overcome the Cook Islands in 2014 to claim the Oceania 1 berth.

Attention then turned to the Pacific Rugby Cup with Fiji's second string to face the best up-and-coming players in Australia and New Zealand. The Warriors' opener against the HSBC Waratahs A side was called off due to poor weather, but they went on to beat the Australian Rugby Union's Brisbane-based Academy team (24–17) and Rebel Rising (27–22). The New Zealand leg began with a 37–37 draw against the Highlanders Development XV before defeats by the Blues Development XV (41–10) and Hurricanes Development XV (38–20) left the Fijians top. With the final series involving the core teams cancelled, the Warriors celebrated another successful title defence.

Buoyed by this success, coach Inoke Male turned his attention to the Pacific Nations Cup. Fiji made an impressive start with a 22–8 victory over Japan in extremely wet conditions in Lautoka.

Four days later Fiji took on Canada in Ottawa in a match that went right down to the wire, their impressive captain Akapusi Qera's late try not enough to prevent the Canadians from recording a first victory over the Islanders since 1995. The only compensation for the 20–18 defeat was a losing bonus point.

After a two-week break the Pacific Nations Cup concluded in Japan. A strong second-half display saw Fiji beat the USA 35–10, crucially securing a try bonus point in the driving rain. That win – allied with Canada's loss to Japan – meant Fiji were one of three nations in contention for the title going into the final round. Their destiny was in their own hands: beat Tonga and they would be crowned champions. Tonga started the brighter and led 11–0 but Fiji recovered to win 34–21 with Qera proclaiming it "a touching achievement as it's been a big year for Fiji rugby".

Less than a week later, the rugby-loving Fijians had their sights set on Moscow for Rugby World Cup Sevens. Fiji's men were among the favourites, bidding to lift the Melrose Cup for the third time, while their women were making their World Cup debut. It was the Fijiana, though, who returned home with silverware as Bowl winners having shown the new-look team's potential.

"I am really proud for all of our girls. We played with a lot of hunger and we are going to get better," said coach Timoci Wainiqolo.

Fiji's men, meanwhile, having scraped into the Cup quarter-finals as the second-best runner-up, beat South Africa 12–10 and were trailing New Zealand in the semi-final when heavy rain began to fall and lightning lit up the sky, forcing the teams off and an hour delay. New Zealand went on to win 17–0 with Fiji having to settle for third after beating Kenya 29–5.

The HSBC Sevens World Series had begun perfectly for Fiji in October 2012 with victory on Australia's Gold Coast, but it would be round six in Hong Kong before they would reach another final. Trailing 19–0 at half-time against Wales, super-sub Osea Kolinisau scored three tries to secure a thrilling 26–19 win for Fiji. Failure to progress beyond the Cup quarter-finals in the remaining three events, however, meant Fiji finished third.

Without doubt, though, the biggest story in 2013 was the induction of Fiji's favourite son Waisale Serevi into the IRB Hall of Fame during the Hong Kong Sevens. "I am honoured and humbled by this recognition from the IRB. The game of rugby has given my family and me so much and it is a privilege to join so many amazing players in the Hall of Fame," said Serevi.

FIJI INTERNATIONAL STATISTICS

MATCH RECORDS UP TO 10 OCTOBER 2013

WINNING MARGIN

Date	Opponent	Result	Winning Margin
10/09/1983	Niue Island	120–4	**116**
21/08/1969	Solomon Islands	113–13	**100**
08/09/1983	Solomon Islands	86–0	**86**
30/08/1979	Papua New Guinea	86–0	**86**
23/08/1969	Papua New Guinea	88–3	**85**

MOST POINTS IN A MATCH

BY THE TEAM

Date	Opponent	Result	Points
10/09/1983	Niue Island	120–4	**120**
21/08/1969	Solomon Islands	113–13	**113**
23/08/1969	Papua New Guinea	88–3	**88**
08/09/1983	Solomon Islands	86–0	**86**
30/08/1979	Papua New Guinea	86–0	**86**

BY A PLAYER

Date	Player	Opponent	Points
10/09/1983	Severo Koroduadua	Niue Island	**36**
21/08/1969	Semesa Sikivou	Solomon Islands	**27**
28/08/1999	Nicky Little	Italy	**25**

MOST TRIES IN A MATCH

BY THE TEAM

Date	Opponent	Result	Tries
21/08/1969	Solomon Islands	113–13	**25**
10/09/1983	Niue Island	120–4	**21**
23/08/1969	Papua New Guinea	88–3	**20**
18/08/1969	Papua New Guinea	79–0	**19**
30/08/1979	Papua New Guinea	86–0	**18**

BY A PLAYER

Date	Player	Opponent	Tries
30/08/1979	Tevita Makutu	Papua New Guinea	**6**
18/08/1969	George Sailosi	Papua New Guinea	**5**

MOST CONVERSIONS IN A MATCH

BY THE TEAM

Date	Opponent	Result	Cons
21/08/1969	Solomon Islands	113–13	**19**
10/09/1983	Niue Island	120–4	**18**
23/08/1969	Papua New Guinea	88–3	**14**

BY A PLAYER

Date	Player	Opponent	Cons
10/09/1983	Severo Koroduadua	Niue Island	**18**
21/08/1969	Semesa Sikivou	Solomon Islands	**12**
07/10/1989	Severo Koroduadua	Belgium	**10**

MOST PENALTIES IN A MATCH

BY THE TEAM

Date	Opponent	Result	Pens
08/07/2001	Samoa	28–17	**7**

BY A PLAYER

Date	Player	Opponent	Pens
08/07/2001	Nicky Little	Samoa	**7**
26/05/2000	Nicky Little	Tonga	**6**
25/05/2001	Nicky Little	Tonga	**6**
05/10/1996	Nicky Little	Hong Kong	**6**
08/07/1967	Inoke Tabualevu	Tonga	**6**

MOST DROP GOALS IN A MATCH

BY THE TEAM

Date	Opponent	Result	DGs
02/07/1994	Samoa	20–13	**3**
12/10/1991	Romania	15–17	**3**

BY A PLAYER

Date	Player	Opponent	DGs
02/07/1994	Opeti Turuva	Samoa	**3**

MOST CAPPED PLAYERS

Name	Caps
Nicky Little	71
Jacob Rauluni	50
Joeli Veitayaki	49
Emori Katalau	47
Norman Ligairi	47

LEADING TRY SCORERS

Name	Tries
Senivalati Laulau	18
Norman Ligairi	16
Viliame Satala	16
Fero Lasagavibau	16

LEADING CONVERSION SCORERS

Name	Cons
Nicky Little	117
Severo Koroduadua	56
Seremaia Bai	47

LEADING PENALTY SCORERS

Name	Pens
Nicky Little	140
Seremaia Bai	51
Severo Koroduadua	47
Waisale Serevi	27

LEADING DROP GOAL SCORERS

Name	DGs
Opeti Turuva	5
Severo Koroduadua	5
Waisale Serevi	3

LEADING POINT SCORERS

Name	Points
Nicky Little	670
Seremaia Bai	270
Severo Koroduadua	268
Waisale Serevi	221

FIJI INTERNATIONAL PLAYERS
UP TO 10 OCTOBER 2013

A Apimeleki 1924 *Sa, Tg, Tg, Tg, Sa,* 1926 *Tg, Tg*
S Aria 1986 *W,* 1988 *Tg, Sa, E, Tg,* 1991 *C, F,* 1993 *Sa, Tg,* 1994 *J*

S Baikeinuku 2000 *J, US, C, It,* 2001 *Tg, Sa, Tg,* 2002 *W, I, S,* 2004 *Tg, Sa,* 2005 *M, NZ, Tg, Sa, Tg, Sa, W, It,* 2006 *Tg, It, Sa, J,* 2007 *J, C, A, W, SA,* 2009 *Sa, J, S, I,* 2010 *F, W, It,* 2011 *J, NZ, Tg, Nm, SA, Sa, W,* 2013 *CAB, US, Tg*
EM Bakaniceva 2010 *J, Tg*
J Bale 2004 *Tg, Sa,* 2005 *M, NZ, Tg, Sa, Tg, Sa, W, It,* 2006 *Tg, It, Sa, J*
P Bale 1995 *C, Sa, Tg, W, I*
S Baleca 1951 *M,* 1952 *A, A,* 1954 *A, A*
DV Baleinadogo 2001 *Tg, Sa, Tg, Sa, C, Sa,* 2002 *Sa, Tg,* 2007 *Sa, J*
K Baleisawani 2004 *Tg, Sa*
N Baleiverata 1988 *Tg, Sa, E,* 1990 *J*
D Baleiwai 1990 *J, HK,* 1991 *Tg, C, F, R*
J Balewai 1926 *Tg, Tg,* 1928 *Tg, Tg, Tg, Sa,* 1932 *Tg, Tg, Tg*
S Banuve 1990 *Tg*
S Baravilala 1934 *Tg, Tg, Tg,* 1947 *Tg, Tg,* 1948 *M, M*
M Bari 1995 *Sa, Tg, W, I,* 1996 *Sa, Tg, HK, HK, M,* 1997 *NZ, Coo, Sa,* 1998 *S, US, A, Tg,* 1999 *Ur, F*
G Barley 1964 *W, F,* 1970 *M, C*
I Basiyalo 1994 *J*
S Basiyalo 1976 *I*
A Batibasaga 1967 *Tg,* 1968 *Tg, Tg,* 1969 *W, PNG, SI, PNG*
I Batibasaga 1974 *M*
I Batibasaga 1970 *C,* 1972 *Tg, Tg, Tg, A,* 1973 *Tg, E,* 1974 *M, M,* 1976 *I,* 1977 *Tg, Tg,* 1979 *M*
A Batikaciwa 1932 *Tg, Tg, Tg,* 1934 *Tg, Tg, Tg*
E Batimala 1994 *J, J, M, W, Sa, Tg,* 1995 *C, Sa, Tg,* 1996 *HK,* 1998 *S*
J Bibi 1928 *Tg, Tg, Tg, Sa*
TM Biumaiwai 1954 *A, A, M, M*
PTQ Biu 1999 *Sp, Ur,* 2000 *J, Tg, Sa,* 2001 *It, F,* 2002 *Sa, Tg, Sa, NZ, Tg,* 2003 *CHL*
M Black 1996 *SA, Sa, Tg, HK*
S Bobo 2004 *Tg, Sa,* 2005 *M, NZ, Tg, W, Pt,* 2007 *W, SA,* 2010 *A,* 2013 *J, CAB, US, Tg*
R Bogisa 1994 *J, W,* 1995 *C, W*
K Bogiwalu 1924 *Sa, Tg, Tg, Tg, Sa,* 1926 *Tg, Tg*
A Boko 2009 *S, I, R*
A Bola 1934 *Tg*
D Bola 1983 *Sa, Niu, Tg,* 1984 *A, Sa, NZ*
E Bola 1939 *M*
IC Bolakoro 2009 *Sa,* 2011 *Sa*
K Bola 2009 *R,* 2010 *Tg, Sa,* 2012 *J, Sa, Tg, E, Geo*
MS Bola 2009 *Tg, Sa, J, S, I, R,* 2010 *A, J, Tg, Sa,* 2011 *Tg, Sa,* 2012 *J, Sa, Tg, Geo*
FV Bolavucu 2009 *Tg, J*
E Bolawaqatabu 1963 *Sa, Tg, Sa, Tg,* 1969 *W, PNG, SI, PNG,* 1970 *M, M,* 1972 *Tg, Tg, Tg, A,* 1973 *M, M*
P Bolea 2001 *Sa*
P Bosco 1968 *Tg, Tg,* 1970 *M, M,* 1972 *Tg, Tg, Tg, A,* 1973 *M, M, Tg, E,* 1977 *Tg, Tg, Tg, BI,* 1979 *M, E*
A Bose 1932 *Tg, Tg, Tg,* 1934 *Tg, Tg, Tg*
E Bose 1998 *Sa*
K Bose 1958 *Tg, Tg, Tg,* 1959 *Tg,* 1961 *A, A, A*
V Bose 1980 *A*
I Buadromo 1970 *C*
VT Buatava 2007 *Sa, J, A,* 2010 *A,* 2011 *Tg, Sa, J, NZ, Tg, Tg, Nm, SA, Sa, W*
T Bucaonadi 1983 *Tg, Sa*
S Bueta 1986 *Tg*
V Bueta 1982 *Sa, Sa, E*
V Buli 1963 *Sa, Tg, Sa, Tg*
A Burogolevu 1954 *A, A*
A Buto 2012 *J, Sa, S*

I Cagilaba 1974 *M,* 1976 *I,* 1977 *Tg, Tg,* 1979 *M, E, F, PNG, Sa*
GK Cakobau 1939 *M*
J Cama 1987 *NZ*
T Cama 1985 *A, A, I, W,* 1987 *Ar, NZ, It, F, Sa, Tg,* 1989 *Tg, Tg,* 1990 *Sa*
A Camaibau 1948 *M, M*
J Campbell 1994 *J, J, M, W, Sa, Tg*
R Caucau 2003 *Ar, CHL, F, S,* 2006 *It, Sa,* 2010 *A*
J Cavalevu 1951 *M,* 1952 *A, A,* 1954 *A, A, M, M, M*
S Cavu 1958 *Tg,* 1961 *A,* 1963 *Sa, Tg, Sa, Tg,* 1964 *M, W, F, C,* 1967 *Tg, Tg,* 1968 *NZ*
VB Cavubati 1995 *Sa, Tg,* 1997 *NZ, Tg, Coo, Sa,* 1998 *F,* 1999 *C, US,* 2001 *Sa, C, Sa, It, F,* 2002 *NZ, Tg, W, I, S,* 2004 *Tg, Sa,* 2005 *M, NZ, Tg, Sa, Tg, Sa*
TGN Cavubati 2011 *Tg, J*

R Cavubuka 1985 *Tg*, 1986 *Sa*, *Tg*
K Cavuilati 1948 *M*, *M*, 1951 *M*, 1952 *A*
ST Cavuilati 1974 *NZ*, *M*, 1976 *A*, *A*
R Cavukubu 1986 *W*
I Cawa 1952 *A*, 1957 *M*, *M*
RI Cawa 1928 *Tg*, *Tg*, 1932 *Tg*, *Tg*, *Tg*, 1934 *Tg*, *Tg*, *Tg*, 1938 *M*, *M*, *M*
I Cerelala 1980 *NZ*, *Ar*
M M Cevalawa 1948 *M*, *M*
I Cobitu 1947 *Tg*, *Tg*, 1948 *M*, *M*, *M*

S Dakuiyaco 2000 *C*
J Dakuvula 2010 *J*
J Damu 1985 *I*, *W*, 1986 *W*, 1987 *F*
P Damu 2000 *J*, *Sa*, *US*, *C*, *It*, 2001 *Tg*, *Sa*, *Tg*, *C*, *Sa*
P Dau 1991 *Tg*, 1992 *Tg*
V Daunibau 1932 *Tg*, *Tg*, *Tg*
S Daunitutu 1963 *Sa*, *Tg*, *Sa*, *Tg*, 1964 *M*, *W*, *F*, *C*
J Daunivucu 2007 *A*, *W*, 2009 *Tg*, *Sa*
I Daveta 1932 *Tg*, *Tg*, *Tg*, 1934 *Tg*, *Tg*, *Tg*
M Davu 2001 *It*, *F*
E Dawai 1947 *Tg*
L Dawai 1947 *Tg*, *Tg*
O Dawai 1954 *A*, *M*, *M*, *M*, 1957 *M*, *M*, 1958 *Tg*, *Tg*, *Tg*, 1959 *Tg*, 1961 *A*, *A*
A Delai 2011 *Tg*, *Sa*, *Tg*, 2013 *J*, *C*, *Tg*
Delana 1926 *Tg*
V Delasau 2000 *US*, *C*, *It*, 2001 *Tg*, *Tg*, *Sa*, *C*, *Sa*, *It*, *F*, 2002 *Sa*, *NZ*, 2003 *Tg*, *F*, *US*, *J*, *S*, 2005 *M*, *NZ*, *Tg*, *Sa*, 2007 *J*, *C*, *A*, *W*, *SA*, 2008 *Sa*, *M*
A Dere 1986 *W*, 1989 *Bel*, *S*, *E*, 1990 *J*, *HK*, 1991 *Tg*, *E*, *C*, *F*, *R*
I Derenalagi 2001 *F*
V Devo 1924 *Sa*, *Tg*, *Tg*, *Tg*, *Sa*
GC Dewes 2007 *J*, *A*, *Tg*, *J*, *C*, *W*, *SA*, 2008 *Sa*, *M*, *Tg*, 2009 *Tg*, *Sa*, *J*, *S*, *I*, *R*, 2010 *A*, *J*, *Tg*, *Sa*, *F*, *W*, 2011 *Tg*, *J*, 2012 *J*, *Tg*
I Domolailai 2001 *It*, *F*, 2005 *M*, *NZ*, *Tg*, *Sa*, *Sa*, *W*, 2006 *Tg*, *It*, *Sa*, *J*, 2007 *A*
JU Domolailai 2008 *Tg*, 2009 *Tg*, *Sa*, *J*, *S*, 2011 *Tg*, *Sa*, *NZ*, *Tg*, 2012 *Sa*, *S*, *Tg*, *Geo*
S Domoni 1952 *A*, 1954 *A*, 1957 *M*
SR Domoni 1990 *HK*, 1991 *Tg*, *Tg*, *E*, *C*, *F*
JAR Dovi 1938 *M*, *M*, *M*
RAR Doviverata 1999 *Sp*, 2000 *J*, *Tg*, *Sa*, *US*, *C*, *It*, 2001 *Tg*, *Sa*, *Tg*, *Sa*, *C*, *Sa*, *It*, *F*, 2002 *Sa*, *Tg*, *Sa*, *NZ*, *Tg*, *W*, *I*, 2003 *Tg*, *Tg*, *F*, *US*, *J*, *S*, 2004 *Tg*, *Sa*, 2005 *W*, *It*, 2006 *It*, *Sa*, *J*, 2007 *Sa*, *J*, *A*, *Tg*
A Doviverata 1948 *M*
A Durusolo 1928 *Tg*, *Tg*

A Eastgate 1968 *NZ*
J Edwards 1988 *Tg*
A Elder 1994 *J*
L Erenavula 1989 *Tg*, *Bel*, *S*, *E*, 1990 *J*, *Sa*, 1992 *M*

RS Fatiaki 2009 *J*, 2011 *Sa*, *J*, *NZ*, *Tg*, *Tg*, *SA*, *W*, 2012 *E*
I Finau 1980 *A*, *It*, *NZ*, *Ar*, *Ar*, 1983 *Tg*, *Sa*, *SI*, *Niu*, *Sa*, 1984 *A*, *Tg*, *NZ*, 1985 *Sa*, *A*, *I*, *W*, 1986 *Tg*
S Fuli 2004 *Sa*

VT Gadolo 2000 *J*, 2002 *Tg*, *S*, 2003 *Tg*, *Tg*, *Ar*, *CHL*, *J*, 2005 *M*, *NZ*, *Tg*, *Sa*, *Tg*, *Sa*, *W*, *Pt*, *It*, 2007 *J*, *A*, *SA*
P Gale 1984 *Tg*, 1985 *Sa*, *Tg*, *A*, *A*, *I*, *W*, 1987 *Ar*, *Sa*, *Tg*, 1988 *Sa*, *E*
RP Ganilau 1939 *M*
R Ganilau 1979 *M*, *E*, *Tg*
S Ganilau 1951 *M*, 1952 *A*
E Gaunavou 1961 *A*, *A*, *A*
I Gavidi 2005 *Pt*, *It*
R Gavidi 1934 *Tg*, *Tg*, *Tg*, 1938 *M*
W Gavidi 1972 *Tg*, *Tg*, *A*, 1973 *M*, *E*, 1974 *NZ*, *M*, *M*, 1976 *A*, *A*, 1977 *Tg*, *Tg*, *Tg*, *BI*, 1979 *M*, *E*, *F*, 1980 *A*, *It*, *NZ*
V Goneva 2007 *Sa*, *J*, *A*, *Tg*, 2008 *J*, *Tg*, 2009 *Sa*, *J*, *S*, *I*, *R*, 2010 *W*, *It*, 2011 *Tg*, *Sa*, *NZ*, *Tg*, *Tg*, *Nm*, *SA*, *Sa*, *W*, 2012 *J*, *Sa*, *S*, *Tg*, *E*, *Geo*
A Gutugutuwai 1967 *Tg*, 1968 *NZ*, *Tg*, 1969 *PNG*
S Gutugutuwai 1982 *Sa*, 1983 *Tg*, *Sa*, *Niu*, *Tg*, *Sa*, 1984 *A*, *Sa*, *Tg*, *NZ*, 1985 *Sa*, *Tg*

R Howard 1977 *Tg*, *Tg*, *Tg*
P Hughes 1973 *Tg*, *E*
APT Hughes 1985 *Sa*, *Tg*, *A*, *I*, *W*, 1986 *Sa*, *Tg*

M Kafoa 1994 *J*, *J*
S Kalou 2010 *A*, *J*, *Tg*, *Sa*, *F*, *W*, *It*, 2011 *Tg*, *Sa*, *NZ*, *Nm*, *Sa*, 2012 *E*
E Katalau 1995 *C*, *Sa*, *Tg*, *W*, *I*, 1996 *SA*, *Sa*, *Tg*, *HK*, *HK*, *M*, 1997 *NZ*, *Tg*, *Coo*, *Sa*, 1998 *S*, *F*, *US*, *A*, 1999 *C*, *US*, *J*, *Tg*, *Sa*, *M*, *Ur*, *It*, *Nm*, *C*, *F*, *E*, 2000 *J*, *Tg*, *Sa*, *US*, *C*, *It*, 2001 *Tg*, *Tg*, *Sa*, *C*, *It*, *F*, 2002 *S*, 2003 *Tg*, *Ar*, *J*
L Katowale 1991 *Tg*, *Tg*, *C*, *F*
IC Katonibau 2012 *J*, *Sa*, *Tg*
E Katonitabua 1984 *A*, *Sa*, *Tg*, *Tg*, *NZ*, 1985 *Sa*
P Kean 1982 *Sa*, 1983 *Tg*, *SI*, *Niu*, 1984 *A*
AR Kenatale 1988 *Tg*
A Kenatale 2013 *C*
NS Kenatale 2008 *J*, *Tg*, 2009 *Tg*, *Sa*, *J*, 2010 *F*, *W*, *It*, 2011 *Tg*, *Sa*, *NZ*, *Tg*, *Nm*, *SA*, *Sa*, *W*, 2012 *Sa*, *S*, 2013 *J*, *C*, *CAB*, *US*, *Tg*
S Kepa 1961 *A*
ILR Keresoni 2008 *Tg*, 2009 *Sa*, *J*, 2010 *J*, *Sa*, 2011 *J*, *NZ*, *Tg*, *Tg*, *Nm*, *W*
KR Ketedromo 2010 *J*, *Tg*, 2012 *J*, *S*, *Tg*
P Kewa Nacuva 1979 *F*, *PNG*, *Sa*, *Tg*, 1980 *NZ*, *M*, *Ar*
K Kida 1926 *Tg*, *Tg*, *Tg*
L Kididromo 1987 *NZ*, *F*, 1988 *Sa*, *Tg*
A Kikau 1948 *M*
O Kililoa 1986 *Sa*, *Tg*
P Kina 1976 *A*, *A*, *A*, 1979 *M*, *E*, *F*, 1980 *A*, *It*, *NZ*, *M*, *NZ*, *Ar*, *Ar*
E Kobiti 1924 *Sa*, *Tg*, *Tg*, *Tg*, *Sa*, 1926 *Tg*, *Tg*, *Tg*
O Koliloa 1986 *Tg*
Ratu Komaitai 1992 *M*, 1993 *S*, *Tg*
SS Koniferedi 2012 *J*, *S*, *Tg*, *E*, 2013 *J*, *C*, *CAB*
S Koroduadua 1982 *S*, *E*, 1983 *Tg*, *Sa*, *Niu*, *Tg*, *Sa*, 1985 *Sa*, *Tg*, *A*, *A*, 1987 *Ar*, *NZ*, *It*, *F*, *Sa*, *Tg*, 1988 *E*, *Tg*, 1989 *Sa*, *Tg*, *Tg*, *Bel*, *S*, *E*, 1990 *Sa*, 1991 *C*, *F*
A Koroi 1932 *Tg*, *Tg*, *Tg*, 1934 *Tg*
B Koroi 2012 *J*, *Tg*
L Koroi 1992 *Sa*, *Tg*, 1998 *US*, *A*
J Koroibanuve 1926 *Tg*
S Koroibanuve 1924 *Sa*, *Tg*, *Tg*, *Tg*, *Sa*
STR Koroilagilagi 2012 *J*, *Sa*, 2013 *J*, *C*, *US*, *Tg*
A Koroitamana 1992 *Tg*
S Koroitamuda 1924 *Sa*, *Tg*, *Tg*, *Tg*, *Sa*
I Koroiyadi 2001 *Tg*
A Kororua 1938 *M*, *M*, *M*
N Korovata 1990 *HK*, 1991 *Sa*, *Tg*
M Korovou 1994 *W*, *Tg*, 1995 *C*, *Tg*
I Korovulavula 1938 *M*, *M*, 1939 *M*
SD Koyamaibole 2001 *Tg*, *Sa*, *C*, *Sa*, *It*, *F*, 2002 *Sa*, *Tg*, *Sa*, *NZ*, *Tg*, *W*, *I*, *S*, 2003 *Tg*, *Tg*, *Ar*, *CHL*, *F*, *US*, *J*, *S*, 2004 *Tg*, *Sa*, 2005 *M*, *NZ*, *Tg*, *Sa*, *Sa*, *W*, *Pt*, *It*, 2007 *Tg*, *J*, *C*, *A*, *W*, *SA*, 2010 *F*, *W*, *It*, 2011 *J*, *Tg*, *Tg*, *SA*, *Sa*
SK Koto 2005 *M*, *Tg*, *Sa*, *Tg*, *W*, *It*, 2006 *Tg*, *It*, *Sa*, *J*, 2007 *Sa*, *J*, *A*, *Tg*, *J*, *C*, *W*, *SA*, 2008 *Sa*, *M*, *J*, *Tg*, 2009 *Tg*, *Sa*, *J*, 2011 *J*, *NZ*, *Tg*, *Tg*, *Nm*, *SA*, *Sa*, *W*
J Kubu 1985 *W*, 1986 *W*, *Tg*, *Sa*, *Tg*, 1987 *NZ*, *It*, *F*, *Sa*, *Tg*, 1988 *E*
P Kubuwai 1991 *Sa*, *Tg*
J Kuinikoro 1977 *Tg*, *Tg*, *Tg*, *BI*, 1979 *M*, *E*, *PNG*, *Sa*, *Tg*, 1980 *A*, *NZ*
I Kunagogo 1980 *A*, *NZ*, *M*
E Kunavore 1963 *Tg*, *Sa*
M Kunavore 2005 *Sa*, *Pt*, *It*, 2006 *It*, *J*, 2007 *C*, *A*
W Kunavula 1951 *M*
A Kunawave 1957 *M*, *M*, 1958 *Tg*, *Tg*, *Tg*, 1959 *Tg*
M Kurisaru 1968 *Tg*, *Tg*, *Tg*, 1969 *PNG*, *SI*, *PNG*, 1970 *M*, *C*, 1972 *Tg*, *Tg*, *Tg*, 1973 *M*, *Tg*, *E*, 1976 *A*
A Kuruisaqila 1957 *M*, 1959 *Tg*
R Kuruisiga 1926 *Tg*, *Tg*, *Tg*

M Labaibure 1948 *M*, *M*, *M*, 1952 *A*, 1954 *A*, *M*, *M*, *M*
E Labalaba 1979 *E*, *F*, *PNG*, *Sa*, *Tg*, 1980 *M*, 1981 *Tg*, *Tg*, *Tg*
P Lagilagi 1939 *M*
S Lala Ragata 1999 *Ur*, 2000 *J*, *Tg*, *Sa*, *US*
A Laqeretabua 1924 *Sa*, *Tg*, *Tg*, *Tg*, *Sa*, 1926 *Tg*, *Tg*, *Tg*, 1928 *Tg*, *Tg*, *Tg*, *Sa*, 1932 *Tg*, *Tg*, *Tg*, 1934 *Tg*, *Tg*, *Tg*, 1938 *M*, *M*
F Lasagavibau 1997 *NZ*, *Tg*, *Coo*, *Sa*, 1998 *S*, *F*, *US*, *Sa*, *Tg*, 1999 *C*, *US*, *Tg*, *Sa*, *M*, *Sp*, *Nm*, *C*, *F*, 2001 *It*, *F*, 2002 *W*, *I*, *S*
T Latianara 2002 *Sa*, *Tg*
T Latianara 1976 *I*
R Latilevu 1970 *C*, 1972 *Tg*, *Tg*, 1973 *E*, 1974 *NZ*, 1976 *A*, *A*
S Laulau 1980 *A*, *It*, *M*, *NZ*, *Ar*, *Ar*, 1981 *Sa*, *Sa*, *Tg*, *Tg*, *Tg*, 1982 *Sa*, *Sa*, *Sa*, *Tg*, 1983 *Tg*, *Sa*, *SI*, *Niu*, *Tg*, *Sa*, 1984 *A*, *Sa*, *Tg*, *Tg*, *NZ*, 1985 *Sa*, *Tg*, *A*, *A*, *I*, *W*
K Leawere 2002 *S*, 2003 *Tg*, *Tg*, *Ar*, *CHL*, *F*, *J*, 2004 *Tg*, *Sa*, 2005 *W*, *Pt*, *It*, 2007 *Sa*, *A*, *Tg*, *J*, *C*, *W*, *SA*, 2008 *Sa*, *M*, *J*, *Tg*, 2009 *Tg*, *Sa*, *J*
S Leawere 2003 *Tg*, *Ar*, *CHL*, 2006 *Tg*, *J*
I Ledua 2009 *Tg*, *Sa*, *J*, *S*, *I*, *R*
P Lese 1951 *M*
J Levula 1951 *M*, 1952 *A*, *A*, 1954 *A*, *A*, *M*, *M*, *M*, 1957 *M*, *M*, 1958 *Tg*, *Tg*, *Tg*, 1959 *Tg*, 1961 *A*, *A*, *A*

RWG Lewaravu 2007 *Sa, J, A, J, A, SA*, 2008 *Sa, M*, 2009 *S, I*, 2010 *F, It*, 2011 *Tg, Tg, Nm, SA, W*, 2013 *J, C, CAB, Tg*
I Leweniqila 1984 *Tg*
NAS Ligairi 2000 *Tg, Sa, US, C, It*, 2001 *Sa, Tg, Sa, C, Sa*, 2002 *Sa, Tg, Sa, NZ, Tg, W, I, S*, 2003 *Ar, CHL, F, J, S*, 2004 *Tg, Sa*, 2005 *M, NZ, Tg, Sa, Tg, Sa, W, It*, 2006 *Tg, It, Sa, J*, 2007 *Tg, J, C, A, W, SA*, 2009 *I, R*, 2010 *F, It*
S Ligamamada 1970 *C*, 1977 *Tg*
V Lilidamu 1986 *Tg, Tg*, 1988 *Tg*
L Little 1995 *C, Sa, Tg, W, I*, 1996 *SA, M*, 1997 *Tg, Coo, Sa*, 1998 *S*, 1999 *US, Tg, Sp*
N Little 1996 *SA, Sa, Tg, HK, HK, M*, 1997 *NZ, Tg, Coo, Sa*, 1998 *S, F, US, Sa*, 1999 *C, US, J, Tg, Sa, Sp, It, Nm, C, F, E*, 2000 *J, Tg, Sa, US, C, It*, 2001 *Tg, Sa, Tg, Sa, C, Sa, It, F*, 2002 *Sa, Tg, Sa, NZ, W, I*, 2003 *Tg, Tg, Ar, CHL, F, US, J, S*, 2005 *M, NZ, Tg, Sa, Tg, Sa, It*, 2007 *J, C, W*, 2009 *S, I*, 2011 *Tg, Sa, Tg, SA, Sa, W*
Livai 1926 *Tg*
V Loba 1939 *M*
D Lobendhan 1973 *M, Tg*, 1976 *A*
J Lotawa 2004 *Tg, Sa*, 2006 *Tg, J*
T Lovo 1989 *S, E*, 1990 *HK*, 1991 *Tg, C, F*, 1993 *S, Sa, Tg*
GV Lovobalavu 2007 *J, A, Tg, A, SA*, 2009 *S, I, R*, 2010 *F, W, It*, 2011 *Tg, Nm, SA, Sa, W*
E Lovodua 1958 *Tg, Tg, Tg*, 1961 *A, A, A*, 1963 *Sa, Tg, Sa, Tg*, 1964 *M*
S Lovokuru 1986 *W, Sa, Tg*, 1987 *NZ*
I Lutumailagi 1979 *F, PNG*, 1980 *It, NZ, M, Ar, Ar*, 1982 *Tg*
JB Lutumailagi 2013 *J, C, CAB*
M Luveitasau 2005 *Sa, Tg, Sa, W, It*, 2006 *Tg, It, Sa*, 2007 *A*
WS Luveniyali 2007 *Tg, A*, 2008 *Sa, M, J, Tg*, 2009 *Sa, J*, 2010 *A*, 2011 *Sa, J, Tg, Tg, Nm, SA, Sa*

GDC Ma'afu 2010 *A, J, Tg, Sa, W, It*, 2011 *Sa, NZ, Tg, Tg, Nm, SA, Sa, W*, 2013 *J, C, CAB, US, Tg*
V Maimuri 2003 *Ar, F, US, J, S*
I Makutu 1976 *A, A, A*
RPN Makutu 2011 *Tg, Sa, J*, 2012 *E*
T Makutu 1979 *PNG, Sa, Tg*, 1980 *NZ, M, NZ, Ar, Ar*, 1981 *Sa, Sa, Tg, Tg, Tg*, 1982 *Sa, Sa*
K Malai 1988 *Tg, Sa, Tg*
IM Male 1998 *A*, 1999 *Ur, E*, 2000 *J, Tg, Sa, US, C, It*, 2001 *Tg, Sa, Tg, Sa, C, Sa*
E Malele 1973 *Tg*, 1976 *I*
D Manaseitava 1981 *Sa*, 1983 *Niu, Sa*, 1985 *Sa, Tg*
DT Manu 2009 *S*, 2010 *A, F, W, It*, 2011 *Tg, Sa, NZ, Tg, Nm, SA, Sa*, 2012 *E*
A Mara 1928 *Tg, Tg, Tg, Sa*
W Masirewa 1995 *Sa, W, I*, 1998 *A*
M Masitabua 1974 *M*
MS Matadigo 2006 *Tg*, 2009 *Tg*, 2011 *Sa, NZ, Tg, SA, W*, 2013 *CAB, US*
E Matalau 1976 *A, A*
S Matalulu 1994 *M, W, Sa*
J Matanatabu 1993 *Sa, Tg*
A Matanibuka 1932 *Tg, Tg, Tg*, 1934 *Tg, Tg, Tg*
A Matanibukaca 2005 *M, NZ, Tg, Tg*
S Matasarasara 1928 *Tg, Tg*
JL Matavesi 2009 *S, I, R*, 2010 *F, W*, 2012 *E*
S Matavesi 2013 *C*
NL Matawalu 2010 *J, Tg, Sa*, 2012 *J, S, Tg, E, Geo*, 2013 *J, CAB, US, Tg*
L Matea 1924 *Sa, Tg, Tg, Tg, Sa*
W Mateiwai 1993 *Sa, Tg, Tg*
N Matirawa 1984 *Tg*, 1989 *Tg, Tg, E*
JTF Matson 1999 *M, Ur*
J McLennan 1994 *M, W, Sa, Tg*, 1995 *C*, 1996 *HK*
T Mitchell 1986 *Tg, Tg*, 1987 *It, F, Sa, Tg*, 1988 *Tg, Sa, E, Tg, Tg*
AM Mocelutu 1994 *J, J, M, W, Sa, Tg*, 1995 *C, Sa*, 1997 *Tg, Coo, Sa*, 1998 *S, US, Sa, Tg*, 1999 *M, Ur, It, Nm, C, F*, 2001 *Tg*, 2002 *Sa, Tg, Sa, NZ, W, I, S*, 2003 *Tg, Ar, CHL, US, J*
V Mocelutu 1974 *NZ, M, M*
M Mocetadra 2012 *Tg*
S Morrell 2009 *J*
I Mow 2002 *Sa, Tg, Sa, Tg*, 2003 *Tg*
A Mucunabita 1994 *J, J*
J Mucunabitu 1957 *M, M*, 1959 *Tg*, 1964 *M, W, F*, 1968 *NZ, Tg, Tg*
K Murimurivalu 2011 *Tg, Tg, Tg, Nm, SA, Sa*
I Musanamasi 1982 *Sa, Sa, E*, 1983 *SI*
K Musunamasi 1977 *Tg, Tg, Tg, BI*, 1979 *M, E, PNG, Sa*

L Nabaro 1976 *I*
N Nabaro 1957 *M, M*, 1959 *Tg*, 1961 *A, A, A*, 1964 *M*
M Nabati 1985 *A, A, W*
O Nabavu 1926 *Tg, Tg*
K Nabili 1926 *Tg*, 1928 *Tg, Tg, Tg, Sa*
K Nabili 1985 *Tg*
I Nabobo 1976 *I*
G Naborisi 1992 *Tg*
G Naborisi 1954 *A*
I Nabou 1961 *A, A, A*
M Nabuta 1967 *Tg, Tg*, 1968 *NZ, Tg, Tg, Tg*, 1969 *PNG, SI, PNG*
S Nacaka 1981 *Tg*, 1982 *Sa, Tg, S*
F Naceba 1924 *Sa, Tg, Tg, Tg, Sa*
I Nacewa 2003 *S*
S Nacolai 1968 *NZ, Tg, Tg*, 1969 *W, SI, PNG*
V Nadaku 1934 *Tg, Tg*, 1938 *M, M, M*
A Nadolo 1987 *It, F, Sa, Tg*, 1988 *E, Tg, Tg*, 1989 *Tg, Tg*, 1991 *Sa, Tg, Tg, R*, 1992 *Sa, Tg*, 1993 *S, Sa, Tg, Tg*, 1995 *C, Sa, Tg, I*
J Nadolo 2000 *Tg, Sa, US, C, It*
A Nadredre 1964 *F, C*, 1968 *Tg*
M Nadridri 2004 *Sa*, 2005 *Sa, Tg*
N Nadruku 1988 *Tg, Sa, E, Tg, Tg*, 1989 *Tg, Bel, S, E*, 1990 *J, HK*, 1991 *C, R*
S Nadruku 1981 *Sa, Sa, Tg, Tg*, 1982 *Sa, Sa, Sa, Tg, S, E*, 1983 *SI, Tg*, 1984 *Sa, Tg, NZ*
A Naevo 1996 *HK, HK, M*, 1997 *NZ, Tg, Sa*, 1998 *S, F, US, Sa, Tg*, 1999 *J, Tg, Sa, M, Sp, Ur, It, Nm, C*, 2001 *Tg, Sa, Tg, Sa, C, Sa*, 2002 *W, I, S*, 2003 *Tg, Tg, F, US, S*
RMS Naevo 2006 *Sa, J*, 2007 *J, C, W, SA*, 2008 *Sa, M, J*, 2009 *Tg, Sa*, 2010 *F, W, It*
I Nagatalevu 1939 *M*
A Nagi 2001 *It, F*, 2004 *Tg, Sa*, 2005 *W, Pt, It*, 2006 *Tg, It, Sa, J*
A Nagicu 1996 *HK*
N Nagusa 2012 *Geo*, 2013 *CAB*
T Nagusa 2008 *Sa, M, J*, 2009 *Tg, I, R*, 2010 *A, J*, 2011 *Tg, J, NZ*, 2013 *US*
Naibuka 1968 *Tg*
T Naidole 1954 *M*, 1957 *M, M*, 1958 *Tg, Tg, Tg*, 1959 *Tg*
S Naiduki 1979 *PNG, Sa, Tg*
J Naikadawa 2009 *R*, 2010 *A, J, It*, 2011 *J*
AN Naikatini 2012 *J, Sa, S, Tg, E, Geo*, 2013 *J, C, CAB, US, Tg*
J Naikidi 1982 *S*
M Naikovu 1957 *M, M*, 1958 *Tg, Tg, Tg*
O Naikovu 1947 *Tg, Tg*, 1948 *M*, 1954 *M*
W Daveta Nailago 2011 *J, Tg, Tg, Nm, SA, W*, 2012 *J, Sa, S*
M Nailumu 1976 *I*
J Naisilisili 2010 *Tg, Sa*
K Naisoro 1991 *Sa, Tg, Tg, F, R*
V Naisoro 1938 *M, M, M*
S Naitau 1968 *Tg, Tg*
S Naiteqe 2000 *J, Tg, Sa, US, It*, 2001 *Sa*
T Naitini 1947 *Tg, Tg*
E Naituivau 1990 *Tg, Sa, HK*, 1991 *Tg, E, C, R*, 1992 *M*, 1995 *W, I*, 1996 *SA, Sa, Tg, HK, M*, 1997 *NZ, Tg, Coo, Sa*, 1999 *Nm, E*
E Naituku 1987 *Ar, It*
I Naituku 1988 *Tg, Sa, E, Tg*, 1990 *Sa*, 1993 *S*
R Naituku 1986 *W*
S Naituku 1983 *SI*, 1985 *A, A, I*, 1986 *Sa*, 1987 *Ar, It, F, Sa, Tg*, 1988 *Tg*, 1989 *Tg, Tg, Bel, S, E*, 1990 *J*
A Naituyaga 1997 *NZ, Tg, Coo, Sa*
A Naituyaga 1972 *A*, 1974 *NZ, M, M*, 1976 *A*
S Naivilawasa 1986 *Tg*, 1987 *Ar, It, F, Tg*, 1988 *Tg, Sa, E, Tg, Tg*, 1989 *Tg, Tg, Bel, S, E*, 1990 *Tg*, 1991 *Sa, Tg, E, C*
L Nakarawa 2009 *I, R*, 2010 *Tg, Sa*, 2011 *Tg, Sa, Tg, Nm, SA, Sa, W*, 2012 *J, Sa, S, Tg, E, Geo*
M Nakauta 1998 *F, US, Sa*, 1999 *Sp, Ur, It, Nm, F, E*
T Nakauta 1987 *Sa, Tg*, 1988 *Tg*
K Nalaga 1986 *Sa*, 1987 *Ar*, 1989 *Tg*
N Nalaga 2009 *S*, 2010 *F, It*, 2011 *J, NZ, Nm, SA, Sa*, 2013 *CAB, US, Tg*
K Nalatu 1967 *Tg, Tg*, 1970 *M, M*, 1973 *M, M*
V Nalio 1961 *A*, 1963 *Sa, Tg, Tg*, 1964 *M, W*, 1967 *Tg*, 1968 *NZ*
L Namadila 1973 *E*, 1974 *M*, 1976 *I*, 1980 *It*
R Namoro 1982 *Sa, S, E*, 1983 *Tg, Sa, Sa*, 1984 *A, Sa, Tg, Tg, NZ*, 1985 *Sa, A, A, I, W*, 1986 *W, Tg, Tg*, 1987 *Ar, F*
I Namua 1969 *PNG*
N Nanuku 2005 *Pt*
A Naqaya 2000 *J, Tg*
S Naqelevuki 1967 *Tg, Tg*, 1968 *Tg, Tg, Tg*, 1969 *W, PNG, SI, PNG*, 1970 *M, M*, 1972 *A*
SM Naqelevuki 2008 *Sa, M, J, Tg*, 2010 *Tg, Sa, F*, 2012 *E*
J Narisia 1972 *A*, 1973 *Tg*
V Narisia 1977 *Tg, Tg, Tg, BI*, 1979 *F, PNG, Sa, Tg*
V Narisia 1990 *J, Tg*
A Nariva 2002 *S*, 2003 *Tg, Tg*
J Narruhn 2002 *Sa, Tg, Sa, NZ, Tg, W, I, S*

P Naruma 1988 Tg, Sa, E, Tg, 1989 Tg, Tg, S, 1990 Tg, Sa, 1991 F, R, 1992 Sa, M, 1993 S, Sa
P Nasalo 1968 Tg, Tg, 1969 W, 1970 M
W Nasalo 1974 NZ, 1976 A, A
S Nasau 1998 S
S Nasave 1969 W, SI, 1970 M, 1972 Tg, Tg, 1973 M, M, 1974 NZ, M, M, 1976 A, A, A, 1977 BI, 1979 M, E, F, PNG, Sa, Tg
R Nasiga 2008 Tg, 2010 A, J, Sa, 2011 Sa, J, NZ, Tg, Tg, Sa, W, 2013 J, CAB, Tg
RND Nadolo 2010 A, J, Tg, 2013 J, C, CAB, US, Tg
S Nasilasila 1996 HK
J Nasova 1963 Sa, 1964 M, W, C, 1967 Tg, Tg, Tg, 1968 NZ, Tg, Tg
K Natoba 2000 US, C, It, 2001 Tg, Tg, Sa
AK Natoga 2012 Geo, 2013 J, C, CAB, Tg
M Natuilagilagi 1989 E, 1990 Tg, 1991 Sa, Tg, 1992 Sa, M, 1993 Sa, Tg
S Natuna 1924 Sa, Tg, Tg, Tg, Sa, 1928 Tg, Tg, Tg, Sa
W Natuna 1982 Sa, Tg
J Naucabalavu 1961 A, A, A, 1963 Sa, 1964 W, F, C, 1967 Tg
J Naucabalavu 1963 Sa, Tg, Sa, Tg, 1964 M, W, F, C, 1967 Tg, Tg, Tg, 1968 NZ, Tg, Tg, Tg, 1969 PNG, SI, PNG, 1970 M
J Naucabalavu 1972 Tg, Tg, Tg, A, 1973 M, E, 1974 NZ, M, 1976 A, A, 1980 A, It
E Nauga 1992 M, 1993 S, 1994 J, J, M, W, Sa
B Naulago 1985 Sa, Tg
S Naureure 2012 J, Sa, Tg, E, Geo
S Naurisau 1954 M, 1959 Tg
M Navugona 1992 Sa, Tg
A Nawalu 1954 A, A, M, M
P Nawalu 1983 Tg, SI, Sa, 1984 Tg, Tg, NZ, 1985 Sa, Tg, A, A, I, W, 1986 W, 1987 Ar, NZ, It, F, Sa
P Nayacakalou 1957 M
A Nayacalagilagi 1926 Tg
K Nayacalevu 1980 M, NZ
WN Nayacalevu 2012 J, Sa, S
TR Nayate 1979 M
I Neivua 2007 Sa, J, A, Tg, J, C, A, W
P Nicuvu 1980 NZ
E Nima 1947 Tg, Tg, 1948 M
S Niqara 1996 M
AS Niuqila 1983 Sa, SI, Tg, Sa, 1984 A, Sa, Tg, NZ, 1985 Sa, Tg, A, A, I, W, 1986 W
M Nukuvou 1947 Tg, Tg, 1948 M, M, 1952 A
R Nyholt 2001 F, 2002 Sa, Tg, Sa, NZ, Tg, W, I, 2003 Tg, Ar, CHL, F, US

M Olsson 1988 Tg, 1990 Tg, Sa, HK, 1991 Sa, E, R
S Ose 1967 Tg

S Pe 1951 M, 1954 A, M, M, M
G Penjueli 1994 J
L Peters 2005 Sa, Tg, Sa, 2007 Sa, J
LD Politini 1982 Sa, E, 1983 Sa, Tg
JJV Prasad 2004 Tg, Sa, 2005 Tg, Tg, Sa, Pt, 2007 Sa, J, A
E Puamau 1976 I

R Qalo 1968 NZ, Tg
R Qaraniqio 1972 A, 1973 M, M, 1974 NZ, M, 1976 I, 1977 Tg, Tg, BI, 1979 M, E, 1980 A, It, NZ, 1981 Sa, Sa, Tg, Tg, Tg
I Qauqau 1999 Sa
A Qera 2005 Sa, Tg, Pt, 2006 Tg, It, J, 2007 Sa, J, A, J, C, W, SA, 2008 Sa, 2009 S, I, 2010 F, W, It, 2011 J, NZ, Tg, Nm, SA, Sa, W, 2012 E, 2013 J, C, CAB, US, Tg
A Qio 1926 Tg, Tg, Tg
AQ Qiodravu 2000 US, C, It, 2001 Tg, Sa, Tg, Sa, C, Sa, It, F, 2007 A, Tg, J, C, A, W, SA
I Qio Ravoka 1947 Tg, Tg, 1948 M, M
J Qoro 1985 Tg
J Qoro 1968 Tg, Tg, 1969 W, PNG, SI, PNG, 1970 M, M, 1972 Tg, Tg, Tg, 1973 M
M Qoro 1987 Ar, It, F, Sa, 1989 Bel
N Qoro 1998 A, 1999 C, US, J, Tg, Sa, M, Sp
JQ Qovu 2005 M, NZ, Tg, Sa, Tg, Sa, Pt, It, 2007 A, 2010 A, F, W, It
S Qurai 1938 M, M, M, 1939 M

S Rabaka 1992 Sa, M, 1993 Tg, 1994 J, J, 1998 S, US, 1999 C, US, J, Tg, Sa, 2001 Tg, Tg, Sa, C, Sa, It, F, 2002 Sa, Tg, Sa, NZ, Tg, W, I, 2003 Tg, F, J
T Rabaka 1991 Sa, Tg, Tg, R
RS Rabeni 2000 J, 2002 Sa, Tg, Sa, NZ, Tg, W, 2003 Tg, Tg, Ar, CHL, F, US, J, S, 2004 Tg, Sa, 2006 Tg, It, Sa, J, 2007 J, C, A, W, SA, 2009 Tg, 2010 F, It, 2011 J
S Rabici 1926 Tg, Tg, 1928 Tg, Tg, Tg
A Rabitu 1990 J, Sa, 1993 S, Sa, Tg
S Rabitu 1932 Tg, Tg, Tg, 1934 Tg, Tg, Tg
S Rabonaqica 2008 J, Tg
T Rabuli 1972 Tg, 1973 M, Tg, E, 1974 M, M, 1976 A, A, A
A Racika 1969 SI, 1970 M, M, C, 1972 Tg, Tg, Tg, A, 1973 M, M, Tg, E, 1974 NZ, M, M, 1976 A, A, 1977 Tg, Tg, Tg, BI, 1979 M, E, F, PNG, Sa, Tg, 1980 A, It, NZ
S Radidi 2008 M, Tg, 2010 A, 2012 Geo, 2013 Tg
U Radike 1959 Tg
U Radike 1938 M, M, M
A Radrado 1989 Tg, Tg
M Radrekusa 1988 Tg
I Radrodo 1951 M
I Radrodro 1957 M, 1958 Tg, Tg, Tg
I Radrodro 1980 A, It, NZ
J Radrodro 1970 M, M, C
J Raikuna 1963 Sa, Tg, Tg, 1964 M, C, 1967 Tg, Tg, 1968 NZ, Tg, Tg, Tg, 1969 W, SI, PNG, 1970 M
JR Railomo 2005 NZ, 2007 J, C, A, W, SA, 2008 Sa, M, J, Tg
L Raitilava 1968 NZ, 1969 W, PNG, SI, PNG, 1972 Tg, Tg, Tg, A, 1976 A, A
S Raiwalui 1997 NZ, Tg, Coo, Sa, 1998 S, F, US, A, Sa, Tg, 1999 C, US, J, Tg, Sa, M, Sp, It, Nm, C, F, E, 2000 J, Tg, Sa, US, C, It, 2001 Sa, C, Sa, 2002 Sa, Tg, Sa, NZ, Tg, W, I, S, 2006 Tg, It, Sa, J
E Rakai 1983 SI, Tg, Sa, 1984 A, Sa, Tg, 1985 Sa, Tg, A, A, I, W, 1986 W, Sa, Tg, 1987 NZ, F
K Rakoroi 1983 Tg, SI, Niu, Tg, 1984 A, Sa, Tg, 1985 A, A, I, W, 1986 W, Tg, Sa, Tg, 1987 Ar, NZ, It, F, Sa, Tg
S Ralagi 1951 M, 1952 A, A, 1954 A, A
S Ralawa 1934 Tg, Tg, Tg, 1938 M, M, M, 1939 M
J Ralulu 2008 Sa, Tg, 2010 J, Tg, Sa, 2012 S, Tg, Geo
TD Ralumu 1979 E, F
T Ranavue 1947 Tg, Tg, 1952 A, A, 1954 A, A, M, M, M
S Rarasea 1961 A
V Rarawa 2010 It
L Rasala 1994 J, J
M Rasari 1988 Tg, Sa, E, Tg, 1989 Bel, S, E, 1990 Sa, 1991 Sa, Tg
I Rasila 1992 Sa, M, 1998 S, F, A, 1999 C, US, Sp, Ur, E, 2000 J, Tg, Sa, US, C, It, 2001 Tg, Sa, Tg, Sa, C, Sa, It, 2002 Sa, Tg, Sa, NZ, S, 2003 Tg, Tg, Ar, CHL, J, S
P Rasiosateki 1963 Sa, Tg, 1964 M, W, F, C
S Rasolea 1984 Tg, NZ, 1985 Sa, Tg, A
S Rasua 1961 A, A, A
J Ratu 1980 NZ, Ar, Ar, 1981 Sa, Tg, Tg, Tg, 1982 Sa, Tg, S, E
Q Ratu 1976 I, 1977 Tg, Tg, Tg, BI
R Ratu 2009 Sa, J, 2010 A, J, Tg, Sa, W
S Ratu 1968 Tg
J Ratu 2009 S, R
N Ratudina 1972 Tg, Tg, 1973 M, M, E, 1974 NZ, M, M, 1977 Tg, Tg, Tg, BI, 1979 M, F
E Ratudradra 1980 A, M, NZ, Ar, Ar, 1981 Tg, Tg, Tg
V Ratudradra 1976 A, A, 1977 Tg, BI, 1979 M, E, 1980 NZ, M, 1981 Sa, Sa, 1982 Sa, 1984 Tg
S Ratumaiyali 1947 Tg
K Ratumuri 1980 M, 1981 Sa, Sa
E Ratuniata 2001 Sa, Tg, 2002 Sa, Sa
A Ratuniyarawa 2012 E, Geo, 2013 J, C, CAB, US, Tg
RARG Ratuva 2005 M, NZ, Tg, Tg, Sa, W, It, 2006 Sa, J, 2007 Tg, J, A, W, SA, 2008 Sa, M, J, Tg
I Ratuva 2012 J, Sa, S, Tg, E, Geo, 2013 C, US
N Ratuveilawa 1961 A, 1963 Sa, Tg, Sa, Tg, 1964 C
K Ratuvou 2005 Sa, W, Pt, It, 2006 Tg, It, Sa, J, 2007 Tg, J, C, W, SA, 2008 Sa, M, J, 2012 Sa, S
SD Raulini 1997 Sa
T Raulumi 1973 M
J Rauluni 1995 C, Sa, Tg, W, I, 1996 SA, Sa, Tg, 1997 NZ, Tg, 1998 S, F, US, Sa, Tg, 1999 J, M, Ur, It, Nm, C, F, E, 2000 Sa, C, It, 2001 Sa, Tg, Sa, C, Sa, 2002 Sa, Tg, Sa, NZ, Tg, W, I, S, 2003 Tg, Tg, S, 2005 M, NZ, Tg, Sa, Tg, 2006 It, Sa, J
MN Rauluni 1996 M, 1997 Tg, Coo, Sa, 1998 A, 1999 Sp, It, C, E, 2000 J, Tg, US, C, It, 2001 Tg, 2003 Ar, CHL, F, US, J, S, 2004 Tg, Sa, 2005 M, NZ, Tg, Sa, Tg, Sa, W, Pt, It, 2007 A, Tg, J, C, A, W, SA, 2008 Sa, M, 2009 S, I
P Rauluni 1984 A, Sa, Tg, 1986 Sa, Tg
T Rauluni 1968 Tg, 1972 Tg, 1974 NZ, M
V Rauluni 1990 Sa, 1991 Sa, Tg, E
V Rauluni 2007 Sa, J, A
V Rauluni 1992 Sa, 1993 S, Tg
J Rauto 1976 A, A, A, 1977 Tg, Tg, BI, 1979 M, E, 1980 Ar, Ar, 1981 Sa, Sa, Tg, Tg, Tg, 1982 Sa, Sa, Tg, E, 1984 Tg, NZ
P Ravaga 1926 Tg, Tg, 1928 Tg, Tg, Tg, Sa

J Ravai 1928 *Tg, Tg, Tg, Sa*
M Ravai 1928 *Tg, Tg*
E Ravi 1961 *A, A, A*
E Ravouvou 1928 *Tg, Tg, Tg, Sa*
I Ravouvou 1958 *Tg, Tg, Tg*, 1959 *Tg*
I Ravouvou 1986 *Sa, Tg*, 1987 *Sa, Tg*
J Ravouvou 1979 *PNG, Sa, Tg*, 1980 *NZ, M, NZ, Ar, Ar*
N Ravouvou 1967 *Tg, Tg, Tg*, 1968 *NZ, Tg, Tg*, 1969 *W, PNG, SI, PNG*, 1970 *M, M, C*, 1972 *A*, 1973 *M, M, Tg, E*
T Ravouvou 1948 *M*
J Ravu 1948 *M, M*, 1954 *M, M, M*
T Ravualala 1976 *I*
M Ravula 1958 *Tg, Tg, Tg*
RMM Ravulo 2010 *F, W*, 2011 *Tg, Sa, NZ, Tg, Nm, Sa, W*, 2012 *J, Sa, S, E, Geo*, 2013 *J, C, CAB, US, Tg*
I Rawaqa 2002 *Sa, Tg, Sa, NZ, Tg, I*, 2003 *Ar, CHL, F, US, S*, 2004 *Tg, Sa*, 2005 *M, NZ, Tg, Sa, Tg, Sa, W, Pt, It*, 2006 *Tg, It*, 2007 *J, A, Tg, C, A, W, SA*, 2008 *Sa, M, J*, 2009 *Sa, S, I*, 2010 *W*, 2011 *J*
RT Rawaqa 2007 *Sa, J, A*, 2008 *Sa, M, J, Tg*, 2009 *Tg, Sa, J*, 2010 *A, Tg, Sa, W*, 2011 *Sa, J, NZ*
F Rayasi 1994 *M, W, Sa, Tg*, 1995 *C, Sa, Tg, W, I*, 1996 *SA, HK, HK*, 1997 *NZ*
E Rayawa 1961 *A*
J Rayawa 1979 *F, PNG, Sa, Tg*
P Rika 1958 *Tg, Tg*
A Rinakama 2001 *Sa, C, Sa*
A Robe 1964 *W, F, C*
S Rokini 2000 *J, Tg, Sa, US*, 2001 *Sa, Tg, Sa, C, Sa, It*, 2003 *CHL*
S Rokobaro 2004 *Tg, Sa*, 2005 *M, NZ*
N Rokobiau 2009 *I, R*
E Rokowailoa 1982 *Sa, Tg, S*, 1983 *Tg, Niu, Tg, Sa*, 1987 *Ar, NZ, It*, 1990 *J, Tg, Sa*, 1992 *M*, 1993 *S, Sa, Tg, Tg*
D Rouse 1995 *C, Tg, W*, 1996 *SA, Sa, Tg, HK, HK, M*, 1997 *NZ, Tg, Coo, Sa*, 1998 *US, A, Sa, Tg*, 1999 *US, J, Tg, Sa, M, Ur, It, Nm, C, F, E*
S Rovuaka 1947 *Tg, Tg*
E Ruivadra 2002 *Tg, Tg, W, S*, 2003 *Tg, J, S*, 2005 *M, NZ, Tg, Sa, Tg, W, Pt, It*, 2006 *Tg, J*, 2010 *J, Sa*

S Sacere 1968 *Tg*
S Sadria 1991 *Sa, Tg, Tg*, 1993 *Sa, Tg*, 1994 *J, J, M*
P Sailasa 1934 *Tg*
G Sailosi 1969 *W, PNG, PNG*
K Salabogi 2005 *W, Pt, It*, 2006 *It*
W Salabogi 1951 *M*, 1952 *A, A*, 1954 *A, A*
L Saladoka 1947 *Tg*
K Salawa 2003 *Tg, Tg, Ar, CHL, F, S*
I Salusalu 2012 *Sa*, 2013 *C*
K Salusalu 1982 *Tg, S, E*, 1983 *Tg, Sa, SI, Niu, Tg, Sa*, 1987 *It, F, Sa, Tg*, 1990 *Sa*
R Samo 2005 *Tg, Tg*, 2006 *Tg, It, Sa, J*
R Samuels 1973 *M, M, Tg, E*, 1974 *NZ, M, M*
J Sanday 1987 *Ar, It*
K Sarai 1988 *Tg, Sa, Tg*
M Sarasau 1976 *I*
A Sassen 1993 *Tg*
A Satala 2005 *Tg, Sa, Tg*, 2007 *A*, 2009 *I, R*
V Satala 1999 *C, US, J, Tg, Sa, M, Sp, It, Nm, C, F, E*, 2000 *C, It*, 2001 *Tg, Sa, Tg, C, Sa, It, F*, 2002 *Tg, Sa, NZ, Tg, I, S*, 2005 *M, NZ*
I Saukuru 1994 *J, J, M*
J Saukuru 1954 *A, A, M, M, M*, 1957 *M, M*, 1958 *Tg, Tg, Tg*, 1959 *Tg*, 1963 *Sa, Tg, Sa, Tg*
WR Saukuru 2010 *Tg, Sa*
RMS Saulo 2012 *E, Geo*, 2013 *J, C, CAB, US, Tg*
S Saumaisue 1998 *S, F, US*
M Saunaki 1984 *NZ*
S Sautu 1957 *M, M*, 1958 *Tg, Tg, Tg*
V Sauturaga 2007 *Tg, C, A, W*, 2008 *Sa, M, J*, 2009 *R*
I Savai 1984 *A, Sa, Tg, Tg, NZ*, 1985 *Sa, Tg, A*, 1987 *Ar, NZ, It, F*, 1989 *Tg, Tg, Bel, S, E*, 1990 *J, Tg, Sa, HK*, 1991 *Sa, Tg, E, C, F, R*, 1992 *Sa, Tg, M*, 1993 *Tg*, 1994 *J, J, M, W, Sa, Tg*, 1995 *C*
M Seavula 1988 *Sa*, 1989 *Tg, Bel*
A Secake 1957 *M*, 1958 *Tg*, 1959 *Tg*
N Senilagakali 1980 *NZ, Ar, Ar*
M Seniloli 1926 *Tg, Tg, Tg*, 1928 *Tg, Sa*
R Seniloli 1934 *Tg, Tg, Tg*
T Seniloli 1926 *Tg*, 1928 *Sa*
I Senivau 1968 *NZ*
W Serevi 1989 *Bel, S*, 1990 *J, Sa*, 1991 *Tg, E, C, F*, 1992 *Sa*, 1993 *S*, 1996 *SA, Tg, M*, 1998 *S, F, US, A, Sa, Tg*, 1999 *Tg, Sa, M, Sp, Ur, It, Nm, C, E*, 2001 *It, F*, 2002 *W, I, S*, 2003 *Tg, Ar, CHL, F, J*
F Seru 1990 *Tg, Sa, HK*, 1991 *Tg, E, C, F, R*, 1992 *Sa*, 1993 *Tg*
N Seru 2003 *Ar, CHL, F, US, J, S*
S Seru 1980 *M, NZ*
S Seruvakula 2002 *Sa*
SG Seruvatu 1952 *A, A*, 1954 *A, M, M, M*, 1959 *Tg*
V Seuseu 2008 *Sa, M, J, Tg*, 2009 *Tg, Sa, I, R*
S Sevu 2001 *Sa*
K Sewabu 1999 *C, US, J, Tg, Sa, M, Sp, It, Nm, C, F, E*, 2000 *US, C, It*, 2002 *Sa, NZ, Tg*, 2003 *Tg, Tg, Ar, US, J, S*
S Sikivou 1968 *Tg*, 1969 *W, PNG, SI, PNG*, 1970 *M, M*, 1973 *M*
R Silotolu 1954 *M, M, M*
M Sisiwa 1994 *J*
G Smith 1995 *W, I*, 1996 *SA, Sa, Tg, HK, HK, M*, 1997 *NZ, Tg, Coo, Sa*, 1998 *US, Sa, Tg*, 1999 *J, Tg, Sa, M, It, Nm, C, F, E*, 2000 *US, C, It*, 2001 *Tg, Sa, Tg, Sa, C, Sa*, 2002 *Sa, Tg, Sa, NZ, Tg, W, I, S*, 2003 *F, US, J, S*
J Sokovata 1963 *Sa, Tg, Tg*, 1964 *M*
S Somoca 2011 *J, NZ, Tg, Sa, W*, 2012 *J, Sa, S, Tg, E, Geo*, 2013 *J, C, CAB, US, Tg*
TN Soqeta 2007 *Sa, J, A*
A Soqosoqo 1964 *M, W, F, C*
SC Sorovaki 1995 *C, Sa, Tg, W, I*, 1996 *SA, Sa, Tg, HK, HK, M*, 1997 *NZ, Tg, Coo, Sa*, 1998 *S, F, US, A, Sa, Tg*
W Sotutu 1999 *C, US, J, Tg, M, Sp, Ur, It, Nm, C, F, E*
V Sovalevu 1992 *Sa, Tg*
J Sovau 1970 *M, M, C*, 1972 *A*, 1973 *M*, 1974 *M*, 1976 *A, A*, 1979 *PNG, Sa, Tg*
Sovu 1928 *Sa*
W Suka 1990 *HK*, 1993 *Sa, Tg*
WS Suka 2009 *Tg, J*
J Suluaqalo 1932 *Tg, Tg, Tg*
A Suluoqalo 1964 *M*
J Susu 1948 *M, M, M*, 1951 *M*, 1952 *A, A*

J Tabaiwalu 1957 *M, M*, 1958 *Tg, Tg, Tg*, 1959 *Tg*, 1961 *A, A, A*, 1963 *Sa, Sa*
S Tabua 2005 *M, NZ*
I Tabualevu 1984 *Sa, Tg*
I Tabualevu 1958 *Tg, Tg, Tg*, 1967 *Tg, Tg, Tg*
S Tabualevu 1983 *Sa*
L Tabuarua 2013 *J, C, US*
M Tabukaci 1947 *Tg, Tg*
P Tabulutu 1986 *Tg, Sa, Tg*, 1987 *Ar, Sa, Tg*, 1988 *Tg, E, Tg, Tg*, 1990 *J, Sa*, 1991 *Sa, Tg, E, C, F, R*
S Tadulala 2009 *R*
MV Taga 1987 *NZ*, 1988 *Tg, Sa, E, Tg*, 1989 *Tg, Tg, Bel, S, E*, 1990 *J, Tg, HK*, 1991 *Sa, Tg, E, C, F*, 1992 *Sa, Tg, M*, 1993 *S, Sa, Tg, Tg*, 1996 *HK, M*, 1997 *NZ, Coo*, 1998 *S, F, A*
N Taga 1952 *A*
N Tagi 2004 *Tg, Sa*
ML Tagicakibau 2007 *Tg*, 2008 *J*, 2010 *W*, 2011 *Tg, W*
MS Tagivetaua 1981 *Tg, Tg*, 1982 *Sa, Sa*, 1983 *Tg, Sa*
S Taka 2006 *Tg*, 2007 *Sa, J*, 2010 *F, W*
S Talawadua 1985 *A*
M Talebula 2012 *S, Tg, E, Geo*
NE Talei 2006 *Tg, It, Sa, J*, 2007 *Sa, J, J, C, A*, 2008 *Sa, M, J, Tg*, 2009 *Tg, Sa, J*, 2011 *Tg, Nm, SA, Sa, W*, 2012 *J, Sa, S*, 2013 *J, CAB, US, Tg*
V Taliga 1928 *Tg, Sa*
S Tamanibeka 1924 *Sa, Tg, Tg, Tg, Sa*, 1926 *Tg*, 1928 *Tg, Tg, Tg, Sa*
M Tamanitoakula 1998 *S, F, A*
I Tabua 1990 *J, Tg*, 1995 *W*, 1998 *F, A, Sa, Tg*, 1999 *C, US, J, Tg, Sa, M, Sp, It, C, F*
S Tamanivalu 1967 *Tg, Tg, Tg*
T Tamanivalu 1995 *I*, 1996 *SA, Sa, Tg, HK, HK, M*
M Tamata 1981 *Sa, Sa, Tg, Tg, Tg*, 1982 *Tg, S, E*
N Tamaya 1981 *Sa*
A Tani 2009 *Tg*
B Tanivukavu 1957 *M*
I Taoba 1974 *M*, 1976 *A, A, A*, 1977 *Tg, Tg, Tg, BI*, 1980 *A, It, NZ*, 1981 *Sa, Sa, Tg, Tg, Tg*, 1982 *Tg, S, E*
J Taqaiwai 1991 *Tg, E*
J Taqiri 1976 *A*
A Tarogi 2009 *J, I, R*
I Tasere 1974 *NZ, M, M*
E Tatawaqa 1981 *Tg, Tg, Tg*, 1982 *Sa, Sa, Sa, Tg, S*
P Tatukivei 1958 *Tg*
E Tauga 1994 *Tg*
I Taukei 1924 *Sa, Tg, Tg, Tg, Sa*, 1926 *Tg*
I Tawake 1986 *W*, 1987 *Sa, Tg*, 1988 *Tg, Tg*, 1990 *J*, 1991 *Tg, E, C, F, R*, 1992 *Sa, Tg, M*, 1993 *S, Sa, Tg*, 1994 *J, J, M, W, Sa, Tg*, 1995 *C, Sa, Tg, W, I*, 1996 *SA, Sa, Tg, HK, M*, 1997 *NZ, Coo, Sa*, 1998 *S, F, US, A*, 1999 *C, US, Tg, Sp, Ur, E*

S Tawake 1992 *Sa, M,* 1998 *Sa, Tg,* 1999 *C, US, J, M, It, Nm, C, F, E,* 2002 *Sa, NZ, Tg, W, I, S,* 2003 *CHL*
S Tawase 1961 *A, A*
E Teleni 1982 *Sa, Sa, S, E,* 1983 *Tg, Sa, Niu, Tg, Sa,* 1984 *A, Sa, Tg,* 1985 *A, A, I, W,* 1986 *W,* 1988 *Tg,* 1989 *Tg, Tg, Bel, S, E*
L Temani 1924 *Sa, Tg, Tg, Tg, Sa*
DD Thomas 2007 *Tg,* 2008 *M, Tg*
I Tikoduadua 1982 *S, E,* 1983 *Sa*
T Matawalu 2005 *Pt,* 2007 *Sa, J*
E Tikoidraubuta 1992 *Tg*
I Tikomaimakogai 1999 *US, J, Tg, Sa, M, Ur, It, Nm, E,* 2000 *J, Tg*
K Tilalati 2000 *J, Sa*
A Toga 1963 *Tg, Sa, Tg*
S Toga 1964 *W, C,* 1967 *Tg, Tg, Tg,* 1968 *NZ, Tg,* 1969 *W, PNG, SI, PNG,* 1970 *C*
A Tokairavua 1967 *Tg,* 1970 *M, C,* 1972 *Tg, Tg, Tg, A,* 1973 *M, Tg,* 1977 *Tg, Tg*
J Toloi 1994 *M, W, Sa, Tg*
S Tolotu 1964 *F*
RDT Tonawai 2007 *Tg,* 2010 *Tg, Sa*
J Tora 2005 *Tg, Sa, Tg, Sa, Pt,* 2006 *Tg, J*
P Tora 1986 *Sa, Tg*
P Tove 1951 *M*
TD Tuapati 2010 *A, J, Tg, Sa, F, W, It,* 2011 *Tg, Sa, Tg, SA, Sa,* 2012 *Sa, S, Tg, Geo,* 2013 *J, C, CAB, US, Tg*
T Tubananitu 1980 *A, It, NZ,* 1981 *Sa, Sa, Tg, Tg, Tg,* 1982 *Sa, Sa, Sa, Tg, S,* 1983 *Niu, Tg, Sa,* 1984 *Tg, NZ,* 1985 *A*
W Tubu 1967 *Tg*
P Tubui 1981 *Sa, Sa*
S Tubuna 1932 *Tg, Tg, Tg*
N Tubutubu 1924 *Sa, Tg, Tg, Tg, Sa*
E Tudia 1973 *Tg*
P Tuidraki 1994 *J, J, M, W, Sa, Tg*
P Tuidraki 1932 *Tg, Tg, Tg*
J Tuikabe 1999 *US, Sa, Ur,* 2000 *J, Tg, Sa, US, C, It,* 2001 *Tg, Sa, Tg, Sa, C, Sa, It, F*
A Tuilevu 1996 *SA, Sa, Tg, HK,* 1997 *Tg, Coo, Sa,* 1998 *S, F, A, Sa,* 2003 *Tg, Tg, Ar, F, US, J, S,* 2004 *Tg*
J Tuilevu 2008 *Tg*
W Tuinagiagia 1968 *Tg,* 1976 *I*
E Tuisese 2001 *F*
I Tuisese 1969 *W, SI,* 1970 *M, M, C,* 1972 *Tg, Tg, Tg,* 1973 *E,* 1974 *NZ, M, M,* 1976 *A, A,* 1977 *Tg, Tg, BI*
I Tuisese 2000 *J, Sa*
S Tuisese 1958 *Tg,* 1963 *Sa, Tg, Sa, Tg,* 1964 *M, W, F*
W Tuisese 1947 *Tg,* 1948 *M, M, M*
A Tuitavua 1938 *M, M, M,* 1939 *M,* 1947 *Tg, Tg,* 1948 *M, M, M,* 1952 *A, A,* 1954 *A, A, M, M, M*
E Tuivunivono 1993 *Tg*
N Tuiyau 1948 *M, M, M*
T Tukaitabua 1968 *NZ, Tg, Tg, Tg,* 1972 *Tg*
U Tukana 1963 *Sa, Sa, Tg,* 1964 *M, W, F, C*
T Tukunia 1984 *Tg*
W Turaga 1986 *Tg*
A Turagacoko 1968 *NZ, Tg, Tg,* 1969 *W*
A Turukawa 2004 *Sa,* 2005 *Pt,* 2007 *Sa, J, A, Tg*
E Turuva 1984 *A,* 1985 *A, I*
O Turuva 1990 *HK,* 1991 *E, R,* 1994 *Sa, Tg,* 1995 *C, Sa, Tg,* 1998 *A,* 1999 *C, US*
S Tuva 1959 *Tg,* 1961 *A, A, A*
M Tuvoli 1951 *M*
S Tuvula 1985 *A, I, W,* 1986 *W,* 1987 *Ar, NZ, It*
E Tuvunivono 1992 *M,* 1993 *S, Tg,* 1997 *NZ*

T Uliuviti 1926 *Tg, Tg, Tg,* 1928 *Tg*
A Uluinayau 1996 *SA, Sa, Tg, HK, HK, M,* 1997 *NZ, Tg, Coo, Sa,* 1998 *F, Sa, Tg,* 1999 *C, J, Tg, Sa, Nm, C, F, E,* 2001 *Tg, C, Sa,* 2002 *Sa, Tg, Sa, NZ,* 2003 *Tg, US*
N Uluiviti 1957 *M, M,* 1959 *Tg*
N Uluvula 1976 *I,* 1979 *M, E, F, PNG, Tg,* 1980 *Ar, Ar,* 1982 *Sa, Sa,* 1983 *Tg, Sa, SI, Sa,* 1984 *A, Tg, NZ,* 1986 *Tg*

J Vadugu 1961 *A, A*
I Vai 1979 *Tg*
RMT Vakacegu 2004 *Sa,* 2007 *Sa, A,* 2008 *Sa, M, J*
F Vakadrano 1986 *Tg*
J Vakalomaloma 1996 *HK*
S Vakarua 1926 *Tg, Tg*
M Vakatawabai 1967 *Tg*
S Valewai 1948 *M, M, M,* 1951 *M,* 1952 *A, A*
S Vanini 1964 *F*
S Varo 1982 *Sa,* 1984 *A, Tg, Tg, NZ*
V Varo 1970 *C,* 1972 *Tg, Tg, Tg, A,* 1973 *M, Tg*
L Vasuvulagi 1989 *S, E,* 1990 *Tg*
AV Vata 2005 *It,* 2008 *Sa, J, Tg*
J Vatubua 1992 *Tg*
S Vatubua 1951 *M,* 1952 *A, A,* 1954 *A, A, M, M, M,* 1958 *Tg, Tg*
W Vatubua 1988 *Tg, Tg*
S Vatudau 1939 *M*
WNNM Vatuvoka 2009 *S, R,* 2011 *J, Tg*
V Vatuwaliwali 1980 *M, NZ, Ar, Ar,* 1981 *Tg, Tg, Tg,* 1982 *Sa, Sa, Sa, Tg, S, E,* 1983 *Niu, Tg, Sa*
E Vavaitamana 1934 *Tg, Tg*
E Vavaitamana 1934 *Tg,* 1938 *M, M, M,* 1947 *Tg, Tg,* 1948 *M, M, M*
V Vavaitamana 1932 *Tg, Tg, Tg,* 1934 *Tg, Tg, Tg,* 1938 *M, M, M,* 1939 *M*
J Veidreyaki 1976 *A*
A Veikoso 1947 *Tg, Tg,* 1948 *M, M, M*
V Veikoso 2009 *S, I,* 2010 *A, J, Tg, Sa, F, W, It,* 2011 *Tg, Sa, NZ, Tg, Nm, W,* 2012 *J, S, E, Geo,* 2013 *J, C, CAB, US, Tg*
J Veitayaki 1994 *M, W, Sa, Tg,* 1995 *C, Sa, Tg, W, I,* 1996 *SA, Sa, Tg, HK, HK, M,* 1997 *NZ,* 1998 *S, F, US, Sa, Tg,* 1999 *C, US, J, Tg, Sa, M, Sp, Ur, It, Nm, C, F, E,* 2000 *J, Tg, Sa, US, C, It,* 2001 *Tg,* 2003 *Tg, Tg, Ar, CHL, F, US, J, S*
S Verevuni 1992 *Sa, Tg*
J Vidiri 1994 *J, J, M, W, Sa, Tg,* 1995 *C*
SN Viriviri 1976 *A, A,* 1977 *Tg, Tg, BI,* 1979 *E, F, PNG, Sa, Tg,* 1980 *NZ, M, NZ, Ar, Ar,* 1981 *Sa, Sa, Tg, Tg, Tg,* 1982 *Sa, Sa, S, E*
J Visei 1970 *M, C,* 1972 *Tg,* 1973 *M, M, Tg, E,* 1974 *M,* 1976 *I*
N Vitau 1994 *J,* 1996 *M*
S Vodivodi 1967 *Tg, Tg, Tg*
S Vola 1964 *C*
I Volavola 1968 *Tg, Tg, Tg,* 1969 *W, PNG, SI, PNG*
L Volavola 1976 *I*
M Volavola 2005 *W, Pt, It,* 2010 *Tg, Sa*
P Volavola 1985 *W,* 1986 *W, Tg, Sa, Tg,* 1987 *NZ, It, Tg,* 1991 *F, R*
S Vonolagi 1988 *Tg, Sa, E, Tg, Tg,* 1990 *Tg, Sa,* 1992 *Tg,* 1993 *S, Sa, Tg*
T Vonolagi 1989 *Tg, Bel, E,* 1990 *J, HK,* 1991 *Sa, Tg, E, R,* 1992 *M,* 1993 *S, Sa, Tg, Tg*
J Voreqe 1938 *M, M, M,* 1939 *M,* 1947 *Tg*
U Vosabalavu 1924 *Sa, Tg, Tg, Tg, Sa*
T Vosaicake 1938 *M, M, M,* 1939 *M*
K Vosailagi 1979 *F, Sa, Tg,* 1980 *A, It, NZ, M, Ar, Ar,* 1981 *Sa, Sa*
M Vosanibole 1991 *Tg, F*
W Votu 2012 *J, Sa, S, Tg, E, Geo*
AW Vuaviri 2012 *Tg*
E Vucago 2006 *Tg,* 2010 *A, J*
L Vuetaki 1980 *A, It, Ar*
S Vuetaki 1982 *Sa, Sa,* 1983 *SI, Niu, Tg,* 1984 *Sa,* 1985 *Tg*
I Vuivuda 1948 *M, M, M*
B Vukiwai 1984 *Tg*
J Vulakoro 2004 *Tg, Sa,* 2005 *W, Pt*
J Vulavou 1989 *Tg*
N Vuli 1991 *F, R,* 1992 *Sa, Tg,* 1993 *Tg*
AJ Vulivuli 2010 *F, W, It,* 2011 *Tg, Sa, NZ, Tg, Tg, Nm, Sa, W*
R Vunakece 1954 *M, M*
M Vunibaka 1999 *C, J, M, Sp, It, C, E,* 2000 *Sa, US, C, It,* 2001 *It, F,* 2003 *Tg, F, US, J*
S Vunivalu 1987 *Ar, NZ, F*
R Vuruya 1951 *M,* 1952 *A*

P Wadali 1957 *M*
T Wainiqolo 1990 *J, Tg, HK,* 1993 *Tg, Tg*
P Waisake 1976 *A,* 1980 *A, It, M*
V Waka 1967 *Tg, Tg, Tg*
S Walisoliso 1963 *Tg,* 1964 *W, F, C,* 1967 *Tg, Tg, Tg*
P Waqa 1926 *Tg,* 1928 *Tg, Sa,* 1932 *Tg, Tg, Tg,* 1934 *Tg, Tg*
J Waqabitu 1995 *W, I,* 1996 *Sa,* 1997 *NZ, Coo, Sa,* 1998 *S, F, US, Sa, Tg,* 2000 *J, Tg, Sa,* 2001 *It, F*
A Waqaliti 1985 *A*
DM Waqaniburotu 2010 *A, J, Tg, Sa,* 2011 *Tg, J, NZ, Tg, Nm, SA*
I Waqavatu 1989 *Tg, Tg, Bel, S*
S Wara 2012 *E, Geo*
I Wea 1938 *M*
J Wesele 1934 *Tg,* 1939 *M*
R Williams 1994 *W, Sa, Tg,* 1995 *C*
AE Wise 2009 *J,* 2010 *A, J*

T Yacabula 2002 *Tg, Sa, Tg*
K Yacalevu 1980 *Ar,* 1981 *Sa, Sa, Tg, Tg, Tg,* 1982 *Sa, Sa, Sa, Tg, S,* 1983 *SI, Niu*
S Yalayala 1983 *Tg, SI, Tg,* 1984 *Sa, Tg, NZ,* 1985 *Sa, Tg,* 1986 *Tg, Sa*
A Yalayalatabua 2007 *Sa, A,* 2008 *J,* 2009 *Sa, J, S, R,* 2010 *J, Tg, Sa*
JNBN Yanuyanutawa 2012 *Sa, S, Tg, Geo,* 2013 *J, C, CAB, US, Tg*

FRANCE

FRANCE'S 2012–13 TEST RECORD

Australia	10 Nov	H	Won 33–6
Argentina	17 Nov	H	Won 39–22
Samoa	24 Nov	H	Won 22–14
Italy	3 Feb	A	Lost 23–18
Wales	9 Feb	H	Lost 6–16
England	23 Feb	A	Lost 23–13
Ireland	9 Mar	A	Drew 13–13
Scotland	16 Mar	H	Won 23–16
New Zealand	8 Jun	A	Lost 23–13
New Zealand	15 Jun	A	Lost 30–0
New Zealand	22 Jun	A	Lost 24–9

LES BLEUS STRUGGLE UNDER SAINT-ANDRÉ

By Iain Spragg

Getty Images

Maxime Médard's try against Scotland was a rare highlight in France's disappointing Six Nations campaign.

Unpredictable is an epitaph which has long been associated with French rugby and so it proved again as Philippe Saint-André's side began their season with a bang against Australia but unravelled through a Championship campaign in which they collected the Wooden Spoon for the first time since 1999 and climaxed with a demoralising series whitewash in New Zealand.

When Les Bleus comprehensively demolished the Wallabies 33–6 in November in Paris, hopes of a successful year soared. Argentina and Samoa were subsequently despatched but the cracks began to appear in February when they lost their Six Nations opener against Italy in Rome, a result which precipitated their worst showing in the Championship for 14 years.

The French headed to New Zealand in June to face the world champions and, although they were competitive against the All Blacks in both the first and third Tests, their 24–9 defeat in New Plymouth in the final match of the tour was a sobering conclusion to what had been an arduous and ultimately disappointing campaign.

"It is never easy to play three Tests at the end of a long season, especially against a team like New Zealand," conceded Saint-André after the third Test loss. "What I am pleased about is we played against the best in the world and fought with very good spirit. I think this is very important. We had seven new caps in the last three games so that was also important for us.

"In the first Test we were close but the scrum was very poor. In the second Test it was our lineout. The third was our discipline so each time we had something wrong. I think that it is a learning process and it is painful given the players' involvement and their state of mind during this tour. The key factor was our lack of efficiency during our stronger moments."

Eight uncapped players made the cut for Saint-André's 35-man squad for the November internationals but France were rocked by the loss of Thierry Dusautoir with a knee injury and veteran second row Pascal Papé temporarily assumed the captaincy for the clash against Australia.

France hadn't beaten the Wallabies since a 26–16 win in Marseille in 2005, a five-match losing sequence, but they were utterly dominant in the Stade de France as they swept Robbie Deans's team aside. Louis Picamoles went over for the first try of the match after 12 minutes, Wesley Fofana crossed for the second midway through the second half and, when referee Nigel Owens awarded a penalty try nine minutes later after a collapsed scrum, Australia's misery was complete and France lifted the Trophée des Bicentenaires.

"I'm proud of my players," said Saint-André. "It was a quality game. We went into it wanting to play in a confrontational way. We produced a great defence, moving up quickly and were very aggressive at the ruck. That was the key to the match.

"When you see what other southern hemisphere countries did today, South Africa beating Ireland and Argentina beating Wales, I've told my players to enjoy the win because it's not often you beat Australia, especially by 30 points."

France were less explosive in their 39–22 win over Argentina in Lille and a 22–14 triumph against Samoa in Paris the following week but nonetheless looked ahead to the Six Nations buoyed by three victories in three Tests.

The Championship, however, started in the worst possible fashion as the side slumped to a 23–18 defeat against Italy at the Stadio Olimpico, paying a heavy price for losing the battle for both territory and possession against a passionate Azzurri team.

Italy were quicker out of the blocks than France and, although Benjamin Fall's 33rd-minute try saw the visitors take a slender 15–13 lead, the home side hit back with a Martin Castrogiovanni score midway through the second half and a late Kris Burton drop goal sealed a famous Italian victory.

"We need to congratulate Italy," Saint-André said. "They played very well, with a lot of passion and kept the ball well. We had control of the game when we were five points in front but we lost the ball too many times and were not precise. When you are not precise in the Six Nations, you are punished. The players are very, very disappointed. We prepared well for the game and we respect the Italian team. They improve each year."

The head coach resisted the temptation to make wholesale changes for the Wales game in the Stade de France six days later but his show of faith in his players failed to elicit a significantly improved performance. A late try from George North saw the Welsh register a 16–6 win and their first success in Paris for eight years.

"Losing at home is not good but you cannot expect to win if you cannot convert your opportunities," admitted Dusautoir. "If we can't score when we have the ball then there is always the risk of the other team scoring."

It was now time for change and Saint-André made seven for the encounter with England at Twickenham. An early Fofana try fleetingly raised the prospect of a first Championship win in London in eight years before the home side came surging back in the second half to record a 23–13 victory.

A degree of respite for Saint-André and his beleaguered troops was to come in the shape of a 13–13 draw with Ireland in Dublin in March courtesy of a late Picamoles try and Frédéric Michalak conversion, and they prepared for their final game against Scotland in the knowledge they could still escape finishing bottom of the final table.

Ireland's 22–15 defeat to Italy in Rome earlier in the day meant Les Bleus required a 16-point winning margin against the Scots in Paris. Although tries from Fofana and Maxime Médard provided the platform for a 23–16 triumph and a first win of the Championship, it was not enough to avoid the ignominy of the Wooden Spoon.

"It was a difficult match but it had been a reflection of where we had been in the tournament this year," Saint-André said. "We made many opportunities in the first half but we were not patient enough. In the second half we scored two great tries but we are still last in the tournament and we have to accept that."

An exacting tour of New Zealand would probably not have been top of the coach's wish list after his team's travails in the Six Nations. He named eight uncapped players in his 35-man squad and two of the newcomers – fly half Camille Lopez and wing Adrien Plante – made Saint-André's starting XV for the first Test against the All Blacks in Auckland.

The French drew first blood at Eden Park with a ninth-minute score from Fofana, the centre's eighth try in his first 16 Test appearances, but the All Blacks hit back with a two-try salvo from Aaron Smith and Sam Cane in the 10 minutes before the break. In the second half France cut the arrears with a successful Lopez penalty but, despite pushing their hosts all the way, the All Blacks eventually closed out a tense 23–13 win with two penalties from Aaron Cruden.

"The difference was that we weren't able to score when we were on top," said hooker Dimitri Szarzewski after the game. "It's a shame but, to win against New Zealand, you must convert opportunities. We know against New Zealand, when you lose the ball in the ruck or in contact, every player can make a difference every time."

A 38–15 midweek victory over the Blues in Albany for the French second-string side briefly brightened the mood in the camp, but the team for the second Test was unable to emulate the achievement and slumped to a 30–0 defeat in Christchurch.

Les Bleus lacked the intensity they had displayed in the first Test and conceded three tries without troubling the scoreboard, the first time the team had failed to score a point against New Zealand in 53 meetings between the two countries.

With the series now beyond France, Saint-André opted to shuffle the deck and named a new-look team for the third Test in New Plymouth, selecting the inexperienced Jean-Marc Doussain and Rémi Talès as his half backs and including second row Alexandre Flanquart, flanker Antonie Claassen and number 8 Damien Chouly in the pack.

The newcomers acquitted themselves well in the Yarrow Stadium and they took an early lead with a Florian Fritz drop goal. The All Blacks responded with a Ben Smith try but two penalties from Doussain either side of half-time kept France in contention. Dan Carter re-established the All Blacks' supremacy with three second-half penalties but the visitors refused to buckle and a last-minute try from New Zealand replacement Beauden Barrett gave the final 24–9 scoreline a gloss that didn't do justice to the French display.

"At the start of the second half they were trailing us by two points but we lost two balls in our 30 metres and we got immediately punished," Saint-André said at the end of a season in which his side won just four of their 11 Tests.

FRANCE INTERNATIONAL STATISTICS

MATCH RECORDS UP TO 10 OCTOBER 2013

MOST CONSECUTIVE TEST WINS

10	1931 E, G, 1932 G, 1933 G, 1934 G, 1935 G, 1936 G1,2, 1937 G, It
8	1998 E, S, I, W, Arg1,2, Fj, Arg3
8	2001 SA3, A, Fj 2002 It, W, E, S, I
8	2004 I, It, W, S, E, US, C, A

MOST CONSECUTIVE TESTS WITHOUT DEFEAT

Matches	Wins	Draws	Period
10	10	0	1931 to 1938
10	8	2	1958 to 1959
10	9	1	1986 to 1987

MOST POINTS IN A MATCH

BY THE TEAM

Pts	Opponents	Venue	Year
87	Namibia	Toulouse	2007
77	Fiji	Saint Etienne	2001
70	Zimbabwe	Auckland	1987
67	Romania	Bucharest	2000
64	Romania	Aurillac	1996
64	Georgia	Marseilles	2007
62	Romania	Castres	1999
62	Romania	Bucharest	2006
61	Fiji	Brisbane	2003
60	Italy	Toulon	1967
59	Romania	Paris	1924
56	Romania	Lens	2003
56	Italy	Rome	2005

BY A PLAYER

Pts	Player	Opponents	Venue	Year
30	D Camberabero	Zimbabwe	Auckland	1987
28	C Lamaison	New Zealand	Twickenham	1999
28	F Michalak	Scotland	Sydney	2003
27	G Camberabero	Italy	Toulon	1967
27	C Lamaison	New Zealand	Marseilles	2000
27	G Merceron	South Africa	Johannesburg	2001
27	J-B Elissalde	Namibia	Toulouse	2007
26	T Lacroix	Ireland	Durban	1995
26	F Michalak	Fiji	Brisbane	2003
25	J-P Romeu	United States	Chicago	1976
25	P Berot	Romania	Agen	1987
25	T Lacroix	Tonga	Pretoria	1995

MOST TRIES IN A MATCH

BY THE TEAM

Tries	Opponents	Venue	Year
13	Romania	Paris	1924
13	Zimbabwe	Auckland	1987
13	Namibia	Toulouse	2007
12	Fiji	Saint Etienne	2001
11	Italy	Toulon	1967
10	Romania	Aurillac	1996
10	Romania	Bucharest	2000

BY A PLAYER

Tries	Player	Opponents	Venue	Year
4	A Jauréguy	Romania	Paris	1924
4	M Celhay	Italy	Paris	1937

MOST CONVERSIONS IN A MATCH

BY THE TEAM

Cons	Opponents	Venue	Year
11	Namibia	Toulouse	2007
9	Italy	Toulon	1967
9	Zimbabwe	Auckland	1987
8	Romania	Wellington	1987
8	Romania	Lens	2003

BY A PLAYER

Cons	Player	Opponents	Venue	Year
11	J-B Elissalde	Namibia	Toulouse	2007
9	G Camberabero	Italy	Toulon	1967
9	D Camberabero	Zimbabwe	Auckland	1987
8	G Laporte	Romania	Wellington	1987

MOST PENALTIES IN A MATCH

BY THE TEAM

Penalties	Opponents	Venue	Year
8	Ireland	Durban	1995
7	Wales	Paris	2001
7	Italy	Paris	2002
6	Argentina	Buenos Aires	1977
6	Scotland	Paris	1997
6	Italy	Auch	1997
6	Ireland	Paris	2000
6	South Africa	Johannesburg	2001
6	Argentina	Buenos Aires	2003
6	Fiji	Brisbane	2003
6	England	Twickenham	2005
6	Wales	Paris	2007
6	England	Twickenham	2007
6	Ireland	Dublin	2011

BY A PLAYER

Penalties	Player	Opponents	Venue	Year
8	T Lacroix	Ireland	Durban	1995
7	G Merceron	Italy	Paris	2002
6	J-M Aguirre	Argentina	Buenos Aires	1977
6	C Lamaison	Scotland	Paris	1997
6	C Lamaison	Italy	Auch	1997
6	G Merceron	Ireland	Paris	2000
6	G Merceron	South Africa	Johannesburg	2001
6	F Michalak	Fiji	Brisbane	2003
6	D Yachvili	England	Twickenham	2005

MOST DROP GOALS IN A MATCH

BY THE TEAM

Drops	Opponents	Venue	Year
3	Ireland	Paris	1960
3	England	Twickenham	1985
3	New Zealand	Christchurch	1986
3	Australia	Sydney	1990
3	Scotland	Paris	1991
3	New Zealand	Christchurch	1994

BY A PLAYER

Drops	Player	Opponents	Venue	Year
3	P Albaladejo	Ireland	Paris	1960
3	J-P Lescarboura	England	Twickenham	1985
3	J-P Lescarboura	New Zealand	Christchurch	1986
3	D Camberabero	Australia	Sydney	1990

CAREER RECORDS

MOST CAPPED PLAYERS

Caps	Player	Career Span
118	F Pelous	1995 to 2007
111	P Sella	1982 to 1995
98	R Ibañez	1996 to 2007
93	S Blanco	1980 to 1991
89	O Magne	1997 to 2007
86	D Traille	2001 to 2011
84	S Marconnet	1998 to 2011
82	I Harinordoquy	2002 to 2012
78	A Benazzi	1990 to 2001
76	A Rougerie	2001 to 2012
75	J Bonnaire	2004 to 2012
74	L Nallet	2000 to 2012
73	Y Jauzion	2001 to 2011
72	D Szarzewski	2004 to 2013
71	J-L Sadourny	1991 to 2001
71	O Brouzet	1994 to 2003
71	C Califano	1994 to 2007
69	R Bertranne	1971 to 1981
69	P Saint-André	1990 to 1997
69	P de Villiers	1999 to 2007
67	C Dominici	1998 to 2007
67	V Clerc	2002 to 2013
66	F Michalak	2001 to 2013

MOST CONSECUTIVE TESTS

Tests	Player	Span
46	R Bertranne	1973 to 1979
45	P Sella	1982 to 1987
44	M Crauste	1960 to 1966
42	M Parra	2009 to 2013
35	B Dauga	1964 to 1968

MOST TESTS AS CAPTAIN

Tests	Captain	Span
42	F Pelous	1997 to 2006
41	R Ibanez	1998 to 2007
38	T Dusautoir	2009 to 2013
34	J-P Rives	1978 to 1984
34	P Saint-André	1994 to 1997
25	D Dubroca	1986 to 1988
25	F Galthié	1999 to 2003
24	G Basquet	1948 to 1952
22	M Crauste	1961 to 1966

MOST POINTS IN TESTS

Points	Player	Tests	Career
380	C Lamaison	37	1996 to 2001
373	D Yachvili	61	2002 to 2012
367	T Lacroix	43	1989 to 1997
362	F Michalak	66	2001 to 2013
354	D Camberabero	36	1982 to 1993
288	M Parra	51	2008 to 2013
267	G Merceron	32	1999 to 2003
265	J-P Romeu	34	1972 to 1977
247	T Castaignède	54	1995 to 2007
233	S Blanco	93	1980 to 1991
214	J-B Elissalde	35	2000 to 2008
200	J-P Lescarboura	28	1982 to 1990

MOST CONVERSIONS IN TESTS

Cons	Player	Tests	Career
59	C Lamaison	37	1996 to 2001
51	D Yachvili	61	2002 to 2012
51	F Michalak	66	2001 to 2013
48	D Camberabero	36	1982 to 1993
45	M Vannier	43	1953 to 1961
42	T Castaignède	54	1995 to 2007
40	J-B Elissalde	35	2000 to 2008
37	M Parra	51	2008 to 2013
36	R Dourthe	31	1995 to 2001
36	G Merceron	32	1999 to 2003
32	T Lacroix	43	1989 to 1997
29	P Villepreux	34	1967 to 1972

MOST TRIES IN TESTS

Tries	Player	Tests	Career
38	S Blanco	93	1980 to 1991
34	V Clerc	67	2002 to 2013
33*	P Saint-André	69	1990 to 1997
30	P Sella	111	1982 to 1995
26	E Ntamack	46	1994 to 2000
26	P Bernat Salles	41	1992 to 2001
25	C Dominici	67	1998 to 2007
23	C Darrouy	40	1957 to 1967
23	A Rougerie	76	2001 to 2012

* Saint-André's total includes a penalty try against Romania in 1992

MOST PENALTY GOALS IN TESTS

Penalties	Player	Tests	Career
89	T Lacroix	43	1989 to 1997
85	D Yachvili	61	2002 to 2012
78	C Lamaison	37	1996 to 2001
67	M Parra	51	2008 to 2013
62	F Michalak	66	2001 to 2013
59	D Camberabero	36	1982 to 1993
57	G Merceron	32	1999 to 2003
56	J-P Romeu	34	1972 to 1977
38	J-B Elissalde	35	2000 to 2008
33	P Villepreux	34	1967 to 1972
33	P Bérot	19	1986 to 1989

MOST DROP GOALS IN TESTS

Drops	Player	Tests	Career
15	J-P Lescarboura	28	1982 to 1990
12	P Albaladejo	30	1954 to 1964
11	G Camberabero	14	1961 to 1968
11	D Camberabero	36	1982 to 1993
9	J-P Romeu	34	1972 to 1977

INTERNATIONAL CHAMPIONSHIP RECORDS

RECORD	DETAIL	HOLDER	SET
Most points in season	156	in five matches	2002
Most tries in season	18	in four matches	1998
	18	in five matches	2006
Highest score	56	56–13 v Italy	2005
Biggest win	51	51–0 v Wales	1998
Highest score conceded	49	14–49 v Wales	1910
Biggest defeat	37	0–37 v England	1911
Most appearances	50	P Sella	1983–1995
Most points in matches	217	D Yachvili	2003–2012
Most points in season	80	G Merceron	2002
Most points in match	24	S Viars	v Ireland, 1992
	24	C Lamaison	v Scotland, 1997
	24	J-B Elissalde	v Wales, 2004
Most tries in matches	14	S Blanco	1981–1991
	14	P Sella	1983–1995
Most tries in season	5	P Estève	1983
	5	E Bonneval	1987
	5	E Ntamack	1999
	5	P Bernat Salles	2001
	5	V Clerc	2008
Most tries in match	3	M Crauste	v England, 1962
	3	C Darrouy	v Ireland, 1963
	3	E Bonneval	v Scotland, 1987
	3	D Venditti	v Ireland, 1997
	3	E Ntamack	v Wales, 1999
	3	V Clerc	v Ireland, 2008
Most cons in matches	30	D Yachvili	2003–2012
Most cons in season	11	M Parra	2010
Most cons in match	6	D Yachvili	v Italy, 2003
Most pens in matches	49	D Yachvili	2003–2012
Most pens in season	18	G Merceron	2002
Most pens in match	7	G Merceron	v Italy, 2002
Most drops in matches	9	J-P Lescarboura	1982–1988
Most drops in season	5	G Camberabero	1967
Most drops in match	3	P Albaladejo	v Ireland, 1960
	3	J-P Lescarboura	v England, 1985

MISCELLANEOUS RECORDS

RECORD	HOLDER	DETAIL
Longest Test Career	F Haget	1974 to 1987
	C Califano	1994 to 2007
	S Marconnet	1998 to 2011
Youngest Test Cap	C Dourthe	18 yrs 7 days in 1966
Oldest Test Cap	A Roques	37 yrs 329 days in 1963

CAREER RECORDS OF FRANCE INTERNATIONAL PLAYERS

UP TO 10 OCTOBER 2013

PLAYER BACKS:	DEBUT	CAPS	T	C	P	D	PTS
M Andreu	2010 v W	7	2	0	0	0	10
M Bastareaud	2009 v W	16	2	0	0	0	10
J-M Buttin	2012 v W	2	0	0	0	0	0
V Clerc	2002 v SA	67	34	0	0	0	170
J-M Doussain	2011 v NZ	3	0	0	2	0	6
B Dulin	2012 v Arg	7	0	0	0	0	0
B Fall	2009 v Sm	6	3	0	0	0	15
G Fickou	2013 v S	1	0	0	0	0	0
W Fofana	2012 v It	18	8	0	0	0	40
F Fritz	2005 v SA	32	3	0	0	3	24
Y Huget	2010 v Arg	20	2	0	0	0	10
C Lopez	2013 v NZ	2	0	0	1	0	3
M Machenaud	2012 v Arg	11	1	2	1	0	12
J Malzieu	2008 v S	20	5	0	0	0	25
M Médard	2008 v Arg	34	11	0	0	1	58
M Mermoz	2008 v A	25	2	0	0	0	10
F Michalak	2001 v SA	66	10	51	62	8	362
M Parra	2008 v S	51	2	37	67	1	288
A Plante	2013 v NZ	2	0	0	0	0	0
R Talès	2013 v NZ	2	0	0	0	0	0
F Trinh-Duc	2008 v S	48	9	2	1	6	70

2012/13 IN PICTURES

Lift-off: Bath's Francois Louw scores a spectacular try against Leicester Tigers.

Sea of red: Alun-Wyn Jones and Jamie Roberts enjoy the British & Irish Lions' series win over Australia.

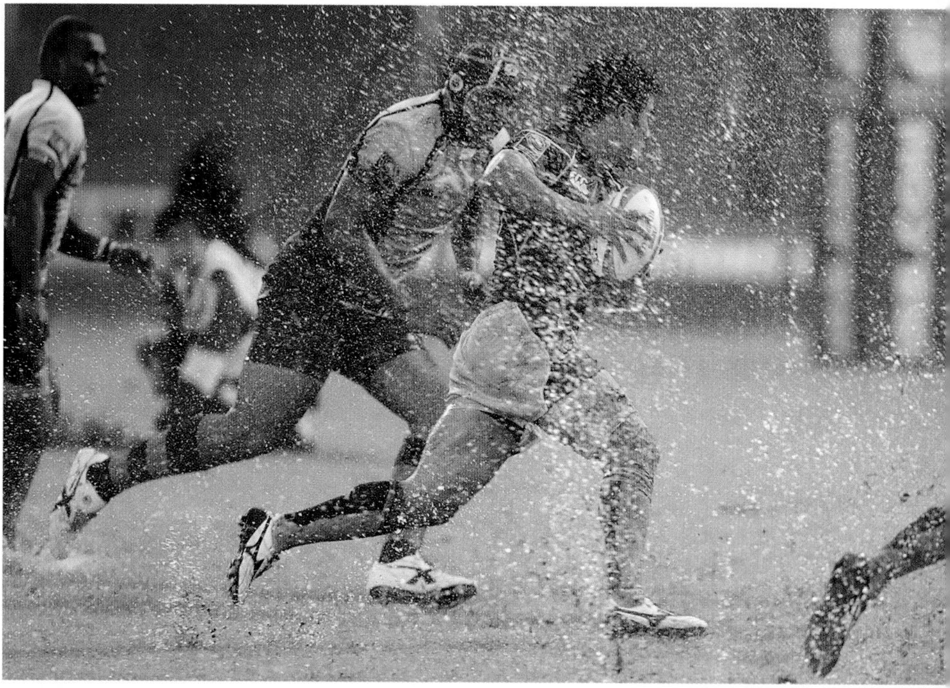

Rain or shine: Japan and Fiji battle the elements in the IRB Pacific Nations Cup.

Standing tall: Richie McCaw leads the All Blacks in the haka.

n the rise: Samoa's win over Sweden helped book their place at Women's Rugby World Cup 2014.

wo's company: South Africa's Bryan Habana tries to escape the clutches of two Argentina tacklers.

Heineken Cup winners: Toulon

Super Rugby winners: Chiefs

RBS Six Nations winners: Wales

Getty Images

The Rugby Championship winners: New Zealand

IRB Junior World Championship winners: England

Mixed emotions: Elation for Fiji but despair for Wales as the referee blows his whistle at the end of the HSBC Sevens World Series final in Hong Kong.

Getty Images

Emerging force: Russia's Ekaterina Kazakova breaks a New Zealand tackle in the IRB Women's Sevens World Series in Amsterdam.

Fist-pumping: South Africa's Chris D
celebrates beating New Zealand in the fina
of the Glasgow round of the World Series.

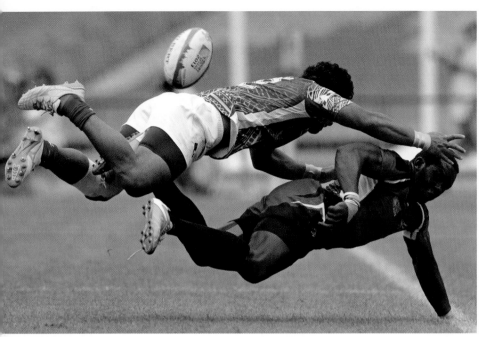

ilky skills: Kenya's Oscar Ouma flicks a pass in a Rugby World Cup Sevens match against Samoa.

ouble champions: Huriana Manuel and Tomasi Cama toast New Zealand's dual success at
ıgby World Cup Sevens 2013 in Moscow.

Devotion: Fijian fans show their support for their team in the HSBC Sevens World Series.

Overpowering: Samoa's Joe Tekori breaks through a Welsh tackle during his country's memorab
victory at the Millennium Stadium.

FORWARDS:							
E Ben Arous	2013 v NZ	1	0	0	0	0	0
D Chouly	2007 v NZ	10	0	0	0	0	0
A D Claassen	2013 v E	4	0	0	0	0	0
V Debaty	2006 v R	18	0	0	0	0	0
T Domingo	2009 v W	27	1	0	0	0	5
L Ducalcon	2010 v S	17	0	0	0	0	0
T Dusautoir	2006 v R	62	6	0	0	0	30
A Flanquart	2013 v NZ	2	0	0	0	0	0
Y Forestier	2012 v A	5	0	0	0	0	0
G Guirado	2008 v It	18	0	0	0	0	0
B Kayser	2008 v A	19	0	0	0	0	0
D M Kotze	2013 v NZ	1	0	0	0	0	0
B Le Roux	2013 v NZ	2	0	0	0	0	0
Y Maestri	2012 v It	17	0	0	0	0	0
N Mas	2003 v NZ	63	0	0	0	0	0
Y Nyanga	2004 v US	33	5	0	0	0	25
F Ouedraogo	2007 v NZ	33	1	0	0	0	5
P Papé	2004 v I	46	3	0	0	0	15
L Picamoles	2008 v I	38	5	0	0	0	25
C Samson	2012 v Arg	5	0	0	0	0	0
J Suta	2012 v A	5	0	0	0	0	0
D Szarzewski	2004 v C	72	6	0	0	0	30
R Taofifenua	2012 v Arg	3	0	0	0	0	0
C-E Tolofua	2012 v Arg	2	0	0	0	0	0
S Vahaamahina	2012 v A	6	0	0	0	0	0
Y Watremez	2012 v Arg	1	0	0	0	0	0

FRENCH INTERNATIONAL PLAYERS
UP TO 10 OCTOBER 2013

Note: Years given for International Championship matches are for second half of season; e.g. 1972 means season 1971–72. Years for all other matches refer to the actual year of the match. Entries in square brackets denote matches played in RWC Finals.

Abadie, A (Pau) 1964 I
Abadie, A (Graulhet) 1965 R, 1967 SA 1, 3, 4, NZ, 1968 S, I
Abadie, L (Tarbes) 1963 R
Accoceberry, G (Bègles) 1994 NZ 1, 2, C 2, 1995 W, E, S, I, R 1, [Iv, S], It, 1996 I, W 1, R, Arg 1, W 2(R), SA 2, 1997 S, It 1
Aguerre, R (Biarritz O) 1979 S
Aguilar, D (Pau) 1937 G
Aguirre, J-M (Bagnères) 1971 A 2, 1972 S, 1973 W, I, J, R, 1974 I, W, Arg 2, R, SA 1, 1976 W (R), E, US, A 2, R, 1977 W, E, S, I, Arg 1, 2, NZ 1, 2, R, 1978 E, S, I, W, R, 1979 I, W, E, S, NZ 1, 2, R, 1980 W, I
Ainciart, E (Bayonne) 1933 G, 1934 G, 1935 G, 1937 G, It, 1938 G 1
Albaladéjo, P (Dax) 1954 E, It, 1960 W, I, It, R, 1961 S, SA, E, W, I, NZ 1, 2, A, 1962 S, E, W, I, 1963 S, I, E, W, It, 1964 S, NZ, W, It, I, SA, Fj
Albouy, A (Castres) 2002 It (R)
Alvarez, A-J (Tyrosse) 1945 B2, 1946 B, I, K, W, 1947 S, I, W, E, 1948 I, A, S, W, E, 1949 I, E, W, 1951 S, E, W
Amand, H (SF) 1906 NZ

Ambert, A (Toulouse) 1930 S, I, E, G, W
Amestoy, J-B (Mont-de-Marsan) 1964 NZ, E
André, G (RCF) 1913 SA, E, W, I, 1914 I, W, E
Andreu, M (Castres) 2010 W(R), It, E, SA(R), Arg2, A(R), 2013 NZ3
Andrieu, M (Nîmes) 1986 Arg 2, NZ 1, R 2, NZ 2, 1987 [R, Z], R, 1988 E, S, I, W, Arg 1, 2, 3, 4, R, 1989 I, W, E, S, NZ 2, B, A 2, 1990 W, E, I (R)
Anduran, J (SCUF) 1910 W
Aqua, J-L (Toulon) 1999 R, Tg, NZ 1(R)
Araou, R (Narbonne) 1924 R
Arcalis, , R (Brive) 1950 S, I, 1951 I, E, W
Arias, J (SF) 2009 A(R), 2010 Fj
Arino, M (Agen) 1962 R
Aristouy, P (Pau) 1948 S, 1949 Arg 2, 1950 S, I, E, W
Arlettaz, P (Perpignan) 1995 R 2
Armary, L (Lourdes) 1987 [R], R, 1988 S, I, W, Arg 3, 4, R, 1989 W, S, A 1, 2, 1990 W, E, S, I, A 1, 2, 3, NZ 1, 1991 W 2, 1992 S, I, R, Arg 1, 2, SA 1, 2, Arg, 1993 E, S, I, W, SA 1, 2, R 2, A 1, 2, 1994 I, W, NZ 1(t), 2(t), 1995 I, R 1 [Tg, I, SA]
Arnal, J-M (RCF) 1914 I, W
Arnaudet, M (Lourdes) 1964 I, 1967 It, W
Arotca, R (Bayonne) 1938 R
Arrieta, J (SF) 1953 E, W
Arthapignet, P (see Harislur-Arthapignet)
Artiguste, E (Castres) 1999 WS
Astre, R (Béziers) 1971 R, 1972 I 1, 1973 E (R), 1975 E, S, I, SA 1, 2, Arg 2, 1976 A 2, R
Attoub, D (Castres, SF) 2006 R, 2012 W, Arg 1, 2
Aucagne, D (Pau) 1997 W (R), S, It 1, R 1(R), A 1, R 2(R), SA 2(R), 1998 S (R), W (R), Arg 2(R), Fj (R), Arg 3, A, 1999 W 1(R), S (R)
Audebert, A (Montferrand) 2000 R, 2002 W (R)
Aué, J-M (Castres) 1998 W (R)
Augé, J (Dax) 1929 S, W
Augras-Fabre, L (Agen) 1931 I, S, W
August, B (Biarritz) 2007 W1(R)
Auradou, D (SF) 1999 E (R), S (R), WS (R), Tg, NZ 1, W 2(R), [Arg (R)], 2000 A (R), NZ 1, 2, 2001 S, I, It, W, E (R), SA 1, 2, NZ (R), SA 3, A, Fj, 2002 It, E, I (R), C (R), 2003 S (R), It (R), W (R), Arg, 1, 2, NZ (R), R (R), E 2(R), 3, [J(R), US, NZ] , 2004 I(R), It(R), S(R), E(R)
Averous, J-L (La Voulte) 1975 S, I, SA 1, 2, 1976 I, W, E, US, A 1, 2, R, 1977 W, E, S, I, Arg 1, R, 1978 E, S, I, 1979 NZ 1, 2, 1980 E, S, 1981 A 2
Avril, D (Biarritz) 2005 A1
Azam, O (Montferrand, Gloucester) 1995 R 2, Arg (R), 2000 A (R), NZ 2(R), 2001 SA 2(R), NZ, 2002 E (R), I (R), Arg (R), A 1
Azarete, J-L (Dax, St Jean-de-Luz) 1969 W, R, 1970 S, I, W, R, 1971 S, I, E, SA 1, 2, A 1, 1972 E, W, I 2, A 1, R, 1973 NZ, W, I, R, 1974 I, R, SA 1, 2, 1975 W

Baby, B (Toulouse, Clermont-Auvergne) 2005 I, SA2(R), A1, 2008 Arg, Pl, A3, 2009 I(R), S, W
Bacqué, N (Pau) 1997 R 2
Bader, E (Primevères) 1926 M, 1927 I, S
Badin, C (Chalon) 1973 W, I, 1975 Arg 1
Baillette, M (Perpignan) 1925 I, NZ, S, 1926 W, M, 1927 I, W, G 2, 1929 G, 1930 S, I, E, G, 1931 I, S, E, 1932 G
Baladie, G (Agen) 1945 B 1, 2, W, 1946 B, I, K
Ballarin, J (Tarbes) 1924 E, 1925 NZ, S
Baquey, J (Toulouse) 1921 I
Barbazanges, A (Roanne) 1932 G, 1933 G
Barcella, F (Auch, Biarritz) 2008 It, W, Arg, 2009 S, W, It, NZ1, 2, A, SA, NZ3, 2010 Arg1, 2011 I3(R), [J, C(t&R), NZ1(R), Tg(R), E(R), W(R), NZ2(R)]
Barrau, M (Beaumont, Toulouse) 1971 S, E, W, 1972 E, W, A 1, 2, 1973 S, NZ, E, I, J, R, 1974 I, S
Barrau, M (Agen) 2004 US, C(R), NZ(R)
Barrère, P (Toulon) 1929 G, 1931 W
Barrière, R (Béziers) 1960 R
Barthe, F (SBUC) 1925 W, E
Barthe, J (Lourdes) 1954 Arg 1, 2, 1955 S, 1956 I, W, It, E, Cz, 1957 S, I, E, W, R 1, 2, 1958 S, E, A, W, It, I, SA 1, 2, 1959 S, E, It, W

Basauri, R (Albi) 1954 Arg 1
Bascou, P (Bayonne) 1914 E
Basquet, G (Agen) 1945 W, 1946 B, I, K, W, 1947 S, I, W, E, 1948 I, A, S, W, E, 1949 S, I, E, W, Arg 1, 1950 S, I, E, W, 1951 S, I, E, W, 1952 S, I, SA, W, E, It
Bastareaud, M (SF, Toulon) 2009 W, E, It(R), NZ1, 2010 S, I, W, It(R), E, 2013 It(R), W, E, I(t&R), S, NZ2(R), 3(t&R)
Bastiat, J-P (Dax) 1969 R, 1970 S, I, W, 1971 S, I, SA 2, 1972 S, A 1, 1973 E, 1974 Arg 1, 2, SA 2, 1975 W, Arg 1, 2, R, 1976 S, I, W, E, A 1, 2, R, 1977 W, E, S, I, 1978 E, S, I, W
Baudry, N (Montferrand) 1949 S, I, W, Arg 1, 2
Baulon, R (Vienne, Bayonne) 1954 S, NZ, W, E, It, 1955 I, E, W, It, 1956 S, I, W, It, E, Cz, 1957 S, I, It
Baux, J-P (Lannemezan) 1968 NZ 1, 2, SA 1, 2
Bavozet, J (Lyon) 1911 S, E, W
Bayard, J (Toulouse) 1923 S, W, E, 1924 W, R, US
Bayardon, J (Chalon) 1964 S, NZ, E
Beaurin-Gressier, C (SF) 1907 E, 1908 E
Beauxis, L (SF, Toulouse) 2007 It(R), I(R), W1(R), E1(R), S, W2, [Nm(R), I(R), Gg, NZ, E, Arg 2(R)], 2009 I, S, A, 2012 It(R), S(R), I(R), E, W
Bégu, J (Dax) 1982 Arg 2(R), 1984 E, S
Béguerie, C (Agen) 1979 NZ 1
Béguet, L (RCF) 1922 I, 1923 S, W, E, I, 1924 S, I, E, R, US
Béhotéguy, A (Bayonne, Cognac) 1923 E, 1924 S, I, E, W, R, US, 1926 E, 1927 E, G 1, 2, 1928 A, I, E, G, W, 1929 S, W, E
Béhotéguy, H (RCF, Cognac) 1923 W, 1928 A, I, E, G, W
Bélascain, C (Bayonne) 1977 R, 1978 E, S, I, W, R, 1979 I, W, E, S, 1982 W, E, S, I, 1983 E, S, I, W
Belletante, G (Nantes) 1951 I, E, W
Belot, F (Toulouse) 2000 I (R)
Ben Arous, E (Racing Métro) 2013 NZ3(R)
Benazzi, A (Agen) 1990 A 1, 2, 3, NZ 1, 2, 1991 E, US 1(R), 2, [R, Fj, C], 1992 SA 1(R), 2, Arg, 1993 E, S, I, W, A 1, 2, 1994 I, W, E, S, C 1, NZ 1, 2, C 2, 1995 W, E, S, I, [Tg, Iv, S, I, SA, E], NZ 1, 2, 1996 E, S, I, W 1, Arg 1, 2, W 2, SA 1, 2, 1997 I, W, E, S, R 1, A 1, 2, It 2, R 2(R), Arg, SA 1, 2, 1999 R, WS, W 2, [C, Nm (R), Fj, Arg, NZ 2, A], 2000 W, E, I, It (R), R, 2001 S (R), I (t&R), E
Bénésis, R (Narbonne) 1969 W, R, 1970 S, I, W, E, R, 1971 S, I, E, W, A 2, R, 1972 S, I 1, E, W, I 2, A 1, R, 1973 NZ, E, W, I, J, R, 1974 I, W, E, S
Benetière, J (Roanne) 1954 It, Arg 1
Benetton, P (Agen) 1989 B, 1990 NZ 2, 1991 US 2, 1992 Arg 1, 2(R), SA 1(R), 2, Arg, 1993 E, S, I, W, SA 1, 2, R 2, A 1, 2, 1994 I, W, E, S, C 1, NZ 1, 2, C 2, 1995 W, E, S, I, [Tg, Iv (R), S], It, R 2(R), Arg, NZ 1, 2, 1996 Arg 1, 2, W 2, SA 1, 2, 1997 I, It 1, 2(R), R 2, Arg, SA 1, 2 1998 E, S (R), I (R), W (R), Arg 1(R), 2(R), Fj (R), 1999 I, W 1, S (R)
Benezech, L (RCF) 1994 E, S, C 1, NZ 1, 2, C 2, 1995 W, E, [Iv, S, E], R 2, Arg, NZ 1, 2
Berbizier, P (Lourdes, Agen) 1981 S, I, W, E, NZ 1, 2, 1982 I, R, 1983 S, I, 1984 S (R), NZ 1, 2, 1985 Arg 1, 2, 1986 S, I, W, E, R 1, Arg 1, A, NZ 1, R 2, NZ 2, 3, 1987 W, E, S, I, [S, R, Fj, A, NZ], R, 1988 E, S, I, W, Arg 1, 2, 1989 I, W, E, S, NZ 1, 2, B, A 1, 1990 W, E, 1991 S, I, W 1, E
Berejnoï, J-C (Tulle) 1963 R, 1964 S, W, It, I, SA, Fj, R, 1965 S, I, E, W, It, R, 1966 S, I, E, W, It, R, 1967 S, A, E, It, W, I, R
Bergès, B (Toulouse) 1926 I
Berges-Cau, R (Lourdes) 1976 E (R)
Bergese, F (Bayonne) 1936 G 2, 1937 G, It, 1938 G 1, R, G 2
Bergougnan, Y (Toulouse) 1945 B 1, W, 1946 B, I, K, W, 1947 S, I, W, E, 1948 S, W, E, 1949 S, E, Arg 1, 2
Bernard, R (Bergerac) 1951 S, I, E, W
Bernat-Salles, P (Pau, Bègles-Bordeaux, Biarritz) 1992 Arg, 1993 R 1, SA 1, 2, R 2, A 1, 2, 1994 I, 1995 E, S, 1996 E (R), 1997 R 1, A 1, 2, 1998 E, S, I, W, Arg 1, 2, Fj, Arg 3(R), A 1999 I, W 1, R, Tg, [Nm, Fj, Arg, NZ 2, A], 2000 I, It, NZ 1(R), 2, 2001 S, I, It, W, E
Bernon, J (Lourdes) 1922 I, 1923 S
Bérot, J-L (Toulouse) 1968 NZ 3, A, 1969 S, I, 1970 E, R, 1971 S, I, E, W, SA 1, 2, A 1, 2, R, 1972 S, I 1, E, W, A 1, 1974 I

Bérot, P (Agen) 1986 R 2, NZ 2, 3, 1987 W, E, S, I, R, 1988 E, S, I, Arg 1, 2, 3, 4, R, 1989 S, NZ 1, 2
Bertrand, P (Bourg) 1951 I, E, W, 1953 S, I, E, W, It
Bertranne, R (Bagnères) 1971 E, W, SA 2, A 1, 2, 1972 S, I 1, 1973 NZ, E, J, R, 1974 I, W, E, S, Arg 1, 2, R, SA 1, 2, 1975 W, E, S, I, SA 1, 2, Arg 1, 2, R, 1976 S, I, W, E, US, A 1, 2, R, 1977 W, E, S, I, Arg 1, 2, NZ 1, 2, R, 1978 E, S, I, W, R, 1979 I, W, E, S, R, 1980 W, E, S, I, SA, R, 1981 S, I, W, E, R, NZ 1, 2
Berty, D (Toulouse) 1990 NZ 2, 1992 R (R), 1993 R 2, 1995 NZ 1(R), 1996 W 2(R), SA 1
Besset, E (Grenoble) 1924 S
Besset, L (SCUF) 1914 W, E
Besson, M (CASG) 1924 I, 1925 I, E, 1926 S, W, 1927 I
Besson, P (Brive) 1963 S, I, E, 1965 R, 1968 SA 1
Betsen, S (Biarritz) 1997 It 1(R), 2000 W (R), E (R), A (R), NZ 1(R), 2(R), 2001 S (R), I (R), It (R), W (R), SA 3(R), A, Fj, 2002 It, W, E, S, I, Arg, A 1, 2, SA, NZ, C, 2003 E 1, S, I, It, W, R, E 2, [Fj, J, S, I, E], 2004 I, It, W, S, E, A, Arg, NZ, 2005 E, W, I, It, 2006 SA, NZ2(R), Arg(R), 2007 It, I, W1, E1, S, E2, W2, [Arg 1, I, Gg, NZ, E]
Bianchi, J (Toulon) 1986 Arg 1
Bichindaritz, J (Biarritz O) 1954 It, Arg 1, 2
Bidabé, P (Biarritz) 2004 C, 2006 R
Bidart, L (La Rochelle) 1953 W
Biémouret, P (Agen) 1969 E, W, 1970 I, W, E, 1971 W, SA 1, 2, A 1, 1972 E, W, I 2, A 2, R, 1973 S, NZ, E, W, I
Biénès, R (Cognac) 1950 S, I, E, W, 1951 S, I, E, W, 1952 S, I, SA, W, E, It, 1953 S, I, E, 1954 S, I, NZ, W, E, Arg 1, 2, 1956 S, I, W, It, E
Bigot, C (Quillan) 1930 S, E, 1931 I, S
Bilbao, L (St Jean-de-Luz) 1978 I, 1979 I
Billac, E (Bayonne) 1920 S, E, W, I, US, 1921 S, W, 1922 W, 1923 E
Billière, M (Toulouse) 1968 NZ 3
Bioussa, A (Toulouse) 1924 W, US, 1925 I, NZ, S, E, 1926 S, I, E, 1928 E, G, W, 1929 I, S, W, E, 1930 S, I, E, G, W
Bioussa, C (Toulouse) 1913 W, I, 1914 I
Biraben, M (Dax) 1920 W, I, US, 1921 S, W, E, I, 1922 S, E, I
Blain, A (Carcassonne) 1934 G
Blanco, S (Biarritz O) 1980 SA, R, 1981 S, W, E, A 1, 2, R, NZ 1, 2, 1982 W, E, S, I, R, Arg 1, 2, 1983 E, S, I, W, 1984 I, W, E, S, NZ 1, 2, R, 1985 E, S, I, W, Arg 1, 2, 1986 S, I, W, E, R 1, Arg 2, A, NZ 1, R 2, NZ 2, 3, 1987 W, E, S, I, [S, R, Fj, A, NZ], R, 1988 E, S, I, W, Arg 1, 2, 3, 4, R, 1989 I, W, E, S, NZ 1, 2, B, A 1, 1990 E, S, I, R, A 1, 2, 3, NZ 1, 2, 1991 S, I, W 1, E, R, US 1, 2, W 2, [R, Fj, C, E]
Blond, J (SF) 1935 G, 1936 G 2, 1937 G, 1938 G 1, R, G 2
Blond, X (RCF) 1990 A 3, 1991 S, I, W 1, E, 1994 NZ 2(R)
Boffelli, V (Aurillac) 1971 A 2, R, 1972 S, I 1, 1973 J, R, 1974 I, W, E, S, Arg 1, 2, R, SA 1, 2, 1975 W, S, I
Bonal, J-M (Toulouse) 1968 E, W, Cz, NZ 2, 3, SA 1, 2, R, 1969 S, I, E, R, 1970 W, E
Bonamy, R (SB) 1928 A, I
Bondouy, P (Narbonne, Toulouse) 1997 S (R), It 1, A 2(R), R 2, 2000 R (R)
Bonetti, S (Biarritz) 2001 It, W, NZ (R)
Boniface, A (Mont-de-Marsan) 1954 I, NZ, W, E, It, Arg 1, 2, 1955 S, I, 1956 S, I, W, It, Cz, 1957 S, I, W, R 2, 1958 S, E, 1959 E, 1961 NZ 1, 3, A, R, 1962 E, W, I, It, R, 1963 S, I, E, W, It, R, 1964 S, NZ, E, W, It, 1965 W, It, R, 1966 S, I, E, W
Boniface, G (Mont-de-Marsan) 1960 W, I, It, R, Arg 1, 2, 3, 1961 S, SA, E, W, It, I, NZ 1, 2, 3, R, 1962 R, 1963 S, I, E, W, It, R, 1964 S, 1965 S, I, E, W, It, R, 1966 S, I, E, W
Bonnaire, J (Bourgoin, Clermont-Auvergne) 2004 S(t&R), A(R), NZ(R), 2005 S, E, W, I, It, SA1, 2, A1, C, Tg, SA3, 2006 S, I, It(R), E(R), W, R, SA(R), NZ1, 2, Arg, 2007 It, I(R), W1, E1, S, E2, 3(R), [Arg1(R), Nm, I, Gg, NZ, E], 2008 S(R), I, E, It(R), W, 2009 E(R), It, SA(R), Sm, NZ3, 2010 S(R), I(R), W, It, E, SA, Arg1, 2, A(R), 2011 S, I1, E(R), It, W, I2(R), 3, [J(R), C, NZ1, Tg, E, W, NZ2], 2012 It, S(R), I, E, W
Bonnes, E (Narbonne) 1924 W, R, US
Bonneval, E (Toulouse) 1984 NZ 2(R), 1985 W, Arg 1, 1986 W, E, R 1, Arg 1, 2, A, R 2, NZ 2, 3, 1987 W, E, S, I, [Z], 1988 E
Bonnus, F (Toulon) 1950 S, I, E, W
Bonnus, M (Toulon) 1937 It, 1938 G 1, R, G 2, 1940 B
Bontemps, D (La Rochelle) 1968 SA 2
Borchard, G (RCF) 1908 E, 1909 E, W, I, 1911 I
Borde, F (RCF) 1920 I, US, 1921 S, W, E, 1922 S, W, 1923 S, I, 1924 E, 1925 I, 1926 E
Bordenave, L (Toulon) 1948 A, S, W, E, 1949 S
Bory, D (Montferrand) 2000 I, It, A, NZ 1, 2001 S, I, SA 1, 2, 3, A, Fj, 2002 It, E, S, I, C, 2003 [US, NZ]
Boubée, J (Tarbes) 1921 S, E, I, 1922 E, W, 1923 E, I, 1925 NZ, S
Boudreaux, R (SCUF) 1910 W, S
Bouet, D (Dax) 1989 NZ 1, 2, B, A 2, 1990 A 3
Bouguyon, G (Grenoble) 1961 SA, E, W, It, I, NZ 1, 2, 3, A
Bouic, G (Agen) 1996 SA 1
Bouilhou, J (Toulouse) 2001 NZ, 2003 Arg 1
Boujet, C (Grenoble) 1968 NZ 2, A (R), SA 1
Bouquet, J (Bourgoin, Vienne) 1954 S, 1955 E, 1956 S, I, W, It, E, Cz, 1957 S, E, W, R 2, 1958 S, E, 1959 S, It, W, I, 1960 S, E, W, I, R, 1961 S, SA, E, W, It, I, R, 1962 S, E, W, I
Bourdeu, J-R (Lourdes) 1952 S, I, SA, W, E, It, 1953 S, I, E
Bourgarel, R (Toulouse) 1969 R, 1970 S, I, E, R, 1971 W, SA 1, 2, 1973 S
Bourguignon, G (Narbonne) 1988 Arg 3, 1989 I, E, B, A 1, 1990 R
Bousquet, A (Béziers) 1921 E, I, 1924 R
Bousquet, R (Albi) 1926 M, 1927 I, S, W, E, G 1, 1929 W, E, 1930 W
Bousses, G (Bourgoin) 2006 S(R)
Boyau, M (SBUC) 1912 I, S, W, E, 1913 W, I
Boyer, P (Toulon) 1935 G
Boyet, B (Bourgoin) 2006 I(R), 2007 NZ1, 2, 2008 A1, 2(R)
Boyoud, R (Dax) 2008 A1(R), 2, 2009 S(R)
Branca, G (SF) 1928 S, 1929 I, S
Branlat, A (RCF) 1906 NZ, E, 1908 W
Bréjassou, R (Tarbes) 1952 S, I, SA, W, E, 1953 W, E, 1954 S, I, NZ, 1955 S, I, E, W, It
Brèthes, R (St Séver) 1960 Arg 2
Bringeon, A (Biarritz O) 1925 W
Brouzet, O (Grenoble, Bègles, Northampton, Montferrand) 1994 S, NZ 2(R), 1995 E, S, I, R 1, [Tg, Iv, E (t)], It, Arg (R), 1996 W 1(R), 1997 R 1, A 1, 2, It 2, Arg, SA 1, 2, 1998 E, S, I, W, Arg 1, 2, Fj, Arg 3, A, 1999 I, W 1, E, S, R, [C (R), Nm, Fj (R), Arg, NZ 2(R), A (R)], 2000 W, E, S, I, It, A, NZ 1(R), 2(R), 2001 SA 1, 2, NZ, 2002 W, E, S, I, Arg, A 1(R), 2, SA, NZ, C, 2003 E 1, S, I, It, W, E 3, [Fj(R), J, S(R), US, I(R)]
Bru, Y (Toulouse) 2001 A (R), Fj (R), 2002 It, 2003 Arg 2, NZ, R, E 2, 3(R), [J, S(R), US, I(t&R), NZ], 2004 I(R), It(R), W(R), S(R), E(R)
Brugnaut, J (Dax) 2008 S, I(R)
Brun, G (Vienne) 1950 E, W, 1951 S, E, W, 1952 S, I, SA, W, E, It, 1953 E, W, It
Bruneau, M (SBUC) 1910 W, E, 1913 SA, E
Brunet, Y (Perpignan) 1975 SA 1, 1977 Arg 1
Bruno, S (Béziers, Sale) 2002 W (R), 2004 A(R), NZ(t&R), 2005 S(R), E, W, I, It, SA1, 2(R), A1(R), 2(R), C, SA3(R), 2006 S(R), I(R), 2007 I(R), E1(R), NZ1, 2, E3(R), W2(R), [Gg, Arg 2(t&R)], 2008 A1, 2
Brusque, N (Pau, Biarritz) 1997 R 2(R), 2002 W, E, S, I, Arg, A 2, SA, NZ, C, 2003 E 2, [Fj, S, I, E, NZ(R)], 2004 I, It, W, S, E, A, Arg, 2005 SA1(R), 2, A1, 2006 S
Buchet, E (Nice) 1980 R, 1982 E, R (R), Arg 1, 2
Buisson, H (see Empereur-Buisson)
Buonomo, Y (Béziers) 1971 A 2, R, 1972 I 1
Burgun, M (RCF) 1909 I, 1910 W, S, I, 1911 S, E, 1912 I, S, 1913 S, E, 1914 E
Bustaffa, D (Carcassonne) 1977 Arg 1, 2, NZ 1, 2, 1978 W, R, 1980 W, E, S, SA, R
Buttin, J-M (Clermont-Auvergne) 2012 W(R), Arg 1
Buzy, C-E (Lourdes) 1946 K, W, 1947 S, I, W, E, 1948 I, A, S, W, E, 1949 S, I, E, W, Arg 1, 2

Caballero, Y (Montauban) 2008 A2(R)
Cabanier, J-M (Montauban) 1963 R, 1964 S, Fj, 1965 S, I, W, It, R, 1966 S, I, E, W, It, R, 1967 S, A, E, It, W, I, SA 1, 3, NZ, R, 1968 S, I
Cabannes, L (RCF, Harlequins) 1990 NZ 2(R), 1991 S, I, W 1, E, US 2, W 2, [R, Fj, C, E], 1992 W, E, S, I, R, Arg 2, SA 1, 2, 1993 E, S, I, W, R 1, SA 1, 2, 1994 E, S, C 1, NZ 1, 2, 1995 W, E, S, R 1, [Tg (R), Iv, S, I, SA, E], 1996 E, S, I, W 1, 1997 It 2, Arg, SA 1, 2
Cabrol, H (Béziers) 1972 A 1(R), 2, 1973 J, 1974 SA 2
Cadenat, J (SCUF) 1910 S, E, 1911 W, I, 1912 W, E, 1913 I
Cadieu, J-M (Toulouse) 1991 R, US 1, [R, Fj, C, E], 1992 W, I, R, Arg 1, 2, SA 1
Cahuc, F (St Girons) 1922 S
Califano, C (Toulouse, Saracens, Gloucester) 1994 NZ 1, 2, C 2, 1995 W, E, S, I, [Iv, S, I, SA, E], It, Arg, NZ 1, 2, 1996 E, S, I, W 1, R, Arg 1, 2, SA 1, 2, 1997 I, W, E, A 1, 2, It 2, R 2(R), Arg, SA 1, 2, 1998 E, S, I, W, 1999 I, W 1, E (R), S, WS, Tg (R), NZ 1, W 2, [C, Nm, Fj], 2000 W, E, S, I, It, R, A, NZ 1, 2(R), 2001 S (R), I (R), It, W, SA 1(R), 2(R), NZ, 2003 E 1, S (R), I (R), 2007 NZ1, 2
Cals, R (RCF) 1938 G 1
Calvo, G (Lourdes) 1961 NZ 1, 3
Camberabero, D (La Voulte, Béziers) 1982 R, Arg 1, 2, 1983 E, W, 1987 [R (R), Z, Fj (R), A, NZ], 1988 I, 1989 B, A 1, 1990 W, S, I, R, A 1, 2, 3, NZ 1, 2, 1991 S, I, W 1, E, R, US 1, 2, W 2, [R, Fj, C], 1993 E, S, I
Camberabero, G (La Voulte) 1961 NZ 3, 1962 R, 1964 R, 1967 A, E, It, W, I, SA 1, 3, 4, 1968 S, E, W
Camberabero, L (La Voulte) 1964 R, 1965 S, I, 1966 E, W, 1967 A, E, It, W, I, 1968 S, E, W
Cambré, T (Oloron) 1920 E, W, I, US
Camel, A (Toulouse) 1928 S, A, I, E, G, W, 1929 W, E, G, 1930 S, I, E, G, W, 1935 G
Camel, M (Toulouse) 1929 S, W, E
Camicas, F (Tarbes) 1927 G 2, 1928 S, I, E, G, W, 1929 I, S, W, E
Camo, E (Villeneuve) 1931 I, S, W, E, G, 1932 G
Campaès, A (Lourdes) 1965 W, 1967 NZ, 1968 S, I, E, W, Cz, NZ 1, 2, A, 1969 S, W, 1972 R, 1973 NZ
Campan, O (Agen) 1993 SA 1(R), 2(R), R 2(R), 1996 I, W 1, R
Candelon, J (Narbonne) 2005 SA1, A1(R)
Cantoni, J (Béziers) 1970 W, R, 1971 S, I, E, W, SA 1, 2, R, 1972 S, I 1, 1973 S, NZ, W, I, 1975 W (R)
Capdouze, J (Pau) 1964 SA, Fj, R, 1965 S, I, E
Capendeguy, J-M (Bègles) 1967 NZ, R
Capitani, P (Toulon) 1954 Arg 1, 2
Capmau, J-L (Toulouse) 1914 E
Carabignac, G (Agen) 1951 S, I, 1952 SA, W, E, 1953 S, I
Carbonne, J (Perpignan) 1927 W
Carbonneau, P (Toulouse, Brive, Pau) 1995 R 2, Arg, NZ 1, 2, 1996 E, S, R (R), Arg 2, W 2, SA 1, 1997 I (R), W, E, S (R), R 1(R), A 1, 2, 1998 E, S, I, W, Arg 1, 2, Fj, Arg 3, A, 1999 I, W 1, E, S, 2000 NZ 2(R), 2001 I
Carminati, A (Béziers, Brive) 1986 R 2, NZ 2, 1987 [R, Z], 1988 I, W, Arg 1, 2, 1989 I, W, S, NZ 1(R), 2, A 2, 1990 S, 1995 It, R 2, Arg, NZ 1, 2
Caron, L (Lyon O, Castres) 1947 E, 1948 I, A, W, E, 1949 S, I, E, W, Arg 1
Carpentier, M (Lourdes) 1980 E, SA, R, 1981 S, I, A 1, 1982 E, S
Carrère, C (Toulon) 1966 R, 1967 S, A, E, W, I, SA 1, 3, 4, NZ, R, 1968 S, I, E, W, Cz, NZ 3, A, R, 1969 S, I, 1970 S, I, W, E, 1971 E, W
Carrère, J (Vichy, Toulon) 1956 S, 1957 E, W, R 2, 1958 S, SA 1, 2, 1959 I
Carrère, R (Mont-de-Marsan) 1953 E, It
Casadei, D (Brive) 1997 S, R 1, SA 2(R)
Casaux, L (Tarbes) 1959 I, It, 1962 S
Cassagne, P (Pau) 1957 It
Cassayet-Armagnac, A (Tarbes, Narbonne) 1920 S, E, W, US, 1921 W, E, I, 1922 S, E, W, 1923 S, W, E, I, 1924 S, E, W, R, US, 1925 I, NZ, S, W, 1926 S, I, E, W, M, 1927 I, S, W
Cassiède, M (Dax) 1961 NZ 3, A, R
Castaignède, S (Mont-de-Marsan) 1999 W 2, [C (R), Nm (R), Fj, Arg (R), NZ 2(R), A (R)]
Castaignède, T (Toulouse, Castres, Saracens) 1995 R 2, Arg, NZ 1, 2, 1996 E, S, I, W 1, Arg 1, 2, 1997 I, A 1, 2, It 2, 1998 E, S, I, W, Arg 1, 2, Fj, 1999 I, W 1, E, S, R, WS, Tg (R), NZ 1, W 2, [C], 2000 W, E, S, It, 2002 SA, NZ, C, 2003 E 1(R), S (R), It, W, Arg 1, 2005 A2(R), C, Tg, SA3, 2006 It, E, W, R, SA(R), 2007 NZ1, 2
Castel, R (Toulouse, Béziers) 1996 I, W 1, W 2, SA 1(R), 2, 1997 I (R), W, E (R), S (R), A 1(R), 1998 Arg 3(R), A (R), 1999 W 1(R), E, S
Castets, J (Toulon) 1923 W, E, I
Caujolle, J (Tarbes) 1909 E, 1913 SA, E, 1914 W, E
Caunègre, R (SB) 1938 R, G 2
Caussade, A (Lourdes) 1978 R, 1979 I, W, E, NZ 1, 2, R, 1980 W, E, S, 1981 S (R), I
Caussarieu, G (Pau) 1929 I
Cayrefourcq, E (Tarbes) 1921 E
Cazalbou, J (Toulouse) 1997 It 2(R), R 2, Arg, SA 2(R)
Cazals, P (Mont-de-Marsan) 1961 NZ 1, A, R
Cazenave, A (Pau) 1927 E, G 1, 1928 S, A, G
Cazenave, F (RCF) 1950 E, 1952 S, 1954 I, NZ, W, E
Cécillon, M (Bourgoin) 1988 I, W, Arg 2, 3, 4, R, 1989 I, E, NZ 1, 2, A 1, 1991 S, I, E (R), R, US 1, W 2, [E], 1992 W, E, S, I, R, Arg 1, 2, SA 1, 2, 1993 E, S, I, W, R 1, SA 1, 2, R 2, A 1, 2, 1994 I, W, NZ 1(R), 1995 I, R 1, [Tg, S (R), I, SA]
Celaya, M (Biarritz O, SBUC) 1953 E, W, It, 1954 I, E, It, Arg 1, 2, 1955 S, I, E, W, It, 1956 S, I, W, It, E, Cz 1957 S, I, E, W, R 2, 1958 S, E, A, W, It, 1959 S, E, 1960 S, E, W, I, R, Arg 1, 2, 3, 1961 S, SA, E, W, It, I, NZ 1, 2, 3, A, R
Celhay, M (Bayonne) 1935 G, 1936 G 1, 1937 G, It, 1938 G 1, 1940 B
Cermeno, F (Perpignan) 2000 R
Cessieux, N (Lyon) 1906 NZ
Cester, E (TOEC, Valence) 1966 S, I, E, 1967 W, 1968 S, I, E, W, Cz, NZ 1, 3, A, SA 1, 2, R, 1969 S, I, E, W, 1970 S, I, W, E, 1971 A 1, 1972 R, 1973 S, NZ, W, I, J, R, 1974 I, W, E, S
Chabal, S (Bourgoin, Sale, Racing-Metro) 2000 S, 2001 SA 1, 2, NZ (R), Fj (R), 2002 Arg (R), A 2, SA (R), NZ (t), C (R), 2003 E 1(R), S (R), I (R), Arg 2, NZ (R), E 2(R), 3, [J(R), US, NZ], 2005 S, E, A2(R), Tg, 2007 It, I, E1, NZ1, 2, E2(R), W2, [Arg1(R), Nm, I, NZ(R), E(R), Arg 2(R)], 2008 A1, 2, Arg(R), PI(R), A3, 2009 I, S(R), W, E, It, NZ1(R), 2, SA(R), Sm, NZ3, 2010 W(R), It(R), E(R), Fj(R), Arg2, A, 2011 S(R), I1(R), E, It
Chaban-Delmas, J (CASG) 1945 B 2
Chabowski, H (Nice, Bourgoin) 1985 Arg 2, 1986 R 2, NZ 2, 1989 B (R)
Chadebech, P (Brive) 1982 R, Arg 1, 2, 1986 S, I
Champ, E (Toulon) 1985 Arg 1, 2, 1986 I, W, E, R 1, Arg 1, 2, A, NZ 1, R 2, NZ 2, 3, 1987 W, E, S, I, [S, R, Fj, A, NZ], R, 1988 E, S, Arg 1, 3, 4, R, 1989 W, S, A 1, 2, 1990 W, E, NZ 1, 1991 R, US 1, [R, Fj, C, E]
Chapuy, L (SF) 1926 S
Charpentier, G (SF) 1911 E, 1912 W, E
Charton, P (Montferrand) 1940 B
Charvet, D (Toulouse) 1986 W, E, R 1, Arg 1, A, NZ 1, 3, 1987 W, E, S, I, [S, R, Z, Fj, A, NZ], R, 1989 E (R), 1990 W, E, 1991 S, I
Chassagne, J (Montferrand) 1938 G 1
Chatau, A (Bayonne) 1913 SA
Chaud, E (Toulon) 1932 G, 1934 G, 1935 G
Chazalet, A (Bourgoin) 1999 Tg
Chenevay, C (Grenoble) 1968 SA 1
Chevallier, B (Montferrand) 1952 S, I, SA, W, E, It, 1953 E, W, It, 1954 S, I, NZ, W, Arg 1, 1955 S, I, E, W, It, 1956 S, I, W, It, E, Cz, 1957 S
Chiberry, J (Chambéry) 1955 It
Chilo, A (RCF) 1920 S, W, 1925 I, NZ
Cholley, G (Castres) 1975 E, S, I, SA 1, 2, Arg 1, 2, R, 1976 S, I, W, E, A 1, 2, R, 1977 W, E, S, I, Arg 1, 2, NZ 1, 2, R, 1978 E, S, I, W, R, 1979 I, S
Chouly, D (Brive, Perpignan, Clermont-Auvergne) 2007 NZ1(R), 2, 2009 NZ2(R), A(R), 2012 A(R), Arg3(R), Sm(R), 2013 It(R), W(R), NZ3
Choy J (Narbonne) 1930 S, I, E, G, W, 1931 I, 1933 G, 1934 G, 1935 G, 1936 G 2

THE COUNTRIES

Cigagna, A (Toulouse) 1995 [E]
Cimarosti, J (Castres) 1976 US (R)
Cistacq, J-C (Agen) 2000 R (R)
Claassen, A D (Castres) 2013 E(R), I(R), S, NZ3
Clady, A (Lezignan) 1929 G, 1931 I, S, E, G
Clarac, H (St Girons) 1938 G 1
Claudel, R (Lyon) 1932 G, 1934 G
Clauzel, F (Béziers) 1924 E, W, 1925 W
Clavé, J (Agen) 1936 G 2, 1938 R, G 2
Claverie, H (Lourdes) 1954 NZ, W
Cléda, T (Pau) 1998 E (R), S (R), I (R), W (R), Arg 1(R), Fj (R), Arg 3(R), 1999 I (R), S
Clément, G (RCF) 1931 W
Clément, J (RCF) 1921 S, W, E, 1922 S, E, W, I, 1923 S, W, I
Clemente, M (Oloron) 1978 R, 1980 S, I
Clerc, V (Toulouse) 2002 SA, NZ, C, 2003 E 1, S, I, It (R), W (R), Arg 2, NZ, 2004 I, It, W, 2005 SA2, Tg, 2006 SA, 2007 I, W1, E1, S, E2, W2, [Nm, I, Gg(R), NZ, E, Arg 2(R)], 2008 S, I, E, It(t), W, 2009 NZ1, 2, A(R), SA, Sm, NZ3, 2010 S(R), I, SA, Arg1, 2011 S(R), I1(R), E, It, W, I2, 3(R), [J, C, NZ1, Tg, E, W, NZ2], 2012 It, S, I, E, A, Arg3, Sm, 2013 E, I, S
Cluchague, L (Biarritz O) 1924 S, 1925 E
Coderc, J (Chalon) 1932 G, 1933 G, 1934 G, 1935 G, 1936 G 1
Codorniou, D (Narbonne) 1979 NZ 1, 2, R, 1980 W, E, S, I, 1981 S, W, E, A 2, 1983 E, S, I, W, A 1, 2, R, 1984 I, W, E, S, NZ 1, 2, R, 1985 E, S, I, W, Arg 1, 2
Coeurveille, C (Agen) 1992 Arg 1(R), 2
Cognet, L (Montferrand) 1932 G, 1936 G 1, 2, 1937 G, It
Collazo, P (Bègles) 2000 R
Colombier, J (St Junien) 1952 SA, W, E
Colomine, G (Narbonne) 1979 NZ 1
Comba, F (SF) 1998 Arg 1, 2, Fj, Arg 3, 1999 I, W 1, E, S, 2000 A, NZ 1, 2, 2001 S, I
Combe, J (SF) 1910 S, E, I, 1911 S
Combes, G (Fumel) 1945 B 2
Communeau, M (SF) 1906 NZ, E, 1907 E, 1908 E, W, 1909 E, W, I, 1910 S, E, I, 1911 S, E, I, 1912 I, S, W, E, 1913 SA, E, W
Condom, J (Boucau, Biarritz O) 1982 R, 1983 E, S, I, W, A 1, 2, R, 1984 I, W, E, S, NZ 1, 2, R, 1985 E, S, I, W, Arg 1, 2, 1986 S, I, W, E, R 1, Arg 1, 2, NZ 1, R 2, NZ 2, 3, 1987 W, E, S, I, [S, R, Z, A, NZ], R, 1988 E, S, W, Arg 1, 2, 3, 4, R, 1989 I, W, E, S, NZ 1, 2, A 1, 1990 I, R, A 2, 3(R)
Conilh de Beyssac, J-J (SBUC) 1912 I, S, 1914 I, W, E
Constant, G (Perpignan) 1920 W
Correia, P (Albi) 2008 A2
Coscolla, G (Béziers) 1921 S, W
Costantino, J (Montferrand) 1973 R
Costes, A (Montferrand) 1994 C 2, 1995 R 1, [Iv], 1997 It 1, 1999 WS, Tg (R), NZ 1, [Nm (R), Fj (R), Arg (R), NZ 2(R), A (t&R)], 2000 S (R), I
Costes, F (Montferrand) 1979 E, S, NZ 1, 2, R, 1980 W, I
Couffignal, H (Colomiers) 1993 R 1
Coulon, E (Grenoble) 1928 S
Courtiols, M (Bègles) 1991 R, US 1, W 2
Coux, J-F (Bourgoin) 2007 NZ1, 2
Couzinet, D (Biarritz) 2004 US, C(R), 2008 A1(R)
Crabos, R (RCF) 1920 S, E, W, I, US, 1921 S, W, E, I, 1922 S, E, W, I, 1923 S, I, 1924 S, I
Crampagne, J (Bègles) 1967 SA 4
Crancée, R (Lourdes) 1960 Arg 3, 1961 S
Crauste, M (RCF, Lourdes) 1957 R 1, 2, 1958 S, E, A, W, It, I, 1959 E, It, W, I, 1960 S, E, W, I, It, R, Arg 1, 3, 1961 S, SA, E, W, It, I, NZ 1, 2, 3, A, R, 1962 S, E, W, I, It, R, 1963 S, I, E, W, It, R, 1964 S, NZ, E, W, It, I, SA, Fj, R, 1965 S, I, E, W, It, R, 1966 S, I, E, W, It
Cremaschi, M (Lourdes) 1980 R, 1981 R, NZ 1, 2, 1982 W, S, 1983 A 1, 2, R, 1984 I, W
Crenca, J-J (Agen) 1996 SA 2(R), 1999 R, Tg, WS (R), NZ 1(R), 2001 SA 1, 2, NZ (R), SA 3, A, Fj, 2002 It, W, E, S, I, Arg, A 2, SA, NZ, C, 2003 E 1, S, I, It, W, R, E 2, [Fj, J(t&R), S, I, E, NZ(R)], 2004 I(R), It(R), W(R), S(R), E(R)
Crichton, W H (Le Havre) 1906 NZ, E
Cristina, J (Montferrand) 1979 R
Cussac, P (Biarritz O) 1934 G
Cutzach, A (Quillan) 1929 G

Daguerre, F (Biarritz O) 1936 G 1
Daguerre, J (CASG) 1933 G
Dal Maso, M (Mont-de-Marsan, Agen, Colomiers) 1988 R (R), 1990 NZ 2, 1996 SA 1(R), 2, 1997 I, W, E, S, It 1, R 1(R), A 1, 2, It 2, Arg, SA 1, 2, 1998 W (R), Arg 1(t), Fj (R), 1999 R (R), WS (R), Tg, NZ 1(R), W 2(R), [Nm (R), Fj (R), Arg (R), A (R)], 2000 W, E, S, I, It
Danion, J (Toulon) 1924 I
Danos, P (Toulon, Béziers) 1954 Arg 1, 2, 1957 R 2, 1958 S, E, W, It, I, SA 1, 2, 1959 S, E, It, W, I, 1960 S, E
Dantiacq, D (Pau) 1997 R 1
Darbos, P (Dax) 1969 R
Darracq, R (Dax) 1957 It
Darrieussecq, A (Biarritz O) 1973 E
Darrieussecq, J (Mont-de-Marsan) 1953 It
Darrouy, C (Mont-de-Marsan) 1957 I, E, W, It, R 1, 1959 E, 1961 R, 1963 S, I, E, W, It, 1964 NZ, E, W, It, I, SA, Fj, R, 1965 S, I, E, It, R, 1966 S, I, E, W, It, R, 1967 S, A, E, It, W, I, SA 1, 2, 4
Daudé, J (Bourgoin) 2000 S
Daudignon, G (SF) 1928 S
Dauga, B (Mont-de-Marsan) 1964 S, NZ, E, W, It, I, SA, Fj, R, 1965 S, I, E, W, It, R, 1966 S, I, E, W, It, R, 1967 S, A, E, It, W, I, SA 1, 2, 3, 4, NZ, R, 1968 S, I, NZ 1, 2, 3, A, SA 1, 2, R, 1969 S, I, E, R, 1970 S, I, W, E, R, 1971 S, I, E, W, SA 1, 2, A 1, 2, R, 1972 S, I 1, W
Dauger, J (Bayonne) 1945 B 1, 2, 1953 S
Daulouède, P (Tyrosse) 1937 G, It, 1938 G 1, 1940 B
David, Y (Bourgoin, Toulouse) 2008 It, 2009 SA, Sm(R), NZ3(R)
Debaty, V (Perpignan, Clermont-Auvergne) 2006 R(R), 2012 It, S(R), I(R), E(R), W(R), Arg 1(R), 2, A(R), Arg3(R), Sm(R), 2013 It(R), W(R), E(R), I(R), S(R), NZ1(R), 2(R)
De Besombes, S (Perpignan) 1998 Arg 1(R), Fj (R)
Decamps, P (RCF) 1911 S
Dedet, J (SF) 1910 S, E, I, 1911 W, I, 1912 S, 1913 E, I
Dedeyn, P (RCF) 1906 NZ
Dedieu, P (Béziers) 1963 E, It, 1964 W, It, I, SA, Fj, R, 1965 S, I, E, W
De Gregorio, J (Grenoble) 1960 S, E, W, I, It, R, Arg 1, 2, 1961 S, SA, E, W, It, I, 1962 S, E, W, 1963 S, W, It, 1964 NZ, E
Dehez, J-L (Agen) 1967 SA 2, 1969 R
De Jouvencel, E (SF) 1909 W, I
De Laborderie, M (RCF) 1921 I, 1922 I, 1925 W, E
Delage, C (Agen) 1983 S, I
De Malherbe, H (CASG) 1932 G, 1933 G
De Malmann, R (RCF) 1908 E, W, 1909 E, W, I, 1910 E, I
De Muizon, J J (SF) 1910 I
Delaigue, G (Toulon) 1973 J, R
Delaigue, Y (Toulon, Toulouse, Castres) 1994 S, NZ 2(R), C 2, 1995 I, R 1, [Tg, Iv], It, R 2(R), 1997 It 1, 2003 Arg 1, 2, 2005 S, E, W, I, It, A2(R), Tg, SA3(R)
Delmotte, G (Toulon) 1999 R, Tg
Delque, A (Toulouse) 1937 It, 1938 G 1, R, G 2
De Rougemont, M (Toulon) 1995 E (t), R 1(t), [Iv], NZ 1, 2, 1996 I (R), Arg 1, 2, W 2, SA 1, 1997 E (R), S (R), It 1
Desbrosse, C (Toulouse) 1999 [Nm (R)], 2000 I
Descamps, P (SB) 1927 G 2
Desclaux, F (RCF) 1949 Arg 1, 2, 1953 It
Desclaux, J (Perpignan) 1934 G, 1935 G, 1936 G 1, 2, 1937 G, It, 1938 G 1, R, G 2, 1945 B 1
Deslandes, C (RCF) 1990 A 1, NZ 2, 1991 W 1, 1992 R, Arg 1, 2
Desnoyer, L (Brive) 1974 R
Destarac, L (Tarbes) 1926 S, I, E, W, M, 1927 W, E, G 1, 2
Desvouges, R (SF) 1914 W
Detrez, P-E (Nîmes) 1983 A 2(R), 1986 Arg 1(R), 2, A (R), NZ1
Devergie, T (Nîmes) 1988 R, 1989 NZ 1, 2, B, A 2, 1990 W, E, S, I, R, A 1, 2, 3, 1991 US 2, W 2, 1992 R (R), Arg 2(R)
De Villiers, P (SF) 1999 W 2, [Arg (R), NZ 2(R), A (R)], 2000 W (R), E (R), S (R), I (R), It (R), NZ 1(R), 2, 2001 S, I, It, W, E, SA 1, 2, NZ (R), SA 3, A, Fj, 2002 It, W, E, I, SA, NZ, C, 2003 Arg 1, 2, NZ (R), 2004 I, It, W, S, E, US, C, NZ,

2005 S, I(R), It(R), SA1(R), 2, A1(R), 2, C, Tg(R), SA3, 2006 S, I, It, E, W, SA, NZ1, 2, Arg, 2007 It, I, E1, S, W2, [Arg1, Nm, I, NZ, E]
Deygas, M (Vienne) 1937 It
Deylaud, C (Toulouse) 1992 R, Arg 1, 2, SA 1, 1994 C 1, NZ 1, 2, 1995 W, E, S, [Iv (R), S, I, SA], It, Arg
Diarra, I (Montauban) 2008 It
Dintrans, P (Tarbes) 1979 NZ 1, 2, R, 1980 E, S, I, SA, R, 1981 S, I, W, E, A 1, 2, R, NZ 1, 2, 1982 W, E, S, I, R, Arg 1, 2, 1983 E, W, A 1, 2, R, 1984 I, W, E, S, NZ 1, 2, R, 1985 E, S, I, W, Arg 1, 2, 1987 [R], 1988 Arg 1, 2, 3, 1989 W, E, S, 1990 R
Dispagne, S (Toulouse) 1996 I (R), W 1
Dizabo, P (Tyrosse) 1948 A, S, E, 1949 S, I, E, W, Arg 2, 1950 S, I, 1960 Arg 1, 2, 3
Domec, A (Carcassonne) 1929 W
Domec, H (Lourdes) 1953 W, It, 1954 S, I, NZ, W, E, It, 1955 S, I, E, W, 1956 I, W, It, 1958 E, A, W, It, I
Domenech, A (Vichy, Brive) 1954 W, E, It, 1955 S, I, E, W, 1956 S, I, W, It, E, Cz, 1957 S, I, E, W, It, R 1, 2, 1958 S, E, It, 1959 It, 1960 S, E, W, I, It, R, Arg 1, 2, 3, 1961 S, SA, E, W, It, I, NZ 1, 2, 3, A, R, 1962 S, E, W, I, It, R, 1963 W, It
Domercq, J (Bayonne) 1912 I, S
Domingo, T (Clermont-Auvergne) 2009 W(R), E(R), It(R), NZ2(R), Sm, 2010 S, I, W, It, E, SA, Arg2, A, 2011 S, I1, E, W, 2012 Arg 2(R), A(R), Arg3(R), Sm, 2013 E, I, S, NZ1, 2, 3
Dominici, C (SF) 1998 E, S, Arg 1, 2, 1999 E, S, WS, NZ 1, W 2, [C, Fj, Arg, NZ 2, A], 2000 W, E, S, R, 2001 I (R), It, W, E, SA 1, 2, NZ, Fj, 2003 Arg 1, R, E 2, 3, [Fj, J, S, I, E], 2004 I, It, W, S, E, A(R), NZ(R), 2005 S, E, W, I, It, 2006 S, I, It, E, W, NZ1, 2(R), Arg, 2007 It, I, W1, E1, S(R), E3, W2(R), [Arg 1, Gg, NZ(R), E(R), Arg 2]
Dorot, J (RCF) 1935 G
Dospital, P (Bayonne) 1977 R, 1980 I, 1981 S, I, W, E, 1982 I, R, Arg 1, 2, 1983 E, S, I, W, 1984 E, S, NZ 1, 2, R, 1985 E, S, I, W, Arg 1
Dourthe, C (Dax) 1966 R, 1967 S, A, E, W, I, SA 1, 2, 3, NZ, 1968 W, NZ 3, SA 1, 2, 1969 W, 1971 SA 2(R), R, 1972 I 1, 2, A 1, 2, R, 1973 S, NZ, E, 1974 I, Arg 1, 2, SA 1, 2, 1975 W, E, S
Dourthe, M (Dax) 2000 NZ 2(t)
Dourthe, R (Dax, SF, Béziers) 1995 R 2, Arg, NZ 1, 2, 1996 E, R, 1996 Arg 1, 2, W 2, SA 1, 2, 1997 W, A 1, 1999 I, W 1, 2, [C, Nm, Fj, Arg, NZ 2, A], 2000 W, E, It, R, A, NZ 1, 2, 2001 S, I
Doussain, J-M (Toulouse) 2011 [NZ2(R)], 2013 NZ1(R), 3
Doussau, E (Angoulême) 1938 R
Droitecourt, M (Montferrand) 1972 R, 1973 NZ (R), E, 1974 E, S, Arg 1, SA 2, 1975 SA 1, 2, Arg 1, 2, R, 1976 S, I, W, A 1, 1977 Arg 2
Dubertrand, A (Montferrand) 1971 A 1, 2, R, 1972 I 2, 1974 I, W, E, SA 2, 1975 Arg 1, 2, R, 1976 S, US
Dubois, D (Bègles) 1971 S
Dubroca, D (Agen) 1979 NZ 2, 1981 NZ 2(R), 1982 E, S, 1984 W, E, S, 1985 Arg 2, 1986 S, I, W, E, R 1, Arg 2, A, NZ 1, R 2, NZ 2, 3, 1987 W, E, S, I, [S, Z, Fj, A, NZ], R, 1988 E, S, I, W
Ducalcon, L (Castres, Racing Métro) 2010 S(R), Fj, Arg2(R), 2011 S(R), It(R), W(R), I2, [C, NZ1, Tg], 2013 It(R), W(R), E(R), S(R), NZ1, 2(R), 3(R)
Duché, A (Limoges) 1929 G
Duclos, A (Lourdes) 1931 S
Ducousso, J (Tarbes) 1925 S, W, E
Dufau, G (RCF) 1948 I, A, 1949 I, W, 1950 S, E, W, 1951 S, I, E, W, 1952 SA, W, 1953 S, I, E, W, 1954 S, I, NZ, W, E, It, 1955 S, I, E, W, It, 1956 S, I, W, It, 1957 S, I, E, W, It, R 1
Dufau, J (Biarritz) 1912 I, S, W, E
Duffaut, Y (Agen) 1954 Arg 1, 2
Duffour, R (Tarbes) 1911 W
Dufourcq, J (SBUC) 1906 NZ, E, 1907 E, 1908 W
Duhard, Y (Bagnères) 1980 E
Duhau, J (SF) 1928 I, 1930 I, G, 1931 I, S, W, 1933 G
Dulaurens, C (Toulouse) 1926 I, 1928 S, 1929 W
Dulin, B (Agen, Castres) 2012 Arg 1, 2, A, Arg3, Sm, 2013 NZ2(R), 3
Duluc, A (Béziers) 1934 G
Du Manoir, Y le P (RCF) 1925 I, NZ, S, W, E, 1926 S, 1927 I, S
Dupont, C (Lourdes) 1923 S, W, I, 1924 S, I, W, R, US, 1925 S, 1927 E, G 1, 2, 1928 A, G, W, 1929 I
Dupont, J-L (Agen) 1983 S
Dupont, L (RCF) 1934 G, 1935 G, 1936 G 1, 2, 1938 R, G 2
Dupouy, A (SB) 1924 W, R
Duprat, B (Bayonne) 1966 E, W, It, R, 1967 S, A, E, SA 2, 3, 1968 S, I, 1972 E, W, I 2, A 1
Dupré, P (RCF) 1909 W
Dupuy, J (Leicester, SF) 2009 NZ1, 2, A(R), SA, Sm(R), NZ3, 2012 S(R), E
Dupuy, J-V (Tarbes) 1956 S, I, W, It, E, Cz, 1957 S, I, E, W, It, R 2, 1958 S, E, SA 1, 2, 1959 S, E, It, W, I, 1960 W, I, It, Arg 1, 3, 1961 S, SA, E, NZ 2, R, 1962 S, E, W, I, It, 1963 W, It, R, 1964 S
Durand, N (Perpignan) 2007 NZ1, 2
Dusautoir, T (Biarritz, Toulouse) 2006 R, SA, NZ1, 2007 E3, W2(R), [Nm, I, NZ, E, Arg 2], 2008 S, I, E, W, Arg, PI, A3, 2009 I, S, W, E, It, NZ1, 2, A, SA, Sm, NZ3, 2010 S, I, W, It, E, SA, Arg1, 2, A, 2011 S, I1, E, It, W, I2, [J, NZ1, Tg, E, W, NZ2], 2012 It, S, I, E, W, 2013 It, W, E, I, S, NZ1, 2, 3
Du Souich, C J (see Judas du Souich)
Dutin, B (Mont-de-Marsan) 1968 NZ 2, A, SA 2, R
Dutour, F X (Toulouse) 1911 E, I, 1912 S, W, E, 1913 S
Dutrain, H (Toulouse) 1945 W, 1946 B, I, 1947 E, 1949 I, E, W, Arg 1
Dutrey, J (Lourdes) 1940 B
Duval, R (SF) 1908 E, W, 1909 E, 1911 E, W, I

Echavé, L (Agen) 1961 S
Elhorga, P (Agen) 2001 NZ, 2002 A 1, 2, 2003 Arg 2, NZ (R), R, [Fj(R), US, I(R), NZ], 2004 I(R), It(R), S, E, 2005 S, E, 2006 NZ2, Arg, 2008 A1
Elissalde, E (Bayonne) 1936 G 2, 1940 B
Elissalde, J-B (La Rochelle, Toulouse) 2000 S (R), R (R), 2003 It (R), W (R), 2004 I, It, W, A, Arg, 2005 SA1, 2(R), A1, 2, SA3, 2006 S, I, It, W(R), NZ1(R), 2, 2007 E2(R), 3, W2(R), [Arg 1(R), Nm, I, Gg(R), NZ, E, Arg 2], 2008 S, I, W, Arg, PI
Elissalde, J-P (La Rochelle) 1980 SA, R, 1981 A 1, 2, R
Empereur-Buisson, H (Béziers) 1931 E, G
Erbani, D (Agen) 1981 A 1, 2, NZ 1, 2, 1982 Arg 1, 2, 1983 S (R), I, W, A 1, 2, R, 1984 W, E, R, 1985 E, W (R), Arg 2, 1986 S, I, W, E, R 1, Arg 2, NZ 1, 2(R), 3, 1987 W, E, S, I, [S, R, Fj, A, NZ], 1988 E, S, 1989 I (R), W, E, S, NZ 1, A 2, 1990 W, E
Escaffre, P (Narbonne) 1933 G, 1934 G
Escommier, M (Montelimar) 1955 It
Esponda, J-M (RCF) 1967 SA 1, 2, R, 1968 NZ 1, 2, SA 2, R, 1969 S, I (R), E
Estebanez, F (Brive, Racing Metro) 2010 Fj, Arg2(R), A(R), 2011 W(R), I3, [J, NZ1(R), Tg(R)]
Estève, A (Béziers) 1971 SA 1, 1972 I 1, E, W, I 2, A 2, R, 1973 S, NZ, E, I, 1974 I, W, E, S, R, SA 1, 2, 1975 W, E
Estève, P (Narbonne, Lavelanet) 1982 R, Arg 1, 2, 1983 E, S, I, W, A 1, 2, R, 1984 I, W, E, S, NZ 1, 2, R, 1985 E, S, I, W, 1986 S, I, 1987 [S, Z]
Etcheberry, J (Rochefort, Cognac) 1923 W, I, 1924 S, I, E, W, R, US, 1926 S, I, E, M, 1927 I, S, W, G 2
Etchenique, J-M (Biarritz O) 1974 R, SA 1, 1975 E, Arg 2
Etchepare, A (Bayonne) 1922 I
Etcheverry, M (Pau) 1971 S, I
Eutrope, A (SCUF) 1913 I

Fabre, E (Toulouse) 1937 It, 1938 G 1, 2
Fabre, J (Toulouse) 1963 S, I, E, W, It, 1964 S, NZ, E
Fabre, L (Lezignan) 1930 G
Fabre, M (Béziers) 1981 A 1, R, NZ 1, 2, 1982 I, R
Failliot, P (RCF) 1911 S, W, I, 1912 I, S, E, 1913 E, W
Fall, B (Bayonne, Racing Métro) 2009 Sm, 2010 S, 2012 Arg 2, 2013 It, W, E
Fargues, G (Dax) 1923 I
Fauré, F (Tarbes) 1914 I, W, E

THE COUNTRIES

Faure, L (Sale) 2008 S, I, E, A1, PI, A3, 2009 I, E
Fauvel, J-P (Tulle) 1980 R
Favre, M (Lyon) 1913 E, W
Ferrand, L (Chalon) 1940 B
Ferrien, R (Tarbes) 1950 S, I, E, W
Fickou, G (Toulouse) 2013 S(R)
Finat, R (CASG) 1932 G, 1933 G
Fite, R (Brive) 1963 W, It
Flanquart, A (SF) 2013 NZ1(R), 3
Floch, A (Clermont-Auvergne) 2008 E(R), It, W
Fofana, W (Clermont-Auvergne) 2012 It, S, I, E, W, Arg 1, 2(R), A, Arg3, Sm, 2013 It, W, E, I, S, NZ1, 2, 3
Forest, M (Bourgoin) 2007 NZ1(R), 2(R)
Forestier, J (SCUF) 1912 W
Forestier, Y (Castres) 2012 A, Arg3, Sm(R), 2013 It, W
Forgues, F (Bayonne) 1911 S, E, W, 1912 I, W, E, 1913 S, SA, W, 1914 I, E
Fort, J (Agen) 1967 It, W, I, SA 1, 2, 3, 4
Fourcade, G (BEC) 1909 E, W
Foures, H (Toulouse) 1951 S, I, E, W
Fournet, F (Montferrand) 1950 W
Fouroux, J (La Voulte) 1972 I 2, R, 1974 W, E, Arg 1, 2, R, SA 1, 2, 1975 W, Arg 1, R, 1976 S, I, W, E, US, A 1, 1977 W, E, S, I, Arg 1, 2, NZ 1, 2, R
Francquenelle, A (Vaugirard) 1911 S, 1913 W, I
Fritz, F (Toulouse) 2005 SA1, A2, SA3, 2006 S, I, It, E, W, SA, NZ1, 2, Arg, 2007 It, 2009 I, E(R), It, NZ2(R), A, 2010 Arg1, 2012 W, Arg 1, 2, A, Arg3, Sm, 2013 It, W(R), E(R), I, NZ1, 2, 3
Froment, R (Castres) 2004 US(R)
Furcade, R (Perpignan) 1952 S

Gabernet, S (Toulouse) 1980 E, S, 1981 S, I, W, E, A 1, 2, R, NZ 1, 2, 1982 I, 1983 A 2, R
Gachassin, J (Lourdes) 1961 S, I, 1963 R, 1964 S, NZ, E, W, It, I, SA, Fj, R, 1965 S, I, E, W, It, R, 1966 S, I, E, W, 1967 S, A, It, W, I, NZ, 1968 I, E, 1969 S, I
Galasso, A (Toulon, Montferrand) 2000 R (R), 2001 E (R)
Galau, H (Toulouse) 1924 S, I, E, W, US
Galia, J (Quillan) 1927 E, G 1, 2, 1928 S, A, I, E, W, 1929 I, E, G, 1930 S, I, E, G, W, 1931 S, W, E, G
Gallart, P (Béziers) 1990 R, A 1, 2(R), 3, 1992 S, I, R, Arg 1, 2, SA 1, 2, Arg, 1994 I, W, E, 1995 I (t), R 1, [Tg]
Gallion, J (Toulon) 1978 E, S, I, W, 1979 I, W, E, S, NZ 2, R, 1980 W, E, S, I, 1983 A 1, 2, R, 1984 I, W, E, S, R, 1985 E, S, I, W, 1986 Arg 2
Galthié, F (Colomiers, SF) 1991 R, US 1, [R, Fj, C, E], 1992 W, E, S, R, Arg, 1994 I, W, E, 1995 [SA, E], 1996 W 1(R), 1997 I, It 2, SA 1, 2, 1998 W (R), Fj (R), 1999 R, WS (R), Tg, NZ 1(R), [Fj (R), Arg, NZ 2, A], 2000 W, E, A, NZ 1, 2, 2001 S, It, W, E, SA 1, 2, NZ, SA 3, A, Fj, 2002 E, S, I, SA, NZ, C, 2003 E 1, S, Arg 1, 2, NZ, R, E 2, [Fj, J, S, I, E]
Galy, J (Perpignan) 1953 W
Garbajosa, X (Toulouse) 1998 I, W, Arg 2(R), Fj, 1999 W 1(R), E, S, WS, NZ 1, W 2, [C, Nm (R), Fj (R), Arg, NZ 2, A], 2000 A, NZ 1, 2, 2001 S, I, E, 2002 It (R), W, SA (R), C (R), 2003 E 1, S, I, It, W, E 3
Garuet-Lempirou, J-P (Lourdes) 1983 A 1, 2, R, 1984 I, NZ 1, 2, R, 1985 E, S, I, W, Arg 1, 1986 S, I, W, E, R 1, Arg 1, NZ 1, R 2, NZ 2, 3, 1987 W, E, S, I, [S, R, Fj, A, NZ], 1988 E, S, Arg 1, 2, R, 1989 E (R), S, NZ 1, 2, 1990 W, E
Gasc, J (Graulhet) 1977 NZ 2
Gasparotto, G (Montferrand) 1976 A 2, R
Gauby, G (Perpignan) 1956 Cz
Gaudermen, P (RCF) 1906 E
Gayraud, W (Toulouse) 1920 I
Gelez, F (Agen) 2001 SA 3, 2002 I (R), A 1, SA, NZ, C (R), 2003 S, I
Geneste, R (BEC) 1945 B 1, 1949 Arg 2
Genet, J-P (RCF) 1992 S, I, R
Gensane, R (Béziers) 1962 S, E, W, I, It, R, 1963 S
Gérald, G (RCF) 1927 E, G 2, 1928 S, 1929 I, S, W, E, G, 1930 S, I, E, G, W, 1931 I, S, E, G
Gérard, D (Bègles) 1999 Tg
Gérintes, G (CASG) 1924 R, 1925 I, 1926 W
Geschwind, P (RCF) 1936 G 1, 2

Giacardy, M (SBUC) 1907 E
Gimbert, P (Bègles) 1991 R, US 1, 1992 W, E
Giordani, P (Dax) 1999 E, S
Glas, S (Bourgoin) 1996 S (t), I (R), W 1, R, Arg 2(R), W 2, SA 1, 2, 1997 I, W, E, S, It 2(R), R 2, Arg, SA 1, 2, 1998 E, S, I, W, Arg 1, 2, Fj, Arg 3, A, 1999 W 2, [C, Nm, Arg (R), NZ 2(R), A (t&R)], 2000 I, 2001 E, SA 1, 2, NZ
Gomès, A (SF) 1998 Arg 1, 2, Fj, Arg 3, A, 1999 I (R)
Gommes, J (RCF) 1909 I
Gonnet, C-A (Albi) 1921 E, I, 1922 E, W, 1924 S, E, 1926 S, I, E, W, M, 1927 I, S, W, E, G 1
Gonzalez, J-M (Bayonne) 1992 Arg 1, 2, SA 1, 2, Arg, 1993 R 1, SA 1, 2, R 2, A 1, 2, 1994 I, W, E, S, C 1, NZ 1, 2, C 2, 1995 W, E, S, I, R 1, [Tg, S, I, SA, E], It, Arg, 1996 E, S, I, W 1
Got, R (Perpignan) 1920 I, US, 1921 S, W, 1922 S, E, W, I, 1924 I, E, W, R, US
Gourdon, J-F (RCF, Bagnères) 1974 S, Arg 1, 2, R, SA 1, 2, 1975 W, E, S, I, R, 1976 S, I, W, E, 1978 E, S, 1979 W, E, S, R, 1980 I
Gourragne, J-F (Béziers) 1990 NZ 2, 1991 W 1
Goutta, B (Perpignan) 2004 C
Goyard, A (Lyon U) 1936 G 1, 2, 1937 G, It, 1938 G 1, R, G 2
Graciet, R (SBUC) 1926 I, W, 1927 S, G 1, 1929 E, 1930 W
Grandclaude, J-P (Perpignan) 2005 E(R), W(R), 2007 NZ1
Graou, S (Auch, Colomiers) 1992 Arg (R), 1993 SA 1, 2, R 2, A 2(R), 1995 R 2, Arg (t), NZ 2(R)
Gratton, J (Agen) 1984 NZ 2, R, 1985 E, S, I, W, Arg 1, 2, 1986 S, NZ 1
Graule, V (Arl Perpignan) 1926 I, E, W, 1927 S, W, 1931 G
Greffe, M (Grenoble) 1968 W, Cz, NZ 1, 2, SA 1
Griffard, J (Lyon U) 1932 G, 1933 G, 1934 G
Gruarin, A (Toulon) 1964 W, It, I, SA, Fj, R, 1965 S, I, E, W, It, 1966 S, I, E, W, It, R, 1967 S, A, E, It, W, I, NZ, 1968 S, I
Guélorget, P (RCF) 1931 E, G
Guichemerre, A (Dax) 1920 E, 1921 E, I, 1923 S
Guilbert, A (Toulon) 1975 E, S, I, SA 1, 2, 1976 A 1, 1977 Arg 1, 2, NZ 1, 2, R, 1979 I, W, E
Guillemin, P (RCF) 1908 E, W, 1909 E, I, 1910 W, S, E, I, 1911 S, E, W
Guilleux, P (Agen) 1952 SA, It
Guirado, G (Perpignan) 2008 It(R), 2009 A(R), Sm(R), 2010 SA(R), Arg1(R), Fj, Arg2(R), A(R), 2011 S(R), E(R), It(R), W(R), I2(R), 3(R), [C(R)], 2013 I(R), S(R), NZ1(R)
Guiral, M (Agen) 1931 G, 1932 G, 1933 G
Guiraud, H (Nîmes) 1996 R

Haget, A (PUC) 1953 E, 1954 I, NZ, E, Arg 2, 1955 E, W, It, 1957 I, E, It, R 1, 1958 It, SA 2
Haget, F (Agen, Biarritz O) 1974 Arg 1, 2, 1975 SA 2, Arg 1, 2, R, 1976 S, 1978 S, I, W, R, 1979 I, W, E, S, NZ 1, 2, R, 1980 W, S, I, 1984 S, NZ 1, 2, R, 1985 E, S, I, 1986 S, I, W, E, R 1, Arg 1, A, NZ 1, 1987 S, I, [R, Fj]
Haget, H (CASG) 1928 S, 1930 G
Halet, R (Strasbourg) 1925 NZ, S, W
Hall, S (Béziers) 2002 It, W
Harinordoquy, I (Pau, Biarritz)) 2002 W, E, S, I, A 1, 2, SA, NZ, C, 2003 E 1, S, I, It, W, Arg 1(R), 2, NZ, R, E 2, 3(R), [Fj, S, I, E], 2004 I, It, W, E, A, Arg, NZ, 2005 W(R), 2006 R(R), SA, 2007 It(R), I, W1(R), E1(R), S, E3, W2, [Arg 1, Nm(R), NZ(R), E(R), Arg 2], 2008 A1, 2, Arg, PI, A3, 2009 I, S, W, E, It, SA, 2010 S, I, W, It, E, Fj, Arg2(R), 2011 S, I1, E, It(R), W, I2, [J, C(R), NZ1(R), Tg(R), E, W, NZ2], 2012 It(R), S, I, E, W
Harislur-Arthapignet, P (Tarbes) 1988 Arg 4(R)
Harize, D (Cahors, Toulouse) 1975 SA 1, 2, 1976 A 1, 2, R, 1977 W, E, S, I
Hauc, J (Toulon) 1928 E, G, 1929 I, S, G
Hauser, M (Lourdes) 1969 E
Hedembaigt, M (Bayonne) 1913 S, SA, 1914 W
Hericé, D (Bègles) 1950 I
Herrero, A (Toulon) 1963 R, 1964 NZ, E, W, It, I, SA, Fj, R, 1965 S, I, E, W, 1966 W, It, R, 1967 S, A, E, It, I, R
Herrero, B (Nice) 1983 I, 1986 Arg 1
Heyer, F (Montferrand) 1990 A 2

Heymans, C (Agen, Toulouse, Bayonne) 2000 It (R) R, 2002 A 2(R), SA, NZ, 2004 W(R), US, C(R), A, Arg, NZ, 2005 I, It, SA1, 2, A1, 2, C, SA3, 2006 S, I, W(R), R, SA, NZ2, Arg, 2007 It, I(R), E1(R), S, E3, W2, [Arg 1, Nm, I, NZ, E], 2008 S, I, E, W(R), Arg, PI, A3, 2009 I(R), S, W, E, It, NZ1, 2, A, SA, NZ3(R), 2011 I3, [J, NZ1(R), Tg(R), E(R)]
Hiquet, J-C (Agen) 1964 E
Hoche, M (PUC) 1957 I, E, W, It, R 1
Hondagné-Monge, M (Tarbes) 1988 Arg 2(R)
Hontas, P (Biarritz) 1990 S, I, R, 1991 R, 1992 Arg, 1993 E, S, I, W
Hortoland, J-P (Béziers) 1971 A 2
Houblain, H (SCUF) 1909 E, 1910 W
Houdet, R (SF) 1927 S, W, G 1, 1928 G, W, 1929 I, S, E, 1930 S, E
Hourdebaigt, A (SBUC) 1909 I, 1910 W, S, E, I
Hubert, A (ASF) 1906 E, 1907 E, 1908 E, W, 1909 E, W, I
Hueber, A (Lourdes, Toulon) 1990 A 3, NZ 1, 1991 US 2, 1992 I, Arg 1, 2, SA 1, 2, 1993 E, S, I, W, R 1, SA 1, 2, R 2, A 1, 2, 1995 [Tg, S (R), I], 2000 It, R
Huget, Y (Bayonne, Toulouse) 2010 Arg2, A, 2011 S, I1, E, It, W(R), 2012 Arg 1, 2, A(R), Arg3(R), Sm(R), 2013 It, W, E, I, S, NZ1, 2, 3
Hutin, R (CASG) 1927 I, S, W
Hyardet, A (Castres) 1995 It, Arg (R)

Ibañez, R (Dax, Perpignan, Castres, Saracens, Wasps) 1996 W 1(R), 1997 It 1(R), R 1, It 2(R), R 2, SA 2(R), 1998 E, S, I, W, Arg 1, 2, Fj, Arg 3, A, 1999 I, W 1, E, S, R, WS, Tg (R), NZ 1, W 2, [C, Nm, Fj, Arg, NZ 2, A], 2000 W (R), E (R), S (R), I (R), It (R), R, 2001 S, I, It, W, E, SA 1, 2, NZ (R), SA 3, A, Fj, 2002 It (R), W, E, S, I, Arg, A 1(R), 2, SA, NZ, C, 2003 E 1, S, I, It, W, R (R), E 2(R), 3, [Fj, J(R), S, I, E, NZ(R)], 2005 C(R), Tg, 2006 I, It, E, W, R, SA(R), NZ1(R), 2, Arg, 2007 It, I, W1, E1, S, NZ1(R), 2(R), E2, 3, [Arg 1, Nm(R), I, NZ, E, Arg 2]
Icard, J (SF) 1909 E, W
Iguiniz, E (Bayonne) 1914 E
Ihingoué, D (BEC) 1912 I, S
Imbernon, J-F (Perpignan) 1976 I, W, E, US, A 1, 1977 W, E, S, I, Arg 1, 2, NZ 1, 2, 1978 E, R, 1979 I, 1981 S, I, W, E, 1982 I, 1983 I, W
Iraçabal, J (Bayonne) 1968 NZ 1, 2, SA 1, 1969 S, I, W, R, 1970 S, I, W, E, R, 1971 W, SA 1, 2, A 1, 1972 E, W, I 2, A 2, R, 1973 S, NZ, E, W, I, J, 1974 I, W, E, S, Arg 1, 2, SA 2(R)
Isaac, H (RCF) 1907 E, 1908 E
Ithurra, E (Biarritz O) 1936 G 1, 2, 1937 G

Jacquet, L (Clermont-Auvergne) 2006 NZ2(R), Arg, 2008 S, I(t&R)
Janeczek, T (Tarbes) 1982 Arg 1, 2, 1990 R
Janik, K (Toulouse) 1987 R
Janin, D (Bourgoin) 2008 A1(R), 2
Jarasse, A (Brive) 1945 B 1
Jardel, J (SB) 1928 I, E
Jauréguy, A (RCF, Toulouse, SF) 1920 S, E, W, I, US, 1922 S, W, 1923 S, W, E, I, 1924 S, W, R, US, 1925 I, NZ, 1926 S, E, W, M, 1927 I, E, 1928 S, A, E, G, W, 1929 I, S, E
Jauréguy, P (Toulouse) 1913 S, SA, W, I
Jauzion, Y (Colomiers, Toulouse) 2001 SA 1, 2, NZ, 2002 A 1(R), 2(R), 2003 Arg 2, NZ, R, E 2, 3, [Fj, S, I, E], 2004 I, It, W, S, E, A, Arg, NZ(t), 2005 W, I, It, SA1, 2, A1, 2, C, Tg(R), SA3, 2006 R, SA, NZ1, 2, Arg, 2007 It, I, W1, E1, S, E3, W2, [Arg 1, Nm(R), I(R), Gg, NZ, E], 2008 It, W, Arg, PI, A3, 2009 I, S, W, E, It, NZ1(R), Sm, NZ3, 2010 S, I, W, It, E, Arg2, A, 2011 I1(R), E, It
Jeangrand, M-H (Tarbes) 1921 I
Jeanjean, N (Toulouse) 2001 SA 1, 2, NZ, SA 3(R), A (R), Fj (R), 2002 It, Arg, A 1
Jeanjean, P (Toulon) 1948 I
Jérôme, G (SF) 1906 NZ, E
Joinel, J-L (Brive) 1977 NZ 1, 1978 R, 1979 I, W, E, S, NZ 1, 2, R, 1980 W, E, S, I, SA, 1981 S, I, W, E, R, NZ 1, 2, 1982 E, S, I, R, 1983 E, S, I, W, A 1, 2, R, 1984 I, W, E, S, NZ 1, 2, 1985 S, I, W, Arg 1, 1986 S, I, W, E, R 1, Arg 1, 2, A, 1987 [Z]
Jol, M (Biarritz O) 1947 S, I, W, E, 1949 S, I, E, W, Arg 1, 2
Jordana, J-L (Pau, Toulouse) 1996 R (R), Arg 1(t), 2, W 2, 1997 I (t), W, S (R)
Judas du Souich, C (SCUF) 1911 W, I
Juillet, C (Montferrand, SF) 1995 R 2, Arg, 1999 E, S, WS, NZ 1, [C, Fj, Arg, NZ 2, A], 2000 A, NZ 1, 2, 2001 S, I, It, W
Junquas, L (Tyrosse) 1945 B 1, 2, W, 1946 B, I, K, W, 1947 S, I, W, E, 1948 S, W

Kaczorowski, D (Le Creusot) 1974 I (R)
Kaempf, A (St Jean-de-Luz) 1946 B
Kayser, B (Leicester, Clermont-Auvergne) 2008 A1(R), 2(R), Arg(R), PI(R), A3(R), 2009 I(R), S(R), W(R), E(R), 2012 A(R), Arg3(R), Sm, 2013 It(R), W(R), E, I, S, NZ2(R), 3
Kotze, D M (Clermont-Auvergne) 2013 NZ1(R)

Labadie, P (Bayonne) 1952 S, I, SA, W, E, It, 1953 S, I, It, 1954 S, I, NZ, W, E, Arg 2, 1955 S, I, E, W, 1956 I, 1957 I
Labarthète, R (Pau) 1952 S
Labazuy, A (Lourdes) 1952 I, 1954 S, W, 1956 E, 1958 A, W, I, 1959 S, E, It, W
Labit, C (Toulouse) 1999 S, R (R), WS (R), Tg, 2000 R (R), 2002 Arg, A 1(R), 2003 Arg 1, 2, NZ (R), R (R), E 3, [Fj(R), J, US, E(R), NZ]
Laborde, C (RCF) 1962 It, R, 1963 R, 1964 SA, 1965 E
Labrousse, T (Brive) 1996 R, SA 1
Lacans, P (Béziers) 1980 SA, 1981 W, E, A 2, R, 1982 W
Lacassagne, H (SBUC) 1906 NZ, 1907 E
Lacaussade, R (Bègles) 1948 A, S
Lacaze, C (Lourdes, Angoulême) 1961 NZ 2, 3, A, R, 1962 E, W, I, It, 1963 W, R, 1964 S, NZ, E, 1965 It, R, 1966 S, I, E, W, It, R, 1967 S, E, SA 1, 3, 4, R, 1968 S, E, W, Cz, NZ 1, 1969 E
Lacaze, H (Périgueux) 1928 I, G, W, 1929 I, W
Lacaze, P (Lourdes) 1958 SA 1, 2, 1959 S, E, It, W, I
Lacazedieu, C (Dax) 1923 W, I, 1928 A, I, 1929 S
Lacombe, B (Agen) 1989 B, 1990 A 2
Lacome, M (Pau) 1960 Arg 2
Lacoste, R (Tarbes) 1914 I, W, E
Lacrampe, F (Béziers) 1949 Arg 2
Lacroix, P (Mont-de-Marsan, Agen) 1958 A, 1960 W, I, It, R, Arg 1, 2, 3, 1961 S, SA, E, W, I, NZ 1, 2, 3, A, R, 1962 S, E, W, I, R, 1963 S, I, E, W
Lacroix, T (Dax, Harlequins) 1989 A 1(R), 2, 1991 W 1(R), 2(R), [R, C (R), E], 1992 SA 2, 1993 E, S, I, W, SA 1, 2, R 2, A 1, 2, 1994 I, W, E, S, C 1, NZ 1, 2, C 2, 1995 W, E, S, R 1, [Tg, Iv, S, I, SA, E], 1996 E, S, I, 1997 It 2, R 2, Arg, SA 1, 2
Lacroix, T (Albi) 2008 A1(R), 2
Lafarge, Y (Montferrand) 1978 R, 1979 NZ 1, 1981 I (R)
Laffitte, R (SCUF) 1910 W, S
Laffont, H (Narbonne) 1926 W
Lafond, A (Bayonne) 1922 E
Lafond, J-B (RCF) 1983 A 1, 1985 Arg 1, 2 1986 S, I, W, E, R 1, 1987 I (R), 1988 W, 1989 I, W, E, 1990 W, A 3(R), NZ 2, 1991 S, I, W 1, E, R, US 1, W 2, [R (R), Fj, C, E], 1992 W, E, S, I (R), SA 2, 1993 E, S, I, W
Lagisquet, P (Bayonne) 1983 A 1, 2, R, 1984 I, W, NZ 1, 2, 1986 R 1(R), Arg 1, 2, A, NZ 1, 1987 [S, R, Fj, A, NZ], R, 1988 S, I, W, Arg 1, 2, 3, 4, R, 1989 I, W, E, S, NZ 1, 2, B, A 1, 2, 1990 W, E, S, I, A 1, 2, 3, 1991 S, I, US 2, [R]
Lagrange, J-C (RCF) 1966 It
Laharrague, J (Brive, Perpignan, Sale) 2005 W, I, It, SA1, A1, 2, C(R), Tg, 2006 R(R), SA, NZ1, 2007 NZ2
Laharrague, N (Perpignan) 2007 NZ1(R), 2(R)
Lakafia, R (Biarritz) 2011 I2, [J, Tg]
Lalande, M (RCF) 1923 S, W, I
Lalanne, F (Mont-de-Marsan) 2000 R
Lamaison, C (Brive, Agen) 1996 SA 1(R), 2, 1997 W, E, S, R 1, A 2, It 2, R 2, Arg, SA 1, 2, 1998 E, S, I, W, Arg 3(R), A, 1999 R, WS (R), Tg, NZ 1(R), W 2(R), [C (R), Nm, Fj, Arg, NZ 2, A], 2000 W, A, NZ 1, 2, 2001 S, I, It, W (R)
Lamboley, G (Toulouse) 2005 S(R), E(R), W(R), I(R), It(R),

THE COUNTRIES

SA1(R), 2(R), A1, 2(R), C(R), Tg, SA3(R), 2007 W1(R), 2010 Arg1(R)
Landreau, F (SF) 2000 A, NZ 1, 2, 2001 E (R)
Lane, G (RCF) 1906 NZ, E, 1907 E, 1908 E, W, 1909 E, W, I, 1910 W, E, 1911 S, W, 1912 I, W, E, 1913 S
Langlade, J-C (Hyères) 1990 R, A 1, NZ 1
Lapandry, A (Clermont-Auvergne) 2009 Sm, 2010 W(R), It(R), E(R), Fj, 2011 W(R), 2012 Arg 1(R), 2
Laperne, D (Dax) 1997 R 1(R)
Laporte, G (Graulhet) 1981 I, W, E, R, NZ 1, 2, 1986 S, I, W, E, R 1, Arg 1, A (R), 1987 [R, Z (R), Fj]
Larreguy, G (Bayonne) 1954 It
Larribau, J (Périgueux) 1912 I, S, W, E, 1913 S, 1914 I, E
Larrieu, J (Tarbes) 1920 I, US, 1921 W, 1923 S, W, E, I
Larrieux, M (SBUC) 1927 G 2
Larrue, H (Carmaux) 1960 W, I, It, R, Arg 1, 2, 3
Lasaosa, P (Dax) 1950 I, 1952 S, I, E, It, 1955 It
Lascubé, G (Agen) 1991 S, I, W 1, E, US 2, W 2, [R, Fj, C, E], 1992 W, E
Lassegue, J-B (Toulouse) 1946 W, 1947 S, I, W, 1948 W, 1949 I, E, W, Arg 1
Lasserre, F (René) (Bayonne, Cognac, Grenoble) 1914 I, 1920 S, 1921 S, W, I, 1922 S, E, W, I, 1923 W, E, 1924 S, I, R, US
Lasserre, J-C (Dax) 1963 It, 1964 S, NZ, E, W, It, I, Fj, 1965 W, It, R, 1966 R, 1967 S
Lasserre, M (Agen) 1967 SA 2, 3, 1968 E, W, Cz, NZ 3, A, SA 1, 2, 1969 S, I, E, 1970 E, 1971 E, W
Laterrade, G (Tarbes) 1910 E, I, 1911 S, E, I
Laudouar, J (Soustons, SBUC) 1961 NZ 1, 2, R, 1962 I, R
Lauga, P (Vichy) 1950 S, I, E, W
Laurent, A (Biarritz O) 1925 NZ, S, W, E, 1926 W
Laurent, J (Bayonne) 1920 S, E, W
Laurent, M (Auch) 1932 G, 1933 G, 1934 G, 1935 G, 1936 G 1
Lauret, W (Biarritz) 2010 SA, 2012 Arg 1, 2(R)
Laussucq, C (SF) 1999 S (R), 2000 W (R), S, I
Lavail, G (Perpignan) 1937 G, 1940 B
Lavaud, R (Carcassonne) 1914 I, W
Lavergne, P (Limoges) 1950 S
Lavigne, B (Agen) 1984 R, 1985 E
Lavigne, J (Dax) 1920 E, W
Laziès, H (Auch) 1954 Arg 2, 1955 It, 1956 E, 1957 S
Le Bourhis, R (La Rochelle) 1961 R
Lecointre, M (Nantes) 1952 It
Le Corvec, G (Perpignan) 2007 NZ1
Lecouls, B (Biarritz) 2008 A1, 2(R), Arg, PI(R), A3(R), 2009 I
Le Droff, J (Auch) 1963 It, R, 1964 S, NZ, E, 1970 E, R, 1971 S, I
Lefèvre, R (Brive) 1961 NZ 2
Leflamand, L (Bourgoin) 1996 SA 2, 1997 W, E, S, It 2, Arg, SA 1, 2(R)
Lefort, J-B (Biarritz O) 1938 G 1
Le Goff, R (Métro) 1938 R, G 2
Legrain, M (SF) 1909 I, 1910 I, 1911 S, E, W, I, 1913 S, SA, E, I, 1914 I, W
Lemeur, Y (RCF) 1993 R 1
Lenient, J-J (Vichy) 1967 R
Lepatey, J (Mazamet) 1954 It, 1955 S, I, E, W
Lepatey, L (Mazamet) 1924 S, I, E
Le Roux, B (Racing Métro) 2013 NZ2, 3(R)
Lescarboura, J-P (Dax) 1982 W, E, S, I, 1983 A 1, 2, R, 1984 I, W, E, S, NZ 1, 2, R, 1985 E, S, I, W, Arg 1, 2, 1986 Arg 2, A, NZ 1, R 2, NZ 2, 1988 S, W, 1990 R
Lesieur, E (SF) 1906 E, 1908 E, W, 1909 E, W, I, 1910 S, E, I, 1911 E, I, 1912 W
Leuvielle, M (SBUC) 1908 W, 1913 S, SA, E, W, 1914 W, E
Levasseur, R (SF) 1925 W, E
Levée, H (RCF) 1906 NZ
Lewis, E W (Le Havre) 1906 E
Lhermet, J-M (Montferrand) 1990 S, I, 1993 R 1
Libaros, G (Tarbes) 1936 G 1, 1940 B
Liebenberg, B (SF) 2003 R (R), E 2(R), 3, [US, I(R), NZ(R)], 2004 I(R), US, C, NZ, 2005 S, E
Lièvremont, M (Perpignan, SF) 1995 It, R 2, Arg (R), NZ 2(R), 1996 R, Arg 1(R), SA 2(R), 1997 R 1, A 2(R), 1998 E (R), S, I, W, Arg 1, 2, Fj, Arg 3, A, 1999 W 2, [C, Nm, Fj, Arg, NZ 2, A]
Lièvremont, M (Dax) 2008 A1(R), 2
Lièvremont, T (Perpignan, SF, Biarritz) 1996 W 2(R), 1998 E, S, I, W, Arg 1, 2, Fj, Arg 3, A, 1999 I, W 1, E, W 2, [Nm], 2000 W (R), E (R), S (R), I, It, 2001 E (R), 2004 I(R), It(R), W, S, US, C, 2005 A2, C, Tg(t&R), SA3(R), 2006 S(R), It, E, W
Lira, M (La Voulte) 1962 R, 1963 I, E, W, It, R, 1964 W, It, I, SA, 1965 S, I, R
Llari, R (Carcassonne) 1926 S
Lobies, J (RCF) 1921 S, W, E
Lombard, F (Narbonne) 1934 G, 1937 It
Lombard, T (SF) 1998 Arg 3, A, 1999 I, W 1, S (R), 2000 W, E, S, A, NZ 1, 2001 It, W
Lombarteix, R (Montferrand) 1938 R, G 2
Londios, J (Montauban) 1967 SA 3
Lopez, C (Bordeaux Begles) 2013 NZ1, 3(R)
Loppy, L (Toulon) 1993 R 2
Lorieux, A (Grenoble, Aix) 1981 A 1, R, NZ 1, 2, 1982 W, 1983 A 2, R, 1984 I, W, E, 1985 Arg 1, 2(R), 1986 R 2, NZ 2, 3, 1987 W, E, [S, Z, Fj, A, NZ], 1988 S, I, W, Arg 1, 2, 4, 1989 W, A 2
Loury, A (RCF) 1927 E, G 1, 2, 1928 S, A, I
Loustau, L (Perpignan) 2004 C
Loustau, M (Dax) 1923 E
Lubin-Lebrère, M-F (Toulouse) 1914 I, W, E, 1920 S, E, W, I, US, 1921 S, 1922 S, E, W, 1924 W, US, 1925 I
Lubrano, A (Béziers) 1972 A 2, 1973 S
Lux, J-P (Tyrosse, Dax) 1967 E, It, W, I, SA 1, 2, 4, R, 1968 I, E, Cz, NZ 3, A, SA 1, 2, 1969 S, I, E, 1970 S, I, W, E, R, 1971 S, I, E, W, A 1, 2, 1972 S, I 1, E, W, I 2, A 1, 2, R, 1973 S, NZ, E, 1974 I, W, E, S, Arg 1, 2, 1975 W

Macabiau, A (Perpignan) 1994 S, C 1
Machenaud, M (Agen, Racing Métro) 2012 Arg 2, A, Arg3, Sm(R), 2013 It, W, E(R), S(R), NZ1, 2, 3(R)
Maclos, P (SF) 1906 E, 1907 E
Maestri, Y (Toulouse) 2012 It(R), S, I, E, W, Arg 1, 2, Arg3, Sm, 2013 It, W, E, I, S, NZ1, 2, 3
Magne, O (Dax, Brive, Montferrand, Clermont-Auvergne, London Irish) 1997 W (R), E, S, R 1(R), A 1, 2, It 2(R), R 2, Arg (R), 1998 E, S, I, W, Arg 1, 2, Fj, Arg 3, A, 1999 I, R, WS, NZ 1, W 2, [C, Nm, Fj, Arg, NZ 2, A], 2000 W, E, S, It, R, A, NZ 1, 2, 2001 S, I, It, W, E, SA 1, 2, NZ, SA 3, A, Fj, 2002 It, E, S, I, Arg, A 1, 2(R), SA, NZ, C, 2003 E 1, S, I, It, W, R, E 2, 3(R), [Fj, J, S, I, E, NZ(R)], 2004 I, It, W(R), S, E, A, Arg, NZ, 2005 SA1, 2(R), A1, 2006 I, It, E, W(R), 2007 NZ1, 2
Magnanou, C (RCF) 1923 E, 1925 W, E, 1926 S, 1929 S, W, 1930 S, I, E, W
Magnol, L (Toulouse) 1928 S, 1929 S, W, E
Magois, H (La Rochelle) 1968 SA 1, 2, R
Majérus, R (SF) 1928 W, 1929 I, S, 1930 S, I, E, G, W
Malbet, J-C (Agen) 1967 SA 2, 4
Maleig, A (Oloron) 1979 W, E, NZ 2, 1980 W, E, SA, R
Mallier, L (Brive) 1999 R, W 2(R), [C (R)], 2000 I (R), It
Malquier, Y (Narbonne) 1979 S
Malzieu, J (Clermont-Auvergne) 2008 S, It, W, Arg, PI, A3, 2009 I, S(R), W, E, It(R), 2010 I(R), W, It(R), E(R), Arg1, 2012 It, S, I, E
Manterola, T (Lourdes) 1955 It, 1957 R 1
Mantoulan, C (Pau) 1959 I
Marcet, J (Albi) 1925 I, NZ, S, W, E, 1926 I, E
Marchal, J-F (Lourdes) 1979 S, R, 1980 W, S, I
Marconnet, S (SF, Biarritz) 1998 Arg 3, A, 1999 I (R), W 1(R), E, S (R), R, Tg, 2000 A, NZ 1, 2, 2001 S, I, It (R), W (R), E, 2002 S (R), Arg (R), A 1, 2, SA (R), C (R), 2003 E1(R), S, I, It, W, Arg 1(t+R), 2, NZ, R, E 2, 3(t+R), [S, US(R), I, E, NZ], 2004 I, It, W, S, E, A, Arg, NZ, 2005 S, E, W, I, It, SA1, 2, A1(R), 2(R), C, Tg, SA3(R), 2006 S, I(R), It(R), E, W, R, SA, NZ1, 2(R), Arg(R), 2007 It(R), I, W1(R), 2009 W, E, It, NZ1, A, SA(R), Sm, NZ3, 2010 I(R), 2011 I1(R), E(R), It, I2
Marchand, R (Poitiers) 1920 S, W
Marfaing, M (Toulouse) 1992 R, Arg 1
Marlu, J (Montferrand, Biarritz)) 1998 Fj (R), 2002 S (R), I (R), 2005 E

Marocco, P (Montferrand) 1968 S, I, W, E, R 1, Arg 1, 2, A, 1988 Arg 4, 1989 I, 1990 E (R), NZ 1(R), 1991 S, I, W 1, E, US 2, [R, Fj, C, E]
Marot, A (Brive) 1969 R, 1970 S, I, W, 1971 SA 1, 1972 I 2, 1976 A 1
Marquesuzaa, A (RCF) 1958 It, SA 1, 2, 1959 S, E, It, W, 1960 S, E, Arg 1
Marracq, H (Pau) 1961 R
Marsh, T (Montferrand) 2001 SA 3, A, Fj, 2002 It, W, E, S, I, Arg, A 1, 2, 2003 [Fj, J, S, I, E, NZ], 2004 C, A, Arg, NZ
Martin, C (Lyon) 1909 I, 1910 W, S
Martin, H (SBUC) 1907 E, 1908 W
Martin, J-L (Béziers) 1971 A 2, R, 1972 S, I 1
Martin, L (Pau) 1948 I, A, S, W, E, 1950 S
Martin, R (SF, Bayonne) 2002 E (t+R), S (R), I (R), 2005 SA1(t&R), 2, A1, 2, C, SA3, 2006 S, I(t&R), R, SA(R), NZ1(R), 2, Arg, 2007 E2, W2, [Arg 1, Gg(R), Arg 2(R)], 2009 NZ2(R), A(R)
Martine, R (Lourdes) 1952 S, I, It, 1953 It, 1954 S, I, NZ, W, E, It, Arg 2, 1955 S, I, W, 1958 A, W, It, I, SA 1, 2, 1960 S, E, Arg 3, 1961 S, It
Martinez, A (Narbonne) 2002 A 1, 2004 C
Martinez, G (Toulouse) 1982 W, E, S, Arg 1, 2, 1983 E, W
Marty, D (Perpignan) 2005 It, C, Tg, 2006 I, It(R), R(R), NZ1(R), Arg(R), 2007 I, W1, E1, S, E2, [Nm, I, Gg, NZ, E, Arg 2], 2008 S, I, E, 2009 SA(R), Sm, NZ3, 2010 S(R), I(R), W(R), It, E(R), SA, Fj, 2011 W, I2, [J(R), C, E(R)]
Mas, F (Béziers) 1962 R, 1963 S, I, E, W
Mas, N (Perpignan) 2003 NZ, 2005 E, W, I, It, 2007 W1, NZ1, 2(R), E2(R), 3(R), W2, [Nm(R), Gg(R), Arg 2], 2008 S(R), I, E, It, W, Arg(R), PI, A3, 2009 I(R), S, NZ1(R), 2, A(R), SA, Sm(R), NZ3(R), 2010 S, I, W, It, E, SA, Arg1, 2, A, 2011 S, I1, E, It, W, I3, [J, E, W, NZ2], 2012 It, S, I, E, A, Arg3, Sm, 2013 It, W, E, I, S, NZ2, 3
Maso, J (Perpignan, Narbonne) 1966 It, R, 1967 S, R, 1968 S, W, Cz, NZ 1, 2, 3, A, R, 1969 S, I, W, 1971 SA 1, 2, R, 1972 E, W, A 2, 1973 W, I, J, R
Massare, J (PUC) 1945 B 1, 2, W, 1946 B, I, W
Massé, A (SBUC) 1908 W, 1909 E, W, 1910 W, S, E, I
Masse, H (Grenoble) 1937 G
Matheu-Cambas, J (Agen) 1945 W, 1946 B, I, K, W, 1947 S, I, W, E, 1948 I, A, S, W, E, 1949 S, I, E, W, Arg 1, 2, 1950 E, W, 1951 S, I
Matiu, L (Biarritz) 2000 W, E
Mauduy, G (Périgueux) 1957 It, R 1, 2, 1958 S, E, 1961 W, It
Mauran, J (Castres) 1952 SA, W, E, It, 1953 I, E
Mauriat, P (Lyon) 1907 E, 1908 E, W, 1909 W, I, 1910 W, S, E, I, 1911 S, E, W, I, 1912 I, S, 1913 S, SA, W, I
Maurin, G (ASF) 1906 E
Maury, A (Toulouse) 1925 I, NZ, S, W, E, 1926 S, I, E
Mayssonnié, A (Toulouse) 1908 E, W, 1910 W
Mazars, L (Narbonne, Bayonne) 2007 NZ2, 2010 Arg1
Mazas, L (Colomiers, Biarritz) 1992 Arg, 1996 SA 1
Médard, M (Toulouse) 2008 Arg, PI, A3, 2009 I, S, W, E, It, NZ1, 2, A, SA(R), Sm, NZ3, 2010 Fj, 2011 S, I1, It, W, I2(R), 3, [J, C(R), NZ1, Tg, E, W, NZ2], 2012 It, S, 2013 I, S, NZ1, 2
Mela, A (Albi) 2008 S(R), I, It(R), W(R)
Melville, E (Toulon) 1990 I (R), A 1, 2, 3, NZ 1, 1991 US 2
Menrath, R (SCUF) 1910 W
Menthiller, Y (Romans) 1964 W, It, SA, R, 1965 E
Merceron, G (Montferrand) 1999 R (R), Tg, 2000 S, I, R, 2001 S (R), W, E, SA 1, 2, NZ (R), Fj, 2002 It, W, E, S, I, Arg, A 2, C, 2003 E 1, It (R), W (R), NZ (t+R), R (R), E 3, [Fj(R), J(R), S(R), US, E(R), NZ]
Meret, F (Tarbes) 1940 B
Mericq, S (Agen) 1959 I, 1960 S, E, W, 1961 I
Merle, O (Grenoble, Montferrand) 1993 SA 1, 2, R 2, A 1, 2, 1994 I, W, E, S, C 1, NZ 1, 2, C 2, 1995 W, I, R 1, [Tg, S, I, SA, E], It, R 2, Arg, NZ 1, 2, 1996 E, S, R, Arg 1, 2, W 2, SA 2, 1997 I, W, E, S, It 1, R 1, A 1, 2, It 2, R 2, SA 1(R), 2
Mermoz, M (Toulouse, Perpignan, Toulon) 2008 A2, 2009 S(R), NZ2, A, SA, 2010 SA, Arg1(R), 2011 S, I2, [C, NZ1, Tg, E, W, NZ2], 2012 It(R), E(R), Arg 1(R), 2, A, Arg3, Sm, 2013 It, W, NZ1(R)
Merquey, J (Toulon) 1950 S, I, E, W
Mesnel, F (RCF) 1986 NZ 2(R), 3, 1987 W, E, S, I, [S, Z, Fj, A, NZ], R, 1988 E, Arg 1, 2, 3, 4, R, 1989 I, W, E, S, NZ 1, A 1, 2, 1990 E, S, I, A 2, 3, NZ 1, 2, 1991 S, I, W 1, E, R, US 1, 2, W 2, [R, Fj, C, E], 1992 W, E, S, I, SA 1, 2, 1993 E (R), W, 1995 I, R 1, [Iv, E]
Mesny, P (RCF, Grenoble) 1979 NZ 1, 2, 1980 SA, R, 1981 I, W (R), A 1, 2, R, NZ 1, 2, 1982 I, Arg 1, 2
Meyer, G-S (Périgueux) 1960 S, E, It, R, Arg 2
Meynard, J (Cognac) 1954 Arg 1, 1956 Cz
Mias, L (Mazamet) 1951 S, I, E, W, 1952 I, SA, W, E, It, 1953 S, I, W, It, 1954 S, I, NZ, W, 1957 R 2, 1958 S, E, A, W, I, SA 1, 2, 1959 S, It, W, I
Michalak, F (Toulouse, Natal Sharks, Toulon) 2001 SA 3(R), A, Fj (R), 2002 It, A 1, 2, 2003 It, W, Arg 2(R), NZ, R, E 2, [Fj, J, S, I, E, NZ(R)], 2004 I, W, S, E, A, Arg, NZ, 2005 S(R), E(R), W(R), I(R), It(R), SA1, 2, A1, 2, C, Tg(R), SA3, 2006 S, I, It, E, W, 2007 E2(R), 3, [Arg1(t&R), Nm, I, NZ(R), E(R), Arg 2], 2009 It(R), 2010 S(R), I(R), W(R), 2012 Arg 1(R), 2, A, Arg3, Sm, 2013 It, W, E(R), I, S, NZ1(R), 2
Mignardi, A (Agen) 2007 NZ1, 2
Mignoni, P (Béziers, Clermont-Auvergne)) 1997 R 2(R), Arg (t), 1999 R (R), WS, NZ 1, W 2(R), [C, Nm], 2002 W, E (R), I (R), Arg, A 2(R), 2005 S, It(R), C(R), 2006 R, 2007 It, I, W1, E1(R), S, E2, 3(R), W2, [Arg 1, Gg, Arg 2(R)]
Milhères, C (Biarritz) 2001 E
Milliand, P (Grenoble) 1936 G 2, 1937 G, It
Millo-Chluski, R (Toulouse) 2005 SA1, 2008 Arg, PI, A3(R), 2009 I(R), S, W(R), NZ1, 2, A, SA, Sm(R), NZ3, 2010 SA, Fj, A(R), 2011 I2, [C]
Milloud, O (Bourgoin) 2000 R (R), 2001 NZ, 2002 W (R), E (R), 2003 It (R), W (R), Arg 1, R (R), E 2(t+R), 3, [J, S(R), US, I(R), E(R)], 2004 US, C(R), A, Arg, NZ(R), 2005 S(R), E(R), W(R), SA1, 2(R), A1, 2, C(R), Tg, SA3, 2006 S(R), I, It, E(R), W(R), NZ1(R), 2, Arg, 2007 It, I(R), W1, E1, S, E2, 3, [Arg 1, I, Gg, NZ, E]
Minjat, R (Lyon) 1945 B 1
Miorin, H (Toulouse) 1996 R, SA 1, 1997 I, W, E, S, It 1, 2000 It (R), R (R)
Mir, J-H (Lourdes) 1967 R, 1968 I
Mir, J-P (Lourdes) 1967 A
Modin, R (Brive) 1987 [Z]
Moga, A-M-A (Bègles) 1945 B 1, 2, W, 1946 B, I, K, W, 1947 S, I, W, E, 1948 I, A, S, W, E, 1949 S, I, E, W, Arg 1, 2
Mola, U (Dax, Castres) 1997 S (R), 1999 R (R), WS, Tg (R), NZ 1, W 2, [C, Nm, Fj, Arg (R), NZ 2(R), A (R)]
Momméjat, B (Cahors, Albi) 1958 It, I, SA 1, 2, 1959 S, E, It, W, I, 1960 S, E, I, R, 1962 S, E, W, I, It, R, 1963 S, I, W
Moncla, F (RCF, Pau) 1956 Cz, 1957 I, E, W, It, R 1, 1958 SA 1, 2, 1959 S, E, It, W, I, 1960 S, E, W, I, It, R, Arg 1, 2, 3, 1961 S, SA, E, W, It, I, NZ 1, 2, 3
Moni, C (Nice, SF) 1996 R, 2000 A, NZ 1, 2, 2001 S, I, It, W
Monié, R (Perpignan) 1956 Cz, 1957 E
Monier, R (SBUC) 1911 I, 1912 S
Monniot, M (RCF) 1912 W, E
Montade, A (Perpignan) 1925 I, NZ, S, W, 1926 W
Montanella, F (Auch) 2007 NZ1(R)
Montlaur, P (Agen) 1992 E (R), 1994 S (R)
Moraitis, B (Toulon) 1969 E, W
Morel, A (Grenoble) 1954 Arg 2
Morère, J (Toulouse) 1927 E, G 1, 1928 S, A
Moscato, V (Bègles) 1991 R, US 1, 1992 W, E
Mougeot, C (Bègles) 1992 W, E, Arg
Mouniq, P (Toulouse) 1911 S, E, W, I, 1912 I, E, 1913 S, SA, E
Moure, H (SCUF) 1908 E
Moureu, P (Béziers) 1920 I, US, 1921 W, E, I, 1922 S, W, I, 1923 S, W, E, I, 1924 S, I, E, W, 1925 E
Mournet, A (Bagnères) 1981 A 1(R)
Mouronval, F (SF) 1909 I
Muhr, A H (RCF) 1906 NZ, E, 1907 E
Murillo, G (Dijon) 1954 It, Arg 1

Nallet, L (Bourgoin, Castres, Racing-Métro) 2000 R, 2001 E, SA 1(R), 2(R), NZ, SA3(R), A (R), Fj (R), 2003 NZ, 2005 A2(R), C, Tg(R), SA3, 2006 I(R), It(R), E(R), W(R), R, SA(R), NZ1(R),

2, Arg, 2007 It, I, W1, E1, S, E3(R), [Nm, I(R), Gg, Arg 2], 2008 S, I, E, It, W, A1, 2, Arg, PI, A3, 2009 I, S, W, E, It, SA, NZ3(R), 2010 S, I, W, It, E, SA, Arg1, 2, 2011 S, I1, E, It, W, I2(R), 3, [J, NZ1, Tg, E, W, NZ2], 2012 It, S(R), I(R), E(R)
Namur, R (Toulon) 1931 E, G
Noble, J-C (La Voulte) 1968 E, W, Cz, NZ 3, A, R
Noirot, B (Racing Metro) 2010 Fj(R)
Normand, A (Toulouse) 1957 R 1
Novès, G (Toulouse) 1977 NZ 1, 2, R, 1978 W, R, 1979 I, W
Ntamack, E (Toulouse) 1994 W, C 1, NZ 1, 2, C 2, 1995 W, I, R 1, [Tg, S, I, SA, E], It, R 2, Arg, NZ 1, 2, 1996 E, S, I, W 1, R (R), Arg 1, 2, W 2, 1997 I, 1998 Arg 3, 1999 I, W 1, E, S, WS, NZ 1, W 2(R), [C (R), Nm, Fj, Arg, NZ 2, A], 2000 W, E, S, I, It
Ntamack F (Colomiers) 2001 SA 3
Nyanga, Y (Béziers, Toulouse) 2004 US, C, 2005 S(R), E(R), W, I, It, SA1, 2, A1(R), 2, C(t&R), Tg, SA3, 2006 S, I, It, E, W, 2007 E2(R), 3, [Nm, I(R), Gg, Arg 2], 2012 A, Arg3, Sm, 2013 E, I, S(t&R), NZ1(R), 2(R)

Olibeau, O (Perpignan) 2007 NZ1(R), 2(R)
Olive, D (Montferrand) 1951 I, 1952 I
Ondarts, P (Biarritz O) 1986 NZ 3, 1987 W, E, S, I, [S, Z, Fj, A, NZ], R, 1988 E, I, W, Arg 1, 2, 3, 4, R, 1989 I, W, E, NZ 1, 2, A 2, 1990 W, E, S, I, R (R), NZ 1, 2, 1991 S, I, W 1, E, US 2, W 2, [R, Fj, C, E]
Orso, J-C (Nice, Toulon) 1982 Arg 1, 2, 1983 E, S, A 1, 1984 E (R), S, NZ 1, 1985 I (R), W, 1988 I
Othats, J (Dax) 1960 Arg 2, 3
Ouedraogo, F (Montpellier) 2007 NZ2(R), 2008 S, I, E(R), It, W, A1, 2, Arg(R), PI, A3, 2009 I, S, W, NZ1, 2, A, NZ3, 2010 S, I, Fj, A, 2011 I3, [C, W(R)], 2012 Arg 1, 2, A, Arg3, Sm, 2013 It, W, NZ1
Ougier, S (Toulouse) 1992 R, Arg 1, 1993 E (R), 1997 It 1

Paco, A (Béziers) 1974 Arg 1, 2, R, SA 1, 2, 1975 W, E, Arg 1, 2, R, 1976 S, I, W, E, US, A 1, 2, R, 1977 W, E, S, I, NZ 1, 2, R, 1978 E, S, I, W, R, 1979 I, W, E, S, 1980 W
Palat, J (Perpignan) 1938 G 2
Palisson, A (Brive, Toulon) 2008 A1, 2, Arg(R), PI(R), A3(R), 2010 I, W, It, E, Fj(R), Arg2, A, 2011 E(R), W, I2, 3, [Tg, E, W, NZ2], 2012 W
Palmié, M (Béziers) 1975 SA 1, 2, Arg 1, 2, R, 1976 S, I, W, E, US, 1977 W, E, S, I, Arg 1, 2, NZ 1, 2, R, 1978 E, S, I, W
Paoli, R (see Simonpaoli)
Paparemborde, R (Pau) 1975 SA 1, 2, Arg 1, 2, R, 1976 S, I, W, E, US, A 1, 2, R, 1977 W, E, S, I, Arg 1, NZ 1, 2, 1978 E, S, I, W, R, 1979 I, W, E, S, NZ 1, 2, R, 1980 W, E, S, SA, R, 1981 S, I, W, E, A 1, 2, R, NZ 1, 2, 1982 W, I, R, Arg 1, 2 1983 E, S, I, W
Papé, P (Bourgoin, Castres, SF) 2004 I, It, W, S, E, C, NZ(R), 2005 I(R), It(R), SA1, 2, A1, 2006 NZ1, 2, 2007 It(R), I, S(R), NZ1, 2, 2008 E, 2009 NZ1, A, Sm, 2010 S, I, Arg1, 2011 W(R), I3, [J(R), C, NZ1, Tg, E, W, NZ2], 2012 It, S, I, E, W, Arg 1, 2, A, Arg3, Sm, 2013 It
Pardo, L (Hendaye) 1924 I, E
Pardo, L (Bayonne) 1980 SA, R, 1981 S, I, W, E, A 1, 1982 W, E, S, 1983 A 1(R), 1985 S, I, Arg 2
Pargade, J-H (Lyon U) 1953 It
Pariès, L (Biarritz O) 1968 SA 2, R, 1970 S, I, W, 1975 E, S, I
Parra, M (Bourgoin, Clermont-Auvergne) 2008 S(R), I(R), E, Arg(R), 2009 I(R), S(R), W, E, It, SA(R), Sm, NZ3(R), 2010 S, I, W, It, E, SA, Arg1, Fj(R), Arg2, A, 2011 S, I1, E(R), It, W, I2(R), 3, [J(R), C, NZ1, Tg, E, W, NZ2], 2012 It(R), S, I, E(R), W(R), Arg 1, 2(R), A(R), Arg3(R), Sm, 2013 It(R), W(R), E, I, S
Pascalin, P (Mont-de-Marsan) 1950 I, E, W, 1951 S, I, E, W
Pascarel, J-R (TOEC) 1912 W, E, 1913 S, SA, E, I
Pascot, J (Perpignan) 1922 S, E, I, 1923 S, 1926 I, 1927 G 2
Paul, R (Montferrand) 1940 B
Pauthe, G (Graulhet) 1956 E
Pebeyre, E-J (Fumel, Brive) 1945 W, 1946 I, K, W, 1947 S, I, W, E
Pebeyre, M (Vichy, Montferrand) 1970 E, R, 1971 I, SA 1, 2, A 1, 1973 W
Péclier, A (Bourgoin) 2004 US, C
Pécune, J (Tarbes) 1974 W, E, S, 1975 Arg 1, 2, R, 1976 I, W, E, US
Pédeutour, P (Bègles) 1980 I
Pellissier, L (RCF) 1928 A, I, E, G, W
Pelous, F (Dax, Toulouse) 1995 R 2, Arg, NZ 1, 2, 1996 E, S, I, R (R), Arg 1, 2, W 2, SA 1, 2, 1997 I, W, E, S, It 1, R 1, A 1, 2, It 2, R 2, Arg, SA 1, 2(R), 1998 E, S, I, W, Arg 1, 2, Fj, Arg 3, A, 1999 I, W 1, E, R (R), WS, Tg (R), NZ 1, W 2, [C, Nm, Fj, NZ 2, A], 2000 W, E, S, I, It, A, NZ 1, 2, 2001 S, I, It, W, E, 2002 It (R), W (R), E (R), S, I, Arg, A 1, 2, SA, NZ, C, 2003 E 1, S, I, It, W, R, E 2, 3(R), [Fj, J, S, I, E, NZ(R)], 2004 I, It, W, S, E, US, C, A, Arg, NZ, 2005 S, E, W, I, It, A2, 2006 S, I, It, E, W, R, SA, NZ1, 2007 E2, 3, W2(R), [Arg1, Nm(R), Gg(R), NZ, E]
Penaud, A (Brive, Toulouse) 1992 W, E, S, I, R, Arg 1, 2, SA 1, 2, Arg, 1993 R 1, SA 1, 2, R 2, A 1, 2, 1994 I, W, E, 1995 NZ 1, 2, 1996 S, R, Arg 1, 2, W 2, 1997 I, E, R 1, A 2, 2000 W (R), It
Périé, M (Toulon) 1996 E, S, I (R)
Péron, P (RCF) 1975 SA 1, 2
Perrier, P (Bayonne) 1982 W, E, S, I (R)
Pesteil, J-P (Béziers) 1975 SA 1, 1976 A 2, R
Petit, C (Lorrain) 1931 W
Peyras, J-B (Bayonne) 2008 A2(R)
Peyrelade, H (Tarbes) 1940 B
Peyrelongue, J (Biarritz) 2004 It, S(R), C(R), A(R), Arg(R), NZ
Peyroutou, G (Périgueux) 1911 S, E
Phliponeau, J-F (Montferrand) 1973 W, I
Piazza, A (Montauban) 1968 NZ 1, A
Picamoles, L (Montpellier, Toulouse) 2008 I(R), E, It, A1, 2(t&R), Arg, PI(R), A3(R), 2009 I(R), S(R), E(R), It(R), NZ1, 2, SA, 2010 SA(R), Arg1, 2011 I3, [C, NZ1, E(R)], 2012 It, S, I(R), E(R), W(R), Arg 1, 2, A, Arg3, Sm, 2013 It, W, E, I, S, NZ1, 2
Picard, T (Montferrand) 1985 Arg 2, 1986 R 1(R), Arg 2
Pierre, J (Bourgoin, Clermont-Auvergne) 2007 NZ1, 2, 2010 S(R), I(R), W, It, E, SA(R), Arg1(R), Fj(R), Arg2, A, 2011 S, I1, E, It, W, I2, 3(R), [J, C(R), NZ1(R), Tg(R), E(R), W(R), NZ2(R)], 2012 W(R)
Pierrot, G (Pau) 1914 I, W, E
Pilon, J (Périgueux) 1949 E, 1950 E
Piqué, J (Pau) 1961 NZ 2, 3, A, 1962 S, It, 1964 NZ, E, W, It, I, SA, Fj, R, 1965 S, I, E, W, It
Piquemal, M (Tarbes) 1927 I, S, 1929 I, G, 1930 S, I, E, G, W
Piquiral, E (RCF) 1924 S, I, E, W, R, US, 1925 E, 1926 S, I, E, W, M, 1927 I, S, W, E, G 1, 2, 1928 E
Piteu, R (Pau) 1921 S, W, E, I, 1922 S, E, W, I, 1923 E, 1924 E, 1925 I, NZ, W, E, 1926 E
Plante, A (Perpignan) 2013 NZ1, 2
Plantefol, A (RCF) 1967 SA 2, 3, 4, NZ, R, 1968 E, W, Cz, NZ 2, 1969 E, W
Plantey, S (RCF) 1961 A, 1962 It
Podevin, G (SF) 1913 W, I
Poeydebasque, F (Bayonne) 1914 I, W
Poirier, A (SCUF) 1907 E
Poitrenaud, C (Toulouse) 2001 SA 3, A, Fj, 2003 E 1, S, I, It, W, Arg 1, NZ, E 3, [J, US, E(R), NZ], 2004 E(R), US, C, Arg(R), NZ, 2006 R, 2007 It, I, W1, E1, S, E2, 3, [Nm, I, Gg, Arg 2], 2009 I, S, 2010 S, I, W, It, E, SA, Arg1(R), 2011 S(R), I1, E, 2012 I, E, W
Pomathios, M (Agen, Lyon U, Bourg) 1948 I, A, S, W, E, 1949 S, I, E, W, Arg 1, 2, 1950 S, I, W, 1951 S, I, E, W, 1952 W, E, 1953 S, I, W, 1954 S
Pons, P (Toulouse) 1920 S, E, W, 1921 S, W, 1922 S
Porcu, C (Agen) 2002 Arg (R), A 1, 2(R)
Porical, J (Perpignan) 2010 Arg1, Fj, Arg2(R), A
Porra, M (Lyon) 1931 I
Porthault, A (RCF) 1951 S, E, W, 1952 I, 1953 S, I, It
Portolan, C (Toulouse) 1986 A, 1989 I, E
Potel, A (Begles) 1932 G
Poux, J-B (Narbonne, Toulouse) 2001 Fj (R), 2002 S, I (R), Arg, A 1(R), 2(R), 2003 E 3, [Fj, J, US, NZ], 2007 E2, 3, W2(R), [Nm, I(R), Gg, NZ(R), E(R), Arg 2], 2008 E(R), It(R), W(R), 2010 W(R), It(R), E(R), SA(R), Arg1(R), 2011 I2(R), 3, [J(R), C, NZ1, Tg, E, W, NZ2], 2012 It(R), S, I, E, W

Prat, J (Lourdes) 1945 B 1, 2, W, 1946 B, I, K, W, 1947 S, I, W, E, 1948 I, A, S, W, E, 1949 S, I, E, W, Arg 1, 2, 1950 S, I, E, W, 1951 S, E, W, 1952 S, I, SA, W, E, It, 1953 S, I, E, W, It, 1954 S, I, NZ, W, E, It, 1955 S, I, E, W, It
Prat, M (Lourdes) 1951 I, 1952 S, I, SA, W, E, 1953 S, I, E, 1954 I, NZ, W, E, It, 1955 S, I, E, W, It, 1956 I, W, It, Cz, 1957 S, I, W, It, R 1, 1958 A, W, I
Prévost, A (Albi) 1926 M, 1927 I, S, W
Prin-Clary, J (Cavaillon, Brive) 1945 B 1, 2, W, 1946 B, I, K, W, 1947 S, I, W
Privat, T (Béziers, Clermont-Auvergne) 2001 SA 3, A, Fj, 2002 It, W, S (R), SA (R), 2003 [NZ], 2005 SA2, A1(R)
Puech, L (Toulouse) 1920 S, E, I, 1921 E, I
Puget, M (Toulouse) 1961 It, 1966 S, I, It, 1967 SA 1, 3, 4, NZ, 1968 Cz, NZ 1, 2, SA 1, 2, R, 1969 E, R, 1970 W
Puig, A (Perpignan) 1926 S, E
Pujol, A (SOE Toulouse) 1906 NZ
Pujolle, M (Nice) 1989 B, A 1, 1990 S, I, R, A 1, 2, NZ 2
Puricelli, J (Bayonne) 2009 NZ1(R), A, Sm(R), NZ3(R)

Quaglio, A (Mazamet) 1957 R 2, 1958 S, E, A, W, I, SA 1, 2, 1959 S, E, It, W, I
Quilis, A (Narbonne) 1967 SA 1, 4, NZ, 1970 R, 1971 I

Rabadan, P (SF) 2004 US(R), C(R)
Ramis, R (Perpignan) 1922 E, I, 1923 W
Rancoule, H (Lourdes, Toulon, Tarbes) 1955 E, W, It, 1958 A, W, It, I, SA 1, 1959 S, It, W, 1960 I, It, R, Arg 1, 2, 1961 SA, E, W, It, NZ 1, 2, 1962 S, E, W, I, It
Rapin, A (SBUC) 1938 R
Raymond, F (Toulouse) 1925 S, 1927 W, 1928 I
Raynal, F (Perpignan) 1935 G, 1936 G 1, 2, 1937 G, It
Raynaud, F (Carcassonne) 1933 G
Raynaud, M (Narbonne) 1999 W 1, E (R)
Razat, J-P (Agen) 1962 R, 1963 S, I, R
Rebujent, R (RCF) 1963 E
Revailler, D (Graulhet) 1981 S, I, W, E, A 1, 2, R, NZ 1, 2, 1982 W, S, I, R, Arg 1
Revillon, J (RCF) 1926 I, E, 1927 S
Ribère, E (Perpignan, Quillan) 1924 I, 1925, I, NZ, S, 1926 S, I, W, M, 1927 I, S, W, E, G 1, 2, 1928 S, A, I, E, G, W, 1929 I, E, G, 1930 S, I, E, W, 1931 I, S, W, E, G, 1932 G, 1933 G
Rives, J-P (Toulouse, RCF) 1975 E, S, I, Arg 1, 2, R, 1976 S, I, W, E, US, A 1, 2, R, 1977 W, E, S, I, Arg 1, 2, R, 1978 E, S, I, W, R, 1979 I, W, E, S, NZ 1, 2, R, 1980 W, E, S, I, SA, 1981 S, I, W, E, A 2, 1982 W, E, S, I, R, 1983 E, S, I, W, A 1, 2, R, 1984 I, W, E, S
Rochon, A (Montferrand) 1936 G 1
Rodrigo, M (Mauléon) 1931 I, W
Rodriguez, L (Mont-de-Marsan, Montferrand, Dax) 1981 A 1, 2, R, NZ 1, 2, 1982 W, E, S, I, R, 1983 E, S, 1984 I, NZ 1, 2, R, 1985 E, S, I, W, 1986 Arg 1, A, R 2, NZ 2, 3, 1987 W, E, S, I, [S, Z, Fj, A, NZ], R, 1988 E, S, I, W, Arg 1, 2, 3, 4, R, 1989 I, E, S, NZ 1, 2, B, A 1, 1990 W, E, S, I, NZ 1
Rogé, L (Béziers) 1952 It, 1953 E, W, It, 1954 S, Arg 1, 2, 1955 S, I, 1956 W, It, E, 1957 S, 1960 S, E
Rollet, J (Bayonne) 1960 Arg 3, 1961 NZ 3, A, 1962 It, 1963 I
Romero, H (Montauban) 1962 S, E, W, I, It, R, 1963 E
Romeu, J-P (Montferrand) 1972 R, 1973 S, NZ, E, W, I, R, 1974 W, E, S, Arg 1, 2, R, SA 1, 2(R), 1975 W, SA 2, Arg 1, 2, R, 1976 S, I, W, E, US, 1977 W, E, S, I, Arg 1, 2, NZ 1, 2, R
Roques, A (Cahors) 1958 A, W, It, I, SA 1, 2, 1959 S, E, W, I, 1960 S, E, W, I, It, Arg 1, 2, 3, 1961 S, SA, E, W, It, I, 1962 S, E, W, I, It, 1963 S
Roques, J-C (Brive) 1966 S, I, It, R
Rossignol, J-C (Brive) 1972 A 2
Rouan, J (Narbonne) 1953 S, I
Roucariès, G (Perpignan) 1956 S
Rouffia, L (Narbonne) 1945 B 2, W, 1946 W, 1948 I
Rougerie, A (Montferrand, Clermont-Auvergne) 2001 SA 3, A, Fj (R), 2002 It, W, E, S, I, Arg, A 1, 2, 2003 E 1, S, I, It, W, Arg 1, 2, NZ, R, E 2, 3(R), [Fj, J, S, I, E], 2004 US, C, A, Arg, NZ, 2005 S, W, A2, C, Tg, SA3, 2006 I, It, E, W, NZ1, 2, 2007 E2, W2, [Arg1, Nm(R), I(R), Gg, Arg 2], 2008 S(R), I, E, It, 2010 S, SA, Arg2, A, 2011 S, I1, E, It, I3, [J, C, NZ1, Tg, E, W, NZ2], 2012 It, S, I, E, W
Rougerie, J (Montferrand) 1973 J
Rougé-Thomas, P (Toulouse) 1989 NZ 1, 2
Roujas, F (Tarbes) 1910 I
Roumat, O (Dax) 1989 NZ 2(R), B, 1990 W, E, S, I, R, A 1, 2, 3, NZ 1, 2, 1991 S, I, W 1, E, R, US 1, W 2, [R, Fj, C, E], 1992 W (R), E (R), S, I, SA 1, 2, Arg, 1993 E, S, I, W, R 1, SA 1, 2, R 2, A 1, 2, 1994 I, W, E, C 1, NZ 1, 2, C 2, 1995 W, E, S, [Iv, S, I, SA, E], 1996 E, S, I, W 1, Arg 1, 2
Rousie, M (Villeneuve) 1931 S, G, 1932 G, 1933 G
Rousset, G (Béziers) 1975 SA 1, 1976 US
Rué, J-B (Agen) 2002 SA (R), C (R), 2003 E 1(R), S (R), It (R), W (R), Arg 1, 2(R)
Ruiz, A (Tarbes) 1968 SA 2, R
Rupert, J-J (Tyrosse) 1963 R, 1964 S, Fj, 1965 E, W, It, 1966 S, I, E, W, It, 1967 It, R, 1968 S

Sadourny, J-L (Colomiers) 1991 W 2(R), [C (R)], 1992 E (R), S, I, Arg 1(R), 2, SA 1, 2, 1993 R 1, SA 1, 2, R 2, A 1, 2, 1994 I, W, E, S, C 1, NZ 1, 2, C 2, 1995 W, E, S, I, R 1, [Tg, S, I, SA, E], It, R 2, Arg, NZ 1, 2, 1996 E, S, I, W 1, Arg 1, 2, W 2, SA 1, 2, 1997 I, W, E, S, It 1, R 1, A 1, 2, It 2, R 2, Arg, SA 1, 2, 1998 E, S, I, W, 1999 R, Tg, NZ 1(R), 2000 NZ 2, 2001 It, W, E
Sagot, P (SF) 1906 NZ, 1908 E, 1909 W
Sahuc, A (Métro) 1945 B 1, 2
Sahuc, F (Toulouse) 1936 G 2
Saint-André, P (Montferrand, Gloucester) 1990 R, A 3, NZ 1, 2, 1991 I (R), W 1, E, US 1, 2, W 2, [R, Fj, C, E], 1992 W, E, S, I, R, Arg 1, 2, SA 1, 2, 1993 E, S, I, W, SA 1, 2, A 1, 2, 1994 I, W, E, S, C 1, NZ 1, 2, C 2, 1995 W, E, S, I, R 1, [Tg, Iv, S, I, SA, E], It, R 2, Arg, NZ 1, 2, 1996 E, S, I, W 1, R, Arg 1, 2, W 2, 1997 It 1, 2, R 2, Arg, SA 1, 2
Saisset, O (Béziers) 1971 R, 1972 S, I 1, A 1, 2, 1973 S, NZ, E, W, I, J, R, 1974 I, Arg 2, SA 1, 2, 1975 W
Salas, P (Narbonne) 1979 NZ 1, 2, R, 1980 W, E, 1981 A 1, 1982 Arg 2
Salinié, R (Perpignan) 1923 E
Sallefranque, M (Dax) 1981 A 2, 1982 W, E, S
Salut, J (TOEC) 1966 R, 1967 S, 1968 I, E, Cz, NZ 1, 1969 I
Samatan, R (Agen) 1930 S, I, E, G, W, 1931 I, S, W, E, G
Samson, C (Toulon, Castres) 2012 Arg 2(R), 2013 E, I, S(R), NZ2
Sanac, A (Perpignan) 1952 It, 1953 S, I, 1954 E, 1956 Cz, 1957 S, I, E, W, It
Sangalli, F (Narbonne) 1975 I, SA 1, 2, 1976 S, A 1, 2, R, 1977 W, E, S, I, Arg 1, 2, NZ 1, 2
Sanz, H (Narbonne) 1988 Arg 3, 4, R, 1989 A 2, 1990 S, I, R, A 1, 2, NZ 2, 1991 W 2
Sappa, M (Nice) 1973 J, R, 1977 R
Sarrade, R (Pau) 1929 I
Sarraméa, O (Castres) 1999 R, WS (R), Tg, NZ 1
Saux, J-P (Pau) 1960 W, It, Arg 1, 2, 1961 SA, E, W, It, I, NZ 1, 2, 3, A, 1962 S, E, W, I, It, 1963 S, I, E, It
Savitsky, M (La Voulte) 1969 R
Savy, M (Montferrand) 1931 I, S, W, E, 1936 G 1
Sayrou, J (Perpignan) 1926 W, M, 1928 E, G, W, 1929 S, W, E, G
Schuster, J (Perpignan) 2010 Fj, A(R)
Scohy, R (BEC) 1931 S, W, E, G
Sébedio, J (Tarbes) 1913 S, E, 1914 I, 1920 S, I, US, 1922 S, E, 1923 S
Séguier, R (Béziers) 1973 J, R
Seigne, L (Agen, Merignac) 1989 B, A 1, 1990 NZ 1, 1993 E, S, I, W, R 1, A 1, 2, 1994 S, C 1, 1995 E (R), S
Sella, P (Agen) 1982 R, Arg 1, 2, 1983 E, S, I, W, A 1, 2, R, 1984 I, W, E, S, NZ 1, 2, R, 1985 E, S, I, W, Arg 1, 2, 1986 S, I, W, E, R 1, Arg 1, 2, A, NZ 1, R 2, NZ 2, 3, 1987 W, E, S, I, [S, R, Z (R), Fj, A, NZ], 1988 E, S, I, W, Arg 1, 2, 3, 4, R, 1989 I, W, E, S, NZ 1, 2, B, A 1, 2, 1990 W, E, S, I, A 1, 2, 3, 1991 W 1, E, R, US 1, 2, W 2, [Fj, C, E], 1992 W, E, S, I, Arg, 1993 E, S, I, W, R 1, SA 1, 2, R 2, A 1, 2, 1994 I, W, E, S, C 1, NZ 1, 2, C 2, 1995 W, E, S, I, [Tg, S, I, SA, E]

Semmartin, J (SCUF) 1913 W, I
Sénal, G (Béziers) 1974 Arg 1, 2, R, SA 1, 2, 1975 W
Sentilles, J (Tarbes) 1912 W, E, 1913 S, SA
Serin, L (Béziers) 1928 E, 1929 W, E, G, 1930 S, I, E, G, W, 1931 I, W, E
Serre, P (Perpignan) 1920 S, E
Serrière, P (RCF) 1986 A, 1987 R, 1988 E
Servat, W (Toulouse) 2004 I, It, W, S, E, US, C, A, Arg, NZ 2005 S, E(R), W(R), It(R), SA1(R), 2, 2008 S, I(R), E(R), W(R), 2009 It(R), NZ1, 2, SA, NZ3, 2010 S, I, W, It, E, Arg2, A, 2011 S, I1, E, It, W, [J, C, NZ1(R), Tg, E, W, NZ2], 2012 It, S(R), I(R), E(R), W
Servole, L (Toulon) 1931 I, S, W, E, G, 1934 G, 1935 G
Sicart, N (Perpignan) 1922 I
Sillières, J (Tarbes) 1968 R, 1970 S, I, 1971 S, I, E, 1972 E, W
Siman, M (Montferrand) 1948 E, 1949 S, 1950 S, I, E, W
Simon, S (Bègles) 1991 R, US 1
Simonpaoli, R (SF) 1911 I, 1912 I, S
Sitjar, M (Agen) 1964 W, It, I, R, 1965 It, R, 1967 A, E, It, W, I, SA 1, 2
Skrela, D (Colomiers, SF, Toulouse) 2001 NZ, 2007 It, I, W1, E1, 2, 3(R), W2, [Arg 1, Gg(R), Arg 2], 2008 S(R), I, E(R), W, Arg, PI, A3, 2010 SA(R), Fj(R), 2011 I2(R), 3, [J(R)]
Skrela, J-C (Toulouse) 1971 SA 2, A 1, 2, 1972 I 1(R), E, W, I 2, A 1, 1973 W, J, R, 1974 W, E, S, Arg 1, R, 1975 W (R), E, S, I, SA 1, 2, Arg 1, 2, R, 1976 S, I, W, E, US, A 1, 2, R, 1977 W, E, S, I, Arg 1, 2, NZ 1, 2, R, 1978 E, S, I, W
Soler, M (Quillan) 1929 G
Soro, R (Lourdes, Romans) 1945 B 1, 2, W, 1946 B, I, K, 1947 S, I, W, E, 1948 I, A, S, W, E, 1949 S, I, E, W, Arg 1, 2
Sorondo, L-M (Montauban) 1946 K, 1947 S, I, W, E, 1948 I
Soulette, C (Béziers, Toulouse) 1997 R 2, 1998 S (R), I (R), W (R), Arg 1, 2, Fj, 1999 W 2(R), [C (R), Nm (R), Arg, NZ 2, A]
Soulié, E (CASG) 1920 E, I, US, 1921 S, E, I, 1922 E, W, I
Sourgens, J (Bègles) 1926 M
Sourgens, O (Bourgoin) 2007 NZ2
Souverbie, J-M (Bègles) 2000 R
Spanghero, C (Narbonne) 1971 E, W, SA 1, 2, A 1, 2, R, 1972 S, E, W, I 2, A 1, 2, 1974 I, W, E, S, R, SA 1, 1975 E, S, I
Spanghero, W (Narbonne) 1964 SA, Fj, R, 1965 S, I, E, W, It, R, 1966 S, I, E, W, It, R, 1967 S, A, E, SA 1, 2, 3, 4, NZ, 1968 S, I, E, W, NZ 1, 2, 3, A, SA 1, 2, R, 1969 S, I, W, 1970 R, 1971 E, W, SA 1, 1972 E, I 2, A 1, 2, R, 1973 S, NZ, E, W, I
Stener, G (PUC) 1956 S, I, E, 1958 SA 1, 2
Struxiano, P (Toulouse) 1913 W, I, 1920 S, E, W, I, US
Suta, J (Toulon) 2012 A, Arg3(R), Sm(R), 2013 W, E(R)
Sutra, G (Narbonne) 1967 SA 2, 1969 W, 1970 S, I
Swierczinski, C (Bègles) 1969 E, 1977 Arg 2
Szarzewski, D (Béziers, SF, Racing Métro) 2004 C(R), 2005 I(R), A1, 2, SA3, 2006 S, E(R), W(t&R), R(R), SA, NZ1, 2(R), Arg(R), 2007 It(R), E2(R), W2, [Arg1(R), Nm, I(R), Gg(R), NZ(R), E(R)], 2008 S(R), I, E, It, W, Arg, PI, A3, 2009 I, S, W, E, It, NZ1(R), 2(R), A, SA(R), Sm, NZ3(R), 2010 S(R), I(R), W(R), It(R), E(R), SA, Arg1, 2011 I2, 3, [J(R), NZ1, Tg(R), E(R), W(R), NZ2(R)], 2012 It(R), S, I, E, W(R), Arg 1, 2, A, Arg3, Sm(R), 2013 It, W, E(R), NZ1, 2, 3(R)

Tabacco, P (SF) 2001 SA 1, 2, NZ, SA 3, A, Fj, 2003 It (R), W (R), Arg 1, NZ, E 2(R), 3, [S(R), US, I(R), NZ], 2004 US, 2005 S
Tachdjian, M (RCF) 1991 S, I, E
Taffary, M (RCF) 1975 W, E, S, I
Taillantou, J (Pau) 1930 I, G, W
Tales, R (Castres) 2013 NZ2(R), 3
Taofifenua, R (Perpignan) 2012 Arg 1(R), 2013 It(R), W(R)
Tarricq, P (Lourdes) 1958 A, W, It, I
Tavernier, H (Toulouse) 1913 I
Téchoueyres, W (SBUC) 1994 E, S, 1995 [Iv]
Terreau, M-M (Bourg) 1945 W, 1946 B, I, K, W, 1947 S, I, W, E, 1948 I, A, W, E, 1949 S, Arg 1, 2, 1951 S
Theuriet, A (SCUF) 1909 E, W, 1910 S, 1911 W, 1913 E
Thevenot, M (SCUF) 1910 W, E, I
Thierry, R (RCF) 1920 S, E, W, US
Thiers, P (Montferrand) 1936 G 1, 2, 1937 G, It, 1938 G 1, 2, 1940 B, 1945 B, 1, 2
Thiéry, B (Bayonne, Biarritz) 2007 NZ1, 2(R), 2008 A1, 2
Thion, J (Perpignan, Biarritz) 2003 Arg 1, 2, NZ, R, E 2, [Fj, S, I, E], 2004 A, Arg, NZ 2005 S, E, W, I, It, A2, C, Tg, SA3, 2006 S, I, It, E, W, R(R), SA, 2007 It, I(R), W1, E1, S, E2, 3, W2, [Arg 1, I, Gg, NZ, E, Arg 2], 2008 E(R), It, W, 2009 E, It(R), 2010 Fj, Arg2(R), A, 2011 S(R), I1(R), E(R), It(R)
Tignol, P (Toulouse) 1953 S, I
Tilh, H (Nantes) 1912 W, E, 1913 S, SA, E, W
Tillous-Borde, S (Castres) 2008 A1(R), 2, PI(R), A3, 2009 I, S, W(R), E(R)
Tolofua, C-E (Toulouse) 2012 Arg 1(R), 2(R)
Tolot, J-L (Agen) 1987 [Z]
Tomas, J (Clermont-Auvergne, Montpellier) 2008 It(R), A3(R), 2011 W(R)
Tordo, J-F (Nice) 1991 US 1(R), 1992 W, E, S, I, R, Arg 1, 2, SA 1, Arg, 1993 E, S, I, W, R 1
Torossian, F (Pau) 1997 R 1
Torreilles, S (Perpignan) 1956 S
Tournaire, F (Narbonne, Toulouse) 1995 It, 1996 I, W 1, R, Arg 1, 2(R), W 2, SA 1, 2, 1997 I, E, S, It 1, R 1, A 1, 2, It 2, R 2, Arg, SA 1, 2, 1998 E, S, I, W, Arg 1, 2, Fj, Arg 3, A, 1999 I, W 1, E, S, R (R), WS, NZ 1, [C, Nm, Fj, Arg, NZ 2, A], 2000 W, E, S, I, It, A (R)
Tourte, R (St Girons) 1940 B
Traille, D (Pau, Biarritz) 2001 SA 3, A, Fj, 2002 It, W, E, S, I, Arg, A 1, 2, SA, NZ, C, 2003 E 1, S, I, It, W, Arg, 1, 2, NZ, R, E 2, [Fj(R), J, S(R), US, NZ], 2004 I, It, W, S, E, 2005 S, E, W, It(R), SA1(R), 2, A1(R), 2006 It, E, W, R, SA, NZ1, 2, Arg, 2007 S(R), E2, 3, W2(R), [Arg 1, Nm, I, NZ, E], 2008 S, I, E, It(R), W, A1, PI(R), A3(R), 2009 E(R), It, NZ1, 2, A, SA, Sm(R), NZ3, 2010 Fj, Arg2, A, 2011 S, I1, E(R), It(R), W, I2, [C, NZ1, 2(R)]
Trillo, J (Bègles) 1967 SA 3, 4, NZ, R, 1968 S, I, NZ 1, 2, 3, A, 1969 I, E, W, R, 1970 E, R, 1971 S, I, SA 1, 2, A 1, 2, 1972 S, A 1, 2, R, 1973 S, E
Trinh-Duc, F (Montpellier) 2008 S, I(R), E, It, W(R), A1, 2, 2009 W(R), E, It, NZ1, 2, SA, Sm, NZ3, 2010 S, I, W, It, E, SA, Arg1, 2011 S, I1, E, It, W, I2, 3(R), [J, C, NZ1(R), Tg(R), E(R), NZ2(t&R)], 2012 It, S, I, E(R), W(R), Arg 1, 2(R), A(R), Arg3(R), 2013 It(R), W(R), E, S(R)
Triviaux, R (Cognac) 1931 E, G
Tucco-Chala, M (PUC) 1940 B

Ugartemendia, J-L (St Jean-de-Luz) 1975 S, I

Vahaamahina, S (Perpignan) 2012 A(R), 2013 I(R), S, NZ1, 2(R), 3(R)
Vaills, G (Perpignan) 1928 A, 1929 G
Valbon, L (Brive) 2004 US, 2005 S(R), 2006 S, E(R), 2007 NZ1(R)
Vallot, C (SCUF) 1912 S
Van Heerden, A (Tarbes) 1992 E, S
Vannier, M (RCF, Chalon) 1953 W, 1954 S, I, Arg 1, 2, 1955 S, I, E, W, It, 1956 S, I, W, It, E, 1957 S, I, E, W, It, R 1, 2, 1958 S, E, A, W, It, I, 1960 S, E, W, I, It, R, Arg 1, 3, 1961 SA, E, W, It, I, NZ 1, A
Vaquer, F (Perpignan) 1921 S, W, 1922 W
Vaquerin, A (Béziers) 1971 R, 1972 S, I 1, A 1, 1973 S, 1974 W, E, S, Arg 1, 2, R, SA 1, 2, 1975 W, E, S, I, 1976 US, A 1(R), 2, R, 1977 Arg 2, 1979 W, E, 1980 S, I
Vareilles, C (SF) 1907 E, 1908 E, W, 1910 S, E
Varenne, F (RCF) 1952 S
Varvier, T (RCF) 1906 E, 1909 E, W, 1911 E, W, 1912 I
Vassal, G (Carcassonne) 1938 R, G 2
Vaysse, J (Albi) 1924 US, 1926 M
Vellat, E (Grenoble) 1927 I, E, G 1, 2, 1928 A
Venditti, D (Bourgoin, Brive) 1996 R, SA 1(R), 2, 1997 I, W, E, S, R 1, A 1, SA 2, 2000 W (R), E, S, It (R)
Vergé, L (Bègles) 1993 R 1(R)
Verger, A (SF) 1927 W, E, G 1, 1928 I, E, G, W
Verges, S-A (SF) 1906 NZ, E, 1907 E
Vermeulen, E (Brive, Montferrand, Clermont-Auvergne) 2001

SA 1(R), 2(R), 2003 NZ, 2006 NZ1, 2, Arg, 2007 W1, S(R), 2008 S, W(R)

Viard, G (Narbonne) 1969 W, 1970 S, R, 1971 S, I

Viars, S (Brive) 1992 W, E, I, R, Arg 1, 2, SA 1, 2(R), Arg, 1993 R 1, 1994 C 1(R), NZ 1(t), 1995 E (R), [Iv], 1997 R 1(R), A 1(R), 2

Vigerie, M (Agen) 1931 W

Vigier, R (Montferrand) 1956 S, W, It, E, Cz, 1957 S, E, W, It, R 1, 2, 1958 S, E, A, W, It, I, SA 1, 2, 1959 S, E, It, W, I

Vigneau, A (Bayonne) 1935 G

Vignes, C (RCF) 1957 R 1, 2, 1958 S, E

Vila, E (Tarbes) 1926 M

Vilagra, J (Vienne) 1945 B 2

Villepreux, P (Toulouse) 1967 It, I, SA 2, NZ, 1968 I, Cz, NZ 1, 2, 3, A, 1969 S, I, E, W, R, 1970 S, I, W, E, R, 1971 S, I, E, W, A 1, 2, R, 1972 S, I 1, E, W, I 2, A 1, 2

Viviès, B (Agen) 1978 E, S, I, W, 1980 SA, R, 1981 S, A 1, 1983 A 1(R)

Volot, M (SF) 1945 W, 1946 B, I, K, W

Watremez, Y (Biarritz) 2012 Arg 1

Weller, S (Grenoble) 1989 A 1, 2, 1990 A 1, NZ 1

Wolf, J-P (Béziers) 1980 SA, R, 1981 A 2, 1982 E

Yachvili, D (Biarritz) 2002 C (R), 2003 S (R), I, It, W, R (R), E 3, [US, NZ], 2004 I(R), It(R), W(R), S, E, 2005 S(R), E, W, I, It, SA1(R), 2, C, Tg, 2006 S(R), I(R), It(R), E, W, SA, NZ1, 2(R), Arg, 2007 E1, 2008 E(R), It, W(R), A1, 2(R), 2009 NZ1(R), 2(R), A, 2010 It(R), SA(R), Arg1(R), Fj, Arg2(R), A(R), 2011 S(R), I1(R), E, I2, 3(R), [J, C(R), NZ1, Tg, E, W, NZ2], 2012 It, W

Yachvili, M (Tulle, Brive) 1968 E, W, Cz, NZ 3, A, R, 1969 S, I, R, 1971 E, SA 1, 2 A 1, 1972 R, 1975 SA 2

Zago, F (Montauban) 1963 I, E

THE COUNTRIES

Getty Images

Wesley Fofana's thrilling try against England was one of several personal highlights in 2012/13.

GEORGIA

GEORGIA'S 2012–13 TEST RECORD

OPPONENTS	DATE	VENUE	RESULT
Japan	17 Nov	H	Lost 22–25
Fiji	24 Nov	H	Lost 19–24
Belgium	2 Feb	A	Won 17–13
Portugal	9 Feb	H	Won 25–12
Russia	23 Feb	A	Won 23–9
Spain	9 Mar	H	Won 61–18
Romania	16 Mar	A	Drew 9–9
Uruguay	11 Jun	H	Won 27–3
Argentina	22 Jun	A	Lost 29–18

GEORGIA RISING TO THE CHALLENGE

By Lúcás Ó'Ceallacháin

Tamar Kulumbegashvili

Georgia beat Russia on the way to an unbeaten start to the European Nations Cup 2014.

The season kicked off in November 2012 with Georgia hosting two Tests against Fiji and Japan in the Mikheil Meskhi Stadium in Tbilisi. The games provided head coach Milton Haig with an excellent opportunity to build a squad and solid performances ahead of the European Nations Cup campaign.

With Fiji ranked 13th in the world and Japan 14th, the scalp of beating higher ranked opposition was tempting, but ultimately proved elusive. Against Japan, discipline was to cost the Lelos dear. Despite the best efforts of Merab Kvirikashvili, who scored a try, conversion and five penalties for a personal haul of 22 points, the Brave Blossoms edged the match 25–22. A week later only five points separated Georgia from the Flying Fijians, with the boot of Jonetani Ralulu proving decisive in the 24–19 win.

In early 2013 the Lelos built on those performances to produce some fine form in the European Nations Cup, going undefeated in all five matches, which also doubled up as Rugby World Cup 2015 qualifiers. Georgia's title defence began against newcomers Belgium at the Stade Roi Baudouin. Belgium were highly motivated on their debut in the top division and gave the Lelos a tough test. With neither team conceding anything in the physical battles, the early exchanges led to a red card for each side and a disjointed performance as a result. Georgia's experience at this level helped them to recover from an early Belgian lead to win 17–13 through a Levan Chilachava try in the 71st minute.

A week later Georgia took on Portugal in Tbilisi. The Lelos looked much more comfortable at home, easing their way to a 25–12 victory over Os Lobos. A solid platform from the Georgian pack allowed the backs to put some excellent play together, with tries from full back Lasha Khmaladze and centre Tedo Zibzibadze. Portugal tried to stay in touch with four penalties from Pedro Leal, but they could not crack the solid Georgian defence.

A trip to Sochi to face Russia is always a difficult prospect, but Georgia hold the upper hand in meetings between the teams. While there seems to be a psychological barrier for Russia against the Lelos, it was nothing compared to the physical one that the Georgian pack posed. Georgia comprehensively dominated the set piece and the breakdown, starving the Russian backline of quality ball. Russia threw everything they had at their opponents and it was not until the 60th minute that Georgia finally scored their first try through replacement Viktor Kolelishvili. The boot of Kvirikashvili kept the scoreboard ticking over before the final flourish was applied by prop Davit Kubriashvili with a try in the final minute as Georgia secured a 23–9 victory.

When Spain arrived in Tbilisi to take on the Lelos a fortnight later, they faced a side who were flying and full of confidence. Georgia ran riot, outclassing the Spaniards 61–18 in a one-sided affair. A standout performance from much improved Edinburgh number 8 Dimitri Basilaia was the highlight of the rout.

In the final round of the European Nations Cup for the season, Georgia travelled to Bucharest to take on the other unbeaten side, Romania. Similarly to Georgia, the Oaks have benefited from a mixture of their players being based at French clubs and coming from the vastly improved domestic structures. In a game for the purists, Florin Vlaicu and Kvirikashvili exchanged kicks as Georgia held a 9–6 lead until the 52nd minute when the Romanian slotted another kick under pressure to tie the scores. Neither team would budge, with the 9–9 draw meaning that Georgia ended the season on top of the table on points difference and in pole position for the Europe 1 qualifying spot for RWC 2015.

The IRB Tbilisi Cup, a joint initiative by the Georgian Rugby Union and the International Rugby Board, offered an excellent opportunity for the GRU to showcase their new stadia, development work progress and performance of their national team. Stiff opposition was provided in the form of Emerging Ireland, Uruguay and a South Africa President's XV.

The first game against Emerging Ireland had an all too familiar feeling for Georgia, as it played out in a similar fashion to the Rugby World Cup 2007 match against Ireland. Georgia used the game to try several new combinations and received just reward for their abrasive style, going into the break 10–6 in front. As at RWC 2007, though, the Irish dug deep, with a David Kearney try and five Ian Keatley penalties denying the Lelos a famous victory as they fell to a 20–15 loss.

Georgia channelled that disappointment into a commanding performance against Uruguay four days later, winning easily 27–3. Buoyed by their vocal home support, the Lelos were never in trouble and deserved their win.

In their final match against the SA President's XV, a well-organised Georgian team showed how much they had improved with an excellent defensive display in a hugely physical encounter. Trailing to two early Carl Bezuidenhout penalties, Georgia worked their way back into the match thanks to the boot of Beka Tsiklauri. The Lelos then pushed on to score the opening try through Chilachava. Both sides continued to trade penalties until the South Africans turned the tide with a try from Rosko Specman. With momentum on their side, the visitors scored a second try when second row Eduan van der Walt crashed over. This was to prove the difference between the sides as the President's XV won 21–16 to be crowned champions.

Despite the loss Haig was pleased with how his players dealt with the step up in class. "I was pleased with the commitment the boys showed," he admitted. "I know there were a lot of people that thought we would lose convincingly today and that hasn't happened. The players went out there and equipped themselves really well."

The season ended with an opportunity for Georgia to show their improvement on a global level when they faced Argentina in a one-off Test in San Juan. The IRB's strategy of increasing the competition schedule for Tier Two nations has shown how quickly teams can improve when given the opportunity.

Argentina rested some frontline players, but Georgia were also missing several stars, including Mamuka Gorgodze. Despite this, Georgia led 12–9 at the break, with all their points coming from the boot of Tsiklauri, including a sweetly struck drop goal. However, poor discipline in the second half as a result of relentless Puma pressure allowed Martín Bustos Moyano to kick Argentina to safety and a 29–18 victory.

As they have done on several occasions, Georgia gave a Tier One nation a terrible fright. If they continue to develop in such a positive fashion, the big result their performances deserve may not be too far away.

GEORGIA INTERNATIONAL STATISTICS

MATCH RECORDS UP TO 10 OCTOBER 2013

WINNING MARGIN

Date	Opponent	Result	Winning Margin
07/04/2007	Czech Republic	98–3	**95**
03/02/2002	Netherlands	88–0	**88**
06/02/2010	Germany	77–3	**74**
26/02/2005	Ukraine	65–0	**65**
12/06/2005	Czech Republic	75–10	**65**

MOST TRIES IN A MATCH

BY THE TEAM

Date	Opponent	Result	Tries
07/04/2007	Czech Republic	98–3	**16**
03/02/2002	Netherlands	88–0	**14**
23/03/1995	Bulgaria	70–8	**11**
26/02/2005	Ukraine	65–0	**11**
12/06/2005	Czech Republic	75–10	**11**
06/02/2010	Germany	77–3	**11**

BY A PLAYER

Date	Player	Opponent	Tries
23/03/1995	Pavle Jimsheladze	Bulgaria	**3**
23/03/1995	Archil Kavtarashvili	Bulgaria	**3**
12/06/2005	Mamuka Gorgodze	Czech Republic	**3**
07/04/2007	David Dadunashvili	Czech Republic	**3**
07/04/2007	Malkhaz Urjukashvili	Czech Republic	**3**
26/04/2008	Mamuka Gorgodze	Spain	**3**

MOST POINTS IN A MATCH

BY THE TEAM

Date	Opponent	Result	Points
07/04/2007	Czech Republic	98–3	**98**
03/02/2002	Netherlands	88–0	**88**
06/02/2010	Germany	77–3	**77**
12/06/2005	Czech Republic	75–10	**75**

BY A PLAYER

Date	Player	Opponent	Points
06/02/2010	Merab Kvirikashvili	Germany	**32**
08/03/2003	Pavle Jimsheladze	Russia	**23**
07/04/2007	Merab Kvirikashvili	Czech Republic	**23**
17/11/2012	Merab Kvirikashvili	Japan	**22**

MOST CONVERSIONS IN A MATCH

BY THE TEAM

Date	Opponent	Result	Cons
06/02/2010	Germany	77–3	**11**
03/02/2002	Netherlands	88–0	**9**
07/04/2007	Czech Republic	98–3	**9**
12/06/2005	Czech Republic	75–10	**7**

BY A PLAYER

Date	Player	Opponent	Cons
06/02/2010	Merab Kvirikashvili	Germany	**11**
03/02/2002	Pavle Jimsheladze	Netherlands	**9**
07/04/2007	Merab Kvirikashvili	Czech Republic	**9**
12/06/2005	Malkhaz Urjukashvili	Czech Republic	**7**

MOST PENALTIES IN A MATCH

BY THE TEAM

Date	Opponent	Result	Pens
08/03/2003	Russia	23–17	6
28/09/2011	Romania	25–9	6
11/06/2010	Scotland A	22–21	5
17/11/2012	Japan	22–25	5
22/06/2013	Argentina	29–18	5

BY A PLAYER

Date	Player	Opponent	Pens
08/03/2003	Pavle Jimsheladze	Russia	6
28/09/2011	Merab Kvirikashvili	Romania	5
11/06/2010	Irakli Kiasashvili	Scotland A	5
17/11/2012	Merab Kvirikashvili	Japan	5
03/02/2002	Pavle Jimsheladze	Netherlands	9
07/04/2007	Merab Kvirikashvili	Czech Republic	9
12/06/2005	Malkhaz Urjukashvili	Czech Republic	7

MOST DROP GOALS IN A MATCH

BY THE TEAM

Date	Opponent	Result	DGs
20/10/1996	Russia	29–20	2
21/11/1991	Ukraine	19–15	2
15/07/1992	Ukraine	15–0	2
04/06/1994	Switzerland	22–21	2

BY A PLAYER

Date	Player	Opponent	DGs
15/07/1992	Davit Chavleishvili	Ukraine	2

MOST CAPPED PLAYERS

Player	Caps
Irakli Abuseridze	85
Malkhaz Urjukashvili	69
Merab Kvirikashvili	69
Tedo Zibzibadze	68
Gia Labadze	67

LEADING TRY SCORERS

Player	Tries
Irakli Machkhaneli	22
Mamuka Gorgodze	21
Malkhaz Urjukashvili	18
Tedo Zibzibadze	18

LEADING CONVERSION SCORERS

Player	Cons
Merab Kvirikashvili	89
Pavle Jimsheladze	61
Malkhaz Urjukashvili	45

LEADING PENALTY SCORERS

Player	Pens
Merab Kvirikashvili	72
Pavle Jimsheladze	48
Malkhaz Urjukashvili	45

LEADING DROP GOAL SCORERS

Player	DGs
Kakha Machitidze	4
Nugzar Dzagnidze	3
Pavle Jimsheladze	3
Lasha Malaguradze	3

LEADING POINT SCORERS

Player	Points
Merab Kvirikashvili	435
Pavle Jimsheladze	320
Malkhaz Urjukashvili	318
Irakli Machkhaneli	110

GEORGIA INTERNATIONAL PLAYERS

UP TO 10 OCTOBER 2013

V Abashidze 1998 It, Ukr, I, 1999 Tg, Tg, 2000 It, Mor, Sp, 2001 H, Pt, Rus, Sp, R, 2006 J

N Abdaladze 1997 Cro, De

I Abuseridze 2000 It, Pt, Mor, Sp, H, R, 2001 H, Pt, Rus, Sp, R, 2002 Pt, Rus, Sp, R, I, Rus, 2003 Pt, Rus, CZR, R, It, E, Sa, SA, 2004 Rus, 2005 Pt, Ukr, R, 2006 Rus, R, Pt, Ukr, J, R, Sp, Pt, Pt, 2007 R, Rus, CZR, Nm, ESp, ItA, Ar, I, Nm, F, 2008 Pt, R, Pt, Rus, Sp, S, 2009 Ger, Pt, Sp, R, Rus, ArJ, ItA, 2010 Pt, Sp, R, Rus, C, US, 2011 Ukr, Sp, Pt, R, Rus, S, E, R, Ar, 2012 Sp, R, Rus, Ukr, US, C, J, Fj, 2013 Sp

V Akhvlediani 2007 CZR

K Alania 1993 Lux, 1994 Swi, 1996 CZR, CZR, Rus, 1997 Pt, Pol, Cro, De, 1998 It, 2001 H, Pt, Sp, F, SA, 2002 H, Pt, Rus, Sp, R, I, Rus, 2003 Rus, 2004 Pt, Sp

N Andghuladze 1997 Pol, 2000 It, Pt, Mor, Sp, H, R, 2004 Sp, Rus, CZR, R

D Ashvetia 1998 Ukr, 2005 Pt, 2006 R, 2007 Sp

K Asieshvili 2008 ItA, 2010 S, ItA, Nm, 2012 Sp

G Babunashvili 1992 Ukr, Ukr, Lat, 1993 Rus, Pol, Lux, 1996 CZR

Z Bakuradze 1989 Z, 1990 Z, 1991 Ukr, Ukr, 1993 Rus, Pol

D Baramidze 2000 H

O Barkalaia 2002 I, 2004 Sp, Rus, CZR, R, Ur, CHL, Rus, 2005 Pt, Ukr, R, CZR, CHL, 2006 Rus, R, Pt, Ukr, J, Bb, R, Sp, 2007 Nm, ItA, I, F, 2008 Pt, R, Pt, Rus, Sp, ESp, Ur, ItA, S, 2009 Ger, Sp, R

D Basilaia 2008 Pt, R, Pt, CZR, Rus, Sp, S, 2009 Ger, Sp, R, C, US, ItA, 2011 Nm, S, E, R, 2012 Sp, Pt, R, Rus, 2013 Bel, Pt, Rus, Sp, R

G Begadze 2012 Pt, R, Rus, Ukr, US, J, 2013 Bel, Pt, Rus, R, Ur, Ar

R Belkania 2004 Sp, 2005 CHL, 2007 Sp, Rus, 2012 Pt, R, Rus, Ukr, US, C, 2013 Bel, Pt, Sp, Ur, Ar

G Beriashvili 1993 Rus, Pol, 1995 Ger

G Berishvili 2011 Nm, E, R, 2012 Sp, Pt, R, Rus, US, C, 2013 Ur

M Besselia 1991 Ukr, 1993 Rus, Pol, 1996 Rus, 1997 Pt

B Bitsadze 2012 Ukr, US, C, Fj, 2013 Pt, Ur, Ar

D Bolgashvili 2000 It, Pt, H, R, 2001 H, Pt, Rus, Sp, R, F, SA, 2002 H, Pt, Rus, I, 2003 Pt, Sp, Rus, CZR, R, E, Sa, SA, 2004 Rus, Ur, CHL, Rus, 2005 CZR, 2007 Sp, 2010 ItA

J Bregvadze 2008 ESp, ItA, 2009 C, IrA, 2010 Sp, R, S, Nm, 2011 Ukr, Sp, R, Rus, Nm, S, E, R, Ar, 2013 R, Ar

G Buguianishvili 1996 CZR, Rus, 1997 Pol, 1998 It, Rus, I, R, 2000 Sp, H, R, 2001 H, F, SA, 2002 Rus

D Chavleishvili 1990 Z, Z, 1992 Ukr, Ukr, Lat, 1993 Pol, Lux

D Chichua 2008 CZR

I Chikava 1993 Pol, Lux, 1994 Swi, 1995 Bul, Mol, H, 1996 CZR, CZR, 1997 Pol, 1998 I

R Chikvaidze 2004 Ur, CHL

L Chikvinidze 1994 Swi, 1995 Bul, Mol, Ger, H, 1996 CZR, Rus

L Chilachava 2012 Sp, C, 2013 Bel, Ur, Ar

G Chkhaidze 2002 H, R, I, Rus, 2003 Pt, CZR, It, E, SA, Ur, 2004 CZR, R, 2006 Pt, Ukr, 2007 R, Rus, CZR, Nm, ESp, ItA, Ar, I, Nm, F, 2008 R, Pt, CZR, Rus, Sp, 2009 Ger, Pt, Sp, R, Rus, ArJ, ItA, 2010 Ger, Pt, Sp, R, Rus, C, US, 2011 Ukr, Sp, Pt, R, Rus, S, E, R, Ar, 2012 Sp, Pt, R, Rus, Ukr, US, C, 2013 Bel, Pt, Rus, Sp, R, Ur, Ar

S Chkhenkeli 1997 Pol

I Chkhikvadze 2005 CHL, 2007 Sp, 2008 Pt, R, Pt, CZR, Rus, ESp, Ur, ItA, S, 2009 Ger, Sp, ItA, 2010 Sp, Rus, S, ItA, Nm, C, US, 2011 Pt, Nm, R, 2012 Pt

I Chkonia 2007 ESp, ItA

D Dadunashvili 2003 It, E, SA, Ur, 2004 Sp, Rus, CZR, R, 2005 CHL, 2007 Sp, Rus, CZR, Nm, ItA, 2008 Pt, R, Pt, CZR, Rus, Sp, S, 2009 C, IrA, US, ItA, 2010 Sp, S, ItA, Nm

L Datunashvili 2004 Sp, 2005 Pt, Ukr, R, CZR, 2006 Rus, R, Pt, Ukr, J, Bb, CZR, Pt, Pt, 2007 R, Rus, Nm, ESp, ItA, I, Nm, F, 2008 Pt, Pt, 2009 Sp, R, Rus, C, US, ArJ, 2010 Ger, Pt, Sp, R, Rus, C, US, 2011 Ukr, Sp, Pt, R, Rus, S, E, R, Ar, 2012 Sp, Pt, Rus, J, Fj, 2013 Sp, R, Ar

V Didebulidze 1991 Ukr, 1994 Kaz, 1995 Bul, Mol, 1996 CZR, 1997 De, 1999 Tg, 2000 H, 2001 H, Pt, Rus, Sp, R, F, SA, 2002 H, Pt, Rus, Sp, R, I, Rus, 2003 Pt, Sp, Rus, CZR, R, It, E, Sa, SA, 2004 Rus, 2005 Pt, 2006 R, R, 2007 R, Sp, Rus, CZR, Nm, ESp, ItA, Ar, Nm, F

E Dzagnidze 1992 Ukr, Ukr, Lat, 1993 Rus, Pol, 1995 Bul, Mol, Ger, H, 1998 I

N Dzagnidze 1989 Z, 1990 Z, Z, 1991 Ukr, 1992 Ukr, Ukr, Lat, 1993 Rus, Pol, 1994 Swi, 1995 Ger, H

T Dzagnidze 2008 ESp

D Dzneladze 1992 Ukr, Lat, 1993 Lux, 1994 Kaz

P Dzotsenidze 1995 Ger, H, 1997 Pt, Pol

G Elizbarashvili 2002 Rus, 2003 Sp, 2004 CHL, 2005 CZR, 2006 Pt, Ukr, J, Bb, CZR, Sp, Pt, 2007 R, Sp, Rus, I, F, 2009 C, IrA

O Eloshvili 2002 H, 2003 SA, 2006 Bb, CZR, 2007 Sp, CZR, Nm, ESp, ItA, I, F

S Essakia 1999 Tg, Tg, 2000 It, Mor, Sp, H, 2004 CZR, R

M Gagnidze 1991 Ukr, Ukr

D Gasviani 2004 Sp, Rus, 2005 CZR, CHL, 2006 Ukr, J, 2007 Rus, CZR, 2008 ESp, Ur, ItA, S

A Ghibradze 1992 Ukr, Ukr, Lat, 1994 Swi, 1995 Bul, Mol, Ger, 1996 CZR

D Ghudushauri 1989 Z, 1991 Ukr, Ukr

L Ghvaberidze 2004 Pt

R Gigauri 2006 Ukr, J, Bb, CZR, Sp, Pt, Pt, 2007 R, Nm, ESp, ItA, Ar, Nm, F, 2008 Pt, R, Pt, Rus, Sp, ESp, Ur, 2009 C, IrA, US, ArJ, ItA, 2010 S, ItA, Nm, 2011 Nm, S, E, R, 2012 Sp

A Giorgadze 1996 CZR, 1998 It, Ukr, Rus, R, 1999 Tg, Tg, 2000 It, Pt, Mor, H, R, 2001 H, Pt, Rus, Sp, R, F, SA, 2002 H, Pt, Rus, Sp, R, I, Rus, 2003 Pt, Sp, Rus, R, It, E, Sa, SA, Ur, 2005 Pt, Ukr, R, CZR, 2006 Rus, R, Pt, Bb, CZR, Sp, Pt, 2007 R, Ar, I, Nm, F, 2009 Ger, Pt, Sp, ArJ, 2010 Ger, Pt, C, US, 2011 Pt, S, Ar

I Giorgadze 2001 F, SA, 2003 Pt, Sp, Rus, R, It, E, Sa, Ur, 2004 Rus, 2005 Pt, R, CZR, 2006 Rus, R, Pt, Bb, CZR, R, Sp, Pt, Pt, 2007 R, Sp, Rus, CZR, Ar, Nm, F, 2008 R, 2009 Ger, Pt, Sp, Rus, 2010 Ger, Sp, R, Rus, 2011 Ukr

M Gorgodze 2003 Sp, Rus, 2004 Pt, Sp, Rus, CZR, R, Ur, CHL, Rus, 2005 Pt, Ukr, R, CZR, CHL, 2006 Rus, Pt, Bb, CZR, R, Sp, Pt, Pt, 2007 Ar, I, Nm, 2008 R, Rus, Sp, 2009 Ger, Pt, Sp, R, Rus, ArJ, 2011 R, Rus, S, E, R, Ar, 2012 Pt, R, Rus, J, Fj, 2013 Bel, Pt, Rus, Sp, R

E Gueguchadze 1990 Z, Z

L Gugava 2004 Sp, Rus, CZR, Ur, CHL, Rus, 2005 Pt, Ukr, 2006 Bb, CZR, 2009 C, IrA, US, 2010 C, US, 2011 Ukr, Sp, Pt, R, Rus, Nm, Ar, 2012 Ukr, C

I Guiorkhelidze 1998 R, 1999 Tg, Tg

G Guiunashvili 1989 Z, 1990 Z, 1991 Ukr, Ukr, 1992 Ukr, Ukr, Lat, 1993 Rus, Pol, Lux, 1994 Swi, 1996 Rus, 1997 Pt

K Guiunashvili 1990 Z, Z, 1991 Ukr, Ukr, 1992 Ukr, Ukr, Lat

B Gujaraidze 2008 ESp, 2012 Ukr

S Gujaraidze 2003 SA, Ur

I Gundishvili 2002 I, 2003 Pt, Sp, Rus, CZR, 2008 ESp, Ur, ItA, 2009 C, US

D Gurgenidze 2007 Sp, ItA

A Gusharashvili 1998 Ukr

D Iobidze 1993 Rus, Pol

E Iovadze 1993 Lux, 1994 Kaz, 1995 Bul, Mol, Ger, H, 2001 Sp, F, SA, 2002 H, Rus, Sp, R, I

A Issakadze 1989 Z

N Iurini 1991 Ukr, 1994 Swi, 1995 Ger, H, 1996 CZR, CZR, Rus, 1997 Pt, Pol, Cro, De, 1998 Ukr, Rus, 2000 It, Sp, H, R

S Janelidze 1991 *Ukr, Ukr*, 1993 *Rus*, 1994 *Kaz*, 1995 *Ger*, 1997 *Pt*, 1998 *Ukr, I, R*, 1999 *Tg*, 2000 *R*
R Japarashvili 1992 *Ukr, Ukr, Lat*, 1993 *Pol, Lux*, 1996 *CZR*, 1997 *Pt*
L Javelidze 1997 *Cro*, 1998 *I*, 2001 *H, R, F, SA*, 2002 *H, R*, 2004 *R*, 2005 *Ukr*, 2007 *Sp*
G Jgenti 2004 *Ur*, 2005 *CHL*, 2007 *Sp, CZR, Nm, ESp, ItA*, 2009 *C, IrA, US*, 2011 *R*
D Jghenti 2004 *CZR, R*
D Jhamutashvili 2005 *CHL*
P Jimsheladze 1995 *Bul, Mol, H*, 1996 *CZR, CZR, Rus*, 1997 *De*, 1998 *It, Ukr, Rus, I, R*, 1999 *Tg, Tg*, 2000 *Pt, Mor, Sp, H, R*, 2001 *H, Pt, Rus, Sp, R, F, SA*, 2002 *H, Pt, Rus, Sp, I, Rus*, 2003 *Pt, Sp, Rus, CZR, R, It, E, Sa, SA, Ur*, 2004 *Rus*, 2005 *R*, 2006 *Rus, R, Pt, Ukr, J, Bb, CZR, Pt, Pt*, 2007 *R, Rus, CZR, Ar*
K Jintcharadze 1993 *Rus, Pol*, 2000 *It, Mor*

D Kacharava 2006 *Ukr, J, R, Sp, Pt*, 2007 *R, Sp, Rus, CZR, Nm, ESp, ItA, I, Nm*, 2008 *Pt, R, Pt, CZR, Rus, Sp, S*, 2009 *Ger, Pt, Sp, R, Rus, C, IrA, US, ArJ, ItA*, 2010 *Ger, Pt, Sp, R, Rus, C, US*, 2011 *Ukr, Sp, Pt, R, Rus, S, E, R, Ar*, 2012 *Sp, Pt, R, Rus, Ukr, US, C, J, Fj*, 2013 *Bel, Pt, Rus, Sp, R, Ur, Ar*
G Kacharava 2005 *Ukr*, 2006 *J, Bb, CZR, R*, 2007 *Sp*, 2008 *CZR*
G Kakhiani 1995 *Bul, Mol*
V Kakovin 2008 *S*, 2009 *C, IrA, US, ItA*, 2010 *S, ItA, Nm*, 2011 *Ukr, Sp, Pt, Rus, Nm, R, Ar*, 2012 *Pt, R, Rus*, 2013 *Rus, Sp, R, Ar*
G Kalmakhelidze 2012 *Sp, Ukr*
V Katsadze 1997 *Pol*, 1998 *It, Ukr, Rus, I, R*, 1999 *Tg, Tg*, 2000 *Pt, Mor, Sp, H, R*, 2001 *H, Pt, Rus, Sp, R*, 2002 *Pt, Rus, Sp, R, I, Rus*, 2003 *Pt, Sp, CZR, R, E, Sa, SA, Ur*, 2004 *Sp*, 2005 *Ukr*
A Kavtarashvili 1994 *Swi*, 1995 *Bul, Mol, Ger*, 1996 *CZR, Rus*, 1997 *Pt, Cro, De*, 1998 *It, Rus, I, R*, 1999 *Tg, Tg*, 2000 *It, H, R*, 2001 *H*, 2003 *SA, Ur*
G Kavtidze 2008 *S*
I Kerauli 1991 *Ukr, Ukr*, 1992 *Ukr, Ukr*
L Khachirashvili 2005 *Ukr*
T Khakhaleishili 1994 *Kaz*
B Khamashuridze 1989 *Z*
B Khamashuridze 1998 *It, Ukr, Rus, I, R*, 1999 *Tg, Tg*, 2000 *It, Pt, Sp, H, R*, 2001 *Pt, Rus, Sp, R, F, SA*, 2002 *H, Pt, Rus, Sp, R, I, Rus*, 2003 *Pt, CZR, R, It, E, Sa, SA, Ur*, 2004 *Pt, Rus, Rus*, 2005 *Pt, Ukr, CHL*, 2006 *Rus, R, Pt, R, Sp, Pt, Pt*, 2007 *Rus, CZR, ESp, Ar, Nm, F*, 2008 *Pt*, 2010 *US*, 2011 *Ukr, Sp, R, Rus, Nm*
M Kharshiladze 1991 *Ukr*
B Khekhelashvili 1999 *Tg, Tg*, 2000 *It, Pt, Mor, Sp, H, R*, 2001 *H, Pt, R, F, SA*, 2002 *H, Pt, Rus, Sp, R, I*, 2003 *Sp, Rus, CZR, R, E, Sa*, 2004 *Sp*
D Khinchagishvili 2003 *Sp, CZR*, 2004 *Pt, Sp, Rus*, 2006 *Bb, CZR, Sp, Pt, Pt*, 2007 *R, Rus, Nm, ESp, ItA, Ar, I, Nm*, 2009 *Ger, Pt, Sp, R, Rus, ArJ, ItA*, 2010 *Ger, Pt, R, Rus, C*, 2011 *Ukr, Pt, R, Rus, S, E, R*, 2012 *Rus, J, Fj*, 2013 *Bel, Pt*
L Khmaladze 2008 *ESp, ItA*, 2009 *ItA*, 2010 *S, ItA, Nm*, 2011 *Nm, E, R, Ar*, 2012 *Ukr, US, J, Fj*, 2013 *Bel, Pt, Rus, Sp, R, Ur, Ar*
G Khonelidze 2003 *SA*
G Khositashvili 2008 *ESp, Ur, ItA*
N Khuade 1989 *Z*, 1990 *Z, Z*, 1991 *Ukr, Ukr*, 1993 *Rus, Pol, Lux*, 1994 *Swi*, 1995 *Ger*
V Khutsishvili 2013 *Rus, Sp, R, Ur, Ar*
Z Khutsishvili 1993 *Lux*, 1994 *Kaz, Swi*, 1995 *Bul*, 1996 *CZR*
A Khvedelidze 1989 *Z*, 1990 *Z, Z*, 1991 *Ukr, Ukr*, 1992 *Ukr, Ukr, Lat*, 1993 *Rus, Pol*
I Kiasashvili 2008 *Pt, CZR, Ur*, 2010 *S, Nm*, 2012 *Rus, Ukr, US, C, J, Fj*, 2013 *Pt, Ar*
D Kiknadze 2004 *Rus*, 2005 *Pt, Ukr*
A Kobakhidze 1997 *Cro*, 1998 *I*
K Kobakhidze 1995 *Ger, H*, 1996 *Rus*, 1997 *Pt*, 1998 *It, Ukr, Rus, I, R*, 1999 *Tg*, 2000 *It*
Z Koberidze 2004 *Ur*
V Kolelishvili 2008 *ItA*, 2010 *S, ItA, Nm, US*, 2011 *Pt, Rus, Nm, S, Ar*, 2012 *Pt, R, J, Fj*, 2013 *Bel, Rus, Sp, R, Ur, Ar*
A Kopaleishvili 2004 *Ur*
A Kopaliani 2003 *It, SA, Ur*, 2004 *Pt*, 2005 *Ukr, R*, 2006 *Rus, R, Ukr, J, Bb, CZR, R, Sp, Pt*, 2007 *R, Sp, Rus, CZR, Ar, I, Nm, F*
G Korkelia 2010 *S, ItA*
D Kubriashvili 2008 *Pt, R, Pt, Rus, Sp*, 2009 *Pt, Sp, R, Rus, ArJ, ItA*, 2010 *Ger, Pt, Sp, US*, 2011 *Nm, S, E, Ar*, 2012 *Pt, R, Rus, J, Fj*, 2013 *Bel, Rus, Sp, R*
E Kuparadze 2007 *ESp*
G Kutarashvili 2004 *Pt, Sp, CZR, R*, 2005 *CHL*, 2006 *Rus, R, Pt, Ukr, J, R*
B Kvinikhidze 2002 *R*, 2004 *Pt, Sp, CZR, R*, 2005 *CHL*
M Kvirikashvili 2003 *Pt, Sp, CZR, E, Sa, SA, Ur*, 2004 *Rus, CZR, R, CHL*, 2005 *CZR, CHL*, 2007 *R, Sp, Rus, CZR, Nm, ESp, ItA, Ar, I, Nm, F*, 2008 *Pt, CZR, Rus, Sp, S*, 2009 *Ger, Pt, R, Rus, C, IrA, US, ArJ, ItA*, 2010 *Ger, Pt, Sp, R, Rus, ItA, Nm, C, US*, 2011 *Ukr, Sp, Pt, R, Rus, S, E, R, Ar*, 2012 *Sp, Pt, R, Rus, US, C, J, Fj*, 2013 *Bel, Pt, Rus, Sp, R*

G Labadze 1996 *CZR, Rus*, 1997 *Pt, Pol, Cro, De*, 1998 *It, Ukr, Rus, I, R*, 1999 *Tg, Tg*, 2000 *It, Pt, Sp, H, R*, 2001 *H, Pt, Rus, Sp, F, SA*, 2002 *Pt, Rus, Sp, R, Rus*, 2003 *Rus, CZR, R, It, E, Sa*, 2004 *Rus*, 2005 *R*, 2006 *Rus, R, Pt, J, R, Pt, Pt*, 2007 *Rus, Ar, Nm*, 2009 *Ger, Pt, Sp, R, Rus, C, IrA, US, ArJ*, 2010 *Ger, Pt, Sp, R, Rus, C*, 2011 *Ukr, Sp, R*, 2012 *US, C*
I Lezhava 1991 *Ukr, Ukr*, 1992 *Ukr*, 1995 *Bul*
Z Lezhava 1991 *Ukr*, 1995 *Ger*, 1996 *CZR, CZR, Rus*, 1997 *Pt, Cro, De*, 1998 *It, Rus, R*, 1999 *Tg*
L Liluashvili 1997 *Pt*
V Liluashvili 1989 *Z*, 1990 *Z, Z*
O Liparteliani 1989 *Z*, 1990 *Z, Z*
S Liparteliani 1991 *Ukr*, 1994 *Kaz, Swi*, 1996 *CZR*
Z Liparteliani 1994 *Kaz, Swi*, 1995 *Bul, Mol, Ger, H*
G Lomgadze 2009 *US*
L Lomidze 2013 *Rus*
D Losaberidze 2009 *IrA*
M Lossaberidze 1989 *Z*

K Machitidze 1989 *Z*, 1993 *Rus*, 1995 *Bul, Mol, Ger, H*, 1996 *CZR, CZR, Rus*, 1997 *Pt, Pol, Cro, De*, 1998 *It, Ukr, Rus, R*, 1999 *Tg*
I Machkhaneli 2002 *H, R*, 2003 *It, E, Sa, SA, Ur*, 2004 *Pt, Ur, CHL, Rus*, 2005 *Pt, Ukr, R, CZR, CHL*, 2006 *Rus, R, Pt, Bb, CZR, R, Pt*, 2007 *R, Ar, I, Nm*, 2008 *S*, 2009 *Ger, Pt, Sp, R, Rus, US, ArJ, ItA*, 2010 *Ger, Pt, Sp, R, Rus, C, US*, 2011 *Ukr, Sp, Pt, R, Rus, S, E*, 2012 *Sp, Pt, R, Rus, Ukr, US, C, J, Fj*, 2013 *Pt, Rus, Sp, R, Ur, Ar*
M Magrakvelidze 1998 *Ukr*, 2000 *Mor*, 2001 *F*, 2002 *Pt, Sp, R*, 2004 *Rus*, 2005 *Pt, R*, 2006 *Bb, CZR, Pt, Pt*, 2007 *R, CZR, Nm, ESp, ItA, I, F*
I Maisuradze 1997 *Cro*, 1998 *It, Ukr*, 1999 *Tg, Tg*, 2004 *Rus, R*, 2005 *CZR*, 2006 *Bb, CZR, R, Pt, Pt*, 2007 *R, Sp, Rus, CZR, ESp, ItA, I, F*
S Maisuradze 2008 *Pt, CZR, Rus, Sp, ESp, Ur, ItA, S*, 2009 *IrA, US, ItA*, 2010 *S, Nm, C, US*, 2011 *Pt*, 2013 *Ur*
V Maisuradze 2011 *Ukr, Sp, Pt, R, Rus, Nm, S, E, R, Ar*, 2012 *Ukr, US, C, J, Fj*, 2013 *Pt, Ur, Ar*
Z Maisuradze 2004 *Pt, Sp, CZR, Ur, CHL, Rus*, 2005 *Ukr, R*, 2006 *Rus, R, Pt, Ukr, J, Bb, CZR, Sp*, 2007 *Nm, ESp, ItA, Ar, I, F*, 2008 *Pt*, 2009 *C, IrA, US*, 2011 *Ukr, Sp, Nm*, 2012 *Ukr, US*
L Malaguradze 2008 *Pt, R, Pt, CZR, Rus, Sp, ESp, Ur, ItA, S*, 2009 *Ger, Pt, Sp, R, Rus, C, IrA, US, ArJ, ItA*, 2010 *Ger, Pt, Sp, R, Rus, C, US*, 2011 *Ukr, Sp, Pt, Rus, Ar*, 2012 *R, Rus, Ukr, US, C*, 2013 *Ur, Ar*
S Mamukashvili 2012 *Sp, Pt, Ukr, US, C, J, Fj*, 2013 *Bel, Pt, Rus*
K Margvelashvili 2003 *It, E, Sa, SA*
M Marjanishvili 1990 *Z, Z*, 1992 *Ukr, Ukr, Lat*, 1993 *Rus, Pol, Lux*
A Matchutadze 1993 *Lux*, 1994 *Kaz*, 1995 *Bul, Mol*, 1997 *Pt, Pol, Cro, De*
Z Matiashvili 2003 *Sp*, 2005 *CHL*
G Mchedlishvili 2008 *CZR*
S Melikidze 2008 *CZR, Sp, ESp, ItA*
L Mgueladze 1992 *Ukr, Ukr*
N Mgueladze 1995 *Bul, Mol, H*, 1997 *Pol*
K Mikautadze 2010 *S, ItA, Nm*, 2012 *Sp, Fj*, 2013 *Bel, Pt, Rus, Sp, R*
I Mirtskhulava 2012 *Ukr, US*, 2013 *Pt, Ur*
I Modebadze 2003 *SA, Ur*, 2004 *Sp*
S Modebadze 1994 *Kaz*, 1995 *Mol*, 1996 *CZR, CZR, Rus*, 1997 *Pt, Pol, Cro, De*, 1998 *It, Ukr, Rus*, 1999 *Tg*, 2000 *It, Pt*, 2001 *Sp, F, SA*, 2002 *H, Pt, Rus, Sp, R*
T Mtchedlidze 2013 *Bel, Pt, Rus, Sp, R, Ar*
A Mtchedlishvili 2004 *Ur, CHL*, 2008 *CZR*
S Mtchedlishvili 2000 *It*, 2007 *Sp*
Z Mtchedlishvili 1995 *Mol*, 1996 *CZR*, 1997 *Cro, De*, 1998 *It, Ukr, Rus, I, R*, 1999 *Tg, Tg*, 2000 *Pt, Mor, Sp, H, R*, 2001 *Rus, Sp, R, F, SA*, 2002 *H, Pt, Rus, I, Rus*, 2003 *Pt, Sp, Rus, CZR, R, It, E, Sa, Ur*, 2004 *Pt, Rus*, 2005 *Pt*, 2006 *J*, 2007 *Rus, CZR, Nm, ESp, ItA, F*
M Mtiulishvili 1991 *Ukr*, 1994 *Kaz*, 1996 *CZR, CZR, Rus*, 1997 *Pt, Pol, Cro, De*, 1998 *It, Ukr, Rus, R*, 2001 *H, Pt, Rus, Sp,*

R, 2002 H, Pt, Rus, Sp, R, I, 2003 Rus, CZR, R, 2004 Rus, CZR, R

V Nadiradze 1994 Kaz, Swi, 1995 H, 1996 Rus, 1997 Pt, De, 1998 I, R, 1999 Tg, 2000 Pt, Mor, Sp, H, R, 2001 H, Pt, Rus, Sp, R, F, SA, 2002 H, Pt, Rus, Sp, R, I, Rus, 2003 Rus, CZR, R, It, E, Sa
M Nariashvili 2012 Sp, Pt, R, Ukr, US, C, J, Fj, 2013 Bel, Pt, Rus
A Natchqebia 1990 Z, Z
I Natriashvili 2006 Ukr, J, 2007 ItA, 2008 Pt, R, Pt, Rus, Sp, ESp, Ur, ItA, S, 2009 Ger, Pt, Sp, R, Rus, C, IrA, US, ArJ, ItA, 2010 Ger, R, Rus, ItA, Nm, US, 2011 Ukr, Sp, Pt, R, 2012 R, Rus, J, Fj, 2013 Rus, Sp, R
N Natroshvili 1992 Ukr, Ukr, Lat
G Nemsadze 2005 CHL, 2006 Ukr, 2007 Sp, 2008 CZR, Sp, ESp, Ur, ItA, 2009 IrA, US, ArJ, ItA, 2010 Ger, Pt, R, Rus, US, 2011 R, Rus, Nm, Ar, 2012 Sp, R, Rus, J, 2013 Ur, Ar
A Nijaradze 2008 CZR
I Nikolaenko 1999 Tg, Tg, 2000 It, Mor, Sp, H, R, 2001 R, F, 2003 Pt, Sp, E, Sa, SA, Ur
I Ninidze 2004 Ur, CHL
M Ninidze 2010 S, Nm

D Oboladze 1993 Rus, Pol, Lux, 1994 Swi, 1995 Bul, Mol, Ger, H, 1996 CZR, CZR, Rus, 1997 Pt, Pol, 1998 It, Ukr
T Odisharia 1989 Z, 1994 Kaz

S Papashvili 2001 SA, 2004 CZR, R, 2006 Bb, CZR, 2007 Sp
S Partsikanashvili 1994 Kaz, 1996 CZR, Rus, 1997 Pol, 1999 Tg, Tg, 2000 It, Pt, Mor
A Peikrishvili 2008 Pt, Pt, 2009 R, 2010 Pt, R, Rus, 2011 Sp, 2013 Ar
G Peradze 1991 Ukr
Z Peradze 1997 Pol, 1998 Rus
Z Petriashvili 2009 C
D Pinchukovi 2004 CZR
L Pirpilashvili 2004 Rus, CZR, R, Ur, CHL, 2005 Ukr, R, CZR
G Pirtskhalava 1989 Z, 1995 Ger, 1996 CZR, Rus, 1997 Pt, Pol
T Pkhakadze 1989 Z, 1990 Z, Z, 1993 Rus, Pol, Lux, 1994 Kaz, 1996 CZR

G Rapava-Ruskini 1990 Z, 1992 Ukr, Lat, 1994 Kaz, 1996 Rus, 1997 Pt, Cro, De, 1998 It, Ukr, Rus, R, 1999 Tg
T Ratianidze 2000 It, 2001 H, Pt, Sp, R, SA, 2002 Pt, Rus, Sp, R, I, Rus, 2003 Pt, Sp, Rus, CZR, R
Z Rekhviashvili 1995 H, 1997 Pt, Pol
G Rokhvadze 2008 ItA, 2009 C, IrA, US, 2010 S, ItA

S Sakandelidze 1996 CZR, 1998 Ukr
S Sakvarelidze 2010 S, ItA
B Samkharadze 2004 Pt, Sp, Rus, CZR, R, Ur, CHL, 2005 CZR, CHL, 2006 Rus, R, Pt, Ukr, Bb, CZR, R, Sp, Pt, Pt, 2007 R, Sp, Rus, CZR, Nm, ESp, Ar, I, Nm, F, 2008 Pt, R, Pt, Sp, ESp, Ur, ItA, S, 2009 Ger, Sp, R, ArJ, ItA, 2010 Ger, Pt, Sp, R, S, ItA, Nm, C, 2011 Ukr, Sp, Pt, Nm, E, R, Ar, 2012 Pt, C
A Sanadze 2004 CHL
P Saneblidze 1994 Kaz
G Sanikidze 2004 Ur, CHL
B Sardanashvili 2004 CHL
V Satseradze 1989 Z, 1990 Z, 1991 Ukr, 1992 Ukr, Ukr, Lat
E Shanidze 1994 Swi
M Sharikadze 2012 Sp, Pt, R, Rus, Ukr, US, J, Fj, 2013 Bel, Pt, Rus, Sp, R, Ur, Ar
B Sheklashvili 2010 S, ItA, Nm, 2011 Sp, 2012 Sp
G Shkinin 2004 CZR, R, CHL, 2005 CHL, 2006 Rus, R, Ukr, J, R, Sp, Pt, Pt, 2007 R, Sp, Rus, CZR, Nm, ESp, ItA, Ar, I, Nm, 2008 R, Pt, CZR, Rus, Sp, ESp, Ur, ItA, S, 2009 Pt, 2012 Sp, Pt, R
B Shvanguiradze 1990 Z, Z, 1992 Ukr, Ukr, Lat, 1993 Rus, Pol, Lux
G Shvelidze 1998 I, R, 1999 Tg, Tg, 2000 It, Pt, Sp, H, R, 2001 H, Pt, Sp, F, SA, 2002 H, Rus, I, Rus, 2003 Pt, Sp, Rus, CZR, R, It, E, Sa, Ur, 2004 Rus, 2005 Pt, CZR, 2006 Rus, R, Pt, R, Sp, Pt, Pt, 2007 Ar, I, Nm, F, 2008 Pt, R, Pt, CZR, Rus, 2009 Ger, Pt, Sp, R, Rus, ArJ, 2010 Sp, R, Rus, C, US, 2011 Pt, Nm, E, R, Ar
I Sikharulidze 1994 Kaz
T Sokhadze 2005 CZR, 2006 Rus, R, Pt, Ukr, J, Pt, Pt, 2009 C, IrA
M Sujashvili 2004 Pt, Rus, 2005 Pt, Ukr, R, CZR, 2006 Pt, Ukr, J, Bb, CZR
S Sultanishvili 1998 Ukr
S Sutiashvili 2005 CHL, 2006 Ukr, 2007 CZR, Nm, ESp, 2008 Pt, R, CZR, Rus, S, 2010 S, ItA, Nm, C, US, 2011 Ukr, Sp, Pt, R, Rus, S, E, 2012 Pt, R, Rus, C, J, Fj, 2013 Bel, Pt, Rus, Sp, R, Ur, Ar
P Svanidze 1992 Ukr

T Tavadze 1991 Ukr, Ukr
L Tavartkiladze 2009 ItA, 2010 Ger, Sp, R, Rus, S, ItA, Nm, 2011 Sp
N Tchavtchavadze 1998 It, Ukr, 2004 CZR, R, Ur, CHL
M Tcheishvili 1989 Z, 1990 Z, Z, 1995 H
B Tepnadze 1995 H, 1996 CZR, 1997 Cro, 1998 I, R, 1999 Tg
G Tkhilaishvili 2012 Ukr, US, C, J
A Todua 2008 CZR, Rus, Sp, ESp, Ur, ItA, S, 2009 Sp, R, C, IrA, US, ArJ, ItA, 2010 Ger, Pt, R, Rus, S, ItA, Nm, 2011 Nm, S, E, R, Ar, 2012 Sp, Pt, R, Rus, US, C, J, Fj, 2013 Bel, Ur
P Tqabladze 1993 Lux, 1995 Bul
L Tsabadze 1994 Kaz, Swi, 1995 Bul, Ger, H, 1996 CZR, Rus, 1997 Cro, De, 1998 It, Rus, I, R, 1999 Tg, Tg, 2000 Pt, Mor, Sp, R, 2001 H, Pt, Rus, Sp, R, F, SA, 2002 H, Pt, Rus, Sp, R, I, Rus
B Tsiklauri 2008 ItA, 2012 Pt, Ukr, 2013 Bel, Rus, Sp, Ur, Ar
G Tsiklauri 2003 SA, Ur
D Tskhvediani 1998 Ukr
V Tskitishvili 1994 Swi, 1995 Bul, Mol
T Turdzeladze 1989 Z, 1990 Z, Z, 1991 Ukr, 1995 Ger, H

K Uchava 2002 Sp, 2004 Sp, 2008 Pt, R, Pt, Rus, Sp, ESp, Ur, ItA, S, 2009 Ger, Pt, R, C, IrA, 2010 S, ItA, Nm
B Udesiani 2001 Sp, F, 2002 H, 2004 Pt, Sp, CZR, R, Rus, 2005 Pt, Ukr, R, CZR, CHL, 2006 Rus, R, Ukr, J, Bb, CZR, R, Sp, Pt, Pt, 2007 R, Rus, CZR, Ar, Nm, 2008 CZR, Sp, ESp, Ur, ItA, S, 2010 Ger, Pt, Sp, R, Rus, C, US, 2011 Ukr
B Urjukashvili 2011 Ukr, Sp, Pt, Rus, Nm
M Urjukashvili 1997 Cro, De, 1998 Ukr, Rus, R, 1999 Tg, Tg, 2000 It, Pt, Mor, Sp, 2001 Pt, Rus, Sp, R, F, SA, 2002 H, Pt, Sp, R, I, Rus, 2003 Pt, Sp, Rus, R, It, E, Sa, Ur, 2004 Pt, Rus, Ur, CHL, Rus, 2005 Pt, R, CZR, 2006 Rus, R, Pt, Ukr, J, R, Sp, 2007 Rus, CZR, Nm, ESp, ItA, Ar, I, Nm, F, 2008 Sp, 2009 R, Rus, 2010 Ger, Sp, R, Rus, ItA, Nm, C, 2011 Nm, S, R, Ar
R Urushadze 1997 Pol, 2002 R, 2004 Pt, Rus, Rus, 2005 Pt, Ukr, R, CZR, CHL, 2006 Rus, R, Pt, Bb, CZR, R, Sp, Pt, Pt, 2007 Nm, ESp, ItA, I, Nm, F, 2008 Pt, R, Pt, Rus, Sp, S, 2009 Ger, Pt, Sp, R, Rus, C, IrA, US, ArJ, ItA

Z Valishvili 2004 CHL
D Vartaniani 1991 Ukr, Ukr, 1992 Ukr, Ukr, Lat, 1997 Pol, 2000 Sp, H, R
L Vashadze 1991 Ukr, 1992 Ukr, Ukr, Lat

G Yachvili 2001 H, Pt, R, 2003 Pt, Sp, Rus, CZR, R, It, E, Sa, Ur

I Zedginidze 1998 I, 2000 It, Pt, Mor, Sp, H, R, 2001 H, Pt, Rus, Sp, R, 2002 H, Rus, Sp, I, Rus, 2003 Pt, Sp, Rus, CZR, R, It, Sa, SA, Ur, 2004 Pt, Sp, Rus, CZR, R, Rus, 2005 Pt, Ukr, R, CZR, 2006 Rus, R, Pt, Ukr, CZR, R, Sp, Pt, Pt, 2007 R, Ar, I, 2008 S, 2009 Ger, Pt, Sp, Rus, ArJ, ItA, 2010 Ger, Pt, Sp, R, Rus, 2011 Nm, E, R, Ar
Z Zhvania 2013 Sp, R
T Zibzibadze 2000 It, Pt, Mor, Sp, 2001 H, Pt, Rus, Sp, R, F, SA, 2002 H, Pt, Rus, Sp, R, I, Rus, 2003 Pt, Sp, Rus, CZR, R, It, E, Sa, Ur, 2004 Pt, Sp, Rus, CZR, R, Rus, 2005 Pt, Ukr, R, CZR, 2009 Ger, Pt, Sp, R, ArJ, 2010 Ger, Pt, Sp, R, Rus, S, ItA, Nm, C, US, 2011 Sp, Pt, R, Rus, S, E, R, Ar, 2012 R, Rus, C, J, 2013 Pt, Rus, R, Ur
D Zirakashvili 2004 Ur, CHL, Rus, 2005 Ukr, R, CZR, 2006 Rus, R, Pt, R, Sp, Pt, 2007 R, Ar, Nm, F, 2008 R, 2009 Ger, 2010 Ger, Pt, Sp, Rus, C, US, 2011 Ukr, Pt, R, Rus, S, E, R, 2012 Ukr, US, C, J, Fj, 2013 Pt, Rus, Sp, R, Ur, Ar

Paddy Jackson was one of several youngsters blooded by Ireland in 2013.

Getty Images

IRELAND

IRELAND'S 2012–13 TEST RECORD

South Africa	10 Nov	H	Lost 12–16
Argentina	24 Nov	H	Won 46–24
Wales	2 Feb	A	Won 30–22
England	10 Feb	H	Lost 6–12
Scotland	24 Feb	A	Lost 12–8
France	9 Mar	H	Drew 13–13
Italy	16 Mar	A	Lost 22–15
USA	8 Jun	A	Won 15–12
Canada	15 Jun	A	Won 40–14

NEW COACH HERALDS A NEW DAWN FOR IRELAND

By Ruaidhri O'Connor

Getty Images

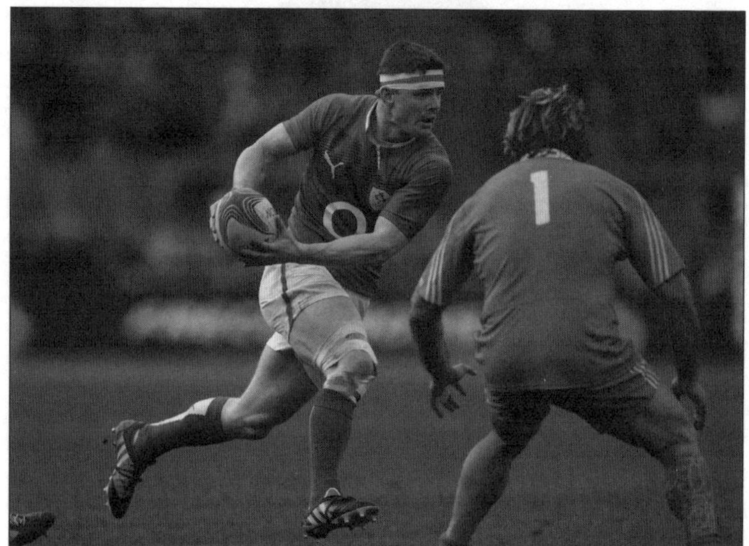

The inspirational Brian O'Driscoll committed to play one more season for Leinster and Ireland.

Irish rugby needs a break from drama after a tumultuous season that began in the shadow of a record defeat and ended with a new coach and the fallout of Brian O'Driscoll's omission from the British & Irish Lions match-day squad for their third Test win over Australia.

Declan Kidney's term as coach came to an end as he paid the price for a hugely disappointing Six Nations in which his side were decimated with injuries as they won just one game.

Their season was summed up in Rome where their backline suffered to such an extent that blindside flanker Peter O'Mahony was forced to play on the wing for an hour. Ireland lost to Italy for the first time in the competition at the Stadio Olimpico and it would prove one defeat too many for the 2009 Grand Slam-winning coach.

Kidney's contract was due to expire after the summer tour of the USA and Canada, but the Irish Rugby Football Union acted swiftly and announced his departure on 2 April, with his assistant Les Kiss remaining to take charge of the summer tour. By the end of the month Leinster coach Joe Schmidt was installed as Kidney's successor after guiding the province to back-to-back Heineken Cups in 2011 and 2012, and signing off with the Amlin Challenge Cup and RaboDirect PRO12 double for good measure.

As if that wasn't enough excitement, there was plenty more drama to take in. Kidney's decision to replace O'Driscoll as captain with Jamie Heaslip ahead of the Six Nations, his call to discard his most capped player and highest points scorer in Ronan O'Gara and replace him with the inexperienced Paddy Jackson, and the fallout over Jonathan Sexton's big-money move to Racing Métro all dominated the sports pages.

The main talking point, however, was the continuation of the national side's underperformance. In their last game of 2011/12, Kidney's side went down 60–0 to New Zealand in Hamilton. That biggest-ever loss hung over the new campaign.

First up were South Africa in November and the under-pressure coach went into the games without key men in the injured O'Driscoll, Rory Best, Paul O'Connell, Sean O'Brien, Stephen Ferris and Rob Kearney.

In difficult conditions they led the Boks 12–3 at half-time, but could not build on that score as Ulster's Ruan Pienaar took advantage of Heaslip's sin-binning on his first outing as captain to score a try as the Rugby World Cup 2007 champions ran out 16–12 winners. The number 8 took responsibility for his ill-discipline after he was yellow-carded for hauling down a maul near the Irish line.

"We came out in the second half and, as captain, I should lead by example, but being yellow-carded wasn't a good example," he said. "I put my hand up straight away when we came in afterwards. I'm a better servant on the field than off it. We were a little bit frustrated we weren't further ahead at half-time."

That frustration would soon be released as a young Irish XV ran in eight tries and Craig Gilroy scored a hat-trick against Fiji in a non-capped international at Thomond Park.

The young Ulster wing kept his place when Argentina visited the Aviva Stadium a week later and opened the scoring with a fine try. The tired Pumas were overwhelmed as Ireland seemed to usher in a new dawn with a scintillating 46–24 win. It would prove false come spring.

In the meantime, Leinster's Heineken Cup three-in-a-row bid was falling to pieces with back-to-back defeats against Clermont Auvergne before Christmas. Munster, too, were in trouble after losing to Racing Métro and Saracens, but the Reds recovered to win their final two games against Edinburgh and Racing and book their place in the quarter-finals at the expense of old rivals Leinster, who finished with wins over the Scarlets and Exeter Chiefs but had given themselves too much to do.

Ulster, meanwhile, looked the form team and qualified for the quarter-finals by topping their pool, although their surprise defeat to Northampton Saints, a week after hammering them away from home, left them without a home tie in the last eight. That would come back to haunt them. Connacht, meanwhile, were competitive in their second season in the competition and beat Biarritz at home.

With qualification dealt with, it was back to the international squad for some players and Ireland opened in Cardiff against their old friends Wales. Their record against Warren Gatland's side was a poor one, but with O'Driscoll, Kearney and O'Brien back they tore into the hosts and led 30–3 after 43 minutes. The defending champions fought back to 30–22 but could get no closer. Ireland were up and running and the Grand Slam was suddenly being talked about as a possibility.

Eight days later that dream was gone as a brutal English pack took advantage of an awful day in Dublin by beating Ireland into submission. Owen Farrell kicked his side to a 12–6 win as Sexton and Simon Zebo limped off early. It was a portent of things to come.

Two weeks on Kidney made his boldest call yet, opting for the uncapped Jackson to play against Scotland ahead of O'Gara. The young Ulsterman had been instrumental in that win over Fiji but he wilted at Murrayfield, missing a series of kicks as the lineout malfunctioned. Ireland lost 12–8 despite dominating territory and possession.

A fortnight later O'Gara had been culled from the squad altogether, with Jackson remaining in situ and Leinster's Ian Madigan on the bench as Ireland drew with France for the second season in a row. Louis Picamoles scored a crucial late try in a dour game as both O'Driscoll and Luke Marshall needed attention for head injuries.

Then came Rome and a debacle that saw Ireland lose Marshall, Keith Earls and Luke Fitzgerald before half-time and then three players – O'Driscoll, Donnacha Ryan and Conor Murray – to the sin-bin. Italy won 22–15 and Kidney was done for.

"I wasn't thinking that this could be my last match as coach; all I was concentrating on was getting the win," Kidney said in the aftermath. "I wanted to get a result out of today, we didn't manage to do that and we'll reflect on it over the coming days and weeks. I'd have to sit down and think about whether I want a new contract. These guys are a pleasure to work with, but beyond that I'd have to sit back and think about it."

He wouldn't get the option as the IRFU decided enough was enough.

The failure of the men's team was compounded by the success of the women's national team, who completed a first-ever Six Nations Grand Slam with a hard-fought 6–3 win over Italy a day after their men's team had slumped to defeat.

Having been appointed to the national job, Schmidt set about signing off from Leinster on a high and he did so by beating Stade Français in the Amlin Challenge Cup final, before completing the double with a hard-fought 24–18 win over Ulster in the RaboDirect PRO12 final in front of a packed RDS.

It was a disappointing end to Ulster's season. They had looked so good but crashed out in the last eight at the hands of Saracens at Twickenham. Munster, however, reached the semi-finals and put in a huge display in defeat to Clermont in what would prove to be O'Gara's final game. It was a fine end to a difficult first season for New Zealander Rob Penney, who is managing huge transition at the province.

Lansdowne ran away with the All-Ireland League Division 1A title, while the most successful club in Irish history, Shannon, were relegated for the first time.

After all that, there was the small matter of the end-of-season tours. With nine players called up to the original Lions squad, Kiss headed for North America with a young squad, captained by O'Mahony. They won both games, edging the USA 15–12 in Houston and Canada 40–14 in Toronto with Schmidt in attendance. An Emerging Ireland team then travelled to Georgia for the inaugural IRB Tbilisi Cup and under Allen Clarke's guidance won two out of three, beating Georgia and Uruguay.

After handing out six new caps on tour and with three other players making their first international starts, Kiss was happy with the progress made.

"Without a doubt we found out a little about ourselves as players," he said. "From a coaching perspective it was certainly encouraging on a lot of fronts. Sometimes the perception is you can come and get these Tier Two nations and run it away easily but they were both tough affairs."

Between the Tests, Schmidt asked fans to be patient in his first year as his success with Leinster brings great expectations.

"Even at the finish of Leinster, a lot of people said, 'I can't wait to see you do that with Ireland.' It is not like that, it is a whole new ball game, a whole new level and it is a different group. You have to start from scratch," he said.

The season finished with the massive news that O'Driscoll had been omitted from Gatland's match-day 23 for the final Lions Test against Australia, which was won with four Irish players on the field as the tourists won the series.

It summed up the year but, with the great centre pledging to continue for one last season and Schmidt at the helm, there is hope for improvement in 2013/14. Irish fans would probably settle for a little less drama.

IRELAND INTERNATIONAL STATISTICS

MATCH RECORDS UP TO 10 OCTOBER 2013

MOST CONSECUTIVE TEST WINS

10	2002 R, Ru, Gg, A, Fj, Arg, 2003 S1, It1, F, W1
8	2003 Tg, Sm,W2 ,It2, S2, R ,Nm, Arg
8	2008 Arg, 2009 F, It, E, S, W ,C, US
6	1968 S, W, A, 1969 F, E, S
6	2004 SA, US, Arg, 2005 It, S, E

MOST CONSECUTIVE TESTS WITHOUT DEFEAT

Matches	Wins	Draws	Period
12	11	1	2008 to 2010
10	10	0	2002 to 2003
8	8	0	2003
7	6	1	1968 to 1969
6	6	0	2004 to 2005

MOST POINTS IN A MATCH

BY THE TEAM

Pts	Opponents	Venue	Year
83	United States	Manchester (NH)	2000
78	Japan	Dublin	2000
70	Georgia	Dublin	1998
64	Fiji	Dublin	2002
64	Namibia	Sydney	2003
63	Georgia	Dublin	2002
62	Russia	Rotorua	2011
61	Italy	Limerick	2003
61	Pacific Islands	Dublin	2006
60	Romania	Dublin	1986
60	Italy	Dublin	2000
55	Zimbabwe	Dublin	1991
55	United States	Dublin	2004
55	Canada	Limerick	2008
54	Wales	Dublin	2002
53	Romania	Dublin	1998
53	United States	Dublin	1999
51	Italy	Rome	2007
50	Japan	Bloemfontein	1995

BY A PLAYER

Pts	Player	Opponents	Venue	Year
32	RJR O'Gara	Samoa	Apia	2003
30	RJR O'Gara	Italy	Dublin	2000
26	DG Humphreys	Scotland	Murrayfield	2003
26	DG Humphreys	Italy	Limerick	2003
26	P Wallace	Pacific Islands	Dublin	2006
24	PA Burke	Italy	Dublin	1997
24	DG Humphreys	Argentina	Lens	1999
23	RP Keyes	Zimbabwe	Dublin	1991
23	RJR O'Gara	Japan	Dublin	2000
22	DG Humphreys	Wales	Dublin	2002
21	SO Campbell	Scotland	Dublin	1982
21	SO Campbell	England	Dublin	1983
21	RJR O'Gara	Italy	Rome	2001
21	RJR O'Gara	Argentina	Dublin	2004
21	RJR O'Gara	England	Dublin	2007
20	MJ Kiernan	Romania	Dublin	1986
20	EP Elwood	Romania	Dublin	1993
20	SJP Mason	Samoa	Dublin	1996
20	EP Elwood	Georgia	Dublin	1998
20	KGM Wood	United States	Dublin	1999
20	DA Hickie	Italy	Limerick	2003
20	DG Humphreys	United States	Dublin	2004

MOST TRIES IN A MATCH

BY THE TEAM

Tries	Opponents	Venue	Year
13	United States	Manchester (NH)	2000
11	Japan	Dublin	2000
10	Romania	Dublin	1986
10	Georgia	Dublin	1998
10	Namibia	Sydney	2003
9	Fiji	Dublin	2003
9	Russia	Rotorua	2011
8	Western Samoa	Dublin	1988
8	Zimbabwe	Dublin	1991
8	Georgia	Dublin	2002
8	Italy	Limerick	2003
8	Pacific Islands	Dublin	2006
8	Italy	Rome	2007
8	Canada	Limerick	2008
7	Japan	Bloemfontein	1995
7	Romania	Dublin	1998
7	United States	Dublin	1999
7	United States	Dublin	2004
7	Japan	Tokyo	2005
7	Argentina	Dublin	2012

BY A PLAYER

Tries	Player	Opponents	Venue	Year
4	BF Robinson	Zimbabwe	Dublin	1991
4	KGM Wood	United States	Dublin	1999
4	DA Hickie	Italy	Limerick	2003
3	R Montgomery	Wales	Birkenhead	1887
3	JP Quinn	France	Cork	1913
3	EO'D Davy	Scotland	Murrayfield	1930
3	SJ Byrne	Scotland	Murrayfield	1953
3	KD Crossan	Romania	Dublin	1986
3	BJ Mullin	Tonga	Brisbane	1987
3	MR Mostyn	Argentina	Dublin	1999
3	BG O'Driscoll	France	Paris	2000
3	MJ Mullins	United States	Manchester (NH)	2000
3	DA Hickie	Japan	Dublin	2000
3	RAJ Henderson	Italy	Rome	2001
3	BG O'Driscoll	Scotland	Dublin	2002
3	KM Maggs	Fiji	Dublin	2002
3	FL McFadden	Canada	Toronto	2013

MOST CONVERSIONS IN A MATCH

BY THE TEAM

Cons	Opponents	Venue	Year
10	Georgia	Dublin	1998
10	Japan	Dublin	2000
9	United States	Manchester (NH)	2000
7	Romania	Dublin	1986
7	Georgia	Dublin	2002
7	Namibia	Sydney	2003
7	United States	Dublin	2004
7	Russia	Rotorua	2011
6	Japan	Bloemfontein	1995
6	Romania	Dublin	1998
6	United States	Dublin	1999
6	Italy	Dublin	2000
6	Italy	Limerick	2003
6	Japan	Tokyo	2005
6	Pacific Islands	Dublin	2006
6	Canada	Limerick	2008

BY A PLAYER

Cons	Player	Opponents	Venue	Year
10	EP Elwood	Georgia	Dublin	1998
10	RJR O'Gara	Japan	Dublin	2000
8	RJR O'Gara	United States	Manchester (NH)	2000
7	MJ Kiernan	Romania	Dublin	1986
7	RJR O'Gara	Namibia	Sydney	2003
7	DG Humphreys	United States	Dublin	2004
6	PA Burke	Japan	Bloemfontein	1995
6	RJR O'Gara	Italy	Dublin	2000
6	DG Humphreys	Italy	Limerick	2003
6	DG Humphreys	Japan	Tokyo	2005
6	P Wallace	Pacific Islands	Dublin	2006
6	RJR O'Gara	Russia	Rotorua	2011
5	MJ Kiernan	Canada	Dunedin	1987
5	EP Elwood	Romania	Dublin	1999
5	RJR O'Gara	Georgia	Dublin	2002
5	DG Humphreys	Fiji	Dublin	2002
5	DG Humphreys	Romania	Dublin	2005
5	RJR O'Gara	Canada	Limerick	2008
5	J Sexton	Fiji	Dublin	2009

MOST PENALTIES IN A MATCH

BY THE TEAM

Penalties	Opponents	Venue	Year
8	Italy	Dublin	1997
7	Argentina	Lens	1999
6	Scotland	Dublin	1982
6	Romania	Dublin	1993
6	United States	Atlanta	1996
6	Western Samoa	Dublin	1996
6	Italy	Dublin	2000
6	Wales	Dublin	2002
6	Australia	Dublin	2002
6	Samoa	Apia	2003
6	Japan	Osaka	2005

BY A PLAYER

Penalties	Player	Opponents	Venue	Year
8	PA Burke	Italy	Dublin	1997
7	DG Humphreys	Argentina	Lens	1999
6	SO Campbell	Scotland	Dublin	1982
6	EP Elwood	Romania	Dublin	1993
6	SJP Mason	Western Samoa	Dublin	1996
6	RJR O'Gara	Italy	Dublin	2000
6	DG Humphreys	Wales	Dublin	2002
6	RJR O'Gara	Australia	Dublin	2002

MOST DROP GOALS IN A MATCH

BY THE TEAM

Drops	Opponents	Venue	Year
2	Australia	Dublin	1967
2	France	Dublin	1975
2	Australia	Sydney	1979
2	England	Dublin	1981
2	Canada	Dunedin	1987
2	England	Dublin	1993
2	Wales	Wembley	1999
2	New Zealand	Dublin	2001
2	Argentina	Dublin	2004
2	England	Dublin	2005

BY A PLAYER

Drops	Player	Opponents	Venue	Year
2	CMH Gibson	Australia	Dublin	1967
2	WM McCombe	France	Dublin	1975
2	SO Campbell	Australia	Sydney	1979
2	EP Elwood	England	Dublin	1993
2	DG Humphreys	Wales	Wembley	1999
2	DG Humphreys	New Zealand	Dublin	2001
2	RJR O'Gara	Argentina	Dublin	2004
2	RJR O'Gara	England	Dublin	2005

CAREER RECORDS

MOST CAPPED PLAYERS

Caps	Player	Career Span
128	RJR O'Gara	2000 to 2013
125	BG O'Driscoll	1999 to 2013
105	JJ Hayes	2000 to 2011
98	PA Stringer	2000 to 2011
94	DP O'Callaghan	2003 to 2013
92	ME O'Kelly	1997 to 2009
85	PJ O'Connell	2002 to 2012
82	GT Dempsey	1998 to 2008
73	GW D'Arcy	1999 to 2013
72	DG Humphreys	1996 to 2005
72	DP Wallace	2000 to 2011
72	GEA Murphy	2000 to 2011
70	KM Maggs	1997 to 2005
69	CMH Gibson	1964 to 1979
67	MJ Horan	2000 to 2011
67	RD Best	2005 to 2013
65	SH Easterby	2000 to 2008
65	SP Horgan	2000 to 2009
63	WJ McBride	1962 to 1975
62	AG Foley	1995 to 2005
62	DA Hickie	1997 to 2007
61	JF Slattery	1970 to 1984
59	PS Johns	1990 to 2000
58	PA Orr	1976 to 1987
58	KGM Wood	1994 to 2003
57	DP Leamy	2004 to 2011
57	JPR Heaslip	2006 to 2013
55	BJ Mullin	1984 to 1995

MOST CONSECUTIVE TESTS

Tests	Player	Span
52	WJ McBride	1964 to 1975
49	PA Orr	1976 to 1986
43	DG Lenihan	1981 to 1989
39	MI Keane	1974 to 1981
38	PA Stringer	2003 to 2007
37	GV Stephenson	1920 to 1929

MOST TESTS AS CAPTAIN

Tests	Captain	Span
83	BG O'Driscoll	2002 to 2012
36	KGM Wood	1996 to 2003
24	TJ Kiernan	1963 to 1973
19	CF Fitzgerald	1982 to 1986
17	JF Slattery	1979 to 1981
17	DG Lenihan	1986 to 1990

MOST POINTS IN TESTS

Points	Player	Tests	Career
1083	RJR O'Gara	128	2000 to 2013
565*	DG Humphreys	72	1996 to 2005
308	MJ Kiernan	43	1982 to 1991
296	EP Elwood	35	1993 to 1999
282	JJ Sexton	36	2009 to 2013
245	BG O'Driscoll	125	1999 to 2013
217	SO Campbell	22	1976 to 1984
158	TJ Kiernan	54	1960 to 1973
145	DA Hickie	62	1997 to 2007
130	TJ Bowe	51	2004 to 2012
113	AJP Ward	19	1978 to 1987

* Humphreys's total includes a penalty try against Scotland in 1999

MOST PENALTY GOALS IN TESTS

Penalties	Player	Tests	Career
202	RJR O'Gara	128	2000 to 2013
110	DG Humphreys	72	1996 to 2005
68	EP Elwood	35	1993 to 1999
65	JJ Sexton	36	2009 to 2013
62	MJ Kiernan	43	1982 to 1991
54	SO Campbell	22	1976 to 1984
31	TJ Kiernan	54	1960 to 1973
29	AJP Ward	19	1978 to 1987

MOST TRIES IN TESTS

Tries	Player	Tests	Career
46	BG O'Driscoll	125	1999 to 2013
29	DA Hickie	62	1997 to 2007
26	TJ Bowe	51	2004 to 2012
21	SP Horgan	65	2000 to 2009
19	GT Dempsey	82	1998 to 2008
18	GEA Murphy	72	2000 to 2011
17	BJ Mullin	55	1984 to 1995
16	RJR O'Gara	128	2000 to 2013
15	KGM Wood	58	1994 to 2003
15	KM Maggs	70	1997 to 2005
14	GV Stephenson	42	1920 to 1930
12	KD Crossan	41	1982 to 1992
12	DP Wallace	72	2000 to 2011
12	KG Earls	39	2008 to 2013
12	AD Trimble	50	2005 to 2013

MOST DROP GOALS IN TESTS

Drops	Player	Tests	Career
15	RJR O'Gara	128	2000 to 2013
8	DG Humphreys	72	1996 to 2005
7	RA Lloyd	19	1910 to 1920
7	SO Campbell	22	1976 to 1984
6	CMH Gibson	69	1964 to 1979
6	BJ McGann	25	1969 to 1976
6	MJ Kiernan	43	1982 to 1991

MOST CONVERSIONS IN TESTS

Cons	Player	Tests	Career
176	RJR O'Gara	128	2000 to 2013
88	DG Humphreys	72	1996 to 2005
43	EP Elwood	35	1993 to 1999
40	MJ Kiernan	43	1982 to 1991
33	JJ Sexton	36	2009 to 2013
26	TJ Kiernan	54	1960 to 1973
16	RA Lloyd	19	1910 to 1920
15	SO Campbell	22	1976 to 1984

INTERNATIONAL CHAMPIONSHIP RECORDS

RECORD	DETAIL	HOLDER	SET
Most points in season	168	in five matches	2000
Most tries in season	17	in five matches	2000
	17	in five matches	2004
	17	In five matches	2007
Highest score	60	60–13 v Italy	2000
Biggest win	47	60–13 v Italy	2000
Highest score conceded	50	18–50 v England	2000
Biggest defeat	40	6–46 v England	1997
Most appearances	63	RJR O'Gara	2000–2013
Most points in matches	557	RJR O'Gara	2000–2013
Most points in season	82	RJR O'Gara	2007
Most points in match	30	RJR O'Gara	v Italy, 2000
Most tries in matches	26	BG O'Driscoll	2000–2013
Most tries in season	5	JE Arigho	1928
	5	BG O'Driscoll	2000
	5	TJ Bowe	2012
Most tries in match	3	R Montgomery	v Wales, 1887
	3	JP Quinn	v France, 1913
	3	EO'D Davy	v Scotland, 1930
	3	SJ Byrne	v Scotland, 1953
	3	BG O'Driscoll	v France, 2000
	3	RAJ Henderson	v Italy, 2001
	3	BG O'Driscoll	v Scotland, 2002
Most cons in matches	81	RJR O'Gara	2000–2013
Most cons in season	11	RJR O'Gara	2000
	11	RJR O'Gara	2004
Most cons in match	6	RJR O'Gara	v Italy, 2000
Most pens in matches	109	RJR O'Gara	2000–2013
Most pens in season	17	RJR O'Gara	2006
Most pens in match	6	SO Campbell	v Scotland, 1982
	6	RJR O'Gara	v Italy, 2000
	6	DG Humphreys	v Wales, 2002
Most drops in matches	7	RA Lloyd	1910–1920
Most drops in season	2	on several	occasions
Most drops in match	2	WM McCombe	v France, 1975
	2	EP Elwood	v England, 1993
	2	DG Humphreys	v Wales, 1999
	2	RJR O'Gara	v England, 2005

MISCELLANEOUS RECORDS

RECORD	HOLDER	DETAIL
Longest Test career	AJF O'Reilly	1955 to 1970
	CMH Gibson	1964 to 1979
Youngest Test cap	FS Hewitt	17 yrs 157 days in 1924
Oldest Test cap	JJ Hayes	37 yrs 277 days in 2011

CAREER RECORDS OF IRELAND INTERNATIONAL PLAYERS

UP TO 10 OCTOBER 2013

PLAYER BACKS:	DEBUT	CAPS	T	C	P	D	PTS
IJ Boss	2006 v NZ	17	3	0	0	0	15
TJ Bowe	2004 v US	51	26	0	0	0	130
DM Cave	2009 v C	5	1	0	0	0	5
GW D'Arcy	1999 v R	73	7	0	0	0	35
J Downey	2013 v C	1	0	0	0	0	0
KG Earls	2008 v C	39	12	0	0	0	60
LM Fitzgerald	2006 v PI	26	2	0	0	0	10
CJH Gilroy	2012 v Arg	5	2	0	0	0	10
R Henshaw	2013 v US	2	0	0	0	0	0
DP Jackson	2013 v S	4	0	3	8	0	30
FA Jones	2011 v S	5	0	0	0	0	0
RDJ Kearney	2007 v Arg	46	7	1	0	0	37
I Madigan	2013 v F	4	0	3	5	0	21
LD Marshall	2013 v S	3	0	0	0	0	0
P Marshall	2013 v It	3	0	0	0	0	0
FL McFadden	2011 v It	19	7	0	0	0	35
C Murray	2011 v F	19	1	0	0	0	5
BG O'Driscoll	1999 v A	125	46	0	0	5	245
RJR O'Gara	2000 v S	128	16	176	202	15	1083
S Olding	2013 v US	1	0	0	0	0	0
EG Reddan	2006 F	50	2	0	0	0	10
JJ Sexton	2009 v Fj	36	3	33	65	2	282
AD Trimble	2005 v A	50	12	0	0	0	60
SR Zebo	2012 v NZ	6	2	0	0	0	10

FORWARDS:

S Archer	2013 v It	1	0	0	0	0	0
M Bent	2012 v SA	2	0	0	0	0	0
RD Best	2005 v NZ	67	7	0	0	0	35
TG Court	2009 v It	32	1	0	0	0	5
SM Cronin	2009 v Fj	27	0	0	0	0	0
S Ferris	2006 v PI	35	2	0	0	0	10
DJ Fitzpatrick	2012 v NZ	5	0	0	0	0	0
JR Hagan	2013 v US	1	0	0	0	0	0
CE Healy	2009 v A	39	2	0	0	0	10
JPR Heaslip	2006 v PI	57	8	0	0	0	40
WI Henderson	2012 v SA	6	0	0	0	0	0
CG Henry	2010 v A	8	0	0	0	0	0
D Kilcoyne	2012 v SA	8	0	0	0	0	0
MP McCarthy	2011 v S	12	0	0	0	0	0
KR McLaughlin	2010 v It	6	0	0	0	0	0
SK O'Brien	2009 v Fj	27	2	0	0	0	10
DP O'Callaghan	2003 v W	94	1	0	0	0	5
PJ O'Connell	2002 v W	85	6	0	0	0	30
T O'Donnell	2013 v US	2	1	0	0	0	5
P O'Mahony	2012 v It	16	0	0	0	0	0
MR Ross	2009 v C	31	0	0	0	0	0
RJ Ruddock	2010 v A	1	0	0	0	0	0
DC Ryan	2008 v Arg	28	0	0	0	0	0
M Sherry	2013 v US	1	0	0	0	0	0
CR Strauss	2012 v SA	4	1	0	0	0	5
D Toner	2010 v Sm	7	0	0	0	0	0
DM Tuohy	2010 v NZ	7	1	0	0	0	5
DA Varley	2010 v A	2	0	0	0	0	0

IRELAND INTERNATIONAL PLAYERS

UP TO 10 OCTOBER 2013

Note: Years given for International Championship matches are for second half of season; e.g. 1972 means season 1971–72. Years for all other matches refer to the actual year of the match. Entries in square brackets denote matches played in RWC Finals.

Abraham, M (Bective Rangers) 1912 E, S, W, SA, 1914 W
Adams, C (Old Wesley), 1908 E, 1909 E, F, 1910 F, 1911 E, S, W, F, 1912 S, W, SA, 1913 W, F, 1914 F, E, S
Agar, R D (Malone) 1947 F, E, S, W, 1948 F, 1949 S, W, 1950 F, E, W
Agnew, P J (CIYMS) 1974 F (R), 1976 A
Ahearne, T (Queen's Coll, Cork) 1899 E
Aherne, L F P (Dolphin, Lansdowne) 1988 E 2, WS, It, 1989 F, W, E, S, NZ, 1990 E, S, F, W (R), 1992 E, S, F, A
Alexander, R (NIFC, Police Union) 1936 E, S, W, 1937 E, S, W, 1938 E, S, 1939 E, S, W
Allen, C E (Derry, Liverpool) 1900 E, S, W, 1901 E, S, W, 1903 S, W, 1904 E, S, W, 1905 E, S, W, NZ, 1906 E, S, W, SA, 1907 S, W
Allen, G G (Derry, Liverpool) 1896 E, S, W, 1897 E, S, 1898 E, S, 1899 E, W
Allen, T C (NIFC) 1885 E, S 1
Allen, W S (Wanderers) 1875 E
Allison, J B (Edinburgh U) 1899 E, S, 1900 E, S, W, 1901 E, S, W, 1902 E, S, W, 1903 S
Anderson, F E (Queen's U, Belfast, NIFC) 1953 F, E, S, W, 1954 NZ, F, E, S, W, 1955 F, E, S, W
Anderson, H J (Old Wesley) 1903 E, S, 1906 E, S
Anderson, W A (Dungannon) 1984 A, 1985 S, F, W, E, 1986 F, S, R, 1987 E, S, F, W, [W, C, Tg, A], 1988 S, F, W, E 1, 2, 1989 F, W, E, NZ, 1990 E, S
Andrews, G (NIFC) 1875 E, 1876 E
Andrews, H W (NIFC) 1888 M, 1889 S, W
Archer, A M (Dublin U, NIFC) 1879 S
Archer, S (Munster) 2013 It(R)
Arigho, J E (Lansdowne) 1928 F, E, W, 1929 F, E, S, W, 1930 F, E, S, W, 1931 F, E, S, W, SA
Armstrong, W K (NIFC) 1960 SA, 1961 E
Arnott, D T (Lansdowne) 1876 E
Ash, W H (NIFC) 1875 E, 1876 E, 1877 S
Aston, H R (Dublin U) 1908 E, W
Atkins, A P (Bective Rangers) 1924 F
Atkinson, J M (NIFC) 1927 F, A
Atkinson, J R (Dublin U) 1882 W, S

Bagot, J C (Dublin U, Lansdowne) 1879 S, E, 1880 E, S, 1881 S
Bailey, A H (UC Dublin, Lansdowne) 1934 W, 1935 E, S, W, NZ, 1936 E, S, W, 1937 E, S, W, 1938 E, S
Bailey, N (Northampton) 1952 E
Bardon, M E (Bohemians) 1934 E
Barlow, M (Wanderers) 1875 E
Barnes, R J (Dublin U, Armagh) 1933 W
Barr, A (Belfast Collegians) 1898 W, 1899 S, 1901 E, S
Barry, N J (Garryowen) 1991 Nm 2(R)
Beamish, C E St J (RAF, Leicester) 1933 W, S, 1934 S, W, 1935 E, S, W, NZ, 1936 E, S, W, 1938 W
Beamish, G R (RAF, Leicester) 1925 E, S, W, 1928 F, E, S, W, 1929 F, E, S, W, 1930 F, S, W, 1931 F, E, S, W, SA, 1932 E, S, W, 1933 E, W, S
Beatty, W J (NIFC, Richmond) 1910 F, 1912 F, W
Becker, V A (Lansdowne) 1974 F, W
Beckett, G G P (Dublin U) 1908 E, S, W
Bell, J C (Ballymena, Northampton, Dungannon) 1994 A 1, 2, US, 1995 S, It, [NZ, W, F], Fj, 1996 US, S, F, W, E, WS, A, 1997 It 1, F, W, E, S, 1998 Gg, R, SA 3, 1999 F, W, S It (R), A 2, [US (R), A 3(R), R], 2001 R (R), 2003 Tg, Sm, It 2(R)
Bell, R J (NIFC) 1875 E, 1876 E
Bell, W E (Belfast Collegians) 1953 F, E, S, W
Bennett, F (Belfast Collegians) 1913 S
Bent, G C (Dublin U) 1882 W, E
Bent, M (Leinster) 2012 SA(R), Arg(R)
Berkery, P J (Lansdowne) 1954 W, 1955 W, 1956 S, W, 1957 F, E, S, W, 1958 A, E, S
Bermingham, J J C (Blackrock Coll) 1921 E, S, W, F
Best, N A (Ulster) 2005 NZ(R), R, 2006 NZ1, 2, A1, SA, A2, 2007 F(R), E(R), S1(R), Arg1, 2(R), S2, It2, [Nm(R), Gg(R), F(R), Arg(t&R]
Best, R D (Ulster) 2005 NZ(R), A(t), 2006 W(R), A1(R), SA, A2, PI(R), 2007 W, F, E, S1, It1, S2(R), It2, [Nm, Gg, Arg(R)], 2008 It, F(R), S(R), W, E, NZ1(R), A, C(R), NZ2, Arg(R), 2009 F(R), It(R), E(R), S, W(R), C, US, 2010 It(R), F(R), E, W, S, SA, Sm(R), NZ2, 2011 It, F1, S1, W, E1, F2, 3, E2(R), [US, A, It, W], 2012 W, It, F, S, E, NZ 1, 2, 3, 2013 W, E, S, F, It
Best, S J (Belfast Harlequins, Ulster) 2003 Tg (R), W 2, S 2(R), 2003 [Nm(R)], 2004 W(R), US(R), 2005 J1, 2, NZ(R), R, 2006 F(R), W(R), PI(R), 2007 E(R), S1, It1(R), Arg1, 2, S2, It2(R), [Nm(R), Gg(R), F(R)]
Bishop, J P (London Irish) 1998 SA, 1, 2, Gg, R, SA 3, 1999 F, W, E, S, It, A 1, 2, Arg 1, [US, A 3, Arg 2], 2000 E, Arg, C, 2002 NZ 1, 2, Fj, Arg, 2003 W 1, E
Blackham, J C (Queen's Coll, Cork) 1909 S, W, F, 1910 E, S, W
Blake-Knox, S E F (NIFC) 1976 E, S, 1977 F (R)
Blayney, J J (Wanderers) 1950 S
Bond, A T W (Derry) 1894 S, W
Bornemann, W W (Wanderers) 1960 E, S, W, SA
Boss, I J (Ulster, Leinster) 2006 NZ2(R), A1(R), SA(R), A2, PI(R), 2007 F, E(R), Arg1, S2, It2(R), [Gg(R), Arg(R)], 2010 Sm(R), 2011 S2(R), [Ru], 2013 US, C
Bowe, T J (Ulster, Ospreys) 2004 US, 2005 J1, 2, NZ, A, R, 2006 It, F, 2007 Arg1, S2, 2008 S, W, E, NZ1, A, C, NZ2, Arg, 2009 F, It, E, S, W, A, SA, 2010 It, F, E, W, S, NZ1, A, SA, Sm, NZ2, Arg, 2011 S1, W, E1, 2, [US, A, It, W], 2012 W, It, F, S, E, SA, Arg
Bowen, D St J (Cork Const) 1977 W, E, S
Boyd, C A (Dublin U) 1900 S, 1901 S, W
Boyle, C V (Dublin U) 1935 NZ, 1936 E, S, W, 1937 E, S, W, 1938 W, 1939 W
Brabazon, H M (Dublin U) 1884 E, 1885 S 1, 1886 E
Bradley, M J (Dolphin) 1920 W, F, 1922 E, S, W, F, 1923 E, S, W, F, 1925 F, S, W, 1926 F, E, S, W, 1927 F, W
Bradley, M T (Cork Constitution) 1984 A, 1985 S, F, W, E, 1986 F, W, E, S, R, 1987 E, S, F, W, [W, C, Tg, A], 1988 S, F, W, E 1, 1990 W, 1992 NZ 1, 2, 1993 S, F, W, E, R, 1994 F, W, E, S, A 1, 2, US, 1995 S, F, [NZ]
Bradshaw, G (Belfast Collegians) 1903 W
Bradshaw, R M (Wanderers) 1885 E, S 1, 2
Brady, A M (UC Dublin, Malone) 1966 S, 1968 E, S, W
Brady, J A (Wanderers) 1976 E, S
Brady, J R (CIYMS) 1951 S, W, 1953 F, E, S, W, 1954 W, 1956 W, 1957 F, E, S, W
Bramwell, T (NIFC) 1928 F
Brand, T N (NIFC) 1924 NZ
Brennan, J I (CIYMS) 1957 S, W
Brennan, T (St Mary's Coll, Barnhall) 1998 SA 1(R), 2(R), 1999 F (R), S (R), It, A 2, Arg 1, [US, A 3], 2000 E (R), 2001 W (R), E (R), Sm (R)
Bresnihan, F P K (UC Dublin, Lansdowne, London Irish) 1966 E, W, 1967 A 1, E, S, W, F, 1968 F, E, S, W, A, 1969 F, E, S, W, 1970 SA, F, E, S, W, 1971 F, E, S, W
Brett, J T (Monkstown) 1914 W
Bristow, J R (NIFC) 1879 E
Brophy, N H (Blackrock Coll, UC Dublin, London Irish) 1957 F, E, 1959 E, S, W, F, 1960 F, SA, 1961 S, W, 1962 E, S, W, 1963 E, W, 1967 E, S, W, F, A 2
Brown, E L (Instonians) 1958 F

Brown, G S (Monkstown, United Services) 1912 S, W, SA
Brown, H (Windsor) 1877 E
Brown, T (Windsor) 1877 E, S
Brown, W H (Dublin U) 1899 E
Brown, W J (Malone) 1970 SA, F, S, W
Brown, W S (Dublin U) 1893 S, W, 1894 E, S, W
Browne, A W (Dublin U) 1951 SA
Browne, D (Blackrock Coll) 1920 F
Browne, H C (United Services and RN) 1929 E, S, W
Browne, W F (United Services and Army) 1925 E, S, W, 1926 S, W, 1927 F, E, S, W, A, 1928 E, S
Browning, D R (Wanderers) 1881 E, S
Bruce, S A M (NIFC) 1883 E, S, 1884 E
Brunker, A A (Lansdowne) 1895 E, W
Bryant, C H (Cardiff) 1920 E, S
Buchanan, A McM (Dublin U) 1926 E, S, W, 1927 S, W, A
Buchanan, J W B (Dublin U) 1882 S, 1884 E, S
Buckley, J H (Sunday's Well) 1973 E, S
Buckley, T D (Munster, Sale) 2007 Arg1(R), 2(R), 2008 It(R), F(R), S(R), W(R), E(R), NZ1(R), A(R), C, NZ2(R), 2009 C, US, Fj(R), 2010 E(R), W(R), S(R), NZ1, A, SA, Arg, 2011 S2, F2(R), [US(R), Ru]
Bulger, L Q (Lansdowne) 1896 E, S, W, 1897 E, S, 1898 E, S, W
Bulger, M J (Dublin U) 1888 M
Burges, J H (Rosslyn Park) 1950 F, E
Burgess, R B (Dublin U) 1912 SA
Burke, P A (Cork Constitution, Bristol, Harlequins) 1995 E, S, W (R), It, [J], Fj, 1996 US (R), A, 1997 It 1, S (R), 2001 R (R), 2003 S 1(R), Sm (R)
Burkitt, J C S (Queen's Coll, Cork) 1881 E
Burns, I J (Wanderers) 1980 E (R)
Butler, L G (Blackrock Coll) 1960 W
Butler, N (Bective Rangers) 1920 E
Byers, R M (NIFC) 1928 S, W, 1929 E, S, W
Byrne, E (St Mary's Coll) 2001 It (R), F (R), S (R), W (R), E (R), Sm, NZ (R), 2003 A (R), Sm (R)
Byrne, E M J (Blackrock Coll) 1977 S, F, 1978 F, W, E, NZ
Byrne, J S (Blackrock Coll, Leinster, Saracens) 2001 R (R), 2002 W (R), E (R), S (R), It, NZ 2(R), R, Ru (R), Gg, A, Arg, 2003 S 1, It 1, F, W 1, E, A, Tg, Sm, W 2(R), It 2, S2(R), [R(R), Nm(R)], 2004 F, W, E, It, S, SA1, 2, 3, Arg, 2005 It, S, E, F, W, NZ, A, R
Byrne, N F (UC Dublin) 1962 F
Byrne, S J (UC Dublin, Lansdowne) 1953 S, W, 1955 F
Byron, W G (NIFC) 1896 E, S, W, 1897 E, S, 1898 E, S, W, 1899 E, S, W

Caddell, E D (Dublin U, Wanderers) 1904 S, 1905 E, S, W, NZ, 1906 E, S, W, SA, 1907 E, S, 1908 S, W
Cagney, S J (London Irish) 1925 W, 1926 F, E, S, W, 1927 F, 1928 E, S, W, 1929 F, E, S, W
Caldwell, R (Ulster) 2009 C(R), US(R)
Callan, C P (Lansdowne) 1947 F, E, S, W, 1948 F, E, S, W, 1949 F, E
Cameron, E D (Bective Rangers) 1891 S, W
Campbell, C E (Old Wesley) 1970 SA
Campbell, E F (Monkstown) 1899 S, W, 1900 E, W
Campbell, K P (Ulster) 2005 J1(R), 2(R), R
Campbell, S B B (Derry) 1911 E, S, W, F, 1912 F, E, S, W, SA, 1913 E, S, F
Campbell, S O (Old Belvedere) 1976 A, 1979 A 1, 2, 1980 E, S, F, W, 1981 F, W, E, S, SA 1, 1982 W, E, S, F, 1983 S, F, W, E, 1984 F, W
Canniffe, D M (Lansdowne) 1976 W, E
Cantrell, J L (UC Dublin, Blackrock Coll) 1976 A, F, W, E, S, 1981 S, SA 1, 2, A
Carey, R W (Dungannon) 1992 NZ 1, 2
Carney, B B (Munster) 2007 Arg1, 2, S2, It2(R)
Carpendale, M J (Monkstown) 1886 S, 1887 W, 1888 W, S
Carr, N J (Ards) 1985 S, F, W, E, 1986 W, E, S, R, 1987 E, S, W
Carroll, C (Bective Rangers) 1930 F
Carroll, R (Lansdowne) 1947 F, 1950 S, W
Casement, B N (Dublin U) 1875 E, 1876 E, 1879 E
Casement, F (Dublin U) 1906 E, S, W
Casey, J C (Young Munster) 1930 S, 1932 E
Casey, P J (UC Dublin, Lansdowne) 1963 F, E, S, W, NZ, 1964 E, S, W, F, 1965 F, E, S
Casey, R E (Blackrock Coll, London Irish) 1999 [A 3(t), Arg 2(R)], 2000 E, US (R), C (R), 2009 C, US
Cave, D M (Ulster) 2009 C, US, 2012 NZ 1(R), 2013 US, C
Chambers, J (Dublin U) 1886 E, S, 1887 E, S, W
Chambers, R R (Instonians) 1951 F, E, S, W, 1952 F, W
Clancy, T P J (Lansdowne) 1988 W, E 1, 2, WS, It, 1989 F, W, E, S

Clarke, A T H (Northampton, Dungannon) 1995 Fj (R), 1996 W, E, WS, 1997 F (R), It 2(R), 1998 Gg (R), R
Clarke, C P (Terenure Coll) 1993 F, W, E, 1998 W, E
Clarke, D J (Dolphin) 1991 W, Nm 1, 2, [J, A], 1992 NZ 2(R)
Clarke, J A B (Bective Rangers) 1922 S, W, F, 1923 F, 1924 E, S, W
Clegg, R J (Bangor) 1973 F, 1975 E, S, F, W
Clifford, J T (Young Munster) 1949 F, E, S, W, 1950 F, E, S, W, 1951 F, E, SA, 1952 F, S, W
Clinch, A D (Dublin U, Wanderers) 1892 S, 1893 W, 1895 E, S, W, 1896 E, S, W, 1897 E, S
Clinch, J D (Wanderers, Dublin U) 1923 W, 1924 F, E, S, W, NZ, 1925 F, E, S, 1926 E, S, W, 1927 F, 1928 F, E, S, W, 1929 F, E, S, W, 1930 F, E, S, W, 1931 F, E, S, W, SA
Clohessy, P M (Young Munster) 1993 F, W, E, 1994 F, W, E, S, A 1, 2, US, 1995 E, S, F, W, 1996 S, F, 1997 It 2, 1998 F (R), W (R), SA 2(R), Gg, R, SA 3, 1999 F, W, E, S, It, A 1, 2 Arg 1, [US, A 3(R)], 2000 E, S, It, F, W, Arg, J, SA, 2001 It, F, R, S, W, E, Sm (R), NZ, 2002 W, E, S, It, F
Clune, J J (Blackrock Coll) 1912 SA, 1913 W, F, 1914 F, E, W
Coffey, J J (Lansdowne) 1900 E, 1901 W, 1902 E, S, W, 1903 E, S, W, 1905 E, S, W, NZ, 1906 E, S, W, SA, 1907 E, 1908 W, 1910 F
Cogan, W St J (Queen's Coll, Cork) 1907 E, S
Collier, S R (Queen's Coll, Belfast) 1883 S
Collins, P C (Lansdowne, London Irish) 1987 [C], 1990 S (R)
Collis, W R F (KCH, Harlequins) 1924 F, W, NZ, 1925 F, E, S, 1926 F
Collis, W S (Wanderers) 1884 W
Collopy, G (Bective Rangers) 1891 S, 1892 S
Collopy, R (Bective Rangers) 1923 E, S, W, F, 1924 F, E, S, W, NZ, 1925 F, E, S, W
Collopy, W P (Bective Rangers) 1914 F, E, S, W, 1921 E, S, W, F, 1922 E, S, W, F, 1923 S, W, F, 1924 F, E, S, W
Combe, A (NIFC) 1875 E
Condon, H C (London Irish) 1984 S (R)
Cook, H G (Lansdowne) 1884 W
Coote, P B (RAF, Leicester) 1933 S
Corcoran, J C (London Irish) 1947 A, 1948 F
Corken, T S (Belfast Collegians) 1937 E, S, W
Corkery, D S (Cork Constitution, Bristol) 1994 A 1, 2, US, 1995 E, [NZ, J, W, F], Fj, 1996 US, S, F, W, E, WS, A, 1997 It 1, F, W, E, S, 1998 S, F, W, E, 1999 A 1(R), 2(R)
Corley, H H (Dublin U, Wanderers) 1902 E, S, W, 1903 E, S, W, 1904 E, S
Cormac, H S T (Clontarf) 1921 E, S, W
Corrigan, R (Greystones, Lansdowne, Leinster) 1997 C (R), It 2, 1998 S, F, W, E, SA 3(R), 1999 A 1(R), 2(R), [Arg 2], 2002 NZ 1, 2, R, Ru, Gg, A, Fj (R), Arg, 2003 S 1, It 1, A, Tg, Sm, W 2, It 2, S 2, [R, Arg, A, F], 2004 F, W, E, It, S, SA1, 2, 3, Arg, 2005 It, S, E, F, W, J1(R), 2(R), 2006 F
Costello, P (Bective Rangers) 1960 F
Costello, R A (Garryowen) 1993 S
Costello, V C P (St Mary's Coll, London Irish) 1996 US, F, W, E. WS (R), 1997 C, It 2(R), 1998 S (R), F, W, E, SA 1, 2, Gg, R, SA 3, 1999 F, W (R), E, S (R), It, A 1, 2002 R (R), A, Arg, 2003 S 1, It 1, F, E, A, It 2, S 2, [R, Arg, F], 2004 F(R), W(R), It(R), S(R)
Cotton, J (Wanderers) 1889 W
Coulter, H H (Queen's U, Belfast) 1920 E, S, W
Court, T G (Ulster) 2009 It(R), W(t), C, US(R), Fj, 2010 It(R), F(t&R), NZ1(R), A(R), SA(R), Sm, NZ2, Arg(R), 2011 It(R), F1(R), S1(R), W(R), E1(R), S2, F3(R), E2(R), [US, A(R), It(R)], 2012 W(R), It(R), F(R), S(t&R), E(R), 2013 S, US(R), C
Courtney, A W (UC Dublin) 1920 S, W, F, 1921 E, S, W, F
Cox, H L (Dublin U) 1875 E, 1876 E, 1877 E, S
Craig, R G (Queen's U, Belfast) 1938 S, W
Crawford, E C (Dublin U) 1885 E, S 1
Crawford, W E (Lansdowne) 1920 E, S, W, F, 1921 E, S, W, F, 1922 E, S, 1923 E, S, W, F, 1924 F, E, W, NZ, 1925 F, E, S, W, 1926 F, E, S, W, 1927 F, E, S, W
Crean, T J (Wanderers) 1894 E, S, W, 1895 E, S, W, 1896 E, S, W
Crichton, R Y (Dublin U) 1920 E, S, W, F, 1921 F, 1922 E, 1923 W, F, 1924 F, E, S, W, NZ, 1925 E, S
Croker, E W D (Limerick) 1878 E
Cromey, G E (Queen's U, Belfast) 1937 E, S, W, 1938 E, S, W, 1939 E, S, W
Cronin, B M (Garryowen) 1995 S, 1997 S
Cronin, S M (Connacht, Leinster) 2009 Fj(R), 2010 W(R), NZ1, A, Sm, NZ2(R), Arg, 2011 It(R), F1(R), S1(R), W(R), E1(R), S2, [Ru, It(R)], 2012 It(R), F(R), S(R), E(R), NZ 1(R), 3(R), SA(t&R), Arg(R), 2013 E(R), F(R), It(R), C(R)
Cronyn, A P (Dublin U, Lansdowne) 1875 E, 1876 E, 1880 S
Crossan, K D (Instonians) 1982 S, 1984 F, W, E, S, 1985 S, F, W,

THE COUNTRIES

E, 1986 E, S, R, 1987 E, S, F, W, [W, C, Tg, A], 1988 S, F, W, E 1, WS, It, 1989 W, S, NZ, 1990 E, S, F, W, Arg, 1991 E, S, Nm 2 [Z, J, S], 1992 W
Crotty, D J (Garryowen) 1996 A, 1997 It 1, F, W, 2000 C
Crowe, J F (UC Dublin) 1974 NZ
Crowe, L (Old Belvedere) 1950 E, S, W
Crowe, M P (Lansdowne) 1929 W, 1930 E, S, W, 1931 F, S, W, SA, 1932 S, W, 1933 W, S, 1934 E
Crowe, P M (Blackrock Coll) 1935 E, 1938 E
Cullen, L F M (Blackrock Coll, Leinster, Leicester) 2002 NZ 2(R), R (R), Ru (R), Gg (R), A (R), Fj, Arg (R), 2003 S 1(R), It 1(R), F (R), W 1, Tg, Sm, It 2, 2004 US(R), 2005 J1, 2, R, 2007 Arg2, 2009 Fj, 2010 It, F, E(R), W(R), 2011 It(R), F1(R), S1(R), W(R), E1(R), S2, F2, [Ru]
Cullen, T J (UC Dublin) 1949 F
Cullen, W J (Monkstown and Manchester) 1920 E
Culliton, M G (Wanderers) 1959 E, S, W, F, 1960 E, S, W, F, SA, 1961 E, S, W, F, 1962 S, F, 1964 E, S, W, F
Cummins, W E A (Queen's Coll, Cork) 1879 S, 1881 E, 1882 E
Cunningham, D McC (NIFC) 1923 E, S, W, 1925 F, E, W
Cunningham, M J (UC Cork) 1955 F, E, S, W, 1956 F, S, W
Cunningham, V J G (St Mary's Coll) 1988 E 2, It, 1990 Arg (R), 1991 Nm 1, 2, [Z, J(R)], 1992 NZ 1, 2, A, 1993 S, F, W, E, R, 1994 F
Cunningham, W A (Lansdowne) 1920 W, 1921 E, S, W, F, 1922 E, 1923 S, W
Cuppaidge, J L (Dublin U) 1879 E, 1880 E, S
Currell, J (NIFC) 1877 S
Curtis, A B (Oxford U) 1950 F, E, S
Curtis, D M (London Irish) 1991 W, E, S, Nm 1, 2, [Z, J, S, A], 1992 W, E, S (R), F
Cuscaden, W A (Dublin U, Bray) 1876 E
Cussen, D J (Dublin U) 1921 E, S, W, F, 1922 E, 1923 E, S, W, F, 1926 F, E, S, W, 1927 F, E

Daly, J C (London Irish) 1947 F, E, S, W, 1948 E, S, W
Daly, M J (Harlequins) 1938 E
Danaher, P P A (Lansdowne, Garryowen) 1988 S, F, W, WS, It, 1989 F, NZ (R), 1990 F, 1992 S, F, NZ 1, A, 1993 S, F, W, E, R, 1994 F, W, E, S, A 1, 2, US, 1995 E, S, F, W
D'Arcy, G W (Lansdowne, Leinster) 1999 [R (R)], 2002 Fj (R), 2003 Tg (R), Sm (R), W 2(R), 2004 F, W, E, It, S, SA1, 2005 It, NZ, A, R, 2006 It, F, W, S, E, NZ1, 2, A1, SA, A2, PI(R), 2007 W, F, E, S1, It1, 2, [Nm, Gg, F, Arg], 2008 It, 2009 F(t&R), It(R), S, W, Fj, SA(R), 2010 It, F, E, W, S, NZ1, SA, NZ2, Arg, 2011 It, F1, S1, W, E1, F3, E2, [US, A, It, W], 2012 W, It, F, S, E, NZ2, SA, Arg, 2013 W, E
Dargan, M J (Old Belvedere) 1952 S, W
Davidson, C T (NIFC) 1921 F
Davidson, I G (NIFC) 1899 E, 1900 S, W, 1901 E, S, W, 1902 E, S, W
Davidson, J C (Dungannon) 1969 F, E, S, W, 1973 NZ, 1976 NZ
Davidson, J W (Dungannon, London Irish, Castres) 1995 Fj, 1996 S, F, W, E, WS, A, 1997 It 1, F, W, E, S, 1998 Gg (R), R (R), SA 3(R), 1999 F, W, E, S, It, A 1, 2(R), Arg 1, [US, R (R), Arg 2], 2000 S (R), W (R), US, C, 2001 It (R), S
Davies, F E (Lansdowne) 1892 S, W, 1893 E, S, W
Davis, J L (Monkstown) 1898 E, S
Davis, W J N (Edinburgh U, Bessbrook) 1890 S, W, E, 1891 E, S, W, 1892 E, S, 1895 S
Davison, W (Belfast Academy) 1887 W
Davy, E O'D (UC Dublin, Lansdowne) 1925 W, 1926 F, E, S, W, 1927 F, E, S, W, A, 1928 F, E, S, W, 1929 F, E, S, W, 1930 F, E, S, W, 1931 F, E, S, W, SA, 1932 E, S, W, 1933 E, W, S, 1934 E
Dawson, A R (Wanderers) 1958 A, E, S, W, F, 1959 E, S, W, F, 1960 F, SA, 1961 E, S, W, F, SA, 1962 S, F, W, 1963 F, E, S, W, NZ, 1964 E, S, F
Dawson, K (London Irish) 1997 NZ, C, 1998 S, 1999 [R, Arg 2], 2000 E, S, It, F, W, J, SA, 2001 R, S, W (R), E (R), Sm, 2002 Fj, 2003 Tg, It 2(R), S 2(R)
Dean, P M (St Mary's Coll) 1981 SA 1, 2, A, 1982 W, E, S, F, 1984 A, 1985 S, F, W, E, 1986 F, W, R, 1987 E, S, F, W, [W, A], 1988 S, F, W, E 1, 2, WS, It, 1989 F, W, E, S
Deane, E C (Monkstown) 1909 E
Deering, M J (Bective Rangers) 1929 W
Deering, S J (Bective Rangers) 1935 E, S, W, NZ, 1936 E, S, W, 1937 E, S
Deering, S M (Garryowen, St Mary's Coll) 1974 W, 1976 F, W, E, S, 1977 W, E, 1978 NZ
De Lacy, H (Harlequins) 1948 E, S
Delany, M G (Bective Rangers) 1895 W
Dempsey, G T (Terenure Coll, Leinster) 1998 Gg (R). SA 3, 1999 F, E, S, It, A 2, 2000 E (R), S, It, F, W, SA, 2001 It, F, S, W, E, NZ, 2002 W, E, S, It, F, NZ 1, 2, R, Ru, Gg, A, Arg, 2003 S 1, E (R), A, Sm, W 2(R), It 2, S 2(R), [R, Nm, Arg, A, F], 2004 F, W, E, It, S, SA1, 2, 3, US(R), Arg, 2005 It(R), S, E, F, W, J1, 2, NZ(R), R(R), 2006 E(R), NZ1(R), 2(t&R), A1, SA, A2(R), PI, 2007 W, F, E, S1, It1, 2, [Nm, Gg, F], 2008 It, F, A(R), NZ2
Dennison, S P (Garryowen) 1973 F, 1975 E, S
Dick, C J (Ballymena) 1961 W, F, SA, 1962 W, 1963 F, E, S, W
Dick, J S (Queen's U, Belfast) 1962 E
Dick, J S (Queen's U, Cork) 1887 E, S, W
Dickson, J A N (Dublin U) 1920 E, W, F
Doherty, A E (Old Wesley) 1974 P (R)
Doherty, W D (Guy's Hospital) 1920 E, S, W, 1921 E, S, W, F
Donaldson, J A (Belfast Collegians) 1958 A, E, S, W
Donovan, T M (Queen's Coll, Cork) 1889 S
Dooley, J F (Galwegians) 1959 E, S, W
Doran, B R W (Lansdowne) 1900 S, W, 1901 E, S, W, 1902 E, S, W
Doran, E F (Lansdowne) 1890 S, W
Doran, G P (Lansdowne) 1899 S, W, 1900 E, S, 1902 S, W, 1903 W, 1904 E
Douglas, A C (Instonians) 1923 F, 1924 E, S, 1927 A, 1928 S
Dowling, I (Munster) 2009 C, US
Downey, J (Munster) 2013 C
Downing, A J (Dublin U) 1882 W
Dowse, J C A (Monkstown) 1914 F, S, W
Doyle, J A P (Greystones) 1984 E, S
Doyle, J T (Bective Rangers) 1935 W
Doyle, M G (Blackrock Coll, UC Dublin, Cambridge U, Edinburgh Wands) 1965 F, E, S, W, SA, 1966 F, E, S, W, 1967 A 1, E, S, W, F, A 2, 1968 F, E, S, W, A
Doyle, T J (Wanderers) 1968 E, S, W
Duffy, G W (Harlequins, Connacht) 2004 SA 2(R), 2005 S(R), J1, 2, 2007 Arg1, 2, S2, [Arg(R)], 2009 C, US
Duggan, A T A (Lansdowne) 1963 NZ, 1964 F, 1966 W, 1967 A 1, S, W, A 2, 1968 F, E, S, W, 1969 F, E, S, W, 1970 SA, F, E, S, W, 1971 F, E, S, W, 1972 F 2
Duggan, W (UC Cork) 1920 S, W
Duggan, W P (Blackrock Coll) 1975 E, S, F, W, 1976 A, F, W, S, NZ, 1977 W, E, S, F, 1978 S, F, W, E, NZ, 1979 E, S, A 1, 2, 1980 E, 1981 F, W, E, S, SA 1, 2, A, 1982 W, E, S, 1983 S, F, W, E, 1984 F, W, E, S
Duignan, P (Galwegians) 1998 Gg, R
Duncan, W R (Malone) 1984 W, E
Dunlea, F J (Lansdowne) 1989 W, E, S
Dunlop, R (Dublin U) 1889 W, 1890 S, W, E, 1891 E, S, W, 1892 E, S, 1893 W, 1894 W
Dunn, P E F (Bective Rangers) 1923 S
Dunn, T B (NIFC) 1935 NZ
Dunne, M J (Lansdowne) 1929 F, E, S, 1930 F, E, S, W, 1932 E, S, W, 1933 E, W, S, 1934 E, S, W
Dwyer, P J (UC Dublin) 1962 W, 1963 F, NZ, 1964 S, W

Earls, K G (Munster) 2008 C, NZ2(R), 2009 A(R), Fj, SA, 2010 It(R), F, E, W, S, SA(R), NZ2(R), Arg(R), 2011 It, F1, S1, W, E1, F2, 3, E2, [US, A, Ru, It, W], 2012 It, F, S, E, NZ 1, 3, SA, Arg, 2013 W(R), E(R), S, F, It
Easterby, S H (Llanelli Scarlets) 2000 S, It, F, W, Arg, US, C, 2001 S, Sm (R), 2002 W, E (R), S (R), It, F, NZ 1, 2, R, Ru, Gg, 2003 Tg, Sm, It 2, S 2(t+R), [Nm, Arg, A, F], 2004 F, W, E, It, S, SA1, 2, 3, US, Arg, 2005 It, S, E, F, W, NZ, A, 2006 It, F, W, S, E, SA(R), A2(R), PI, 2007 W, F, E, S1, It1, 2, [Nm, Gg, F, Arg], 2008 It, S(R), E(R)
Easterby, W G (Ebbw Vale, Ballynahinch, Llanelli, Leinster) 2000 US, C (R), 2001 R (R), S, W (R), Sm (R), 2002 W (R), S (R), R (R), Ru (R), Gg (R), Fj, 2003 S 1(R), It 1(R), Tg, Sm, W 2(R), It 2, S 2(R), [R(R), Nm(R), F(R)], 2004 W(R), It(R), S(R), SA2(R), US, 2005 S(R)
Edwards, H G (Dublin U) 1877 E, 1878 E
Edwards, R W (Malone) 1904 W
Edwards, T (Lansdowne) 1888 M, 1890 S, W, E, 1892 W, 1893 E
Edwards, W V (Malone) 1912 F, E
Egan, J D (Bective Rangers) 1922 S
Egan, J T (Cork Constitution) 1931 F, E, SA
Egan, M S (Garryowen) 1893 E, 1895 S
Ekin, W (Queen's Coll, Belfast) 1888 W, S
Elliott, W R J (Bangor) 1979 S
Elwood, E P (Lansdowne, Galwegians) 1993 W, E, R, 1994 F, W, E, S, A 1, 2, 1995 F, W, [NZ, W, F], 1996 US, S, 1997 F, W, E, NZ, C, It 2(R), 1998 F, W, E, SA 1, 2, Gg, R, SA 3, 1999 It, Arg 1(R), [US (R), A 3(R), R]
English, M A F (Lansdowne, Limerick Bohemians) 1958 W, F, 1959 E, S, F, 1960 E, S, 1961 S, W, F, 1962 F, W, 1963 E, S, W, NZ

Ennis, F N G (Wanderers) 1979 A 1(R)
Ensor, A H (Wanderers) 1973 W, F, 1974 F, W, E, S, P, NZ, 1975 E, S, F, W, 1976 A, F, W, E, NZ, 1977 E, 1978 S, F, W, E
Entrican, J C (Queen's U, Belfast) 1931 S
Erskine, D J (Sale) 1997 NZ (R), C, It 2

Fagan, G L (Kingstown School) 1878 E
Fagan, W B C (Wanderers) 1956 F, E, S
Farrell, J L (Bective Rangers) 1926 F, E, S, W, 1927 F, E, S, W, A, 1928 F, E, S, W, 1929 F, E, S, W, 1930 F, E, S, W, 1931 F, E, S, W, SA, 1932 E, S, W
Feddis, N (Lansdowne) 1956 E
Feighery, C F P (Lansdowne) 1972 F 1, E, F 2
Feighery, T A O (St Mary's Coll) 1977 W, E
Ferris, H H (Queen's Coll, Belfast) 1901 W
Ferris, J H (Queen's Coll, Belfast) 1900 E, S, W
Ferris, S (Ulster) 2006 PI, 2007 Arg1(R), 2, S2, 2008 A(R), C, NZ2(R), Arg, 2009 F, It, E, S, W, A, Fj, SA, 2010 F, E, W, S, SA, Sm(R), NZ2, Arg, 2011 F3(R), E2, [US, A, It, W], 2012 W, It, F, S, E
Field, M J (Malone) 1994 E, S, A 1(R), 1995 F (R), W (t), It (R), [NZ(t + R), J], Fj, 1996 F (R), W, E, A (R), 1997 F, W, E, S
Finlay, J E (Queen's Coll, Belfast) 1913 E, S, W, 1920 E, S, W
Finlay, W (NIFC) 1876 E, 1877 E, S, 1878 E, 1879 S, E, 1880 S, 1882 S
Finn, M C (UC Cork, Cork Constitution) 1979 E, 1982 W, E, S, F, 1983 S, F, W, E, 1984 E, S, A, 1986 F, W
Finn, R G A (UC Dublin) 1977 F
Fitzgerald, C C (Glasgow U, Dungannon) 1902 E, 1903 E, S
Fitzgerald, C F (St Mary's Coll) 1979 A 1, 2, 1980 E, S, F, W, 1982 W, E, S, F, 1983 S, F, W, E, 1984 F, W, A, 1985 S, F, W, E, 1986 F, W, E, S
Fitzgerald, D C (Lansdowne, De La Salle Palmerston) 1984 E, S, 1986 W, E, S, R, 1987 E, S, F, W, [W, C, A], 1988 S, F, W, E 1, 1989 NZ (R), 1990 E, S, F, W, Arg, 1991 F, W, E, S, Nm 1, 2, [Z, S, A], 1992 W, S (R)
Fitzgerald, J (Wanderers) 1884 W
Fitzgerald, J J (Young Munster) 1988 S, F, 1990 S, F, W, 1991 F, W, E, S, [J], 1994 A 1, 2
Fitzgerald, L M (Leinster) 2006 PI, 2007 Arg2(R), 2008 W(R), E(R), C, NZ2, Arg, 2009 F, It, E, S, W, A, 2010 SA, Sm, NZ2, 2011 It, F1, S1, W, S2, F2, 3(R), 2013 S(R), F(R), It(R)
Fitzgibbon, M J J (Shannon) 1992 W, E, S, F, NZ 1, 2
Fitzpatrick, D J (Ulster) 2012 NZ 1, 3(R), 2013 W(R), E(R), C(R)
Fitzpatrick, J M (Dungannon) 1998 SA 1, 2 Gg (R), R (R), SA 3, 1999 F (R), W (R), E (R), It, Arg 1(R), [US (R), A 3, R, Arg 2(t&R)], 2000 S (R), It (R), Arg (R), US, C, SA (t&R), 2001 R (R), 2003 W 1(R), E (R), Tg, W 2(R), It 2(R)
Fitzpatrick, M P (Wanderers) 1978 S, 1980 S, F, W, 1981 F, W, E, S, A, 1985 F (R)
Flannery, J P (Munster) 2005 R(R), 2006 It, F, W, S, E, NZ1, 2, A1, 2007 W(R), F(R), E(R), S1(R), It1(R), Arg1, S2, It2(R), [Nm(R), Gg(R), F, Arg], 2008 NZ1, A(R), C, NZ2(R), Arg, 2009 F, It, E, S(R), W, A, Fj, SA, 2010 It, F, 2011 S2(R), F2(R), 3(R), E2, [US(R)]
Flavin, P (Blackrock Coll) 1997 F (R), S
Fletcher, W W (Kingstown) 1882 W, S, 1883 E
Flood, R S (Dublin U) 1925 W
Flynn, M K (Wanderers) 1959 F, 1960 F, 1962 E, S, F, W, 1964 E, S, W, F, 1965 F, E, S, W, SA, 1966 F, E, S, 1972 F 1, E, F 2, 1973 NZ
Fogarty, J (Leinster) 2010 NZ1(R)
Fogarty, T (Garryowen) 1891 W
Foley, A G (Shannon, Munster) 1995 E, S, F, W, It, [J(t + R)], 1996 A, 1997 It 1, E (R), 2000 E, S, It, F, W, Arg, C, J, SA, 2001 It, F, R, S, W, E, Sm, NZ, 2002 W, E, S, It, F, NZ 1, 2, R, Ru, Gg, A, Fj, Arg, 2003 S 1, It 1, F, W 1, E, W 2, [R, A], 2004 F, W, E, It, S, SA1, 2, 3, US(R), Arg, 2005 It, S, E, F, W
Foley, B O (Shannon) 1976 F, E, 1977 W (R), 1980 F, W, 1981 F, E, S, SA 1, 2, A
Forbes, R E (Malone) 1907 E
Forrest, A J (Wanderers) 1880 E, S, 1881 E, S, 1882 W, E, 1883 E, 1885 S 2
Forrest, E G (Wanderers) 1888 M, 1889 S, W, 1890 S, E, 1891 E, 1893 S, W, 1894 E, S, W, 1895 W, 1897 E, S
Forrest, H (Wanderers) 1893 S, W
Fortune, J J (Clontarf) 1963 NZ, 1964 E
Foster, A R (Derry) 1910 E, S, F, 1911 E, S, W, F, 1912 F, E, S, W, 1914 E, S, W, 1921 E, S, W
Francis, N P J (Blackrock Coll, London Irish, Old Belvedere) 1987 [Tg, A], 1988 WS, It, 1989 S, 1990 E, F, W, 1991 E, S, Nm 1, 2, [Z, J, S, A], 1992 W, E, S, 1993 F, R, 1994 F, W, E, S, A 1, 2, US, 1995 E, [NZ, J, W, F], Fj, 1996 US, S
Franks, J G (Dublin U) 1898 E, S, W
Frazer, E F (Bective Rangers) 1891 S, 1892 S
Freer, A E (Lansdowne) 1901 E, S, W
Fulcher, G M (Cork Constitution, London Irish) 1994 A 2, US, 1995 E (R), S, F, W, It, [NZ, W, F], Fj, 1996 US, S, F, W, E, A, 1997 It 1, W (R), 1998 SA 1(R)
Fulton, J (NIFC) 1895 S, W, 1896 E, 1897 E, 1898 W, 1899 E, 1900 W, 1901 E, 1902 E, S, W, 1903 E, S, W, 1904 E, S
Furlong, J N (UC Galway) 1992 NZ 1, 2

Gaffikin, W (Windsor) 1875 E
Gage, J H (Queen's U, Belfast) 1926 S, W, 1927 S, W
Galbraith, E (Dublin U) 1875 E
Galbraith, H T (Belfast Acad) 1890 W
Galbraith, R (Dublin U) 1875 E, 1876 E, 1877 E
Galwey, M J (Shannon) 1991 F, W, Nm 2(R), [J], 1992 E, S, F, NZ 1, 2, A, 1993 F, W, E, R, 1994 F, W, E, S, A 1, US (R), 1995 E, 1996 WS, 1998 F (R), 1999 W (R), 2000 E (R), S, It, F, W, Arg, C, 2001 It, F, R, W, E, Sm, NZ, 2002 W, E, S
Ganly, J B (Monkstown) 1927 F, E, S, W, A, 1928 F, E, S, W, 1929 F, S, 1930 F
Gardiner, F (NIFC) 1900 E, S, 1901 E, W, 1902 E, S, W, 1903 E, W, 1904 E, S, W, 1906 E, S, W, 1907 S, W, 1908 S, W, 1909 E, S, F
Gardiner, J B (NIFC) 1923 E, S, W, F, 1924 F, E, S, W, NZ, 1925 F, E, S, W
Gardiner, S (Belfast Albion) 1893 E, S
Gardiner, W (NIFC) 1892 E, S, 1893 E, S, W, 1894 E, S, W, 1895 E, S, W, 1896 E, S, W, 1897 E, S, 1898 W
Garry, M G (Bective Rangers) 1909 E, S, W, F, 1911 E, S, W
Gaston, J T (Dublin U) 1954 NZ, F, E, S, W, 1955 W 1956 F, E
Gavin, T J (Moseley, London Irish) 1949 F, E
Geoghegan, S P (London Irish, Bath) 1991 F, W, E, S, Nm 1, [Z, S, A], 1992 E, S, F, A, 1993 S, F, W, E, R, 1994 F, W, E, S, A 1, 2, US, 1995 E, S, F, W, [NZ, J, W, F], Fj, 1996 US, S, W, E
Gibson, C M H (Cambridge U, NIFC) 1964 E, S, W, F, 1965 F, E, S, W, SA, 1966 F, E, S, W, 1967 A 1, E, S, W, F, A 2, 1968 E, S, W, A, 1969 E, S, W, 1970 SA, F, E, S, W, 1971 F, E, S, W, 1972 F 1, E, F 2, 1973 NZ, E, S, W, F, 1974 F, W, E, S, P, 1975 E, S, F, W, 1976 A, F, W, E, S, NZ, 1977 W, E, S, F, 1978 F, W, E, NZ, 1979 S, A 1, 2
Gibson, M E (Lansdowne, London Irish) 1979 F, W, E, S, 1981 W (R), 1986 R, 1988 S, F, W, E 2
Gifford, H P (Wanderers) 1890 S
Gillespie, J C (Dublin U) 1922 W, F
Gilpin, F G (Queen's U, Belfast) 1962 E, S, F
Gilroy, C J H (Ulster) 2012 Arg, 2013 W, E, S, It
Glass, D C (Belfast Collegians) 1958 F, 1960 W, 1961 W, SA
Gleeson, K D (St Mary's Coll, Leinster) 2002 W (R), F (R), NZ 1, 2, R, Ru, Gg, A, Arg, 2003 S 1, It 1, F, W 1, E, A, W 2, [R, A, F], 2004 F, W, E, It, 2006 NZ1(R), A1(R), 2007 Arg1, S2(R)
Glennon, B T (Lansdowne) 1993 F (R)
Glennon, J J (Skerries) 1980 E, S, 1987 E, S, F, [W (R)]
Godfrey, R P (UC Dublin) 1954 S, W
Goodall, K G (City of Derry, Newcastle U) 1967 A 1, E, S, W, F, A 2, 1968 F, E, S, W, A, 1969 F, E, S, 1970 SA, F, E, S, W
Gordon, A (Dublin U) 1884 S
Gordon, T G (NIFC) 1877 E, S, 1878 E
Gotto, R P C (NIFC) 1906 SA
Goulding, W J (Cork) 1879 S
Grace, T O (UC Dublin, St Mary's Coll) 1972 F 1, E, 1973 NZ, E, S, W, 1974 E, S, P, NZ, 1975 E, S, F, W, 1976 A, F, W, E, S, NZ, 1977 W, E, S, F, 1978 S
Graham, R I (Dublin U) 1911 F
Grant, E L (CIYMS) 1971 F, E, S, W
Grant, P J (Bective Rangers) 1894 S, W
Graves, C R A (Wanderers) 1934 E, S, W, 1935 E, S, W, NZ, 1936 E, S, W, 1937 E, S, 1938 E, S, W
Gray, R D (Old Wesley) 1923 E, S, 1925 F, 1926 F
Greene, E H (Dublin U, Kingstown) 1882 W, 1884 W, 1885 E, S 2, 1886 E
Greer, R (Kingstown) 1876 E
Greeves, T J (NIFC) 1907 E, S, W, 1909 W, F
Gregg, R J (Queen's U, Belfast) 1953 F, E, S, W, 1954 F, E, S
Griffin, C S (London Irish) 1951 F, E
Griffin, J L (Wanderers) 1949 S, W
Griffiths, W (Limerick) 1878 E
Grimshaw, C (Queen's U, Belfast) 1969 E (R)
Guerin, B N (Galwegians) 1956 S
Gwynn, A P (Dublin U) 1895 W
Gwynn, L H (Dublin U) 1893 S, 1894 E, S, W, 1897 S, 1898 E, S

Hagan, J R (Leinster) 2013 US(R)
Hakin, R F (CIYMS) 1976 W, S, NZ, 1977 W, E, F

Hall, R O N (Dublin U) 1884 W
Hall, W H (Instonians) 1923 E, S, W, F, 1924 F, S
Hallaran, C F G T (Royal Navy) 1921 E, S, W, 1922 E, S, W, 1923 E, F, 1924 F, E, S, W, 1925 F, 1926 F, E
Halpin, G F (Wanderers, London Irish) 1990 E, 1991 [J], 1992 E, S, F, 1993 R, 1994 F (R), 1995 It, [NZ, W, F]
Halpin, T (Garryowen) 1909 S, W, F, 1910 E, S, W, 1911 E, S, W, F, 1912 F, E, S
Halvey, E O (Shannon) 1995 F, W, It, [J, W (t), F (R)], 1997 NZ, C (R)
Hamilton, A J (Lansdowne) 1884 W
Hamilton, G F (NIFC) 1991 F, W, E, S, Nm 2, [Z, J, S, A], 1992 A
Hamilton, R L (NIFC) 1926 F
Hamilton, R W (Wanderers) 1893 W
Hamilton, W J (Dublin U) 1877 E
Hamlet, G T (Old Wesley) 1902 E, S, W, 1903 E, S, W, 1904 S, W, 1905 E, S, W, NZ, 1906 SA, 1907 E, S, W, 1908 E, S, W, 1909 E, S, W, F, 1910 E, S, F, 1911 E, S, W, F
Hanrahan, C J (Dolphin) 1926 S, W, 1927 E, S, W, A, 1928 F, E, S, 1929 F, E, S, W, 1930 F, E, S, W, 1931 F, 1932 S, W
Harbison, H T (Bective Rangers) 1984 W (R), E, S, 1986 R, 1987 E, S, F, W
Hardy, G G (Bective Rangers) 1962 S
Harman, G R A (Dublin U) 1899 E, W
Harper, J (Instonians) 1947 F, E, S
Harpur, T G (Dublin U) 1908 E, S, W
Harrison, T (Cork) 1879 S, 1880 S, 1881 E
Harvey, F M W (Wanderers) 1907 W, 1911 F
Harvey, G A D (Wanderers) 1903 E, S, 1904 W, 1905 E, S
Harvey, T A (Dublin U) 1900 W, 1901 S, W, 1902 E, S, W, 1903 E, W
Haycock, P P (Terenure Coll) 1989 E
Hayes, J J (Shannon, Munster) 2000 S, It, F, W, Arg, C, J, SA, 2001 It, F, R, S, W, E, Sm, NZ, 2002 W, E, S, It, F, NZ 1, 2, R, Ru, Gg, A, Fj, Arg, 2003 S 1, It 1, F, W 1, E, [R(R), Nm, Arg, A, F], 2004 F, W, E, It, S, SA1, 2, 3, US, Arg, 2005 It, S, E, F, W, NZ, A, R(R), 2006 It, F, W, S, E, NZ1, 2, A1, SA, A2, PI, 2007 W, F, E, S1, It1, S2(R), It2, [Nm, Gg, F, Arg], 2008 It, F, S, W, E, NZ1, A, C(R), NZ2, Arg, 2009 F, It, E, S, W, A, Fj, SA, 2010 It, F, E, W, S, Sm, NZ2(R), 2011 S2(R)
Headon, T A (UC Dublin) 1939 S, W
Healey, P (Limerick) 1901 E, S, W, 1902 E, S, W, 1903 E, S, W, 1904 S
Healy, C E (Leinster) 2009 A, SA, 2010 It, F, E, W, S, NZ1, A, SA, Sm(R), NZ2, Arg, 2011 It, F1, S1, W, E1, F2, 3, E2, [A, Ru, It, W], 2012 W, It, F, S, E, NZ 1, 2, 3, SA, Arg, 2013 W, E, F, It
Heaslip, J P R (Leinster) 2006 PI, 2007 Arg1, S2, 2008 It(R), F, S, W, E, NZ1, A, C, NZ2, Arg, 2009 F, It, E, S(R), W, A, Fj, SA, 2010 It, F, E, W, S, NZ1, SA, Sm, NZ2, Arg, 2011 F1, S1, W, E1, F2(R), 3, E2, [US, A, Ru, It, W], 2012 W, It, F, S, E, NZ 1, 2, SA, Arg, 2013 W, E, S, F, It
Heffernan, M R (Cork Constitution) 1911 E, S, W, F
Hemphill, R (Dublin U) 1912 F, E, S, W
Henderson, N J (Queen's U, Belfast, NIFC) 1949 S, W, 1950 F, 1951 F, E, S, W, SA, 1952 F, S, W, E, 1953 F, E, S, W, 1954 NZ, F, E, S, W, 1955 F, E, S, W, 1956 S, W, 1957 F, E, S, W, 1958 A, E, S, W, F, 1959 E, S, W, F
Henderson R A J (London Irish, Wasps, Young Munster) 1996 WS, 1997 NZ, C, 1998 F, W, SA 1(R), 2(R), 1999 F (R), E, S (R), It, 2000 S (R), It (R), F, W, Arg, US, J (R), SA, 2001 It, F, 2002 W (R), E (R), F, R (R), Ru (t), Gg (R), 2003 It 1(R), 2
Henderson, W I (Ulster) 2012 SA(R), Arg(R), 2013 S(R), F(R), It(R), US
Henebrey, G J (Garryowen) 1906 E, S, W, SA, 1909 W, F
Henry, C G (Ulster) 2010 A, 2012 NZ 3(R), SA, Arg, 2013 W(R), E(R), US, C(R)
Henshaw, R (Connacht) 2013 US, C(R)
Heron, A G (Queen's Coll, Belfast) 1901 E
Heron, J (NIFC) 1877 S, 1879 E
Heron, W T (NIFC) 1880 E, S
Herrick, R W (Dublin U) 1886 S
Heuston, F S (Kingstown) 1882 W, 1883 E, S
Hewitt, D (Queen's U, Belfast, Instonians) 1958 A, E, S, F, 1959 S, W, F, 1960 E, S, W, F, 1961 E, S, W, F, 1962 S, F, 1965 W
Hewitt, F S (Instonians) 1924 W, NZ, 1925 F, E, S, 1926 E, 1927 E, S, W
Hewitt, J A (NIFC) 1981 SA 1(R), 2(R)
Hewitt, T R (Queen's U, Belfast) 1924 W, NZ, 1925 F, E, S, 1926 F, E, S, W
Hewitt, V A (Instonians) 1935 S, W, NZ, 1936 E, S, W
Hewitt, W J (Instonians) 1954 E, 1956 S, 1959 W, 1961 SA
Hewson, F T (Wanderers) 1875 E
Hickie, D A (St Mary's Coll, Leinster) 1997 W, E, S, NZ, C, It 2, 1998 S, F, W, E, SA 1, 2, 2000 S, It, F, W, J, SA, 2001 F, R, S, W, E, NZ, 2002 W, E, S, It, F, R, Ru, Gg, A, 2003 S 1, It 1, F, W 1, E, It 2, S 2, [R, Nm, Arg, A], 2004 SA3, Arg, 2005 It, S, E, F, W, 2006 A2, PI, 2007 W, F, E, S1, It1, 2, [Nm, Gg, Arg]
Hickie, D J (St Mary's Coll) 1971 F, E, S, W, 1972 F 1, E
Higgins, J A D (Civil Service) 1947 S, W, A, 1948 F, S, W
Higgins, W W (NIFC) 1884 E, S
Hillary, M F (UC Dublin) 1952 E
Hingerty, D J (UC Dublin) 1947 F, E, S, W
Hinton, W P (Old Wesley) 1907 W, 1908 E, S, W, 1909 E, S, 1910 E, S, W, F, 1911 E, S, W, 1912 F, E, W
Hipwell, M L (Terenure Coll) 1962 E, S, 1968 F, A, 1969 F (R), S (R), W, 1971 F, E, S, W, 1972 F 2
Hobbs, T H M (Dublin U) 1884 S, 1885 E
Hobson, E W (Dublin U) 1876 E
Hogan, N A (Terenure Coll, London Irish) 1995 E, W, [J, W, F], 1996 F, W, E, WS, 1997 F, W, E, It 2
Hogan, P (Garryowen) 1992 F
Hogan, T (Munster, Leinster) 2005 J1(R), 2(R), 2007 It1(R), Arg1
Hogg, W (Dublin U) 1885 S 2
Holland, J J (Wanderers) 1981 SA 1, 2, 1986 W
Holmes, G W (Dublin U) 1912 SA, 1913 E, S
Holmes, L J (Lisburn) 1889 S, W
Hooks, K J (Queen's U, Belfast, Ards, Bangor) 1981 S, 1989 NZ, 1990 F, W, Arg, 1991 F
Horan, A K (Blackheath) 1920 E, W
Horan, M J (Shannon, Munster) 2000 US (R), 2002 Fj, Arg (R), 2003 S 1(R), It 1(R), F, W 1, E, A, Sm, It 2, S 2, [R, Nm, Arg(t&R), A(R), F(R)], 2004 It(R), S(R), SA1(R), 2(t&R), 3(R), US, 2005 It(R), S(R), E(R), F(R), W(R), J1, 2, NZ, A, R, 2006 It, W, S, E, NZ1, 2, A1, SA, A2(R), 2007 W, F, E, It1, 2, [Nm, Gg, F, Arg], 2008 It, F, S, W, E, NZ1, A, C, NZ2, Arg, 2009 F, It, E, S, W, 2011 S2(R)
Horgan, A P (Cork Const, Munster) 2003 Sm, W 2, S 2, 2004 F(R), 2005 J1, 2, NZ
Horgan, S P (Lansdowne, Leinster) 2000 S, It, W, Arg, C, J, SA (R), 2001 It, S, W, E, NZ, 2002 S, It, F, A, Fj, Arg, 2003 S 1, [R, Nm, Arg, A, F], 2004 F, W, E, It, S, SA1, 2, 3, US, Arg, 2005 It, S, E, NZ, A, R, 2006 It, F, W, S, E, NZ1, 2, A1, SA, A2, PI, 2007 F, E, S1, It1, [Gg, F, Arg], 2008 S(R), W, E, NZ1, A, C(R), 2009 Fj
Houston, K J (Oxford U, London Irish) 1961 SA, 1964 S, W, 1965 F, E, SA
Howe, T G (Dungannon, Ballymena, Ulster) 2000 US, J, SA, 2001 It, F, R, Sm, 2002 It (R), 2003 Tg, W 2, 2004 F, W, E, SA2
Hughes, R W (NIFC) 1878 E, 1880 E, S, 1881 S, 1882 E, S, 1883 E, S, 1884 E, S, 1885 E, 1886 E
Humphreys, D G (London Irish, Dungannon, Ulster) 1996 F, W, E, WS, 1997 E (R), S, It 2, 1998 S, E (R), SA 2(t + R), R (R), 1999 F, W, E, S, A 1, 2, Arg 1, [US, A 3, Arg 2], 2000 E, S (R), F (t&R), W (R), Arg, US (R), C, J (R), SA (R), 2001 It (R), R, S (R), W, E, NZ, 2002 W, E, S, It, F, NZ 1(R), 2(R), R (t+R), Ru (R), Gg (R), Fj, 2003 S 1, It 1, F, W 1, E, A, W 2, It 2, S 2(R), [R, Arg, A(R), F(R)], 2004W(R), It(R), S(R), SA2(R), US, 2005 S(R), W(R), J1, 2, NZ(R), A(R), R
Hunt, E W F de Vere (Army, Rosslyn Park) 1930 F, 1932 E, S, W, 1933 E
Hunter, D V (Dublin U) 1885 S 2
Hunter, L M (Civil Service) 1968 W, A
Hunter, W R (CIYMS) 1962 E, S, W, F, 1963 F, E, S, 1966 F, E, S
Hurley, D (Munster) 2009 US(t&R)
Hurley, H D (Old Wesley, Moseley) 1995 Fj (t), 1996 WS
Hutton, S A (Malone) 1967 S, W, F, A 2

Ireland J (Windsor) 1876 E, 1877 E
Irvine, H A S (Collegians) 1901 S
Irwin, D G (Queen's U, Belfast, Instonians) 1980 F, W, 1981 F, W, E, S, SA 1, 2, A, 1982 W, 1983 S, F, W, E, 1984 F, W, 1987 [Tg, A (R)], 1989 F, W, E, S, NZ, 1990 E, S
Irwin, J W S (NIFC) 1938 E, S, 1939 E, S, W
Irwin, S T (Queen's Coll, Belfast) 1900 E, S, W, 1901 E, W, 1902 E, S, W, 1903 S

Jack, H W (UC Cork) 1914 S, W, 1921 W
Jackman, B J (Leinster) 2005 J1(R), 2(R), 2007 Arg1(R), 2(R), 2008 It(R), F, S, W(R), E(R)
Jackson, A R V (Wanderers) 1911 E, S, W, F, 1913 W, F, 1914 F, E, S, W
Jackson, D P (Ulster) 2013 S, F, It, C(R)
Jackson, F (NIFC) 1923 E
Jackson, H W (Dublin U) 1877 E
Jameson, J S (Lansdowne) 1888 M, 1889 S, W, 1891 W, 1892 E, W, 1893 S

Jeffares, E W (Wanderers) 1913 E, S
Jennings, S (Leicester, Leinster) 2007 Arg 2, 2008 NZ1(R), A, C, NZ2(R), 2010 E(R), W(R), NZ1(R), A, 2011 F3, [US, Ru(R)], 2012 S(R)
Johns, P S (Dublin U, Dungannon, Saracens) 1990 Arg, 1992 NZ 1, 2, A, 1993 S, F, W, E, R, 1994 F, W, E, S, A 1, 2, US, 1995 E, S, W, It, [NZ, J, W, F], Fj, 1996 US, S, F, WS, 1997 It 1(R), F, W, E, S, NZ, C, It 2, 1998 S, F, W, E, SA 1, 2, Gg, R, SA 3, 1999 F, W, E, S, It, A 1, 2, Arg 1, [US, A 3, R], 2000 F (R), J
Johnston, J (Belfast Acad) 1881 S, 1882 S, 1884 S, 1885 S 1, 2, 1886 E, 1887 E, S, W
Johnston, M (Dublin U) 1880 E, S, 1881 E, S, 1882 E, 1884 E, S, 1886 E
Johnston, R (Wanderers) 1893 E, W
Johnston, R W (Dublin U) 1890 S, W, E
Johnston, T J (Queen's Coll, Belfast) 1892 E, S, W, 1893 E, S, 1895 E
Johnstone, W E (Dublin U) 1884 W
Johnstone-Smyth, T R (Lansdowne) 1882 E
Jones, F A (Munster) 2011 S2(R), F2(R), 3, 2013 US(t&R), C

Kavanagh, J R (UC Dublin, Wanderers) 1953 F, E, S, W, 1954 NZ, S, W, 1955 F, E, 1956 E, S, W, 1957 F, E, S, W, 1958 A, E, S, W, 1959 E, S, W, F, 1960 E, S, W, F, SA, 1961 E, S, W, F, SA, 1962 F
Kavanagh, P J (UC Dublin, Wanderers) 1952 E, 1955 W
Keane, K P (Garryowen) 1998 E (R)
Keane, M I (Lansdowne) 1974 F, W, E, S, P, NZ, 1975 E, S, F, W, 1976 A, F, W, E, S, NZ, 1977 W, E, S, F, 1978 S, F, W, E, NZ, 1979 F, W, E, S, A 1, 2, 1980 E, S, F, W, 1981 F, W, E, S, 1982 W, E, S, F, 1983 S, F, W, E, 1984 F, W, E, S
Kearney, R D J (Leinster) 2007 Arg 2, 2008 It(R), F, S, W, E, NZ1, A, C, NZ2, Arg, 2009 F, It, E, S, W, A, Fj, SA, 2010 It, F, W(R), S(R), NZ1, A, SA, NZ2, 2011 S2, F2, [A, Ru, It, W], 2012 W, It, F, S, E, NZ 1, 2, 3, 2013 W, E, S, F, It
Kearney, R K (Wanderers) 1982 F, 1984 A, 1986 F, W
Keatley, I J (Connacht) 2009 C, US
Keeffe, E (Sunday's Well) 1947 F, E, S, W, A, 1948 F
Kelly, H C (NIFC) 1877 E, S, 1878 E, 1879 S, 1880 E, S
Kelly, J C (UC Dublin) 1962 F, W, 1963 F, E, S, W, NZ, 1964 E, S, W, F
Kelly, J P (Cork Constitution) 2002 It, NZ 1, 2, R, Ru, Gg, A (R), 2003 It 1, F, A, Tg, Sm, It 2, [R(R), Nm(R), A(R), F]
Kelly, S (Lansdowne) 1954 S, W, 1955 S, 1960 W, F
Kelly, W (Wanderers) 1884 S
Kennedy, A G (Belfast Collegians) 1956 F
Kennedy, A P (London Irish) 1986 W, E
Kennedy, F (Wanderers) 1880 E, 1881 E, 1882 W
Kennedy, F A (Wanderers) 1904 E, W
Kennedy, H (Bradford) 1938 S, W
Kennedy, J M (Wanderers) 1882 W, 1884 W
Kennedy, K W (Queen's U, Belfast, London Irish) 1965 F, E, S, W, SA, 1966 F, E, W, 1967 A 1, E, S, W, F, A 2, 1968 F, A, 1969 F, E, S, W, 1970 SA, F, E, S, W, 1971 F, E, S, W, 1972 F 1, E, F 2, 1973 NZ, E, S, W, F, 1974 F, W, E, S, P, NZ, 1975 F, W
Kennedy, T J (St Mary's Coll) 1978 NZ, 1979 F, W, E (R), A 1, 2, 1980 E, S, F, W, 1981 SA 1, 2, A
Kenny, P (Wanderers) 1992 NZ 2(R)
Keogh, F S (Bective Rangers) 1964 W, F
Keon, J J (Limerick) 1879 E
Keyes, R P (Cork Constitution) 1986 E, 1991 [Z, J, S, A], 1992 W, E, S
Kidd, F W (Dublin U, Lansdowne) 1877 E, S, 1878 E
Kiely, M D (Lansdowne) 1962 W, 1963 F, E, S, W
Kiernan, M J (Dolphin, Lansdowne) 1982 W (R), E, S, F, 1983 S, F, W, E, 1984 E, S, A, 1985 S, F, W, E, 1986 F, W, E, S, R, 1987 E, S, F, W, [W, C, A], 1988 S, F, W, E 1, 2, WS, 1989 F, W, E, S, 1990 E, S, F, W, Arg, 1991 F
Kiernan, T J (UC Cork, Cork Const) 1960 E, S, W, F, SA, 1961 E, S, W, F, SA, 1962 E, W, 1963 F, S, W, NZ, 1964 E, S, 1965 F, E, S, W, SA, 1966 F, E, S, W, 1967 A 1, E, S, W, F, A 2, 1968 F, E, S, W, A, 1969 F, E, S, W, 1970 SA, F, E, S, W, 1971 F, 1972 F 1, E, F 2, 1973 NZ, E, S
Kilcoyne, D (Munster) 2012 SA(t), Arg(R), 2013 W(R), E(R), S(R), It(R), US, C(R)
Killeen, G V (Garryowen) 1912 E, S, W, 1913 E, S, W, F, 1914 E, S, W
King, H (Dublin U) 1883 E, S
Kingston, T J (Dolphin) 1987 [W, Tg, A], 1988 S, F, W, E 1, 1990 F, W, 1991 [J], 1993 F, W, E, R, 1994 F, W, E, S, 1995 F, W, It, [NZ, J (R), W, F], Fj, 1996 US, S, F
Knox, J H (Dublin U, Lansdowne) 1904 W, 1905 E, S, W, NZ, 1906 E, S, W, 1907 W, 1908 S

Kyle, J W (Queen's U, Belfast, NIFC) 1947 F, E, S, W, A, 1948 F, E, S, W, 1949 F, E, S, W, 1950 F, E, S, W, 1951 F, E, S, W, SA, 1952 F, S, W, E, 1953 F, E, S, W, 1954 NZ, F, 1955 F, E, W, 1956 F, E, S, W, 1957 F, E, S, W, 1958 A, E, S

Lambert, N H (Lansdowne) 1934 S, W
Lamont, R A (Instonians) 1965 F, E, SA, 1966 F, E, S, W, 1970 SA, F, E, S, W
Landers, M F (Cork Const) 1904 W, 1905 E, S, W, NZ
Lane, D J (UC Cork) 1934 S, W, 1935 E, S
Lane, M F (UC Cork) 1947 W, 1949 F, E, S, W, 1950 F, E, S, W, 1951 F, S, W, SA, 1952 F, S, 1953 F, E
Lane, P (Old Crescent) 1964 W
Langan, D J (Clontarf) 1934 W
Langbroek, J A (Blackrock Coll) 1987 [Tg]
Lavery, P (London Irish) 1974 W, 1976 W
Lawlor, P J (Clontarf) 1951 S, SA, 1952 F, S, W, E, 1953 F, 1954 NZ, E, S, 1956 F, E
Lawlor, P J (Bective Rangers) 1935 E, S, W, 1937 E, S, W
Lawlor, P J (Bective Rangers) 1990 Arg, 1992 A, 1993 S
Leahy, K T (Wanderers) 1992 NZ 1
Leahy, M W (UC Cork) 1964 W
Leamy, D P (Munster) 2004 US, 2005 It, J2, NZ, A, R, 2006 It, F, W, S, E, NZ1, 2, A1, SA, A2, PI(R), 2007 W, F, E, S1, It1, 2, [Nm, Gg, F, Arg], 2008 It, F, S, W, E, NZ1, A, 2009 F(R), It(t&R), E(R), S, W(R), C, US, A(t&R), Fj, 2010 Sm, NZ2(R), Arg(R), 2011 It, S1(R), W(R), E1(R), S2, F2, E2(R), [US(R), Ru(R), It(R), W(R)]
Lee, S (NIFC) 1891 E, S, W, 1892 E, S, W, 1893 E, S, W, 1894 E, S, W, 1895 E, W, 1896 E, S, W, 1897 E, 1898 E
Le Fanu, V C (Cambridge U, Lansdowne) 1886 E, S, 1887 E, W, 1888 S, 1889 W, 1890 E, 1891 E, 1892 E, S, W
Lenihan, D G (UC Cork, Cork Const) 1981 A, 1982 W, E, S, F, 1983 S, F, W, E, 1984 F, W, E, S, A, 1985 S, F, W, E, 1986 F, W, E, S, R, 1987 E, S, F, W, [W, C, Tg, A], 1988 S, F, W, E 1, 2, WS, It, 1989 F, W, E, S, NZ, 1990 S, F, W, Arg, 1991 Nm 2, [Z, S, A], 1992 W
L'Estrange, L P F (Dublin U) 1962 E
Levis, F H (Wanderers) 1884 E
Lewis, K P (Leinster) 2005 J2(R), 2007 Arg1, 2(R)
Lightfoot, E J (Lansdowne) 1931 F, E, S, W, SA, 1932 E, S, W, 1933 E, W, S
Lindsay, H (Dublin U, Armagh) 1893 E, S, W, 1894 E, S, W, 1895 E, 1896 E, S, W, 1898 E, S, W
Little, T J (Bective Rangers) 1898 W, 1899 S, W, 1900 S, W, 1901 E, S
Lloyd, R A (Dublin U, Liverpool) 1910 E, S, 1911 E, S, W, F, 1912 F, E, S, W, SA, 1913 E, S, W, F, 1914 F, E, 1920 E, F
Longwell, G W (Ballymena) 2000 J (R), SA, 2001 F (R), R, S (R), Sm, NZ (R), 2002 W (R), E (R), S (R), It, F, NZ 1, 2, R, Ru, Gg, A, Arg, 2003 S 1, It 1, F, E, A, It 2, 2004 It(R)
Loughney, R (Connacht) 2012 NZ 1(R)
Lydon, C T J (Galwegians) 1956 S
Lyle, R K (Dublin U) 1910 W, F
Lyle, T R (Dublin U) 1885 E, S 1, 2, 1886 E, 1887 E, S
Lynch, J F (St Mary's Coll) 1971 F, E, S, W, 1972 F 1, E, F 2, 1973 NZ, E, S, W, 1974 F, W, E, S, P, NZ
Lynch, L M (Lansdowne) 1956 S
Lytle, J H (NIFC) 1894 E, S, W, 1895 W, 1896 E, S, W, 1897 E, S, 1898 E, S, 1899 S
Lytle, J N (NIFC) 1888 M, 1889 W, 1890 E, 1891 E, S, 1894 E, S, W
Lyttle, V J (Collegians, Bedford) 1938 E, 1939 E, S

McAleese, D R (Ballymena) 1992 F
McAllan, G H (Dungannon) 1896 S, W
Macauley, J (Limerick) 1887 E, S
McBride, W D (Malone) 1988 W, E 1, WS, It, 1989 S, 1990 F, W, Arg, 1993 S, F, W, E, R, 1994 W, E, S, A 1(R), 1995 S, F, [NZ, W, F], Fj (R), 1996 W, E, WS, A, 1997 It 1(R), F, W, E, S
McBride, W J (Ballymena) 1962 E, S, F, W, 1963 F, E, S, W, NZ, 1964 E, S, F, 1965 F, E, S, W, SA, 1966 F, E, S, W, 1967 A 1, E, S, W, F, A 2, 1968 F, E, S, W, A, 1969 F, E, S, W, 1970 SA, F, E, S, W, 1971 F, E, S, W, 1972 F 1, E, F 2, 1973 NZ, E, S, W, F, 1974 F, W, E, S, P, NZ, 1975 E, S, F, W
McCahill, S A (Sunday's Well) 1995 Fj (t)
McCall, B W (London Irish) 1985 F (R), 1986 E, S
McCall, M C (Bangor, Dungannon, London Irish) 1992 NZ 1(R), 2, 1994 W, 1996 E (R), A, 1997 It 1, NZ, C, It 2, 1998 S, E, SA 1, 2
McCallan, B (Ballymena) 1960 E, S
McCarten, R J (London Irish) 1961 E, W, F
McCarthy, E A (Kingstown) 1882 W

McCarthy, J S (Dolphin) 1948 F, E, S, W, 1949 F, E, S, W, 1950 W, 1951 F, E, S, W, SA, 1952 F, S, W, E, 1953 F, E, S, 1954 NZ, F, E, S, W, 1955 F, E
McCarthy, M P (Connacht) 2011 S2, F3(R), 2012 S(R), E(R), SA, Arg, 2013 W, E, F, It, US, C(R)
McCarthy, P D (Cork Const) 1992 NZ 1, 2, A, 1993 S, R (R)
MacCarthy, St G (Dublin U) 1882 W
McCarthy, T (Cork) 1898 W
McClelland, T A (Queen's U, Belfast) 1921 E, S, W, F, 1922 E, W, F, 1923 E, S, W, F, 1924 F, E, S, W, NZ
McClenahan, R O (Instonians) 1923 E, S, W
McClinton, A N (NIFC) 1910 W, F
McCombe, W McM (Dublin U, Bangor) 1968 F, 1975 E, S, F, W
McConnell, A A (Collegians) 1947 A, 1948 F, E, S, W, 1949 F, E
McConnell, G (Derry, Edinburgh U) 1912 F, E, 1913 W, F
McConnell, J W (Lansdowne) 1913 S
McCormac, F M (Wanderers) 1909 W, 1910 W, F
McCormick, W J (Wanderers) 1930 E
McCoull, H C (Belfast Albion) 1895 E, S, W, 1899 E
McCourt, D (Queen's U, Belfast) 1947 A
McCoy, J J (Dungannon, Bangor, Ballymena) 1984 W, A, 1985 S, F, W, E, 1986 F, 1987 [Tg], 1988 E 2, WS, It, 1989 F, W, E, S, NZ
McCracken, H (NIFC) 1954 W
McCullen, A (Lansdowne) 2003 Sm
McCullough, M T (Ulster) 2005 J1, 2, NZ(R), A(R)
McDermott, S J (London Irish) 1955 S, W
Macdonald, J A (Methodist Coll, Belfast) 1875 E, 1876 E, 1877 S, 1878 E, 1879 S, 1880 E, 1881 S, 1882 E, S, 1883 E, S, 1884 E, S
McDonald, J P (Malone) 1987 [C], 1990 E (R), S, Arg
McDonnell, A C (Dublin U) 1889 W, 1890 S, W, 1891 E
McDowell, J C (Instonians) 1924 F, NZ
McFadden, F L (Leinster) 2011 It, F1, S2, F2(R), E2(R), [Ru], 2012 W, It(R), F(R), S(R), E(R), NZ 1, 2, 3, SA(R), Arg(R), 2013 F, US, C
McFarland, B A T (Derry) 1920 S, W, F, 1922 W
McGann, B J (Lansdowne) 1969 F, E, S, W, 1970 SA, F, E, S, W, 1971 F, E, S, W, 1972 F 1, E, F 2, 1973 NZ, E, S, W, 1976 F, W, E, S, NZ
McGowan, A N (Blackrock Coll) 1994 US
McGown, T M W (NIFC) 1899 E, S, 1901 S
McGrath, D G (UC Dublin, Cork Const) 1984 S, 1987 [W, C, Tg, A]
McGrath, N F (Oxford U, London Irish) 1934 W
McGrath, P J (UC Cork) 1965 E, S, W, SA, 1966 F, E, S, W, 1967 A 1, A 2
McGrath, R J M (Wanderers) 1977 W, E, F (R), 1981 SA 1, 2, A, 1982 W, E, S, F, 1983 S, F, W, E, 1984 F, W
McGrath, T (Garryowen) 1956 W, 1958 F, 1960 E, S, W, F, 1961 SA
McGuinness, C D (St Mary's Coll) 1997 NZ, C, 1998 F, W, E, SA 1, 2, Gg, R (R), SA 3, 1999 F, W, E, S
McGuire, E P (UC Galway) 1963 E, S, W, NZ, 1964 E, S, W, F
MacHale, S (Lansdowne) 1965 F, E, S, W, SA, 1966 F, E, S, W, 1967 S, W, F
McHugh, M (St Mary's Coll) 2003 Tg
McIldowie, G (Malone) 1906 SA, 1910 E, S, W
McIlrath, J A (Ballymena) 1976 A, F, NZ, 1977 W, E
McIlwaine, E H (NIFC) 1895 S, W
McIlwaine, E N (NIFC) 1875 E, 1876 E
McIlwaine, J E (NIFC) 1897 E, S, 1898 E, S, W, 1899 E, W
McIntosh, L M (Dublin U) 1884 S
MacIvor, C V (Dublin U) 1912 F, E, S, W, 1913 E, S, F
McIvor, S C (Garryowen) 1996 A, 1997 It 1, S (R)
McKay, J W (Queen's U, Belfast) 1947 F, E, S, W, A, 1948 F, E, S, W, 1949 F, E, S, W, 1950 F, E, S, W, 1951 F, E, S, W, SA, 1952 F
McKee, W D (NIFC) 1947 A, 1948 F, E, S, W, 1949 F, E, S, W, 1950 F, E, 1951 SA
McKeen, A J W (Lansdowne) 1999 [R (R)]
McKelvey, J M (Queen's U, Belfast) 1956 F, E
McKenna, P (St Mary's Coll) 2000 Arg
McKibbin, A R (Instonians, London Irish) 1977 W, E, S, 1978 S, F, W, E, NZ, 1979 F, W, E, S, 1980 E, S
McKibbin, C H (Instonians) 1976 S (R)
McKibbin, D (Instonians) 1950 F, E, S, W, 1951 F, E, S, W
McKibbin, H R (Queen's U, Belfast) 1938 W, 1939 E, S, W
McKinney, S A (Dungannon) 1972 F 1, E, F 2, 1973 W, F, 1974 F, E, S, P, NZ, 1975 E, S, 1976 A, F, W, E, S, NZ, 1977 W, E, S, 1978 S (R), F, W, E
McLaughlin, J H (Derry) 1887 E, S, 1888 W, S
McLaughlin, K R (Leinster) 2010 It, 2011 S2(R), 2012 NZ 1(R), 2, 3, 2013 C
McLean, R E (Dublin U) 1881 S, 1882 W, E, S, 1883 E, S, 1884 E, S, 1885 E, S 1
Maclear, B (Cork County, Monkstown) 1905 E, S, W, NZ, 1906 E, S, W, SA, 1907 E, S, W
McLennan, A C (Wanderers) 1977 F, 1978 S, F, W, E, NZ, 1979 F, W, E, S, 1980 E, F, 1981 F, W, E, S, SA 1, 2
McLoughlin, F M (Northern) 1976 A
McLoughlin, G A J (Shannon) 1979 F, W, E, S, A 1, 2, 1980 E, 1981 SA 1, 2, 1982 W, E, S, F, 1983 S, F, W, E, 1984 F
McLoughlin, R J (UC Dublin, Blackrock Coll, Gosforth) 1962 E, S, F, 1963 E, S, W, NZ, 1964 E, S, 1965 F, E, S, W, SA, 1966 F, E, S, W, 1971 F, E, S, W, 1972 F 1, E, F 2, 1973 NZ, E, S, W, F, 1974 F, W, E, S, P, NZ, 1975 E, S, F, W
McMahon, L B (Blackrock Coll, UC Dublin) 1931 E, SA, 1933 E, 1934 E, 1936 E, S, W, 1937 E, S, W, 1938 E, S
McMaster, A W (Ballymena) 1972 F 1, E, F 2, 1973 NZ, E, S, W, F, 1974 F, E, S, P, 1975 F, W, 1976 A, F, W, NZ
McMordie, J (Queen's Coll, Belfast) 1886 S
McMorrow, A (Garryowen) 1951 W
McMullen, A R (Cork) 1881 E, S
McNamara, V (UC Cork) 1914 E, S, W
McNaughton, P P (Greystones) 1978 S, F, W, E, 1979 F, W, E, S, A 1, 2, 1980 E, S, F, W, 1981 F
MacNeill, H P (Dublin U, Oxford U, Blackrock Coll, London Irish) 1981 F, W, E, S, A, 1982 W, E, S, F, 1983 S, F, W, E, 1984 F, W, E, A, 1985 S, F, W, E, 1986 F, W, E, S, R, 1987 E, S, F, W, [W, C, Tg, A], 1988 S (R), E 1, 2
McQuilkin, K P (Bective Rangers, Lansdowne) 1996 US, S, F, 1997 F (t & R), S
MacSweeney, D A (Blackrock Coll) 1955 S
McVicker, H (Army, Richmond) 1927 E, S, W, A, 1928 F
McVicker, J (Collegians) 1924 F, E, S, W, NZ, 1925 F, E, S, W, 1926 F, E, S, W, 1927 F, E, S, W, A, 1928 W, 1930 F
McVicker, S (Queen's U, Belfast) 1922 E, S, W, F
McWeeney, J P J (St Mary's Coll) 1997 NZ
Madden, M N (Sunday's Well) 1955 E, S, W
Madigan, I (Leinster) 2013 F(R), It(R), US, C
Magee, A M (Louis) (Bective Rangers, London Irish) 1895 E, S, W, 1896 E, S, W, 1897 E, S, 1898 E, S, W, 1899 E, S, W, 1900 E, S, W, 1901 E, S, W, 1902 E, S, W, 1903 E, S, W, 1904 W
Magee, J T (Bective Rangers) 1895 E, S
Maggs, K M (Bristol, Bath, Ulster) 1997 NZ (R), C, It 2, 1998 S, F, W, E, SA 1, 2, Gg, R (R), SA 3, 1999 F, W, E, S, It, A 1, 2, Arg 1, [US, A 3, Arg 2], 2000 E, F, Arg, US (R), C, 2001 It (R), F (R), R, S (R), W, E, Sm, NZ, 2002 W, E, S, R, Ru, Gg, A, Fj, Arg, 2003 S 1, It 1, F, W 1, E, A, W 2, S 2, [R, Nm, Arg, A, F], 2004 F, W(R), E(R), It(R), S(R), SA1(R), 2, US, 2005 S, F, W, J1
Maginiss, R M (Dublin U) 1875 E, 1876 E
Magrath, R M (Cork Constitution) 1909 S
Maguire, J F (Cork) 1884 S
Mahoney, J (Dolphin) 1923 E
Malcolmson, G L (RAF, NIFC) 1935 NZ, 1936 E, S, W, 1937 E, S, W
Malone, N G (Oxford U, Leicester) 1993 S, F, 1994 US (R)
Mannion, N P (Corinthians, Lansdowne, Wanderers) 1988 WS, It, 1989 F, W, E, S, NZ, 1990 E, S, F, W, Arg, 1991 Nm 1(R), 2, [J], 1993 S
Marshall, B D E (Queen's U, Belfast) 1963 E
Marshall, L D (Ulster) 2013 S, F, It
Marshall, P (Ulster) 2013 It(R), US(R), C(R)
Mason, S J P (Orrell, Richmond) 1996 W, E, WS
Massey-Westropp, R H (Limerick, Monkstown) 1886 E
Matier, R N (NIFC) 1878 E, 1879 S
Matthews, P M (Ards, Wanderers) 1984 A, 1985 S, F, W, E, 1986 R, 1987 E, S, F, W, [W, Tg, A], 1988 S, F, W, E 1, 2, WS, It, 1989 F, W, E, S, NZ, 1990 E, S, 1991 F, W, E, S, Nm 1 [Z, S, A], 1992 W, E, S
Mattsson, J (Wanderers) 1948 E
Mayne, R B (Queen's U, Belfast) 1937 W, 1938 E, W, 1939 E, S, W
Mayne, R H (Belfast Academy) 1888 W, S
Mayne, T (NIFC) 1921 E, S, F
Mays, K M A (UC Dublin) 1973 NZ, E, S, W
Meares, A W D (Dublin U) 1899 S, W, 1900 E, W
Megaw, J (Richmond, Instonians) 1934 W, 1938 E
Millar, A (Kingstown) 1880 E, S, 1883 E
Millar, H J (Monkstown) 1904 W, 1905 E, S, W
Millar, S (Ballymena) 1958 F, 1959 E, S, W, F, 1960 E, S, W, F, SA, 1961 E, S, W, F, SA, 1962 E, S, F, 1963 F, E, S, W, 1964 F, 1968 F, E, S, W, A, 1969 F, E, S, W, 1970 SA, F, E, S, W
Millar, W H J (Queen's U, Belfast) 1951 E, S, W, 1952 S, W

Miller, E R P (Leicester, Tererure Coll, Leinster) 1997 It 1, F, W, E, NZ, It 2, 1998 S, W (R), Gg, R, 1999 F, W, E (R), S, Arg 1(R), [US (R), A 3(t&R), Arg 2(R)], 2000 US, C (R), SA, 2001 R, W, E, Sm, NZ, 2002 E, S, It (R), Fj (R), 2003 W 1(t+R), Tg, Sm, It 2, S 2, [Nm, Arg(R), A(t&R), F(R)], 2004 SA3(R), US, Arg(R), 2005 It(R), S(R), F(R), W(R), J1(R), 2
Miller, F H (Wanderers) 1886 S
Milliken, R A (Bangor) 1973 E, S, W, F, 1974 F, W, E, S, P, NZ, 1975 E, S, F, W
Millin, T J (Dublin U) 1925 W
Minch, J B (Bective Rangers) 1912 SA, 1913 E, S, 1914 E, S
Moffat, J (Belfast Academy) 1888 W, S, M, 1889 S, 1890 S, W, 1891 S
Moffatt, J E (Old Wesley) 1904 S, 1905 E, S, W
Moffett, J W (Ballymena) 1961 E, S
Molloy, M G (UC Galway, London Irish) 1966 F, E, 1967 A 1, E, S, W, F, A 2, 1968 F, E, S, W, A, 1969 F, E, S, W, 1970 F, E, S, W, 1971 F, E, S, W, 1973 F, 1976 A
Moloney, J J (St Mary's Coll) 1972 F 1, E, F 2, 1973 NZ, E, S, W, F, 1974 F, W, E, S, P, NZ, 1975 E, S, F, W, 1976 S, 1978 S, F, W, E, 1979 A 1, 2, 1980 S, W
Moloney, L A (Garryowen) 1976 W (R), S, 1978 S (R), NZ
Molony, J U (UC Dublin) 1950 S
Monteith, J D E (Queen's U, Belfast) 1947 E, S, W
Montgomery, A (NIFC) 1895 S
Montgomery, F P (Queen's U, Belfast) 1914 E, S, W
Montgomery, R (Cambridge U) 1887 E, S, W, 1891 E, 1892 W
Moore, C M (Dublin U) 1887 S, 1888 W, S
Moore, D F (Wanderers) 1883 E, S, 1884 E, W
Moore, F W (Wanderers) 1884 W, 1885 E, S 2, 1886 S
Moore, H (Windsor) 1876 E, 1877 S
Moore, H (Queen's U, Belfast) 1910 S, 1911 W, F, 1912 F, E, S, W, SA
Moore, T A P (Highfield) 1967 A 2, 1973 NZ, E, S, W, F, 1974 F, W, E, S, P, NZ
Moore, W D (Queen's Coll, Belfast) 1878 E
Moran, F G (Clontarf) 1936 E, 1937 E, S, W, 1938 S, W, 1939 E, S, W
Morell, H B (Dublin U) 1881 E, S, 1882 W, E
Morgan, G J (Clontarf) 1934 E, S, W, 1935 E, S, W, NZ, 1936 E, S, W, 1937 E, S, W, 1938 E, S, W, 1939 E, S, W
Moriarty, C C H (Monkstown) 1899 W
Moroney, J C M (Garryowen) 1968 W, A, 1969 F, E, S, W
Moroney, R J M (Lansdowne) 1984 F, W, 1985 F
Moroney, T A (UC Dublin) 1964 W, 1967 A 1, E
Morphy, E McG (Dublin U) 1908 E
Morris, D P (Bective Rangers) 1931 W, 1932 E, 1935 E, S, W, NZ
Morrow, J W R (Queen's Coll, Belfast) 1882 S, 1883 E, S, 1884 E, W, 1885 S 1, 2, 1886 E, S, 1888 S
Morrow, R D (Bangor) 1986 F, E, S
Mortell, M (Bective Rangers, Dolphin) 1953 F, E, S, W, 1954 NZ, F, E, S, W
Morton, W A (Dublin U) 1888 S
Mostyn, M R (Galwegians) 1999 A 1, Arg 1, [US, A 3, R, Arg 2]
Moyers, L W (Dublin U) 1884 W
Moylett, M M F (Shannon) 1988 E 1
Mulcahy, W A (UC Dublin, Bective Rangers, Bohemians) 1958 A, E, S, W, F, 1959 E, S, W, F, 1960 E, S, W, SA, 1961 E, S, W, SA, 1962 E, S, F, W, 1963 F, E, S, W, NZ, 1964 E, S, W, F, 1965 F, E, S, W, SA
Muldoon, J (Connacht) 2009 C, US, 2010 NZ1
Mullan, B (Clontarf) 1947 F, E, S, W, 1948 F, E, S, W
Mullane, J P (Limerick Bohemians) 1928 W, 1929 F
Mullen, K D (Old Belvedere) 1947 F, E, S, W, A, 1948 F, E, S, W, 1949 F, E, S, W, 1950 F, E, S, W, 1951 F, E, S, W, SA, 1952 F, S, W
Mulligan, A A (Wanderers) 1956 F, E, 1957 F, E, S, W, 1958 A, E, S, F, 1959 E, S, W, F, 1960 E, S, W, F, SA, 1961 W, F, SA
Mullin, B J (Dublin U, Oxford U, Blackrock Coll, London Irish) 1984 A, 1985 S, W, E, 1986 F, W, E, S, R, 1987 E, S, F, W, [W, C, Tg, A], 1988 S, F, W, E 1, 2, WS, It, 1989 F, W, E, S, NZ, 1990 E, S, W, Arg, 1991 F, W, E, S, Nm 1, 2, [J, S, A], 1992 W, E, S, 1994 US, 1995 E, S, F, W, It, [NZ, J, W, F]
Mullins, M J (Young Munster, Old Crescent) 1999 Arg 1(R), [R], 2000 E, S, It, Arg (t&R), US, C, 2001 It, R, W (R), E (R), Sm (R), NZ (R), 2003 Tg, Sm
Murphy, B J (Munster) 2007 Arg 1(R), 2, 2009 C, US
Murphy, C J (Lansdowne) 1939 E, S, W, 1947 F, E
Murphy, G E A (Leicester) 2000 US, C (R), J, 2001 R, S, Sm, 2002 W, E, NZ 1, 2, Fj, 2003 S 1(R), It 1, F, W 1, E, A, W 2, It 2(R), S 2, 2004 It, S, SA1, 3, US, Arg, 2005 It, S, E, F, W, NZ, A, R, 2006 It, F, W, S, E, NZ1, 2, A1(R), SA(R), A2, 2007 W(t&R), F, Arg1(t&R), 2, S2, It2, [Nm(R), Arg], 2008 It, F, S, E, NZ1(R), A(R), Arg, 2009 F(R), It(R), S(R), W(R), 2010 E, W, S, NZ1(R), A(R), Arg, 2011 E2, [US, Ru(R)]
Murphy, J G M W (London Irish) 1951 SA, 1952 S, W, E, 1954 NZ, 1958 W
Murphy, J J (Greystones) 1981 SA 1, 1982 W (R), 1984 S
Murphy, J N (Greystones) 1992 A
Murphy, K J (Cork Constitution) 1990 E, S, F, W, Arg, 1991 F, W (R), S (R), 1992 S, F, NZ 2(R)
Murphy, N A A (Cork Constitution) 1958 A, E, S, W, F, 1959 E, S, W, F, 1960 E, S, W, F, SA, 1961 E, S, W, 1962 E, 1963 NZ, 1964 E, S, W, F, 1965 F, E, S, W, SA, 1966 F, E, S, W, 1967 A 1, E, S, W, F, 1969 F, E, S, W
Murphy, N F (Cork Constitution) 1930 E, W, 1931 F, E, S, W, SA, 1932 E, S, W, 1933 E
Murphy-O'Connor, J (Bective Rangers) 1954 E
Murray, C (Munster) 2011 F2(R), E2(R), [US, A(R), It, W], 2012 W, It, F, NZ 1, 2, 3, SA, Arg, 2013 W, E, S, F, It
Murray, H W (Dublin U) 1877 S, 1878 E, 1879 E
Murray, J B (UC Dublin) 1963 F
Murray, P F (Wanderers) 1927 F, 1929 F, E, S, 1930 F, E, S, W, 1931 F, E, S, W, SA, 1932 E, S, W, 1933 E, W, S
Murtagh, C W (Portadown) 1977 S
Myles, J (Dublin U) 1875 E

Nash, L C (Queen's Coll, Cork) 1889 S, 1890 W, E, 1891 E, S, W
Neely, M R (Collegians) 1947 F, E, S, W
Neill, H J (NIFC) 1885 E, S 1, 2, 1886 S, 1887 E, S, W, 1888 W, S
Neill, J McF (Instonians) 1926 F
Nelson, J E (Malone) 1947 A, 1948 E, S, W, 1949 F, E, S, W, 1950 F, E, S, W, 1951 F, E, W, 1954 F
Nelson, R (Queen's Coll, Belfast) 1882 E, S, 1883 S, 1886 S
Nesdale, R P (Newcastle) 1997 W, E, S, NZ (R), C, 1998 F (R), W (R), Gg, SA 3(R), 1999 It, A 2(R), [US (R), R]
Nesdale, T J (Garryowen) 1961 F
Neville, W C (Dublin U) 1879 S, E
Nicholson, P C (Dublin U) 1900 E, S, W
Norton, G W (Bective Rangers) 1949 F, E, S, W, 1950 F, E, S, W, 1951 F, E, S
Notley, J R (Wanderers) 1952 F, S
Nowlan, K W (St Mary's Coll) 1997 NZ, C, It 2

O'Brien, B (Derry) 1893 S, W
O'Brien, B A P (Shannon) 1968 F, E, S
O'Brien, D J (London Irish, Cardiff, Old Belvedere) 1948 E, S, W, 1949 F, E, S, W, 1950 F, E, S, W, 1951 F, E, S, W, SA, 1952 F, S, W, E
O'Brien, K A (Broughton Park) 1980 E, 1981 SA 1(R), 2
O'Brien, S K (Leinster) 2009 Fj(R), SA(R), 2010 It(R), Sm, 2011 It, F1, S1, W, E1, F2, 3, [A, Ru, It, W], 2012 W, It, F, E, NZ 1, 2, 3, 2013 W, E, S, F, It
O'Brien-Butler, P E (Monkstown) 1897 S, 1898 E, S, 1899 S, W, 1900 E
O'Callaghan, C T (Carlow) 1910 W, F, 1911 E, S, W, F, 1912 F
O'Callaghan, D P (Cork Const, Munster) 2003 W 1(R), Tg (R), Sm (R), W 2(R), It2(R), [R(R), A(t&R)], 2004 F(t&R), W, It, S(t&R), SA2(R), US, 2005 It(R), S(R), W(R), NZ, A, R, 2006 It(R), F(R), W, S(R), E(R), NZ1, 2, A1, SA, A2, PI(R), 2007 W, F, E, S1, It1, 2, [Nm, Gg, F, Arg], 2008 It, F, S, W, E, NZ1, A, C, NZ2, Arg, 2009 F, It, E, S, W, A, Fj(R), SA, 2010 E, W, S, NZ1, A, SA, Sm, NZ2, Arg, 2011 It, F1, S1, W, E1, F2, 3, E2, [US, A, Ru, It, W], 2012 W, It, F, S, E, NZ 1(R), 2(R), 3(R), SA(t&R), Arg(R), 2013 W(R), E(R), S, F(R)
O'Callaghan, M P (Sunday's Well) 1962 W, 1964 E, F
O'Callaghan, P (Dolphin) 1967 A 1, E, A 2, 1968 F, E, S, W, 1969 F, E, S, W, 1970 SA, F, E, S, W, 1976 F, W, E, S, NZ
O'Connell, K D (Sunday's Well) 1994 F, E (t)
O'Connell, P (Bective Rangers) 1913 W, F, 1914 F, E, S, W
O'Connell, P J (Young Munster, Munster) 2002 W, It (R), F (R), NZ 1, 2003 E (R), A (R), Tg, Sm, W 2, S 2, [R, Nm, Arg, A, F], 2004 F, W, E, S, SA1, 2, 3, US, Arg, 2005 It, S, E, F, W, 2006 It, F, S, E, NZ1, 2, A1, SA, A2, PI, 2007 W, F, E, S1, 2, It2, [Nm, Gg, F, Arg], 2008 S(R), W, E, NZ1, A, C, NZ2, Arg, 2009 F, It, E, S, W, A, Fj, SA, 2010 It, F, E, W, S, 2011 It, F1, S1, W, E1, F2(R), 3, E2, [US, A, It, W], 2012 W, It, F
O'Connell, W J (Lansdowne) 1955 F
O'Connor, H S (Dublin U) 1957 F, E, S, W
O'Connor, J (Garryowen) 1895 S
O'Connor, J H (Bective Rangers) 1888 M, 1890 S, W, E, 1891 E, S, 1892 E, W, 1893 E, S, 1894 E, S, W, 1895 E, 1896 E, S, W
O'Connor, J H (Wasps) 2004 SA3, Arg, 2005 S, E, F, W, J1, NZ, A, R, 2006 W(R), E(t&R)
O'Connor, J J (Garryowen) 1909 F

THE COUNTRIES

O'Connor, J J (UC Cork) 1933 S, 1934 E, S, W, 1935 E, S, W, NZ, 1936 S, W, 1938 S
O'Connor, P J (Lansdowne) 1887 W
O'Cuinneagain, D (Sale, Ballymena) 1998 SA 1, 2, Gg (R), R (R), SA 3, 1999 F, W, E, S, It, A 1, 2, Arg 1, [US, A 3, R, Arg 2], 2000 E, It (R)
Odbert, R V M (RAF) 1928 F
O'Donnell, R C (St Mary's Coll) 1979 A 1, 2, 1980 S, F, W
O'Donnell, T (Munster) 2013 US(t&R), C
O'Donoghue, P J (Bective Rangers) 1955 F, E, S, W, 1956 W, 1957 F, E, 1958 A, E, S, W
O'Driscoll, B G (Blackrock Coll, Leinster) 1999 A 1, 2, Arg 1, [US, A 3, R (R), Arg 2], 2000 E, S, It, F, W, J, SA, 2001 F, S, W, E, Sm, NZ, 2002 W, E, S, It, F, NZ 1, 2, R, Ru, Gg, A, Fj, Arg, 2003 S 1, It 1, F, W 1, E, W 2, It 2, S 2, [R, Nm, Arg, A, F], 2004 W, E, It, S, SA1, 2, 3, US, Arg, 2005 It, E, F, W, 2006 It, F, W, S, E, NZ1, 2, A1, SA, A2, Pl, 2007 W, E, S1, It1, S2, [Nm, Gg, F, Arg], 2008 It, F, S, W, NZ1, A, C, NZ2, Arg, 2009 F, It, E, S, W, A, Fj, SA, 2010 It, F, E, W, S, NZ1, A, SA, Sm, NZ2, Arg, 2011 It, F1, S1, W, E1, F3, [US, A, It, W], 2012 NZ 1, 2, 3, 2013 W, E, S, F, It
O'Driscoll, B J (Manchester) 1971 F (R), E, S, W
O'Driscoll, J B (London Irish, Manchester) 1978 S, 1979 A 1, 2, 1980 E, S, F, W, 1981 F, W, E, S, SA 1, 2, A, 1982 W, E, S, F, 1983 S, F, W, E, 1984 F, W, E, S
O'Driscoll, M R (Cork Const, Munster) 2001 R (R), 2002 Fj (R), 2005 R(R), 2006 W(R), NZ1(R), 2(R), A1(R), 2007 E(R), It1, Arg1(t&R), 2, 2008 It(R), F(R), S, E(R), 2009 C, US, 2010 NZ1, A, SA, NZ2, Arg, 2011 S2(R)
O'Flanagan, K P (London Irish) 1947 A
O'Flanagan, M (Lansdowne) 1948 S
O'Gara, R J R (Cork Const, Munster) 2000 S, It, F, W, Arg (R), US, C (R), J, SA, 2001 It, F, S, W (R), E (R), Sm, 2002 W (R), E (R), S (R), It (t), F (R), NZ 1, 2, R, Ru, Gg, A, Arg, 2003 W 1(R), E (R), A (t+R), Tg, Sm, S 2, [R(R), Nm, Arg(R), A, F], 2004 F, W, E, It, S, SA1, 2, 3, Arg, 2005 It, S, E, F, W, NZ, A, R(R), 2006 It, F, W, S, E, NZ1, 2, A1, SA, A2, Pl(R), 2007 W, F, E, S1, It1, S2(R), It2, [Nm, Gg, F, Arg], 2008 It, F, S, W, E, NZ1, A, C, NZ2, Arg, 2009 F, It, E, S, W, A, 2010 It, F, E(R), W(R), S(R), NZ1, SA(R), Sm, NZ2(R), Arg(R), 2011 It(R), F1(R), S1, W, E1(R), F2, 3(R), E2, [US(R), A(R), Ru, It, W], 2012 W(R), It(R), F(R), S(R), E(R), NZ 1(R), 2(R), 3(R), SA(R), Arg(R), 2013 E(R), S(R)
O'Grady, D (Sale) 1997 It 2
O'Hanlon, B (Dolphin) 1947 E, S, W, 1948 F, E, S, W, 1949 F, E, S, W, 1950 F
O'Hara, P T J (Sunday's Well, Cork Const) 1988 WS (R), 1989 F, W, E, NZ, 1990 E, S, F, W, 1991 Nm 1, [J], 1993 F, W, E, 1994 US
O'Kelly, M E (London Irish, St Mary's Coll, Leinster) 1997 NZ, C, It 2, 1998 S, F, W, E, SA 1, 2, Gg, R, SA 3, 1999 A 1(R), 2, Arg 1(R), [US (R), A 3, R, Arg 2], 2000 E, S, It, F, W, Arg, US, J, SA, 2001 It, F, S, W, E, NZ, 2002 E, S, It, F, NZ 1(R), 2, R, Ru, Gg, A, Fj, Arg, 2003 S 1, It 1, F, W 1, E, A, W 2, S 2, [R, Nm, Arg, A, F], 2004 F, W(R), E, It, S, SA1, 2, 3, Arg, 2005 It, S, E, F, W, NZ, A, 2006 It, F, W, S, E, SA(R), A2(R), Pl, 2007 Arg1, 2(R), S2, It2(R), [F(R), Arg(R)], 2008 It, F, 2009 It(R)
Olding, S (Ulster) 2013 US
O'Leary, A (Cork Constitution) 1952 S, W, E
O'Leary, T G (Munster) 2007 Arg1(R), 2008 NZ2, Arg, 2009 F, It, E, S(R), W, A, Fj(R), SA, 2010 It, F, E, W, S, NZ1, A, 2011 It, F1, S2, F3, 2012 S(R), E(R)
O'Loughlin, D B (UC Cork) 1938 E, S, W, 1939 E, S, W
O'Mahony, David (Cork Constitution) 1995 It
O'Mahony, D W (UC Dublin, Moseley, Bedford) 1995 It, [F], 1997 It 2, 1998 R
O'Mahony, P (Munster) 2012 It(R), F(R), S, E(R), NZ 1, 2(R), 3, SA, Arg, 2013 W, E, S, F, It, US, C
O'Meara, B T (Cork Constitution) 1997 E (R), S, NZ (R), 1998 S, 1999 [US (R), R (R)], 2001 It (R), 2003 Sm (R), It 2(R)
O'Meara, J A (UC Cork, Dolphin) 1951 F, E, S, W, SA, 1952 F, S, W, E, 1953 F, E, S, W, 1954 NZ, F, E, S, 1955 F, E, 1956 S, W, 1958 W
O'Neill, H O'H (Queen's U, Belfast, UC Cork) 1930 E, S, W, 1933 E, S, W
O'Neill, J B (Queen's U, Belfast) 1920 S
O'Neill, W A (UC Dublin, Wanderers) 1952 E, 1953 F, E, S, W, 1954 NZ
O'Reilly, A J F (Old Belvedere, Leicester) 1955 F, E, S, W, 1956 F, E, S, W, 1957 F, E, S, W, 1958 A, E, S, W, F, 1959 E, S, W, F, 1960 E, 1961 E, F, SA, 1963 F, S, W, 1970 E
Orr, P A (Old Wesley) 1976 F, W, E, S, NZ, 1977 W, E, S, F, 1978 S, F, W, E, NZ, 1979 F, W, E, S, A 1, 2, 1980 E, S, F, W, 1981 F, W, E, S, SA 1, 2, A, 1982 W, E, S, F, 1983 S, F, W, E, 1984 F, W, E, S, A, 1985 S, F, W, E, 1986 F, S, R, 1987 E, S, F, W, [W, C, A]
O'Shea, C M P (Lansdowne, London Irish) 1993 R, 1994 F, W, E, S, A 1, 2, US, 1995 E, S, [J, W, F], 1997 It 1, F, S (R), 1998 S, F, SA 1, 2, Gg, R, SA 3, 1999 F, W, E, S, It, A 1, Arg 1, [US, A 3, R, Arg 2], 2000 E
O'Sullivan, A C (Dublin U) 1882 S
O'Sullivan, J M (Limerick) 1884 S, 1887 S
O'Sullivan, P J A (Galwegians) 1957 F, E, S, W, 1959 E, S, W, F, 1960 SA, 1961 E, S, 1962 F, W, 1963 F, NZ
O'Sullivan, W (Queen's Coll, Cork) 1895 S
Owens, R H (Dublin U) 1922 E, S

Parfrey, P (UC Cork) 1974 NZ
Parke, J C (Monkstown) 1903 W, 1904 E, S, W, 1905 W, NZ, 1906 E, S, W, SA, 1907 E, S, W, 1908 E, S, W, 1909 E, S, W, F
Parr, J S (Wanderers) 1914 F, E, S, W
Patterson, C S (Instonians) 1978 NZ, 1979 F, W, E, S, A 1, 2, 1980 E, S, F, W
Patterson, R d'A (Wanderers) 1912 F, S, W, SA, 1913 E, S, W, F
Payne, C T (NIFC) 1926 E, 1927 F, E, S, A, 1928 F, E, S, W, 1929 F, E, W, 1930 F, E, S, W
Pedlow, A C (CIYMS) 1953 W, 1954 NZ, F, E, 1955 F, E, S, W, 1956 F, E, S, W, 1957 F, E, S, W, 1958 A, E, S, W, F, 1959 E. 1960 E, S, W, F, SA, 1961 S, 1962 W, 1963 F
Pedlow, J (Bessbrook) 1882 S, 1884 W
Pedlow, R (Bessbrook) 1891 W
Pedlow, T B (Queen's Coll, Belfast) 1889 S, W
Peel, T (Limerick) 1892 E, S, W
Peirce, W (Cork) 1881 E
Phipps, G C (Army) 1950 E, W, 1952 F, W, E
Pike, T O (Lansdowne) 1927 E, S, W, A, 1928 F, E, S, W
Pike, V J (Lansdowne) 1931 E, S, W, SA, 1932 E, S, W, 1933 E, W, S, 1934 E, S, W
Pike, W W (Kingstown) 1879 E, 1881 E, S, 1882 E, 1883 S
Pinion, G (Belfast Collegians) 1909 E, S, W, F
Piper, O J S (Cork Constitution) 1909 E, S, W, F, 1910 E, S, W, F
Polden, S E (Clontarf) 1913 W, F, 1914 F, 1920 F
Popham, I (Cork Constitution) 1922 S, W, F, 1923 F
Popplewell, N J (Greystones, Wasps, Newcastle) 1989 NZ, 1990 Arg, 1991 Nm 1, 2, [Z, S, A], 1992 W, E, S, F, NZ 1, 2, A, 1993 S, F, W, E, R, 1994 F, W, E, S, US, 1995 E, S, F, W, It, [NZ, J, W, F], Fj, 1996 US, S, F, W, E, A, 1997 It 1, F, W, E, NZ, C, 1998 S (t), F (R)
Potterton, H N (Wanderers) 1920 W
Pratt, R H (Dublin U) 1933 E, W, S, 1934 E, S
Price, A H (Dublin U) 1920 S, F
Pringle, J C (NIFC) 1902 S, W
Purcell, N M (Lansdowne) 1921 E, S, W, F
Purdon, H (NIFC) 1879 S, E, 1880 E, 1881 E, S
Purdon, W B (Queen's Coll, Belfast) 1906 E, S, W
Purser, F C (Dublin U) 1898 E, S, W

Quinlan, A N (Shannon, Munster) 1999 [R (R)], 2001 It, F, 2002 NZ 2(R), Ru (R), Gg (R), A (R), Fj, Arg (R), 2003 S 1(R), It 1(R), F (R), W 1, E (R), A, W 2, [R(R), Nm, Arg], 2004 SA1(R), 2(R), 2005 J1, 2(t&R), 2007 Arg2, S2(t&R), 2008 C(R), NZ2
Quinlan, D P (Northampton) 2005 J1(R), 2
Quinlan, S V J (Blackrock Coll) 1956 F, E, W, 1958 W
Quinn, B T (Old Belvedere) 1947 F
Quinn, F P (Old Belvedere) 1981 F, W, E
Quinn, J P (Dublin U) 1910 E, S, 1911 E, S, W, F, 1912 E, S, W, 1913 E, W, F, 1914 F, E, S
Quinn, K (Old Belvedere) 1947 F, A, 1953 F, E, S
Quinn, M A M (Lansdowne) 1973 F, 1974 F, W, E, S, P, NZ, 1977 S, F, 1981 SA 2
Quirke, J M T (Blackrock Coll) 1962 E, S, 1968 S

Rainey, P I (Ballymena) 1989 NZ
Rambaut, D F (Dublin U) 1887 E, S, W, 1888 W
Rea, H H (Edinburgh U) 1967 A 1, 1969 F
Read, H M (Dublin U) 1910 E, S, 1911 E, S, W, F, 1912 F, E, S, W, SA, 1913 E, S
Reardon, J V (Cork Constitution) 1934 E, S
Reddan, E G (Wasps, Leinster) 2006 F(R), 2007 Arg2, S2(R), [F, Arg], 2008 It, F, S, W, E, NZ1, A(R), C, NZ2(R), 2009 C(R), US(R), Fj, 2010 It(R), F(R), W(R), NZ1(R), SA, NZ2, Arg(R), 2011 It(R), F1(R), S1, W, E1, F2, 3(R), E2, [US(R), A, Ru(R), It(R), W(R)], 2012 W(R), It(R), F(R), S, E, NZ 1(R), 2(R), 3(R), SA(R), Arg(R), 2013 W(R), S(R), F(R)
Reid, C (NIFC) 1899 S, W, 1900 E, 1903 W
Reid, J L (Richmond) 1934 S, W

Reid, P J (Garryowen) 1947 A, 1948 F, E, W
Reid, T E (Garryowen) 1953 E, S, W, 1954 NZ, F, 1955 E, S, 1956 F, E, 1957 F, E, S, W
Reidy, C J (London Irish) 1937 W
Reidy, G F (Dolphin, Lansdowne) 1953 W, 1954 F, E, S, W
Richey, H A (Dublin U) 1889 W, 1890 S
Ridgeway, E C (Wanderers) 1932 S, W, 1935 E, S, W
Rigney, B J (Greystones) 1991 F, W, E, S, Nm 1, 1992 F, NZ 1(R), 2
Ringland, T M (Queen's U, Belfast, Ballymena) 1981 A, 1982 W, E, F, 1983 S, F, W, E, 1984 F, W, E, S, A, 1985 S, F, W, E, 1986 F, W, E, S, R, 1987 E, S, F, W, [W, C, Tg, A], 1988 S, F, W, E 1
Riordan, W F (Cork Constitution) 1910 E
Ritchie, J S (London Irish) 1956 F, E
Robb, C G (Queen's Coll, Belfast) 1904 E, S, W, 1905 NZ, 1906 S
Robbie, J C (Dublin U, Greystones) 1976 A, F, NZ, 1977 S, F, 1981 F, W, E, S
Robinson, B F (Ballymena, London Irish) 1991 F, W, E, S, Nm 1, 2, [Z, S, A], 1992 W, E, S, F, NZ 1, 2, A, 1993 W, E, R, 1994 F, W, E, S, A 1, 2
Robinson, T T H (Wanderers) 1904 E, S, 1905 E, S, W, NZ, 1906 SA, 1907 E, S, W
Roche, J (Wanderers) 1890 S, W, E, 1891 E, S, W, 1892 W
Roche, R E (UC Galway) 1955 E, S, 1957 S, W
Roche, W J (UC Cork) 1920 E, S, F
Roddy, P J (Bective Rangers) 1920 S, F
Roe, R (Lansdowne) 1952 E, 1953 F, E, S, W, 1954 F, E, S, W, 1955 F, E, S, W, 1956 F, E, S, W, 1957 F, E, S, W
Rolland, A C (Blackrock Coll) 1990 Arg, 1994 US (R), 1995 It (R)
Ronan, N (Munster) 2009 C, US, 2010 A, 2011 S2
Rooke, C V (Dublin U) 1891 E, W, 1892 E, S, W, 1893 E, S, W, 1894 E, S, W, 1895 E, S, W, 1896 E, S, W, 1897 E, S
Ross, D J (Belfast Academy) 1884 E, 1885 S 1, 2, 1886 E, S
Ross, G R P (CIYMS) 1955 W
Ross, J F (NIFC) 1886 S
Ross, J P (Lansdowne) 1885 E, S 1, 2, 1886 E, S
Ross, M R (Harlequins, Leinster) 2009 C(R), US, 2011 It, F1, S1, W, E1, F2, 3, E2, [US, A, Ru(R), It, W], 2012 W, It, F, S, E, NZ 2, 3, SA, Arg, 2013 W, E, S, F, It, US, C
Ross, N G (Malone) 1927 F, E
Ross, W McC (Queen's U, Belfast) 1932 E, S, W, 1933 E, W, S, 1934 E, S, 1935 NZ
Ruddock, R J (Leinster) 2010 A(R)
Russell, J (UC Cork) 1931 F, E, S, W, SA, 1933 E, W, S, 1934 E, S, W, 1935 E, S, W, 1936 E, S, W, 1937 E, S
Russell, P (Instonians) 1990 E, 1992 NZ 1, 2, A
Rutherford, W G (Tipperary) 1884 E, S, 1885 E, S 1, 1886 E, 1888 W
Ryan, D C (Munster) 2008 Arg(R), 2009 C(R), US(R), 2010 It(R), F(R), SA(R), Sm(R), 2011 S2, F2, E2(R), [Ru, It(R), W(R)], 2012 W(R), It(R), F(R), S, E, NZ 1, 2, 3, SA, Arg, 2013 W, E, S, F, It
Ryan, E (Dolphin) 1937 W, 1938 E, S
Ryan, J (Rockwell Coll) 1897 E, 1898 E, S, W, 1899 E, S, W, 1900 S, W, 1901 E, S, W, 1902 E, 1904 E
Ryan, J G (UC Dublin) 1939 E, S, W
Ryan, M (Rockwell Coll) 1897 E, S, 1898 E, S, W, 1899 E, S, W, 1900 E, S, W, 1901 E, S, W, 1903 E, 1904 E, S

Saunders, R (London Irish) 1991 F, W, E, S, Nm 1, 2, [Z, J, S, A], 1992 W, 1994 F (t)
Saverimutto, C (Sale) 1995 Fj, 1996 US, S
Sayers, H J M (Lansdowne) 1935 E, S, W, 1936 E, S, W, 1938 W, 1939 E, S, W
Scally, C J (U C Dublin) 1998 Gg (R), R, 1999 S (R), It
Schute, F (Wanderers) 1878 E, 1879 E
Schute, F G (Dublin U) 1912 SA, 1913 E, S
Scott, D (Malone) 1961 F, SA, 1962 S
Scott, R D (Queen's U, Belfast) 1967 E, F, 1968 F, E, S
Scovell, R H (Kingstown) 1883 E, 1884 E
Scriven, G (Dublin U) 1879 S, E, 1880 E, S, 1881 E, 1882 S, 1883 E, S
Sealy, J (Dublin U) 1896 E, S, W, 1897 S, 1899 E, S, W, 1900 E, S
Sexton, J F (Dublin U, Lansdowne) 1988 E 2, WS, It, 1989 F
Sexton, J J (Leinster) 2009 Fj, SA, 2010 F(R), E, W, S, NZ1(R), A, SA, NZ2, Arg, 2011 It, F1, S1(R), W(R), E1, S2, F3, E2(R), [US, A, Ru(R), It(R), W(R)], 2012 W, It, F, S, E, NZ 1, 2, 3, SA, Arg, 2013 W, E
Sexton, W J (Garryowen) 1984 A, 1988 S, E 2
Shanahan, T (Lansdowne) 1885 E, S 1, 2, 1886 E, 1888 S, W
Shaw, G M (Windsor) 1877 S
Sheahan, F J (Cork Const, Munster) 2000 US (R), 2001 It (R), R, W (R), Sm, 2002 W, E, S, Gg (R), A (t+R), Fj, 2003 S 1(R), It 1(R), 2004 F(R), W(R), It(R), S(R), SA1(R), US, 2005 It(R), S(R), W(R), J1, 2, 2006 SA(R), A2(R), PI, 2007 Arg2, [F(t&R)]
Sheehan, M D (London Irish) 1932 E
Sherry, B F (Terenure Coll) 1967 A 1, E, S, A 2, 1968 F, E
Sherry, M (Munster) 2013 US(R)
Sherry, M J A (Lansdowne) 1975 F, W
Shields, P M (Ballymena) 2003 Sm (R), It 2(R)
Siggins, J A E (Belfast Collegians) 1931 F, E, S, W, SA, 1932 E, S, W, 1933 E, W, S, 1934 E, S, W, 1935 E, S, W, NZ, 1936 E, S, W, 1937 E, S, W
Slattery, J F (UC Dublin, Blackrock Coll) 1970 SA, F, E, S, W, 1971 F, E, S, W, 1972 F 1, E, F 2, 1973 NZ, E, S, W, F, 1974 F, W, E, S, P, NZ, 1975 E, S, F, W, 1976 A, 1977 S, F, 1978 S, F, W, E, NZ, 1979 F, W, E, S, A 1, 2, 1980 E, S, F, W, 1981 F, W, E, S, SA 1, 2, A, 1982 W, E, S, F, 1983 S, F, W, E, 1984 F
Smartt, F N B (Dublin U) 1908 E, S, 1909 E
Smith, B A (Oxford U, Leicester) 1989 NZ, 1990 S, F, W, Arg, 1991 F, W, E, S
Smith, J H (London Irish) 1951 F, E, S, W, SA, 1952 F, S, W, E, 1954 NZ, W, F
Smith, R E (Lansdowne) 1892 E
Smith, S J (Ballymena) 1988 E 2, WS, It, 1989 F, W, E, S, NZ, 1990 E, 1991 F, W, E, S, Nm 1, 2, [Z, S, A], 1992 W, E, S, F, NZ 1, 2, 1993 S
Smithwick, F F S (Monkstown) 1898 S, W
Smyth, J T (Queen's U, Belfast) 1920 F
Smyth, P J (Belfast Collegians) 1911 E, S, F
Smyth, R S (Dublin U) 1903 E, S, 1904 E
Smyth, T (Malone, Newport) 1908 E, S, W, 1909 E, S, W, 1910 E, S, W, F, 1911 E, S, W, 1912 E
Smyth, W S (Belfast Collegians) 1910 W, F, 1920 E
Solomons, B A H (Dublin U) 1908 E, S, W, 1909 E, S, W, F, 1910 E, S, W
Spain, A W (UC Dublin) 1924 NZ
Sparrow, W (Dublin U) 1893 W, 1894 E
Spillane, B J (Bohemians) 1985 S, F, W, E, 1986 F, W, E, 1987 F, W, [W, C, A (R)], 1989 E (R)
Spring, D E (Dublin U) 1978 S, NZ, 1979 S, 1980 S, F, W, 1981 W
Spring, R M (Lansdowne) 1979 F, W, E
Spunner, H F (Wanderers) 1881 E, S, 1884 W
Stack, C R R (Dublin U) 1889 S
Stack, G H (Dublin U) 1875 E
Staples, J E (London Irish, Harlequins) 1991 W, E, S, Nm 1, 2, [Z, J, S, A], 1992 W, E, NZ 1, 2, A, 1995 F, W, It, [NZ], Fj, 1996 US, S, F, A, 1997 W, E, S
Staunton, J W (Garryowen, Wasps) 2001 Sm, 2005 J1(R), 2(R), 2006 A1(R), 2007 Arg2
Steele, H W (Ballymena) 1976 E, 1977 F, 1978 F, W, E, 1979 F, W, E, A 1, 2
Stephenson, G V (Queen's U, Belfast, London Hosp) 1920 F, 1921 E, S, W, F, 1922 E, S, W, F, 1923 E, S, W, F, 1924 F, E, S, W, NZ, 1925 F, E, S, W, 1926 F, E, S, W, 1927 F, E, S, W, A, 1928 F, E, S, W, 1929 F, E, W, 1930 F, E, S, W
Stephenson, H W V (United Services) 1922 S, W, F, 1924 F, E, S, W, NZ, 1925 F, E, S, W, 1927 A, 1928 E
Stevenson, J (Dungannon) 1888 M, 1889 S
Stevenson, J B (Instonians) 1958 A, E, S, W, F
Stevenson, R (Dungannon) 1887 E, S, W, 1888 M, 1889 S, W, 1890 S, W, E, 1891 W, 1892 W, 1893 E, S, W
Stevenson, T H (Belfast Acad) 1895 E, W, 1896 E, S, W, 1897 E, S
Stewart, A L (NIFC) 1913 W, F, 1914 F
Stewart, J W (Queen's U, Belfast, NIFC) 1922 F, 1924 S, 1928 F, E, S, W, 1929 F, E, S, W
Stoker, E W (Wanderers) 1888 W, S
Stoker, F O (Wanderers) 1886 S, 1888 W, M, 1889 S, 1891 W
Stokes, O S (Cork Bankers) 1882 E, 1884 E
Stokes, P (Garryowen) 1913 E, S, 1914 F, 1920 E, S, W, F, 1921 E, S, F, 1922 W, F
Stokes, R D (Queen's Coll, Cork) 1891 S, W
Strathdee, E (Queen's U, Belfast) 1947 E, S, W, A, 1948 W, F, 1949 E, S, W
Strauss, C R (Leinster) 2012 SA, Arg, 2013 US, C
Stringer, P A (Shannon, Munster) 2000 S, It, F, W, Arg, C, J, SA, 2001 It, F, R, S (R), W, E, Sm, NZ, 2002 W, E, S, It, F, NZ 1, 2, R, Ru, Gg, A, Arg, 2003 S 1, It 1, F, W 1, E, A, W 2, S 2, [R, Nm, Arg, A, F], 2004 F, W, E, It, S, SA1, 2, 3, US(R), Arg, 2005 It, S, E, F, W, J1, 2, NZ, A, R(R), 2006 It, F, W, S, E, NZ1, 2, A1, SA, A2(R), PI, 2007 W, E, S1, It1, 2, [Nm, Gg], 2008 It(R), S(R), E(R), NZ1(R), A, C(R), 2009 It(t&R), E(R), S,

THE COUNTRIES

W(R), C, US, 2010 SA(R), Sm, NZ2(R), Arg, 2011 S1(R), W(R), E1(R)
Stuart, C P (Clontarf) 1912 SA
Stuart, I M B (Dublin U) 1924 E, S
Sugars, H S (Dublin U) 1905 NZ, 1906 SA, 1907 S
Sugden, M (Wanderers) 1925 F, E, S, W, 1926 F, E, S, W, 1927 E, S, W, A, 1928 F, E, S, W, 1929 F, E, S, W, 1930 F, E, S, W, 1931 F, E, S, W
Sullivan, D B (UC Dublin) 1922 E, S, W, F
Sweeney, J A (Blackrock Coll) 1907 E, S, W
Symes, G R (Monkstown) 1895 E
Synge, J S (Lansdowne) 1929 S

Taggart, T (Dublin U) 1887 W
Taylor, A S (Queen's Coll, Belfast) 1910 E, S, W, 1912 F
Taylor, D R (Queen's Coll, Belfast) 1903 E
Taylor, J (Belfast Collegians) 1914 E, S, W
Taylor, J W (NIFC) 1879 S, 1880 E, S, 1881 S, 1882 E, S, 1883 E, S
Tector, W R (Wanderers) 1955 F, E, S
Tedford, A (Malone) 1902 E, S, W, 1903 E, S, W, 1904 E, S, W, 1905 E, S, W, NZ, 1906 E, S, W, SA, 1907 E, S, W, 1908 E, S, W
Teehan, C (UC Cork) 1939 E, S, W
Thompson, C (Belfast Collegians) 1907 E, S, 1908 E, S, W, 1909 E, S, W, F, 1910 E, S, W, F
Thompson, J A (Queen's Coll, Belfast) 1885 S 1, 2
Thompson, J K S (Dublin U) 1921 W, 1922 E, S, F, 1923 E, S, W, F
Thompson, R G (Lansdowne) 1882 W
Thompson, R H (Instonians) 1951 SA, 1952 F, 1954 NZ, F, E, S, W, 1955 F, S, W, 1956 W
Thornhill, T (Wanderers) 1892 E, S, W, 1893 E
Thrift, H (Dublin U) 1904 W, 1905 E, S, W, NZ, 1906 E, W, SA, 1907 E, S, W, 1908 E, S, W, 1909 E, S, W, F
Tierney, D (UC Cork) 1938 S, W, 1939 E
Tierney, T A (Garryowen) 1999 A 1, 2, Arg 1, [US, A 3, R, Arg 2], 2000 E
Tillie, C R (Dublin U) 1887 E, S, 1888 W, S
Todd, A W P (Dublin U) 1913 W, F, 1914 F
Toner, D (Leinster) 2010 Sm, NZ2(R), Arg(R), 2013 S(R), It(R), US, C
Topping, J A (Ballymena) 1996 WS, A, 1997 It 1, F, E, 1999 [R], 2000 US, 2003 A
Torrens, J D (Bohemians) 1938 W, 1939 E, S, W
Trimble, A D (Ulster) 2005 A, R, 2006 F(R), W, S, E, NZ1, 2, A1, SA, 2007 W, F(R), E(R), It1(R), Arg1, S2(R), It2, [Nm, F], 2008 It, F, S, W, E, 2009 Fj(R), 2010 It, E(R), NZ1, A, Sm, Arg, 2011 E1, S2, F2, 3, E2, [US(R), A(t&R), Ru, It(R), W(R)], 2012 W, It, F, S, E, NZ 2, 3(t&R), SA, 2013 C
Tucker, C C (Shannon) 1979 F, W, 1980 F (R)
Tuke, B B (Bective Rangers) 1890 E, 1891 E, S, 1892 E, 1894 E, S, W, 1895 E, S
Tuohy, D M (Ulster) 2010 NZ1(R), A(t&R), 2012 NZ 1, 2, 3, 2013 US(R), C
Turley, N (Blackrock Coll) 1962 E
Tweed, D A (Ballymena) 1995 F, W, It, [J]
Tydings, J J (Young Munster) 1968 A
Tyrrell, W (Queen's U, Belfast) 1910 F, 1913 E, S, W, F, 1914 F, E, S, W

Uprichard, R J H (Harlequins, RAF) 1950 S, W

Varley, D A (Munster) 2010 A(R), Arg(R)

Waide, S L (Oxford U, NIFC) 1932 E, S, W, 1933 E, W
Waites, J (Bective Rangers) 1886 S, 1888 M, 1889 W, 1890 S, W, E, 1891 E
Waldron, O C (Oxford U, London Irish) 1966 S, W, 1968 A
Walker, S (Instonians) 1934 E, S, 1935 E, S, W, NZ, 1936 E, S, W, 1937 E, S, W, 1938 E, S, W
Walkington, D B (NIFC) 1887 E, W, 1888 W, 1890 W, E, 1891 E, S, W
Walkington, R B (NIFC) 1875 E, 1876 E, 1877 E, S, 1878 E, 1879 S, 1880 E, S, 1882 E, S
Wall, H (Dolphin) 1965 S, W
Wallace, D P (Garryowen, Munster) 2000 Arg, US, 2001 It, F, R (R), S (R), W, E, NZ, 2002 W, E, S, It, F, 2003 Tg (R), Sm (R), W 2(t+R), S 2, 2004 S, SA1, 2, 2005 J2, 2006 It, F, W, S, E, NZ1, 2, A1, SA, A2, 2007 W, F, E, S1, It1, [Nm, Gg, F, Arg], 2008 It, F, S, W, E, NZ1, C(R), NZ2, Arg, 2009 F, It, E, S, W, A, SA, 2010 It, F, E, W, S, NZ1, SA, NZ2, Arg, 2011 It, F1, S1, W, E1, 2
Wallace, Jas (Wanderers) 1904 E, S
Wallace, Jos (Wanderers) 1903 S, W, 1904 E, S, W, 1905 E, S, W, NZ, 1906 W
Wallace, P R (Ulster) 2006 SA(R), PI, 2007 E(R), Arg1, S2, [Nm(R)], 2008 S(R), E(R), NZ1, A, C(R), NZ2(R), 2009 F, It, E, W(R), A, Fj(R), SA, 2010 It(R), F(t&R), A, Sm, 2011 It(R), W(R), E1(R), S2, F2, [Ru], 2012 NZ 3
Wallace, P S (Blackrock Coll, Saracens) 1995 [J], Fj, 1996 US, W, E, WS, A, 1997 It 1, F, W, E, S, NZ, C, 1998 S, F, W, E, SA 1, 2, Gg, R, 1999 F, W, E, S, It (R), 1999 A 1, 2, Arg 1, [US, A 3, R, Arg 2], 2000 E, US, C (R), 2002 W (R), E (R), S (R), It (R), F (R), NZ 2(R), Ru (R), Gg (R)
Wallace, R M (Garryowen, Saracens) 1991 Nm 1(R), 1992 W, E, S, F, A, 1993 S, F, W, E, R, 1994 F, W, E, S, 1995 W, It, [NZ, J, W], Fj, 1996 US, S, F, WS, 1998 S, F, W, E
Wallace, T H (Cardiff) 1920 E, S, W
Wallis, A K (Wanderers) 1892 E, S, W, 1893 E, W
Wallis, C O'N (Old Cranleighans, Wanderers) 1935 NZ
Wallis, T G (Wanderers) 1921 F, 1922 E, S, W, F
Wallis, W A (Wanderers) 1880 S, 1881 E, S, 1882 W, 1883 S
Walmsley, G (Bective Rangers) 1894 E
Walpole, A (Dublin U) 1888 S, M
Walsh, E J (Lansdowne) 1887 E, S, W, 1892 E, S, W, 1893 E
Walsh, H D (Dublin U) 1875 E, 1876 E
Walsh, J C (UC Cork, Sunday's Well) 1960 S, SA, 1961 E, S, F, SA, 1963 E, S, W, NZ, 1964 E, S, W, F, 1965 F, S, W, SA, 1966 F, S, W, 1967 E, S, W, F, A 2
Ward, A J (Ballynahinch) 1998 F, W, E, SA 1, 2, Gg, R, SA 3, 1999 W, E, S, It (R), A 1, 2, Arg 1, [US, A 3, R, Arg 2], 2000 F (R), W (t&R), Arg (R), US (R), C, J, SA (R), 2001 It (R), F (R)
Ward, A J P (Garryowen, St Mary's Coll, Greystones) 1978 S, F, W, E, NZ, 1979 F, W, E, S, 1981 W, E, S, A, 1983 E (R), 1984 E, S, 1986 S, 1987 [C, Tg]
Warren, J P (Kingstown) 1883 E
Warren, R G (Lansdowne) 1884 W, 1885 E, S 1, 2, 1886 E, 1887 E, S, W, 1888 W, S, M, 1889 S, W, 1890 S, W, E
Watson, R (Wanderers) 1912 SA
Wells, H G (Bective Rangers) 1891 S, W, 1894 E, S
Westby, A J (Dublin U) 1876 E
Wheeler, G H (Queen's Coll, Belfast) 1884 S, 1885 E
Wheeler, J R (Queen's U, Belfast) 1922 E, S, W, F, 1924 E
Whelan, P C (Garryowen) 1975 E, S, 1976 NZ, 1977 W, E, S, F, 1978 S, F, W, E, NZ, 1979 F, W, E, S, 1981 F, W, E
White, M (Queen's Coll, Cork) 1906 E, S, W, SA, 1907 E, W
Whitestone, A M (Dublin U) 1877 E, 1879 S, E, 1880 E, 1883 S
Whitten, I W (Ulster) 2009 C, US
Whittle, D (Bangor) 1988 F
Wilkinson, C R (Malone) 1993 S
Wilkinson, R W (Wanderers) 1947 A
Williamson, F W (Dolphin) 1930 E, S, W
Willis, W J (Lansdowne) 1879 E
Wilson, F (CIYMS) 1977 W, E, S
Wilson, H G (Glasgow U, Malone) 1905 E, S, W, NZ, 1906 E, S, W, SA, 1907 E, S, W, 1908 E, S, W, 1909 E, S, W, 1910 W
Wilson, R G (Ulster) 2005 J1
Wilson, W H (Bray) 1877 E, S
Withers, H H C (Army, Blackheath) 1931 F, E, S, W, SA
Wolfe, E J (Armagh) 1882 E
Wood, G H (Dublin U) 1913 W, 1914 F
Wood, B G M (Garryowen) 1954 E, S, 1956 F, E, S, W, 1957 F, E, S, W, 1958 A, E, S, W, F, 1959 E, S, W, F, 1960 E, S, W, F, SA, 1961 E, S, W, F, SA
Wood, K G M (Garryowen, Harlequins) 1994 A 1, 2, US, 1995 E, S, [J], 1996 A, 1997 It 1, F, 1997 NZ, It 2, 1998 S, F, W, E, SA 1, 2, R (R), SA 3, 1999 F, W, E, S, It (R), A 1, 2, Arg 1, [US, A 3, R (R), Arg 2], 2000 E, S, It, F, W, Arg, US, C, J, SA, 2001 It, F, S, W, E, NZ, 2002 F, NZ 1, 2, Ru, 2003 W 2, S 2, [R, Nm, Arg, A, F]
Woods, D C (Bessbrook) 1888 M, 1889 S
Woods, N K P J (Blackrock Coll, London Irish) 1994 A 1, 2, 1995 E, F, 1996 F, W, E, 1999 W
Wright, R A (Monkstown) 1912 S

Yeates, R A (Dublin U) 1889 S, W
Young, B G (Ulster) 2006 NZ2(R), A1(R), SA(R), A2, PI, 2007 Arg1, 2, S2
Young, G (UC Cork) 1913 E
Young, R M (Collegians) 1965 F, E, S, W, SA, 1966 F, E, S, W, 1967 W, F, 1968 W, A, 1969 F, E, S, W, 1970 SA, F, E, S, W, 1971 F, E, S, W

Zebo, S R (Munster) 2012 NZ 1, SA, Arg, 2013 W, E, US

Italy prop Martin Castrogiovanni makes himself heard against Wales.

Getty Images

ITALY

ITALY'S 2012–13 TEST RECORD

OPPONENTS	DATE	VENUE	RESULT
Tonga	10 Nov	H	Won 28–23
New Zealand	17 Nov	H	Lost 10–42
Australia	24 Nov	H	Lost 19–22
France	3 Feb	H	Won 23–18
Scotland	9 Feb	A	Lost 34–10
Wales	23 Feb	H	Lost 29–26
England	10 Mar	A	Lost 18–11
Ireland	16 Mar	H	Won 22–15
South Africa	8 Jun	A	Lost 44–10
Samoa	15 Jun	N	Lost 39–10
Scotland	22 Jun	N	Lost 30–29

ITALY'S BEST IS STILL TO COME

With Sergio Parisse

Getty Images

Sergio Parisse led Italy to two wins in a Six Nations campaign for only the second time.

Italy are, without doubt, heading in the right direction under coach Jacques Brunel as memorable wins over France and Ireland in the RBS Six Nations showed. They are not there yet, but there were plenty of positives in a season which also saw them come close to recording first ever victories over Australia and England.

The signs that the Azzurri would enjoy such a season were not evident when they kicked off their November series with a narrow 28–23 win over Tonga at the Stadio Mario Rigamonti in Brescia. Lorenzo Cittadini's early try had given Italy the perfect start and they went into the last 15 minutes with a 12-point lead after being awarded a penalty try. However, they switched off as Tonga ensured a nervous finish for their hosts.

The error-strewn performance was hardly the best preparation for facing New Zealand a week later, but Italy made the world champions work hard for their 42–10 victory, the score only blowing out in the last 20 minutes with tries from Cory Jane and a Julian Savea double.

If the Italians were hoping to go one better against Australia a week later in Florence they gave themselves a mountain to climb by going in 22–6 behind at half-time. That deficit, though, had been cut to just three points by the 55th minute thanks to Luciano Orquera's boot and Robert Barbieri's try. The score remained that way until the final minute, when Orquera had the chance to complete the comeback with a penalty, only to send his kick just wide.

Italy may have come up just short of that maiden victory over the Wallabies, but for captain Sergio Parisse there were still positives to take away from the three outings in November.

"We played a pretty bad game against the Tongans in Brescia, failing to impose our rugby as we wanted to do, but we achieved the result in the end which is good," explained Parisse, back in the Azzurri shirt after missing the June tour through injury. "It's always difficult to play the Pacific Island sides. They're physical and consistent, so the positive from that game was definitely the result.

"One week later, we played a much better game against New Zealand, but unfortunately only for 60 minutes. The final score was pretty severe, which is pretty obvious when you're not challenging an opponent like the All Blacks until the final whistle.

"The last match in Florence was a different story. We underperformed in the first half but we expressed our rugby at its best in the second. We must learn that, if we play to our best, we can effectively challenge any opponent.

"We absolutely drew confidence from those two games, despite the final results. It was frustrating to get so close against Australia, but at the same time it made us understand where we can go. This is the biggest positive from the defeat."

Italy's focus going into the Six Nations was, in Parisse's words, "to keep on improving and we achieved this". The annual competition could certainly not have started better for Italy with a 23–18 victory over France, their second in a row in Rome. Parisse scored Italy's opening try and another talisman, Martin Castrogiovanni, added another as Orquera's performance again suggested that the Azzurri's quest to find the fly half they had sought since Diego Dominguez retired a decade earlier was over.

"When we beat France in 2011 there were more negatives from their performance than positives from ours. This time, we built up our victory thanks to our game plan, we imposed our rugby which is exactly what Jacques Brunel is expecting from us," explained Parisse.

A week later and Italy were brought back down to earth at Murrayfield with a 34–10 defeat by Scotland after failing "to adapt our game plan to the situation" and paying the price for an error-strewn performance.

It was to get worse when Wales came to Rome at the end of February with three Kris Burton penalties all Italy were able to muster in a 26–9 defeat. It was a difficult match for Parisse to watch from the sidelines, the number 8 having been suspended for insulting a referee in a Stade Français match.

"It was probably our worst game in the Six Nations, but we were facing a great team," admitted Parisse, who had his suspension reduced to 20 days on appeal, making him available for the final two matches. "It was frustrating to watch the game from the sideline. We didn't express our rugby at all. We didn't respect the game plan and Wales took advantage of that."

With their talisman back, Italy gave England "a massive scare" in the words of forwards coach Graham Rowntree in losing 18–11 at Twickenham. Italy had suffered a setback with Castrogiovanni forced off before the half-hour mark and England wasted several first-half chances, but the Azzurri came alive after the break with Orquera's boot and the only try of the match by Luke McLean setting up a nervous last quarter for their hosts.

"The first half was a disappointing one and, despite that, we were close to them on the scoreboard (12–3)," recalled Parisse. "We understood that to challenge England was within us, that by playing our rugby we could come back into the game and that was exactly what happened. Minute by minute in the second half we gained confidence in ourselves and delivered a big performance."

A first win over England had slipped through their grasp for a second year running, but the Azzurri ensured a new chapter in their history was written a week later with a 22–15 victory over Ireland, their first in the history of the Six Nations. Ireland suffered a spate of injuries but that took nothing away from the Italian performance which ensured an emotional farewell for prop Andrea Lo Cicero.

"We had never beaten Ireland in the Six Nations before. None of us had ever beaten them in a Test in our careers because the last win was achieved in 1997," explained Parisse. "After the England game we were pretty tired, so we asked our coaches for an extra day off to recover and focus on the Ireland game. We guaranteed them a great performance as payback and we kept to our word.

"From a general point of view, this Six Nations was one our best since we joined the Championship. We won two games, we were close to achieving an historic result at Twickenham, but we also played two poor games in Scotland and at home against Wales. We are growing, but we still need to find continuity."

The fact that Italy's two wins came over sides they will face in the

Rugby World Cup 2015 pool stages was also not lost on Parisse. "No doubt we sent them a message that Italy is growing and wants to reach the knockout stages. Even if it is still a long way until our first RWC 2015 match (against France) at Twickenham, now everybody knows that Italy cannot be underestimated."

Italy therefore headed to South Africa in June full of confidence for the quadrangular tournament involving the Springboks, Samoa and Scotland. However, things did not go according to plan and the Azzurri returned home with three frustrating defeats.

First up was a 44–10 loss to South Africa despite the Azzurri having 57 per cent of possession and dominating in the scrums against a side who scored many of their five tries off turnovers. A week later Samoa were simply too good for Italy on the day despite the efforts of the tireless Parisse, running in five tries in a 39–10 victory in Nelspruit which condemned their opponents to the third place play-off against Scotland the following week. This was a much closer affair with the set-piece battle intense between two strong forward packs. In fact it went right down to the wire, flanker Alasdair Strokosch scoring a try from a quick tap in the dying seconds, which Greig Laidlaw converted to snatch a 30–29 victory in Pretoria.

"It would have been important to build on our Six Nations results and performances but we lacked in continuity during the tour. We lost our focus and we suffered three defeats in a row, which is something we did not expect or want," admitted Parisse.

"We played our rugby for only 25 minutes against the Springboks, and we completely slipped up against Samoa. The Islanders are a high-level team today, mixing individual talent and a solid game plan, but we were poor at the breakdowns, confused and inefficient. It was a really bad game. Scotland, in the end, was disappointing. We were in control of the game and we wasted our efforts with a defensive mistake in injury-time. A win could have changed our tour."

While Italy's senior team disappointed in South Africa, their Under 20s achieved their target of securing an immediate return to the IRB Junior World Championship in 2014 by winning the IRB Junior World Rugby Trophy in Chile, beating Canada 45–23 in the final in early June. It was a fitting finale for coach Gianluca Guidi who admitted he could "retire with the joy of the win", while captain Angelo Espósito said he had "no words to describe this moment". Emerging Italy also performed well in the IRB Nations Cup, having to settle for the runners-up spot again after losing 26–13 in the title decider with defending champions Romania in Bucharest.

The future looks bright and Parisse certainly believes so. "There is no doubt, we're much more confident in ourselves and in our rugby than in the past. We know that, if we play to our best level, we can challenge anybody. Believe me, there's still much work to do from our side and I'm sure the best is yet to come."

ITALY INTERNATIONAL STATISTICS

MATCH RECORDS UP TO 10 OCTOBER 2013

WINNING MARGIN

Date	Opponent	Result	Winning Margin
18/05/1994	Czech Republic	104 –8	**96**
07/10/2006	Portugal	83–0	**83**
17/06/1993	Croatia	76–11	**65**
19/06/1993	Morocco	70–9	**61**
02/03/1996	Portugal	64–3	**61**

MOST POINTS IN A MATCH

BY THE TEAM

Date	Opponent	Result	Points
18/05/1994	Czech Republic	104–8	**104**
07/10/2006	Portugal	83–0	**83**
17/06/1993	Croatia	76–11	**76**
19/06/1993	Morocco	70–9	**70**

BY A PLAYER

Date	Player	Opponent	Points
10/11/2001	Diego Dominguez	Fiji	**29**
05/02/2000	Diego Dominguez	Scotland	**29**
01/07/1983	Stefano Bettarello	Canada	**29**
21/05/1994	Diego Dominguez	Netherlands	**28**
20/12/1997	Diego Dominguez	Ireland	**27**

MOST TRIES IN A MATCH

BY THE TEAM

Date	Opponent	Result	Tries
18/05/1994	Czech Republic	104–8	**16**
07/10/2006	Portugal	83–0	**13**
18/11/1998	Netherlands	67–7	**11**
17/06/1993	Croatia	76–11	**11**

BY A PLAYER

Date	Player	Opponent	Tries
19/06/1993	Ivan Francescato	Morocco	**4**
10/10/1937	Renzo Cova	Belgium	**4**

MOST CONVERSIONS IN A MATCH

BY THE TEAM

Date	Opponent	Result	Cons
18/05/1994	Czech Republic	104–8	**12**
19/06/1993	Morocco	70–9	**10**
17/06/1993	Croatia	76–11	**9**
07/10/2006	Portugal	83–0	**9**

BY A PLAYER

Date	Player	Opponent	Cons
18/05/1994	Luigi Troiani	Czech Republic	**12**
19/06/1993	Gabriel Filizzola	Morocco	**10**
17/06/1993	Luigi Troiani	Croatia	**9**

MOST PENALTIES IN A MATCH

BY THE TEAM

Date	Opponent	Result	Pens
01/10/1994	Romania	24–6	**8**
27/11/2010	Fiji	24–16	**8**
10/11/2001	Fiji	66–10	**7**

BY A PLAYER

Date	Player	Opponent	Pens
01/10/1994	Diego Dominguez	Romania	**8**
27/11/2010	Mirco Bergamasco	Fiji	**8**
10/11/2001	Diego Dominguez	Fiji	**7**

MOST DROP GOALS IN A MATCH

BY THE TEAM

Date	Opponent	Result	DGs
07/10/1990	Romania	29–21	**3**
05/02/2000	Scotland	34–20	**3**
11/07/1973	Transvaal	24–28	**3**

BY A PLAYER

Date	Player	Opponent	DGs
05/02/2000	Diego Dominguez	Scotland	**3**
11/07/1973	Rocco Caligiuri	Transvaal	**3**

MOST CAPPED PLAYERS

Player	Caps
Andrea lo Cicero	103
Alessandro Troncon	101
Martin Castrogiovanni	98
Sergio Parisse	98
Marco Bortolami	97

LEADING PENALTY SCORERS

Player	Pens
Diego Dominguez	209
Stefano Bettarello	106
Luigi Troiani	57
Ramiro Pez	52
Mirco Bergamasco	49

LEADING TRY SCORERS

Player	Tries
Marcello Cuttitta	25
Paolo Vaccari	22
Manrico Marchetto	21
Carlo Checchinato	21
Alessandro Troncon	19

LEADING DROP GOAL SCORERS

Player	DGs
Diego Dominguez	19
Stefano Bettarello	15
Ramiro Pez	6

LEADING CONVERSION SCORERS

Player	Cons
Diego Dominguez	127
Luigi Troiani	57
Stefano Bettarello	46
David Bortolussi	35
Ramiro Pez	33

LEADING POINT SCORERS

Player	Points
Diego Dominguez	983
Stefano Bettarello	483
Luigi Troiani	294
Ramiro Pez	260
Mirco Bergamasco	256

ITALY INTERNATIONAL PLAYERS
UP TO 10 OCTOBER 2013

E Abbiati 1968 *WGe*, 1970 *R*, 1971 *Mor*, *F*, 1972 *Pt*, *Sp*, *Sp*, *Yug*, 1973 *Pt*, *ETv*, 1974 *Leo*
A Agosti 1933 *Cze*
M Aguero 2005 *Tg*, *Ar*, *Fj*, 2006 *Fj*, 2007 *Ur*, *Ar*, *I*, *Pt*, 2008 *A*, *Ar*, *Pl*, 2009 *A*, 2010 *I*, *E*, *S*, *F*, *W*, 2013 *SA*, *S*
A Agujari 1967 *Pt*
E Aio 1974 *WGe*
G Aiolfi 1952 *Sp*, *Ger*, *F*, 1953 *F*, 1955 *Ger*, *F*
A Alacevich 1939 *R*
A Albonico 1934 *R*, 1935 *F*, 1936 *Ger*, *R*, 1937 *Ger*, *R*, *Bel*, *Ger*, *F*, 1938 *Ger*
N Aldorvandi 1994 *Sp*, *CZR*, *H*
M Alfonsetti 1994 *F*
E Allevi 1929 *Sp*, 1933 *Cze*
I Aloisio 1933 *Cze*, *Cze*, 1934 *Cat*, *R*, 1935 *Cat*, 1936 *Ger*, *R*
A Altigeri 1973 *Rho*, *WTv*, *Bor*, *NEC*, *Nat*, *Leo*, *FS*, *Tva*, *Cze*, *Yug*, *A*, 1974 *Pt*, *WGe*, 1975 *F*, *E*, *Pol*, *H*, *Sp*, 1976 *F*, *R*, *J*, 1978 *Ar*, *USS*, *Sp*, 1979 *F*, *Pol*, *R*
T Altissimi 1929 *Sp*
V Ambron 1962 *Ger*, *R*, 1963 *F*, 1964 *Ger*, *F*, 1965 *F*, *Cze*, 1966 *F*, *Ger*, *R*, 1967 *Pt*, *R*, 1968 *Pt*, *WGe*, *Yug*, 1969 *Bul*, *Sp*, *Bel*, 1970 *Mad*, *Mad*, *R*, 1971 *Mor*, 1972 *Sp*, *Sp*
R Ambrosio 1987 *NZ*, *USS*, *Sp*, 1988 *F*, *R*, *A*, *I*, 1989 *R*, *Sp*, *Ar*, *Z*, *USS*
B Ancillotti 1978 *Sp*, 1979 *F*, *Pol*, *R*
E Andina 1952 *F*, 1955 *F*
C Angelozzi 1979 *E*, *Mor*, 1980 *Coo*
A Angioli 1960 *Ger*, *F*, 1961 *Ger*, *F*, 1962 *F*, *Ger*, *R*, 1963 *F*
A Angrisiani 1979 *Mor*, *F*, *Pol*, *USS*, *Mor*, 1980 *Coo*, 1984 *Tun*
S Annibal 1980 *Fj*, *Coo*, *Pol*, *Sp*, 1981 *F*, *WGe*, 1982 *R*, *E*, *WGe*, 1983 *F*, *USS*, *Sp*, *Mor*, *F*, *A*, 1984 *F*, 1985 *F*, *Z*, *Z*, 1986 *Tun*, *F*, *Pt*, 1990 *F*
JM Antoni 2001 *Nm*, *SA*
C Appiani 1976 *Sp*, 1977 *Mor*, *Pol*, *Sp*, 1978 *USS*
S Appiani 1985 *R*, 1986 *Pt*, 1988 *A*, 1989 *F*
O Arancio 1993 *Rus*, 1994 *CZR*, *H*, *A*, *A*, *R*, *W*, *F*, 1995 *S*, *I*, *Sa*, *E*, *Ar*, *F*, *R*, *NZ*, *SA*, 1996 *W*, *Pt*, *W*, *A*, *E*, *S*, 1997 *I*, *I*, 1998 *S*, *Ar*, *E*, 1999 *F*, *W*, *I*, *SA*, *E*, *NZ*
D Armellin 1965 *Cze*, 1966 *Ger*, 1968 *Pt*, *WGe*, *Yug*, 1969 *Bul*, *Sp*, *Bel*, *F*
A Arrigoni 1949 *Cze*
G Artuso 1977 *Pol*, *R*, 1978 *Sp*, 1979 *F*, *E*, *NZ*, *Mor*, 1980 *F*, *R*, *JAB*, 1981 *F*, 1982 *F*, *E*, *Mor*, 1983 *F*, *R*, *USS*, *C*, *C*, 1984 *USS*, 1985 *R*, *EngB*, *USS*, *R*, 1986 *Tun*, *F*, *Tun*, 1987 *Pt*, *F*, *R*, *NZ*
E Augeri 1962 *F*, *Ger*, *R*, 1963 *F*
A Autore 1961 *Ger*, *F*, 1962 *F*, 1964 *Ger*, 1966 *Ger*, 1968 *Pt*, *WGe*, *Yug*, 1969 *Bul*, *Sp*, *Bel*, *F*
L Avigo 1959 *F*, 1962 *F*, *Ger*, *R*, 1963 *F*, 1964 *Ger*, *F*, 1965 *F*, *Cze*, 1966 *Ger*, *R*
R Aymonod 1933 *Cze*, 1934 *Cat*, *R*, 1935 *F*
A Azzali 1981 *WGe*, 1982 *F*, *R*, *WGe*, 1983 *F*, *R*, *USS*, *Sp*, *Mor*, *F*, 1984 *F*, *Mor*, *R*, 1985 *R*, *EngB*, *Sp*

S Babbo 1996 *Pt*
A Bacchetti 2009 *I*, *S*
A Balducci 1929 *Sp*
F Baraldi 1973 *Cze*, *Yug*, 1974 *Mid*, *Sus*, *Oxo*, 1975 *E*, *Pol*, *H*, *Sp*, 1976 *F*, *R*, *A*, 1977 *F*, *Mor*, *Cze*
R Baraldi 1971 *R*
A Barattin 1996 *A*, *E*
S Barba 1985 *R*, *EngB*, 1986 *E*, *A*, 1987 *Pt*, *F*, *R*, *Ar*, *Fj*,

1988 *R, USS, A*, 1990 *F, Pol, Sp, H, R, USS*, 1991 *F, R, Nm, Nm, US, E, USS*, 1992 *Sp, F, R, R, S*, 1993 *Sp, F, Cro, Mor, Sp*
RJ Barbieri 2006 *J, Fj, Pt*, 2007 *Ur, Ar, I*, 2008 *SA*, 2010 *Ar, A, Fj*, 2011 *E, W, F, S, S, A*, 2012 *F, E, I, W, S, Ar, C, US, Tg, NZ, A*, 2013 *E, SA, S*
G Barbini 1978 *USS*
M Barbini 2002 *NZ, Sp, Ar, A*, 2003 *I, NZ*, 2004 *F, I, R, J, NZ, US*, 2005 *W, E*, 2007 *I*
N Barbini 1953 *Ger, R*, 1954 *Sp, F*, 1955 *Ger, F, Sp, Cze*, 1956 *Ger*, 1957 *Ger*, 1958 *R*, 1960 *Ger, F*
F Bargelli 1979 *E, Sp, Mor, F, Pol, USS, NZ, Mor*, 1980 *F, R, Fj, Sp*, 1981 *F, R*
S Barilari 1948 *Cze*, 1953 *Ger, R*
M Baroni 1999 *F, W, I, SA, SA*, 2000 *C*
V Barzaghi 1929 *Sp*, 1930 *Sp*, 1933 *Cze*
JL Basei 1979 *E, Sp, Mor, F, Pol, USS, NZ, Mor*, 1980 *F, R, Fj, JAB, Coo, USS*, 1981 *R*
A Battagion 1948 *F, Cze*
F Battaglini 1948 *F*
M Battaglini 1940 *R, Ger*, 1951 *Sp*, 1953 *F, R*
A Becca 1937 *R*, 1938 *Ger*, 1939 *R*, 1940 *Ger*
E Bellinazzo 1958 *R*, 1959 *F*, 1960 *Ger, F*, 1961 *Ger, F*, 1962 *F, Ger*, 1964 *Ger, F*, 1966 *F, Ger, R*, 1967 *F*
A Benatti 2001 *Fj, SA, Sa*, 2002 *W*, 2003 *NZ*
A Benettin 2012 *C*
C Bentivoglio 1977 *Pol*
T Benvenuti 2010 *Ar, A, Fj*, 2011 *W, F, S, J, S, A, Rus, US, I*, 2012 *F, E, I, W, S, Ar, C, US, Tg, NZ, A*, 2013 *F, S, W, E, I*
D Beretta 1993 *S*
A Bergamasco 1973 *Bor, Tva*, 1977 *Pol*, 1978 *USS*
M Bergamasco 1998 *H, E*, 1999 *SA, E*, 2000 *S, W, I, E, F, C*, 2001 *I, E, F, S, W, Fj, SA, Sa*, 2002 *F, S, W, I, E, NZ, Sp, R, A*, 2003 *W, I, S, I, Geo, NZ, Tg, W*, 2004 *J, C, NZ*, 2005 *I, W, Ar, A, Ar, Fj*, 2006 *I, E, F, J, Fj, Pt, Rus, A, Ar, C*, 2007 *F, S, W, J, NZ, R, Pt, S*, 2008 *I, E, W, Ar, A, Ar, Pl*, 2009 *E, I, S, W, F, A, NZ, NZ, SA, Sa*, 2010 *I, E, S, F, W*, 2011 *J, Rus, US, I*, 2012 *E, Ar, C, US, NZ*, 2013 *Sa*
M Bergamasco 2002 *F, S, W, Ar, A*, 2003 *W, I, E, F, S, S, Geo, NZ, C*, 2004 *E, F, S, I, W*, 2005 *I, W, S, Tg, Ar, Fj*, 2006 *I, E, F, W, S, J, Fj, Pt, Rus, A, Ar, C*, 2007 *F, E, S, W, I, J, I, NZ, R, S*, 2008 *I, E, W, F, S, Ar, A, Ar, Pl*, 2009 *E, I, S, W, F, A, NZ, NZ, SA, Sa*, 2010 *I, E, S, F, W, SA, SA, Ar, A, Fj*, 2011 *I, E, W, F, S, S, A, US, I*, 2012 *W, S, NZ, A*
L Bernabo 1970 *Mad, Mad, R*, 1972 *Sp, Sp*
V Bernabò 2004 *US*, 2005 *Tg, Fj*, 2007 *E, S, W, I, Ur, Ar, J, I, NZ, R*, 2010 *W, SA*, 2011 *I, E, W, S*, 2013 *SA, Sa*
F Berni 1985 *R, Sp, Z, Z*, 1986 *E, A*, 1987 *R, NZ*, 1988 *A*, 1989 *F*
D Bertoli 1967 *R*
V Bertolotto 1936 *Ger, R*, 1937 *Ger, R*, 1942 *R*, 1948 *F*
O Bettarello 1958 *F*, 1959 *F*, 1961 *Ger*
R Bettarello 1953 *Ger, R*
S Bettarello 1979 *Pol, E, Sp, F, NZ, Mor*, 1980 *F, R, Fj, JAB, Coo, Pol, USS, Sp*, 1981 *F, R, USS, WGe*, 1982 *F, R, E, WGe, Mor*, 1983 *F, R, USS, C, Sp, Mor, F, A*, 1984 *F, Mor, R, Tun, USS*, 1985 *F, R, EngB, Sp, Z, USS, R*, 1986 *Tun, F, Pt, E, A, Tun, USS*, 1987 *R, USS, Sp*, 1988 *USS, A*
L Bettella 1969 *Sp, Bel, F*
R Bevilacqua 1937 *Bel, Ger, F*, 1938 *Ger*, 1939 *Ger, R*, 1940 *R, Ger*, 1942 *R*
C Bezzi 2003 *W, I, E, F, S, I, NZ, W*, 2004 *US*, 2005 *Ar, A*
G Biadene 1958 *R*, 1959 *F*
G Bigi 1930 *Sp*, 1933 *Cze*
M Bimbati 1989 *Z*
M Birtig 1998 *H*, 1999 *F*
F Blessano 1975 *F, R, Pol, H, Sp*, 1976 *F, R, J*, 1977 *F, Mor, Pol, R, Cze, R, Sp*, 1978 *F, Ar, Sp*, 1979 *F, Pol, R*
L Boccaletto 1969 *Bul, Bel, F*, 1970 *Cze, Mad, Mad, R*, 1971 *F, R*, 1972 *Pt, Sp, Sp*, 1975 *E*
S Boccazzi 1985 *Z*, 1988 *USS*
R Bocchino 2010 *I, F, W, SA, A, Fj*, 2011 *J, S, A, Rus, US, I*, 2012 *Ar, US*
M Bocconelli 1967 *R*
M Bollesan 1963 *F*, 1964 *F*, 1965 *F*, 1966 *F, Ger*, 1967 *F, Pt*, 1968 *Pt, WGe, Yug*, 1969 *Bul, Sp, Bel, F*, 1970 *Cze, Mad, Mad, R*, 1971 *Mor, F, R*, 1972 *Pt, Pt, Sp, Sp, Yug*, 1973 *Pt, Rho, WTv, Bor, NEC, Nat, ETv, Leo, FS, Tva, Yug, A*, 1974 *Pt, Mid, Sus, Oxo, WGe, Leo*, 1975 *F, Sp, Cze*
A Bona 1972 *Sp, Yug*, 1973 *Rho, WTv, Bor, NEC, Nat, ETv, Leo, FS, Tva, Cze, Yug, A*, 1974 *Pt, WGe, Leo*, 1975 *F, Sp, R, Cze, E, Pol, H, Sp*, 1976 *F, R, J, A, Sp*, 1977 *F, Mor*, 1978 *Ar, USS, Sp*, 1979 *F, Sp, Mor, F, Pol, USS, NZ, Mor*, 1980 *F, R, Fj, JAB, Pol, Sp*, 1981 *F*
L Bonaiti 1979 *R*, 1980 *Pol*
G Bonati 1939 *Ger, R*
S Bonetti 1972 *Yug*, 1973 *Rho, WTv, Bor, NEC, Nat, ETv, Leo, FS, Tva*, 1974 *Pt, Mid, Sus, Oxo, Leo*, 1975 *F, Sp, R, Cze, E, Pol, H, Sp*, 1976 *R, J, A, Sp*, 1977 *F, Mor, R, Sp*, 1978 *F*, 1979 *F*, 1980 *USS*
S Bonfante 1936 *Ger, R*
G Bonino 1949 *F*
M Bonomi 1988 *F, R*, 1990 *Sp, H, R, USS*, 1991 *F, R, Nm, Nm, E, NZ, USS*, 1992 *R, R*, 1993 *Cro, Mor, Sp, F, S*, 1994 *Sp, R, H, A, A, W*, 1995 *S, I, Sa, F, Ar, R, NZ*, 1996 *W*
S Bordon 1990 *R, USS*, 1991 *Nm, USS*, 1992 *F, R*, 1993 *Sp, F, Pt, Rus, F*, 1994 *R, A, A, R, W, F*, 1995 *I, E, Ar, F, Ar, NZ, SA*, 1996 *W, A, E*, 1997 *I, F*
L Borsetto 1977 *Pol*
V Borsetto 1948 *F, Cze*
M Bortolami 2001 *Nm, SA, Fj, SA, Sa*, 2002 *F, S, W, I, E, NZ, Sp, R, Ar, A*, 2003 *W, I, E, S, Geo, Tg, C*, 2004 *E, F, S, I, W, R, J, C, NZ*, 2005 *I, W, S, E, F, Ar, Ar, A, Tg, Ar, Fj*, 2006 *I, E, F, W, S, J, Fj, Pt, Rus, A, Ar, C*, 2007 *F, E, S, W, I, J, I, NZ, R, Pt*, 2008 *W, F, S, A, Ar, Pl*, 2009 *E, S, W, F, A, A, NZ*, 2010 *I, E, S, F, W, SA, SA*, 2011 *J, A, Rus, I*, 2012 *F, E, I, W, S, Ar*, 2013 *SA, Sa, S*
G Bortolini 1933 *Cze*, 1934 *Cat*
D Bortolussi 2006 *J, Fj, Pt, Rus, Ar, C*, 2007 *Ur, Ar, J, I, NZ, R, Pt, S*, 2008 *I, E*
L Boscaino 1967 *Pt*
L Bossi 1940 *R, Ger*
T Botes 2012 *F, E, I, W, S, Tg, NZ, A*, 2013 *F, S, W, E, I, SA, Sa, S*
A Bottacchiara 1991 *NZ, USS*, 1992 *Sp, F, R, R*
G Bottacin 1956 *Cze*
O Bottonelli 1929 *Sp*, 1934 *R*, 1935 *Cat, F*, 1937 *Ger*, 1939 *Ger*
L Bove 1948 *Cze*, 1949 *F, Cze*
O Bracaglia 1939 *R*
M Braga 1958 *R*
L Bricchi 1929 *Sp*, 1930 *Sp*, 1933 *Cze*
L Brighetti 1934 *Cat*
A Brunelli 1969 *Bel*, 1970 *Mad*, 1971 *F*
M Brunello 1988 *I*, 1989 *F*, 1990 *F, Sp, H, R, USS*, 1993 *Pt*
S Brusin 1957 *Ger*
KS Burton 2007 *Ur, Ar*, 2009 *A, NZ*, 2011 *I, E, W, F, S*, 2012 *F, E, I, W, S, Ar, C, US, Tg*, 2013 *F, S, W*
P Buso 2008 *W*
G Busson 1957 *Ger*, 1958 *R*, 1959 *F*, 1960 *Ger, F*, 1961 *Ger, F*, 1962 *F, Ger*, 1963 *F*

F Caccia-Dominioni 1935 *F*, 1937 *Ger*
C Caione 1995 *R*, 1996 *Pt*, 1997 *F, R*, 1998 *Rus, Ar, H, E*, 1999 *F, S, SA, Ur, Sp, Fj, Tg, NZ*, 2000 *Sa, Fj, C, R, NZ*, 2001 *I, E, S, Fj*
R Caligiuri 1969 *F*, 1973 *Pt, Rho, WTv, NEC, Nat, ETv, Leo, FS, Tva*, 1975 *E, Pol, H, Sp*, 1976 *F, R, J, A, Sp*, 1978 *F, Ar, USS, Sp*, 1979 *F, Pol, R*
A Caluzzi 1970 *R*, 1971 *Mor, F*, 1972 *Pt, Pt, Sp, Sp*, 1973 *Pt*, 1974 *Oxo, WGe, Leo*
P Camiscioni 1975 *E*, 1976 *R, J, A, Sp*, 1977 *F*, 1978 *F*
M Campagna 1933 *Cze*, 1934 *Cat*, 1936 *Ger, R*, 1937 *Ger, R, Bel*, 1938 *Ger*
GJ Canale 2003 *S, Geo, NZ, Tg, C, W*, 2004 *S, I, W, R, J, C*, 2005 *I, Ar, Ar, A, Tg, Ar, Fj*, 2006 *I, E, F, W, S, A, Ar, C*, 2007 *F, E, S, W, J, I, R, Pt, S*, 2008 *I, E, W, F, S, A*, 2009 *E, I, S, W, F, A, NZ, NZ, Sa*, 2010 *I, E, S, F, W, SA, SA, Ar, A, Fj*, 2011 *I, E, W, F, S, J, S, A, Rus, US, I*, 2012 *F, E, I, W, S*, 2013 *F, S, W, E, I, Sa, S*
PL Canavosio 2005 *A, Tg, Fj*, 2006 *I, E, F, W, S, Fj, Pt, Rus*,

THE COUNTRIES

A, Ar, 2007 Ar, J, I, Pt, 2008 I, SA, Ar, A, Ar, 2009 S, W, F, A, 2010 E, S, F, W, Ar, A, 2011 I, E, W, S, J, Rus
C Cantoni 1956 *Ger, F, Cze*, 1957 *Ger*
L Capitani 1989 *F, R, Sp, Ar, Z, USS*
M Capuzzoni 1993 *Cro*, 1995 *I*
A Caranci 1989 *R*
M Carli 1955 *Sp, Cze*
C Carloni 1935 *F*
D Carpente 2004 *R, J*
T Carraro 1937 *R*
T Casagrande 1977 *R*
U Cassellato 1990 *Sp*, 1992 *R, S*, 1993 *Sp, F, Pt, Cro, Mor, F, S*
R Cassina 1992 *R, S*
A Castellani 1994 *CZR*, 1995 *Ar, R*, 1996 *W, S*, 1997 *Ar, R, I*, 1998 *S, W, Rus, H, E*, 1999 *F, W, Ur, Sp, Fj, Tg, NZ*
ML Castrogiovanni 2002 *NZ, Sp, R, Ar, A*, 2003 *I, E, F, S, I, Geo, NZ, Tg, C, W*, 2004 *E, F, S, I, W, J*, 2005 *I, W, S, E, F, Ar, A, Ar, Fj*, 2006 *I, E, F, W, S, Pt, Rus, A, Ar, C*, 2007 *F, E, S, J, I, NZ, R, Pt, S*, 2008 *I, E, W, F, S*, 2009 *E, I, S, W, F, NZ, SA, Sa*, 2010 *I, E, S, F, W, SA, Ar, A, Fj*, 2011 *I, E, W, F, S, J, S, A, Rus, US, I*, 2012 *F, E, S, Ar, C, US, Tg, NZ, A*, 2013 *F, S, W, E, SA, Sa, S*
L Catotti 1979 *Pol, E*
A Cazzini 1933 *Cze, Cze*, 1934 *Cat, R*, 1935 *Cat, F*, 1936 *Ger, R*, 1937 *Ger, R, Bel, Ger, F*, 1939 *R*, 1942 *R*
G Cecchetto 1955 *F*
A Cecchetto-Milani 1952 *Sp, Ger, F*
G Cecchin 1970 *Cze, R*, 1971 *F, R*, 1972 *Pt*
G Ceccotti 1972 *Pt, Sp*
L Cedaro 2013 *S*
A Centinari 1930 *Sp*
R Centinari 1935 *F*, 1936 *Ger, R*, 1937 *Bel, F*, 1939 *Ger*
A Cepolino 1999 *Ur, Sp, Fj, Tg, NZ*
L Cesani 1929 *Sp*, 1930 *Sp*, 1935 *Cat, F*
F Ceselin 1989 *F, R*
C Checchinato 1990 *Sp*, 1991 *Nm, Nm, US, NZ, USS*, 1992 *Sp, F, R, S*, 1993 *Pt, Cro, Sp, F, Rus, F, S*, 1994 *Sp, R, CZR, A, A, R, W, F*, 1995 *Sa, F, Ar, R, NZ*, 1996 *W, E*, 1997 *I, F, Ar, R, SA, I*, 1998 *Rus, Ar, H, E*, 1999 *F, S, SA, SA, Ur, Fj, E, Tg, NZ*, 2000 *S, W, I, E, F, Sa, Fj*, 2001 *I, E, F, S, W, Nm, SA, Ur, Ar, Fj, SA, Sa*, 2002 *F, S, W, Sp, R*, 2003 *Geo, NZ, Tg, C, W*, 2004 *E, F, I*
G Chechinato 1973 *Cze, Yug, A*, 1974 *WGe, Leo*
G Cherubini 1949 *Cze*, 1951 *Sp*
A Chillon 2013 *S*
T Ciccio 1992 *R*, 1993 *Sp, F, Mor, F*
E Cicognani 1940 *Ger*
R Cinelli 1968 *Pt*, 1969 *Sp*
G Cinti 1973 *Rho, WTv, ETv*
F Cioni 1967 *Pt, R*, 1968 *Pt*, 1969 *Bul, Sp, Bel*, 1970 *Cze, Mad, Mad, R*
L Cittadini 2008 *I*, 2010 *SA, SA, A*, 2011 *J, S, A, Rus*, 2012 *F, E, I, W, S, Tg, NZ, A*, 2013 *F, S, W, E, I, SA, Sa, S*
L Clerici 1939 *Ger*
A Colella 1983 *R, USS, C, C, Sp, Mor, F, A, USS*, 1984 *R, Tun, USS*, 1985 *F, R, EngB, Sp, Z, Z, USS, R*, 1986 *Tun, F, Pt, E, A, Tun, USS*, 1987 *Pt, F, Ar, Fj, USS, Sp*, 1988 *F, R, USS*, 1989 *R, Sp, Ar*, 1990 *Pol, R*
O Collodo 1977 *Pol, Cze, R, Sp*, 1978 *F*, 1986 *Pt, E, A, USS*, 1987 *Pt, F, R, NZ, Ar, Fj*
S Colombini 1971 *R*
F Colombo 1933 *Cze*
G Colussi 1957 *F*, 1958 *F*, 1964 *Ger, F*, 1965 *F, Cze*, 1968 *Pt*
C Colusso 1982 *F*
A Comin 1955 *Ger, F, Sp, F, Cze*, 1956 *F, Cze*, 1958 *F*
U Conforto 1965 *Cze*, 1966 *Ger, R*, 1967 *F, R*, 1968 *Pt, WGe, Yug*, 1969 *Bul, Sp, Bel, F*, 1970 *Cze*, 1971 *Mor, F*, 1972 *Yug*, 1973 *Pt*
F Coppio 1993 *F, Pt, Cro, Mor, Sp*
L Cornella 1999 *Sp*
R Corvo 1985 *F, Sp, Z*
U Cossara 1971 *Mor, F, R*, 1972 *Pt, Sp*, 1973 *Pt, Rho, NEC, Nat, Leo, FS, Tva, Cze*, 1975 *F, Sp, R, Cze, E, Pol, H*, 1976 *F, J, A*, 1977 *Pol*
A Costa 1940 *R, Ger*, 1942 *R*
S Costanzo 2004 *R, C, NZ, US*
E Cottafava 1973 *Pt*
R Cova 1937 *Bel, Ger, F*, 1938 *Ger*, 1939 *Ger, R*, 1942 *R*
C Covi 1988 *F, R, USS, A, I*, 1989 *F, R, Sp, Ar, Z, USS*, 1990 *F, Pol, R*, 1991 *F, R, Nm, Nm*, 1996 *E*
F Crepaz 1972 *Pt*
M Crescenzo 1984 *R*
U Crespi 1933 *Cze, Cze*, 1934 *Cat, R*, 1935 *Cat*, 1937 *Ger*
W Cristofoletto 1992 *R*, 1993 *Mor, Sp, F*, 1996 *Pt, A, E, S*, 1997 *I, F, F, Ar, SA, I*, 1998 *S, W, Rus, Ar, E*, 1999 *F, S, W, I, SA, SA, Sp, Fj, E, NZ*, 2000 *E, F*
G Croci 1990 *Sp, H, R, USS*, 1991 *F, R, Nm, US, E, NZ, USS*, 1992 *Sp, F*, 1993 *S*, 1996 *S*, 1997 *I, F, F, Ar, R, SA, I*, 1998 *S, W*
R Crotti 1993 *S*, 1995 *SA*
L Cucchiarelli 1966 *R*, 1967 *R*
G Cucchiella 1973 *A*, 1974 *Sus*, 1979 *Sp, F, Pol, USS, NZ, Mor*, 1980 *F, R, Fj, JAB, Coo*, 1985 *USS, R*, 1986 *Tun, F, Pt, E*, 1987 *Pt, F, Fj*
M Cuttitta 1987 *Pt, F, R, NZ, Ar, Fj, USS, Sp*, 1988 *F, R*, 1989 *Z, USS*, 1990 *Pol, R*, 1991 *F, R, Nm, US, E, NZ, USS*, 1992 *Sp, F, R, R, S*, 1993 *Sp, F, Mor, Sp, F, F*, 1994 *Sp, R, H, A, A, F*, 1995 *S, I, Sa*, 1996 *S*, 1997 *I, F, F, Ar, R, SA, I*, 1998 *S, W, Rus, Ar*, 1999 *F*
M Cuttitta 1990 *Pol, R, Sp, H, R, USS*, 1991 *F, Nm, Nm, US, E, NZ, USS*, 1992 *Sp, F, R, R, S*, 1993 *Sp, F, Pt, Cro, Mor, Sp, F, Rus, F, S*, 1994 *Sp, R, CZR, H, A, A, W, F*, 1995 *S, I, Sa, E, Ar, F, Ar, R, NZ, SA*, 1996 *W, Pt, W, E, S*, 1997 *I, F, F, Ar, SA, I*, 1998 *W, Rus, Ar, H, E*, 1999 *F, S, W*, 2000 *S, W, I, E*

G Dagnini 1949 *F*
D Dal Maso 2000 *Sa, Fj*, 2001 *I, E*, 2004 *J, C, NZ, US*, 2005 *I, W, S, E, F, A*
M Dal Sie 1993 *Pt*, 1994 *R, W, F*, 1995 *F, Ar*, 1996 *A*
A D'Alberton 1966 *F, Ger, R*, 1967 *F, R*
D Daldoss 1979 *Pol, R, E, Sp, Mor*
C D'Alessio 1937 *R, Bel, F*, 1938 *Ger*, 1939 *Ger*
D Dallan 1999 *F, S, W*, 2000 *S, W, I, E, F, C, R, NZ*, 2001 *I, E, F, W, Fj, SA, Sa*, 2002 *F, S, I, E, NZ, Sp, R*, 2003 *W, I, E, F, S, Tg, C, W*, 2004 *E, F, S, I, W, C*, 2006 *J*, 2007 *F, E*
M Dallan 1997 *Ar, R, I*, 1998 *Ar, H, E*, 1999 *SA, SA*, 2000 *S, Sa, C*, 2001 *F, S*, 2003 *Tg, C*, 2004 *E, F, S*
A Danieli 1955 *Ger, F, Sp, F, Cze*
V D'Anna 1993 *Rus*
T D'Apice 2011 *J, S, Rus*, 2012 *F, E, I, W, S, C, US*
P Dari 1951 *Sp*, 1952 *Sp, Ger, F*, 1953 *Ger, R*, 1954 *Sp, F*
G De Angelis 1934 *Cat, R*, 1935 *Cat, F*, 1937 *R*
E De Anna 1972 *Yug*, 1973 *Cze, A*, 1975 *F, Sp, R, Cze, E, Pol, H, Sp*, 1976 *F, R*, 1978 *Ar, USS, Sp*, 1979 *F, R, Sp, Mor, F, USS, NZ*, 1980 *F, R, Fj, JAB*
R De Bernardo 1980 *USS, Sp*, 1981 *F, R, USS, WGe*, 1982 *R, E*, 1983 *R, USS, C, C, Sp, Mor, F, A, USS*, 1984 *F, USS*, 1985 *R, EngB*, 1988 *I*, 1989 *Ar, Z*
CF De Biase 1987 *Sp*, 1988 *F, A*
G De Carli 1996 *W*, 1997 *R*, 1998 *S, Rus, Ar, H, E*, 1999 *F, I, SA, SA, Ur, Fj*, 2000 *S, Sa, Fj*, 2001 *I, E, W, SA, Ur, Fj, SA, Sa*, 2002 *F, S, W, I, E*, 2003 *W, I, E*
B de Jager 2006 *J*
L De Joanni 1983 *C, Mor, F, A, USS*, 1984 *R, Tun, USS*, 1985 *F, R, EngB, Sp, Z*, 1986 *A, Tun*, 1989 *F, R, Sp, Ar, Z*, 1990 *R*
A De Marchi 2012 *Ar, US, Tg, NZ*, 2013 *F, S, W, E, I, SA, Sa, S*
R De Marchis 1935 *F*
H De Marco 1993 *Pt*
JR de Marigny 2004 *E, F, S, I, W, US*, 2005 *I, W, S*, 2007 *F, E, S, W, I, Ur, J, I, NZ, Pt*
A de Rossi 1999 *Ur, Sp, E*, 2000 *I, E, F, Sa, C, R, NZ*, 2001 *SA, Ur, Ar*, 2002 *I, E, NZ, Sp, R*, 2003 *W, I, E, F, S, I, Geo, Tg, C, W*, 2004 *E, F, S, I, W, R*
C De Rossi 1994 *Sp, H, R*
L De Santis 1952 *Sp*
M De Stefani 1989 *Z*
C De Vecchi 1948 *F*
G Degli Antoni 1963 *F*, 1965 *F*, 1966 *F, Ger, R*, 1967 *F*

M Del Bono 1960 *Ger, F*, 1961 *Ger, F*, 1962 *F, Ger, R*, 1963 *F*, 1964 *Ger, F*
G Del Bono 1951 *Sp*
CA Del Fava 2004 *W, R, J*, 2005 *I, W, S, E, F, Tg, Ar, Fj*, 2006 *I, E, F, W, S, J, Fj, Pt*, 2007 *Ur, Ar, Pt, S*, 2008 *I, E, W, F, S, SA, Ar, A, Ar*, 2009 *I, S, W, F, A, NZ, NZ, SA, Sa*, 2010 *I, S, F, SA, Ar, A, Fj*, 2011 *I, E, F, S, S, A*
C Della Valle 1968 *WGe, Yug*, 1969 *F*, 1970 *Mad, Mad*, 1971 *F*
S Dellapè 2002 *F, S, I, E, NZ, Sp, Ar*, 2003 *F, S, S, Geo, Tg, C, W*, 2004 *E, F, S, I, W, C, NZ*, 2005 *I, W, S, E, F, Ar*, 2006 *I, E, W, S, J, Fj, Pt, Rus, A, Ar, C*, 2007 *F, E, S, W, I, J, NZ, R, S*, 2008 *I, E, W, SA, Ar*, 2009 *E, I, S, W, F*, 2010 *Ar, A, Fj*, 2011 *I, E, W, F*
G Delli Ficorilli 1969 *F*
PE Derbyshire 2009 *A*, 2010 *E, F, SA, SA, Ar, A, Fj*, 2011 *F, S, J, S, A, Rus, US, I*, 2013 *F, S, W, I*
A Di Bello 1930 *Sp*, 1933 *Cze, Cze*, 1934 *Cat*
A Di Bernardo 2013 *SA, Sa, S*
F Di Carlo 1975 *Sp, R, Cze, Sp*, 1976 *F, Sp*, 1977 *Pol, R, Pol*, 1978 *Ar, USS*
B Di Cola 1973 *A*
G Di Cola 1972 *Sp, Sp*, 1973 *A*
F Di Maura 1971 *Mor*
A Di Zitti 1958 *R*, 1960 *Ger*, 1961 *Ger, F*, 1962 *F, Ger, R*, 1964 *Ger, F*, 1965 *F, Cze*, 1966 *F, Ger, R*, 1967 *F, Pt, R*, 1969 *Bul, Sp, Bel*, 1972 *Pt, Sp*
R Dolfato 1985 *F*, 1986 *A*, 1987 *Pt, Fj, USS, Sp*, 1988 *F, R, USS*
D Dominguez 1991 *F, R, Nm, Nm, US, E, NZ, USS*, 1992 *Sp, F, R, S*, 1993 *Sp, F, Rus, F, S*, 1994 *R, H, R, W*, 1995 *S, I, Sa, E, Ar, SA*, 1996 *W, Pt, W, A, E, S*, 1997 *I, F, F, Ar, R, SA, I*, 1998 *S, W, Rus, Ar, H, E*, 1999 *F, S, W, I, Ur, Sp, Fj, E, Tg, NZ*, 2000 *S, W, I, E, F*, 2001 *F, S, W, Fj, SA, Sa*, 2002 *F, S, I, E, Ar*, 2003 *W, I*
D Dondana 1929 *Sp*, 1930 *Sp*
G Dora 1929 *Sp*
R D'Orazio 1969 *Bul*
M Dotti IV 1939 *R*, 1940 *R, Ger*
F Dotto 1971 *Mor, F*, 1972 *Pt, Pt, Sp*
P Dotto 1993 *Sp, Cro*, 1994 *Sp, R*

J Erasmus 2008 *F, S, SA*

U Faccioli 1948 *F*
A Falancia 1975 *E, Pol*
G Faliva 1999 *SA*, 2002 *NZ, Ar, A*
G Faltiba 1993 *Pt*
G Fanton 1979 *Pol*
P Farina 1987 *F, NZ, Fj*
P Farinelli 1940 *R*, 1949 *F, Cze*, 1951 *Sp*, 1952 *Sp*
T Fattori 1936 *Ger, R*, 1937 *R, Ger, F*, 1938 *Ger*, 1939 *Ger, R*, 1940 *R, Ger*
E Fava 1948 *F, Cze*
P Favaretto 1951 *Sp*
R Favaro 1988 *F, USS, A, I*, 1989 *F, R, Sp, Ar, Z, USS*, 1990 *F, Pol, R, H, R, USS*, 1991 *F, R, Nm, Nm, US, E, NZ, USS*, 1992 *Sp, F, R*, 1993 *Sp, F, Cro, Sp, F*, 1994 *CZR, A, A, R, W, F*, 1995 *S, I, Sa*, 1996 *Pt*
S Favaro 2009 *A, NZ, NZ, SA, Sa*, 2010 *SA*, 2012 *F, I, W, S, Ar, C, US, Tg, NZ, A*, 2013 *F, S, W, E, I*
G Favretto 1948 *Cze*, 1949 *Cze*
A Fedrigo 1972 *Yug*, 1973 *Pt, Rho, WTv, Bor, NEC, Nat, ETv, Leo, FS, Cze, Yug, A*, 1974 *Pt, Mid, Sus, Oxo, WGe, Leo*, 1975 *F, Sp, R, Cze, E, Pol, H, Sp*, 1976 *F, J, A, Sp*, 1977 *F, Pol, R, Cze, R, Sp*, 1978 *F, Ar*, 1979 *Pol, R*
P Fedrigo 1973 *Pt*
I Fernandez- Rouyet 2008 *SA, Ar*, 2009 *A, NZ, NZ, SA, Sa*
P Ferracin 1975 *R, Cze, E, Pol, H, Sp*, 1976 *F*, 1977 *Mor, Pol*, 1978 *USS*
C Festuccia 2003 *W, I, E, F, S, S, I, Geo, NZ, Tg, C, W*, 2004 *E, F, S, I*, 2005 *F, Ar, Ar, A, Tg, Ar*, 2006 *E, F, W, S, Pt, Rus, A, Ar, C*, 2007 *F, E, S, W, I, Ur, Ar, J, NZ, R, S*, 2008 *I, E, W*, 2009 *E, I*, 2010 *A, Fj*, 2011 *F, S*, 2012 *Ar, C, US*
G Figari 1940 *R, Ger*, 1942 *R*
EG Filizzola 1993 *Pt, Mor, Sp, F, Rus, F, S*, 1994 *Sp, CZR, A*, 1995 *R, NZ*
M Finocchi 1968 *Yug*, 1969 *F*, 1970 *Cze, Mad, Mad, R*, 1971 *Mor, R*
G Fornari 1952 *Sp, Ger, F*, 1953 *F, Ger, R*, 1954 *Sp, F*, 1955 *Ger, F, Sp, F, Cze*, 1956 *Ger, F, Cze*
B Francescato 1977 *Cze, R, Sp*, 1978 *F, Sp*, 1979 *F*, 1981 *R*
I Francescato 1990 *R, USS*, 1991 *F, R, US, E, NZ, USS*, 1992 *R, S*, 1993 *Mor, F*, 1994 *Sp, H, R, W, F*, 1995 *S, I, Sa, E, Ar, F, Ar, R, NZ, SA*, 1996 *W, Pt, W, A, E, S*, 1997 *F, F, Ar, R, SA*
N Francescato 1972 *Yug*, 1973 *Rho, WTv, Bor, NEC, Nat, ETv, Leo*, 1974 *Pt*, 1976 *J, A, Sp*, 1977 *F, Mor, Pol, R, R, Sp*, 1978 *F, Ar, USS, Sp*, 1979 *F, R, E, Sp, Mor, F, Pol, USS, NZ*, 1980 *F, R, Fj, JAB, Coo, Pol, USS, Sp*, 1981 *F, R*, 1982 *Mor*
R Francescato 1976 *Sp*, 1978 *Ar, USS*, 1979 *Sp, F, Pol, USS, NZ, Mor*, 1980 *F, R, Fj, JAB, Coo, Pol, USS, Sp*, 1981 *F, R*, 1982 *WGe*, 1983 *F, R, USS, C, C, Sp, Mor, F, A*, 1984 *Mor, R, Tun*, 1985 *F, Sp, Z, USS*, 1986 *Tun, F*
G Franceschini 1975 *H, Sp*, 1976 *F, J*, 1977 *F, Pol, Pol, Cze, R, Sp*
A Francese 1939 *R*, 1940 *R*
J Francesio 2000 *W, I, Sa*, 2001 *Ur*
F Frati 2000 *C, NZ*, 2001 *I, S*
F Frelich 1955 *Cze*, 1957 *F, Ger*, 1958 *F, R*
M Fumei 1984 *F*
J Furno 2011 *S*, 2012 *S, Ar, C, US, Tg*, 2013 *E, I, SA, S*
A Fusco 1982 *E*, 1985 *R*, 1986 *Tun, F, Tun*
E Fusco 1960 *Ger, F*, 1961 *F*, 1962 *F, Ger, R*, 1963 *F*, 1964 *Ger, F*, 1965 *F*, 1966 *F*
M Fuser 2012 *C*

R Gabanella 1951 *Sp*, 1952 *Sp*
P Gabrielli 1948 *Cze*, 1949 *F, Cze*, 1951 *Sp*, 1954 *F*
F Gaetaniello 1980 *Sp*, 1982 *E*, 1984 *USS*, 1985 *R, Sp, Z, Z, USS, R*, 1986 *Pt, E, A, Tun, USS*, 1987 *Pt, F, NZ, Ar, Fj, USS, Sp*, 1988 *F*, 1990 *F, R, Sp, H*, 1991 *Nm, US, E, NZ*
F Gaetaniello 1975 *H*, 1976 *R, A, Sp*, 1977 *F, Pol, R, Pol, R, Sp*, 1978 *Sp*, 1979 *Pol, R, E, Sp, Mor, F, Pol, USS, NZ, Mor*, 1980 *Fj, JAB, Sp*, 1981 *F, R, USS, WGe*, 1982 *F, R, E, WGe, Mor*, 1983 *F, R, USS, C, C, Sp*
A Galante 2007 *Ur, Ar*
A Galeazzo 1985 *Sp*, 1987 *Pt, R, Ar, USS*
M Galletto 1972 *Pt, Sp, Yug*
E Galon 2001 *I*, 2005 *Tg, Ar, Fj*, 2006 *W, S, Rus*, 2007 *I, Ur, Ar, I, NZ, R, S*, 2008 *I, E, W, F, S*
R Ganzerla 1973 *Bor, NEC*
G Garcia 2008 *SA, Ar, A, Ar, Pl*, 2009 *E, I, S, A, NZ, NZ, SA, Sa*, 2010 *I, E, S, F, W*, 2011 *I, E, F, S, A, US, I*, 2013 *W, E, I, Sa*
M Gardin 1981 *USS, WGe*, 1982 *Mor*, 1983 *F, R*, 1984 *Mor, R, USS*, 1985 *EngB, USS, R*, 1986 *Tun, F, Pt, Tun, USS*, 1987 *Pt, F, R, NZ, Ar, Fj, USS, Sp*, 1988 *R*
JM Gardner 1992 *R, S*, 1993 *Rus, F*, 1994 *Sp, R, H, F*, 1995 *S, I, Sa, E, Ar*, 1996 *W*, 1997 *I, F, SA, I*, 1998 *S, W*
P Gargiullo 1973 *FS*, 1974 *Mid, Sus, Oxo*
F Garguillo 1972 *Yug*
F Garguilo 1967 *F, Pt*, 1968 *Yug*, 1974 *Sus*
S Garozzo 2001 *Ur, Ar*, 2002 *Ar*
M Gatto 1967 *Pt, R*
G Gattoni 1933 *Cze, Cze*
Q Geldenhuys 2009 *A, A, NZ, NZ, SA, Sa*, 2010 *I, E, S, F, W, SA, SA, Ar, A, Fj*, 2011 *I, E, W, F, S, J, Rus, US, I*, 2012 *F, E, I, W, S, Tg, NZ, A*, 2013 *F, S, W, E, I*
A Gerardo 1968 *Yug*, 1969 *Sp*, 1970 *Cze, Mad*, 1971 *R*, 1972 *Sp*
F Geremia 1980 *JAB, Pol*
G Geremia 1956 *Cze*
E Gerosa 1952 *Sp, Ger, F*, 1953 *F, Ger, R*, 1954 *Sp*
M Gerosa 1994 *CZR, A, A, R, W*, 1995 *E, Ar*
C Ghezzi 1938 *Ger*, 1939 *Ger, R*, 1940 *R, Ger*
A Ghini 1981 *USS, WGe*, 1982 *F, R, E, Mor*, 1983 *F, R, C, Mor, F, A, USS*, 1984 *F, Mor, R, USS*, 1985 *F, R, EngB, Z, Z, USS*, 1987 *Fj*, 1988 *R, USS*
L Ghiraldini 2006 *J, Fj*, 2007 *I, J, Pt*, 2008 *I, E, W, F, S, SA, Ar, A, Ar, Pl*, 2009 *S, W, F, A, A, NZ, NZ, SA, Sa*, 2010 *I,*

E, S, F, W, SA, SA, Ar, 2011 I, E, W, F, S, J, A, US, I, 2012 F, E, I, W, Tg, NZ, A, 2013 F, S, W, E, I, SA, Sa, S

S Ghizzoni 1977 F, Mor, Pol, R, Pol, Cze, R, Sp, 1978 F, Ar, USS, 1979 F, Pol, Sp, Mor, F, Pol, 1980 R, Fj, JAB, Coo, Pol, USS, Sp, 1981 F, 1982 F, R, E, WGe, Mor, 1983 F, USS, C, C, Sp, Mor, F, A, USS, 1984 F, Mor, R, Tun, USS, 1985 F, R, EngB, Z, Z, USS, R, 1986 F, E, A, Tun, USS, 1987 Pt, F, R, NZ

M Giacheri 1992 R, 1993 Sp, F, Pt, Rus, F, S, 1994 Sp, R, CZR, H, A, A, F, 1995 S, I, E, Ar, F, Ar, R, NZ, SA, 1996 W, 1999 S, W, I, Ur, Fj, E, Tg, NZ, 2001 Nm, SA, Ur, Ar, SA, 2002 F, S, W, I, E, NZ, A, 2003 E, F, S, I

G Giani 1966 Ger, R, 1967 F, Pt, R

D Giazzon 2012 Ar, US, Tg, NZ, A, 2013 F, S, W, E, I, SA, S

G Gini 1968 Pt, WGe, Yug, 1969 Bul, Sp, Bel, F, 1970 Cze, Mad, Mad, R, 1971 Mor, F, 1972 Pt, Pt, 1974 Mid, Oxo

G Giorgio 1968 Pt, WGe

M Giovanelli 1989 Z, USS, 1990 Pol, Sp, H, R, USS, 1991 F, R, Nm, E, NZ, USS, 1992 Sp, F, S, 1993 Sp, F, Pt, Cro, Mor, Sp, F, 1994 R, CZR, H, A, A, 1995 F, Ar, R, NZ, SA, 1996 A, E, S, 1997 F, F, Ar, R, SA, I, 1998 S, W, Rus, Ar, H, E, 1999 S, W, I, SA, SA, Ur, Sp, Fj, E, Tg, NZ, 2000 S

E Giugovaz 1965 Cze, 1966 F

R Giuliani 1951 Sp

E Gori 2010 A, Fj, 2011 I, J, S, A, Rus, US, I, 2012 F, E, I, S, Ar, C, US, Tg, NZ, A, 2013 F, S, W, E, I, SA, Sa

M Gorni 1939 R, 1940 R, Ger

M Goti 1990 H

C Gower 2009 A, A, NZ, NZ, SA, Sa, 2010 I, E, S, F, W, SA, SA, Ar

G Grasselli 1952 Ger

G Grespan 1989 F, Sp, USS, 1990 F, R, 1991 R, NZ, USS, 1992 R, S, 1993 Sp, F, Cro, Sp, F, Rus, 1994 Sp, CZR, R, W

PR Griffen 2004 E, F, S, I, W, R, J, C, NZ, US, 2005 W, S, F, Ar, Ar, A, Tg, Ar, Fj, 2006 I, E, F, W, S, J, Fj, Rus, A, Ar, C, 2007 F, I, Ur, Ar, I, NZ, R, Pt, 2009 I, S, W, F

A Gritti 1996 Pt, 2000 S, W, I, E, F, Sa, Fj, C, R, NZ, 2001 E, F, S, W

G Guidi 1996 Pt, E, 1997 F, Ar, R

T Iannone 2012 Tg, 2013 SA, Sa

M Innocenti 1981 WGe, 1982 F, R, E, WGe, Mor, 1983 F, USS, C, C, Mor, F, A, USS, 1984 F, Mor, Tun, USS, 1985 F, R, EngB, Sp, USS, R, 1986 Tun, F, Pt, E, A, Tun, USS, 1987 Pt, F, R, NZ, Ar, Fj, USS, Sp, 1988 F, R, A

G Intoppa 2004 R, J, C, NZ, 2005 I, W, E

C Jannone 1981 USS, 1982 F, R

S Lanfranchi 1949 F, Cze, 1953 F, Ger, R, 1954 Sp, F, 1955 F, 1956 Ger, Cze, 1957 F, 1958 F, 1959 F, 1960 F, 1961 F, 1962 F, Ger, R, 1963 F, 1964 Ger, F

G Lanzi 1998 Ar, H, E, 1999 Sp, 2000 S, W, I, 2001 I

G Lari 1972 Yug, 1973 Yug, A, 1974 Pt, Mid, Sus, Oxo, Leo

E Lazzarini 1970 Cze, 1971 Mor, F, R, 1972 Pt, Pt, Sp, Sp, 1973 Pt, Rho, WTv, Bor, NEC, Leo, FS, Tva, Cze, Yug, A, 1974 Pt, Mid, Sus, Oxo, WGe

U Levorato 1956 Ger, F, 1957 F, 1958 F, R, 1959 F, 1961 Ger, F, 1962 F, Ger, R, 1963 F, 1964 Ger, F, 1965 F

A Lijoi 1977 Pol, R, 1978 Sp, 1979 R, Mor

G Limone 1979 E, Mor, USS, Mor, 1980 JAB, Sp, 1981 USS, WGe, 1982 E, 1983 USS

A Lo Cicero 2000 E, F, Sa, Fj, C, R, NZ, 2001 I, E, F, S, W, Fj, SA, Sa, 2002 F, S, W, Sp, R, A, 2003 F, S, S, I, Geo, Tg, C, W, 2004 E, F, S, I, W, R, J, C, NZ, US, 2005 I, W, S, E, F, Ar, Ar, A, Tg, Ar, 2006 E, F, W, S, J, Fj, Pt, Rus, A, Ar, C, 2007 F, E, S, W, Ur, Ar, J, NZ, R, Pt, S, 2008 I, E, W, F, S, Ar, Pl, 2010 Ar, A, Fj, 2011 I, E, W, F, S, J, S, A, US, I, 2012 F, E, W, S, Tg, NZ, A, 2013 F, S, W, E, I

C Loranzi 1973 Nat, ETv, Leo, FS, Tva

F Lorigiola 1979 Sp, F, Pol, USS, NZ, Mor, 1980 F, R, Fj, JAB, Pol, USS, Sp, 1981 F, R, USS, 1982 WGe, 1983 R, USS, C, Sp, 1984 Tun, 1985 Sp, 1986 Pt, E, A, Tun, USS, 1987 Pt, F, R, NZ, Ar, 1988 F

G Luchini 1973 Rho, Nat

L Luise 1955 Ger, F, Sp, F, Cze, 1956 Ger, F, Cze, 1957 Ger, 1958 F

R Luise III 1959 F, 1960 Ger, F, 1961 Ger, F, 1962 F, Ger, R, 1965 F, Cze, 1966 F, 1971 R, 1972 Pt, Sp, Sp

T Lupini 1987 R, NZ, Ar, Fj, USS, Sp, 1988 F, R, USS, A, 1989 R

O Maestri 1935 Cat, F, 1937 Ger

R Maffioli 1933 Cze, Cze, 1934 Cat, R, 1935 Cat, 1936 Ger, R, 1937 Ger, R, Bel, Ger

R Maini 1948 F, Cze

G Malosti 1953 F, 1954 Sp, 1955 F, 1956 Ger, F, 1957 F, 1958 F

G Mancini 1952 Ger, F, 1953 F, Ger, R, 1954 Sp, F, 1955 Cze, 1956 Ger, F, Cze, 1957 F

R Mandelli 2004 I, W, R, J, US, 2007 F, E, Ur, Ar

A Manici 2013 Sa

A Mannato 2004 US, 2005 Ar, A

E Manni 1976 J, A, Sp, 1977 Mor

L Manteri 1996 W, A, E, S

A Marcato 2006 J, Pt, 2008 I, E, W, F, S, SA, Ar, A, Ar, Pl, 2009 E, S, W, F

M Marchetto 1972 Yug, 1973 Pt, Cze, Yug, 1974 Pt, Mid, Sus, WGe, Leo, 1975 F, Sp, R, Cze, E, Pol, H, Sp, 1976 F, R, J, A, Sp, 1977 F, Mor, Pol, R, Cze, R, Sp, 1978 F, USS, Sp, 1979 F, Pol, R, E, Pol, USS, NZ, Mor, 1980 F, Coo, 1981 USS

A Marescalchi 1933 Cze, 1935 F, 1937 R

P Mariani 1976 R, A, Sp, 1977 F, Pol, 1978 F, Ar, USS, Sp, 1979 F, Pol, R, Sp, F, Pol, USS, NZ, Mor, 1980 F, R, Fj, JAB

P Marini 1949 F, Cze, 1951 Sp, 1953 F, Ger, R, 1955 Ger

L Martin 1997 F, R, 1998 S, W, Rus, H, E, 1999 F, S, W, I, SA, SA, Ur, Sp, Fj, E, 2000 S, W, I, E, F, Sa, Fj, C, R, NZ, 2001 I, E, S, W, SA, Ar, Fj, SA, Sa, 2002 F, S

F Martinenghi 1952 Sp, Ger

R Martinez-Frugoni 2002 NZ, Sp, R, 2003 W, I, E, F, S, S, NZ

G Martini 1965 F, 1967 F, 1968 Pt

R Martini 1959 F, 1960 Ger, F, 1961 Ger, F, 1964 Ger, F, 1965 F, 1968 WGe, Yug

P Masci 1948 Cze, 1949 F, Cze, 1952 Sp, Ger, F, 1953 F, 1954 Sp, 1955 F

M Mascioletti 1977 Mor, Pol, 1978 Ar, USS, Sp, 1979 Pol, E, Sp, Mor, F, Pol, USS, NZ, Mor, 1980 F, R, Fj, 1981 WGe, 1982 F, R, WGe, 1983 F, R, USS, C, C, Sp, Mor, F, A, USS, 1984 F, Mor, Tun, 1985 F, R, Z, Z, USS, R, 1986 Tun, F, Pt, E, Tun, USS, 1987 NZ, Ar, Fj, 1989 Sp, Ar, Z, USS, 1990 Pol

A Masi 1999 Sp, 2003 E, F, S, S, I, NZ, Tg, C, W, 2004 E, I, W, R, J, C, 2005 I, W, S, E, F, Ar, Ar, A, 2006 J, Fj, Pt, Rus, 2007 F, S, J, NZ, R, Pt, S, 2008 I, E, W, F, S, SA, A, Ar, Pl, 2009 E, I, 2010 I, E, S, F, SA, SA, Ar, A, Fj, 2011 I, E, W, F, S, S, A, Rus, I, 2012 F, E, I, W, S, Tg, NZ, A, 2013 F, S, W, E, I, SA, Sa, S

L Mastrodomenico 2000 Sa, C, NZ, 2001 Nm, Ar

I Matacchini 1948 F, Cze, 1949 F, Cze, 1954 Sp, 1955 Ger, F, Sp, F

L Mattarolo 1973 Bor, Nat, ETv, Leo, FS, Tva, Cze

M Mattei 1967 R

R Mattei 1978 F, USS

F Mazzantini 1965 Cze, 1966 F, 1967 F

M Mazzantini 2000 S, 2001 S, W, 2002 E, NZ, 2003 E, F, Geo, NZ, C

F Mazzariol 1995 F, Ar, R, NZ, 1996 Pt, 1997 F, R, SA, 1998 Ar, H, 1999 F, SA, SA, Sp, E, NZ, 2000 Fj, C, 2001 Nm, SA, Ur, Ar, Fj, SA, 2002 W, NZ, Sp, 2003 S, I, NZ, C, W, 2004 R

G Mazzi 1998 H, 1999 SA, SA, Ur, Sp

N Mazzucato 1995 SA, 1996 Pt, S, 1997 I, 1999 Sp, E, Tg, NZ, 2000 F, Sa, Fj, R, 2001 Nm, SA, Ur, Ar, 2002 W, I, E, NZ, Sp, R, Ar, A, 2003 E, F, S, I, NZ, Tg, W, 2004 E, F, S, I, W, R, J

I Mazzucchelli 1965 F, Cze, 1966 F, Ger, R, 1967 F, 1968 Pt, WGe, 1969 Bul, F, 1971 F, 1972 Pt, Sp, 1974 WGe, 1975 F, R, Cze, Pol, 1976 F, R

LJ McLean 2008 SA, Ar, Pl, 2009 E, I, S, W, F, A, A, NZ,

NZ, SA, Sa, 2010 I, E, S, F, W, SA, SA, Ar, A, Fj, 2011 I, E, W, S, J, A, Rus, US, I, 2012 F, E, I, W, US, Tg, NZ, A, 2013 F, S, W, E, I, SA, Sa, S
P Menapace 1996 Pt
E Michelon 1969 Bel, F, 1970 Cze, Mad, Mad, R, 1971 R
A Miele 1968 Yug, 1970 Mad, 1971 R, 1972 Pt, Sp
GE Milano 1990 USS
F Minto 2012 NZ, A, 2013 F, S, W, E, I
A Mioni 1955 Ger, F, F, 1957 F
A Modonesi 1929 Sp
L Modonesi 1966 Ger, R, 1967 F, Pt, R, 1968 Pt, WGe, 1970 Cze, Mad, Mad, R, 1971 F, 1974 Leo, 1975 F, Sp, R, Cze
N Molari 1957 F, 1958 R
F Molinari 1973 NEC
G Molinari 1948 F
P Monfeli 1970 R, 1971 Mor, F, 1972 Pt, 1976 J, A, Sp, 1977 F, R, Cze, R, Sp, 1978 F
JF Montauriol 2009 E, A
G Morelli 1981 WGe, 1982 R, E, Mor, 1983 USS, 1984 F
G Morelli 1976 F, 1982 F, R, Mor, 1983 R, C, Sp, A, USS, 1984 Mor, R, USS, 1985 R, EngB, Z, Z, USS, R, 1986 Tun, F, E, A, Tun, USS, 1987 F, NZ
G Morelli 1988 I, 1989 F, R
A Moreno 1999 Tg, NZ, 2002 F, S, 2008 Ar
A Moretti 1997 R, 1998 Rus, 1999 Ur, Sp, Tg, NZ, 2002 E, NZ, Sp, R, Ar, A, 2005 Ar
U Moretti 1933 Cze, 1934 R, 1935 Cat, 1937 R, Ger, F, 1942 R
A Morimondi 1930 Sp, 1933 Cze, 1934 Cat, 1935 Cat
LE Morisi 2012 E, US, 2013 SA, S
A Moscardi 1993 Pt, 1995 R, 1996 S, 1998 Ar, H, E, 1999 F, S, W, I, SA, SA, Ur, Fj, E, Tg, NZ, 2000 S, W, I, E, F, Sa, Fj, C, R, NZ, 2001 I, E, F, S, W, Nm, SA, Ur, Ar, Fj, SA, Sa, 2002 F, S, W, I, E
A Muraro 2000 C, R, NZ, 2001 I, E, Nm, SA, Ur, Ar, Fj, SA, Sa, 2002 F

E Nathan 1930 Sp
G Navarini 1957 Ger, 1958 R
M Nicolosi 1982 R
C Nieto 2002 E, 2005 Ar, Ar, A, Tg, Ar, Fj, 2006 I, E, F, W, J, Fj, A, Ar, C, 2007 F, S, W, I, Ar, 2008 E, F, S, SA, Ar, A, Ar, Pl, 2009 E, I, S, W, F
A Nisti 1929 Sp, 1930 Sp
L Nitoglia 2004 C, NZ, US, 2005 I, W, S, E, F, Ar, Tg, Ar, Fj, 2006 I, E, F, W, S

F Ongaro 2000 C, 2001 Nm, SA, Ur, Ar, 2002 Ar, A, 2003 E, F, S, I, Geo, NZ, Tg, C, W, 2004 E, F, S, I, W, R, J, C, NZ, US, 2005 I, W, S, E, F, Tg, Ar, Fj, 2006 I, E, F, W, S, J, Fj, Pt, Rus, Ar, C, 2007 F, S, Ur, Ar, I, NZ, S, 2008 F, S, SA, Ar, A, Ar, Pl, 2009 E, I, NZ, SA, Sa, 2010 I, E, S, F, W, SA, SA, Ar, A, Fj, 2011 I, E, S, Rus, US, I, 2012 S
C Orlandi 1992 S, 1993 Sp, F, Mor, F, Rus, F, S, 1994 Sp, CZR, H, A, A, R, W, 1995 S, I, Sa, E, Ar, F, Ar, R, NZ, SA, 1996 W, Pt, W, A, E, S, 1997 I, F, F, Ar, R, SA, I, 1998 S, W, 2000 W, F
S Orlando 2004 E, S, W, C, NZ, US, 2005 E, F, Ar, A, 2006 J, 2007 Ur, Ar, Pt
L Orquera 2004 C, NZ, US, 2005 I, W, S, E, F, Ar, Tg, 2008 A, Ar, 2009 W, F, 2010 Ar, A, Fj, 2011 I, E, W, F, S, J, S, A, US, I, 2012 NZ, A, 2013 F, S, E, I, SA, Sa
A Osti 1981 F, R, USS, 1982 E, Mor, 1983 R, C, A, USS, 1984 R, USS, 1985 F, 1986 Tun, 1988 R

S Pace 1977 Mor, 1984 R, Tun
S Pace 2001 SA, Sa, 2005 Fj
P Pacifici 1969 Bul, Sp, F, 1970 Cze, Mad, Mad, R, 1971 Mor, F
R Paciucci 1937 R, Ger, F
F Paganelli 1972 Sp
S Palmer 2002 Ar, A, 2003 I, E, F, S, S, NZ, C, W, 2004 I, R
P Paoletti 1972 Pt, Sp, Yug, 1973 Pt, Rho, WTv, Bor, NEC, Nat, ETv, Leo, FS, Tva, 1974 Mid, Oxo, WGe, Leo, 1975 F, Sp, 1976 R
T Paoletti 2000 S, W, I, E, F, Sa, C, R, NZ, 2001 F, Nm, Ur, Ar, Fj, SA
G Paolin 1929 Sp
S Parisse 2002 NZ, Sp, R, Ar, A, 2003 S, I, Geo, NZ, Tg, C, W, 2004 E, F, S, 2005 I, W, S, E, F, Ar, Ar, A, Tg, Ar, Fj, 2006 I, E, F, W, S, Fj, Pt, Rus, A, Ar, C, 2007 F, E, S, W, I, J, I, NZ, R, Pt, S, 2008 I, E, W, F, S, Ar, A, Ar, Pl, 2009 E, I, S, W, F, A, A, NZ, NZ, SA, 2010 SA, SA, Ar, A, Fj, 2011 I, E, W, F, S, J, S, A, Rus, US, I, 2012 F, E, I, W, S, Tg, NZ, A, 2013 F, S, E, I, SA, Sa, S
E Parmiggiani 1942 R, 1948 Cze
P Paselli 1929 Sp, 1930 Sp, 1933 Cze
E Passarotto 1975 Sp
E Patrizio 2007 Ur, 2008 F, S, SA
R Pavan 2008 SA
A Pavanello 2007 Ar, 2009 SA, Sa, 2012 E, I, Ar, C, US, Tg, NZ, A, 2013 F, S, W, E, I, SA, Sa, S
E Pavanello 2002 R, Ar, A, 2004 R, J, C, NZ, US, 2005 Ar, A
P Pavesi 1977 Pol, 1979 Mor, 1980 USS
M Pavin 1980 USS, 1986 F, Pt, E, A, Tun, USS, 1987 Ar
R Pedrazzi 2001 Nm, Ar, 2002 F, S, W, 2005 S, E, F
P Pedroni 1989 Z, USS, 1990 F, Pol, R, 1991 F, R, Nm, 1993 Rus, F, 1994 Sp, R, CZR, H, 1995 I, Sa, E, Ar, F, Ar, R, NZ, SA, 1996 W, W
G Peens 2002 W, I, E, NZ, Sp, R, Ar, A, 2003 E, F, S, S, I, Geo, NZ, 2004 NZ, 2005 E, F, Ar, Ar, A, 2006 Pt, A
L Pelliccione 1983 Sp, Mor, F
L Pelliccione 1977 Pol
M Percudani 1952 F, 1954 F, 1955 Ger, Sp, F, Cze, 1956 Cze, 1957 F, 1958 R
F Perrini 1955 Sp, F, Cze, 1956 Ger, F, Cze, 1957 F, 1958 F, 1959 F, 1962 R, 1963 F
F Perrone 1951 Sp
AR Persico 2000 S, W, E, F, Sa, Fj, 2001 F, S, W, Nm, SA, Ur, Ar, Fj, SA, Sa, 2002 F, S, W, I, E, NZ, Sp, R, Ar, A, 2003 W, I, E, F, S, I, Geo, Tg, C, W, 2004 E, F, S, I, W, R, J, C, NZ, 2005 I, W, S, E, F, Ar, Ar, Tg, Ar, 2006 I, E
J Pertile 1994 R, 1995 Ar, 1996 W, A, E, S, 1997 I, F, SA, 1998 Rus, 1999 S, W, I, SA, SA
S Perugini 2000 I, F, Sa, Fj, 2001 S, W, Nm, SA, Ur, Ar, 2002 W, I, 2003 W, S, Geo, NZ, Tg, W, 2004 E, F, I, W, C, NZ, US, 2005 I, W, S, E, F, 2006 I, E, F, W, S, Pt, Rus, 2007 F, E, S, W, I, J, I, NZ, Pt, S, 2008 I, E, W, F, S, A, Ar, Pl, 2009 E, I, S, W, F, A, A, NZ, NZ, SA, Sa, 2010 I, E, S, F, W, SA, SA, Ar, Fj, 2011 I, E, W, F, S, Rus, US, I
L Perziano 1993 Pt
M Perziano 2000 NZ, 2001 F, S, W, Nm, SA, Ur, Ar, Fj, SA
V Pesce 1988 I, 1989 R
P Pescetto 1956 Ger, Cze, 1957 F
G Petralia 1984 F
R Pez 2000 Sa, Fj, C, R, NZ, 2001 I, 2002 S, W, E, A, 2003 I, E, F, S, S, Geo, 2005 Ar, A, Tg, Ar, Fj, 2006 I, E, F, W, S, J, Fj, Pt, Rus, A, Ar, 2007 F, E, S, W, I, J, R, S
M Phillips 2002 F, S, W, I, E, 2003 W, I, E, F, S, S, I, NZ, W
G Pianna 1934 R, 1935 Cat, F, 1936 Ger, R, 1938 Ger
A Piazza 1990 USS
F Piccini 1963 F, 1964 Ger, 1966 F
S Picone 2004 I, W, 2005 F, 2006 E, F, S, J, Pt, Rus, Ar, C, 2008 E, W, F, S, SA, Ar, 2009 NZ, SA, Sa, 2010 I, SA, SA
F Pietroscanti 1987 USS, Sp, 1988 A, I, 1989 F, R, Sp, Ar, Z, USS, 1990 F, Pol, R, H, 1991 Nm, Nm, 1992 Sp, F, R, 1993 Sp, Mor, Sp, F, Rus, F
F Pignotti 1968 WGe, Yug, 1969 Bul, Sp, Bel
C Pilat 1997 I, 1998 S, W, 2000 E, Sa, 2001 I, W
MJ Pini 1998 H, E, 1999 F, Ur, Fj, E, Tg, NZ, 2000 S, W, I, F
M Piovan 1973 Pt, 1974 Pt, Mid, Sus, Oxo, 1976 A, 1977 F, Mor, R, 1979 F
R Piovan 1996 Pt, 1997 R, 2000 R, NZ
M Piovene 1995 NZ
E Piras 1971 R
M Pisaneschi 1948 Cze, 1949 Cze, 1953 F, Ger, R, 1954 Sp, F, 1955 Ger, F, Sp, F, Cze
F Pitorri 1948 Cze, 1949 F
M Pitorri 1973 NEC
G Pivetta 1979 R, E, Mor, 1980 Coo, USS, 1981 R, USS, WGe, 1982 F, R, WGe, Mor, 1983 F, USS, C, Sp, Mor, F,

USS, 1984 *F*, *Mor*, *R*, *Tun*, 1985 *F*, *R*, *Sp*, *Z*, *Z*, 1986 *Pt*, 1987 *Sp*, 1989 *R*, *Sp*, 1990 *F*, *Pol*, *R*, *Sp*, *R*, *USS*, 1991 *F*, *R*, *Nm*, *Nm*, *US*, *E*, *NZ*, *USS*, 1992 *Sp*, *F*, *R*, *R*, 1993 *Cro*, *Mor*, *Sp*
M Platania 1994 *F*, 1995 *F*, *R*, 1996 *Pt*
I Ponchia 1955 *F*, *Sp*, *F*, *Cze*, 1956 *F*, 1957 *Ger*, 1958 *F*
E Ponzi 1973 *Cze*, *A*, 1974 *WGe*, 1975 *F*, *Sp*, *R*, *Cze*, *E*, *Pol*, *H*, *Sp*, 1976 *F*, *R*, *J*, *A*, *Sp*, 1977 *F*, *Mor*, *Pol*, *R*
G Porcellato 1989 *R*
G Porzio 1970 *Cze*, *Mad*, *Mad*
C Possamai 1970 *Cze*, *Mad*, *Mad*
W Pozzebon 2001 *I*, *E*, *F*, *S*, *W*, *Nm*, *SA*, *Ur*, *Ar*, *Fj*, *SA*, *Sa*, 2002 *NZ*, *Sp*, 2004 *R*, *J*, *C*, *NZ*, *US*, 2005 *W*, *E*, 2006 *C*
A Pratichetti 2012 *C*
C Pratichetti 1988 *R*, 1990 *Pol*
M Pratichetti 2004 *NZ*, 2007 *E*, *W*, *I*, *Ur*, *Ar*, *I*, *Pt*, 2008 *SA*, *Ar*, *Ar*, *PI*, 2009 *E*, *I*, *S*, *W*, *F*, *A*, *NZ*, *SA*, 2010 *W*, *SA*, 2011 *J*, *Rus*
G Preo 1999 *I*, 2000 *I*, *E*, *Sa*, *Fj*, *R*, *NZ*
P Presutti 1974 *Mid*, *Sus*, *Oxo*, 1977 *Pol*, *Cze*, *R*, *Sp*, 1978 *F*
FP Properzi-Curti 1990 *Pol*, *Sp*, *H*, *R*, 1991 *F*, *Nm*, *Nm*, *US*, *E*, *NZ*, 1992 *Sp*, *F*, *R*, 1993 *Cro*, *Mor*, *F*, *Rus*, *F*, *S*, 1994 *Sp*, *R*, *H*, *A*, *A*, 1995 *S*, *I*, *Sa*, *E*, *Ar*, *NZ*, *SA*, 1996 *W*, *Pt*, *W*, *A*, *E*, 1997 *I*, *F*, *F*, *Ar*, *SA*, 1998 *Ar*, 1999 *S*, *W*, *I*, *SA*, *SA*, *Ur*, *E*, *Tg*, *NZ*, 2001 *F*, *S*, *W*
C Prosperini 1966 *R*, 1967 *F*, *Pt*, *R*
F Pucciarello 1999 *Sp*, *Fj*, *E*, 2002 *S*, *W*, *I*, *E*, *Ar*
G Puglisi 1971 *F*, 1972 *Yug*, 1973 *Cze*
M Pulli 1968 *Pt*, 1972 *Pt*, *Pt*
A Puppo 1972 *Pt*, *Pt*, *Sp*, *Sp*, 1973 *Pt*, *Rho*, *WTv*, *Bor*, *NEC*, *Nat*, *ETv*, *Leo*, *FS*, *Tva*, 1974 *Mid*, *Sus*, *Oxo*, *WGe*, *Leo*, 1977 *R*

I Quaglio 1970 *R*, 1971 *R*, 1972 *Pt*, *Sp*, 1973 *WTv*, *Bor*, *NEC*, *Nat*, *Leo*, *FS*, *Tva*, 1975 *H*, *Sp*, 1976 *F*, *R*
M Quaglio 1984 *Tun*, 1988 *F*, *R*
R Quartaroli 2009 *W*, *F*, *A*, 2012 *Ar*, *US*
JM Queirolo 2000 *Sa*, *Fj*, 2001 *E*, *F*, *Fj*, 2002 *NZ*, *Sp*, *A*, 2003 *Geo*
P Quintavala 1958 *R*

C Raffo 1929 *Sp*, 1930 *Sp*, 1933 *Cze*, *Cze*, 1937 *R*, *Bel*
G Raineri 1998 *H*, 2000 *Fj*, *R*, *NZ*, 2001 *I*, *E*, *S*, *W*, *Nm*, *SA*, *Ur*, *Ar*, 2002 *W*, *I*, *E*, *NZ*, 2003 *W*, *I*, *E*, *F*, *S*, *Geo*
G Raisi 1956 *Ger*, *F*, 1957 *F*, *Ger*, 1960 *Ger*, 1964 *Ger*, *F*
R Rampazzo 1996 *W*, 1999 *I*
M Ravazzolo 1993 *Cro*, *Sp*, *F*, *F*, *S*, 1994 *Sp*, *R*, *CZR*, *H*, 1995 *S*, *I*, *Sa*, *F*, *Ar*, *NZ*, 1996 *W*, *Pt*, *W*, *A*, 1997 *F*, *Ar*, *R*, *SA*
A Re Garbagnati 1936 *Ger*, *R*, 1937 *Ger*, *Bel*, *Ger*, *F*, 1938 *Ger*, 1939 *Ger*, *R*, 1940 *R*, *Ger*, 1942 *R*
P Reale 1987 *USS*, *Sp*, 1988 *USS*, *A*, *I*, 1989 *Z*, 1992 *S*
T Reato 2008 *I*, *SA*, *Ar*, *A*, *Ar*, *PI*, 2009 *E*, *I*, *A*
G Riccardi 1955 *Ger*, *F*, *Sp*, *F*, *Cze*, 1956 *F*, *Cze*
G Ricci 1967 *Pt*, 1969 *Bul*, *Sp*, *Bel*, *F*
G Ricciarelli 1962 *Ger*
L Riccioni 1951 *Sp*, 1952 *Sp*, *Ger*, *F*, 1953 *F*, *Ger*, 1954 *F*
S Rigo 1992 *S*, 1993 *Sp*, *F*, *Pt*
A Rinaldo 1977 *Mor*, *Pol*, *R*, *Cze*
W Rista 1968 *Yug*, 1969 *Bul*, *Sp*, *Bel*, *F*
M Rivaro 2000 *S*, *W*, *I*, 2001 *E*
M Rizzo 2005 *A*, 2008 *SA*, 2012 *I*, *C*, *US*, *A*, 2013 *I*, *Sa*
G Rizzoli 1935 *F*, 1936 *Ger*, *R*
C Robazza 1978 *Ar*, *Sp*, 1979 *F*, *Pol*, *R*, *E*, *Sp*, *F*, *Pol*, *USS*, *NZ*, *Mor*, 1980 *F*, *R*, *Fj*, *JAB*, *Coo*, *Pol*, *Sp*, 1981 *F*, *R*, *USS*, *WGe*, 1982 *E*, *WGe*, 1983 *F*, *USS*, *C*, *Mor*, *F*, 1984 *F*, *Tun*, 1985 *F*
KP Robertson 2004 *R*, *J*, *C*, *NZ*, *US*, 2005 *I*, *W*, *S*, *F*, *Ar*, *Ar*, *A*, 2006 *Pt*, *Rus*, 2007 *F*, *E*, *S*, *W*, *I*, *Ur*, *Ar*, *J*, *I*, *NZ*, *R*, *S*, 2008 *I*, *E*, *F*, *S*, *SA*, *Ar*, *A*, *Ar*, *PI*, 2009 *E*, *I*, *A*, *NZ*, *NZ*, *Sa*, 2010 *I*, *E*, *S*, *F*, *W*, *SA*
A Rocca 1973 *WTv*, *Bor*, *NEC*, 1977 *R*
G Romagnoli 1965 *F*, *Cze*, 1967 *Pt*, *R*
S Romagnoli 1982 *Mor*, 1984 *R*, *Tun*, *USS*, 1985 *F*, *Z*, *Z*, 1986 *Tun*, *Pt*, *A*, *Tun*, *USS*, 1987 *Pt*, *F*, *Fj*
G Romano 1942 *R*
L Romano 2012 *Ar*, *C*
P Romano 1942 *R*
F Roselli 1995 *F*, *R*, 1996 *W*, 1998 *Rus*, *Ar*, *H*, *E*, 1999 *F*, *S*, *W*, *I*, *SA*, *SA*, *Ur*, *Fj*, *Tg*
P Rosi 1948 *F*, *Cze*, 1949 *F*, *Cze*, 1951 *Sp*, 1952 *Ger*, *F*, 1953 *F*, *Ger*, *R*, 1954 *Sp*, *F*
G Rossi 1981 *USS*, *WGe*, 1982 *E*, *WGe*, *Mor*, 1983 *F*, *R*, *USS*, *C*, *C*, *Mor*, *F*, *A*, *USS*, 1984 *Mor*, 1985 *F*, *R*, *EngB*, *Sp*, *Z*, *USS*, *R*, 1986 *Tun*, *F*, *E*, *A*, *Tun*, *USS*, 1987 *R*, *NZ*, *Ar*, *USS*, *Sp*, 1988 *USS*, *A*, *I*, 1989 *F*, *R*, *Sp*, *Ar*, *Z*, *USS*, 1990 *F*, *R*, 1991 *R*
N Rossi 1973 *Yug*, 1974 *Pt*, *Mid*, *Sus*, *Oxo*, *WGe*, *Leo*, 1975 *Sp*, *Cze*, *E*, *H*, 1976 *J*, *A*, *Sp*, 1977 *Cze*, 1980 *USS*
Z Rossi 1959 *F*, 1961 *Ger*, *F*, 1962 *F*, *Ger*, *R*
E Rossini 1948 *F*, *Cze*, 1949 *F*, *Cze*, 1951 *Sp*, 1952 *Ger*
B Rovelli 1960 *Ger*, *F*, 1961 *Ger*, *F*
G Rubini 2009 *S*, *W*, *F*, *A*
A Russo 1986 *E*

D Sacca 2003 *I*
R Saetti 1957 *Ger*, 1958 *F*, *R*, 1959 *F*, 1960 *F*, 1961 *Ger*, *F*, 1964 *Ger*, *F*
R Saetti 1988 *USS*, *I*, 1989 *F*, *R*, *Sp*, *Ar*, *Z*, *USS*, 1990 *F*, *Sp*, *H*, *R*, *USS*, 1991 *R*, *Nm*, *Nm*, *US*, *E*, 1992 *R*
A Sagramora 1970 *Mad*, *Mad*, 1971 *R*
E Saibene 1957 *F*, *Ger*
C Salmasco 1965 *F*, 1967 *F*
L Salsi 1971 *Mor*, 1972 *Pt*, *Sp*, *Yug*, 1973 *Pt*, *Rho*, *WTv*, *Nat*, *ETv*, *Leo*, *FS*, *Tva*, *Cze*, *Yug*, *A*, 1974 *Pt*, *Oxo*, *WGe*, *Leo*, 1975 *Sp*, *R*, *Sp*, 1977 *R*, *Pol*, *Cze*, *R*, *Sp*, 1978 *F*
F Salvadego 1985 *Z*
R Salvan 1973 *Yug*, 1974 *Pt*
L Salvati 1987 *USS*, 1988 *USS*, *I*
R Santofadre 1952 *Sp*, *Ger*, *F*, 1954 *Sp*, *F*
Sarto 2013 *S*
F Sartorato 1956 *Ger*, *F*, 1957 *F*
M Savi 2004 *R*, *J*, 2005 *E*
S Saviozzi 1998 *Rus*, *H*, 1999 *W*, *I*, *SA*, *SA*, *Ur*, *Fj*, *Tg*, *NZ*, 2000 *C*, *NZ*, 2002 *NZ*, *Sp*
F Sbaraglini 2009 *S*, *F*, *A*, *NZ*, 2010 *SA*
D Scaglia 1994 *R*, *W*, 1995 *S*, 1996 *W*, *A*, 1999 *W*
E Scalzotto 1974 *Mid*, *Sus*, *Oxo*
A Scanavacca 1999 *Ur*, 2001 *E*, 2002 *Sp*, *R*, 2004 *US*, 2006 *Ar*, *C*, 2007 *F*, *E*, *S*, *I*
R Sciacol 1965 *Cze*
I Scodavolpe 1954 *Sp*
F Screnci 1977 *Cze*, *R*, *Sp*, 1978 *F*, 1979 *Pol*, *R*, *E*, 1982 *F*, 1984 *Mor*
A Selvaggio 1973 *Rho*, *WTv*, *ETv*, *Leo*, *FS*, *Tva*
F Semenzato 2011 *E*, *W*, *F*, *S*, *S*, *A*, *US*, *I*, 2012 *F*, *E*, *I*, *W*
M Sepe 2006 *J*, *Fj*, 2010 *SA*
D Sesenna 1992 *R*, 1993 *Cro*, *Mor*, *F*, 1994 *R*
G Sessa 1930 *Sp*
G Sessi 1942 *R*
A Sgarbi 2008 *E*, *W*, 2009 *A*, *A*, *SA*, 2010 *Ar*, *A*, *Fj*, 2011 *I*, *E*, *W*, *S*, *J*, *Rus*, 2012 *F*, *I*, *W*, *Ar*, *C*, *US*, *Tg*, *NZ*, *A*, 2013 *F*, *SA*, *S*
E Sgorbati 1933 *Cze*, 1934 *Cat*, *R*, 1935 *Cat*, *F*, 1936 *Ger*, 1937 *Ger*, 1938 *Ger*, 1939 *Ger*, 1940 *R*, *Ger*, 1942 *R*
E Sgorbati 1968 *WGe*, *Yug*
A Sgorlon 1993 *Pt*, *Mor*, *Sp*, *F*, *Rus*, *F*, *S*, 1994 *CZR*, *R*, *W*, 1995 *S*, *E*, *Ar*, *F*, *Ar*, *R*, *NZ*, *SA*, 1996 *W*, *Pt*, *W*, *A*, *E*, *S*, 1997 *I*, *F*, *F*, *Ar*, *R*, *SA*, *I*, 1998 *S*, *W*, *Rus*, 1999 *F*, *S*, *W*
P Sguario 1958 *R*, 1959 *F*, 1960 *Ger*, *F*, 1961 *Ger*, 1962 *R*
M Silini 1955 *Ger*, *Sp*, *F*, *Cze*, 1956 *Cze*, 1957 *Ger*, 1958 *F*, 1959 *F*
S Silvestri 1954 *F*
U Silvestri 1949 *F*, *Cze*
U Silvestri 1967 *Pt*, *R*, 1968 *Pt*, *WGe*
L Simonelli 1956 *Ger*, *F*, *Cze*, 1958 *F*, 1960 *Ger*, *F*
F Sinitich 1980 *Fj*, *Coo*, *Pol*, *Sp*, 1981 *R*, 1983 *USS*
JW Sole 2005 *Ar*, *Tg*, *Ar*, 2006 *I*, *E*, *F*, *W*, *S*, *J*, *Fj*, *Rus*, *A*, *Ar*, *C*, 2007 *F*, *E*, *I*, *Ur*, *Ar*, *J*, *I*, *R*, *S*, 2008 *I*, *E*, *W*, *F*, *S*, *SA*, *Ar*, *A*, *Ar*, *PI*, 2009 *E*, *I*, *S*, *W*, *F*, *NZ*, *SA*, *Sa*, 2010 *I*, *E*, *S*, *F*, *W*, 2011 *I*
F Soro 1965 *Cze*, 1966 *F*, *Ger*, *R*
A Spagnoli 1973 *Rho*

E Speziali 1965 *Cze*
W Spragg 2006 *C*
F Staibano 2006 *J, Fj,* 2007 *W, I, Ur, Ar,* 2009 *A, A, NZ,* 2012 *I, W*
MP Stanojevic 2006 *Pt, Rus, A, Ar, C,* 2007 *J, NZ*
U Stenta 1937 *Bel, Ger, F,* 1938 *Ger,* 1939 *Ger, R,* 1940 *R, Ger,* 1942 *R*
P Stievano 1948 *F,* 1952 *F,* 1953 *F, Ger, R,* 1954 *Sp, F,* 1955 *Ger*
S Stocco 1998 *H,* 1999 *S, I,* 2000 *Fj*
CA Stoica 1997 *I, F, SA, I,* 1998 *S, W, Rus, Ar, H, E,* 1999 *S, W, SA, SA, Ur, Sp, Fj, E, Tg, NZ,* 2000 *S, W, I, E, F, Sa, Fj, C, R, NZ,* 2001 *I, E, F, S, W, Fj, SA, Sa,* 2002 *F, S, W, I, E, Sp, R, Ar, A,* 2003 *W, I, S, I, Geo, Tg, C, W,* 2004 *E, F, S, I, W, US,* 2005 *S, Tg, Ar,* 2006 *I, E, F, W, S,* 2007 *Ur, Ar*

L Tagliabue 1930 *Sp,* 1933 *Cze, Cze,* 1934 *Cat, R,* 1935 *F,* 1937 *Ger*
S Tartaglini 1948 *Cze,* 1949 *F, Cze,* 1951 *Sp,* 1952 *Sp, Ger, F,* 1953 *F*
A Tassin 1973 *A*
A Taveggia 1954 *F,* 1955 *Ger, F, Sp, F,* 1956 *Ger, F, Cze,* 1957 *F, Ger,* 1958 *F, R,* 1959 *F,* 1960 *Ger, F,* 1967 *Pt*
D Tebaldi 1985 *Z, Z,* 1987 *R, Ar, Fj, USS, Sp,* 1988 *F, A, I,* 1989 *F,* 1990 *F, Pol, R,* 1991 *Nm*
T Tebaldi 2009 *A, A, NZ, NZ, SA, Sa,* 2010 *I, E, S, F, W, SA, SA, Ar,* 2012 *C, US*
T Tedeschi 1948 *F*
G Testoni 1937 *Bel,* 1938 *Ger,* 1942 *R*
C Tinari 1980 *JAB, Coo, Pol, USS, Sp,* 1981 *USS, WGe,* 1982 *F, WGe,* 1983 *R, USS, C, C, Sp, Mor, A, USS,* 1984 *Mor, R*
M Tommasi 1990 *Pol,* 1992 *R, S,* 1993 *Pt, Cro, Sp, F*
G Toniolatti 2008 *A,* 2009 *E, I, A, NZ,* 2011 *J, Rus, US,* 2012 *W, S, Ar, C*
C Torresan 1980 *F, R, Fj, Coo, Pol, USS,* 1981 *R, USS,* 1982 *R, Mor,* 1983 *C, F, A, USS,* 1984 *F, Mor, Tun, USS,* 1985 *Z, Z, USS*
F Tozzi 1933 *Cze*
P Travagli 2004 *C, NZ,* 2008 *I, E, W, F, S, Ar, PI*
L Travini 1999 *SA, Ur, Sp, Fj,* 2000 *I*
F Trebbi 1933 *Cze, Cze*
F Trentin 1979 *Mor, F, Pol, USS,* 1981 *R*
M Trevisiol 1988 *F, USS, A, I,* 1989 *F, Ar, USS,* 1994 *R*
M Trippiteli 1979 *Pol,* 1980 *Pol, Sp,* 1981 *F, R,* 1982 *F, E, WGe,* 1984 *Tun*
LR Troiani 1985 *R,* 1986 *Tun, F, Pt, A, USS,* 1987 *Pt, F,* 1988 *R, USS, A, I,* 1989 *Sp, Ar, Z, USS,* 1990 *F, Pol, R, Sp, H, R, USS,* 1991 *F, R, Nm, Nm, US, E,* 1992 *Sp, F, R, R, S,* 1993 *Sp, F, Cro, Rus, F,* 1994 *Sp, CZR, A, A, F,* 1995 *S, E, Ar*
A Troncon 1994 *Sp, R, CZR, H, A, A, R, W, F,* 1995 *S, I, Sa, E, Ar, F, Ar, R, NZ, SA,* 1996 *W, W, A, E, S,* 1997 *I, F, F, Ar, SA, I,* 1998 *S, W, Rus, Ar, H, E,* 1999 *F, S, W, I, Ur, Sp, Fj, E, Tg, NZ,* 2000 *S, W, I, E, F, R, NZ,* 2001 *I, F, Nm, SA, Ur, Ar, Fj, SA, Sa,* 2002 *F, S, W, I, E, Sp, R, Ar, A,* 2003 *W, I, E, F, S, S, I, Geo, NZ, Tg, C, W,* 2004 *R, J,* 2005 *I, W, S, E, F,* 2007 *F, E, S, W, I, J, I, NZ, R, Pt, S*
G Troncon 1962 *F, Ger, R,* 1963 *F,* 1964 *Ger, F,* 1965 *Cze,* 1966 *F, R,* 1967 *F,* 1968 *Yug,* 1972 *Pt*
L Turcato 1952 *Sp, Ger, F,* 1953 *Ger, R*
M Turcato 1949 *F,* 1951 *Sp*

P Vaccari 1991 *Nm, Nm, US, E, NZ, USS,* 1992 *Sp, F, R, R, S,* 1993 *Mor, Sp, F, Rus, F, S,* 1994 *Sp, R, CZR, H, A, A, R, W, F,* 1995 *I, Sa, E, Ar, F, Ar, R, NZ, SA,* 1996 *W, W, E, S,* 1997 *I, F, F, Ar, R, SA, I,* 1998 *S, W, Ar,* 1999 *Ur, Sp, E, Tg, NZ,* 2001 *Fj,* 2002 *F, S, Ar, A,* 2003 *W, I, E, F, S*
V Vagnetti 1939 *R,* 1940 *R*
F Valier 1968 *Yug,* 1969 *F,* 1970 *Cze, R,* 1971 *Mor, R,* 1972 *Pt*
L Valtorta 1957 *Ger,* 1958 *F*
C Van Zyl 2011 *J, S, A, Rus, US, I,* 2012 *F, W*
G Venditti 2012 *F, E, I, S, Ar, C, US, NZ, A,* 2013 *F, S, W, E, I, SA, Sa, S*
O Vene 1966 *F*
E Venturi 1983 *C,* 1985 *EngB, Sp,* 1986 *Tun, Pt,* 1988 *USS, A,* 1989 *F, R, Sp, Ar, USS,* 1990 *F, Pol, R, Sp, H, R, USS,* 1991 *F, R, NZ, USS,* 1992 *Sp, F, R,* 1993 *Sp, F*
P Vezzani 1973 *Yug,* 1975 *F, Sp, R, Cze, E, Pol, H, Sp,* 1976 *F*
F Vialetto 1972 *Yug*
V Viccariotto 1948 *F*
S Vigliano 1937 *R, Bel, Ger, F,* 1939 *R,* 1942 *R*
L Villagra 2000 *Sa, Fj*
E Vinci I 1929 *Sp*
P Vinci II 1929 *Sp,* 1930 *Sp,* 1933 *Cze*
F Vinci III 1929 *Sp,* 1930 *Sp,* 1934 *Cat, R,* 1935 *Cat, F,* 1936 *Ger, R,* 1937 *Ger, R, Ger, F,* 1939 *Ger, R,* 1940 *Ger*
P Vinci IV 1929 *Sp,* 1930 *Sp,* 1933 *Cze, Cze,* 1934 *Cat, R,* 1935 *Cat, F,* 1937 *Ger, Bel, Ger, F,* 1939 *Ger*
A Visentin 1970 *R,* 1972 *Pt, Sp,* 1973 *Rho, WTv, Bor, NEC, Nat, ETv, Leo, FS, Tva, Cze, Yug, A,* 1974 *Pt, Leo,* 1975 *F, Sp, R, Cze,* 1976 *R,* 1978 *Ar*
G Visentin 1935 *Cat, F,* 1936 *R,* 1937 *Ger, Bel, Ger, F,* 1938 *Ger,* 1939 *Ger*
T Visentin 1996 *W*
W Visser 1999 *I, SA, SA,* 2000 *S, W, I, F, C, R, NZ,* 2001 *I, E, F, S, W, Nm, SA, Ur, Ar, Fj, SA, Sa*
F Vitadello 1985 *Sp,* 1987 *Pt*
C Vitelli 1973 *Cze, Yug,* 1974 *Pt, Sus*
I Vittorini 1969 *Sp*
RMS Vosawai 2007 *J, I, NZ, R, Pt,* 2010 *W, SA,* 2011 *W,* 2012 *S, A,* 2013 *W, Sa*

RS Wakarua 2003 *Tg, C, W,* 2004 *E, F, S, W, J, C, NZ,* 2005 *Fj*
F Williams 1995 *SA*

M Zaffiri 2000 *Fj, R, NZ,* 2001 *W,* 2003 *S,* 2005 *Tg, Fj,* 2006 *W, S, C,* 2007 *E, S, W, I*
R Zanatta 1954 *Sp, F*
G Zanchi 1953 *Ger, R,* 1955 *Sp, Cze,* 1957 *Ger*
A Zanella 1977 *Mor*
M Zanella 1976 *J, Sp,* 1977 *R, Pol, Cze,* 1978 *Ar,* 1980 *Pol, USS*
E Zanetti 1942 *R*
F Zani 1960 *Ger, F,* 1961 *Ger, F,* 1962 *F, R,* 1963 *F,* 1964 *F,* 1965 *F,* 1966 *Ger, R*
G Zani 1934 *R*
A Zanni 2005 *Tg, Ar, Fj,* 2006 *F, W, S, Pt, Rus, A, Ar, C,* 2007 *S, W, I, Ur, I, NZ,* 2008 *I, E, W, F, S, SA, Ar, A, PI,* 2009 *E, I, S, W, F, A, A, NZ, NZ, SA, Sa,* 2010 *I, E, S, F, W, SA, SA, Ar, A, Fj,* 2011 *I, E, W, F, S, J, S, A, Rus, US, I,* 2012 *F, E, I, W, S, Ar, C, US, Tg, NZ, A,* 2013 *F, S, W, E, I, SA, Sa, S*
C Zanoletti 2001 *Sa,* 2002 *E, NZ, R, Ar, A,* 2005 *A*
G Zanon 1981 *F, R, USS, WGe,* 1982 *R, E, WGe, Mor,* 1983 *F, R, USS, C, C, Sp, Mor, F, A, USS,* 1984 *F, Mor, R, USS,* 1985 *F, R, EngB, Sp, Z, Z, USS,* 1986 *USS,* 1987 *R, Ar, USS,* 1989 *Sp, Ar,* 1990 *F, Pol, R, Sp, H, R, USS,* 1991 *Nm, US, E*
M Zingarelli 1973 *A*
N Zisti 1999 *E, NZ,* 2000 *E, F*
G Zoffoli 1936 *Ger, R,* 1937 *Ger, R, Ger,* 1938 *Ger,* 1939 *R*
S Zorzi 1985 *R,* 1986 *Tun, F,* 1988 *F, R, USS,* 1992 *R*
A Zucchelo 1956 *Ger, F*
C Zucchi 1952 *Sp,* 1953 *F*
L Zuin 1977 *Cze,* 1978 *Ar, USS, Sp,* 1979 *F, Pol, R*

JAPAN

JAPAN'S 2012–13 TEST RECORD

OPPONENTS	DATE	VENUE	RESULT
Romania	10 Nov	A	Won 34–23
Georgia	17 Nov	A	Won 25–22
Philippines	20 Apr	H	Won 121–0
Hong Kong	27 Apr	A	Won 38–0
Korea	4 May	H	Won 64–5
UAE	10 May	A	Won 93–3
Tonga	25 May	H	Lost 17–27
Fiji	1 Jun	A	Lost 22–8
Wales	8 June	H	Lost 18–22
Wales	15 Jun	H	Won 23–8
Canada	19 Jun	H	Won 16–13
USA	23 June	H	Won 38–20

JAPAN MAKE HISTORY AT HOME AND ABROAD

By Rich Freeman

Getty Images

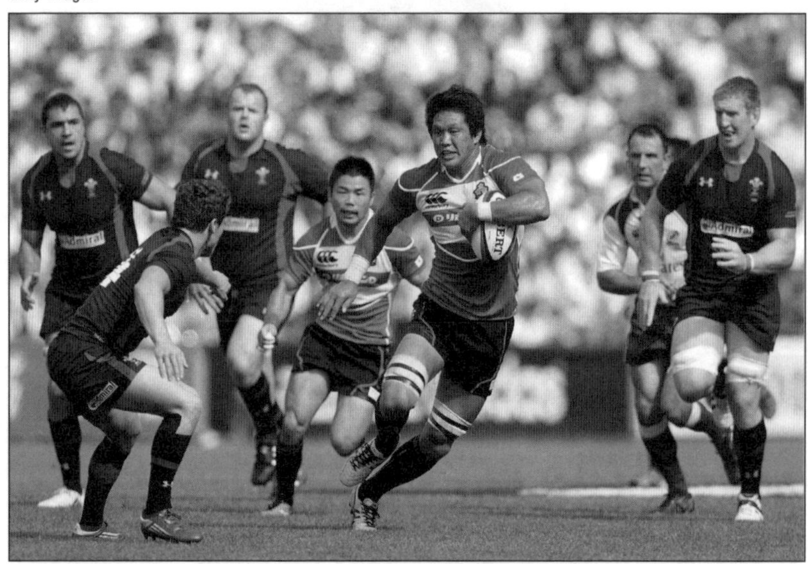

Takashi Kikutani makes a break in Japan's historic win over Wales, their first ever over a top 10 nation.

Japan didn't just enjoy their busiest international year, they also rose to the occasion and had their most successful year on record.

Eddie Jones's side played 12 Tests, winning nine, including a first-ever victory in Europe outside of a Rugby World Cup, and an historic first win over a country ranked in the world's top 10.

They also maintained their perfect record in the HSBC Asian 5 Nations, and finished the year off with three wins in the space of eight days.

"Of our three losses, we could have beaten Wales in the first Test, played badly for the first 40 minutes against Tonga and tactically got things wrong against Fiji. It just shows how far we have come," said Jones.

On top of all that Japan also had their first two representatives in Super Rugby, with Shota Horie and Fumiaki Tanaka doing more than enough to ensure they are likely to be followed by a number of other Brave Blossoms.

"Shota and Fumi have had an enormous impact on the players and a number of our young players have told me they now want to play Super Rugby," said Jones. "As we have seen with soccer, that can only be good for the national team as playing at a higher level soon becomes the norm for the players, not the unusual."

Japan's long year began in eastern Europe in November with Tests against Romania and Georgia. Jones had named a squad that combined experience and youth and it was the former that led the way in Bucharest. Takashi Kikutani scored a try in the first half before Hirotoki Onozawa sealed the 34–23 win with a five-pointer late in the second.

The win marked the first time that Japan had beaten a European country in Europe, their only other win in the continent coming against Zimbabwe in Belfast at Rugby World Cup 1991. They promptly made it two victories in seven days when they defeated Georgia the following week, thanks to a last-minute drop goal from Kosei Ono, who was wearing borrowed boots having left his own pair in Romania.

"I've lost one big game through a drop goal but never won one till now," said Jones, referring to the Rugby World Cup 2003 final when the Australia team that he coached was beaten by England and Jonny Wilkinson.

The remaining two games on the tour – against a Basque Select XV and the French Barbarians – may have been lost, but the Brave Blossoms returned home having done what they had set out to achieve.

"To come away with victories against Romania and Georgia was a real tribute to the resilience of the players," said Jones. "What made the victories all the more remarkable – or miraculous – was that we won just 17 per cent of our own scrum ball in those two games."

Not winning their own scrum ball was never going to be an issue in the Asian 5 Nations, and Japan showed from the outset that they were on a mission to maintain their perfect record in the competition. Jones's side ran in 18 tries in a 121–0 demolition of the Philippines, no mean feat given the game was played in torrential rain.

Five players grabbed a brace of tries, including debutant Kenki Fukuoka, while Ayumu Goromaru ended the day with 36 points, courtesy of a try, a penalty and 14 conversions.

"That was the third-biggest winning score ever for Japan and to do it in conditions where the ball is like a piece of soap is not a bad effort," said Jones. "On a good day we could have scored 160 points, I have no doubt."

A week later in Hong Kong, Japan picked up their 22nd straight bonus point win in the competition as they downed the former British colony 38–0. Captain Toshiaki Hirose led the way with two tries, but it was the locals who did a lap of honour at the end of the game following a valiant defensive effort.

Japan clinched their sixth straight Asian title a week later in Tokyo when they beat Korea 64–5, although they did not pick up the silverware until they completed their campaign with a 93–3 victory over the United Arab Emirates in Dubai.

The win was Japan's sixth straight, matching a national record but, as Jones pointed out, it didn't mean too much in the big scheme of things.

"No disrespect to the UAE but we can't take too much out of that," he said. "We weren't really tested, especially in terms of speed, physicality and speed of decision-making. We've still got a lot of work to do before we take on the likes of Tonga and Wales."

Japan opened the expanded IRB Pacific Nations Cup against Tonga in Yokohama and were brought down to earth by the physical Pacific islanders, who won 27–17.

A week later in monsoon-like conditions in Lautoka, Japan fell to a second consecutive loss as they went down 22–8 to Fiji. Jones later admitted he had got things wrong, both in the build-up to the game, which was marred by a serious leg injury to Michael Leitch, and also in the tactical approach of the team.

The return of Horie and Tanaka, however, seemed to give everyone in the camp a spark and Japan went into the first Test with Wales hoping to produce an upset. And they could have done it were it not for a rare off day from Goromaru, who missed a number of kicks, allowing the Six Nations champions (albeit missing their British & Irish Lions representatives) a 22–18 win.

Seven days later in front of a full house at the Prince Chichibu Memorial Rugby Ground in Tokyo, Goromaru made amends as he knocked over three penalties and converted tries by Craig Wing and Michael Broadhurst as Japan won the second Test 23–8.

"We have created history today," said Jones. "We are the first Japan team to beat a top 10 team in the world. We understand the Welsh didn't have 15 of their best players here. But we played a very good game of Test rugby and it's another step forward for the team."

The game in Tokyo marked the first of three Tests in eight days for the Brave Blossoms and, with Japanese rugby on a high, the local heroes didn't disappoint. A penalty by Goromaru eight minutes from time saw Japan down Canada 16–13, before they rounded off their year with a 38–20 victory over the United States.

"Twenty-two of the 23 players were playing their third Test in eight days, so it's an unbelievable effort," raved Jones, who gave particular praise to spot coaches Steve Borthwick and Marc Dal Maso for their efforts in making the Japan pack a truly competitive outfit.

Earlier in the year, Suntory Sungoliath won the league and cup double, becoming the first team to go through a domestic season unbeaten. Inspired by George Smith, who picked up his second straight MVP award, the Sungoliath downed local rivals Toshiba Brave Lupus 19–3 in the Top League final, before beating Kobe Kobelco Steelers 36–20 in the final of the All-Japan Championship.

JAPAN INTERNATIONAL STATISTICS

MATCH RECORDS UP TO 10 OCTOBER 2013

WINNING MARGIN

Date	Opponent	Result	Winning Margin
06/07/2002	Chinese Taipei	155–3	**152**
27/10/1998	Chinese Taipei	134–6	**128**
20/04/2013	Philippines	121–0	**121**
21/07/2002	Chinese Taipei	120–3	**117**
13/05/2011	United Arab Emirates	111–0	**111**

MOST POINTS IN A MATCH

BY THE TEAM

Date	Opponent	Result	Points
06/07/2002	Chinese Taipei	155–3	**155**
27/10/1998	Chinese Taipei	134–6	**134**
20/04/2013	Philippines	121–0	**121**
21/07/2002	Chinese Taipei	120–3	**120**
03/05/2008	Arabian Gulf	114–6	**114**

BY A PLAYER

Date	Player	Opponent	Points
21/07/2002	Toru Kurihara	Chinese Taipei	**60**
06/07/2002	Daisuke Ohata	Chinese Taipei	**40**
20/04/2013	Ayumu Goromaru	Philippines	**36**
16/06/2002	Toru Kurihara	Korea	**35**
08/05/1999	Keiji Hirose	Tonga	**34**

MOST TRIES IN A MATCH

BY THE TEAM

Date	Opponent	Result	Tries
06/07/2002	Chinese Taipei	155–3	**23**
27/10/1998	Chinese Taipei	134–6	**20**
21/07/2002	Chinese Taipei	120–3	**18**
03/05/2008	Arabian Gulf	114–6	**18**
20/04/2013	Philippines	121–0	**18**

BY A PLAYER

Date	Player	Opponent	Tries
06/07/2002	Daisuke Ohata	Chinese Taipei	**8**
21/07/2002	Toru Kurihara	Chinese Taipei	**6**
08/05/2005	Daisuke Ohata	Hong Kong	**6**
05/05/2012	Yoshikazu Fujita	United Arab Emirates	**6**

MOST CONVERSIONS IN A MATCH

BY THE TEAM

Date	Opponent	Result	Cons
06/07/2002	Chinese Taipei	155–3	**20**
27/10/1998	Chinese Taipei	134–6	**17**
21/07/2002	Chinese Taipei	120–3	**15**
20/04/2013	Philippines	121–0	**14**

BY A PLAYER

Date	Player	Opponent	Cons
21/07/2002	Toru Kurihara	Chinese Taipei	**15**
20/04/2013	Ayumu Goromaru	Philippines	**14**
06/07/2002	Andy Miller	Chinese Taipei	**12**
13/05/2011	James Arlidge	United Arab Emirates	**12**

MOST PENALTIES IN A MATCH

BY THE TEAM

Date	Opponent	Result	Pens
08/05/1999	Tonga	44–17	**9**
08/04/1990	Tonga	28–16	**6**

BY A PLAYER

Date	Player	Opponent	Pens
08/05/1999	Keiji Hirose	Tonga	**9**
08/04/1990	Takahiro Hosokawa	Tonga	**6**

MOST DROP GOALS IN A MATCH

BY THE TEAM

Date	Opponent	Result	DGs
15/09/1998	Argentina	44–29	**2**

BY A PLAYER

Date	Player	Opponent	DGs
15/09/1998	Kensuke Iwabuchi	Argentina	**2**

MOST CAPPED PLAYERS

Name	Caps
Hirotoki Onozawa	81
Yukio Motoki	79
Hitoshi Ono	73
Takashi Kikutani	63
Takeomi Ito	62

LEADING TRY SCORERS

Name	Tries
Daisuke Ohata	69
Hirotoki Onozawa	55
Takashi Kikutani	32
Terunori Masuho	28
Alisi Tupuailai	21

LEADING CONVERSION SCORERS

Name	Cons
James Arlidge	78
Keiji Hirose	77
Ayumu Goromaru	73
Toru Kurihara	71
Ryan Nicholas	53

LEADING PENALTY SCORERS

Name	Pens
Keiji Hirose	76
Toru Kurihara	35
James Arlidge	28
Ayumu Goromaru	28
Takahiro Hosokawa	24

LEADING DROP GOAL SCORERS

Name	DGs
Kyohei Morita	5

LEADING POINT SCORERS

Name	Points
Keiji Hirose	413
Toru Kurihara	347
Daisuke Ohata	345
Ayumu Goromaru	300
James Arlidge	286
Hirotoki Onozawa	275

JAPAN INTERNATIONAL PLAYERS

UP TO 10 OCTOBER 2013

T Adachi 1932 *C, C*
M Aizawa 1984 *Kor*, 1986 *US, C, S, E, Kor*, 1987 *A, NZ, NZ*, 1988 *OU, Kor*
H Akama 1973 *F*, 1975 *A, W*, 1976 *S, E, It, Kor*, 1977 *S*
T Akatsuka 1994 *Fj*, 1995 *Tg, NZ*, 1996 *Kor*, 2005 *Sp*, 2006 *HK, Kor*
J Akune 2001 *W, C*
M Amino 2000 *Kor, C*, 2003 *Rus, AuA, Kor, E, E, S, Fj, US*
E Ando 2006 *AG, Kor, Geo, Tg, Sa, JAB, Fj*, 2007 *HK, Fj, Tg, Sa, JAB, It*
D Anglesey 2002 *Tg, Tai, Tai*
T Aoi 1959 *BCo, BCo, OCC*, 1963 *BCo*
S Aoki 1989 *S*, 1990 *Fj*, 1991 *US, C*, 1993 *W*
Y Aoki 2007 *Kor, AuA, JAB*, 2008 *Kor, Kaz, HK, AuA, Tg, Fj, Sa, US, US*, 2009 *Kaz, Sin, Sa, JAB, Tg, Fj*, 2011 *Sa, Tg, US, NZ*, 2013 *PHP, HK, Kor, UAE, Tg, Fj*
S Arai 1959 *BCo, BCo*
R Arita 2012 *Kaz, UAE, Kor, HK, Fj, Tg, Sa*
JA Arlidge 2007 *Kor*, 2008 *Kor, AG, Kaz, HK, AuA, Tg, Fj, M, Sa*, 2009 *Sa, JAB, Tg, Fj, C, C*, 2010 *Kor, AG, Kaz, HK, Fj, Sa, Tg, Sa, Rus*, 2011 *Kaz, UAE, Tg, It, F, Tg, C*
G Aruga 2006 *HK, Kor*, 2007 *Kor, HK, AuA, Sa, JAB, It, Fj, C*, 2008 *Kor, HK*, 2009 *C, C*, 2011 *UAE, Fj*, 2012 *R, Geo*
K Aruga 1974 *NZU*, 1975 *A, A, W, W*, 1976 *S, E, It, Kor*
T Asahara 2013 *PHP, HK, Kor, UAE, Fj*
R Asano 2003 *AuA, AuA, F, Fj*, 2005 *Ar, HK, Kor, R, C, I, I, Sp*, 2006 *Kor, Geo, Tg, It, HK, Kor*, 2007 *Kor, It, W*
M Atokawa 1969 *HK*, 1970 *Tha, BCo*, 1971 *E, E*
H Atou 1976 *BCo*

T Baba 1932 *C*
GTM Bachop 1999 *C, Tg, Sa, Fj, Sp, Sa, W, Ar*
I Basiyalo 1997 *HK, US, US, C, HK*
D Bickle 1996 *HK, HK, C, US, US, C*
M Broadhurst 2012 *R, Geo*, 2013 *PHP, HK, Kor, UAE, Tg, Fj, W, W, C, US*

KCC Chang 1930 *BCo*, 1932 *C, C*
T Chiba 1930 *BCo*
M Chida 1980 *Kor*, 1982 *HK, C, C, Kor*, 1983 *W*, 1984 *F, F, Kor*, 1985 *US, I, I, F, F*, 1986 *US, C, S, E, Kor*, 1987 *US, E*

H Daimon 2004 *S, W*

K Endo 2004 *It*, 2006 *AG, Kor, Geo, Tg, It, JAB, Fj*, 2007 *HK, Fj, Tg, AuA, Sa, It, Fj, W, C*, 2008 *AuA, Tg, Fj, M, US, US*, 2009 *C, C*, 2010 *Kor, AG, Kaz, HK, Fj, Sa, Tg, Sa, Rus*, 2011 *UAE, Sa, Tg, It, F, Tg, C*
J Enomoto 2005 *Sp*
R Enomoto 1959 *BCo, BCo*

B Ferguson 1993 *W*, 1994 *Fj, Fj, HK, Kor*, 1995 *Tg, Tg, R, W, I, NZ*, 1996 *HK, HK, C, US, US, C*
K Fijii 2000 *Sa*
S Fuchigami 2000 *I*, 2002 *Rus, Tai*, 2003 *US, Rus*
A Fuji 1959 *BCo, BCo*
A Fujii 1956 *AuUn*
J Fujii 2012 *Kaz, UAE, Kor, HK, Fj, Sa*
M Fujii 1930 *BCo*
M Fujikake 1993 *W*, 1994 *HK, Kor*, 1995 *Tg*
T Fujimoto-Kamohara 1969 *HK*, 1970 *BCo*, 1971 *E, E*, 1972 *HK*, 1973 *W*
N Fujita 2010 *Kor, AG, Kaz, Rus*, 2011 *HK, UAE, SL, Fj, It, US, F, NZ, Tg, C*

T Fujita 1980 *H, F*, 1983 *W*, 1984 *F, F, Kor*, 1985 *US, I, I, F, F*, 1986 *US, C, S, E*, 1987 *US, E, A, NZ, NZ*, 1989 *S*, 1990 *Fj, Tg, Kor, Sa*, 1991 *US, US, I*
Y Fujita 2012 *UAE*, 2013 *HK, Kor, UAE, Tg, W, W, C, US*
M Fujiwara 1973 *W*, 1974 *NZU*, 1975 *A, A, W, W*, 1976 *S, E, It*, 1977 *S*, 1978 *F, Kor*, 1979 *HK, E*, 1980 *H, F*
K Fukumuro 1990 *Kor*
K Fukuoka 2013 *PHP, Kor, Tg, Fj, W, W, C*
K Fukuoka 2000 *Fj*
S Fukuoka 1990 *Kor*
R Fukurodate 1976 *BCo, Kor*, 1979 *E, E*, 1980 *H, F, Kor*
T Fumihara 2000 *I*

T Goda 1990 *Fj, Tg, Kor, Sa, US, Kor*, 1991 *US*, 1995 *Tg*
WR Gordon 1997 *HK, C, US, US*, 1998 *C, US, HK, HK, US, C*, 1999 *C, Sa, Fj, Sp, Sa, W, Ar*
A Goromaru 2005 *Ur, R, C, I*, 2009 *Kaz, HK, Kor, Sin, JAB, C*, 2010 *Sa*, 2012 *Kaz, UAE, Kor, HK, Fj, Tg, Sa, R, Geo*, 2013 *PHP, HK, Kor, Tg, Fj, W, W, C, US*
S Goto 2005 *Ur, Ar, Kor, R, C, I, I*, 2006 *HK*

M Hagimoto 1987 *E*
T Hagiwara-Maekawa 1930 *BCo*
K Hamabe 1996 *C, US, US, C, Kor*, 1997 *HK, C, US, US, C*, 2001 *Sa, C*
T Haneda 1995 *Tg*
S Hara 1970 *BCo*, 1971 *E, E*, 1973 *W, F*, 1974 *NZU, SL*, 1975 *A, W*, 1976 *E*
T Harada 1959 *BCo*
S Hasegawa 1997 *HK*, 1998 *C, US, HK, HK, US, C, Ar, Kor, Tai, HK, Kor*, 1999 *C, Tg, Sa, Fj, US, Sa, W, Ar*, 2000 *Fj, US, Tg, Sa, C*, 2001 *W, W, Sa, C*, 2002 *Tg, Kor, Tai, Kor*, 2003 *US, AuA, E, S, F, Fj, US*
D Hashimoto 2012 *UAE*
S Hashimoto 1953 *OCC*
K Hatakeyama 2008 *US, US*, 2009 *HK, Sin, Sa, JAB, Tg, Fj, C, C*, 2010 *Kor, Kaz, Sa, Tg, Sa*, 2011 *Kaz, UAE, SL, Sa, Tg, Fj, It, US, F, NZ, Tg, C*, 2012 *Kaz, UAE, Kor, HK, Fj, Tg, Sa, R, Geo*, 2013 *PHP, HK, Kor, UAE, Tg, Fj, W, W, C, US*
T Hatakeyama 1976 *It, Kor*, 1977 *S*, 1978 *F, Kor*, 1979 *HK, E, E*
T Hayashi 1989 *S*
T Hayashi 1980 *F*, 1982 *C, C, Kor*, 1983 *W*, 1984 *F, F*, 1985 *US, I, I, F, F*, 1986 *US, C, S, E, Kor*, 1987 *US, E, A, IrSt, NZ, NZ*, 1990 *Tg, Sa*, 1991 *US, C, HK, S, I, Z*, 1992 *HK*
T Higashida 1983 *W*
T Hirai 1980 *Kor*, 1982 *HK*
S Hirao 1932 *C, C*
S Hirao 1983 *W*, 1984 *F, F*, 1985 *US, I, I*, 1986 *US, C, S, E*, 1987 *US, E, A, NZ, NZ*, 1988 *Kor*, 1989 *S*, 1990 *Fj, Tg, Kor, US, Kor*, 1991 *US, C, HK, S, I, Z*, 1995 *R, W, I*
T Hirao 1998 *Kor*, 1999 *Tg, Sa, W*, 2001 *Tai, Sa, C*, 2004 *Kor, Rus, C, It*
H Hirashima 2008 *US, US*, 2009 *Kaz, Kor, Sa, JAB, Tg, Fj, C, C*, 2010 *Kor, AG, Kaz, HK, Fj, Sa, Tg, Sa, Rus*, 2011 *Kaz, UAE, Sa, Tg, It, F, Tg, C*
T Hirata 2000 *US, C*
J Hiratsuka 1999 *US*
K Hirose 1994 *Kor*, 1995 *Tg, NZ*, 1996 *HK, HK, C, US, US, Kor*, 1998 *HK, HK, US, C, Kor, Tai, HK, Kor*, 1999 *C, Tg, Sa, Fj, US, Sp, Sa, W, Ar*, 2000 *Fj, US, Kor, C, I*, 2003 *AuA, AuA, Kor, E, E, S*, 2005 *HK, I, Sp*
T Hirose 2007 *HK*, 2012 *Kaz, UAE, Kor, HK, Fj, Tg, Sa, R, Geo*, 2013 *PHP, HK, W, C, US*
T Hirose 1988 *Kor*
E Hirotsu 1995 *Tg*
Y Hisadomi 2002 *Rus*, 2003 *Rus, AuA, Kor, E*, 2004 *Kor, C, It, S, R*, 2005 *Sp*, 2006 *AG, Kor, Geo, Tg, It, Sa, JAB, Fj, HK, Kor*
A Hiwasa 2011 *HK, UAE, Sa, Fj, It, US, F, NZ, Tg, C*, 2012 *Kor, HK, Fj, Tg, Sa, R, Geo*, 2013 *PHP, HK, Kor, UAE, Tg, Fj, W, W, C, US*
M Hohokabe 1978 *F, Kor*
RK Holani 2008 *Kaz, HK, AuA, Fj, M, Sa, US, US*, 2010 *HK, Fj, Sa, Tg, Sa, Rus*, 2011 *HK, UAE, Sa, Tg, It, F*, 2012 *R, Geo*, 2013 *PHP, HK, Kor*
K Honjo 1982 *C, C*, 1985 *US, I, F*
K Horaguchi 1979 *E, E*, 1980 *F*, 1982 *HK, C, C, Kor*, 1983 *W*, 1984 *F*, 1985 *US, I, I, F, F*, 1987 *US, E*
H Hori 1956 *AuUn*
S Horie 2009 *C, C*, 2010 *Kor, Kaz, HK, Fj, Sa, Tg, Sa, Rus*, 2011 *Tg, Fj, It, US, F, Tg, C*, 2012 *R, Geo*, 2013 *W, W, C, US*
M Horikoshi 1988 *Kor*, 1989 *S*, 1990 *Fj, Tg, Kor, US, Kor*, 1991 *US, C, HK, I, Z*, 1992 *HK*, 1993 *Ar, Ar*, 1994 *Kor*, 1995 *Tg, R, W, I*, 1997 *C*, 1998 *C, US, Tai, HK, Kor*
S Hoshino 1975 *W*, 1976 *S*, 1978 *Kor*, 1979 *HK*
T Hosokawa 1990 *Tg, Kor, Sa, US*, 1991 *US, S, I, Z*, 1993 *Ar, Ar*

S Iburi 1972 *HK*
M Iguchi 1973 *F*, 1974 *NZU*, 1975 *A, A, W*
H Ijyuin 1932 *C, C*
W Ikeda 2004 *Kor, Rus, C, It, S, R, W*, 2005 *Sp*, 2006 *AG, Geo, Tg, It, JAB, Fj*
Y Ikeda 1980 *Kor*, 1983 *W*, 1984 *F, F*
Y Ikegaya 2008 *AG, HK, M*
H Ikuta 1987 *US, A, NZ*
K Imaizumi 1988 *Kor*, 1994 *Fj, HK*, 1996 *US*, 1997 *C, US, US, C*
k Imakoma 1988 *Kor*
K Imamura 1959 *BCo, BCo*
R Imamura 1959 *BCo, BCo*
Y Imamura 2006 *AG, Geo, It, Sa, Fj*, 2007 *HK, Fj, Tg, AuA, Sa, JAB, It, Fj, W, C*, 2008 *AG, Kaz, HK, AuA, M*, 2009 *Kaz, Kor, Sin, Sa, JAB, Tg, Fj*, 2010 *Rus*, 2011 *Kaz, SL, Sa, Fj, NZ*, 2013 *HK, Kor, UAE, Fj, US*
R Imazato 1969 *HK*, 1970 *Tha, BCo*, 1971 *E, E*, 1972 *HK*, 1973 *W, F*, 1974 *JAB*, 1975 *CU, A, A, W, W*, 1976 *S, E, It*
T Inokuchi 2007 *It, A, W*, 2008 *AG, HK, AuA, M*
Y Inose 2008 *AG, Kaz, AuA, Tg, M, Sa*
M Inoue 1982 *C, C, Kor*
M Irie 2008 *US*
R Ishi 1999 *Sp*
K Ishii 1986 *S*
J Ishiyama 1980 *H, F, Kor*, 1982 *HK, C, Kor*, 1983 *W*, 1985 *US, I, I, F, F*
K Ishizuka 1963 *BCo*
T Ishizuka 1974 *NZU, SL*, 1975 *A, W, W*, 1978 *F, Kor*, 1979 *HK, E, E*, 1980 *H, F, Kor*, 1982 *HK, C, C, NZU, NZU, EnSt, NZU, Kor*
H Ito 2004 *Kor, Rus*
M Ito 2000 *Tg, Sa, Kor, C, I*, 2004 *Kor, C*, 2005 *Sp*, 2006 *AG, Kor, Geo, Tg, Sa, Fj, HK, Kor*
M Ito 1969 *HK*
S Ito 2012 *Kaz, UAE, Kor, HK, Fj, Tg, Sa*, 2013 *PHP, HK, Kor, UAE, Tg, Fj, W, W, C, US*
T Ito 1963 *BCo*, 1969 *HK*, 1970 *Tha, BCo*, 1971 *E*, 1972 *HK*, 1973 *W, F*, 1974 *NZU*
T Ito 1980 *H, F*, 1982 *HK, C, Kor*
T Ito 1996 *HK, HK, C, US, US, C, Kor*, 1997 *HK, C, US, US*, 1998 *C, US, HK, HK, US, C, Ar, Kor, Tai, HK, Kor*, 1999 *C, Tg, Sa, Fj, US, Sp, Sa, W, Ar*, 2000 *I*, 2001 *Kor, W, Sa, C*, 2002 *Rus, Tg, Kor, Tai, Kor, Tai*, 2003 *US, Rus, AuA, AuA, Kor, E, E, S, F, Fj, US*, 2004 *Kor, Rus, C, It*, 2005 *Ur, Ar, R, C, I*
JT Ives 2011 *HK, Kaz, UAE, SL, Sa, Tg, Fj, It*, 2013 *PHP, HK, Kor, W, C, US*
K Iwabuchi 1997 *HK, C, US, US, C, HK*, 1998 *C, US, Ar, Tai, HK*, 1999 *C*, 2001 *Kor, Tai, W, W, Sa*, 2002 *Tg, Kor, Tai, Kor*
Y Iwama 2000 *US, Tg, Sa, Kor, C*, 2001 *Tai*
H Iwashita 1930 *BCo*
Y Izawa 1970 *Tha, BCo*, 1971 *E, E*, 1972 *HK*, 1973 *W, F*, 1974 *NZU*, 1975 *A, A, W*, 1976 *S, E, It*
K Izawa-Nakamura 1995 *Tg, Tg, I, NZ*, 1996 *US, Kor*, 1997 *HK, C, US, US, C, HK*, 1998 *Ar, Kor, Tai, HK, Kor*

JW Joseph 1999 *C, Tg, Sa, Fj, US, Sp, Sa, W, Ar*

S Ka 1934 *AuUn*
H Kajihara 1989 *S*, 1990 *Fj, Tg, Kor, Sa, US, Kor*, 1991 *US, US, HK, S, I, Z*, 1993 *Ar, Ar*, 1994 *Fj, Fj, Kor*, 1995 *Tg, R, W, I, NZ*, 1996 *HK, HK, C, US, US, C, Kor*, 1997 *C*
S Kaleta 1992 *HK*, 1993 *Ar, Ar, W*
K Kamata 1970 *BCo*
T Kanai 2009 *Kaz, HK, Sin, JAB*
F Kanaya 1980 *F*, 1982 *HK, C, C*, 1983 *W*, 1984 *F, F, Kor*, 1985 *US*
R Kanazawa 2010 *AG, Sa, Tg*
Kanbara 1971 *E*
H Kaneshiro 1993 *Ar*
H Kano 1974 *SL*, 1982 *Kor*
T Kasahara 1932 *C, C*
K Kasai 1999 *C*, 2005 *Ar, HK, Kor, R, C, I, I*, 2006 *AG, Tg*
Y Kasai 1985 *F, F*
Y Katakura 1959 *BCo*
A Kato 2001 *Tai, W*
H Kato 1993 *Ar, Ar*
D Katsuno 2002 *Kor*
T Katsuraguchi 1970 *Tha*
H Kawachi 1980 *H, Kor*, 1982 *C*, 1983 *W*, 1984 *F, F, Kor*
K Kawachi 1984 *Kor*
R Kawai 2000 *I*
N Kawamata 2008 *US*, 2009 *HK, Kor, C, C*, 2010 *HK, Fj, Sa, Tg, Sa, Rus*, 2011 *HK, Kaz, SL, Tg, Fj, US, NZ*
K Kawasaki 1963 *BCo*
M Kawasaki 1970 *Tha*
T Kawasaki 2000 *US, Tg*

Y Kawase 1983 W, 1985 US, I, I, F, 1986 Kor, 1987 A
T Kikutani 2005 Sp, 2006 AG, Kor, Geo, Tg, It, Sa, JAB, Fj, Kor, 2008 Kor, AG, AuA, Tg, Fj, Sa, US, US, 2009 Kaz, HK, Kor, Sin, Sa, JAB, Tg, Fj, C, C, 2010 Kor, AG, Fj, Sa, Tg, Sa, Rus, 2011 HK, Kaz, UAE, SL, Sa, Tg, Fj, It, US, F, NZ, Tg, C, 2012 Fj, Tg, Sa, R, Geo, 2013 PHP, HK, Kor, UAE, Tg, Fj, W, W, C, US
CW Kim 2007 W, C
K Kimura 1996 C
T Kimura 1984 F, F, Kor, 1985 US, 1986 E, Kor, 1987 E, A, NZ
T Kinashita 2002 Tg, Kor
T Kinoshita 1932 C, C
H Kiso 2001 Kor, Tai, 2003 AuA, AuA, Kor, E, E, S, Fj, US, 2004 S, R, W, 2005 HK, I, Sp, 2006 AG, Kor, Geo, It, Sa, JAB, Fj, HK, Kor, 2007 Kor, Fj, AuA, A, W, C, 2008 US
T Kitagawa 2006 HK, 2007 HK, A
T Kitagawa 2005 Sp, 2006 AG, Kor, Tg, Sa, JAB, 2008 Kor, AG, Kaz, HK, AuA, Tg, Fj, M, Sa, US, US, 2009 Kaz, Kor, Sa, JAB, Tg, Fj, C, C, 2010 Kor, AG, HK, Fj, Sa, Tg, Sa, Rus, 2011 HK, Sa, Fj, It, F, NZ, Tg, C, 2013 Fj, W
Y Kitagawa 2007 Kor, 2009 HK, Kor, Sin, JAB, 2011 NZ
T Kitahara 1978 Kor, 1979 HK
H Kitajima 1963 BCo
T Kitano 1930 BCo, 1932 C, C
S Kitaoka 1959 BCo
T Kizu 2009 C, 2010 AG, 2011 HK, Kaz, UAE, Sa, Fj, 2012 Kaz, UAE, Kor, HK, Fj, Tg, Sa, 2013 HK, UAE, Tg, Fj, W, W, C, US
H Kobayashi 1983 W, 1984 F, Kor, 1985 I, F, 1986 Kor
I Kobayashi 1975 A, A, W, W, 1976 BCo, S, E, It, Kor, 1977 S, 1978 F, Kor, 1979 HK, E, E
K Kobayashi 1959 BCo, BCo
K Koizumi 1997 US, C, HK, 2000 Fj, US, Tg, Sa, C, 2001 W, Sa, C, 2002 Tg, Tai
J Komura 1992 HK, 1998 Kor, 2000 Kor, C
GN Konia 2003 US, AuA, AuA, F, Fj, US
K Konishi 1986 US, Kor
Y Konishi 1980 F, Kor, 1982 HK, Kor, 1983 W, 1984 F, F, Kor, 1985 US, I, I, F, F, 1986 US, C, S, E, Kor, 1987 NZ
M Koshiyama 1984 F, F, Kor, 1985 US, I, I, 1986 C, Kor, 1987 NZ, NZ
T Kouda 1988 Kor
O Koyabu 1974 SL
K Kubo 2000 I, 2001 Kor, W, W, Sa, C, 2002 Rus, Kor, Tai, Kor, Kor, 2003 US, Rus, E, F, Fj, 2004 Kor, C, It
K Kubota 2004 S, R, W
T Kudo-Nakayama 1979 E
T Kumagae 2004 Kor, Rus, C, It, S, R, W, 2005 Ur, Ar, Kor, R, C, I, I, Sp, 2006 AG, Kor, Geo, It, Sa, Fj, 2007 HK, Fj, AuA, Sa, A
N Kumagai 1977 S, 1978 F, 1979 HK
M Kunda 1990 Sa, US, Kor, 1991 C, HK, S, I, Z, 1992 HK, 1993 Ar, Ar, W, 1994 Fj, Fj, HK, Kor, 1995 Tg, R, W, I, NZ, 1996 HK, HK, C, 1997 HK, C, US, US, 1998 C, HK, HK, US, C, Ar, Kor, HK, Kor, 1999 Sa, Fj, US, Sp, Sa, W, Ar
S Kurihara 1986 S, E, 1987 E
S Kurihara 1974 SL
T Kurihara 2000 Fj, US, Tg, Sa, Kor, C, 2001 Kor, Tai, W, W, Sa, C, 2002 Rus, Tg, Kor, Tai, Kor, Tai, 2003 US, Rus, AuA, AuA, E, E, S, F, Fj, US
M Kurokawa 1998 Tai, HK, Kor, 2000 Fj, Tg, Sa, Kor, C
T Kurosaka 1970 BCo, 1974 SL, 1975 A, A, W, W
M Kusatsu 1963 BCo
T Kusumi 2007 A, W, 2008 Kor
E Kutsuki 1985 F, 1986 US, C, S, E, 1987 US, E, A, NZ, NZ, 1989 S, 1990 Fj, Tg, Kor, Sa, US, Kor, 1991 US, US, C, HK, S, I, Z, 1992 HK, 1993 W, 1994 Fj, Fj, HK
Y Kuwazuru 2012 UAE, Kor, HK

S Latu 1987 US, A, NZ, NZ, 1989 S, 1990 Fj, Tg, Kor, Sa, US, Kor, 1991 US, C, HK, S, I, Z, 1992 HK, 1993 Ar, Ar, 1994 Fj, Fj, HK, Kor, 1995 Tg, Tg, R, W, I, NZ
ST Latu 1993 W, 1994 Fj, Fj, HK, Kor, 1995 Tg, R, W, I
MG Leitch 2008 US, US, 2009 Kaz, HK, Kor, Sa, JAB, C, C, 2010 HK, Fj, Tg, Rus, 2011 HK, UAE, Tg, Fj, It, F, NZ, Tg, C, 2012 Kaz, Kor, HK, Fj, R, Geo, 2013 Fj
CED Loamanu 2005 Ur, HK, 2007 Kor, Fj, Tg, Sa, JAB, It, Fj, W, C, 2008 AuA, Tg, Fj, M, Sa
ET Luaiufi 1990 Fj, Kor, US, Kor, 1991 US, US, C, HK, S, I, Z

T Madea 1991 US, C, HK, 1995 Tg
P Mafileo 2008 US
S Makabe 2009 C, 2010 Kaz, 2012 Kaz, UAE, Kor, HK, Fj, Tg, Sa, 2013 PHP, HK, Kor, UAE, Tg, W, C, US
HAW Makiri 2005 Ur, Ar, HK, Kor, R, I, I, 2006 AG, Tg, Sa, JAB, 2007 Kor, Tg, AuA, Sa, JAB, It, A, Fj, W, C, 2008 AuA, Tg, Fj, M, Sa
M Mantani 1969 HK, 1970 Tha, BCo, 1971 E, E, 1972 HK
G Marsh 2007 AuA, Sa, JAB
T Masuho 1991 US, C, HK, S, I, Z, 1993 Ar, Ar, 1994 Fj, Fj, Kor, 1995 Tg, W, 1996 HK, C, US, US, C, 1997 HK, C, US, C, HK, 1998 C, US, HK, HK, US, C, Ar, Kor, Tai, HK, 1999 C, US, Sp, Sa, 2000 Fj, US, Tg, Sa, Kor, C, 2001 Kor, W, Sa, C
Y Masutome 1986 Kor
K Matsubara 1930 BCo
T Matsubara 1932 C, C
Y Matsubara 2004 Kor, Rus, C, It, 2005 Sp, 2006 AG, Kor, Geo, Tg, It, Sa, JAB, Fj, Kor, 2007 Kor, Fj, Tg, Sa, JAB, It, Fj, W, C
T Matsuda 1992 HK, 1993 W, 1994 Fj, HK, Kor, 1995 Tg, R, W, I, NZ, 1996 HK, HK, C, US, US, C, Kor, 1998 US, HK, HK, US, C, Ar, Kor, Tai, HK, Kor, 1999 C, Fj, US, Sp, Sa, Ar, 2001 Kor, Tai, W, 2003 US, AuA, Kor, E, S, Fj, US
J Matsumoto 1977 S, 1978 F, 1980 H, 1982 C, C
T Matsunaga 1985 F, F
Y Matsunobu 1963 BCo
H Matsuo 2003 AuA, AuA, Kor, E, E
K Matsuo 1986 US, C, S, E, Kor, 1987 E, NZ, 1988 Kor, 1990 Tg, Kor, Sa, US, 1991 US, HK, S, I, Z, 1993 Ar, Ar, 1994 Fj, Fj, HK, 1995 Tg
Y Matsuo 1974 SL, 1976 BCo, E, It, Kor, 1977 S, 1979 HK, E, E, 1982 HK, C, C, 1983 OCC, W, 1984 F, F, Kor
S Matsuoka 1963 BCo, 1970 Tha
K Matsushita 2008 US, US, 2010 AG, HK, Fj, Sa, Tg
F Mau 2004 Rus, C, It, S, R, W
AF McCormick 1996 HK, HK, US, 1997 HK, C, US, US, C, HK, 1998 C, US, HK, Ar, Kor, Tai, HK, 1999 C, Tg, Sa, Fj, US, Sp, Sa, W, Ar
M Mikami 2013 PHP, HK, UAE, Tg, Fj, W, W, C, US
R Miki 1999 Sp, 2002 Tg, Tai, Kor, Tai, Kor, 2004 S, R, W
A Miller 2002 Rus, Kor, Tai, Kor, Tai, 2003 Kor, S, F, Fj, US
S Miln 1998 C, US, HK, HK, US
Y Minamikawa 1976 BCo, 1978 F, Kor, 1979 HK, E, E, 1980 H, F, Kor, 1982 HK, C, C, Kor
M Mishima 1930 BCo, 1932 C, C
T Miuchi 2002 Rus, Kor, Kor, Tai, Kor, 2003 US, Rus, AuA, Kor, E, E, S, F, Fj, US, 2004 Rus, C, It, S, R, W, 2005 Ur, Ar, HK, Kor, R, C, I, I, 2006 HK, Kor, 2007 Kor, HK, Fj, Tg, Sa, It, Fj, W, C, 2008 Kor, AG, Kaz, HK, AuA, Tg, Fj, Sa
S Miura 1963 BCo
K Miyai 1959 BCo, BCo, 1963 BCo
K Miyaji 1969 HK
K Miyajima 1959 BCo, BCo
H Miyaji-Yoshizawa 1930 BCo
T Miyake 2005 Sp, 2006 Sa, JAB, Fj
K Miyamoto 1986 S, E, 1987 US, E, A, 1988 Kor, 1991 I
K Miyata 1971 E, E, 1972 HK
M Miyauchi 1975 W, 1976 It, Kor
K Mizobe 1997 C
K Mizoguchi 1997 C
K Mizube 1997 HK
H Mizuno 2004 R, 2005 HK, Kor, R, C, I, 2006 AG, Geo, Tg, It, Sa, JAB
M Mizutani 1970 Tha, 1971 E
N Mizuyama 2008 Tg, M, Sa, US
Y Mochizuki 2012 Kaz, UAE, Kor, HK, Fj, Tg, Sa
S Mori 1974 NZU, SL, 1975 A, A, W, W, 1976 BCo, S, E, It, Kor, 1977 S, 1978 F, 1979 HK, E, E, CU, 1980 NZU, H, F, Kor, 1981 AuUn
K Morikawa 2012 UAE
K Morioka 1982 Kor
K Morita 2004 C, It, 2005 Ur, Ar, Kor, R, C, I
A Moriya 2006 Tg, It, Sa, JAB, Fj, 2008 AG, Kaz
Y Motoki 1991 US, US, C, 1992 HK, 1993 Ar, Ar, 1994 Fj, Fj, Kor, 1995 Tg, Tg, R, W, I, NZ, 1996 HK, HK, C, US, US, C, Kor, 1997 HK, C, US, US, C, HK, 1998 C, US, HK, HK, US, C, Ar, Kor, HK, Kor, 1999 C, Tg, Sa, Fj, US, Sp, Sa, W, Ar, 2001 W, W, Sa, C, 2002 Rus, Tg, Kor, Tai, Kor, Tai, Kor, 2003 Kor, E, E, S, Fj, US, 2004 Kor, Rus, C, It, S, R, W, 2005 Ur, Ar, HK, Kor, R, C, I, I
K Motoyoshi 2001 Tai
S Mukai 1985 I, I, F, 1986 US, C, E, Kor, 1987 US, A, NZ, NZ
M Mukoyama 2004 Kor, C, It, S, R, W
K Muraguchi 1976 S, Kor
D Murai 1985 I, I, F, F, 1987 E
K Murata 1963 BCo
W Murata 1991 US, S, 1995 Tg, NZ, 1996 HK, HK, C, US, US, C, Kor, 1997 HK, C, US, US, HK, 1998 HK, HK, US, C, Ar, Kor, Kor, 1999 US, W, 2001 W, W, Sa, 2002 Rus, Tg, Kor, Tai, Kor, Tai, 2003 US, AuA, E, 2005 Ur, Ar, Kor, I, I
Y Murata 1971 E, E, 1972 HK, 1973 W, 1974 NZU, SL

Y Nagae 2012 Kaz, UAE, Kor, HK, Fj, Tg, Sa, R, Geo, 2013 W, W, C, US
M Nagai 1988 Kor
Y Nagatomo 2010 Kor, AG, Kaz, 2012 Kaz, UAE, Kor, HK, Fj, Sa
Y Nagatomo 1993 W, 1994 Fj, HK, 1995 Tg, 1996 US, US, 1997 C

T Naito 1934 *AuUn*
M Nakabayashi 2005 *HK, Kor, R, I*
T Nakai 2005 *Ur, HK, C, I, I, Sp,* 2006 *AG, Kor, Geo, Tg, It, Fj*
T Nakamichi 1996 *HK, HK, US, US, C,* 1998 *Ar, Kor,* 1999 *C, Sa, Fj, Sp, W, Ar,* 2000 *Fj, US, Tg*
N Nakamura 1998 *C, US, HK, HK, US, C, Ar, Kor, Tai, HK, Kor,* 1999 *C, Tg, Sa, Fj, US, Sp, W, Ar,* 2000 *I*
R Nakamura 2013 *UAE*
S Nakamura 2009 *Kaz, Sin,* 2010 *AG, Kaz, HK, Fj*
S Nakashima 1989 *S,* 1990 *Fj, Tg, Kor, Sa, US,* 1991 *US, US, C, HK, S*
T Nakayama 1976 *BCo,* 1978 *F,* 1979 *E,* 1980 *H,* 1982 *C, C*
Y Nakayama 2008 *Kor, AG, Kaz, HK, Tg, M,* 2009 *HK, Kor, Sin, Tg, Fj*
H Namba 2000 *Fj, US, Tg, Sa, Kor, C, I,* 2001 *Tai, W, W, C,* 2002 *Rus, Tg, Kor, Tai, Kor,* 2003 *US, Rus, AuA, AuA, Kor, E, E, F*
RT Nicholas 2008 *Kor, Kaz, HK, AuA, Tg, Fj, Sa, US, US,* 2009 *HK, Kor, Sa, JAB, Tg, Fj, C, C,* 2010 *Kor, Kaz, HK, Fj, Sa, Tg, Sa, Rus,* 2011 *HK, UAE, Sa, Tg, Fj, It, US, F, Tg, C,* 2012 *Fj, Tg, Sa*
H Nishida 1994 *Fj*
S Nishigaki 1932 *C, C*
T Nishihara 2011 *Sa, It, US*
T Nishiura 2004 *W,* 2006 *HK, Kor,* 2007 *Kor, Fj, Tg, Sa, It, Fj, W, C,* 2008 *Kor, HK, AuA, Tg, Fj, Sa*
H Nishizumi 1963 *BCo*
M Niwa 1932 *C*
I Nogami 1932 *C,* 1936 *NZU*
T Nozawa 2000 *Tg, Sa, Kor, C*

M Oda 2000 *US, Tg, Sa, Kor, I*
H Ogasawara 1969 *HK,* 1970 *Tha, BCo,* 1971 *E, E,* 1973 *F,* 1974 *NZU,* 1975 *A, A, W, W,* 1976 *NZU,* 1977 *S*
K Oguchi 1997 *US, C, HK,* 1998 *Tai,* 1999 *Sa, Ar,* 2000 *Fj, Tg, Sa, Kor*
K Ohara 1998 *Kor, Tai,* 2000 *Kor, C, I*
D Ohata 1996 *Kor,* 1997 *HK, C, US,* 1998 *HK, C, Ar, Kor, HK,* 1999 *C, Tg, Sa, Fj, US, Sp, Sa, W, Ar,* 2000 *Fj, US, Kor, C, I,* 2002 *Rus, Kor, Tai, Kor, Tai, Kor,* 2003 *US, Rus, AuA, AuA, Kor, E, E, S, F, Fj, US,* 2004 *Kor, Rus, C, It,* 2005 *Ur, Ar, HK, Kor, R, C, I, I,* 2006 *AG, Kor, Geo, Tg, HK, Kor*
K Ohigashi 1973 *W, F,* 1974 *NZU, SL*
K Ohigashi 2004 *Kor, Rus, C,* 2007 *Kor, HK, AuA, JAB*
K Ohotsuka 1959 *BCo*
S Oikawa 1980 *H*
E Okabe 1963 *BCo,* 1967 *NZU*
Y Okada 1932 *C, C*
M Okidoi 1987 *A, NZ, NZ*
N Okubo 1999 *Tg, Sa, Fj, US, Sp, Sa, W, Ar,* 2000 *Fj, US, Tg, Sa, Kor, C,* 2002 *Rus, Tg, Kor, Tai, Kor, Tai,* 2003 *US, Rus, S, F, Fj, US,* 2004 *S, R, W*
T Omata 1970 *NZU, BCo, NZU*
S Onishi 2000 *Fj, US, Tg, Sa, Kor, C,* 2001 *Kor, Tai, W, C,* 2005 *Sp,* 2006 *AG, Kor, Geo, Tg, It, JAB, HK, Kor,* 2007 *HK, Tg, AuA, Sa, JAB, It, Fj, W, C,* 2008 *Kor, AG, HK, M, Sa*
H Ono 2004 *Kor, Rus, C, S,* 2005 *Ar, Kor, I,* 2006 *Kor, Geo, It, Sa, JAB, Fj, HK, Kor,* 2007 *Kor, Fj, Tg, Sa, JAB, It, Fj, W, C,* 2008 *Kor, AG, AuA, Tg, Fj, US,* 2009 *HK, Sin, Sa, JAB, Tg, C, C,* 2010 *Kor, Kaz, HK, Fj, Sa, Tg, Sa, Rus,* 2011 *Kaz, UAE, SL, Tg, Fj, US, NZ, Tg, C,* 2012 *Kaz, UAE, Kor, HK, Fj, Tg, Sa, R, Geo,* 2013 *PHP, HK, Kor, UAE, Tg, Fj, W, W, C, US*
K Ono 2007 *Kor, AuA, JAB, It, A,* 2012 *Kaz, UAE, Kor, HK, Fj, Tg, Sa, R, Geo,* 2013 *PHP, HK, Kor, Tg*
S Ono 1932 *C, C*
H Onozawa 2001 *W, Sa, C,* 2002 *Rus, Kor, Tai, Kor,* 2003 *Rus, AuA, AuA, Kor, E, E, S, F, Fj, US,* 2004 *Kor, Rus, C, It,* 2005 *Ur, Ar, HK, Kor, R, C, I, Sp,* 2006 *HK, Kor,* 2007 *Kor, Tg, AuA, JAB, A, Fj, W, C,* 2008 *Kor, AG, Kaz, HK, AuA, Tg, Fj, Sa,* 2009 *Kaz, HK, Kor, Sa, Tg, C, C,* 2010 *Fj, Sa, Tg, Sa,* 2011 *HK, SL, Sa, Tg, Fj, US, F, NZ, Tg, C,* 2012 *Kaz, Kor, HK, Fj, Tg, Sa, R, Geo,* 2013 *PHP, UAE, Tg, Fj, W*
S Onuki 1984 *F, F, Kor,* 1985 *US, I, I, F, F,* 1986 *US, C, S, E, Kor,* 1987 *US, E*
PD O'Reilly 2005 *Kor,* 2006 *JAB, Fj, HK, Kor,* 2007 *It, Fj, C,* 2009 *Kaz, C, C*
G Ota 1930 *BCo*
O Ota 1986 *US, S,* 1989 *S,* 1990 *Fj, Tg, Kor, Sa, US, Kor,* 1991 *US, C, HK, S, I, Z,* 1992 *HK,* 1993 *Ar, Ar, W,* 1994 *Fj, HK, Kor,* 1995 *Tg, R, W, I, NZ*
T Otao 2004 *W,* 2009 *Kaz, HK, Kor, Sin, JAB, Tg*
L Oto 1992 *HK,* 1995 *R, W, I, NZ,* 1996 *C,* 1997 *C, HK*
M Oto 1972 *HK*
N Oto 2001 *Kor, Tai, W, Sa,* 2005 *Sp,* 2006 *Kor, Tg, It, Sa, JAB, Fj,* 2007 *A*
K Otukolo 2005 *HK, Kor, C*
F Ouchi 1991 *US*
H Ouchi 1990 *Kor,* 1993 *Ar, W,* 1994 *HK*
N Owashi 1992 *HK*
M Oyabu 1998 *Kor*
A Oyagi 1983 *W,* 1984 *F, F, Kor,* 1985 *US, I, I, F, F,* 1986 *US, C,* 1987 *US, E, NZ, NZ,* 1988 *Kor,* 1989 *S,* 1990 *Fj, Tg, Kor, Sa, US, Kor,* 1991 *US, C, I, Z*
J Oyamada 1997 *HK, US*
A Ozaki 2008 *Kor, AG, HK*
M Ozaki 1963 *BCo,* 1967 *NZU,* 1968 *JAB, NZU,* 1969 *HK*
H Ozeki 1996 *HK, HK, US, C, Kor*

A Parker 2002 *Rus, Tg, Kor, Tai, Kor, Tai,* 2003 *US, Rus, AuA, AuA, Kor, E, E, S, F, Fj, US,* 2004 *It*
R Parkinson 2003 *Rus, AuA, E, S, Fj,* 2005 *Ur, Ar, HK, I, I*

D Quate 2009 *C*

BB Robins 2007 *Kor, Fj, Tg, AuA, Sa, JAB, It, Fj, W, C,* 2008 *Kor, AG, Kaz, HK, AuA, Tg, Fj, M, Sa, US, US,* 2009 *Kaz,* 2010 *Sa, Rus,* 2011 *C*

K Sagawa 1977 *S*
R Saito 1952 *OU,* 1953 *OCC*
Y Saito 2001 *Tai, W, W, Sa, C,* 2002 *Rus, Kor, Tai, Kor,* 2003 *Kor, E, E, US,* 2004 *Kor*
M Sakamoto 1978 *F, Kor,* 1980 *Kor*
M Sakata 1994 *HK,* 1996 *C, US, US, C, Kor,* 1997 *US, US, C, HK,* 1998 *US, HK, Tai,* 1999 *C, Tg, US, Sp, Sa, W, Ar,* 2001 *W, W, Sa, C,* 2002 *Rus, Tg, Kor, Tai, Kor,* 2003 *US, Rus, AuA, S, F, Fj*
Y Sakata 1969 *HK,* 1970 *Tha, BCo,* 1971 *E, E,* 1972 *HK*
Y Sakuraba 1986 *S, E,* 1987 *A, NZ, NZ,* 1988 *Kor,* 1992 *HK,* 1993 *Ar, Ar, W,* 1994 *Fj, HK, Kor,* 1995 *Tg, R, W, I, NZ,* 1996 *HK, Kor,* 1997 *C, US, C, HK,* 1998 *C, US, HK, HK, US, C, Ar, Kor, Tai, HK, Kor,* 1999 *C, Tg, Sa, Fj, W, Ar*
L Samurai Vatuvei 2001 *Kor, Tai, W, W, Sa, C,* 2002 *Rus, Tg, Kor, Kor, Tai,* 2003 *US, Rus, AuA,* 2004 *Kor, Rus, C, It,* 2006 *HK, Kor,* 2007 *It, A, C*
T Saruta 1969 *HK*
M Sasada 1976 *BCo, E, It, Kor,* 1977 *S,* 1979 *HK, E*
Y Sasada 1973 *W, F*
T Sasaki 2007 *HK, Fj, Tg, AuA, JAB, A,* 2012 *Kaz, UAE, Kor, HK, Fj, Tg, Sa*
K Sato 1996 *US, US, C,* 1997 *C*
T Sato 2008 *AG, Kaz, HK*
T Sato 2008 *Kor, AG, Kaz, HK*
T Sato 2005 *Sp,* 2006 *AG, Kor, Geo, Tg, Sa, Fj,* 2007 *Kor, AuA*
Y Sato 1994 *Fj,* 1995 *Tg,* 1996 *C*
M Sau 2013 *PHP, HK, Kor, Tg, Fj, W, W, C, US*
T Sawaguchi 2002 *Kor*
K Sawaki 1998 *Ar, Tai, Kor,* 1999 *Sa,* 2004 *S,* 2006 *HK, Kor*
K Segawa 1982 *HK*
K Sejimo 1980 *H, F,* 1982 *HK, C, C, Kor*
T Senba 2012 *Kaz, UAE, Kor, HK, Fj, Tg, Sa, R, Geo*
K Shibata 1972 *HK,* 1973 *W,* 1974 *SL,* 1975 *A,* 1976 *BCo, S, E*
M Shichinohe 2002 *Tai, Kor*
S Shiga 1959 *BCo, BCo*
F Shimazaki 1970 *Tha, BCo,* 1971 *E, E,* 1972 *HK,* 1973 *W, F*
S Shimizu 1930 *BCo*
S Shimizu 1996 *Kor*
M Shimoji 1979 *HK*
S Shimomura 2004 *S, R,* 2007 *HK,* 2013 *UAE*
M Shimosono 1970 *Tha,* 1971 *E, E,* 1972 *HK,* 1973 *F*
Y Shinomiya 2003 *US, AuA, Kor*
K Shinozuka 2008 *Kor, AG, Kaz, HK, M,* 2012 *Kaz*
K Shomen 2002 *Kor,* 2006 *Kor*
G Smith 1998 *C, US, HK, HK, US, C, Ar, Kor, HK,* 1999 *C, Tg, Sa, Fj, US, Sa, W, Ar*
T Soma 2005 *Sp,* 2006 *AG, Kor, Geo, Tg, It,* 2007 *Kor, HK, Fj, Tg, AuA, Sa, JAB, It, Fj, W, C,* 2008 *Kor, Kaz, AuA, Tg, Fj, M, Sa*
Y Sonoda 2000 *Fj, US, Tg,* 2001 *Tai, W, C,* 2002 *Rus, Kor,* 2003 *US, Rus, AuA, Kor, E, E, S, F, Fj, US*
H Sugarwara 2000 *Fj, US, Tg, I,* 2001 *Tai, W*
T Sugata 1998 *Kor*
H Suzuki 1930 *BCo*
G Tachikawa 1999 *C, Tg,* 2005 *Ur, Ar, Kor, R, C, I, I, Sp,* 2007 *Kor, Fj, Tg,* 2010 *Kor, Kaz, HK,* 2011 *Kaz, UAE, SL, Sa*
H Taione 1986 *US, C, S,* 1988 *Kor*
K Taira 2007 *Kor, Fj, AuA, A, Fj, W, C,* 2008 *Tg, Fj, Sa, US,* 2009 *HK, Sin, Sa, JAB, Tg, Fj, C,* 2010 *Kor, Kaz, HK, Fj, Sa, Rus,* 2011 *HK, Kaz, Tg, Fj, It, US, F, NZ*
H Takafumi 1999 *Fj*
S Takagi 2005 *Ur, HK, R, I, I*
H Takahashi 2005 *Ur, Ar, Kor, C, I*
K Takahashi 1990 *Fj, Sa, Kor,* 1991 *US, US, C,* 1992 *HK,* 1993 *Ar, Ar, W,* 1994 *Fj, HK, Kor,* 1995 *Tg, W, NZ,* 1996 *HK, HK, C,* 1997 *US, C, HK*

Y Takahashi 1952 *OU*
T Takata 1974 *NZU*, 1975 *A, A, W, W*, 1976 *BCo, S, WaCl, E, It, Kor*, 1977 *OU, S*
K Takayangi 2001 *Kor, Tai*
K Takei 2004 *It*, 2006 *AG, Kor, Geo, It, Fj*
T Takeyama 1994 *HK, Kor*, 1995 *Tg*
M Takura 1989 *S*, 1990 *Fj, Tg, Kor, Sa, US*, 1991 *US, HK, S, I, Z*, 1994 *Fj, Kor*, 1995 *Tg, R, I*
H Tamura 1998 *HK, US, C, Ar, Kor, Tai, HK, Kor*, 1999 *C*
Y Tamura 2012 *Kaz, Kor, HK*, 2013 *PHP, HK, Kor, UAE, Tg, Fj, W, W, C, US*
A Tanabe 2010 *Rus*, 2011 *Kaz, SL*
F Tanaka 2008 *AG, HK, AuA, Tg, Fj, Sa, US, US*, 2009 *Kaz, HK, Sin, Sa, Tg, Fj*, 2010 *Kor, Kaz, HK, Fj, Sa, Tg, Sa, Rus*, 2011 *Kaz, UAE, SL, Sa, Tg, It, F, Tg, C*, 2012 *R, Geo*, 2013 *W, W, C, US*
K Tanaka 2004 *S, R, W*
N Tanaka 1974 *SL*, 1975 *A, W*, 1976 *BCo, S, E*, 1977 *S*, 1980 *F, Kor*, 1982 *HK, Kor*
S Tanaka 1959 *BCo, BCo*
N Tanifuji 1979 *HK, E, E*, 1982 *C, C*, 1983 *W*, 1984 *F, Kor*, 1985 *US*
Y Tanigawa 1969 *HK*
I Taniguchi 2010 *Rus*, 2011 *Kaz, SL, Sa, Tg, Fj, US, F, NZ, Tg*
T Taniguchi 2006 *Tg, It, JAB*, 2008 *Kor, Kaz, HK, AuA, Tg, Fj, M, Sa, US*
H Tanuma 1996 *Kor*, 1997 *HK, C, US, US, HK*, 1998 *C, US, HK*, 1999 *Sa, Fj, US, Sp, Sa, W, Ar*, 2000 *Fj, US, Tg, Sa, Kor, C, I*, 2001 *Kor, Tai, W, W, Sa, C*, 2002 *Kor*, 2003 *AuA, E, F*
J Tarrant 2009 *Kaz, HK, Kor, Sa, JAB, Tg, Fj*
H Tatekawa 2012 *Kaz, UAE, Kor, HK, Fj, Tg, Sa, R, Geo*, 2013 *PHP, HK, Kor, UAE, Tg, Fj, W, W, C, US*
M Tatsukawa 2000 *Sa*
T Taufa 2009 *Kaz, Kor, Sin, Sa, JAB, Tg, Fj, C, C*, 2010 *Kor, AG, Kaz, HK, Fj, Sa, Tg, Sa*, 2011 *HK, Kaz, UAE, SL, C*
N Taumoefolau 1985 *F, F*, 1986 *US, C, S, E, Kor*, 1987 *US, E, A, NZ*, 1988 *Kor*, 1989 *S*, 1990 *Fj*
T Terai 1969 *HK*, 1970 *Tha*, 1971 *E, E*, 1972 *HK*, 1973 *W, F*, 1974 *NZU*, 1975 *A, W, W*, 1976 *S, E, It, Kor*
S Teramura 1930 *BCo*
LM Thompson 2007 *HK, Fj, Tg, Sa, JAB, It, Fj, W, C*, 2008 *M, Sa, US, US*, 2009 *Kaz, Kor, Sa, Tg, Fj*, 2010 *Kor, AG, Kaz, HK, Fj, Sa, Tg, Sa, Rus*, 2011 *HK, Kaz, SL, Sa, Tg, It, US, F, Tg, C*, 2012 *R, Geo*
R Thompson 1998 *C, US, HK, HK, US, C*
Z Toba-Nakajima 1930 *BCo*, 1932 *C*
K Todd 2000 *Fj, Sa, I*
H Tominaga 1959 *BCo, BCo*
K Tomioka 2008 *US, US*, 2009 *Kor, Sin, Sa, JAB*
T Tomioka 2005 *I, I*
T Toshi 1932 *C, C*
H Toshima 1980 *H, F*, 1982 *HK, C, C*, 1984 *F, F, Kor*
M Toyoda 2008 *US*
N Toyoda 1982 *HK*
S Toyoda 1974 *SL*
T Toyoda 1978 *Kor*
M Toyota 2009 *Sin, Sa, Tg, Fj*, 2010 *Kor, AG, Kaz, HK*
K Toyoyama 1976 *BCo*, 1979 *E, E*, 1980 *H*
M Toyoyama 2000 *Fj, US, Sa, C*, 2001 *Kor, W, W, Sa, C*, 2002 *Rus, Kor, Tai, Kor, Tai*, 2003 *US, Rus, AuA, Kor, E, E, S, Fj, US*
H Tsuboi 2012 *Kaz, UAE*
M Tsuchida 1985 *F*
T Tsuchiya 1956 *AuUn*, 1959 *BCo, BCo*
E Tsuji 1980 *Kor*, 1982 *Kor*
T Tsuji 2003 *S, Fj, US*, 2005 *HK, R, C*, 2006 *Kor*
Y Tsujimoto 2001 *Kor*
K Tsukagoshi 2002 *Kor*, 2005 *Ur, Ar, HK, Kor, R, C, I, I*
S Tsukda 2001 *Kor, C*, 2002 *Tg, Tai, Kor, Tai, Kor*, 2003 *AuA, E*
T Tsuyama 1976 *BCo, Kor*
H Tui 2012 *Tg, Sa, R, Geo*, 2013 *PHP, HK, Kor, UAE, Tg, Fj, W, W, C, US*
P Tuidraki 1997 *HK, C*, 1998 *C, US, HK, HK, US, C, Tai*, 1999 *Tg, Sa, Fj, Sa, W, Ar*, 2000 *I*, 2001 *Tai, W, W*
A Tupuailai 2009 *C, C*, 2010 *Kor, AG, Kaz, HK, Fj, Sa, Tg, Sa, Rus*, 2011 *HK, Kaz, SL, It, US, F, NZ, Tg, C*

K Uchida 2012 *Kaz, UAE*, 2013 *UAE, Fj*
M Uchida 1969 *HK*
A Ueda 1975 *W*, 1978 *Kor*, 1979 *E, E*
T Ueda 2011 *HK, Kaz, UAE, SL, US, NZ*
S Ueki 1963 *BCo*
R Ueno 2011 *SL*
N Ueyama 1973 *F*, 1974 *NZU, SL*, 1975 *A, A, W, W*, 1976 *BCo, E, It, Kor*, 1978 *F*, 1980 *Kor*
H Ujino 1976 *BCo*, 1977 *S*, 1978 *F, Kor*, 1979 *HK, E, E*, 1980 *H, Kor*, 1982 *HK, Kor*
R Umei 1958 *NZ23, NZ23, NZ23*
Y Uryu 2000 *Sa*, 2001 *Kor*
T Usuzuki 2011 *UAE, SL, Sa, Fj, It, US, NZ*

S Vatuvei 2010 *Kor, AG, Kaz, Sa*, 2011 *US, NZ, Tg, C*

K Wada 1997 *HK, US, US, C, HK*
K Wada 2010 *AG, Kaz, Fj, Tg, Rus*
S Wada 1930 *BCo*
T Wada 1975 *A*, 1976 *S*, 1979 *E, E*
J Washington 2005 *Ur, Ar, HK, Kor, R, C, I*
M Washiya 2000 *Kor, C*
H Watanabe 1990 *Sa*
T Watanabe 2002 *Kor*
Y Watanabe 1996 *HK, HK*, 1998 *C, US, HK, HK, Ar, Kor, Tai, HK*, 1999 *C, Tg, US, Sp, Sa*, 2000 *Fj, US, I*, 2003 *Rus, AuA, AuA, E, S*, 2004 *Kor*, 2005 *HK, R, C*, 2007 *HK, Fj, Tg, Sa, JAB, A, W*
SJ Webb 2008 *AG, Kaz, HK, AuA, Tg, Fj, M, US, US*, 2009 *Kaz, Kor, Sa, Tg, Fj, C, C*, 2010 *Kor, Kaz, HK, Fj, Sa, Tg*, 2011 *HK, Kaz, UAE, SL, Sa, Tg, Fj, It, US, F, NZ, Tg, C*
IM Williams 1993 *W*
MC Williams 2011 *Sa, Fj, US, F, NZ, C*
C Wing 2013 *UAE, Fj, W, W, US*

T Yagai 1930 *BCo*
T Yajima 1978 *Kor*, 1979 *E*
K Yamada 1963 *BCo*
K Yamaguchi 1936 *NZU*
T Yamaguchi 2004 *S, R, W*
Y Yamaguchi 1970 *Tha, BCo*, 1971 *E, E*, 1972 *HK*
E Yamamoto 2001 *Kor, W*, 2002 *Tg, Kor*
I Yamamoto 1973 *W*
M Yamamoto 2002 *Rus, Kor, Tai, Kor*, 2003 *Rus, AuA, AuA, Kor, E, E, Fj, US*, 2004 *Kor, Rus, C, S, R, W*, 2006 *Sa, JAB, Fj*, 2007 *HK, Fj, AuA, JAB, A*
M Yamamoto 2004 *C, S, W*, 2006 *HK, Kor*, 2007 *HK, Fj, Tg, AuA, Sa*
T Yamamoto 1988 *Kor*, 1989 *S*, 1990 *Fj*
R Yamamura 2001 *W*, 2002 *Tg, Tai, Tai*, 2003 *AuA, F*, 2004 *Kor, Rus, C, It, S, R, W*, 2005 *Ur, Ar, HK, Kor, R, C, I, I, Sp*, 2006 *Kor, Geo, It, Sa, JAB, Fj, HK, Kor*, 2007 *Kor, Tg, AuA, Sa, JAB, It, A, Fj, W, C*
R Yamanaka 2010 *AG*
T Yamaoka 2004 *It, S, R, W*, 2005 *Sp*, 2006 *AG, Kor, Geo, Tg, It, Sa, JAB, Fj*
H Yamashita 2009 *Kaz, HK, Kor, Sin, Sa, JAB, Tg, Fj*, 2012 *Kor, HK, Fj, Tg, Sa, R, Geo*, 2013 *PHP, HK, Kor, UAE, Tg, Fj, W, W, C, US*
O Yamashita 1974 *SL*
M Yasuda 1984 *F*
N Yasuda 2000 *Kor, I*
Y Yasue 2009 *HK, Kor*
R Yasui 2013 *UAE, W*
T Yasui 1976 *S, E*, 1977 *S*, 1978 *F, Kor*, 1979 *HK, E*
K Yasumi 1986 *C*, 1987 *US, NZ*
Y Yatomi 2006 *Kor*, 2007 *HK, Fj, Tg, AuA, Sa, JAB, A, Fj*, 2009 *Kaz, Kor, JAB, C*
O Yatsuhashi 1996 *US, C*, 1998 *US, HK, HK, US, C, Ar, Tai, Kor*, 2000 *Kor, C*
A Yokoi 1969 *HK*, 1970 *Tha, NZU, BCo*, 1971 *E*, 1972 *AuUn, AuUn, HK*, 1973 *W, E, F*, 1974 *NZU*
A Yoshida 1995 *R, W, I, NZ*, 1996 *C, US, C, Kor*, 1997 *US, HK*, 1999 *Sa*, 2000 *Fj, US, Tg, Sa, Kor, C*
H Yoshida 2001 *Sa, C*, 2002 *Tg, Tai*, 2004 *R, W*, 2006 *AG, Kor, Geo, Tg, Sa, JAB, Fj, HK, Kor*
H Yoshida 2008 *Kor, AG, Kaz, M*, 2009 *Kaz, HK, Sin*
J Yoshida 1973 *W, F*
M Yoshida 1974 *NZU*, 1975 *A, A, W*, 1976 *BCo, S, E, It, Kor*, 1977 *S*, 1978 *F, Kor*
T Yoshida 2002 *Tg, Tai, Kor*, 2003 *E*
T Yoshida 2007 *Kor, Fj, Tg, Sa, It, Fj, W, C*, 2008 *Kor, Kaz, AuA, Tg, M, Sa, US*, 2009 *Kor, Sa, JAB, C, C*, 2010 *AG, HK, Sa*, 2011 *US, NZ*
Y Yoshida 1988 *Kor*, 1989 *S*, 1990 *Fj, Tg, Kor, Sa, US, Kor*, 1991 *US, US, C, HK, S, I, Z*, 1992 *HK*, 1993 *Ar, Ar, W*, 1994 *Fj, Fj, HK, Kor*, 1995 *Tg, Tg, R, I, NZ*, 1996 *HK*
K Yoshinaga 1986 *Kor*, 1987 *US, A, NZ*, 1990 *Sa*
K Yoshino 1973 *W*
T Yoshino 1985 *US, I, I, F, F*, 1986 *Kor*, 1987 *NZ*
H Yuhara 2010 *Kor, AG, HK, Fj, Rus*, 2011 *HK, UAE, SL, NZ*, 2013 *PHP, Kor*

NAMIBIA

NAMIBIA'S 2012–13 TEST RECORD

OPPONENTS	DATE	VENUE	RESULT
Zimbabwe	10 Nov	H	Won 37–33
Spain	17 Nov	H	Lost 37–38
Senegal	11 Jun	A	Won 35–12
Tunisia	15 Jun	N	Won 45–13

NAMIBIA BACK ON TRACK

By Andrew Poolman

AFP/Getty Images

Namibia's Africa Cup Division 1B success kept their Rugby World Cup 2015 dream alive.

Namibia found themselves in the last-chance saloon in June when they travelled to Senegal for the Africa Cup Division 1B tournament, knowing that only lifting the silverware would suffice because anything less and their hopes of qualifying for a fifth successive Rugby World Cup would be over.

Twelve months earlier they had fallen at the final hurdle after an incredible 57–54 loss to hosts Madagascar before a crowd of 40,000, putting them in a position where they couldn't afford another slip-up if they wanted first to secure promotion back to Division 1A and then win that title in 2014 to qualify for England 2015 as Africa 1.

This time they made no mistake at the Stade Iba Mar Doip in Dakar, seeing off the challenges of their hosts 35–12 and then Tunisia 45–13 in the final. The Welwitschias can now look forward to battling with African champions Kenya, Zimbabwe and Madagascar with the Africa Cup winner in 2014 to join defending champions New Zealand, Argentina, Tonga and the Europe 1 qualifier in Pool C at RWC 2015. The dream will not be over for the runner-up, though, as they will enter the Répechage.

There will be no room for complacency among coach Danie

Vermeulen's men. Kenya and Zimbabwe will have drawn confidence from their exploits on the Sevens circuit – an area where success continues to elude Namibia. Division 1A in 2014 will test the Welwitschias' traditional dominance like never before as those two rivals, coached by ex-Western Province flanker Jerome Paarwater and Brendan Dawson respectively, prepare to upset the applecart.

Namibia will expect to have their inspirational captain Jacques Burger back for that vital Africa Cup campaign, the flanker having not worn the national jersey since major knee and shoulder operations following RWC 2011.

His absence in Senegal, though, offered little respite for Namibia's opponents in a competition which provided opportunities for new players to shine. Full back Chrysander Botha was named player of the tournament, scoring three tries in the two matches and showing why he has developed into a highly-rated attacking force signed by South Africa's Golden Lions.

Fly half Theuns Kotzé, who will always be known for his three drop goals within nine minutes in the RWC 2011 match against Fiji in Rotorua, ended the tournament with 33 points and his reputation as the team's master tactician enhanced.

There was also an influential debut from Jaco Engels. The loosehead prop plied his trade with the Blue Bulls and the Southern Kings for many years before finally playing international rugby for the country of his birth. His 125kg frame added some valuable bulk and experience to the pack.

After years of turning down offers to represent Namibia, Engels admitted before the tour that the timing was finally right. "I still have a few years of good rugby in me and would like to contribute towards the next World Cup. It is important to send a strong team to Senegal and for the team to succeed in the qualifiers, otherwise there would be no Namibian team at the World Cup."

Another Namibian making waves abroad was centre David Philander. The skilful centre showed good form for his New Zealand club Poverty Bay following his move to Rotorua where the Namibians were based during RWC 2011. If he is successful in his aim of being selected by the Hurricanes for their Super Rugby squad in 2014, that would represent a significant breakthrough for Namibian players.

Off the pitch, Sybrand de Beer, a former loose forward and RWC 1999 veteran, was appointed as chief executive of the Namibia Rugby Union late last year and was heavily involved in organising the Tri Nations Rugby Series involving Zimbabwe and Spain in the capital Windhoek in November 2012.

Namibia started the competition at the Hage Geingob Rugby Stadium with a win, 37–33 over Zimbabwe courtesy of tries from Renaud van

Neel, Chrysander Botha, Johan Tromp and Johnny Redelinghuys and 17 points from the boot of Kotzé. Spain also beat Zimbabwe 47–14 a few days later, so they met Namibia in the final match of the round robin on 17 November to determine the inaugural champions.

The Weltwitschias started brightly and led 13–3 after as many minutes before going in with a 26–17 advantage at half-time. The loss of Andre Schlechter just before the break, though, would prove costly as Spain came out firing in the second half and moved ahead before the hour mark. The sides traded scores for the remainder of the match with Kotzé kicking what appeared to be the winning penalty for Namibia to take his personal haul to 22 points in the game. However, Spain were not finished with Jaime Nava's last-gasp penalty snatching a 38–37 victory for the visitors.

Despite the defeat and seeing the title slip through their grasp, there were still positives for Namibia to take away with the tournament having coincided with a visit from South African experts Rassie Erasmus and defence coach Jacques Nienaber, who brought some organisational improvements to the national team's structure.

A second edition of the Tri Nations Rugby Series will take place in November 2013 with Zimbabwe and Kenya the visitors this time and it is sure to prove a competitive event with each nation looking to get one over the sides they will face again in the final stage of African qualifying for RWC 2015.

Away from the senior side, in 2013 Namibia Under 20s returned to the IRB Junior World Rugby Trophy stage as African champions for the first time since 2009. However, the eight-team tournament in the Chilean city of Temuco did not go according to plan with Namibia finishing eighth after losing to eventual champions Italy (33–7), Portugal (26–17) and Chile (23–21) in the pool stages and then Uruguay (40–29) in the seventh place play-off.

They will have a chance to improve on that ranking at the IRB Junior World Rugby Trophy 2014 in Hong Kong after successfully defending their Confédération Africaine de Rugby Under 19 title with victories over Madagascar (64–22) and Kenya (51–8) in Nelspruit, South Africa, in August. Namibia had only led 15–3 at half-time against Kenya, who had upset Zimbabwe 29–20 to reach the final, but tries from Donovan Kandjii, Justin Newman, Janco Venter, Ethan Beukes and Wian Conradie ensured the title was retained with a comfortable victory.

The Namibian Schools team, meanwhile, were in action at the renowned Craven Week in South Africa, where they lost their opening match 38–20 against Border, but then recovered well to beat Griquas (27–10) and Zimbabwe (33–10). Fly half Chris Arries was an all-round star performer, scoring 50 points in the three matches.

NAMIBIA INTERNATIONAL STATISTICS

MATCH RECORDS UP TO 10 OCTOBER 2013

WINNING MARGIN

Date	Opponent	Result	Winning Margin
15/06/2002	Madagascar	112–0	**112**
21/04/1990	Portugal	86–9	**77**
27/05/2006	Kenya	82–12	**70**
26/05/2007	Zambia	80–10	**70**

MOST POINTS IN A MATCH

BY THE TEAM

Date	Opponent	Result	Points
15/06/2002	Madagascar	112–0	**112**
21/04/1990	Portugal	86–9	**86**
31/08/2003	Uganda	82–13	**82**
27/05/2006	Kenya	82–12	**82**

BY A PLAYER

Date	Player	Opponent	Points
06/07/1993	Jaco Coetzee	Kenya	**35**
26/05/2007	Justinus van der Westhuizen	Zambia	**33**
27/06/2009	Chrysander Botha	Cote D'Ivoire	**29**
21/04/1990	Moolman Olivier	Portugal	**26**
15/06/2002	Riaan van Wyk	Madagascar	**25**

MOST TRIES IN A MATCH

BY THE TEAM

Date	Opponent	Result	Tries
15/06/2002	Madagascar	112–0	**18**
21/04/1990	Portugal	86–9	**16**
17/10/1999	Germany	79–13	**13**

BY A PLAYER

Date	Player	Opponent	Tries
21/04/1990	Gerhard Mans	Portugal	**6**
15/06/2002	Riaan van Wyk	Madagascar	**5**
16/05/1992	Eden Meyer	Zimbabwe	**4**
16/08/2003	Melrick Africa	Kenya	**4**

MOST CONVERSIONS IN A MATCH

BY THE TEAM

Date	Opponent	Result	Cons
15/06/2002	Madagascar	112–0	**11**
21/04/1990	Portugal	86–9	**11**
31/08/2003	Uganda	82–13	**11**
27/05/2006	Kenya	82–12	**11**

BY A PLAYER

Date	Player	Opponent	Cons
21/04/1990	Moolman Olivier	Portugal	**11**
27/05/2006	Morne Schreuder	Kenya	**11**
26/05/2007	Justinus van der Westhuizen	Zambia	**9**
31/08/2003	Rudi van Vuuren	Uganda	**8**
04/07/1993	Jaco Coetzee	Arabian Gulf	**8**

MOST PENALTIES IN A MATCH

BY THE TEAM

Date	Opponent	Result	Pens
17/11/2012	Spain	37–38	**6**
	5 on 6 occasions		

BY A PLAYER

Date	Player	Opponent	Pens
17/11/2012	Theuns Kotze	Spain	**6**
22/06/1991	Jaco Coetzee	Italy	**5**
23/01/1998	Rudi van Vuuren	Portugal	**5**
30/06/1990	Shaun McCulley	France A	**5**
28/11/2009	Emile Wessels	Tunisia	**5**
15/06/2011	Theuns Kotze	Portugal	**5**
10/11/2012	Theuns Kotze	Zimbabwe	**5**

MOST DROP GOALS IN A MATCH

BY THE TEAM

Date	Opponent	Result	DGs
10/09/2011	Fiji	25–49	**3**

BY A PLAYER

Date	Player	Opponent	DGs
10/09/2011	Theuns Kotze	Fiji	**3**

MOST CAPPED PLAYERS

Name	Caps
Eugene Jantjies	36
Johnny Redelinghuys	36
Hugo Horn	35
Herman Lindvelt	33
Tinus Du Plessis	33

LEADING PENALTY SCORERS

Name	Pens
Jaco Coetzee	46
Theuns Kotze	27
Emile Wessels	21
Morne Schreuder	18
Rudi van Vuuren	14

LEADING TRY SCORERS

Name	Tries
Gerhard Mans	27
Eden Meyer	21
Melrick Africa	12
Chrysander Botha	12

LEADING DROP GOAL SCORERS

Name	DGs
Theuns Kotze	4
Jaco Coetzee	3
Eugene Jantjies	2

LEADING CONVERSION SCORERS

Name	Cons
Jaco Coetzee	82
Morne Schreuder	36
Rudi van Vuuren	26
Theuns Kotze	20

LEADING POINT SCORERS

Name	Points
Jaco Coetzee	340
Morne Schreuder	146
Theuns Kotze	143
Chrysander Botha	127
Gerhard Mans	118
Rudi van Vuuren	109

AFP/Getty Images

Namibia's victory over Tunisia in Dakar secured their promotion back to Division IA.

NAMIBIA INTERNATIONAL PLAYERS

UP TO 10 OCTOBER 2013

MJ Africa 2003 *Sa, Ken, Uga, Ar, I, A*, 2005 *Mad, Mor*, 2006 *Ken, Tun, Ken, Tun, Mor, Mor*, 2007 *Za, Geo, R, Uga, SA, I, F, Ar, Geo*
W Alberts 1991 *Sp, Pt, It, It, Z, Z, I, I, Z, Z, Z*, 1995 *Z*, 1996 *Z, Z*
H Amakali 2005 *Mad*
J Augustyn 1991 *Z*, 1998 *Iv, Mor, Z*

RS Bardenhorst 2007 *Geo, R*
J Barnard 1990 *Z, Pt, W, W, F, F*, 1991 *Sp, Pt, It, It, Z, Z, I, I, Z, Z, Z*, 1992 *Z, Z*
R Becker 2012 *Z, Sp*, 2013 *Sen*
D Beukes 2000 *Z, Ur*, 2001 *Z, Z*
E Beukes 1990 *Z, F, WGe*
J Beukes 1994 *Z, Mor*, 1995 *Z*
AJ Blaauw 1996 *Z, Z*, 1997 *Tg*, 1998 *Pt, Tun, Z, Iv, Mor, Z*, 1999 *Z, Fj, F, C, Ger*, 2000 *Z, Z, Ur*, 2001 *It*, 2003 *Ar, I, A, R*, 2004 *Mor*
ML Blom 2010 *Sp*, 2011 *Pt, Geo*, 2012 *Sen, Mad*, 2013 *Sen, Tun*
JH Bock 2005 *Mad, Mor*, 2006 *Ken, Tun, Ken, Tun, Mor, Mor*, 2007 *Za, R, SA, I, F, Ar, Geo*, 2009 *Pt, Tun*, 2010 *R, Geo*, 2011 *R, Pt, Geo, SA*
J Bock 2005 *Mad, Mor*, 2009 *Iv, Iv*, 2010 *R, Geo, Pt*
J Booysen 2003 *Sa, Ken, Ar, A*, 2007 *Uga*
M Booysen 1993 *W, AG, Z*, 1994 *Rus, Z, HK*, 1996 *Z, Z*
LW Botes 2006 *Ken, Mor*, 2007 *Za, Geo, R, Uga, SA, F*
CA Botha 2008 *Z*, 2009 *Iv, Iv, Pt, Tun, Tun*, 2010 *Rus, R, Geo, Pt, Sp*, 2011 *R, Pt, Geo, Fj, Sa, SA, W*, 2012 *Sen, Mad, Z*, 2013 *Sen, Tun*
HP Botha 2000 *Z, Z, Ur*
H Botha 2012 *Z, Sp*
AC Bouwer 2012 *Sen, Mad, Sp*, 2013 *Sen, Tun*
H Breedt 1998 *Tun, Z*
H Brink 1992 *Z, Z*, 1993 *W, Ken, Z*, 1994 *Rus, Z, Iv, Mor, HK*
J Britz 1996 *Z*
E Buitenbag 2010 *Rus*, 2013 *Sen, Tun*
B Buitendag 1990 *W, W, F, F, WGe*, 1991 *Sp, Pt, It, It, Z, Z, I, I, Z, Z, Z*, 1992 *Z, Z*, 1993 *W, AG, Ken, Z*
J Burger 2004 *Za, Ken, Z, Mor*, 2006 *Tun, Tun, Mor, Mor*, 2007 *Za, Geo, R, SA, I, F, Ar, Geo*, 2008 *Z*, 2009 *Iv, Iv, Pt, Tun, Tun*, 2010 *R, Geo, Pt*, 2011 *Fj, Sa, SA, W*

B Calitz 1995 *Z*
C Campbell 2008 *Z*
DJ Coetzee 1990 *Pt, W, F, F, WGe*, 1991 *Sp, Pt, It, It, Z, Z, I, I, Z, Z, Z*, 1992 *Z, Z*, 1993 *W, AG, Ken, Z*, 1994 *Z, Iv, Mor, HK*, 1995 *Z, Z*
JC Coetzee 1990 *W*
M Couw 2006 *Ken*
B Cronjé 1994 *Rus*

HDP Dames 2011 *Fj, Sa, SA, W*, 2012 *Sen, Mad*
HDP Dames 2013 *Sen, Tun*
J Dames 1998 *Tun, Z*
D de Beer 2000 *Z*
S de Beer 1995 *Z*, 1997 *Tg*, 1998 *Tun, Z, Iv, Mor, Z*, 1999 *Ger*
AD de Klerk 2009 *Iv, Iv*
CJ De Koe 2010 *Geo, Pt, Sp*
DP De La Harpe 2010 *Rus, R, Geo, Pt, Sp*, 2011 *R, Pt, Geo, Fj, Sa, SA, W*, 2012 *Z, Sp*, 2013 *Sen, Tun*
RCA De La Harpe 2011 *R, Pt, Geo, Fj, SA, W*
SC De La Harpe 2010 *Sp*, 2012 *Z, Sp*
H de Waal 1990 *Z, Pt*
N de Wet 2000 *Ur*
R Dedig 2004 *Mor, Za, Ken, Z, Mor*
CJH Derks 1990 *Z, Pt, W, W, F, F, WGe*, 1991 *Sp, Pt, It, It, Z, Z, I, I, Z, Z, Z*, 1992 *Z, Z*, 1993 *W, AG, Z*, 1994 *Rus, Z, Iv, Mor, HK*
J Deysel 1990 *Z, Pt, W, W*, 1991 *Sp, Pt, It, It, Z, Z, I, I, Z, Z, Z*, 1992 *Z*
VA Dreyer 2002 *Z*, 2003 *Ar, I, R*
J Drotsky 2006 *Ken*, 2008 *Sen*
AJ Du Plessis 2010 *Pt, Sp*
I du Plessis 2005 *Mor*, 2009 *Tun*
M du Plessis 2001 *Z*, 2005 *Mor*
N du Plessis 1993 *Ken*, 1994 *Rus*, 1995 *Z*
O Du Plessis 2008 *Sen*
T Du Plessis 2006 *Ken, Tun, Mor, Mor*, 2007 *Geo, R, Uga, SA, I, F, Ar, Geo*, 2008 *Sen, Z*, 2009 *Iv, Iv, Pt, Tun, Tun*, 2010 *R, Geo, Pt, Sp*, 2011 *R, Pt, Geo, Fj, SA, W*, 2012 *Sen, Sp*, 2013 *Sen, Tun*
P du Plooy 1992 *Z, Z*, 1994 *Z, Mor, HK*
S du Rand 2007 *Geo, R, Uga*
JA Du Toit 2007 *Za, Geo, R, Uga, SA, I, F, Geo*, 2008 *Sen, Z*, 2009 *Pt, Tun, Tun*, 2010 *Rus, R, Geo, Pt, Sp*, 2011 *R, Pt, Geo, Sa, SA, W*
N du Toit 2002 *Tun*, 2003 *Sa, Ar, I, A, R*
V du Toit 1990 *Pt, W, W, F*
JH Duvenhage 2000 *Z, Z*, 2001 *It, Z, Z*, 2002 *Mad*, 2003 *Sa, Uga, Ar, I, R*, 2007 *Za, R, Uga*

A Engelbrecht 2000 *Z*
J Engelbrecht 1990 *WGe*, 1994 *Rus, Z, Iv, Mor, HK*, 1995 *Z, Z*
N Engelbrecht 1996 *Z*
H Engels 1990 *F, WGe*
JB Engels 2013 *Sen, Tun*
E Erasmus 1997 *Tg*
G Esterhuizen 2008 *Sen, Z*
SF Esterhuizen 2008 *Z*, 2009 *Iv, Iv, Pt, Tun, Tun*, 2010 *Rus, R, Geo, Pt, Sp*, 2011 *R, Pt*, 2012 *Sen, Mad*
N Esterhuyse 2006 *Ken, Tun, Mor*, 2007 *Za, Geo, R, Uga, SA, I, F, Ar, Geo*, 2008 *Z*, 2009 *Iv, Iv, Pt, Tun, Tun*, 2010 *Rus, R, Geo, Pt, Sp*, 2011 *R, Pt, Geo, Fj, Sa, SA, W*

D Farmer 1997 *Tg*, 1998 *Pt, Iv, Mor, Z*, 1999 *Z, Fj, Ger*
F Fisch 1999 *Z, Ger*
TR Forbes 2010 *Rus*
HH Franken 2011 *Sa*, 2012 *Sen, Mad*
S Furter 1999 *Z, Fj, F, C, Ger*, 2001 *It*, 2002 *Mad, Z, Tun, Tun*, 2003 *Sa, Ken, Uga, Ar, I, A, R*, 2004 *Mor*, 2006 *Ken, Tun, Ken*

E Gaoab 2005 *Mad, Mor*
I Gaya 2004 *Za, Ken*
J Genis 2000 *Z, Z, Ur*, 2001 *Z*
N Genis 2006 *Mor*
R Gentz 2001 *It*
R Glundeung 2006 *Ken*
CJ Goosen 1991 *Sp, Pt, It, It*, 1993 *W*
D Gouws 2000 *Z, Z, Ur*, 2001 *It, Z, Z*
T Gouws 2003 *Ken, Uga*, 2004 *Za, Ken*, 2006 *Ken, Tun*
A Graham 2001 *It, Z, Z*, 2002 *Mad, Tun*, 2003 *Ken, Uga, I*, 2004 *Mor*
A Greeff 1997 *Tg*
D Grobelaar 2008 *Z*
DP Grobler 2001 *Z*, 2002 *Mad, Tun, Tun*, 2003 *Sa, Ken, Uga, Ar, I, A, R*, 2004 *Mor, Za, Ken, Z, Mor*, 2006 *Ken, Tun, Ken*, 2007 *Za, Geo, R, SA, Ar*
HJ Grobler 1990 *Z, Pt, W, W, F, F, WGe*, 1991 *Sp, Pt, It, It, Z, Z, I, I, Z, Z, Z*, 1992 *Z, Z*

T Grünewald 1990 *Z*
D Grunschloss 2003 *A, R*

F Hartung 1996 *Z, Z*
RJ Herridge 2009 *Pt, Tun, Tun*
L Holtzhausen 1997 *Tg*, 1998 *Pt, Tun, Z, Iv, Mor, Z*, 1999 *Ger*
F Horn 2005 *Mad, Mor*, 2006 *Ken*
H Horn 1997 *Tg*, 1998 *Pt, Iv, Mor, Z*, 1999 *Z, Fj, F, C, Ger*, 2001 *It*, 2002 *Mad, Z, Tun*, 2003 *Sa*, 2007 *Za, Geo, R, Uga, SA, I, F, Ar, Geo*, 2008 *Sen, Z*, 2009 *Iv, Iv, Tun, Tun*, 2010 *Rus*, 2011 *Fj, Sa, SA, W*
K Horn 1997 *Tg*, 1998 *Pt*
Q Hough 1995 *Z, Z*, 1998 *Pt, Tun, Z, Iv, Mor, Z*, 1999 *Z, Fj, F, C*
P Human 2012 *Sen, Mad*
D Husselman 1993 *AG*, 1994 *Z, Mor*, 2002 *Mad, Z, Tun*, 2003 *Sa, Ar, I, A*
JJ Husselman 2004 *Za, Ken*

E Isaacs 1993 *Ken*, 1994 *Iv*
P Isaacs 2000 *Z, Z, Ur*, 2001 *Z, Z*, 2003 *A*, 2005 *Mad, Mor*
E Izaacs 1998 *Pt*, 1999 *Z, Ger*, 2000 *Z, Z, Ur*, 2001 *It, Z, Z*, 2002 *Mad, Z, Tun, Tun*, 2003 *Sa, Ken, Ar, A, R*

M Jacobs 1999 *Z, Fj, F, Ger*
P Jan van Lill 2013 *Sen, Tun*
E Jansen 2006 *Ken*
EA Jantjies 2006 *Ken, Tun, Ken, Tun*, 2007 *Za, Geo, R, Uga, SA, I, F, Ar, Geo*, 2008 *Sen, Z*, 2009 *Iv, Iv, Pt, Tun, Tun*, 2010 *Rus, R, Geo, Pt, Sp*, 2011 *R, Pt, Geo, Fj, Sa, SA, W*, 2012 *Sen, Mad, Z, Sp*
R Jantjies 1994 *HK*, 1995 *Z, Z*, 1996 *Z*, 1998 *Pt, Tun, Iv, Mor, Z*, 1999 *Z, Fj, F, C*, 2000 *Z, Z*
M Jeary 2003 *Uga*, 2004 *Ken, Z, Mor*
R Jeary 2000 *Z, Ur*
D Jeffrey 1990 *F*
J Jenkins 2002 *Mad, Tun*, 2003 *Ken*
AJ Jevu 2012 *Sen*

SM Kaizemi 2012 *Sp*
D Kamonga 2004 *Mor, Za, Ken, Z, Mor*, 2007 *Uga, Geo*
M Kapitako 2000 *Z, Z*, 2001 *It, Z, Z*, 2003 *Uga*, 2004 *Za*, 2006 *Tun*
HI Kasera 2012 *Mad*
M Kasiringwa 2012 *Z, Sp*
M Katjiuanjo 2005 *Mad, Mor*
M Kazombiaze 2006 *Ken, Tun*
U Kazombiaze 2006 *Ken, Tun, Mor, Mor*, 2007 *Za, Uga, SA, I, F, Ar, Geo*, 2008 *Sen, Z*, 2009 *Iv, Iv, Pt, Tun, Tun*, 2010 *Rus, Geo*, 2011 *W*
R Kitshoff 2010 *Pt, Sp*, 2011 *R, Pt, Geo, Fj, Sa, SA, W*, 2013 *Sen, Tun*
DPW Koen 2006 *Tun*
HVW Koll 2009 *Pt, Tun*, 2010 *Rus, R, Geo, Pt, Sp*, 2011 *R, Pt, Geo, Fj, Sa, SA, W*, 2012 *Sen, Mad*
A Kotze 1991 *Sp, Z, Z, I, I*, 1993 *W, AG, Z*
D Kotze 1993 *W, AG, Ken, Z*, 1994 *Rus, HK*
J Kotze 1995 *Z, Z*, 1996 *Z, Z*, 2000 *Z, Z*, 2001 *It, Z, Z*, 2002 *Mad, Z, Tun, Tun*, 2004 *Za, Ken, Z, Mor*
P Kotze 2001 *It*
P Kotze 1996 *Z*
TAW Kotze 2011 *Pt, Fj, Sa, SA, W*, 2012 *Sen, Mad, Z, Sp*, 2013 *Sen, Tun*
L Kotzee 2008 *Z*
JL Kruger 2001 *It, Z, Z*
R Kruger 2003 *Ken, Uga*, 2005 *Mad, Mor*
R Kruger 2004 *Mor, Za, Ken, Mor*

SO Lambert 2000 *Z, Ur*, 2001 *It, Z, Z*, 2003 *Ken, Uga*, 2004 *Mor*, 2005 *Mad*, 2006 *Ken, Tun, Ken*
B Langenhoven 2007 *SA, I, F, Ar, Geo*, 2008 *Sen, Z*, 2009 *Pt, Tun, Tun*, 2010 *Rus*
R Larson 2011 *Fj, Sa, W*
G Lensing 2002 *Mad, Z, Tun, Tun*, 2003 *Sa, Ar, I, A, R*, 2004 *Mor*, 2006 *Ken, Mor, Mor*, 2007 *R, SA, I, F, Ar, Geo*, 2009 *Iv, Iv, Tun, Tun*
C Lesch 2005 *Mad, Mor*

HD Lindvelt 1998 *Iv, Z*, 1999 *F, C, Ger*, 2001 *It, Z, Z*, 2002 *Mad, Z, Tun, Tun*, 2003 *Sa, Ken, Uga, Ar, I, A*, 2004 *Mor, Za, Ken, Z, Mor*, 2006 *Ken, Tun, Ken, Mor, Mor*, 2007 *Za, Geo, SA, F, Ar*
J Lombaard 1996 *Z*
H Loots 1990 *Z*
J Losper 2005 *Mor*
SJ Losper 1990 *Z, Pt, W, W, F, F, WGe*, 1991 *Sp, Pt, It, It, Z, Z, I, I, Z, Z, Z*
TC Losper 2007 *Za, Geo, R, Uga, SA, I, F*, 2008 *Sen*, 2011 *Geo, W*
W Lötter 1990 *Z*
RC Loubser 1999 *F*, 2005 *Mad, Mor*
O Louw 1993 *Ken, Z*, 1994 *Z, Iv*, 1996 *Z*

M MacKenzie 2004 *Mor*, 2006 *Ken, Tun*, 2007 *Uga, I, F, Ar*
B Malgas 1991 *Z, Z, Z*, 1993 *W, AG, Ken, Z*, 1994 *Rus, Z, Iv, Mor, HK*, 1995 *Z, Z*, 1996 *Z*
G Mans 1990 *Z, Pt, W, W, F*, 1991 *Sp, Pt, It, It, Z, Z, I, I, Z, Z, Z*, 1992 *Z, Z*, 1993 *W, AG, Ken, Z*, 1994 *Rus, Z, Iv, Mor, HK*
C Marais 2010 *Pt, Sp*, 2011 *Fj, SA*
M Marais 1992 *Z*, 1993 *W, AG, Z*
W Maritz 1990 *Z*, 1991 *Z, Z, I, I, Z, Z, Z*
S McCulley 1990 *W, W, F, WGe*
E Meyer 1991 *Sp, Pt, It, It, Z, Z, I, I, Z, Z, Z*, 1992 *Z, Z*, 1993 *W*, 1994 *Z, Iv, Mor, HK*, 1995 *Z, Z*, 1996 *Z*
H Meyer 2004 *Za, Ken, Z, Mor*
JM Meyer 2003 *Ken, Uga, Ar, I, R*, 2006 *Ken, Tun, Tun, Mor, Mor*, 2007 *Uga, SA, I, F, Ar, Geo*
P Meyer 2005 *Mad*
M Moore 2013 *Tun*
DA Mouton 1999 *Z, Fj, Ger*, 2000 *Z, Z, Ur*, 2002 *Mad, Z, Tun*, 2003 *Sa, Ken, Uga, Ar, I, A, R*, 2004 *Mor*, 2005 *Mad, Mor*, 2006 *Tun, Ken, Tun, Mor*, 2007 *Ar*, 2008 *Sen*
H Mouton 2000 *Z*
P Mouton 2005 *Mad, Mor*

H Neethling 1993 *Ken*
G Nel 2006 *Mor, Mor*
JA Nel 2012 *Sen, Mad, Z, Sp*, 2013 *Tun*
S Nell 2000 *Z, Z*
S Neustadt 2012 *Z, Sp*, 2013 *Sen, Tun*
J Nienaber 1998 *Pt, Tun, Z, Mor, Z*
J Nieuwenhuis 2007 *Za, Geo, R, Uga, SA, I, F, Geo*, 2008 *Sen, Z*, 2009 *Iv, Iv, Tun, Tun*, 2010 *R, Geo, Sp*, 2011 *R, Pt, Geo, Fj, SA, W*

EB O'Callaghan 2010 *R, Geo, Pt, Sp*, 2011 *R, Pt, Geo, Fj, Sa, SA, W*
J Olivier 1999 *Z, Fj, Ger*, 2000 *Z, Z, Ur*
M Olivier 1990 *Pt, F*
LT Oosthuizen 1990 *Z, Pt, W, W, F, F, WGe*
GJ Opperman 1999 *Z, Fj, F, C, Ger*
T Opperman 2002 *Mad, Z*
WJ Otto 1993 *AG, Z*, 1994 *Rus*

R Pedro 1998 *Z*, 1999 *Ger*, 2000 *Ur*, 2001 *It, Z, Z*, 2003 *Sa, Ken, Uga, Ar, I, A, R*, 2004 *Mor*
DG Philander 2008 *Sen*, 2009 *Iv, Iv, Pt, Tun, Tun*, 2010 *Rus*, 2011 *R, Pt, Geo, W*, 2013 *Sen, Tun*
F Pienaar 2006 *Ken*
D Pieters 2008 *Sen*
L Plaath 2001 *It, Z, Z*
CJ Powell 2001 *It, Z, Z*, 2002 *Mad, Z, Tun, Tun*, 2003 *Sa, Ken, Uga, Ar, I, R*, 2004 *Mor, Ken, Z, Mor*, 2006 *Ken, Tun, Tun, Mor, Mor*, 2007 *Za, Geo, R, Ar, Geo*

JH Redelinghuys 2006 *Ken, Tun, Mor*, 2007 *Za, Geo, R, Uga, SA, I, F, Ar, Geo*, 2008 *Sen, Z*, 2009 *Iv, Iv, Pt, Tun*, 2010 *Rus, R, Geo, Pt, Sp*, 2011 *R, Pt, Geo, Fj, Sa, SA, W*, 2012 *Sen, Mad, Z, Sp*, 2013 *Sen, Tun*
C Redlinghaus 2001 *It*
H Reinders 1996 *Z*
G Rich 1993 *W*
V Rodrigues 2012 *Z, Sp*
C Roets 1995 *Z*

P Rossouw 2004 *Za, Ken, Z, Mor,* 2005 *Mad, Mor,* 2006 *Mor, Mor,* 2007 *Za, Geo, R*

A Samuelson 1995 *Z,* 1996 *Z, Z,* 1997 *Tg,* 1998 *Pt, Tun, Z, Iv, Mor, Z,* 1999 *Z, Fj, F, C, Ger*
A Schlechter 2012 *Z, Sp,* 2013 *Sen, Tun*
M Schreuder 2002 *Mad, Z, Tun, Tun,* 2003 *Sa, Ken, Uga, I, A, R,* 2004 *Mor, Za, Ken, Z, Mor,* 2006 *Ken, Ken,* 2007 *Ar, Geo*
C Schumacher 1995 *Z*
JH Senekal 1998 *Iv, Mor, Z,* 1999 *Z, Fj, F, C, Ger,* 2002 *Mad, Z,* 2003 *Sa, Ken, Uga, Ar, I, A, R,* 2005 *Mad,* 2006 *Ken, Mor, Mor,* 2007 *Geo, R, Uga, I, Ar, Geo*
A Skinner 1990 *Z, Pt, W, W, F, F, WGe*
G Smit 1990 *F*
H Smit 2013 *Sen, Tun*
C Smith 2012 *Sen, Mad, Z, Sp*
E Smith 1998 *Tun, Iv, Mor, Z,* 1999 *Fj, F, C,* 2002 *Mad*
P Smith 1993 *Ken,* 1994 *Iv,* 1995 *Z, Z*
S Smith 1990 *Pt, W, W, F,* 1992 *Z, Z,* 1993 *W, AG, Ken, Z,* 1994 *Rus, Z, Iv, Mor, HK,* 1996 *Z*
W Smith 2002 *Mad, Z, Tun*
D Snyders 2003 *Uga,* 2005 *Mad,* 2012 *Z*
H Snyman 1990 *F, F,* 1991 *Sp, Pt, It, It, Z, Z, I, I, Z, Z, Z,* 1992 *Z, Z,* 1993 *W, AG, Ken, Z,* 1994 *Z, Iv, Mor, HK,* 1995 *Z, Z,* 1996 *Z, Z*
M Snyman 1994 *Rus, Z, Iv, Mor, HK*
D Spangenberg 2005 *Mad, Mor*
A Steenkamp 1994 *Iv, Mor*
C Steenkamp 2007 *Uga*
T Steenkamp 1992 *Z, Z,* 1993 *Ken,* 1994 *Rus, Iv,* 1995 *Z,* 1996 *Z,* 1998 *Pt, Tun, Z*
P Steyn 1996 *Z, Z,* 1997 *Tg,* 1998 *Pt, Tun, Z, Iv, Mor,* 1999 *Z, Fj, F, C*
A Stoop 1990 *Z, Pt, W,* 1991 *Sp, Pt, It, It, Z, I, I, Z*
L Stoop 2012 *Sen, Mad*
L Stoop 1994 *Iv*
H Stroh 2012 *Mad*
G Suze 2005 *Mad*
CI Swanepoel 2012 *Sen, Mad,* 2013 *Sen, Tun*
JC Swanepoel 2013 *Sen, Tun*
N Swanepoel 2003 *Ken, Ar, I, A, R,* 2004 *Mor, Za, Ken, Z, Mor*
H Swart 1995 *Z,* 1996 *Z,* 1997 *Tg,* 1998 *Pt, Tun, Z*
JL Swart 1990 *F, WGe*
BM Swartz 1990 *W, W, F, F, WGe*

R Theart 1998 *Pt*
J Theron 1998 *Iv, Mor, Z,* 1999 *Fj, F, C, Ger,* 2004 *Mor*
A Thompson 2013 *Sen, Tun*
RHR Thompson 2004 *Za, Ken, Mor,* 2005 *Mad,* 2006 *Ken, Tun, Ken, Tun, Mor, Mor*
M Tjuiza 2012 *Z, Sp,* 2013 *Sen, Tun*
D Tredoux 2001 *Z*
JA Tromp 2012 *Z, Sp,* 2013 *Sen*

L van Coller 1993 *AG, Ken,* 1994 *Rus, Iv*
GE van der Berg 2005 *Mor,* 2006 *Ken, Tun, Tun, Mor*
L van der Linde 2006 *Tun*
A van der Merwe 1990 *Pt, W, W, F, F, WGe,* 1991 *Sp, Pt, It, It, Z, Z, I, I, Z, Z, Z,* 1992 *Z, Z*
D van der Merwe 1990 *WGe*
S van der Merwe 1997 *Tg,* 1998 *Iv, Mor, Z,* 1999 *Z, Fj, F, C,* 2002 *Z, Tun, Tun,* 2003 *Sa, Ken, Ar, I, A, R,* 2004 *Za, Ken, Z, Mor,* 2006 *Tun, Mor*
J van der Westhuizen 2007 *Za, Geo*
L van Dyk 1998 *Tun, Z, Iv, Mor, Z,* 1999 *Fj, F, C, Ger,* 2002 *Mad*
JA van Lill 2002 *Mad, Tun, Tun,* 2003 *Sa, Ar, I, A, R,* 2004 *Mor,* 2006 *Tun,* 2007 *Za*
PJ van Lill 2006 *Ken,* 2008 *Sen, Z,* 2009 *Iv, Pt, Tun, Tun,* 2010 *Rus, R, Geo, Pt, Sp,* 2011 *R, Pt, Geo, Fj, Sa, SA,* 2012 *Sen, Mad, Z, Sp*
RE van Neel 2010 *Rus,* 2011 *Sa,* 2012 *Z*
F van Rensburg 1995 *Z,* 1996 *Z, Z,* 1997 *Tg,* 1998 *Tun, Z,* 1999 *Z, Fj, F, C, Ger,* 2000 *Z,* 2001 *It, Z, Z*
SJ van Rensburg 1998 *Z, Iv, Mor, Z,* 1999 *Z, Fj, F, Ger,* 2000 *Z, Ur*
SL van Rooi 2003 *Uga, A,* 2004 *Mor,* 2005 *Mor*
A van Rooyen 1991 *Sp, Pt, It, It, I,* 1992 *Z, Z*
M van Rooyen 1996 *Z,* 1998 *Pt, Tun, Z, Mor, Z,* 1999 *Z, F, C*
C van Schalkwyk 1993 *AG, Z*
A van Tonder 1995 *Z*
CJ van Tonder 2002 *Tun,* 2003 *Sa, Ken, Uga, I, A, R,* 2004 *Mor, Za, Ken, Z, Mor,* 2006 *Ken, Ken,* 2007 *Za,* 2012 *Sp*
JH van Tonder 2004 *Mor, Ken, Z, Mor,* 2006 *Ken, Tun,* 2007 *Uga, SA, I, F, Ar, Geo,* 2008 *Z,* 2009 *Iv, Iv, Pt, Tun*
N van Vuuren 1993 *AG*
RJ van Vuuren 1997 *Tg,* 1998 *Pt, Tun, Z,* 1999 *Z, Ger,* 2000 *Z, Z, Ur,* 2002 *Mad, Z,* 2003 *Ken, Uga, R*
A van Wyk 1993 *W, Ken,* 1994 *Iv, HK*
D van Wyk 2011 *R, Pt, Geo, Fj, Sa, SA, W,* 2012 *Z, Sp*
G van Wyk 1999 *Z, Fj, F, C,* 2000 *Z, Z, Ur,* 2001 *It*
L van Wyk 2004 *Mor*
M van Wyk 2009 *Iv, Iv, Pt,* 2010 *Rus, Geo, Pt,* 2011 *R, Pt, Geo,* 2012 *Sp*
R van Wyk 2004 *Za, Ken, Z, Mor*
R van Wyk 2002 *Mad, Z, Tun, Tun,* 2003 *Sa,* 2004 *Mor, Za, Ken, Z, Mor*
J van Zyl 2008 *Sen*
WP Van Zyl 2007 *SA, I, F, Ar, Geo,* 2008 *Z,* 2009 *Iv, Iv, Pt, Tun, Tun,* 2010 *R, Geo, Pt, Sp,* 2011 *Fj, Sa, SA, W*
R van Zyl 1997 *Tg,* 1998 *Tun, Z, Iv, Mor, Z*
M Venter 2003 *Uga,* 2004 *Mor,* 2008 *Z,* 2009 *Iv, Iv, Pt, Tun, Tun,* 2010 *Rus*
D Vermaak 1998 *Z*
JJ Vermaak 1990 *Pt,* 1994 *Rus,* 1996 *Z*
A Vermeulen 2010 *Rus*
B Vermeulen 1995 *Z*
D Vermeulen 1996 *Z, Z,* 1997 *Tg,* 1998 *Pt*
G Vermeulen 1991 *Z*
M Visser 2007 *Za, Geo, R, Uga, SA, Ar, Geo,* 2009 *Iv, Iv, Pt, Tun, Tun,* 2010 *Rus, R, Geo, Pt, Sp,* 2011 *SA*
CW Viviers 2010 *Sp,* 2011 *R, Pt, Geo*
P von Wielligh 1991 *It, Z,* 1992 *Z,* 1993 *AG, Z,* 1994 *Iv, Mor,* 1995 *Z,* 1996 *Z*

B Walters 2009 *Pt*
GAE Walters 2008 *Z,* 2009 *Iv,* 2010 *R, Geo, Pt, Sp*
W Wentzel 1991 *Sp, Z, Z*
E Wessels 2002 *Tun, Tun,* 2003 *Sa, Ar, I, A, R,* 2006 *Tun, Mor, Mor,* 2007 *SA, I, F,* 2009 *Iv, Pt, Tun, Tun,* 2010 *Rus*
LP Winkler 2008 *Z,* 2009 *Iv, Iv,* 2010 *Rus, R, Geo,* 2011 *R, Pt, Geo, Fj, Sa*
RC Witbooi 2004 *Za, Z,* 2005 *Mor,* 2006 *Ken, Tun, Ken,* 2007 *Za, Geo, R, Uga, I, F, Geo,* 2008 *Sen*
J Wohler 2005 *Mad, Mor*

J Zaayman 1997 *Tg,* 1998 *Pt, Tun, Z, Iv, Mor, Z,* 1999 *Z, Fj, F, C, Ger*

After a seven-month sabbatical Richie McCaw returned to help New Zealand retain the Bledisloe Cup.

AFP/Getty Images

NEW ZEALAND

NEW ZEALAND'S 2012–13 TEST RECORD

OPPONENTS	DATE	VENUE	RESULT
Australia	20 Oct	A	Drew 18–18
Scotland	11 Nov	A	Won 51–22
Italy	17 Nov	A	Won 42–10
Wales	24 Nov	A	Won 33–10
England	1 Dec	A	Lost 38–21
France	8 Jun	H	Won 23–13
France	15 Jun	H	Won 30–0
France	22 Jun	H	Won 24–9
Australia	17 Aug	A	Won 47–29
Australia	24 Aug	H	Won 27–16
Argentina	7 Sep	H	Won 28–13
South Africa	14 Sep	H	Won 29–15
Argentina	28 Sep	A	Won 33–15
South Africa	5 Oct	A	Won 38–27

RECORDS TUMBLE AS ALL BLACKS RETAIN CROWN

By Ian Jones

Getty Images

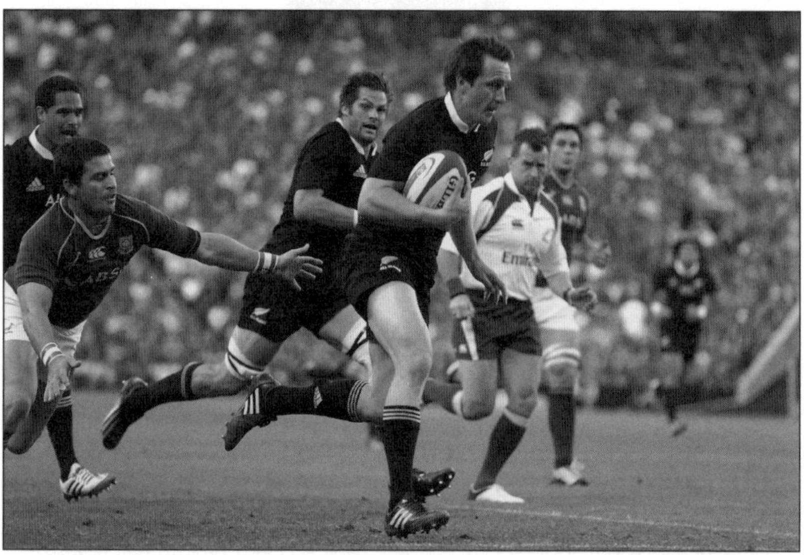

Wing Ben Smith scored a record eight tries for New Zealand in their successful Rugby Championship campaign.

It was another wonderful, hugely impressive 12 months of football from Steve Hansen's All Black team which saw them successfully defend their Rugby Championship crown, a testament to the incredible professionalism as well as ambition that exists within the New Zealand camp. The current group clearly live and breathe rugby, relentlessly pushing themselves every day on the training paddock, and that dedication was reflected in some outstanding performances during the season.

The defeat against England at Twickenham in December may have denied the All Blacks an unbeaten record of 13 wins and a draw from the season but it was, in perspective, a blemish on their record rather than a significant setback and overall I thought they convincingly underlined their status as the number one team in the world.

It was a season of memorable collective and individual milestones.

The team's 47–29 win over Australia in Sydney in August was New Zealand's 100th over the Wallabies while the 38–27 victory in an epic against the Springboks at Ellis Park to claim the Championship title was the All Blacks' 50th in Tests against South Africa. Dan Carter became the first player to score 1,400 Tests points in the match against Argentina in Hamilton and Ma'a Nonu and Conrad Smith have now played a world record 51 games together in the midfield. The 29–15 win against the Springboks in Auckland in September was New Zealand's 383rd Test triumph, taking them past France's previous mark of 382 victories in internationals.

These were all fantastic achievements but perhaps just as satisfying for All Blacks supporters was the style in which the team played, adopting a high-risk strategy that was so entertaining to watch throughout the year. It was an approach that brought big rewards as well as inevitable mistakes, but it was the bedrock of the team's approach and they had the courage to stick to their guns and play with what seemed like little or no fear.

In my opinion, this current side already deserves to be considered as one of the greatest in New Zealand history but they do not seem to be finished creating their own legacy. As a group they are always striving for improvement, regardless of what they have already achieved, and that ethos could yet take them to an even higher level in the future.

The team's autumn opener against Scotland at Murrayfield was a chance to put things right after being held to an 18–18 draw by Australia in October and the boys looked in good shape on the back of a 51–22 win in Edinburgh. Steve Hansen made 14 changes for the Italy game, giving almost all the squad a chance to get their hands dirty, and they were made to work hard in Rome. They were only 13–7 up at the break and it was a timely reminder you have to earn the right to play fast and wide rugby. The boys drafted in did the job in the second half, though, and it finished 42–10 to the All Blacks.

Wales' reputation as Six Nations Grand Slam champions preceded them before the game in Cardiff but New Zealand matched fire with fire, which was crucial in a 33–10 win. To be honest, I thought the side tired a little in the second half after another long, hard season but the defence was solid enough as Wales tried to launch a fightback.

There's no denying the 38–21 loss to England was a shock to the system to everyone involved in All Black rugby. It was the first defeat for Steve since becoming head coach after Rugby World Cup 2011 and there cannot have been many New Zealand sides who have conceded three tries in the space of eight minutes before. It proved form and reputation mean nothing ahead of big Test matches.

There was talk of fatigue and a virus running through the squad before the game but I wouldn't want to take anything away from the English performance. New Zealand simply could not live with them on the day and the better team won.

I spoke to a few of the players after the game and they were all ready to take it on the chin. They were disappointed but they spoke about moving forward and learning from what was an unusual and uncomfortable experience for them. Good sides learn from the past but do not dwell on it.

The summer series against the French was a fascinating contest, not least because New Zealand were without Richie McCaw for the three Tests. Kieran Read stepped up as skipper and showed he is cut from the same cloth as McCaw, leading the team by example on and off the pitch. Steve is a lucky man because he knows he has a readymade replacement in Kieran whenever Richie finally calls it a day and the All Blacks are blessed to have a player with such athleticism and a phenomenal work rate. His subsequent form in The Rugby Championship was incredible.

The three games against France were all different. The French came close in the first Test in Auckland (23–13) but that was probably their big chance and they were outclassed (30–0) in the second match in Christchurch before losing 24–9 in New Plymouth. What was really impressive from a New Zealand perspective was the negatives from the first Test – the kick-chase game, the physicality at the breakdown – became virtues a week later and their ability to adapt and adjust in the space of seven days spoke volumes about the team's preparation and attitude.

What was also pleasing in the games against the French was the direct running of the backs and it was a credit to the hard work obviously put in by backs coach Ian Foster on the training paddock.

The Rugby Championship kicked off with the double-header against the Wallabies and then the visit of Argentina to Hamilton but, as many people had predicted, the competition eventually boiled down to the two games against the Springboks. The first match at Eden Park in September finished in a 29–15 win for Steve and the boys – a 31st consecutive All Black win at the ground – and the stage was then set for the big decider at Ellis Park in October. South Africa needed to score four tries and deny New Zealand a losing bonus point for the title.

I can honestly say the game in Johannesburg was one of the greatest Test matches I've ever seen. Every single player on the pitch was amazing and, in terms of sheer entertainment, I'm struggling to think of a game to rival it. The lead changed hands seven times, there were nine tries and, especially in the second half, it was relentless end-to-end stuff.

The difference between the two teams was ultimately New Zealand's ability to convert chances and play with real intensity for the full 80 minutes. At times the Springboks looked irresistible but, not for the first time, the All Blacks got over the line because they sustained a high-tempo game longer than the opposition.

South Africa's performance, though, was brilliant and I believe they are going to get stronger, which I hope will lead to more matches like the one we saw at Ellis Park. That can only be exciting for world rugby.

Steve can rightly be very happy with his second year in charge. The results, Twickenham aside, were obviously there but I think he also struck a nice balance between winning games and giving new players an opportunity at Test level. He gave 10 players their debuts over the course of the year and although I can't see any of the more senior players volunteering to hang up their boots just yet, it's healthy to blood possible replacements sooner rather than later. The hookers Keven Mealamu and Andrew Hore probably won't make it to Rugby World Cup 2015 but Steve brought Dane Coles into the squad for the northern hemisphere tour and it was no coincidence he went on to play in 10 games during the year as the coach keeps one eye on the future.

New Zealand are a team still evolving after winning RWC 2011 but the emergence since 2011 of players like Julian Savea and Ben Smith, who scored 17 tries between them during the year, is proof of a side that is moving in the right direction. The younger players like Sam Cane, Steven Luatua, Tawera Kerr-Barlow and Beauden Barrett will keep pushing hard for a place in the starting XV and that intense competition for places can only be healthy.

Strength in depth is crucial and it was in evidence in August for the game against Australia in Wellington when Carter, Aaron Cruden and Barrett were all out injured and Tom Taylor came in from the Crusaders and did a job at fly half on debut. He was an unfamiliar face in a key position in the starting XV but the team didn't skip a beat.

Steve is clearly a players' coach. They want to play for him and the confidence he has in his wider squad, his match-day 23 and the high-risk approach he wants has been infectious. The All Blacks produced an ambitious and at the same time no fuss brand of rugby, which made for a wonderful ride as a supporter.

NEW ZEALAND INTERNATIONAL STATISTICS

MATCH RECORDS UP TO 10 OCTOBER 2013

MOST CONSECUTIVE TEST WINS

17 1965 *SA* 4, 1966 *BI* 1,2,3,4, 1967 *A,E,W,F,S,* 1968 *A* 1,2, *F* 1,2,3, 1969 *W* 1,2

16 2011 *Tg, J, F, C, Arg, A, F,* 2012 *I* 1,2,3, *A*1,2, *Arg*1, *SA*1, *Arg*2, *SA*2

15 2005 *A* 1, *SA* 2, *A* 2, *W,I E,S,* 2006 *I* 1,2, *Arg, A* 1, *SA* 1, *A* 2, 3, *SA* 2

15 2009 *A* 3, 4, *W,It E,F* 3, 2010 *I* 1, *W* 1,2, *SA* 1, 2, *A* 1, 2, *SA* 3, *A* 3

12 1988 *A* 3, 1989 *F* 1,2, *Arg* 1,2, *A,W,I,* 1990 *S* 1,2, *A* 1,2

MOST CONSECUTIVE TESTS WITHOUT DEFEAT

Matches	Wins	Draws	Period
23	22	1	1987 to 1990
20	19	1	2011 to 2012
17	17	0	1965 to 1969
17	15	2	1961 to 1964
15	15	0	2005 to 2006
15	15	0	2009 to 2010

MOST POINTS IN A MATCH

BY THE TEAM

Pts	Opponents	Venue	Year
145	Japan	Bloemfontein	1995
108	Portugal	Lyons	2007
102	Tonga	Albany	2000
101	Italy	Huddersfield	1999
101	Samoa	N Plymouth	2008
93	Argentina	Wellington	1997
91	Tonga	Brisbane	2003
91	Fiji	Albany	2005
85	Romania	Toulouse	2007
83	Japan	Hamilton	2011
79	Canada	Wellington	2011
76	Italy	Marseilles	2007
74	Fiji	Christchurch	1987
73	Canada	Auckland	1995
71	Fiji	Albany	1997
71	Samoa	Albany	1999

BY A PLAYER

Pts	Player	Opponents	Venue	Year
45	SD Culhane	Japan	Bloemfontein	1995
36	TE Brown	Italy	Huddersfield	1999
33	CJ Spencer	Argentina	Wellington	1997
33	AP Mehrtens	Ireland	Dublin	1997
33	DW Carter	B&I Lions	Wellington	2005
33	NJ Evans	Portugal	Lyons	2007
32	TE Brown	Tonga	Albany	2000
30	MCG Ellis	Japan	Bloemfontein	1995
30	TE Brown	Samoa	Albany	2001
29	AP Mehrtens	Australia	Auckland	1999
29	AP Mehrtens	France	Paris	2000
29	LR MacDonald	Tonga	Brisbane	2003
29	DW Carter	Canada	Hamilton	2007

MOST TRIES IN A MATCH

BY THE TEAM

Tries	Opponents	Venue	Year
21	Japan	Bloemfontein	1995
16	Portugal	Lyons	2007
15	Tonga	Albany	2000
15	Fiji	Albany	2005
15	Samoa	N Plymouth	2008
14	Argentina	Wellington	1997
14	Italy	Huddersfield	1999
13	USA	Berkeley	1913
13	Tonga	Brisbane	2003
13	Romania	Toulouse	2007
13	Japan	Hamilton	2011
12	Italy	Auckland	1987
12	Fiji	Christchurch	1987
12	Canada	Wellington	2011

BY A PLAYER

Tries	Player	Opponents	Venue	Year
6	MCG Ellis	Japan	Bloemfontein	1995
5	JW Wilson	Fiji	Albany	1997
4	D McGregor	England	Crystal Palace	1905
4	CI Green	Fiji	Christchurch	1987
4	JA Gallagher	Fiji	Christchurch	1987
4	JJ Kirwan	Wales	Christchurch	1988
4	JT Lomu	England	Cape Town	1995
4	CM Cullen	Scotland	Dunedin	1996
4	JW Wilson	Samoa	Albany	1999
4	JM Muliaina	Canada	Melbourne	2003
4	SW Sivivatu	Fiji	Albany	2005
4	ZR Guildford	Canada	Wellington	2011

MOST CONVERSIONS IN A MATCH

BY THE TEAM

Cons	Opponents	Venue	Year
20	Japan	Bloemfontein	1995
14	Portugal	Lyons	2007
13	Tonga	Brisbane	2003
13	Samoa	N Plymouth	2008
12	Tonga	Albany	2000
11	Italy	Huddersfield	1999
10	Fiji	Christchurch	1987
10	Argentina	Wellington	1997
10	Romania	Toulouse	2007
9	Canada	Melbourne	2003
9	Italy	Marseilles	2007
9	Ireland	N Plymouth	2010
9	Japan	Hamilton	2011
8	Italy	Auckland	1987
8	Wales	Auckland	1988
8	Fiji	Albany	1997
8	Italy	Hamilton	2003
8	Fiji	Albany	2005
8	Canada	Wellington	2011

BY A PLAYER

Cons	Player	Opponents	Venue	Year
20	SD Culhane	Japan	Bloemfontein	1995
14	NJ Evans	Portugal	Lyons	2007
12	TE Brown	Tonga	Albany	2000
12	LR MacDonald	Tonga	Brisbane	2003
11	TE Brown	Italy	Huddersfield	1999
10	GJ Fox	Fiji	Christchurch	1987
10	CJ Spencer	Argentina	Wellington	1997
9	DW Carter	Canada	Melbourne	2003
9	CR Slade	Japan	Hamilton	2011
8	GJ Fox	Italy	Auckland	1987
8	GJ Fox	Wales	Auckland	1988
8	AP Mehrtens	Italy	Hamilton	2002

MOST DROP GOALS IN A MATCH

BY THE TEAM

Drops	Opponents	Venue	Year
3	France	Christchurch	1986

BY A PLAYER

Drops	Player	Opponents	Venue	Year
2	OD Bruce	Ireland	Dublin	1978
2	FM Botica	France	Christchurch	1986
2	AP Mehrtens	Australia	Auckland	1995

MOST PENALTIES IN A MATCH

BY THE TEAM

Penalties	Opponents	Venue	Year
9	Australia	Auckland	1999
9	France	Paris	2000
7	Western Samoa	Auckland	1993
7	South Africa	Pretoria	1999
7	South Africa	Wellington	2006
7	Australia	Auckland	2007
7	Argentina	Auckland	2011
6	British/Irish Lions	Dunedin	1959
6	England	Christchurch	1985
6	Argentina	Wellington	1987
6	Scotland	Christchurch	1987
6	France	Paris	1990
6	South Africa	Auckland	1994
6	Australia	Brisbane	1996
6	Ireland	Dublin	1997
6	South Africa	Cardiff	1999
6	Scotland	Murrayfield	2001
6	South Africa	Christchurch	2004
6	Australia	Sydney	2004
6	South Africa	Dunedin	2008
6	Australia	Tokyo	2009
6	Australia	Brisbane	2012

BY A PLAYER

Pens	Player	Opponents	Venue	Year
9	AP Mehrtens	Australia	Auckland	1999
9	AP Mehrtens	France	Paris	2000
7	GJ Fox	Western Samoa	Auckland	1993
7	AP Mehrtens	South Africa	Pretoria	1999
7	DW Carter	South Africa	Wellington	2006
7	DW Carter	Australia	Auckland	2007
7	PAT Weepu	Argentina	Auckland	2011
6	DB Clarke	British/Irish Lions	Dunedin	1959
6	KJ Crowley	England	Christchurch	1985
6	GJ Fox	Argentina	Wellington	1987
6	GJ Fox	Scotland	Christchurch	1987
6	GJ Fox	France	Paris	1990
6	SP Howarth	South Africa	Auckland	1994
6	AP Mehrtens	Australia	Brisbane	1996
6	AP Mehrtens	Ireland	Dublin	1997
6	AP Mehrtens	South Africa	Cardiff	1999
6	AP Mehrtens	Scotland	Murrayfield	2001
6	DW Carter	South Africa	Dunedin	2008
6	DW Carter	Australia	Tokyo	2009
6	DW Carter	Australia	Brisbane	2012

CAREER RECORDS

MOST CAPPED PLAYERS

Caps	Player	Career Span
120	RH McCaw	2001 to 2013
107	KF Mealamu	2002 to 2013
104	TD Woodcock	2002 to 2013
100	JM Muliaina	2003 to 2011
97	DW Carter	2003 to 2013
92	SBT Fitzpatrick	1986 to 1997
84	MA Nonu	2003 to 2013
81	JW Marshall	1995 to 2005
81	AK Hore	2002 to 2013
79	ID Jones	1990 to 1999
77	AJ Williams	2002 to 2012
75	CG Smith	2004 to 2013
74	JF Umaga	1997 to 2005
71	PAT Weepu	2004 to 2013
70	AP Mehrtens	1995 to 2004
68	JT Rokocoko	2003 to 2010
67	CR Jack	2001 to 2007
66	GM Somerville	2000 to 2008
63	JJ Kirwan	1984 to 1994
63	JT Lomu	1994 to 2002
62	RM Brooke	1992 to 1999
62	DC Howlett	2000 to 2007
62	R So'oialo	2002 to 2009
60	C W Dowd	1993 to 2000
60	JW Wilson	1993 to 2001
59	AD Oliver	1997 to 2007
59	BC Thorn	2003 to 2011
58	GW Whetton	1981 to 1991
58	ZV Brooke	1987 to 1997
58	CM Cullen	1996 to 2002
57	BT Kelleher	1999 to 2007
57	KJ Read	2008 to 2013
56	OM Brown	1992 to 1998
56	LR MacDonald	2000 to 2008
55	CE Meads	1957 to 1971
55	FE Bunce	1992 to 1997
55	MN Jones	1987 to 1998

MOST CONSECUTIVE TESTS

Tests	Player	Span
63	SBT Fitzpatrick	1986 to 1995
51	CM Cullen	1996 to 2000
49	RM Brooke	1995 to 1999
41	JW Wilson	1996 to 1999
40	GW Whetton	1986 to 1991

MOST TESTS AS CAPTAIN

Tests	Captain	Span
83	RH McCaw	2004 to 2013
51	SBT Fitzpatrick	1992 to 1997
30	WJ Whineray	1958 to 1965
23	RD Thorne	2002 to 2007
22	TC Randell	1998 to 2002
21	JF Umaga	2004 to 2005
19	GNK Mourie	1977 to 1982
18	BJ Lochore	1966 to 1970
17	AG Dalton	1981 to 1985

MOST POINTS IN TESTS

Points	Player	Tests	Career
1411	DW Carter	97	2003 to 2013
967	AP Mehrtens	70	1995 to 2004
645	GJ Fox	46	1985 to 1993
291	CJ Spencer	35	1997 to 2004
245	DC Howlett	62	2000 to 2007
236	CM Cullen	58	1996 to 2002
234	JW Wilson	60	1993 to 2001
230	JT Rokocoko	68	2003 to 2010
207	DB Clarke	31	1956 to 1964
201	AR Hewson	19	1981 to 1984

MOST TRIES IN TESTS

Tries	Player	Tests	Career
49	DC Howlett	62	2000 to 2007
46	CM Cullen	58	1996 to 2002
46	JT Rokocoko	68	2003 to 2010
44	JW Wilson	60	1993 to 2001
37	JT Lomu	63	1994 to 2002
37*	JF Umaga	74	1997 to 2005
35	JJ Kirwan	63	1984 to 1994
34	JM Muliaina	100	2003 to 2011
29	DW Carter	97	2003 to 2013
29	SW Sivivatu	45	2005 to 2011
25	MA Nonu	84	2003 to 2013
24	JW Marshall	81	1995 to 2005
24	CG Smith	75	2004 to 2013
21*	RH McCaw	120	2001 to 2013
20	FE Bunce	55	1992 to 1997

** Umaga and McCaw's totals each include a penalty try*

MOST CONVERSIONS IN TESTS

Cons	Player	Tests	Career
249	DW Carter	97	2003 to 2013
169	AP Mehrtens	70	1995 to 2004
118	GJ Fox	46	1985 to 1993
49	CJ Spencer	35	1997 to 2004
43	TE Brown	18	1999 to 2001
33	DB Clarke	31	1956 to 1964
32	SD Culhane	6	1995 to 1996

MOST PENALTY GOALS IN TESTS			
Penalties	Player	Tests	Career
250	DW Carter	97	2003 to 2013
188	AP Mehrtens	70	1995 to 2004
128	GJ Fox	46	1985 to 1993
43	AR Hewson	19	1981 to 1984
41	CJ Spencer	35	1997 to 2004
38	DB Clarke	31	1956 to 1964
26	AW Cruden	25	2010 to 2013
24	WF McCormick	16	1965 to 1971

MOST DROP GOALS IN TESTS			
Drops	Player	Tests	Career
10	AP Mehrtens	70	1995 to 2004
7	GJ Fox	46	1985 to 1993
6	DW Carter	97	2003 to 2013
5	DB Clarke	31	1956 to 1964
5	MA Herewini	10	1962 to 1967
5	OD Bruce	14	1976 to 1978

RUGBY CHAMPIONSHIP (FORMERLY TRI-NATIONS) RECORDS

RECORD	DETAIL	HOLDER	SET
Most points in season	202	in six matches	2013
Most tries in season	24	in six matches	2013
Highest score	55	55–35 v S Africa (h)	1997
Biggest win	39	54–15 v Argentina (a)	2012
Highest score conceded	46	40–46 v S Africa (a)	2000
Biggest defeat	21	7–28 v Australia (a)	1999
Most appearances	49	RH McCaw	2002 to 2013
Most points in matches	531	DW Carter	2003 to 2013
Most points in season	99	DW Carter	2006
Most points in match	29	AP Mehrtens	v Australia (h) 1999
Most tries in matches	16	CM Cullen	1996 to 2002
Most tries in season	8	BR Smith	2013
Most tries in match	3	JT Rokocoko	v Australia (a) 2003
	3	DC Howlett	v Australia (h) 2005
	3	CS Jane	v Argentina (a) 2012
	3	BR Smith	v Australia (a) 2013
Most cons in matches	72	DW Carter	2003 to 2013
Most cons in season	14	DW Carter	2006
Most cons in match	4	CJ Spencer	v S Africa (h) 1997
	4	AP Mehrtens	v Australia (a) 2000
	4	AP Mehrtens	v S Africa (a) 2000
	4	CJ Spencer	v S Africa (a) 2003
	4	DW Carter	v S Africa (a) 2006
	4	DW Carter	v Australia (a) 2008
	4	DW Carter	v Australia (a) 2010
Most pens in matches	115	DW Carter	2003 to 2013
Most pens in season	21	DW Carter	2006
Most pens in match	9	AP Mehrtens	v Australia (h) 1999

MISCELLANEOUS RECORDS

RECORD	HOLDER	DETAIL
Longest Test career	E Hughes/CE Meads	1907–21/1957–71
Youngest Test cap	JT Lomu	19 yrs 45 days in 1994
Oldest Test cap	E Hughes	40 yrs 123 days in 1921

CAREER RECORDS OF NEW ZEALAND INTERNATIONAL PLAYERS

UP TO 10 OCTOBER 2013

PLAYER BACKS:	DEBUT	CAPS	T	C	P	D	PTS
BJ Barrett	2012 v I	13	3	9	4	0	45
DW Carter	2003 v W	97	29	249	250	6	1411
RS Crotty	2013 v A	1	0	0	0	0	0
AW Cruden	2010 v I	25	2	27	26	1	145
IJA Dagg	2010 v I	34	12	1	1	0	65
TE Ellison	2009 v It	4	0	0	0	0	0
HE Gear	2008 v A	14	6	0	0	0	30
CS Jane	2008 v A	43	16	0	0	0	80
TNJ Kerr-Barlow	2012 v S	10	0	0	0	0	0
MA Nonu	2003 v E	84	25	0	0	0	125
ST Piutau	2013 v F	6	0	0	0	0	0
RMN Ranger	2010 v W	6	1	0	0	0	5
F Saili	2013 v Arg	1	0	0	0	0	0
SJ Savea	2012 v I	17	15	0	0	0	75
CR Slade	2010 v A	11	3	18	3	0	60
AL Smith	2012 v I	21	7	0	0	0	35
BR Smith	2009 v It	21	12	0	0	0	60
CG Smith	2004 v It	75	24	0	0	0	120
TJ Taylor	2013 v A	1	0	1	4	0	14
PAT Weepu	2004 v W	71	7	10	16	0	103
S Williams	2010 v E	19	6	0	0	0	30

FORWARDS:							
BTP Afeaki	2013 v F	1	0	0	0	0	0
SJ Cane	2012 v I	12	5	0	0	0	25
DS Coles	2012 v S	10	0	0	0	0	0
WWV Crockett	2009 v It	19	1	0	0	0	5
HTP Elliot	2010 v S	3	0	0	0	0	0
CC Faumuina	2012 v Arg	13	0	0	0	0	0
BJ Franks	2010 v I	28	1	0	0	0	5
OT Franks	2009 v It	51	0	0	0	0	0
AK Hore	2002 v E	81	8	0	0	0	40
DS Luatua	2013 v F	7	0	0	0	0	0
RH McCaw	2001 v I	120	21*	0	0	0	105
KF Mealamu	2002 v W	107	12	0	0	0	60
LJ Messam	2008 v S	25	5	0	0	0	25
KJ Read	2008 v S	57	12	0	0	0	60
BA Retallick	2012 v I	20	1	0	0	0	5
L Romano	2012 v I	15	1	0	0	0	5
AJ Thomson	2008 v I	29	6	0	0	0	30
JI Thrush	2013 v F	3	0	0	0	0	0
MB Todd	2013 v F	2	0	0	0	0	0
VVJ Vito	2010 v I	22	2	0	0	0	10
SL Whitelock	2010 v I	47	4	0	0	0	20
AJ Williams	2002 v E	77	7	0	0	0	35
TD Woodcock	2002 v W	104	9	0	0	0	45

NB McCaw's figures include a penalty try awarded against Ireland in 2008.

NEW ZEALAND INTERNATIONAL PLAYERS

UP TO 10 OCTOBER 2013

Entries in square brackets denote matches played in RWC Finals.

Abbott, H L (Taranaki) 1906 F
Afeaki, B T P (North Harbour) 2013 F1(R)
Afoa, I F (Auckland) 2005 I,S, 2006 E(R), 2008 I1, SA2, A1(R), 2(R), SA3(R), A3(R), S, I2(t&R), W(R), E3(R), 2009 F1(R), 2(R), It1,SA2(R), A2(R), SA3(R), A3(R), 4(R), It2(R), E(R), 2010 SA3(R), A3(R), 4(R), E(R), S(R), I2(R), W3(R), 2011 Fj(R), SA1(R), 2, A2(R), [J(R), Arg(R)]
Aitken, G G (Wellington) 1921 SA 1,2
Alatini, P F (Otago) 1999 F 1(R), [It, SA 3(R)], 2000 Tg, S 1, A 1, SA 1, A 2, SA 2, It, 2001 Sm, Arg 1, F, SA 1, A 1, SA 2, A 2
Allen, F R (Auckland) 1946 A 1,2, 1947 A 1,2, 1949 SA 1,2
Allen, M R (Taranaki, Manawatu) 1993 WS (t), 1996 S 2 (t), 1997 Arg 1(R),2(R), SA 2(R), A 3(R), E 2, W (R)
Allen, N H (Counties) 1980 A 3, W
Alley, G T (Canterbury) 1928 SA 1,2,3
Anderson, A (Canterbury) 1983 S, E, 1984 A 1,2,3, 1987 [Fj]
Anderson, B L (Wairarapa-Bush) 1986 A 1
Anesi, S R (Waikato) 2005 Fj(R)
Archer, W R (Otago, Southland) 1955 A 1,2, 1956 SA 1,3
Argus, W G (Canterbury) 1946 A 1,2, 1947 A 1,2
Arnold, D A (Canterbury) 1963 I, W, 1964 E, F
Arnold, K D (Waikato) 1947 A 1,2
Ashby, D L (Southland) 1958 A 2
Asher, A A (Auckland) 1903 A
Ashworth, B G (Auckland) 1978 A 1,2
Ashworth, J C (Canterbury, Hawke's Bay) 1978 A 1, 2, 3, 1980 A 1, 2, 3, 1981 SA 1, 2, 3, 1982 A 1, 2, 1983 BI 1, 2, 3, 4, A, 1984 F 1, 2, A 1, 2, 3, 1985 E 1, 2, A
Atiga, B A C (Auckland) 2003 [Tg(R)]
Atkinson, H (West Coast) 1913 A 1
Avery, H E (Wellington) 1910 A 1,2,3

Bachop, G T M (Canterbury) 1989 W, I, 1990 S 1,2, A 1,2,3, F 1,2, 1991 Arg 1,2, A 1,2, [E, US, C, A, S], 1992 Wld 1, 1994 SA 1,2,3, A, 1995 C, [I, W, S, E, SA], A 1,2
Bachop, S J (Otago) 1994 F 2, SA 1,2,3, A
Badeley, C E O (Auckland) 1921 SA 1,2

Baird, J A S (Otago) 1913 A 2
Ball, N (Wellington) 1931 A, 1932 A 2,3, 1935 W, 1936 E
Barrett, B J (Taranaki) 2012 I 3(R), Arg1(R), S(R), It, W(R), 2013 F1(R), 2(R), 3(R), A1(R), Arg1(R), SA1(R), Arg2(R), SA2(R)
Barrett, J (Auckland) 1913 A 2,3
Barry, E F (Wellington) 1934 A 2
Barry, L J (North Harbour) 1995 F 2
Bates, S P (Waikato) 2004 It(R)
Batty, G B (Wellington, Bay of Plenty) 1972 W, S, 1973 E 1, I, F, E 2, 1974 A 1,3, I, 1975 S, 1976 SA 1,2,3,4, 1977 BI 1
Batty, W (Auckland) 1930 BI 1,3,4, 1931 A
Beatty, G E (Taranaki) 1950 BI 1
Bell, R H (Otago) 1951 A 3, 1952 A 1,2
Bellis, E A (Wanganui) 1921 SA 1,2,3
Bennet, R (Otago) 1905 A
Berghan, T (Otago) 1938 A 1,2,3
Berry, M J (Wairarapa-Bush) 1986 A 3(R)
Berryman, N R (Northland) 1998 SA 2(R)
Bevan, V D (Wellington) 1949 A 1,2, 1950 BI 1,2,3,4
Birtwistle, W M (Canterbury) 1965 SA 1,2,3,4, 1967 E, W, S
Black, J E (Canterbury) 1977 F 1, 1979 A, 1980 A 3
Black, N W (Auckland) 1949 SA 3
Black, R S (Otago) 1914 A 1
Blackadder, T J (Canterbury) 1998 E 1(R),2, 2000 Tg, S 1,2, A 1, SA 1, A 2, SA 2, F 1,2, It
Blair, B A (Canterbury) 2001 S (R), Arg 2, 2002 E, W
Blake, A W (Wairarapa) 1949 A 1
Blowers, A F (Auckland) 1996 SA 2(R),4(R), 1997 I, E 1(R), W (R), 1999 F 1(R), SA 1, A 1(R), SA 2, A 2(R), [It]
Boggs, E G (Auckland) 1946 A 2, 1949 SA 1
Bond, J G (Canterbury) 1949 A 2
Booth, E E (Otago) 1906 F, 1907 A 1,3
Boric, A F (North Harbour) 2008 E1(R), 2(R), SA2, A2(R), SA3(R), Sm, A3(R), 4(R), S, E3(R), 2009 It2, E(R), F3(R), 2010 I1, W1, A3(R), E(R), S(R), I2, W3(R), 2011 [Tg(R), J(R), F1(R), C(R)]
Boroevich, K G (Wellington) 1986 F 1, A 1, F 3(R)
Botica, F M (North Harbour) 1986 F 1, A 1,2,3, F 2,3, 1989 Arg 1(R)
Bowden, N J G (Taranaki) 1952 A 2
Bowers, R G (Wellington) 1954 I, F
Bowman, A W (Hawke's Bay) 1938 A 1,2,3
Braid, D J (Auckland) 2002 W, 2003 [C(R),Tg], 2008 A1, 2010 S(R),W3(R)
Braid, G J (Bay of Plenty) 1983 S, E
Bremner, S G (Auckland, Canterbury) 1952 A 2, 1956 SA 2
Brewer, M R (Otago, Canterbury) 1986 F 1, A 1,2,3, F 2,3, 1988 A 1, 1989 A, W, I, 1990 S 1,2, A 1,2,3, F 1,2, 1992 I 2, A 1, 1994 F 1,2, SA 1,2,3, A, 1995 C, [I, W, E, SA], A 1,2
Briscoe, K C (Taranaki) 1959 BI 2, 1960 SA 1,2,3,4, 1963 I, W, 1964 E, S
Brooke, R M (Auckland) 1992 I 2, A 1,2,3, SA, 1993 BI 1,2,3, A, WS, 1994 SA 2,3, 1995 C, [J, S, E, SA], A 1,2, It, F 1,2, 1996 WS, S 1,2, A 1, SA 1, A 2, SA 2,3,4,5, 1997 Fj, Arg 1,2, A 1, SA 1, A 2, SA 2, A 3, I, E 1, W, E 2, 1998 E 1,2, A 1, SA 1, A 2, SA 2, A 3, 1999 WS, F 1, SA 1, A 1, SA 2, A 2, [Tg, E, It (R), S, F 2]
Brooke, Z V (Auckland) 1987 [Arg], 1989 Arg 2(R), 1990 A 1,2,3, F 1(R), 1991 Arg 2, A 1,2, [E, It, C, A, S], 1992 A 2,3, SA, 1993 BI 1,2,3(R), WS (R), S, E, 1994 F 2, SA 1,2,3, A, 1995 [J, S, E, SA], A 1,2, It, F 1,2, 1996 WS, S 1,2, A 1, SA 1, A 2, SA 2,3,4,5, 1997 Arg 1,2, A 1, SA 1, A 2, SA 2, A 3, I, E 1, W, E 2
Brooke-Cowden, M (Auckland) 1986 F 1, A 1, 1987 [W]
Broomhall, S R (Canterbury) 2002 SA 1(R),2(R), E, F
Brown, C (Taranaki) 1913 A 2,3
Brown, O M (Auckland) 1992 I 2, A 1,2,3, SA, 1993 BI 1,2,3, A, S, E, 1994 F 1,2, SA 1,2,3, A, 1995 C, [I, W, S, E, SA], A 1,2, It, F 1,2, 1996 WS, S 1,2, A 1, SA 1, A 2, SA 2,3,4,5, 1997 Fj, Arg 1,2, A 1, SA 1, A 2, SA 2, A 3, I, E 1, W, E 2, 1998 E 1,2, A 1, SA 1, A 2, SA 2
Brown, R H (Taranaki) 1955 A 3, 1956 SA 1,2,3,4, 1957 A 1,2, 1958 A 1,2,3, 1959 BI 1,3, 1961 F 1,2,3, 1962 A 1
Brown, T E (Otago) 1999 WS, F 1(R), SA 1(R), A 1(R),2(R), [E (R), It, S (R)], 2000 Tg, S 2(R), A 1(R), SA 1(R), A 2(R), 2001 Sm, Arg 1(R), F, SA 1, A 1
Brownlie, C J (Hawke's Bay) 1924 W, 1925 E, F
Brownlie, M J (Hawke's Bay) 1924 I, W, 1925 E, F, 1928 SA 1,2,3,4
Bruce, J A (Auckland) 1914 A 1,2
Bruce, O D (Canterbury) 1976 SA 1,2,4, 1977 BI 2,3,4, F 1,2, 1978 A 1,2, I, W, E, S
Bryers, R F (King Country) 1949 A 1
Budd, T A (Southland) 1946 A 2, 1949 A 2
Bullock-Douglas, G A H (Wanganui) 1932 A 1,2,3, 1934 A 1,2
Bunce, F E (North Harbour) 1992 Wld 1,2,3, I 1,2, A 1,2,3, SA, 1993 BI 1,2,3, A, WS, S, E, 1994 F 1,2, SA 1,2,3, A, 1995 C, [I, W, S, E, SA], A 1,2, It, F 1,2, 1996 WS, S 1,2, A1, SA 1, A 2, SA 2,3,4,5, 1997 Fj, Arg 1,2, A 1, SA 1, A 2, SA 2, A 3, I, E 1, W, E 2
Burgess, G A J (Auckland) 1981 SA 2
Burgess, G F (Southland) 1905 A
Burgess, R E (Manawatu) 1971 BI 1,2,3, 1972 A 3, W, 1973 I, F
Burke, P S (Taranaki) 1955 A 1, 1957 A 1,2
Burns, P J (Canterbury) 1908 AW 2, 1910 A 1,2,3, 1913 A 3
Bush, R G (Otago) 1931 A
Bush, W K (Canterbury) 1974 A 1,2, 1975 S, 1976 I, SA, 2,4, 1977 BI 2,3,4(R), 1978 I, W, 1979 A
Buxton, J B (Canterbury) 1955 A 3, 1956 SA 1

Cain, M J (Taranaki) 1913 US, 1914 A 1,2,3
Callesen, J A (Manawatu) 1974 A 1,2,3, 1975 S
Cameron, D (Taranaki) 1908 AW 1,2,3
Cameron, L M (Manawatu) 1980 A 3, 1981 SA 1(R),2,3, R
Cane, S J (Bay of Plenty) 2012 I 2(R), 3, Arg2(R), It, 2013 F1, 2, 3, A1(R), Arg1(R), SA1, Arg2, SA2(R)
Carleton, S R (Canterbury) 1928 SA 1, 2, 3, 1929 A 1, 2, 3
Carrington, K R (Auckland) 1971 BI 1,3,4
Carter, D W (Canterbury) 2003 W, F, A 1(R),[It, C, Tg, SA(R), F(R)], 2004 E1, 2, PI, A1, SA1, A2, It, W, F, 2005 Fj, BI1, 2, SA1, A1, W, E, 2006 Arg, A1, SA1, A2, 3, SA2, 3, E, F1, 2, W, 2007 F1, C, SA1, A1, SA2, A2, [It, S, F], 2008 I1, E1, 2, SA1, 2,A1, 2, SA3, Sm, A3, 4, S(R), I2, W, E3, 2009 A2, SA3, A3, 4, W, E, F3, 2010 I1, W1, 2, SA1, 2, A1, 2, SA3, A4, E, S, I2, W3, 2011 Fj(R), SA1, A1, 2, [Tg, F1], 2012 I 1, 2, A1, 2, Arg2, SA2, A3, S, E, 2013 F3, Arg1, SA1
Carter, M P (Auckland) 1991 A 2, [It, A], 1997 Fj (R), A 1(R), 1998 E 2(R), A 2
Casey, S T (Otago) 1905 S, I, E, W, 1907 A 1,2,3, 1908 AW 1
Cashmore, A R (Auckland) 1996 S 2(R), 1997 A 2(R)
Catley, E H (Waikato) 1946 A 1, 1947 A 1,2, 1949 SA 1,2,3,4
Caughey, T H C (Auckland) 1932 A 1,3, 1934 A 1,2, 1935 S, I, 1936 E, A 1, 1937 SA 3
Caulton, R W (Wellington) 1959 BI 2,3,4, 1960 SA 1,4, 1961 F 2, 1963 E 1,2, I, W, 1964 E, S, F, A 1,2,3
Cherrington, N P (North Auckland) 1950 BI 1
Christian, D L (Auckland) 1949 SA 4
Clamp, M (Wellington) 1984 A 2,3
Clark, D W (Otago) 1964 A 1,2
Clark, W H (Wellington) 1953 W, 1954 I, E, S, 1955 A 1,2, 1956 SA 2,3,4
Clarke, A H (Auckland) 1958 A 3, 1959 BI 4, 1960 SA 1
Clarke, D B (Waikato) 1956 SA 3,4, 1957 A 1,2, 1958 A 1,3, 1959 BI 1,2,3,4, 1960 SA 1,2,3,4, 1961 F 1,2,3, 1962 A 1,2,3,4,5, 1963 E 1,2, I, W, 1964 E, S, F, A 2,3
Clarke, E (Auckland) 1992 Wld 2,3, I 1,2, 1993 BI 1,2, S (R), E, 1998 SA 2, A 3
Clarke, I J (Waikato) 1953 W, 1955 A 1,2,3, 1956 SA 1,2,3,4, 1957 A 1,2, 1958 A 1,3, 1959 BI 1,2, 1960 SA 2,4, 1961 F 1,2,3, 1962 A 1,2,3, 1963 E 1,2
Clarke, R L (Taranaki) 1932 A 2,3
Cobden, D G (Canterbury) 1937 SA 1
Cockerill, M S (Taranaki) 1951 A 1,2,3
Cockroft, E A P (South Canterbury) 1913 A 3, 1914 A 2,3
Codlin, B W (Counties) 1980 A 1,2,3
Coles, D S (Wellington) 2012 S(R), It(R), W(R), E(R), 2013 F1, 2, A2(R), Arg1(R), SA1, 2(R)
Collins, A H (Taranaki) 1932 A 2,3, 1934 A 1
Collins, J (Wellington) 2001 Arg 1, 2003 E (R), W, F, SA 1, A 1, SA 2, A 2,[It, W, SA, A, F], 2004 E2(R), Arg, PI(R), A1(R), SA1, It, F, 2005 Fj, BI1, 2, 3, SA1, A1, SA2, W, E, 2006 Arg, A1, 2, 3, SA2(R), 3, F1, 2, W, 2007 F2, C, SA1, A1, SA2(R), A2, [It, Pt, R, F]

Collins, J L (Poverty Bay) 1964 A 1, 1965 SA 1,4
Colman, J T H (Taranaki) 1907 A 1,2, 1908 AW 1,3
Connor, D M (Auckland) 1961 F 1, 2, 3, 1962 A 1, 2, 3, 4, 5, 1963 E 1, 2, 1964 A 2, 3
Conway, R J (Otago, Bay of Plenty) 1959 BI 2, 3, 4, 1960 SA 1, 3, 4, 1965 SA 1, 2, 3, 4
Cooke, A E (Auckland, Wellington) 1924 I, W, 1925 E, F, 1930 BI 1,2,3,4
Cooke, R J (Canterbury) 1903 A
Cooksley, M S B (Counties, Waikato) 1992 Wld 1, 1993 BI 2,3(R), A, 1994 F 1,2, SA 1,2, A, 2001 A 1(R), SA 2(t&R)
Cooper, G J L (Auckland, Otago) 1986 F 1, A 1,2, 1992 Wld 1,2,3, I 1
Cooper, M J A (Waikato) 1992 I 2, SA (R), 1993 BI 1(R),3(t), WS (t), S, 1994 F 1,2
Corner, M M N (Auckland) 1930 BI 2,3,4, 1931 A, 1934 A 1, 1936 E
Cossey, R R (Counties) 1958 A 1
Cottrell, A I (Canterbury) 1929 A 1,2,3, 1930 BI 1,2,3,4, 1931 A, 1932 A 1,2,3
Cottrell, W D (Canterbury) 1968 A 1,2, F 2,3, 1970 SA 1, 1971 BI 1,2,3,4
Couch, M B R (Wairarapa) 1947 A 1, 1949 A 1,2
Coughlan, T D (South Canterbury) 1958 A 1
Cowan, Q J (Southland) 2004 It(R), 2005 W(R), I(R), S(R), 2006 I1(R), SA1(R), A2(R), SA2(R), 3, 2008 E1(R), 2(R),SA1(R),A1(t&R),2, SA3, Sm, A3, 4, I2, W, E3, 2009 F1, 2, A1, SA2, A2, SA3, A3, 4, W(R), It2(R), E, F3, 2010 I1, W1, 2, SA1, 2(R), A1, SA3, A3(R), 4, S, W3, 2011 Fj, SA1, 2, [Tg, J(R), C, Arg(R)]
Creighton, J N (Canterbury) 1962 A 4
Cribb, R T (North Harbour) 2000 S 1,2, A 1, SA 1, A 2, SA 2, F 1,2, It, 2001 Sm, F, SA 1, A 1, SA 2, A 2
Crichton, S (Wellington) 1983 S, E
Crockett, W W V (Canterbury) 2009 It1, W, It2, 2011 Fj, SA1, A1, 2012 A2, S, It(R), W(R), E(R), 2013 F1, 2, 3, A2(R), Arg1(R), SA1(R), Arg2(R), SA2(R)
Cross, T (Canterbury) 1904 BI, 1905 A
Crotty, R S (Canterbury) 2013 A1(R)
Crowley, K J (Taranaki) 1985 E 1,2, A, Arg 1,2, 1986 A 3, F 2,3, 1987 [Arg], 1990 S 1,2, A 1,2,3, F 1,2, 1991 Arg 1,2, [A]
Crowley, P J B (Auckland) 1949 SA 3,4, 1950 BI 1,2,3,4
Cruden, A W (Manawatu) 2010 I1(R), W1(R), 2(R), SA2(R), A1(R), 3, 2011 [Arg(R), A, F2], 2012 I 1(R), 3, A2(R), Arg1, SA1, Arg2(R), SA2(R), A3(R), It, W, E(R), 2013 F1, 2, A1, Arg2, SA2
Culhane, S D (Southland) 1995 [J], It, F 1,2, 1996 SA 3,4
Cullen C M (Manawatu, Central Vikings, Wellington) 1996 WS, S 1,2, A 1, SA 1, A 2, SA 2,3,4,5, 1997 Fj, Arg 1,2, A 1, SA 1, A 2, SA 2, A 3, I, E 1, W, E 2, 1998 E 1,2, A 1, SA 1, A 2, SA 2, A 3, 1999 WS, F 1, SA 1, A 1, SA 2, A 2, [Tg, E, It (R), S, F 2, SA 3], 2000 Tg, S 1,2, A 1, SA 1, A 2, SA 2, F 1,2, It, 2001 A 2(R), 2002 It, Fj, A 1, SA 1, A 2, F
Cummings, W (Canterbury) 1913 A 2,3
Cundy, R T (Wairarapa) 1929 A 2(R)
Cunningham, G R (Auckland) 1979 A, S, E, 1980 A 1,2
Cunningham, W (Auckland) 1905 S, I, 1906 F, 1907 A 1, 2, 3, 1908 AW 1,2,3
Cupples, L F (Bay of Plenty) 1924 I, W
Currie, C J (Canterbury) 1978 I, W
Cuthill, J E (Otago) 1913 A 1, US

Dagg, I J A (Hawke's Bay) 2010 I1, W1, SA2(R), A1(R), SA3(R), A3, 2011 SA2, [Tg, F1, C, A, F2], 2012 I 1, 2, 3, A1, 2, Arg1, SA1, Arg2, SA2, A3, S, W, E, 2013 F1, 2, 3, A1, 2, Arg1, SA1, Arg2, SA2
Dalley, W C (Canterbury) 1924 I, 1928 SA 1,2,3,4
Dalton, A G (Counties) 1977 F 2, 1978 A 1,2,3, I, W, E, S, 1979 F 1,2, S, 1981 S 1,2, SA 1,2,3, R, F 1,2, 1982 A 1,2,3, 1983 BI 1,2,3,4, A, 1984 F 1,2, A 1,2,3, 1985 E 1,2, A
Dalton, D (Hawke's Bay) 1935 I, W, 1936 A 1,2, 1937 SA 1,2,3, 1938 A 1,2
Dalton, R A (Wellington) 1947 A 1,2
Dalzell, G N (Canterbury) 1953 W, 1954 I, E, S, F
Davie, M G (Canterbury) 1983 E (R)
Davies, W A (Auckland, Otago) 1960 SA 4, 1962 A 4,5
Davis, K (Auckland) 1952 A 2, 1953 W, 1954 I, E, S, F, 1955 A 2, 1958 A 1,2,3
Davis, L J (Canterbury) 1976 I, 1977 BI 3,4
Davis, W L (Hawke's Bay) 1967 A, E, W, F, S, 1968 A 1,2, F 1, 1969 W 1,2, 1970 SA 2
Deans, I B (Canterbury) 1988 W 1,2, A 1,2,3, 1989 F 1,2, Arg 1,2, A
Deans, R G (Canterbury) 1905 S, I, E, W, 1908 AW 3
Deans, R M (Canterbury) 1983 S, E, 1984 A 1(R),2,3
Delamore, G W (Wellington) 1949 SA 4
Delany, M P (Bay of Plenty) 2009 It 2
De Malmanche, A P (Waikato) 2009 It1(R),A3(R), 2010 I1(R),W1(R),2(R)
Dermody, C (Southland) 2006 I1,2,E(R)
Devine, S J (Auckland) 2002 E, W 2003 E (R), W, F, SA 1, A 1(R), [C,SA(R),F]
Dewar, H (Taranaki) 1913 A 1, US
Diack, E S (Otago) 1959 BI 2
Dick, J (Auckland) 1937 SA 1,2, 1938 A 3
Dick, M J (Auckland) 1963 I, W, 1964 E, S, F, 1965 SA 3, 1966 BI 4, 1967 A, E, W, F, 1969 W 1,2, 1970 SA 1,4
Dixon, M J (Canterbury) 1954 I, E, S, F, 1956 SA 1,2,3,4, 1957 A 1, 2
Dobson, R L (Auckland) 1949 A 1
Dodd, E H (Wellington) 1905 A
Donald, A J (Wanganui) 1983 S, E, 1984 F 1,2, A 1,2,3
Donald, J G (Wairarapa) 1921 SA 1,2
Donald, Q (Wairarapa) 1924 I, W, 1925 E, F
Donald, S R (Waikato) 2008 E1(R), 2(R), A2(R), SA3(R), Sm(R), A3(R), 4, S, I2(R), 2009 F1, 2, A1, SA1, 2, A2(R), SA3, A4(R), It2(R), F3(R), 2010 A4(R), S(R), W3(R), 2011[F2(R)]
Donaldson, M W (Manawatu) 1977 F 1, 2, 1978 A 1, 2, 3, I, E, S, 1979 F 1, 2, A, S (R), 1981 SA 3(R)
Donnelly, T J S (Otago) 2009 A3, 4, W(R), It2, E, F3, 2010 W2, SA1, 2, A1, 2, SA3, A3, 4, I2
Dougan, J P (Wellington) 1972 A 1, 1973 E 2
Dowd, C W (Auckland) 1993 BI 1,2,3, A, WS, S, E, 1994 SA 1(R), 1995 C, [I, W, J, E, SA], A 1,2, It, F 1,2, 1996 WS, S 1,2, A 1, SA 1, A 2, SA 2,3,4,5, 1997 Fj, Arg 1,2, A 1, SA 1, A 2, SA 2, A 3, I, E 1, W, 1998 E 1,2, A 1, SA 1, A 2,3(R), 1999 SA 2(R), A 2(R), [Tg (R), E, It, S, F 2, SA 3], 2000 Tg, S 1(R),2(R), A 1(R), SA 1(R), A 2(R)
Dowd, G W (North Harbour) 1992 I 1(R)
Downing, A J (Auckland) 1913 A 1, US, 1914 A 1,2,3
Drake, J A (Auckland) 1986 F 2,3, 1987 [Fj, Arg, S, W, F], A
Duff, R H (Canterbury) 1951 A 1,2,3, 1952 A 1,2, 1955 A 2,3, 1956 SA 1,2,3,4
Duggan, R J L (Waikato) 1999 [It (R)]
Duncan, J (Otago) 1903 A
Duncan, M G (Hawke's Bay) 1971 BI 3(R),4
Duncan, W D (Otago) 1921 SA 1,2,3
Dunn, E J (North Auckland) 1979 S, 1981 S 1
Dunn, I T W (North Auckland) 1983 BI 1,4, A
Dunn, J M (Auckland) 1946 A 1

Earl, A T (Canterbury) 1986 F 1, A 1, F 3(R), 1987 [Arg], 1989 W, I, 1991 Arg 1(R),2, A 1, [E (R), US, S], 1992 A 2, 3(R)
Eastgate, B P (Canterbury) 1952 A 1,2, 1954 S
Eaton, J J (Taranaki) 2005 I, E(t), S(R), 2006 Arg, A1, 2(R), 3, SA3(R), F1(R), 2(R), 2009 A1(R), SA1(R), A3(R), 4(R), W
Elliot, H T P (Hawke's Bay) 2010 S,I 2, 2012 I 1(R)
Elliott, K G (Wellington) 1946 A 1,2
Ellis, A M (Canterbury) 2006 E(R), F2(R), 2007 [Pt(R), R], 2008 I1, E1, 2, SA1, 2, A1, S(R), 2009 It2, E(R), F3(R), 2010 E(R), S(R), I2, W3(R), 2011 A1(R), SA2(R), A2(R), [J,F1(R), C(R), A(R), F2(R)]
Ellis, M C G (Otago) 1993 S, E, 1995 C, [I (R), W, J, S, SA (R)]
Ellison, T E (Wellington, Otago) 2009 It 2, 2012 I 3(R), SA2(R), S
Elsom, A E G (Canterbury) 1952 A 1,2, 1953 W, 1955 A 1,2,3
Elvidge, R R (Otago) 1946 A 1, 2, 1949 SA 1, 2, 3, 4, 1950 BI 1, 2, 3
Erceg, C P (Auckland) 1951 A 1,2,3, 1952 A 1
Evans, B R (Hawke's Bay) 2009 F1(R),2(R)
Evans, D A (Hawke's Bay) 1910 A 2
Evans, N J (North Harbour, Otago) 2004 E1(R), 2, Arg, PI(R),

2005 I, S, 2006 F2(R), W(R), 2007 F1(R), 2, SA2(R), A2(R), [Pt, S(R), R, F(R)]
Eveleigh, K A (Manawatu) 1976 SA 2,4, 1977 BI 1,2

Fanning, A H N (Canterbury) 1913 A 3
Fanning, B J (Canterbury) 1903 A, 1904 BI
Farrell, C P (Auckland) 1977 BI 1,2
Faumuina, C C (Auckland) 2012 Arg1(R), SA1(R), Arg2(R), A3, It, W(R), E(R), 2013 A1(R), 2(R), Arg1, SA1(R), Arg2(R), SA2
Fawcett, C L (Auckland) 1976 SA 2, 3
Fea, W R (Otago) 1921 SA 3
Feek, G E (Canterbury) 1999 WS (R), A 1(R), SA 2, [E (t), It], 2000 F 1, 2, It, 2001 I, S
Filipo, R A (Wellington) 2007 C, SA1(R), A1(R), 2008 S(R)
Finlay, B E L (Manawatu) 1959 BI 1
Finlay, J (Manawatu) 1946 A 1
Finlayson, I (North Auckland) 1928 SA 1, 2, 3, 4, 1930 BI 1, 2
Fitzgerald, J T (Wellington) 1952 A 1
Fitzpatrick, B B J (Wellington) 1953 W, 1954 I, F
Fitzpatrick, S B T (Auckland) 1986 F 1, A 1, F 2,3, 1987 [It, Fj, Arg, S, W, F], A, 1988 W 1,2, A 1,2,3, 1989 F 1,2, Arg 1,2, A, W, I, 1990 S 1,2, A 1,2,3, F 1,2, 1991 Arg 1,2, A 1,2, [E, US, It, C, A, S], 1992 Wld 1,2,3, I 1,2, A 1,2,3, SA, 1993 BI 1,2,3, A, WS, S, E, 1994 F 1,2, SA 1,2,3, A, 1995 C, [I, W, S, E, SA], A 1,2, It, F 1,2, 1996 WS, S 1,2, A 1, SA 1, A 2, SA 2,3,4,5, 1997 Fj, Arg 1,2, A 1, SA 1, A 2, SA 2, A 3, W (R)
Flavell, T V (North Harbour, Auckland) 2000 Tg, S 1(R), A 1(R), SA 1,2(t), F 1(R),2(R), It, 2001 Sm, Arg 1, F, SA 1, A 1, SA 2, A 2, 2006 I1(R),2, 2007 F1(R),2(R),C,SA1,A1
Fleming, J K (Wellington) 1979 S, E, 1980 A 1,2,3
Fletcher, C J C (North Auckland) 1921 SA 3
Flynn, C R (Canterbury) 2003 [C(R),Tg], 2004 It(R), 2008 S(R), I2(R), 2009 It2,F3(R), 2010 SA1(R), 2(R), A1(R), 2(R), 3(R), 2011 Fj(R), SA1(R), [Tg(R)]
Fogarty, R (Taranaki) 1921 SA 1,3
Ford, B R (Marlborough) 1977 BI 3,4, 1978 I, 1979 E
Forster, S T (Otago) 1993 S, E, 1994 F 1,2, 1995 It, F 1
Fox, G J (Auckland) 1985 Arg 1, 1987 [It, Fj, Arg, S, W, F], A, 1988 W 1,2, A 1,2,3, 1989 F 1,2, Arg 1,2, A, W, I, 1990 S 1,2, A 1,2,3, F 1,2, 1991 Arg 1,2, A 1,2, [E, It, C, A], 1992 Wld 1,2(R), A 1,2,3, SA, 1993 BI 1,2,3, A, WS
Francis, A R H (Auckland) 1905 A, 1907 A 1,2,3, 1908 AW 1,2,3, 1910 A 1,2,3
Francis, W C (Wellington) 1913 A 2,3, 1914 A 1,2,3
Franks, B J (Tasman, Canterbury, Hawkes' Bay) 2010 I1, W1, SA1(R), 2(R), A1(R), 2(R), SA3, 2011 Fj, SA1, A1(R), SA2(R), [Tg(R), F1(R), C(R), A(R)], 2012 I1(R), 2(R), 3(R), A1(R), 2(R), SA2(R), S(R), It(R), 2013 F1(R), 2(R), A1(R), Arg1(R), SA2(R)
Franks, O T (Canterbury) 2009 It1(R), A1(R), SA1(R), 2, A2, SA3, W(R), E, F3(R), 2010 I1, W1, 2(t&R), SA1, 2, A1, 2, 3, 4, E, S, I2, W3, 2011 A1, 2, [Tg, J, F1, C, Arg, A, F2], 2012 I 1, 2, 3, A1, 2, Arg1, SA1, Arg2, SA2, A3(t&R), S, W, E, 2013 F1, 2, 3, A1, 2, SA1, Arg2
Fraser, B G (Wellington) 1979 S, E, 1980 A 3, W, 1981 S 1, 2, SA 1, 2, 3, R, F 1,2, 1982 A 1, 2, 3, 1983 BI 1, 2, 3, 4, A, S, E, 1984 A 1
Frazer, H F (Hawke's Bay) 1946 A 1,2, 1947 A 1,2, 1949 SA 2
Fryer, F C (Canterbury) 1907 A 1,2,3, 1908 AW 2
Fuller, W B (Canterbury) 1910 A 1,2
Furlong, B D M (Hawke's Bay) 1970 SA 4

Gallagher, J A (Wellington) 1987 [It, Fj, S, W, F], A, 1988 W 1,2, A 1,2,3, 1989 F 1,2, Arg 1,2, A, W, I
Gallaher, D (Auckland) 1903 A, 1904 BI, 1905 S, E, W, 1906 F
Gard, P C (North Otago) 1971 BI 4
Gardiner, A J (Taranaki) 1974 A 3
Gear, H E (Wellington) 2008 A4, 2009 A3(R), 2010 E, S, I2, W3, 2011 A1, SA2, 2012 I 3, A1, 2, SA2, A3, It
Gear, R L (North Harbour, Nelson Bays, Tasman) 2004 PI, It, 2005 BI1(R), 2, 3, SA1, A1, SA2, W, S, 2006 Arg, A1, 2, SA2, 3(R), E, W, 2007 C(R), A1
Geddes, J H (Southland) 1929 A 1
Geddes, W McK (Auckland) 1913 A 2
Gemmell, B McL (Auckland) 1974 A 1,2
George, V L (Southland) 1938 A 1,2,3
Gibbes, J B (Waikato) 2004 E1, 2, Arg(R), PI, A1, 2, SA2, 2005 BI2(R)
Gibson, D P E (Canterbury) 1999 WS, F 1, SA 1, A 1, SA 2, A 2, [Tg (R), E (R), It, S (R), F 2(R)], 2000 F 1, 2, 2002 It, I 1(R),2(R), Fj, A 2(R), SA 2(R)
Gilbert, G D M (West Coast) 1935 S, I, W, 1936 E
Gillespie, C T (Wellington) 1913 A 2
Gillespie, W D (Otago) 1958 A 3
Gillett, G A (Canterbury, Auckland) 1905 S, I, E, W, 1907 A 2,3, 1908 AW 1,3
Gillies, C C (Otago) 1936 A 2
Gilray, C M (Otago) 1905 A
Glasgow, F T (Taranaki, Southland) 1905 S, I, E, W, 1906 F, 1908 AW 3
Glenn, W S (Taranaki) 1904 BI, 1906 F
Goddard, M P (South Canterbury) 1946 A 2, 1947 A 1,2, 1949 SA 3,4
Going, S M (North Auckland) 1967 A, F, 1968 F 3, 1969 W 1, 2, 1970 SA 1(R),4, 1971 BI 1, 2, 3, 4, 1972 A 1, 2, 3, W, S, 1973 E 1, I, F, E 2, 1974 I, 1975 S, 1976 I (R), SA 1, 2, 3, 4, 1977 BI 1,2
Gordon, S B (Waikato) 1993 S, E
Graham, D J (Canterbury) 1958 A 1, 2, 1960 SA 2,3, 1961 F 1, 2, 3, 1962 A 1, 2, 3, 4, 5, 1963 E 1,2, I, W, 1964 E, S, F, A 1, 2, 3
Graham, J B (Otago) 1913 US, 1914 A 1,3
Graham, W G (Otago) 1979 F 1(R)
Grant, L A (South Canterbury) 1947 A 1,2, 1949 SA 1,2
Gray, G D (Canterbury) 1908 AW 2, 1913 A 1, US
Gray, K F (Wellington) 1963 I, W, 1964 E, S, F, A 1,2,3, 1965 SA 1,2,3,4, 1966 BI 1,2,3,4, 1967 W, F, S, 1968 A 1, F 2,3, 1969 W 1,2
Gray, W N (Bay of Plenty) 1955 A 2,3, 1956 SA 1,2,3,4
Green, C I (Canterbury) 1983 S (R), E, 1984 A 1,2,3, 1985 E 1,2, A, Arg 1,2, 1986 A 2,3, F 2,3, 1987 [It, Fj, S, W, F], A
Grenside, B A (Hawke's Bay) 1928 SA 1,2,3,4, 1929 A 2,3
Griffiths, J L (Wellington) 1934 A 2, 1935 S, I, W, 1936 A 1,2, 1938 A 3
Guildford, Z R (Hawke's Bay) 2009 W,E, 2010 I1(R),W2, 2011 Fj,SA1,A2,[C], 2012 I 1,2
Guy, R A (North Auckland) 1971 BI 1,2,3,4

Haden, A M (Auckland) 1977 BI 1, 2, 3, 4, F 1,2, 1978 A 1, 2, 3, I, W, E, S, 1979 F 1, 2, A, S, E, 1980 A 1, 2, 3, W, 1981 S 2, SA 1,2,3, R, F 1,2, 1982 A 1, 2, 3, 1983 BI 1, 2, 3, 4, A, 1984 F 1, 2, 1985 Arg 1, 2
Hadley, S (Auckland) 1928 SA 1,2,3,4
Hadley, W E (Auckland) 1934 A 1,2, 1935 S, I, W, 1936 E, A 1,2
Haig, J S (Otago) 1946 A 1,2
Haig, L S (Otago) 1950 BI 2,3,4, 1951 A 1,2,3, 1953 W, 1954 E, S
Hales, D A (Canterbury) 1972 A 1,2,3, W
Hamilton, D C (Southland) 1908 AW 2
Hamilton, S E (Canterbury) 2006 Arg,SA1
Hammett, M G (Canterbury) 1999 F 1(R), SA 2(R), [It, S (R), SA 3], 2000 Tg, S 1(R),2(t&R), A 1(R), SA 1(R), A 2(R), SA 2(R), F 2(R), It (R), 2001 Arg 1(t), 2002 It (R), I 1, 2, A 1, SA 1, 2(R), 2003 SA 1(R), A 1(R), SA 2, [It(R), C, W(R), SA(R), F(R)]
Hammond, I A (Marlborough) 1952 A 2
Harper, E T (Canterbury) 1904 BI, 1906 F
Harding, S (Otago) 2002 Fj
Harris, P C (Manawatu) 1976 SA 3
Hart, A H (Taranaki) 1924 I
Hart, G F (Canterbury) 1930 BI 1, 2, 3, 4, 1931 A, 1934 A 1, 1935 S, I, W, 1936 A 1,2
Harvey, B A (Wairarapa-Bush) 1986 F 1
Harvey, I H (Wairarapa) 1928 SA 4
Harvey, L R (Otago) 1949 SA 1,2,3,4, 1950 BI 1,2,3,4
Harvey, P (Canterbury) 1904 BI
Hasell, E W (Canterbury) 1913 A 2,3
Hayman, C J (Otago) 2001 Sm (R), Arg 1, F (R), A 1(R), SA 2(R), A 2(R), 2002 F (t), W, 2004 E1, 2, PI, A1, 2, SA2, It, W(R), F, 2005 BI1, SA1, A1, SA2, A2, W, E, 2006 I1, 2, A1, SA1, A2, 3, SA3, E, F1, 2, W, 2007 F1, 2, SA1, A1, SA2, A2, [It, Pt(R), S, F]
Hayward, H O (Auckland) 1908 AW 3
Hazlett, E J (Southland) 1966 BI 1,2,3,4, 1967 A, E

Hazlett, W E (Southland) 1928 SA 1,2,3,4, 1930 BI 1,2,3,4
Heeps, T R (Wellington) 1962 A 1,2,3,4,5
Heke, W R (North Auckland) 1929 A 1,2,3
Hemi, R C (Waikato) 1953 W, 1954 I, E, S, F, 1955 A 1,2,3, 1956 SA 1, 3, 4, 1957 A 1, 2, 1959 BI 1, 3, 4
Henderson, P (Wanganui) 1949 SA 1,2,3,4, 1950 BI 2,3,4
Henderson, P W (Otago) 1991 Arg 1, [C], 1992 Wld 1,2,3, I 1, 1995 [J]
Herewini, M A (Auckland) 1962 A 5, 1963 I, 1964 S, F, 1965 SA 4, 1966 BI 1,2,3,4, 1967 A
Hewett, D N (Canterbury) 2001 I (R), S (R), Arg 2, 2002 It (R), I 1,2, A 1, SA 1, A 2, SA 2, 2003 E, F, SA 1, A 1, SA 2, A 2, [It,Tg(R),W,SA,A,F]
Hewett, J A (Auckland) 1991 [It]
Hewitt, N J (Southland) 1995 [I (t), J], 1996 A 1(R), 1997 SA 1(R), I, E 1, W, E 2, 1998 E 2(t + R)
Hewson, A R (Wellington) 1981 S 1,2, SA 1, 2, 3, R, F 1,2, 1982 A 1, 2, 3, 1983 BI 1, 2, 3, 4, A, 1984 F 1, 2, A 1
Higginson, G (Canterbury, Hawke's Bay) 1980 W, 1981 S 1, SA 1, 1982 A 1, 2, 1983 A
Hill, D W (Waikato) 2006 I2(R)
Hill, S F (Canterbury) 1955 A 3, 1956 SA 1, 3, 4, 1957 A 1,2, 1958 A 3, 1959 BI 1, 2, 3, 4
Hines, G R (Waikato) 1980 A 3
Hobbs, M J B (Canterbury) 1983 BI 1, 2, 3, 4, A, S, E, 1984 F 1, 2, A 1, 2, 3, 1985 E 1, 2, A, Arg 1, 2, 1986 A 2, 3, F 2, 3
Hoeata, J M R A (Taranaki) 2011 Fj,SA1(R),2(R)
Hoeft, C H (Otago) 1998 E 2(t + R), A 2(R), SA 2, A 3, 1999 WS, F 1, SA 1, A 1, 2, [Tg,E, S, F 2, SA 3(R)], 2000 S 1,2, A 1, SA 1, A 2, SA 2, 2001 Sm, Arg 1, F, SA 1, A 1, SA 2, A 2, 2003 W, [C,F(R)]
Holah, M R (Waikato) 2001 Sm, Arg 1(t&R), F (R), SA 1(R), A 1(R), SA 2(R), A 2(R), 2002 It, I 2(R), A 2(t), E, F, W (R), 2003 W, F (R), A 1(R), SA 2, [It(R), C, Tg(R), W(R), SA(t&R), A(R), F(t&R)], 2004 E1(R), 2, Arg(R), PI, A1, SA1, A2, SA2, 2005 BI3(R), A1(R), 2006 I1, SA3(t)
Holder, E C (Buller) 1934 A 2
Hook, L S (Auckland) 1929 A 1,2,3
Hooper, J A (Canterbury) 1937 SA 1,2,3
Hopkinson, A E (Canterbury) 1967 S, 1968 A 2, F 1,2,3, 1969 W 2, 1970 SA 1,2,3
Hore, A K (Taranaki) 2002 E, F, 2004 E1(t), 2(R), Arg, A1(t), 2005 W(R), I(R), S(R), 2006 I2(R), Arg(R), A1(R), SA1(R), A2(R), SA3, E(R), F2(R), W(R), 2007 F1(R), C, SA2(R), [Pt, S(R), R(R), F(R)], 2008 I1, E1, 2, SA1, 2, A1, 2, SA3, Sm, A3, 4, 2009 F1, A1, SA1, 2, A2, SA3, A3, 4, W, E, F3, 2010 S(R), I2(R), W3(R), 2011 Fj, SA1, A1(R), SA2(R), A2(R), [Tg,J(R), F1(R), C, Arg(R), A(R), F2(R)], 2012 I1, 2, 3, A1(R), 2(R), Arg1(R), SA1, Arg2, SA2, A3(R), S, W, 2013 F2(R), 3, A1, 2, Arg1, 2, SA2
Hore, J (Otago) 1930 BI 2, 3, 4, 1932 A 1, 2, 3, 1934 A 1, 2, 1935 S, 1936 E
Horsley, R H (Wellington) 1960 SA 2,3,4
Hotop, J (Canterbury) 1952 A 1,2, 1955 A 3
Howarth, S P (Auckland) 1994 SA 1,2,3, A
Howlett, D C (Auckland) 2000 Tg (R), F 1,2, It, 2001 Sm, Arg 1(R), F (R), SA 1, A 1,2, I, S, Arg 2, 2002 It, I 1,2(R), Fj, A 1, SA 1, A 2, SA 2, E, F, W, 2003 E, W, F, SA 1, A 1, SA 2, A 2, [It, C(R), Tg, W, SA, A, F], 2004 E1, A1, SA1, A2, SA2, W, F, 2005 Fj, BI1, A2, I, E, 2006 I1, 2, SA1, A3, SA3, 2007 F2(R), C, SA2, A2, [It, S, R(R)]
Hughes, A M (Auckland) 1949 A 1,2, 1950 BI 1,2,3,4
Hughes, E (Southland, Wellington) 1907 A 1,2,3, 1908 AW 1, 1921 SA 1,2
Hunter, B A (Otago) 1971 BI 1,2,3
Hunter, J (Taranaki) 1905 S, I, E, W, 1906 F, 1907 A 1,2,3, 1908 AW 1,2,3
Hurst, I A (Canterbury) 1973 I, F, E 2, 1974 A 1,2

Ieremia, A (Wellington) 1994 SA 1,2,3, 1995 [J], 1996 SA 2(R),5(R), 1997 A 1(R), SA 1(R), A 2, SA 2, A 3, I, E 1, 1999 WS, F 1, SA 1, A 1, SA 2, A 2, [Tg, E, S, F 2, SA 3], 2000 Tg, S 1,2, A 1,2, SA 2
Ifwersen, K D (Auckland) 1921 SA 3
Innes, C R (Auckland) 1989 W, I, 1990 A 1, 2, 3, F 1,2, 1991 Arg 1, 2, A 1,2, [E, US, It, C, A, S]
Innes, G D (Canterbury) 1932 A 2
Irvine, I B (North Auckland) 1952 A 1
Irvine, J G (Otago) 1914 A 1,2,3
Irvine, W R (Hawke's Bay, Wairarapa) 1924 I, W, 1925 E, F, 1930 BI 1
Irwin, M W (Otago) 1955 A 1,2, 1956 SA 1, 1958 A 2, 1959 BI 3,4, 1960 SA 1

Jack, C R (Canterbury, Tasman) 2001 Arg 1(R), SA 1(R),2, A 2, I, S, Arg 2, 2002 I 1,2, A 1, SA 1, A 2, SA 2, 2003 E, W, F, SA 1, A 1, SA 2(R), A 2, [It, C, SA, A, F], 2004 E1, 2, Arg, PI, A1, SA1, A2, SA2, It, W, F, 2005 Fj(R), BI1, 2, 3, SA1, A1, SA2, A2, W, E, S, 2006 I1, 2, A1, SA1, A2, 3, SA2(R), 3, E, F2, 2007 F1, 2, A1, SA2, A2, [It, Pt, S(R), R(R), F(R)]
Jackson, E S (Hawke's Bay) 1936 A 1,2, 1937 SA 1, 2, 3, 1938 A 3
Jaffray, J L (Otago, South Canterbury) 1972 A 2, 1975 S, 1976 I, SA 1, 1977 BI 2, 1979 F 1,2
Jane, C S (Wellington) 2008 A4(R), S(R), 2009 F1, 2, It1(R), A1, SA3(R), A3, 4, W, It2, F3, 2010 I1, W1, 2, SA1, 2, A1, 2, SA3, A3, 4, I2, 2011 SA1, 2(R), A2, [Tg(R), J, F1, Arg, A, F2], 2012 A1, 2, Arg1, SA1, Arg2, SA2, A3, S, It(R), W, E
Jarden, R A (Wellington) 1951 A 1, 2, 1952 A 1, 2, 1953 W, 1954 I, E, S, F, 1955 A 1,2,3, 1956 SA 1,2,3,4
Jefferd, A C R (East Coast) 1981 S 1,2, SA 1
Jessep, E M (Wellington) 1931 A, 1932 A 1
Johnson, L M (Wellington) 1928 SA 1,2,3,4
Johnston, W (Otago) 1907 A 1,2,3
Johnstone, B R (Auckland) 1976 SA 2, 1977 BI 1,2, F 1,2, 1978 I, W, E, S, 1979 F 1,2, S, E
Johnstone, C R (Canterbury) 2005 Fj(R),BI2(R),3(R)
Johnstone, P (Otago) 1949 SA 2,4, 1950 BI 1,2,3,4, 1951 A 1,2,3
Jones, I D (North Auckland, North Harbour) 1990 S 1,2, A 1,2,3, F 1,2, 1991 Arg 1,2, A 1,2, [E, US, It, C, A, S], 1992 Wld 1,2,3, I 1,2, A 1,2,3, SA, 1993 BI 1,2(R),3, WS, S, E, 1994 F 1,2, SA 1,3, A, 1995 C, [I, W, S, E, SA], A 1,2, It, F 1,2, 1996 WS, S 1,2, A 1, SA 1, A 2, SA 2,3,4,5, 1997 Fj, Arg 1,2, A 1, SA 1, A 2, SA 2, A 3, I, E 1, W, E 2, 1998 E 1,2, A 1, SA 1, A 2,3(R), 1999 F 1(R), [It, S (R)]
Jones, M G (North Auckland) 1973 E 2
Jones, M N (Auckland) 1987 [It, Fj, S, F], A, 1988 W 1,2, A 2,3, 1989 F 1,2, Arg 1,2, 1990 F 1,2, 1991 Arg 1,2, A 1,2, [E, US, S], 1992 Wld 1,3, I 2, A 1,3, SA, 1993 BI 1,2,3, A, WS, 1994 SA 3(R), A, 1995 A 1(R),2, It, F 1,2, 1996 WS, S 1,2, A 1, SA 1, A 2, SA 2,3,4,5, 1997 Fj, 1998 E 1, A 1, SA 1, A 2
Jones, P F H (North Auckland) 1954 E, S, 1955 A 1,2, 1956 SA 3,4, 1958 A 1,2,3, 1959 BI 1, 1960 SA 1
Joseph, H T (Canterbury) 1971 BI 2,3
Joseph, J W (Otago) 1992 Wld 2,3(R), I 1, A 1(R),3, SA, 1993 BI 1,2,3, A, WS, S, E, 1994 SA 2(t), 1995 C, [I, W, J (R), S, SA (R)]

Kahui, R D (Waikato) 2008 E2,A1,2,SA3,Sm,A3,S,W, 2010 W1(R),2,SA1(R), 2011 SA2,[Tg,J,F1,A,F2]
Kaino, J (Auckland) 2006 I1(R),2, 2008 I1, E1, SA1, 2, A1, 2, SA3, Sm, A3, 4, I2, W, E3, 2009 F2, It1, A1, SA1, 2, A2, SA3, W, E(R), F3, 2010 I1, W2, SA1, 2, A1, 2, SA3, A3(R), 4, E, I2, W3, 2011 Fj(R), SA1, A1, SA2, [Tg, J, F1, C, Arg, A, F2]
Karam, J F (Wellington, Horowhenua) 1972 W, S, 1973 E 1, I, F, 1974 A 1,2,3, I, 1975 S
Katene, T (Wellington) 1955 A 2
Kearney, J C (Otago) 1947 A 2, 1949 SA 1,2,3
Kelleher, B T (Otago, Waikato) 1999 WS (R), SA 1(R), A 2(R), [Tg (R), E (R), It, F 2], 2000 S 1, A 1(R),2(R), It (R), 2001 Sm, F (R), A 1(R), SA 2, A 2, I, S, 2002 It, I 2(R), Fj, SA 1(R),2(R), 2003 F (R), [A(R)], 2004 Arg, PI(R), SA1(R), 2(R), It, W(R), F, 2005 Fj, BI1(R), 2, 3, SA1, W, E, 2006 I1, 2, A1, 2, 3, SA3(R), E, F1(R), 2, W, 2007 F2, C, SA1, A1, 2, [It, S, F]
Kelly, J W (Auckland) 1949 A 1,2
Kember, G F (Wellington) 1970 SA 4
Kerr-Barlow, T N J (Waikato) 2012 S(R),It(R), 2013 F1(R), 3(R), A1(R), 2(R), Arg1(R), SA1(R), Arg2(R), SA2(R)

Ketels, R C (Counties) 1980 W, 1981 S 1,2, R, F 1
Kiernan, H A D (Auckland) 1903 A
Kilby, F D (Wellington) 1932 A 1,2,3, 1934 A 2
Killeen, B A (Auckland) 1936 A 1
King, R M (Waikato) 2002 W
King, R R (West Coast) 1934 A 2, 1935 S, I, W, 1936 E, A 1,2, 1937 SA 1,2,3, 1938 A 1,2,3
Kingstone, C N (Taranaki) 1921 SA 1,2,3
Kirk, D E (Auckland) 1985 E 1,2, A, Arg 1, 1986 F 1, A 1,2,3, F 2,3, 1987 [It, Fj, Arg, S, W, F], A
Kirkpatrick, I A (Canterbury, Poverty Bay) 1967 F, 1968 A 1(R),2, F 1,2,3, 1969 W 1,2, 1970 SA 1,2,3,4, 1971 BI 1,2,3,4, 1972 A 1,2,3, W, S, 1973 E 1, I, F, E 2, 1974 A 1,2,3, I 1975 S, 1976 I, SA 1,2,3,4, 1977 BI 1,2,3,4
Kirton, E W (Otago) 1967 E, W, F, S, 1968 A 1,2, F 1,2,3, 1969 W 1,2, 1970 SA 2,3
Kirwan, J J (Auckland) 1984 F 1,2, 1985 E 1,2, A, Arg 1,2, 1986 F 1, A 1,2,3, F 2,3, 1987 [It, Fj, Arg, S, W, F], A, 1988 W 1,2, A 1,2,3, 1989 F 1,2, Arg 1,2, A, 1990 S 1,2, A 1,2,3, F 1,2, 1991 Arg 2, A 1,2, [E, It, C, A, S], 1992 Wld 1,2(R),3, I 1,2, A 1,2,3, SA, 1993 BI 2,3, A, WS, 1994 F 1,2, SA 1,2,3
Kivell, A L (Taranaki) 1929 A 2,3
Knight, A (Auckland) 1934 A 1
Knight, G A (Manawatu) 1977 F 1,2, 1978 A 1, 2, 3, E, S, 1979 F 1,2, A, 1980 A 1,2,3, W, 1981 S 1,2, SA 1, 3, 1982 A 1,2,3, 1983 BI 1, 2, 3, 4, A, 1984 F 1,2, A 1, 2, 3, 1985 E 1,2, A, 1986 A 2,3
Knight, L G (Poverty Bay) 1977 BI 1,2,3,4, F 1,2
Koteka, T T (Waikato) 1981 F 2, 1982 A 3
Kreft, A J (Otago) 1968 A 2
Kronfeld, J A (Otago) 1995 C, [I, W, S, E, SA], A 1,2(R) 1996 WS, S 1,2, A 1, SA 1, A 2, SA 2,3,4,5, 1997 Fj, Arg 1,2, A 1, SA 1, A 2, SA 2, A 3, I (R), E 1, W, E 2, 1998 E 1,2, A 1, SA 1,2 A 3, 1999 WS, F 1, SA 1, A 1, SA 2, A 2, [Tg, E, S, F 2, SA 3], 2000 Tg, S 1(R),2, A 1(R), SA 1, A 2, SA 2

Laidlaw, C R (Otago, Canterbury) 1964 F, A 1, 1965 SA 1,2,3,4, 1966 BI 1, 2, 3, 4, 1967 E, W, S, 1968 A 1, 2, F 1, 2, 1970 SA 1, 2, 3
Laidlaw, K F (Southland) 1960 SA 2,3,4
Lambert, K K (Manawatu) 1972 S (R), 1973 E 1, I, F, E 2, 1974 I, 1976 SA 1,3,4, 1977 BI 1,4
Lambourn, A (Wellington) 1934 A 1, 2, 1935 S, I, W, 1936 E, 1937 SA 1, 2, 3, 1938 A 3
Larsen, B P (North Harbour) 1992 Wld 2, 3, I 1, 1994 F 1, 2, SA 1, 2, 3, A (t), 1995 [I, W, J, E(R)], It, F 1, 1996 S 2(t), SA 4(R)
Latimer, T D (Bay of Plenty) 2009 F1(R),2,It1,2,F3(R)
Lauaki, S T (Waikato) 2005 Fj(R), BI1(R), 2(R), 3, A2, I, S, 2007 [It(R), Pt, S(R), R], 2008 E1(R), 2(R), SA1(R), 2(R), A1(R), Sm(R)
Laulala, C D E (Canterbury) 2004 W, 2006 I2
Le Lievre, J M (Canterbury) 1962 A 4
Lee, D D (Otago) 2002 E (R), F
Lendrum, R N (Counties) 1973 E 2
Leonard, B G (Waikato) 2007 F1(R), 2(R), SA2(R), A2(R), [It(R), Pt, S(R), R(R), F(R)], 2009 It1, SA1, A3(R), W
Leslie, A R (Wellington) 1974 A 1, 2, 3, I, 1975 S, 1976 I, SA 1, 2, 3, 4
Leys, E T (Wellington) 1929 A 3
Lilburne, H T (Canterbury, Wellington) 1928 SA 3, 4, 1929 A 1, 2, 3, 1930 BI 1,4, 1931 A, 1932 A 1, 1934 A 2
Lindsay, D F (Otago) 1928 SA 1,2,3
Lineen, T R (Auckland) 1957 A 1,2, 1958 A 1,2,3, 1959 BI 1, 2, 3, 4, 1960 SA 1, 2, 3
Lister, T N (South Canterbury) 1968 A 1, 2, F 1, 1969 W 1, 2, 1970 SA 1, 4, 1971 BI 4
Little, P F (Auckland) 1961 F 2, 3, 1962 A 2, 3, 5, 1963 I, W, 1964 E, S, F
Little, W K (North Harbour) 1990 S 1,2, A 1,2,3, F 1,2, 1991 Arg 1,2, A 1, [It, S], 1992 Wld 1,2,3, I 1,2, A 1,2,3, SA, 1993 BI 1, WS (R), 1994 SA 2(R), A, 1995 C, [I, W, S, E, SA], A 1,2, It, F 1,2, 1996 S 2, A 1, SA 1, A 2, SA 2,3,4,5, 1997 W, E 2, 1998 E 1, A 1, SA 1, A 2
Loader, C J (Wellington) 1954 I, E, S, F
Lochore, B J (Wairarapa) 1964 E, S, 1965 SA 1,2,3,4, 1966 BI 1,2,3,4, 1967 A, E, W, F, S, 1968 A 1, F 2,3, 1969 W 1,2, 1970 SA 1,2,3,4, 1971 BI 3
Loe, R W (Waikato, Canterbury) 1987 [It, Arg], 1988 W 1,2, A 1,2,3, 1989 F 1,2, Arg 1,2, A, W, I, 1990 S 1,2, A 1,2,3, F 1,2, 1991 Arg 1,2, A 1,2, [E, It, C, A, S], 1992 Wld 1,2,3, I 1, A 1,2,3, SA, 1994 F 1,2, SA 1,2,3, A, 1995 [J, S, SA (R)], A 2(t), F 2(R)
Lomu, J T (Counties Manukau, Wellington) 1994 F 1,2, 1995 [I, W, S, E, SA], A 1,2, It, F 1,2, 1996 WS, S 1, A 1, SA 1, A 2, 1997 E 1, W, E 2, 1998 E 1,2, A 1(R), SA 1, A 2, SA 2, A 3, 1999 WS (R), SA 1(R), A 1(R), SA 2(R), A 2(R), [Tg, E, It, S, F 2, SA 3], 2000 Tg, S 1,2, A 1, SA 1, A 2, SA 2, F 1, 2001 Arg 1, F, SA 1, A 1, SA 2, A 2, I, S, Arg 2, 2002 It (R), I 1(R),2, Fj, SA 1(R), E, F, W
Long, A J (Auckland) 1903 A
Loveridge, D S (Taranaki) 1978 W, 1979 S, E, 1980 A 1,2,3, W, 1981 S 1,2, SA 1,2,3, R, F 1,2, 1982 A 1,2,3, 1983 BI 1,2,3,4, A, 1985 Arg 2
Lowen, K R (Waikato) 2002 E
Luatua, D S (Auckland) 2013 F3(R), A1, 2, Arg1, SA1(R), Arg2(R), SA2(R)
Lucas, F W (Auckland) 1924 I, 1925 F, 1928 SA 4, 1930 BI 1, 2, 3, 4
Lunn, W A (Otago) 1949 A 1,2
Lynch, T W (South Canterbury) 1913 A 1, 1914 A 1,2,3
Lynch, T W (Canterbury) 1951 A 1,2,3

McAlister, C L (North Harbour) 2005 BI3, SA1(R), A1(R), SA2(R), A2(R), 2006 I1, 2, SA1(R), A3, SA2, F1, W, 2007 F2, C, SA1(R), A1, SA2, A2, [It, S, R, F], 2009 F1(R), 2(R), It1, SA1(R), 2(R), A2, It2, F3(R)
McAtamney, F S (Otago) 1956 SA 2
McCahill, B J (Auckland) 1987 [Arg, S (R), W (R)], 1989 Arg 1(R),2(R), 1991 A 2, [E, US, C, A]
McCaw, R H (Canterbury) 2001 I, S, Arg 2, 2002 I 1,2, A 1, SA 1, A 2, SA 2, 2003 E, F, SA 1, A 1,2, [It, C(R), Tg(R), W, SA, A, F], 2004 E1, Arg, It, W, F, 2005 Fj, BI1, 2, SA1, A1, SA2, A2, W(R), I, S, 2006 I1, 2, A1, SA1, A2, 3, SA2, 3, E, F1, 2, W, 2007 F1, 2, C(R), SA1, A1, SA2, A2, [It, S, R(R), F], 2008 I1, E1, 2, A2, SA3, A3, 4, S(R), I2, W, E3, 2009 A1, SA1, 2, A2, SA3, A3, 4, W, E, F3, 2010 I1, W1, 2, SA1, 2, A1, 2, SA3, A3, 4, E, S, I2, W3, 2011 Fj, SA1, A1, 2, [Tg, F1, Arg, A, F2], 2012 I 1, 2, 3, A1, 2, Arg1, SA1, Arg2, SA2, A3, S, W, E, 2013 A1, 2, Arg1, SA2
McCaw, W A (Southland) 1951 A 1,2,3, 1953 W, 1954 F
McCool, M J (Wairarapa-Bush) 1979 A
McCormick, W F (Canterbury) 1965 SA 4, 1967 E, W, F, S, 1968 A 1,2, F 1,2,3, 1969 W 1,2, 1970 SA 1,2,3, 1971 BI 1
McCullough, J F (Taranaki) 1959 BI 2,3,4
McDonald, A (Otago) 1905 S, I, E, W, 1907 A 1, 1908 AW 1, 1913 A 1, US
Macdonald, A J (Auckland) 2005 W(R),S
Macdonald, H H (Canterbury, North Auckland) 1972 W, S, 1973 E 1, I, F, E 2, 1974 I, 1975 S, 1976 I, SA 1,2,3
MacDonald, L R (Canterbury) 2000 S 1(R),2(R), SA 1(t),2(R), 2001 Sm, Arg 1, F, SA 1(R), A 1(R), SA 2, A 2, I, S, 2002 I 1,2, Fj (R), A 2(R), SA 2, 2003 A 2(R), [It(R), C, Tg, W, SA, A, F], 2005 BI1, 2(R), SA1, 2, A2, W(R), I, E(R), S(R), 2006 Arg, A1, SA1, A2, 3(R), SA2, F1, 2, 2007 F1, 2, C(R), SA1(R), [It, Pt(R), S, F], 2008 I1(R), E1(R), 2, SA1(R), 2(R)
McDonnell, J M (Otago) 2002 It, I 1(R),2(R), Fj, SA 1(R), A 2(R), E, F
McDowell, S C (Auckland, Bay of Plenty) 1985 Arg 1,2, 1986 A 2,3, F 2,3, 1987 [It, Fj, S, W, F], A, 1988 W 1,2, A 1,2,3, 1989 F 1,2, Arg 1,2, A, W, I, 1990 S 1,2, A 1,2,3, F 1,2, 1991 Arg 1,2, A 1,2, [E, US, It, C, A, S], 1992 Wld 1,2,3, I 1,2
McEldowney, J T (Taranaki) 1977 BI 3,4
MacEwan, I N (Wellington) 1956 SA 2, 1957 A 1,2, 1958 A 1,2,3, 1959 BI 1,2,3, 1960 SA 1,2,3,4, 1961 F 1,2,3, 1962 A 1,2,3,4
McGrattan, B (Wellington) 1983 S, E, 1985 Arg 1,2, 1986 F 1, A 1
McGregor, A J (Auckland) 1913 A 1, US
McGregor, D (Canterbury, Southland) 1903 A, 1904 BI, 1905 E, W

McGregor, N P (Canterbury) 1924 W, 1925 E
McGregor, R W (Auckland) 1903 A, 1904 BI
McHugh, M J (Auckland) 1946 A 1,2, 1949 SA 3
McIntosh, D N (Wellington) 1956 SA 1,2, 1957 A 1,2
McKay, D W (Auckland) 1961 F 1,2,3, 1963 E 1,2
McKechnie, B J (Southland) 1977 F 1,2, 1978 A 2(R),3, W (R), E, S, 1979 A, 1981 SA 1(R), F 1
McKellar, G F (Wellington) 1910 A 1,2,3
McKenzie, R J (Wellington) 1913 A 1, US, 1914 A 2,3
McKenzie, R McC (Manawatu) 1934 A 1, 1935 S, 1936 A 1, 1937 SA 1,2,3, 1938 A 1,2,3
McLachlan, J S (Auckland) 1974 A 2
McLaren, H C (Waikato) 1952 A 1
McLean, A L (Bay of Plenty) 1921 SA 2,3
McLean, H F (Wellington, Auckland) 1930 BI 3,4, 1932 A 1,2,3, 1934 A 1, 1935 I, W, 1936 E
McLean, J K (King Country, Auckland) 1947 A 1, 1949 A 2
McLeod, B E (Counties) 1964 A 1,2,3, 1965 SA 1,2,3,4, 1966 BI 1,2,3,4, 1967 E, W, F, S, 1968 A 1,2, F 1,2,3, 1969 W 1,2, 1970 SA 1,2
McLeod, S J (Waikato) 1996 WS, S 1, 1997 Fj (R), Arg 2(t + R), I (R), E 1(R), W (t), E 2(R), 1998 A 1, SA 1(R)
McMinn, A F (Wairarapa, Manawatu) 1903 A, 1905 A
McMinn, F A (Manawatu) 1904 BI
McMullen, R F (Auckland) 1957 A 1,2, 1958 A 1,2,3, 1959 BI 1,2,3, 1960 SA 2,3,4
McNab, J R (Otago) 1949 SA 1,2,3, 1950 BI 1,2,3
McNaughton, A M (Bay of Plenty) 1971 BI 1,2,3
McNeece, J (Southland) 1913 A 2,3, 1914 A 1,2,3
McPhail, B E (Canterbury) 1959 BI 1,4
Macpherson, D G (Otago) 1905 A
MacPherson, G L (Otago) 1986 F 1
MacRae, I R (Hawke's Bay) 1966 BI 1,2,3,4, 1967 A, E, W, F, S, 1968 F 1,2, 1969 W 1,2, 1970 SA 1,2,3,4
McRae, J A (Southland) 1946 A 1(R),2
McWilliams, R G (Auckland) 1928 SA 2, 3, 4, 1929 A 1, 2, 3, 1930 BI 1, 2, 3, 4
Mackintosh, J L (Southland) 2008 S
Mackrell, W H C (Auckland) 1906 F
Macky, J V (Auckland) 1913 A 2
Maguire, J R (Auckland) 1910 A 1,2,3
Mahoney, A (Bush) 1935 S, I, W, 1936 E
Mains, L W (Otago) 1971 BI 2,3,4, 1976 I
Major, J (Taranaki) 1967 A
Maka, I (Otago) 1998 E 2(R), A 1(R), SA 1(R),2
Maling, T S (Otago) 2002 It, I 2(R), Fj, A 1, SA 1, A 2, SA 2, 2004 Arg,A1,SA1,2
Manchester, J E (Canterbury) 1932 A 1,2,3, 1934 A 1,2, 1935 S, I, W, 1936 E
Mannix, S J (Wellington) 1994 F 1
Marshall, J W (Southland, Canterbury) 1995 F 2, 1996 WS, S 1,2, A 1, SA 1, A 2, SA 2,3,4,5, 1997 Fj, Arg 1,2, A 1, SA 1, A 2, SA 2, A 3, I, E 1, W, E 2, 1998 A 1, SA 1, A 2, SA 2, A 3, 1999 WS, F 1, SA 1, A 1, SA 2, A 2, [Tg, E, S, F 2(R), SA 3], 2000 Tg, S 2, A 1, SA 1, A 2, SA 2, F 1,2, It, 2001 Arg 1, F, SA 1, A 1,2(R), 2002 I 1,2, Fj (R), A 1, SA 1, A 2, SA 2, 2003 E, SA 1(R), A 1, SA 2, A 2, [It, Tg, W, SA, A], 2004 E1, 2, PI, A1, SA1, A2, SA2, 2005 Fj(R), BI1, 2(R), 3(R)
Masaga, L T C (Counties Manukau) 2009 It1
Masoe, M C (Taranaki, Wellington) 2005 W, E, 2006Arg, A1(R), SA1(R), A2(R), 3(R), SA2, E, F2(R), 2007 F1, 2(R), C, A1(R), SA2(R), [It(R), Pt, S, R, F(R)]
Mason, D F (Wellington) 1947 A 2(R)
Masters, R R (Canterbury) 1924 I, W, 1925 E, F
Mataira, H K (Hawke's Bay) 1934 A 2
Matheson, J D (Otago) 1972 A 1,2,3, W, S
Mathewson, A S (Wellington) 2010 A2(R),4(R),E,I2(R)
Mauger, A J D (Canterbury) 2001 I, S, Arg 2, 2002 It (R), I 1, 2, Fj, A 1, SA 1, A 2, SA 2, 2003 SA 1, A 1, SA 2, A 2, [W, SA, A, F], 2004 SA2(R), It(R), W, F(R), 2005 Fj, BI1, 2, SA1, A1, SA2, A2, I, E, 2006 I1, 2, A1, 2, SA3, E, 2007 F1, C, SA1, A1, [It(R), Pt, R]
Max, D S (Nelson) 1931 A, 1934 A 1,2
Maxwell, N M C (Canterbury) 1999 WS, F 1, SA 1, A 1, SA 2, A 2, [Tg, E, S, F 2, SA 3], 2000 S 1,2, A 1, SA 1(R), A 2, SA 2, F 1,2, It (R), 2001 Sm, Arg 1, F, SA 1, A 1, SA 2, A2, I, S, Arg 2, 2002 It, I 1,2, Fj, 2004 It,F
Mayerhofler, M A (Canterbury) 1998 E 1,2, SA 1, A 2, SA 2, A 3
Meads, C E (King Country) 1957 A 1,2, 1958 A 1,2,3, 1959 BI 2,3,4, 1960 SA 1,2,3,4, 1961 F 1,2,3, 1962 A 1,2,3,5, 1963 E 1,2, I, W, 1964 E, S, F, A 1,2,3, 1965 SA 1,2,3,4, 1966 BI 1,2,3,4, 1967 A, E, W, F, S, 1968 A 1,2, F 1,2,3, 1969 W 1,2, 1970 SA 3,4, 1971 BI 1,2,3,4
Meads, S T (King Country) 1961 F 1, 1962 A 4,5, 1963 I, 1964 A 1,2,3, 1965 SA 1,2,3,4, 1966 BI 1,2,3,4
Mealamu, K F (Auckland) 2002 W, 2003 E (R), W, F (R), SA 1, A 1, SA 2(R), A 2,[It,W,SA,A,F], 2004 E1, 2, PI, A1, SA1, A2, SA2, W, F(R), 2005 Fj(R), BI1, 2, 3, SA1, A1, SA2, A2, I, E, 2006 I1, 2, A1, 2, 3, SA2(R), E, F1(R), 2, 2007 F1, 2(R), SA1(R), A1(R), SA2, A2(R), [It, Pt(R), R], 2008 I1(R), E1(t&R), 2(t&R), SA1(R), 2(R), A1(R), 2(R), SA3(R), Sm(R), A3(R), 4(R), S, I2, W, E3, 2009 F1(R), 2, It1, A1(R), SA1(R), 2(R), 2010 I1, W1, 2, SA1, 2, A1, 2, SA3, A3, 4, E, W3, 2011 A1, SA2, A2, [J, F1, C(R), Arg, A, F2], 2012 I 3(R), A1, 2, Arg1, SA1(R), Arg2(R), SA2(R), A3, It, E, 2013 F1(R), 3(R), A1(R), SA1(R), Arg2(R)
Meates, K F (Canterbury) 1952 A 1,2
Meates, W A (Otago) 1949 SA 2,3,4, 1950 BI 1,2,3,4
Meeuws, K J (Otago, Auckland) 1998 A 3, 1999 WS, F 1, SA 1, A 1, SA 2, A 2, [Tg, It (R), S (R), F 2(R), SA 3], 2000 Tg (R), S 2, A 1, SA 1, A 2, SA 2, 2001 Arg 2, 2002 It, Fj, E, F, W (R), 2003 W, F (R), SA 1(R), A 1(R), SA 2, [It(R), C, Tg, W(R), SA(R), A(R)], 2004 E1, 2, PI, A1, SA1, A2, SA2
Mehrtens, A P (Canterbury) 1995 C, [I, W, S, E, SA], A 1,2, 1996 WS, S 1,2, A 1, SA 1, A 2, SA 2,5, 1997 Fj, SA 2(R), I, E 1, W, E 2, 1998 E 1,2, A 1, SA 1(R), A 2, SA 2, A 3, 1999 F 1, SA 1, A 1, SA 2, A 2, [Tg, E, S, F 2, SA 3], 2000 S 1,2, A 1, SA 1, A 2, SA 2, F 1,2, It (R), 2001 Arg 1, A 1(R), SA 2, A 2, I, S, Arg 2, 2002 It, I 1,2, Fj (R), A 1, SA 1, A 2, SA 2, E (R), F, W, 2004 E2(R),Arg,A2(R),SA2
Messam, L J (Waikato) 2008 S, 2009 F1,It2, 2010 SA1(R),2(R),S, 2011 Fj, SA1(R), 2, 2012 I 3, A1, 2, Arg1(R), SA1, Arg2, SA2, A3, It, W, E, 2013 F1, 2, SA1, Arg2, SA2
Metcalfe, T C (Southland) 1931 A, 1932 A 1
Mexted, G G (Wellington) 1950 BI 4
Mexted, M G (Wellington) 1979 S, E, 1980 A 1,2,3, W, 1981 S 1,2, SA 1,2,3, R, F 1,2, 1982 A 1,2,3, 1983 BI 1,2,3,4, A, S, E, 1984 F 1,2, A 1,2,3, 1985 E 1,2, A, Arg 1,2
Mika, B M (Auckland) 2002 E (R), F, W (R)
Mika, D G (Auckland) 1999 WS, F 1, SA 1(R), A 1,2, [It, SA 3(R)]
Mill, J J (Hawke's Bay, Wairarapa) 1924 W, 1925 E, F, 1930 BI 1
Milliken, H M (Canterbury) 1938 A 1,2,3
Milner, H P (Wanganui) 1970 SA 3
Mitchell, N A (Southland, Otago) 1935 S, I, W, 1936 E, A 2, 1937 SA 3, 1938 A 1,2
Mitchell, T W (Canterbury) 1976 SA 4(R)
Mitchell, W J (Canterbury) 1910 A 2,3
Mitchinson, F E (Wellington) 1907 A 1,2,3, 1908 AW 1,2,3, 1910 A 1,2,3, 1913 A 1(R), US
Moffitt, J E (Wellington) 1921 SA 1,2,3
Moore, G J T (Otago) 1949 A 1
Moreton, R C (Canterbury) 1962 A 3,4, 1964 A 1,2,3, 1965 SA 2,3
Morgan, J E (North Auckland) 1974 A 3, I, 1976 SA 2,3,4
Morris, T J (Nelson Bays) 1972 A 1,2,3
Morrison, T C (South Canterbury) 1938 A 1,2,3
Morrison, T G (Otago) 1973 E 2(R)
Morrissey, P J (Canterbury) 1962 A 3,4,5
Mourie, G N K (Taranaki) 1977 BI 3,4, F 1,2, 1978 I, W, E, S, 1979 F 1,2, A, S, E, 1980 W, 1981 S 1,2, F 1,2, 1982 A 1,2,3
Muliaina, J M (Auckland, Waikato) 2003 E (R), W, F, SA 1, A 1, SA 2, A 2, [It, C, Tg, W, SA, A, F], 2004 E1, 2, Arg, PI, A1, SA1, A2, SA2, It, W, F, 2005 Fj, BI1(R), 2, 3, SA1, A1, SA2, A2, W, E, 2006 I1, 2, A1, SA1, A2, 3, SA2, 3, E, F1(R), 2, W, 2007 C, SA1, A1, SA2, A2, [It, Pt, F], 2008 I1, E1, 2(t), SA1, 2, A1, 2, SA3, Sm, A3, I2, W, E3, 2009 F1, 2, It1, A1, SA1, 2, A2, SA3, A3, 4, W, It2(R), E, F3, 2010 W2, SA1, 2, A1, 2, SA3, A3, 4, E, S, I2, W3, 2011 Fj, SA1, A1, 2, [C, Arg]
Muller, B L (Taranaki) 1967 A, E, W, F, 1968 A 1, F 1, 1969 W 1, 1970 SA 1, 2, 4, 1971 BI 1, 2, 3, 4

Mumm, W J (Buller) 1949 A 1
Murdoch, K (Otago) 1970 SA 4, 1972 A 3, W
Murdoch, P H (Auckland) 1964 A 2,3, 1965 SA 1,2,3
Murray, H V (Canterbury) 1913 A 1, US, 1914 A 2,3
Murray, P C (Wanganui) 1908 AW 2
Myers, R G (Waikato) 1978 A 3
Mynott, H J (Taranaki) 1905 I, W, 1906 F, 1907 A 1,2,3, 1910 A 1,3

Nathan, W J (Auckland) 1962 A 1,2,3,4,5, 1963 E 1,2, W, 1964 F, 1966 BI 1,2,3,4, 1967 A
Nelson, K A (Otago) 1962 A 4,5
Nepia, G (Hawke's Bay, East Coast) 1924 I, W, 1925 E, F, 1929 A 1, 1930 BI 1,2,3,4
Nesbit, S R (Auckland) 1960 SA 2,3
Newby, C A (North Harbour) 2004 E2(t),SA2(R), 2006 I2(R)
Newton, F (Canterbury) 1905 E, W, 1906 F
Nicholls, H E (Wellington) 1921 SA 1
Nicholls, M F (Wellington) 1921 SA 1,2,3, 1924 I, W, 1925 E, F, 1928 SA 4, 1930 BI 2,3
Nicholson, G W (Auckland) 1903 A, 1904 BI, 1907 A 2,3
Nonu, M A (Wellington) 2003 E, [It(R), C, Tg(R)], 2004 It(R), W(R), F(R), 2005 BI2(R), W(R), I, S(R), 2006 I1, E, F1(R), 2, W(R), 2007 F1(R), 2(R), 2008 I1, E1, 2, SA1, 2, A1, 2, SA3, Sm, A3, 4(R), S, I2, W, E3, 2009 F1, 2, It1, A1, SA1, 2, A2(t&R), SA3, A3, 4, W, E, F3, 2010 SA1, 2, A1, 2, SA3, A3, 4, E, I2, W3(R), 2011 Fj, SA1, A1, 2, [Tg, J, F1, Arg, A, F2], 2012 A1, 2, Arg1, SA1, Arg2, SA2, A3, It, W, E, 2013 F1, 2, 3, A1, 2, SA1, Arg2, SA2
Norton, R W (Canterbury) 1971 BI 1,2,3,4, 1972 A 1, 2, 3, W, S, 1973 E 1, I, F, E 2, 1974 A 1, 2, 3, I, 1975 S, 1976 I, SA 1, 2, 3, 4, 1977 BI 1, 2, 3, 4

O'Brien, J G (Auckland) 1914 A 1
O'Callaghan, M W (Manawatu) 1968 F 1,2,3
O'Callaghan, T R (Wellington) 1949 A 2
O'Donnell, D H (Wellington) 1949 A 2
O'Halloran, J D (Wellington) 2000 It (R)
Old, G H (Manawatu) 1981 SA 3, R (R), 1982 A 1(R)
O'Leary, M J (Auckland) 1910 A 1,3, 1913 A 2,3
Oliver, A D (Otago) 1997 Fj (t), 1998 E 1,2, A 1, SA 1, A 2, SA 2, A 3, 1999 WS, F 1, SA 1, A 1, SA 2, A 2, [Tg, E, S, F 2, SA 3(R)], 2000 Tg (R), S 1,2, A 1, SA 1, A 2, SA 2, F 1,2, It, 2001 Sm, Arg 1, F, SA 1, A 1, SA 2, A 2, I, S, Arg 2, 2003 E, F, 2004 It,F, 2005 W,S, 2006 Arg, SA1, 2, 3(R), F1, W, 2007 F2, SA1, A1, 2, [It(R), Pt(R), S, F]
Oliver, C J (Canterbury) 1929 A 1,2, 1934 A 1, 1935 S, I, W, 1936 E
Oliver, D J (Wellington) 1930 BI 1,2
Oliver, D O (Otago) 1954 I, F
Oliver, F J (Southland, Otago, Manawatu) 1976 SA 4, 1977 BI 1,2,3,4, F 1,2, 1978 A 1,2,3, I, W, E, S, 1979 F 1,2, 1981 SA 2
O'Neill, K J (Canterbury) 2008 SA2(R)
Orr, R W (Otago) 1949 A 1
Osborne, G M (North Harbour) 1995 C, [I, W, J, E, SA], A 1,2, F 1(R),2, 1996 SA 2,3,4,5, 1997 Arg 1(R), A 2,3, I, 1999 [It]
Osborne, W M (Wanganui) 1975 S, 1976 SA 2(R),4(R), 1977 BI 1,2,3,4, F 1(R),2, 1978 I, W, E, S, 1980 W, 1982 A 1,3
O'Sullivan, J M (Taranaki) 1905 S, I, E, W, 1907 A 3
O'Sullivan, T P A (Taranaki) 1960 SA 1, 1961 F 1, 1962 A 1,2

Page, J R (Wellington) 1931 A, 1932 A 1,2,3, 1934 A 1,2
Palmer, B P (Auckland) 1929 A 2, 1932 A 2,3
Parker, J H (Canterbury) 1924 I, W, 1925 E
Parkhill, A A (Otago) 1937 SA 1,2,3, 1938 A 1,2,3
Parkinson, R M (Poverty Bay) 1972 A 1,2,3, W, S, 1973 E 1,2
Paterson, A M (Otago) 1908 AW 2,3, 1910 A 1,2,3
Paton, H (Otago) 1910 A 1,3
Pene, A R B (Otago) 1992 Wld 1(R),2,3, I 1,2, A 1,2(R), 1993 BI 3, A, WS, S, E, 1994 F 1,2(R), SA 1(R)
Phillips, W J (King Country) 1937 SA 2, 1938 A 1,2
Philpott, S (Canterbury) 1991 [It (R), S (R)]
Pickering, E A R (Waikato) 1958 A 2, 1959 BI 1,4
Pierce, M J (Wellington) 1985 E 1, 2, A, Arg 1, 1986 A 2,3, F 2, 3, 1987 [It, Arg, S, W, F], A, 1988 W 1, 2, A 1,2,3, 1989 F 1, 2, Arg 1,2, A, W, I

Piutau, S T (Auckland) 2013 F3(R), A2(t&R), Arg1(R), SA1(R), Arg2(R), SA2(R)
Pokere, S T (Southland, Auckland) 1981 SA 3, 1982 A 1,2,3, 1983 BI 1,2,3,4, A, S, E, 1984 F 1,2, A 2,3, 1985 E 1,2, A
Pollock, H R (Wellington) 1932 A 1,2,3, 1936 A 1,2
Porter, C G (Wellington) 1925 F, 1929 A 2,3, 1930 BI 1,2,3,4
Preston, J P (Canterbury, Wellington) 1991 [US, S], 1992 SA (R), 1993 BI 2,3, A, WS, 1996 SA 4(R), 1997 I (R), E 1(R)
Procter, A C (Otago) 1932 A 1
Purdue, C A (Southland) 1905 A
Purdue, E (Southland) 1905 A
Purdue, G B (Southland) 1931 A, 1932 A 1,2,3
Purvis, G H (Waikato) 1991 [US], 1993 WS
Purvis, N A (Otago) 1976 I

Quaid, C E (Otago) 1938 A 1,2

Ralph, C S (Auckland, Canterbury) 1998 E 2, 2002 It, I 1,2, A 1, SA 1, A 2, SA 2, 2003 E, A 1(R), [C, Tg, SA(R), F(t&R)]
Ranby, R M (Waikato) 2001 Sm (R)
Randell, T C (Otago) 1997 Fj, Arg 1,2, A 1, SA 1, A 2, SA 2, A 3, I, E 1, W, E 2, 1998 E 1,2, A 1, SA 1, A 2, SA 2, A 3, 1999 WS, F 1, SA 1, A 1, SA 2, A 2, [Tg, E, It, S, F 2, SA 3], 2000 Tg, S 1,2(R), A 1, SA 1, A 2, SA 2, F 2(R), It (R), 2001 Arg 1, F, SA 1, A 1, SA 2, A 2, 2002 It, Fj, E, F, W
Ranger, R M N (Northland) 2010 W2(R),SA2,A3(R), 2013 F1(R),2(R),3
Rangi, R E (Auckland) 1964 A 2,3, 1965 SA 1,2,3,4, 1966 BI 1,2,3,4
Rankin, J G (Canterbury) 1936 A 1,2, 1937 SA 2
Rawlinson, G P (North Harbour) 2006 I1, 2(R), SA2, 2007 SA1
Read, K J (Canterbury) 2008 S, I2(R), E3(R), 2009 F1, 2, It1, A1(R), SA1(R), 2(R), A2, SA3, A3, 4(R), W, E, F3, 2010 I1, W1, 2, SA1, 2, A1, 2, SA3, A3, 4, E, S, I2, W3, 2011 A1, 2, [C, Arg, A, F2], 2012 I 1, 2, A1, 2, Arg1, SA1, Arg2, SA2, A3, It, W, E, 2013 F1, 2, 3, A1, 2, Arg1, SA1, Arg2, SA2
Reedy, W J (Wellington) 1908 AW 2,3
Reid, A R (Waikato) 1952 A 1, 1956 SA 3,4, 1957 A 1,2
Reid, H R (Bay of Plenty) 1980 A 1,2, W, 1983 S, E, 1985 Arg 1,2, 1986 A 2,3
Reid, K H (Wairarapa) 1929 A 1,3
Reid, S T (Hawke's Bay) 1935 S, I, W, 1936 E, A 1,2, 1937 SA 1,2,3
Reihana, B T (Waikato) 2000 F 2, It
Reside, W B (Wairarapa) 1929 A 1
Retallick, B A (Bay of Plenty) 2012 I1, 2, 3(R), A1(R),2(R), Arg1, SA1(R), Arg2(t&R), SA2, A3, It, W(R), E, 2013 F1, A1(R), 2, Arg1, SA1, Arg2, SA2
Rhind, P K (Canterbury) 1946 A 1,2
Richardson, J (Otago, Southland) 1921 SA 1,2,3, 1924 I, W, 1925 E, F
Rickit, H (Waikato) 1981 S 1,2
Riechelmann, C C (Auckland) 1997 Fj (R), Arg 1(R), A 1(R), SA 2(t), I (R), E 2(t)
Ridland, A J (Southland) 1910 A 1,2,3
Roberts, E J (Wellington) 1914 A 1,2,3, 1921 SA 2,3
Roberts, F (Wellington) 1905 S, I, E, W, 1907 A 1,2,3, 1908 AW 1,3, 1910 A 1,2,3
Roberts, R W (Taranaki) 1913 A 1, US, 1914 A 1,2,3
Robertson, B J (Counties) 1972 A 1,3, S, 1973 E 1, I, F, 1974 A 1,2,3, I, 1976 I, SA 1,2,3,4, 1977 BI 1,3,4, F 1,2, 1978 A 1,2,3, W, E, S, 1979 F 1,2, A, 1980 A 2,3, W, 1981 S 1,2
Robertson, D J (Otago) 1974 A 1,2,3, I, 1975 S, 1976 I, SA 1,3,4, 1977 BI 1
Robertson, S M (Canterbury) 1998 A 2(R), SA 2(R), A 3(R), 1999 [It (R)], 2000 Tg (R), S 1,2(R), A 1, SA 1(R),2(R), F 1,2, It, 2001 I, S, Arg 2, 2002 I 1,2, Fj (R), A 1, SA 1, A 2, SA 2
Robilliard, A C C (Canterbury) 1928 SA 1,2,3,4
Robinson, C E (Southland) 1951 A 1,2,3, 1952 A 1,2
Robinson, K J (Waikato) 2002 E, F (R), W, 2004 E1, 2, PI, 2006 E, W, 2007 SA2, A2, [R, F]
Robinson, M D (North Harbour) 1998 E 1(R), 2001 S (R), Arg 2
Robinson, M P (Canterbury) 2000 S 2, SA 1, 2002 It, I 2, A 1, SA 1, E (t&R), F, W (R)
Rokocoko, J T (Auckland) 2003 E, W, F, SA 1, A 1, SA 2, A 2, [It, W, SA, A, F], 2004 E1, 2,Arg, PI, A1, SA1, A2, SA2, It,

THE COUNTRIES

W, F, 2005 SA1(R), A1, SA2, A2, W, E(R), S, 2006 I1, 2, A1, 2, 3, SA3, E, F1, 2, 2007 F1, 2, SA1, A1, SA2, A2, [Pt, R, F], 2008 S, I2, W, E3, 2009 F1, 2, It1, SA1, 2, A2, SA3, A3, 2010 I1, W1, SA1, A1, 2, SA3, A4, E
Rollerson, D L (Manawatu) 1980 W, 1981 S 2, SA 1,2,3, R, F 1(R),2
Romano, L (Canterbury) 2012 I 3, A1, 2, Arg1, SA1, Arg2, SA2(R), A3(R), S, W, E(R), 2013 F1, 2, 3, A1
Roper, R A (Taranaki) 1949 A 2, 1950 BI 1,2,3,4
Ross, I B (Canterbury) 2009 F1, 2, It1, A1, SA1, 2, A2, SA3
Rowley, H C B (Wanganui) 1949 A 2
Rush, E J (North Harbour) 1995 [W (R), J], It, F 1,2, 1996 S 1(R),2, A 1(t), SA 1(R)
Rush, X J (Auckland) 1998 A 3, 2004 E1, 2, PI, A1, SA1, A2, SA2
Rutledge, L M (Southland) 1978 A 1, 2, 3, I, W, E, S, 1979 F 1,2, A, 1980 A 1,2,3
Ryan, J (Wellington) 1910 A 2, 1914 A 1,2,3
Ryan, J A C (Otago) 2005 Fj, BI3(R), A1(R), SA2(R), A2(R), W, S, 2006 F1, W(R)

Sadler, B S (Wellington) 1935 S, I, W, 1936 A 1,2
Saili, F (North Harbour) 2013 Arg1
Salmon, J L B (Wellington) 1981 R, F 1,2(R)
Savage, L T (Canterbury) 1949 SA 1,2,4
Savea, S J (Wellington) 2012 I 1, 2, Arg1, SA1, Arg2, S, It, W, E, 2013 F1, 2, A1, 2, Arg1, SA1, Arg2, SA2
Saxton, C K (South Canterbury) 1938 A 1, 2, 3
Schuler, K J (Manawatu, North Harbour) 1990 A 2(R), 1992 A 2, 1995 [I (R), J]
Schuster, N J (Wellington) 1988 A 1,2,3, 1989 F 1,2, Arg 1,2, A, W, I
Schwalger, J E (Wellington) 2007 C, 2008 I1(R)
Scott, R W H (Auckland) 1946 A 1,2, 1947 A 1,2, 1949 SA 1,2,3,4, 1950 BI 1,2,3,4, 1953 W, 1954 I, E, S, F
Scown, A I (Taranaki) 1972 A 1,2,3, W (R), S
Scrimshaw, G (Canterbury) 1928 SA 1
Seear, G A (Otago) 1977 F 1,2, 1978 A 1,2,3, I, W, E, S, 1979 F 1,2, A
Seeling, C E (Auckland) 1904 BI, 1905 S, I, E, W, 1906 F, 1907 A 1,2, 1908 AW 1,2,3
Sellars, G M V (Auckland) 1913 A 1, US
Senio, K (Bay of Plenty) 2005 A2(R)
Shaw, M W (Manawatu, Hawke's Bay) 1980 A 1,2,3(R), W, 1981 S 1,2, SA 1,2, R, F 1,2, 1982 A 1,2,3, 1983 BI 1,2,3,4, A, S, E, 1984 F 1,2, A 1, 1985 E 1,2, A, Arg 1,2, 1986 A 3
Shelford, F N K (Bay of Plenty) 1981 SA 3, R, 1984 A 2,3
Shelford, W T (North Harbour) 1986 F 2,3, 1987 [It, Fj, S, W, F], A, 1988 W 1,2, A 1,2,3, 1989 F 1,2, Arg 1,2, A, W, I, 1990 S 1,2
Siddells, S K (Wellington) 1921 SA 3
Simon, H J (Otago) 1937 SA 1,2,3
Simpson, J G (Auckland) 1947 A 1,2, 1949 SA 1,2,3,4, 1950 BI 1,2,3
Simpson, V L J (Canterbury) 1985 Arg 1,2
Sims, G S (Otago) 1972 A 2
Sivivatu, S W (Waikato) 2005 Fj, BI1, 2, 3, I, E, 2006 SA2, 3, E(R), F1, 2, W, 2007 F1, 2, C, SA1, A1(R), [It, S, R, F], 2008 I1, E1, 2, SA1, 2, A1, 2, SA3, A3, 4, I2, W, E3, 2009 A1, SA1, 2, A2, SA3, A4, It2, E, F3, 2011 Fj, A1
Skeen, J R (Auckland) 1952 A 2
Skinner, K L (Otago, Counties) 1949 SA 1, 2, 3, 4, 1950 BI 1, 2, 3, 4, 1951 A 1, 2, 3, 1952 A 1, 2, 1953 W, 1954 I, E, S, F, 1956 SA 3,4
Skudder, G R (Waikato) 1969 W 2
Slade, C R (Canterbury) 2010 A3(R), 2011 Fj, SA1(R), A1(R), SA2, [Tg(R), J, F1(R), C, Arg], 2013 A2(R)
Slater, G L (Taranaki) 2000 F 1(R),2(R), It (R)
Sloane, P H (North Auckland) 1979 E
Smith, A E (Taranaki) 1969 W 1,2, 1970 SA 1
Smith, A L (Manawatu) 2012 I 1, 2, 3, A1, 2, Arg1, SA1(R), Arg2, SA2, A3, It, W, E, 2013 F1, 2, A1, 2, Arg1, SA1, Arg2, SA2
Smith, B R (Otago) 2009 It 2, 2011 Fj(R), 2012 I 1(R), 2(R), 3, A2(R), Arg1(R), 2(R), A3(R), S, W(R), E(R), 2013 F1, 2, 3, A1, 2, Arg1, SA1, Arg2, SA2
Smith, B W (Waikato) 1984 F 1,2, A 1
Smith, C G (Wellington) 2004 It,F, 2005 Fj(R),BI3,W,S, 2006 F1,W, 2007 SA2(R), [Pt,S,R(R)], 2008 I1, E1, SA1, 2, A1(R), 2, SA3, Sm, A3, 4, I2, E3, 2009 F2, A1, SA1, 2, A2, 4, W, E, F3, 2010 I1, W1, SA1, 2, A1, 2, SA3, A3, 4, S, I2, W3, 2011 Fj, SA1, A1, 2, [J, F1, C, Arg, A, F2], 2012 I 1, 2, 3, Arg1, SA1, Arg2, SA2, A3, It, W, E, 2013 F1, 2, 3, A1, 2, Arg1, SA1, Arg2, SA2
Smith, G W (Auckland) 1905 S, I
Smith, I S T (Otago, North Otago) 1964 A 1,2,3, 1965 SA 1,2,4, 1966 BI 1,2,3
Smith, J B (North Auckland) 1946 A 1, 1947 A 2, 1949 A 1,2
Smith, R M (Canterbury) 1955 A 1
Smith, W E (Nelson) 1905 A
Smith, W R (Canterbury) 1980 A 1, 1982 A 1,2,3, 1983 BI 2,3, S, E, 1984 F 1,2, A 1,2,3, 1985 E 1,2, A, Arg 2
Snow, E M (Nelson) 1929 A 1,2,3
Solomon, F (Auckland) 1931 A, 1932 A 2,3
Somerville, G M (Canterbury) 2000 Tg, S 1, SA 2(R), F 1,2, It, 2001 Sm, Arg 1(R), F, SA 1, A 1, SA 2, A 2, I, S, Arg 2(t+R), 2002 I 1,2, A 1, SA 1, A 2, SA 2, 2003 E, F, SA 1, A 1, SA 2(R), A 2, [It, Tg, W, SA, A, F], 2004 Arg, SA1, A2(R), SA2(R), It(R), W, F(R), 2005 Fj, BI1(R)2, 3, SA1(R), A1(R), SA2(R), A2(R), 2006 Arg, A1(R), SA1(R), A2(R), 3(R), SA2, 2007 [Pt, R], 2008 E1, 2, SA1, A1, 2, SA3, Sm, A3, 4(R)
Sonntag, W T C (Otago) 1929 A 1,2,3
So'oialo, R (Wellington) 2002 W, 2003 E, SA 1(R), [It(R), C, Tg, W(t)], 2004 W, F, 2005 Fj, BI1, 2, 3, SA1, A1, SA2, A2, W, I(R), E, 2006 I1, 2, A1, SA1, A2, 3, SA3, E(R), F1, 2, W, 2007 F1(R), 2, SA1, A1, SA2, A2, [It, Pt(R), S, F], 2008 I1, E1, 2, SA1, 2, A1, 2, SA3, Sm, A3, 4, I2, W, E3, 2009 A1, SA1, 2, A2(R), 3(R), 4, It2
Speight, M W (Waikato) 1986 A 1
Spencer, C J (Auckland) 1997 Arg 1,2, A 1, SA 1, A 2, SA 2, A 3, E 2(R), 1998 E 2(R), A 1(R), SA 1, A 3(R), 2000 F 1(t&R), It, 2002 E, 2003 E, W, F, SA 1, A 1, SA 2, A 2, [It, C, Tg, W, SA, A, F], 2004 E1, 2, PI, A1, SA1, A2
Spencer, J C (Wellington) 1905 A, 1907 A 1(R)
Spiers, J E (Counties) 1979 S, E, 1981 R, F 1,2
Spillane, A P (South Canterbury) 1913 A 2,3
Stanley, B J (Auckland) 2010 I1,W1,2
Stanley, J T (Auckland) 1986 F 1, A 1,2,3, F 2,3, 1987 [It, Fj, Arg, S, W, F], A, 1988 W 1,2, A 1,2,3, 1989 F 1,2, Arg 1,2, A, W, I, 1990 S 1,2
Stead, J W (Southland) 1904 BI, 1905 S, I, E, 1906 F, 1908 AW 1,3
Steel, A G (Canterbury) 1966 BI 1,2,3,4, 1967 A, F, S, 1968 A 1,2
Steel, J (West Coast) 1921 SA 1,2,3, 1924 W, 1925 E, F
Steele, L B (Wellington) 1951 A 1,2,3
Steere, E R G (Hawke's Bay) 1930 BI 1,2,3,4, 1931 A, 1932 A 1
Steinmetz, P C (Wellington) 2002 W (R)
Stensness, L (Auckland) 1993 BI 3, A, WS, 1997 Fj, Arg 1,2, A 1, SA 1
Stephens, O G (Wellington) 1968 F 3
Stevens, I N (Wellington) 1972 S, 1973 E 1, 1974 A 3
Stewart, A J (Canterbury, South Canterbury) 1963 E 1,2, I, W, 1964 E, S, F, A 3
Stewart, J D (Auckland) 1913 A 2,3
Stewart, K W (Southland) 1973 E 2, 1974 A 1,2,3, I, 1975 S, 1976 I, SA 1,3, 1979 S, E, 1981 SA 1,2
Stewart, R T (South Canterbury, Canterbury) 1928 SA 1,2,3,4, 1930 BI 2
Stohr, L B (Taranaki) 1910 A 1,2,3
Stone, A M (Waikato, Bay of Plenty) 1981 F 1,2, 1983 BI 3(R), 1984 A 3, 1986 F 1, A 1,3, F 2,3
Storey, P W (South Canterbury) 1921 SA 1,2
Strachan, A D (Auckland, North Harbour) 1992 Wld 2,3, I 1,2, A 1,2,3, SA, 1993 BI 1, 1995 [J, SA (t)]
Strahan, S C (Manawatu) 1967 A, E, W, F, S, 1968 A 1,2, F 1,2,3, 1970 SA 1,2,3, 1972 A 1,2,3, 1973 E 2
Strang, W A (South Canterbury) 1928 SA 1,2, 1930 BI 3,4, 1931 A
Stringfellow, J C (Wairarapa) 1929 A 1(R),3
Stuart, K C (Canterbury) 1955 A 1
Stuart, R C (Canterbury) 1949 A 1,2, 1953 W, 1954 I, E, S, F
Stuart, R L (Hawke's Bay) 1977 F 1(R)

Sullivan, J L (Taranaki) 1937 SA 1,2,3, 1938 A 1,2,3
Sutherland, A R (Marlborough) 1970 SA 2,4, 1971 BI 1, 1972 A 1,2,3, W, 1973 E 1, I, F
Svenson, K S (Wellington) 1924 I, W, 1925 E, F
Swain, J P (Hawke's Bay) 1928 SA 1,2,3,4

Tanner, J M (Auckland) 1950 BI 4, 1951 A 1,2,3, 1953 W
Tanner, K J (Canterbury) 1974 A 1,2,3, I, 1975 S, 1976 I, SA 1
Taumoepeau, S (Auckland) 2004 It, 2005 I(R),S
Taylor, G L (Northland) 1996 SA 5(R)
Taylor, H M (Canterbury) 1913 A 1, US, 1914 A 1,2,3
Taylor, J M (Otago) 1937 SA 1,2,3, 1938 A 1,2,3
Taylor, M B (Waikato) 1979 F 1,2, A, S, E, 1980 A 1,2
Taylor, N M (Bay of Plenty, Hawke's Bay) 1977 BI 2,4(R), F 1,2, 1978 A 1,2,3, I, 1982 A 2
Taylor, R (Taranaki) 1913 A 2,3
Taylor, T J (Canterbury) 2013 A2
Taylor, W T (Canterbury) 1983 BI 1,2,3,4, A, S, 1984 F 1,2, A 1,2, 1985 E 1,2, A, Arg 1,2, 1986 A 2, 1987 [It, Fj, S, W, F], A, 1988 W 1,2
Tetzlaff, P L (Auckland) 1947 A 1,2
Thimbleby, N W (Hawke's Bay) 1970 SA 3
Thomas, B T (Auckland, Wellington) 1962 A 5, 1964 A 1,2,3
Thomson, A J (Otago) 2008 I1(t&R), E2, SA1, 2, A2(R), SA3(R), Sm, A4(t&R), S, 2009 F1, SA3(R), A3, 4, W(R), E, 2010 W1(R), 2(R), 2011 Fj, SA1, A1(R), SA2, A2, [J, F1], 2012 I1(R), 2, 3(R), SA2(R), S
Thomson, H D (Wellington) 1908 AW 1
Thorn, B C (Canterbury, Tasman) 2003 W (R), F (R), SA 1(R), A 1(R), SA 2,[It, C, Tg, W, SA(R), A(R), F(R)], 2008 I1, E1, 2, SA1, A1, 2, SA3, A3, 4, I2, W, E3, 2009 F1, 2, It1, A1, SA1, 2, A2,S A3, A3, 4, W, E, F3, 2010 I1, W1, 2, SA1, 2, A1, 2, SA3, A3, 4, E, S, W3, 2011 A1, 2, [Tg, J, F1, C(R), Arg, A, F2]
Thorne, G S (Auckland) 1968 A 1,2, F 1,2,3, 1969 W 1, 1970 SA 1, 2, 3, 4
Thorne, R D (Canterbury) 1999 SA 2(R), [Tg, E, S, F 2, SA 3], 2000 Tg, S 2, A 2(R), F 1,2, 2001 Sm, Arg 1, F, SA 1, A 1, I, S, Arg 2, 2002 It, I 1,2, Fj, A 1, SA 1, A2, SA 2, 2003 E, W, F, SA 1, A 1, SA 2, A 2, [It, C, Tg, W, SA, A, F], 2006 SA1, 2, E, W(R), 2007 F1, C, SA2, [S, R]
Thornton, N H (Auckland) 1947 A 1,2, 1949 SA 1
Thrush, J I (Wellington) 2013 F2(R),Arg1(R),2(R)
Tialata, N S (Wellington) 2005 W, E(t), S(R), 2006 I1(R), 2(R), Arg(R), SA1, 2, 3(R), F1(R), 2(R), W, 2007 F1(R), 2(R), C, A1(R), SA2(R), [It(t&R), Pt, S(R), R], 2008 I1, E1, 2, SA1(R), 2(R), Sm(R), A4, S(R), I2, W, E3, 2009 F1, 2, A1, SA1, A3, 4, W, It2, F3, 2010 I1(R), W2
Tiatia, F I (Wellington) 2000 Tg (R), It
Tilyard, J T (Wellington) 1913 A 3
Timu, J K R (Otago) 1991 Arg 1, A 1,2, [E, US, C, A], 1992 Wld 2, I 2, A 1, 2, 3, SA, 1993 BI 1, 2, 3, A, WS, S, E, 1994 F 1, 2, SA 1, 2, 3, A
Tindill, E W T (Wellington) 1936 E
Todd, M B (Canterbury) 2013 F3(R),SA1(t)
Toeava, I (Auckland) 2005 S, 2006 Arg, A1(t&R), A3, SA2(R), 2007 F1, 2, SA1, 2, A2, [It(R), Pt, S(R), R, F(R)], 2008 SA3(R), Sm(R), A4, S, I2(R), E3(R), 2009 F1, 2(R), It1, SA3(R), A3, 2010 A4(R), E(R), S, W3, 2011 SA2, A2(R), [Tg, J, C(R), Arg(R)]
Tonu'u, O F J (Auckland) 1997 Fj (R), A 3(R), 1998 E 1, 2, SA 1(R)
Townsend, L J (Otago) 1955 A 1,3
Tremain, K R (Canterbury, Hawke's Bay) 1959 BI 2, 3, 4, 1960 SA 1, 2, 3, 4, 1961 F 2, 3 1962 A 1, 2, 3, 1963 E 1,2, I, W, 1964 E, S, F, A 1, 2, 3, 1965 SA 1, 2, 3, 4, 1966 BI 1, 2, 3, 4, 1967 A, E, W, S, 1968 A 1, F 1, 2, 3
Trevathan, D (Otago) 1937 SA 1,2,3
Tuck, J M (Waikato) 1929 A 1, 2, 3
Tuiali'i, M M (Auckland) 2004 Arg, A2(R), SA2(R), It, W, 2005 I, E(R), S(R), 2006 Arg
Tuigamala, V L (Auckland) 1991 [US, It, C, S], 1992 Wld 1,2,3, I 1, A 1, 2, 3, SA, 1993 BI 1, 2, 3, A, WS, S, E
Tuitavake, A S M (North Harbour) 2008 I1, E1, A1, 2(R), Sm, S
Tuitupou, S (Auckland) 2004 E1(R), 2(R), Arg, SA1(R), A2(R), SA2, 2006 Arg, SA1, 2(R)
Turner, R S (North Harbour) 1992 Wld 1,2(R)
Turtill, H S (Canterbury) 1905 A
Twigden, T M (Auckland) 1980 A 2,3
Tyler, G A (Auckland) 1903 A, 1904 BI, 1905 S, I, E, W, 1906 F

Udy, D K (Wairarapa) 1903 A
Umaga, J F (Wellington) 1997 Fj, Arg 1,2, A 1, SA 1,2, 1999 WS, F 1, SA 1, A 1, SA 2, A 2, [Tg, E, S, F 2, SA 3], 2000 Tg, S 1,2, A 1, SA 1, A 2, SA 2, F 1,2, It, 2001 Sm, Arg 1, F, SA 1, A 1, SA 2, A 2, I, S, Arg 2, 2002 I 1, Fj, SA 1(R), A 2, SA 2, E, F, W, 2003 E, W, F, SA 1, A 1, SA 2, A 2, [It], 2004 E1, 2, Arg, PI, A1, SA1, A2, SA2, It, F, 2005 Fj, BI1, 2, 3, SA1, A1, SA2, A2, W, E, S
Urbahn, R J (Taranaki) 1959 BI 1,3,4
Urlich, R A (Auckland) 1970 SA 3,4
Uttley, I N (Wellington) 1963 E 1,2

Vidiri, J (Counties Manukau) 1998 E 2(R), A 1
Vincent, P B (Canterbury) 1956 SA 1,2
Vito, V V J (Wellington) 2010 I1(R), W1, A1(R), 2(R), SA3(R), A3, 2011 SA2(R), A2(R), [Tg, J, C, Arg(R), A(R)], 2012 I 1, A2(R), Arg1, A3(R), S, W(R), E(R), 2013 F2(R),3
Vodanovich, I M H (Wellington) 1955 A 1, 2, 3

Wallace, W J (Wellington) 1903 A, 1904 BI, 1905 S, I, E, W, 1906 F, 1907 A 1, 2, 3, 1908 AW 2
Waller, D A G (Wellington) 2001 Arg 2(t)
Walsh, P T (Counties) 1955 A 1, 2, 3, 1956 SA 1, 2, 4, 1957 A 1,2, 1958 A 1, 2, 3, 1959 BI 1, 1963 E 2
Ward, R H (Southland) 1936 A 2, 1937 SA 1,3
Waterman, A C (North Auckland) 1929 A 1,2
Watkins, E L (Wellington) 1905 A
Watt, B A (Canterbury) 1962 A 1,4, 1963 E 1,2, W, 1964 E, S, A 1
Watt, J M (Otago) 1936 A 1,2
Watt, J R (Wellington) 1958 A 2, 1960 SA 1,2,3,4, 1961 F 1,3, 1962 A 1,2
Watts, M G (Taranaki) 1979 F 1,2, 1980 A 1,2,3(R)
Webb, D S (North Auckland) 1959 BI 2
Weepu, P A T (Wellington, Auckland) 2004 W, 2005 SA1(R), A1, SA2, A2, I, E(R), S, 2006 Arg, A1(R), SA1, A3(R), SA2, F1, W(R), 2007 F1, C(R), SA1(R), A1(R), SA2, 2008 A2(R), SA3(R), Sm(R), A3(R), 4(R), S, I2(R), W(R), E3(R), 2009 F1(R), 2(R), It1(R), A1(R), SA1(R), 2(R), 2010 I1(R), W1(R), 2(R), SA1(R), 2, A1(R), 2, SA3(R), A3, 2011 Fj(R), SA1(R), A1, SA2(R), A2, [Tg(R), J(R), F1, C(R), Arg, A, F2], 2012 I 1(R), 2(R), 3(R), A1(R), 2(R), Arg1(R), SA1, Arg2(R), SA2(R), A3(R), S, W(R), E(R), 2013 F2(R), 3
Wells, J (Wellington) 1936 A 1,2
West, A H (Taranaki) 1921 SA 2,3
Whetton, A J (Auckland) 1984 A 1(R),3(R), 1985 A (R), Arg 1(R), 1986 A 2, 1987 [It, Fj, Arg, S, W, F], A, 1988 W 1,2, A 1,2,3, 1989 F 1,2, Arg 1,2, A, 1990 S 1,2, A 1,2,3, F 1,2, 1991 Arg 1, [E, US, It, C, A]
Whetton, G W (Auckland) 1981 SA 3, R, F 1,2, 1982 A 3, 1983 BI 1,2,3,4, 1984 F 1,2, A 1,2,3, 1985 E 1,2, A, Arg 2, 1986 A 2,3, F 2,3, 1987 [It, Fj, Arg, S, W, F], A, 1988 W 1,2, A 1,2,3, 1989 F 1,2, Arg 1,2, A, W, I, 1990 S 1,2, A 1,2,3, F 1,2, 1991 Arg 1,2, A 1,2, [E, US, It, C, A, S]
Whineray, W J (Canterbury, Waikato, Auckland) 1957 A 1,2, 1958 A 1,2,3, 1959 BI 1,2,3,4, 1960 SA 1,2,3,4, 1961 F 1,2,3, 1962 A 1,2,3,4,5, 1963 E 1,2, I, W, 1964 E, S, F, 1965 SA 1,2,3,4
White, A (Southland) 1921 SA 1, 1924 I, 1925 E, F
White, H L (Auckland) 1954 I, E, F, 1955 A 3
White, R A (Poverty Bay) 1949 A 1,2, 1950 BI 1,2,3,4, 1951 A 1,2,3, 1952 A 1,2, 1953 W, 1954 I, E, S, F, 1955 A 1,2,3, 1956 SA 1,2,3,4
White, R M (Wellington) 1946 A 1,2, 1947 A 1,2
Whitelock, G B (Canterbury) 2009 It1(R)
Whitelock, S L (Canterbury) 2010 I1(R), W1(R), 2(R), SA1(R), 2(R), A1(R), 2(R), SA3(R), A4(R), E, S, I2(R), W3, 2011 Fj(R), SA1, A1(R), SA2, A2, [Tg(R), J, F1, C, Arg, A, F2], 2012 I 1, 2, 3, A1, 2, Arg1(R), SA1, Arg2, SA2, A3, S, It(R), W, E, 2013 F2, 3, A1, 2, Arg1, SA1, Arg2, SA2
Whiting, G J (King Country) 1972 A 1,2, S, 1973 E 1, I, F

Whiting, P J (Auckland) 1971 BI 1,2,4, 1972 A 1,2,3, W, S, 1973 E 1, I, F, 1974 A 1,2,3, I, 1976 I, SA 1,2,3,4

Williams, A J (Auckland, Tasman) 2002 E, F, W, 2003 E, W, F, SA 1, A 1, SA 2, A 2, [Tg, W, SA, A, F], 2004 SA1(R), A2, It(R), W, F(R), 2005 Fj, BI1, 2, 3, SA1, A1, SA2, A2, I, E, 2006 Arg, A1(R), SA1, A2, 3(R), SA2, 3, F1, 2, W, 2007 F1, 2, [It, Pt, S, F], 2008 I1, E1, 2, SA1, 2, A1, 2, SA3, Sm, A3, 4, S, I2, W, E3, 2011 Fj, SA1, A1, SA2, A2(R), [Tg, J(R), F1(R), C, Arg(R), A(R), F2(R)], 2012 I 1(R), 2(R), S(R), It

Williams, B G (Auckland) 1970 SA 1,2,3,4, 1971 BI 1,2,4, 1972 A 1,2,3, W, S, 1973 E 1, I, F, E 2, 1974 A 1,2,3, I, 1975 S, 1976 I, SA 1,2,3,4, 1977 BI 1,2,3,4, F 1, 1978 A 1,2,3, I (R), W, E, S

Williams, G C (Wellington) 1967 E, W, F, S, 1968 A 2

Williams, P (Otago) 1913 A 1

Williams, S (Canterbury) 2010 E, S, I2(R), W3, 2011 SA1(R), A1(R), SA2, [Tg, J(R), F1(R), C, Arg, A(R), F2(R)], 2012 I 1, 2, 3, A1, 2

Williment, M (Wellington) 1964 A 1, 1965 SA 1,2,3, 1966 BI 1,2,3,4, 1967 A

Willis, R K (Waikato) 1998 SA 2, A 3, 1999 SA 1(R), A 1(R), SA 2(R), A 2(R), [Tg (R), E (R), It, F 2(R), SA 3], 2002 SA 1(R)

Willis, T E (Otago) 2002 It, Fj, SA 2(R), A 2, SA 2

Willocks, C (Otago) 1946 A 1,2, 1949 SA 1,3,4

Wilson, B W (Otago) 1977 BI 3,4, 1978 A 1,2,3, 1979 F 1,2, A

Wilson, D D (Canterbury) 1954 E, S

Wilson, H W (Otago) 1949 A 1, 1950 BI 4, 1951 A 1,2,3

Wilson, J W (Otago) 1993 S, E, 1994 A, 1995 C, [I, J, S, E, SA], A 1,2, It, F 1, 1996 WS, S 1,2, A 1, SA 1, A 2, SA 2,3,4,5, 1997 Fj, Arg 1,2, A 1, SA 1, A 2, SA 2, A 3, I, E 1, W, E 2, 1998 E 1,2, A 1, SA 1, A 2, SA 2, A 3, 1999 WS, F 1, SA 1, A 1, SA 2, A 2, [Tg, E, It, S, F 2, SA 3], 2001 Sm, Arg 1, F, SA 1, A 1, SA 2

Wilson, N A (Wellington) 1908 AW 1,2, 1910 A 1,2,3, 1913 A 2,3, 1914 A 1,2,3

Wilson, N L (Otago) 1951 A 1,2,3

Wilson, R G (Canterbury) 1979 S, E

Wilson, S S (Wellington) 1977 F 1,2, 1978 A 1,2,3, I, W, E, S, 1979 F 1,2, A, S, E, 1980 A 1, W, 1981 S 1,2, SA 1,2,3, R, F 1,2, 1982 A 1,2,3, 1983 BI 1,2,3,4, A, S, E

Witcombe, D J C (Auckland) 2005 Fj,BI1(R),2(R),SA1(R),A1(R)

Wolfe, T N (Wellington, Taranaki) 1961 F 1, 2, 3, 1962 A 2, 3, 1963 E 1

Wood, M E (Canterbury, Auckland) 1903 A, 1904 BI

Woodcock, T D (North Harbour) 2002 W, 2004 E1(t&R), 2(t&R), Arg, W, F, 2005 Fj, BI1, 2, 3, SA1, A1, SA2, A2, W(R), I, E, 2006 Arg, A1, 2, 3, SA2(R), 3, E, F1, 2, W(R), 2007 F1, 2, SA1, A1, SA2, A2, [It, Pt(R), S, F], 2008 E2(R), SA1, 2, A1, 2, SA3, Sm, A3, 4, I2, W, E3, 2009 F1, 2, It1(R), A1, SA1, 2, A2, SA3, A3, 4, E, F3, 2010 W1(R), 2, SA1, 2, A1, 2, SA3, A3, 4, E, S, I2, W3, 2011 SA2, A2, [Tg, J, F1, C, Arg, A, F2], 2012 I 1, 2, 3, A1, Arg1, SA1, Arg2, SA2, A3, S(R), It, W, E, 2013 F2(R), 3(R), A1, 2, Arg1, SA1, Arg2, SA2

Woodman, F A (North Auckland) 1981 SA 1,2, F 2

Wrigley, E (Wairarapa) 1905 A

Wright, T J (Auckland) 1986 F 1, A 1, 1987 [Arg], 1988 W 1, 2, A 1, 2, 3, 1989 F 1, 2, Arg 1, 2, A, W, I, 1990 S 1, 2, A 1, 2, 3, F 1,2, 1991 Arg 1, 2, A 1, 2, [E, US, It, S]

Wulf, R N (North Harbour) 2008 E2, SA1, 2, Sm(R)

Wylie, J T (Auckland) 1913 A 1, US

Wyllie, A J (Canterbury) 1970 SA 2, 3, 1971 BI 2, 3, 4, 1972 W, S, 1973 E 1, I, F, E 2

Yates, V M (North Auckland) 1961 F 1,2,3

Young, D (Canterbury) 1956 SA 2, 1958 A 1, 2, 3, 1960 SA 1, 2, 3, 4, 1961 F 1, 2, 3, 1962 A 1, 2, 3, 5, 1963 E 1, 2, I, W, 1964 E, S, F

Oyonnax second row Valentin Ursache is one of several Romanians playing club rugby in France.

AFP/Getty Images

ROMANIA

ROMANIA'S 2012–13 TEST RECORD

OPPONENTS	DATE	VENUE	RESULT
Japan	10 Nov	H	Lost 23–34
USA	24 Nov	H	Lost 3–34
Portugal	2 Feb	A	Won 19–13
Russia	9 Feb	H	Won 29–14
Spain	23 Feb	A	Won 25–15
Belgium	9 Mar	A	Won 32–14
Georgia	16 Mar	H	Drew 9–9
Russia	8 Jun	H	Won 30–20

HOWELLS TAKES THE REINS

By Chris Thau

Razvan Pasarica

Romania beat Russia 30–20 on their way to winning the IRB Nations Cup for a second successive year.

By the end of November 2012, the euphoria that had engulfed Romanian rugby in the aftermath of their IRB Nations Cup success in June had dissipated under the heat generated by defeats to Japan and the USA.

Romania were pumped up for the first Test against Japan, but the Brave Blossoms' coach Eddie Jones had prepared his side well for the traditional forward strength of their hosts. So, time and time again, the Romanians, led by flanker Mihai Macovei, ran into a well-organised Japanese defence and were rarely able to dent it, often left bemused and disheartened by their opponents' pace and guile in the 34–23 win.

The second Test against the Eagles added insult to injury, with Romania out-muscled, out-thought and outplayed by a fitter, stronger and faster team. The 34–3 defeat in itself was not a disaster, but the manner of it must have given the Federaţia Română de Rugby's senior management food for thought with the Rugby World Cup 2015 qualifying process looming large on the horizon. It was duly decided that coach Haralambie Dumitras should step down after less than a year in charge, with the Union's director of rugby Lynn Howells taking over as head coach.

Having been around for several months as director of rugby, the appointment did not come as a complete change of scenery for Howells or the players. It was more a subtle act of rearranging priorities with the European Nations Cup 2014 – which doubled as the region's qualifying process for England 2015 – becoming the main objective. The best players available were selected for the matches and Romania played to win, which they did in increasingly confident fashion.

By the end of March and the halfway stage of the qualification process, it was mission accomplished with Romania lying second to Georgia on points differential after both recorded four wins and a draw. A similar return in February and March 2014 will be enough to secure Romania one of Europe's two direct qualification places at RWC 2015 and ensure they do not have to negotiate the Répechage as they did to take their place at New Zealand 2011.

Romania began their European Nations Cup campaign in Lisbon against a Portugal side who are always a tough nut to crack on home soil, and so it proved with the Oaks triumphing 19–13. A week later, at home in Bucharest, Romania overcame Russia 29–14, although the score did somewhat flatter the Oaks who will expect a strong backlash when the sides meet again on Russian soil.

With the Division 1A teams all ranked so closely together in the IRB World Rankings – they occupied 16th to 21st when the competition kicked off – there are no easy matches nowadays. Romania's third match took them to Spain, and this time it was Florin Vlaicu's boot that did most of the damage, complemented by a brilliant try by Catalin Fercu, in the 25–15 victory.

A fortnight later Romania travelled to Brussels to face Belgium and found the match less demanding than initially thought, running out 32–14 winners and collecting their first try-bonus point of the campaign. The final act in part one was the visit of table-toppers Georgia, but nothing could split the teams and the match was far more exciting than the 9–9 score suggests. Vlaicu turned the Romanian labour up front into points, but Georgia retained the Antim Cup, which is played for every time the two nations cross swords.

With RWC 2015 qualification on track, Howells's next priority was to widen the selection base for the national team. "If we want to do ourselves justice in the Rugby World Cup we need at least 40 players of a reasonable high standard," he explained. "We need competition for positions. My role is to find these players and, because I cannot speak Romanian, I have to rely on what I see rather than what I am told. I am pleased to say that I have seen talent and have acted accordingly.

"At the same time I am trying to free players from the fear factor that is still so strong in Romanian rugby. I want them to try things, to feel free to play what's in front of them, without fear of making mistakes. This is why I want to give youngsters opportunities, rather than look for established players."

Indeed the IRB Nations Cup in June enabled Howells to experiment by giving seven players the opportunity to experience the intensity of Test rugby for the first time in props Constantin Pristavita, Alex Tarus and Silviu Suciu, teenage flanker Vlad Nistor, and backs Ionut Dumitru, Florin Ionita and Stephen Hihetah, the latter the first UK-born player to wear the Romanian jersey. More and probably better will follow, as the group gets stronger and more confident.

A full house of nearly 6,000 at the Stadionul National Arcul de Triumf in Bucharest cheered on Romania in the winner-takes-all match against the unbeaten Emerging Italy on the final day of the Nations Cup. Full back Fercu was the star of the show with two tries as Romania prevailed 26–13 to defend the title successfully. Romania had earlier opened their Nations Cup campaign with an error-strewn 30–20 victory over Russia and then produced a more coherent display to see off the Argentina Jaguars 30–8 to battle with Emerging Italy once again for the silverware.

Only time will tell if the feel-good factor from this IRB Nations Cup success will last and allow Romania to build momentum through the November internationals and into the climax of the European Nations Cup as they look to preserve their ever-present record on the RWC stage.

On the domestic front, the Romanian season had begun in April 2012 and ended in early December with the CEC Bank Super League final. After a 40-year wait Timisoara University, coached by Springbok legend Chester Williams, won the National Championship title, challenged all the way by former champions Baia Mare, the winners of the FRR Cup. Baia Mare finished the regular season on top of the table with 57 points, followed by Timisoara (56) and the Army club Steaua (46). In the play-offs Baia Mare topped the table from Timisoara, but in the final the students managed to turn the tables on their Baia Mare counterparts to win 16–6, with 21-year-old sensation Gabriel Conache coming off the bench to score 13 of Timisoara's points.

ROMANIA INTERNATIONAL STATISTICS

MATCH RECORDS UP TO 10 OCTOBER 2013

WINNING MARGIN

Date	Opponent	Result	Winning Margin
21/09/1976	Bulgaria	100–0	**100**
19/03/2005	Ukraine	97–0	**97**
13/04/1996	Portugal	92–0	**92**
17/11/1976	Morocco	89–0	**89**
19/04/1996	Belgium	83–5	**78**

MOST POINTS IN A MATCH

BY THE TEAM

Date	Opponent	Result	Points
21/09/1976	Bulgaria	100–0	**100**
19/03/2005	Ukraine	97–0	**97**
13/04/1996	Portugal	92–0	**92**
17/11/1976	Morocco	89–0	**89**

BY A PLAYER

Date	Player	Opponent	Points
05/10/2002	Ionut Tofan	Spain	**30**
13/04/1996	Virgil Popisteanu	Portugal	**27**
04/02/2001	Petre Mitu	Portugal	**27**
13/04/1996	Ionel Rotaru	Portugal	**25**

MOST TRIES IN A MATCH

BY THE TEAM

Date	Opponent	Result	Tries
17/11/1976	Morocco	89–0	**17**
21/10/1951	East Germany	64–26	**16**
19/03/2005	Ukraine	97–0	**15**
16/04/1978	Spain	74–3	**14**

BY A PLAYER

Date	Player	Opponent	Tries
30/04/1972	Gheorghe Rascanu	Morocco	**5**
18/10/1986	Cornel Popescu	Portugal	**5**
13/04/1996	Ionel Rotaru	Portugal	**5**

MOST CONVERSIONS IN A MATCH

BY THE TEAM

Date	Opponent	Result	Cons
13/04/1996	Portugal	92–0	**12**
19/03/2005	Ukraine	97–0	**11**
04/10/1997	Belgium	83–13	**10**

BY A PLAYER

Date	Player	Opponent	Cons
13/04/1996	Virgil Popisteanu	Portugal	**12**
04/10/1997	Serban Guranescu	Belgium	**10**
19/03/2005	Marin Danut Dumbrava	Ukraine	**8**
22/03/2008	Florin Adrian Vlaicu	Czech Republic	**8**

MOST PENALTIES IN A MATCH

BY THE TEAM

Date	Opponent	Result	Pens
15/06/2010	Argentina Jaguars	24–8	**7**
14/05/1994	Italy	26–12	**6**
04/02/2001	Portugal	47–0	**6**
23/02/2013	Spain	25–15	**6**

BY A PLAYER

Date	Player	Opponent	Pens
14/05/1994	Neculai Nichitean	Italy	**6**
04/02/2001	Petre Mitu	Portugal	**6**
23/02/2013	Florin Vlaicu	Spain	**6**

MOST DROP GOALS IN A MATCH

BY THE TEAM

Date	Opponent	Result	DGs
29/10/1967	West Germany	27–5	**4**
14/11/1965	West Germany	9–8	**3**
17/10/1976	Poland	38–8	**3**
03/10/1990	Spain	19–6	**3**

BY A PLAYER

Date	Player	Opponent	DGs
29/10/1967	Valeriu Irimescu	West Germany	**3**
17/10/1976	Alexandru Dumitru	Poland	**3**

MOST CAPPED PLAYERS

Player	Caps
Cristian Petre	91
Adrian Lungu	77
Romeo Stefan Gontineac	77
Lucian Mihai Sirbu	77
Gabriel Brezoianu	72

LEADING PENALTY SCORERS

Player	Pens
Danut Dumbrava	70
Florin Vlaicu	63
Neculai Nichitean	53
Petre Mitu	53

LEADING TRY SCORERS

Player	Tries
Petre Motrescu	33
Gabriel Brezoianu	28
Florica Murariu	27

LEADING DROP GOAL SCORERS

Player	DGs
Alexandru Dumitru	14
Neculai Nichitean	10
Valeriu Irimescu	10
Gelu Ignat	8

LEADING CONVERSION SCORERS

Player	Cons
Danut Dumbrava	69
Florin Vlaicu	69
Petre Mitu	53
Ionut Tofan	52

LEADING POINT SCORERS

Player	Points
Marin Danut Dumbrava	369
Florin Vlaicu	358
Petre Mitu	335
Ionut Tofan	322
Neculai Nichitean	257

ROMANIA INTERNATIONAL PLAYERS

UP TO 10 OCTOBER 2013

A Achim 1974 *Pol*, 1976 *Pol*, *Mor*
M Adascalitei 2007 *Rus*, 2009 *Pt*, *Ur*, *F*, *ItA*, 2012 *Ukr*, *Ur*
Ailenei 2012 *Ukr*
M Aldea 1979 *USS*, *W*, *Pol*, *F*, 1980 *It*, *USS*, *I*, *F*, 1981 *It*, *Sp*, *USS*, *S*, *NZ*, *F*, 1982 *WGe*, *It*, *USS*, *Z*, *Z*, *F*, 1983 *Mor*, *WGe*, *It*, *USS*, *Pol*, *W*, *USS*, *F*, 1984 *It*, *S*, *F*, 1985 *E*, *USS*
C Alexandrescu 1934 *It*
N Anastasiade 1927 *Cze*, 1934 *It*
V Anastasiade 1939 *It*
I Andrei 2003 *W*, *I*, *Ar*, *Nm*, 2004 *CZR*, *Pt*, *Sp*, *Rus*, *Geo*, *It*, *W*, *J*, *CZR*, 2005 *Rus*, *US*, *S*, *Pt*, 2006 *CZR*, 2007 *Pt*, 2008 *Sp*, *Pt*, *Rus*
I Andriesi 1937 *It*, *H*, *Ger*, 1938 *F*, *Ger*, 1939 *It*, 1940 *It*
E Apjok 1996 *Bel*, 2000 *It*, 2001 *Pt*
AM Apostol 2011 *Nm*, *E*, 2012 *Rus*, *Geo*, *Sp*, 2013 *Pt*, *Sp*, *Bel*, *Geo*
D Armasel 1924 *F*, *US*
A Atanasiu 1970 *It*, *F*, 1971 *It*, *Mor*, *F*, 1972 *Mor*, *Cze*, *WGe*, 1973 *Sp*, *Mor*, *Ar*, *Ar*, *WGe*, 1974 *Pol*

I Bacioiu 1976 *USS*, *Bul*, *Pol*, *F*, *Mor*
N Baciu 1964 *Cze*, *EGe*, 1967 *It*, *F*, 1968 *Cze*, *Cze*, *F*, 1969 *Pol*, *WGe*, *F*, 1970 *It*, 1971 *It*, *Mor*, *F*, 1972 *Mor*, *Cze*, *WGe*, 1973 *Ar*, *Ar*, 1974 *Cze*, *EGe*
VC Badalicescu 2012 *Pt*, *J*
B Balan 2003 *Pt*, *Sp*, *Geo*, 2004 *W*, 2005 *Rus*, *Ukr*, *J*, *US*, *S*, *Pt*, 2006 *Geo*, *Pt*, *Ukr*, *Rus*, *F*, *Geo*, *Sp*, *S*, 2007 *Sp*, *ESp*, *ItA*, *Nm*, *It*, *S*, *Pt*, *NZ*, 2009 *Fj*, 2010 *Ger*, *Rus*, *Ur*, *Ur*, 2011 *Pt*
D Balan 1983 *F*
PV Balan 1998 *H*, *Pol*, *Ukr*, *Ar*, *Geo*, *I*, 1999 *F*, *S*, *A*, *US*, *I*, 2000 *Mor*, *H*, *Pt*, *Sp*, *Geo*, *F*, *It*, 2001 *Pt*, *Sp*, *H*, *Rus*, *Geo*, *I*, *E*, 2002 *Pt*, *Sp*, *H*, *Rus*, *Geo*, *Sp*, *S*, *S*, 2003 *CZR*, *F*, *W*, *I*, *Nm*, 2004 *It*, *W*, *J*, *CZR*, 2005 *Geo*, *C*, *I*, 2006 *Geo*, *Pt*, *F*, *Geo*, *Sp*, *S*, 2007 *Geo*, 2009 *Ur*, *F*
L Balcan 1963 *Bul*, *EGe*, *Cze*
F Balmus 2000 *Mor*, *H*, *Pt*
S Bals 1927 *F*, *Ger*, *Cze*
G Baltaretu 1965 *WGe*, *F*
C Barascu 1957 *F*
M Baraulea 2004 *CZR*, *Pt*, *Geo*
A Barbu 1958 *WGe*, *It*, 1959 *EGe*, *Pol*, *Cze*, *EGe*, 1960 *F*
A Barbuliceanu 2008 *Rus*, *ESp*, 2009 *Sp*, *Ger*, *Rus*, *Geo*, *Pt*
S Bargaunas 1971 *It*, *Mor*, 1972 *F*, 1974 *Cze*, 1975 *It*
S Barsan 1934 *It*, 1936 *F*, *It*, 1937 *It*, *H*, *F*, *Ger*, 1938 *F*, *Ger*, 1939 *It*, 1940 *It*, 1942 *It*
RC Basalau 2007 *Pt*, 2008 *Geo*, *Pt*, *Rus*, *CZR*, *Ur*, *Rus*, *ESp*, 2010 *ItA*, *Tun*
CD Beca 2009 *Sp*, *Ger*, *Rus*, *Geo*, *Pt*, 2011 *Pt*
E Beches 1979 *It*, *Sp*, *USS*, 1982 *WGe*, *It*, 1983 *Pol*
M Bejan 2001 *I*, *W*, 2002 *Pt*, 2003 *Geo*, *CZR*, 2004 *It*
C Beju 1936 *F*, *It*, *Ger*
G Bentia 1919 *US Army*, *F Army*, 1924 *F*, *US*
V Bezarau 1995 *Ar*, *F*, *It*
R Bezuscu 1985 *It*, 1987 *F*
G Bigiu 2007 *Pt*, 2008 *Geo*, *Sp*, *Pt*, *Rus*, *CZR*, *Ur*, *Rus*
M Blagescu 1952 *EGe*, *EGe*, 1953 *It*, 1955 *Cze*, 1957 *F*, *Cze*, *Bel*, *F*
G Blasek 1937 *It*, *H*, *F*, *Ger*, 1940 *It*, 1942 *It*
A Bogheanu 1980 *Mor*

D Boldor 1988 *It, Sp, US, USS, USS, W,* 1989 *It, E, Sp, Z*
A Boroi 1975 *Sp*
P Bors 1975 *JAB,* 1976 *Sp,* 1977 *It,* 1980 *It, USS, I, Pol, F,* 1981 *It, Sp, USS, S, NZ, F,* 1982 *WGe,* 1983 *Mor, WGe, It, USS,* 1984 *It*
IC Botezatu 2009 *Ger, Rus, Geo, ItA,* 2010 *Ger, Rus, Ukr, Ukr, Nm, ArJ,* 2011 *Pt,* 2012 *Ur, J, US*
D Bozian 1997 *Bel,* 1998 *H, Pol, Ukr*
V Brabateanu 1919 *US Army, F Army*
M Braga 1970 *It, F*
C Branescu 1994 *It, E,* 1997 *F*
I Bratulescu 1927 *Ger, Cze*
G Brezoianu 1996 *Bel,* 1997 *F,* 1998 *H, Pol, Ukr, Ar, Geo, I,* 1999 *F, S, A, US, I,* 2000 *H, Pt, Sp, Geo, F, It,* 2001 *Sp, Rus, Geo, I, W, E,* 2002 *Pt, Sp, H, Rus, Geo, I, It, Sp, W, S, S,* 2003 *Pt, Sp, Rus, Geo, CZR, F, W, I, A, Ar, Nm,* 2005 *Rus, Ukr, J, US, S, Pt, C, I,* 2006 *CZR, Pt, Ukr, Rus, F, Geo, Sp, S,* 2007 *Geo, Sp, CZR, ESp, ItA, Nm, It, S, NZ*
V Brici 1991 *NZ,* 1992 *USS, F, It,* 1993 *Tun, F, Sp, I,* 1994 *Sp, Ger, Rus, It, W, It, E,* 1995 *F, S, J, J, SA, A,* 1996 *Pt, F,* 1997 *WalA, F*
TE Brinza 1990 *It, USS,* 1991 *C,* 1992 *It, Ar,* 1993 *Pt, Tun, F, F, I,* 1994 *Sp, Ger, It, W, It, E,* 1995 *F, S, J, J, SA, A,* 1996 *Pt, F, Pol,* 1997 *WalA, F, W, Ar, F, It,* 1998 *Ukr,* 1999 *A, US, I,* 2000 *H, Geo,* 2002 *H*
I Bucan 1976 *Bul,* 1977 *Sp,* 1978 *Cze,* 1979 *F,* 1980 *It, USS, I, Pol, F,* 1981 *It, Sp, USS, S, NZ, F,* 1982 *WGe, It, USS, Z, Z, F,* 1983 *Mor, WGe, It, USS, Pol, W, USS, F,* 1984 *It, S, F, Sp,* 1985 *E, Tun, USS, USS, It,* 1986 *Pt, S, F, Pt,* 1987 *It, USS, Z, S, USS, F*
M Bucos 1972 *Mor, Cze, WGe,* 1973 *Sp,* 1975 *JAB, Pol, F,* 1976 *H, It, Sp, USS, Bul, Pol, F, Mor,* 1977 *Sp, It, F, Pol, It, F,* 1978 *Pol, F,* 1979 *W,* 1980 *It, Mor*
P Buda 1953 *It,* 1955 *Cze,* 1957 *F, Cze*
C Budica 1974 *Cze, EGe, Cze*
SS Burcea 2006 *F,* 2007 *ESp, ItA, Nm, Rus, Pt,* 2008 *Geo, Pt, CZR, Ur, Rus, ESp,* 2009 *Sp, Ger, Rus, Geo, Pt, ItA, Fj,* 2010 *Ger, Rus, Geo, Pt, Ukr, Ukr, Nm, ArJ, ItA, Tun, Ur, Ur,* 2011 *Rus, ArJ, Ukr, S, E*
M Burghelea 1974 *Cze, EGe, F,* 1975 *It*
S Burlescu 1936 *F, It, Ger,* 1938 *F, Ger,* 1939 *It*
M Butugan 2003 *Pt*

VN Calafeteanu 2004 *J,* 2005 *Ukr,* 2006 *CZR, Pt, Ukr, F, Sp, S,* 2007 *Geo, Sp, CZR, ESp, ItA, Nm, It, S, Pt, NZ,* 2008 *Geo, Sp, Pt, CZR,* 2009 *Ger, Geo, Pt, Ur, F, ItA, ItA, Fj,* 2010 *Ger, Rus, Tun, Ur, Ur,* 2011 *Pt, Geo, Sp, Nm, ArJ, Ar, E, Geo,* 2012 *Pt, Rus, Geo, Sp, Ukr, Ur,* 2013 *Rus*
A Caligari 1951 *EGe,* 1953 *It*
S Caliman 1958 *EGe,* 1960 *Pol, EGe, Cze*
P Calistrat 1940 *It,* 1942 *It*
Ion Camenita 1939 *It*
ME Capatana 2012 *Ukr,* 2013 *Pt, Rus, Sp, Bel, Geo, Rus*
CF Caplescu 2007 *Sp, CZR, Rus, Pt,* 2008 *Rus, CZR, Ur,* 2013 *Rus, Sp, Bel*
C Capmare 1983 *Pol,* 1984 *It*
N Capusan 1960 *F,* 1961 *Pol, Cze, EGe, F,* 1962 *Cze, EGe, Pol, It*
R Capusan 1963 *Bul, EGe, Cze*
G Caracostea 1919 *US Army, F Army*
G Caragea 1980 *I, Pol, F,* 1981 *It, Sp, USS, S, NZ, F,* 1982 *WGe, It, USS, Z, Z, F,* 1983 *Mor, WGe, It, USS, Pol, W, F,* 1984 *F, Sp,* 1985 *E, Tun,* 1986 *S, F, Tun, Tun, Pt, F, I,* 1988 *It, Sp, US, USS,* 1989 *E*
C Carp 1989 *Z, Sa, USS*
D Carpo 2008 *Sp, Pt, Rus, CZR, Ur, Rus, ESp,* 2009 *Sp, Ger, Rus, Geo, Pt, Ur, F,* 2010 *Ger, Rus, Geo, Pt, Sp, ArJ, ItA, Tun, Ur, Ur,* 2011 *Pt, Rus, Geo, Sp, Nm, ArJ, Ukr, S, Ar, Geo,* 2012 *Pt, Rus, Geo,* 2013 *Pt, Rus, Sp, Bel, Geo, Rus*
GA Catuna 2009 *ItA,* 2012 *Pt*
I Cazan 2010 *ItA, Tun, Ur,* 2011 *Pt, Rus, Geo, Sp, Nm, ArJ, S, Ar, E,* 2012 *J, US*
G Celea 1963 *EGe*
D Chiriac 1999 *S, A, I,* 2001 *H*
G Chiriac 1996 *Bel,* 2001 *Pt, Rus,* 2002 *Sp, H, Rus, Geo, I, Sp, W, S, S,* 2003 *Sp, Rus, Geo, F, W, I, A, Ar, Nm*
R Chiriac 1952 *EGe,* 1955 *Cze,* 1957 *F, Bel, F,* 1958 *Sp, WGe,* 1960 *F,* 1961 *Pol, EGe, Cze, EGe, F,* 1962 *Cze, EGe, Pol, It, F,* 1963 *Bul, EGe, Cze, F,* 1964 *Cze, EGe, WGe, F*
M Chiricencu 1980 *It, Pol*
S Chirila 1989 *Sp, S,* 1990 *F, H, Sp, It, USS,* 1991 *It*
V Chirita 1999 *S*
G Cilinca 1993 *Pt*
N Cioarec 1974 *Pol,* 1976 *It,* 1979 *Pol*
P Ciobanel 1961 *Pol, EGe, Cze, EGe, F,* 1962 *Cze, EGe, Pol, It, F,* 1963 *F,* 1964 *Cze, EGe, WGe, F,* 1965 *WGe, F,* 1966 *Cze, It, F,* 1967 *F,* 1968 *Cze, Cze, F,* 1969 *Pol, WGe, Cze, F,* 1970 *F,* 1971 *F*
I Ciobanu 1952 *EGe*
M Ciobanu 1949 *Cze,* 1951 *EGe*
R Cioca 1994 *Sp, Ger, Rus, It, It, E,* 1995 *S,* 1996 *Bel*
I Ciofu 2000 *It,* 2003 *Pt*
ML Ciolacu 1998 *Ukr, Ar, Geo, I,* 1999 *F,* 2001 *Sp, H, Rus, Geo, W, E*
S Ciorascu 1988 *US, USS, USS, F, W,* 1989 *It, E, Sp, Z, Sa, USS, S,* 1990 *It, F, H, Sp, USS,* 1991 *It, NZ, S, F, C, Fj,* 1992 *Sp, It, It, Ar,* 1994 *Ger, Rus, It, W,* 1995 *F, S, J, C, SA, A,* 1996 *F,* 1997 *F, It,* 1999 *F*
M Ciornei 1972 *WGe, F,* 1973 *Ar, Ar, WGe, F,* 1974 *Mor, Pol, EGe, F, Cze,* 1975 *It, Sp*
SE Ciuntu 2007 *NZ, Rus, Pt,* 2008 *Geo, Sp, Pt, Rus, CZR, Ur, ESp,* 2009 *Sp, Ger, Rus, Geo, Pt, Ur, F, ItA, Fj,* 2010 *Ger, Rus, Geo, Pt, Sp, Ukr, Ukr, Nm, ArJ, ItA, Tun,* 2011 *Ukr, S, E, Geo*
C Cocor 1940 *It,* 1949 *Cze*
M Codea 1998 *Ukr,* 2001 *E*
L Codoi 1980 *I, Pol,* 1984 *F,* 1985 *Tun, USS*
C Cojocariu 1990 *It, F, H, Sp, It, USS,* 1991 *It, NZ, F, S, F, C, Fj,* 1992 *Sp, It, USS, F, Ar,* 1993 *Pt, F, F, I,* 1994 *Sp, Ger, Rus, It, W, It, E,* 1995 *F, S, J, J, C, SA, A, Ar, F, It,* 1996 *F*
L Colceriu 1991 *S, Fj,* 1992 *Sp, It, It,* 1993 *I,* 1994 *Sp, Ger, Rus, It, W, It,* 1995 *F, J, J, C, SA, A,* 1997 *WalA, F, W, Bel, Ar, F, It,* 1998 *Pol, Ukr*
D Coliba 1987 *USS, F*
M Coltuneac 2002 *Sp, W, S*
T Coman 1984 *Sp,* 1986 *F, Tun, Tun, I,* 1988 *Sp, US, USS, USS,* 1989 *It,* 1992 *F*
F Constantin 1972 *Mor, Cze, WGe,* 1973 *Ar, Ar, WGe,* 1980 *Mor,* 1982 *It*
I Constantin 1971 *Mor,* 1972 *WGe,* 1973 *Ar, Ar, WGe, F,* 1974 *Mor, Pol, Sp, F, Cze,* 1975 *It, Sp, JAB, Pol, F,* 1976 *H, It, Sp, USS, Bul, Pol,* 1977 *It, F,* 1978 *Pol, F,* 1979 *It, Sp, USS, W, Pol, F,* 1980 *It, USS, I, Pol, F,* 1981 *It, Sp, USS, S, NZ, F,* 1982 *WGe, It, USS, Z, Z,* 1983 *WGe, USS,* 1985 *It*
L Constantin 1983 *USS, F,* 1984 *It, S, F, Sp,* 1985 *E, It, Tun, USS, USS, It,* 1986 *Pt, S, F, Tun, Tun, Pt, F, I,* 1987 *It, USS, Z, F, S, USS, F,* 1991 *It, NZ, F*
LT Constantin 1985 *USS*
C Constantin 2001 *Pt,* 2002 *Geo, W*
S Constantin 1980 *Mor,* 1982 *Z, Z,* 1983 *Pol, W, USS, F,* 1984 *S, F,* 1985 *USS,* 1986 *Pt, S, F, Tun,* 1987 *It, Z, S*
T Constantin 1992 *USS, F, It,* 1993 *Pt, F, Sp,* 1996 *Pt,* 1997 *It,* 1999 *F, US, I,* 2000 *Pt, Sp, Geo, F,* 2002 *Rus, Geo*
T Constantin 1985 *USS*
N Copil 1985 *USS, It,* 1986 *S*
D Coravu 1968 *F*
N Cordos 1958 *EGe,* 1961 *EGe,* 1963 *Bul, Cze,* 1964 *Cze, EGe*
V Cornel 1977 *F,* 1978 *Cze, Sp*
G Corneliu 1980 *Mor, USS,* 1982 *WGe, It, Z, Z,* 1986 *Tun, Pt, F,* 1993 *I,* 1994 *W*
M Corneliu 1979 *USS*
G Corneliu 1976 *USS, Bul,* 1977 *F,* 1979 *It,* 1981 *S,* 1982 *Z*
F Corodeanu 1997 *WalA, F, W,* 1998 *H, Pol, Ar, Geo,* 1999 *F, S, A, US, I,* 2000 *H, Sp, Geo, F, It,* 2001 *Pt, Sp, H, Rus, Geo, I, E,* 2002 *Pt, Sp, Rus, Geo, It, Sp, W, S, S,* 2003 *Sp,* 2005 *Geo, J, US, S, Pt, C, I,* 2006 *Geo, CZR, Pt, Geo, Sp, S,* 2007 *Geo, ESp, ItA, Nm, It, S, Pt, NZ,* 2008 *Ur, Rus, ESp,* 2009 *Sp, Ger, Rus, Pt*
Coste 2007 *Pt,* 2008 *Geo, Sp, Pt, Rus, CZR, Ur,* 2009 *Sp, Rus, Geo, Pt, F,* 2010 *Ukr,* 2012 *Pt, Rus, Geo, Ur, J, US,* 2013 *Rus, Bel, Geo*

L Costea 1994 *E*, 1995 *S*, *J*, *J*, *Ar*, *F*, 1997 *WalA*, *F*
L Coter 1957 *F*, *Cze*, 1959 *EGe*, *Pol*, *Cze*, 1960 *F*
F Covaci 1936 *Ger*, 1937 *H*, *F*, *Ger*, 1940 *It*, 1942 *It*
C Cratunescu 1919 *US Army*, *F Army*
N Crissoveloni 1936 *F*, *It*, 1937 *H*, *F*, *Ger*, 1938 *F*, *Ger*
S Cristea 1973 *Mor*
C Cristoloveanu 1952 *EGe*
G Crivat 1938 *F*, *Ger*
V Csoma 1983 *WGe*
D Curea 2005 *Rus*, *Ukr*, *J*, *US*, *S*, *Pt*

V Daiciulescu 1966 *Cze*, *F*, 1967 *It*, *Pol*, 1968 *F*, 1969 *Pol*
A Damian 1934 *It*, 1936 *F*, *It*, *Ger*, 1937 *It*, 1938 *F*, *Ger*, 1939 *It*, 1949 *Cze*
M Danila 2012 *Ukr*
G Daraban 1969 *Cze*, 1972 *Mor*, *Cze*, *WGe*, *F*, 1973 *Sp*, *Mor*, *Ar*, *Ar*, 1974 *Cze*, *EGe*, *F*, *Cze*, 1975 *It*, *Sp*, *JAB*, *Pol*, *F*, 1976 *H*, *It*, *Sp*, *USS*, *Bul*, *Pol*, *F*, *Mor*, 1977 *Sp*, *It*, *F*, 1978 *Cze*, *Sp*, *Pol*, *F*, 1982 *F*, 1983 *Mor*, *WGe*, *It*, *USS*, *W*
CR Dascalu 2006 *Ukr*, *F*, *Geo*, *Sp*, *S*, 2007 *Sp*, *CZR*, *ESp*, *NZ*, *Rus*, *Pt*, 2008 *Geo*, *Rus*, *Ur*, *Rus*, *ESp*, 2009 *Sp*, *Rus*, *Geo*, *Ur*, *ItA*, *ItA*, 2010 *Ger*, *Rus*, *Geo*, *Sp*, *Ukr*, *Ukr*, *Nm*, 2011 *Pt*, *Rus*, *Geo*, 2013 *Pt*, *Rus*, *Sp*, *Bel*, *Geo*
V David 1984 *Sp*, 1986 *Pt*, *S*, *F*, *Tun*, 1987 *USS*, *Z*, *F*, 1992 *USS*
S Demci 1998 *Ar*, 2001 *H*, *Rus*, *Geo*, *I*, *W*
R Demian 1959 *EGe*, 1960 *F*, 1961 *Pol*, *EGe*, *Cze*, *EGe*, *F*, 1962 *Cze*, *Pol*, *It*, *F*, 1963 *Bul*, *EGe*, *Cze*, *F*, 1964 *WGe*, *F*, 1965 *WGe*, *F*, 1966 *Cze*, *It*, *F*, 1967 *It*, *Pt*, *Pol*, *WGe*, *F*, 1968 *Cze*, *F*, 1969 *Pol*, *WGe*, *F*, 1971 *It*, *Mor*
E Denischi 1949 *Cze*, 1952 *EGe*, *EGe*
I Diaconu 1942 *It*
C Diamandi-Telu 1938 *Ger*, 1939 *It*
ND Dima 1999 *A*, *US*, *I*, 2000 *H*, *Pt*, *Geo*, *F*, *It*, 2001 *Sp*, *H*, *Rus*, *Geo*, *W*, *E*, 2002 *Pt*, *Sp*, *Rus*, *W*, *S*, *S*, 2004 *CZR*, *Pt*, *Sp*, *Rus*, *Geo*, 2009 *ItA*, *ItA*, 2010 *Ger*, *Geo*, *Pt*, *Sp*, *Nm*, *ArJ*, *Ur*, *Ur*, 2011 *Geo*, *Sp*, *Nm*, *Ukr*
TI Dimofte 2004 *It*, *W*, *CZR*, 2005 *C*, *I*, 2006 *Geo*, *CZR*, *Pt*, *Ukr*, *Rus*, *F*, *Geo*, *Sp*, *S*, 2007 *ESp*, *ItA*, *Nm*, *It*, *S*, *Pt*, *NZ*, *Rus*, *Pt*, 2008 *Geo*, *Sp*, *Pt*, *Rus*, *CZR*, *Ur*, *Rus*, *ESp*, 2009 *Sp*, *Ger*, *Rus*, *Geo*, *Pt*, *Ur*, *F*, *ItA*, *Fj*, 2010 *Ger*, *Rus*, *Geo*, *Pt*, *Sp*, *Ukr*, *Ukr*, *Nm*, *ItA*, *Tun*, *Ur*, *Ur*, 2011 *Sp*, *Nm*, *ArJ*, *Ukr*, *S*, *Ar*, *Geo*, 2013 *Bel*, *Geo*, *Rus*
C Dinescu 1934 *It*, 1936 *F*, *It*, *Ger*, 1937 *It*, *H*, *F*, *Ger*, 1938 *F*, *Ger*, 1940 *It*, 1942 *It*
IC Dinis 2012 *Pt*, *Rus*, *Geo*, *Sp*, *Ukr*, *Ur*
C Dinu 1965 *WGe*, *F*, 1966 *Cze*, *It*, *F*, 1967 *It*, *Pt*, *Pol*, *WGe*, 1968 *F*, 1969 *Pol*, *WGe*, *Cze*, *F*, 1970 *It*, *F*, 1971 *Mor*, *F*, 1972 *Mor*, *Cze*, *WGe*, *F*, 1973 *Sp*, *Mor*, *Ar*, *Ar*, *WGe*, *F*, 1974 *Mor*, *Pol*, *Sp*, *Cze*, *F*, *Cze*, 1975 *It*, *Sp*, 1976 *H*, *It*, *Sp*, *Pol*, *F*, *Mor*, 1977 *Sp*, *It*, *F*, *Pol*, *It*, *F*, 1978 *Sp*, *Pol*, *F*, 1979 *Sp*, *USS*, *W*, *Pol*, 1980 *I*, *Pol*, *F*, 1981 *It*, *Sp*, *USS*, *NZ*, *F*, 1982 *F*, 1983 *Mor*, *WGe*, *It*, *USS*
F Dinu 2000 *Mor*, *H*
G Dinu 1975 *Pol*, 1979 *It*, *Sp*, 1983 *Pol*, *USS*
G Dinu 1990 *It*, *F*, *H*, *Sp*, *It*, *USS*, 1991 *It*, *S*, *F*, *C*, *Fj*, 1992 *Sp*, *It*, *USS*, *F*, *It*, 1993 *F*
F Dobre 2001 *E*, 2004 *W*, *CZR*, 2007 *Pt*, 2008 *CZR*, 2012 *Rus*, *Ukr*, *Ur*
I Dobre 1951 *EGe*, 1952 *EGe*, 1953 *It*, 1955 *Cze*, 1957 *Cze*, *Bel*, *F*, 1958 *Sp*
I Doja 1986 *Tun*, *Pt*, *F*, *I*, 1988 *F*, *W*, 1989 *Sp*, *Z*, *Sa*, *S*, 1990 *It*, 1991 *It*, *NZ*, *F*, *C*, 1992 *Sp*
V Doja 1997 *Bel*, 1998 *Pol*, *Geo*, *I*
A Domocos 1989 *Z*, *Sa*, *USS*
I Dorutiu 1957 *Cze*, *Bel*, *F*, 1958 *Sp*, *WGe*
A Draghici 1919 *US*
C Dragnea 1995 *F*, 1996 *Pol*, 1997 *WalA*, *F*, *Bel*, *Ar*, *F*, *It*, 1998 *H*, *Pol*, 1999 *F*, 2000 *F*
I Dragnea 1985 *Tun*
S Dragnea 2002 *S*
M Dragomir 2001 *H*, *Geo*, 2002 *I*
M Dragomir 1996 *Bel*, 1997 *Bel*, 1998 *H*, *Pol*, *Ukr*, *Geo*, *I*, 2001 *I*, *W*, *E*
V Dragomir 1964 *Cze*, *EGe*, 1966 *It*, 1967 *Pol*, *WGe*
G Dragomirescu 1919 *F Army*
G Dragomirescu-Rahtopol 1963 *Bul*, *EGe*, *Cze*, *F*, 1964 *Cze*, *EGe*, *WGe*, *F*, 1965 *WGe*, *F*, 1966 *Cze*, 1967 *It*, *Pt*, *Pol*, *WGe*, *F*, 1968 *Cze*, *Cze*, *F*, 1969 *Pol*, *WGe*, *Cze*, *F*, 1970 *It*, *F*, 1971 *It*, *Mor*, 1972 *Mor*, *Cze*, *WGe*, *F*, 1973 *WGe*, *F*
N Dragos 1995 *Ar*, *It*, 1997 *WalA*, *F*, *Ar*, *F*, *It*, 1998 *H*, *Pol*, *Ukr*, *Ar*, *Geo*, *I*, 1999 *F*, *S*, 2000 *Sp*, *Geo*, *F*
CS Draguceanu 1994 *Sp*, *Ger*, *Rus*, *It*, *W*, *It*, *E*, 1995 *S*, *J*, *Ar*, *F*, *It*, 1996 *Bel*, 1997 *W*, *Bel*, *Ar*, *F*, *It*, 1998 *H*, *Pol*, *Ukr*, *Ar*, *Geo*, *I*, 1999 *S*, *A*, *US*, *I*, 2000 *Mor*, *H*, *Pt*, *Sp*, *Geo*, *F*, *It*
C Dragulescu 1969 *Cze*, 1970 *F*, 1971 *It*, 1972 *Cze*
G Drobota 1960 *Pol*, *Cze*, 1961 *EGe*, *EGe*, *F*, 1962 *Cze*, *EGe*, *Pol*, *F*, 1964 *Cze*, *EGe*, *F*
MD Dumbrava 2002 *W*, *S*, 2003 *Sp*, *Rus*, *Geo*, *CZR*, *F*, *W*, *I*, *A*, *Nm*, 2004 *CZR*, *Pt*, *Sp*, *Rus*, *Geo*, *It*, *J*, *CZR*, 2005 *Rus*, *Geo*, *Ukr*, *J*, *US*, *S*, *Pt*, *C*, 2006 *Geo*, *Pt*, *Rus*, 2007 *Sp*, *CZR*, *Pt*, *Rus*, *Pt*, 2008 *Sp*, *Pt*, *Rus*, *CZR*, *Ur*, *Rus*, *ESp*, 2009 *Fj*, 2010 *Geo*, *Pt*, *Sp*, *Ukr*, *Ukr*, *Nm*, *ArJ*, *ItA*, *Tun*, *Ur*, *Ur*, 2011 *Pt*, *Rus*, *Geo*, *Sp*, *Nm*, *Ukr*, *S*, *E*, *Geo*, 2012 *Pt*
H Dumitras 1984 *It*, 1985 *E*, *It*, *USS*, 1986 *Pt*, *F*, *I*, 1987 *It*, *USS*, *Z*, *S*, *USS*, *F*, 1988 *It*, *Sp*, *US*, *USS*, *USS*, *F*, *W*, 1989 *It*, *E*, *Z*, *Sa*, *USS*, *S*, 1990 *It*, *F*, *H*, *Sp*, *USS*, 1991 *It*, *NZ*, *F*, *S*, *F*, *C*, *Fj*, 1992 *Sp*, *USS*, *F*, *Ar*, 1993 *Pt*, *Tun*, *F*, *Sp*, *F*, *I*
I Dumitras 2002 *H*, 2006 *Geo*, *CZR*, *Ukr*, *Rus*, *F*, 2007 *Geo*, *Sp*, *CZR*, *ESp*, *ItA*, *Nm*, *It*, *S*, *Pt*, *NZ*, 2009 *Ur*, *F*, *ItA*, *ItA*, *Fj*, 2010 *Ger*, *Rus*, *Geo*, *Pt*, *Sp*, *Ur*, *Ur*, 2011 *Pt*, *Rus*, *Geo*, *Sp*, *ArJ*, *Ukr*, *S*, *Ar*, *E*, *Geo*, 2012 *Pt*, *Rus*, *Geo*, *Sp*, *Ur*
E Dumitrescu 1953 *It*, 1958 *Sp*, *WGe*
G Dumitrescu 1988 *It*, *Sp*, *F*, *W*, 1989 *It*, *E*, *Sp*, *Z*, *Sa*, *USS*, *S*, 1990 *It*, *F*, *H*, *Sp*, *It*, *USS*, 1991 *It*, *NZ*, *F*, 1997 *It*
L Dumitrescu 1997 *Bel*, *Ar*, 2001 *W*
G Dumitriu 1937 *H*, *F*, *Ger*
A Dumitru 1974 *Pol*, 1975 *Sp*, *JAB*, 1976 *Sp*, *USS*, *Bul*, *Pol*, *F*, *Mor*, 1977 *Sp*, *It*, *F*, *Pol*, *F*, 1978 *Cze*, *Sp*, 1979 *It*, *Sp*, *USS*, *W*, *F*, 1980 *It*, *I*, *Pol*, *F*, 1981 *Sp*, *USS*, *S*, *NZ*, *F*, 1982 *Z*, 1983 *It*, *USS*, *Pol*, *W*, 1984 *It*, *S*, *F*, *Sp*, 1985 *E*, 1987 *It*, *USS*, *Z*, *S*, *USS*, *F*, 1988 *USS*
D Dumitru 2002 *S*, 2009 *Ur*, *F*, *ItA*, *ItA*, *Fj*
G Dumitru 1973 *Sp*, *Mor*, *Ar*, *Ar*, *WGe*, *F*, 1974 *Mor*, *Sp*, *Cze*, *EGe*, *F*, 1975 *JAB*, *Pol*, *F*, 1976 *H*, *It*, *Sp*, 1977 *Sp*, *Pol*, *F*, 1978 *Cze*, *Sp*, *Pol*, *F*, 1979 *It*, *Sp*, *USS*, *W*, *Pol*, *F*, 1980 *It*, *Mor*, *USS*, *I*, *Pol*, *F*, 1981 *It*, *Sp*, *USS*, *S*, *NZ*, *F*, 1982 *WGe*, *It*, *USS*, *Z*, *Z*, *F*, 1983 *Mor*, *WGe*, *It*, *USS*, *Pol*, *USS*, *F*, 1984 *It*, *S*, *F*, 1985 *E*, *It*, *Tun*, *USS*, 1986 *F*, *I*, 1987 *USS*, *F*, *S*, *USS*, *F*
I Dumitru 2013 *Rus*
M Dumitru 1990 *F*, *H*, *Sp*, *It*, *USS*, 1991 *NZ*, *F*, *F*, *C*, 1992 *F*, 1993 *F*, *Sp*, *F*
M Dumitru 1997 *WalA*, 1998 *Ar*, 1999 *F*, 2000 *Mor*, *H*, *Pt*, *Sp*, *Geo*, *F*, 2002 *H*, 2003 *Sp*
M Dumitru 2002 *Pt*, *Sp*, *H*, *I*
S Dumitru 2004 *It*, 2005 *Rus*, *Ukr*, *US*, *S*, *Pt*
R Durbac 1968 *Cze*, 1969 *WGe*, *Cze*, 1970 *It*, *F*, 1971 *It*, *Mor*, *F*, 1972 *WGe*, *F*, 1973 *Ar*, *Ar*, *WGe*, *F*, 1974 *Mor*, *Pol*, *Sp*, *Cze*, *EGe*, *F*, *Cze*, 1975 *It*, *Sp*, *JAB*, *Pol*, *F*
A Duta 1973 *Ar*

R Eckert 1927 *F*, *Ger*, *Cze*
I Enache 1977 *It*
M Ezaru 2000 *Pt*, *Geo*, *F*

V Falcusanu 1974 *Sp*, *Cze*
G Fantaneanu 1934 *It*, 1936 *F*, *It*, *Ger*, 1937 *It*, *H*, *F*, *Ger*
C Fercu 2005 *C*, *I*, 2006 *Geo*, *CZR*, *Pt*, *Ukr*, *Rus*, *F*, *Geo*, *Sp*, 2007 *Geo*, *Sp*, *CZR*, *ESp*, *ItA*, *Nm*, *It*, *S*, *Pt*, 2008 *Geo*, *Sp*, *Pt*, *Rus*, *CZR*, *Ur*, *Rus*, *ESp*, 2009 *Sp*, *Ger*, *Rus*, *Pt*, *Ur*, *F*, 2010 *Ger*, *Rus*, *Geo*, *Pt*, *Sp*, *Ukr*, *Nm*, *ArJ*, *ItA*, *Tun*, *Ur*, *Ur*, 2011 *Rus*, *Geo*, *Sp*, *Nm*, *ArJ*, *Ukr*, 2012 *Ur*, *J*, *US*, 2013 *Pt*, *Rus*, *Sp*, *Bel*, *Geo*, *Rus*
Filip 2012 *J*, *US*
C Florea 1937 *It*, *F*, *Ger*
G Florea 1981 *S*, *NZ*, *F*, 1982 *WGe*, *It*, *USS*, *Z*, *Z*, 1984 *Sp*, 1985 *USS*, 1986 *Pt*, *F*
IM Florea 2012 *J*, *US*
S Florea 2000 *It*, 2001 *Sp*, *Geo*, *I*, *E*, 2002 *It*, *Sp*, *W*, 2003 *Sp*, *Rus*, *Geo*, *CZR*, *A*, *Ar*, *Nm*, 2007 *Sp*, *CZR*, *S*, *NZ*, 2009 *Sp*, *Ger*, 2010 *Rus*, *Ukr*, *Ukr*, *Nm*, 2011 *S*, *Ar*, *E*, *Geo*

I Florescu 1957 *F, Cze*
M Florescu 1995 *F*
P Florescu 1967 *It, Pt, Pol, WGe, F*, 1968 *Cze, Cze, F*, 1969 *Pol, WGe, Cze, F*, 1971 *Mor*, 1973 *Sp, Mor, Ar, Ar*, 1974 *Cze, EGe, F*
P Florian 1927 *F*, 1934 *It*
T Florian 1927 *F, Ger*
V Flutur 1994 *Ger*, 1995 *J, J, C, SA, A, Ar, F, It*, 1996 *Bel, Pol*, 1997 *WalA, F*
M Foca 1992 *It, USS, It, Ar*, 1993 *Pt, Tun, F*
C Fugigi 1992 *Ar*
C Fugigi 1964 *Cze*, 1969 *Cze*, 1972 *Mor, Cze, WGe, F*, 1973 *Sp, Ar, Ar, WGe, F*, 1974 *Mor, Sp, Cze, EGe*, 1975 *It, Sp, JAB*
R Fugigi 1995 *It*, 1996 *Pt, F, Pol*, 1998 *Ukr, Ar, I*, 1999 *S, I*
S Fuicu 1976 *H*, 1980 *USS, I, Pol, F*, 1981 *It, Sp, USS, S, NZ, F*, 1982 *Z, Z, F*, 1983 *Mor, WGe, It, USS, W*, 1984 *It*
N Fulina 1988 *F, W*, 1989 *It, E, Sp, Sa, USS*, 1990 *It, F, H, Sp, USS*, 1991 *NZ, C, Fj*, 1992 *It, It*, 1993 *Pt, F, Sp, F, I*, 1994 *Sp, Ger, Rus, It, W, It*

CM Gal 2005 *I*, 2006 *Geo, CZR, Pt, S*, 2007 *Geo, CZR, ESp, ItA, Nm, It, S, NZ, Rus, Pt*, 2008 *Geo, Sp, Pt, Rus*, 2009 *Ger, Pt, ItA, ItA, Fj*, 2010 *Geo, Pt, Sp, Ukr, Ukr, Nm, ArJ, ItA, Tun, Ur, Ur*, 2011 *Pt, Geo, Sp, Nm, ArJ, S, Ar, E, Geo*, 2012 *Pt, Rus, Geo, Sp, Ukr, Ur, J, US*, 2013 *Rus, Sp, Bel, Geo, Rus*
S Galan 1985 *It, It*
I Garlesteanu 1924 *F, US*, 1927 *F, Cze*
A Gealapu 1994 *It, E*, 1995 *F, S, J, J, C, SA, A, Ar, F, It*, 1996 *Pt, F, Pol*
C Gheara 2004 *CZR, Sp, Rus, Geo*, 2010 *Ger*, 2011 *Rus, Ukr, Ar, Geo*, 2012 *Pt, Rus, Geo, Ukr, Ur, J, US*
C Gheorghe 1992 *It*, 1993 *Tun, F, Sp*, 1994 *Sp, Ger, E*
D Gherasim 1959 *Cze*
V Ghiata 1951 *EGe*
S Ghica 1937 *H, F*, 1942 *It*
V Ghioc 2000 *It*, 2001 *Pt, Sp, Rus, Geo, I, W, E*, 2002 *Pt, Sp, H, W, S, S*, 2003 *CZR, Ar*, 2004 *It, W, CZR*, 2005 *Ukr, J, S*, 2008 *Pt*
N Ghiondea 1949 *Cze*, 1951 *EGe*
D Ghiuzelea 1951 *EGe*, 1952 *EGe, EGe*, 1953 *It*, 1955 *Cze*, 1957 *Cze*
A Girbu 1992 *Ar*, 1993 *Tun, Sp, F, I*, 1994 *Sp*, 1995 *Ar, F, It*, 1996 *Pt, F, Pol*, 1997 *WalA, F, Ar, F, It*, 1998 *H, Pol, Geo, I*
L Giucal 2009 *Sp, Ger*
M Giucal 1985 *It, Tun, USS, It*, 1986 *Pt, F, Tun*
A Giugiuc 1963 *Bul, EGe, Cze*, 1964 *Cze, EGe*, 1966 *Cze*
V Giuglea 1986 *S, Tun*
I Glavan 1942 *It*
RS Gontineac 1995 *F, S, J, J, C, SA, A*, 1996 *Pt, F, Pol*, 1997 *F, W, Ar, F, It*, 1998 *H, Pol, Ukr, Ar, Geo, I*, 1999 *F, S, A, US, I*, 2000 *H, Sp, Geo, F*, 2001 *Rus, Geo*, 2002 *Pt, Sp, Rus, Geo, I, It, Sp, W, S, S*, 2003 *Pt, Sp, Geo, CZR, F, W, I, A, Ar, Nm*, 2004 *CZR, Pt, Rus, Geo, It, W, J, CZR*, 2005 *Geo, C*, 2006 *Geo, Pt, Ukr, Rus, F, Geo, Sp, S*, 2007 *Geo, Sp, It, S, Pt, NZ*, 2008 *ESp*
A Gorcioaia 2009 *Ger*, 2012 *Rus, Geo, Sp*
M Gorcioaia 2012 *Ukr*
G Graur 1958 *It*, 1959 *EGe, Pol, Cze, EGe*, 1960 *Pol, EGe, Cze*, 1961 *EGe*, 1962 *EGe, It*
E Grigore 1982 *WGe*, 1984 *Sp*, 1985 *E, Tun*, 1987 *It, USS, Z, F, S*
V Grigorescu 1936 *F, It, Ger*, 1939 *It*
M Guramare 1982 *WGe, It*, 1983 *Mor, WGe*, 1988 *Sp*
A Guranescu 1991 *S, F*, 1992 *USS, It*, 1993 *Pt, Tun, I*, 1994 *Ger, Rus, It, W, E*, 1995 *SA, A, Ar, F, It*
S Guranescu 1997 *W, Bel, Ar*, 2001 *Sp, H, Rus, I*

A Hariton 1973 *Mor, Ar, Ar*, 1978 *Cze, Sp*
T Hell 1958 *EGe*
CN Hildan 1998 *H, Pol, Geo*, 1999 *S*
L Hodorca 1984 *It*, 1985 *Tun*, 1986 *Pt, S, F, Tun, Tun, I*, 1987 *It, Z*, 1988 *F*
M Holban 1980 *Mor*, 1982 *F*, 1985 *It, USS*, 1986 *Pt, I*
J Hussar 1919 *US*

D Iacob 1996 *Bel*, 2001 *Pt, Sp, H, Geo, W*
ML Iacob 1997 *W, Bel, Ar, F, It*, 1999 *S*
DG Ianus 2009 *Sp*, 2010 *Ukr, Nm, ItA, Tun*, 2011 *Rus, Geo, Sp, Nm, Ar, E, Geo*
P Ianusevici 1974 *Pol, Cze, EGe, Cze*, 1975 *It*, 1976 *USS, Bul, Pol, F, Mor*, 1977 *Sp, Pol, It, F*, 1978 *F*
I Iconomu 1919 *US Army, F Army*
M Iconomu 1919 *US Army, F Army*
N Ifrim 1937 *F, Ger*
G Ignat 1986 *Pt, S, F, Tun*, 1988 *It, Sp, US, USS, USS, F, W*, 1989 *It, E, Sp, S*, 1990 *It, F, H, Sp*, 1991 *It, NZ*, 1992 *Sp, It, USS, F*
V Ilca 1987 *F*
I Ilie 1952 *EGe, EGe*, 1953 *It*, 1955 *Cze*, 1957 *F, Cze, Bel, F*, 1958 *It*, 1959 *EGe*
M Iliescu 1961 *EGe*, 1963 *Bul, EGe, Cze, F*, 1965 *WGe, F*, 1967 *WGe*
T Ioan 1937 *H, F, Ger*
V Ioan 1927 *Ger, Cze*, 1937 *It*
A Ion 2012 *Sp, Ukr*
F Ion 1991 *S*, 1992 *Sp*, 1993 *F*
G Ion 1984 *Sp*, 1986 *F, I*, 1988 *USS, F, W*, 1989 *It, E, Sp, Sa, USS, S*, 1990 *It, F, H, Sp, It, USS*, 1991 *It, NZ, F, S, F, C, Fj*, 1992 *Sp, It, USS, F, Ar*, 1993 *Pt, F, Sp, F*, 1994 *Sp, Rus, It, W, It*, 1997 *WalA*
P Ion 2003 *Ar*, 2004 *It*, 2005 *Rus, Ukr, J, US, S*, 2006 *Geo, CZR, Pt, Ukr, Rus, F, Geo, S*, 2007 *Geo, Sp, CZR, ESp, ItA, Pt, NZ, Rus*, 2008 *Geo, Sp, Rus, Ur, Rus, ESp*, 2009 *Sp, Ger, Rus, Geo, Pt, Ur, F, ItA, ItA, Fj*, 2010 *Ger, Rus, Geo, Pt*, 2011 *ArJ, Ukr, S, Ar, E, Geo*, 2012 *Geo, Sp*, 2013 *Pt, Rus, Sp, Bel, Geo, Rus*
V Ion 1980 *Mor, USS*, 1982 *Z, Z, F*, 1983 *Mor, It, USS, W, USS, F*, 1984 *S*, 1985 *It*, 1987 *It, USS, Z, F, S*
A Ionescu 1958 *EGe, It*, 1959 *EGe, Pol, Cze*, 1960 *Pol, EGe, Cze*, 1961 *Pol, Cze, EGe, F*, 1962 *EGe, It, F*, 1963 *F*, 1964 *Cze, EGe, F*, 1965 *WGe*, 1966 *Cze, It, F*
D Ionescu 1949 *Cze*, 1951 *EGe*, 1952 *EGe, EGe*, 1953 *It*, 1955 *Cze*, 1957 *F, Cze, F*, 1958 *Sp, It*
G Ionescu 1949 *Cze*
G Ionescu 1934 *It*, 1936 *F, It, Ger*, 1937 *It, F*, 1938 *F, Ger*, 1940 *It*, 1942 *It*
M Ionescu 1972 *Mor*, 1976 *USS, Bul, Pol, F*, 1977 *It, F, Pol, It, F*, 1978 *Cze, Sp, Pol, F*, 1979 *It, Sp, USS, W, Pol, F*, 1980 *I*, 1981 *NZ*, 1983 *USS*
R Ionescu 1968 *Cze, Cze*, 1971 *F*
S Ionescu 1936 *It, Ger*, 1937 *It*
V Ionescu 1992 *It*
V Ionescu 1993 *Tun, F*, 1994 *Ger, Rus*, 1998 *Ukr*
F Ionita 1974 *Sp*, 1978 *Pol, F*
P Iordachescu 1957 *F, Cze, Bel, F*, 1958 *Sp, WGe, EGe, It*, 1959 *EGe, Pol, Cze, EGe*, 1960 *Pol, EGe, Cze*, 1961 *EGe*, 1963 *F*, 1964 *Cze, EGe, WGe*, 1965 *WGe, F*, 1966 *Cze*
M Iordan 1980 *Mor*
P Iordanescu 1949 *Cze*
V Iorgulescu 1967 *WGe*, 1968 *Cze, F*, 1969 *Pol, WGe, Cze*, 1970 *It, F*, 1971 *F*, 1973 *Ar, Ar*
V Irimescu 1960 *F*, 1961 *Pol, Cze, EGe, F*, 1962 *Cze, EGe, Pol, It, F*, 1963 *F*, 1964 *F*, 1965 *WGe, F*, 1966 *Cze, It, F*, 1967 *It, Pt, Pol, WGe, F*, 1968 *Cze, Cze, F*, 1969 *Pol, WGe, Cze, F*, 1970 *It, F*, 1971 *F*
I Irimia 1936 *F, It, Ger*, 1937 *It, H, Ger*, 1938 *F, Ger*, 1939 *It*, 1940 *It*
G Irisescu 1993 *Sp*
A Iulian 2003 *CZR*
VM Ivan 2010 *Geo, Pt, Sp, Ukr, Ukr, Tun*
I Ivanciuc 1991 *Fj*, 1994 *E*, 1995 *J, C, SA, A*

I Jipescu 1927 *F*

C Kramer 1955 *Cze*, 1958 *Sp, WGe, It*, 1960 *Pol, EGe, Cze*
T Krantz 1940 *It*, 1942 *It*
C Kurtzbauer 1939 *It*

C Lapusneanu 1934 *It*
D Lazar 2013 *Rus*
MA Lazar 2008 *CZR, Ur, Rus, ESp*, 2009 *Geo*, 2010 *Geo*,

Pt, Sp, Tun, Ur, Ur, 2011 Rus, Sp, Nm, ArJ, Ukr, S, Ar, Geo, 2012 Pt, Rus, Geo, Sp, US, 2013 Pt, Rus, Bel, Geo

MV Lemnaru 2009 Sp, Rus, 2010 Ur, Ur, 2011 Rus, Geo, Sp, ArJ, S, Ar, Geo, 2012 Pt, Rus, Geo, Sp, Ukr, Ur, J, US

G Leonte 1984 S, F, 1985 E, It, USS, 1987 It, USS, Z, S, USS, F, 1988 It, Sp, US, USS, USS, F, W, 1989 It, E, Sp, Z, Sa, USS, S, 1990 It, F, H, Sp, It, 1991 It, NZ, F, S, F, C, 1992 USS, F, It, Ar, 1993 Tun, F, Sp, F, I, 1994 Sp, Ger, Rus, It, W, It, 1995 F, S, J, J, C, SA, A

M Leuciuc 1987 F

T Luca 1995 Ar, F, It, 1996 F

V Lucaci 1996 Bel

V Lucaci 2009 Fj, 2010 Sp, Ukr, 2011 Pt, Sp, 2012 Pt, Rus, Geo, Ukr, Ur, J, US, 2013 Pt, Rus, Sp, Bel, Geo, Rus

A Lungu 1980 It, USS, 1981 It, Sp, USS, S, NZ, F, 1982 WGe, It, USS, Z, Z, F, 1983 Mor, WGe, It, USS, Pol, W, USS, F, 1984 It, S, F, Sp, 1985 E, It, Tun, USS, USS, It, 1986 Pt, S, F, Tun, Tun, Pt, F, I, 1987 It, USS, Z, F, S, USS, F, 1988 It, Sp, US, USS, USS, F, W, 1989 It, E, Sp, Z, Sa, USS, S, 1990 It, F, It, 1991 It, NZ, F, S, F, C, Fj, 1992 Sp, It, USS, F, Ar, 1995 A

R Lungu 2002 Pt, H, It, Sp, W, S, 2003 Pt

A Lupu 2006 S

C Lupu 1998 Pol, I, 1999 F, 2000 Mor, It, 2001 Pt, H, Rus, W, 2002 H, Rus

S Luric 1951 EGe, 1952 EGe, EGe, 1953 It, 1955 Cze

V Luscal 1958 Sp, WGe, EGe

F Macaneata 1983 USS

M Macovei 2006 Ukr, Rus, 2007 Geo, Rus, Pt, 2008 Geo, Rus, CZR, Ur, Rus, ESp, 2009 Rus, Geo, ItA, 2010 Ger, Geo, Sp, Ukr, 2011 Pt, Geo, Nm, Ukr, S, Ar, E, Geo, 2012 Pt, Rus, Geo, Sp, Ukr, Ur, J, US, 2013 Pt, Rus, Sp, Bel, Geo, Rus

V Maftei 1995 Ar, F, It, 1996 Bel, 1997 WalA, W, F, 1998 Ar, 2001 Pt, Sp, H, Geo, I, 2002 Pt, Sp, Rus, Geo, I, It, Sp, S, 2003 Pt, Geo, CZR, F, W, I, A, Ar, Nm, 2004 Pt, Sp, Rus, Geo, W, J, CZR, 2005 Rus, Geo, Ukr, C, I, 2006 CZR

G Malancu 1976 H, It, USS, Bul

A Man 1988 US

V Man 1988 USS, USS

D Manoileanu 1949 Cze

DG Manole 2009 Ger, 2012 Rus, Geo, Sp, Ur, 2013 Pt, Rus, Sp, Bel

G Manole 1959 Pol, 1960 Pol, EGe, Cze

AV Manta 1996 Bel, 1997 F, 1998 Ar, Geo, I, 2000 F, 2001 Pt, Sp, Rus, Geo, 2002 Sp, H, Rus, I, It, Sp, 2003 Pt, Rus, 2005 C, I, 2006 Geo, CZR, Pt, Geo, 2007 It, S, NZ, 2009 Pt, Ur, F, ItA, 2010 Rus, Pt, Ukr, Tun, Ur, Ur, 2012 J, US

H Manu 1919 US Army, F Army, 1927 F, Ger

N Marascu 1919 US Army, F Army, 1924 F, US, 1927 F, Cze

A Marasescu 1927 F, Ger, 1936 It, Ger

E Marculescu 1936 F, It, Ger, 1937 It, 1939 It, 1940 It

A Marghescu 1980 Pol, 1981 It, 1983 W, USS, F, 1984 S, F, Sp, 1985 E

I Marica 1972 WGe, F, 1973 Sp, Mor, WGe, F, 1974 Mor, Sp, Cze, EGe, F, Cze, 1975 It, Sp

A Marin 1978 Cze, Sp, Pol, 1979 F, 1980 Pol, 1982 USS, 1983 Pol, 1984 Sp, 1985 USS, It, 1986 Pt, 1987 USS, Z

A Marin 2008 CZR

N Marin 1991 Fj, 1992 Sp, It, 1993 F, I, 1995 Ar, F, It

A Marinache 1949 Cze, 1951 EGe, 1952 EGe, EGe, 1955 Cze, 1957 F, Bel, F, 1960 F, 1961 Pol, EGe, Cze, EGe, F, 1962 Cze, Pol

V Marinescu 1967 Pt, WGe, 1968 Cze, 1969 Cze, F

F Marioara 1994 E, 1996 Pol, 1998 Geo, I

S Maris 2010 Ukr, Ukr, Nm, ArJ, ItA, Tun

V Mariscaru 2011 Rus, Geo

A Mateescu 1959 EGe, Pol, Cze, EGe, 1960 Pol, EGe, Cze, 1962 EGe, Pol, 1963 Bul, EGe, Cze, 1964 Cze, EGe, 1965 WGe, F, 1966 F, 1970 It, F, 1973 Sp, WGe, F, 1974 Mor, Pol, Sp

AT Matei 2013 Geo, Rus

A Mateiescu 1934 It, 1936 F, Ger

R Mavrodin 1998 Geo, I, 1999 F, A, US, I, 2000 H, Pt, Sp, Geo, F, It, 2002 Pt, Sp, H, I, It, Sp, W, 2003 I, A, Ar, Nm, 2004 Pt, Sp, Rus, Geo, W, J, CZR, 2005 Rus, J, US, S, Pt, 2006 Ukr, Rus, F, Geo, Sp, S, 2007 Geo, ESp, ItA, Nm, It, S, Pt, NZ, 2009 Ur

F Maxim 2007 Rus

G Mazilu 1958 Sp, WGe, 1959 EGe, Pol, Cze

S Mehedinti 1951 EGe, 1953 It

G Melinte 1958 EGe, It

P Mergisescu 1960 Pol, EGe, Cze

C Mersoiu 2000 Mor, Pt, 2001 I, 2002 S, S, 2003 Pt, Sp, Geo, CZR, F, W, 2004 CZR, Pt, Sp, Rus, It, W, J, CZR, 2005 Rus, Geo, Ukr, I, 2006 CZR, Pt, Geo, Sp, 2007 Geo, Sp, CZR, Rus, Pt, 2008 Geo, Sp, Pt, Rus, CZR, Ur, Rus, ESp, 2009 Geo

A Miclescu 1971 Mor

S Mihailescu 1919 F Army, 1924 F, US, 1927 F

D Mihalache 1973 Mor

M Mihalache 2007 Pt, 2008 Geo, Sp, Rus

V Mihalascu 1967 Pol, WGe

A Mitocaru 1992 Ar, 1993 Pt, Sp, F

A Mitu 2013 Sp, Bel, Geo

P Mitu 1996 Bel, Pol, 1997 W, Bel, Ar, It, 1998 H, Pol, Ukr, Ar, Geo, I, 1999 F, S, A, US, I, 2000 H, Pt, Sp, Geo, It, 2001 Pt, Sp, H, Rus, 2002 Pt, Sp, H, Rus, Geo, Sp, W, S, S, 2003 Geo, 2005 I, 2006 Geo, 2009 Sp, Ger, Rus, Pt

M Miu 2003 Pt, Sp

V Mladin 1955 Cze, 1957 Bel, F, 1958 Sp, WGe, It, 1959 EGe, 1960 F

S Mocanu 1996 Bel, 1998 H, Pol, Ukr, 2000 Mor, Pt

T Moldoveanu 1937 F, Ger, 1938 F, Ger, 1939 It, 1940 It

O Morariu 1984 Sp, 1985 Tun

V Morariu 1952 EGe, EGe, 1953 It, 1955 Cze, 1957 F, Cze, Bel, F, 1959 EGe, 1960 F, 1961 Pol, Cze, EGe, F, 1962 Cze, EGe, Pol, It, F, 1963 F, 1964 WGe, F

C Moscu 1934 It, 1937 It

M Mot 1980 Mor, 1982 It, USS, Z, 1985 It, It, 1986 F, Tun, 1988 US, USS

M Motoc 1988 US, 1989 S

P Motrescu 1973 Mor, Ar, Ar, 1974 Mor, Pol, Sp, Cze, 1975 JAB, Pol, F, 1976 H, It, Sp, Bul, Pol, F, Mor, 1977 Sp, It, F, Pol, It, F, 1978 Cze, Sp, Pol, F, 1979 It, Sp, USS, W, Pol, 1980 It, Mor

B Munteanu 2000 It

IC Munteanu 1940 It, 1942 It

M Munteanu 1973 WGe, F, 1974 Mor, Sp, Cze, EGe, F, Cze, 1975 It, Sp, JAB, Pol, F, 1976 H, It, Sp, Pol, Mor, 1978 Pol, F, 1979 It, Sp, W, Pol, 1980 It, I, Pol, F, 1981 It, Sp, USS, S, NZ, F, 1982 F, 1983 Mor, WGe, It, USS, Pol, W, USS, F, 1984 It, S, F, 1985 USS, 1986 S, Tun, Pt, F, 1988 It, Sp

T Munteanu 2003 CZR, 2004 CZR

F Murariu 1976 H, USS, Bul, Pol, F, Mor, 1977 Sp, It, F, Pol, It, F, 1978 Cze, Sp, Pol, F, 1979 It, Sp, USS, W, Pol, F, 1980 It, I, Pol, F, 1981 USS, NZ, 1982 USS, Z, Z, F, 1983 Mor, WGe, It, USS, Pol, W, F, 1984 It, S, F, Sp, 1985 E, It, Tun, USS, USS, It, 1986 Pt, S, F, Tun, 1987 It, USS, Z, S, USS, F, 1988 It, Sp, US, USS, USS, F, W, 1989 It, E, Sp, Z

D Musat 1974 Sp, Cze, EGe, Cze, 1975 It, JAB, Pol, F, 1976 Mor, 1980 Mor

M Nache 1980 Mor

M Nagel 1958 EGe, 1960 Pol, EGe, Cze

R Nanu 1952 EGe, EGe, 1953 It, 1955 Cze, 1957 F, Bel, F

V Nastase 1985 Tun, USS, 1986 Tun, Pt, F, I

D Neaga 1988 It, Sp, USS, F, W, 1989 It, E, Sp, Z, Sa, USS, S, 1990 It, F, H, Sp, USS, 1991 It, F, S, F, C, Fj, 1993 Tun, F, Sp, I, 1994 Sp, Ger, Rus, It, W, It, E, 1995 F, S, J, J, C, 1996 Pt, F

I Neagu 1972 Mor, Cze

E Necula 1987 It, F

P Nedelcovici 1924 F

C Nedelcu 1964 Cze, EGe

M Nedelcu 1993 Pt, Tun, F, 1994 Sp, It, 1995 Ar, F, It

V Nedelcu 1996 Pol, 1997 WalA, F, W, Ar, F, 1998 H, Pol, Ukr, Ar, 2000 H, 2001 I, W, E, 2002 Rus, Geo

I Negreci 1994 E, 1995 F, J, C, SA, A, Ar, F, It

I Nemes 1924 F, US, 1927 Ger, Cze

N Nere 2006 *CZR*, 2007 *CZR*, *Rus*, *Pt*, 2008 *Sp*, *Pt*, *Rus*, 2009 *Sp*, *Ger*, *Rus*, *Geo*, *Pt*, 2011 *Pt*, *Rus*, *Geo*, *Sp*, *Nm*, *E*
I Niacsu 2012 *Sp*, *Ukr*, 2013 *Sp*, *Bel*, *Geo*
G Nica 1964 *Cze*, *EGe*, *WGe*, 1966 *It*, *F*, 1967 *Pol*, *F*, 1969 *Pol*, *WGe*, *Cze*, *F*, 1970 *It*, *F*, 1971 *It*, *Mor*, *F*, 1972 *Mor*, *Cze*, *WGe*, *F*, 1973 *Sp*, *Mor*, *Ar*, *Ar*, *WGe*, *F*, 1974 *Mor*, *Pol*, *Sp*, *Cze*, *EGe*, *F*, *Cze*, 1975 *It*, *Sp*, *JAB*, *Pol*, *F*, 1976 *H*, *It*, *Sp*, *USS*, *Bul*, *Pol*, *F*, *Mor*, 1977 *Sp*, *It*, *F*, *Pol*, *It*, *F*, 1978 *Pol*, *F*
N Nichitean 1990 *It*, *Sp*, *It*, *USS*, 1991 *It*, *F*, *F*, *C*, *Fj*, 1992 *USS*, *It*, *Ar*, 1993 *Pt*, *Tun*, *F*, *Sp*, 1994 *Sp*, *Ger*, *Rus*, *It*, *W*, *It*, 1995 *F*, *S*, *J*, *J*, *C*, 1997 *WalA*, *F*
G Nicola 1927 *F*, *Ger*, *Cze*
C Nicolae 2003 *Pt*, *Rus*, 2006 *Sp*, 2007 *ItA*, *Nm*, *Pt*, *Rus*, 2009 *Geo*, *Pt*, *Ur*, *F*, *ItA*, *Fj*, 2010 *Pt*, *Ukr*, *Nm*, *ArJ*, *Tun*, *Ur*, 2011 *Pt*, *Nm*, *ArJ*, *Ukr*, *E*
M Nicolae 2003 *I*, *A*
N Nicolau 1940 *It*
M Nicolescu 1969 *Pol*, *WGe*, *Cze*, *F*, 1971 *It*, *Mor*, *F*, 1972 *Mor*, *Cze*, *WGe*, *F*, 1973 *Sp*, *Mor*, *Ar*, *Ar*, *WGe*, *F*, 1974 *Mor*, *Cze*, *EGe*, *F*, *Cze*, 1975 *It*, *Sp*, *Pol*, *F*
P Niculescu 1958 *It*, 1959 *EGe*, *Cze*
V Niculescu 1938 *F*, *Ger*
F Nistor 1986 *Tun*
V Nistor 1959 *EGe*, *Pol*, *EGe*
Nistor 2013 *Rus*

M Oblomenco 1967 *It*, *Pt*, *WGe*, *F*
G Olarasu 2000 *Mor*, *H*
M Olarasu 2000 *Mor*
V Onutu 1967 *It*, *Pt*, *Pol*, *WGe*, *F*, 1968 *Cze*, 1969 *F*, 1971 *It*, *Mor*
N Oprea 2000 *It*, 2001 *Pt*, *Sp*, *H*, *Rus*, *Geo*, *I*, *W*, *E*
F Opris 1986 *F*, *Tun*, *Tun*, *Pt*, *F*, *I*, 1987 *F*
G Oprisor 2004 *W*, *J*, *CZR*, 2005 *Rus*, *Ukr*, *J*, *US*, *S*, *Pt*
T Oroian 1988 *F*, *W*, 1989 *It*, *E*, *Sp*, *Z*, *USS*, 1990 *Sp*, *It*, 1993 *Pt*, *Tun*, *F*, *Sp*, *I*, 1994 *Sp*, *Ger*, *Rus*, *It*, *W*, *It*, *E*, 1995 *F*, *S*, *J*, *J*, *C*
M Ortelecan 1972 *Mor*, *Cze*, *WGe*, *F*, 1974 *Pol*, 1976 *It*, *Sp*, *USS*, *Bul*, *F*, 1977 *Sp*, *It*, *F*, *Pol*, *It*, *F*, 1978 *Cze*, *Sp*, 1979 *F*, 1980 *USS*

A Palosanu 1952 *EGe*, *EGe*, 1955 *Cze*, 1957 *F*, *Cze*
E Pana 1937 *F*, *Ger*
M Paraschiv 1975 *Sp*, *JAB*, *Pol*, *F*, 1976 *H*, *It*, *Sp*, *USS*, *Bul*, *F*, *Mor*, 1977 *Sp*, *It*, *Pol*, *F*, 1978 *Cze*, *Sp*, *Pol*, *F*, 1979 *It*, *Sp*, *W*, 1980 *It*, *I*, *F*, 1981 *It*, *USS*, *S*, *NZ*, *F*, 1982 *WGe*, *It*, *USS*, *Z*, *Z*, *F*, 1983 *Mor*, *WGe*, *It*, *USS*, *Pol*, *W*, *USS*, *F*, 1984 *It*, *S*, *F*, 1985 *E*, *It*, *Tun*, *USS*, *USS*, *It*, 1986 *Pt*, *S*, *Tun*, 1987 *It*, *USS*, *Z*, *F*, *S*, *USS*, *F*
G Parcalabescu 1940 *It*, 1942 *It*, 1949 *Cze*, 1951 *EGe*, 1952 *EGe*, *EGe*, 1953 *It*, 1955 *Cze*, 1957 *Cze*, *Bel*, *F*, 1958 *It*, 1959 *EGe*, *Pol*, *Cze*, 1960 *Pol*, *EGe*, *Cze*
G Pasache 2001 *E*
V Pascu 1983 *It*, *Pol*, *W*, *USS*, *F*, 1984 *It*, 1985 *USS*, 1986 *Pt*, *S*, *F*, *Tun*, *I*, 1987 *F*, 1988 *It*
C Patrichi 1993 *Pt*, *Tun*
A Pavlovici 1972 *Mor*, *Cze*
A Penciu 1955 *Cze*, 1957 *F*, *Cze*, *Bel*, *F*, 1958 *Sp*, *WGe*, *EGe*, *It*, 1959 *EGe*, *Pol*, *Cze*, *EGe*, 1960 *F*, 1961 *Pol*, *EGe*, *Cze*, *EGe*, *F*, 1962 *Cze*, *EGe*, *Pol*, *It*, *F*, 1963 *Bul*, *Cze*, *F*, 1964 *WGe*, *F*, 1965 *WGe*, *F*, 1966 *It*, *F*, 1967 *F*
I Peter 1973 *Sp*, *Mor*
AA Petrache 1998 *H*, *Pol*, 1999 *F*, *S*, *A*, *US*, *I*, 2000 *Mor*, *H*, *Pt*, *Sp*, *Geo*, *F*, 2001 *W*, *E*, 2002 *Pt*, *Sp*, *H*, *Rus*, *I*, *It*, *Sp*, *W*, *S*, *S*, 2003 *Pt*, *Sp*, *Rus*, 2004 *It*, *W*, *J*, *CZR*
CC Petre 2001 *E*, 2002 *Pt*, *Sp*, *H*, *Rus*, *Geo*, *I*, *It*, *Sp*, *W*, *S*, *S*, 2003 *Pt*, *Rus*, *Geo*, *CZR*, *F*, *W*, *I*, *A*, *Ar*, *Nm*, 2004 *CZR*, *Pt*, *Sp*, *Rus*, *Geo*, *It*, *W*, *J*, *CZR*, 2005 *Rus*, *Geo*, *Ukr*, *J*, *US*, *S*, *Pt*, *C*, *I*, 2006 *Geo*, *CZR*, *Pt*, *Ukr*, *Rus*, *F*, *Geo*, *Sp*, *S*, 2007 *Geo*, *Sp*, *CZR*, *ESp*, *ItA*, *Nm*, *It*, *S*, *Pt*, *NZ*, 2008 *Sp*, *Rus*, 2009 *Ger*, *Pt*, *Ur*, *F*, *ItA*, *ItA*, 2010 *Ger*, *Rus*, *Geo*, *Pt*, *Sp*, *Tun*, *Ur*, *Ur*, 2011 *Pt*, *Rus*, *Geo*, *Sp*, *Nm*, *ArJ*, *Ukr*, *S*, *Ar*, *E*, *Geo*, 2012 *Pt*, *Rus*, *Geo*, *Sp*, *Ur*
SA Petrichei 2002 *I*, *S*, *S*, 2003 *Sp*, *Rus*, *Geo*, *CZR*, *F*, *W*, *I*, *Ar*, *Nm*, 2004 *Pt*, *Sp*, *Rus*, *Geo*, 2007 *ESp*, *Nm*, 2009 *Ur*, *ItA*, *ItA*, *Fj*
P Petrisor 1985 *It*, 1987 *USS*
H Peuciulescu 1927 *F*
M Picoiu 2001 *Pt*, *H*, 2002 *Pt*, *Sp*, *H*, *Rus*, *I*, *It*, *Sp*, *W*
A Pilotschi 1985 *It*, *Tun*, 1987 *S*
C Pinghert 1996 *Bel*
I Pintea 1974 *Pol*, 1976 *Pol*, *F*, *Mor*, 1977 *Sp*, *It*, *F*, *Pol*, *It*, *F*, 1979 *It*, *Sp*, *USS*, *W*, *Pol*, *F*, 1980 *It*, *USS*
D Piti 1987 *USS*, *F*, 1988 *It*, *Sp*, *US*, 1991 *S*
T Pllotschi 2011 *Sp*
Plumea 1927 *Ger*
S Podarescu 1979 *Pol*, *F*, 1980 *USS*, 1982 *WGe*, *It*, *USS*, *F*, 1983 *Mor*, *WGe*, *USS*, *F*, 1984 *It*, 1985 *E*, *It*
C Podea 2001 *Geo*, *I*, 2002 *I*, *It*, *Sp*, *W*, *S*, 2003 *Pt*, *Sp*, *Rus*, *F*, *A*
R Polizu 1919 *US*
A Pop 1970 *It*, 1971 *It*, *Mor*, 1972 *Mor*, *Cze*, *F*, 1973 *WGe*, *F*, 1974 *Mor*, *Pol*, *Sp*, *EGe*, *F*, *Cze*, 1975 *It*, *Sp*, *JAB*, *Pol*, *F*
D Popa 1993 *Tun*, *F*, *Sp*
I Popa 1934 *It*, 1936 *F*, *It*, *Ger*, 1937 *H*, *F*, 1938 *F*, *Ger*, 1939 *It*, 1940 *It*, 1942 *It*
M Popa 1962 *EGe*
N Popa 1952 *EGe*
V Poparlan 2007 *Nm*, *Pt*, 2008 *Geo*, *Sp*, *Pt*, *Ur*, *Rus*, *ESp*, 2009 *Sp*, *Ger*, *Rus*, *Geo*, 2011 *Pt*, *Rus*, *Geo*, *Sp*, *ArJ*, *Ukr*, *S*, *Ar*, *E*, *Geo*, 2012 *Ukr*, 2013 *Rus*
A Popean 1999 *S*, 2001 *Pt*, *H*
CD Popescu 1997 *Bel*, 2003 *CZR*, *F*, *W*, *I*, *A*, *Ar*, *Nm*, 2004 *CZR*, *Pt*, *Sp*, *Rus*, *Geo*, *J*, *CZR*, 2005 *Rus*, *S*, *Pt*, *C*, 2006 *CZR*, *Ukr*, *Rus*, *F*, *Geo*, *Sp*, *S*, 2007 *Geo*, *Sp*, *CZR*, *ESp*, *ItA*, *Nm*, *It*, *Pt*, 2009 *Ur*, *F*, *ItA*, 2010 *Geo*, *Pt*, *Sp*, *Ukr*, *Ukr*, *ArJ*, *ItA*, *Tun*, *Ur*, *Ur*, 2011 *Pt*, *Rus*, *ArJ*
C Popescu 1986 *Tun*, *Pt*, *F*
I Popescu 1958 *EGe*
I Popescu 2001 *Pt*, *Sp*, *H*, *Rus*, *Geo*
C Popescu-Colibasi 1934 *It*
V Popisteanu 1996 *Pt*, *F*, *Pol*
F Popovici 1973 *Sp*, *Mor*
N Postolache 1972 *WGe*, *F*, 1973 *Sp*, *Mor*, *WGe*, *F*, 1974 *Mor*, *Pol*, *Sp*, *EGe*, *F*, *Cze*, 1975 *It*, *Sp*, *Pol*, *F*, 1976 *H*, *It*
C Preda 1961 *Pol*, *Cze*, 1962 *EGe*, *F*, 1963 *Bul*, *EGe*, *Cze*, *F*, 1964 *Cze*, *EGe*, *WGe*, *F*
C Pristavita 2013 *Rus*
H Pungea 2012 *J*, *US*, 2013 *Sp*, *Bel*, *Geo*, *Rus*

NF Racean 1988 *USS*, *USS*, *F*, *W*, 1989 *It*, *E*, *Z*, *Sa*, *USS*, 1990 *H*, *Sp*, *It*, *USS*, 1991 *NZ*, *F*, *F*, *C*, *Fj*, 1992 *Sp*, *It*, *USS*, *F*, *It*, *Ar*, 1993 *Pt*, *Tun*, *F*, *Sp*, 1994 *Ger*, *Rus*, *It*, *W*, 1995 *F*, *S*, *J*, *J*, *C*, *SA*, *A*
A Radoi 2008 *CZR*, 2009 *ItA*, *Fj*, 2010 *Sp*, *Ukr*, *Ukr*, *Nm*, *ArJ*, *ItA*, *Tun*, 2011 *Geo*, *Sp*, *ArJ*, *Ukr*, 2012 *Rus*, *Sp*, *Ukr*, *Ur*, *US*, 2013 *Pt*, *Rus*, *Sp*, *Bel*, *Geo*, *Rus*
M Radoi 1995 *F*, 1996 *Pt*, *Pol*, 1997 *WalA*, *F*, *W*, *Bel*, *Ar*, *F*, *It*, 1998 *H*, *Pol*, *Ukr*
P Radoi 1980 *Mor*
T Radu 1991 *NZ*
C Raducanu 1985 *It*, 1987 *It*, *USS*, *Z*, *F*, *S*, 1989 *It*, *E*, *Sp*, *Z*
A Radulescu 1980 *USS*, *Pol*, 1981 *It*, *Sp*, *USS*, *S*, *F*, 1982 *WGe*, *It*, *USS*, *Z*, *Z*, 1983 *Pol*, *W*, *USS*, *F*, 1984 *It*, *S*, *F*, *Sp*, 1985 *E*, *USS*, 1988 *It*, *Sp*, *US*, *USS*, *USS*, *F*, *W*, 1989 *It*, *E*, *Sa*, *USS*, 1990 *It*, *F*, *H*, *Sp*, *It*, *USS*
T Radulescu 1958 *Sp*, *WGe*, 1959 *EGe*, *Pol*, *Cze*, *EGe*, 1963 *Bul*, *EGe*, *Cze*, 1964 *F*, 1965 *WGe*, *F*, 1966 *Cze*
D Rascanu 1972 *WGe*, *F*
G Rascanu 1966 *It*, *F*, 1967 *It*, *Pt*, *Pol*, *WGe*, *F*, 1968 *Cze*, *Cze*, *F*, 1969 *Pol*, *WGe*, *Cze*, *F*, 1970 *It*, *F*, 1971 *It*, *Mor*, *F*, 1972 *Mor*, *Cze*, *WGe*, *F*, 1974 *Sp*
CA Ratiu 2003 *CZR*, 2005 *J*, *US*, *S*, *Pt*, *C*, *I*, 2006 *CZR*, *Pt*, *Ukr*, *Rus*, *F*, *Geo*, *Sp*, *S*, 2007 *Sp*, *CZR*, *ESp*, *It*, *S*, *Pt*, *NZ*, *Rus*, *Pt*, 2009 *Geo*, *Pt*, 2010 *Sp*, 2011 *Nm*, *ArJ*, *Ukr*, *E*, 2012 *Ur*, *US*
I Ratiu 1992 *It*
S Rentea 2000 *Mor*
I Roman 1976 *Bul*
AM Rosca 2013 *Rus*
M Rosca 2012 *Ukr*, 2013 *Pt*, *Rus*, *Sp*

C Rosu 1993 *I*
I Rotaru 1995 *J, J, C, Ar, It,* 1996 *Pt, F, Pol,* 1997 *W, Bel, Ar, F*
L Rotaru 1999 *F, A, I*
N Rus 2007 *Rus*
VS Rus 2007 *Rus, Pt,* 2008 *Geo, Pt, Rus,* 2009 *F, ItA, Fj,* 2012 *Ur, J, US*
M Rusu 1959 *EGe,* 1960 *F,* 1961 *Pol, Cze,* 1962 *Cze, EGe, Pol, It, F,* 1963 *Bul, EGe, Cze, F,* 1964 *WGe, F,* 1965 *WGe, F,* 1966 *Cze, It, F,* 1967 *It, Pt, Pol*
V Rusu 1960 *Pol, EGe, Cze,* 1961 *EGe, F,* 1962 *Cze, EGe, Pol, It, F,* 1964 *Cze, EGe, WGe, F,* 1965 *WGe,* 1966 *It, F,* 1967 *WGe,* 1968 *Cze*

I Sadoveanu 1939 *It,* 1942 *It*
AA Salageanu 1995 *Ar, F, It,* 1996 *Pt, F, Pol,* 1997 *W, Bel, F*
V Samuil 2000 *It,* 2001 *Pt, E,* 2002 *Pt, Sp, Geo*
C Sasu 1989 *Z,* 1991 *It, NZ, F, S, F, C, Fj,* 1993 *I*
C Sauan 1999 *S, A, US, I,* 2000 *It,* 2002 *Geo, I, It, Sp,* 2003 *Pt, Rus, Geo, CZR, F, W, I, A, Ar, Nm,* 2004 *CZR, Pt, Sp, Rus, Geo, It, W, J, CZR,* 2005 *Rus, Geo, Ukr, J, US, S, Pt,* 2006 *Rus,* 2007 *Geo*
G Sava 1989 *Z, S,* 1990 *H, Sp, It, USS,* 1991 *It, F, S, F, C,* 1992 *Sp*
I Sava 1959 *EGe, Pol, Cze, EGe,* 1960 *F,* 1961 *Pol, EGe, Cze, EGe, F,* 1962 *Cze, Pol, It, F*
C Scarlat 1976 *H, Sp,* 1977 *F,* 1978 *Cze, Sp,* 1979 *It, Sp, USS, W, Pol, F,* 1980 *It, USS,* 1982 *USS*
R Schmettau 1919 *US Army, F Army*
V Sebe 1960 *Pol, EGe, Cze*
I Seceleanu 1992 *It, USS, F, It, Ar,* 1993 *Pt, Tun, F, Sp, F*
S Seceleanu 1986 *Pt, F, I,* 1990 *It*
E Septar 1996 *Bel, Pol,* 1997 *WalA, W,* 1998 *Pol, Ukr, I,* 1999 *F, S, A, US, I,* 2000 *It*
B Serban 1989 *Sa, USS, S,* 1990 *It,* 1992 *It, USS*
C Serban 1964 *Cze, EGe, WGe,* 1967 *Pol,* 1968 *Cze, F,* 1969 *Pol, WGe, Cze, F,* 1970 *It, F,* 1971 *It, Mor, F,* 1972 *F,* 1973 *WGe, F,* 1974 *Mor*
M Serbu 1967 *It*
E Sfetescu 1924 *F, US,* 1927 *Cze*
E Sfetescu 1934 *It,* 1936 *F, Ger,* 1937 *It*
G Sfetescu 1927 *F, Ger*
M Sfetescu 1924 *F, US,* 1927 *Ger, Cze*
N Sfetescu 1927 *F, Ger, Cze*
G Simion 1998 *H*
G Simion 1919 *US*
I Simion 1976 *H, It, Sp,* 1979 *Pol, F,* 1980 *F*
ML Sirbe 2008 *CZR,* 2010 *Ukr, Ukr, Nm, ArJ, Tun,* 2011 *Pt, Nm,* 2012 *Ur, J,* 2013 *Pt, Rus, Sp, Bel, Geo, Rus*
L Sirbu 1996 *Pt,* 2000 *Mor, H, Pt, Geo, F,* 2001 *H, Rus, Geo, I, W, E,* 2002 *Pt, Sp, H, Rus, I, It, S, S,* 2003 *Pt, Sp, CZR, F, W, I, A, Ar, Nm,* 2004 *Pt, Sp, Rus, Geo, It, W, CZR,* 2005 *Rus, Geo, Ukr, J, US, S, Pt, C,* 2006 *Geo, Pt, Ukr, Rus, F, Geo, Sp,* 2007 *Geo, ItA, It, S, Pt, NZ,* 2009 *Ur, F, ItA, ItA, Fj,* 2010 *Ger, Rus, Geo, Pt, Sp, Nm, ArJ, ItA, Ur, Ur,* 2011 *Rus, Nm, Ukr, S, E*
M Slobozeanu 1936 *F,* 1937 *H, F, Ger,* 1938 *F, Ger*
OS Slusariuc 1993 *Tun,* 1995 *J, J, C,* 1996 *Pt, F,* 1997 *Bel, Ar, F,* 1998 *H, Ar, Geo, I,* 1999 *F, S, A*
S Soare 2001 *I, W,* 2002 *Geo*
S Soare 1924 *F, US*
M Socaciu 2000 *It,* 2001 *I, W, E,* 2002 *It, W, S, S,* 2003 *Pt, Sp, Rus, Geo, CZR, F, W, I, A, Nm,* 2004 *CZR, Pt, Sp, Rus, Geo, It, W, J, CZR,* 2005 *Rus, Geo, Ukr, J, US, Pt, C, I,* 2006 *CZR*
S Socol 2001 *Sp, H, Rus, Geo,* 2002 *Pt, It, Sp, W,* 2003 *Sp, Rus, Geo, F, W, I, A, Ar, Nm,* 2004 *CZR, Pt, Sp, Rus, Geo,* 2005 *Rus, Geo, Ukr, C, I,* 2006 *Geo, CZR, Pt, Ukr, Rus, F, Geo, Sp, S,* 2007 *Geo, Sp, CZR, It, S, Pt, NZ,* 2009 *Ur, F, ItA, Fj,* 2010 *Ger, Rus, Geo, Pt, Sp, Ukr, Ukr, Nm, ArJ, ItA, Ur, Ur,* 2011 *Rus, Geo*
N Soculescu 1949 *Cze,* 1951 *EGe,* 1952 *EGe, EGe,* 1953 *It,* 1955 *Cze*
N Soculescu 1927 *Ger*
V Soculescu 1927 *Cze*
GL Solomie 1992 *Sp, F, It, Ar,* 1993 *Pt, Tun, F, Sp, F, I,* 1994 *Sp, Ger, W, It, E,* 1995 *F, S, J, J, C, SA, A, Ar, F, It,* 1996 *Pt, F, Pol,* 1997 *WalA, F, W, Bel, Ar, F, It,* 1998 *H, Pol, Ukr, Ar, Geo, I,* 1999 *S, A, US, I,* 2000 *Sp, F, It,* 2001 *Sp, H, Rus*
C Stan 1990 *H, USS,* 1991 *It, F, S, F, C, Fj,* 1992 *Sp, It, It, Ar,* 1996 *Pt, Bel, F, Pol,* 1997 *WalA, F, W, Bel,* 1998 *Ar, Geo,* 1999 *F, S, A, US, I*
A Stanca 1996 *Pt, Pol*
R Stanca 1997 *F,* 2003 *Sp, Rus,* 2009 *Geo, Pt*
A Stanciu 1958 *EGe, It*
G Stanciu 1958 *EGe, It*
C Stanescu 1957 *Bel,* 1958 *WGe,* 1959 *EGe,* 1960 *F,* 1961 *Pol, EGe, Cze,* 1962 *Cze, It, F,* 1963 *Bul, EGe, Cze, F,* 1964 *WGe, F,* 1966 *Cze, It*
C Stefan 1951 *EGe,* 1952 *EGe*
E Stoian 1927 *Cze*
E Stoica 1973 *Ar, Ar,* 1974 *Cze,* 1975 *Sp, Pol, F,* 1976 *Sp, USS, Bul, F, Mor,* 1977 *Sp, It, F, Pol, It, F,* 1978 *Cze, Sp, Pol, F,* 1979 *It, Sp, USS, W, Pol, F,* 1980 *It, USS, I, Pol, F,* 1981 *It, Sp, USS, S, NZ, F,* 1982 *WGe, It, USS, Z, Z, F*
G Stoica 1963 *Bul, Cze,* 1964 *WGe,* 1966 *It, F,* 1967 *Pt, F,* 1968 *Cze, Cze, F,* 1969 *Pol*
I Stroe 1986 *Pt*
E Suciu 1976 *Bul, Pol,* 1977 *It, F, It,* 1979 *USS, Pol, F,* 1981 *Sp*
M Suciu 1968 *F,* 1969 *Pol, WGe, Cze,* 1970 *It, F,* 1971 *It, Mor, F,* 1972 *Mor, F*
O Sugar 1983 *It,* 1989 *Z, Sa, USS, S,* 1991 *NZ, F*
K Suiogan 1996 *Bel*
F Surugiu 2008 *Ur, Rus, ESp,* 2010 *Ukr, Ukr, Nm, ArJ, ItA,* 2011 *Pt, Rus, Geo, Sp, ArJ, Ukr, S, Ar, Geo,* 2012 *Pt, Rus, Geo, Ukr, Ur, J, US,* 2013 *Pt, Rus, Sp, Bel, Geo*

D Talaba 1996 *Bel,* 1997 *F, It*
P Tamba 2012 *J, US,* 2013 *Bel*
C Tanase 1938 *F, Ger,* 1939 *It,* 1940 *It*
A Tanasescu 1919 *US Army, F Army,* 1924 *F, US*
N Tanoviceanu 1937 *It, H, F,* 1939 *It*
I Tarabega 1934 *It,* 1936 *It*
F Tasca 2008 *Ur, Rus, ESp,* 2009 *Sp, Ger, Rus, Geo, Pt*
V Tata 1971 *F,* 1973 *Ar, Ar*
CF Tatu 2003 *Ar,* 2004 *CZR, Pt, Sp, Rus, Geo, It, W,* 2005 *Ukr, J,* 2013 *Rus, Sp*
I Tatucu 1973 *Sp, Mor,* 1974 *Cze, F*
D Teleasa 1971 *It,* 1973 *Sp, Ar, Ar*
D Tenescu 1951 *EGe*
I Teodorescu 2001 *I, W, E,* 2002 *Pt, Sp, S, S,* 2003 *Pt, Sp, Rus, W, I, A, Ar, Nm,* 2004 *CZR, Pt, Sp, Rus, Geo, W, J, CZR,* 2005 *Rus, Geo, Ukr, J, US, S, Pt, C, I,* 2006 *Geo, CZR, Pt, Ukr, F, Geo, S,* 2007 *ESp, ItA*
I Teodorescu 1958 *Sp, WGe, EGe, It,* 1960 *Pol, EGe, Cze,* 1963 *Bul, EGe, Cze,* 1965 *WGe, F*
A Teofilovici 1957 *F, Cze, Bel, F,* 1958 *Sp, WGe,* 1959 *EGe,* 1960 *F,* 1961 *Pol, EGe, Cze, EGe, F,* 1962 *Cze, Pol, It, F,* 1963 *Bul, EGe, Cze, F,* 1964 *WGe*
O Tepurica 1985 *USS*
M Tibuleac 1957 *Bel, F,* 1959 *Pol, Cze,* 1966 *Cze,* 1967 *It, Pt, Pol, WGe,* 1968 *Cze, Cze*
G Ticleanu 1919 *F Army*
M Tigora 2004 *CZR*
A Tinca 1987 *USS, F*
VM Tincu 2002 *Pt, Sp, H, Rus, Geo, I, It, Sp, S, S,* 2003 *Pt, Sp, Rus, Geo, F, W,* 2004 *Sp,* 2005 *Geo, Ukr, C, I,* 2006 *Geo, CZR, F, S,* 2007 *Geo, Sp, CZR, ESp, ItA, Nm, It, S, Pt, NZ,* 2008 *Geo,* 2009 *F, ItA, ItA,* 2010 *Ger, Rus, Geo, Pt, Ur, Ur,* 2011 *Nm, S, Ar, E, Geo,* 2012 *Pt, Rus, Geo, Sp*
M Toader 1982 *WGe,* 1984 *Sp,* 1985 *E, It, Tun, USS,* 1986 *S, F, Tun, Tun, Pt, F, I,* 1987 *It, USS, Z, F, S, USS, F,* 1988 *F, W,* 1989 *It, E, Sp, Sa, USS, S,* 1990 *It, F, It*
P Toderasc 2000 *It,* 2001 *Pt, Rus, Geo, W, E,* 2002 *H, Rus, Geo, I, It, Sp, W, S, S,* 2003 *Sp, Rus, Geo, CZR, F, W, I, A, Ar, Nm,* 2004 *CZR, Pt, Sp, Rus, Geo, It, J, CZR,* 2005 *J, US, S, Pt, C, I,* 2006 *Geo, Pt, Ukr, Sp,* 2007 *Geo, ESp, ItA, Nm, It, S,* 2009 *ItA, Fj*
IR Tofan 1997 *Bel, Ar, F, It,* 1998 *H, Ar,* 1999 *I,* 2000 *Mor, Sp, Geo,* 2001 *Pt, Sp, H, Geo, I, W, E,* 2002 *Pt, Sp, H, Rus, Geo, I, It, Sp, W, S, S,* 2003 *Pt, Sp, Rus, Geo, CZR,*

F, W, I, A, Ar, Nm, 2004 Sp, Geo, It, W, J, 2005 Rus, Geo, Ukr, J, US, I, 2006 Geo, CZR, Pt, Geo, Sp, S, 2007 Geo, ESp, ItA, Nm, S
S Tofan 1985 USS, It, 1986 Tun, Pt, F, I, 1987 It, USS, Z, F, S, USS, F, 1988 It, Sp, US, USS, 1991 NZ, 1992 Ar, 1993 Pt, 1994 It, E
O Tonita 2000 Mor, H, Pt, Sp, Geo, F, 2001 Pt, Sp, H, Rus, Geo, I, 2002 Sp, It, Sp, W, 2003 Rus, Geo, F, W, I, A, Ar, Nm, 2004 Sp, Rus, Geo, It, 2005 Rus, Pt, C, I, 2006 Geo, Pt, Geo, Sp, S, 2007 Sp, CZR, It, S, Pt, NZ, 2009 Ur, F, ItA, ItA, Fj, 2010 Ger, Rus, Geo, Pt, Nm, ArJ, ItA, Ur, Ur, 2011 Pt, Rus, ArJ, Ukr, S, Ar, E, Geo, 2012 US, 2013 Pt, Rus
Traian 1942 It
N Tranca 1992 Sp
B Tudor 2003 CZR, A
F Tudor 1924 F, US
M Tudor 1924 F, US
AM Tudori 2003 F, W, I, A, Ar, Nm, 2004 Sp, Rus, Geo, W, J, CZR, 2005 Rus, Geo, Ukr, J, US, S, Pt, 2006 Geo, CZR, Ukr, Rus, F, 2007 Sp, CZR, ESp, ItA, Nm, It, S, Pt, 2009 Geo, Ur, ItA
D Tudosa 1999 S, 2002 Geo, I, It, 2003 Pt, W
T Tudose 1977 It, 1978 Cze, Sp, Pol, F, 1979 It, Sp, USS, 1980 USS
V Tufa 1985 USS, 1986 Pt, S, 1990 It, 1991 F, 1995 F, S, J, J, SA, A, 1996 Pt, F, Pol
D Tunaru 1985 It
O Turashvili 2012 Ur, J, US
V Turlea 1974 Sp, 1975 JAB, Pol, F, 1977 Pol
C Turut 1937 H, 1938 F
I Tutuianu 1960 Pol, EGe, 1963 Bul, EGe, Cze, 1964 Cze, EGe, WGe, 1965 WGe, F, 1966 Cze, It, F, 1967 Pt, Pol, WGe, F, 1968 Cze, Cze, F, 1969 Pol, WGe, Cze, F, 1970 It, F, 1971 F
G Tutunea 1992 Sp

M Ungur 1996 Bel
V Ungureanu 1979 It
V Urdea 1979 F
A Ursache 2012 Pt, Rus, Geo, Sp, Ukr, Ur, 2013 Pt, Sp, Geo
SF Ursache 2009 ItA, 2010 Ukr, Nm
VN Ursache 2004 It, W, CZR, 2005 S, C, 2006 Geo, Ukr, Rus, F, S, 2007 Geo, Sp, CZR, ESp, ItA, Nm, Pt, NZ, Rus, 2008 Pt, Rus, CZR, Rus, 2009 ItA, Fj, 2010 Ger, Rus, Geo, Pt, Sp, Ukr, Ukr, Nm, ArJ, ItA, Tun, Ur, Ur, 2011 Geo, Sp, Nm, ArJ, S, Ar, Geo, 2012 Pt, Rus, Geo, Sp, J, 2013 Pt, Sp, Bel, Geo

R Vacioiu 1977 It, F, It
E Valeriu 1949 Cze, 1952 EGe
M Vardala 1924 F, US
N Vardela 1927 F, Ger
G Varga 1976 It, USS, Bul, Pol, F, Mor, 1977 Sp, It, F, Pol, 1978 Sp
N Varta 1958 EGe
G Varzaru 1980 Mor, I, Pol, F, 1981 It, Sp, USS, F, 1983 Mor, WGe, It, USS, F, 1984 S, F, 1985 Tun, USS, 1986 F, 1988 It, Sp, US, USS, USS
Z Vasluianu 1989 Sp, Z, Sa
P Veluda 1967 It, Pt, Pol, WGe, F
R Veluda 1949 Cze, 1952 EGe
R Veluda 1968 Cze, Cze
N Veres 1986 Tun, Pt, 1987 F, USS, F, 1988 It, Sp, USS
M Vidrascu 1919 US Army, F Army
P Vidrascu 1924 F, US, 1927 Cze
M Vioreanu 1994 E, 1998 H, Pol, Ukr, Ar, Geo, I, 1999 F, S, A, US, I, 2000 Mor, Pt, Sp, Geo, F, 2001 Geo, 2002 Rus, Geo, I, It, Sp, 2003 Sp, Rus, F, I, A, Ar, Nm
A Visan 1949 Cze
D Vlad 2005 US, S, C, I, 2006 Rus, 2007 Sp, CZR, It, Rus, Pt, 2008 Sp, CZR
G Vlad 1991 C, Fj, 1992 Sp, It, USS, F, It, Ar, 1993 Pt, F, I, 1994 Sp, Ger, Rus, It, W, It, E, 1995 F, C, SA, A, Ar, It, 1996 Pt, F, 1997 W, Ar, F, It, 1998 Ar
V Vlad 1980 Mor
FA Vlaicu 2006 Ukr, F, Geo, Sp, S, 2007 Geo, Sp, CZR, ESp, ItA, Nm, S, NZ, Pt, 2008 Geo, Pt, Rus, CZR, Ur, 2009 Sp, Ger, Rus, Geo, Pt, Ur, F, ItA, ItA, Fj, 2010 Ger, Rus, Geo, Sp, Ukr, Ukr, ArJ, ItA, Tun, Ur, 2011 Pt, Rus, Geo, Sp, Nm, ArJ, Ukr, S, Ar, E, Geo, 2012 Pt, Rus, Geo, Ukr, 2013 Pt, Rus, Sp, Bel, Geo, Rus
C Vlasceanu 2000 Mor, Pt, Sp, Geo, F
B Voicu 2003 CZR, 2004 CZR, Pt, Sp, Rus, It, J, 2005 J, Pt
M Voicu 1979 Pol
M Voicu 2002 Pt
V Voicu 1951 EGe, 1952 EGe, EGe, 1953 It, 1955 Cze
R Voinov 1985 It, 1986 Pt, S, F, Tun
P Volvoreanu 1924 US
G Vraca 1919 US Army, F Army
M Vusec 1959 EGe, Pol, Cze, EGe, 1960 F, 1961 Pol, EGe, Cze, EGe, F, 1962 Cze, EGe, Pol, It, F, 1963 Bul, EGe, Cze, F, 1964 WGe, F, 1965 WGe, F, 1966 It, F, 1967 It, Pt, Pol, WGe, F, 1968 Cze, Cze, F, 1969 Pol, F
RL Vusec 1998 Geo, I, 1999 F, S, A, US, I, 2000 Mor, H, Pt, Sp, F, 2002 H, Rus, I

F Wirth 1934 It

I Zafiescu 1979 W, Pol, F
M Zafiescu 1980 Mor, 1986 I
D Zamfir 1949 Cze
B Zebega Suman 2004 CZR, Pt, Rus, Geo, It, W, CZR, 2005 Rus, Ukr, US, S, 2006 Ukr, Sp, 2007 Rus, Pt, 2008 Geo, Pt, Rus, CZR, Ur, 2010 Ger, Sp, Ukr, Ukr, Nm, ArJ, 2011 Pt, Rus, Geo, Sp, Nm, ArJ, Ukr, S, E
D Zlatoianu 1958 Sp, WGe, EGe, It, 1959 EGe, 1960 Pol, EGe, Cze, 1961 EGe, EGe, F, 1964 Cze, EGe, 1966 Cze

www.irb.com/laws

The IRB's Law Education web site

English • French • Spanish • Russian • Chinese • Japanese • Italian • Romanian • Dutch

- Read the Laws of the Game and the IRB Playing Charter
- Watch video clips and digital animations of the Laws in practice
- Take the self-test Law exam and download your awareness certificate
- Download PDF files of the Law Book

Get the free IRB Laws iPhone/iPad app - out now

RUSSIA

RUSSIA'S 2012–13 TEST RECORD

OPPONENTS	DATE	VENUE	RESULT
USA	9 Nov	N	Lost 26–40
Canada	17 Nov	N	Lost 3–35
Spain	2 Feb	H	Won 13–9
Romania	9 Feb	A	Lost 29–14
Georgia	23 Feb	H	Lost 9–23
Portugal	9 Mar	A	Won 31–23
Belgium	16 Mar	H	Won 43–32
Romania	8 Jun	A	Lost 30–20

ATTACKING BEARS SHOW THEIR STRENGTH

By Lúcás Ó'Ceallacháin

Getty Images

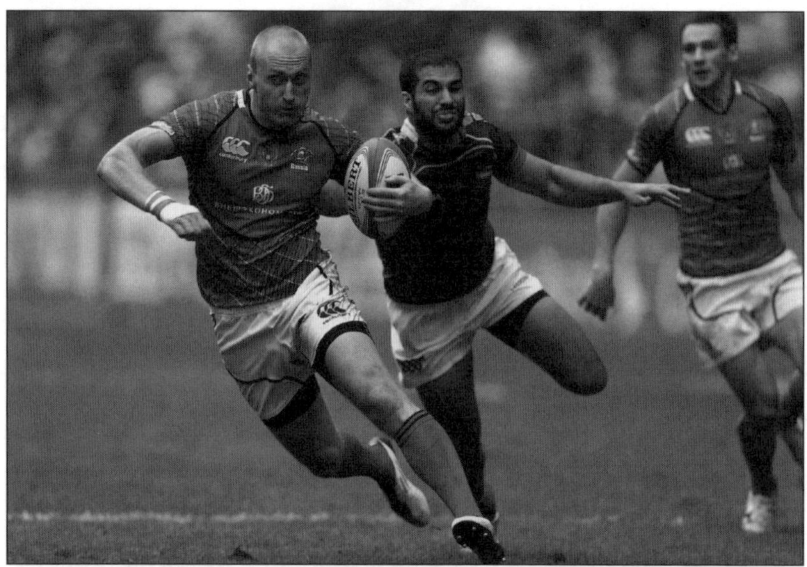

Russian Sevens continues to go from strength to strength after several positive performances in 2012/13.

It was a mixed year for the Russian Bears in Test rugby. The free-scoring backline that excited so many fans during Rugby World Cup 2011 continued to deliver a number of explosive performances, running in tries for fun with speed, power and panache. It was to be the defensive game, however, which frustrated so many Russian fans.

The season kicked off with a mouth-watering double-header against Canada and USA. The teams converged on Parc Eirias in Colwyn Bay, Wales, to face each other as part of an IRB initiative to provide Tier Two nations with more competitive matches ahead of Rugby World Cup 2015.

First up for Russia in the IRB International Rugby Series were USA and a rematch of the two nations' RWC 2011 clash and a strong rugby rivalry. Russia prepared for the Test with a 29–15 victory over Oxford University with Denis Simplikevich running riot. Despite all their attacking flair, though, conceding 15 points was a concern for Russia head coach Kingsley Jones going into the Test.

USA were clearly the hungrier of the two teams and their forward pack dominated the set pieces and breakdown. Under new coach Mike Tolkin, the Eagles ran up a 21–9 half-time lead through tries from prop Eric Fry, fly half Toby L'Estrange and second row Brian Doyle. Igor Klyuchnikov kept Russia in touch through his kicking but two yellow cards for the Bears proved costly. With Alexey Shcherban and Victor Gresev both going to the bin, USA continued to exploit gaps in the Russian defence, with scrum half Robbie Shaw crossing twice and veteran Chris Wyles once. Wyles added to his personal tally with five successful conversions, giving him 15 points for the match.

Russia continued to fight and there were encouraging signs when Vladimir Ostroushko, who impressed throughout, scored an excellent try. Livewire flanker Andrey Temnov chipped in with two tries in a tireless display. It was a case of too little too late for the Bears, however, as USA had built an unassailable lead in the first 60 minutes. The Eagles eventually ran out 40–26 winners, a result which will no doubt add more fuel to the fire for the next round of this rivalry.

There was little time for the Bears to lick their wounds as they faced Canada a week later. The Canucks were coming into the game on the back of a heavy 42–12 defeat to Samoa the previous week.

It was clear that Canada's preparation for the fixture in facing the Samoans was to be a great advantage in taking on the physicality of Russia's pack. A Canadian team looking to restore some pride proved too strong for the Russians with powerful running and set-piece dominance setting up a victory – their third in a row over their opponents.

It was Canada's backline who shone brightest in this game with tries from right wing Taylor Paris, centre Nick Blevins and two from man of the match Jeff Hassler. James Pritchard kept the pressure on the Bears with the boot, kicking three penalties and three conversions.

Undeterred, Russia pounded away at the Canadian line in the final quarter and only a tremendous defensive effort kept them at bay. Despite all their hard work, a solitary penalty from full back Klyuchnikov was the only reward as Russia went down 35–3.

Following a winter break and time to digest their performances, Russia returned to European Nations Cup action in February. Russia needed to consolidate their place in the top division and the games had the added spice of doubling up as RWC 2015 qualifiers.

First up was the visit of Spain to Sochi, host city for the 2014 Winter Olympic Games. A nervy performance saw Russia do just enough through a solitary Mikhail Babaev try and the trusty boot of Klyuchnikov to nick a 13–9 victory. Two sets of brothers took to the field for the Bears

– the front row pairing of Grigory and Valery Tsnobiladze and the half-back pairing of Alexander and Sergey Yanyushkin. The return of Alexander Yanyushkin was pivotal as the high-octane scrum half had been sorely missed by the Russian pack.

Romania, Russia's closest rivals in the competition, proved too hard a nut to crack with the resurgent home side winning a tough encounter in Bucharest 29–14. Too many penalties as a result of pressure from the Romanian Oaks allowed Florin Vlaicu to win his kicking duel with Klyuchnikov on this occasion.

A fortnight later, against defending champions Georgia, Klyuchnikov was outfoxed in another kicking duel, this time by Merab Kvirikashvili. The 23–9 defeat must have been difficult for the Russian team to take and means they may have to beat Georgia and Romania in 2014 if they are to qualify directly for RWC 2015 and avoid the Repechage.

Russia comprehensively outplayed Portugal next to win 31–23, scoring tries through backs Ostroushko and Vasily Artemyev, and forwards Kirill Kulemin and Temnov. This result paved the way for a six-try, 43–32 victory over Division 1A newcomers Belgium. While the Russians didn't have it all their own way in Sochi, Belgium were outclassed by an exciting brand of attacking rugby.

Russia took this playing style into the IRB Nations Cup in Bucharest in June, where they had the opportunity to pit themselves against another level of opposition. Building on their form, Russia put in a much-improved display against Romania, losing 30–20. Despite following that up with a 27–19 loss to Emerging Italy and 30–17 defeat to the Argentina Jaguars, the performances were much improved from the autumn.

While the fortunes of the Test team were mixed, there is no doubt that the season finished in Sevens heaven for Russian rugby. Building up to RWC Sevens 2013 in Moscow at the end of June, it was the Russian women's team who grabbed the headlines by winning their first ever European Sevens title. They clinched the European Women's Grand Prix Series ahead of fierce rivals and favourites, England.

The women then proved that was not a one-off when they dispatched them for a memorable 17–15 victory in front of their home fans to reach the RWC Sevens quarter-finals and secure core team status on the 2013/14 IRB Women's Sevens World Series. The men's team were not to be outdone, winning the Bowl final against Japan.

The Sevens momentum continued into the Kazan Universiade in July where many of the players from the men's and women's teams helped Russia win both gold medals. The success of the Sevens teams and tournaments will no doubt set a bright future for the game in Russia.

RUSSIA INTERNATIONAL STATISTICS

MATCH RECORDS UP TO 10 OCTOBER 2013

WINNING MARGIN

Date	Opponent	Result	Winning Margin
13/05/2000	Denmark	104–7	**97**
16/04/2000	Germany	89–6	**83**
11/06/2005	Ukraine	72–0	**72**
25/05/1995	Norway	66–0	**66**
18/09/1999	Ukraine	71–5	**66**

MOST POINTS IN A MATCH

BY THE TEAM

Date	Opponent	Result	Points
13/05/2000	Denmark	104–7	**104**
16/04/2000	Germany	89–6	**89**
17/02/2002	Netherlands	73–10	**73**
15/05/1999	Poland	72–13	**72**
11/06/2005	Ukraine	72–0	**72**

BY A PLAYER

Date	Player	Opponent	Points
16/04/2000	Konstantin Rachkov	Germany	**29**
15/05/1999	Konstantin Rachkov	Poland	**27**
16/02/2003	Konstantin Rachkov	Spain	**27**
02/06/2002	Werner Pieterse	Netherlands	**25**
19/07/2003	Konstantin Rachkov	USA A	**25**

MOST TRIES IN A MATCH

BY THE TEAM

Date	Opponent	Result	Tries
13/05/2000	Denmark	104–7	**17**
16/04/2000	Germany	89–6	**15**
02/10/1997	Poland	70–26	**12**

BY A PLAYER

Date	Player	Opponent	Tries
18/09/1999	Sergey Sergeev	Ukraine	**4**
13/05/2000	Andrey Kuzin	Denmark	**4**
21/04/2007	Igor Galinovskiy	Czech Republic	**4**

MOST CONVERSIONS IN A MATCH

BY THE TEAM

Date	Opponent	Result	Cons
18/09/1999	Ukraine	71–5	**8**
15/05/1999	Poland	72–13	**8**
13/05/2000	Denmark	104–7	**8**

BY A PLAYER

Date	Player	Opponent	Cons
15/05/1999	Konstantin Rachkov	Poland	**8**
13/05/2000	Konstantin Rachkov	Denmark	**8**
16/04/2000	Konstantin Rachkov	Germany	**7**

MOST PENALTIES IN A MATCH

BY THE TEAM

Date	Opponent	Result	Pens
16/02/2003	Spain	52–19	**6**
19/07/2003	USA A	30–21	**6**
08/03/2008	Spain	42–16	**6**

BY A PLAYER

Date	Player	Opponent	Pens
16/02/2003	Konstantin Rachkov	Spain	**6**
19/07/2003	Konstantin Rachkov	USA A	**6**
20/10/1996	Sergey Boldakov	Georgia	**5**
25/05/1993	Viktor Yakovlev	Georgia	**5**
19/05/2012	Yury Kushnarev	Spain	**5**

MOST DROP GOALS IN A MATCH

BY THE TEAM

Date	Opponent	Result	DGs
08/03/2003	Georgia	17–23	**2**

BY A PLAYER

Date	Player	Opponent	DGs
08/03/2003	Konstantin Rachkov	Georgia	**2**

MOST CAPPED PLAYERS

Name	Caps
Andrey Kuzin	**78**
Alexander Khrokin	**75**
Vyacheslav Grachev	**73**
Igor Klyuchnikov	**62**

LEADING TRY SCORERS

Name	Tries
Vyacheslav Grachev	**31**
Andrey Kuzin	**25**
Konstantin Rachkov	**16**
Alexander Gvozdovsky	**15**
Alexander Zakarlyuk	**14**

LEADING CONVERSION SCORERS

Name	Cons
Konstantin Rachkov	54
Yury Kushnarev	50
Vladimir Simonov	25
Victor Motorin	24

LEADING PENALTY SCORERS

Name	Pens
Yury Kushnarev	83
Konstantin Rachkov	47
Vladimir Simonov	21

LEADING DROP GOAL SCORERS

Name	DGs
Konstantin Rachkov	6
Werner Pieterse	2

LEADING POINT SCORERS

Name	Points
Yury Kushnarev	384
Konstantin Rachkov	347
Vladimir Simonov	178
Vyacheslav Grachev	155
Andrey Kuzin	125

RUSSIA INTERNATIONAL PLAYERS

UP TO 10 OCTOBER 2013

D Akulov 2003 *Pt, J, CZR, USAA*, 2004 *Sp, Geo, R, J, Geo*, 2005 *R, CZR, Pt, CZR*
A Andreev 2008 *ItA*
D Antonov 2011 *ItA, US, US, It, I*, 2012 *Pt, R, Ukr, Geo, Sp, Ur, ArJ*, 2013 *R, Elt, ArJ*
V Artemyev 2009 *Pt, R, Geo, Ger, C*, 2010 *Nm, Pt, Sp, R, Ger, Geo, US, E, Ur, ArJ, ArJ, J*, 2011 *Sp, Pt, R, Ukr, Geo, C, ItA, US, US, It, I, A*, 2012 *Sp, US, C*, 2013 *Sp, R, Geo, Pt, Bel*
V Ashurka 1993 *Geo*, 1994 *Nm, Ger, R, H*
O Azarenko 1999 *Ukr, Pol*, 2002 *Geo, Sp, Sp*, 2003 *CZR*, 2006 *Ukr, It*

M Babaev 2006 *Pt*, 2007 *Sp, CZR, Pt, R*, 2008 *Pt, CZR, ItA, R, Ur, Sp*, 2009 *Pt, R, Geo, Ger, S, ItA, C*, 2010 *Nm, Pt, Sp, R, Ger, Geo, US, E, Ur*, 2011 *Sp, Pt, R, Geo, ItA, US, I, A*, 2012 *Pt, R, Ukr, Geo, Elt, Ur, ArJ*, 2013 *Sp, R, Geo*
G Babkin 2012 *US*
V Balashov 1996 *CZR*, 1997 *Tun, Mor, Ukr, Cro*, 1998 *Sp, It, De*
P Baranovsky 1992 *Bel, F*, 1993 *Mor*, 1994 *F, Swe*, 1995 *Pol, Nor, De*, 1997 *Ukr, Pol*
S Bazhenov 2008 *ItA, Ur, Sp*, 2009 *Ur, C*
S Belousov 2006 *Ukr, Ukr, It*, 2007 *Geo*, 2008 *CZR, Ur*
R Bikbov 1993 *Mor, Geo, Pol*, 1994 *Nm, Sp, Ger, R, F, H*, 1996 *Geo, CZR*, 1997 *Tun, Mor, Ukr, Pol, Cro*, 1998 *Sp, It, De, Geo*, 1999 *Ukr, Pol, CZR, Ukr*, 2000 *De*, 2001 *H, Pt*, 2002 *H, Geo, CZR*, 2003 *J*
V Bogdanov 1992 *Ger*
S Boldakov 1992 *Bel, F*, 1996 *Mor, Geo*
V Boltenkov 2010 *ArJ*, 2011 *C*, 2012 *Pt, R, Geo, US*
V Bondarev 1993 *It*, 1994 *Nm, R*
S Borisov 1992 *Bel, F, Ger*, 1993 *Mor, Pol, It*, 1994 *Nm, Sp, Ger, F, H*, 1995 *Tun, Bel, Pol, F*, 1996 *Sp, Mor*, 2001 *Sp, H, R*
V Botvinnikov 2008 *Pt, Sp, Geo, CZR, ItA, R, Ur, Sp*, 2009 *Pt, S, ItA, Ur, C*, 2010 *Ger, Geo, E, Ur*, 2011 *US, It, A*, 2012 *Pt, R, Ukr, Elt*
C Breytenbach 2002 *Geo, R*
S Budnikov 1996 *CZR*, 1997 *Tun, Mor, Cro*, 2000 *Ger, De*, 2002 *Sp, H, Geo, R, Pt, CZR, H*
P Butenko 2012 *Ukr, Geo, Elt, ArJ, US, C*, 2013 *Sp, R, Geo, Pt, Bel, R, Elt, ArJ*
A Bychkov 1992 *Bel, F*, 1996 *Geo*, 1997 *Mor*
A Bykanov 2003 *J*, 2005 *R, CZR, Ukr, CZR*, 2006 *Geo*, 2011 *C, ItA, I*
A Byrnes 2011 *US, It, I, A*, 2012 *Elt, Ur*

A Chebotaryov 1992 *Bel, F, Ger*, 1994 *F*
V Chernykh 1997 *Cro*, 1998 *It*
A Chernyshev 2008 *Pt, Sp, Geo, CZR, ItA, R, Ur*, 2011 *ItA, US*
A Chupin 1999 *CZR, Ukr*, 2001 *R, Pt*, 2002 *H, CZR, H*, 2003 *CZR*

K Djincharadze 1995 *Tun, Bel, Pol*, 1997 *Pol*
D Dyatlov 1996 *CZR*, 1997 *Tun, Mor, Cro*, 1998 *Sp, It, De, Geo*, 1999 *Ukr, Pol, CZR, Ukr*, 2000 *De*, 2001 *R, Pt*, 2002 *Sp, H*, 2003 *CZR, USAA*, 2004 *Geo, R, J, US*
I Dymchenko 1994 *Swe*, 1995 *Nor, De*, 1996 *Sp*, 1997 *Pol*, 2002 *H, Geo, R, CZR, J, I, Geo*, 2003 *Sp, Geo, R, Pt*, 2004 *J, US*

A Emelyanov 1992 *Bel, F*
A Epimakhov 1998 *Sp*, 1999 *Ukr, Pol, CZR*, 2000 *De*
D Eskin 1998 *De*
A Evdokimov 1993 *Mor*, 1994 *Swe*, 1995 *Nor, De*, 1999 *CZR, Ukr*, 2000 *Ger, De*, 2001 *Sp*

A Fatakhov 2005 *CZR*, 2006 *Pt, Ukr, R, ArA, ItA, Ukr, Ukr, It, Pt*, 2007 *Sp, Geo, CZR*, 2008 *ItA, Ur*, 2009 *R, Geo, Ger, S, ItA, Ur, C*, 2010 *Nm, Sp, R, Ger, Geo, US, E, Ur, ArJ, J*, 2011 *Sp, Pt, R, Ukr, Geo, US, It, I, A*, 2012 *Pt, Ukr, Geo, Sp, Elt, Ur, ArJ*, 2013 *Sp, R, Geo, Pt, R, Elt, ArJ*
V Fedchenko 2002 *Sp, H, Geo, R, Pt, I, Geo, Sp, Sp*, 2003 *Sp, Geo, R, J, USAA*, 2004 *Sp, Geo, R, Pt, Geo*, 2006 *Pt, ArA, ItA, Pt*, 2007 *CZR, R*, 2008 *Pt, Sp, R, Geo, CZR*
V Fedorov 1994 *Swe*, 1995 *De*
R Fedotov 2004 *J, US*
I Frantsuzov 1992 *Bel*, 1993 *Geo*

I Galinovskiy 2006 *Ukr, Ukr*, 2007 *Sp, Geo, CZR, Pt*, 2008 *Pt, Sp, R, Geo*, 2009 *ItA, Ur*, 2010 *ArJ*, 2011 *Sp, Pt, R, Ukr, Geo, C*
A Garbuzov 2005 *R, CZR, Pt, Ukr, CZR*, 2006 *Geo, Pt, Ukr, R, Pt, ArA, ItA*, 2007 *Sp, Geo, Pt, R*, 2008 *Pt, Sp, R, Geo, CZR*, 2009 *Pt, Geo, Ger, C*, 2010 *Nm*, 2011 *Sp, Pt, R, Ukr, Geo, C, ItA, US, US, It, I, A*, 2012 *Pt, R, Geo, Sp, US, C*, 2013 *Sp, R, R, Elt, ArJ*
N Gasanov 2008 *CZR*, 2012 *Ukr, Geo*
R Gaysin 2012 *C*
D Gerasimov 2008 *Sp*, 2009 *Pt, R, S, Ur*, 2010 *US, E*, 2012 *Pt, R, Geo, Elt, ArJ, US, C*, 2013 *R, Geo, Pt, Bel*
G Godlyuk 2012 *Ukr*
V Grachev 1993 *It*, 1994 *Nm, Sp, Ger, F, Swe, H*, 1995 *Tun, Bel, Pol, F*, 1996 *Sp, Mor, Geo, CZR*, 1997 *Tun, Mor, Ukr, Pol, Cro*, 1998 *Sp, It, Geo*, 1999 *Ukr, Pol, CZR, Ukr*, 2000 *Ger, De*, 2001

Sp, H, Geo, 2002 Sp, H, Geo, R, Pt, J, I, Geo, Sp, 2003 Sp, Geo, R, Pt, J, USAA, 2004 Sp, Geo, R, Pt, Geo, 2005 R, CZR, Pt, 2006 Geo, Pt, R, Pt, ArA, ItA, It, Pt, 2007 Geo, 2008 Geo, 2011 Ukr, Geo, C, ItA, US, US, It, A

V Gresev 2006 It, 2007 Geo, CZR, Pt, 2008 Pt, Geo, CZR, Sp, 2009 Pt, R, Geo, Ger, S, ItA, Ur, C, 2010 Nm, Pt, Sp, R, Geo, US, E, Ur, ArJ, ArJ, J, 2011 Sp, Pt, R, Geo, C, ItA, US, US, It, I, A, 2012 Pt, Geo, Sp, Elt, Ur, ArJ, US, C, 2013 Sp, R, Geo, Pt, Bel

A Gvozdovsky 2005 R, CZR, CZR, 2006 Geo, Pt, Ukr, R, Pt, ArA, 2007 Sp, Geo, CZR, Pt, R, 2008 Pt, R, Geo, CZR, Sp, 2009 Pt, R, Geo, Ger, S, ItA, Ur, C, 2010 Nm, Pt, Sp, R

J Hendriks 2002 Geo, Pt, CZR, J, H, I, Geo, Sp, Sp

V Ignatev 2006 R, Pt, ArA, ItA, Ukr, Ukr, 2007 CZR, Pt, 2008 R, Ur

A Igretsov 2006 Pt, Ukr, Ukr, 2007 CZR, Pt, 2012 R, Sp, 2013 Sp, Geo, Bel

V Ilarionov 2001 H, Pt, 2002 Sp, H, Pt, CZR, 2003 Geo, R, Pt

P Ilvovsky 1998 Sp, It, Geo, 1999 Ukr, Pol, CZR, Ukr

S Kashcheev 1993 Mor, 1995 Tun, De, 1996 Sp, Mor, Geo, CZR, 1997 Tun, Mor, Cro, 1998 It, De, 1999 Ukr, Pol, CZR, Ukr, 2000 Ger, De, 2001 Geo, R, Pt

A Kazantsev 2003 USAA, 2004 R, Pt, J, US, Geo, 2005 R, CZR, Pt, Ukr

V Kazydub 1992 Bel

I Khohlov 1994 Nm, R, 1995 F, 1996 Sp, Mor, Geo, CZR, 1997 Ukr, Cro, 1998 Sp, It, De, Geo, 1999 Ukr, Pol, CZR, Ukr

A Khrokin 1994 Swe, 1995 Nor, De, 2000 Ger, 2002 Sp, CZR, J, I, Geo, Sp, Sp, 2003 Sp, Geo, R, Pt, J, CZR, USAA, 2004 Sp, Geo, R, Pt, J, US, Geo, 2005 R, Pt, Ukr, CZR, 2006 Geo, Pt, Ukr, R, ArA, ItA, Ukr, Ukr, It, Pt, 2007 Sp, Geo, CZR, Pt, R, 2008 Pt, Sp, R, Geo, ItA, R, Ur, Sp, 2009 Pt, R, Geo, Ger, C, 2010 Nm, Pt, Sp, R, Ger, Geo, US, E, Ur, ArJ, ArJ, J, 2011 Sp, Pt, Ukr, Geo, It, I

A Khudyakov 2013 R, Elt, ArJ

A Khvorostyanoy 2008 Pt, CZR

E Kiselev 1994 Nm, Sp, H

M Kiselev 2007 CZR

N Kiselev 1993 Geo, Pol, 1994 Nm, Sp, Ger, 1995 F, 1996 Mor, Geo, CZR, 1997 Tun, 1998 Sp, It, De

S Klimenko 1992 F, 1994 Ger, R, H, 2001 Sp, H, Geo, R

I Klyuchnikov 2003 Geo, J, USAA, 2004 Sp, R, Pt, J, Geo, 2005 Pt, Ukr, CZR, 2006 Geo, Ukr, ArA, Ukr, Ukr, It, 2007 Sp, Geo, R, 2008 Pt, Sp, R, Geo, Sp, 2009 Pt, R, Geo, Ger, S, ItA, Ur, C, 2010 Nm, Pt, Sp, R, Ger, Geo, E, Ur, ArJ, ArJ, J, 2011 Sp, Pt, R, Ukr, Geo, C, ItA, US, US, It, 2012 Sp, US, C, 2013 Sp, R, Geo, Pt, Bel

O Kobzev 2005 R, CZR, Ukr, 2006 Geo, Ukr, Ukr, 2007 CZR, Pt, 2008 Sp, CZR, ItA, R, Ur, Sp, 2010 ArJ, J

V Kobzev 2008 R, Ur

R Kochetov 1992 Ger

A Komarov 1994 Swe, 1995 Nor, De

K Kopeshkin 2012 Ukr

A Korobeynikov 1996 Sp, 2002 Sp, H, Geo, R, Pt, CZR, J, H, I, Geo, Sp, Sp, 2003 Sp, Geo, R, Pt, J, CZR, USAA, 2004 Sp, Geo, R, Pt, J, US, Geo, 2005 Pt, CZR, 2006 Ukr, R, Pt, ArA, ItA, Pt, 2007 Pt, 2008 Pt, Sp, CZR, 2009 C, 2010 Nm, Sp, R, Ger, Geo, US, E, Ur, ArJ, ArJ, J

V Korshunov 2002 H, Sp, 2003 R, Pt, J, 2004 Sp, Geo, R, J, US, Geo, 2005 Pt, Ukr, CZR, 2006 Geo, Pt, Ukr, R, Pt, ArA, It, Pt, 2007 Pt, R, 2008 Pt, Sp, R, Geo, ItA, R, Sp, 2009 Pt, R, Geo, Ger, C, 2010 Nm, Pt, Sp, R, Ger, Geo, US, E, Ur, ArJ, ArJ, J, 2011 Sp, R, Ukr, Geo, C, ItA, US, US, It, A, 2012 Sp, US, C

Y Koshelev 2002 H

E Kosolapov 1992 Bel, F, 2000 De

I Kotov 2012 Elt, Ur, ArJ, 2013 R, Elt, ArJ

Y Krasnobaev 1993 It, 1997 Ukr, Pol, 1998 Sp, It, De, Geo, 2000 De, 2001 Sp, R, Pt

S Krechun 1997 Ukr, Pol, Cro, 1998 Sp, 1999 Ukr, Pol, CZR, Ukr

A Krinitsa 1994 Swe

S Kryksa 1993 Geo, Pol, It, 1994 Nm, Sp, Ger, R, F, H, 1995 Tun, Bel, Pol, F, 1996 Sp, Mor, Geo, CZR

K Kulemin 2006 Pt, R, Pt, 2007 Sp, Pt, 2008 R, Geo, Sp, 2009 Pt, R, Geo, 2010 Pt, Sp, R, 2012 R, Ukr, Geo, Sp, US, C, 2013 Sp, R, Geo, Pt, Bel

I Kuperman 1993 Geo, Pol

I Kurashov 2006 Ukr, 2007 CZR, 2013 R, ArJ

K Kushnarev 2004 J, Geo, 2005 Pt, Ukr, CZR, 2006 Geo, Ukr, Pt, ArA, ItA, Ukr, 2007 Sp, Geo, Pt, R, 2008 Pt, Sp, R, ItA, R, Ur, 2009 Ger, S, Ur, 2010 Ger, Geo, US, E, Ur, ArJ, J, 2011 Pt, R

V Kushnarev 1992 Bel, F

Y Kushnarev 2005 CZR, 2006 Geo, Pt, ArA, ItA, Ukr, Ukr, It, 2007 Sp, Geo, CZR, Pt, R, 2008 Pt, Sp, R, Geo, CZR, Sp, 2009 Pt, R, Geo, Ger, S, ItA, Ur, C, 2010 Nm, Pt, Sp, R, Ger, Geo, US, E, Ur, 2011 Sp, Pt, R, Ukr, Geo, C, ItA, US, US, It, A, 2012 Pt, R, Ukr, Geo, Sp, 2013 Pt, Bel, R, Elt, ArJ

A Kuzin 1997 Tun, Mor, Cro, 1998 Sp, It, De, Geo, 1999 Ukr, Pol, CZR, Ukr, 2000 Ger, De, 2001 Sp, H, Geo, R, 2002 H, Geo, R, Pt, J, I, Geo, Sp, 2003 Sp, Geo, R, USAA, 2004 Sp, Geo, Pt, 2005 Pt, Ukr, CZR, 2006 Geo, Pt, Ukr, R, ArA, ItA, Ukr, It, Pt, 2007 Sp, Geo, CZR, R, 2008 Pt, Sp, R, Geo, CZR, 2009 Pt, R, Geo, Ger, S, ItA, C, 2010 Nm, Sp, R, Ger, Geo, US, E, Ur, ArJ, ArJ, J, 2011 Sp, Pt, R, Ukr, It, I, A

S Kuzmenko 2002 Sp, Sp, 2005 Ukr, 2008 R, Ur

L Kuzmin 1998 Geo

P Kvernadze 2012 R, Ukr, Geo, Elt, Ur, ArJ, 2013 Geo, Pt, Bel

D Loskutov 2004 R, US, Geo, 2005 R

A Lubkov 2003 CZR, 2005 R, CZR

A Lugin 2004 US, 2005 R, CZR, 2008 ItA, R, Ur, Sp, 2009 S, ItA, Ur

S Lysko 1994 Swe

K Maglakelidze 2009 S, ItA, Ur, 2010 Nm, Pt, Sp, R, E, ArJ, 2011 Sp, Pt, R

A Makovetskiy 2010 Nm, Ger, Geo, US, E, Ur, ArJ, J, 2011 Ukr, C, US, US, It, A, 2012 Pt, R, Ukr, Geo, Sp, Elt, Ur, ArJ, US, 2013 Sp, R, Geo, Pt, Bel, R, Elt, ArJ

A Malinin 1993 Pol, 1994 Ger, H

D Malyakin 2005 R

R Mamin 1998 De, Geo, 1999 Pol

D Mananikov 1994 F, 1995 Pol

V Marchenko 1992 Bel, F, 1997 Tun, Mor, Ukr, Pol, 1999 Ukr, 2001 Sp, H, R, Pt, 2006 Ukr, Pt, Ukr, Ukr, It, Pt, 2007 Sp, Geo, Pt, R, 2008 Pt, Sp, Geo, ItA, R, Ur, 2009 R, Ger

E Matveev 2007 CZR, R, 2008 Geo, CZR, Sp, 2009 Pt, R, Geo, Ger, S, ItA, C, 2010 Nm, Pt, Sp, R, Ger, Geo, US, E, Ur, ArJ, ArJ, J, 2011 Sp, Pt, R, Ukr, Geo, I, A, 2012 Pt, R, 2013 R, Elt, ArJ

N Medkov 2007 CZR, 2010 Ger, E, Ur, ArJ, J, 2012 R

G Minadze 2009 ItA, 2010 Ger, US

I Mironov 1992 F

E Mochnev 1993 Geo, Pol

V Motorin 1999 Ukr, Pol, CZR, Ukr, 2001 Sp, H, Geo, 2002 Sp, CZR, J, I, Geo, 2003 Sp, J, CZR, USAA, 2004 Sp, R, Geo, 2006 Pt, ArA, ItA, Ukr, Ukr, It, Pt, 2007 Sp, CZR, Pt, R, 2008 Pt, Sp, R, Geo, CZR, ItA, R, Sp, 2009 Pt, Ger, S

I Naumenko 2002 H, 2003 CZR, 2007 Sp, Geo, CZR

V Negodin 1993 Geo, Pol, It, 1994 Nm, Sp, R, 1995 F, 1996 Geo, CZR, 1997 Pol, Cro, 1998 Sp, It, De, Geo, 1999 Ukr, Pol, CZR, 2001 Geo

Y Nikolaev 1993 Pol, It, 1994 Nm, Sp, R, 1997 Tun, Ukr, Pol, 1998 It

I Nikolaychuk 1993 Mor, Geo, Pol, It, 1994 Nm, Sp, Ger, R, F, H, 1995 Tun, Bel, Pol, F, 1996 Sp, Mor, Geo, CZR, 1997 Tun, Mor, Pol, 1998 Sp, It, De, Geo, 1999 Ukr, Pol, CZR, Ukr, 2000 Ger, De, 2001 Sp, H, Geo, R, Pt, 2002 H, Geo, Pt, CZR, H, I, Geo, Sp, 2003 Geo, R, J, CZR, USAA, 2005 CZR

I Novikov 1994 Nm, Sp, R, H

P Novikov 2004 Geo, 2005 Pt, Ukr, CZR, 2006 Geo, Pt, Ukr, R, Pt, ArA

S Novoselov 1997 Pol, 2000 Ger, 2001 H, 2003 CZR, 2004 R, J, 2006 Ukr, Pt, ArA, ItA, 2007 Sp, Pt, R

I Osminko 2013 R, ArJ

A Ostrikov 2008 Pt, Sp, R, Geo, 2009 Pt, R, Geo, Ger, 2010 Pt, Sp, R, 2011 Sp, Pt, R, Geo

V Ostroushko 2006 It, Pt, 2007 Geo, 2009 ItA, Ur, 2010 Ger, ArJ, ArJ, J, 2011 Sp, Pt, R, Ukr, Geo, C, US, US, It, I, A, 2012 Pt, R, Sp, US, C, 2013 Pt

A Otrokov 2012 Ukr, Geo, Elt, Ur, ArJ, 2013 R, Elt, ArJ

A Panasenko 2004 Geo, 2005 Pt, CZR, 2006 Geo, Ukr, R, 2007 Sp, Geo, Pt, R, 2008 Geo, CZR, Sp, 2009 R, S, ItA, Ur, C, 2010 Nm, Ger, Geo, US, ArJ, J, 2011 Ukr, C, ItA, US

S Patlasov 1997 Tun, Mor, Ukr, Cro, 1998 Sp, It, Geo, 1999 Ukr

S Perepyolkin 1993 It

A Petrovetz 1996 CZR, 1997 Pol

W Pieterse 2002 Pt, CZR, J, H, I, Sp, Sp

A Podshibiakin 1995 Nor, De

A Polivalov 2013 Geo, R, Elt

D Polovykh 2006 Ukr, Ukr

S Popov 2003 *CZR*, 2004 *Sp*, *J*, 2005 *Ukr*, *CZR*, 2006 *Ukr*, *ArA*, *ItA*, *Ukr*, *It*, 2007 *Geo*, 2010 *US*, *J*, 2011 *Ukr*, *Geo*, *C*, *US*, *US*, *I*, *A*, 2012 *Sp*, *Elt*, *Ur*, *ArJ*
V Postnikov 1995 *Nor*, *De*
I Povesma 2007 *Pt*, *R*
I Prishchepenko 2003 *USAA*, 2004 *Sp*, *Geo*, *R*, 2005 *CZR*, 2006 *Geo*, *Pt*, *Ukr*, *R*, *Pt*, *ArA*, *ItA*, *Ukr*, *Ukr*, *It*, 2007 *Sp*, *Geo*, *CZR*, *R*, 2008 *Pt*, *Sp*, *R*, 2009 *R*, *Geo*, *Ger*, 2010 *ArJ*, *ArJ*, *J*, 2011 *R*, *Ukr*, *Geo*, *C*, *ItA*, *US*, *US*, *It*, *I*, *A*
E Pronenko 2009 *Pt*, *S*, *ItA*, *Ur*, *C*, 2010 *Nm*, *Pt*, *Sp*, *R*, *Ger*, *Geo*, *US*, *E*, *Ur*, *ArJ*, *ArJ*, *J*, 2011 *Sp*, *Pt*, *R*, 2012 *Elt*, *Ur*, *ArJ*, *US*, *C*, 2013 *Sp*, *R*, *Geo*, *Pt*, *Bel*, *R*, *ArJ*
A Protasov 2002 *H*

K Rachkov 1997 *Pol*, *Cro*, 1998 *Sp*, *It*, *De*, *Geo*, 1999 *Ukr*, *Pol*, *CZR*, *Ukr*, 2000 *Ger*, *De*, 2001 *H*, *Geo*, *R*, *Pt*, 2002 *Sp*, *H*, *Geo*, *R*, *Pt*, *I*, *Geo*, 2003 *Sp*, *Geo*, *R*, *J*, *CZR*, *USAA*, 2004 *Sp*, *Geo*, 2006 *Pt*, *R*, *It*, *Pt*, 2011 *Sp*, *Pt*, *R*, *Ukr*, *Geo*, *US*, *It*, *I*, *A*
A Rechnev 2001 *H*, *R*, *Pt*, 2003 *Pt*, 2004 *Geo*, 2005 *CZR*, 2006 *Geo*, *Ukr*, *Ukr*, *Ukr*
Y Rechnev 2003 *J*, 2004 *Sp*, *Geo*, *R*, *Pt*, *J*, *US*, *Geo*, 2006 *Pt*, *ArA*, *ItA*, 2007 *Sp*, 2013 *Bel*, *R*, *Elt*, *ArJ*
R Romak 2001 *Pt*, 2002 *Sp*, *H*, *Geo*, *R*, *Pt*, *CZR*, *J*, *H*, *I*, *Geo*, *Sp*, *Sp*, 2003 *Sp*, *Geo*, *USAA*, 2004 *Sp*, *Geo*, *R*, *Pt*, *J*, *US*, *Geo*, 2005 *R*, *CZR*, *Pt*, *Ukr*, *CZR*, 2006 *Geo*, *Pt*, *Ukr*, *R*, *ArA*, *ItA*, *Ukr*, *Pt*
S Romanov 1992 *Bel*, *F*, *Ger*, 1994 *Ger*, *F*, *H*, 1995 *Tun*, *Pol*, *F*
O Rudenok 1995 *Tun*, *Bel*, *Pol*, 1996 *Sp*
A Ryabov 2011 *ItA*, 2012 *Pt*, *R*, *Ukr*, *Geo*, *Sp*, *Elt*, *ArJ*, 2013 *Elt*, *ArJ*

R Sagdeev 2002 *Pt*, *CZR*, *J*, *H*, *Sp*, 2004 *Geo*, 2005 *Pt*, *Ukr*
A Sarychev 1999 *Ukr*, *Pol*, *CZR*, 2000 *De*, 2001 *Sp*, *H*, *R*, 2002 *Sp*, *Sp*, 2003 *Geo*, *R*, *Pt*, *J*, *CZR*, *USAA*, 2004 *Sp*, *Geo*, *R*, *Pt*, *J*, *US*, 2005 *R*, *CZR*, *Pt*, 2006 *Pt*, *Ukr*, *Ukr*, *Pt*
S Sekisov 2013 *Elt*, *ArJ*
S Selskiy 2012 *Elt*
A Sergeev 1992 *Ger*, 1993 *Mor*, 1995 *Tun*, *Bel*, *F*, 1996 *Mor*, 2000 *De*, 2001 *Sp*, *H*, *Geo*, *R*, *Pt*, 2002 *H*, *I*, *Geo*, *Sp*, *Sp*, 2003 *Sp*
O Sergeev 1993 *Mor*
S Sergeev 1998 *Geo*, 1999 *Ukr*, 2000 *Ger*, 2001 *Sp*, *Geo*, *Pt*, 2002 *Sp*, *H*, *Geo*, *R*, *J*, *I*, *Geo*, *Sp*, 2003 *Sp*, *Geo*, *R*, *Pt*, *J*, *USAA*, 2004 *Sp*, *Geo*, *R*, *Pt*, 2006 *ItA*, *It*, *Pt*
S Sergeev Jnr 2010 *US*, *E*, *Ur*, *ArJ*, *ArJ*
A Shabolin 1993 *It*
A Shakirov 2004 *Geo*, *R*, *Pt*, *J*, *US*, 2005 *R*, *Pt*, *Ukr*, *CZR*, 2006 *Ukr*, *R*, *ArA*, *ItA*, *Ukr*, *Pt*, 2007 *Sp*, *Geo*, *R*, 2008 *R*, *Geo*, *CZR*, *Sp*, 2009 *R*, *Geo*, *Ger*, *S*, *ItA*, *Ur*, *C*, 2010 *Pt*, *Sp*, *R*, *Ger*, *Geo*, *US*, *E*, *Ur*, *ArJ*, *ArJ*, *J*, 2011 *Sp*, *Pt*, *R*, *Ukr*, *Geo*, *C*, *ItA*, *US*, *US*, *It*, *A*, 2012 *Ukr*, *Geo*, *Sp*, *Elt*, *Ur*, *ArJ*
A Shalyuta 1992 *Bel*, *F*, *Ger*, 1993 *Mor*, *Pol*, *It*, 1994 *Nm*, *Sp*, *Ger*, *R*, *Swe*, *H*, 1995 *Tun*, *Bel*, *Pol*, *Nor*, *De*, *F*, 1996 *Mor*, *Geo*
A Shcherban 2010 *ArJ*, 2012 *Elt*, *Ur*, *ArJ*, *US*, *C*, 2013 *Pt*, *R*, *ArJ*
R Shelepkov 1997 *Mor*, *Ukr*, *Pol*, *Cro*, 1998 *De*, 2000 *Ger*, 2002 *H*, *R*, *Pt*, *CZR*, *H*, 2003 *Sp*, *Geo*, *R*
Y Shelepkov 2000 *De*, 2001 *Sp*, *H*, *Geo*, *R*, *Pt*, 2004 *Sp*, *Geo*, *R*, *Pt*, *J*, *US*
O Sheviakov 1996 *Geo*, *CZR*, 1997 *Pol*
S Shirakovski 1992 *Ger*
S Shishkov 2008 *ItA*, *R*, *Ur*
O Shukaylov 1994 *Swe*, 1995 *Nor*, *De*, 2000 *Ger*, *De*, 2001 *H*, *Geo*, *R*, *Pt*, 2002 *Sp*, *H*, *Geo*, *R*, *Pt*, *CZR*, *J*, *H*, *I*, *Geo*, *Sp*, *Sp*, 2003 *Geo*, *R*, *Pt*, *J*, *USAA*, 2004 *Sp*, *Geo*, *R*, *Pt*, *J*, *US*, *Geo*, 2005 *R*, *CZR*, *Pt*, *Ukr*, 2006 *Geo*, *Ukr*, *Ukr*, *It*, *Pt*, 2008 *Sp*
M Sidorov 2011 *ItA*, *It*, *I*
V Simonov 2001 *Sp*, *H*, *Geo*, *Pt*, 2002 *Sp*, *H*, *Geo*, *R*, *Pt*, *CZR*, *J*, *Geo*, *Sp*, *Sp*, 2003 *J*, 2004 *Sp*, *Geo*, *R*, *Pt*, *J*, *US*, *Geo*
D Simplikevich 2011 *I*, *A*, 2012 *Pt*, *Ukr*, *US*, *C*
A Sinitsyn 2012 *Ukr*
V Smirnov 1997 *Ukr*, 1998 *De*, 1999 *Ukr*, *Pol*, *CZR*, *Ukr*, 2000 *Ger*
A Sobolevsky 1994 *Swe*
D Soldatov 2007 *CZR*
A Sorokin 1992 *Bel*, *F*, *Ger*, 1993 *Geo*, *It*, 1994 *Nm*, *Sp*, *Swe*, *H*, 1995 *Tun*, *Bel*, *Pol*, *Nor*, *De*, *F*, 1996 *Mor*, *Geo*, *CZR*, 1997 *Tun*, *Mor*, 2008 *ItA*, *R*, *Ur*
V Sorokin 1992 *Bel*, *F*, *Ger*, 1993 *Mor*, *Geo*, *Pol*, *It*, 1994 *Nm*, *Sp*, *Ger*, *R*, *F*, *H*, 1995 *Tun*, *Bel*, *Pol*, *F*, 1996 *Sp*, *Mor*, *Geo*, 1997 *Tun*, 2000 *De*, 2001 *Sp*, *Pt*
S Starovatov 1993 *Mor*, *Pol*, 1994 *Sp*, *Ger*, *H*, 1995 *Bel*, *Pol*, *F*, 1996 *Sp*, *Mor*, *Geo*, *CZR*
M Sturza 2012 *Geo*, *ArJ*
S Sugrobov 2005 *R*, *CZR*, *Ukr*, 2006 *Ukr*, 2012 *Elt*, *Ur*, *ArJ*, *US*, *C*, 2013 *Geo*, *Pt*, *Bel*, *R*, *Elt*, *ArJ*
A Suhov 1992 *Bel*, *F*, *Ger*, 1993 *Pol*, 1994 *Ger*, *R*, *F*, 1997 *Pol*
S Sysoev 1995 *De*

A Temnov 2005 *Ukr*, 2006 *Ukr*, *Ukr*, 2007 *Sp*, 2010 *Nm*, *Pt*, *Sp*, *R*, *Geo*, 2011 *Sp*, *Ukr*, *Geo*, *C*, *US*, 2012 *Pt*, *R*, *Sp*, *Elt*, *Ur*, *US*, *C*, 2013 *Sp*, *R*, *Geo*, *Pt*, *Bel*, *R*, *Elt*, *ArJ*
A Tikhonov 1992 *F*, 1994 *Ger*, *R*
R Timerbulatov 2008 *CZR*, *ItA*, *R*
M Timoshchuk 2013 *Geo*
N Timosyuk 2007 *CZR*
E Titov 2010 *ArJ*, 2012 *Ukr*
A Tolstykh 2010 *Nm*
A Travkin 2001 *Sp*, *H*, *Geo*, *R*, *Pt*, 2002 *Sp*, *H*, *Geo*, *R*, *Pt*, *CZR*, *J*, *Geo*, *Sp*, 2003 *Sp*, *Geo*, *R*, *Pt*, *J*, *CZR*, *USAA*, 2004 *Geo*, 2005 *R*, *CZR*, *Pt*, *Ukr*, 2008 *Geo*, *CZR*, *ItA*, *R*, *Ur*, *Sp*, 2009 *Pt*, *R*, *Geo*, *S*, *ItA*, *Ur*, *C*, 2010 *Nm*, *Pt*, *Sp*, *R*, *Ger*, *Geo*, *US*, *Ur*, *ArJ*, 2011 *Sp*, *Pt*, *R*, *Ukr*, *Geo*, *C*, *ItA*, *I*, *A*
S Trishin 2005 *CZR*, 2006 *Geo*, *Pt*, *Ukr*, *R*, *Pt*, 2007 *Pt*, *R*, 2008 *Pt*, *Sp*, *R*, *Geo*, *CZR*, *ItA*, *R*, *Sp*, 2009 *Pt*, *R*, *Geo*, *Ger*, *S*, *ItA*, *Ur*, *C*, 2010 *Pt*, *Sp*, *R*, *Geo*, *US*, *ArJ*, *ArJ*, *J*, 2011 *C*, *ItA*, *I*, 2012 *Pt*, *R*, *Ukr*, *Geo*, *Sp*, *Ur*, *ArJ*, *C*, 2013 *Sp*, *Geo*
G Tsnobiladze 2011 *ItA*, 2012 *Pt*, *US*, *C*, 2013 *Sp*, *R*, *Pt*, *Bel*
V Tsnobiladze 2010 *ArJ*, 2011 *Pt*, *C*, *ItA*, *It*, *I*, 2012 *Pt*, *R*, *Ur*, *ArJ*, *US*, *C*, 2013 *Sp*, *R*, *Pt*, *Bel*, *R*, *Elt*, *ArJ*
M Tumenev 1995 *Tun*, *Bel*, *Pol*, 1996 *Sp*

M Uanbayev 1998 *Geo*, 1999 *Ukr*, 2001 *Sp*, *H*, *Geo*, *Pt*, 2002 *I*, 2003 *USAA*, 2004 *Geo*
M Uskov 2005 *R*, *CZR*, 2006 *ItA*

E Valiev 1992 *Ger*
A Vasiliev 1995 *Nor*, *De*
N Vasiliev 1993 *Mor*, 1996 *CZR*, 1997 *Ukr*, *Cro*
S Vasiliev 2004 *J*, *US*, 2005 *R*
Y Vengerov 2013 *Elt*
A Vergun 1995 *Tun*, *Bel*, *Pol*
A Voinov 1992 *Ger*
A Volkov 2008 *CZR*, *ItA*, *R*, *Ur*, 2009 *ItA*, *Ur*, 2012 *R*, *Ukr*, *Geo*, *Sp*, *Elt*, *Ur*, *ArJ*, *US*, *C*, 2013 *Sp*, *R*, *Geo*, *Pt*, *Bel*, *R*, *Elt*, *ArJ*
R Volschenk 2002 *Geo*, *R*, *CZR*, *J*, *H*, *I*, *Geo*, *Sp*, *Sp*
V Vorapaev 1992 *Bel*, *F*, 1993 *Geo*, *Pol*, *It*, 1994 *Nm*, *Sp*, *Ger*, *R*, *H*
A Voytov 2003 *CZR*, 2004 *Sp*, *J*, *US*, 2005 *R*, *CZR*, *Pt*, *Ukr*, *CZR*, 2006 *Geo*, *Pt*, *Ukr*, *R*, *ArA*, 2007 *R*, 2008 *ItA*, *R*, *Sp*, 2009 *Pt*, *R*, *Geo*, *Ger*, *S*, *ItA*, *Ur*, *C*, 2010 *Nm*, *Pt*, *Sp*, *R*, *Ger*, *Geo*, *E*, *Ur*, *ArJ*, *ArJ*, *J*, 2011 *Sp*, *Pt*, *R*, *Ukr*, *Geo*, *C*, *US*, *US*, *It*, *I*, *A*, 2012 *Sp*, *Elt*, *Ur*, *ArJ*, *US*, *C*, 2013 *Sp*, *R*, *Geo*, *Pt*, *Bel*

R Yagudin 2011 *ItA*
A Yanyushkin 2002 *CZR*, *H*, *Sp*, *Sp*, 2003 *Sp*, *Geo*, *R*, *Pt*, *USAA*, 2004 *Sp*, *Geo*, *J*, *US*, *Geo*, 2006 *Geo*, *Pt*, *R*, 2007 *Geo*, *Pt*, 2008 *Pt*, *Sp*, *ItA*, *R*, *Ur*, 2009 *R*, *Geo*, *Ger*, *S*, *ItA*, *Ur*, *C*, 2010 *Nm*, *Pt*, *Sp*, *R*, *Ger*, *Geo*, *US*, *E*, *Ur*, *ArJ*, *J*, 2011 *Sp*, *Pt*, *R*, *Ukr*, *Geo*, *It*, *I*, *A*, 2012 *Pt*, *R*, *Geo*, 2013 *Sp*, *R*, *Geo*, *Pt*, *Bel*
V Yakovlev 1992 *Ger*, 1993 *Mor*, *Geo*, *Pol*, 1994 *Nm*, *Ger*, *F*, *Swe*, *H*, 1995 *Tun*, *Bel*, *Pol*, *Nor*, *De*, *F*, 1996 *Sp*, 1997 *Pol*, 1999 *Ukr*, 2000 *Ger*, 2001 *R*, *Pt*
S Yanyushkin 2013 *Sp*, *R*, *Geo*, *Pt*, *Bel*

A Zaitzev 1992 *Ger*, 1994 *F*
A Zakarlyuk 1993 *Mor*, *Geo*, *It*, 1994 *Nm*, *Sp*, *Ger*, *F*, *H*, 1995 *Tun*, *Bel*, *Pol*, *F*, 1996 *Mor*, *Geo*, *CZR*, 1997 *Tun*, *Mor*, *Ukr*, *Cro*, 1998 *Sp*, *It*, *De*, *Geo*, 1999 *Ukr*, *Pol*, *CZR*, *Ukr*, 2000 *Ger*, *De*, 2001 *Sp*, *H*, *Geo*, 2002 *CZR*, *J*, *H*, *I*, *Geo*, *Sp*, *Sp*
V Zdanovich 1999 *Ukr*, *Pol*, *CZR*, 2000 *Ger*, *De*, 2006 *R*, *Pt*
S Zedin 1994 *Swe*, 1995 *Nor*, *De*
V Zeer 1995 *Pol*, 1996 *Sp*, *Mor*, *Geo*, 1997 *Mor*, *Ukr*, *Pol*, *Cro*, 1998 *Sp*, *Geo*, 1999 *Pol*, *CZR*, *Ukr*, 2002 *Sp*, 2003 *Geo*, *R*, *Pt*, *J*, *CZR*, *USAA*
O Zhukov 2000 *De*, 2001 *Sp*, *H*, *Geo*, *R*, *Pt*, 2002 *H*, *Pt*, *J*, *H*, 2003 *Pt*, 2006 *Ukr*
A Zhuravliov 2008 *Sp*
D Zubarev 2006 *Ukr*, *ItA*, *Pt*, 2008 *ItA*, *R*, *Ur*
A Zubov 1994 *Swe*, 1995 *Nor*, *De*
A Zukrov 1994 *Swe*, 1995 *Tun*, *Pol*, *Nor*, *De*
I Zykov 2012 *Pt*, *Ukr*, *Geo*, *Elt*, *Ur*, *ArJ*, *US*, *C*, 2013 *Sp*, *R*, *Elt*, *ArJ*
V Zykov 1993 *Mor*, *Geo*, *Pol*, *It*, 1994 *Nm*, *Sp*, *Ger*, *R*, *F*, *H*, 1995 *Tun*, 1996 *Sp*, 1997 *Ukr*, *Pol*, *Cro*, 1998 *Sp*, 2002 *Sp*, *H*, *Geo*, *R*, *Pt*, *CZR*, *J*, *I*, *Geo*, *Sp*, 2003 *Sp*, *Geo*, *R*, *Pt*, *J*, *USAA*, 2004 *Geo*, *R*
V Zyrianov 1996 *Sp*

SAMOA

SAMOA'S 2012–13 TEST RECORD

OPPONENTS	DATE	VENUE	RESULT
Canada	9 Nov	N	Won 42–12
Wales	16 Nov	A	Won 26–19
France	24 Nov	A	Lost 22–14
Scotland	8 Jun	N	Won 27–17
Italy	15 Jun	N	Won 39–10
South Africa	22 Jun	A	Lost 56–23

SAMOA SOAR TO A NEW HIGH

Getty Images

Alesana Tuilagi scores a try as Samoa beat Scotland for the first time in their history in the quadrangular tournament.

The season began with good performances during the November tour, survived Cyclone Evans and ended with Samoa making the final of the quadrangular tournament in South Africa.

The performance of the Manu Samoa continues to improve with the team reducing losing margins against Tier One nations from less than a converted try on average to victories against Wales, Scotland and Italy. This improvement also saw the team outscore Tier One opposition by 13 tries to four until playing South Africa in that final.

The November tour started well with a convincing 42–12 defeat of Canada in the inaugural IRB International Rugby Series in Colwyn Bay, north Wales. It was the perfect preparation for the much-anticipated re-match with Wales in Cardiff, a year on from the 17–10 loss in the Rugby World Cup 2011 pool stages, and the match didn't disappoint. Samoa emerged victorious this time, tries from Fa'atoina Autagavaia, George Pisi and Johnny Leota securing a 26–19 victory over the Six Nations champions in front of 58,000 people at the Millennium Stadium.

Samoa then travelled to France on a high, but were unable to complete a clean sweep in November with four Frédéric Michalak penalties in the last 22 minutes enough to see France to a 22–14 victory at the Stade de France. Samoa could take some comfort, though, after outscoring their hosts by two tries to one with David Lemi and Joe Tekori crossing Les Bleus' try-line.

Change continues to be the nature for Samoa. In April 2012 the Samoa Rugby Union recruited a new Manu Samoa head coach in Stephen Betham who, with his management team, has brought significant success in the last 12 months. One of the highly-praised aspects of Samoa's RWC 2011 campaign had been its coaching team, but despite the majority of that team being unavailable and an ageing playing squad it has not stopped the Manu from continuing their progress and reaching their highest ever position of seventh in the IRB World Rankings, above the likes of Ireland, Argentina, Scotland and Italy.

Betham, the former Samoa Sevens coach, has been able to manage the number of retiring players with the integration of new players from the National Academy in Samoa, such as the exciting new talent of Robert Lilomaiava, who scored four tries on his Test debut against Canada.

Samoa's results in November, after winning the IRB Pacific Nations Cup earlier that year, ensured they were the highest ranked Tier Two nation in 2012, earning their place in the quadrangular tournament in South Africa in June 2013.

With a successful November tour under their belts, there was expectation that the Samoans would continue to develop and compete well against South Africa, Scotland and Italy. This was all thrown into question after a humiliating defeat against the Golden Lions, the South African side relegated from Super Rugby to allow the Southern Kings' entry. Samoa came unstuck in the set pieces and defensively as they crashed to a 74–14 defeat at Ellis Park on 1 June. The Lions scored 10 tries, most of them coming from a long way out, especially in the second half when they built on a 27–14 half-time lead.

Samoa bounced back from this defeat with a physically dominant performance to record their first ever win over Scotland, tries from James So'oialo and an Alesana Tuilagi brace securing the 27–17 win in Durban. A number of players had their tournament cut short by injury but it did not derail Samoa as another impressive display earned them a 39–10 victory over Italy with Paul Williams, Alapati Leiua, Johnny Leota, Taiasina Tuifua and Brando Va'aulu all touching down.

Those wins set up a final against South Africa, the first meeting between the sides since the Springboks won their RWC 2011 pool encounter 13–5. There was to be no second historic result for Samoa, though, as South Africa ran out comfortable 56–23 winners at Loftus Versfeld in Pretoria.

The challenge now, though, is for Samoa to continue to build on their wins in South Africa in November when they will face Ireland, the French Barbarians and Georgia.

There was also cause for the Samoan women's team to celebrate in 2013 after they booked their place at Women's Rugby World Cup 2014 in France. Something of an unknown quantity having not played an international in four years, Samoa arrived in Spain for a six-team qualifier in April in determined mood. With Samoan great Peter Fatialofa as coach, the Manusina bounced back from an opening 65–22 loss to Italy to beat Sweden 29–0 and the Netherlands 33–14 to finish as runners-up and join hosts Spain in qualifying for the 2014 showpiece event.

"We came here to do our best and to qualify. We've achieved that and I'm delighted for the girls," admitted Fatialofa. "The fact is that we're now representing the Pacific Islands in the Women's Rugby World Cup in 2014. That's a great honour and I wish to thank the IRB for its help and investment in the game. We have to go back now and focus on the tough work ahead because we're going to be playing some incredible teams in France."

The Samoa Sevens programme in 2012/13 undertook a redevelopment phase with a large proportion of young, emerging players being blooded after a number of years in the National Licenced Training Centre. This regeneration saw a mixed bag of results and a decline in performances in the second half of the season leading into RWC Sevens 2013, but the highlight was the success in Dubai in round two and finishing fourth overall on the HSBC Sevens World Series standings.

Samoa's Under 20s travelled to France in June for the IRB Junior World Championship with the target of bettering their 10th place finish of 2012. They lost all three pool matches to Wales, Argentina and Scotland, but bounced back to beat Fiji 19–18 – albeit only after two tries in the dying minutes – and then the Scots 33–24 to finish ninth and achieve their goal.

The Samoa A team again came up short in their bid to wrestle the IRB Pacific Rugby Cup crown away from Fiji Warriors, although this time the margin between the two was significantly reduced from 18 points to just four. Samoa A lost two matches in Australia, beating only the ARU's Sydney Academy, but then edged the Blues Development XV 19–17 and lost narrowly to the Crusaders Knights and Chiefs Development XV in the New Zealand series.

Off the field, 2013 also saw the high performance programme develop the first medical clinic on site at the high performance unit in Tuanaimato. The clinic is now staffed by two full-time physiotherapists and two strength and conditioning coaches. This programme will expand further before the end of 2013 with an additional two interns to be recruited to support it.

SAMOA INTERNATIONAL STATISTICS

MATCH RECORDS UP TO 10 OCTOBER 2013

WINNING MARGIN

Date	Opponent	Result	Winning Margin
11/07/2009	PNG	115–7	**108**
08/04/1990	Korea	74–7	**67**
18/07/2009	PNG	73–12	**61**
10/06/2000	Japan	68–9	**59**
29/06/1997	Tonga	62–13	**49**

MOST POINTS IN A MATCH

BY THE TEAM

Date	Opponent	Result	Points
11/07/2009	PNG	115–7	**115**
08/04/1990	Korea	74–7	**74**
18/07/2009	PNG	73–12	**73**
10/06/2000	Japan	68–9	**68**
29/06/1997	Tonga	62–13	**62**

BY A PLAYER

Date	Player	Opponent	Points
11/07/2009	Gavin Williams	PNG	**30**
29/05/2004	Roger Warren	Tonga	**24**
03/10/1999	Silao Leaega	Japan	**23**
08/04/1990	Andy Aiolupo	Korea	**23**
08/07/2000	Toa Samania	Italy	**23**

MOST POINTS IN A MATCH

BY THE TEAM

Date	Opponent	Result	Points
11/07/2009	PNG	115–7	**115**
08/04/1990	Korea	74–7	**74**
18/07/2009	PNG	73–12	**73**
10/06/2000	Japan	68–9	**68**
29/06/1997	Tonga	62–13	**62**

BY A PLAYER

Date	Player	Opponent	Points
11/07/2009	Gavin Williams	PNG	**30**
29/05/2004	Roger Warren	Tonga	**24**
03/10/1999	Silao Leaega	Japan	**23**
08/04/1990	Andy Aiolupo	Korea	**23**
08/07/2000	Toa Samania	Italy	**23**

MOST TRIES IN A MATCH

BY THE TEAM

Date	Opponent	Result	Tries
11/07/2009	PNG	115–7	**17**
08/04/1990	Korea	74–7	**13**
18/07/2009	PNG	73–12	**11**

BY A PLAYER

Date	Player	Opponent	Tries
28/05/1991	Tupo Fa'amasino	Tonga	**4**
10/06/2000	Elvis Seveali'I	Japan	**4**
02/07/2005	Alesana Tuilagi	Tonga	**4**
11/07/2009	Esera Lauina	PNG	**4**
09/11/2012	Robert Lilomaiava	Canada	**4**

MOST CONVERSIONS IN A MATCH

BY THE TEAM

Date	Opponent	Result	Cons
11/07/2009	PNG	115–7	**15**
18/07/2009	PNG	73–12	**9**
08/04/1990	Korea	74–7	**8**

BY A PLAYER

Date	Player	Opponent	Cons
11/07/2009	Gavin Williams	PNG	**10**
18/07/2009	Titi Jnr Esau	PNG	**9**
08/04/1990	Andy Aiolupo	Korea	**8**

MOST PENALTIES IN A MATCH

BY THE TEAM

Date	Opponent	Result	Pens
29/05/2004	Tonga	24–14	**8**

BY A PLAYER

Date	Player	Opponent	Pens
29/05/2004	Roger Warren	Tonga	**8**

MOST DROP GOALS IN A MATCH

BY THE TEAM

1 on 11 occasions

BY A PLAYER

1 on 11 occasions

MOST CAPPED PLAYERS

Name	Caps
Brian Lima	65
To'o Vaega	60
Semo Sititi	59
Opeta Palepoi	42
Census Johnston	42

LEADING PENALTY SCORERS

Name	Pens
Darren Kellett	35
Earl Va'a	31
Silao Leaega	31
Roger Warren	29
Andy Aiolupo	24

LEADING TRY SCORERS

Name	Tries
Brian Lima	31
Semo Sititi	17
Alesana Tuilagi	17
Afato So'oialo	15
To'o Vaega	15

LEADING DROP GOAL SCORERS

Name	DGs
Darren Kellet	2
Roger Warren	2
Steve Bachop	2
Tusi Pisi	2

LEADING CONVERSION SCORERS

Name	Cons
Andy Aiolupo	35
Earl Va'a	33
Silao Leaega	26
Tanner Vili	21
Gavin Williams	18

LEADING POINT SCORERS

Name	Points
Earl Va'a	184
Andy Aiolupo	172
Silao Leaega	160
Darren Kellett	155
Brian Lima	150

SAMOA INTERNATIONAL PLAYERS
UP TO 10 OCTOBER 2013

A'ati 1932 *Tg*
V Afatia 2012 *Tg, C*
JT Afoa 2010 *Tg, J*
Agnew 1924 *Fj, Fj*
S Ah Fook 1947 *Tg*
F Ah Long 1955 *Fj*
Ah Mu 1932 *Tg*
T Aialupo 1986 *W*
F Aima'asu 1981 *Fj*, 1982 *Fj, Fj, Fj, Tg*, 1988 *Tg, Fj*
AA Aiolupo 1983 *Tg*, 1984 *Fj, Tg*, 1985 *Fj, Tg, Tg*, 1986 *Fj, Tg*, 1987 *Fj, Tg*, 1988 *Tg, Fj, I, W*, 1989 *Fj, WGe, Bel, R*, 1990 *Kor, Tg, J, Tg, Fj*, 1991 *W, A, Ar, S*, 1992 *Tg, Fj*, 1993 *Tg, Fj, NZ*, 1994 *Tg, W, A*
A Aiono 2009 *PNG*, 2010 *J, I, E, S*, 2011 *Tg*, 2012 *Tg, S*
Aitofele 1924 *Fj, Fj*
P Alalatoa 1986 *W*
V Alalatoa 1988 *I, W*, 1989 *Fj*, 1991 *Tg, W, A, Ar, S*, 1992 *Tg, Fj*
P Alauni 2009 *PNG*
R Ale 1997 *Tg, Fj*, 1999 *J, Ar, W, S*
A Alelupo 1994 *Fj*
T Aleni 1982 *Tg*, 1983 *Tg*, 1985 *Tg*, 1986 *W, Fj, Tg*, 1987 *Fj*
S Alesana 1979 *Tg, Fj*, 1980 *Tg*, 1981 *Fj, Fj*, 1982 *Fj, Tg*, 1983 *Tg, Fj*, 1984 *Fj, Tg*, 1985 *Fj, Tg*
T Allen 1924 *Fj, Fj*
K Anufe 2009 *Tg*, 2012 *Tg, Fj, J, F*, 2013 *It*
L Aoelua 2008 *NZ*
T Aoese 1981 *Fj, Fj*, 1982 *Fj, Fj, Fj, Tg*, 1983 *Tg*
J Apelu 1985 *Tg*
F Asi 1975 *Tg*
F Asi 1963 *Fj, Fj, Tg*
SP Asi 1999 *S*, 2000 *Fj, J, Tg, C, It, US, W, S*, 2001 *Tg, Fj, NZ, Fj, Tg, Fj*
L Asi 2010 *J*
Atiga 1924 *Fj*
S Ati'ifale 1979 *Tg*, 1980 *Tg*, 1981 *Fj, Fj*
J Atoa 1975 *Tg*, 1981 *Fj*
F Autagavaia 2012 *Tg, Fj, J, S, C, W*
WO Avei 2011 *J, Tg, SA*, 2012 *Tg, Fj, J, S, C, W, F*, 2013 *S, It, SA*

SJ Bachop 1991 *Tg, Fj, W, A, Ar, S*, 1998 *Tg, Fj*, 1999 *J, C, F, NZ, US, Fj, J, Ar, W, S*
C Betham 1955 *Fj*
ML Birtwistle 1991 *Fj, W, A, Ar, S*, 1993 *Fj, NZ*, 1994 *Tg, W, Fj, A*, 1996 *I*
W Brame 2009 *J, Fj*
FE Bunce 1991 *W, A, Ar, S*

CH Capper 1924 *Fj*
J Cavanagh 1955 *Fj, Fj, Fj*
J Clarke 1997 *Tg*, 1998 *A*, 1999 *US, Fj, J*
A Collins 2005 *S, Ar*
A Cortz 2007 *Fj*

G Cowley 2005 *S, Ar*, 2006 *J, Tg*
T Cowley 2000 *J, C, It*
O Crichton 1955 *Fj, Fj, Fj*, 1957 *Tg, Tg*
D Crichton 2012 *Tg, Fj, J, S*
L Crichton 2006 *Fj, Tg*, 2007 *Fj, SA, J, Tg, SA, Tg, E, US*
O Crichton 1988 *Tg*
T Curtis 2000 *Fj, J, Tg, C, It, US*

H Ekeroma 1972 *Tg, Tg*
G Elisara 2003 *I, Nm*
S Enari 1975 *Tg*
S Epati 1972 *Tg*
T Esau 2009 *PNG, PNG, F, It*
K Ese 1947 *Tg*
S Esera 1981 *Fj*
L Eves 1957 *Tg, Tg*

H Fa'afili 2008 *Fj, Tg, J*, 2009 *J, Tg, Fj, PNG, W, F, It*
T Fa'afou 2007 *Fj*
P Fa'alogo 1963 *Fj*
Fa'amaile 1947 *Tg*
T Fa'amasino 1988 *W*, 1989 *Bel, R*, 1990 *Kor, Tg, J, Tg, Fj*, 1991 *Tg, Fj, A*, 1995 *It, Ar, E, SA, Fj, Tg*, 1996 *NZ, Tg, Fj*
JS Fa'amatuainu 2005 *S, Ar*, 2008 *Fj, J*, 2009 *J, Tg, Fj, PNG, W, F, It*, 2011 *Tg*
S Fa'aofo 1990 *Tg*
P Faasalele 2013 *It*
Fa'asalele 1957 *Tg, Tg*
F Fa'asau 1963 *Fj, Tg*
M Faasavalu 2002 *SA*, 2003 *I, Nm, Ur, Geo, E, SA*, 2011 *J, Fj, A, Nm, W, Fj, SA*, 2012 *Fj, J, S, W, F*
V Faasua 1987 *Fj*, 1988 *Tg, Fj, W*
S Fa'asua 2000 *W*
F Fa'asuaga 1947 *Tg*
L Fa'atau 2000 *Fj, Tg, C, US*, 2001 *I, It*, 2002 *Fj, Tg, Fj, Tg, SA*, 2003 *I, Ur, E, SA*, 2004 *Tg, S, Fj*, 2005 *A, Tg, Tg, Fj, S, E, Ar*, 2006 *J, Fj, Tg*, 2007 *Fj, SA, J, Tg, SA, US*
F Fagasoaia 2010 *J*
K Faiva'ai 1998 *Tg, Fj, A*, 1999 *J, C, Tg, NZ, US, Fj*
L Falaniko 1990 *Tg, Fj*, 1991 *Tg*, 1993 *Tg, Fj, NZ*, 1995 *SA, It, Ar, E, SA, Fj, Tg, S, E*, 1996 *NZ*, 1999 *US, Fj, W, S*
E Fale 2008 *Tg*
S Fale 1955 *Fj*
S Fanolua 1990 *Tg, Fj*, 1991 *Tg, Fj*
TL Fanolua 1996 *NZ, Fj*, 1997 *Tg*, 1998 *Tg, Fj, A*, 1999 *W, S*, 2000 *J, Tg, C, It, US*, 2001 *Tg, Fj, NZ, Fj, Tg, J, Fj*, 2002 *Fj*, 2003 *Nm, Ur, Geo, E*, 2005 *A, Tg, Fj, Fj*
R Fanuatanu 2003 *I, Geo*
M Faoagali 1999 *J, C*
A Faosiliva 2006 *J, Tg*, 2008 *Tg, NZ*, 2010 *Tg, J, Fj*, 2012 *Tg, Fj, J, C*, 2013 *SA*
DS Farani 2005 *Tg, Fj, S, E, Ar*, 2006 *J, Fj, Tg*
J Fatialofa 2009 *F*
M Fatialofa 1996 *Tg*
PM Fatialofa 1988 *I, W*, 1989 *Bel, R*, 1990 *Kor, Tg, J*, 1991 *Tg, Fj, W, A, Ar, S*, 1992 *Tg, Fj*, 1993 *Tg, Fj, NZ*, 1994 *Tg, W, Fj, A*, 1995 *SA, It, Ar, E, SA, Fj, Tg, S, E*, 1996 *NZ, Fj*
Fatu 1947 *Tg*
E Feagai 1963 *Fj, Tg*
S Feagai 1963 *Fj, Fj*
D Feaunati 2003 *Nm, Ur, Geo, E, SA*
I Fea'unati 1996 *I*, 1997 *Tg*, 1999 *Tg, NZ, Fj, Ar*, 2000 *Fj, J, Tg, C, It, US*, 2006 *Fj, Tg*
M Fepuleai 1957 *Tg*
V Fepuleai 1988 *W*, 1989 *Fj, WGe, R*
I Fesuiai'i 1985 *Fj, Tg*
JA Filemu 1995 *S, E*, 1996 *NZ, Tg, Fj, I*, 1997 *Fj*, 1999 *J, C, Tg, F, NZ*, 2000 *Fj, J, Tg, C, It, US*, 2001 *Tg, Fj, Tg, J*
F Fili 2003 *I, Nm*, 2009 *W, F*, 2011 *Tg*
F Filisoa 2005 *Tg*
T Fomai 2012 *C, W, F*
T Fong 1983 *Tg, Fj*, 1984 *Fj, Tg*, 1986 *W, Fj, Tg*, 1987 *Fj, Tg*
K Fotuali'i 2010 *J, I, E, S*, 2011 *A, Nm, W, Fj, SA*, 2012 *J, S, C, W, F*
S Fretton 1947 *Tg*
J Fruean 1972 *Tg*, 1975 *Tg*
Fruean 1932 *Tg*
S Fruean 1955 *Fj, Fj*
P Fualau 2012 *Tg, Fj*
S Fuatai 1972 *Tg*
P Fuatai 1988 *Tg, Fj*, 1989 *Fj, WGe, R*
T Fuga 1999 *F, NZ, US*, 2000 *Fj, J, Tg, C, It, US*, 2007 *SA, Tg*
ES Fuimaono Sapolu 2005 *S, E, Ar*, 2006 *Fj, Tg*, 2007 *SA, E, US*, 2008 *Fj, Tg, J*, 2009 *J, Fj, PNG, PNG, F, It*, 2011 *Fj, A, Nm, W, Fj, SA*

T Galuvao 1972 *Tg*
N George 2004 *Tg, Fj*
C Glendinning 1999 *J, C, Tg, F, NZ, US, Fj, J, W, S*, 2000 *Fj, J, Tg, C, It, US*, 2001 *Tg, Fj, NZ, Fj, Tg, Fj*
P Grey 1975 *Tg*, 1979 *Tg, Fj*, 1980 *Tg*
A Grey 1957 *Tg, Tg*
I Grey 1985 *Fj, Tg*

G Harder 1995 *SA, It, Ar, SA*
Hellesoe 1932 *Tg*
B Helleur 2011 *Tg, A*
J Helleur 2010 *Tg, J, Fj, J*
M Hewitt 1955 *Fj, Fj*
J Huch 1982 *Fj, Fj*, 1986 *Fj, Tg*
J Hunt 1957 *Tg, Tg*

A Ieremia 1992 *Tg, Fj*, 1993 *Tg, Fj, NZ*
I Imo 1924 *Fj*
T Imo 1955 *Fj, Fj, Fj*, 1957 *Tg, Tg*
A Ioane 1957 *Tg, Tg, Tg*
E Ioane 1990 *Tg, Fj*, 1991 *Tg, Fj, S*
T Iona 1975 *Tg*
T Iosua 2006 *J*, 2011 *J, Fj, Tg*
Iupati 1924 *Fj*
M Iupeli 1988 *Tg, Fj, I, W*, 1989 *Fj, WGe, R*, 1993 *Tg, NZ*, 1994 *Tg, W, Fj, A*, 1995 *SA, E*
S Iuta 1947 *Tg*

T Jensen 1987 *Tg*, 1989 *Bel*
CAI Johnston 2005 *A, Tg, Fj, S, E, Ar*, 2006 *Fj, Tg*, 2007 *SA, J, Tg, SA, Tg, E, US*, 2008 *Fj, J*, 2009 *J, Tg, Fj, PNG, W, F, It*, 2010 *J, Fj, E, S*, 2011 *Tg, A, Nm, W, Fj, SA*, 2012 *J, S, C, W, F*, 2013 *S, It, SA*
JVI Johnston 2008 *Tg, J*, 2011 *Tg*, 2012 *Fj, C, W, F*, 2013 *S, It, SA*
MN Jones 1986 *W*

S Kalapu 1957 *Tg*
D Kaleopa 1990 *Kor, Tg, J*, 1991 *A*, 1992 *Fj*, 1993 *Tg, Fj*
S Kaleta 1994 *Tg, W*, 1995 *S, E*, 1996 *NZ*, 1997 *Tg, Fj*
T Kali 1975 *Tg*
L Kamu 1955 *Fj, Fj, Fj*
MG Keenan 1991 *W, A, Ar*, 1992 *Tg, Fj*, 1993 *NZ*, 1994 *Tg, W, Fj, A*
JR Keil 2010 *J, J*
F Kelemete 1984 *Fj, Tg*, 1985 *Tg*, 1986 *W*
DK Kellet 1993 *Tg, Fj, NZ*, 1994 *Tg, W, Fj, A*, 1995 *It, Ar, Fj, Tg, S, E*
DA Kerslake 2005 *Tg, Fj, Tg, Fj*, 2006 *J, Tg*, 2007 *Fj, SA, J, Tg*
A Koko 1999 *J*
R Koko 1983 *Tg, Fj, Fj*, 1984 *Fj, Tg*, 1985 *Fj, Tg, Tg*, 1986 *W, Fj, Tg*, 1987 *Fj, Tg*, 1988 *Tg, Fj, I, W*, 1989 *WGe, R*, 1993 *Tg, NZ*, 1994 *Tg*
M Krause 1984 *Tg*, 1986 *W*
H Kruse 1963 *Fj, Fj, Tg*
JA Kuoi 1987 *Fj, Tg*, 1988 *I, W*, 1990 *Kor, Tg*

B Laban 1955 *Fj*, 1957 *Tg, Tg*
SL Lafaiali'I 2001 *Tg, Fj, NZ, Tg*, 2002 *Fj, Tg, Fj, Tg, SA*, 2003 *I, Nm, Ur, Geo, E, SA*, 2004 *Tg, S, Fj*, 2005 *A, S, E*, 2007 *Fj, J, Tg, Tg, US*
IR Lafo 2012 *C*
I Laga'aia 1975 *Tg*, 1979 *Tg, Fj*
F Lalomilo 2001 *I, It*
J Lam 2013 *S, It, SA*
PR Lam 1991 *W, Ar, S*, 1994 *W, Fj, A*, 1995 *SA, Ar, E, SA, Fj, Tg, S, E*, 1996 *NZ, Tg, Fj, I*, 1997 *Tg, Fj*, 1998 *Tg, Fj, A*, 1999 *J, C, Tg, F, NZ, US, Fj, J, Ar, W, S*
S Lameta 1982 *Fj*
F Lameta 1990 *Tg, Fj*
G Latu 1994 *Tg, W, Fj, A*, 1995 *SA, Ar, E, SA, Fj, Tg*
E Lauina 2008 *Fj, Tg, J, NZ*, 2009 *J, Tg, Fj, PNG, PNG*
M Lautau 1985 *Fj*

T Lavea 2010 *I, E, S*, 2011 *J, Fj, Nm, W*
FH Lavea Levi 2007 *Fj, SA, J, Tg*, 2008 *Fj, J, NZ*, 2009 *J, Tg, Fj, PNG, W, F, It*, 2010 *Tg, J, Fj, I, E, S*, 2011 *J, Fj, Tg, A, Fj*
S Leaega 1997 *Tg, Fj*, 1999 *J, J, Ar, W, S*, 2001 *Tg, Fj, NZ, Fj, Tg, Fj, I, It*, 2002 *Fj, Tg, SA*
K Lealamanua 2000 *Fj, J, Tg, C, It*, 2001 *NZ, Fj, Tg, J, Fj*, 2002 *Fj, Tg, Fj, Tg, SA*, 2003 *I, Nm, Ur, Geo, E, SA*, 2004 *Tg, S, Fj*, 2005 *S, E*, 2007 *SA, Tg, E, US*
S Leaupepe 1979 *Tg, Fj*, 1980 *Tg*
GE Leaupepe 1995 *SA, Ar, E, Fj, Tg, S, E*, 1996 *NZ, Tg, Fj, I*, 1997 *Tg, Fj*, 1998 *Tg, A*, 1999 *J, C, Tg, F, NZ, US, Fj, J, Ar, W*, 2005 *A*
P Leavai 1990 *J*
A Leavasa 1979 *Tg, Fj*, 1980 *Tg*
MP Leavasa 1993 *Tg, Fj*, 1995 *It, Ar, E, S, E*, 1996 *NZ, Tg, Fj, I*, 1997 *Tg, Fj*, 2002 *Tg, Fj, Tg, SA*
P Leavasa 1955 *Fj, Fj, Fj*, 1957 *Tg, Tg, Tg*
S Leavasa 1955 *Fj, Fj, Fj*, 1957 *Tg*
T Leiasamaivao 1993 *Tg, NZ*, 1994 *Tg, W, Fj*, 1995 *SA, It, Ar, E, SA, S, E*, 1996 *NZ, Tg, Fj, I*, 1997 *Tg, Fj*
M Leiataua 2013 *S*
A Leiua 2013 *S, It, SA*
N Leleimalefaga 2007 *Fj, US*
F Lemalu 2012 *Tg, Fj, J, S, C, F*, 2013 *S*
S Lemalu 2003 *Ur, Geo, E*, 2004 *Tg, S, Fj*, 2008 *Tg, J, NZ*, 2010 *J, I*, 2011 *Fj, Tg*
S Lemamea 1988 *I, W*, 1989 *Fj, WGe, Bel, R*, 1990 *J*, 1992 *Tg, Fj*, 1995 *E, SA, Fj, Tg*
D Lemi 2004 *Tg, S, Fj*, 2005 *Tg, Fj, Tg, Fj*, 2007 *Fj, SA, J, Tg, SA, Tg, E, US*, 2008 *Fj, Tg, J*, 2009 *W, F, It*, 2010 *Tg, J, Fj, I, E, S*, 2011 *Fj, Tg, SA*, 2012 *Tg, Fj, J, S, W, F*
DA Leo 2005 *A, Tg, Fj, Tg, Fj, S, E, Ar*, 2006 *J, Fj, Tg*, 2007 *SA, J, Tg, SA, Tg, E*, 2008 *Tg, J*, 2009 *J, Fj, PNG*, 2010 *S*, 2011 *J, Fj, A, Nm, W, Fj, SA*, 2012 *W*, 2013 *S, It, SA*
J Leota 2011 *Fj, Tg*, 2012 *C, W, F*, 2013 *S, It, SA*
M Leota 2000 *Fj, Tg, C*
P Leata 1990 *Kor, Tg, J*
T Leota 1997 *Tg, Fj*, 1998 *Tg, Fj, A*, 1999 *J, C, Tg, F, Fj, J, Ar, W, S*, 2000 *Fj, J*, 2001 *Tg, Fj, NZ, Fj, J, Fj*, 2002 *Fj, Tg, Fj, Tg, SA*, 2003 *I*, 2005 *A*
A Le'u 1987 *Fj, Tg*, 1989 *WGe, R*, 1990 *Kor, J, Tg, Fj*, 1993 *Tg, Fj, NZ*, 1996 *I*
T Leupolu 2001 *I, It*, 2002 *Fj, Tg, Fj, Tg, SA*, 2003 *I, Nm, SA*, 2004 *Tg, S, Fj*, 2005 *Ar*
R Levasa 2008 *NZ*, 2009 *J, PNG*, 2010 *J, Fj*
A Liaina 1963 *Fj, Fj, Tg*
S Liaina 1963 *Fj, Fj, Tg*
P Lilomaiava 1993 *NZ*
R Lilomaiava 2012 *C, F*
M Lima 1982 *Fj, Fj*
MBP Lima 1991 *Tg, Fj, W, A, Ar, S*, 1992 *Tg, Fj*, 1993 *Fj, NZ*, 1994 *Tg, W, Fj, A*, 1995 *SA, It, Ar, E, SA, Fj, Tg, S, E*, 1996 *NZ, Tg, Fj*, 1997 *Fj*, 1998 *Tg, Fj, A*, 1999 *Tg, F, NZ, US, J, Ar, W, S*, 2000 *C, It, US*, 2001 *Fj, Tg, Fj, I, It*, 2002 *Fj, Tg*, 2003 *I, Nm, Ur, Geo, E, SA*, 2004 *Tg, S, Fj*, 2005 *A, Fj*, 2006 *J, Fj*, 2007 *Fj, Tg, SA, E*
F Lima 1981 *Fj*
M Lome 1957 *Tg, Tg, Tg*, 1963 *Fj*
M Luafalealo 1999 *J*, 2000 *It, US*, 2001 *Tg, Fj, NZ, Fj, J, Fj*
E Lua'iufi 1987 *Fj, Tg*, 1988 *Tg, Fj*
Lui 1932 *Tg*
LS Lui 2004 *Fj*, 2005 *Tg, Fj, Ar*, 2006 *J, Tg*, 2007 *Tg, Tg, E, US*, 2009 *J, Tg, Fj, PNG, PNG, W, F*, 2010 *Tg, J, Fj, J*, 2012 *Tg, Fj, J, S*
M Lupeli 1993 *Fj*

A Macdonald 1924 *Fj, Fj*, 1932 *Tg*
T Magele 1988 *Tg*
M Magele 2009 *PNG*
U Mai 2008 *Tg, J, NZ*, 2009 *J, Fj, PNG, PNG, W, F, It*, 2010 *Tg, J, Fj*, 2011 *J, Fj, Tg*
F Mailei 1963 *Fj, Tg*
F Malele 1979 *Tg, Fj*, 1980 *Tg*
J Maligi 2000 *W, S*
P Maligi 1982 *Fj, Tg*, 1983 *Tg, Fj*, 1984 *Fj, Tg*, 1985 *Fj, Tg, Tg*, 1986 *Fj, Tg*
L Malo 1979 *Fj*
J Mamea 2000 *W, S*
L Mano 1988 *Fj, I, W*
C Manu 2002 *Fj, Tg, Tg, SA*
S Mapusua 2006 *J, Fj, Tg*, 2007 *SA, J, Tg, Tg, E, US*, 2009 *Tg, Fj, W, F, It*, 2010 *I, E, S*, 2011 *J, A, Nm, W, Fj, SA*, 2013 *S, It, SA*
P Mareko 1979 *Fj*
K Mariner 2005 *Ar*
BF Masoe 2012 *Tg, Fj, J, S*
M Mata'afa 1947 *Tg*
P Matailina 1957 *Tg, Tg, Tg*
O Matauiau 1996 *Tg, Fj*, 1999 *Ar, W, S*, 2000 *It, W, S*
K Mavaega 1985 *Tg*
M McFadyen 1957 *Tg*
K McFall 1983 *Fj*
J Meafou 2007 *Tg, SA, E*, 2008 *NZ*
L Mealamu 2000 *W, S*
I Melei 1972 *Tg*
O Meredith 1947 *Tg*
C Meredith 1932 *Tg*
J Meredith 1963 *Fj, Fj, Tg*
J Meredith 2001 *I, It*, 2002 *Fj, Tg, Fj, Tg, SA*, 2003 *I, Nm, Ur, Geo, E, SA*, 2004 *Tg, S, Fj*, 2005 *A, Tg, Fj, Fj*
A Mika 2000 *S*
D Mika 1994 *W, A*
MAN Mika 1995 *SA, It, Ar, E, SA, S, E*, 1997 *Tg, Fj*, 1999 *Tg, F, NZ, J, Ar, W*
S Mika 2004 *Fj*, 2005 *A, Tg, Fj, Tg, Fj*
S Mikaele 2008 *NZ*, 2009 *PNG, PNG*, 2010 *J*
P Misa 2000 *W, S*
S Moala 2008 *Fj*
F Moamanu 1989 *WGe*
S Moamanu 1985 *Fj*, 1986 *Fj, Tg*
M Moke 1990 *Kor, Tg, J, Tg, Fj*
P Momoisea 1972 *Tg, Tg*
H Moors 1924 *Fj, Fj*
R Moors 1994 *Tg*
Mose 1932 *Tg*
S Motoi 1984 *Tg*
F Motusagu 2000 *Tg, It*, 2005 *A*
RR Muagututia 2010 *J*
L Mulipola 2009 *PNG*, 2010 *J*, 2011 *J, Fj, Tg, SA*, 2012 *Tg, Fj, J, S*, 2013 *S, It, SA*
L Mulipola 2009 *F, It*

P Neenee 1987 *Fj, Tg*, 1991 *Tg, Fj*
O Nelson 1955 *Fj, Fj, Fj*, 1957 *Tg, Tg*
N Ngapaku 2000 *J, C, US*
F Nickel 1957 *Tg*
N Nifo 2009 *PNG*
Nimmo 1957 *Tg*
T Nu'uali'itia 1994 *Tg, A*, 1995 *SA, It, Ar, E, SA*, 1996 *NZ*

R Ofisa 2011 *Tg*
A Olive 2008 *Tg*
F Otto 2010 *Tg, Fj, E, S*, 2011 *Tg*, 2012 *Fj, S*

FJP Palaamo 1998 *Tg, Fj, A*, 1999 *J, C, F, NZ, US, Fj*, 2007 *Fj, E*, 2009 *Fj, PNG, PNG*
S Pala'amo 1955 *Fj, Fj, Fj*, 1957 *Tg*
T Palamo 1972 *Tg*
A Palamo 1979 *Tg, Fj*, 1980 *Tg*, 1981 *Fj, Fj*, 1982 *Fj, Fj, Fj, Tg*
LN Palamo 1979 *Tg, Fj*, 1981 *Fj, Fj*, 1982 *Fj, Fj, Fj, Tg*, 1984 *Fj, Tg*, 1985 *Tg*, 1986 *W, Fj, Tg*
O Palepoi 1998 *Tg, Fj, A*, 1999 *J, F, NZ, US, Fj, J, Ar*, 2000 *J, C, It, US, W*, 2001 *Tg, Fj, NZ, Fj, Tg, J, Fj, I, It*, 2002 *Fj, Tg, Fj, Tg, SA*, 2003 *I, Nm, Ur, Geo, E, SA*, 2004 *Tg, S*, 2005 *A, Tg, Fj, Tg, Fj*
Panapa 1932 *Tg*
P Papali'I 1924 *Fj, Fj*
M Papali'I 1955 *Fj, Fj*
PJ Paramore 1991 *Tg, Fj, A*, 1992 *Fj*, 1994 *Tg*, 1995 *SA, It, Ar, SA, Fj, Tg*, 1996 *I*, 1997 *Tg, Fj*, 1998 *Tg, Fj, A*, 1999 *J, Ar, W*, 2001 *Tg, Fj, NZ, Fj, Tg, J, Fj*
J Parkinson 2005 *A, Tg*
T Pati 1997 *Tg*
M Patolo 1986 *W, Fj, Tg*
T Patu 1979 *Tg, Fj*, 1980 *Tg*, 1981 *Fj, Fj*
O Patu 1980 *Tg*
HV Patu 1995 *S, E*, 1996 *I*, 2000 *W, S*
P Paul 1955 *Fj, Fj, Fj*
M Paulino 2008 *NZ*, 2010 *J*, 2012 *Tg, Fj*
P Paulo 1989 *Bel*, 1990 *Tg, Fj*

T Paulo 2012 *C, W, F*, 2013 *S, It, SA*
T Paulo 2010 *E, S*, 2011 *J, Fj, Tg, A, Nm, W, Fj*, 2012 *J, S, W, F*, 2013 *It, SA*
A Perelini 1991 *Tg, Fj, W, A, Ar, S*, 1992 *Tg, Fj*, 1993 *NZ*
AI Perenise 2010 *Tg, J, Fj, J, I, E, S*, 2011 *J, Fj, A, Nm, W, Fj, SA*
PL Perez 2012 *Tg, Fj, J, S, C, W, F*
S Perez 1963 *Fj, Fj, Tg*
MS Pesamino 2009 *PNG, PNG*, 2010 *Tg, J, Fj, J*
N Petaia 1963 *Fj*
Petelo 1932 *Tg*
T Petelo 1985 *Fj*
P Petia 2003 *Nm*
O Pifeleti 1987 *Fj*
K Pisi 2012 *Tg, Fj*
TG Pisi 2010 *Tg, Fj, I, E, S*, 2011 *J, A, Nm, W, Fj*, 2012 *C, W, F*
T Pisi 2011 *J, Fj, A, Nm, Fj, SA*, 2012 *S, C, W, F*, 2013 *S, It, SA*
S Po Ching 1990 *Kor, Tg*, 1991 *Tg*
S Poching 2000 *W, S*, 2001 *Tg*
AJ Poluleuligaga 2007 *SA, J, Tg, SA, Tg, E, US*, 2008 *NZ*, 2009 *J, Tg, Fj, W, F, It*, 2010 *Tg, J, I, E*, 2011 *Nm*, 2013 *It, SA*
HA Porter 2011 *Tg*
P Poulos 2003 *Ur, Geo, E, SA*
E Puleitu 1995 *SA, E*
S Punivalu 1981 *Fj, Fj*, 1982 *Fj, Fj, Fj*, 1983 *Tg, Fj*
JEP Purdie 2007 *Fj, SA, J, Tg, SA, Tg, E, US*

I Railey 1924 *Fj, Fj*
D Rasmussen 2003 *I, Ur, Geo, E, SA*, 2004 *Tg, S, Fj*
R Rasmussen 1997 *Tg*
B Reidy 1995 *SA, Fj, Tg*, 1996 *NZ, Tg, Fj, I*, 1998 *Fj, A*, 1999 *Tg, F, NZ, US, Fj, J, Ar, W, S*
K Roberts 1972 *Tg*
F Ropati 1982 *Fj, Fj, Fj*, 1984 *Fj, Tg*
R Ropati 2003 *SA*, 2008 *NZ*
W Ryan 1983 *Fj*, 1985 *Tg*

S Sa 2012 *C*
E Sa'aga 1924 *Fj, Fj*, 1932 *Tg*
PD Saena 1988 *Tg, Fj, I*, 1989 *Fj, Bel, R*, 1990 *Kor, Tg, J, Tg, Fj*, 1991 *Tg, Fj*, 1992 *Tg, Fj*, 1993 *Tg, Fj*
L Sagaga 1963 *Fj, Tg*
K Saifoloi 1979 *Tg, Fj*, 1980 *Tg*, 1982 *Fj, Fj*, 1984 *Fj, Tg*
P Saili 1957 *Tg, Tg, Tg*
M Salanoa 2005 *Tg, Fj*, 2006 *J, Fj, Tg*, 2007 *Fj, SA, J, Tg, Tg*
M Salavea 2010 *Tg, Fj, I, E, S*, 2011 *J, Tg, A, W, Fj*
T Salesa 1979 *Tg, Fj*, 1980 *Tg*, 1981 *Fj, Fj*, 1982 *Fj, Fj, Fj, Tg*, 1983 *Tg, Fj, Fj*, 1984 *Fj, Tg*, 1985 *Fj, Tg, Tg*, 1986 *Fj, Tg*, 1987 *Fj, Tg*, 1988 *Tg, Fj, I*, 1989 *Fj, WGe, R*
G Salima 2008 *Fj*
T Samania 1994 *W, Fj, A*, 1996 *NZ*, 2000 *Fj, J, C, It*, 2001 *Tg*
D Sanft 2006 *J*
Q Sanft 2000 *W, S*
L Sasi 1982 *Fj, Tg*, 1983 *Tg, Fj*, 1984 *Fj, Tg*, 1985 *Tg*, 1986 *W, Fj, Tg*, 1987 *Fj, Tg*, 1988 *Tg, Fj*
B Sasulu 2008 *Fj*
S Sauila 1989 *Bel*
L Savai'inaea 1957 *Tg, Tg*
J Schaafhausen 1947 *Tg*
W Schaafhausen 1947 *Tg*
P Schmidt 1980 *Tg*, 1985 *Tg*
P Schmidt 1989 *Fj, WGe*
R Schmidt 1979 *Tg*, 1980 *Tg*
D Schuster 1982 *Tg*, 1983 *Tg, Fj, Fj*
H Schuster 1989 *Fj*, 1990 *Kor, Tg, J*
J Schuster 1985 *Fj, Tg, Tg*
NSJ Schuster 1999 *Tg, F, US*
M Schuster 2000 *S*, 2004 *Tg, S, Fj*
P Schuster 1975 *Tg*
M Schwalger 2000 *W, S*, 2001 *It*, 2003 *Nm, Ur, Geo, E*, 2005 *S, E, Ar*, 2006 *J, Fj, Tg*, 2007 *Fj, SA, Tg, SA, Tg, E, US*, 2008 *Fj*, 2009 *J, Tg, Fj, PNG, W, F, It*, 2010 *Tg, J, Fj, I, E, S*, 2011 *Fj, A, Nm, W, Fj, SA*
Sefo 1932 *Tg*
E Sefo 1984 *Fj*
T Sefo 1987 *Tg*, 1988 *I*
P Segi 2001 *Fj, NZ, Fj, Tg, J, I, It*, 2002 *Fj, Tg, Fj, Tg*
K Seinafo 1992 *Tg*
F Selesele 2010 *Tg, J, J*
S Semeane 2009 *It*
J Senio 2004 *Tg, S, Fj*, 2005 *Tg, Fj, Tg, Fj*, 2006 *J, Fj, Tg*
U Setu 2010 *Tg, J*
T Seumanutafa 1981 *Fj*
E Seveali'I 2000 *Fj, J, Tg, C*, 2001 *Tg, NZ, J, Fj, It*, 2002 *Fj, Tg, Fj, Tg, SA*, 2005 *E*, 2007 *SA, J, Tg, SA, Tg, US*
F Sililoto 1980 *Tg*, 1981 *Fj, Fj*, 1982 *Fj, Fj, Fj*
Simanu 1932 *Tg*
A Simanu 1975 *Tg*, 1981 *Fj*
Sinaumea 1924 *Fj*
F Sini 1995 *SA, Ar, E, SA*
S Sinoti 2010 *J*
T Sio 1990 *Tg*, 1992 *Fj*
K Sio 1988 *Tg, Fj, I, W*, 1989 *Fj, WGe, R*, 1990 *J, Tg, Fj*, 1992 *Tg, Fj*, 1993 *NZ*, 1994 *Tg*
P Sioa 1981 *Fj, Fj*
S Sititi 1999 *J, C, F, J, W, S*, 2000 *Fj, J, Tg, C, US*, 2001 *Tg, Fj, NZ, Fj, Tg, J, Fj, I, It*, 2002 *Fj, Tg, Fj, Tg, SA*, 2003 *I, Nm, Ur, Geo, E, SA*, 2004 *Tg, S, Fj*, 2005 *A, Fj, Tg, Fj, S, E, Ar*, 2006 *J, Fj, Tg*, 2007 *Fj, SA, J, Tg, SA, Tg, E, US*, 2008 *Fj, Tg, J, NZ*, 2009 *J, PNG, PNG*
F Siu 1975 *Tg*
P Siu 1963 *Fj, Fj, Tg*
S Skelton 1982 *Fj*
E Skelton 2009 *J, Tg, PNG, PNG*
R Slade 1972 *Tg*
C Slade 2006 *J, Fj, Tg*, 2008 *Fj, Tg, NZ*
S Smith 1995 *S, E*, 1996 *Tg, Fj*, 1999 *C, Tg, F, NZ*
P Solia 1955 *Fj, Fj*
I Solipo 1981 *Fj*
F Solomona 1985 *Tg*
JS Sooialo 2011 *J, Fj, Tg, W*, 2012 *C*, 2013 *S, SA*
A So'oialo 1996 *I*, 1997 *Tg, Fj*, 1998 *Tg*, 1999 *Tg, F, NZ, US, Fj, J, Ar*, 2000 *Tg, It*, 2001 *Tg, Fj, NZ, Fj, Tg, J, I*
S So'oialo 1998 *Tg, Fj*, 1999 *NZ, US, Fj, J, Ar, W, S*, 2000 *W, S*, 2001 *Tg, Fj, NZ, Fj, J, Fj, I*, 2002 *Tg, Fj, Tg, SA*, 2003 *I, Nm, Ur, Geo, E, SA*, 2004 *Tg, S, Fj*, 2005 *E*, 2007 *Fj, SA, J, Tg, E, US*
F So'olefai 1999 *C, Tg*, 2000 *W, S*, 2001 *Tg, Fj, NZ, Fj, J*
V Stet 1963 *Fj*
A Stewart 2005 *A, Tg*
G Stowers 2001 *I*, 2008 *Fj, Tg, J, NZ*, 2009 *J, Tg, Fj, PNG, W, It*, 2010 *Tg, J, Fj, I, E, S*, 2011 *Fj, A, Nm, W, Fj, SA*
R Stowers 2008 *Fj*
F Sua 1982 *Fj, Fj, Fj, Tg*, 1983 *Tg, Fj*, 1984 *Fj*, 1985 *Fj, Tg, Tg*, 1986 *Fj, Tg*, 1987 *Fj*
JI Sua 2011 *W, Fj*, 2012 *Tg, Fj, J, S, C, W, F*, 2013 *S, It, SA*
P Swepson 1957 *Tg*

S Ta'ala 1996 *Tg, Fj, I*, 1997 *Tg, Fj*, 1998 *Tg, Fj, A*, 1999 *J, C, Tg, US, Fj, J, Ar, W, S*, 2001 *J*
T Taega 1997 *Fj*
PI Taele 2005 *Tg, Fj, E, Ar*, 2006 *J, Fj, Tg*, 2010 *J*
D Tafeamalii 2000 *W, S*
T Tafua 1981 *Fj, Fj*, 1982 *Fj, Fj, Fj, Tg*, 1983 *Tg, Fj*, 1985 *Fj, Tg, Tg*, 1986 *W, Fj, Tg*, 1987 *Tg*, 1989 *Fj, WGe, R*
L Tafunai 2004 *Tg, Fj*, 2005 *Tg, Fj, Tg, Fj, S, Ar*, 2008 *Tg, J, NZ*
TDL Tagaloa 1990 *Kor, Tg, J, Tg, Fj*, 1991 *W, A, Ar, S*
S Tagicakibau 2003 *Nm, Ur, Geo, E, SA*, 2004 *Tg, S, Fj*, 2005 *S, E, Ar*, 2007 *Tg*, 2009 *J, Tg, Fj*, 2011 *J, Fj, A, Nm, W, Fj*
Tagimanu 1924 *Fj*
I Taina 2005 *Tg, Fj, Tg, Fj, S*
F Taiomaivao 1989 *Bel*
F Talapusi 1979 *Tg, Fj*, 1980 *Tg*
F Talapusi 2005 *A, Fj, Tg, Fj*
Tamalua 1932 *Tg*
F Tanoa'i 1996 *Tg, Fj*
S Tanuko 1987 *Tg*
P Tapelu 2002 *SA*
V Tasi 1981 *Fj*, 1982 *Fj, Fj, Fj, Tg*, 1983 *Tg, Fj*, 1984 *Fj, Tg*
J Tatupu 2010 *J*
S Tatupu 1990 *Tg*, 1993 *Tg, Fj, NZ*, 1995 *It, Ar, E, SA, Fj, Tg*
N Tauafao 2005 *A, Tg, Fj, Tg, Fj, S, Ar*, 2007 *Fj*, 2008 *Fj, Tg, J, NZ*, 2009 *J, Fj, PNG, PNG*
S Taulafo 2009 *W, F, It*, 2010 *Tg, Fj, I, E, S*, 2011 *J, A, Nm, W, Fj, SA*, 2012 *Tg, Fj, J, S, C, W, F*, 2013 *S, It, SA*
I Tautau 1985 *Fj, Tg*, 1986 *W*
A Tavana 2012 *Tg*

T Tavita 1984 *Fj, Tg*
E Taylor 2011 *J, Fj*
HL Tea 2008 *Fj, Tg, J, NZ,* 2009 *PNG*
I Tekori 2007 *SA, J, SA, Tg, E, US,* 2009 *Tg, Fj, W, F,* 2010 *Tg, J, Fj, I, E, S,* 2011 *J, Nm, W, SA,* 2012 *J, S, C, W, F*
S Telea 1989 *Bel*
AT Telea 1995 *S, E,* 1996 *NZ, Tg, Fj*
E Telea 2008 *Fj*
V Teo 1957 *Tg, Tg*
F Teo 1955 *Fj*
A Teo 1947 *Tg*
KG Thompson 2007 *Fj, SA, Tg, SA, Tg, E, US,* 2008 *Tg, J,* 2009 *W, F, It,* 2010 *Tg, Fj, I, E, S,* 2011 *A, Nm, W, Fj, SA,* 2012 *J, S,* 2013 *It, SA*
H Thomson 1947 *Tg*
R Tiatia 1972 *Tg*
A Tiatia 2001 *Tg, Fj, NZ, Fj, Tg, J, Fj*
S Tilialo 1972 *Tg*
MM Timoteo 2009 *Tg, F, It,* 2012 *Tg, Fj*
F Tipi 1998 *Fj, A,* 1999 *J, C, F, NZ, Fj*
F Toala 1998 *Fj,* 1999 *J, C, S,* 2000 *W, S*
L Toelupe 1979 *Fj*
P Toelupe 2008 *Fj, J, NZ*
T Tofaeono 1989 *Fj, Bel*
A Toleafoa 2000 *W, S,* 2002 *Tg, SA*
K Toleafoa 1955 *Fj, Fj*
PL Toleafoa 2006 *J, Fj*
K Tole'afoa 1998 *Tg, A,* 1999 *Ar*
F Toloa 1979 *Tg,* 1980 *Tg*
R Tolufale 2008 *NZ,* 2009 *PNG*
J Tomuli 2001 *I, It,* 2002 *Fj, Tg, Fj, Tg, SA,* 2003 *I, Nm, Ur, Geo, E, SA,* 2006 *J*
L Tone 1998 *Tg, Fj, A,* 1999 *J, C, Tg, F, NZ, US, J, Ar, W, S,* 2000 *Fj, J, Tg, C, It, US, S,* 2001 *NZ, Fj, Tg, J, Fj*
S Tone 2000 *W*
Toni 1924 *Fj*
OFJ Tonu'u 1992 *Tg,* 1993 *Tg, Fj, NZ*
F To'omalatai 1989 *Bel*
PS To'omalatai 1985 *Fj, Tg,* 1986 *W, Fj, Tg,* 1988 *Tg, Fj, I, W,* 1989 *Fj, WGe, Bel, R,* 1990 *Kor, Tg, J, Tg, Fj,* 1991 *Tg, Fj, W, A, Ar, S,* 1992 *Tg, Fj,* 1993 *Fj,* 1994 *A,* 1995 *Fj*
O Treviranus 2009 *J, Tg, Fj, PNG, PNG, W, F, It,* 2010 *J, Fj, J, I, E, S,* 2011 *Fj, Tg, Nm, W, SA,* 2012 *C, W, F,* 2013 *S, It, SA*
Tualai 1924 *Fj, Fj*
I Tualaulelei 1963 *Fj, Fj, Tg*
F Tuatagaloa 1957 *Tg*
V Tuatagaloa 1963 *Fj, Tg*
K Tuatagaloa 1963 *Fj, Fj, Tg,* 1972 *Tg*
Tufele 1924 *Fj*
D Tuiavi'I 2003 *I, Nm, Ur, E, SA*
T Tuifua 2011 *J, Fj, A, Nm, Fj, SA,* 2012 *C, W, F,* 2013 *S, It, SA*
G Tuigamala 2012 *Tg, Fj*
VL Tuigamala 1996 *Fj, I,* 1997 *Tg, Fj,* 1998 *Tg, Fj, A,* 1999 *F, NZ, US, Fj, J, Ar, W, S,* 2000 *Fj, J, Tg, US,* 2001 *J, Fj, I, It*
AT Tuilagi 2002 *Fj, Tg, SA,* 2005 *A, Tg, Fj, Tg, Fj, S, E,* 2007 *SA, J, Tg, SA, Tg, E, US,* 2010 *I, E, S,* 2011 *J, A, Nm, W, Fj, SA,* 2013 *S, It, SA*
AF Tuilagi 2005 *Tg, Fj, Tg, Fj, S, Ar,* 2006 *J, Tg,* 2007 *Fj, SA, J,* 2008 *Tg, J,* 2009 *W*
F Tuilagi 1992 *Tg,* 1994 *W, Fj, A,* 1995 *SA, SA, Fj,* 2000 *W, S,* 2001 *Fj, NZ, Tg,* 2002 *Fj, Tg, Fj, Tg, SA*
H Tuilagi 2002 *Fj, Tg, Fj, Tg,* 2007 *SA, E,* 2008 *J,* 2009 *W, F, It*
T Tuisaula 1947 *Tg*
R Tuivaiti 2004 *Fj*
A Tunupopo 1963 *Fj*
P Tupa'i 2005 *A, Tg, S, E, Ar*
A Tupou 2008 *NZ,* 2009 *PNG*
S Tupuola 1982 *Fj, Fj, Fj, Tg,* 1983 *Tg, Fj,* 1985 *Tg,* 1986 *Fj, Tg,* 1987 *Fj, Tg,* 1988 *W,* 1989 *R*
P Tu'uau 1972 *Tg, Tg,* 1975 *Tg*
D Tyrrell 2000 *Fj, J, C,* 2001 *It,* 2002 *Fj, Tg, SA,* 2003 *I, Nm, Ur, Geo, E, SA*

S Uati 1988 *Tg, Fj*
T Ugapo 1988 *Tg, Fj, I, W,* 1989 *Fj, WGe, Bel*
U Ulia 2004 *Tg, S, Fj,* 2005 *Ar,* 2006 *J, Fj, Tg,* 2007 *Fj, Tg, Tg, US*
J Ulugia 1985 *Fj, Tg*
M Umaga 1995 *SA, It, Ar, E, SA,* 1998 *Tg, Fj, A,* 1999 *Tg, F, NZ, US, Fj*
L Utu'utu 1975 *Tg*
A Utu'utu 1979 *Tg, Fj*

E Va'a 1996 *I,* 1997 *Fj,* 1998 *A,* 1999 *Tg, NZ, Fj, J, W, S,* 2001 *Tg, Fj, NZ, Fj, Tg, J, Fj, I,* 2002 *Fj, Tg, Fj, Tg, SA,* 2003 *I, Nm, Ur, Geo, E, SA*
JH Va'a 2005 *A, Fj, Tg, Fj, S, E, Ar,* 2006 *Fj, Tg,* 2007 *SA, J, Tg, SA,* 2009 *J, Tg, Fj, W, It*
B Vaaulu 2013 *S, It, SA*
M Vaea 1991 *Tg, Fj, W, A, Ar, S,* 1992 *Fj,* 1995 *S*
K Vaega 1982 *Fj, Tg,* 1983 *Fj*
TM Vaega 1986 *W,* 1989 *WGe, Bel, R,* 1990 *Kor, Tg, J, Tg, Fj,* 1991 *Tg, Fj, W, A, Ar, S,* 1992 *Tg, Fj,* 1993 *Tg, Fj, NZ,* 1994 *Tg, W, Fj, A,* 1995 *SA, It, Ar, E, SA, Fj, Tg, S, E,* 1996 *NZ, Tg, Fj, I,* 1997 *Tg,* 1998 *Fj, A,* 1999 *J, C, F, NZ, Fj, J, Ar, W, S,* 2000 *Fj, J, Tg, C, It, US,* 2001 *Fj, Tg, J, Fj, I*
A Vaeluaga 2000 *W, S,* 2001 *Tg, Fj, Tg, J, Fj, I,* 2007 *SA, J, SA, E, US*
F Vagaia 1972 *Tg*
K Vai 1987 *Fj, Tg,* 1989 *Bel*
TS Vaifale 1989 *R,* 1990 *Kor, Tg, J, Tg, Fj,* 1991 *Tg, Fj, W, Ar, S,* 1992 *Tg, Fj,* 1993 *NZ,* 1994 *Tg, W, Fj, A,* 1995 *SA, It, SA, Fj, S, E,* 1996 *NZ, Tg,* 1997 *Tg, Fj*
S Vaili 2001 *I, It,* 2002 *Fj, Tg, Fj, Tg,* 2003 *Geo,* 2004 *Tg, S, Fj*
L Vailoaloa 2005 *A,* 2011 *J, Fj, Tg*
S Vaisola Sefo 2007 *US*
T Veiru 2000 *W, S*
M Vili 1975 *Tg*
M Vili 1957 *Tg*
T Vili 1999 *C, Tg, US, Ar,* 2000 *Fj, J, Tg, C, It, US,* 2001 *Tg, Fj, J, Fj, I, It,* 2003 *Ur, Geo, E, SA,* 2004 *Tg, S, Fj,* 2005 *A, Tg, Fj, S, E,* 2006 *J, Fj, Tg*
T Viliamu 1947 *Tg*
K Viliamu 2001 *I, It,* 2002 *Fj, SA,* 2003 *I, Ur, Geo, E, SA,* 2004 *S*
Visesio 1932 *Tg*
FV Vitale 1994 *W, Fj, A,* 1995 *Fj, Tg*
F Vito 1972 *Tg,* 1975 *Tg*
M von Dincklage 2004 *S*

R Warren 2004 *Tg, S,* 2005 *Tg, Fj, Tg, Fj, S, Ar,* 2008 *Fj, Tg, J, NZ*
S Wendt 1955 *Fj, Fj, Fj*
AF Williams 2009 *J, Fj, PNG, PNG, F, It,* 2010 *J, J*
DR Williams 1988 *I, W,* 1995 *SA, It, E*
G Williams 2007 *Fj, SA, SA, Tg,* 2008 *Tg, J,* 2009 *J, Tg, Fj, PNG, PNG, W, It,* 2010 *J, I, E*
H Williams 2001 *Tg, Tg, J*
PB Williams 2010 *Tg, J, Fj, I, E, S,* 2011 *A, Nm, W, Fj, SA,* 2012 *Fj, J, S, W,* 2013 *S, It, SA*

P Young 1988 *I,* 1989 *Bel*

SCOTLAND

SCOTLAND'S 2012–13 TEST RECORD

OPPONENTS	DATE	VENUE	RESULT
New Zealand	11 Nov	H	Lost 22–51
South Africa	17 Nov	H	Lost 10–21
Tonga	24 Nov	H	Lost 15–21
England	2 Feb	A	Lost 38–18
Italy	9 Feb	H	Won 34–10
Ireland	24 Feb	H	Won 12–8
Wales	9 Mar	H	Lost 18–28
France	16 Mar	A	Lost 23–16
Samoa	8 Jun	N	Lost 27–17
South Africa	15 Jun	A	Lost 30–17
Italy	22 Jun	N	Won 30–29

A SEASON OF CHANGE

By Chris Paterson

Getty Images

Stuart Hogg cheers Matthew Scott over the try-line in Scotland's emphatic Six Nations win over Italy.

The 2012/13 season in Scotland was one of change. Yes, there was some consistency, not least in the performances of Ryan Grant, Alasdair Strokosch, Greig Laidlaw, Matt Scott and Stuart Hogg in the national team. The five had earned plaudits in the spring and summer of 2012, and wind the clock forward a year and their reputation as the 'go-to' men was enhanced.

There was, however, the familiar challenge for Scottish rugby: to produce back-to-back performances, rather than roller-coaster peaks and troughs. There was also the requirement to broaden the base of the national squad, a familiar tale for Scottish rugby as a whole.

The international season began with a tangible air of optimism. Murrayfield attracted a capacity crowd for the first Test of the season against New Zealand. Scotland scored the first try through the prolific Tim Visser on his home debut but, ultimately, the hosts were well-beaten by a clinical New Zealand side. Still, the fact that Scotland crossed the New Zealand whitewash on three occasions – their first tries against the All Blacks in seven years – did little to diminish a general upbeat mood.

Six days was a short turnaround to face South Africa and the

Springboks brought their most physical game to Murrayfield, dominating the first half and pretty much controlling the match. It turned out to be Mike Blair's last match for Scotland, the country's most-capped scrum half bowing out after a 10-year international career.

His replacement in that game, Henry Pyrgos – who had won his first cap as a substitute against New Zealand the week previously – scored a second-half try but there was to be no repeat of the 2010 victory against South Africa. Pyrgos, incidentally, was the first of 15 new caps Scotland fielded throughout the season, a statistic that underlined the transitional nature of the nation's rugby year.

The autumn series concluded against Tonga in Aberdeen. It was a hugely disappointing game in front of a big and loyal north-east crowd. Scotland were second-best to the islanders, who showed great desire and physicality, especially in the breakdown and in defence.

That defeat was the lowest point of the season and the performance and result triggered immediate consequences as head coach Andy Robinson, who had been part of England's coaching team for their Rugby World Cup 2003 success, departed. It also transpired that the Tonga match was the last appearance of another redoubtable Scotland number nine, Rory Lawson.

Come the RBS Six Nations the optimism of the autumn had been replaced by uncertainty. The national coaching team was headed up by Scott Johnson, whom Robinson had recruited as his attack coach but also with a responsibility to lead Scotland's talent identification programme.

Specialist coaches Matt Taylor (defence), Massimo Cuttitta (scrum) and Duncan Hodge (kicking and catching) were joined by one gnarled new face in Dean Ryan, the former Gloucester director of rugby and England international who would pilot the forwards alongside Stevie Scott, the former Scotland hooker who had been part of the national set-up before and had returned north after a spell at Sale Sharks. It was asking a lot of this management team to deliver a turnaround in fortunes given such a short preparation time.

There was another factor at play, mind you, among the pro-clubs, with Glasgow Warriors, under the guidance of head coach Gregor Townsend, putting together some impressive displays in the RaboDirect PRO12 built around aggression and accuracy up front, uncompromising defence and wit and imagination in their back play.

The opening Six Nations game saw Scotland head to Twickenham for the Calcutta Cup clash, which proved to be a disappointment. Yes, there were positives in the two tries – an early one from debutant Sean Maitland and an absolute long-range cracker from Hogg – but what misfired badly in that game was the contact area.

Scotland put that right seven days later to win their game against

Italy 34–10, scoring four tries through Visser, Scott, Hogg and Sean Lamont. One win from two in the Six Nations, playing some really good rugby and with the top try scorers in the tournament at that point – it was a long way from the mood just six weeks beforehand!

The fixture scheduling had been kind to Scotland and the fact that they had three home games in a row – Italy, Ireland and Wales – meant they could target further success.

The Ireland match was very different from the game against the Azzurri. I played in Scotland games where neutrals would look at the stats the opposition enjoyed in terms of territory and possession and would be incredulous how Scotland had won.

Here was a game where Scotland had almost no possession and almost no territory but the desire and attitude instilled by the new coaching team won the game – a first Six Nations triumph against Ireland at Murrayfield in 12 years.

Next up was Wales and from a Scottish perspective this was a depressing game. Conditions were poor and scrum infringements dominated. It was stop-start with no tempo and was frustrating.

The Six Nations campaign ended with a trip to the Stade de France in Paris. As a player I always looked forward massively to this game, more so when it was the last game of the Championship. On this occasion, Scotland's mistakes allowed France back into the game, though a late try from Visser was a reminder of the potency of their attack if they could get things right.

The 2013 Championship had been played out as the backdrop to selection for the British & Irish Lions tour to Australia. As Scotland finished third in the Six Nations and there had been some terrific individual performances, debate began as to how many Scots would make the tour party. As matters transpired, three were rewarded with call-ups initially – Hogg, Maitland and Richie Gray, and a fourth, Grant, was quite rightly in my view added later on. Another two or three Scots had every right to be disappointed that they were not included.

Attention for the national team turned to the quadrangular tournament in June that involved South Africa, Samoa, Italy and Scotland in Durban, Nelspruit and Pretoria. The tour party contained nine uncapped players and, by the end of the trip, all nine (plus a 10th who had travelled out as an injury replacement given a sizable casualty count) had won caps, thus Johnson's intention to find out about players was played out in greater detail than perhaps he had at first imagined.

Those who were capped on the tour were backs Alex Dunbar, Peter Horne, Peter Murchie and Tommy Seymour (all Glasgow Warriors) plus Greig Tonks (Edinburgh Rugby) and Duncan Taylor (Saracens), and forwards Pat MacArthur, Tim Swinson and Fraser Brown (Glasgow Warriors) and Steve Lawrie (Edinburgh Rugby).

The tour was perhaps Scotland's season in microcosm. They were slow to start and suffered as a consequence against a powerful Samoan side. They delivered a passionate and brave display, led by Laidlaw with notable contributions from new cap Swinson and Strokosch, against South Africa, and it took a late, last-minute try against Italy for a win but, in that game, the result mattered more than the performance.

Joining the new caps I've mentioned already over the course of the season were Tom Heathcote, the Bath fly half, Ryan Wilson, the Glasgow Warriors number 8, and Edinburgh Rugby second row Grant Gilchrist, all of whom also featured on the tour. The stars of the month in South Africa, though, were Scott, Strokosch and Laidlaw. Just as we had seen the year before, Strokosch was, by some distance, the player of the tour.

Elsewhere within Scottish Rugby, reorganisation is underway for the Scotland Women's team, the Scotland Under 20 side retained their place among the top tier countries who compete in the IRB Junior World Championship, while the men's national Sevens team secured their core status on the HSBC Sevens World Series for another year, but left it late within the final qualifying competition at Twickenham.

With the 2014 Commonwealth Games in Glasgow and, looking further ahead, the return of rugby to the 2016 Olympic Games in Rio, the focus on the abbreviated game will intensify and much will be expected of head coach Stephen Gemmell and his squad.

While Glasgow Warriors reached the play-offs of the RaboDirect PRO12, only to be thwarted by Leinster away, it was a poor season for Edinburgh Rugby, which resulted in an entire new coaching team being brought in to point the way forward for the new season.

On the club scene, Ayr completed the RBS Cup and Premiership double, while the competition for places in the British & Irish Cup raised the standard generally among the top 10 club sides with Gala, Stirling County and Edinburgh Accies joining Ayr in the cross-border competition for 2013/14.

Looking ahead, the national team will have a new head coach in the shape of New Zealander Vern Cotter (currently at Clermont Auvergne), who is scheduled to take the reins after the Six Nations. Johnson will remain involved with the national team, though his duties will focus sharply on his Director of Performance Rugby remit, and all supporters will hope that this particular trans-Tasman alliance will inspire Scotland for the next major global test, Rugby World Cup 2015 in England.

SCOTLAND INTERNATIONAL STATISTICS

MATCH RECORDS UP TO 10 OCTOBER 2013

MOST CONSECUTIVE TEST WINS

6 1925 F, W, I, E, 1926 F, W
6 1989 Fj, R, 1990 I, F, W, E

MOST CONSECUTIVE TESTS WITHOUT DEFEAT

Matches	Wins	Draws	Period
9	6*	3	1885 to 1887
6	6	0	1925 to 1926
6	6	0	1989 to 1990
6	4	2	1877 to 1880
6	5	1	1983 to 1984

* includes an abandoned match

MOST POINTS IN A MATCH

BY THE TEAM

Pts	Opponents	Venue	Year
100	Japan	Perth	2004
89	Ivory Coast	Rustenburg	1995
65	United States	San Francisco	2002
60	Zimbabwe	Wellington	1987
60	Romania	Hampden Park	1999
56	Portugal	Saint Etienne	2007
55	Romania	Dunedin	1987
53	United States	Murrayfield	2000
51	Zimbabwe	Murrayfield	1991
49	Argentina	Murrayfield	1990
49	Romania	Murrayfield	1995

BY A PLAYER

Pts	Player	Opponents	Venue	Year
44	AG Hastings	Ivory Coast	Rustenburg	1995
40	CD Paterson	Japan	Perth	2004
33	GPJ Townsend	United States	Murrayfield	2000
31	AG Hastings	Tonga	Pretoria	1995
27	AG Hastings	Romania	Dunedin	1987
26	KM Logan	Romania	Hampden Park	1999
24	BJ Laney	Italy	Rome	2002
24	DA Parks	Argentina	Tucumán	2010
23	G Ross	Tonga	Murrayfield	2001
22	GD Laidlaw	Fiji	Lautoka	2012
21	AG Hastings	England	Murrayfield	1986
21	AG Hastings	Romania	Bucharest	1986
21	CD Paterson	Wales	Murrayfield	2007
21	DA Parks	South Africa	Murrayfield	2010

MOST TRIES IN A MATCH

BY THE TEAM

Tries	Opponents	Venue	Year
15	Japan	Perth	2004
13	Ivory Coast	Rustenburg	1995
12	Wales	Raeburn Place	1887
11	Zimbabwe	Wellington	1987
10	United States	San Francisco	2002
9	Romania	Dunedin	1987
9	Argentina	Murrayfield	1990

BY A PLAYER

Tries	Player	Opponents	Venue	Year
5	GC Lindsay	Wales	Raeburn Place	1887
4	WA Stewart	Ireland	Inverleith	1913
4	IS Smith	France	Inverleith	1925
4	IS Smith	Wales	Swansea	1925
4	AG Hastings	Ivory Coast	Rustenburg	1995

MOST CONVERSIONS IN A MATCH

BY THE TEAM

Cons	Opponents	Venue	Year
11	Japan	Perth	2004
9	Ivory Coast	Rustenburg	1995
8	Zimbabwe	Wellington	1987
8	Romania	Dunedin	1987
8	Portugal	Saint Etienne	2007

BY A PLAYER

Cons	Player	Opponents	Venue	Year
11	CD Paterson	Japan	Perth	2004
9	AG Hastings	Ivory Coast	Rustenburg	1995
8	AG Hastings	Zimbabwe	Wellington	1987
8	AG Hastings	Romania	Dunedin	1987

MOST PENALTIES IN A MATCH

BY THE TEAM

Penalties	Opponents	Venue	Year
8	Tonga	Pretoria	1995
7	Wales	Murrayfield	2007
6	France	Murrayfield	1986
6	Italy	Murrayfield	2005
6	Ireland	Murrayfield	2007
6	Italy	Saint Etienne	2007
6	Argentina	Tucumán	2010
6	South Africa	Murrayfield	2010
6	Wales	Murrayfield	2013

BY A PLAYER

Penalties	Player	Opponents	Venue	Year
8	AG Hastings	Tonga	Pretoria	1995
7	CD Paterson	Wales	Murrayfield	2007
6	AG Hastings	France	Murrayfield	1986
6	CD Paterson	Italy	Murrayfield	2005
6	CD Paterson	Ireland	Murrayfield	2007
6	CD Paterson	Italy	Saint Etienne	2007
6	DA Parks	Argentina	Tucumán	2010
6	DA Parks	South Africa	Murrayfield	2010
6	GD Laidlaw	Wales	Murrayfield	2013

MOST DROP GOALS IN A MATCH

BY THE TEAM

Drops	Opponents	Venue	Year
3	Ireland	Murrayfield	1973
2	on several	occasions	

BY A PLAYER

Drops	Player	Opponents	Venue	Year
2	RC MacKenzie	Ireland	Belfast	1877
2	NJ Finlay	Ireland	Glasgow	1880
2	BM Simmers	Wales	Murrayfield	1965
2	DW Morgan	Ireland	Murrayfield	1973
2	BM Gossman	France	Parc des Princes	1983
2	JY Rutherford	New Zealand	Murrayfield	1983
2	JY Rutherford	Wales	Murrayfield	1985
2	JY Rutherford	Ireland	Murrayfield	1987
2	CM Chalmers	England	Twickenham	1995
2	DA Parks	Wales	Cardiff	2010
2	DA Parks	Argentina	Tucumán	2010

CAREER RECORDS

MOST CAPPED PLAYERS

Caps	Player	Career Span
109	CD Paterson	1999 to 2011
87	S Murray	1997 to 2007
85	MRL Blair	2002 to 2012
82	GPJ Townsend	1993 to 2003
79	SF Lamont	2004 to 2013
77	JPR White	2000 to 2009
77	NJ Hines	2000 to 2011
75	GC Bulloch	1997 to 2005
71	SB Grimes	1997 to 2005
70	KM Logan	1992 to 2003
68	RW Ford	2004 to 2013
67	DA Parks	2004 to 2012
66	SM Taylor	2000 to 2009
65	S Hastings	1986 to 1997
65	AF Jacobsen	2002 to 2012
62	CP Cusiter	2004 to 2012
61	AG Hastings	1986 to 1995
61	GW Weir	1990 to 2000
61	TJ Smith	1997 to 2005
60	CM Chalmers	1989 to 1999
60	BW Redpath	1993 to 2003
59	HFG Southwell	2004 to 2011

MOST CONSECUTIVE TESTS

Tests	Player	Span
49	AB Carmichael	1967 to 1978
44	CD Paterson	2004 to 2008
40	HF McLeod	1954 to 1962
37	JM Bannerman	1921 to 1929
35	AG Stanger	1989 to 1994

MOST TESTS AS CAPTAIN

Tests	Captain	Span
25	DMB Sole	1989 to 1992
21	BW Redpath	1998 to 2003
20	AG Hastings	1993 to 1995
19	J McLauchlan	1973 to 1979
19	JPR White	2005 to 2008
16	RI Wainwright	1995 to 1998
15	MC Morrison	1899 to 1904
15	AR Smith	1957 to 1962
15	AR Irvine	1980 to 1982

MOST POINTS IN TESTS

Points	Player	Tests	Career
809	CD Paterson	109	1999 to 2011
667	AG Hastings	61	1986 to 1995
273	AR Irvine	51	1972 to 1982
266	DA Parks	67	2004 to 2012
220	KM Logan	70	1992 to 2003
210	PW Dods	23	1983 to 1991
193	GD Laidlaw	21	2010 to 2013
166	CM Chalmers	60	1989 to 1999
164	GPJ Townsend	82	1993 to 2003
141	BJ Laney	20	2001 to 2004
123	DW Hodge	26	1997 to 2002
106	AG Stanger	52	1989 to 1998

MOST TRIES IN TESTS

Tries	Player	Tests	Career
24	IS Smith	32	1924 to 1933
24	AG Stanger	52	1989 to 1998
22	CD Paterson	109	1999 to 2011
17	AG Hastings	61	1986 to 1995
17	AV Tait	27	1987 to 1999
17	GPJ Townsend	82	1993 to 2003
15	I Tukalo	37	1985 to 1992
13	KM Logan	70	1992 to 2003
12	AR Smith	33	1955 to 1962

MOST CONVERSIONS IN TESTS

Cons	Player	Tests	Career
90	CD Paterson	109	1999 to 2011
86	AG Hastings	61	1986 to 1995
34	KM Logan	70	1992 to 2003
26	PW Dods	23	1983 to 1991
25	AR Irvine	51	1972 to 1982
21	GD Laidlaw	21	2010 to 2013
19	D Drysdale	26	1923 to 1929
17	BJ Laney	20	2001 to 2004
15	DW Hodge	26	1997 to 2002
15	DA Parks	67	2004 to 2012
14	FH Turner	15	1911 to 1914
14	RJS Shepherd	20	1995 to 1998

MOST PENALTY GOALS IN TESTS

Penalties	Player	Tests	Career
170	CD Paterson	109	1999 to 2011
140	AG Hastings	61	1986 to 1995
61	AR Irvine	51	1972 to 1982
55	DA Parks	67	2004 to 2012
50	PW Dods	23	1983 to 1991
47	GD Laidlaw	21	2010 to 2013
32	CM Chalmers	60	1989 to 1999
29	KM Logan	70	1992 to 2003
29	BJ Laney	20	2001 to 2004
21	M Dods	8	1994 to 1996
21	RJS Shepherd	20	1995 to 1998

MOST DROP GOALS IN TESTS

Drops	Player	Tests	Career
17	DA Parks	67	2004 to 2012
12	JY Rutherford	42	1979 to 1987
9	CM Chalmers	60	1989 to 1999
7	IR McGeechan	32	1972 to 1979
7	GPJ Townsend	82	1993 to 2003
6	DW Morgan	21	1973 to 1978
5	H Waddell	15	1924 to 1930

INTERNATIONAL CHAMPIONSHIP RECORDS

RECORD	DETAIL	HOLDER	SET
Most points in season	120	in four matches	1999
Most tries in season	17	in four matches	1925
Highest score	38	38–10 v Ireland	1997
Biggest win	28	31–3 v France	1912
	28	38–10 v Ireland	1997
Highest score conceded	51	16–51 v France	1998
Biggest defeat	40	3–43 v England	2001
Most appearances	53	CD Paterson	2000–2011
Most points in matches	403	CD Paterson	2000–2011
Most points in season	65	CD Paterson	2007
Most points in match	24	BJ Laney	v Italy, 2002
Most tries in matches	24	IS Smith	1924–1933
Most tries in season	8	IS Smith	1925
Most tries in match	5	GC Lindsay	v Wales, 1887
Most cons in matches	34	CD Paterson	2000–2011
Most cons in season	11	KM Logan	1999
Most cons in match	5	FH Turner	v France, 1912
	5	JW Allan	v England, 1931
	5	RJS Shepherd	v Ireland, 1997
Most pens in matches	99	CD Paterson	2000–2011
Most pens in season	17	GD Laidlaw	2013
Most pens in match	7	CD Paterson	v Wales, 2007
Most drops in matches	9	DA Parks	2004–2012
Most drops in season	5	DA Parks	2010
Most drops in match	2	on several	occasions

SCOTLAND

MISCELLANEOUS RECORDS

RECORD	HOLDER	DETAIL
Longest Test career	WCW Murdoch	1935 to 1948
Youngest Test cap	NJ Finlay	17 yrs 36 days in 1875*
Oldest Test cap	J McLauchlan	37 yrs 210 days in 1979

** C Reid, also 17 yrs 36 days on debut in 1881, was a day older than Finlay, having lived through an extra leap-year day.*

CAREER RECORDS OF SCOTLAND INTERNATIONAL PLAYERS

UP TO 10 OCTOBER 2013

PLAYER	DEBUT	CAPS	T	C	P	D	PTS
BACKS:							
MRL Blair	2002 v C	85	7	0	0	0	35
NJ de Luca	2008 v F	38	1	0	0	0	5
AJ Dunbar	2013 v Sm	3	1	0	0	0	5
MB Evans	2008 v C	35	3	0	0	0	15
TA Heathcote	2012 v Tg	3	0	0	0	0	0
SW Hogg	2012 v W	15	3	0	0	0	15
P Horne	2013 v Sm	2	0	0	0	0	0
RJH Jackson	2010 v NZ	21	0	3	2	2	18
GD Laidlaw	2010 v NZ	21	2	21	47	0	193
SF Lamont	2004 v Sm	79	11	0	0	0	55
RGM Lawson	2006 v A	31	0	0	0	0	0
SD Maitland	2013 v E	5	1	0	0	0	5
PE Murchie	2013 v SA	2	0	0	0	0	0
HB Pyrgos	2012 v NZ	9	1	0	0	0	5
MCM Scott	2012 v I	15	3	0	0	0	15
TSF Seymour	2013 v SA	2	0	0	0	0	0
DM Taylor	2013 v Sm	3	0	0	0	0	0
GA Tonks	2013 v Sm	1	0	0	0	0	0
TJW Visser	2012 v Fj	12	6	0	0	0	30
D Weir	2012 v F	5	0	1	0	0	2
FORWARDS:							
JA Barclay	2007 v NZ	41	2	0	0	0	10
JW Beattie	2006 v R	24	3	0	0	0	15
F Brown	2013 v It	1	0	0	0	0	0
KDR Brown	2005 v R	58	4	0	0	0	20
GDS Cross	2009 v W	22	1	0	0	0	5
DK Denton	2011 v I	14	0	0	0	0	0
AG Dickinson	2007 v NZ	27	1	0	0	0	5
RW Ford	2004 v A	68	2	0	0	0	10
GS Gilchrist	2013 v F	3	0	0	0	0	0
R Grant	2012 v A	10	0	0	0	0	0
RJ Gray	2010 v F	31	1	0	0	0	5
DWH Hall	2003 v W	42	1	0	0	0	5
JL Hamilton	2006 v R	48	1	0	0	0	5
RJ Harley	2012 v Sm	5	1	0	0	0	5
AF Jacobsen	2002 v C	65	0	0	0	0	0

AD Kellock	2004 v A	55	1	0	0	0	5
S Lawrie	2013 v Sm	1	0	0	0	0	0
S Lawson	2005 v R	38	2	0	0	0	10
MJ Low	2009 v F	21	0	0	0	0	0
PC MacArthur	2013 v Sm	1	0	0	0	0	0
EA Murray	2005 v R	56	2	0	0	0	10
RM Rennie	2008 v I	20	0	0	0	0	0
AK Strokosch	2006 v A	35	2	0	0	0	10
TJM Swinson	2013 v SA	2	0	0	0	0	0
K Traynor	2009 v Fj	4	0	0	0	0	0
J Welsh	2012 v It	2	0	0	0	0	0
R Wilson	2013 v W	4	0	0	0	0	0

SCOTLAND INTERNATIONAL PLAYERS

UP TO 10 OCTOBER 2013

Note: Years given for International Championship matches are for second half of season; e.g. 1972 means season 1971–72. Years for all other matches refer to the actual year of the match. Entries in square brackets denote matches played in RWC Finals.

Abercrombie, C H (United Services) 1910 I, E, 1911 F, W, 1913 F, W
Abercrombie, J G (Edinburgh U) 1949 F, W, I, 1950 F, W, I, E
Agnew, W C (Stewart's Coll FP) 1930 W, I
Ainslie, R (Edinburgh Inst FP) 1879 I, E, 1880 I, E, 1881 E, 1882 I, E
Ainslie, T (Edinburgh Inst FP) 1881 E, 1882 I, E, 1883 W, I, E, 1884 W, I, E, 1885 W, I 1, 2
Aitchison, G R (Edinburgh Wands) 1883 I
Aitchison, T G (Gala) 1929 W, I, E
Aitken, A I (Edinburgh Inst FP) 1889 I
Aitken, G G (Oxford U) 1924 W, I, E, 1925 F, W, I, E, 1929 F
Aitken, J (Gala) 1977 E, I, F, 1981 F, W, E, I, NZ 1, 2, R, A, 1982 E, I, F, W, 1983 F, W, E, NZ, 1984 W, E, I, F, R
Aitken, R (London Scottish) 1947 W
Allan, B (Glasgow Acads) 1881 I
Allan, J (Edinburgh Acads) 1990 NZ 1, 1991, W, I, R, [J, I, WS, E, NZ]
Allan, J L (Melrose) 1952 F, W, I, 1953 W
Allan, J L F (Cambridge U) 1957 I, E
Allan, J W (Melrose) 1927 F, 1928 I, 1929 F, W, I, E, 1930 F, E, 1931 F, W, I, E, 1932 SA, W, I, 1934 I, E
Allan, R C (Hutchesons' GSFP) 1969 I
Allardice, W D (Aberdeen GSFP) 1947 A, 1948 F, W, I, 1949 F, W, I, E
Allen, H W (Glasgow Acads) 1873 E
Anderson, A H (Glasgow Acads) 1894 I
Anderson, D G (London Scottish) 1889 I, 1890 W, I, E, 1891 W, E, 1892 W, E
Anderson, E (Stewart's Coll FP) 1947 I, E
Anderson, J W (W of Scotland) 1872 E
Anderson, T (Merchiston Castle School) 1882 I
Angus, A W (Watsonians) 1909 W, 1910 F, W, E, 1911 W, I, 1912 F, W, I, E, SA, 1913 F, W, 1914 E, 1920 F, W, I, E
Ansbro, J A (Northampton, London Irish) 2010 SA, Sm, 2011 F, W, E, It1, I2, [R, E], 2012 A, Sm
Anton, P A (St Andrew's U) 1873 E
Armstrong, G (Jedforest, Newcastle) 1988 A, 1989 W, E, I, F, Fj, R, 1990 I, F, W, E, NZ 1, 2, Arg, 1991 F, W, E, I, R, [J, I, WS, E, NZ], 1993 I, F, W, E, 1994 E, I, 1996 NZ, 1, 2, A, 1997 W, SA (R), 1998 It, I, F, W, E, SA (R), 1999 W, E, I, F, Arg, R, [SA, U, Sm, NZ]
Arneil, R J (Edinburgh Acads, Leicester and Northampton) 1968 I, E, A, 1969 F, W, I, E, SA, 1970 F, W, I, E, A, 1971 F, W, I, E (2[1C]), 1972 F, W, E, NZ
Arthur, A (Glasgow Acads) 1875 E, 1876 E
Arthur, J W (Glasgow Acads) 1871 E, 1872 E
Asher, A G G (Oxford U) 1882 I, 1884 W, I, E, 1885 W, 1886 I, E
Auld, W (W of Scotland) 1889 W, 1890 W
Auldjo, L J (Abertay) 1878 E

Bain, D McL (Oxford U) 1911 E, 1912 F, W, E, SA, 1913 F, W, I, E, 1914 W, I
Baird, G R T (Kelso) 1981 A, 1982 E, I, F, W, A 1, 2, 1983 I, F, W, E, NZ, 1984 W, E, I, F, A, 1985 I, W, E, 1986 F, W, E, I, R, 1987 E, 1988 I
Balfour, A (Watsonians) 1896 W, I, E, 1897 E
Balfour, L M (Edinburgh Acads) 1872 E
Bannerman, E M (Edinburgh Acads) 1872 E, 1873 E
Bannerman, J M (Glasgow HSFP) 1921 F, W, I, E, 1922 F, W, I, E, 1923 F, W, I, E, 1924 F, W, I, E, 1925 F, W, I, E, 1926 F, W, I, E, 1927 F, W, I, E, A, 1928 F, W, I, E, 1929 F, W, I, E
Barclay, J A (Glasgow Warriors) 2007 [NZ], 2008 F, W, Arg 2, NZ, SA, C, 2009 W, F, It, I, Fj, A, 2010 F, W, It, E, I, Arg 1, 2, NZ, SA, Sm, 2011 F, W, I1, E, It1, 2, [R, Arg, E], 2012 E(R), W(R), F, I, It, A, Fj, SA, Tg(R)
Barnes, I A (Hawick) 1972 W, 1974 F (R), 1975 E (R), NZ, 1977 I, F, W
Barrie, R W (Hawick) 1936 E
Bearne, K R F (Cambridge U, London Scottish) 1960 F, W

Beattie, J A (Hawick) 1929 F, W, 1930 W, 1931 F, W, I, E, 1932 SA, W, I, E, 1933 W, E, I, 1934 I, E, 1935 W, I, E, NZ, 1936 W, I, E

Beattie, J R (Glasgow Acads) 1980 I, F, W, E, 1981 F, W, E, I, 1983 F, W, E, NZ, 1984 E (R), R, A, 1985 I, 1986 F, W, E, I, R, 1987 I, F, W, E

Beattie, J W (Glasgow Warriors, Montpellier) 2006 R, PI, 2007 F, 2008 Arg 1, 2009 Fj, A, Arg, 2010 F, W, It, E, I, Arg 1, 2, 2011 I1, 2, 2013 E, It1, I, W, F, Sm, SA, It2

Beattie, R S (Newcastle, Bristol) 2000 NZ 1, 2(R), Sm (R), 2003 E(R), It(R), I 2, [J(R), US, Fj]

Bedell-Sivright, D R (Cambridge U, Edinburgh U) 1900 W, 1901 W, I, E, 1902 W, I, E, 1903 W, I, 1904 W, I, E, 1905 NZ, 1906 W, I, E, SA, 1907 W, I, E, 1908 W, I

Bedell-Sivright, J V (Cambridge U) 1902 W

Begbie, T A (Edinburgh Wands) 1881 I, E

Bell, D L (Watsonians) 1975 I, F, W, E

Bell, J A (Clydesdale) 1901 W, I, E, 1902 W, I, E

Bell, L H I (Edinburgh Acads) 1900 E, 1904 W, I

Berkeley, W V (Oxford U) 1926 F, 1929 F, W, I

Berry, C W (Fettesian-Lorettonians) 1884 I, E, 1885 W, I 1, 1887 I, W, E, 1888 W, I

Bertram, D M (Watsonians) 1922 F, W, I, E, 1923 F, W, I, E, 1924 W, I, E

Beveridge, G (Glasgow) 2000 NZ 2(R), US (R), Sm (R), 2002 Fj(R), 2003 W 2, 2005 R(R)

Biggar, A G (London Scottish) 1969 SA, 1970 F, I, E, A, 1971 F, W, I, E (2[1C]), 1972 F, W

Biggar, M A (London Scottish) 1975 I, F, W, E, 1976 W, E, I, 1977 I, F, W, 1978 I, F, W, E, NZ, 1979 W, E, I, F, NZ, 1980 I, F, W, E

Birkett, G A (Harlequins, London Scottish) 1975 NZ

Bishop, J M (Glasgow Acads) 1893 I

Bisset, A A (RIE Coll) 1904 W

Black, A W (Edinburgh U) 1947 F, W, 1948 E, 1950 W, I, E

Black, W P (Glasgow HSFP) 1948 F, W, I, E, 1951 E

Blackadder, W F (W of Scotland) 1938 E

Blaikie, C F (Heriot's FP) 1963 I, E, 1966 E, 1968 A, 1969 F, W, I, E

Blair, M R L (Edinburgh, Brive) 2002 C, US, 2003 F(t+R), W 1(R), SA 2(R), It 2, I 2, [US], 2004 W(R), E(R), It(R), F(R), I(R), Sm(R), A1(R), 3(R), J(R), A4(R), SA(R), 2005 I(t&R), It(R), W(R), E, R, Arg, Sm(R), NZ(R), 2006 F, W, E, I, It(R), SA 1, 2, R, PI(R), A, 2007 I2, SA, [Pt, R, It, Arg], 2008 F, W, I, E, It, Arg 1, 2, NZ, SA, C, 2009 W, F, It, I, E, Fj(R), 2010 W(R), It(R), I(R), Arg 1(R), 2(R), NZ, Sm(R), 2011 F(R), W(R), I1, E(R), It1(R), 2, [R, Arg(R), E], 2012 E(R), W(R), F, I, It, A, Fj, Sm(R), NZ, SA

Blair, P C B (Cambridge U) 1912 SA, 1913 F, W, I, E

Bolton, W H (W of Scotland) 1876 E

Borthwick, J B (Stewart's Coll FP) 1938 W, I

Bos, F H ten (Oxford U, London Scottish) 1959 E, 1960 F, W, SA, 1961 F, SA, W, I, E, 1962 F, W, I, E, 1963 F, W, I, E

Boswell, J D (W of Scotland) 1889 W, I, 1890 W, I, E, 1891 W, I, E, 1892 W, I, E, 1893 I, E, 1894 I, E

Bowie, T C (Watsonians) 1913 I, E, 1914 I, E

Boyd, G M (Glasgow HSFP) 1926 E

Boyd, J L (United Services) 1912 E, SA

Boyle, A C W (London Scottish) 1963 F, W, I

Boyle, A H W (St Thomas's Hospital, London Scottish) 1966 A, 1967 F, NZ, 1968 F, W, I

Brash, J C (Cambridge U) 1961 E

Breakey, R W (Gosforth) 1978 E

Brewis, N T (Edinburgh Inst FP) 1876 E, 1878 E, 1879 I, E, 1880 I, E

Brewster, A K (Stewart's-Melville FP) 1977 E, 1980 I, F, 1986 E, I, R

Brotherstone, S J (Melrose, Brive, Newcastle) 1999 I (R), 2000 F, W, E, US, A, Sm, 2002 C (R)

Brown, A H (Heriot's FP) 1928 E, 1929 F, W

Brown, A R (Gala) 1971 E (2[1C]), 1972 F, W, E

Brown, C H C (Dunfermline) 1929 E

Brown, D I (Cambridge U) 1933 W, E, I

Brown, F (Glasgow Warriors) 2013 It2(R)

Brown, G L (W of Scotland) 1969 SA, 1970 F, W (R), I, E, A, 1971 F, W, I, E (2[1C]), 1972 F, W, E, NZ, 1973 E (R), P, 1974 W, E, I, F, 1975 I, F, W, E, A, 1976 F, W, E, I

Brown, J A (Glasgow Acads) 1908 W, I

Brown, J B (Glasgow Acads) 1879 I, E, 1880 I, E, 1881 I, E, 1882 I, E, 1883 W, I, E, 1884 W, I, E, 1885 I 1, 2, 1886 W, I, E

Brown, K D R (Borders, Glasgow Warriors, Saracens) 2005 R, Sm(R), NZ(R), 2006 SA 1(R), 2(R), R, PI, A, 2007 E, W, It, I1, 2(R), SA, [Pt(R), R(R), NZ, It(R), Arg(R)], 2008 F(R), W, I, E(R), It(R), Arg 1(R), 2(R), 2009 W(R), F(R), It(R), E(R), 2010 F, W, It, E, I, Arg 1, 2, NZ, SA, Sm, 2011 F, W, I1, E, It1, 2, [R, Gg, Arg], 2012 NZ, SA, Tg, 2013 E, It1, I, W, F, Sm

Brown, P C (W of Scotland, Gala) 1964 F, NZ, W, I, E, 1965 I, E, SA, 1966 A, 1969 I, E, 1970 W, E, 1971 F, W, I, E (2[1C]), 1972 F, W, E, NZ, 1973 F, W, I, E, P

Brown, T G (Heriot's FP) 1929 W

Brown, T G (Edinburgh) 2012 A(R)

Brown, W D (Glasgow Acads) 1871 E, 1872 E, 1873 E, 1874 E, 1875 E

Brown, W S (Edinburgh Inst FP) 1880 I, E, 1882 I, E, 1883 W, E

Browning, A (Glasgow HSFP) 1920 I, 1922 F, W, I, 1923 W, I, E

Bruce, C R (Glasgow Acads) 1947 F, W, I, E, 1949 F, W, I, E

Bruce, N S (Blackheath, Army and London Scottish) 1958 F, A, I, E, 1959 F, W, I, E, 1960 F, W, I, E, SA, 1961 F, SA, W, I, E, 1962 F, W, I, E, 1963 F, W, I, E, 1964 F, NZ, W, I, E

Bruce, R M (Gordonians) 1947 A, 1948 F, W, I

Bruce-Lockhart, J H (London Scottish) 1913 W, 1920 E

Bruce-Lockhart, L (London Scottish) 1948 E, 1950 F, W, 1953 I, E

Bruce-Lockhart, R B (Cambridge U and London Scottish) 1937 I, 1939 I, E

Bryce, C C (Glasgow Acads) 1873 E, 1874 E

Bryce, R D H (W of Scotland) 1973 I (R)

Bryce, W E (Selkirk) 1922 W, I, E, 1923 F, W, I, E, 1924 F, W, I, E

Brydon, W R C (Heriot's FP) 1939 W

Buchanan, A (Royal HSFP) 1871 E

Buchanan, F G (Kelvinside Acads and Oxford U) 1910 F, 1911 F, W

Buchanan, J C R (Stewart's Coll FP) 1921 W, I, E, 1922 W, I, E, 1923 F, W, I, E, 1924 F, W, I, E, 1925 F, I

Buchanan-Smith, G A E (London Scottish, Heriot's FP) 1989 Fj (R), 1990 Arg

Bucher, A M (Edinburgh Acads) 1897 E

Budge, G M (Edinburgh Wands) 1950 F, W, I, E

Bullmore, H H (Edinburgh U) 1902 I

Bulloch, A J (Glasgow) 2000 US, A, Sm, 2001 F (t+R), E

Bulloch, G C (West of Scotland, Glasgow) 1997 SA, 1998 It, I, F, W, E, Fj, A 1, SA, 1999 W, E, It, I, F, Arg, [SA, U, Sm, NZ], 2000 It, I, W (R), NZ 1, 2, A (R), Sm (R), 2001 F, W, E, It, I, Tg, Arg, NZ, 2002 E, It, I, F, W, C, US, R, SA, Fj, 2003 I 1, F, W 1, E, It 1, SA 1, 2, It 2(R), W2, I 2, [US, F, Fj, A], 2004 W, E, It, F, I, Sm, A1, 2, 3, J, A4, SA, 2005 F, I, It, W, E

Burnell, A P (London Scottish, Montferrand) 1989 E, I, F, Fj, R, 1990 I, F, W, E, Arg, 1991 F, W, E, I, R, [J, Z, I, WS, E, NZ], 1992 E, I, F, W, 1993 I, F, W, E, NZ, 1994 W, E, I, F, Arg 1, 2, SA, 1995 [Iv, Tg (R), F (R)], WS, 1998 E, SA, 1999 W, E, It, I, F, Arg, [Sp, Sm (R), NZ]

Burnet, P J (London Scottish and Edinburgh Acads) 1960 SA

Burnet, W (Hawick) 1912 E

Burnet, W A (W of Scotland) 1934 W, 1935 W, I, E, NZ, 1936 W, I, E

Burnett, J N (Heriot's FP) 1980 I, F, W, E

Burns, G G (Watsonians, Edinburgh) 1999 It (R), 2001 Tg (R), NZ (R), 2002 US (R)

Burrell, G (Gala) 1950 F, W, I, 1951 SA

Cairns, A G (Watsonians) 1903 W, I, E, 1904 W, I, E, 1905 W, I, E, 1906 W, I, E

Cairns, B J (Edinburgh) 2008 Arg 1, 2, NZ, SA, C, 2009 W, Arg

Calder, F (Stewart's-Melville FP) 1986 F, W, E, I, R, 1987 I, F, W, E, [F, Z, R, NZ], 1988 I, F, W, E, 1989 W, E, I, F, R, 1990 I, F, W, E, NZ 1, 2, 1991 R, [J, I, WS, E, NZ]

Calder, J H (Stewart's-Melville FP) 1981 F, W, E, I, NZ 1, 2, R, A, 1982 E, I, F, W, A 1, 2, 1983 I, F, W, E, NZ, 1984 W, E, I, F, A, 1985 I, F, W

Callam, D A (Edinburgh) 2006 R(R), PI(R), A, 2007 E, W, It, I1, F(R), SA, [NZ], 2008 F
Callander, G J (Kelso) 1984 R, 1988 I, F, W, E, A
Cameron, A (Glasgow HSFP) 1948 W, 1950 I, E, 1951 F, W, I, E, SA, 1953 I, E, 1955 F, W, I, E, 1956 F, W, I
Cameron, A D (Hillhead HSFP) 1951 F, 1954 F, W
Cameron, A W C (Watsonians) 1887 W, 1893 W, 1894 I
Cameron, D (Glasgow HSFP) 1953 I, E, 1954 F, NZ, I, E
Cameron, N W (Glasgow U) 1952 E, 1953 F, W
Campbell, A J (Hawick) 1984 I, F, R, 1985 I, F, W, E, 1986 F, W, E, I, R, 1988 F, W, A
Campbell, G T (London Scottish) 1892 W, I, E, 1893 I, E, 1894 W, I, E, 1895 W, I, E, 1896 W, I, E, 1897 I, 1899 I, 1900 E
Campbell, H H (Cambridge U, London Scottish) 1947 I, E, 1948 I, E
Campbell, J A (W of Scotland) 1878 E, 1879 I, E, 1881 I, E
Campbell, J A (Cambridge U) 1900 I
Campbell, N M (London Scottish) 1956 F, W
Campbell, S J (Dundee HSFP) 1995 C, I, F, W, E, R, [Iv, NZ (R)], WS (t), 1996 I, F, W, E, 1997 A, SA, 1998 Fj (R), A 2(R)
Campbell-Lamerton, J R E (London Scottish) 1986 F, 1987 [Z, R(R)]
Campbell-Lamerton, M J (Halifax, Army, London Scottish) 1961 F, SA, W, I, 1962 F, W, I, E, 1963 F, W, I, E, 1964 I, E, 1965 F, W, I, E, SA, 1966 F, W, I, E
Carmichael, A B (W of Scotland) 1967 I, NZ, 1968 F, W, I, E, A, 1969 F, W, I, E, SA, 1970 F, W, I, E, A, 1971 F, W, I, E (2[1C]), 1972 F, W, E, NZ, 1973 F, W, I, E, P, 1974 W, E, I, F, 1975 I, F, W, E, NZ, A, 1976 F, W, E, I, 1977 E, I (R), F, W, 1978 I
Carmichael, J H (Watsonians) 1921 F, W, I
Carrick, J S (Glasgow Acads) 1876 E, 1877 E
Cassels, D Y (W of Scotland) 1880 E, 1881 I, 1882 I, E, 1883 W, I, E
Cathcart, C W (Edinburgh U) 1872 E, 1873 E, 1876 E
Cawkwell, G L (Oxford U) 1947 F
Chalmers, C M (Melrose) 1989 W, E, I, F, Fj, 1990 I, F, W, E, NZ 1, 2, Arg, 1991 F, W, E, I, R, [J, Z (R), I, WS, E, NZ], 1992 E, I, F, W, A 1, 2, 1993 I, F, W, E, NZ, 1994 W, SA, 1995 C, I, F, W, E, R, [Iv, Tg, F, NZ], WS, 1996 A, It, 1997 W, I, F, A (R), SA, 1998 It, I, F, W, E, 1999 Arg (R)
Chalmers, T (Glasgow Acads) 1871 E, 1872 E, 1873 E, 1874 E, 1875 E, 1876 E
Chambers, H F T (Edinburgh U) 1888 W, I, 1889 W, I
Charters, R G (Hawick) 1955 W, I, E
Chisholm, D H (Melrose) 1964 I, E, 1965 E, SA, 1966 F, I, E, A, 1967 F, W, NZ, 1968 F, W, I
Chisholm, R W T (Melrose) 1955 I, E, 1956 F, W, I, E, 1958 F, W, A, I, 1960 SA
Church, W C (Glasgow Acads) 1906 W
Clark, R L (Edinburgh Wands, Royal Navy) 1972 F, W, E, NZ, 1973 F, W, I, E, P
Clauss, P R A (Oxford U) 1891 W, I, E, 1892 W, E, 1895 I
Clay, A T (Edinburgh Acads) 1886 W, I, E, 1887 I, W, E, 1888 W
Clunies-Ross, A (St Andrew's U) 1871 E
Coltman, S (Hawick) 1948 I, 1949 F, W, I, E
Colville, A G (Merchistonians, Blackheath) 1871 E, 1872 E
Connell, G C (Trinity Acads and London Scottish) 1968 E, A, 1969 F, E, 1970 F
Cooper, M McG (Oxford U) 1936 W, I
Corcoran, I (Gala) 1992 A 1(R)
Cordial, I F (Edinburgh Wands) 1952 F, W, I, E
Cotter, J L (Hillhead HSFP) 1934 I, E
Cottington, G S (Kelso) 1934 I, E, 1935 W, I, 1936 E
Coughtrie, S (Edinburgh Acads) 1959 F, W, I, E, 1962 W, I, E, 1963 F, W, I, E
Couper, J H (W of Scotland) 1896 W, I, 1899 I
Coutts, F H (Melrose, Army) 1947 W, I, E
Coutts, I D F (Old Alleynians) 1951 F, 1952 E
Cowan, R C (Selkirk) 1961 F, 1962 F, W, I, E
Cowie, W L K (Edinburgh Wands) 1953 E
Cownie, W B (Watsonians) 1893 W, I, E, 1894 W, I, E, 1895 W, I, E
Crabbie, G E (Edinburgh Acads) 1904 W
Crabbie, J E (Edinburgh Acads, Oxford U) 1900 W, 1902 I, 1903 W, I, 1904 E, 1905 W
Craig, A (Orrell, Glasgow) 2002 C, US, R, SA, Fj, 2003 I 1, F(R), W 1(R), E, It 1, SA 1, 2, W 2, I 2, [J, US, F], 2004 A3(R), 2005 F, I, It, W, E
Craig, J B (Heriot's FP) 1939 W
Craig, J M (West of Scotland, Glasgow) 1997 A, 2001 W (R), E (R), It
Cramb, R I (Harlequins) 1987 [R(R)], 1988 I, F, A
Cranston, A G (Hawick) 1976 W, E, I, 1977 E, W, 1978 F (R), W, E, NZ, 1981 NZ 1, 2
Crawford, J A (Army, London Scottish) 1934 I
Crawford, W H (United Services, RN) 1938 W, I, E, 1939 W, E
Crichton-Miller, D (Gloucester) 1931 W, I, E
Crole, G B (Oxford U) 1920 F, W, I, E
Cronin, D F (Bath, London Scottish, Bourges, Wasps) 1988 I, F, W, E, A, 1989 W, E, I, F, Fj, R, 1990 I, F, W, E, NZ 1, 2, 1991 F, W, E, I, R, [Z], 1992 A 2, 1993 I, F, W, E, NZ, 1995 C, I, F, [Tg, F, NZ], WS, 1996 NZ 1, 2, A, It, 1997 F (R), 1998 I, F, W, E
Cross, G D S (Edinburgh) 2009 W, 2010 E(R), 2011 I1(t&R), E(R), It1, I2, [R, Arg], 2012 E(R), W, F, I, It, Fj(R), NZ, SA(R), Tg(t), 2013 It1(R), I, W(R), F(R), Sm(R)
Cross, M (Merchistonians) 1875 E, 1876 E, 1877 I, E, 1878 E, 1879 I, E, 1880 I, E
Cross, W (Merchistonians) 1871 E, 1872 E
Cumming, R S (Aberdeen U) 1921 F, W
Cunningham, G (Oxford U) 1908 W, I, 1909 W, E, 1910 F, I, E, 1911 E
Cunningham, R F (Gala) 1978 NZ, 1979 W, E
Currie, L R (Dunfermline) 1947 A, 1948 F, W, I, 1949 F, W, I, E
Cusiter, C P (Borders, Perpignan, Glasgow Warriors) 2004 W, E, It, F, I, Sm, A1, 2, 3, J, A4, SA, 2005 F, I, It, W, Arg(R), Sm, NZ, 2006 F(R), W(R), E(R), I(R), It, R(R), PI, 2007 E, W, It, I1, F(R), I2(R), [R(R), NZ, It(R), Arg(R)], 2008 F(R), W(R), I(R), 2009 W(R), F(R), It(R), I(R), E(R), Fj, A, Arg, 2010 F, W, It, E, I, 2011 It2(R), [R(R), E(R)], 2012 E, W, F(R), I(R), A(R), Fj(R), Sm
Cuthbert, J E (Bath) 2011 I2(R)
Cuthbertson, W (Kilmarnock, Harlequins) 1980 I, 1981 W, E, I, NZ 1, 2, R, A, 1982 E, I, F, W, A 1, 2, 1983 I, F, W, NZ, 1984 W, E, A

Dalgleish, A (Gala) 1890 W, E, 1891 W, I, 1892 W, 1893 W, 1894 W, I
Dalgleish, K J (Edinburgh Wands, Cambridge U) 1951 I, E, 1953 F, W
Dall, A K (Edinburgh) 2003 W 2(R)
Dallas, J D (Watsonians) 1903 E
Danielli, S C J (Bath, Borders, Ulster) 2003 It 2, W 2, [J(R), US, Fj, A], 2004 W, E, It, F, I, 2005 F, I, 2008 W(R), It, Arg 1, 2009 F, It, I, E, Fj, A, 2010 It, E(R), I(R), Arg 2, 2011 I1(R), E, It1, 2, [R, E]
Davidson, J A (London Scottish, Edinburgh Wands) 1959 E, 1960 I, E
Davidson, J N G (Edinburgh U) 1952 F, W, I, E, 1953 F, W, 1954 F
Davidson, J P (RIE Coll) 1873 E, 1874 E
Davidson, R S (Royal HSFP) 1893 E
Davies, D S (Hawick) 1922 F, W, I, E, 1923 F, W, I, E, 1924 F, E, 1925 W, I, E, 1926 F, W, I, E, 1927 F, W, I
Dawson, J C (Glasgow Acads) 1947 A, 1948 F, W, 1949 F, W, I, 1950 F, W, I, E, 1951 F, W, I, E, SA, 1952 F, W, I, E, 1953 E
Deans, C T (Hawick) 1978 F, W, E, NZ, 1979 W, E, I, F, NZ, 1980 I, F, 1981 F, W, E, I, NZ 1, 2, R, A, 1982 E, I, F, W, A 1, 2, 1983 I, F, W, E, NZ, 1984 W, E, I, F, A, 1985 I, F, W, E, 1986 F, W, E, I, R, 1987 I, F, W, E, [F, Z, R, NZ]
Deans, D T (Hawick) 1968 E
Deas, D W (Heriot's FP) 1947 F, W
De Luca, N J (Edinburgh) 2008 F, W, I(t&R), Arg 2(R), NZ, SA, C, 2009 F(R), It(R), I(R), E(R), Fj(R), A(R), Arg(R), 2010 It(R), E, I, Arg 1, 2(R), 2011 F, W, I1, E(R), It1(R), I2(R), It2, [Gg, Arg, E(R)], 2012 E, W, F(R), It, A, Fj, NZ, SA, Tg(R)
Denton, D K (Edinburgh) 2011 I2(R), 2012 E, W, F, I, It, NZ(R), SA, Tg, 2013 E(R), It1(R), I(t&R), SA(R), It2
Dewey, R E (Edinburgh, Ulster) 2006 R, 2007 E(R), W, It, I1, F, I2, SA, [Pt, R, NZ(R), It, Arg]
Dick, L G (Loughborough Colls, Jordanhill, Swansea) 1972 W

(R), E, 1974 W, E, I, F, 1975 I, F, W, E, NZ, A, 1976 F, 1977 E

Dick, R C S (Cambridge U, Guy's Hospital) 1934 W, I, E, 1935 W, I, E, NZ, 1936 W, I, E, 1937 W, 1938 W, I, E

Dickinson, A G (Gloucester, Sale) 2007 [NZ], 2008 E(R), It(R), Arg 1(R), 2(t&R), NZ(R), SA(R), C(R), 2009 W(t&R), F, It(R), I, E, 2010 F, W, It(R), I(R), Arg 2(R), NZ(t&R), 2011 I2(R), It2, [R(R), Arg(R), E(R)], 2013 Sm, SA, It2

Dickson, G (Gala) 1978 NZ, 1979 W, E, I, F, NZ, 1980 W, 1981 F, 1982 W (R)

Dickson, M R (Edinburgh U) 1905 I

Dickson, W M (Blackheath, Oxford U) 1912 F, W, E, SA, 1913 F, W, I

Di Rollo, M P (Edinburgh) 2002 US (R), 2005 R, Arg, Sm, NZ, 2006 F, E, I, It, SA 1, 2, R, PI,
A, 2007 E, W, It, I1, F(R), [Pt, NZ]

Dobson, J (Glasgow Acads) 1911 E, 1912 F, W, I, E, SA

Dobson, J D (Glasgow Acads) 1910 I

Dobson, W G (Heriot's FP) 1922 W, I, E

Docherty, J T (Glasgow HSFP) 1955 F, W, 1956 E, 1958 F, W, A, I, E

Dods, F P (Edinburgh Acads) 1901 I

Dods, J H (Edinburgh Acads) 1895 W, I, E, 1896 W, I, E, 1897 I, E

Dods, M (Gala, Northampton) 1994 I (t), Arg 1, 2, 1995 WS, 1996 I, F, W, E

Dods, P W (Gala) 1983 I, F, W, E, NZ, 1984 W, E, I, F, R, A, 1985 I, F, W, E, 1989 W, E, I, F, 1991 I (R), R, [Z, NZ (R)]

Donald, D G (Oxford U) 1914 W, I

Donald, R L H (Glasgow HSFP) 1921 W, I, E

Donaldson, W P (Oxford U, W of Scotland) 1893 I, 1894 I, 1895 E, 1896 I, E, 1899 I

Don-Wauchope, A R (Fettesian-Lorettonians) 1881 E, 1882 E, 1883 W, 1884 W, I, E, 1885 W, I 1, 2, 1886 W, I, E, 1888 I

Don-Wauchope, P H (Fettesian-Lorettonians) 1885 I 1, 2, 1886 W, 1887 I, W, E

Dorward, A F (Cambridge U, Gala) 1950 F, 1951 SA, 1952 W, I, E, 1953 F, W, E, 1955 F, 1956 I, E, 1957 F, W, I, E

Dorward, T F (Gala) 1938 W, I, E, 1939 I, E

Douglas, B A F (Borders) 2002 R, SA, Fj, 2003 I 1, F, W 1, E, It 1, SA 1, 2, It 2, W 2, [J, US(t&R), F(R), Fj, A], 2004 W, E, It, F, I, Sm, A1, 2, 3, A4(R), SA(R), 2005 F(R), I(R), It(R), W(R), E(R), R, Arg, NZ, 2006 F, W, E, I, It, SA 1, 2(R)

Douglas, G (Jedforest) 1921 W

Douglas, J (Stewart's Coll FP) 1961 F, SA, W, I, E, 1962 F, W, I, E, 1963 F, W, I

Douty, P S (London Scottish) 1927 A, 1928 F, W

Drew, D (Glasgow Acads) 1871 E, 1876 E

Druitt, W A H (London Scottish) 1936 W, I, E

Drummond, A H (Kelvinside Acads) 1938 W, I

Drummond, C W (Melrose) 1947 F, W, I, E, 1948 F, I, E, 1950 F, W, I, E

Drybrough, A S (Edinburgh Wands, Merchistonians) 1902 I, 1903 I

Dryden, R H (Watsonians) 1937 E

Drysdale, D (Heriot's FP) 1923 F, W, I, E, 1924 F, W, I, E, 1925 F, W, I, E, 1926 F, W, I, E, 1927 F, W, I, E, A, 1928 F, W, I, E, 1929 F

Duff, P L (Glasgow Acads) 1936 W, I, 1938 W, I, E, 1939 W

Duffy, H (Jedforest) 1955 F

Duke, A (Royal HSFP) 1888 W, I, 1889 W, I, 1890 W, I

Dunbar, A J (Glasgow Warriors) 2013 Sm, SA, It2

Dunbar, J P A (Leeds) 2005 F(R), It(R)

Duncan, A W (Edinburgh U) 1901 W, I, E, 1902 W, I, E

Duncan, D D (Oxford U) 1920 F, W, I, E

Duncan, M D F (W of Scotland) 1986 F, W, E, R, 1987 I, F, W, E, [F, Z, R, NZ], 1988 I, F, W, E, A, 1989 W

Duncan, M M (Fettesian-Lorettonians) 1888 W

Dunlop, J W (W of Scotland) 1875 E

Dunlop, Q (W of Scotland) 1971 E (2[1C])

Dykes, A S (Glasgow Acads) 1932 E

Dykes, J C (Glasgow Acads) 1922 F, E, 1924 I, 1925 F, W, I, 1926 F, W, I, E, 1927 F, W, I, E, A, 1928 F, I, 1929 F, W, I

Dykes, J M (Clydesdale, Glasgow HSFP) 1898 I, E, 1899 W, E, 1900 W, I, 1901 W, I, E, 1902 E

Edwards, D B (Heriot's FP) 1960 I, E, SA

Edwards, N G B (Harlequins, Northampton) 1992 E, I, F, W, A 1, 1994 W

Elgie, M K (London Scottish) 1954 NZ, I, E, W, 1955 F, W, I, E

Elliot, C (Langholm) 1958 E, 1959 F, 1960 F, 1963 E, 1964 F, NZ, W, I, E, 1965 F, W, I

Elliot, M (Hawick) 1895 W, 1896 E, 1897 I, E, 1898 I, E

Elliot, T (Gala) 1905 E

Elliot, T (Gala) 1955 W, I, E, 1956 F, W, I, E, 1957 F, W, I, E, 1958 W, A, I

Elliot, T G (Langholm) 1968 W, A, 1969 F, W, 1970 E

Elliot, W I D (Edinburgh Acads) 1947 F, W, E, A, 1948 F, W, I, E, 1949 F, W, I, E, 1950 F, W, I, E, 1951 F, W, I, E, SA, 1952 F, W, I, E, 1954 NZ, I, E, W

Ellis, D G (Currie) 1997 W, E, I, F

Emslie, W D (Royal HSFP) 1930 F, 1932 I

Eriksson, B R S (London Scottish) 1996 NZ 1, A, 1997 E

Evans, H L (Edinburgh U) 1885 I 1, 2

Evans, M B (Glasgow Warriors, Castres) 2008 C(R), 2009 W(R), F, It, I, E, 2010 F, W(t&R), It, E, I, Arg 1, 2, NZ, Sm(R), 2011 F, W, I1, E, It2, [R, Gg, Arg, E], 2012 E, W, I, It, Fj, Sm(R), NZ(R), Tg, 2013 E(R), It1(R), F(R)

Evans, T H (Glasgow Warriors) 2008 Arg 1, NZ, SA, 2009 F, It, I, E, Arg, 2010 F, W

Ewart, E N (Glasgow Acads) 1879 E, 1880 I, E

Fahmy, E C (Abertillery) 1920 F, W, I, E

Fairley, I T (Kelso, Edinburgh) 1999 It, I (R), [Sp (R)]

Fasson, F H (London Scottish, Edinburgh Wands) 1900 W, 1901 W, I, 1902 W, E

Fell, A N (Edinburgh U) 1901 W, I, E, 1902 W, E, 1903 W, E

Ferguson, J H (Gala) 1928 W

Ferguson, W G (Royal HSFP) 1927 A, 1928 F, W, I, E

Fergusson, E A J (Oxford U) 1954 F, NZ, I, E, W

Finlay, A B (Edinburgh Acads) 1875 E

Finlay, J F (Edinburgh Acads) 1871 E, 1872 E, 1874 E, 1875 E

Finlay, N J (Edinburgh Acads) 1875 E, 1876 E, 1878 E, 1879 I, E, 1880 I, E, 1881 I, E

Finlay, R (Watsonians) 1948 E

Fisher, A T (Waterloo, Watsonians) 1947 I, E

Fisher, C D (Waterloo) 1975 NZ, A, 1976 W, E, I

Fisher, D (W of Scotland) 1893 I

Fisher, J P (Royal HSFP, London Scottish) 1963 E, 1964 F, NZ, W, I, E, 1965 F, W, I, E, SA, 1966 F, W, I, E, A, 1967 F, W, I, E, NZ, 1968 F, W, I, E

Fleming, C J N (Edinburgh Wands) 1896 I, E, 1897 I

Fleming, G R (Glasgow Acads) 1875 E, 1876 E

Fletcher, H N (Edinburgh U) 1904 E, 1905 W

Flett, A B (Edinburgh U) 1901 W, I, E, 1902 W, I

Forbes, J L (Watsonians) 1905 W, 1906 I, E

Ford, D St C (United Services, RN) 1930 I, E, 1931 E, 1932 W, I

Ford, J R (Gala) 1893 I

Ford, R W (Borders, Glasgow, Edinburgh) 2004 A3(R), 2006 W(R), E(R), PI(R), A(R), 2007 E(R), W(R), It(R), I1(R), F, I2, SA, [Pt(R), R, It, Arg], 2008 F, W, I, E, Arg 1, 2, NZ, SA, C, 2009 W, F, It, I, E, Fj, A, Arg, 2010 F, W, It, E, I, Arg 1, 2, NZ, SA, Sm, 2011 F, W, I1, E, It1, I2, [R, Gg, Arg, E], 2012 E, W, F, I, It, A, Fj, Sm, NZ, SA, 2013 E(R), It1, I, W, F

Forrest, J E (Glasgow Acads) 1932 SA, 1935 E, NZ

Forrest, J G S (Cambridge U) 1938 W, I, E

Forrest, W T (Hawick) 1903 W, I, E, 1904 W, I, E, 1905 W, I

Forsayth, H H (Oxford U) 1921 F, W, I, E, 1922 W, I, E

Forsyth, I W (Stewart's Coll FP) 1972 NZ, 1973 F, W, I, E, P

Forsyth, J (Edinburgh U) 1871 E

Foster, R A (Hawick) 1930 W, 1932 SA, I, E

Fox, J (Gala) 1952 F, W, I, E

Frame, J N M (Edinburgh U, Gala) 1967 NZ, 1968 F, W, I, E, 1969 W, I, E, SA, 1970 F, W, I, E, A, 1971 F, W, I, E (2[1C]), 1972 F, W, E, 1973 P (R)

France, C (Kelvinside Acads) 1903 I

Fraser, C F P (Glasgow U) 1888 W, 1889 W

Fraser, J W (Edinburgh Inst FP) 1881 E

Fraser, R (Cambridge U) 1911 F, W, I, E

French, J (Glasgow Acads) 1886 W, 1887 I, W, E

Frew, A (Edinburgh U) 1901 W, I, E

Frew, G M (Glasgow HSFP) 1906 SA, 1907 W, I, E, 1908 W, I, E, 1909 W, I, E, 1910 F, W, I, 1911 I, E
Friebe, J P (Glasgow HSFP) 1952 E
Fullarton, I A (Edinburgh) 2000 NZ 1(R), 2, 2001 NZ (R), 2003 It 2(R), I 2(t), 2004 Sm(R), A1(R), 2
Fulton, A K (Edinburgh U, Dollar Acads) 1952 F, 1954 F
Fyfe, K C (Cambridge U, Sale, London Scottish) 1933 W, E, 1934 E, 1935 W, I, E, NZ, 1936 W, E, 1939 I

Gallie, G H (Edinburgh Acads) 1939 W
Gallie, R A (Glasgow Acads) 1920 F, W, I, E, 1921 F, W, I, E
Gammell, W B B (Edinburgh Wands) 1977 I, F, W, 1978 W, E
Geddes, I C (London Scottish) 1906 SA, 1907 W, I, E, 1908 W, E
Geddes, K I (London Scottish) 1947 F, W, I, E
Gedge, H T S (Oxford U, London Scottish, Edinburgh Wands) 1894 W, I, E, 1896 E, 1899 W, E
Gedge, P M S (Edinburgh Wands) 1933 I
Gemmill, R (Glasgow HSFP) 1950 F, W, I, E, 1951 F, W, I
Gibson, W R (Royal HSFP) 1891 I, E, 1892 W, I, E, 1893 W, I, E, 1894 W, I, E, 1895 W, I, E
Gilbert-Smith, D S (London Scottish) 1952 E
Gilchrist, G S (Edinburgh) 2013 F, Sm, It2(R)
Gilchrist, J (Glasgow Acads) 1925 F
Gill, A D (Gala) 1973 P, 1974 W, E, I, F
Gillespie, J I (Edinburgh Acads) 1899 E, 1900 W, E, 1901 W, I, E, 1902 W, I, 1904 I, E
Gillies, A C (Watsonians) 1924 W, I, E, 1925 F, W, E, 1926 F, W, 1927 F, W, I, E
Gilmour, H R (Heriot's FP) 1998 Fj
Gilray, C M (Oxford U, London Scottish) 1908 E, 1909 W, E, 1912 I
Glasgow, I C (Heriot's FP) 1997 F (R)
Glasgow, R J C (Dunfermline) 1962 F, W, I, E, 1963 I, E, 1964 I, E, 1965 W, I
Glen, W S (Edinburgh Wands) 1955 W
Gloag, L G (Cambridge U) 1949 F, W, I, E
Godman, P J (Edinburgh) 2005 R(R), Sm(R), NZ(R), 2006 R, PI(R), A(t&R), 2007 W, It, 2008 Arg 2, NZ, SA, C, 2009 W, F, It, I, E, Fj, A, Arg, 2010 F, W(R), E(R)
Goodfellow, J (Langholm) 1928 W, I, E
Goodhue, F W J (London Scottish) 1890 W, I, E, 1891 W, I, E, 1892 W, I, E
Gordon, R (Edinburgh Wands) 1951 W, 1952 F, W, I, E, 1953 W
Gordon, R E (Royal Artillery) 1913 F, W, I
Gordon, R J (London Scottish) 1982 A 1, 2
Gore, A C (London Scottish) 1882 I
Gossman, B M (W of Scotland) 1980 W, 1983 F, W
Gossman, J S (W of Scotland) 1980 E (R)
Gowans, J J (Cambridge U, London Scottish) 1893 W, 1894 W, E, 1895 W, I, E, 1896 I, E
Gowlland, G C (London Scottish) 1908 W, 1909 W, E, 1910 F, W, I, E
Gracie, A L (Harlequins) 1921 F, W, I, E, 1922 F, W, I, E, 1923 F, W, I, E, 1924 F
Graham, G (Newcastle) 1997 A (R), SA (R), 1998 I, F (R), W (R), 1999 F (R), Arg (R), R, [SA, U, Sm, NZ (R)], 2000 I (R), US, A, Sm, 2001 I (R), Tg (R), Arg (R), NZ (R), 2002 E (R), It (R), I (R), F (R), W (R)
Graham, I N (Edinburgh Acads) 1939 I, E
Graham, J (Kelso) 1926 I, E, 1927 F, W, I, E, A, 1928 F, W, I, E, 1930 I, E, 1932 SA, W
Graham, J H S (Edinburgh Acads) 1876 E, 1877 I, E, 1878 E, 1879 I, E, 1880 I, E, 1881 I, E
Grant, D (Hawick) 1965 F, E, SA, 1966 F, W, I, E, A, 1967 F, W, I, E, NZ, 1968 F
Grant, D M (East Midlands) 1911 W, I
Grant, M L (Harlequins) 1955 F, 1956 F, W, 1957 F
Grant, R (Glasgow Warriors) 2012 A, Fj, Sm, NZ, SA, 2013 E, It1, I, W, F
Grant, T O (Hawick) 1960 I, E, SA, 1964 F, NZ, W
Grant, W St C (Craigmount) 1873 E, 1874 E
Gray, C A (Nottingham) 1989 W, E, I, F, Fj, R, 1990 I, F, W, E, NZ 1, 2, Arg, 1991 F, W, E, I, [J, I, WS, E, NZ]
Gray, D (W of Scotland) 1978 E, 1979 I, F, NZ, 1980 I, F, W, E, 1981 F
Gray, G L (Gala) 1935 NZ, 1937 W, I, E
Gray, R J (Glasgow Warriors, Sale) 2010 F(R), W(R), I(R), NZ, SA, Sm, 2011 F, I1, E, It1, I2, It2(R), [R, Gg(R), Arg, E], 2012 E, W, F, I, It, A, Fj, Sm, NZ, SA, Tg, 2013 E, It1, I, W
Gray, S D (Borders, Northampton) 2004 A3, 2008 NZ(R), SA(R), C(R), 2009 W(R), It(R), I(R), E
Gray, T (Northampton, Heriot's FP) 1950 E, 1951 F, E
Greenlees, H D (Leicester) 1927 A, 1928 F, W, 1929 I, E, 1930 E
Greenlees, J R C (Cambridge U, Kelvinside Acads) 1900 I, 1902 W, I, E, 1903 W, I, E
Greenwood, J T (Dunfermline and Perthshire Acads) 1952 F, 1955 F, W, I, E, 1956 F, W, I, E, 1957 F, W, E, 1958 F, W, A, I, E, 1959 F, W, I
Greig, A (Glasgow HSFP) 1911 I
Greig, L L (Glasgow Acads, United Services) 1905 NZ, 1906 SA, 1907 W, 1908 W, I
Greig, R C (Glasgow Acads) 1893 W, 1897 I
Grieve, C F (Oxford U) 1935 W, 1936 E
Grieve, R M (Kelso) 1935 W, I, E, NZ, 1936 W, I, E
Grimes, S B (Watsonians, Newcastle) 1997 A (t+R), 1998 I (R), F (R), W (R), E (R), Fj, A 1, 2, 1999 W (R), E, It, I, F, Arg, R, [SA, U, Sm (R), NZ (R)], 2000 It, I, F (R), W, US, A, Sm (R), 2001 F (R), W (R), E (R), It, I (R), Tg, Arg, NZ, 2002 E, It, I, F (R), W (R), C, US, R, SA, Fj, 2003 I 1, F, W 1, E(R), It 1(R), W 2, I 2, [J, US, F, Fj, A], 2004 W, E, It, F, I, Sm, A1, J, A4, SA, 2005 F, I, It, W, E(R)
Grove, A (Worcester) 2009 Fj, A, Arg
Gunn, A W (Royal HSFP) 1912 F, W, I, SA, 1913 F

Hall, A J A (Glasgow) 2002 US (R)
Hall, D W H (Edinburgh, Glasgow Warriors) 2003 W 2(R), 2005 R(R), Arg, Sm(R), NZ(R), 2006 F, E, I, It(R), SA 1(R), 2, R, PI, A, 2007 E, W, It, I1, F(R), 2008 Arg 2(R), NZ(R), SA(R), C(R), 2009 W(R), F(R), It(R), I(R), E(R), Fj(R), A(R), Arg(R), 2010 SA(R), Sm(R), 2011 F(R), I2(R), It2(R), [Arg(R)], 2012 SA(R), Tg(R), 2013 E, I(R), F(R)
Hamilton, A S (Headingley) 1914 W, 1920 F
Hamilton, C P (Newcastle) 2004 A2(R), 2005 R, Arg, Sm, NZ
Hamilton, H M (W of Scotland) 1874 E, 1875 E
Hamilton, J L (Leicester, Edinburgh, Gloucester) 2006 R(R), A(R), 2007 E, W, It(R), I1(R), F(R), I2, SA, [R, NZ(R), It, Arg], 2008 F, W, I(R), NZ, SA, C, 2009 W, F, I, E, 2010 W, It, E, I, Arg 1, 2, NZ, Sm(R), 2011 I2, [Gg, Arg], 2012 E, W, F, I, It, NZ, SA, 2013 E, It1, I, W, F, Sm(R), SA
Hannah, R S M (W of Scotland) 1971 I
Harley, R J (Glasgow Warriors) 2012 Sm(R), 2013 It1, I, W, It2(R)
Harrower, P R (London Scottish) 1885 W
Hart, J G M (London Scottish) 1951 SA
Hart, T M (Glasgow U) 1930 W, I
Hart, W (Melrose) 1960 SA
Harvey, L (Greenock Wands) 1899 I
Hastie, A J (Melrose) 1961 W, I, E, 1964 I, E, 1965 E, SA, 1966 F, W, I, E, A, 1967 F, W, I, NZ, 1968 F, W
Hastie, I R (Kelso) 1955 F, 1958 F, E, 1959 F, W, I
Hastie, J D H (Melrose) 1938 W, I, E
Hastings, A G (Cambridge U, Watsonians, London Scottish) 1986 F, W, E, I, R, 1987 I, F, W, E, [F, Z, R, NZ], 1988 I, F, W, E, A, 1989 Fj, R, 1990 I, F, W, E, NZ 1, 2, Arg, 1991 F, W, E, I, [J, I, WS, E, NZ], 1992 E, I, F, W, A 1, 1993 I, F, W, E, NZ, 1994 W, E, I, F, SA, 1995 C, I, F, W, E, R, [Iv, Tg, F, NZ]
Hastings, S (Watsonians) 1986 F, W, E, I, R, 1987 I, F, W, [R], 1988 I, F, W, A, 1989 W, E, I, F, Fj, R, 1990 I, F, W, E, NZ 1, 2, Arg, 1991 F, W, E, I, [J, Z, I, WS, E, NZ], 1992 E, I, F, W, A 1, 2, 1993 I, F, W, E, NZ, 1994 E, I, F, SA, 1995 W, E, R (R), [Tg, F, NZ], 1996 I, F, W, E, NZ 2, It, 1997 W, E (R)
Hay, B H (Boroughmuir) 1975 NZ, A, 1976 F, 1978 I, F, W, E, NZ, 1979 W, E, I, F, NZ, 1980 I, F, W, E, 1981 F, W, E, I, NZ 1, 2
Hay, J A (Hawick) 1995 WS
Hay-Gordon, J R (Edinburgh Acads) 1875 E, 1877 I, E
Heathcote, T A (Bath) 2012 Tg(R), 2013 Sm, It2
Hegarty, C B (Hawick) 1978 I, F, W, E
Hegarty, J J (Hawick) 1951 F, 1953 F, W, I, E, 1955 F

Henderson, A R (Glasgow Warriors) 2001 I (R), Tg (R), NZ (R), 2002 It, I, US (R), 2003 SA 1, 2, It 2, I 2, [US, F, Fj, A], 2004 W, E(t&R), It(R), F, I, Sm, A1, 2, 3, J, A4, SA, 2005 W(R), R, Arg, Sm, NZ, 2006 F, W, E, I, It, SA 1, 2, PI, A, 2007 E, It(R), I1(R), F, I2, SA, [NZ, It(R), Arg(R)], 2008 F, W, I, It(R)
Henderson, B C (Edinburgh Wands) 1963 E, 1964 F, I, E, 1965 F, W, I, E, 1966 F, W, I, E
Henderson, F W (London Scottish) 1900 W, I
Henderson, I C (Edinburgh Acads) 1939 I, E, 1947 F, W, E, A, 1948 I, E
Henderson, J H (Oxford U, Richmond) 1953 F, W, I, E, 1954 F, NZ, I, E, W
Henderson, J M (Edinburgh Acads) 1933 W, E, I
Henderson, J Y M (Watsonians) 1911 E
Henderson, M M (Dunfermline) 1937 W, I, E
Henderson, N F (London Scottish) 1892 I
Henderson, R G (Newcastle Northern) 1924 I, E
Hendrie, K G P (Heriot's FP) 1924 F, W, I
Hendry, T L (Clydesdale) 1893 W, I, E, 1895 I
Henriksen, E H (Royal HSFP) 1953 I
Hepburn, D P (Woodford) 1947 A, 1948 F, W, I, E, 1949 F, W, I, E
Heron, G (Glasgow Acads) 1874 E, 1875 E
Hill, C C P (St Andrew's U) 1912 F, I
Hilton, D I W (Bath, Glasgow) 1995 C, I, F, W, E, R, [Tg, F, NZ], WS, 1996 I, F, W, E, NZ 1, 2, A, It, 1997 W, A, SA, 1998 It, I (R), F, W, E, A 1, 2, SA (R), 1999 W (R), E (R), It (R), I (R), F, R (R), [SA (R), U (R), Sp], 2000 It (R), F (R), W (R), 2002 SA(R)
Hines, N J (Edinburgh, Glasgow, Perpignan, Leinster, Clermont-Auvergne) 2000 NZ 2(R), 2002 C, US, R(R), SA(R), Fj(R), 2003 W 1(R), E, It 1, SA 1, 2, It 2, W 2(R), I 2, [US, F(R), Fj, A], 2004 E(R), It(R), F(R), I(R), A3, J, A4, SA, 2005 F(R), I(R), It(R), W(R), E, 2006 E(R), I, It, SA 1, 2, R, PI, 2007 W(R), It, I1, F, I2, SA, [Pt, R, It, Arg], 2008 F, W, I, E, It, NZ, SA, C, 2009 I(R), E(R), Fj, A, Arg, 2010 F, It(R), E(R), NZ(R), SA, Sm, 2011 F, W, I1(R), E, It1, 2, [R(R), Gg, Arg(R), E(R)]
Hinshelwood, A J W (London Scottish) 1966 F, W, I, E, A, 1967 F, W, I, E, NZ, 1968 F, W, I, E, A, 1969 F, W, I, SA, 1970 F, W
Hinshelwood, B G (Worcester) 2002 C (R), R(R), SA(R), Fj, 2003 It 2, [J, US(R), Fj(R), A(R)], 2004 W, E, It, Sm, A1, 2, J, A4, SA, 2005 It(R)
Hodge D W (Watsonians, Edinburgh) 1997 F (R), A, SA (t+R), 1998 A 2(R), SA, 1999 W, Arg, R, [Sp, Sm (R)], 2000 F (R), W, E, NZ 1, 2, US (R), Sm (R), 2001 F (R), W, E, It, I (R), 2002 E, W (R), C, US
Hodgson, C G (London Scottish) 1968 I, E
Hogg, A (Edinburgh) 2004 W, E(R), It, F(R), I, Sm, A1, 2, 3, J, A4, SA, 2005 F, I, It, W, E, R, Arg, Sm, NZ, 2006 F, W, E, I, It, SA 1, 2, 2007 E(R), W(R), It(R), I1(R), F, I2, SA(t&R), [Pt, R, It, Arg], 2008 W(R), I, E, It, Arg 1, 2, NZ, SA, 2009 W
Hogg, C D (Melrose) 1992 A 1, 2, 1993 NZ (R), 1994 Arg 1, 2
Hogg, C G (Boroughmuir) 1978 F (R), W (R)
Hogg, S W (Glasgow Warriors) 2012 W(R), F, I, It, A, Fj, Sm, NZ, SA, Tg, 2013 E, It1, I, W, F
Holmes, S D (London Scottish) 1998 It, I, F
Holms, W F (RIE Coll) 1886 W, E, 1887 I, E, 1889 W, I
Horne, P (Glasgow Warriors) 2013 Sm(R), SA(R)
Horsburgh, G B (London Scottish) 1937 W, I, E, 1938 W, I, E, 1939 W, I, E
Howie, D D (Kirkcaldy) 1912 F, W, I, E, SA, 1913 F, W
Howie, R A (Kirkcaldy) 1924 F, W, I, E, 1925 W, I, E
Hoyer-Millar, G C (Oxford U) 1953 I
Huggan, J L (London Scottish) 1914 E
Hume, J (Royal HSFP) 1912 F, 1920 F, 1921 F, W, I, E, 1922 F
Hume, J W G (Oxford U, Edinburgh Wands) 1928 I, 1930 F
Hunter, F (Edinburgh U) 1882 I
Hunter, I G (Selkirk) 1984 I (R), 1985 F (R), W, E
Hunter, J M (Cambridge U) 1947 F
Hunter, M D (Glasgow High) 1974 F
Hunter, W J (Hawick) 1964 F, NZ, W, 1967 F, W, I, E
Hutchison, W R (Glasgow HSFP) 1911 E
Hutton, A H M (Dunfermline) 1932 I
Hutton, J E (Harlequins) 1930 E, 1931 F

Inglis, H M (Edinburgh Acads) 1951 F, W, I, E, SA, 1952 W, I
Inglis, J M (Selkirk) 1952 E
Inglis, W M (Cambridge U, Royal Engineers) 1937 W, I, E, 1938 W, I, E
Innes, J R S (Aberdeen GSFP) 1939 W, I, E, 1947 A, 1948 F, W, I, E
Ireland, J C H (Glasgow HSFP) 1925 W, I, E, 1926 F, W, I, E, 1927 F, W, I, E
Irvine, A R (Heriot's FP) 1972 NZ, 1973 F, W, I, E, P, 1974 W, E, I, F, 1975 I, F, W, E, NZ, A, 1976 F, W, E, I, 1977 E, I, F, W, 1978 I, F, E, NZ, 1979 W, E, I, F, NZ, 1980 I, F, W, E, 1981 F, W, E, I, NZ 1, 2, R, A, 1982 E, I, F, W, A 1, 2
Irvine, D R (Edinburgh Acads) 1878 E, 1879 I, E
Irvine, R W (Edinburgh Acads) 1871 E, 1872 E, 1873 E, 1874 E, 1875 E, 1876 E, 1877 I, E, 1878 E, 1879 I, E, 1880 I, E
Irvine T W (Edinburgh Acads) 1885 I 1, 2, 1886 W, I, E, 1887 I, W, E, 1888 W, I, 1889 I

Jackson, R J H (Glasgow Warriors) 2010 NZ(R), Sm(R), 2011 F(R), I1, E, It1, I2, It2(R), [R, Arg, E], 2012 I(R), It(R), NZ(R), SA(R), 2013 E, It1, I, W(R), F(R), SA
Jackson, K L T (Oxford U) 1933 W, E, I, 1934 W
Jackson, T G H (Army) 1947 F, W, E, A, 1948 F, W, I, E, 1949 F, W, I, E
Jackson, W D (Hawick) 1964 I, 1965 E, SA, 1968 A, 1969 F, W, I, E
Jacobsen, A F (Edinburgh) 2002 C (R), US, 2003 I 2, 2004 It, F, I, A3, J, A4, SA, 2005 R, Arg(R), Sm, 2006 R(R), PI(R), A(R), 2007 E(R), W(R), It(t&R), I1(R), F(R), I2, SA(R), [Pt], 2008 F, W, I, E, It, Arg 1, 2, NZ, SA, C, 2009 W, F, It, Fj, A, Arg, 2010 F(R), W(R), It, E, I, Arg 1, 2, NZ, SA, Sm, 2011 F, W, I1, E, It1, I2, [R, Gg, Arg, E], 2012 E, W, F, I, NZ(R)
Jamieson, J (W of Scotland) 1883 W, I, E, 1884 W, I, E, 1885 W, I 1, 2
Jardine, I C (Stirling County) 1993 NZ, 1994 W, E (R), Arg 1, 2, 1995 C, I, F, [Tg, F (t & R), NZ (R)], 1996 I, F, W, E, NZ 1, 2, 1998 Fj
Jeffrey, J (Kelso) 1984 A, 1985 I, E, 1986 F, W, E, I, R, 1987 I, F, W, E, [F, Z, R], 1988 I, W, A, 1989 W, E, I, F, Fj, R, 1990 I, F, W, E, NZ 1, 2, Arg, 1991 F, W, E, I, [J, I, WS, E, NZ]
Johnston, D I (Watsonians) 1979 NZ, 1980 I, F, W, E, 1981 R, A, 1982 E, I, F, W, A 1, 2, 1983 I, F, W, NZ, 1984 W, E, I, F, R, 1986 F, W, E, I, R
Johnston, H H (Edinburgh Collegian FP) 1877 I, E
Johnston, J (Melrose) 1951 SA, 1952 F, W, I, E
Johnston, W C (Glasgow HSFP) 1922 F
Johnston, W G S (Cambridge U) 1935 W, I, 1937 W, I, E
Joiner, C A (Melrose, Leicester) 1994 Arg 1, 2, 1995 C, I, F, W, E, R, [Iv, Tg, F, NZ], 1996 I, F, W, E, NZ 1, 1997 SA, 1998 It, I, A 2(R), 2000 NZ 1(R), 2, US (R)
Jones, L (Edinburgh) 2012 E, W, F, I
Jones, P M (Gloucester) 1992 W (R)
Junor, J E (Glasgow Acads) 1876 E, 1877 I, E, 1878 E, 1879 E, 1881 I

Kalman, E D (Glasgow Warriors) 2012 W(R), F(R)
Keddie, R R (Watsonians) 1967 NZ
Keith, G J (Wasps) 1968 F, W
Keller, D H (London Scottish) 1949 F, W, I, E, 1950 F, W, I
Kellock, A D (Edinburgh, Glasgow Warriors) 2004 A3(t&R), 2005 R(R), Arg(R), Sm(R), NZ(R), 2006 F, W, E, It(R), SA 1(R), 2, PI(R), A, 2007 E, 2008 Arg 1(t&R), 2(R), 2009 It, Fj, A, Arg, 2010 F, W, It, E, I, Arg 1, 2, 2011 F, W, I1, E, It1, I2(R), It2, [R, E], 2012 E(R), W(R), F(R), I(R), It(R), A, Fj, Sm, NZ(R), SA(R), Tg, 2013 E(R), It1(R), I(R), W(R), F(R), Sm, SA(R), It2
Kelly, R F (Watsonians) 1927 A, 1928 F, W, E
Kemp, J W Y (Glasgow HSFP) 1954 W, 1955 F, W, I, E, 1956 F, W, I, E, 1957 F, W, I, E, 1958 F, W, A, I, E, 1959 F, W, I, E, 1960 F, W, I, E, SA
Kennedy, A E (Watsonians) 1983 NZ, 1984 W, E, A
Kennedy, F (Stewart's Coll FP) 1920 F, W, I, E, 1921 E
Kennedy, N (W of Scotland) 1903 W, I, E
Ker, A B M (Kelso) 1988 W, E

Ker, H T (Glasgow Acads) 1887 I, W, E, 1888 I, 1889 W, 1890 I, E
Kerr, D S (Heriot's FP) 1923 F, W, 1924 F, 1926 I, E, 1927 W, I, E, 1928 I, E
Kerr, G (Leeds, Borders, Glasgow, Edinburgh) 2003 I 1(R), F(R), W 1(R), E(R), SA 1, 2, W 2, [J(R), US, F], 2004 W(R), E(R), It(R), F(R), I(R), J, A4, SA, 2005 F, I, It, W, E, Arg, Sm(R), NZ, 2006 F, W, E, I, It, SA 1, 2, R, PI, A, 2007 E, W, It, I1, F, SA, [Pt(R), R, NZ(R), It, Arg], 2008 F(R), W(R), I(R)
Kerr, G C (Old Dunelmians, Edinburgh Wands) 1898 I, E, 1899 I, W, E, 1900 W, I, E
Kerr, J M (Heriot's FP) 1935 NZ, 1936 I, E, 1937 W, I
Kerr, R C (Glasgow) 2002 C, US, 2003 W 2
Kerr, W (London Scottish) 1953 E
Kidston, D W (Glasgow Acads) 1883 W, E
Kidston, W H (W of Scotland) 1874 E
Kilgour, I J (RMC Sandhurst) 1921 F
King, J H F (Selkirk) 1953 F, W, E, 1954 E
Kininmonth, P W (Oxford U, Richmond) 1949 F, W, I, E, 1950 F, W, I, E, 1951 F, W, I, E, SA, 1952 F, W, I, 1954 F, NZ, I, E, W
Kinnear, R M (Heriot's FP) 1926 F, W, I
Knox, J (Kelvinside Acads) 1903 W, I, E
Kyle, W E (Hawick) 1902 W, I, E, 1903 W, I, E, 1904 W, I, E, 1905 W, I, E, NZ, 1906 W, I, E, 1908 E, 1909 W, I, E, 1910 W

Laidlaw, A S (Hawick) 1897 I
Laidlaw, F A L (Melrose) 1965 F, W, I, E, SA, 1966 F, W, I, E, A, 1967 F, W, I, E, NZ, 1968 F, W, I, A, 1969 F, W, I, E, SA, 1970 F, W, I, E, A, 1971 F, W, I
Laidlaw, G D (Edinburgh) 2010 NZ(R), 2011 I2(R), 2012 E(R), W, F, I, It, A, Fj, Sm, NZ, SA, Tg, 2013 E, It1, I, W, F, Sm, SA, It2
Laidlaw, R J (Jedforest) 1980 I, F, W, E, 1981 F, W, E, I, NZ 1, 2, R, A, 1982 E, I, F, W, A 1, 2, 1983 I, F, W, E, NZ, 1984 W, E, I, F, R, A, 1985 I, F, 1986 F, W, E, I, R, 1987 I, F, W, E, [F, R, NZ], 1988 I, F, W, E
Laing, A D (Royal HSFP) 1914 W, I, E, 1920 F, W, I, 1921 F
Lambie, I K (Watsonians) 1978 NZ (R), 1979 W, E, NZ
Lambie, L B (Glasgow HSFP) 1934 W, I, E, 1935 W, I, E, NZ
Lamond, G A W (Kelvinside Acads) 1899 W, E, 1905 E
Lamont, R P (Glasgow, Sale, Toulon, Glasgow Warriors) 2005 W, E, R, Arg, Sm, 2007 E(R), I1(R), F(R), I2, SA, [Pt, R, It, Arg], 2008 F, I, E, SA, C, 2009 Fj, A, Arg, 2010 W, NZ, 2011 It2, [Gg], 2012 E, W, F
Lamont, S F (Glasgow, Northampton, Llanelli Scarlets, Glasgow Warriors) 2004 Sm, A1, 2, 3, J, A4, SA, 2005 F, I, It, W, E, R, Arg, Sm, NZ, 2006 F, W, E, I, It, SA1, R, PI, A, 2007 E, W, It, I1, F, I2, [Pt, R, It, Arg], 2008 NZ, 2009 W, Fj, A, Arg, 2010 F, W, It, E, I, Arg1, 2, NZ, SA, Sm, 2011 F(R), W(R), I1, E, It1, I2, [R, Gg, Arg, E], 2012 E, W, F, I, It, A, Fj(R), Sm, NZ, SA, Tg, 2013 E, It1, I, W, F, Sm, SA, It2
Laney, B J (Edinburgh) 2001 NZ, 2002 E, It, I, F, W, C, US, R, SA, Fj, 2003 I 1, F, SA 2(R), It 2(R), W 2, 2004 W, E, It, I(R)
Lang, D (Paisley) 1876 E, 1877 I
Langrish, R W (London Scottish) 1930 F, 1931 F, W, I
Lauder, W (Neath) 1969 I, E, SA, 1970 F, W, I, A, 1973 F, 1974 W, E, I, F, 1975 I, F, NZ, A, 1976 F, 1977 E
Laughland, I H P (London Scottish) 1959 F, 1960 F, W, I, E, 1961 SA, W, I, E, 1962 F, W, I, E, 1963 F, W, I, 1964 F, NZ, W, I, E, 1965 F, W, I, E, SA, 1966 F, W, I, E, 1967 E
Lawrie, J R (Melrose) 1922 F, W, I, E, 1923 F, W, I, E, 1924 W, I, E
Lawrie, K G (Gala) 1980 F (R), W, E
Lawrie, S (Edinburgh) 2013 Sm(R)
Lawson, A J M (Edinburgh Wands, London Scottish) 1972 F (R), E, 1973 F, 1974 W, E, 1976 E, I, 1977 E, 1978 NZ, 1979 W, E, I, F, NZ, 1980 W (R)
Lawson, R G M (Gloucester, Newcastle) 2006 A(R), 2007 E(R), W(R), It(R), I1(R), F, SA(R), [Pt(R), NZ(R)], 2008 E(R), Arg1(R), 2(R), NZ(R), SA(R), C(R), 2009 A(R), Arg(R), 2010 E(R), Arg 1, 2, SA, Sm, 2011 F, W, I1(R), E, It1, I2, [Gg, Arg], 2012 Tg(R)
Lawson, S (Glasgow, Sale, Gloucester, London Irish, Newcastle) 2005 R, Arg(R), Sm, NZ, 2006 F(R), W, I(R), It, SA 1, 2(R), R(R), 2007 [Pt, R(R), NZ, Arg(R)], 2008 It(R), 2010 F(R), W(R), E(R), I(R), Arg1(R), 2(R), NZ(R), 2011 W(R), I1(R), E(R), It1(R), 2, [R(R)], 2012 E(R), W(R), F(R), Fj(R), Sm(R), NZ(R), Tg, 2013 SA, It2
Lawther, T H B (Old Millhillians) 1932 SA, W
Ledingham, G A (Aberdeen GSFP) 1913 F
Lee, D J (London Scottish, Edinburgh) 1998 I (R), F, W, E, Fj, A 1, 2, SA, 2001 Arg, 2004 It(R), F, I(R)
Lees, J B (Gala) 1947 I, A, 1948 F, W, E
Leggatt, H T O (Watsonians) 1891 W, I, E, 1892 W, I, 1893 W, E, 1894 I, E
Lely, W G (Cambridge U, London Scottish) 1909 I
Leslie, D G (Dundee HSFP, W of Scotland, Gala) 1975 I, F, W, E, NZ, A, 1976 F, W, E, I, 1978 NZ, 1980 E, 1981 W, E, I, NZ 1, 2, R, A, 1982 E, 1983 I, F, W, E, 1984 W, E, I, F, R, 1985 F, W, E
Leslie, J A (Glasgow, Northampton) 1998 SA, 1999 W, E, It, I, F, [SA], 2000 It, F, W, US, A, Sm, 2001 F, W, E, It, I, Tg, Arg, NZ, 2002 F, W
Leslie, M D (Glasgow, Edinburgh) 1998 SA (R), 1999 W, E, It, I, F, R, [SA, U, Sm, NZ], 2000 It, I, F, W, E, NZ 1, 2, 2001 F, W, E, It, 2002 It (R), I (R), F, W, R, SA, Fj(R), 2003 I 1, F, SA 1(R), 2 (R), It 2(R), W 2, [J(R), US(R)]
Liddell, E H (Edinburgh U) 1922 F, W, I, 1923 F, W, I, E
Lind, H (Dunfermline) 1928 I, 1931 F, W, I, E, 1932 SA, W, E, 1933 W, E, I, 1934 W, I, E, 1935 I, 1936 E
Lindsay, A B (London Hospital) 1910 I, 1911 I
Lindsay, G C (London Scottish) 1884 W, 1885 I 1, 1887 W, E
Lindsay-Watson, R H (Hawick) 1909 I
Lineen, S R P (Boroughmuir) 1989 W, E, I, F, Fj, R, 1990 I, F, W, E, NZ 1, 2, Arg, 1991 F, W, E, I, R, [J, Z, I, E, NZ], 1992 E, I, F, W, A 1, 2
Little, A W (Hawick) 1905 W
Logan, K M (Stirling County, Wasps) 1992 A 2, 1993 E (R), NZ (t), 1994 W, E, I, F, Arg 1, 2, SA, 1995 C, I, F, W, E, R, [Iv, Tg, F, NZ], WS, 1996 W (R), NZ 1, 2, A, It, 1997 W, E, I, F, A, 1998 I, F, SA (R), 1999 W, E, It, I, F, Arg, R, [SA, U, Sm, NZ], 2000 It, I, F, Sm, 2001 F, W, E, It, 2002 I (R), F (R), W, 2003 I 1, F, W 1, E, It 1, SA 1, 2, It 2, I 2, [J, US(R), F, Fj, A]
Logan, W R (Edinburgh U, Edinburgh Wands) 1931 E, 1932 SA, W, I, 1933 W, E, I, 1934 W, I, E, 1935 W, I, E, NZ, 1936 W, I, E, 1937 W, I, E
Longstaff, S L (Dundee HSFP, Glasgow) 1998 F (R), W, E, Fj, A 1, 2 1999 It (R), I (R), Arg (R), R, [U (R), Sp], 2000 It, I, NZ 1
Lorraine, H D B (Oxford U) 1933 W, E, I
Loudoun-Shand, E G (Oxford U) 1913 E
Low, M J (Glasgow Warriors) 2009 F(R), E(R), Fj, A, Arg, 2010 F, Arg 1, 2, SA(R), Sm(R), 2011 F(R), W(R), I1, E, It2, 2013 It1(R), I(t&R), F(R), Sm(R), SA(R), It2(R)
Lowe, J D (Heriot's FP) 1934 W
Lumsden, I J M (Bath, Watsonians) 1947 F, W, A, 1949 F, W, I, E
Lyall, G G (Gala) 1947 A, 1948 F, W, I, E
Lyall, W J C (Edinburgh Acads) 1871 E

Mabon, J T (Jedforest) 1898 I, E, 1899 I, 1900 I
Macarthur, J P (Waterloo) 1932 E
MacArthur, P C (Glasgow Warriors) 2013 Sm
MacCallum, J C (Watsonians) 1905 E, NZ, 1906 W, I, E, SA, 1907 W, I, E, 1908 W, I, E, 1909 W, I, E, 1910 F, W, I, E, 1911 F, I, E, 1912 F, W, I, E
McClung, T (Edinburgh Acads) 1956 I, E, 1957 W, I, E, 1959 F, W, I, 1960 W
McClure, G B (W of Scotland) 1873 E
McClure, J H (W of Scotland) 1872 E
McCowan, D (W of Scotland) 1880 I, E, 1881 I, E, 1882 I, E, 1883 I, E, 1884 I, E
McCowat, R H (Glasgow Acads) 1905 I
McCrae, I G (Gordonians) 1967 E, 1968 I, 1969 F (R), W, 1972 F, NZ
McCrow, J W S (Edinburgh Acads) 1921 I
Macdonald, A E D (Heriot's FP) 1993 NZ
MacDonald, A R (Edinburgh) 2009 Arg, 2010 W(t&R), E(R), I(t)
McDonald, C (Jedforest) 1947 A
Macdonald, D C (Edinburgh U) 1953 F, W, 1958 I, E
Macdonald, D S M (Oxford U, London Scottish, W of Scotland) 1977 E, I, F, W, 1978 I, W, E

Macdonald, J D (London Scottish, Army) 1966 F, W, I, E, 1967 F, W, I, E
Macdonald, J M (Edinburgh Wands) 1911 W
Macdonald, J S (Edinburgh U) 1903 E, 1904 W, I, E, 1905 W
Macdonald, K R (Stewart's Coll FP) 1956 F, W, I, 1957 W, I, E
Macdonald, R (Edinburgh U) 1950 F, W, I, E
McDonald, W A (Glasgow U) 1889 W, 1892 I, E
Macdonald, W G (London Scottish) 1969 I (R)
MacDougall, B (Borders) 2006 W, SA2(R)
Macdougall, J B (Greenock Wands, Wakefield) 1913 F, 1914 I, 1921 F, I, E
McEwan, M C (Edinburgh Acads) 1886 E, 1887 I, W, E, 1888 W, I, 1889 W, I, 1890 W, I, E, 1891 W, I, E, 1892 E
MacEwan, N A (Gala, Highland) 1971 F, W, I, E (2[1C]), 1972 F, W, E, NZ, 1973 F, W, I, E, P, 1974 W, E, I, F, 1975 W, E
McEwan, W M C (Edinburgh Acads) 1894 W, E, 1895 W, E, 1896 W, I, E, 1897 I, E, 1898 I, E, 1899 I, W, E, 1900 W, E
MacEwen, R K G (Cambridge U, London Scottish) 1954 F, NZ, I, W, 1956 F, W, I, E, 1957 F, W, I, E, 1958 W
Macfadyen, D J H (Glasgow) 2002 C (R), US, 2004 Sm, A1, 2, 3, J, A4, SA, 2006 SA 1, 2(R)
Macfarlan, D J (London Scottish) 1883 W, 1884 W, I, E, 1886 W, I, 1887 I, 1888 I
McFarlane, J L H (Edinburgh U) 1871 E, 1872 E, 1873 E
McGaughey, S K (Hawick) 1984 R
McGeechan, I R (Headingley) 1972 NZ, 1973 F, W, I, E, P, 1974 W, E, I, F, 1975 I, F, W, E, NZ, A, 1976 F, W, E, I, 1977 E, I, F, W, 1978 I, F, W, NZ, 1979 W, E, I, F
McGlashan, T P L (Royal HSFP) 1947 F, I, E, 1954 F, NZ, I, E, W
MacGregor, D G (Watsonians, Pontypridd) 1907 W, I, E
MacGregor, G (Cambridge U) 1890 W, I, E, 1891 W, I, E, 1893 W, I, E, 1894 W, I, E, 1896 E
MacGregor, I A A (Hillhead HSFP, Llanelli) 1955 I, E, 1956 F, W, I, E, 1957 F, W, I
MacGregor, J R (Edinburgh U) 1909 I
McGuinness, G M (W of Scotland) 1982 A 1, 2, 1983 I, 1985 I, F, W, E
McHarg, A F (W of Scotland, London Scottish) 1968 I, E, A, 1969 F, W, I, E, 1971 F, W, I, E (2[1C]), 1972 F, E, NZ, 1973 F, W, I, E, P, 1974 W, E, I, F, 1975 I, F, W, E, NZ, A, 1976 F, W, E, I, 1977 E, I, F, W, 1978 I, F, W, NZ, 1979 W, E
McIlwham, G R (Glasgow Hawks, Glasgow, Bordeaux-Bègles) 1998 Fj, A 2(R), 2000 E (R), NZ 2(R), US (R), A (R), Sm (R), 2001 F (R), W (R), E (R), It (R), 2003 SA 2(R), It 2(R), W 2(R), I 2, [A(R)]
McIndoe, F J (Glasgow Acads) 1886 W, I
MacIntyre, I (Edinburgh Wands) 1890 W, I, E, 1891 W, I, E
McIvor, D J (Edinburgh Acads) 1992 E, I, F, W, 1993 NZ, 1994 SA
Mackay, E B (Glasgow Acads) 1920 W, 1922 E
McKeating, E (Heriot's FP) 1957 F, W, 1961 SA, W, I, E
McKelvey, G (Watsonians) 1997 A
McKendrick, J G (W of Scotland) 1889 I
Mackenzie, A D G (Selkirk) 1984 A
Mackenzie, C J G (United Services) 1921 E
Mackenzie, D D (Edinburgh U) 1947 W, I, E, 1948 F, W, I
Mackenzie, D K A (Edinburgh Wands) 1939 I, E
Mackenzie, J M (Edinburgh U) 1905 NZ, 1909 W, I, E, 1910 W, I, E, 1911 W, I
McKenzie, K D (Stirling County) 1994 Arg 1, 2, 1995 R, [Iv], 1996 I, F, W, E, NZ 1, 2, A, It, 1998 A 1(R), 2
Mackenzie, R C (Glasgow Acads) 1877 I, E, 1881 I, E
Mackie, G Y (Highland) 1975 A, 1976 F, W, 1978 F
MacKinnon, A (London Scottish) 1898 I, E, 1899 I, W, E, 1900 E
Mackintosh, C E W C (London Scottish) 1924 F
Mackintosh, H S (Glasgow U, W of Scotland) 1929 F, W, I, E, 1930 F, W, I, E, 1931 F, W, I, E, 1932 SA, W, I, E
MacLachlan, L P (Oxford U, London Scottish) 1954 NZ, I, E, W
Maclagan, W E (Edinburgh Acads) 1878 E, 1879 I, E, 1880 I, E, 1881 I, E, 1882 I, E, 1883 W, I, E, 1884 W, I, E, 1885 W, I 1, 2, 1887 I, W, E, 1888 W, I, 1890 W, I, E
McLaren, A (Durham County) 1931 F
McLaren, E (London Scottish, Royal HSFP) 1923 F, W, I, E, 1924 F
McLaren, J G (Bourgoin, Glasgow, Bordeaux-Bègles, Castres) 1999 Arg, R, [Sp, Sm], 2000 It (R), F, E, NZ 1, 2001 F, W, E (R), I, Tg, Arg, NZ, 2002 E, It, I, F, W, 2003 W 1, E, It 1, SA 1(R), It 2, I 2(R), [J, F(R), Fj(t&R), A(R)]
McLauchlan, J (Jordanhill) 1969 E, SA, 1970 F, W, 1971 F, W, I, E (2[1C]), 1972 F, W, E, NZ, 1973 F, W, I, E, P, 1974 W, E, I, F, 1975 I, F, W, E, NZ, A, 1976 F, W, E, I, 1977 W, 1978 I, F, W, E, NZ, 1979 W, E, I, F, NZ
McLean, D I (Royal HSFP) 1947 I, E
Maclennan, W D (Watsonians) 1947 F, I
MacLeod, D A (Glasgow U) 1886 I, E
MacLeod, G (Edinburgh Acads) 1878 E, 1882 I
McLeod, H F (Hawick) 1954 F, NZ, I, E, W, 1955 F, W, I, E, 1956 F, W, I, E, 1957 F, W, I, E, 1958 F, W, A, I, E, 1959 F, W, I, E, 1960 F, W, I, E, SA, 1961 F, SA, W, I, E, 1962 F, W, I, E
MacLeod, K G (Cambridge U) 1905 NZ, 1906 W, I, E, SA, 1907 W, I, E, 1908 I, E
MacLeod, L M (Cambridge U) 1904 W, I, E, 1905 W, I, NZ
MacLeod, S J (Borders, Llanelli Scarlets, Edinburgh) 2004 A3, J(t&R), A4(R), SA(R), 2006 F(R), W(R), E, SA2(R), 2007 I2(R), [Pt(R), R(R), NZ, It(R), Arg(R)], 2008 F(R), W(R), I, E, It, Arg 1, 2, 2010 Arg 2(t&R), SA, 2011 W(R)
Macleod, W M (Fettesian-Lorettonians, Edinburgh Wands) 1886 W, I
McMillan, K H D (Sale) 1953 F, W, I, E
MacMillan, R G (London Scottish) 1887 W, I, E, 1890 W, I, E, 1891 W, E, 1892 W, I, E, 1893 W, E, 1894 W, I, E, 1895 W, I, E, 1897 I, E
MacMyn, D J (Cambridge U, London Scottish) 1925 F, W, I, E, 1926 F, W, I, E, 1927 E, A, 1928 F
McNeil, A S B (Watsonians) 1935 I
McPartlin, J J (Harlequins, Oxford U) 1960 F, W, 1962 F, W, I, E
Macphail, J A R (Edinburgh Acads) 1949 E, 1951 SA
Macpherson, D G (London Hospital) 1910 I, E
Macpherson, G P S (Oxford U, Edinburgh Acads) 1922 F, W, I, E, 1924 W, E, 1925 F, W, E, 1927 F, W, I, E, 1928 F, W, E, 1929 I, E, 1930 F, W, I, E, 1931 W, E, 1932 SA, E
Macpherson, N C (Newport) 1920 W, I, E, 1921 F, E, 1923 I, E
McQueen, S B (Waterloo) 1923 F, W, I, E
Macrae, D J (St Andrew's U) 1937 W, I, E, 1938 W, I, E, 1939 W, I, E
Madsen, D F (Gosforth) 1974 W, E, I, F, 1975 I, F, W, E, 1976 F, 1977 E, I, F, W, 1978 I
Mair, N G R (Edinburgh U) 1951 F, W, I, E
Maitland, G (Edinburgh Inst FP) 1885 W, I 2
Maitland, R (Edinburgh Inst FP) 1881 E, 1882 I, E, 1884 W, 1885 W
Maitland, R P (Royal Artillery) 1872 E
Maitland, S D (Glasgow Warriors) 2013 E, It1, I, W, F
Malcolm, A G (Glasgow U) 1888 I
Manson, J J (Dundee HSFP) 1995 E (R)
Marsh, J (Edinburgh Inst FP) 1889 W, I
Marshall, A (Edinburgh Acads) 1875 E
Marshall, G R (Selkirk) 1988 A (R), 1989 Fj, 1990 Arg, 1991 [Z]
Marshall, J C (London Scottish) 1954 F, NZ, I, E, W
Marshall, K W (Edinburgh Acads) 1934 W, I, E, 1935 W, I, E, 1936 W, 1937 E
Marshall, T R (Edinburgh Acads) 1871 E, 1872 E, 1873 E, 1874 E
Marshall, W (Edinburgh Acads) 1872 E
Martin, H (Edinburgh Acads, Oxford U) 1908 W, I, E, 1909 W, E
Masters, W H (Edinburgh Inst FP) 1879 I, 1880 I, E
Mather, C G (Edinburgh, Glasgow) 1999 R (R), [Sp, Sm (R)], 2000 F (t), 2003 [F, Fj, A], 2004 W, E, F
Maxwell, F T (Royal Engineers) 1872 E
Maxwell, G H H P (Edinburgh Acads, RAF, London Scottish) 1913 I, E, 1914 W, I, E, 1920 W, E, 1921 F, W, I, E, 1922 F, E
Maxwell, J M (Langholm) 1957 I
Mayer, M J M (Watsonians, Edinburgh) 1998 SA, 1999 [SA (R), U, Sp, Sm, NZ], 2000 It, I
Mein, J (Edinburgh Acads) 1871 E, 1872 E, 1873 E, 1874 E, 1875 E
Melville, C L (Army) 1937 W, I, E
Menzies, H F (W of Scotland) 1893 W, I, 1894 W, E

THE COUNTRIES

Metcalfe, G H (Glasgow Hawks, Glasgow) 1998 A 1, 2, 1999 W, E, It, I, F, Arg, R, [SA, U, Sm, NZ], 2000 It, I, F, W, E, 2001 I, Tg, 2002 E, It, I, F, W (R), C, US, 2003 I 1, F, W 1, E, It 1, SA 1, 2, W 2, I 2, [US, F, Fj, A]
Metcalfe, R (Northampton, Edinburgh) 2000 E, NZ 1, 2, US (R), A (R), Sm, 2001 F, W, E
Methuen, A (London Scottish) 1889 W, I
Michie, E J S (Aberdeen U, Aberdeen GSFP) 1954 F, NZ, I, E, 1955 W, I, E, 1956 F, W, I, E, 1957 F, W, I, E
Millar, J N (W of Scotland) 1892 W, I, E, 1893 W, 1895 I, E
Millar, R K (London Scottish) 1924 I
Millican, J G (Edinburgh U) 1973 W, I, E
Milne, C J B (Fettesian-Lorettonians, W of Scotland) 1886 W, I, E
Milne, D F (Heriot's FP) 1991 [J(R)]
Milne, I G (Heriot's FP, Harlequins) 1979 I, F, NZ, 1980 I, F, 1981 NZ 1, 2, R, A, 1982 E, I, F, W, A 1, 2, 1983 I, F, W, E, NZ, 1984 W, E, I, F, A, 1985 F, W, E, 1986 F, W, E, I, R, 1987 I, F, W, E, [F, Z, NZ], 1988 A, 1989 W, 1990 NZ 1, 2
Milne, K S (Heriot's FP) 1989 W, E, I, F, Fj, R, 1990 I, F, W, E, NZ 2, Arg, 1991 F, W (R), E, [Z], 1992 E, I, F, W, A 1, 1993 I, F, W, E, NZ, 1994 W, E, I, F, SA, 1995 C, I, F, W, E, [Tg, F, NZ]
Milne, W M (Glasgow Acads) 1904 I, E, 1905 W, I
Milroy, E (Watsonians) 1910 W, 1911 E, 1912 W, I, E, SA, 1913 F, W, I, E, 1914 I, E
Mitchell, G W E (Edinburgh Wands) 1967 NZ, 1968 F, W
Mitchell, J G (W of Scotland) 1885 W, I 1, 2
Moffat, J S D (Edinburgh, Borders) 2002 R, SA, Fj(R), 2004 A3
Moir, C C (Northampton) 2000 W, E, NZ 1
Moncreiff, F J (Edinburgh Acads) 1871 E, 1872 E, 1873 E
Monteith, H G (Cambridge U, London Scottish) 1905 E, 1906 W, I, E, SA, 1907 W, I, 1908 E
Monypenny, D B (London Scottish) 1899 I, W, E
Moodie, A R (St Andrew's U) 1909 E, 1910 F, 1911 F
Moore, A (Edinburgh Acads) 1990 NZ 2, Arg, 1991 F, W, E
Morgan, D W (Stewart's-Melville FP) 1973 W, I, E, P, 1974 I, F, 1975 I, F, W, E, NZ, A, 1976 F, W, 1977 I, F, W, 1978 I, F, W, E
Morrison, G A (Glasgow Warriors) 2004 A1(R), 2(R), 3, J(R), A4(R), SA(R), 2008 W(R), E, It, Arg 1, 2, 2009 W, F, It, I, E, Fj, A, 2010 F, W, It, E, I, Arg 1, 2, NZ, SA, Sm, 2011 I2, It2, [Gg, Arg], 2012 F, I, It
Morrison, I R (London Scottish) 1993 I, F, W, E, 1994 W, SA, 1995 C, I, F, W, E, R, [Tg, F, NZ]
Morrison, M C (Royal HSFP) 1896 W, I, E, 1897 I, E, 1898 I, E, 1899 I, W, E, 1900 W, E, 1901 W, I, E, 1902 W, I, E, 1903 W, I, 1904 W, I, E
Morrison, R H (Edinburgh U) 1886 W, I, E
Morrison, W H (Edinburgh Acads) 1900 W
Morton, D S (W of Scotland) 1887 I, W, E, 1888 W, I, 1889 W, I, 1890 I, E
Mowat, J G (Glasgow Acads) 1883 W, E
Mower, A L (Newcastle) 2001 Tg, Arg, NZ, 2002 It, 2003 I 1, F, W 1, E, It 1, SA 1, 2, W 2, I 2
Muir, D E (Heriot's FP) 1950 F, W, I, E, 1952 W, I, E
Munnoch, N M (Watsonians) 1952 F, W, I
Munro, D S (Glasgow High Kelvinside) 1994 W, E, I, F, Arg 1, 2, 1997 W (R)
Munro, P (Oxford U, London Scottish) 1905 W, I, E, NZ, 1906 W, I, E, SA, 1907 I, E, 1911 F, W, I
Munro, R (St Andrew's U) 1871 E
Munro, S (Ayr, W of Scotland) 1980 I, F, 1981 F, W, E, I, NZ 1, 2, R, 1984 W
Munro, W H (Glasgow HSFP) 1947 I, E
Murchie, P E (Glasgow Warriors) 2013 SA, It2
Murdoch, W C W (Hillhead HSFP) 1935 E, NZ, 1936 W, I, 1939 E, 1948 F, W, I, E
Murray, C A (Hawick, Edinburgh) 1998 E (R), Fj, A 1, 2, SA, 1999 W, E, It, I, F, Arg, [SA, U, Sp, Sm, NZ], 2000 NZ 2, US, A, Sm, 2001 F, W, E, It (R), Tg, Arg
Murray, E A (Glasgow, Northampton, Newcastle, Worcester Warriors) 2005 R(R), 2006 R, Pl, A, 2007 E, W, It, I1, F, I2, SA, [Pt, R, It, Arg], 2008 F, W, I, E, It, Arg 1, 2, NZ, SA, C, 2009 It, I, E, 2010 W, It, E, I, NZ, SA, Sm, 2011 F, W, It1(R), 2(R), [Gg, E], 2012 E, I(R), It(R), A, Fj, Sm, SA, Tg, 2013 E, It1, W, F, Sm, SA, It2
Murray, G M (Glasgow Acads) 1921 I, 1926 W
Murray, H M (Glasgow U) 1936 W, I
Murray, K T (Hawick) 1985 I, F, W
Murray, R O (Cambridge U) 1935 W, E
Murray, S (Bedford, Saracens, Edinburgh) 1997 A, SA, 1998 It, Fj, A 1, 2, SA, 1999 W, E, It, I, F, Arg, R, [SA, U, Sm, NZ], 2000 It, I, F, W, E, NZ 1, US, A, Sm, 2001 F, W, E, It, I, Tg, Arg, NZ, 2002 E, It, I, F, W, R, SA, 2003 I 1, F, W 1, E, It 1, SA 1, 2, It 2, W 2, [J, F, A(R)], 2004 W, E, It, F, I, Sm, A1, 2, 2005 F, I, It, W, E, R, Arg, Sm, NZ, 2006 F, W, I, It, SA1, R, Pl, A, 2007 E(t&R), W, It, I1, F, SA(R), [Pt, NZ]
Murray, W A K (London Scottish) 1920 F, I, 1921 F
Mustchin, M L (Edinburgh) 2008 Arg 1, 2, NZ(R), SA(R), C(R)

Napier, H M (W of Scotland) 1877 I, E, 1878 E, 1879 I, E
Neill, J B (Edinburgh Acads) 1963 E, 1964 F, NZ, W, I, E, 1965 F
Neill, R M (Edinburgh Acads) 1901 E, 1902 I
Neilson, G T (W of Scotland) 1891 W, I, E, 1892 W, E, 1893 W, 1894 W, I, 1895 W, I, E, 1896 W, I, E
Neilson, J A (Glasgow Acads) 1878 E, 1879 E
Neilson, R T (W of Scotland) 1898 I, E, 1899 I, W, 1900 I, E
Neilson, T (W of Scotland) 1874 E
Neilson, W (Merchiston Castle School, Cambridge U, London Scottish) 1891 W, E, 1892 W, I, E, 1893 I, E, 1894 E, 1895 W, I, E, 1896 I, 1897 I, E
Neilson, W G (Merchistonians) 1894 E
Nelson, J B (Glasgow Acads) 1925 F, W, I, E, 1926 F, W, I, E, 1927 F, W, I, E, 1928 I, E, 1929 F, W, I, E, 1930 F, W, I, E, 1931 F, W, I
Nelson, T A (Oxford U) 1898 E
Nichol, J A (Royal HSFP) 1955 W, I, E
Nichol, S A (Selkirk) 1994 Arg 2(R)
Nicol, A D (Dundee HSFP, Bath, Glasgow) 1992 E, I, F, W, A 1, 2, 1993 NZ, 1994 W, 1997 A, SA, 2000 I (R), F, W, E, NZ 1, 2, 2001 F, W, E, I (R), Tg, Arg, NZ
Nimmo, C S (Watsonians) 1920 E

Ogilvy, C (Hawick) 1911 I, E, 1912 I
Oliver, G H (Hawick) 1987 [Z], 1990 NZ 2(R), 1991 [Z]
Oliver, G K (Gala) 1970 A
Orr, C E (W of Scotland) 1887 I, E, W, 1888 W, I, 1889 W, I, 1890 W, I, E, 1891 W, I, E, 1892 W, I, E
Orr, H J (London Scottish) 1903 W, I, E, 1904 W, I
Orr, J E (W of Scotland) 1889 I, 1890 W, I, E, 1891 W, I, E, 1892 W, I, E, 1893 I, E
Orr, J H (Edinburgh City Police) 1947 F, W
Osler, F L (Edinburgh U) 1911 F, W

Park, J (Royal HSFP) 1934 W
Parks, D A (Glasgow Warriors, Cardiff Blues) 2004 W(R), E(R), F(R), I, Sm(t&R), A1, 2, 3, J, A4, SA, 2005 F, I, It, W, R, Arg, Sm, NZ, 2006 F, W, E, I, It(R), SA1, Pl, A, 2007 E, I1, F, I2(R), SA(R), [Pt, R, NZ(R), It, Arg], 2008 F, W, I(R), E(R), It, Arg 1, 2(R), NZ(R), SA(t), C(R), 2010 W, It, E, I, Arg 1, 2, NZ, SA, Sm, 2011 F, W, I1(R), E(R), It1(R), 2, [R(R), Gg, Arg(R), E(R)], 2012 E
Paterson, C D (Edinburgh, Gloucester) 1999 [Sp], 2000 F, W, E, NZ 1, 2, US, A, Sm, 2001 F, W, E, It, I, NZ, 2002 E, It, I, F, W, C, US, R, SA, Fj, 2003 I 1, F, W 1, E, It 1, SA 1, 2, It 2(R), W 2(R), I 2, [J, US, F, Fj, A], 2004 W, E, It, F, I, Sm, A3, J, A4, SA, 2005 F, I, It, W, E, R, Arg, Sm, NZ, 2006 F, W, E, I, It, SA 1, 2, R(R), Pl, A, 2007 E, W, It, I1, F, I2, SA, [Pt(R), R, NZ, It, Arg], 2008 F(R), W, I, E, It, Arg 1, 2, NZ, SA, 2009 W(R), F(R), It(t&R), I, E, Fj(R), A(R), Arg(R), 2010 F, W, SA(R), 2011 I1, E, It1, I2, [R, Gg(R), Arg, E]
Paterson, D S (Gala) 1969 SA, 1970 I, E, A, 1971 F, W, I, E (2[1C]), 1972 W
Paterson, G Q (Edinburgh Acads) 1876 E
Paterson, J R (Birkenhead Park) 1925 F, W, I, E, 1926 F, W, I, E, 1927 F, W, I, E, A, 1928 F, W, I, E, 1929 F, W, I, E
Patterson, D (Hawick) 1896 W
Patterson, D W (West Hartlepool) 1994 SA, 1995 [Tg]
Pattullo, G L (Panmure) 1920 F, W, I, E
Paxton, I A M (Selkirk) 1981 NZ 1, 2, R, A, 1982 E, I, F, W, A 1, 2, 1983 I, E, NZ, 1984 W, E, I, F, 1985 I (R), F, W, E, 1986 W, E, I, R, 1987 I, F, W, E, [F, Z, R, NZ], 1988 I, E, A

Paxton, R E (Kelso) 1982 I, A 2(R)
Pearson, J (Watsonians) 1909 I, E, 1910 F, W, I, E, 1911 F, 1912 F, W, SA, 1913 I, E
Pender, I M (London Scottish) 1914 E
Pender, N E K (Hawick) 1977 I, 1978 F, W, E
Penman, W M (RAF) 1939 I
Peterkin, W A (Edinburgh U) 1881 E, 1883 I, 1884 W, I, E, 1885 W, I 1, 2
Peters, E W (Bath) 1995 C, I, F, W, E, R, [Tg, F, NZ], 1996 I, F, W, E, NZ 1, 2, A, It, 1997 A, SA, 1998 W, E, Fj, A 1, 2, SA, 1999 W, E, It, I
Petrie, A G (Royal HSFP) 1873 E, 1874 E, 1875 E, 1876 E, 1877 I, E, 1878 E, 1879 I, E, 1880 I, E
Petrie, J M (Glasgow) 2000 NZ 2, US, A, Sm, 2001 F, W, It (R), I (R), Tg, Arg, 2002 F (t), W (R), C, R(R), Fj, 2003 F(t+R), W 1(R), SA 1(R), 2 (R), It 2, W 2, I 2(R), [J, US, F(t&R), A(R)], 2004 It(R), I(R), Sm(R), A1(R), 2(t&R), 3(R), J, A4, SA(R), 2005 F, I, It, W, E(R), R, 2006 F(R), W(R), I(R), SA 2
Philip, T K (Edinburgh) 2004 W, E, It, F, I
Philp, A (Edinburgh Inst FP) 1882 E
Pinder, S J (Glasgow) 2006 SA 1(R), 2(R)
Pocock, E I (Edinburgh Wands) 1877 I, E
Pollock, J A (Gosforth) 1982 W, 1983 E, NZ, 1984 E (R), I, F, R, 1985 F
Polson, A H (Gala) 1930 E
Pountney, A C (Northhampton) 1998 SA, 1999 W (t+R), E (R), It (t+R), I (R), F, Arg, [SA, U, Sm, NZ], 2000 It, I, F, W, E, US, A, Sm, 2001 F, W, E, It, I, 2002 E, I, F, W, R, SA, Fj
Proudfoot, M C (Melrose, Glasgow) 1998 Fj, A 1, 2, 2003 I 2(R)
Purdie, W (Jedforest) 1939 W, I, E
Purves, A B H L (London Scottish) 1906 W, I, E, SA, 1907 W, I, E, 1908 W, I, E
Purves, W D C L (London Scottish) 1912 F, W, I, SA, 1913 I, E
Pyrgos, H B (Glasgow Warriors) 2012 NZ(R), SA(R), Tg, 2013 E(R), It1(R), F(R), Sm(R), SA(R), It2(R)

Rea, C W W (W of Scotland, Headingley) 1968 A, 1969 F, W, I, SA, 1970 F, W, I, A, 1971 F, W, E (2[1C])
Redpath, B W (Melrose, Narbonne, Sale) 1993 NZ (t), 1994 E(t), F, Arg 1, 2, 1995 C, I, F, W, E, R, [Iv, F, NZ], WS, 1996 I, F, W, E. A (R), It, 1997 E, I, F, 1998 Fj, A 1, 2, SA, 1999 R (R), [U (R), Sp], 2000 It, I, US, A, Sm, 2001 F (R), E (R), It, I, 2002 E, It, I, F, W, R, SA, Fj, 2003 I 1, F, W 1, E, It 1, SA 1, 2, [J, US(R), F, Fj, A]
Reed, A I (Bath, Wasps) 1993 I, F, W, E, 1994 E, I, F, Arg 1, 2, SA, 1996 It, 1997 W, E, I, F, 1999 It (R), F (R), [Sp]
Reid, C (Edinburgh Acads) 1881 I, E, 1882 I, E, 1883 W, I, E, 1884 W, I, E, 1885 W, I 1, 2, 1886 W, I, E, 1887 I, W, E, 1888 W, I
Reid, J (Edinburgh Wands) 1874 E, 1875 E, 1876 E, 1877 I, E
Reid, J M (Edinburgh Acads) 1898 I, E, 1899 I
Reid, M F (Loretto) 1883 I, E
Reid, R E (Glasgow) 2001 Tg (R), Arg
Reid, S J (Boroughmuir, Leeds, Narbonne) 1995 WS, 1999 F, Arg, [Sp], 2000 It (t), F, W, E (t)
Reid-Kerr, J (Greenock Wand) 1909 E
Relph, W K L (Stewart's Coll FP) 1955 F, W, I, E
Rennie, R M (Edinburgh) 2008 I(R), 2010 NZ(R), SA(R), Sm(R), 2011 F(R), W(R), I2, It2(R), [R(R), Gg, E(R)], 2012 E, W, F, I, It, A, Fj, Sm, NZ
Renny-Tailyour, H W (Royal Engineers) 1872 E
Renwick, J M (Hawick) 1972 F, W, E, NZ, 1973 F, 1974 W, E, I, F, 1975 I, F, W, E, NZ, A, 1976 F, W, E (R), 1977 I, F, W, 1978 I, F, W, E, NZ, 1979 W, E, I, F, NZ, 1980 I, F, W, E, 1981 F, W, E, I, NZ 1, 2, R, A, 1982 E, I, F, W, 1983 I, F, W, E, 1984 R
Renwick, W L (London Scottish) 1989 R
Renwick, W N (London Scottish, Edinburgh Wands) 1938 E, 1939 W
Richardson, J F (Edinburgh Acads) 1994 SA
Ritchie, G (Merchistonians) 1871 E
Ritchie, G F (Dundee HSFP) 1932 E
Ritchie, J M (Watsonians) 1933 W, E, I, 1934 W, I, E
Ritchie, W T (Cambridge U) 1905 I, E
Robb, G H (Glasgow U) 1881 I, 1885 W
Roberts, G (Watsonians) 1938 W, I, E, 1939 W, E
Robertson, A H (W of Scotland) 1871 E
Robertson, A W (Edinburgh Acads) 1897 E
Robertson, D (Edinburgh Acads) 1875 E
Robertson, D D (Cambridge U) 1893 W
Robertson, I (London Scottish, Watsonians) 1968 E, 1969 E, SA, 1970 F, W, I, E, A
Robertson, I P M (Watsonians) 1910 F
Robertson, J (Clydesdale) 1908 E
Robertson, K W (Melrose) 1978 NZ, 1979 W, E, I, F, NZ, 1980 W, E, 1981 F, W, E, I, R, A, 1982 E, I, F, A 1, 2, 1983 I, F, W, E, 1984 E, I, F, R, A, 1985 I, F, W, E, 1986 I, 1987 F (R), W, E, [F, Z, NZ], 1988 E, A, 1989 E, I, F
Robertson, L (London Scottish United Services) 1908 E, 1911 W, 1912 W, I, E, SA, 1913 W, I, E
Robertson, M A (Gala) 1958 F
Robertson, R D (London Scottish) 1912 F
Robson, A (Hawick) 1954 F, 1955 F, W, I, E, 1956 F, W, I, E, 1957 F, W, I, E, 1958 W, A, I, E, 1959 F, W, I, E, 1960 F
Rodd, J A T (United Services, RN, London Scottish) 1958 F, W, A, I, E, 1960 F, W, 1962 F, 1964 F, NZ, W, 1965 F, W, I
Rogerson, J (Kelvinside Acads) 1894 W
Roland, E T (Edinburgh Acads) 1884 I, E
Rollo, D M D (Howe of Fife) 1959 E, 1960 F, W, I, E, SA, 1961 F, SA, W, I, E, 1962 F, W, E, 1963 F, W, I, E, 1964 F, NZ, W, I, E, 1965 F, W, I, E, SA, 1966 F, W, I, E, A, 1967 F, W, E, NZ, 1968 F, W, I
Rose, D M (Jedforest) 1951 F, W, I, E, SA, 1953 F, W
Ross, A (Kilmarnock) 1924 F, W
Ross, A (Royal HSFP) 1905 W, I, E, 1909 W, I
Ross, A R (Edinburgh U) 1911 W, 1914 W, I, E
Ross, E J (London Scottish) 1904 W
Ross, G (Edinburgh, Leeds) 2001 Tg, 2002 R, SA, Fj(R), 2003 I 1, W 1(R), SA 2(R), It 2, I 2, [J], 2004 Sm, A1(R), 2(R), J(R), SA(R), 2005 It(R), W(R), E, 2006 F(R), W(R), E(R), I(R), It, SA 1(R), 2
Ross, G T (Watsonians) 1954 NZ, I, E, W
Ross, I A (Hillhead HSFP) 1951 F, W, I, E
Ross, J (London Scottish) 1901 W, I, E, 1902 W, 1903 E
Ross, K I (Boroughmuir FP) 1961 SA, W, I, E, 1962 F, W, I, E, 1963 F, W, E
Ross, W A (Hillhead HSFP) 1937 W, E
Rottenburg, H (Cambridge U, London Scottish) 1899 W, E, 1900 W, I, E
Roughead, W N (Edinburgh Acads, London Scottish) 1927 A, 1928 F, W, I, E, 1930 I, E, 1931 F, W, I, E, 1932 W
Rowan, N A (Boroughmuir) 1980 W, E, 1981 F, W, E, I, 1984 R, 1985 I, 1987 [R], 1988 I, F, W, E
Rowand, R (Glasgow HSFP) 1930 F, W, 1932 E, 1933 W, E, I, 1934 W
Roxburgh, A J (Kelso) 1997 A, 1998 It, F (R), W, E, Fj, A 1(R), 2(R)
Roy, A (Waterloo) 1938 W, I, E, 1939 W, I, E
Russell, R R (Saracens, London Irish) 1999 R, [U (R), Sp, Sm (R), NZ (R)], 2000 I (R), 2001 F (R), 2002 F (R), W (R), 2003 W 1(R), It 1(R), SA 1 (R), 2 (R), It 2, I 2(R), [J, F(R), Fj(t), A(R)] , 2004 W(R), E(R), F(R), I(R), J(R), A4(R), SA(R), 2005 It(R)
Russell, W L (Glasgow Acads) 1905 NZ, 1906 W, I, E
Rutherford, J Y (Selkirk) 1979 W, E, I, F, NZ, 1980 I, F, E, 1981 F, W, E, I, NZ 1, 2, A, 1982 E, I, F, W, A 1, 2, 1983 E, NZ, 1984 W, E, I, F, R, 1985 I, F, W, E, 1986 F, W, E, I, R, 1987 I, F, W, E, [F]
Ryder, T P (Glasgow Warriors) 2012 Fj(R), Sm(R)

Sampson, R W F (London Scottish) 1939 W, 1947 W
Sanderson, G A (Royal HSFP) 1907 W, I, E, 1908 I
Sanderson, J L P (Edinburgh Acads) 1873 E
Schulze, D G (London Scottish) 1905 E, 1907 I, E, 1908 W, I, E, 1909 W, I, E, 1910 W, I, E, 1911 W
Scobie, R M (Royal Military Coll) 1914 W, I, E
Scotland, K J F (Heriot's FP, Cambridge U, Leicester) 1957 F, W, I, E, 1958 E, 1959 F, W, I, E, 1960 F, W, I, E, 1961 F, SA, W, I, E, 1962 F, W, I, E, 1963 F, W, I, E, 1965 F
Scott, D M (Langholm, Watsonians) 1950 I, E, 1951 W, I, E, SA, 1952 F, W, I, 1953 F
Scott, J M B (Edinburgh Acads) 1907 E, 1908 W, I, E, 1909 W, I, E, 1910 F, W, I, E, 1911 F, W, I, 1912 W, I, E, SA, 1913 W, I, E

Scott, J S (St Andrew's U) 1950 E
Scott, J W (Stewart's Coll FP) 1925 F, W, I, E, 1926 F, W, I, E, 1927 F, W, I, E, A, 1928 F, W, E, 1929 E, 1930 F
Scott, M (Dunfermline) 1992 A 2
Scott, M C M (Edinburgh) 2012 I(R), A, Fj, Sm, NZ, SA, Tg, 2013 E, It1, I, W, F, Sm, SA, It2
Scott, R (Hawick) 1898 I, 1900 I, E
Scott, S (Edinburgh, Borders) 2000 NZ 2 (R), US (t+R), 2001 It (R), I (R), Tg (R), NZ (R), 2002 US (R), R(R), Fj(R), 2004 Sm(R), A1(R)
Scott, T (Langholm, Hawick) 1896 W, 1897 I, E, 1898 I, E, 1899 I, W, E, 1900 W, I, E
Scott, T M (Hawick) 1893 E, 1895 W, I, E, 1896 W, E, 1897 I, E, 1898 I, E, 1900 W, I
Scott, W P (W of Scotland) 1900 I, E, 1902 I, E, 1903 W, I, E, 1904 W, I, E, 1905 W, I, E, NZ, 1906 W, I, E, SA, 1907 W, I, E
Scoular, J G (Cambridge U) 1905 NZ, 1906 W, I, E, SA
Selby, J A R (Watsonians) 1920 W, I
Seymour, T S F (Glasgow Warriors) 2013 SA, It2
Shackleton, J A P (London Scottish) 1959 E, 1963 F, W, 1964 NZ, W, 1965 I, SA
Sharp, A V (Bristol) 1994 E, I, F, Arg 1, 2 SA
Sharp, G (Stewart's FP, Army) 1960 F, 1964 F, NZ, W
Shaw, G D (Sale) 1935 NZ, 1936 W, 1937 W, I, E, 1939 I
Shaw, I (Glasgow HSFP) 1937 I
Shaw, J N (Edinburgh Acads) 1921 W, I
Shaw, R W (Glasgow HSFP) 1934 W, I, E, 1935 W, I, E, NZ, 1936 W, I, E, 1937 W, I, E, 1938 W, I, E, 1939 W, I, E
Shedden, D (W of Scotland) 1972 NZ, 1973 F, W, I, E, P, 1976 W, E, I, 1977 I, F, W, 1978 I, F, W
Shepherd, R J S (Melrose) 1995 WS, 1996 I, F, W, E, NZ 1, 2, A, It, 1997 W, E, I, F, SA, 1998 It, I, W (R), Fj (t), A 1, 2
Shiel, A G (Melrose, Edinburgh) 1991 [I (R), WS], 1993 I, F, W, E, NZ, 1994 Arg 1, 2, SA, 1995 R, [Iv, F, NZ], WS, 2000 I, NZ 1(R), 2
Shillinglaw, R B (Gala, Army) 1960 I, E, SA, 1961 F, SA
Simmers, B M (Glasgow Acads) 1965 F, W, 1966 A, 1967 F, W, I, 1971 F (R)
Simmers, W M (Glasgow Acads) 1926 W, I, E, 1927 F, W, I, E, A, 1928 F, W, I, E, 1929 F, W, I, E, 1930 F, W, I, E, 1931 F, W, I, E, 1932 SA, W, I, E
Simpson, G L (Kirkcaldy, Glasgow) 1998 A 1, 2, 1999 Arg (R), R, [SA, U, Sm, NZ], 2000 It, I, NZ 1(R), 2001 I, Tg (R), Arg (R), NZ
Simpson, J W (Royal HSFP) 1893 I, E, 1894 W, I, E, 1895 W, I, E, 1896 W, I, 1897 E, 1899 W, E
Simpson, R S (Glasgow Acads) 1923 I
Simson, E D (Edinburgh U, London Scottish) 1902 E, 1903 W, I, E, 1904 W, I, E, 1905 W, I, E, NZ, 1906 W, I, E, 1907 W, I, E
Simson, J T (Watsonians) 1905 NZ, 1909 W, I, E, 1910 F, W, 1911 I
Simson, R F (London Scottish) 1911 E
Sloan, A T (Edinburgh Acads) 1914 W, 1920 F, W, I, E, 1921 F, W, I, E
Sloan, D A (Edinburgh Acads, London Scottish) 1950 F, W, E, 1951 W, I, E, 1953 F
Sloan, T (Glasgow Acads, Oxford U) 1905 NZ, 1906 W, SA, 1907 W, E, 1908 W, 1909 I
Smeaton, P W (Edinburgh Acads) 1881 I, 1883 I, E
Smith, A R (Oxford U) 1895 W, I, E, 1896 W, I, 1897 I, E, 1898 I, E, 1900 I, E
Smith, A R (Cambridge U, Gosforth, Ebbw Vale, Edinburgh Wands) 1955 W, I, E, 1956 F, W, I, E, 1957 F, W, I, E, 1958 F, W, A, I, 1959 F, W, I, E, 1960 F, W, I, E, SA, 1961 F, SA, W, I, E, 1962 F, W, I, E
Smith, C J (Edinburgh) 2002 C, US (R), 2004 Sm(t&R), A1(R), 2(R), 3(R), J(R), 2005 Arg(R), Sm, NZ(R), 2006 F(R), W(R), E(R), I(R), It(R), SA 1(R), 2, R(R), 2007 I2(R), [R(R), NZ, It(R), Arg(R)], 2008 E(R), It(R)
Smith, D W C (London Scottish) 1949 F, W, I, E, 1950 F, W, I, 1953 I
Smith, E R (Edinburgh Acads) 1879 I
Smith, G K (Kelso) 1957 I, E, 1958 F, W, A, 1959 F, W, I, E, 1960 F, W, I, E, 1961 F, SA, W, I, E
Smith, H O (Watsonians) 1895 W, 1896 W, I, E, 1898 I, E, 1899 W, I, E, 1900 E, 1902 E
Smith, I R (Gloucester, Moseley) 1992 E, I, W, A 1, 2, 1994 E (R), I, F, Arg 1, 2, 1995 [Iv], WS, 1996 I, F, W, E, NZ 1, 2, A, It, 1997 E, I, F, A, SA
Smith, I S (Oxford U, Edinburgh U) 1924 W, I, E, 1925 F, W, I, E, 1926 F, W, I, E, 1927 F, I, E, 1929 F, W, I, E, 1930 F, W, I, 1931 F, W, I, E, 1932 SA, W, I, E, 1933 W, E, I
Smith I S G (London Scottish) 1969 SA, 1970 F, W, I, E, 1971 F, W, I
Smith, M A (London Scottish) 1970 W, I, E, A
Smith, R T (Kelso) 1929 F, W, I, E, 1930 F, W, I
Smith, S H (Glasgow Acads) 1877 I, 1878 E
Smith, T J (Gala) 1983 E, NZ, 1985 I, F
Smith T J (Watsonians, Dundee HSFP, Glasgow, Brive, Northampton) 1997 E, I, F, 1998 SA, 1999 W, E, It, I, Arg, R, [SA, U, Sm, NZ], 2000 It, I, F, W, E, NZ 1, 2, US, A, Sm, 2001 F, W, E, It, I, Tg, Arg, NZ, 2002 E, It, I, F, W, R, SA, Fj, 2003 I 1, F, W 1, E, It 1, 2, [J, US, F, Fj, A], 2004 W, E, Sm, A1, 2, 2005 F, I, It, W, E
Sole, D M B (Bath, Edinburgh Acads) 1986 F, W, 1987 I, F, W, E, [F, Z, R, NZ], 1988 I, F, W, E, A, 1989 W, E, I, F, Fj, R, 1990 I, F, W, E, NZ 1, 2, Arg, 1991 F, W, E, I, R, [J, I, WS, E, NZ], 1992 E, I, F, W, A 1, 2
Somerville, D (Edinburgh Inst FP) 1879 I, 1882 I, 1883 W, I, E, 1884 W
Southwell, H F G (Edinburgh, Stade Français) 2004 Sm(t&R), A1, 2, 3(R), J, A4, SA, 2005 F, I, It, W, E, R(R), Arg(R), Sm(R), NZ, 2006 F, W, E, I, It, SA 1, 2, 2006 R, PI(t&R), A(R), 2007 E, W, It, I1, SA(R), [Pt(R), R(R), NZ, It(R), Arg(R)], 2008 F(R), W, I, E, It, Arg 2, NZ(R), SA(R), 2009 W, F, It, E(R), 2010 F(R), It, E, I, Arg 1, 2, NZ, SA, Sm, 2011 F, W
Speirs, L M (Watsonians) 1906 SA, 1907 W, I, E, 1908 W, I, E, 1910 F, W, E
Spence, K M (Oxford U) 1953 I
Spencer, E (Clydesdale) 1898 I
Stagg, P K (Sale) 1965 F, W, E, SA, 1966 F, W, I, E, A, 1967 F, W, I, E, NZ, 1968 F, W, I, E, A, 1969 F, W, I (R), SA, 1970 F, W, I, E, A
Stanger, A G (Hawick) 1989 Fj, R, 1990 I, F, W, E, NZ 1, 2, Arg, 1991 F, W, E, I, R, [J, Z, I, WS, E, NZ], 1992 E, I, F, W, A 1, 2, 1993 I, F, W, E, NZ, 1994 W, E, I, F, SA, 1995 R, [Iv], 1996 NZ 2, A, It, 1997 W, E, I, F, A, SA, 1998 It, I (R), F, W, E
Stark, D A (Boroughmuir, Melrose, Glasgow Hawks) 1993 I, F, W, E, 1996 NZ 2(R), It (R), 1997 W (R), E, SA
Steel, J F (Glasgow) 2000 US, A, 2001 I, Tg, NZ
Steele, W C C (Langholm, Bedford, RAF, London Scottish) 1969 E, 1971 F, W, I, E (2[1C]), 1972 F, W, E, NZ, 1973 F, W, I, E, 1975 I, F, W, E, NZ (R), 1976 W, E, I, 1977 E
Stephen, A E (W of Scotland) 1885 W, 1886 I
Steven, P D (Heriot's FP) 1984 A, 1985 F, W, E
Steven, R (Edinburgh Wands) 1962 I
Stevenson, A K (Glasgow Acads) 1922 F, 1923 F, W, E
Stevenson, A M (Glasgow U) 1911 F
Stevenson, G D (Hawick) 1956 E, 1957 F, 1958 F, W, A, I, E, 1959 W, I, E, 1960 W, I, E, SA, 1961 F, SA, W, I, E, 1963 F, W, I, 1964 E, 1965 F
Stevenson, H J (Edinburgh Acads) 1888 W, I, 1889 W, I, 1890 W, I, E, 1891 W, I, E, 1892 W, I, E, 1893 I, E
Stevenson, L E (Edinburgh U) 1888 W
Stevenson, R C (London Scottish) 1897 I, E, 1898 E, 1899 I, W, E
Stevenson, R C (St Andrew's U) 1910 F, I, E, 1911 F, W, I
Stevenson, W H (Glasgow Acads) 1925 F
Stewart, A K (Edinburgh U) 1874 E, 1876 E
Stewart, A M (Edinburgh Acads) 1914 W
Stewart, B D (Edinburgh Acads, Edinburgh) 1996 NZ 2, A, 2000 NZ 1, 2
Stewart, C A R (W of Scotland) 1880 I, E
Stewart, C E B (Kelso) 1960 W, 1961 F
Stewart, J (Glasgow HSFP) 1930 F
Stewart, J L (Edinburgh Acads) 1921 I
Stewart M J (Northampton) 1996 It, 1997 W, E, I, F, A, SA, 1998 It, I, F, W, Fj (R), 2000 It, I, F, W, E, NZ 1(R), 2001 F, W, E, It, I, Tg, Arg, NZ, 2002 E, It, I, F, W, C, US, R(R)
Stewart, M S (Stewart's Coll FP) 1932 SA, W, I, 1933 W, E, I, 1934 W, I, E

Stewart, W A (London Hospital) 1913 F, W, I, 1914 W
Steyn, S S L (Oxford U) 1911 E, 1912 I
Strachan, G M (Jordanhill) 1971 E (C) (R), 1973 W, I, E, P
Strokosch, A K (Edinburgh, Gloucester, Perpignan) 2006 A(R), 2008 I, E, It, Arg 1, 2, C, 2009 F, It, I, E, Fj, A, Arg, 2010 It(R), Arg 1(R), 2(R), 2011 E(R), It1(R), I2, [Gg, Arg, E], 2012 E, W, A, Fj, Sm, NZ, Tg, 2013 E, F, Sm, SA, It2
Stronach, R S (Glasgow Acads) 1901 W, E, 1905 W, I, E
Stuart, C D (W of Scotland) 1909 I, 1910 F, W, I, E, 1911 I, E
Stuart, L M (Glasgow HSFP) 1923 F, W, I, E, 1924 F, 1928 E, 1930 I, E
Suddon, N (Hawick) 1965 W, I, E, SA, 1966 A, 1968 E, A, 1969 F, W, I, 1970 I, E, A
Sutherland, W R (Hawick) 1910 W, E, 1911 F, E, 1912 F, W, E, SA, 1913 F, W, I, E, 1914 W
Swan, J S (Army, London Scottish, Leicester) 1953 E, 1954 F, NZ, I, E, W, 1955 F, W, I, E, 1956 F, W, I, E, 1957 F, W, 1958 F
Swan, M W (Oxford U, London Scottish) 1958 F, W, A, I, E, 1959 F, W, I
Sweet, J B (Glasgow HSFP) 1913 E, 1914 I
Swinson, T J M (Glasgow Warriors) 2013 SA, It2
Symington, A W (Cambridge U) 1914 W, E

Tait, A V (Kelso, Newcastle, Edinburgh) 1987 [F(R), Z, R, NZ], 1988 I, F, W, E, 1997 I, F, A, 1998 It, I, F, W, E, SA, 1999 W (R), E, It, I, F, Arg, R, [A, U, NZ]
Tait, J G (Edinburgh Acads) 1880 I, 1885 I 2
Tait, P W (Royal HSFP) 1935 E
Taylor, D M (Saracens) 2013 Sm(R), SA(R), It2(R)
Taylor, E G (Oxford U) 1927 W, A
Taylor, R C (Kelvinside-West) 1951 W, I, E, SA
Taylor, S M (Edinburgh, Stade Français) 2000 US, A, 2001 E, It, I, NZ (R), 2002 E, It, I, F, W, C, US, R, SA, Fj, 2003 I 1, F, W 1, E, It 1, SA 1, 2, It 2, I 2, [J, US, F, Fj, A], 2004 W, E, It, F, I, 2005 It, W, E, Arg, Sm, NZ, 2006 F, W, E, I, It, PI, A, 2007 E, W, It, I1, F, I2, [Pt, R, It, Arg], 2008 E, It, C, 2009 W, F, It, I, E
Telfer, C M (Hawick) 1968 A, 1969 F, W, I, E, 1972 F, W, E, 1973 W, I, E, P, 1974 W, E, I, 1975 A, 1976 F
Telfer, J W (Melrose) 1964 F, NZ, W, I, E, 1965 F, W, I, 1966 F, W, I, E, 1967 W, I, E, 1968 E, A, 1969 F, W, I, E, SA, 1970 F, W, I
Tennent, J M (W of Scotland) 1909 W, I, E, 1910 F, W, E
Thom, D A (London Scottish) 1934 W, 1935 W, I, E, NZ
Thom, G (Kirkcaldy) 1920 F, W, I, E
Thom, J R (Watsonians) 1933 W, E, I
Thomson, A E (United Services) 1921 F, W, E
Thomson, A M (St Andrew's U) 1949 I
Thomson, B E (Oxford U) 1953 F, W, I
Thomson, F M A (Glasgow Warriors) 2007 I2(t&R), SA(R), [NZ(R)], 2008 F(R), W(R), I(R), E(R), It
Thomson, I H M (Heriot's FP, Army) 1951 W, I, 1952 F, W, I, 1953 I, E
Thomson, J S (Glasgow Acads) 1871 E
Thomson, R H (London Scottish, PUC) 1960 I, E, SA, 1961 F, SA, W, I, E, 1963 F, W, I, E, 1964 F, NZ, W
Thomson, W H (W of Scotland) 1906 SA
Thomson, W J (W of Scotland) 1899 W, E, 1900 W
Timms, A B (Edinburgh U, Edinburgh Wands) 1896 W, 1900 W, I, 1901 W, I, E, 1902 W, E, 1903 W, E, 1904 I, E, 1905 I, E
Tod, H B (Gala) 1911 F
Tod, J (Watsonians) 1884 W, I, E, 1885 W, I 1, 2, 1886 W, I, E
Todd, J K (Glasgow Acads) 1874 E, 1875 E
Tolmie, J M (Glasgow HSFP) 1922 E
Tomes, A J (Hawick) 1976 E, I, 1977 E, 1978 I, F, W, E, NZ, 1979 W, E, I, F, NZ, 1980 F, W, E, 1981 F, W, E, I, NZ 1, 2, R, A, 1982 E, I, F, W, A 1, 2, 1983 I, F, W, 1984 W, E, I, F, R, A, 1985 W, E, 1987 I, F, E (R), [F, Z, R, NZ]
Tonks, G A (Edinburgh) 2013 Sm
Torrie, T J (Edinburgh Acads) 1877 E
Townsend, G P J (Gala, Northampton, Brive, Castres, Borders) 1993 E (R), 1994 W, E, I, F, Arg 1, 2, 1995 C, I, F, W, E, WS, 1996 I, F, W, E, NZ 1, 2, A, It, 1997 W, E, I, F, A, SA, 1998 It, I, F, W, E, Fj, A 1, 2, SA (R), 1999 W, E, It, I, F, [SA, U, Sp (R), Sm, NZ], 2000 It, I, F, W, E, NZ 1, 2, US, A, Sm, 2001 F, It, I, Arg, NZ, 2002 E, It, I, F, W, R(R), SA(R), Fj, 2003 I 1(R), F, W 1, E, It 1, SA 1, 2, W 2, [J(R), US, F, Fj, A]
Traynor, K (Edinburgh, Bristol) 2009 Fj(R), A(R), Arg(R), 2012 Tg
Tukalo, I (Selkirk) 1985 I, 1987 I, F, W, E, [F, Z, R, NZ], 1988 F, W, E, A, 1989 W, E, I, F, Fj, 1990 I, F, W, E, NZ 1, 1991 I, R, [J, Z, I, WS, E, NZ], 1992 E, I, F, W, A 1, 2
Turk, A S (Langholm) 1971 E (R)
Turnbull, D J (Hawick) 1987 [NZ], 1988 F, E, 1990 E (R), 1991 F, W, E, I, R, [Z], 1993 I, F, W, E, 1994 W
Turnbull, F O (Kelso) 1951 F, SA
Turnbull, G O (W of Scotland) 1896 I, E, 1897 I, E, 1904 W
Turnbull, P (Edinburgh Acads) 1901 W, I, E, 1902 W, I, E
Turner, F H (Oxford U, Liverpool) 1911 F, W, I, E, 1912 F, W, I, E, SA, 1913 F, W, I, E, 1914 I, E
Turner, J W C (Gala) 1966 W, A, 1967 F, W, I, E, NZ, 1968 F, W, I, E, A, 1969 F, 1970 E, A, 1971 F, W, I, E (2[1C])

Usher, C M (United Services, Edinburgh Wands) 1912 E, 1913 F, W, I, E, 1914 E, 1920 F, W, I, E, 1921 W, E, 1922 F, W, I, E
Utterson, K N (Borders) 2003 F, W 1, E(R)

Valentine, A R (RNAS, Anthorn) 1953 F, W, I
Valentine, D D (Hawick) 1947 I, E
Veitch, J P (Royal HSFP) 1882 E, 1883 I, 1884 W, I, E, 1885 I 1, 2, 1886 E
Vernon, R J (Glasgow Warriors, Sale) 2009 Fj(R), A(R), Arg(R), 2010 NZ, SA(R), Sm, 2011 F(R), W, I1(R), E(R), It1(R), 2, [R, Arg(R), E], 2012 F(R), I(R), It(R), Fj(R), Sm
Villar, C (Edinburgh Wands) 1876 E, 1877 I, E
Visser, T J W (Edinburgh) 2012 Fj, Sm, NZ, SA, Tg, 2013 E, It1, I, W, F, Sm, It2(R)

Waddell, G H (London Scottish, Cambridge U) 1957 E, 1958 F, W, A, I, E, 1959 F, W, I, E, 1960 I, E, SA, 1961 F, 1962 F, W, I, E
Waddell, H (Glasgow Acads) 1924 F, W, I, E, 1925 I, E, 1926 F, W, I, E, 1927 F, W, I, E, 1930 W
Wade, A L (London Scottish) 1908 E
Wainwright, R I (Edinburgh Acads, West Hartlepool, Watsonians, Army, Dundee HSFP) 1992 I (R), F, A 1, 2, 1993 NZ, 1994 W, E, 1995 C, I, F, W, E, R, [Iv, Tg, F, NZ], WS, 1996 I, F, W, E, NZ 1, 2, 1997 W, E, I, F, SA, 1998 It, I, F, W, E, Fj, A 1, 2
Walker, A (W of Scotland) 1881 I, 1882 E, 1883 W, I, E
Walker, A W (Cambridge U, Birkenhead Park) 1931 F, W, I, E, 1932 I
Walker, J G (W of Scotland) 1882 E, 1883 W
Walker, M (Oxford U) 1952 F
Walker, N (Borders, Ospreys) 2002 R, SA, Fj, 2007 W(R), It(R), F, I2(R), SA, [R(R), NZ], 2008 F, W, I, E, C, 2010 NZ(R), SA, Sm, 2011 F, W, I1, It1, I2, It2(R)
Wallace, A C (Oxford U) 1923 F, 1924 F, W, E, 1925 F, W, I, E, 1926 F
Wallace, W M (Cambridge U) 1913 E, 1914 W, I, E
Wallace, M I (Glasgow High Kelvinside) 1996 A, It, 1997 W
Walls, W A (Glasgow Acads) 1882 E, 1883 W, I, E, 1884 W, I, E, 1886 W, I, E
Walter, M W (London Scottish) 1906 I, E, SA, 1907 W, I, 1908 W, I, 1910 I
Walton, P (Northampton, Newcastle) 1994 E, I, F, Arg 1, 2, 1995 [Iv], 1997 W, E, I, F, SA (R), 1998 I, F, SA, 1999 W, E, It, I, F (R), Arg, R, [SA (R), U (R), Sp]
Warren, J R (Glasgow Acads) 1914 I
Warren, R C (Glasgow Acads) 1922 W, I, 1930 W, I, E
Waters, F H (Cambridge U, London Scottish) 1930 F, W, I, E, 1932 SA, W, I
Waters, J A (Selkirk) 1933 W, E, I, 1934 W, I, E, 1935 W, I, E, NZ, 1936 W, I, E, 1937 W, I, E
Waters, J B (Cambridge U) 1904 I, E
Watherston, J G (Edinburgh Wands) 1934 I, E
Watherston, W R A (London Scottish) 1963 F, W, I
Watson, D H (Glasgow Acads) 1876 E, 1877 I, E
Watson, W S (Boroughmuir) 1974 W, E, I, F, 1975 NZ, 1977 I, F, W, 1979 I, F

Watt, A G J (Glasgow High Kelvinside) 1991 [Z], 1993 I, NZ, 1994 Arg 2(t & R)
Watt, A G M (Edinburgh Acads) 1947 F, W, I, A, 1948 F, W
Weatherstone, T G (Stewart's Coll FP) 1952 E, 1953 I, E, 1954 F, NZ, I, E, W, 1955 F, 1958 W, A, I, E, 1959 W, I, E
Webster, S L (Edinburgh) 2003 I 2(R), 2004 W(R), E, It, F, I, Sm, A1, 2, 2005 It, NZ(R), 2006 F(R), W(R), E(R), I(R), It(R), SA 1(R), 2, R, PI, A, 2007 W(R), I2, SA, [Pt, R, NZ, It, Arg], 2008 F, I, E, It, Arg 1(R), 2, C, 2009 W
Weir, D (Glasgow Warriors) 2012 F(R), Fj(R), 2013 I(R), W, F
Weir, G W (Melrose, Newcastle) 1990 Arg, 1991 R, [J, Z, I, WS, E, NZ], 1992 E, I, F, W, A 1, 2, 1993 I, F, W, E, NZ, 1994 W (R), E, I, F, SA, 1995 F (R), W, E, R, [Iv, Tg, F, NZ], WS, 1996 I, F, W, E, NZ 1, 2, A, It (R), 1997 W, E, I, F, 1998 It, I, F, W, E, SA, 1999 W, Arg (R), R (R), [SA (R), Sp, Sm, NZ], 2000 It (R), I (R), F
Welsh, J (Glasgow Warriors) 2012 It, 2013 It2(R)
Welsh, R (Watsonians) 1895 W, I, E, 1896 W
Welsh, R B (Hawick) 1967 I, E
Welsh, W B (Hawick) 1927 A, 1928 F, W, I, 1929 I, E, 1930 F, W, I, E, 1931 F, W, I, E, 1932 SA, W, I, E, 1933 W, E, I
Welsh, W H (Edinburgh U) 1900 I, E, 1901 W, I, E, 1902 W, I, E
Wemyss, A (Gala, Edinburgh Wands) 1914 W, I, 1920 F, E, 1922 F, W, I
West, L (Edinburgh U, West Hartlepool) 1903 W, I, E, 1905 I, E, NZ, 1906 W, I, E
Weston, V G (Kelvinside Acads) 1936 I, E
White, D B (Gala, London Scottish) 1982 F, W, A 1, 2, 1987 W, E, [F, R, NZ], 1988 I, F, W, E, A, 1989 W, E, I, F, Fj, R, 1990 I, F, W, E, NZ 1, 2, 1991 F, W, E, I, R, [J, Z, I, WS, E, NZ], 1992 E, I, F, W
White, D M (Kelvinside Acads) 1963 F, W, I, E
White, J P R (Glasgow, Sale, Clermont-Auvergne) 2000 E, NZ 1, 2, US (R), A (R), Sm, 2001 F (R), I, Tg, Arg, NZ, 2002 E, It, I, F, W, C, US, SA(R), Fj, 2003 F(R), W 1, E, It 1, SA 1, 2, It 2, [J, US(R), F, Fj(R), A], 2004 W(R), E, It, F, I, Sm, A1, 2, J(R), A4(R), SA, 2005 F, I, E, Arg, Sm, NZ, 2006 F, W, E, I, It, SA 1, 2, R, 2007 I2, SA, [Pt, R, It, Arg], 2008 F, W, E(R), It(R), NZ, SA, 2009 W, F, It, I, E, Fj(R), A(R), Arg(R)
White, T B (Edinburgh Acads) 1888 W, I, 1889 W
Whittington, T P (Merchistonians) 1873 E
Whitworth, R J E (London Scottish) 1936 I
Whyte, D J (Edinburgh Wands) 1965 W, I, E, SA, 1966 F, W, I, E, A, 1967 F, W, I, E
Will, J G (Cambridge U) 1912 F, W, I, E, 1914 W, I, E
Wilson, A W (Dunfermline) 1931 F, I, E
Wilson, A W (Glasgow) 2005 R(R)
Wilson, G A (Oxford U) 1949 F, W, E
Wilson, G R (Royal HSFP) 1886 E, 1890 W, I, E, 1891 I
Wilson, J H (Watsonians) 1953 I
Wilson, J S (St Andrew's U) 1931 F, W, I, E, 1932 E
Wilson, J S (United Services, London Scottish) 1908 I, 1909 W
Wilson, R (London Scottish) 1976 E, I, 1977 E, I, F, 1978 I, F, 1981 R, 1983 I
Wilson, R (Glasgow Warriors) 2013 W(R), F(R), Sm(R), SA
Wilson, R L (Gala) 1951 F, W, I, E, SA, 1953 F, W, E
Wilson, R W (W of Scotland) 1873 E, 1874 E
Wilson, S (Oxford U, London Scottish) 1964 F, NZ, W, I, E, 1965 W, I, E, SA, 1966 F, W, I, A, 1967 F, W, I, E, NZ, 1968 F, W, I, E
Wood, A (Royal HSFP) 1873 E, 1874 E, 1875 E
Wood, G (Gala) 1931 W, I, 1932 W, I, E
Woodburn, J C (Kelvinside Acads) 1892 I
Woodrow, A N (Glasgow Acads) 1887 I, W, E
Wotherspoon, W (W of Scotland) 1891 I, 1892 I, 1893 W, E, 1894 W, I, E
Wright, F A (Edinburgh Acads) 1932 E
Wright, H B (Watsonians) 1894 W
Wright, K M (London Scottish) 1929 F, W, I, E
Wright, P H (Boroughmuir) 1992 A 1, 2, 1993 F, W, E, 1994 W, 1995 C, I, F, W, E, R, [Iv, Tg, F, NZ], 1996 W, E, NZ 1
Wright, R W J (Edinburgh Wands) 1973 F
Wright, S T H (Stewart's Coll FP) 1949 E
Wright, T (Hawick) 1947 A
Wyllie, D S (Stewart's-Melville FP) 1984 A, 1985 W (R), E, 1987 I, F, [F, Z, R, NZ], 1989 R, 1991 R, [J (R), Z], 1993 NZ (R), 1994 W (R), E, I, F

Young, A H (Edinburgh Acads) 1874 E
Young, E T (Glasgow Acads) 1914 E
Young, R G (Watsonians) 1970 W
Young, T E B (Durham) 1911 F
Young, W B (Cambridge U, London Scottish) 1937 W, I, E, 1938 W, I, E, 1939 W, I, E, 1948 E

South Africa fly half Morné Steyn delivers some instructions against New Zealand.

Getty Images

SOUTH AFRICA

SOUTH AFRICA'S 2012–13 TEST RECORD

OPPONENTS	DATE	VENUE	RESULT
Ireland	10 Nov	A	Won 16–12
Scotland	17 Nov	A	Won 21–10
England	24 Nov	A	Won 16–15
Italy	8 Jun	H	Won 44–10
Scotland	15 Jun	H	Won 30–17
Samoa	22 Jun	H	Won 56–23
Argentina	17 Aug	H	Won 73–13
Argentina	24 Aug	A	Won 22–17
Australia	7 Sep	A	Won 38–12
New Zealand	14 Sep	A	Lost 29–15
Australia	28 Sep	H	Won 28–8
New Zealand	5 Oct	H	Lost 27–38

SPRINGBOKS EMERGE AS MAJOR FORCE

By Joel Stransky

AFP/Getty Images

Captain Jean de Villiers proved an inspirational leader for South Africa during their Rugby Championship campaign.

When Heyneke Meyer became head coach at the start of 2012, he arrived with a reputation for playing conservative rugby and following the South African Rugby Union's decision to give him the job, the feeling was he would mould the Springboks in his own image. After a season in which South Africa won 10 of their 12 Tests and played some increasingly expansive rugby, he proved a lot of the sceptics wrong.

During Heyneke's five years in charge at Loftus Versfeld, his Bulls side did score tries in Super Rugby but they gained a reputation for a reliance on physical domination and a confrontational style as they tried to bully opponents into submission. South Africa were expected to follow the same path but I think he took a long, hard look at modern Super Rugby and realised teams now have to do much more than just win the battle up front to be successful.

As a result, the Springboks are a team trying to reinvent themselves, with a degree of success, and I think overall Heyneke did a good job in beginning the process of changing the side's mindset. It was never going to be an overnight fix but it was clear to me in The Rugby Championship in particular that the players were looking to put more width on the ball.

The end-of-year tour of Europe was not, though, the ideal time to begin throwing the ball around and South Africa played more traditional, simple and smart rugby. Heading to the northern hemisphere in the autumn is a double challenge because of the sudden change in the weather and the fatigue factor and I believe any Test win is a good one.

Ireland was first up and the side had to recover from a 12–3 half-time deficit in Dublin to get the 16–12 win. It was a gritty rather than particularly fluid performance but they showed character and deserved credit to come away from the Aviva Stadium with something. I thought this was a particularly strong show of character and mental strength as not many teams come back when trailing against the Irish!

I'm sure the team was acutely conscious that South Africa had lost on their last visit to Edinburgh in 2010 as they prepared to face Scotland. The Springboks have struggled at Murrayfield on recent visits and that made their 21–10 victory very satisfying. Defence was key in the second half as Scotland came back into it strongly but the Springboks again showed tremendous determination and got the job done.

There's no doubt there was an element of luck in the 16–15 win over England at Twickenham the following week. Willem Alberts's try early in the second half came from a series of mistakes and ricochets but I think it would be too simplistic to say it was the score that settled the match.

It was another narrow victory but, to put it into context, the English smashed the All Blacks at Twickenham seven days later and I'm sure Heyneke was delighted with the win. It was an unbeaten tour and it is the sign of a strong team who can win when they're not firing on all cylinders. To concede only one try in the three Tests was also a big plus.

The more ambitious style of rugby I talked about began to come through in the summer's quadrangular tournament that featured South Africa, Italy, Scotland and Samoa.

There was a lot of debate about how worthwhile the tournament, against what the fans perceived as weaker sides, would be in terms of preparation for The Rugby Championship. Many dismissed it as a waste of time but in hindsight I thought it proved a positive exercise in which the Springboks were able to go through the phases and embrace a new game plan. Heyneke made the most of the opportunity by blooding seven new players and it was also a chance for him to take a look at some new combinations.

South Africa won the title by beating Samoa 56–23 in Pretoria after wins against Italy and Scotland. The Springboks scored eight tries and it was no surprise that Bryan Habana crossed twice, taking him to 50 Test tries and fifth on the all-time list.

It's difficult to know what more you can say about Bryan. His try-scoring record speaks for itself but I think his all-round contribution on the park is often overlooked. He's tactically very astute, his defence is underestimated and sometimes it's only when he's off the pitch that you realise how important he is to the side. Playing on the wing in Test rugby is a young man's game but Bryan's powers have not diminished even though he's now in his 30s.

The Rugby Championship campaign began against Argentina in Johannesburg and I was a little surprised that the Springboks ran away with it so comprehensively, beating the Pumas 73–13. There were eight different try scorers plus a penalty try and South Africa were very clinical, sustaining the tempo of the match for the full 80 minutes.

Argentina were more gutsy in the return game in Mendoza but Morné Steyn was in great form with the boot, kicking 15 points in a 22–17 win. It was great to see Morné do the business on the road because he has a bit of a reputation for struggling away from home and that performance for me settled the debate about the No.10 shirt.

Pat Lambie played on the European tour and there was a school of thought that he was more suited to the wide game Heyneke wanted to play. His form in Super Rugby for the Sharks dipped while Morné was in good nick for the Bulls and his display in Mendoza I think put that particular selection issue to bed.

South Africa went to Brisbane to face Australia in their third game on the back of seven defeats in seven previous visits to Suncorp Stadium but in the end came away with a fantastic 38–12 win. The team had to be patient after an early try from Coenie Oosthuizen but they ripped the Wallabies to shreds in the second half with three more tries and overall it was a polished and accurate display. It would have to rank as one of the best results of Heyneke's Springboks career so far.

The game against the All Blacks in Auckland in September was certainly a controversial one. Bismarck du Plessis picked up two yellow cards and was sent off in the 42nd minute and South Africa were a man down for rest of the second half. Bismarck's first sin bin was undoubtedly a refereeing error as it was a perfectly legal tackle on Dan Carter and the sense of injustice in the Springbok camp after the 29–15 defeat at Eden Park was understandable.

I can understand the anger. The fact there was an official apology after the match says it all but just as it's impossible to say England would have won at Twickenham had it not been for Alberts's lucky try, you can't definitively argue South Africa would have won in Auckland if Bismarck had stayed on the pitch. I'd also say that players on a yellow card, however unjustified, have a responsibility to the team to be more conservative in approach and ensure that they do not pick up a second one.

The team recovered to beat Australia 28–8 in the penultimate game of the Championship in Cape Town. It was a wet and slippery afternoon and tries at Newlands in these conditions are notoriously difficult to come by. Nonetheless it was a good performance but South Africa should have secured the bonus point which would have made their task in the last game against the All Blacks at Ellis Park a lot easier. In the end, the Boks needed to win, score four tries and deny New Zealand a bonus point to take the title.

It was an unbelievable game of rugby in Johannesburg. When Jean de Villiers scored in the 57th minute, the team went 27–24 up and it seemed like they might pull it off but the All Blacks are a dangerous animal and they breached the defence for two more tries in the final quarter for what was a thrilling but, from a South African perspective, disappointing 38–27 victory.

It would be harsh to criticise the team for losing an epic match against the best side in the world. They gave it their all but paid the price for the game becoming more open and loose earlier than they would have liked. Surprisingly the lineout struggled and they missed one or two important tackles, which you just cannot afford to do against the Kiwis.

It was overall, though, a year in which the team made real progress in both results and performance. Heyneke's first year in charge brought a modest four wins in nine Tests, so 10 victories in 12 matches was a marked and measurable improvement. That those two defeats came against the All Blacks tells its own story.

I have already mentioned Habana in terms of standout individual performers but I was equally impressed with the captaincy of Jean de Villiers, who stood up more than anyone expected. No one doubted his qualities as a player but he really grew into his new leadership role and clearly galvanised the players around him. The two hookers – Bismarck and Adriaan Strauss – were both outstanding throughout the year and Francois Louw was enormous in the back row in every single game he played. Willie le Roux on the wing is an exciting addition to the squad and vital to the future of the team if they are to progress with a more expansive game plan.

South Africa now appear to be in a position to move forward off a solid base and challenge New Zealand for the number one ranking in the future. Heyneke has work to do but his platform is strong, he has plenty of talent to work with and his team is certainly moving in the right direction.

SOUTH AFRICA INTERNATIONAL STATISTICS

MATCH RECORDS UP TO 10 OCTOBER 2013

MOST CONSECUTIVE TEST WINS

17 1997 *A*2,*It*, *F* 1,2, *E*,*S*, 1998 *I* 1,2,*W* 1,*E* 1, *A* 1,*NZ* 1,2, *A* 2, *W* 2, *S*, *I* 3

15 1994 *Arg* 1,2, *S*, *W* 1995 *WS*, *A*, *R*, *C*, *WS*, *F*, *NZ*, *W*, *It*, *E*, 1996 *Fj*

MOST CONSECUTIVE TESTS WITHOUT DEFEAT

Matches	Wins	Draws	Period
17	17	0	1997 to 1998
16	15	1	1994 to 1996
15	12	3	1960 to 1963

MOST POINTS IN A MATCH

BY THE TEAM

Pts	Opponents	Venue	Year
134	Uruguay	E London	2005
105	Namibia	Cape Town	2007
101	Italy	Durban	1999
96	Wales	Pretoria	1998
87	Namibia	Albany	2011
74	Tonga	Cape Town	1997
74	Italy	Port Elizabeth	1999
73	Argentina	Soweto	2013
72	Uruguay	Perth	2003
68	Scotland	Murrayfield	1997
64	USA	Montpellier	2007
63	Argentina	Johannesburg	2008
62	Italy	Bologna	1997
61	Australia	Pretoria	1997

BY A PLAYER

Pts	Player	Opponents	Venue	Year
35	PC Montgomery	Namibia	Cape Town	2007
34	JH de Beer	England	Paris	1999
31	PC Montgomery	Wales	Pretoria	1998
31	M Steyn	N Zealand	Durban	2009
30	T Chavhanga	Uruguay	E London	2005
29	GS du Toit	Italy	Port Elizabeth	1999
29	PC Montgomery	Samoa	Paris	2007
28	GK Johnson	W Samoa	Johannesburg	1995
28	M Steyn	Argentina	Soweto	2013
26	JH de Beer	Australia	Pretoria	1997
26	PC Montgomery	Scotland	Murrayfield	1997
26	M Steyn	Italy	East London	2010
25	JT Stransky	Australia	Bloemfontein	1996
25	CS Terblanche	Italy	Durban	1999

MOST TRIES IN A MATCH

BY THE TEAM

Tries	Opponents	Venue	Year
21	Uruguay	E London	2005
15	Wales	Pretoria	1998
15	Italy	Durban	1999
15	Namibia	Cape Town	2007
12	Tonga	Cape Town	1997
12	Uruguay	Perth	2003
12	Namibia	Albany	2011
11	Italy	Port Elizabeth	1999
10	Ireland	Dublin	1912
10	Scotland	Murrayfield	1997

BY A PLAYER

Tries	Player	Opponents	Venue	Year
6	T Chavhanga	Uruguay	E London	2005
5	CS Terblanche	Italy	Durban	1999
4	CM Williams	W Samoa	Johannesburg	1995
4	PWG Rossouw	France	Parc des Princes	1997
4	CS Terblanche	Ireland	Bloemfontein	1998
4	BG Habana	Samoa	Paris	2007
4	JL Nokwe	Australia	Johannesburg	2008

MOST CONVERSIONS IN A MATCH

BY THE TEAM

Cons	Opponents	Venue	Year
13	Italy	Durban	1999
13	Uruguay	E London	2005
12	Namibia	Cape Town	2007
12	Namibia	Albany	2011
9	Scotland	Murrayfield	1997
9	Wales	Pretoria	1998
9	Argentina	Johannesburg	2008
8	Italy	Port Elizabeth	1999
8	USA	Montpellier	2007
8	Argentina	Soweto	2013
7	Scotland	Murrayfield	1951
7	Tonga	Cape Town	1997
7	Italy	Bologna	1997
7	France	Parc des Princes	1997
7	Italy	Genoa	2001
7	Samoa	Pretoria	2002
7	Samoa	Brisbane	2003
7	England	Bloemfontein	2007
7	Italy	East London	2010

BY A PLAYER

Cons	Player	Opponents	Venue	Year
12	PC Montgomery	Namibia	Cape Town	2007
9	PC Montgomery	Wales	Pretoria	1998
9	AD James	Argentina	Johannesburg	2008
8	PC Montgomery	Scotland	Murrayfield	1997
8	GS du Toit	Italy	Port Elizabeth	1999
8	GS du Toit	Italy	Durban	1999
8	M Steyn	Argentina	Soweto	2013
7	AO Geffin	Scotland	Murrayfield	1951
7	JMF Lubbe	Tonga	Cape Town	1997
7	HW Honiball	Italy	Bologna	1997
7	HW Honiball	France	Parc des Princes	1997
7	AS Pretorius	Samoa	Pretoria	2002
7	JNB van der Westhuyzen	Uruguay	E London	2005
7	PC Montgomery	England	Bloemfontein	2007

MOST PENALTIES IN A MATCH

BY THE TEAM

Pens	Opponents	Venue	Year
8	Scotland	Port Elizabeth	2006
8	N Zealand	Durban	2009
7	France	Pretoria	1975
7	France	Cape Town	2006
7	Australia	Cape Town	2009
6	Australia	Bloemfontein	1996
6	Australia	Twickenham	1999
6	England	Pretoria	2000
6	Australia	Durban	2000
6	France	Johannesburg	2001
6	Scotland	Johannesburg	2003
6	N Zealand	Bloemfontein	2009
6	Australia	Bloemfontein	2010

MOST PENALTIES IN A MATCH

BY A PLAYER

Pens	Player	Opponents	Venue	Year
8	M Steyn	N Zealand	Durban	2009
7	PC Montgomery	Scotland	Port Elizabeth	2006
7	PC Montgomery	France	Cape Town	2006
7	M Steyn	Australia	Cape Town	2009
6	GR Bosch	France	Pretoria	1975
6	JT Stransky	Australia	Bloemfontein	1996
6	JH de Beer	Australia	Twickenham	1999
6	AJJ van Straaten	England	Pretoria	2000
6	AJJ van Straaten	Australia	Durban	2000
6	PC Montgomery	France	Johannesburg	2001
6	LJ Koen	Scotland	Johannesburg	2003
6	M Steyn	Australia	Bloemfontein	2010

MOST DROP GOALS IN A MATCH

BY THE TEAM

Drops	Opponents	Venue	Year
5	England	Paris	1999
4	England	Twickenham	2006
3	S America	Durban	1980
3	Ireland	Durban	1981
3	Scotland	Murrayfield	2004

BY A PLAYER

Drops	Player	Opponents	Venue	Year
5	JH de Beer	England	Paris	1999
4	AS Pretorius	England	Twickenham	2006
3	HE Botha	S America	Durban	1980
3	HE Botha	Ireland	Durban	1981
3	JNB van der Westhuyzen	Scotland	Murrayfield	2004
2	BL Osler	N Zealand	Durban	1928
2	HE Botha	NZ Cavaliers	Cape Town	1986
2	JT Stransky	N Zealand	Johannesburg	1995
2	JH de Beer	N Zealand	Johannesburg	1997
2	PC Montgomery	N Zealand	Cardiff	1999
2	FPL Steyn	Australia	Cape Town	2007

CAREER RECORDS

MOST CAPPED PLAYERS

Caps	Player	Career Span
111	JW Smit	2000 to 2011
110	V Matfield	2001 to 2011
102	PC Montgomery	1997 to 2008
93	J de Villiers	2002 to 2013
92	BG Habana	2004 to 2013
89	JH van der Westhuizen	1993 to 2003
80	JP du Randt	1994 to 2007
77	MG Andrews	1994 to 2001
76	JP Botha	2002 to 2011
75	CJ van der Linde	2002 to 2012
71	R Pienaar	2006 to 2013
69	JH Smith	2003 to 2010
69	J Fourie	2003 to 2011
68	SWP Burger	2003 to 2011
66	AG Venter	1996 to 2001
65	PF du Preez	2004 to 2013
64	BJ Paulse	1999 to 2007
63	D J Rossouw	2003 to 2011
54	A-H le Roux	1994 to 2002
54	BW du Plessis	2007 to 2013
53	FPL Steyn	2006 to 2012
53	PJ Spies	2006 to 2013
52	JC van Niekerk	2001 to 2010
51	PA van den Berg	1999 to 2007
51	M Steyn	2009 to 2013
51	JN du Plessis	2007 to 2013
50	T Mtawarira	2008 to 2013

MOST CONSECUTIVE TESTS

Tests	Player	Span
46	JW Smit	2003 to 2007
39	GH Teichmann	1996 to 1999
28	V Matfield	2008 to 2010
26	AH Snyman	1996 to 1998
26	AN Vos	1999 to 2001
25	SH Nomis	1967 to 1972
25	AG Venter	1997 to 1999
25	A-H le Roux	1998 to 1999

MOST POINTS IN TESTS

Points	Player	Tests	Career
893	PC Montgomery	102	1997 to 2008
618	M Steyn	51	2009 to 2013
312	HE Botha	28	1980 to 1992
265	BG Habana	92	2004 to 2013
240	JT Stransky	22	1993 to 1996
221	AJJ van Straaten	21	1999 to 2001
190	JH van der Westhuizen	89	1993 to 2003
181	JH de Beer	13	1997 to 1999
171	AS Pretorius	31	2002 to 2007
160	J Fourie	69	2003 to 2011
156	HW Honiball	35	1993 to 1999
154	AD James	42	2001 to 2011
145	LJ Koen	15	2000 to 2003
135*	BJ Paulse	64	1999 to 2007
132	FPL Steyn	53	2006 to 2012
130	PJ Visagie	25	1967 to 1971
130	R Pienaar	71	2006 to 2013

* includes a penalty try

MOST TESTS AS CAPTAIN

Tests	Captain	Span
83	JW Smit	2003 to 2011
36	GH Teichmann	1996 to 1999
29	JF Pienaar	1993 to 1996
22	DJ de Villiers	1965 to 1970
21	J de Villiers	2012 to 2013
18	CPJ Krigé	1999 to 2003
17	V Matfield	2007 to 2011
16	AN Vos	1999 to 2001
15	M du Plessis	1975 to 1980
12	RB Skinstad	2001 to 2007
11	JFK Marais	1971 to 1974

MOST TRIES IN TESTS

Tries	Player	Tests	Career
53	BG Habana	92	2004 to 2013
38	JH van der Westhuizen	89	1993 to 2003
32	J Fourie	69	2003 to 2011
27*	BJ Paulse	64	1999 to 2007
25	PC Montgomery	102	1997 to 2008
24	J de Villiers	93	2002 to 2013
21	PWG Rossouw	43	1997 to 2003
20	JT Small	47	1992 to 1997
19	DM Gerber	24	1980 to 1992
19	CS Terblanche	37	1998 to 2003
14	CM Williams	27	1993 to 2000
14	J-PR Pietersen	48	2006 to 2012
14	PF du Preez	65	2004 to 2013

* includes a penalty try

MOST PENALTY GOALS IN TESTS

Penalties	Player	Tests	Career
148	PC Montgomery	102	1997 to 2008
128	M Steyn	51	2009 to 2013
55	AJJ van Straaten	21	1999 to 2001
50	HE Botha	28	1980 to 1992
47	JT Stransky	22	1993 to 1996
31	LJ Koen	15	2000 to 2003
28	AD James	42	2001 to 2011
27	JH de Beer	13	1997 to 1999
25	HW Honiball	35	1993 to 1999
25	AS Pretorius	31	2002 to 2007
23	GR Bosch	9	1974 to 1976
21	FPL Steyn	53	2006 to 2012
19	PJ Visagie	25	1967 to 1971

MOST CONVERSIONS IN TESTS

Cons	Player	Tests	Career
153	PC Montgomery	102	1997 to 2008
85	M Steyn	51	2009 to 2013
50	HE Botha	28	1980 to 1992
38	HW Honiball	35	1993 to 1999
33	JH de Beer	13	1997 to 1999
31	AS Pretorius	31	2002 to 2007
30	JT Stransky	22	1993 to 1996
26	AD James	42	2001 to 2011
25	GS du Toit	14	1998 to 2006
23	AJJ van Straaten	21	1999 to 2001
23	LJ Koen	15	2000 to 2003
22	R Pienaar	71	2006 to 2013
20	PJ Visagie	25	1967 to 1971

MOST DROP GOALS IN TESTS

Drops	Player	Tests	Career
18	HE Botha	28	1980 to 1992
8	JH de Beer	13	1997 to 1999
8	AS Pretorius	31	2002 to 2007
8	M Steyn	51	2009 to 2013
6	PC Montgomery	102	1997 to 2008
5	JD Brewis	10	1949 to 1953
5	PJ Visagie	25	1967 to 1971
4	BL Osler	17	1924 to 1933

RUGBY CHAMPIONSHIP (FORMERLY TRI-NATIONS) RECORDS

RECORD	DETAIL	HOLDER	SET
Most points in season	203	in six matches	2013
Most tries in season	23	in six matches	2013
Highest score	73	73–13 v Argentina (h)	2013
Biggest win	60	73–13 v Argentina (h)	2013
Highest score conceded	55	35–55 v N Zealand (a)	1997
Biggest defeat	49	0–49 v Australia (a)	2006
Most appearances	44	V Matfield	2001 to 2011
	44	J de Villiers	2004 to 2013
Most points in matches	320	M Steyn	2009 to 2013
Most points in season	95	M Steyn	2009
Most points in match	31	M Steyn	v N Zealand (h) 2009
Most tries in matches	17	BG Habana	2005 to 2013
Most tries in season	7	BG Habana	2012
Most tries in match	4	JL Nokwe	v Australia (h) 2008
Most cons in matches	39	M Steyn	2009 to 2013
Most cons in season	17	M Steyn	2013
Most cons in match	8	M Steyn	v Argentina (h) 2013
Most pens in matches	75	M Steyn	2009 to 2013
Most pens in season	23	M Steyn	2009
Most pens in match	8	M Steyn	v N Zealand (h) 2009

MISCELLANEOUS RECORDS

RECORD	HOLDER	DETAIL
Longest Test career	JP du Randt	1994–2007
Youngest Test cap	AJ Hartley	18 yrs 18 days in 1891
Oldest Test cap	JN Ackermann	37 yrs 34 days in 2007

CAREER RECORDS OF SOUTH AFRICA INTERNATIONAL PLAYERS

UP TO 10 OCTOBER 2013

PLAYER	DEBUT	CAPS	T	C	P	D	PTS
BACKS:							
BA Basson	2010 v W	11	3	0	0	0	15
JL de Jongh	2010 v W	14	3	0	0	0	15
J de Villiers	2002 v F	93	24	0	0	0	120
PF du Preez	2004 v I	65	14	0	0	0	70
JJ Engelbrecht	2012 v Arg	10	4	0	0	0	20
BG Habana	2004 v E	92	53	0	0	0	265
F Hougaard	2009 v It	27	4	0	0	0	20
ET Jantjies	2012 v A	2	0	0	2	0	6
Z Kirchner	2009 v BI	28	5	0	0	0	25
PJ Lambie	2010 v I	29	1	10	10	0	55
WJ Le Roux	2013 v It	9	3	0	0	0	15
LN Mvovo	2010 v S	7	1	0	0	0	5
R Pienaar	2006 v NZ	71	7	22	17	0	130
J-PR Pietersen	2006 v A	48	14	0	0	0	70
JL Serfontein	2013 v It	9	1	0	0	0	5
FPL Steyn	2006 v I	53	10	5	21	3	132
M Steyn	2009 v BI	51	8	85	128	8	618
JJ Taute	2012 v A	3	0	0	0	0	0
PE van Zyl	2013 v S	2	0	0	0	0	0
J Vermaak	2013 v It	3	0	0	0	0	0
FORWARDS:							
WS Alberts	2010 v W	27	6	0	0	0	30
AF Botha	2013 v It	2	0	0	0	0	0
SB Brits	2008 v It	5	0	0	0	0	0
PM Cilliers	2012 v Arg	6	0	0	0	0	0
MC Coetzee	2012 v E	14	1	0	0	0	5
BW du Plessis	2007 v A	54	8	0	0	0	40
JN du Plessis	2007 v A	51	1	0	0	0	5
E Etzebeth	2012 v E	20	0	0	0	0	0
S Kolisi	2013 v S	8	0	0	0	0	0
PJJ Kruger	2012 v E	17	0	0	0	0	0
L-FP Louw	2010 v W	25	5	0	0	0	25
T Mtawarira	2008 v W	50	2	0	0	0	10
TN Nyakane	2013 v It	3	1	0	0	0	5
CV Oosthuizen	2012 v E	11	1	0	0	0	5
UJ Potgieter	2012 v E	3	0	0	0	0	0
MC Ralepelle	2006 v NZ	22	1	0	0	0	5

PJ Spies	2006 v A	53	7	0	0	0	35
GG Steenkamp	2004 v S	46	6	0	0	0	30
JA Strauss	2008 v A	30	5	0	0	0	25
CJ van der Linde	2002 v S	75	4	0	0	0	20
F van der Merwe	2013 v NZ	1	0	0	0	0	0
HS van der Merwe	2007 v W	4	0	0	0	0	0
PR van der Merwe	2010 v F	31	1	0	0	0	5
DJ Vermeulen	2012 v A	13	1	0	0	0	5

SOUTH AFRICAN INTERNATIONAL PLAYERS

UP TO 10 OCTOBER 2013

Entries in square brackets denote matches played in RWC Finals.

Ackermann, D S P (WP) 1955 BI 2,3,4, 1956 A 1,2, NZ 1,3, 1958 F 2

Ackermann, J N (NT, BB, N) 1996 Fj, A 1, NZ 1, A 2, 2001 F 2(R), It 1, NZ 1(R), A 1, 2006 I, E1,2, 2007 Sm, A2

Aitken, A D (WP) 1997 F 2(R), E, 1998 I 2(R), W 1(R), NZ 1,2(R), A 2(R)

Alberts, W S (NS) 2010 W2(R), S(t&R), E(R), 2011 NZ2, [W(R), Fj(R), Nm, Sm(t&R), A(t&R)], 2012 E1, 2, Arg1, 2, A1, NZ1, A2, NZ2, I, S, E4, 2013 Sm, Arg1, 2, A1, NZ1, A2, NZ2

Albertyn, P K (SWD) 1924 BI 1,2,3,4

Alexander, F A (GW) 1891 BI 1,2

Allan, J (N) 1993 A 1(R), Arg 1,2(R), 1994 E 1,2, NZ 1,2,3, 1996 Fj, A 1, NZ 1, A 2, NZ 2

Allen, P B (EP) 1960 S

Allport, P H (WP) 1910 BI 2,3

Anderson, J W (WP) 1903 BI 3

Anderson, J H (WP) 1896 BI 1,3,4

Andrew, J B (Tvl) 1896 BI 2

Andrews, E P (WP) 2004 I1,2,W1(t&R),PI,NZ1,A1,NZ2,A2,W2,I3,E, 2005 F1,A2, NZ2(t), Arg(R), F3(R), 2006 S1, 2, F, A1(R), NZ1(t), 2007 A2(R), NZ2(R)

Andrews, K S (WP) 1992 E, 1993 F 1,2, A 1(R), 2,3, Arg 1(R), 2, 1994 NZ 3

Andrews, M G (N) 1994 E 2, NZ 1,2,3, Arg 1,2, S, W, 1995 WS, [A, WS, F, NZ], W, It, E, 1996 Fj, A 1, NZ 1, A 2, NZ 2,3,4,5, Arg 1,2, F 1,2, W, 1997 Tg (R), BI 1,2, NZ 1, A 1, NZ 2, A 2, It, F 1,2, E, S, 1998 I 1,2, W 1, E 1, A 1, NZ 1,2, A 2, W 2, S, I 3, E 2, 1999 NZ 1,2(R), A 2(R), [S, U, E, A 3, NZ 3], 2000 A 2, NZ 2, A 3, Arg, I, W, E 3, 2001 F 1,2, It 1, NZ 1, A 1,2, NZ 2, F 3, E

Antelme, J G M (Tvl) 1960 NZ 1,2,3,4, 1961 F

Apsey, J T (WP) 1933 A 4,5, 1938 BI 2

Aplon, G G (WP) 2010 W1, F, It 1, 2, NZ1(R), 2(R), A1, NZ3, A3(R), I, W2, S, E, 2011 A1, 2(R), [Nm], 2012 E3

Ashley, S (WP) 1903 BI 2

Aston, F T D (Tvl) 1896 BI 1,2,3,4

Atherton, S (N) 1993 Arg 1,2, 1994 E 1,2, NZ 1,2,3, 1996 NZ 2

Aucamp, J (WT) 1924 BI 1,2

Baard, A P (WP) 1960 I

Babrow, L (WP) 1937 A 1,2, NZ 1,2,3

Badenhorst, C (OFS) 1994 Arg 2, 1995 WS (R)

Bands, R E (BB) 2003 S 1,2, Arg (R), A 1, NZ 1, A 2, NZ 2, [U,E,Sm(R),NZ(R)]

Barnard, A S (EP) 1984 S Am 1,2, 1986 Cv 1,2

Barnard, J H (Tvl) 1965 S, A 1,2, NZ 3,4

Barnard, R W (Tvl) 1970 NZ 2(R)

Barnard, W H M (NT) 1949 NZ 4, 1951 W

Barry, D W (WP) 2000 C, E 1,2, A 1(R), NZ 1, A 2, 2001 F 1,2, US (R), 2002 W 2, Arg, Sm, NZ 1, A 1, NZ 2, A 2, 2003 A 1, NZ 1, A 2, [U, E, Sm, NZ], 2004 PI, NZ1, A1, NZ2, A2, W2, I3, E, Arg(t), 2005 F1, 2, A1, NZ2, W(R), F3(R), 2006 F

Barry, J (WP) 1903 BI 1,2,3

Bartmann, W J (Tvl, N) 1986 Cv 1, 2, 3, 4, 1992 NZ, A, F, 1, 2

Basson, B A (GW, BB) 2010 W1(R), It 1(R), I, W2, 2011 A1, NZ1, 2013 It, S1, Sm, Arg1,2

Bastard, W E (N) 1937 A 1, NZ 1,2,3, 1938 BI 1,3

Bates, A J (WT) 1969 E, 1970 NZ 1,2, 1972 E

Bayvel, P C R (Tvl) 1974 BI 2,4, F 1,2, 1975 F 1,2, 1976 NZ 1,2,3,4

Beck, J J (WP) 1981 NZ 2(R), 3(R), US

Bedford, T P (N) 1963 A 1, 2, 3, 4, 1964 W, F, 1965 I, A 1,2, 1968 BI 1, 2, 3, 4, F 1, 2, 1969 A 1, 2, 3, 4, S, E, 1970 I, W, 1971 F 1, 2

Bekker, A (WP) 2008 W1, 2(R), It(R), NZ1(R), 2(t&R), A1(t&R), Arg(R), NZ3, A2, 3, W3(R), S(R), E(R), 2009 BI 1(R), 2(R), NZ2(R), A1(R), 2(R), F(t&R), It, I, 2010 It2, NZ1(R), 2(R), 2012 Arg1, 2, NZ1(t&R), A2, NZ2

Bekker, H J (WP) 1981 NZ 1,3

Bekker, H P J (NT) 1952 E, F, 1953 A 1,2,3,4, 1955 BI 2,3,4, 1956 A 1,2, NZ 1,2,3,4

Bekker, M J (NT) 1960 S

Bekker, R P (NT) 1953 A 3,4

Bekker, S (NT) 1997 A 2(t)

Bennett, R G (Border) 1997 Tg (R), BI 1(R), 3, NZ 1, A 1, NZ 2

Bergh, W F (SWD) 1931 W, I, 1932 E, S, 1933 A 1,2,3,4,5, 1937 A 1,2, NZ 1,2,3, 1938 BI 1,2,3

Bestbier, A (OFS) 1974 F 2(R)

Bester, J J N (WP) 1924 BI 2,4

Bester, J L A (WP) 1938 BI 2,3

Beswick, A M (Bor) 1896 BI 2,3,4

Bezuidenhout, C E (NT) 1962 BI 2,3,4

Bezuidenhout, C J (MP) 2003 NZ 2(R), [E,Sm,NZ]

Bezuidenhout, N S E (NT) 1972 E, 1974 BI 2,3,4, F 1,2, 1975 F 1,2, 1977 Wld

Bierman, J N (Tvl) 1931 I

Bisset, W M (WP) 1891 BI 1,3

Blair, R (WP) 1977 Wld

Bobo, G (GL, WP) 2003 S 2(R), Arg, A 1(R), NZ 2, 2004 S(R), 2008 It

Boome, C S (WP) 1999 It 1,2, W, NZ 1(R), A 1, NZ 2, A 2, 2000 C, E 1,2, 2003 S 1(R),2(R), Arg (R), A 1(R), NZ 1(R), A 2, NZ 2(R), [U(R),Gg,NZ(R)]

Bosch, G R (Tvl) 1974 BI 2, F 1,2, 1975 F 1,2, 1976 NZ 1,2,3,4
Bosman, H M (FS) 2005 W,F3, 2006 A1(R)
Bosman, N J S (Tvl) 1924 BI 2,3,4
Botha, A F (BB) 2013 It,S1
Botha, B J (N, Ulster) 2006 NZ2(R), 3, A3, I(R), E1, 2, 2007 E1, Sm, A1, NZ1, Nm(R), S(t&R), [Sm(R), E1, Tg(R), US], 2008 W2, 2009 It(R), I, 2010 W1, F, It 2(R), NZ1(R), 2(R), A1
Botha, D S (NT) 1981 NZ 1
Botha, G van G (BB) 2005 A3(R), F3(R), 2007 E1(R), 2(R), Sm(R), A1(R), NZ1, A2, NZ2(R), Nm, S, [Tg]
Botha, H E (NT) 1980 S Am 1,2, BI 1,2,3,4, S Am 3,4, F, 1981 I 1,2, NZ 1,2,3, US, 1982 S Am 1,2, 1986 Cv 1, 2, 3, 4, 1989 Wld 1,2, 1992 NZ, A, F 1,2, E
Botha, J A (Tvl) 1903 BI 3
Botha, J P (BB) 2002 F, 2003 S 1,2, A 1, NZ 1, A 2(R), [U, E, Gg, Sm, NZ], 2004 I1, PI, NZ1, A1, NZ2, A2, W2, I3, E, S, Arg, 2005 A1, 2, 3, NZ1, A4, NZ2, Arg, W, F3, 2007 E1, 2, A1, NZ1, Nm,S, [Sm, E1, Tg, US(R), Fj, Arg, E2], W, 2008 W1, 2, It, NZ1, 2, A1, Arg, W3, S, E, 2009 BI 1, 2, NZ1, 2, A1, 2, 3, NZ3, F, It, 2010 It 1, 2, NZ1, I, W2, S, E, 2011 A2, NZ2, [Fj, Nm]
Botha, J P F (NT) 1962 BI 2,3,4
Botha, P H (Tvl) 1965 A 1,2
Boyes, H C (GW) 1891 BI 1,2
Brand, G H (WP) 1928 NZ 2,3, 1931 W, I, 1932 E, S, 1933 A 1,2,3,4,5, 1937 A 1,2, NZ 2,3, 1938 BI 1
Bredenkamp, M J (GW) 1896 BI 1,3
Breedt, J C (Tvl) 1986 Cv 1,2,3,4, 1989 Wld 1,2, 1992 NZ, A
Brewis, J D (NT) 1949 NZ 1,2,3,4, 1951 S, I, W, 1952 E, F, 1953 A 1
Briers, T P D (WP) 1955 BI 1,2,3,4, 1956 NZ 2,3,4
Brink D J (WP) 1906 S, W, E
Brink, R (WP) 1995 [R, C]
Brits, S B (WP, Saracens) 2008 It(R),NZ2(R),A1, 2012 S(R),E4(R)
Britz, G J J (FS, WP) 2004 I1(R), 2(R), W1(R), PI, A1, NZ2, A 2(R), I3(t), S(t&R), Arg(R), 2005 U, 2006 E2(R), 2007 NZ2(R)
Britz, W K (N) 2002 W 1
Brooks, D (Bor) 1906 S
Brosnihan, W (GL, N) 1997 A 2, 2000 NZ 1(t+R), A 2(t+R), NZ 2(R), A 3(R), E 3(R)
Brown, C B (WP) 1903 BI 1,2,3
Brüssow, H W (FS) 2008 E(R), 2009 BI 1, 2(R), 3, NZ1, 2, A1, 2, 3, NZ3, F, It, I, 2011 A2, NZ2, [W, Fj, Nm(R), Sm, A]
Brynard, G S (WP) 1965 A 1, NZ 1,2,3,4, 1968 BI 3,4
Buchler, J U (Tvl) 1951 S, I, W, 1952 E, F, 1953 A 1,2,3,4, 1956 A 2
Burdett, A F (WP) 1906 S, I
Burger, J M (WP) 1989 Wld 1,2
Burger, M B (NT) 1980 BI 2(R), S Am 3, 1981 US (R)
Burger, S W P (WP) 1984 E 1,2, 1986 Cv 1,2,3,4
Burger, S W P (WP) 2003 [Gg(R), Sm(R), NZ(R)], 2004 I1, 2, W1, PI, NZ1, A1, NZ2, A2, W2, I3, E, 2005 F1, 2, A1, 2(R), 3(R), NZ1, A4, NZ2, Arg(R), W, F3, 2006 S1, 2, 2007 E1, 2, A1, NZ1, Nm, S, [Sm, US, Fj, Arg, E2], W, 2008 It(R), NZ1, 2, A1, NZ3, A2, 3, W3, S, E, 2009 BI 2, A2(R), 3(R), NZ3, F, I, 2010 F, It2, NZ1, 2, A1, NZ3, A2, 3, 2011 [W, Fj, Nm, Sm, A]
Burger, W A G (Bor) 1906 S, I, W, 1910 BI 2

Carelse, G (EP) 1964 W, F, 1965 I, S, 1967 F 1,2,3, 1968 F 1,2, 1969 A 1,2,3,4, S
Carlson, R A (WP) 1972 E
Carolin, H W (WP) 1903 BI 3, 1906 S, I
Carstens, P D (NS) 2002 S, E, 2006 E1(t&R),2(R), 2007 E1,2(t&R),Sm(R), 2009 BI 1(R),3(t)
Castens, H H (WP) 1891 BI 1
Chavhanga, T (WP) 2005 U, 2007 NZ2(R), 2008 W1,2
Chignell, T W (WP) 1891 BI 3
Cilliers, G D (OFS) 1963 A 1,3,4
Cilliers, N V (WP) 1996 NZ 3(t)
Cilliers, P M (GL) 2012 Arg1(t&R),2(R),A1(t&R),2(R),I(R),E4(R)
Claassen, J T (WT) 1955 BI 1,2,3,4, 1956 A 1,2, NZ 1,2,3,4, 1958 F 1,2, 1960 S, NZ 1,2,3, W, I, 1961 E, S, F, I, A 1,2, 1962 BI 1,2,3,4
Claassen, W (N) 1981 I 1,2, NZ 2,3, US, 1982 S Am 1,2
Claassens, M (FS) 2004 W2(R), S(R), Arg(R), 2005 Arg(R), W, F3, 2007 A2(R), NZ2(R)
Clark, W H G (Tvl) 1933 A 3
Clarkson, W A (N) 1921 NZ 1,2, 1924 BI 1
Cloete, H A (WP) 1896 BI 4
Cockrell, C H (WP) 1969 S, 1970 I, W
Cockrell, R J (WP) 1974 F 1,2, 1975 F 1,2, 1976 NZ 1,2, 1977 Wld, 1981 NZ 1,2(R), 3, US
Coetzee, D (BB) 2002 Sm, 2003 S 1,2, Arg, A 1, NZ 1, A 2, NZ 2, [U, E, Sm(R), NZ(R)], 2004 S(R), Arg(R), 2006 A1(R)
Coetzee, J H H (WP) 1974 BI 1, 1975 F 2(R), 1976 NZ 1,2,3,4
Coetzee, M C (NS) 2012 E1, 2, 3, Arg1, 2, A1, NZ1(R), A2(R), NZ2(t&R), I(R), S(R), E4(R), 2013 It(t&R), S1
Conradie, J H (WP) 2002 W 1,2, Arg (R), Sm, NZ 1, A 1, NZ 2(R), A 2(R), S, E, 2004 W1(R), PI, NZ2, A2, 2005 Arg, 2008 W1, 2(R), NZ1(R)
Cope, D K (Tvl) 1896 BI 2
Cotty, W (GW) 1896 BI 3
Crampton, G (GW) 1903 BI 2
Craven, D H (WP) 1931 W, I, 1932 S, 1933 A 1,2,3,4,5, 1937 A 1,2, NZ 1,2,3, 1938 BI 1,2,3,
Cronjé, G (BB) 2003 NZ 2, 2004 I2(R),W1(R)
Cronjé, J (BB, GL) 2004 I1, 2, W1, PI, NZ1, A1, NZ2(R), A2(t&R), S(t&R), Arg, 2005 U, F1, 2, A1, 3, NZ1(R), 2(t), Arg, W, F3, 2006 S2(R), F(R), A1(t&R), NZ1, A2, NZ2, A3(R), I(R), E1, 2007 A2(R), NZ2, Nm
Cronje, P A (Tvl) 1971 F 1,2, A 1, 2, 3, 1974 BI 3,4
Crosby, J H (Tvl) 1896 BI 2
Crosby, N J (Tvl) 1910 BI 1,3
Currie, C (GW) 1903 BI 2

D'Alton, G (WP) 1933 A 1
Dalton, J (Tvl, GL, Falcons) 1994 Arg 1(R), 1995 [A, C], W, It, E, 1996 NZ 4(R),5, Arg 1,2, F 1,2, W, 1997 Tg (R), BI 3, NZ 2, A 2, It, F 1, 2, E, S, 1998 I 1,2, W 1, E 1, A 1, NZ 1,2, A 2, W 2, S, I 3, E 2, 2002 W 1,2, Arg, NZ 1, A 1, NZ 2, A 2, F, E
Daneel, G M (WP) 1928 NZ 1,2,3,4, 1931 W, I, 1932 E, S
Daneel, H J (WP) 1906 S, I, W, E
Daniel, K R (NS) 2010 I(R), 2012 E1(R),2(R),Arg1,2(R)
Davidson, C D (N) 2002 W 2(R), Arg, 2003 Arg, NZ 1(R), A 2
Davids, Q (WP) 2002 W 2, Arg (R), Sm (R), 2003 Arg, 2004 I1(R), 2, W1, PI(t&R), NZ1(R)
Davison, P M (EP) 1910 BI 1
De Beer, J H (OFS) 1997 BI 3, NZ 1, A 1, NZ 2, A 2, F 2(R), S, 1999 A 2, [S, Sp, U, E, A 3]
De Bruyn, J (OFS) 1974 BI 3
De Jongh, H P K (WP) 1928 NZ 3
De Jongh, J L (WP) 2010 W1, F(R), It 1(R), 2, A1(R), NZ3, 2011 A1, NZ1, [Fj(R), Nm(R)], 2012 A2(R), NZ2(R), S, E4
De Klerk, I J (Tvl) 1969 E, 1970 I, W
De Klerk, K B H (Tvl) 1974 BI 1, 2, 3(R), 1975 F 1,2, 1976 NZ 2(R), 3, 4, 1980 S Am 1, 2, BI 2, 1981 I 1,2
De Kock, A N (GW) 1891 BI 2
De Kock, D (Falcons) 2001 It 2(R), US
De Kock, J S (WP) 1921 NZ 3, 1924 BI 3
De Kock, N A (WP) 2001 It 1, 2002 Sm (R), NZ 1(R), 2, A 2, F, 2003 [U(R), Gg, Sm(R), NZ(R)]
Delport, G M (GL, Worcester) 2000 C (R), E 1(t+R), A 1, NZ 1, A 2, NZ 2, A 3, Arg, I, W, 2001 F 2, It 1, 2003 A 1, NZ 2, [U, E, Sm, NZ]
Delport, W H (EP) 1951 S, I, W, 1952 E, F, 1953 A 1,2,3,4
De Melker, S C (GW) 1903 BI 2, 1906 E
Devenish, C E (GW) 1896 BI 2
Devenish, G St L (Tvl) 1896 BI 2
Devenish, G E (Tvl) 1891 BI 1
De Villiers, D I (Tvl) 1910 BI 1,2,3
De Villiers, D J (WP, Bol) 1962 BI 2,3, 1965 I, NZ 1,3,4, 1967 F 1,2,3,4, 1968 BI 1,2,3,4, F 1,2, 1969 A 1,4, E, 1970 I, W, NZ 1,2,3,4
De Villiers, H A (WP) 1906 S, W, E
De Villiers, H O (WP) 1967 F 1,2,3,4, 1968 F 1,2, 1969 A 1,2,3,4, S, E, 1970 I, W
De Villiers, J (WP, Munster) 2002 F, 2004 PI, NZ1, A1, NZ2, A2, W2(R), E, 2005 U, F1, 2, A1, 2, 3, NZ1, A4, NZ2, Arg, W, F3, 2006 S1,NZ2, 3, A3, I, E1, 2, 2007 E1, 2, A1, NZ1, Nm, [Sm], 2008 W1, 2, It, NZ1, 2, A1, Arg, NZ3, A2, 3, W3, S, E, 2009 BI 1, 2, NZ1, 2, A1, 2, 3, NZ3, I(R), 2010 F(t&R), It1, 2, NZ1, 2, 3, A2, 3, I, W2, S, E, 2011 A2, NZ2, [W, Sm(R), A], 2012 E1, 2, 3, Arg1, 2, A1, NZ1, A2, NZ2, I, S, E4, 2013 It, S1, Sm, Arg1, 2, A1, NZ1, A2, NZ2

De Villiers, P du P (WP) 1928 NZ 1,3,4, 1932 E, 1933 A 4, 1937 A 1,2, NZ 1
Devine, D (Tvl) 1924 BI 3, 1928 NZ 2
De Vos, D J J (WP) 1965 S, 1969 A 3, S
De Waal, A N (WP) 1967 F 1,2,3,4
De Waal, P J (WP) 1896 BI 4
De Wet, A E (WP) 1969 A 3,4, E
De Wet, P J (WP) 1938 BI 1,2,3
Deysel, J R (NS) 2009 It(R), 2011 A1(R),NZ1,A2(R)
Dinkelmann, E E (NT) 1951 S, I, 1952 E, F, 1953 A 1,2
Dirksen, C W (NT) 1963 A 4, 1964 W, 1965 I, S, 1967 F 1,2,3,4, 1968 BI 1,2
Dlulane, V T (MP) 2004 W2(R)
Dobbin, F J (GW) 1903 BI 1,2, 1906 S, W, E, 1910 BI 1, 1912 S, I, W
Dobie, J A R (Tvl) 1928 NZ 2
Dormehl, P J (WP) 1896 BI 3,4
Douglass, F W (EP) 1896 BI 1
Drotské, A E (OFS) 1993 Arg 2, 1995 [WS (R)], 1996 A 1(R), 1997 Tg, BI 1,2,3(R), NZ 1, A 1, NZ 2(R), 1998 I 2(R), W 1(R), I 3(R), 1999 It 1,2, W, NZ 1, A 1, NZ 2, A 2, [S, Sp (R), U, E, A 3, NZ 3]
Dryburgh, R G (WP) 1955 BI 2,3,4, 1956 A 2, NZ 1,4, 1960 NZ 1,2
Duff, B R (WP) 1891 BI 1,2,3
Duffy, B A (Bor) 1928 NZ 1
Du Plessis, B W (NS) 2007 A2(t&R), NZ2, Nm(R), S(R), [Sm(R), E1(R), US(R), Arg(R), E2(t)], W(R), 2008 W1(R), 2(R), It, NZ1(R), 2, Arg, NZ3, A2, 3, W3, S, 2009 BI 1, 2, 3(R), NZ1, 2, A1, 2, 3, NZ3, F, I(R), 2010 I, W2, S, E, 2011 A2(R), NZ2, [W(R), Fj(R), Sm, A(R)], 2012 E1, 2, 3, Arg1, 2013 S1(R), Sm(R), Arg1(R), 2(R), A1, NZ1, A2(R), NZ2
Du Plessis, C J (WP) 1982 S Am 1,2, 1984 E 1,2, S Am 1,2, 1986 Cv 1,2,3,4, 1989 Wld 1,2
Du Plessis, D C (NT) 1977 Wld, 1980 S Am 2
Du Plessis, F (Tvl) 1949 NZ 1,2,3
Du Plessis, J N (FS, NS) 2007 A2,NZ2, [Fj,Arg(t&R)],W, 2008 A3(R),E, 2009 NZ1(t), 2(R), A1(R), 2(R), NZ3(R), 2010 W1(R), F(R), It 1, 2, NZ1, 3, A2, 3, I, W2, S, E, 2011 A2, NZ2, [W, Fj, Sm, A], 2012 E1, 2, 3, Arg1, 2, A1, NZ1, A2, NZ2, I, S, E4, 2013 It, S1, Sm, Arg1, 2, A1, NZ1, A2, NZ2
Du Plessis, M (WP) 1971 A 1,2,3, 1974 BI 1,2, F 1,2, 1975 F 1,2, 1976 NZ 1,2,3,4, 1977 Wld, 1980 S Am 1,2, BI 1,2,3,4, S Am 4, F
Du Plessis, M J (WP) 1984 S Am 1,2, 1986 Cv 1, 2, 3, 4, 1989 Wld 1,2
Du Plessis, N J (WT) 1921 NZ 2,3, 1924 BI 1,2,3
Du Plessis, P G (NT) 1972 E
Du Plessis, T D (NT) 1980 S Am 1,2
Du Plessis, W (WP) 1980 S Am 1,2, BI 1,2,3,4, S Am 3,4, F, 1981 NZ 1,2,3, 1982 S Am 1,2
Du Plooy, A J J (EP) 1955 BI 1
Du Preez, F C H (NT) 1961 E, S, A 1,2, 1962 BI 1,2,3,4, 1963 A 1, 1964 W, F, 1965 A 1,2, NZ 1,2,3,4, 1967 F 4, 1968 BI 1,2,3,4, F 1,2, 1969 A 1,2, S, 1970 I, W, NZ 1,2,3,4, 1971 F 1,2, A 1,2,3
Du Preez, G J D (GL) 2002 Sm (R), A 1(R)
Du Preez, J G H (WP) 1956 NZ 1
Du Preez, P F (BB, Suntory Sungoliaths) 2004 I1, 2, W1, PI(R), NZ1, A1, NZ2(R), A2(R), W2, I3, E, S, Arg, 2005 U(R), F1, 2(R), A1(R), 2(R), 3, NZ1(R), A4(R), 2006 S1, 2, F, A1(R), NZ1, A2, NZ2, 3, A3, 2007 Nm, S, [Sm, E1, US, Fj, Arg, E2], 2008 Arg(R), NZ3, A2, 3, W3, 2009 BI 1, 2, 3, NZ1, 2, A1, 2, 3, NZ3, F, It, I, 2011 A2, NZ2, [W, Fj, Nm(R), Sm, A], 2013 Arg1(R), A2, NZ2
Du Preez, R J (N) 1992 NZ, A, 1993 F 1,2, A 1,2,3
Du Preez, W H (FS) 2009 It
Du Rand, J A (R, NT) 1949 NZ 2,3, 1951 S, I, W, 1952 E, F, 1953 A 1,2,3,4, 1955 BI 1,2,3,4, 1956 A 1,2, NZ 1,2,3,4
Du Randt, J P (OFS, FS) 1994 Arg 1,2, S, W, 1995 WS, [A, WS, F, NZ], 1996 Fj, A 1, NZ 1, A 2, NZ 2,3,4, 1997 Tg, BI 1,2,3, NZ 1, A 1, NZ 2, A 2, It, F 1,2, E, S, 1999 NZ 1, A 1, NZ 2, A 2, [S, Sp (R), U, E, A 3, NZ 3], 2004 I1,2,W1,PI,NZ1,A1,NZ2, A2, W2, I3, E, S(R), Arg(R), 2005 U(R), F1, A1, NZ1, A4, NZ2, Arg, W(R), F3, 2006 S1, 2, F, A1, NZ1, A2, NZ2, 3, A3, 2007 Sm, NZ1, Nm, S, [Sm, E1, US, Fj, Arg, E2]
Du Toit, A F (WP) 1928 NZ 3,4
Du Toit, B A (Tvl) 1938 BI 1,2,3
Du Toit, G S (GW, WP) 1998 I 1, 1999 It 1,2, W (R), NZ 1, 2, 2004 I1, W1(R), A1(R), S(R), Arg, 2006 S1(R), 2(R), F(R)
Du Toit, P A (NT) 1949 NZ 2,3,4, 1951 S, I, W, 1952 E, F
Du Toit, P G (WP) 1981 NZ 1, 1982 S Am 1,2, 1984 E 1,2
Du Toit, P S (WP) 1958 F 1,2, 1960 NZ 1,2,3,4, W, I, 1961 E, S, F, I, A 1,2
Duvenhage, F P (GW) 1949 NZ 1,3

Edwards, P (NT) 1980 S Am 1,2
Ellis, J H (SWA) 1965 NZ 1,2,3,4, 1967 F 1,2,3,4, 1968 BI 1,2,3,4, F 1,2, 1969 A 1,2,3,4, S, 1970 I, W, NZ 1,2,3,4, 1971 F 1,2, A 1,2,3, 1972 E, 1974 BI 1,2,3,4, F 1,2, 1976 NZ 1
Ellis, M C (Tvl) 1921 NZ 2,3, 1924 BI 1,2,3,4
Els, W W (OFS) 1997 A 2(R)
Engelbrecht, J J (BB) 2012 Arg1(R), 2013 It, S1, Sm, Arg1, 2, A1, NZ1, A2, NZ2
Engelbrecht, J P (WP) 1960 S, W, I, 1961 E, S, F, A 1,2, 1962 BI 2,3,4, 1963 A 2,3, 1964 W, F, 1965 I, S, A 1,2, NZ 1,2,3,4, 1967 F 1,2,3,4, 1968 BI 1,2, F 1,2, 1969 A 1,2
Erasmus, F S (NT, EP) 1986 Cv 3,4, 1989 Wld 2
Erasmus, J C (OFS, GL) 1997 BI 3, A 2, It, F 1,2, S, 1998 I 1,2, W 1, E 1, A 1, NZ 2, A 2, S, W 2, I 3, E 2, 1999 It 1,2, W, A 1, NZ 2, A 2, [S, U, E, A 3, NZ 3], 2000 C, E 1, A 1, NZ 1,2, A 3, 2001 F 1,2
Esterhuizen, G (GL) 2000 NZ 1(R),2, A 3, Arg, I, W (R), E 3(t)
Etlinger, T E (WP) 1896 BI 4
Etzebeth, E (WP) 2012 E1, 2, 3, Arg1, 2, A1, 2, NZ2, I, S, E4, 2013 It, S1, Sm, Arg1, 2, A1, NZ1, A2, NZ2

Ferreira, C (OFS) 1986 Cv 1,2
Ferreira, P S (WP) 1984 S Am 1,2
Ferris, H H (Tvl) 1903 BI 3
Fleck R F (WP) 1999 It 1,2, NZ 1(R), A 1, NZ 2(R), A 2, [S, U, E, A 3, NZ 3], 2000 C, E 1,2, A 1, NZ 1, A 2, NZ 2, A 3, Arg, I, W, E 3, 2001 F 1(R),2, It 1, NZ 1, A 1,2, 2002 S, E
Floors, L (FS) 2006 E2
Forbes, H H (Tvl) 1896 BI 2
Fortuin, B A (FS) 2006 I, 2007 A2
Fourie, C (EP) 1974 F 1,2, 1975 F 1,2
Fourie, J (GL, WP) 2003 [U, Gg, Sm(R), NZ(R)], 2004 I2, E(R), S, Arg, 2005 U(R), F2(R), A1(R), 2, 3, NZ1, A4, NZ2, Arg, W, F3, 2006 S1, A1, NZ1, A2, NZ2, 3, A3, 2007 Sm(R), A1, NZ1, Nm, S, [Sm, E1, US, Fj, Arg, E2], W, 2008 Arg(R), W3(R), S(R), E(R), 2009 BI 1(R), 2(R), 3, NZ1, 2, A1, 2, 3, NZ3, F, It, I, 2010 W1, F, It2, NZ1, 2, A1, 2, 3, 2011 A2, NZ2, [W, Fj, Nm, Sm, A]
Fourie, T T (SET) 1974 BI 3
Fourie, W L (SWA) 1958 F 1,2
Francis, J A J (Tvl) 1912 S, I, W, 1913 E, F
Frederickson, C A (Tvl) 1974 BI 2, 1980 S Am 1,2
Frew, A (Tvl) 1903 BI 1
Froneman, D C (OFS) 1977 Wld
Froneman, I L (Bor) 1933 A 1
Fuls, H T (Tvl, EP) 1992 NZ (R), 1993 F 1,2, A 1,2,3, Arg 1,2
Fry, S P (WP) 1951 S, I, W, 1952 E, F, 1953 A 1,2,3,4, 1955 BI 1,2,3,4
Fynn, E E (N) 2001 F 1, It 1(R)
Fyvie, W (N) 1996 NZ 4(t & R), 5(R), Arg 2(R)

Gage, J H (OFS) 1933 A 1
Gainsford, J L (WP) 1960 S, NZ 1,2,3,4, W, I, 1961 E, S, F, A 1,2, 1962 BI 1,2,3,4, 1963 A 1,2,3,4, 1964 W, F, 1965 I, S, A 1,2, NZ 1,2,3,4, 1967 F 1,2,3
Garvey, A C (N) 1996 Arg 1,2, F 1,2, W, 1997 Tg, BI 1,2,3(R), A 1(t), It, F 1,2, E, S, 1998 I 1,2, W 1, E1, A 1, NZ 1,2 A 2, W 2, S, I 3, E 2, 1999 [Sp]
Geel, P J (OFS) 1949 NZ 3
Geere, V (Tvl) 1933 A 1,2,3,4,5
Geffin, A O (Tvl) 1949 NZ 1,2,3,4, 1951 S, I, W
Geldenhuys, A (EP) 1992 NZ, A, F 1,2
Geldenhuys, S B (NT) 1981 NZ 2,3, US, 1982 S Am 1,2, 1989 Wld 1,2
Gentles, T A (WP) 1955 BI 1,2,4, 1956 NZ 2,3, 1958 F 2
Geraghty, E M (Bor) 1949 NZ 4
Gerber, D M (EP, WP) 1980 S Am 3,4, F, 1981 I 1,2, NZ 1,2,3, US, 1982 S Am 1,2, 1984 E 1,2, S Am 1,2, 1986 Cv 1,2,3,4, 1992 NZ, A, F 1,2, E

Gerber, H J (WP) 2003 S 1,2
Gerber, M C (EP) 1958 F 1,2, 1960 S
Gericke, F W (Tvl) 1960 S
Germishuys, J S (OFS, Tvl) 1974 BI 2, 1976 NZ 1,2,3,4, 1977 Wld, 1980 S Am 1,2, BI 1,2,3,4, S Am 3,4, F, 1981 I 1,2, NZ 2,3, US
Gibbs, B (GW) 1903 BI 2
Goosen, C P (OFS) 1965 NZ 2
Goosen, J L (FS) 2012 A1(R),NZ1(R),A2,NZ2
Gorton, H C (Tvl) 1896 BI 1
Gould, R L (N) 1968 BI 1,2,3,4
Grant, P J (WP) 2007 A2(R),NZ2(R), 2008 W1(t&R),It(R),A1(R)
Gray, B G (WP) 1931 W, 1932 E, S, 1933 A 5
Greeff, W W (WP) 2002 Arg (R), Sm, NZ 1, A 1, NZ 2, A 2, F, S, E, 2003 [U,Gg]
Greenwood, C M (WP) 1961 I
Greyling, M D (BB) 2011 A1,NZ1, 2012 NZ1(R)
Greyling, P J F (OFS) 1967 F 1,2,3,4, 1968 BI 1, F 1,2, 1969 A 1,2,3,4, S, E, 1970 I, W, NZ 1,2,3,4, 1971 F 1,2, A 1,2,3, 1972 E
Grobler, C J (OFS) 1974 BI 4, 1975 F 1,2
Guthrie, F H (WP) 1891 BI 1,3, 1896 BI 1

Habana, B G (GL, BB, WP, Toulon) 2004 E(R),S,Arg, 2005 U, F1, 2, A1, 2, 3, NZ1, A4, NZ2, Arg, W, F3, 2006 S2, F, A1, NZ1, A2, NZ2, 3, I, E1, 2, 2007 E1, 2, S, [Sm, E1, Tg(R), US, Fj, Arg, E2], W, 2008 W1, 2, It, NZ1, 2, A1, NZ3, W3, S, E, 2009 BI 1, 2, NZ1, 2, A1, 2, 3, NZ3, F, It, I, 2010 F, It 1, 2, NZ1, 2, A1, NZ3, A2, 3, I, W2, 2011 A2, NZ2, [W, Nm, Sm, A], 2012 E1, 2, 3, Arg1, 2, A1, NZ1, A2, NZ2, 2013 It, S1, Sm, Arg1, 2, A1, NZ1, A2, NZ2
Hahn, C H L (Tvl) 1910 BI 1,2,3
Hall, D B (GL) 2001 F 1,2, NZ 1, A 1,2, NZ 2, It 2, E, US, 2002 Sm, NZ 1,2, A 2
Halstead, T M (N) 2001 F 3, It 2, E, US (R), 2003 S 1,2
Hamilton, F (EP) 1891 BI 1
Hargreaves, A J (NS) 2010 W1(R),It 1(R), 2011 A1,NZ1
Harris, T A (Tvl) 1937 NZ 2,3, 1938 BI 1,2,3
Hartley, A J (WP) 1891 BI 3
Hattingh, H (NT) 1992 A (R), F 2(R), E, 1994 Arg 1,2
Hattingh, L B (OFS) 1933 A 2
Heatlie, B H (WP) 1891 BI 2,3, 1896 BI 1,4, 1903 BI 1,3
Hendricks, M (Bol) 1998 I 2(R), W 1(R)
Hendriks, P (Tvl) 1992 NZ, A, 1994 S, W, 1995 [A, R, C], 1996 A 1, NZ 1, A 2, NZ 2,3,4,5
Hepburn, T B (WP) 1896 BI 4
Heunis, J W (NT) 1981 NZ 3(R), US, 1982 S Am 1,2, 1984 E 1,2, S Am 1,2, 1986 Cv 1,2,3,4, 1989 Wld 1,2
Hill, R A (R) 1960 W, I, 1961 I, A 1,2, 1962 BI 4, 1963 A 3
Hills, W G (NT) 1992 F 1,2, E, 1993 F 1,2, A 1
Hirsch, J G (EP) 1906 I, 1910 BI 1
Hobson, T E C (WP) 1903 BI 3
Hoffman, R S (Bol) 1953 A 3
Holton, D N (EP) 1960 S
Honiball, H W (N) 1993 A 3(R), Arg 2, 1995 WS (R), 1996 Fj, A 1, NZ 5, Arg 1,2, F 1,2, W, 1997 Tg, BI 1,2,3(R), NZ 1(R), A 1(R), NZ 2, A 2, It, F 1,2, E, 1998 W 1(R), E 1, A 1, NZ 1,2, A 2, W 2, S, I 3, E 2, 1999 [A 3(R), NZ 3]
Hopwood, D J (WP) 1960 S, NZ 3,4, W, 1961 E, S, F, I, A 1,2, 1962 BI 1,2,3,4, 1963 A 1,2,4, 1964 W, F, 1965 S, NZ 3,4
Hougaard, D J (BB) 2003 [U(R), E(R), Gg, Sm,NZ], 2007 Sm, A2, NZ2
Hougaard, F (BB) 2009 It(R), 2010 A1(R), NZ3, A2, 3, W2(R), S, E(t&R), 2011 A2(t), NZ2(R), [W(R), Fj(R), Nm, Sm(R), A(R)], 2012 E1, 2, 3, Arg1, 2, A1, NZ1, A2, NZ2, I, S, E4
Howe, B F (Bor) 1956 NZ 1,4
Howe-Browne, N R F G (WP) 1910 BI 1,2,3
Hugo, D P (WP) 1989 Wld 1,2
Human, D C F (WP) 2002 W 1,2, Arg (R), Sm (R)
Hurter, M H (NT) 1995 [R, C], W, 1996 Fj, A 1, NZ 1,2,3,4,5, 1997 NZ 1,2, A 2

Immelman, J H (WP) 1913 F

Jackson, D C (WP) 1906 I, W, E
Jackson, J S (WP) 1903 BI 2
Jacobs, A A (Falcons, NS) 2001 It 2(R), US, 2002 W 1(R), Arg, Sm (R), NZ 1(t+R), A 1(R), F, S, E (R), 2008 W1, 2, NZ1, 2, Arg, NZ3, A2, 3, W3, S, E, 2009 BI 1, 2, NZ2(R), A1(R), 2(R), 3(R), NZ3(R), F, It, 2010 I(R), E(R), 2011 A1(R), NZ1
James, A D (N, Bath, GL) 2001 F 1,2, NZ 1, A 1,2, NZ 2, 2002 F (R), S, E, 2006 NZ1, A2, NZ2, 3(R), E1, 2007 E1, 2, A1, NZ1, Nm, S, [Sm, E1, US, Fj, Arg, E2], 2008 W1, 2, NZ1, 2, A1, Arg, NZ3, A2, 3, 2010 It1, 2(R), NZ1(R), A1(R), 2(R), 2011 A2, [W(R)]
Jansen, E (OFS) 1981 NZ 1
Jansen, J S (OFS) 1970 NZ 1,2,3,4, 1971 F 1,2, A 1,2,3, 1972 E
Jantjes, C A (GL, WP) 2001 It 1, A 1,2, NZ 2, F 3, It 2, E, US, 2005 Arg, W, 2007 W(R), 2008 W1, 2, It, NZ1, 2(R), A1, Arg, NZ3(R), A2, 3, W3, S, E
Jantjies, E T (GL) 2012 A2(R),NZ2(R)
Januarie, E R (GL, WP) 2005 U, F2, A1, 2, 3(R), NZ1, A4, NZ2, 2006 S1(R), 2(R), F(R), A1, I, E1, 2, 2007 E1, 2, Sm, Nm(R), [Sm(R), Tg], W, 2008 W2, It, NZ1, 2, A1, Arg, NZ3(R), A2(R), 3(R), W3(R), S, E, 2009 BI 1(R), NZ1(R), 2(R), A1(R), 2(R), NZ3(R), 2010 W1, F, It 1, 2, NZ1, 2, 3(R)
Jennings, C B (Bor) 1937 NZ 1
Johnson, A F (FS) 2011 A1,NZ1(t&R),2(t&R)
Johnson, G K (Tvl) 1993 Arg 2, 1994 NZ 3, Arg 1, 1995 WS, [R, C, WS]
Johnstone, P G A (WP) 1951 S, I, W, 1952 E, F, 1956 A 1, NZ 1,2,4
Jones, C H (Tvl) 1903 BI 1,2
Jones, P S T (WP) 1896 BI 1,3,4
Jordaan, N (BB) 2002 E (R)
Jordaan, R P (NT) 1949 NZ 1,2,3,4
Joubert, A J (OFS, N) 1989 Wld 1(R), 1993 A 3, Arg 1, 1994 E 1,2, NZ 1,2(R), 3, Arg 2, S, W, 1995 [A, C, WS, F, NZ], W, It, E, 1996 Fj, A 1, NZ 1,3,4,5, Arg 1,2, F 1,2, W, 1997 Tg, BI 1,2, A 2
Joubert, M C (Bol, WP) 2001 NZ 1, 2002 W 1,2, Arg (R), Sm, NZ 1, A1, NZ 2, A 2, F (R), 2003 S 2, Arg, A 1, 2004 I1, 2, W1, PI, NZ1, A1, NZ2, A2, W2, I3, E, S, Arg, 2005 U, F1, 2, A1
Joubert, S J (WP) 1906 I, W, E
Julies, W (Bol, SWD, GL) 1999 [Sp], 2004 I1,2,W1,S,Arg, 2005 A2(R),3(t), 2006 F(R), 2007 Sm, [Tg]

Kahts, W J H (NT) 1980 BI 1,2,3, S Am 3,4, F, 1981 I 1,2, NZ 2, 1982 S Am 1,2
Kaminer, J (Tvl) 1958 F 2
Kankowski, R (NS) 2007 W, 2008 W2(R), It, A1(R), W3(R), S(R), E(R), 2009 BI3, NZ3(R), F, It, 2010 W1(R), It 1(R), NZ2(R), A1, 3(R), S, 2011 A1(R), NZ1(R), 2012 E3(R)
Kayser, D J (EP, N) 1999 It 2(R), A 1(R), NZ 2, A 2, [S, Sp (R), U, E, A 3], 2001 It 1(R), NZ 1(R), A 2(R), NZ 2(R)
Kebble, G R (N) 1993 Arg 1,2, 1994 NZ 1(R), 2
Kelly, E W (GW) 1896 BI 3
Kempson, R B (N, WP, Ulster) 1998 I 2(R), W 1, E 1, A 1, NZ 1,2 A 2, W 2, S, I 3, E 2, 1999 It 1,2, W, 2000 C, E 1,2, A 1, NZ 1, A 2,3, Arg, I, W, E 3, 2001 F 1,2(R), NZ 1, A 1,2, NZ 2, 2003 S 1(R),2(R), Arg, A 1(R), NZ 1(R), A 2
Kenyon, B J (Bor) 1949 NZ 4
Kipling, H G (GW) 1931 W, I, 1932 E, S, 1933 A 1,2,3,4,5
Kirchner, Z (BB, Leinster) 2009 BI 3, F, It, I, 2010 W1(R), F, It1,NZ1, 2, A1, I, W2(R), S, E, 2012 E1, Arg1, 2, A1, NZ1, A2, NZ2, I, S, E4, 2013 A1, NZ1, A2, NZ2
Kirkpatrick, A I (GW) 1953 A 2, 1956 NZ 2, 1958 F 1, 1960 S, NZ 1,2,3,4, W, I, 1961 E, S, F
Knight, A S (Tvl) 1912 S, I, W, 1913 E, F
Knoetze, F (WP) 1989 Wld 1,2
Koch, A C (Bol) 1949 NZ 2, 3, 4, 1951 S, I, W, 1952 E, F, 1953 A 1, 2, 4, 1955 BI 1, 2, 3, 4, 1956 A 1, NZ 2, 3, 1958 F 1, 2, 1960 NZ 1, 2
Koch, H V (WP) 1949 NZ 1,2,3,4
Koen, L J (GL, BB) 2000 A 1, 2001 It 2, E, US, 2003 S 1, 2, Arg, A 1, NZ 1, A 2, NZ 2, [U, E, Sm(R), NZ(R)]
Kolisi, S (WP) 2013 S1(R), Sm(R), Arg1(R), 2(R), A1(R), NZ1(R), A2(R), NZ2(R)
Kotze, G J M (WP) 1967 F 1,2,3,4
Krantz, E F W (OFS) 1976 NZ 1, 1981 I 1,
Krige, C P J (WP) 1999 It 2, W, NZ 1, 2000 C (R), E 1(R),2, A 1(R), NZ 1, A 2, NZ 2, A 3, Arg, I, W, E 3, 2001 F 1,2, It 1(R), A 1(t+R), It 2(R), E (R), 2002 W 2, Arg, Sm, NZ 1, A

1, NZ 2, A 2, F, S, E, 2003 Arg, A 1, NZ 1, A 2, NZ 2, [E, Sm, NZ]

Krige, J D (WP) 1903 BI 1,3, 1906 S, I, W

Kritzinger, J L (Tvl) 1974 BI 3,4, F 1,2, 1975 F 1,2, 1976 NZ 4

Kroon, C M (EP) 1955 BI 1

Kruger, P E (Tvl) 1986 Cv 3,4

Kruger, P J J (BB, Racing Metro) 2012 E1, 2, 3, A1, NZ1, I, S, E4, 2013 It, S1, Sm(t&R), Arg1, 2, A1(R), NZ1(R), A2(R), NZ2

Kruger, R J (NT, BB) 1993 Arg 1,2, 1994 S, W, 1995 WS, [A, R, WS, F, NZ], W, It, E, 1996 Fj, A 1, NZ 1, A 2, NZ 2,3,4,5, Arg 1,2, F 1,2, W, 1997 Tg, BI 1,2, NZ 1, A 1, NZ 2, 1999 NZ 2, A 2(R), [Sp, NZ 3(R)]

Kruger, T L (Tvl) 1921 NZ 1,2, 1924 BI 1,2,3,4, 1928 NZ 1,2

Kruger, W (BB) 2011 A1,NZ1, 2012 E2(R),3(R)

Kuhn, S P (Tvl) 1960 NZ 3,4, W, I, 1961 E, S, F, I, A 1,2, 1962 BI 1,2,3,4, 1963 A 1,2,3, 1965 I, S

Labuschagne, J J (GL) 2000 NZ 1(R), 2002 W 1,2, Arg, NZ 1, A 1, NZ 2, A2, F, S, E

La Grange, J B (WP) 1924 BI 3,4

Lambie, P J (NS) 2010 I(R), W2(R), S(R), E(R), 2011 A1(R), NZ1, 2, [Fj, Nm, Sm, A], 2012 E1(R), 2, A1(R), NZ1(R), A2(R), NZ2(R), I, S, E4, 2013 It(R), S1(R), Sm(R), Arg1(R), 2(R), A1(R), NZ1(R), A2(R), NZ2(R)

Larard, A (Tvl) 1896 BI 2,4

Lategan, M T (WP) 1949 NZ 1,2,3,4, 1951 S, I, W, 1952 E, F, 1953 A 1,2

Laubscher, T G (WP) 1994 Arg 1,2, S, W, 1995 It, E

Lawless, M J (WP) 1964 F, 1969 E (R), 1970 I, W

Ledger, S H (GW) 1912 S, I, 1913 E, F

Leonard, A (WP, SWD) 1999 A 1, [Sp]

Le Roux, A H (OFS, N) 1994 E 1, 1998 I 1,2, W 1(R), E 1(R), A 1(R), NZ 1(R),2(R), A 2(R), W 2(R), S (R), I 3(R), E 2(t+R), 1999 It 1(R),2(R), W (R), NZ 1(R), A 1(R), NZ 2(R), A 2(R), [S(R), Sp, U (R), E (R), A 3(R), NZ 3(R)], 2000 E 1(t+R),2(R), A 1(R),2(R), NZ 2, A 3(R), Arg (R), I (t), W (R), E 3(R), 2001 F 1(R),2, It 1, NZ 1(R), A 1(R),2(R), NZ 2(R), F 3, It 2, E, US (R), 2002 W 1(R),2(R), Arg, NZ 1(R), A 1(R), NZ 2(R), A 2(R)

Le Roux, H P (Tvl) 1993 F 1,2, 1994 E 1,2, NZ 1,2,3, Arg 2, S, W, 1995 WS [A, R, C (R), WS, F, NZ], W, It, E, 1996 Fj, NZ 2, Arg 1,2, F 1,2, W

Le Roux, J H S (Tvl) 1994 E 2, NZ 1,2

Le Roux, M (OFS) 1980 BI 1,2,3,4, S Am 3,4, F, 1981 I 1

Le Roux, P A (WP) 1906 I, W, E

Le Roux, W J (Griquas) 2013 It,S1,Sm,Arg1,2,A1,NZ1,A2,NZ2

Liebenberg, C R (WP) 2012 Arg2(R), A1(R), NZ1(R), A2(R), NZ2(R)

Little, E M (GW) 1891 BI 1,3

Lobberts, H (BB) 2006 E1(R), 2007 NZ2(R)

Lochner, G P (WP) 1955 BI 3, 1956 A 1,2, NZ 1,2,3,4, 1958 F 1,2

Lochner, G P (EP) 1937 NZ 3, 1938 BI 1,2

Lockyear, R J (GW) 1960 NZ 1,2,3,4, 1960 I, 1961 F

Lombard, A C (EP) 1910 BI 2

Lombard, F (FS) 2002 S, E

Lötter, D (Tvl) 1993 F 2, A 1,2

Lotz, J W (Tvl) 1937 A 1,2, NZ 1,2,3, 1938 BI 1,2,3

Loubscher, R I P (EP, N) 2002 W 1, 2003 S 1, [U(R),Gg]

Loubser, J A (WP) 1903 BI 3, 1906 S, I, W, E, 1910 BI 1,3

Lourens, M J (NT) 1968 BI 2,3,4

Louw, F H (WP) 2002 W 2(R), Arg, Sm

Louw, J S (Tvl) 1891 BI 1,2,3

Louw, L-F P (WP, Bath) 2010 W1, F, It 1, 2, NZ1, 2, 3(R), 2011 [Fj(t), Nm(t&R), A(R)], 2012 A1(R), NZ1, A2, NZ2, I, S, E4, 2013 It, Sm, Arg1, 2, A1, NZ1, A2, NZ2

Louw, M J (Tvl) 1971 A 2,3

Louw, M M (WP) 1928 NZ 3,4, 1931 W, I, 1932 E, S, 1933 A 1, 2, 3, 4, 5, 1937 A 1, 2, NZ 2,3, 1938 BI 1, 2, 3

Louw, R J (WP) 1980 S Am 1,2, BI 1,2,3,4 S Am 3,4, F, 1981 I 1,2, NZ 1,3, 1982 S Am 1,2, 1984 E 1,2, S Am 1,2

Louw, S C (WP) 1933 A 1, 2, 3, 4, 5, 1937 A 1, NZ 1, 2, 3, 1938 BI 1, 2, 3

Lubbe, E (GW) 1997 Tg, BI 1

Luyt, F P (WP) 1910 BI 1,2,3, 1912 S, I, W, 1913 E

Luyt, J D (EP) 1912 S, W, 1913 E, F

Luyt, R R (W P) 1910 BI 2,3, 1912 S, I, W, 1913 E, F

Lyons, D J (EP) 1896 BI 1

Lyster, P J (N) 1933 A 2,5, 1937 NZ 1

McCallum, I D (WP) 1970 NZ 1,2,3,4, 1971 F 1,2, A 1,2,3, 1974 BI 1,2

McCallum, R J (WP) 1974 BI 1

McCulloch, J D (GW) 1913 E, F

MacDonald, A W (R) 1965 A 1, NZ 1,2,3,4

Macdonald, D A (WP) 1974 BI 2

Macdonald, I (Tvl) 1992 NZ, A, 1993 F 1, A 3, 1994 E 2, 1995 WS (R)

McDonald, J A J (WP) 1931 W, I, 1932 E, S

McEwan, W M C (Tvl) 1903 BI 1,3

McHardy, E E (OFS) 1912 S, I, W, 1913 E, F

McKendrick, J A (WP) 1891 BI 3

McLeod, C (NS) 2011 NZ1(R)

Maku, B G (BB) 2010 It1(R)

Malan, A S (Tvl) 1960 NZ 1,2,3,4, W, I, 1961 E, S, F, 1962 BI 1, 1963 A 1,2,3, 1964 W, 1965 I, S

Malan, A W (NT) 1989 Wld 1,2, 1992 NZ, A, F 1,2, E

Malan, E (NT) 1980 BI 3(R), 4

Malan, G F (WP) 1958 F 2, 1960 NZ 1,3,4, 1961 E, S, F, 1962 BI 1,2,3, 1963 A 1,2,4, 1964 W, 1965 A 1,2, NZ 1,2

Malan, P (Tvl) 1949 NZ 4

Mallett, N V H (WP) 1984 S Am 1,2

Malotana, K (Bor) 1999 [Sp]

Mans, W J (WP) 1965 I, S

Marais, C F (WP) 1999 It 1(R),2(R), 2000 C, E 1,2, A 1, NZ 1, A 2, NZ 2, A 3, Arg (R), W (R)

Marais, F P (Bol) 1949 NZ 1,2, 1951 S, 1953 A 1,2

Marais, J F K (WP) 1963 A 3, 1964 W, F, 1965 I, S, A 2, 1968 BI, 1,2,3,4, F 1,2, 1969 A 1,2,3,4, S, E, 1970 I, W, NZ 1,2,3,4, 1971 F 1,2, A 1,2,3, 1974 BI 1,2,3,4, F 1,2

Maré, D S (Tvl) 1906 S

Marsberg, A F W (GW) 1906 S, W, E

Marsberg, P A (GW) 1910 BI 1

Martheze, W C (GW) 1903 BI 2, 1906 I, W

Martin, H J (Tvl) 1937 A 2

Matfield, V (BB) 2001 It 1(R), NZ 1, A 2, NZ 2, F 3, It 2, E, US, 2002 W 1, Sm, NZ 1, A 1, NZ 2(R), 2003 S 1,2, Arg, A 1, NZ 1, A 2, NZ 2, [U, E, Sm, NZ], 2004 I1, 2, W1, NZ2, A2, W2, I3, E, S, Arg, 2005 F1, 2, A1, 2, 3, NZ1, A4, NZ2, Arg, W, F3, 2006 S1, 2, F, A1, NZ1, A2, NZ2, 3, A3, 2007 E1, 2, A1, NZ1, Nm, S, [Sm, E1, Tg(R), US, Fj, Arg, E2], 2008 W1(R), 2, It, NZ1, 2, A1, Arg, NZ3, A2, 3, W3, S, E, 2009 BI 1, 2, 3, NZ1, 2, A1, 2, 3, NZ3, F, It(R), I, 2010 W1, F, It 1, NZ1, 2, A1, NZ3, A2, 3, I, W2, S, E, 2011 A2, NZ2, [W, Sm, A]

Mellet, T B (GW) 1896 BI 2

Mellish, F W (WP) 1921 NZ 1,3, 1924 BI 1,2,3,4

Mentz, H (N) 2004 I1,W1(R)

Merry, J (EP) 1891 BI 1

Metcalf, H D (Bor) 1903 BI 2

Meyer, C du P (WP) 1921 NZ 1,2,3

Meyer, P J (GW) 1896 BI 1

Meyer, W (OFS, GL) 1997 S (R), 1999 It 2, NZ 1(R), A 1(R), 2000 C (R), E 1, NZ 1(R),2(R), Arg, I, W, E 3, 2001 F 1(R),2, It 1, F 3(R), It 2, E, US (t+R), 2002 W 1,2, Arg, NZ 1,2, A 2, F

Michau, J M (Tvl) 1921 NZ 1

Michau, J P (WP) 1921 NZ 1,2,3

Millar, W A (WP) 1906 E, 1910 BI 2,3, 1912 I, W, 1913 F

Mills, W J (WP) 1910 BI 2

Moll, T (Tvl) 1910 BI 2

Montini, P E (WP) 1956 A 1,2

Montgomery, P C (WP, Newport, N, Perpignan) 1997 BI 2,3, NZ 1, A 1, NZ 2, A 2, F 1,2, E, S, 1998 I 1,2, W 1, E 1, A 1, NZ 1,2, A 2, W 2, S, I 3, E 2, 1999 It 1,2, W, NZ 1, A 1, NZ 2, A 2, [S, U, E, A 3, NZ 3], 2000 C, E 1,2, A 1, NZ 1, A 2(R), Arg, I, W, E 3, 2001 F 1, 2(t), It 1, NZ 1, F 3(R), It 2(R), 2004 I2, W1, PI, NZ1, A1, NZ2, A2, W2, I3, E, S, 2005 U, F1, 2, A1, 2, 3, NZ1, A4, NZ2, Arg, W, F3, 2006 S1, 2, F, A1, NZ1, A2, NZ2, 2007 E1, 2, Sm(R), A1, NZ1, Nm, S, [Sm, E1, Tg(R), US, Fj, Arg, E2], 2008 W1(R), 2(R), NZ1(R), 2, Arg(R), NZ3, A2(R), 3(R)

Moolman, L C (NT) 1977 Wld, 1980 S Am 1,2, BI 1,2,3,4, S Am 3,4, F, 1981 I 1,2, NZ 1,2,3, US, 1982 S Am 1,2, 1984 S Am 1,2, 1986 Cv 1,2,3,4

Mordt, R H (Z-R, NT) 1980 S Am 1,2, BI 1,2,3,4, S Am 3,4, F, 1981 I 2, NZ 1,2,3, US, 1982 S Am 1,2, 1984 S Am 1,2

Morkel, D A (Tvl) 1903 BI 1

Morkel, D F T (Tvl) 1906 I, E, 1910 BI 1,3, 1912 S, I, W, 1913 E, F

Morkel, H J (WP) 1921 NZ 1
Morkel, H W (WP) 1921 NZ 1,2
Morkel, J A (WP) 1921 NZ 2,3
Morkel, J W H (WP) 1912 S, I, W, 1913 E, F
Morkel, P G (WP) 1912 S, I, W, 1913 E, F, 1921 NZ 1,2,3
Morkel, P K (WP) 1928 NZ 4
Morkel, W H (WP) 1910 BI 3, 1912 S, I, W, 1913 E, F, 1921 NZ 1,2,3
Morkel, W S (Tvl) 1906 S, I, W, E
Moss, C (N) 1949 NZ 1,2,3,4
Mostert, G (Stade Français) 2011 NZ1,A2(R)
Mostert, P J (WP) 1921 NZ 1,2,3, 1924 BI 1,2,4, 1928 NZ 1,2,3,4, 1931 W, I, 1932 E, S
Mtawarira, T (NS) 2008 W2, It, A1(R), Arg, NZ3, A2, 3, W3, S, E, 2009 BI 1, 2, 3, NZ1, 2, A1, 2, 3, NZ3, F, It(R), I, 2010 I, W2, S, E, 2011 A2, NZ2(R), [W, Fj(R), Nm(R), Sm], 2012 E1, 2, 3, Arg1, 2, A1, NZ1, A2, NZ2, 2013 It, S1, Sm, Arg1, 2, A1, NZ1, A2, NZ2
Muir, D J (WP) 1997 It, F 1,2, E, S
Mujati, B V (WP) 2008 W1, It(R), NZ1(R), 2(t), A1(R), Arg(R), NZ3(R), A2(R), 3, W3(t), S(R), E(R)
Mulder, J C (Tvl, GL) 1994 NZ 2,3, S, W, 1995 WS, [A, WS, F, NZ], W, It, E, 1996 Fj, A 1, NZ 1, A 2, NZ 2,5, Arg 1,2, F 1,2, W, 1997 Tg, BI 1, 1999 It 1(R),2, W, NZ 1, 2000 C(R), A 1, E 3, 2001 F 1, It 1
Muller, G H (WP) 1969 A 3,4, S, 1970 W, NZ 1,2,3,4, 1971 F 1,2, 1972 E, 1974 BI 1,3,4
Muller, G J (NS, Ulster) 2006 S1(R), NZ1(R), A2, NZ2, 3, A3, I(R), E1, 2, 2007 E1(R), 2(R), Sm(R), A1(R), NZ1(R), A2, NZ2, Nm(R), [Sm(R), E1(R), Fj(t&R), Arg(t&R)], W, 2009 BI 3, 2011 [W(R)]
Muller, G P (GL) 2003 A 2, NZ 2, [E,Gg(R),Sm,NZ]
Muller, H L (OFS) 1986 Cv 4(R), 1989 Wld 1(R)
Muller, H S V (Tvl) 1949 NZ 1,2,3,4, 1951 S, I, W, 1952 E, F, 1953 A 1,2,3,4
Muller, L J J (N) 1992 NZ, A
Muller, P G (N) 1992 NZ, A, F 1,2, E, 1993 F 1,2, A 1,2,3, Arg 1,2, 1994 E 1,2, NZ 1, S, W, 1998 I 1,2, W 1, E 1, A 1, NZ 1,2, A 2, 1999 It 1, W, NZ 1, A 1, [Sp, E, A 3, NZ 3]
Murray, W M (N) 2007 Sm,A2,NZ2
Mvovo, L N (NS) 2010 S,E, 2011 A1,NZ1, 2012 Arg1,2,A1(R)
Myburgh, F R (EP) 1896 BI 1
Myburgh, J L (NT) 1962 BI 1, 1963 A 4, 1964 W, F, 1968 BI 1,2,3, F 1,2, 1969 A 1,2,3,4, E, 1970 I, W, NZ 3,4
Myburgh, W H (WT) 1924 BI 1

Naude, J P (WP) 1963 A 4, 1965 A 1,2, NZ 1,3,4, 1967 F 1,2,3,4, 1968 BI 1,2,3,4
Ndungane, A Z (BB) 2006 A1,2,NZ2,3,A3, E1,2, 2007 E2,Nm(R), [US],W(R)
Ndungane, O M (NS) 2008 It,NZ1,A3, 2009 BI 3,A3,NZ3, 2010 W1, 2011 NZ1(R),[Fj]
Neethling, J B (WP) 1967 F 1,2,3,4, 1968 BI 4, 1969 S, 1970 NZ 1,2
Nel, J A (Tvl) 1960 NZ 1,2, 1963 A 1,2, 1965 A 2, NZ 1,2,3,4, 1970 NZ 3,4
Nel, J J (WP) 1956 A 1,2, NZ 1,2,3,4, 1958 F 1,2
Nel, P A R O (Tvl) 1903 BI 1,2,3
Nel, P J (N) 1928 NZ 1,2,3,4, 1931 W, I, 1932 E, S, 1933 A 1,3,4,5, 1937 A 1,2, NZ 2,3
Nimb, C F (WP) 1961 I
Nokwe, J L (FS) 2008 Arg,A2,3, 2009 BI 3
Nomis, S H (Tvl) 1967 F 4, 1968 BI 1,2,3,4, F 1,2, 1969 A 1,2,3,4, S, E, 1970 I, W, NZ 1,2,3,4, 1971 F 1,2, A 1,2,3, 1972 E
Nyakane, T N (FSC) 2013 It(R),S1(R),Sm(R)
Nykamp, J L (Tvl) 1933 A 2

Ochse, J K (WP) 1951 I, W, 1952 E, F, 1953 A 1,2,4
Oelofse, J S A (Tvl) 1953 A 1,2,3,4
Oliver, J F (Tvl) 1928 NZ 3,4
Olivier, E (WP) 1967 F 1,2,3,4, 1968 BI 1,2,3,4, F 1,2, 1969 A 1,2,3,4, S, E
Olivier, J (NT) 1992 F 1,2, E, 1993 F 1,2 A 1,2,3, Arg 1, 1995 W, It (R), E, 1996 Arg 1,2, F 1,2, W
Olivier, W (BB) 2006 S1(R), 2, F, A1, NZ1, A2, NZ2(R), 3, A3, I(R), E1, 2, 2007 E1, 2, NZ1(R), A2, NZ2, [E1(R), Tg, Arg(R)], W(R), 2009 BI 3, NZ1(R), 2(R), F(R), It(R), I, 2010 F, It2(R), NZ1, 2, A1, 2011 A1, NZ1(R), 2012 E1(t), 2(R), 3
Olver, E (EP) 1896 BI 1
Oosthuizen, C V (FSC) 2012 E1(t&R), NZ2(R), 2013 It(R), S1(R), Sm(R), Arg1(R), 2(R), A1(t&R), NZ1(R), A2(R), NZ2(R)
Oosthuizen, J J (WP) 1974 BI 1, F 1,2, 1975 F 1,2, 1976 NZ 1,2,3,4
Oosthuizen, O W (NT, Tvl) 1981 I 1(R), 2, NZ 2,3, US, 1982 S Am 1,2, 1984 E 1,2
Osler, B L (WP) 1924 BI 1,2,3,4, 1928 NZ 1,2,3,4, 1931 W, I, 1932 E, S, 1933 A 1,2,3,4,5
Osler, S G (WP) 1928 NZ 1
Otto, K (NT, BB) 1995 [R, C (R), WS (R)], 1997 BI 3, NZ 1, A 1, NZ 2, It, F 1,2, E, S, 1998 I 1,2, W 1, E 1, A 1, NZ 1,2, A 2, W 2, S, I 3, E 2, 1999 It 1, W, NZ 1, A 1, [S (R), Sp, U, E, A 3, NZ 3], 2000 C, E 1,2, A 1
Oxlee, K (N) 1960 NZ 1,2,3,4, W, I, 1961 S, A 1,2, 1962 BI 1,2,3,4, 1963 A 1,2,4, 1964 W, 1965 NZ 1,2

Pagel, G L (WP) 1995 [A (R), R, C, NZ (R)], 1996 NZ 5(R)
Parker, W H (EP) 1965 A 1,2
Partridge, J E C (Tvl) 1903 BI 1
Paulse, B J (WP) 1999 It 1,2, NZ 1, A 1,2(R), [S (R), Sp, NZ 3], 2000 C, E 1,2, A 1, NZ 1, A 2, NZ 2, A 3, Arg, W, E 3, 2001 F 1,2, It 1, NZ 1, A 1,2, NZ 2, F 3, It 2, E, 2002 W 1,2, Arg, Sm (R), A 1, NZ 2, A 2, F, S, E, 2003 [Gg], 2004 I1, 2, W1, PI, NZ1, A1, NZ2, A2, W2, I3, E, 2005 A2, 3, NZ1, A4, F3, 2006 S1, 2, A1(R), NZ1, 3(R), A3(R), 2007 A2,NZ2
Payn, C (N) 1924 BI 1,2
Pelser, H J M (Tvl) 1958 F 1, 1960 NZ 1,2,3,4, W, I, 1961 F, I, A 1,2
Pfaff, B D (WP) 1956 A 1
Pickard, J A J (WP) 1953 A 3,4, 1956 NZ 2, 1958 F 2
Pienaar, J F (Tvl) 1993 F 1,2, A 1,2,3, Arg 1,2, 1994 E 1,2, NZ 2,3, Arg 1,2, S, W, 1995 WS, [A, C, WS, F, NZ], W, It, E, 1996 Fj, A 1, NZ 1, A 2, NZ 2
Pienaar, R (NS, Ulster) 2006 NZ2(R), 3(R), A3(R), I(t), E1(R), 2007 E1(R), 2(R), Sm(R), A1, NZ1, A2, NZ2, Nm(R), S(R), [E1(t&R), Tg, US(R), Arg(R)], W, 2008 W1(R), It(R), NZ2(R), A1(R), 3(R), W3, S, E, 2009 BI 1, 2, 3(R), NZ1, A1(R), 2, 3, It(R), I(R), 2010 W1, F(R), It 1(R), 2(R), NZ1(R), 2(R), A1, I, W2, S(R), E, 2011 A1, NZ1, [Fj(R), Nm(R)], 2012 E1(R), 2(R), 3(R), Arg1(R), 2(R), A1, NZ1, A2, NZ2, I, S, E4, 2013 It(R), S1, Sm, Arg1, 2, A1, NZ1, 2(R)
Pienaar, Z M J (OFS) 1980 S Am 2(R), BI 1,2,3,4, S Am 3,4, F, 1981 I 1,2, NZ 1,2,3
Pietersen, J-P R (NS) 2006 A3, 2007 Sm, A1, NZ1, A2, NZ2, Nm, S, [Sm, E1, Tg, US(R), Fj, Arg, E2], W, 2008 NZ2, A1, Arg, NZ3, A2, W3, S, E, 2009 BI 1, 2, NZ1, 2, A1, 2, F, It, I, 2010 NZ3, A2, 3, 2011 A2, NZ2, [W, Fj, Sm, A], 2012 E1, 2, 3, I, S, E4
Pitzer, G (NT) 1967 F 1,2,3,4, 1968 BI 1,2,3,4, F 1,2, 1969 A 3,4
Pope, C F (WP) 1974 BI 1,2,3,4, 1975 F 1,2, 1976 NZ 2,3,4
Potgieter, D J (BB) 2009 I(t), 2010 W1,F(t&R),It 1,2(R),A1(R)
Potgieter, H J (OFS) 1928 NZ 1,2
Potgieter, H L (OFS) 1977 Wld
Potgieter, U J (BB) 2012 E3,Arg1(R),2
Powell, A W (GW) 1896 BI 3
Powell, J M (GW) 1891 BI 2, 1896 BI 3, 1903 BI 1,2
Prentis, R B (Tvl) 1980 S Am 1,2, BI 1,2,3,4, S Am 3,4, F, 1981 I 1,2
Pretorius, A S (GL) 2002 W 1,2, Arg, Sm, NZ 1, A 1, NZ 2, F, S (R), E, 2003 NZ 1(R), A 1, 2005 A2, 3, NZ1, A4, NZ2, Arg, 2006 NZ2(R), 3, A3, I, E1(t&R), 2, 2007 S(R), [Sm(R), E1(R), Tg, US(R), Arg(R)], W
Pretorius, J C (GL) 2006 I, 2007 NZ2
Pretorius, N F (Tvl) 1928 NZ 1,2,3,4
Prinsloo, J (Tvl) 1958 F 1,2
Prinsloo, J (NT) 1963 A 3
Prinsloo, J P (Tvl) 1928 NZ 1
Putter, D J (WT) 1963 A 1,2,4

Raaff, J W E (GW) 1903 BI 1,2, 1906 S, W, E, 1910 BI 1
Ralepelle, M C (BB) 2006 NZ2(R), E2(R), 2008 E(t&R), 2009 BI 3, NZ1(R), 2(R), A2(R), NZ3(R), 2010 W1(R), F(R), It 1, 2(R), NZ1(R), 2(R), A1(R), 2(R), 3(R), W2(R), 2011 A1(R), NZ1(R), [Nm(R)], 2013 It(R)
Ras, W J de Wet (OFS) 1976 NZ 1(R), 1980 S Am 2(R)
Rautenbach, S J (WP) 2002 W 1(R),2(t+R), Arg (R), Sm, NZ 1(R), A 1, NZ 2(R), A 2(R), 2003 [U(R), Gg, Sm, NZ], 2004 W1,NZ1(R)

Reece-Edwards, H (N) 1992 F 1,2, 1993 A 2
Reid, A (WP) 1903 BI 3
Reid, B C (Bor) 1933 A 4
Reinach, J (OFS) 1986 Cv 1,2,3,4
Rens, I J (Tvl) 1953 A 3,4
Retief, D F (NT) 1955 BI 1,2,4, 1956 A 1,2, NZ 1,2,3,4
Reyneke, H J (WP) 1910 BI 3
Richards, A R (WP) 1891 BI 1,2,3
Richter, A (NT) 1992 F 1,2, E, 1994 E 2, NZ 1,2,3, 1995 [R, C, WS (R)]
Riley, N M (ET) 1963 A 3
Riordan, C A (Tvl) 1910 BI 1,2
Robertson, I W (R) 1974 F 1,2, 1976 NZ 1,2,4
Rodgers, P H (NT, Tvl) 1989 Wld 1,2, 1992 NZ, F 1,2
Rogers, C D (Tvl) 1984 E 1,2, S Am 1,2
Roos, G D (WP) 1910 BI 2,3
Roos, P J (WP) 1903 BI 3, 1906 I, W, E
Rosenberg, W (Tvl) 1955 BI 2,3,4, 1956 NZ 3, 1958 F 1
Rossouw, C L C (Tvl, N) 1995 WS, [R, WS, F, NZ], 1999 NZ 2(R), A 2(t), [Sp, NZ 3(R)]
Rossouw, D H (WP) 1953 A 3, 4
Rossouw, D J (BB) 2003 [U, Gg, Sm(R), NZ], 2004 E(R), S, Arg, 2005 U, F1, 2, A1, W(R), F3(R), 2006 S1, 2, F, A1, I, E1, 2, 2007 E1, Sm, A1(R), NZ1, S, [Sm, E1, Tg, Fj, Arg, E2], 2008 W1(t&R), NZ3(R), A3(R), S(R), E, 2009 BI 1(R), 2(R), NZ1(R), 2(R), A1(R), 3(R), NZ3(R), F(R), It, I, 2010 W1, F, NZ1(R), 2, A1, NZ3(t&R), A2(R), 3, 2011 A1, NZ1, A2, NZ2(t&R), [W, Fj, Nm, Sm, A]
Rossouw, P W G (WP) 1997 BI 2,3, NZ 1, A 1, NZ 2(R), A 2(R), It, F 1,2, E, S, 1998 I 1,2, W 1, E 1, A 1, NZ 1,2, A 2, W 2, S, I 3, E 2, 1999 It 1, W, NZ 1, A 1(R), NZ 2, A 2, [S, U, E, A 3], 2000 C, E 1,2, A 2, Arg (R), I, W, 2001 F 3, US, 2003 Arg
Rousseau, W P (WP) 1928 NZ 3,4
Roux, F du T (WP) 1960 W, 1961 A 1,2, 1962 BI 1,2,3,4, 1963 A 2, 1965 A 1,2, NZ 1,2,3,4, 1968 BI 3,4, F 1,2 1969 A 1,2,3,4, 1970 I, NZ 1,2,3,4
Roux, J P (Tvl) 1994 E 2, NZ 1,2,3, Arg 1, 1995 [R, C, F (R)], 1996 A 1(R), NZ 1, A 2, NZ 3
Roux, O A (NT) 1969 S, E, 1970 I, W, 1972 E, 1974 BI 3,4
Roux, W G (BB) 2002 F (R), S, E
Russell, R B (MP, N) 2002 W 1(R),2, Arg, A 1(R), NZ 2(R), A 2, F, E (R), 2003 Arg (R), A 1(R), NZ 1, A 2(R), 2004 I2(t&R), W1, NZ1(R), W2(R), Arg(R), 2005 U(R), F2(R), A1(t), Arg(R), W(R), 2006 F

Samuels, T A (GW) 1896 BI 2,3,4
Santon, D (Bol) 2003 A 1(R), NZ 1(R), A 2(t), [Gg(R)]
Sauermann, J T (Tvl) 1971 F 1,2, A 1, 1972 E, 1974 BI 1
Schlebusch, J J J (OFS) 1974 BI 3,4, 1975 F 2
Schmidt, L U (NT) 1958 F 2, 1962 BI 2
Schmidt, U L (NT, Tvl) 1986 Cv 1,2,3,4, 1989 Wld 1,2, 1992 NZ, A, 1993 F 1,2, A 1,2,3, 1994 Arg 1,2, S, W
Schoeman, J (WP) 1963 A 3,4, 1965 I, S, A 1, NZ 1,2
Scholtz, C P (WP, Tvl) 1994 Arg 1, 1995 [R, C, WS]
Scholtz, H (FS) 2002 A 1(R), NZ 2(R), A 2(R), 2003 [U(R),Gg]
Scholtz, H H (WP) 1921 NZ 1,2
Schutte, P J W (Tvl) 1994 S, W
Scott, P A (Tvl) 1896 BI 1,2,3,4
Sendin, W D (GW) 1921 NZ 2
Sephaka, L D (GL) 2001 US, 2002 Sm, NZ 1, A 1, NZ 2, A 2, F, 2003 S 1,2, A 1, NZ 1, A 2(t+R), NZ 2, [U, E(t&R),Gg], 2005 F2, A1, 2(R), W, 2006 S1(R), NZ3(t&R), A3(R), I
Serfontein, D J (WP) 1980 BI 1,2,3,4, S Am 3,4, F, 1981 I 1,2, NZ 1,2,3, US, 1982 S Am 1,2, 1984 E 1,2, S Am 1,2
Serfontein, J L (BB) 2013 It(R), S1(R), Sm(R), Arg1(R), 2(R), A1(R), NZ1(t&R), A2(R), NZ2(R)
Shand, R (GW) 1891 BI 2,3
Sheriff, A R (Tvl) 1938 BI 1,2,3
Shimange, M H (FS, WP) 2004 W1(R), NZ2(R), A2(R), W2(R), 2005 U(R), A1(R), 2(R), Arg(R), 2006 S1(R)
Shum, E H (Tvl) 1913 E
Sinclair, D J (Tvl) 1955 BI 1,2,3,4
Sinclair, J H (Tvl) 1903 BI 1
Skene, A L (WP) 1958 F 2
Skinstad, R B (WP, GL, N) 1997 E (t), 1998 W 1(R), E 1(t), NZ 1(R),2(R), A 2(R), W 2(R), S, I 3, E 2, 1999 [S, Sp (R), U, E, A 3], 2001 F 1(R),2(R), It 1, NZ 1, A 1,2, NZ 2, F 3, It 2, E, 2002 W 1,2, Arg, Sm, NZ 1, A 1, NZ 2, A 2, 2003 Arg (R), 2007 E2(t&R), Sm, NZ1, A2, [E1(R), Tg, US(R), Arg(R)]
Slater, J T (EP) 1924 BI 3,4, 1928 NZ 1
Smal, G P (WP) 1986 Cv 1,2,3,4, 1989 Wld 1,2
Small, J T (Tvl, N, WP) 1992 NZ, A, F 1,2, E, 1993 F 1,2, A 1,2,3, Arg 1,2, 1994 E 1,2, NZ 1,2,3(t), Arg 1, 1995 WS, [A, R, F, NZ], W, It, E (R), 1996 Fj, A 1, NZ 1, A 2, NZ 2, Arg 1,2, F 1,2, W, 1997 Tg, BI 1, NZ 1(R), A 1(R), NZ 2, A 2, It, F 1,2, E, S
Smit, F C (WP) 1992 E
Smit, J W (NS, Clermont-Auvergne) 2000 C (t), A 1(R), NZ 1(t+R), A 2(R), NZ 2(R), A 3(R), Arg, I, W, E 3, 2001 F 1,2, It 1, NZ 1(R), A 1(R),2(R), NZ 2(R), F 3(R), It 2, E, US (R), 2003 [U(R), E(t&R), Gg, Sm, NZ], 2004 I1, 2, W1, PI, NZ1, A1, NZ2, A2, W2, I3, E, S, Arg, 2005 U, F1, 2, A1, 2, 3, NZ1, A4, NZ2, Arg, W, F3, 2006 S1, 2, F, A1, NZ1, A2, NZ2, 3, A3, I, E1, 2, 2007 E1, 2, Sm, A1, [Sm, E1, Tg(R), US, Fj, Arg, E2], W, 2008 W1, 2, NZ1, W3, S, E, 2009 BI 1, 2, 3, NZ1, 2, A1, 2, 3, NZ3, F, It, I, 2010 W1, F, It 2, NZ1, 2, A1, NZ3, A2, 3, 2011 A1, NZ1, A2, NZ2(R), [W, Fj, Nm, Sm(R), A]
Smith, C M (OFS) 1963 A 3,4, 1964 W, F, 1965 A 1,2, NZ 2
Smith, C W (GW) 1891 BI 2, 1896 BI 2,3
Smith, D (GW) 1891 BI 2
Smith D J (Z-R) 1980 BI 1,2,3,4
Smith, G A C (EP) 1938 BI 3
Smith, J H (FS) 2003 S 1(R), 2(R), A 1, NZ 1, A 2, NZ 2, [U, E, Sm, NZ], 2004 W2, 2005 U(R), F2(R), A2, 3, NZ1, A4, NZ2, Arg, W, F3, 2006 S1, 2, F, A1, NZ1, A2, I, E2, 2007 E1, 2, A1, Nm, S, [Sm, E1, Tg(t&R), US, Fj, Arg, E2], W, 2008 W1, 2, It, NZ1, 2, A1, Arg, NZ3, A2, 3, W3, S, 2009 BI 1, 2, 3, NZ1, 2, A1, 2, 3, 2010 NZ3, A2, 3, I, W2, S, E
Smith, P F (GW) 1997 S (R), 1998 I 1(t), 2, W 1, NZ 1(R), 2(R), A 2(R), W 2, 1999 NZ 2
Smollan, F C (Tvl) 1933 A 3,4,5
Snedden, R C D (GW) 1891 BI 2
Snyman, A H (NT, BB, N) 1996 NZ 3,4, Arg 2(R), W (R), 1997 Tg, BI 1,2,3, NZ 1, A 1, NZ 2, A 2, It, F 1,2, E, S, 1998 I 1,2, W 1, E 1, A 1, NZ 1,2, A 2, W 2, S, I 3, E 2, 1999 NZ 2, 2001 NZ 2, F 3, US, 2002 W 1, 2003 S 1, NZ 1, 2006 S1,2
Snyman, D S L (WP) 1972 E, 1974 BI 1,2(R), F 1,2, 1975 F 1,2, 1976 NZ 2,3, 1977 Wld
Snyman, J C P (OFS) 1974 BI 2,3,4
Sonnekus, G H H (OFS) 1974 BI 3, 1984 E 1,2
Sowerby, R S (N) 2002 Sm (R)
Spies, J J (NT) 1970 NZ 1,2,3,4
Spies, P J (BB) 2006 A1, NZ2, 3, A3, I, E1, 2007 E1(R), 2, A1, 2008 W1, 2, A1, Arg, NZ3, A2, 3, W3, S, E, 2009 BI 1, 2, 3(R), NZ1, 2, A1, 2, 3, NZ3, 2010 F, It 1, 2, NZ1, 2, A1, NZ3, A2, 3, I, W2, E, 2011 A2, NZ2, [W, Fj, Nm, Sm, A], 2012 E1, 2, 3, 2013 It, S1, Sm
Stander, J C J (OFS) 1974 BI 4(R), 1976 NZ 1,2,3,4
Stapelberg, W P (NT) 1974 F 1,2
Starke, J J (WP) 1956 NZ 4
Starke, K T (WP) 1924 BI 1,2,3,4
Steenekamp, J G A (Tvl) 1958 F 1
Steenkamp, G G (FS, BB, Toulouse) 2004 S,Arg, 2005 U, F2(R), A2, 3, NZ1(R), A4(R), 2007 E1(R), 2, A1, [Tg, Fj(R)], 2008 W1, 2(R), NZ1, 2, A1, W3(R), S(R), 2009 BI 1(R), 3(R), 2010 F, It 1, 2, NZ1, 2, A1, NZ3, A2, 3, 2011 A2(R), NZ2, [W(R), Fj, Nm, Sm(R), A], 2012 S, E4, 2013 Arg1(R), 2(R), A1(R), NZ1(R), A2(R), NZ2(R)
Stegmann, A C (WP) 1906 S, I
Stegmann, G J (BB) 2010 I,W2,S,E, 2011 A1,NZ1
Stegmann, J A (Tvl) 1912 S, I, W, 1913 E, F
Stewart, C (WP) 1998 S, I 3, E 2
Stewart, D A (WP) 1960 S, 1961 E, S, F, I, 1963 A 1,3,4, 1964 W, F, 1965 I
Steyn, F P L (NS, Racing Metro) 2006 I,E1,2, 2007 E1(R), 2(R), Sm, A1(R), NZ1(R), S, [Sm(R), E1, Tg(R), US, Fj, Arg, E2], W, 2008 W2(R), It, NZ1(R), 2(R), A1, NZ3(R), A2(R), W3(R), S(R), E(R), 2009 BI 1, 2, 3(t&R), NZ1, 2, A1, 2(R), 3(R), NZ3, 2010 W1, A2, 3, W2, S, E, 2011 A2,[W, Fj, Nm, Sm], 2012 E1, 2, Arg1, 2, A1, NZ1
Steyn, M (BB, SF) 2009 BI 1(t&R), 2(R), 3, NZ1(R), 2, A1, 2, 3, NZ3, F, It, I, 2010 F,It 1, 2, NZ1, 2, A1, NZ3, A2, 3, I, W2, S, E, 2011 A1, NZ1, A2(R), NZ2, [W, Fj, Nm, Sm, A], 2012 E1,

THE COUNTRIES

2, 3, Arg1, 2, A1, NZ1, S(R), 2013 It, S1, Sm, Arg1, 2, A1, NZ1, A2, NZ2

Stofberg, M T S (OFS, NT, WP) 1976 NZ 2,3, 1977 Wld, 1980 S Am 1,2, BI 1,2,3,4, S Am 3,4, F, 1981 I 1,2, NZ 1,2, US, 1982 S Am 1,2, 1984 E 1,2

Strachan, L C (Tvl) 1932 E, S, 1937 A 1,2, NZ 1,2,3, 1938 BI 1,2,3

Stransky, J T (N, WP) 1993 A 1,2,3, Arg 1, 1994 Arg 1,2, 1995 WS, [A, R (t), C, F, NZ], W, It, E, 1996 Fj (R), NZ 1, A 2, NZ 2,3,4,5(R)

Straeuli, R A W (Tvl) 1994 NZ 1, Arg 1,2, S, W, 1995 WS, [A, WS, NZ (R)], E (R)

Strauss, C P (WP) 1992 F 1,2, E, 1993 F 1,2, A 1,2,3, Arg 1,2, 1994 E 1, NZ 1,2, Arg 1,2

Strauss, J A (WP) 1984 S Am 1,2

Strauss, J A (FSC) 2008 A1(R), Arg(R), NZ3(R), A2(R), 3(R), 2009 F(R), It, 2010 S(R), E(R), 2012 E1(R), 2(R), 3(R), Arg1(R), 2, A1, NZ1, A2, NZ2, I, S, E4, 2013 It, S1, Sm, Arg1, 2, A1(R), NZ1(t&R), A2, NZ2(R)

Strauss, J H P (Tvl) 1976 NZ 3,4, 1980 S Am 1

Strauss, S S F (GW) 1921 NZ 3

Strydom, C F (OFS) 1955 BI 3, 1956 A 1,2, NZ 1,4, 1958 F 1,

Strydom, J J (Tvl, GL) 1993 F 2, A 1,2,3, Arg 1,2, 1994 E 1, 1995 [A, C, F, NZ], 1996 A 2(R), NZ 2(R), 3,4, W (R), 1997 Tg, BI 1,2,3, A 2

Strydom, L J (NT) 1949 NZ 1,2

Styger, J J (OFS) 1992 NZ (R), A, F 1,2, E, 1993 F 2(R), A 3(R)

Suter, M R (N) 1965 I, S

Swanepoel, W (OFS, GL) 1997 BI 3(R), A 2(R), F 1(R), 2, E, S, 1998 I 2(R), W 1(R), E 2(R), 1999 It 1,2(R), W, A 1, [Sp, NZ 3(t)], 2000 A 1, NZ 1, A 2, NZ 2, A 3

Swart, J (WP) 1996 Fj, NZ 1(R), A 2, NZ 2,3,4,5, 1997 BI 3(R), It, S (R)

Swart, J J N (SWA) 1955 BI 1

Swart, I S (Tvl) 1993 A 1,2,3, Arg 1, 1994 E 1,2, NZ 1,3, Arg 2(R), 1995 WS, [A, WS, F, NZ], W, 1996 A 2

Taberer, W S (GW) 1896 BI 2

Taute, J J (GL) 2012 A2,NZ2,I

Taylor, O B (N) 1962 BI 1

Terblanche, C S (Bol, N) 1998 I 1,2, W 1, E 1, A 1, NZ 1,2, A 2, W 2, S, I 3, E 2, 1999 It 1(R),2, W, A 1, NZ 2(R), [Sp, E (R), A 3(R), NZ 3], 2000 E 3, 2002 W 1,2, Arg, Sm, NZ 1, A 1,2(R), 2003 S 1,2, Arg, A 1, NZ 1, A 2, NZ 2, [Gg]

Teichmann, G H (N) 1995 W, 1996 Fj, A 1, NZ 1, A 2, NZ 2,3,4,5, Arg 1,2, F 1,2, W, 1997 Tg, BI 1,2,3, NZ 1, A 1, NZ 2, A 2, It, F 1,2 E, S, 1998 I 1,2, W 1, E 1, A 1, NZ 1,2, A 2, W 2, S, I 3, E 2, 1999 It 1, W, NZ 1

Theron, D F (GW) 1996 A 2(R), NZ 2(R), 5, Arg 1,2, F 1,2, W, 1997 BI 2(R), 3, NZ 1(R), A 1, NZ 2(R)

Theunissen, D J (GW) 1896 BI 3

Thompson, G (WP) 1912 S, I, W

Tindall, J C (WP) 1924 BI 1, 1928 NZ 1,2,3,4

Tobias, E G (SARF, Bol) 1981 I 1,2, 1984 E 1,2, S Am 1,2

Tod, N S (N) 1928 NZ 2

Townsend, W H (N) 1921 NZ 1

Trenery, W E (GW) 1891 BI 2

Tromp, H (NT) 1996 NZ3,4, Arg 2(R), F 1(R)

Truter, D R (WP) 1924 BI 2,4

Truter, J T (N) 1963 A 1, 1964 F, 1965 A 2

Turner, F G (EP) 1933 A 1,2,3, 1937 A 1,2, NZ 1,2,3, 1938 BI 1,2,3

Twigge, R J (NT) 1960 S

Tyibilika, S (N) 2004 S,Arg, 2005 U,A2,Arg, 2006 NZ1,A2,NZ2

Ulyate, C A (Tvl) 1955 BI 1,2,3,4, 1956 NZ 1,2,3

Uys, P de W (NT) 1960 W, 1961 E, S, I, A 1,2, 1962 BI 1,4, 1963 A 1,2, 1969 A 1(R), 2

Uys, P J (Pumas) 2002 S

Van Aswegen, H J (WP) 1981 NZ 1, 1982 S Am 2(R)

Van Biljon, L (N) 2001 It 1(R), NZ 1, A 1,2, NZ 2, F 3, It 2(R), E (R), US, 2002 F (R), S, E (R), 2003 NZ 2(R)

Van Broekhuizen, H D (WP) 1896 BI 4

Van Buuren, M C (Tvl) 1891 BI 1

Van de Vyver, D F (WP) 1937 A 2

Van den Berg, D S (N) 1975 F 1,2, 1976 NZ 1,2

Van den Berg, M A (WP) 1937 A 1, NZ 1,2,3

Van den Berg, P A (WP, GW, N) 1999 It 1(R),2, NZ 2, A 2, [S, U (t+R), E (R), A 3(R), NZ 3(R)], 2000 E 1(R), A 1, NZ 1, A 2, NZ 2(R), A 3(t+R), Arg, I, W, E 3, 2001 F 1(R),2, A 2(R), NZ 2(R), US, 2004 NZ1, 2005 U, F1, 2, A1(R), 2(R), 3(R), 4(R), Arg(R), F3(R), 2006 S2(R), A1(R), NZ1, A2(R), NZ2(R), A3(R), I, E1(R), 2(R), 2007 Sm, A2(R), NZ2, Nm(t&R), S(R), [Tg, US], W(R)

Van den Bergh, E (EP) 1994 Arg 2(t & R)

Van der Linde, A (WP) 1995 It, E, 1996 Arg 1(R), 2(R), F 1(R), W (R), 2001 F 3(R)

Van der Linde, C J (FS, Leinster, WP, GL) 2002 S (R), E(R), 2004 I1(R), 2(R), PI(R), A1(R), NZ2(t&R), A2(R), W2(R), I3(R), E(t&R), S, Arg, 2005 U, F1(R), 2, A1(R), 3, NZ1, A4, NZ2, Arg, W, F3, 2006 S2(R), F(R), A1, NZ1, A2, NZ2, I, E1, 2, 2007 E1(R), 2, A1(R), NZ1(R), A2, NZ2, Nm, S, [Sm, E1(R), Tg, US(R), Arg, E2], W, 2008 W1(t&R), It, NZ1, 2, A1, Arg, NZ3, A2, 2009 F(R), I(t), 2010 W1, It1(R), NZ2, A1(t&R), NZ3(R), A2(R), 3(R), I(R), W2(R), S(R), E(R), 2011 A1(t&R), NZ1(R), 2(R), [Nm], 2012 I, S(R)

Van der Merwe, A J (Bol) 1955 BI 2,3,4, 1956 A 1,2, NZ 1,2,3,4, 1958 F 1, 1960 S, NZ 2

Van der Merwe, A V (WP) 1931 W

Van der Merwe, B S (NT) 1949 NZ 1

Van der Merwe, F (GL) 2013 NZ 2(R)

Van der Merwe, H S (NT) 1960 NZ 4, 1963 A 2,3,4, 1964 F

Van der Merwe, H S (GL, Leinster) 2007 W(t+R), 2012 I(R),S(R),E4(R)

Van der Merwe, J P (WP) 1970 W

Van der Merwe, P R (SWD, WT, GW) 1981 NZ 2,3, US, 1986 Cv 1,2, 1989 Wld 1

Van der Merwe, P R (BB) 2010 F(R),It 2(R), A1(R), NZ3, A2, 3(R), I(R), W2(R), S(R), E(R), 2011 A1, 2012 E1(R), 2(R), 3(R), Arg1(R), 2(R), A1(R), NZ1, A2(R), NZ2(R), I(R), S(R), E4(R), 2013 It(R),S1(R), Sm, Arg1(R), 2(R), A1, NZ1, A2

Vanderplank, B E (N) 1924 BI 3,4

Van der Schyff, J H (GW) 1949 NZ 1,2,3,4, 1955 BI 1

Van der Watt, A E (WP) 1969 S (R), E, 1970 I

Van der Westhuizen, J C (WP) 1928 NZ 2,3,4, 1931 I

Van der Westhuizen, J H (WP) 1931 I, 1932 E, S

Van der Westhuizen, J H (NT, BB) 1993 Arg 1,2, 1994 E 1,2(R), Arg 2, S, W, 1995 WS, [A, C (R), WS, F, NZ], W, It, E, 1996 Fj, A 1,2(R), NZ 2,3(R), 4,5, Arg 1,2, F 1,2, W, 1997 Tg, BI 1,2,3, NZ 1, A 1, NZ 2, A 2, It, F 1, 1998 I 1,2, W 1, E 1, A 1, NZ 1,2, A 2, W 2, S, I 3, E 2, 1999 NZ 2, A 2, [S, Sp (R), U, E, A 3, NZ 3], 2000 C, E 1,2, A 1(R), NZ 1(R), A 2(R), Arg, I, W, E 3, 2001 F 1,2, It 1(R), NZ 1, A 1,2, NZ 2, F 3, It 2, E, US (R), 2003 S 1,2, A 1, NZ 1, A 2(R), NZ 2, [U, E, Sm, NZ]

Van der Westhuyzen, J N B (MP, BB) 2000 NZ 2(R), 2001 It 1(R), 2003 S 1(R),2, Arg, A 1, 2003 [E, Sm, NZ], 2004 I1, 2, W1, PI, NZ1, A1, NZ2, A2, W2, I3, E, S, Arg, 2005 U, F1, 2, A1, 4(R), NZ2(R), 2006 S1, 2, F, A1

Van Druten, N J V (Tvl) 1924 BI 1,2,3,4, 1928 NZ 1,2,3,4

Van Heerden, A J (Tvl) 1921 NZ 1,3

Van Heerden, F J (WP) 1994 E 1,2(R), NZ 3, 1995 It, E, 1996 NZ 5(R), Arg 1(R), 2(R), 1997 Tg, BI 2(t+R), 3(R), NZ 1(R), 2(R), 1999 [Sp]

Van Heerden, J L (NT, Tvl) 1974 BI 3,4, F 1,2, 1975 F 1,2, 1976 NZ 1,2,3,4, 1977 Wld, 1980 BI 1,3,4, S Am 3,4, F

Van Heerden, J L (BB) 2003 S 1,2, A 1, NZ 1, A 2(t), 2007 A2, NZ2, S(R), [Sm(R), E1, Tg, US, Fj(R), E2(R)]

Van Jaarsveld, C J (Tvl) 1949 NZ 1

Van Jaarsveldt, D C (R) 1960 S

Van Niekerk, J A (WP) 1928 NZ 4

Van Niekerk, J C (GL, WP, Toulon) 2001 NZ 1(R), A 1(R), NZ 2(t+R), F 3(R), It2, US, 2002 W 1(R),2(R), Arg (R), Sm, NZ 1, A 1, NZ 2, A 2, F, S, E, 2003 A 2, NZ 2, [U, E, Gg, Sm], 2004 NZ1(R), A1(t), NZ2, A2, W2, I3, E, S, Arg(R), 2005 U(R), F2(R), A1(R), 2, 3, NZ1, A4, NZ2, 2006 S1, 2, F, A1, NZ1(R), A2(R), 2008 It(R), NZ1, 2, Arg(R), A2(R), 2010 W1

Van Reenen, G L (WP) 1937 A 2, NZ 1

Van Renen, C G (WP) 1891 BI 3, 1896 BI 1,4

Van Renen, W (WP) 1903 BI 1,3

Van Rensburg, J T J (Tvl) 1992 NZ, A, E, 1993 F 1,2, A 1, 1994 NZ 2

Van Rooyen, G W (Tvl) 1921 NZ 2,3

Van Ryneveld, R C B (WP) 1910 BI 2,3

Van Schalkwyk, D (NT) 1996 Fj (R), NZ 3,4,5, 1997 BI 2,3, NZ 1, A 1
Van Schoor, R A M (R) 1949 NZ 2,3,4, 1951 S, I, W, 1952 E, F, 1953 A 1,2,3,4
Van Straaten, A J J (WP) 1999 It 2(R), W, NZ 1(R), A 1, 2000 C, E 1,2, NZ 1, A 2, NZ 2, A 3, Arg (R), I (R), W, E 3, 2001 A 1,2, NZ 2, F 3, It 2, E
Van Vollenhoven, K T (NT) 1955 BI 1,2,3,4, 1956 A 1,2, NZ 3
Van Vuuren, T F (EP) 1912 S, I, W, 1913 E, F
Van Wyk, C J (Tvl) 1951 S, I, W, 1952 E, F, 1953 A 1,2,3,4, 1955 BI 1
Van Wyk, J F B (NT) 1970 NZ 1,2,3,4, 1971 F 1,2, A 1,2,3, 1972 E, 1974 BI 1,3,4, 1976 NZ 3,4
Van Wyk, S P (WP) 1928 NZ 1,2
Van Zyl, B P (WP) 1961 I
Van Zyl, C G P (OFS) 1965 NZ 1,2,3,4
Van Zyl, D J (WP) 2000 E 3(R)
Van Zyl, G H (WP) 1958 F 1, 1960 S, NZ 1,2,3,4, W, I, 1961 E, S, F, I, A 1,2, 1962 BI 1,3,4
Van Zyl, H J (Tvl) 1960 NZ 1,2,3,4, I, 1961 E, S, I, A 1,2
Van Zyl, P J (Bol) 1961 I
Van Zyl, P E (FSC) 2013 S1(R),Sm(R)
Veldsman, P E (WP) 1977 Wld
Venter, A G (OFS) 1996 NZ 3,4,5, Arg 1,2, F 1,2, W, 1997 Tg, BI 1,2,3, NZ 1, A 1, NZ 2, It, F 1,2, E, S, 1998 I 1,2, W 1, E 1, A 1, NZ 1,2, A 2, W 2, S (R), I 3(R), E 2(R), 1999 It 1,2(R), W (R), NZ 1, A 1, NZ 2, A 2, [S, U, E, A 3, NZ 3], 2000 C, E 1,2, A 1, NZ 1, A 2, NZ 2, A 3, Arg, I, W, E 3, 2001 F 1, It 1, NZ 1, A 1,2, NZ 2, F 3(R), It 2(R), E (t+R), US (R)
Venter, A J (N) 2000 W (R), E 3(R), 2001 F 3, It 2, E, US, 2002 W 1,2, Arg, NZ 1(R),2, A 2, F, S (R), E, 2003 Arg, 2004 PI, NZ1, A1, NZ2(R), A2, I3, E, 2006 NZ3, A3
Venter, B (OFS) 1994 E 1,2, NZ 1,2,3, Arg 1,2, 1995 [R, C, WS (R), NZ (R)], 1996 A 1, NZ 1, A 2, 1999 A 2, [S, U]
Venter, F D (Tvl) 1931 W, 1932 S, 1933 A 3
Vermaak, J (BB) 2013 It,A1(R),NZ1(R)
Vermeulen, D J (WP) 2012 A1,NZ1,A2,NZ2,I,S,E4, 2013 Arg1,2,A1,NZ1,A2,NZ2
Versfeld, C (WP) 1891 BI 3
Versfeld, M (WP) 1891 BI 1,2,3
Vigne, J T (Tvl) 1891 BI 1,2,3
Viljoen, J F (GW) 1971 F 1,2, A 1,2,3, 1972 E
Viljoen, J T (N) 1971 A 1,2,3
Villet, J V (WP) 1984 E 1,2
Visagie, I J (WP) 1999 It 1, W, NZ 1, A 1, NZ 2, A 2, [S, U, E, A 3, NZ 3], 2000 C, E 2, A 1, NZ 1, A 2, NZ 2, A 3, 2001 NZ 1, A 1,2, NZ 2, F 3, It 2(R), E (t+R), US, 2003 S 1(R),2(R), Arg
Visagie, P J (GW) 1967 F 1,2,3,4, 1968 BI 1,2,3,4, F 1,2, 1969 A 1,2,3,4, S, E, 1970 NZ 1,2,3,4, 1971 F 1,2, A 1,2,3
Visagie, R G (OFS, N) 1984 E 1,2, S Am 1,2, 1993 F 1
Visser, J de V (WP) 1981 NZ 2, US
Visser, M (WP) 1995 WS (R)
Visser, P J (Tvl) 1933 A 2
Viviers, S S (OFS) 1956 A 1,2, NZ 2,3,4
Vogel, M L (OFS) 1974 BI 2(R)
Von Hoesslin, D J B (GW) 1999 It 1(R),2, W (R), NZ 1, A 1(R)
Vos, A N (GL) 1999 It 1(t+R),2, NZ 1(R),2(R), A 2, [S (R), Sp, E (R), A 3(R), NZ 3], 2000 C, E 1,2, A 1, NZ 1, A 2, NZ 2, A 3, Arg, I, W, E 3, 2001 F 1,2, It 1, NZ 1, A 1,2, NZ 2, F 3, It 2, E, US

Wagenaar, C (NT) 1977 Wld
Wahl, J J (WP) 1949 NZ 1
Walker, A P (N) 1921 NZ 1,3, 1924 BI 1,2,3,4
Walker, H N (OFS) 1953 A 3, 1956 A 2, NZ 1,4
Walker, H W (Tvl) 1910 BI 1,2,3
Walton, D C (N) 1964 F, 1965 I, S, NZ 3,4, 1969 A 1,2, E
Wannenburg, P J (BB) 2002 F (R), E, 2003 S 1, 2, Arg, A 1(t+R), NZ 1(R), 2004 I1, 2,W1, PI(R), 2006 S1(R), F, NZ2(R), 3, A3, 2007 Sm(R), NZ1(R), A2, NZ2
Waring, F W (WP) 1931 I, 1932 E, 1933 A 1,2,3,4,5
Watson, L A (WP) 2007 Sm, 2008 W1, 2, It, NZ1(R), 2(R), Arg, NZ3(R), A2(R), 3(t&R)
Wegner, N (WP) 1993 F 2, A 1,2,3
Wentzel, M van Z (Pumas) 2002 F (R), S
Wessels, J J (WP) 1896 BI 1,2,3
Whipp, P J M (WP) 1974 BI 1,2, 1975 F 1, 1976 NZ 1,3,4, 1980 S Am 1,2
White, J (Bor) 1931 W, 1933 A 1,2,3,4,5, 1937 A 1,2, NZ 1,2
Wiese, J J (Tvl) 1993 F 1, 1995 WS, [R, C, WS, F, NZ], W, It, E, 1996 NZ 3(R), 4(R), 5, Arg 1,2, F 1,2, W
Willemse, A K (GL) 2003 S 1, 2, NZ 1, A 2, NZ 2, [U, E, Sm, NZ], 2004 W2, I3, 2007 E1, 2(R), Sm, A1, NZ1, Nm, S(R), [Tg]
Williams, A E (GW) 1910 BI 1
Williams, A P (WP) 1984 E 1,2
Williams, C M (WP, GL) 1993 Arg 2, 1994 E 1,2, NZ 1,2,3, Arg 1,2, S, W, 1995 WS, [WS, F, NZ], It, E, 1998 A 1(t), NZ 1(t), 2000 C (R), E 1(t),2(R), A 1(R), NZ 2, A 3, Arg, I, W (R)
Williams, D O (WP) 1937 A 1,2, NZ 1,2,3, 1938 BI 1,2,3
Williams, J G (NT) 1971 F 1,2, A 1,2,3, 1972 E, 1974 BI 1,2,4, F 1,2, 1976 NZ 1,2
Wilson, L G (WP) 1960 NZ 3,4, W, I, 1961 E, F, I, A 1,2, 1962 BI 1,2,3,4, 1963 A 1, 2, 3, 4, 1964 W, F, 1965 I, S, A 1,2, NZ 1,2,3,4
Wolmarans, B J (OFS) 1977 Wld
Wright, G D (EP, Tvl) 1986 Cv 3,4, 1989 Wld 1,2, 1992 F 1,2, E
Wyness, M R K (WP) 1962 BI 1,2,3,4, 1963 A 2

Zeller, W C (N) 1921 NZ 2,3
Zimerman, M (WP) 1931 W, I, 1932 E, S

TONGA

TONGA'S 2012–13 TEST RECORD

OPPONENTS	DATE	VENUE	RESULT
Italy	10 Nov	A	Lost 28–23
USA	17 Nov	N	Won 22–13
Scotland	24 Nov	A	Won 21–15
Japan	25 May	A	Won 27–17
Canada	8 Jun	A	Lost 36–27
USA	14 Jun	A	Won 18–9
Fiji	23 Jun	N	Lost 34–21

TONGA BUILDING FOR THE FUTURE

AFP/Getty Images

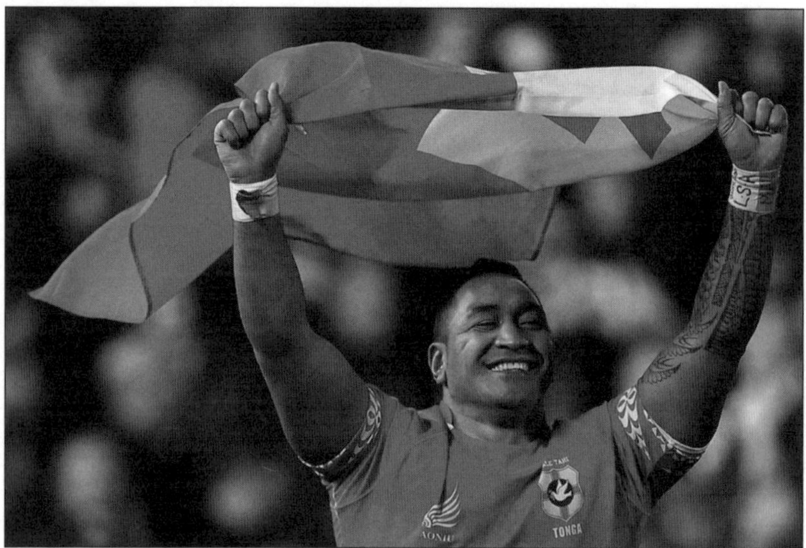

A delighted Halani Aulika celebrates Tonga's first ever win against Scotland in November 2012.

A number of important milestones, at both ends of the participation spectrum, were achieved in the 2012/13 season by the Tonga Rugby Union. In November 2012, with the scent of French blood still fresh in the minds of players and fans alike, the Ikale Tahi recorded their first ever win over Scotland.

Despite the historical magnitude of Tonga's 21–15 win in Aberdeen, head coach Mana 'Otai was not getting carried away. "It was a pretty good performance in alien conditions, but it could have been better. There were aspects of the match we did not execute properly so we have work to do," he said.

After a disappointing start to their first European tour since Rugby World Cup 2011, Tonga's win capped off what should be considered a successful first foray under the guidance of their RWC 1995 captain. An opening 28–23 loss to Italy in Brescia was redeemed somewhat by a 22–13 win over USA at the inaugural IRB International Rugby Series in Colwyn Bay, Wales.

Three months later Tonga A assembled for the increasingly popular IRB Pacific Rugby Cup in Australia and New Zealand. Once again, the competition posed by the development teams from Australian and New Zealand Super Rugby franchises, as well as the Australian Rugby Union's own Academy programme, proved a tough test for the best locally based players from the Kingdom.

Losses to the Brumby Runners (62–12), the ARU Sydney Academy (32–18), Reds College XV (24–3), Hurricanes Development XV (68–3), Chiefs Development XV (50–18) and Crusaders Knights (70–19) suggest it was a torrid tour for the young Tongan team. Yet this is precisely why the IRB Pacific Rugby Cup was established – to expose the best home-based players from Fiji, Samoa and Tonga to the next generation of Super Rugby stars from Australia and New Zealand – and the benefit of the tournament became evident with the selection of three Tonga A players in the national team for the IRB Pacific Nations Cup in May.

The tough PRC schedule of six matches in four weeks was the perfect dress rehearsal for those three players and the Ikale Tahi management team for what was going to be a demanding schedule in the expanded Pacific Nations Cup.

For the first time, the Pacific Nations Cup featured Canada and USA. With defending champions Samoa participating in a quadrangular tournament in South Africa with Italy and Scotland, and after the success of the European tour the previous November, the Ikale Tahi entered the tournament with their eyes firmly on securing a maiden PNC title.

A first-up 27–17 win over Japan in Yokohama was the perfect start for Tonga ahead of an exhausting three-week tour of North America which saw the team travel from Japan to San Francisco to Ontario and finally to Los Angeles before returning to Tokyo for the final leg of the tournament. After a week-long training camp in San Francisco, the Tongans travelled to Canada for the first meeting between the sides since the Canucks recorded what many considered a 25–20 upset at RWC 2011.

The Tongans were keen to avenge that defeat, but sent out a relatively inexperienced team, with just 149 caps, to do so. Canada ran out 36–27 winners, aided considerably by their opponents' ill-disciplined performance that at one stage in the second half saw them reduced to just 12 men.

"Our discipline let us down today, we can't afford to have men sent off and sin-binned; that's an area we've got to work on," admitted Tonga captain Nili Latu.

Next stop was Los Angeles for the first PNC match on American soil. In a scrappy affair a brace of tries by centre Sione Piukala helped Tonga get back to winning ways with an 18–9 win over the Eagles.

Tonga then travelled to Tokyo for their final match of the tournament against Fiji – the 86th Test between the two Pacific Island rivals. Japan's 16–13 win over Canada earlier in the week meant that the PNC title would be decided by this battle at the Prince Chichibu Memorial Stadium.

Latu could hardly wait for game day. "Tomorrow is the most important game of the year for us. It's really exciting. We've never had the trophy before so we are going to give it our all. We're hungry to win, but we need to control our discipline, back our game and not give silly penalties away."

By establishing an 11–0 lead after only 10 minutes Tonga made their intentions known. But a late first-half Fijian surge, sparked by some brilliance by veteran Sireli Bobo, saw the teams head into the break locked at 14–14. The second half, however, was all Fiji – the sheer pace of the Fijians' game had Tonga out on their legs for the final quarter – and tries from Nemani Nadolo and Napolioni Nalaga gave them a 34–21 win and a first PNC title.

"We were very disappointed not to win," admitted Latu. "We wanted so bad to win but we weren't good enough. Fiji deserved to win."

In the Sevens format, the Tonga Rugby Union had set out to achieve core team status on the HSBC Sevens World Series and their bold recruitment of Fiji's assistant coach, Eddie Waqa, signalled how serious they were in achieving this.

Tonga booked their place at the pre-qualifier in Hong Kong by finishing third at the 2012 Oceania Sevens Championship in Sydney. A strong performance in Hong Kong, where they finished second behind Zimbabwe, ensured Tonga would have a shot at securing core team status at the London Sevens for the 2013/14 season. Unfortunately for Tonga, they came up against a superior Scottish outfit in the Cup quarter-finals, a 31–0 loss meaning they fell short of their goal.

There was better news off the pitch as the TRU – after participating in the regional development workshop in Fiji in May – launched its mass participation strategy in the second half of 2013, aimed at providing opportunities for more boys and girls to take part in rugby. Using the IRB's Get Into Rugby framework, the TRU Development Unit delivered the curriculum in every primary school in the capital Nuku'alofa and, in the first three months of operation, achieved a participation rate of 5,000 children.

The expansion of the programme into secondary schools on the main island Tongatapu and the primary schools of the outer island groups in 2014 will provide an opportunity for more children, inspired by their Ikale Tahi heroes, to experience the joys of rugby in the Kingdom.

TONGA INTERNATIONAL STATISTICS

MATCH RECORDS UP TO 10 OCTOBER 2013

WINNING MARGIN

Date	Opponent	Result	Winning Margin
21/03/2003	Korea	119–0	**119**
08/07/2006	Cook Islands	90–0	**90**
01/01/1979	Solomon Islands	92–3	**89**
10/02/2007	Korea	83–3	**80**
15/03/2003	Korea	75–0	**75**

MOST POINTS IN A MATCH

BY THE TEAM

Date	Opponent	Result	Points
21/03/2003	Korea	119–0	**119**
01/01/1979	Solomon Islands	92–3	**92**
08/07/2006	Cook Islands	90–0	**90**
06/12/2002	Papua New Guinea	84–12	**84**
10/02/2007	Korea	83–3	**83**

BY A PLAYER

Date	Player	Opponent	Points
21/03/2003	Pierre Hola	Korea	**39**
10/02/2007	Fangatapu Apikotoa	Korea	**28**
04/05/1999	Sateki Tuipulotu	Korea	**27**
21/03/2003	Benhur Kivalu	Korea	**25**
06/12/2002	Pierre Hola	Papua New Guinea	**24**

MOST TRIES IN A MATCH

BY THE TEAM

Date	Opponent	Result	Tries
21/03/2003	Korea	119–0	**17**
08/07/2006	Cook Islands	90–0	**14**
10/02/2007	Korea	83–3	**13**
24/06/2006	Cook Islands	77–10	**13**

BY A PLAYER

Date	Player	Opponent	Tries
21/03/2003	Benhur Kivalu	Korea	**5**
08/06/2011	Viliame Iongi	USA	**4**

MOST CONVERSIONS IN A MATCH

BY THE TEAM

Date	Opponent	Result	Cons
21/03/2003	Korea	119–0	**17**
08/07/2006	Cook Islands	90–0	**10**

BY A PLAYER

Date	Player	Opponent	Cons
21/03/2003	Pierre Hola	Korea	**17**
08/07/2006	Fangatapu Apikotoa	Cook Islands	**9**
10/02/2007	Fangatapu Apikotoa	Korea	**9**
06/12/2002	Pierre Hola	Papua New Guinea	**9**
05/07/1997	Kusitafu Tonga	Cook Islands	**9**

MOST PENALTIES IN A MATCH

BY THE TEAM

Date	Opponent	Result	Pens
05/06/2012	Samoa	18–20	**6**
10/11/2001	Scotland	20–43	**5**
28/06/2008	Samoa	15–20	**5**
13/07/2011	Samoa	29–19	**5**
19/08/2011	Fiji	32–20	**5**

BY A PLAYER

Date	Player	Opponent	Pens
05/06/2012	Kurt Morath	Samoa	**6**
13/07/2011	Kurt Morath	Samoa	**5**
19/08/2011	Kurt Morath	Fiji	**5**

MOST DROP GOALS IN A MATCH

BY THE TEAM

1 on 8 occasions

BY A PLAYER

1 on 8 occasions

MOST CAPPED PLAYERS

Name	Caps
'Elisi Vunipola	41
Benhur Kivalu	38
Pierre Hola	37
Manu Vunipola	35
Aleki Lutui	33

LEADING TRY SCORERS

Name	Tries
Siua Taumalolo	12
Fepikou Tatafu	11
Benhur Kivalu	10

LEADING CONVERSION SCORERS

Name	Cons
Pierre Hola	65
Fangatapu Apikotoa	38
Kurt Morath	34
Sateki Tuipulotu	33

LEADING PENALTY SCORERS

Name	Pens
Kurt Morath	52
Pierre Hola	35
Sateki Tuipulotu	32

LEADING DROP GOAL SCORERS

Name	DGs
Pierre Hola	3

LEADING POINT SCORERS

Name	Points
Pierre Hola	289
Kurt Morath	231
Sateki Tuipulotu	190
Fangatapu Apikotoa	139
Siua Taumalolo	108

TONGA INTERNATIONAL PLAYERS

UP TO 10 OCTOBER 2013

I Afeaki 1995 *F*, *S*, *Iv*, 1997 *Fj*, 2001 *S*, *W*, 2002 *J*, *Fj*, *Sa*, *Fj*, 2003 *Kor*, *Kor*, *I*, *Fj*, *Fj*, *It*, *C*, 2004 *Sa*, *Fj*, 2005 *It*, 2007 *Sa*, *SA*, *E*
P Afeaki 1983 *Fj*, *Sa*
S Afeaki 2002 *Fj*, *Sa*, *Fj*, *PNG*, *PNG*, 2003 *Kor*, *Kor*, *I*, *Fj*, *It*, *W*, *NZ*
V Afeaki 1997 *Sa*, 2002 *Sa*, *Fj*
JL Afu 2008 *J*, *Sa*, *Fj*, 2009 *Fj*, *Sa*, *J*, 2011 *US*, 2012 *Sa*, *J*, *Fj*, *US*, 2013 *J*, *C*, *US*, *Fj*
T Afu Fifita 1924 *Fj*, *Fj*, *Fj*
A Afu Fungavaka 1982 *Sa*, 1984 *Fj*, *Fj*, 1985 *Fj*, 1986 *W*, *Fj*, *Fj*, 1987 *C*, *W*, *I*, *Sa*, *Fj*
S 'Aho 1974 *S*, *W*
T Ahoafi 2007 *AuA*, *Sa*
P Ahofono 1990 *Sa*
E Aholelei 2013 *J*, *C*
K Ahota'e'iloa 1999 *Sa*, *F*, *Fj*, 2000 *C*, *Fj*, *J*
M Ahota'e'iloa 2010 *Sa*, *Fj*, *J*
S Aisake 1934 *Fj*
M Akau'ola 1934 *Fj*
P 'Ake 1926 *Fj*, *Fj*, *Fj*
M Alatini 1969 *M*, 1972 *Fj*, *Fj*, 1973 *M*, *A*, *A*, *Fj*, 1974 *S*, *W*, *C*, 1975 *M*, 1977 *Fj*
PF Alatini 1995 *Sa*
S Alatini 1994 *Sa*, *Fj*, 1998 *Sa*, *Fj*, 2000 *NZ*, *US*
S Alatini 1977 *Fj*, 1979 *NC*, *M*, *E*
T Alatini 1932 *Fj*
A Alatini 2001 *S*, 2002 *J*, *Sa*, *Fj*, 2003 *I*, *Fj*
V 'Alipate 1967 *Fj*, 1968 *Fj*, *Fj*, *Fj*, 1969 *M*
A Amone 1987 *W*, *I*, *Sa*, *Fj*
A Amore 1988 *Fj*
F Anderson 2013 *US*, *Fj*
V Anitoni 1990 *Sa*
T Anitoni 1995 *J*, *Sa*, *Fj*, 1996 *Sa*, *Fj*
F Apikotoa 2004 *Sa*, *Fj*, 2005 *Fj*, *Sa*, *Fj*, *Sa*, *It*, *F*, 2006 *Coo*, *Coo*, 2007 *Kor*, *AuA*, *J*, *JAB*, 2008 *J*, *Sa*, *Fj*, 2009 *Fj*, *J*, 2010 *Fj*, *CHL*, 2012 *It*, *US*, *S*, 2013 *J*
T Apitani 1947 *Fj*, *Fj*
S Asi 1987 *C*
T Asi 1996 *Sa*
H 'Asi 2000 *C*
S Ata 1928 *Fj*
S Atiola 1987 *Sa*, *Fj*, 1988 *Fj*, *Fj*, 1989 *Fj*, *Fj*, 1990 *Fj*, *J*
H Aulika 2011 *Fj*, *Fj*, *C*, *J*, *F*, 2012 *It*, *US*, *S*

K Bakewa 2002 *PNG*, *PNG*, 2003 *Fj*
O Beba 1932 *Fj*, *Fj*, *Fj*
O Blake 1983 *M*, *M*, 1987 *Sa*, *Fj*, 1988 *Sa*, *Fj*, *Fj*
T Bloomfield 1973 *M*, *A*, *A*, *Fj*, 1986 *W*
D Briggs 1997 *W*
J Buloka 1932 *Fj*, *Fj*

D Edwards 1998 *A*, 1999 *Geo*, *Geo*, *Kor*, *US*, *Sa*, *F*, *Fj*, *C*, *NZ*, *It*, *E*
T Ete'aki 1984 *Fj*, 1986 *W*, *Fj*, *Fj*, 1987 *C*, *W*, *I*, 1990 *Fj*, *J*, *Sa*, *Kor*, *Sa*, 1991 *Sa*

U Fa'a 1994 *Sa*, *W*, 1995 *J*, 1998 *Sa*, *A*, *Fj*
L Fa'aoso 2004 *Sa*, *Fj*, 2005 *Fj*, *Sa*, *Fj*, *Sa*, 2007 *US*, *E*, 2009 *Pt*, 2011 *Fj*, *J*, *Fj*

P Fa'apoi 1963 *Fj*
V Fa'aumu 1986 *Fj*, *Fj*
SSA Fahiua 2013 *US*, *Fj*
V Faingaa 2012 *Sa*, *Fj*
OHL Faingaanuku 2011 *US*, 2012 *Fj*
T Fainga'anuku 1999 *NZ*, *It*, *E*, 2000 *C*, *Fj*, *J*, *NZ*, 2001 *Fj*, *Sa*, *Fj*, *Sa*
S Faka 'osi'folau 1997 *Z*, *Nm*, *SA*, *Fj*, *Sa*, *Coo*, *W*, 1998 *A*, *Fj*, 1999 *Geo*, *Kor*, *Fj*, 2001 *Sa*
DAT Fakafanua 2010 *CHL*, 2012 *Sa*
P Fakalelu 2005 *It*, 2006 *Coo*, *Coo*, 2009 *Sa*, *J*, 2013 *US*, *Fj*
J Fakalolo 1926 *Fj*, *Fj*, *Fj*
P Fakana 1963 *Fj*, *Fj*
F Fakaongo 1993 *S*, *Fj*, 1995 *Iv*, *Sa*, *Fj*, 2000 *Fj*, *J*, *NZ*, *Sa*, 2001 *S*, *W*, 2002 *J*, *Fj*, *Sa*
V Fakatou 1998 *Sa*, *A*, *Fj*, 1999 *Kor*, *NZ*
V Fakatulolo 1975 *M*
S Fakaua 2005 *Sa*
P Faka'ua 1967 *Fj*, *Fj*, *Fj*, 1968 *Fj*, *Fj*, *Fj*, 1969 *M*, *M*, 1972 *Fj*
N Fakauho 1977 *Fj*, *Fj*
P Fakava 1988 *Sa*, *Fj*
DT Faleafa 2013 *US*, *Fj*
K Faletau 1988 *Sa*, *Fj*, 1989 *Fj*, *Fj*, 1990 *Sa*, 1991 *Fj*, 1992 *Fj*, 1997 *Nm*, *SA*, *Fj*, *Sa*, *Coo*, *W*, 1999 *Sa*, *F*, *Fj*, *C*
FP Faletau 1999 *Geo*, *Kor*, *Kor*, *J*, *US*, *Sa*, *F*, *Fj*, *C*
M Fanga'uta 1982 *Fj*
K Fangupo 2009 *Pt*
MU Fangupo 2009 *Sa*, *J*, 2010 *J*, *CHL*
F Faotusa 1990 *Sa*
LAHN Fatafehi 2009 *Fj*, *Sa*, *Pt*, 2010 *Sa*, *Fj*, *J*, 2011 *Fj*, *NZ*, *C*, *J*, *F*, 2012 *Sa*, *J*, *Fj*, *It*, *US*, *S*
IT Fatani 1992 *Fj*, 1993 *Sa*, *S*, *Fj*, *A*, *Fj*, 1997 *Fj*, *Coo*, 1999 *Geo*, *Kor*, *Kor*, *J*, *US*, *Sa*, *F*, *Fj*, *C*, *NZ*, *It*, *E*, 2000 *C*, *Fj*, *J*, *NZ*, *Sa*, *US*
O Faupula 1924 *Fj*, *Fj*, *Fj*
SLJ Faupula 2010 *CHL*
AOM Feao 2010 *Sa*, *Fj*
S Fe'ao 1995 *F*, *S*
SL Fekau 1983 *M*, *M*
K Feke 1988 *Fj*, *Fj*, 1989 *Fj*, 1990 *Fj*, *Sa*
SH Fekitoa 2010 *Sa*, *J*
T Feleola 1934 *Fj*
M Felise 1987 *W*, *I*
I Fenukitau 1993 *Sa*, *S*, *Fj*, *A*, *Fj*, 1994 *Sa*, *Fj*, 1995 *J*, *J*, *F*, *S*, 2002 *J*, *Fj*, *Sa*, 2003 *It*, *W*, *NZ*, *C*
Fetu'ulele 1967 *Fj*
K Fielea 1987 *C*, *W*, *I*, *Sa*, *Fj*, 1990 *J*, *Sa*, *Kor*, *Sa*, 1991 *Sa*
L Fifita 1934 *Fj*
P Fifita 1983 *Fj*
P Fifita 2003 *C*
S Fifita 1974 *S*, *W*, *C*, 1975 *M*
T Fifita 1984 *Fj*, *Fj*, 1986 *W*, *Fj*, *Fj*, 1987 *C*, *W*, *I*, 1991 *Sa*, *Fj*, *Fj*
T Fifita 2001 *Fj*, *Fj*, 2003 *Fj*, 2006 *J*, 2008 *J*
V Fifita 1982 *Fj*
V Fifita 2005 *F*
V Fihaki 2013 *J*, *C*, *Fj*
F Filikitonga 1990 *Fj*, *Sa*
L Fililava 1960 *M*
M Filimoehala 1968 *Fj*, 1974 *W*, *C*, 1975 *M*, *M*
OAML Filipine 2000 *C*, 2006 *J*, *Fj*, *Coo*, *Sa*, 2007 *US*, *SA*, 2008 *J*
M Filise 1986 *Fj*, *Fj*
T Filise 2001 *Fj*, *Fj*, *S*, *W*, 2002 *Sa*, *Fj*, 2004 *Sa*, *Fj*, 2005 *Fj*, *Sa*, *Fj*, *Sa*, 2007 *Fj*, *Sa*, *E*, 2011 *NZ*, *J*
S Filo 2004 *Sa*, *Fj*
I Finau 1987 *Sa*, *Fj*, 1990 *Fj*, *J*, *Sa*
M Finau 2007 *AuA*, 2008 *J*, 2009 *Fj*, *J*, 2010 *J*, *CHL*
M Finau 1979 *NC*, *M*, *E*, *Sa*, 1980 *Sa*, 1984 *Fj*
S Finau 1998 *Sa*, 1999 *Geo*, *Sa*, *F*, *Fj*, *C*, *E*, 2001 *Fj*, *Fj*, *S*, 2005 *It*, *F*
S Finau 1924 *Fj*, *Fj*, *Fj*, 1926 *Fj*, *Fj*, *Fj*
S Finau 1989 *Fj*, *Fj*, 1990 *Fj*, *J*, *Sa*, *Kor*, *Sa*
T Finau 1967 *Fj*
T Finau 1924 *Fj*, *Fj*, *Fj*
V Finau 1987 *Sa*, *Fj*
I Fine 2007 *Kor*, *AuA*, *JAB*, *Sa*
K Fine 1987 *C*, *W*, *I*, 1988 *Fj*
L Fineanganofo 1924 *Fj*, *Fj*, *Fj*
J Finisi 1932 *Fj*, *Fj*, *Fj*
S Finisi 1928 *Fj*
P Fisi'iahi 1992 *Sa*
K Fisilau 1999 *J*, *US*, 2000 *C*, 2005 *Fj*, *Sa*, *It*
S Fisilau 2010 *Sa*, *Fj*, *J*, 2011 *Fj*, *J*, *Sa*, *Fj*, *NZ*, *J*, 2012 *It*
K Fokofuka 1995 *Sa*
K Folea 1991 *Fj*
S Foliaki 1973 *A*, *A*, 1977 *Fj*
Fololisi 1991 *Fj*
U Fono 2005 *Sa*, *Fj*, *It*, *F*
H Fonua 1973 *M*, *A*, *A*, *Fj*, 1974 *S*, *W*, *C*
O Fonua 2009 *Fj*, *Sa*, *Pt*
S Fonua 1928 *Fj*, *Fj*, *Fj*
SO Fonua 2002 *Sa*, *Sa*, 2003 *It*, *W*, *NZ*, *C*, 2007 *Kor*, *AuA*, *J*, *JAB*, *Fj*, *Sa*
T Fonua 2007 *Kor*
K Fotu 1990 *Fj*, *Sa*, *Kor*, *Sa*
TK Fotu 1987 *C*, 1988 *Sa*, *Fj*, 1989 *Fj*, 1990 *J*
L Fotu 1991 *Sa*, 1992 *Fj*, 1993 *S*, *Fj*
R Fotu 1979 *M*, 1983 *Fj*, *Sa*
S Fotu 1947 *Fj*
S Fotu 1968 *Fj*, *Fj*, *Fj*, 1969 *M*, *M*
P Fua'ava 1985 *Fj*
T Fuataimi 1928 *Fj*, 1932 *Fj*, *Fj*, *Fj*
F Fukofuka 1926 *Fj*, *Fj*, *Fj*, 1928 *Fj*
T Fukofuka 1993 *Fj*, 1995 *J*, *J*, *F*, *S*, *Iv*, *Fj*
A Fungavaka 1982 *Fj*
L Fusimalohi 1987 *Fj*, 1988 *Fj*, 1990 *J*, *Sa*

W Gibbons 2002 *PNG*, 2003 *Fj*

F Hafoka 1932 *Fj*, *Fj*, *Fj*
I Hafoka 1928 *Fj*, *Fj*, 1932 *Fj*, *Fj*, *Fj*, 1934 *Fj*
K Hafoka 1967 *Fj*, *Fj*, 1968 *Fj*, *Fj*, *Fj*
M Hafoka 1977 *Fj*, *Fj*, 1979 *M*, 1980 *Sa*
S Hafoka 1997 *W*
T Hafoka 1987 *Fj*
VA Hakalo 2006 *J*, *Coo*, *Sa*, 2010 *CHL*, 2013 *C*, *US*
S Hala 1999 *Geo*, *Geo*, *Kor*, 2002 *J*, *Fj*, *Sa*, *Sa*, *Fj*, 2003 *Kor*, *Kor*
H Halaeua 2010 *Fj*, *J*
M Halafatu 1989 *Fj*
KM Halafihi 2010 *Sa*, *J*
T Halafihi 1982 *Sa*, *Fj*, 1983 *Sa*, 1985 *Fj*
S Halahingano 1924 *Fj*, *Fj*, *Fj*
T Halaifonua 2009 *Fj*, *J*, 2013 *J*, *C*
A Halangahu 2007 *Kor*, 2011 *US*
A Halangahu 2007 *Kor*, 2011 *US*
C Halangi 2002 *Fj*
T Halasika 1988 *Fj*, *Fj*
C Hala'ufia 2000 *C*, 2001 *Fj*, *Sa*, *Fj*, *Sa*, *W*, 2002 *Sa*, 2004 *Sa*, *Fj*, 2005 *Fj*, *Fj*, *Sa*, *It*, *F*, 2006 *J*, *Fj*, *Coo*, *Sa*, *Coo*, 2007 *JAB*, *Fj*, 2009 *Fj*
S Hala'ufia 1977 *Fj*, 1979 *NC*, *M*, *E*, *Sa*, 1981 *Fj*
L Halavatau 1982 *Sa*, *Fj*
N Hau 2002 *Sa*
T Haumono 1924 *Fj*, *Fj*, *Fj*, 1926 *Fj*, *Fj*, *Fj*, 1928 *Fj*, 1932 *Fj*, *Fj*, *Fj*
T Havea 1924 *Fj*, *Fj*, *Fj*
SP Havea 2000 *NZ*, *US*, 2004 *Sa*, *Fj*, 2005 *Fj*, *Sa*, *Fj*, *Sa*, *It*, *F*, 2006 *J*, *Fj*, *Coo*, *Sa*, 2007 *Kor*, *JAB*, *Fj*, *Sa*, *US*, *SA*, *E*, 2008 *J*, *Sa*, *Fj*, 2010 *CHL*, 2011 *US*, *J*, *Sa*
M Havili 1987 *Sa*, 1988 *Fj*
P Havili 1981 *Fj*, *Fj*, *Fj*
R Havili 2013 *Fj*
AP Havili 2000 *C*, *Fj*, *J*, *Sa*, *US*, 2001 *Fj*, *Sa*, *Fj*, 2007 *AuA*, *J*, *JAB*, *US*, *SA*, *E*
KP Hehea 2006 *J*, *Fj*, *JAB*, *Coo*, *Sa*, *Coo*, 2007 *US*, *Sa*, *SA*, 2008 *Sa*, *Fj*, 2009 *Pt*, 2011 *Fj*, *J*, *Sa*, *Fj*, *NZ*, *J*, *F*
SE Hehepoto 1972 *Fj*, 1973 *M*, *A*, *A*, *Fj*
M Hekeheke 1986 *Fj*, *Fj*, 1988 *Fj*
Helehele 1985 *Fj*
T Helu 1967 *Fj*, *Fj*

VFUA Helu 2010 *Fj, J*, 2011 *US, Fj, J, Sa, Fj, C*, 2012 *It, US, S*, 2013 *J, C, US, Fj*
T Hikila 2010 *CHL*
O Hiko 1979 *E*
RP Hola 1998 *Sa, A, Fj*, 2001 *W*, 2002 *J, Fj, Sa, Sa, Fj, PNG, PNG*, 2003 *Kor, Kor, I, Fj, It, W, NZ, C*, 2005 *Fj*, 2006 *J, Fj, JAB, Coo, Sa, Coo*, 2007 *Sa, US, Sa, SA, E*, 2008 *J, Sa, Fj*, 2009 *Sa, J, Pt*
S Hola 1979 *Fj*
L Hopoate 1986 *W*
V Hosea 1967 *Fj, Fj*
F Hufanga 1973 *M*
S Hufanga 2003 *Fj, W, NZ, C*, 2004 *Sa, Fj*, 2005 *It, F*, 2006 *J, Fj, JAB*, 2007 *Fj, US, Sa, SA, E*, 2008 *Sa*, 2009 *Pt*, 2011 *US, Sa, Fj, Fj, NZ, J, F*, 2012 *It, US, S*

F Ika 1988 *Sa, Fj, Fj, Fj*, 1989 *Fj, Fj*
S Ika 2008 *J*, 2009 *Sa, J*
R Iloalahia 2010 *CHL*
M Ilolahia 1947 *Fj*
Inoke 1947 *Fj*
K 'Inoke 1967 *Fj, Fj, Fj*, 1968 *Fj, Fj, Fj*, 1969 *M, M*, 1972 *Fj*, 1973 *A*, 1975 *M*
V Iongi 2011 *US, Fj, J, Sa, Fj, Fj, NZ, C, F*, 2012 *Sa, J, Fj, It, US, S*, 2013 *C, US, Fj*
K 'Iongi 1967 *Fj, Fj, Fj*, 1968 *Fj, Fj, Fj*, 1969 *M, M*, 1972 *Fj*, 1973 *M, A, Fj*
T 'Isitolo 1995 *Iv, Sa, Fj*

M Kafatolu 2002 *J, Fj, Sa*
PNA Kaho 2011 *US*, 2012 *Sa, J, Fj, It*, 2013 *J, C, US*
T Kaho 1973 *A*
J Kaihau 1932 *Fj, Fj*
P Kaihau 1975 *M*, 1977 *Fj, Fj, Fj*
S Kaihau 1934 *Fj*
M Kaihea 1999 *Geo, Kor, Kor, J, Sa, F*
L Kainga 1928 *Fj, Fj*
L Kaiqa 1928 *Fj*
'A Kaitu'u 2000 *C*
J Kalaivalu 1996 *Sa*
SM Kalamafoni 2007 *Kor, AuA, J, JAB, Fj, Sa*, 2010 *Sa, Fj, J*, 2011 *Fj, J, Sa, Fj, Fj, NZ, C, J, F*
N Kalaniuvalu 1963 *Fj*
R Kapeli 1992 *Sa, Fj*, 1993 *Fj, A*
S Kapeli 2005 *Sa*
T Kapeli 1982 *Sa*
PF Kata 2009 *Pt*, 2010 *Sa, Fj, J*
FKM Katoa 2009 *J*
L Katoa 1996 *Sa, Fj*, 1997 *Nm, Fj, Sa*
P Katoa 1977 *Fj, Fj, Fj*, 1979 *NC, M, E, Sa, Fj*, 1981 *Fj, Fj, Fj*
P Katoa 1924 *Fj*
T Kaufana 1947 *Fj*
T Kaufusi 2007 *Kor, AuA, J, JAB, Fj, Sa*, 2009 *Sa, J*
L Kauhalaniua 1984 *Fj*
S Kauhenga 2002 *Sa, Sa, Fj*, 2003 *Fj*, 2006 *J*, 2007 *SA*, 2008 *J*, 2009 *Sa, J, Pt*, 2011 *US*, 2013 *J, C, US, Fj*
S Kava 1967 *Fj*
T Kavapalu 1967 *Fj*, 1968 *Fj, Fj, Fj*, 1969 *M, M*, 1972 *Fj*, 1973 *M, A, Fj*, 1974 *W*, 1975 *M, M*
A Kefu 1926 *Fj, Fj, Fj*, 1928 *Fj, Fj*
F Kefu 1972 *Fj, Fj*, 1973 *A*, 1974 *W, C*, 1975 *M*
M Kefu 2012 *Sa, J, Fj*
M Kefu 1959 *Fj*, 1960 *M*, 1963 *Fj, Fj*
E Kelemeni 1967 *Fj, Fj, Fj*
K Kioa 1959 *Fj*, 1960 *M*
P Kiole 1977 *Fj, Fj, Fj*, 1979 *M, E, Fj*, 1980 *Sa*
S Kiole 2005 *Fj, Fj, Sa*, 2007 *AuA, J, JAB, Fj, Sa*, 2008 *Fj*
FT Kitekei'aho 1987 *C, W, I*
T Kitekei'aho 1979 *Fj*
DJB Kivalu 1998 *Sa, A*, 1999 *Geo, Geo, Kor, Sa, F, Fj, C, NZ, It, E*, 2000 *C, Fj, J, NZ, Sa, US*, 2002 *J, Sa, Sa, Fj, PNG, PNG*, 2003 *Kor, Kor, Fj, Fj, It, W, NZ, C*, 2004 *Sa, Fj*, 2005 *Fj, Sa, Fj, Sa*
T Kolo 1993 *A*, 1995 *Sa, Fj*
OPV Koloamatangi 2011 *US*, 2012 *Sa, J*
C Koloi 1999 *US*
S Koloi 1998 *Sa, Fj*, 1999 *Geo, Geo, Kor, Kor, J, C, NZ, It, E*, 2000 *NZ, Sa, US*, 2001 *Sa*
K Kolokihakaufiji 2010 *CHL*
E Koloto 1986 *W*

F Lagilagi 1991 *Fj*
Jione Laiseni 1932 *Fj, Fj*
P Langi 1986 *W, Fj*
E Langi 2003 *NZ*
F Langi 1990 *Fj, J*
O Latu 2006 *J, Fj, JAB, Coo, Sa, Coo*, 2007 *Kor, AuA, J, JAB, Fj, Sa, US, Sa, SA, E*, 2008 *J, Sa, Fj*, 2009 *Fj, Sa, J*, 2012 *US, S*, 2013 *J, C, US, Fj*
F Lani 1986 *Fj*
TA Latailakepa 1992 *Sa, Fj*, 1993 *Sa*
K Latu 1987 *Fj*
MKM Latu 2011 *J*
P Latu 1994 *W*, 1995 *J, J, F, S, Iv, Sa, Fj*
S Latu 1972 *Fj*, 1973 *M, A, A, Fj*, 1974 *S, W, C*, 1975 *M, M*
S Latu 1992 *Fj*, 1993 *Fj, A*
S Latu 1984 *Fj, Fj*
U Latu 1997 *W*, 1998 *Sa*, 2002 *PNG, PNG*, 2003 *Kor, Kor, I, It, W, NZ, C*
U Latufeku 1959 *Fj*, 1960 *M*, 1963 *Fj*, 1968 *Fj, Fj, Fj*
P Latukefu 1995 *J, J, S, Iv, Sa, Fj*, 1998 *A, Fj*
T Latukefu 1967 *Fj, Fj, Fj*, 1968 *Fj, Fj, Fj*
M Latunipulu 1926 *Fj, Fj, Fj*
F Latusela 2003 *Kor, Kor*
F Lauei 1985 *Fj*
H Lavaka 1996 *Sa*, 1997 *SA, Fj, Sa, Coo, W*, 2003 *I, Fj, Fj, It, W, NZ, C*
K Lavaka 1996 *Fj*
M Lavaka 1993 *S, Fj, A, Fj*
S Lavaka 2008 *J*
T Lavaki 1990 *J, Kor*, 1993 *S*
F Lavemai 1984 *Fj, Fj*, 1985 *Fj*, 1986 *W*
M Lavulo 1979 *E*
T Lea'aetoa 2002 *PNG, PNG*, 2003 *Kor, Kor, I, It, W, NZ, C*, 2005 *It, F*, 2006 *J, Fj, JAB, Coo, Sa, Coo*, 2008 *J, Sa, Fj*, 2011 *US, Fj, Fj, Fj*
J Leba 1932 *Fj, Fj, Fj*
G Leger 2001 *S, W*, 2002 *J, Fj, Sa, Sa, Fj*, 2003 *Kor, Kor, I, Fj, It, NZ, C*
T Leger 1967 *Fj, Fj*
T Leha 1983 *M, M*
S Leilani 1981 *Fj*, 1983 *Fj, Sa*
FVMH Lemoto 2007 *Fj*
S Lepa 1928 *Fj, Fj*
A Liava'a 1979 *E*, 1981 *Fj, Fj, Fj*, 1983 *Fj, Sa, M, M*, 1984 *Fj, Fj*, 1985 *Fj*, 1987 *C, W, I*
S Liava'a 1979 *M, E*, 1981 *Fj, Fj*
V Likio 1947 *Fj, Fj*
L Lile 2002 *Sa, Fj*, 2003 *Fj*
VF Lilo 2007 *Kor, J, JAB, US, Sa, SA, E*, 2008 *J, Sa, Fj*, 2009 *Fj, Sa, J, Pt*, 2010 *Sa, Fj, J*, 2011 *Fj, J, Sa, Fj, NZ, J, F*, 2012 *It, US, S*
J Lino 1926 *Fj, Fj, Fj*
M Liongitau 1924 *Fj, Fj, Fj*
S Lisala 2005 *Sa, Fj*
S Lo'amanu 1926 *Fj, Fj, Fj*, 1928 *Fj, Fj, Fj*
T Lokotui 2001 *W*, 2011 *Fj, J, Sa, Fj, C, J, F*, 2012 *Fj, It, US, S*, 2013 *C, US, Fj*
S Lolo 1993 *Sa*
T Lolo'ahea 1987 *Sa*, 1990 *J, Sa, Kor, Sa*, 1991 *Sa, Fj, Fj*
L Lolohea 2007 *JAB*
P Lolohea 1983 *M, M*
K Lomu 1979 *Fj*
W Lose 1995 *F, S, Iv*
L Loto'ahea 1994 *Sa*
T Loto'ahea 1987 *Fj*, 1988 *Fj, Fj*, 1989 *Fj, Fj*, 1993 *S, Fj*, 1994 *W, Fj*
T Lovo 1982 *Sa*, 1986 *W, Fj, Fj*, 1987 *Sa*, 1988 *Fj*, 1989 *Fj, Fj*, 1990 *Sa*
S Luau 2007 *AuA*
I Lupina 1969 *M*, 1972 *Fj*
T Lutua 1990 *Kor*, 1992 *Fj*, 1994 *Sa, W, Fj*, 1995 *J, J, Iv*
V Lutua 1981 *Fj, Fj, Fj*, 1987 *W, I*, 1988 *Fj, Fj*

AA Lutui 1999 *Geo, J, Sa, F*, 2001 *Fj, Fj, S, W*, 2004 *Sa, Fj*, 2005 *Fj, Sa, Fj, Sa*, 2006 *Fj, JAB*, 2007 *AuA, J, JAB, Fj, Sa, US, Sa, SA, E*, 2010 *Sa, Fj, J*, 2011 *Fj, Fj, NZ, J, F*

F Ma'afa 1981 *Fj, Fj*
F Ma'afu 1985 *Fj*, 1986 *Fj, Fj*, 1988 *Sa, Fj, Fj, Fj*
P Ma'afu 1959 *Fj*, 1960 *M*, 1963 *Fj*
P Ma'afu 1979 *M, E, Sa, Fj*, 1980 *Sa*, 1981 *Fj, Fj*, 1983 *M, M*
T Ma'afu 1983 *M, M*
VS Ma'afu 2011 *US, J, Sa, Fj, Fj, NZ, C, J, F*, 2012 *J, It, US, S*
V Ma'ake 1973 *M, A, A, Fj*, 1974 *S, W, C*, 1975 *M, M*, 1977 *Fj, Fj, Fj*, 1979 *NC, M, E, Sa, Fj*, 1980 *Sa*
SM Maama 2010 *Sa, Fj*
AI Ma'asi 2009 *Fj, Sa, J*, 2011 *US, J, Sa, Fj, C, J*, 2012 *Sa, J, Fj, It, S*, 2013 *J, C, US, Fj*
V Ma'asi 1997 *W*, 2000 *C, J, Sa, US*, 2001 *Fj, Fj, Sa, S, W*, 2002 *J, Fj, Sa, Sa*, 2003 *I, Fj, Fj, It, W, NZ, C*, 2005 *Fj, Sa, It, F*, 2008 *J, Sa, Fj*, 2009 *Fj, Sa, J*
S Mafana 1959 *Fj*, 1960 *M*, 1963 *Fj, Fj*
A Mafi 1995 *Iv*
F Mafi 1993 *A, Fj*, 1994 *Sa, W, Fj*, 1995 *J, J, F*, 1996 *Sa, Fj*, 1998 *Sa, A*, 1999 *Geo, Geo, Kor, J, US, NZ, It, E*
S Mafi 1988 *Fj*, 1989 *Fj*, 1990 *Fj, Kor*, 1993 *Sa*
S Mafi 1969 *M, M*, 1972 *Fj, Fj, Fj*, 1973 *M, A, A, Fj*, 1974 *S, W, C*, 1975 *M, M*
S Mafi 2010 *Sa, Fj, J*, 2012 *Sa, J, Fj, It, US, S*
S Mafile'o 1995 *Iv, Sa, Fj*, 1997 *Z, Nm, SA*, 2002 *J*, 2003 *Kor, Kor, I, Fj*
R Mahe 2005 *Sa, It, F*, 2006 *Fj, JAB, Coo, Coo*, 2007 *Kor*
S Mahe 1981 *Fj, Fj, Fj*
F Mahoni 1993 *Sa, A, Fj*, 1995 *J, J, F, Sa, Fj*, 1996 *Sa, Fj*, 1999 *Geo, J*
F Mailangi 1928 *Fj, Fj*
A Mailangi 2010 *J*
F Mailangi 1968 *Fj, Fj, Fj*, 1969 *M*
L Mailangi 1959 *Fj*, 1960 *M*, 1963 *Fj, Fj*
TS Mailau 2012 *Sa, J, It, US, S*
P Mailefihi 1979 *E*, 1982 *Fj*
AK Ma'ilei 2002 *J, Fj, Sa, Sa, Fj, PNG, PNG*, 2003 *Kor, Kor*, 2005 *Fj, Sa, F*, 2010 *Sa, J*, 2011 *Fj, J, Fj, Fj, NZ, J, F*
T Mak 1988 *Fj*
A Maka 2005 *F*
F Maka 2007 *US, Sa, SA, E*, 2011 *Fj, NZ, C, F*
L Maka 1997 *Z*, 1999 *Geo, J, US, F, NZ, It, E*, 2000 *C, Fj, J, NZ, US*, 2002 *J, Sa, Sa, Fj*, 2003 *Kor, Kor*
P Maka 1985 *Fj*
T Maka 1979 *NC, Sa*, 1981 *Fj, Fj*
V Maka 1983 *Fj, Sa*, 1984 *Fj, Fj*
H Makahoi 1974 *C*, 1975 *M, M*, 1977 *Fj, Fj, Fj*, 1979 *Sa, Fj*, 1980 *Sa*
S Makalo 1975 *M*
M Makasini 2005 *Fj, Sa, Fj, Sa*
T Makisi 1983 *M, M*, 1989 *Fj, Fj*
M Malu 1979 *NC, Sa*
Malu 1947 *Fj*
MV Malupo 2009 *Sa*, 2011 *US, Sa*
L Manako 2000 *NZ, Sa*
T Manako 1995 *J, J*
T Manako 2000 *J*
C Manu 1987 *Sa, Fj*, 1989 *Fj, Fj*
E Manu 1996 *Sa, Fj*, 1999 *Kor, J, US*
F Manukia 1993 *A, Fj*, 1994 *Sa, W, Fj*, 1995 *J, J*
M Manukia 1993 *Sa, S, Fj, A, Fj*, 1994 *Fj*
T Mapa 1967 *Fj, Fj*
P Mapakaitolo 1977 *Fj, Fj*
VP Mapakaitolo 2009 *Fj, J*, 2011 *US*
S Martens 1998 *A, Fj*, 1999 *Geo, Geo, Kor, Kor, J, US, Sa, F, Fj, C, NZ, It, E*, 2001 *S, W*, 2002 *Fj, Sa, Sa, Fj*, 2003 *Kor, Kor, It, W, NZ, C*, 2009 *Fj, Sa, J*
S Masi 1989 *Fj*
F Masila 1990 *J*, 1991 *Fj*, 1993 *Sa, S, A, Fj*, 1994 *W*, 1995 *F, Fj*, 1998 *Sa, A*
Masili 1991 *Fj*
SK Masima 2005 *Fj*
SFL Masima 2013 *J, Fj*
T Matakaiongo 1997 *W*
S Matangi 2000 *J, Sa*, 2001 *Fj, Sa*, 2002 *Fj, PNG*, 2004 *Sa, Fj*
S Matapule 1973 *M*, 1975 *M*
SH Mata'u 2007 *AuA*, 2008 *J*
S Mateaki 1928 *Fj, Fj*
P Mateo 2010 *CHL*
K Ma'u 1981 *Fj*, 1983 *Fj, Sa, M*, 1984 *Fj, Fj*
T Ma'u 1947 *Fj, Fj*
V Ma'u 1947 *Fj*
O Misa 2004 *Sa, Fj*
S Misa 1926 *Fj, Fj, Fj*
S Moa 1928 *Fj*
U Moa 1998 *A, Fj*, 1999 *Geo*
UV Moa 2011 *Fj, Fj, NZ, C, J, F*, 2012 *Sa, J, Fj, It, US, S*, 2013 *J, C, US, Fj*
V Moa 1993 *Sa, S*, 1998 *Sa*
M Moala 1986 *W, Fj, Fj*
F Moala 1982 *Sa*, 1983 *Sa*, 1985 *Fj*
F Moala 1982 *Sa, Fj*, 1983 *Fj, Sa, M, M*, 1984 *Fj, Fj*, 1985 *Fj*
F Moala 1963 *Fj, Fj*, 1968 *Fj, Fj, Fj*
K Moala 1959 *Fj*, 1960 *M*, 1963 *Fj*, 1967 *Fj, Fj*
M Moala 2004 *Sa, Fj*, 2009 *Pt*
P Moala 1981 *Fj, Fj, Fj*
P Moala 1982 *Sa*, 1983 *M*, 1986 *W, Fj, Fj*, 1987 *Sa, Fj*
S Moala 1988 *Fj*
T Moala 1972 *Fj*
V Moala'eua 1977 *Fj, Fj, Fj*, 1979 *NC, M, Sa, Fj*, 1981 *Fj, Fj*
V Moeaki 1934 *Fj*
Mofuike 1986 *Fj*
S Mohi 1986 *W, Fj, Fj*, 1987 *C, W, I*
S Moimoi 2001 *W*
S Moli 1992 *Fj*
F Molitika 2000 *C, J*, 2001 *Fj, Sa, S*, 2005 *It, F*
MK Molitika 1997 *Nm, SA, Fj, Sa, Coo, W*, 2000 *NZ, Sa, US*, 2001 *S*, 2005 *It*, 2006 *Fj, JAB, Coo, Sa*, 2007 *E*
DW Morath 2010 *Sa, Fj*, 2011 *US*
KS Morath 2009 *Pt*, 2010 *Sa, Fj, J*, 2011 *US, Fj, J, Sa, Fj, NZ, C, J, F*, 2012 *Sa, J, Fj*, 2013 *J, C*
K Motu'apuaka 1972 *Fj*
S Motu'apuaka 1969 *M, M*, 1972 *Fj*
S Moto'apuaka 1980 *Sa*, 1987 *C*
S Motu'apuka 1979 *Fj*
S Motuliki 1967 *Fj*
Mounga 1947 *Fj*
E Mo'ungaloa 1924 *Fj, Fj, Fj*
F Muller 1967 *Fj*, 1968 *Fj, Fj, Fj*, 1969 *M, M*, 1972 *Fj, Fj*

S Na'a Tovo 1924 *Fj, Fj, Fj*
T Na'aniumotu 2006 *J, JAB, Coo, Sa, Coo*, 2010 *CHL*
F Naitoko 2005 *Sa*
S Napa'a 1934 *Fj*
S Nau 2000 *C, Fj, J*, 2001 *Fj*, 2003 *Fj*, 2005 *It, F*, 2006 *JAB, Coo, Sa*
N Naufahu 2001 *Fj, Sa, Fj, W*, 2002 *J, Sa, Sa, Fj, PNG, PNG*, 2003 *Kor, Kor, I, W, C*
S Nauvai 1960 *M*
T Ngaluafe 1974 *S, W, C*, 1975 *M, M*
J Ngauamo 2003 *Kor, I, Fj, It, C*, 2005 *It*
MM Ngauamo 2002 *PNG, PNG*, 2003 *Kor, I, Fj, It, W, NZ, C*, 2005 *F*, 2006 *Fj, JAB*, 2008 *Sa, Fj*
S Ngauamo 1997 *Coo*, 1998 *A*
T Nisa 1991 *Fj*, 1992 *Fj*
U Niuila 1990 *Sa*
S Nuku 1981 *Fj, Fj, Fj*, 1984 *Fj, Fj*

L Ofa 1983 *Fj, Sa, M, M*, 1984 *Fj*
A Olosoni 2010 *Sa, Fj, J*
I Omani 1928 *Fj*, 1932 *Fj, Fj, Fj*
M Otai 1995 *J, J, F, S, Iv*
M 'Ota'ota 2000 *C*, 2005 *Fj, Sa, Fj*

E Paea 2011 *US*, 2012 *Fj*
H Paea 2007 *Kor*
L Pahulu 1973 *A, Fj*, 1974 *S*
V Pahulu 1967 *Fj, Fj, Fj*, 1968 *Fj, Fj, Fj*, 1969 *M, M*, 1973 *M*

P Palavi 1924 *Fj, Fj, Fj*
U Palavi 1960 *M*, 1963 *Fj, Fj*
J Pale 2001 *S, W*, 2002 *J, Fj, Sa, Sa, Fj*, 2003 *Fj*
M Pale 1998 *A*, 1999 *Geo*, 2002 *J, Fj*, 2006 *J, Coo, Sa*
SW Palei 2009 *J*
S Palenapa 1990 *Fj, J, Sa, Kor, Sa*, 1996 *Sa, Fj*
D Palu 2002 *PNG, PNG*, 2003 *Kor, Kor, I, Fj, C*, 2006 *J, JAB, Coo*, 2007 *AuA, J, JAB*
P Palu 1979 *NC*, 1981 *Fj*
TT Palu 2011 *Sa, Fj, Fj, C, F*, 2012 *Fj*, 2013 *J, US, Fj*
TM Palu 2008 *J*
S Panelapa 1988 *Fj*
H Pau'u 1983 *Fj, Sa*
T Pau'u 1992 *Fj*
J Payne 2002 *PNG, PNG*, 2003 *Kor, Kor, I, Fj, It, W, NZ, C*
D Penisini 1997 *Nm, Coo*, 1999 *Geo, Kor, C*
'O Pepa 1928 *Fj, Fj, Fj*
H Petelo 1982 *Fj*
H Pierra 2005 *Sa*
O Pifeleti 1983 *Fj, Sa, M, M*, 1984 *Fj, Fj*, 1985 *Fj*, 1989 *Fj, Fj*, 1990 *Sa*, 1991 *Sa, Fj, Fj*
S Piukala 2012 *It, US, S*, 2013 *J, C, US, Fj*
T Piukala 1934 *Fj*
SV Piutau 2011 *Fj, Fj, NZ, C, J, F*, 2012 *Sa, J, Fj*, 2013 *J, C*
H Pohiva 1997 *W*, 1998 *Sa, Fj*
VV Pola 2010 *Fj, CHL*, 2012 *Sa, Fj*
THN Pole 2007 *Kor, AuA, J, JAB, Fj, Sa, US, Sa, E*, 2008 *Sa, Fj*, 2009 *Fj, Sa, J*, 2012 *It, US, S*, 2013 *J, C, US, Fj*
S Pone 2008 *Sa, Fj*, 2013 *US*
S Pongi 1990 *Sa*
SE Poteki 2007 *Kor*
VT Poteki 2007 *Kor*
S Pouanga 1947 *Fj, Fj*
E Pou'uhila 1988 *Fj*
SKV Puafisi 2011 *J, Sa*, 2012 *Fj*, 2013 *C, US, Fj*
ST Puloka 1928 *Fj, Fj*, 1934 *Fj*
K Pulu 2002 *Fj, PNG, PNG*, 2003 *Kor, Kor, I, Fj, It, W, NZ*, 2005 *Fj, Sa, Fj, Sa*, 2006 *J*, 2007 *US, Sa, SA, E*, 2008 *Fj*, 2009 *Sa, J*, 2011 *US, NZ, C, F*, 2012 *Sa, J, Fj*
M Pulumu 1979 *NC, Sa, Fj*, 1980 *Sa*, 1981 *Fj, Fj, Fj*
T Pulumufila 1974 *S, W, C*

H Saafi 2000 *NZ*
K Sakalia 2010 *CHL*, 2013 *J, C, US, Fj*
T Samiu 1947 *Fj*
Sanilaita 1981 *Fj*
S Satui 2009 *Pt*
A Saulala 1991 *Fj*
C Schaumkel 1992 *Sa, Fj*, 1997 *SA, Fj*
S Selupe 1963 *Fj, Fj*, 1967 *Fj, Fj*, 1969 *M, M*, 1972 *Fj*, 1973 *M, A, Fj*
S Selupe 1967 *Fj*, 1969 *M*, 1972 *Fj*
S Selupe 1924 *Fj, Fj, Fj*, 1928 *Fj*
T Siale 1997 *Nm, Sa*
M Sifa 1947 *Fj*
S Sika 1968 *Fj, Fj, Fj*, 1969 *M, M*
AH Sikalu 2007 *AuA, J*, 2010 *Sa, Fj*
T Sime 1963 *Fj*
T Sitanilei 1932 *Fj*
J Sitoa 1998 *A*
E Siua 2009 *Pt*, 2010 *CHL*, 2011 *US*
PIL Siulangapo 2010 *CHL*
T Soaiti 1932 *Fj, Fj, Fj*
T Soane 1982 *Sa, Fj*, 1983 *Fj, Sa*, 1984 *Fj, Fj*, 1985 *Fj*
L Stanley 1985 *Fj*
L Susimalofi 1989 *Fj*

L Tafa 2007 *J*
S Tahaafe 1987 *C*
P Taholo 1983 *M*
S Tai 1997 *W*, 1998 *A*
U Tai 1969 *M*, 1972 *Fj*
E Taione 2012 *It, US, S*, 2013 *J, C, US, Fj*
E Taione 1999 *It, E*, 2000 *Fj, J*, 2001 *S, W*, 2005 *F*, 2006 *JAB, Sa*, 2007 *Fj, Sa, US, Sa, SA, E*, 2008 *Sa, Fj*, 2009 *Fj*
K Take 1989 *Fj*
E Talakai 1993 *Sa, S, Fj, Fj*, 1995 *S, Iv, Sa, Fj*
H Taliai 1934 *Fj*
P Tanginoa 1995 *Fj*, 1997 *W*, 1998 *Sa, A*, 1999 *Geo*
T Tanginoa 2007 *AuA, J*
F Taniela 1982 *Fj*
I Tapueluelu 1990 *Fj, J, Sa, Sa*, 1993 *Sa, S*, 1999 *Kor, Kor, J, US, NZ, It, E*
F Tatafu 1996 *Fj*, 1997 *Z, Nm, Fj, Sa, Coo, W*, 1999 *Geo, Kor, Kor, J, Sa, Fj, C, NZ, E*, 2002 *J, Fj, Sa, PNG, PNG*
S Tatafu 1967 *Fj*
T Tatafu 1963 *Fj*
V Tau 1999 *US*
A Taufa 1993 *A*, 1995 *J, J, F, S*
AN Taufa 2010 *Sa, Fj, J*, 2011 *Fj, J, C*, 2012 *Sa, J, Fj*, 2013 *Fj*
E Taufa 2007 *Sa*, 2008 *J, Sa, Fj*
I Taufa 1972 *Fj*
S Taufa 1984 *Fj*
S Taufa 2005 *Fj, Sa, Fj, Sa*
T Taufa 1990 *Fj*
T Taufahema 1998 *Sa, A, Fj*, 1999 *Sa, F, NZ, It*, 2000 *C, Fj, J, NZ, Sa*, 2001 *Fj, Sa, Fj, S, W*
M Taufateau 1983 *M, M*, 1984 *Fj*, 1987 *Fj*
V Taufatofua 1926 *Fj, Fj, Fj*
A Ta'ufo'ou 1997 *Nm, SA, Fj, Sa, Coo*
E Ta'ufo'ou 2000 *C, Fj, J, NZ, Sa, US*
N Taufo'ou 1996 *Sa, Fj*, 1997 *Nm, SA, Fj, Sa, Coo, W*, 1998 *Sa, A, Fj*, 1999 *Geo, Kor, F, Fj, NZ, It, E*, 2000 *NZ, Sa, US*
E Taukafa 2002 *PNG, PNG*, 2003 *Kor, Kor, I, Fj, Fj, It, W, NZ, C*, 2005 *Fj, Sa, It, F*, 2006 *J, Fj, Coo, Sa, Coo*, 2007 *US, Sa, SA, E*, 2008 *Sa, Fj*, 2011 *Fj, J, Sa, Fj, NZ, C*
S Taukapo 2005 *Sa*
P Taukolo 1982 *Sa, Fj*
P Taula 2009 *Fj, Pt*, 2010 *Sa, Fj, J*
FKA Taumalolo 2011 *Fj, J, Sa, Fj, NZ, C, J, F*, 2012 *It, US, S*
S Taumalolo 1996 *Sa, Fj*, 1997 *Z, Nm, SA, Coo, W*, 1999 *Geo, Geo, Sa, F, Fj, C, NZ*, 2000 *NZ, Sa, US*, 2001 *Fj, Sa, S, W*, 2006 *J*, 2007 *JAB, Fj, Sa*
P Taumiuvao 1986 *Fj*
N Taumoefolau 1979 *NC, E, Sa, Fj*
P Taumoepeau 1928 *Fj, Fj, Fj*
SS Taumoepeau 2011 *US*
T Taumoepeau 1988 *Fj*
T Taumoepeau 1999 *Geo, Kor, Kor, J, US, NZ, E*, 2000 *Fj, J, NZ, Sa, US*, 2001 *Fj, Sa, Sa, S, W*, 2002 *J, Fj, Sa*, 2006 *J, Fj, JAB, Coo, Sa, Coo*, 2007 *AuA, J, Fj, Sa*
V Taumoepeau 1994 *Sa, W*, 1995 *Sa, Fj*
P Taumoua 2007 *J*
S Taupeaafe 1994 *W, Fj*, 1998 *Sa, A, Fj*, 1999 *Kor, J, NZ, It, E*, 2000 *NZ, US*, 2001 *Fj, Sa*
F Tautau'a 2007 *Kor*
S Tavo 1959 *Fj*, 1960 *M*, 1963 *Fj, Fj*, 1967 *Fj, Fj, Fj*, 1968 *Fj, Fj, Fj*, 1969 *M, M*
M Te Pou 1998 *A, Fj*, 1999 *Geo, Geo, Kor, Kor, J, US, F, NZ, It*, 2001 *S, W*
Telanisi 1967 *Fj*
SF Telefoni 2008 *J, Sa, Fj*, 2009 *Pt*, 2011 *Fj*
Teri 1991 *Fj*
Teutau 1991 *Fj*
SLN Timani 2008 *J*, 2009 *Fj*, 2011 *US, Fj, Fj, NZ, C*, 2012 *S*
D Tiueti 1997 *Fj, Sa, W*, 1999 *Geo, Geo, Kor, Sa, F, Fj, C, NZ, It, E*, 2000 *C, Fj, J, NZ, Sa, US*, 2001 *S, W*
T Tofua 1924 *Fj, Fj, Fj*, 1926 *Fj, Fj, Fj*
T Toga 1968 *Fj*
T Tohi 1997 *Nm, SA*
T Toke 2007 *Kor, J, JAB, Fj, Sa, US, Sa*, 2009 *Fj*, 2010 *Sa, Fj, J*
M Toloke 2010 *CHL*
V Toloke 1995 *J, Sa, Fj*, 1996 *Sa, Fj*, 1999 *Geo, Geo, Kor, Kor, US, NZ, E*, 2000 *NZ, Sa, US*, 2002 *J, Sa, Sa*
M Toma 1988 *Sa, Fj, Fj*, 1991 *Sa, Fj, Fj*
T Tonga 1990 *Sa*
G Tonga 1997 *Z, W*
K Tonga 2003 *Fj, C*, 2004 *Sa, Fj*, 2005 *Fj, Fj*
K Tonga 1947 *Fj, Fj*

K Tonga 1996 *Fj*, 1997 *Nm*, *SA*, *Fj*, *Sa*, *Coo*, 1999 *Geo*, *Geo*, *Kor*, 2001 *Fj*, *Sa*
M Tonga 1947 *Fj*, *Fj*
M Tonga 2001 *Fj*, *Sa*, *Fj*, *Sa*, 2003 *Kor*, *Kor*
P Tonga 1973 *A*
S Tonga 2005 *Sa*, *Fj*, *Sa*
S Tonga Simiki 1924 *Fj*, 1926 *Fj*, *Fj*, *Fj*
H Tonga'uiha 2005 *Fj*, *Sa*, *Sa*, 2006 *J*, *Fj*, *JAB*, *Coo*, *Sa*, *Coo*, 2007 *Kor*, *AuA*, *J*, *JAB*, *Fj*, *Sa*, *E*, 2008 *J*, *Sa*, *Fj*, 2009 *Fj*, *Sa*, *J*, 2011 *J*, *Sa*
SL Tonga'uiha 2005 *It*, *F*, 2007 *JAB*, *US*, *Sa*, *SA*, *E*, 2011 *Fj*, *NZ*, *C*, *J*, *F*, 2012 *It*
'O Topeni 2000 *J*
J Tuamoheloa 2003 *Fj*
S Tuamoheloa 2003 *Fj*, *C*, 2005 *Fj*
T Tuavao 1986 *Fj*
N Tufui 1990 *Fj*, *J*, *Sa*, *Sa*, 1992 *Fj*, 1994 *Fj*, 1995 *S*, *Iv*
S Tufui 1926 *Fj*, *Fj*, *Fj*, 1928 *Fj*, *Fj*, *Fj*, 1932 *Fj*, *Fj*, *Fj*, 1934 *Fj*
TH Tu'ifua 2003 *Fj*, *It*, *W*, *NZ*, 2006 *J*, *Fj*, *JAB*, *Coo*, *Sa*, 2007 *Fj*, *Sa*, *US*, *Sa*, *SA*, *E*
P Tu'ihalamaka 1972 *Fj*, 1973 *M*, *A*, *A*, *Fj*, 1974 *S*, *C*, 1975 *M*, *M*, 1977 *Fj*, *Fj*, 1979 *NC*, 1981 *Fj*, *Fj*, *Fj*, 1987 *C*
S Tu'ihalamaka 1999 *Kor*, *Kor*, *J*, *US*, 2001 *Sa*, *Fj*
Tu'ikolovatu 1983 *Fj*
JML Tuineau 2011 *Fj*, *J*, *Sa*, *Fj*, *NZ*, *J*, *F*, 2012 *Sa*, *J*, *Fj*, *It*, *US*, *S*
T Tu'ineua 1992 *Fj*, 1993 *Sa*, *S*, *Fj*, *A*, *Fj*
E Tu'ipolotu 1926 *Fj*, *Fj*, *Fj*, 1928 *Fj*, *Fj*
S Tu'ipolotu 1981 *Fj*
S Tu'ipolotu 1947 *Fj*, *Fj*
K Tuipulotu 1994 *Fj*, 1997 *Fj*, *Sa*, *Coo*
S Tuipulotu 1993 *Fj*, 1994 *Sa*, *W*, *Fj*, 1995 *J*, *J*, *F*, *S*, *Iv*, 1999 *Kor*, *F*, *Fj*, *C*, *It*, *E*, 2001 *S*, 2003 *Fj*, *Fj*, *It*, *NZ*
K Tu'ipulotu 1994 *W*, 1997 *SA*, *Fj*, *Coo*, *W*, 1999 *Kor*, *Kor*, *J*, *US*, *Fj*, *It*, *E*, 2000 *Fj*, *J*, 2001 *Fj*
M Tu'ipulotu 1977 *Fj*, *Fj*, *Fj*
P Tu'ipulotu 1979 *Sa*, 1980 *Sa*
SM Tu'ipulotu 1997 *W*, 1998 *Sa*, *A*, 1999 *Sa*, *F*, *NZ*, *E*, 2000 *C*, *NZ*, *Sa*, *US*, 2001 *Fj*, *Fj*, *Sa*, 2005 *Fj*, *Sa*, *It*, *F*, 2006 *J*, *Fj*, *JAB*, *Coo*, *Sa*, 2007 *US*, *Sa*, *SA*, *E*, 2008 *J*, *Sa*
V Tu'ipulotu 1977 *Fj*, *Fj*, *Fj*, 1979 *M*, *E*, *Fj*
J Tu'itavake 1932 *Fj*
L Tu'itavake 1959 *Fj*, 1960 *M*, 1963 *Fj*, *Fj*
P Tu'itavake 1995 *Fj*
I Tuivai 1993 *Sa*
K Tuivailala 1987 *Sa*, 1988 *Sa*, *Fj*, *Fj*, 1989 *Fj*, *Fj*, 1990 *Fj*, *J*, *Sa*, *Kor*, 1991 *Fj*
K Tuivailala 1988 *Fj*
M Tuku'aho 1979 *NC*, *Sa*, 1980 *Sa*, 1982 *Sa*
M Tuku'aho 1979 *Fj*
T Tulia 2002 *PNG*, 2003 *Kor*, *Kor*, *I*, *Fj*, 2004 *Sa*, *Fj*, 2005 *Fj*, *Sa*
A Tulikaki 1993 *S*
S Tulikifanga 1997 *SA*, *Fj*, *Sa*, *Coo*
S Tunufa'i 1934 *Fj*
F Tupi 1973 *A*, *A*, *Fj*, 1974 *S*, *W*, 1975 *M*, *M*
H Tupou 1982 *Sa*, *Fj*, 1983 *M*, *M*, 1984 *Fj*, *Fj*, 1987 *C*, *W*, *I*
J Tupou 1994 *Fj*
IM Tupou 2006 *Coo*, *Coo*, 2007 *Kor*, *AuA*, *J*, *JAB*, *US*, *Sa*, *SA*, 2008 *J*, 2009 *Fj*, *Sa*
M Tupou 2005 *Fj*, *Fj*, *Sa*, 2010 *CHL*
P Tupou 1984 *Fj*, 1986 *W*, 1988 *Fj*
S Tupou 1975 *M*
M Tu'ungafasi 1986 *W*, *Fj*, 1987 *W*, *I*
L Tu'uta 1928 *Fj*, *Fj*
T Tu'utu Kakato 1987 *C*, *W*, *I*, 1990 *Sa*, *Kor*, 1991 *Sa*, *Fj*, 1992 *Fj*

A Uasi 1993 *S*, 1994 *Sa*, *Fj*
L Uhatafe 1987 *Sa*, *Fj*
V Uhi 1997 *Z*, *Nm*, *SA*, *Fj*, *Sa*, *Coo*
S Ula 1959 *Fj*, 1960 *M*, 1963 *Fj*, *Fj*
T Ula 2011 *Fj*
L Ulufonua 2002 *PNG*, 2003 *Kor*, *Kor*, *Fj*
T Unga 1934 *Fj*

S Vaea 1928 *Fj*, *Fj*, *Fj*
S Vaea 1974 *S*, *W*, *C*, 1975 *M*, 1977 *Fj*, *Fj*
S Vaeno 1991 *Sa*
L Vaeno 1986 *Fj*
L Va'eono 1987 *W*
S Vaenuku 2003 *Fj*, *It*, *W*, *NZ*, 2004 *Sa*, *Fj*, 2005 *Sa*, *Fj*, *Sa*, *It*, 2007 *AuA*, *Sa*
T Va'enuku 1991 *Sa*, *Fj*, 1992 *Sa*, *Fj*, 1993 *S*, *Fj*, *A*, *Fj*, 1994 *Sa*, *W*, *Fj*, 1995 *F*, *S*, *Iv*
U Va'enuku 1995 *F*, *S*, *Iv*
L Vaeuo 1985 *Fj*
S Vaha'akolo 1990 *J*, *Kor*
SK Vahafolau 2007 *J*, *Fj*, *Sa*, 2008 *Sa*, *Fj*, 2009 *Pt*, 2011 *Fj*, *Sa*, *Fj*, *Fj*, *NZ*, *C*, *J*, *F*
N Vahe 1977 *Fj*, *Fj*
S Vai 1981 *Fj*, *Fj*, 1988 *Sa*, *Fj*
A Vaihu 1975 *M*
T Vaikona 2006 *J*, *Fj*, *JAB*, *Coo*
H Vaingalo 1988 *Fj*
F Vainikolo 2011 *Fj*, *Fj*, *C*, *J*, 2012 *It*, *US*, *S*, 2013 *J*, *C*
SAF Vaioleti 2010 *CHL*
T Vaioleti 2005 *F*, 2010 *CHL*
SFKHF Vaiomounga 2009 *Pt*, 2010 *Sa*, *Fj*, *J*, 2011 *Fj*, *Sa*, *Fj*, *C*, *J*, 2012 *Sa*, *J*, *Fj*, *It*
L Vaipulu 1987 *C*
JW Vaka 2004 *Sa*, *Fj*, 2005 *Sa*, 2007 *US*, *Sa*, *SA*, *E*, 2009 *Fj*, *Sa*, *J*, 2012 *Sa*, *J*, *Fj*
PM Vakaloa 2009 *Pt*
P Vakamalolo 1993 *Sa*
S Vaka'uta 1924 *Fj*, *Fj*, *Fj*
I Vaka'uta 1959 *Fj*, 1963 *Fj*, *Fj*
V Vaka'uta 1959 *Fj*, 1960 *M*
V Vake 1932 *Fj*
VL Vaki 2001 *Fj*, *Sa*, *Fj*, *Sa*, *S*, *W*, 2002 *J*, *Fj*, *Sa*, *Sa*, *Fj*, *PNG*, 2003 *I*, *Fj*, *Fj*, *It*, *W*, *NZ*, *C*, 2005 *Fj*, *Sa*, *It*, *F*, 2006 *JAB*, *Coo*, *Sa*, *Coo*, 2007 *US*, *Sa*, *SA*, *E*, 2008 *Fj*
Valeli 1947 *Fj*
F Valu 1973 *M*, *A*, *A*, *Fj*, 1974 *S*, *W*, *C*, 1975 *M*, *M*, 1977 *Fj*, *Fj*, *Fj*, 1979 *NC*, *M*, *E*, *Sa*, *Fj*, 1980 *Sa*, 1981 *Fj*, 1983 *Fj*, *Sa*, *M*, *M*, 1987 *C*, *W*, *I*
V Vanisi 1969 *M*, *M*
L Vano 1986 *Fj*
A Vasi 1993 *Fj*
I Vave 1973 *A*, *A*, *Fj*, 1974 *S*, *C*
T Vave 1993 *A*
M Vea 1992 *Fj*
T Vea 2013 *J*, *C*, *US*, *Fj*
S Veehala 1987 *Sa*, *Fj*, 1988 *Fj*, *Fj*, 1989 *Fj*, 1990 *J*, *Kor*, 1991 *Sa*, *Fj*, *Fj*
J Vikilani 1932 *Fj*, *Fj*
T Vikilani 1992 *Fj*, 1994 *Sa*, *W*
T Viliame 1979 *M*
O Vitelefi 1986 *W*
F Vuna 1977 *Fj*, *Fj*, *Fj*, 1979 *NC*, *M*, *Sa*, 1981 *Fj*
V Vuni 1932 *Fj*, *Fj*, *Fj*, 1934 *Fj*
A Vunipola 1982 *Fj*
E Vunipola 1990 *Fj*, *Kor*, 1993 *Sa*, *S*, *Fj*, *A*, *Fj*, 1994 *Sa*, *W*, 1995 *J*, *J*, *F*, *S*, *Iv*, 1996 *Sa*, *Fj*, 1997 *Z*, 1999 *Geo*, *Geo*, *Kor*, *Kor*, *J*, *F*, *Fj*, *NZ*, *It*, *E*, 2000 *C*, *Fj*, *J*, *NZ*, *Sa*, *US*, 2001 *Fj*, *Sa*, *Fj*, *Sa*, *S*, 2004 *Sa*, *Fj*, 2005 *F*
F Vunipola 1988 *Fj*, 1991 *Sa*, *Fj*, *Fj*, 1994 *Sa*, *W*, *Fj*, 1995 *J*, *J*, *F*, *S*, *Iv*, *Sa*, *Fj*, 1996 *Sa*, *Fj*, 1997 *SA*, *Fj*, *Coo*, 1998 *Sa*, *Fj*, 1999 *Geo*, *Kor*, *Kor*, *Fj*, *C*, *NZ*, *E*, 2000 *NZ*, *Sa*, *US*, 2001 *Sa*
K Vunipola 1982 *Sa*, *Fj*, 1983 *Fj*, *Sa*, *M*, *M*
M Vunipola 1987 *W*, *Sa*, 1988 *Sa*, *Fj*, *Fj*, *Fj*, 1989 *Fj*, *Fj*, 1990 *Kor*, 1991 *Fj*, *Fj*, 1992 *Sa*, 1993 *Sa*, *S*, *Fj*, *A*, *Fj*, 1994 *Sa*, *W*, 1995 *J*, *J*, *F*, *S*, *Sa*, *Fj*, 1996 *Sa*, *Fj*, 1997 *Nm*, *SA*, *Coo*, 1999 *Geo*, *Kor*, *Kor*, *US*, *Fj*
S Vunipola 1977 *Fj*, 1981 *Fj*, 1982 *Sa*
V Vunipola 1982 *Fj*
VS Vunipola 2004 *Sa*, *Fj*, 2005 *It*
S Vunipoli 1960 *M*, 1963 *Fj*

B Woolley 1998 *Sa*, *Fj*, 1999 *Geo*, *Geo*, *Kor*, *J*, *US*, *Sa*, *C*, *It*

A strong performance in Tokyo helped the USA retain their core status in the HSBC Sevens World Series.

AFP/Getty Images

USA

USA'S 2012–13 TEST RECORD

OPPONENTS	DATE	VENUE	RESULT
Russia	9 Nov	N	Won 40–26
Tonga	17 Nov	N	Lost 22–13
Romania	24 Nov	A	Won 34–3
Canada	25 May	A	Lost 16–9
Ireland	8 Jun	H	Lost 12–15
Tonga	14 Jun	H	Lost 9–18
Fiji	19 Jun	N	Lost 35–10
Japan	23 Jun	A	Lost 38–20
Canada	17 Aug	H	Lost 9–27
Canada	24 Aug	A	Lost 13–11

EAGLES READY TO SOAR AGAIN

By Ian Gilbert

AFP/Getty Images

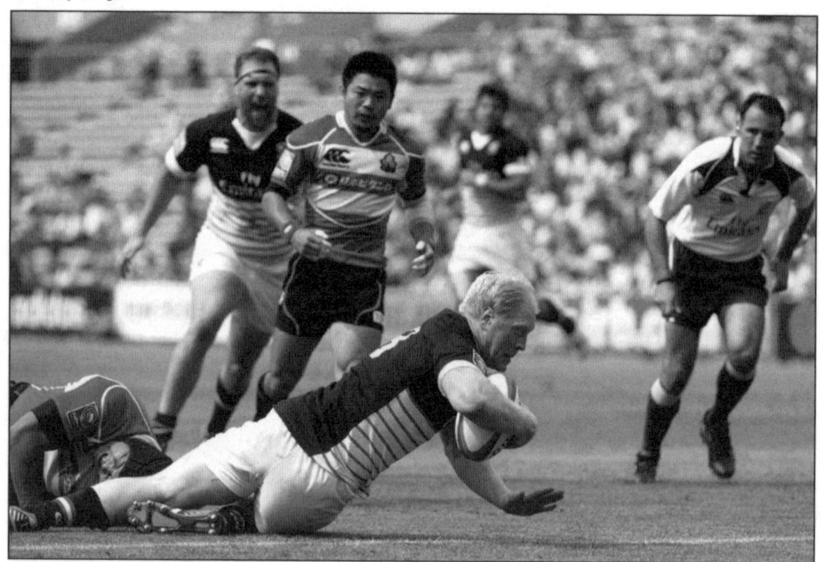

Eric Fry stretches to score a try for the USA against Japan in their IRB Pacific Nations Cup match in Tokyo.

The USA started their 2012/13 season against Russia, a foe they had faced the year before in New Zealand when Rugby World Cup honours were at stake. This time the setting was the less familiar surrounds of the north Wales coastal town of Colwyn Bay as the sides joined Tonga, Canada and Samoa in the inaugural IRB International Rugby Series in November.

They had won all but one of their five previous clashes against Russia, whose solitary victory came back in 1988, and on neutral territory the Eagles continued their dominance of the fixture by scoring six tries on their way to a 40–26 victory. However, any expectations that the win may have raised for a successful season proved unfounded. Nor did the result that day give any indication of the mid-season try drought that would hamper the Eagles' efforts to boost their win tally.

A 22–13 defeat by Tonga in their next match completed the Eagles' International Rugby Series and victory over Romania later in November would be the last USA win for the season as they lost the next seven matches.

One of those reverses was perhaps the most creditworthy performance of the year as the USA came within a whisker of registering their first-ever win against Ireland in eight attempts. The Irish, who were admittedly shorn of their British & Irish Lions, edged home 15–12 in Houston but it was the smallest losing margin that the Eagles had posted against the tourists.

That performance, against one of the top-eight seeded sides for Rugby World Cup 2015, gave the USA every reason to feel confident for the remainder of the season, starting with the resumption of their debut season in the IRB Pacific Nations Cup. However the Eagles, who had already been beaten 16–9 by Canada, failed to build on their near-miss against the Irish, losing again to Tonga.

Among the more frustrating statistics for USA head coach Mike Tolkin was the realisation that the 18–9 defeat was the third consecutive match in which his side had failed to score a try. "Obviously our attacking is spluttering and we need to figure that out," admitted Tolkin.

Figure it out they did in their next match against Fiji with Andrew Suniula touching down. However, the Flying Fijians scored four tries of their own for a 35–10 victory. That result, in the Japanese city of Nagoya, set up Fiji's Pacific Nations Cup-clinching win against Tonga four days later, while the USA endured another defeat, 38–20 against their hosts.

It was hardly ideal preparation for the two-match series against Canada in August. While the stakes are high whenever the two North American rivals play each other, these Tests carried added weight as the aggregate winner would qualify for RWC 2015 as Americas 1 and join RWC 2011 runners-up France, Ireland, Italy and the Europe 2 qualifier in Pool D.

The first game was held in Charleston, South Carolina, where home advantage counted for little as the Canadians laid solid foundations with a 27–9 victory. In the return leg, in Toronto, Suniula impressed for the Eagles with his surging runs and the Eagles' Biarritz-based wing Takudzwa Ngwenya crossed for the game's first try. The Canadians struck back and, with the score 8–8 at half-time, the Eagles still needed to overhaul the 18-point deficit from the first game. Canada added a second try and, although a penalty kept the USA in touch on the day, they were not near enough in the aggregate total. Such calculations proved academic as Canada claimed the match with a 13–11 win.

The Eagles, who have lost their past seven games against Canada, must now focus on the home and away tie against Uruguay in 2014 with the winner securing the Americas 2 place in Pool B alongside South Africa, Samoa, Scotland and the Asia 1 qualifier.

One player who will not be involved is veteran centre Paul Emerick who called time on his international career in August. The win over Romania was Emerick's last game in national colours, with the ankle injury sustained during that match ultimately forcing him to retire as his country's fourth most-capped player with 53 Tests and second on their all-time list of try-scorers with 17.

The Women's Eagles fared a little better than their male counterparts, winning five of their 10 Tests over the last 12 months, including impressive wins over Canada and France. They did suffer four defeats across two series with France, but the margins of defeat had reduced significantly between November's series in Europe and the return in Colorado in June as the side continues to build towards Women's Rugby World Cup 2014 in France.

The Junior All-Americans returned to the IRB Junior World Championship stage in 2013 but found the step up from winning the IRB Junior World Rugby Trophy to be too big, suffering record defeats against South Africa (97–0) and England (109–0). They failed to win a match in France and will return to the second tier, the Junior World Rugby Trophy, in 2014.

In Sevens, the women led the way by finishing third at RWC Sevens in Moscow, beating Spain 10–5 after extra-time. The Americans progressed well through the tournament, accounting for Brazil, Fiji and Spain to book a quarter-final with Ireland. There, they scored two late tries to defeat Ireland 14–5 and their progress was only checked by New Zealand in the semi-final.

The men's team made the Plate quarter-finals, losing 28–5 to Argentina in an anti-climactic finish to a campaign that had provided several bright notes. The Eagles coughed up a 10-point head-start to Canada but came back to within a point, and then raced to a 19–5 lead over New Zealand before allowing the eventual champions to emerge 26–19 winners. USA finished 11th in the 2012/13 HSBC Sevens World Series, finishing strongly in the last three events with two Plate successes to guarantee their core team status for next season. They also registered a first-ever win over South Africa in London.

On the domestic scene, the restructured national club competition saw San Francisco Golden Gate claim the inaugural Elite Cup, which is structured along regional lines, by beating Life University 31–26. Life University made amends by securing the Division One Championship, edging a 27–26 thriller against Seattle Old Puget Sound Beach in their second title decider in consecutive weekends.

The Women's Premier League was played at the start of the season, with Berkeley All-Blues securing the title in November against Glendale Raptors 39–5. Atlanta Harlequins gained promotion after winning the Division One National Championship.

USA INTERNATIONAL STATISTICS

MATCH RECORDS UP TO 10 OCTOBER 2013

WINNING MARGIN

Date	Opponent	Result	Winning Margin
01/07/2006	Barbados	91–0	91
06/07/1996	Japan	74–5	69
07/11/1989	Uruguay	60–3	57
12/03/1994	Bermuda	60–3	57

MOST POINTS IN A MATCH

BY THE TEAM

Date	Opponent	Result	Points
01/07/2006	Barbados	91–0	91
06/07/1996	Japan	74–5	74
17/05/2003	Japan	69–27	69
12/04/2003	Spain	62–13	62
08/04/1998	Portugal	61–5	61

BY A PLAYER

Date	Player	Opponent	Points
07/11/1989	Chris O'Brien	Uruguay	26
31/05/2004	Mike Hercus	Russia	26
01/07/2006	Mike Hercus	Barbados	26
12/03/1994	Chris O'Brien	Bermuda	25
06/07/1996	Matt Alexander	Japan	24

MOST TRIES IN A MATCH

BY THE TEAM

Date	Opponent	Result	Tries
01/07/2006	Barbados	91–0	13
17/05/2003	Japan	69–27	11
07/11/1989	Uruguay	60–3	11
06/07/1996	Japan	74–5	11

BY A PLAYER

Date	Player	Opponent	Tries
11/05/1924	Dick Hyland	Romania	5
06/07/1996	Vaea Anitoni	Japan	4
07/06/1997	Brian Hightower	Japan	4
08/04/1998	Vaea Anitoni	Portugal	4
11/05/1924	John Patrick	Romania	4

MOST CONVERSIONS IN A MATCH

BY THE TEAM

Date	Opponent	Result	Cons
01/07/2006	Barbados	91–0	13
07/11/1989	Uruguay	60–3	8
06/07/1996	Japan	74–5	8

BY A PLAYER

Date	Player	Opponent	Cons
01/07/2006	Mike Hercus	Barbados	13
06/07/1996	Matt Alexander	Japan	8
07/11/1989	Chris O'Brien	Uruguay	7
17/05/2003	Mike Hercus	Japan	7

MOST PENALTIES IN A MATCH

BY THE TEAM

Date	Opponent	Result	Pens
18/09/1996	Canada	18–23	6

BY A PLAYER

Date	Player	Opponent	Pens
18/09/1996	Matt Alexander	Canada	6
21/09/1996	Matt Alexander	Uruguay	5
02/10/1993	Chris O'Brien	Australia	5
20/10/2003	Mike Hercus	Scotland	5
22/05/1999	Kevin Dalzell	Fiji	5
09/06/1984	Ray Nelson	Canada	5

MOST DROP GOALS IN A MATCH

BY THE TEAM

Date	Opponent	Result	DGs
27/11/2010	Georgia	17–19	2

BY A PLAYER

1 on 18 occasions

MOST CAPPED PLAYERS

Name	Caps
Mike MacDonald	67
Luke Gross	62
Alec Parker	57
Dave Hodges	53
Paul Emerick	53

LEADING TRY SCORERS

Name	Tries
Vaea Anitoni	26
Paul Emerick	17
Todd Clever	11
Philip Eloff	10
Takudzwa Ngwenya	10
Riaan van Zyl	10
Chris Wyles	10

LEADING CONVERSION SCORERS

Name	Cons
Mike Hercus	90
Matt Alexander	45
Chris O'Brien	24
Nese Malifa	17

LEADING PENALTY SCORERS

Name	Pens
Mike Hercus	76
Matt Alexander	55
Mark Williams	35

LEADING DROP GOAL SCORERS

Name	DGs
Mike Hercus	4

LEADING POINT SCORERS

Name	Points
Mike Hercus	465
Matt Alexander	286
Chris Wyles	147
Chris O'Brien	144
Mark Williams	143

USA INTERNATIONAL PLAYERS
UP TO 10 OCTOBER 2013

M Alexander 1995 *C*, 1996 *I*, *C*, *HK*, *J*, *HK*, *J*, *Ar*, *C*, *Ur*, 1997 *W*, *C*, *HK*, *J*, *J*, *HK*, *C*, *W*, *W*, 1998 *Pt*, *Sp*, *J*, *HK*, *C*
AE Allen 1912 *A*
S Allen 1996 *J*, 1997 *HK*, *J*, *J*, *C*, *W*, *W*
T Altemeier 1978 *C*
D Anderson 2002 *S*
B Andrews 1978 *C*, 1979 *C*
VN Anitoni 1992 *C*, 1994 *C*, *Ar*, *Ar*, *I*, 1995 *C*, 1996 *I*, *C*, *C*, *HK*, *J*, *HK*, *J*, *Ar*, *C*, *Ur*, 1997 *W*, *C*, *J*, *HK*, *C*, *W*, *W*, 1998 *Pt*, *Sp*, *J*, *HK*, *C*, *C*, *J*, *HK*, *Fj*, *Ar*, *C*, *Ur*, 1999 *Tg*, *Fj*, *J*, *C*, *Sa*, *E*, *I*, *R*, *A*, 2000 *Fj*, *Sa*
J Arrell 1912 *A*
D Asbun 2012 *Geo*, *It*, *Tg*, *R*, 2013 *C*
S Auerbach 1976 *A*
CA Austin 1912 *A*, 1913 *NZ*
M Aylor 2006 *IrA*, *M*, *C*, *Bar*, *Ur*, *Ur*, 2007 *S*, *C*, *Sa*, *SA*, 2008 *IrA*

A Bachelet 1993 *C*, *A*, 1994 *Ber*, *C*, *Ar*, *Ar*, *I*, 1995 *C*, 1996 *I*, *C*, *C*, *HK*, *J*, *HK*, *J*, *Ar*, *C*, 1997 *W*, *C*, *HK*, *J*, *J*, *HK*, *C*, *W*, *W*, 1998 *Pt*, *Sp*, *J*, *HK*, *C*, *C*, *J*
R Bailey 1979 *C*, 1980 *NZ*, 1981 *C*, *SA*, 1982 *C*, 1983 *C*, *A*, 1987 *Tun*, *C*, *J*, *E*
B Barnard 2006 *IrA*, *M*, *Bar*, *C*
JI Basauri 2007 *S*, *E*, *Tg*, 2008 *Ur*, *J*, *J*, 2010 *Pt*, *Geo*, 2011 *Tg*, *Rus*, *C*, *A*, 2012 *Rus*, *Tg*, *R*
D Bateman 1982 *C*, *E*, 1983 *A*, 1985 *J*, *C*
P Bell 2006 *IrA*, *M*, *C*, *Bar*, *C*, *Ur*, *Ur*
W Bernhard 1987 *Tun*
CM Biller 2009 *I*, *W*, *Geo*, *C*, *C*, 2010 *Rus*, *Pt*, *Geo*, 2011 *Tg*, *Rus*, *C*, *C*, *J*, *I*, *Rus*, *It*, 2012 *C*, *Geo*, *It*, *Rus*, *Tg*, *R*, 2013 *I*, *Tg*, *Fj*, *J*, *C*, *C*
TW Billups 1993 *C*, *A*, 1994 *Ber*, *C*, *Ar*, *Ar*, *I*, 1995 *C*, 1996 *I*, *C*, *C*, *HK*, *HK*, *J*, *Ar*, *C*, *Ur*, 1997 *W*, *C*, *HK*, *HK*, *W*, *W*, 1998 *Pt*, *Sp*, *J*, *HK*, *C*, *C*, *J*, *HK*, *Fj*, *Ar*, *C*, *Ur*, 1999 *Tg*, *Fj*, *J*, *C*, *Sa*, *E*, *I*, *R*, *A*
RR Blasé 1913 *NZ*
A Blom 1998 *Sp*, *J*, *HK*, *C*, *C*, *HK*, *Fj*, *Ar*, *Ur*, 1999 *Sa*, 2000 *J*, *C*, *I*
H Bloomfield 2007 *E*, *Tg*, *SA*, 2008 *E*, *C*
R Bordley 1976 *A*, *F*, 1977 *C*, *E*, 1978 *C*
J Boyd 2008 *IrA*, 2009 *I*
S Bracken 1994 *Ar*, 1995 *C*
G Brackett 1976 *A*, *F*, 1977 *E*
N Brendel 1983 *A*, 1984 *C*, 1985 *J*, *C*, 1987 *Tun*, *E*
D Briley 1979 *C*, 1980 *W*, *C*, *NZ*
J Buchholz 2001 *C*, 2002 *S*, 2003 *Sp*, *EngA*, *Ar*, *Fj*, *J*, *F*, 2004 *C*
B Burdette 2006 *Ur*, *Ur*, 2007 *E*, *S*, *C*, *E*, *Tg*, *Sa*, *SA*
JR Burke 1990 *C*, *J*, 1991 *J*, *J*, *S*, *C*, *F*, *NZ*, 1992 *C*
J Burke 2000 *C*, *I*
J Burkhardt 1983 *C*, 1985 *C*
E Burlingham 1980 *NZ*, 1981 *C*, *SA*, 1982 *C*, *E*, 1983 *C*, *A*, 1984 *C*, 1985 *C*, 1986 *J*, 1987 *Tun*, *C*, *J*, *E*

C Campbell 1993 *C*, *A*, 1994 *Ber*, *C*, *Ar*
D Care 1998 *Pt*, *J*, *C*
M Carlson 1987 *W*, *C*

DB Carroll 1913 *NZ*, 1920 *F*, *F*
L Cass 1913 *NZ*
M Caulder 1984 *C*, 1985 *C*, 1989 *C*
R Causey 1977 *C*, 1981 *C*, *SA*, 1982 *C*, *E*, 1984 *C*, 1986 *J*, 1987 *E*
W Chai 1993 *C*
R Chapman 2011 *J*
D Chipman 1976 *A*, 1978 *C*
JE Clark 1979 *C*, 1980 *C*
P Clark 1924 *R*
J Clarkson 1986 *J*, 1987 *Tun*, *C*, *J*, *E*
J Clayton 1999 *C*, *R*, *A*, 2000 *J*, *C*, *I*, *Fj*, *Tg*, *Sa*, *S*, *W*
N Cleveland 1924 *R*, *F*
TS Clever 2003 *Ar*, 2005 *C*, *R*, *W*, *ArA*, *C*, 2006 *IrA*, *M*, *C*, *Bar*, *C*, *Ur*, *Ur*, 2007 *E*, *S*, *C*, *E*, *Tg*, *Sa*, *SA*, 2008 *E*, *IrA*, *C*, *Ur*, *J*, *J*, 2009 *Geo*, *C*, *C*, *Ur*, *Ur*, 2010 *Pt*, *Geo*, 2011 *Tg*, *Rus*, *C*, *C*, *I*, *Rus*, *It*, 2012 *C*, *Geo*, *It*, *Rus*, *Tg*, *R*, 2013 *C*, *I*, *Tg*, *J*, *C*, *C*
R Cooke 1979 *C*, 1980 *W*, *C*, *NZ*, 1981 *C*, *SA*
B Corcoran 1989 *Ur*, *Ar*, 1990 *Ar*
J Coulson 1999 *A*
M Crick 2007 *E*, *S*, *C*, 2008 *E*, *IrA*, *C*, *Ur*, *J*, *J*
R Crivellone 1983 *C*, 1986 *C*, 1987 *C*
K Cross 2003 *Sp*, *Sp*, *J*, *C*, *EngA*, *EngA*, *Ar*, *C*, *Fj*, *S*, 2004 *C*, *Rus*
C Culpepper 1977 *E*, 1978 *C*
C Curtis 1997 *C*, *HK*, *J*, 1999 *Sa*, 2001 *Ar*

P Dahl 2009 *I*, *W*, 2012 *Rus*, *Tg*, *R*, 2013 *C*, *I*, *Tg*, *Fj*, *J*, *C*, *C*
B Daily 1989 *Ur*, *Ar*, 1990 *Ar*, *C*, *A*, *J*, 1991 *J*, *J*, *S*, *F*, *F*, *It*
K Dalzell 1996 *Ur*, 1998 *Sp*, *C*, *HK*, *C*, *Ur*, 1999 *Tg*, *Fj*, *J*, *C*, *Sa*, *E*, *I*, *R*, *A*, 2000 *J*, *C*, *I*, *Fj*, *Tg*, *Sa*, *S*, *W*, 2001 *C*, *E*, *SA*, 2002 *S*, *C*, *C*, *CHL*, *Ur*, 2003 *Sp*, *Sp*, *J*, *C*, *EngA*, *C*, *Ur*, *Fj*, *S*, *J*, *F*
PJ Danahy 2009 *Ur*, 2010 *Rus*, 2011 *Tg*, *Rus*, *J*, *A*
WP Darsie 1913 *NZ*
G Davis 1920 *F*
G De Bartolo 2008 *E*, *C*, *Ur*, *J*, *J*, 2009 *W*
D de Groot 1924 *F*
MG de Jong 1990 *C*, 1991 *J*, *J*, *S*, *C*, *F*, *F*, *It*, *E*
M Deaton 1983 *A*, 1984 *C*, 1985 *J*
M Delai 1996 *I*, *HK*, *J*, 1997 *HK*, 1998 *HK*, 2000 *J*, *C*, *I*, *Fj*, *Tg*, *Sa*, *S*, *W*, 2001 *C*, *Ar*, *Ur*
RH Devereaux 1924 *R*, *F*
D Dickson 1986 *J*, 1987 *A*
CW Dirksen 2012 *Rus*, *Tg*
G Dixon 1924 *R*, *F*
C Doe 1920 *F*, *F*, 1924 *R*, *F*
C Doherty 1987 *W*
CA Dolan 2013 *Fj*, *J*, *C*, *C*
D Dorsey 2001 *SA*, 2002 *S*, *C*, *C*, *CHL*, *Ur*, *CHL*, *Ur*, 2003 *Sp*, *Sp*, *J*, *C*, *EngA*, *Ar*, *C*, *Ur*, *Fj*, *S*, *J*, *F*, 2004 *C*, *Rus*, *C*, *F*
G Downes 1992 *HK*
BG Doyle 2008 *E*, *IrA*, *C*, 2012 *C*, *Geo*, *It*, *Rus*, *Tg*, 2013 *C*, *I*, *Tg*, *Fj*, *J*, *C*, *C*
R Duncanson 1977 *E*
A Durutalo 2012 *C*, *It*

P Eloff 2000 *J*, *C*, *I*, *Fj*, *Tg*, *Sa*, *S*, *W*, 2001 *C*, *Ar*, *Ur*, *E*, *SA*, 2002 *S*, *C*, *CHL*, *Ur*, 2003 *Sp*, *Sp*, *J*, *C*, *EngA*, *C*, *Ur*, *Fj*, *S*, *J*, *F*, 2006 *Bar*, *C*, *Ur*, *Ur*, 2007 *Tg*, *Sa*, *SA*
PL Emerick 2003 *Sp*, *EngA*, *Ar*, *C*, *Ur*, *Fj*, *S*, *J*, 2004 *C*, *F*, *I*, *It*, 2005 *C*, *R*, *W*, *ArA*, *C*, 2006 *C*, *Bar*, *C*, *Ur*, *Ur*, 2007 *S*, *C*, *E*, 2008 *E*, *IrA*, *C*, *Ur*, *J*, *J*, 2009 *Geo*, *C*, *C*, *Ur*, *Ur*, 2010 *Rus*, *Pt*, *Geo*, 2011 *Tg*, *Rus*, *C*, *C*, *J*, *I*, *Rus*, *It*, 2012 *C*, *Geo*, *It*, *Rus*, *Tg*, *R*
TV Enosa 2011 *Tg*, *Rus*, *C*, *C*, *J*, *A*
BE Erb 1912 *A*
C Erskine 2006 *C*, *Ur*, *Ur*, 2007 *E*, *Tg*, *Sa*, *SA*, 2008 *Ur*, *J*, *J*
V Esikia 2006 *IrA*, *M*, *Bar*, *C*, *Ur*, *Ur*, 2007 *E*, *E*, *Tg*, *Sa*, *SA*, 2008 *E*, *IrA*
J Everett 1984 *C*, 1985 *J*, 1986 *J*, *C*, 1987 *Tun*, *J*, *E*
W Everett 1985 *J*, 1986 *J*, *C*

M Fabling 1995 *C*
M Fanucchi 1979 *C*, 1980 *W*
R Farley 1989 *I*, *Ur*, *Ar*, 1990 *Ar*, *C*, *A*, *J*, 1991 *J*, *J*, *S*, *C*, *F*, *F*, *It*, *E*, 1992 *C*
P Farner 1999 *Tg*, *Fj*, *J*, *C*, 2000 *J*, *C*, *I*, *Fj*, *Tg*, *Sa*, *S*, *W*, 2002 *C*, *C*, *CHL*, *Ur*, *CHL*, *Ur*
L Farrish 1924 *F*
D Fee 2002 *C*, *C*, *CHL*, *Ur*, *CHL*, *Ur*, 2003 *Sp*, *Sp*, *J*, *C*, *EngA*, *C*, *Ur*, *Fj*, *S*, *J*, *F*, 2004 *C*, *Rus*, *C*, *F*, *I*, *It*, 2005 *C*, *R*, *W*, *ArA*, *C*
ZT Fenoglio 2012 *Rus*, 2013 *C*, *Tg*, *Fj*, *J*, *C*, *C*
O Fifita 2000 *Fj*, *Tg*, *Sa*, *S*, *W*, 2001 *C*, *Ar*, *Ur*, *E*, *SA*, 2002 *C*, *C*, 2003 *Sp*, *EngA*, *EngA*, *Ar*, *S*
S Finkel 1981 *C*, 1983 *C*, *A*, 1986 *C*, 1987 *A*, *E*
G Fish 1920 *F*
J Fitzpatrick 1920 *F*
AW Flay 1990 *J*, 1991 *J*, *J*, *S*, *F*, *It*, *E*
R Flynn 2000 *C*, *I*, *Fj*, *Tg*, *Sa*, *W*, 2001 *C*, *Ar*
J Fowler 1980 *W*, *C*, *NZ*, 1981 *C*, *SA*, 1982 *C*, *E*
W Fraumann 1976 *F*, 1977 *E*
A Freeman 1995 *C*, 1996 *I*
M French 2005 *W*, *ArA*, 2006 *IrA*, *M*, *Ur*, *Ur*, 2007 *E*, *C*
EC Fry 2011 *Tg*, *Rus*, *C*, *C*, *J*, *A*, 2012 *C*, *Geo*, *It*, *Rus*, *Tg*, *R*, 2013 *C*, *I*, *Tg*, *Fj*, *J*, *C*, *C*
B Furrow 1998 *C*, *C*, *J*, *HK*

JR Gagiano 2008 *Ur*, *J*, *J*, 2009 *I*, *W*, *Geo*, *C*, *C*, *Ur*, *Ur*, 2010 *Rus*, *Pt*, 2011 *J*, *A*
M Gale 1992 *C*
FJ Gard 1912 *A*, 1913 *NZ*
B Geraghty 1993 *C*
J Gillam 2000 *Tg*
D Gillies 1998 *Ar*, 1999 *Tg*
G Glasscock 1913 *NZ*
D Gonzalez 1990 *A*, 1993 *C*
G Goodman 1992 *C*
J Gouws 2003 *EngA*, *EngA*, *Ar*, *C*, *Ur*, *S*, *F*, 2004 *I*, *It*
E Graff 1924 *R*, *F*
J Grant 1981 *SA*
R Grant 2000 *Tg*
S Gray 1976 *F*, 1977 *E*, 1979 *C*, 1980 *W*, *NZ*, 1981 *SA*
R Green 1994 *I*, 1995 *C*, 1996 *I*, *C*, *C*, *HK*, *J*, *HK*, *J*, 1998 *Fj*, *Ar*
M Griffin 2003 *Sp*, *J*, *EngA*, 2004 *Rus*, *C*, *F*, 2005 *C*, *R*
J Grobler 1996 *Ar*, *C*, *Ur*, 1997 *C*, *J*, *J*, 1998 *J*, *Fj*, *C*, *Ur*, 1999 *Fj*, *J*, *C*, *Sa*, *E*, *I*, *R*, *A*, 2000 *J*, *C*, *I*, *Tg*, *Sa*, *S*, *W*, 2001 *C*, *Ar*, *Ur*, *E*, *SA*, 2002 *C*, *CHL*, *Ur*
LJ Gross 1996 *I*, *C*, *C*, *HK*, *J*, *HK*, *J*, *C*, *Ur*, 1997 *C*, *HK*, *J*, *J*, *HK*, *C*, *W*, *W*, 1998 *Pt*, *Sp*, *J*, *HK*, *C*, *C*, *J*, *HK*, *Fj*, *Ar*, *C*, *Ur*, 1999 *Tg*, *Fj*, *J*, *C*, *Sa*, *E*, *I*, *R*, *A*, 2000 *Fj*, *Tg*, *Sa*, *S*, *W*, 2001 *C*, *Ar*, *E*, *SA*, 2002 *S*, *C*, 2003 *Sp*, *Sp*, *J*, *C*, *EngA*, *EngA*, *Ar*, *C*, *Ur*, *Fj*, *S*, *J*, *F*
D Guest 1976 *F*, 1977 *C*
I Gunn 1982 *E*

EB Hall 1913 *NZ*
T Hall 2011 *Tg*, 2013 *C*
M Halliday 1977 *E*, 1978 *C*, 1980 *W*, *C*, 1982 *C*, *E*
C Hansen 2005 *C*, 2006 *IrA*, *M*, *C*
J Hanson 1977 *C*, *E*, 1980 *W*, *C*, 1981 *C*, 1983 *C*, *A*
PR Harrigan 1912 *A*
GW Harriman 2012 *R*, 2013 *Fj*
J Hartman 1983 *A*, 1984 *C*
J Hartman 2005 *C*, *ArA*
MTB Hawkins 2010 *Rus*
CC Hawley 2009 *Geo*, 2011 *Tg*, *Rus*, *C*, *A*, 2012 *Geo*, *It*
W Hayward 1991 *J*, *C*
GM Hein 1987 *Tun*, *C*, *J*, *A*, *E*, *W*, *C*, 1988 *R*, *USS*, 1989 *I*, *C*, *Ur*, *Ar*, 1990 *Ar*, *A*, 1991 *J*, *F*, *F*, *It*, *NZ*, *E*, 1992 *HK*, 1993 *C*, *A*, 1994 *Ber*
R Helu 1981 *C*, *SA*, 1982 *C*, *E*, 1983 *C*, *A*, 1985 *J*, *C*, 1987 *Tun*, *C*, *J*, *A*
B Henderson 1977 *C*
M Hercus 2002 *S*, *C*, *C*, *CHL*, *Ur*, *CHL*, *Ur*, 2003 *Sp*, *Sp*, *J*, *C*, *Ur*, *Fj*, *S*, *J*, *F*, 2004 *C*, *Rus*, *C*, *F*, *I*, *It*, 2005 *C*, *R*, *W*, *ArA*, *C*, 2006 *Bar*, *C*, *Ur*, *Ur*, 2007 *E*, *Tg*, *Sa*, *SA*, 2008 *E*, *IrA*, *C*, *Ur*, *J*, *J*, 2009 *I*, *W*, *Geo*, *C*, *C*, *Ur*, *Ur*

SJ Hiatt 1993 *A*, 1998 *Ar*, *C*
KG Higgins 1985 *J*, *C*, 1986 *J*, *C*, 1987 *Tun*, *C*, *J*, *A*, *E*, *W*, *C*, 1988 *C*, *R*, *USS*, 1989 *I*, *C*, *Ur*, *Ar*, 1990 *Ar*, *A*, *J*, 1991 *J*, *J*, *S*, *C*, *F*, *It*, *E*
B Hightower 1997 *W*, *J*, *HK*, *C*, *W*, *W*, 1998 *Fj*, *C*, *Ur*, 1999 *Tg*, *Fj*, *J*, *C*, *Sa*, *I*, *R*, *A*
D Hobson 1991 *J*
M Hobson 2005 *R*
DT Hodges 1996 *Ur*, 1997 *W*, *W*, 1998 *Pt*, *Sp*, *J*, *HK*, *C*, *J*, *HK*, *Fj*, *Ar*, *C*, *Ur*, 1999 *Tg*, *Fj*, *J*, *C*, *Sa*, *E*, *I*, *R*, *A*, 2000 *J*, *C*, *I*, *Fj*, *Tg*, *Sa*, *S*, *W*, 2001 *C*, *Ar*, *Ur*, *E*, *SA*, 2002 *S*, *C*, *C*, *CHL*, *Ur*, *CHL*, *Ur*, 2003 *Sp*, *J*, *C*, *EngA*, *Fj*, *S*, *J*, *F*, 2004 *C*, *F*
C Hodgson 2002 *S*, *C*, *CHL*, *CHL*, 2003 *Sp*, *Sp*, *J*, *C*, *EngA*, *C*, 2004 *C*, *Rus*
W Holder 2012 *C*, *Geo*, *It*
J Hollings 1979 *C*, 1980 *NZ*
J Holtzman 1995 *C*, 1997 *HK*, *J*, 1998 *Ar*
J Hopkins 1996 *HK*
D Horton 1986 *C*, 1987 *A*, *C*
B Horwath 1984 *C*, 1985 *J*, *C*, 1986 *C*, 1987 *A*, *W*, 1990 *J*
B Hough 1991 *C*, 1992 *HK*, 1994 *Ar*
B Howard 1998 *HK*, *Fj*, *Ar*, 1999 *Sa*
C Howard 1980 *NZ*
J Hullinger 2006 *IrA*, *C*, *Bar*, *Ur*, *Ur*
L Hume 2012 *C*, *Geo*, *It*, *Rus*, *Tg*, *R*, 2013 *C*, *I*, *Fj*, *J*, *C*
J Hunter 1920 *F*
RF Hyland 1924 *R*, *F*

M Inns 1985 *J*, *C*, 1986 *C*
R Isaac 1989 *C*, *Ar*

D Jablonski 1977 *C*, 1978 *C*, 1979 *C*, 1980 *W*
DW James 1990 *C*, *A*, 1993 *C*, *A*, 1994 *Ber*, *C*, *Ar*, *Ar*, *I*
WL Jefferson 1985 *J*, *C*, 1986 *C*, 1987 *W*, *C*, 1989 *I*
J Jellaco 1982 *C*, *E*
D Jenkinson 1984 *C*, 1985 *C*, 1986 *J*
NS Johnson 2009 *I*, *W*, *Geo*, *C*, *C*, *Ur*, 2010 *Rus*, *Pt*, *Geo*, 2011 *Tg*, *Rus*, *C*, *C*, *J*, *I*, *Rus*, *A*, *It*
PW Johnson 1987 *C*, *A*, *W*, *C*, 1988 *C*, *R*, *USS*, 1989 *I*, *C*, *Ar*, 1990 *A*, 1991 *F*, *F*, *NZ*, 1992 *HK*, *C*
WD Johnson 2009 *I*, *W*, *Ur*, *Ur*
S Jones 2005 *ArA*, 2006 *Ur*
G Judge 1991 *C*, 1992 *HK*

M Kane 2000 *J*, *I*, *Fj*, 2004 *C*, *F*, 2005 *ArA*, *C*
J Kelleher 1978 *C*, 1979 *C*
T Kelleher 2000 *C*, *I*, 2001 *C*, *Ar*, *Ur*
J Keller 1992 *HK*, *C*
J Kelly 2006 *M*, *C*, *Bar*
S Kelly 2013 *C*, *I*, *Tg*, *Fj*, *J*, *C*
S Kelso 1977 *C*, *E*, 1978 *C*
D Kennedy 1997 *HK*, 1998 *Pt*, *Sp*, *J*, *HK*
J Keyter 2000 *W*, 2001 *SA*, 2002 *S*, *C*, *C*, *CHL*, *Ur*, *CHL*, *Ur*, 2003 *C*, *EngA*, *Ar*, *C*, *Ur*, *S*, *F*
F Khasigian 1976 *A*
K Khasigian 1998 *Ar*, 1999 *J*, *E*, *I*, *R*, *A*, 2000 *J*, *C*, *I*, *Fj*, *Sa*, *S*, *W*, 2001 *C*, *Ar*, *Ur*, *E*, *SA*, 2002 *S*, *C*, *C*, *CHL*, *Ur*, *CHL*, *Ur*, 2003 *Sp*, *Sp*, *J*, *C*, *EngA*, *Ar*, *C*, *Ur*, *Fj*, *S*, *J*, *F*
EN King 1912 *A*, 1913 *NZ*
M Kirksey 1920 *F*
K Kjar 2001 *Ar*, *SA*, 2002 *S*, *C*, *C*, *CHL*, *Ur*, *CHL*, 2003 *EngA*, *EngA*, *Ar*, *S*, *J*, 2005 *ArA*, *C*, 2006 *C*, 2007 *E*, *S*, *C*
T Klein 1976 *A*, 1977 *C*, 1978 *C*
S Klerck 2003 *Ar*, *Ur*, *J*, 2004 *C*, *Rus*, *C*, *I*, *It*
T Kluempers 1996 *J*, 2000 *W*, 2001 *C*, *Ar*, *Ur*
A Knowles 1913 *NZ*
J Knutson 1988 *USS*

CD Labounty 1998 *C*, *J*
A Lakomskis 2002 *CHL*, *Ur*, 2004 *I*, *It*
G Lambert 1981 *C*, *SA*, 1982 *C*, *E*, 1984 *C*, 1985 *C*, 1987 *Tun*, *C*, *J*, *A*, *E*, 1988 *C*, *R*, *USS*, 1989 *C*, *Ur*, *Ar*, 1990 *Ar*
T Lamositele 2013 *C*, *C*
S Laporta 1989 *Ur*, *Ar*
M Laulaupealu 2008 *E*, *IrA*, *C*
SC LaValla 2010 *Rus*, *Pt*, 2011 *Tg*, *Rus*, *C*, *J*, *Rus*, *A*, *It*, 2012 *C*, *Geo*, *It*, *Rus*, *Tg*, *R*, 2013 *I*, *Tg*, *J*, *C*, *C*
S Lawrence 2006 *C*, *Bar*, *C*, *Ur*, *Ur*
R Le Clerc 1998 *C*, *Ur*
B Le May 2008 *J*
PW LeClerc 1996 *HK*, *J*, 1997 *W*, *J*, *HK*, *C*, 1998 *C*, 1999 *Tg*, *Fj*, *J*, *C*, *Sa*
R Lehner 1995 *C*, 1996 *C*, *C*, *HK*, *J*, *HK*, *J*, *Ar*, *C*, 1997 *W*, *C*, *J*, *J*, *HK*, *C*, *W*, *W*, 1998 *Pt*, *Sp*, *J*, *HK*, *C*, *C*, *Ar*, *Ur*, 1999 *Tg*, *Fj*, *J*, *Sa*, *E*, *I*, *R*, 2000 *J*, *C*, *I*, *Fj*, *Tg*, *Sa*
O Lentz 2006 *IrA*, *M*, *Bar*, 2007 *E*, *Tg*, *Sa*, *SA*
T L'Estrange 2012 *Rus*, *Tg*, *R*, 2013 *C*, *I*, *Tg*, *Fj*, *J*, *C*, *C*
J Lett 2008 *E*, *IrA*, *C*
WN Leversee 1988 *R*, 1989 *I*, *Ur*, 1990 *Ar*, *C*, *A*, *J*, 1991 *J*, *J*, *S*, *F*, *It*, 1994 *Ar*, *I*, 1996 *Ar*
R Lewis 1990 *C*, 1991 *S*
M L'Huillier 1999 *E*, *A*
R Liddington 2003 *Ar*, *C*, *S*, 2004 *Rus*, *C*
J Lik 2005 *C*, *R*, *ArA*
S Lipman 1988 *C*, *R*, *USS*, 1990 *C*, *J*, 1991 *F*, *It*, *NZ*, *E*
C Lippert 1989 *C*, *Ur*, *Ar*, 1990 *Ar*, *C*, *A*, *J*, 1991 *J*, *S*, *C*, *F*, *F*, *It*, *NZ*, 1993 *A*, 1994 *Ber*, *C*, *Ar*, *Ar*, *I*, 1996 *HK*, *J*, *Ar*, *C*, *Ur*, 1997 *C*, *HK*, *J*, *J*, *HK*, *W*, *W*, 1998 *J*, *HK*, *C*, *C*, *J*, *HK*
M Liscovitz 1977 *C*, *E*, 1978 *C*
THA Liufau 2012 *It*
R Lockerem 1996 *C*, *Ur*
J Lombard 1977 *C*, *E*, 1979 *C*
C Long 2003 *Sp*
J Lopez 1978 *C*
I Loveseth 1983 *A*
RA Lumkong 1994 *Ber*, *C*, *Ar*, *Ar*, *I*, 1996 *C*, *C*, *HK*, *J*, *HK*, *J*, *Ar*, *C*, *Ur*, 1997 *W*, 1998 *Pt*, *Sp*, *J*, *HK*, *C*, *C*, *J*, *HK*, *Fj*, *C*, *Ur*, 1999 *E*, *R*, *A*
D Lyle 1994 *I*, 1995 *C*, 1996 *I*, *C*, *C*, *HK*, *J*, *HK*, *J*, 1997 *W*, *C*, *HK*, *J*, *J*, *HK*, *C*, *W*, *W*, 1999 *Tg*, *Fj*, *J*, *C*, *Sa*, *E*, *I*, *R*, 2000 *S*, *W*, 2001 *C*, *Ar*, *E*, *SA*, 2002 *CHL*, *Ur*, 2003 *Sp*, *Sp*, *J*, *C*, *EngA*, *C*, *Ur*, *Fj*, *S*, *J*, *F*

MS MacDonald 2000 *Fj*, 2001 *C*, *Ar*, *Ur*, *E*, *SA*, 2002 *S*, *C*, *C*, *CHL*, *Ur*, *CHL*, *Ur*, 2003 *Sp*, *Sp*, *J*, *C*, *EngA*, *EngA*, *C*, *Ur*, *Fj*, *S*, *J*, *F*, 2004 *C*, *Rus*, *F*, *I*, *It*, 2005 *C*, *R*, *W*, *ArA*, *C*, 2006 *IrA*, *C*, *Bar*, *C*, *Ur*, *Ur*, 2007 *S*, *C*, *E*, *Tg*, *Sa*, *SA*, 2008 *E*, *IrA*, *C*, *Ur*, *J*, *J*, 2009 *I*, *W*, *Geo*, *C*, *C*, 2010 *Pt*, *Geo*, 2011 *C*, *J*, *I*, *Rus*, *It*, 2012 *C*, *It*
C Mackay 2008 *J*, 2009 *I*, *W*
A Magleby 2000 *W*, 2001 *Ar*, *Ur*, *E*
A Malifa 2009 *I*, *W*, *Geo*, *C*
VL Malifa 2007 *E*, *S*, *C*, *E*, *SA*, 2008 *IrA*, *C*, *Ur*, *J*, *J*, 2009 *Ur*, *Ur*, 2010 *Rus*, *Pt*, *Geo*, 2011 *Tg*, *Rus*, *C*, *C*, *J*, *I*, *A*, *It*
P Malloy 1995 *C*
C Manelli 1924 *R*, *F*
L Manga 1986 *J*, 1989 *Ar*, 1991 *J*, *C*, *NZ*, *E*, 1992 *HK*, *C*
M Mangan 2005 *C*, *R*, *W*, *ArA*, *C*, 2006 *IrA*, *M*, *C*, *Bar*, *C*, *Ur*, 2007 *E*, *S*, *C*, *E*, *Tg*, *SA*
S Manoa 2010 *Geo*, 2013 *I*, *C*
J McBride 1998 *Pt*, *Sp*, *C*, *Fj*, *Ar*, *C*, *Ur*, 2000 *J*, *C*, *I*, *Tg*, *Sa*
BR McClenahan 2009 *W*, *Ur*, 2011 *A*
T McCormack 1989 *Ur*, *Ar*, 1990 *Ar*, *C*
G McDonald 1989 *I*, 1996 *I*, *C*
A McGarry 2002 *S*, *CHL*
JL McKim 1912 *A*, 1913 *NZ*
M McLeod 1997 *J*, *HK*, *C*
C Meehan 1920 *F*, *F*
T Meek 2006 *IrA*, *M*, *C*, *Bar*
H Mexted 2006 *Bar*, *Ur*, *Ur*, 2007 *E*, *S*, *C*, *E*, *Sa*
J Meyersieck 1982 *C*, 1983 *C*, *A*, 1985 *J*, 1986 *C*
J Mickel 1986 *C*
K Miles 1982 *C*, *E*
C Miller 2002 *CHL*, *Ur*
MM Mitchell 1913 *NZ*
M Moeakiola 2007 *E*, *Tg*, *Sa*, *SA*, 2008 *E*, *IrA*, *C*, *Ur*, *J*, *J*, 2009 *I*, *W*, *Geo*, *C*, *C*, *Ur*, *Ur*, 2010 *Rus*, *Pt*, *Geo*, 2011 *Tg*, *Rus*, *C*, *I*, *Rus*, *It*
TJ Mokate 2012 *C*, *Geo*, *It*
E Momson 1912 *A*
B Monroe 1985 *C*

A Montgomery 1986 *C*, 1987 *W*, *C*, 1988 *C*, 1989 *I*, *C*
LM Morris 1912 *A*
B Morrison 1979 *C*, 1980 *W*
C Morrow 1997 *W*, *C*, *HK*, *C*, *W*, *W*, 1998 *Pt*, *C*, *C*, 1999 *Tg*, *C*, *E*
T Moser 1980 *W*
N Mottram 1990 *Ar*, *J*, 1991 *J*, *S*, *C*, *F*, *NZ*, *E*, 1992 *C*
F Mounga 1998 *C*, *J*, *HK*, *Fj*, *C*, *Ur*, 1999 *Sa*, *E*, *I*, *R*, *A*, 2003 *Sp*, *J*, 2004 *F*, *I*, *It*, 2005 *R*, 2007 *E*, *C*, *Sa*
J Muldoon 1920 *F*, *F*
D Murphy 1976 *F*
LP Murphy 2013 *C*, *J*

J Naivalu 2000 *Sa*, *S*, *W*, 2001 *C*, *Ur*, *E*, 2004 *C*, *Rus*, *C*, *F*
J Naqica 2001 *E*, *SA*, 2002 *S*, *C*, *C*, *CHL*, *Ur*, 2003 *Ar*
J Nash 2006 *M*, *C*
RB Nelson 1983 *C*, *A*, 1984 *C*, 1985 *C*, 1986 *J*, 1987 *C*, *J*, *A*, *E*, 1988 *R*, *USS*, 1989 *I*, *Ur*, *Ar*, 1990 *Ar*, *C*, *A*, *J*, 1991 *J*, *S*, *C*, *F*, *F*, *It*, *E*
T Ngwenya 2007 *E*, *Tg*, *Sa*, *SA*, 2008 *IrA*, *C*, *Ur*, *J*, *J*, 2009 *Geo*, *C*, *C*, *Ur*, *Ur*, 2010 *Rus*, *Pt*, *Geo*, 2011 *C*, *C*, *I*, *Rus*, *It*, 2012 *R*, 2013 *I*, *Tg*, *C*, *C*
C Nicolau 2002 *C*, 2003 *J*, *C*, *EngA*
S Niebauer 1976 *A*, 1979 *C*, 1980 *W*, *C*, *NZ*, 1981 *C*, *SA*, 1982 *C*, *E*
D Niu 1999 *Tg*, *Fj*, *J*, *C*, *E*, *I*, *R*, *A*
F Niua 2013 *C*, *C*
RM Noble 1912 *A*

CP O'Brien 1988 *C*, *R*, *USS*, 1989 *I*, *C*, *Ur*, *Ar*, 1990 *Ar*, *A*, *J*, 1991 *S*, *C*, *F*, *F*, *NZ*, *E*, 1992 *HK*, 1993 *C*, *A*, 1994 *Ber*
T O'Brien 1980 *NZ*, 1983 *C*, *A*
M O'Donnell 1976 *F*
C Okezie 1979 *C*, 1980 *C*, *NZ*, 1981 *C*, 1982 *C*, *E*
JT O'Neill 1920 *F*, *F*, 1924 *R*, *F*
M Ording 1976 *A*, *F*, 1977 *E*, 1978 *C*
M Ormsby 1983 *C*
A Osborne 2007 *C*
C Osentowski 2004 *It*, 2005 *C*, *R*, *W*, 2006 *IrA*, *M*, *C*, *Bar*, *C*, *Ur*, *Ur*, 2007 *E*, *S*, *C*, *E*, *Tg*, *Sa*, *SA*
K Oxman 1976 *A*

S Paga 1998 *C*, *C*, 1999 *C*, *Sa*, *E*, *I*, *R*, *A*, 2002 *CHL*, *Ur*, *CHL*, *Ur*, 2003 *J*, 2004 *C*, *Rus*, *F*
TD Palamo 2007 *SA*, 2008 *J*
MJ Palefau 2005 *C*, *R*, *W*, *ArA*, *C*, 2006 *IrA*, *M*, *C*, 2007 *E*, *S*, 2008 *E*
ZJ Pangelinan 2012 *Tg*, *R*
AF Paoli 1982 *E*, 1983 *C*, 1985 *J*, 1986 *J*, *C*, 1987 *C*, *J*, *A*, *W*, *C*, 1988 *C*, *R*, *USS*, 1989 *I*, *C*, *Ur*, *Ar*, 1991 *J*, *F*, *It*
AJ Parker 1996 *HK*, *J*, *HK*, *J*, *Ar*, *C*, *Ur*, 1997 *W*, 1998 *Pt*, *Sp*, *J*, *HK*, *C*, *C*, *J*, *HK*, *Fj*, 1999 *Fj*, *C*, *Sa*, *E*, *I*, *R*, *A*, 2002 *CHL*, *Ur*, *CHL*, *Ur*, 2003 *Sp*, *Sp*, *C*, *EngA*, *C*, *Ur*, *Fj*, *S*, *F*, 2004 *C*, *Rus*, *C*, *I*, *It*, 2005 *W*, 2006 *C*, *Ur*, *Ur*, 2007 *E*, *Tg*, *Sa*, *SA*, 2008 *Ur*, *J*, 2009 *Geo*, *C*, *C*, *Ur*, *Ur*
D Parks 1980 *C*
E Parthmore 1977 *E*
JD Paterson 2011 *J*, *I*, *Rus*, *It*, 2012 *C*, *Geo*, *It*, 2013 *C*, *I*, *Tg*, *Fj*, *J*
J Patrick 1920 *F*, *F*, 1924 *R*, *F*
DT Payne 2007 *S*, *SA*
SB Peart 1912 *A*, 1913 *NZ*
J Peter 1987 *W*, *C*
T Petersen 1993 *C*
MZ Petri 2007 *SA*, 2008 *E*, *IrA*, *C*, *Ur*, *J*, *J*, 2009 *I*, *W*, *Geo*, *C*, *C*, *Ur*, *Ur*, 2010 *Rus*, *Pt*, *Geo*, 2011 *Tg*, *Rus*, *C*, *C*, *J*, *I*, *Rus*, *A*, *It*, 2012 *C*, *Geo*, *It*, *Rus*, *Tg*, *R*, 2013 *I*, *Tg*, *Fj*, *J*, *C*, *C*
A Petruzzella 2004 *C*, *F*, *I*, 2005 *W*, *ArA*, *C*, 2006 *IrA*, *M*, *Bar*
MD Pidcock 1991 *C*, *NZ*, *E*
ST Pittman 2008 *Ur*, *J*, 2009 *Geo*, *C*, *C*, 2010 *Rus*, *Pt*, *Geo*, 2011 *Tg*, *Rus*, *C*, *C*, *J*, *I*, *Rus*, *A*, *It*, 2012 *C*, *Geo*, *It*, *Rus*, *Tg*, *R*, 2013 *C*, *I*, *Tg*, *Fj*, *J*, *C*, *C*
M Purcell 1980 *W*, 1981 *C*, *SA*, 1982 *C*, *E*, 1983 *C*, *A*, 1984 *C*, 1986 *J*, *C*, 1987 *Tun*, *C*, *J*, *E*
TJ Purpura 2010 *Rus*
J Pye 2005 *ArA*, *C*

JF Quill 2012 *Rus*, *Tg*, *R*, 2013 *C*, *Tg*, *Fj*
P Quinn 2007 *E*, 2008 *Ur*, *J*, *J*

JA Ramage 1913 *NZ*
RR Randell 1993 *A*, 1994 *Ber*, *C*, *Ar*, *I*, 1995 *C*, 1996 *I*, *HK*, *J*, *Ar*, *C*, 1997 *C*
J Raven 1998 *C*, *J*
E Reed 1999 *A*, 2001 *Ur*, *E*, *SA*, 2002 *S*, *C*, *C*
AM Ridnell 1987 *A*, 1988 *C*, *R*, *USS*, 1991 *J*, *S*, *C*, *F*, *F*, *It*, *NZ*, *E*, 1992 *HK*, 1993 *C*
C Righter 1920 *F*
J Rissone 1996 *I*, *C*, *C*, *HK*, *Ur*
WL Rogers 1924 *F*
R Rosser 2006 *Ur*, *Ur*
VR Rouse 2010 *Rus*
D Rowe 2005 *R*, *W*
A Russell 2006 *C*, *Ur*
A Ryland 2005 *C*, *R*, *W*, *C*

R Samaniego 1992 *HK*
AM Sanborn 1912 *A*
L Sanft 1996 *J*
J Santos 1995 *C*, 1996 *C*, *C*, *HK*
A Satchwell 2002 *S*, 2003 *Ur*
A Saulala 1997 *C*, *HK*, *C*, *W*, *W*, 1998 *Pt*, *Sp*, *HK*, *C*, *J*, *HK*, 1999 *Tg*, *Fj*, *J*, *C*, *Sa*, *E*, *A*, 2000 *Fj*, *Tg*
M Saunders 1987 *Tun*, *C*, *J*, *A*, *E*, *W*, *C*, 1988 *C*, *R*, *USS*, 1989 *I*, *C*
MH Sawicki 1990 *Ar*, *J*, 1991 *J*, *F*, *NZ*
MA Scharrenberg 1993 *A*, 1994 *Ber*, *C*, *Ar*, *Ar*, 1995 *C*, 1996 *I*, *J*, *HK*, *J*, *Ar*, *C*, *Ur*, 1997 *W*, *C*, *HK*, *J*, *J*, *HK*, *C*, *W*, *W*, 1998 *Pt*, *Sp*, *J*, *HK*, *C*, *C*, *Ar*, *C*, *Ur*, 1999 *Tg*, *Fj*, *J*, *C*, *Sa*, *I*, *R*, *A*
KL Schaupp 1912 *A*
J Scheitlin 1979 *C*
CJ Schlereth 1993 *C*, 1994 *I*, 1998 *J*
G Schneeweis 1976 *A*, 1977 *E*
B Schoener 2006 *IrA*, *M*, *C*
RS Scholz 1920 *F*, *F*, 1924 *R*, *F*
E Schram 1993 *A*, 1994 *Ber*, *C*, *Ar*, *Ar*, 1996 *J*, *Ar*
J Schraml 1991 *C*, 1992 *HK*, 1993 *C*
K Schubert 2000 *J*, *C*, *I*, *Fj*, *Tg*, *Sa*, 2001 *C*, *Ar*, *Ur*, *E*, *SA*, 2002 *S*, *C*, *C*, *CHL*, *Ur*, *CHL*, *Ur*, 2003 *Sp*, *Sp*, *J*, *C*, *EngA*, *Ar*, *C*, *Ur*, *Fj*, *S*, *J*, *F*, 2004 *C*, *Rus*, *C*, *F*, *I*, *It*, 2005 *C*, *R*, *W*, *ArA*, *C*, 2006 *IrA*, *M*, *C*, *Bar*, *C*, 2008 *IrA*, *C*
RE Schurfeld 1992 *HK*, *C*, 1993 *A*, 1994 *Ber*, *C*
T Scott 1976 *F*
BH Scully 2011 *Rus*, *C*, *C*, *J*, *I*, *Rus*, *A*, *It*, 2013 *C*, *Fj*, *J*, *C*, *C*
T Selfridge 1976 *A*, *F*, 1977 *C*, 1980 *W*, *C*
D Shanagher 1980 *NZ*, 1981 *C*, *SA*, 1982 *C*, *E*, 1984 *C*, 1985 *J*, 1986 *J*, 1987 *W*
RC Shaw 2008 *IrA*, *C*, 2012 *Rus*, *Tg*, *R*, 2013 *C*, *Tg*, *Fj*, *J*, *C*, *C*
P Sheehy 1991 *NZ*, *E*, 1992 *HK*, *C*
M Sherlock 1977 *C*
MM Sherman 2003 *EngA*, *Ar*, *F*, 2004 *Rus*, 2005 *C*, *W*, *ArA*
W Shiflet 1983 *C*, *A*, 1985 *J*, 1987 *A*
K Shuman 1997 *HK*, *J*, *J*, *W*, 1998 *J*, *HK*, *C*, *C*, *J*, *Ar*, 1999 *Tg*, *Fj*, *J*, *E*, *I*, *R*, *A*, 2000 *J*, *C*, *I*, *Fj*, *Tg*, *Sa*, *S*, *W*, 2001 *Ar*, *Ur*, *E*, *SA*
M Siano 1989 *I*, *C*, *Ur*, *Ar*
A Siddall 2013 *C*, *Tg*, *Fj*, *J*
L Sifa 2008 *Ur*, *J*, 2009 *I*, *W*, *Ur*, *Ur*, 2010 *Rus*, 2011 *A*
MK Sika 1993 *C*, *A*, 1994 *Ber*, *C*, *Ar*, *Ar*, *I*, 1996 *C*, *C*, *J*, *HK*, *J*, *Ar*, *C*, *Ur*, 1997 *J*, *W*
S Sika 2003 *Fj*, *J*, *F*, 2004 *C*, *F*, *I*, *It*, 2005 *W*, *C*, 2006 *IrA*, *M*, 2007 *S*, *C*, *E*, *Tg*, *Sa*, *SA*, 2008 *IrA*, *C*, *Ur*, 2009 *Geo*, *C*
C Slaby 2008 *E*, *C*
C Slater 1920 *F*, *F*, 1924 *F*
N Slater 1924 *R*
WL Smith 1912 *A*
H Smith 2008 *Ur*, *J*, *J*, 2009 *I*, *W*, *Geo*, *C*, *C*, *Ur*, *Ur*, 2010 *Geo*, 2011 *C*, *C*, *J*, *I*, *Rus*, *A*, *It*

M Smith 1988 *C*
T Smith 1980 *C*, 1981 *C*, *SA*, 1982 *E*
B Smoot 1992 *C*
J Sprague 2009 *Ur*, *Ur*
M Stanaway 1997 *C*, *HK*, *J*, *C*, 1998 *HK*
LE Stanfill 2005 *C*, 2006 *C*, 2007 *E*, *S*, *C*, *E*, *Tg*, *Sa*, *SA*, 2008 *E*, *IrA*, 2009 *I*, *W*, *Geo*, *C*, *C*, *Ur*, *Ur*, 2010 *Rus*, *Pt*, *Geo*, 2011 *Tg*, *Rus*, *C*, *C*, *J*, *I*, *Rus*, *A*, *It*, 2012 *C*, *Geo*, *It*, *Rus*, *Tg*, *R*, 2013 *C*, *I*, *Tg*, *Fj*, *J*, *C*, *C*
D Steinbauer 1992 *C*, 1993 *C*
J Stencel 2006 *C*
D Stephenson 1976 *A*, *F*, 1977 *C*
I Stevens 1998 *C*
P Still 2000 *S*, *W*, 2001 *C*, *Ar*, *Ur*, *E*, *SA*
HR Stolz 1913 *NZ*
W Stone 1976 *F*
D Straehley 1983 *C*, 1984 *C*
G Sucher 1998 *C*, *J*, *HK*, *Fj*, *C*, *Ur*, 1999 *Tg*, *Fj*, *J*, *C*, *Sa*, *E*, *I*, *R*, *A*
A Suniula 2008 *J*, 2010 *Rus*, *Pt*, *Geo*, 2011 *Tg*, *Rus*, *C*, *C*, *J*, *I*, *Rus*, *It*, 2012 *C*, *Geo*, *It*, *Rus*, *Tg*, *R*, 2013 *C*, *I*, *Tg*, *Fj*, *J*, *C*, *C*
RPJ Suniula 2009 *I*, *W*, *C*, *C*, 2011 *Tg*, *C*, *C*, *J*, *I*, *Rus*, *It*, 2012 *Geo*, *It*, *Rus*, *Tg*, *R*, 2013 *C*
B Surgener 2001 *SA*, 2002 *C*, *Ur*, 2003 *Sp*, *EngA*, *EngA*, 2004 *C*, *F*, *I*, *It*, 2005 *W*
E Swanson 1976 *A*
C Sweeney 1976 *A*, *F*, 1977 *C*, *E*
M Swiderski 1976 *A*
K Swiryn 2009 *I*, *W*, *C*, *C*, *Ur*, *Ur*, 2010 *Pt*, *Geo*, 2011 *Tg*, *Rus*, *C*, *J*, *A*
B Swords 1980 *W*, *C*, *NZ*
KR Swords 1985 *J*, *C*, 1986 *C*, 1987 *Tun*, *C*, *J*, *A*, *W*, *C*, 1988 *C*, *R*, *USS*, 1989 *I*, *C*, *Ur*, *Ar*, 1990 *Ar*, *C*, *A*, *J*, 1991 *J*, *J*, *S*, *C*, *F*, *F*, *It*, *NZ*, *E*, 1992 *C*, 1993 *C*, *A*, 1994 *Ber*, *C*, *Ar*, *Ar*

TK Takau 1994 *Ar*, *Ar*, *I*, 1996 *C*, *C*, *HK*, *J*, *HK*, 1997 *C*, *HK*, *J*, *HK*, *W*, *W*, 1998 *Sp*, *HK*, *C*, *C*, *J*, *HK*, *Ur*, 1999 *E*, *I*, *R*, *A*
R Tardits 1993 *A*, 1994 *Ber*, *C*, *Ar*, *Ar*, *I*, 1995 *C*, 1996 *I*, *C*, *C*, *J*, *Ar*, 1997 *W*, *C*, 1998 *Sp*, *HK*, *Fj*, 1999 *Tg*, *Fj*, *J*, *C*, *Sa*, *I*, *R*
J Tarpoff 2002 *S*, *C*, *C*, *CHL*, 2003 *Sp*, *Sp*, *C*, *EngA*, *EngA*, 2006 *IrA*, *M*, *C*, *Bar*
R Templeton 1920 *F*
P Thiel 2009 *Ur*, *Ur*, 2010 *Rus*, *Pt*, *Geo*, 2011 *Tg*, *C*, *C*, *J*, *I*, *A*, *It*, 2013 *Fj*, *J*, *C*
C Tilden Jr 1920 *F*, *F*
M Timoteo 2000 *Tg*, 2001 *C*, *Ar*, *Ur*, *SA*, 2002 *S*, *C*, *C*, *CHL*, *Ur*, *CHL*, 2003 *Sp*, *Sp*, *J*, *EngA*, *Ar*, *C*, *F*, 2004 *C*, *Rus*, *C*, *F*, *I*, *It*, 2005 *C*, *R*, 2006 *IrA*, *M*, *C*, *Bar*, 2012 *It*
AEO Tuilevuka 2006 *IrA*, *M*, *C*, 2009 *I*, *W*, *Geo*, *C*, *Ur*, *Ur*, 2010 *Rus*
STV Tuilevuka 2010 *Pt*
A Tuipulotu 2004 *C*, *Rus*, *C*, *I*, *It*, 2005 *C*, *R*, *W*, 2006 *C*, *Bar*, *C*, *Ur*, *Ur*, 2007 *E*, *S*, *C*, *Tg*, *Sa*, 2008 *E*
CE Tunnacliffe 1991 *F*, *NZ*, *E*, 1992 *HK*
E Turkington 1924 *R*

JC Urban 1913 *NZ*
TD Usasz 2009 *I*, *W*, *Geo*, *C*, *C*, *Ur*, *Ur*, 2010 *Rus*, *Pt*, *Geo*, 2011 *Tg*, *Rus*, *C*, *C*, *J*, *I*, *Rus*, *A*, *It*

Vaka 1987 *C*
AC Valentine 1924 *R*, *F*
JL Van Der Giessen 2008 *E*, *C*, *Ur*, *J*, *J*, 2009 *I*, *W*, *Geo*, *C*, *C*, *Ur*, *Ur*, 2010 *Rus*, *Pt*, 2011 *Tg*, *Rus*, *C*, *C*, *I*, *Rus*, *It*
M van der Molen 1992 *C*
R van Zyl 2003 *Sp*, *Sp*, *J*, *C*, *EngA*, *C*, *Ur*, *Fj*, *S*, *J*, *F*, 2004 *C*, *F*
EL Vidal 1920 *F*
F Viljoen 2004 *Rus*, *C*, *F*, *I*, *It*, 2005 *C*, *R*, *W*, *ArA*, *C*, 2006 *IrA*, *M*, *C*, *Ur*, *Ur*, 2007 *E*, *S*, *C*
T Vinick 1986 *C*, 1987 *A*, *E*
J Vitale 2006 *C*, *Ur*, 2007 *E*, 2008 *IrA*
BG Vizard 1986 *J*, *C*, 1987 *Tun*, *C*, *J*, *A*, *E*, *W*, *C*, 1988 *C*, *R*, *USS*, 1989 *I*, *C*, 1990 *C*, *A*, 1991 *J*, *J*, *S*, *C*, *F*, *It*
C Vogl 1996 *C*, *C*, 1997 *W*, *C*, *HK*, *J*, *J*, *HK*, *C*, 1998 *HK*, *Fj*, *Ar*
G Voight 1913 *NZ*
H von Schmidt 1920 *F*

J Waasdorp 2003 *J*, *EngA*, *Ar*, *Ur*, *J*, *F*, 2004 *C*, *Rus*, *C*, *F*, *I*, *It*, 2005 *C*, *ArA*, *C*
D Wack 1976 *F*, 1977 *C*, 1978 *C*, 1980 *C*
B Waite 1976 *F*
J Walker 1996 *I*, *C*, *HK*, *J*, *Ar*, *C*, *Ur*, 1997 *W*, *J*, *HK*, *C*, *W*, *W*, 1998 *Sp*, *J*, *HK*, *C*, *C*, *J*, *HK*, *Ar*, *C*, *Ur*, 1999 *Tg*, *J*
D Wallace 1920 *F*
NS Wallace 2013 *Tg*, *Fj*, *J*
L Walton 1980 *C*, *NZ*, 1981 *C*, *SA*
A Ward 1980 *NZ*, 1983 *C*
B Warhurst 1983 *C*, *A*, 1984 *C*, 1985 *J*, *C*, 1986 *J*, 1987 *Tun*, *C*, *J*
M Waterman 1992 *C*
J Welch 2008 *J*, *J*, 2009 *I*, *Geo*, *C*
G Wells 2000 *J*, *C*, *I*, *Fj*, *Tg*, *Sa*, *S*, *W*, 2001 *C*, *Ar*, *Ur*, *E*
T Whelan 1982 *E*, 1987 *C*, 1988 *C*, *R*, *USS*
EA Whitaker 1990 *J*, 1991 *F*, *F*, *It*, *NZ*
B Wiedemer 2007 *E*, 2008 *E*, *IrA*, *C*
L Wilfley 2000 *I*, *Tg*, *W*, 2001 *Ar*, *Ur*, *SA*, 2002 *S*, *C*, *C*, *CHL*, *Ur*, *CHL*, *Ur*, 2003 *Sp*, *Sp*, *J*, *C*, *EngA*, *EngA*, *S*
JP Wilkerson 1991 *E*, 1993 *A*, 1994 *C*, 1996 *C*, *Ur*, 1997 *W*, *C*, *HK*, *J*, *J*, *C*, *W*, *W*, 1998 *Pt*, *Sp*, *J*, *HK*
A Williams 1924 *R*
B Williams 1988 *C*, *R*, *USS*, 1989 *C*, 1992 *C*
C Williams 1990 *C*, *A*, *J*, 1991 *J*, *S*, *C*
D Williams 2004 *C*, *Rus*, *C*, *F*, *I*, *It*, 2005 *ArA*, 2006 *Ur*, *Ur*, 2007 *E*, *C*
MA Williams 1987 *W*, *C*, 1988 *C*, *R*, *USS*, 1989 *I*, *Ur*, *Ar*, 1990 *Ar*, *C*, *A*, 1991 *J*, *J*, *F*, *F*, *It*, *NZ*, *E*, 1992 *HK*, 1994 *C*, *Ar*, *Ar*, *I*, 1996 *I*, *C*, *C*, *HK*, 1997 *W*, 1998 *Fj*, *Ar*, *Ur*, 1999 *Tg*, *J*, *C*, *Sa*, *E*, *I*
G Wilson 1978 *C*, 1980 *W*, *C*, 1981 *C*, *SA*
J Winston 1920 *F*
H Wrenn 1920 *F*, *F*
M Wyatt 2003 *Ar*, *C*, *Ur*, *J*, *F*, 2004 *C*, *Rus*, *C*, *F*, *I*, *It*, 2005 *W*, *ArA*, *C*, 2006 *C*
CT Wyles 2007 *E*, *S*, *C*, *E*, *Tg*, *Sa*, *SA*, 2008 *E*, *IrA*, *C*, *Ur*, *J*, *J*, 2009 *I*, *W*, *Geo*, *C*, *C*, *Ur*, *Ur*, 2010 *Rus*, *Pt*, *Geo*, 2011 *Rus*, *A*, *It*, 2012 *C*, *Geo*, *It*, *Rus*, *R*, 2013 *I*, *Tg*, *Fj*, *J*, *C*, *C*

D Younger 2000 *J*, *C*, *I*, *Fj*
S Yungling 1997 *HK*, *W*

R Zenker 1987 *W*, *C*

WALES

WALES' 2012–13 TEST RECORD

OPPONENTS	DATE	VENUE	RESULT
Argentina	10 Nov	H	Lost 12–26
Samoa	16 Nov	H	Lost 19–26
New Zealand	24 Nov	H	Lost 10–33
Australia	1 Dec	H	Lost 12–14
Ireland	2 Feb	H	Lost 22–30
France	9 Feb	A	Won 16–6
Italy	23 Feb	A	Won 26–9
Scotland	9 Mar	A	Won 28–18
England	16 Mar	H	Won 30–3
Japan	8 Jun	A	Won 22–18
Japan	15 Jun	A	Lost 23–8

DESPAIR TURNS TO DELIGHT

By Martyn Williams

Getty Images

George North evades François Trinh-Duc to score the match-winning try in Wales' victory over France.

It was by anyone's standards a roller-coaster of a season for the Wales team. The misery of four defeats in the four November internationals was a bitter blow for Welsh rugby but the successful, seemingly impossible defence of the Six Nations title transformed the mood of the country and the contrasting fortunes which the side experienced once again proved how fickle sport can be.

For me it was a classic, typical Welsh campaign. Wales have enjoyed plenty of success in the last eight years, winning three Grand Slams and reaching the Rugby World Cup 2011 semi-final. But Welsh rugby always seems to be one defeat away from a crisis or one victory from glory and it was a familiar story again as they went through agonies in the autumn and then ecstasy in Cardiff in March after the 30–3 win over England that sealed the Championship. Following the Wales team is rarely a smooth ride.

Expectations at the start of the season were high. After winning the Grand Slam in 2012, there was a sense of real optimism and a lot of people were talking about winning three of the four autumn games at the Millennium Stadium.

However, Wales came crashing back down to earth after losing 26–12 to Argentina and then going down 26–19 to Samoa, and very quickly the optimism turned to negativity. It's no secret that Wales follow a rigid game plan and, when it works, it's incredibly difficult to counter but against the Pumas and the Samoans they struggled to get over the gain-line and dominate the breakdown and it was clear there wasn't really a plan B. Both teams matched Wales physically and scoring one try in the two Tests – an intercept from Ashley Beck – highlighted the lack of Welsh creativity.

The Samoa game saw Ryan Jones captain the side. It was his 29th Test as Wales skipper, breaking Ieuan Evans's record for wearing the armband, and it's a milestone that deserves recognition. Ryan has had his critics and at times certain people have looked for any excuse to drop him, but he's a phenomenal player and has been a brilliant ambassador for Welsh rugby throughout his career.

The third game of the series was against the All Blacks. In previous seasons there has been serious talk of beating New Zealand in Cardiff but there were no such hopes in 2012 and in truth the team were second best in a 33–10 defeat.

A second-half fightback gave the scoreline a more flattering look from a Welsh perspective but the match was won and lost by half-time. On the positive side, young players like Liam Williams and Scott Andrews can only improve after being given the opportunity to play against world-class opposition.

Wales wrapped up the Tests against Australia and, after the June series Down Under, it was a sense of frustrating déjà vu as the Wallabies edged it when Kurtley Beale scored the only try of the match in the final minute. It was a horrible way to lose and condemned the team to a seventh straight Test defeat.

Everyone had an opinion on how Wales had again conspired to snatch defeat from the jaws of victory against Australia. Some argued the team didn't have the mental strength and self-belief to get over the line against southern hemisphere opposition but that ignored the brilliance of Beale's try and the Wallaby counter-attack. The Australians never give up and, credit where it is due, it was a superb score.

The result meant Wales dropped out of the top eight for the Rugby World Cup 2015 draw. The media made a lot out of that and Wales subsequently drew Australia and England in Pool A for 2015 and I think it was actually a good result for them. The Rugby Championship has proved the Wallabies are currently the weakest of the 'big three' in the southern hemisphere and the boys have shown they know how to beat the English, so there's no reason why they cannot get out of the pool. I would have been more worried if they'd come out in the same pot as South Africa and Samoa.

The defeat also heaped the pressure on Rob Howley, deputising as head coach while Warren Gatland was on his British & Irish Lions sabbatical. It was a rough time for Rob but he didn't blink and the way the side subsequently performed in the Championship more than vindicated him.

To be honest, I was surprised how well Rob reacted to the criticism. I saw him before the start of the Six Nations and he was incredibly calm and philosophical about what had happened in November. His belief in the players didn't waver and he was very upbeat about the team's prospects for the Championship. Rob was a shrewd and conscientious player and he's shown the same qualities as a coach and has now proved he has the credentials to become Wales head coach whenever Warren steps aside.

The Six Nations began badly with a 30–22 defeat against Ireland in Cardiff, making it eight Tests losses on the bounce. The confidence drained out of the players after Ireland scored early through Simon Zebo and, although they staged an exciting second-half revival and scored three tries, the match was effectively over after 40 minutes. I was commentating on the match and the difference between the two teams was the impact of Sean O'Brien and Peter O'Mahony at the breakdown. Wales just couldn't find an answer to their physicality.

The French in Paris in the next game was probably the ideal fixture for Wales because they were written off before kick-off. Everyone was expecting a French backlash after they had lost to Italy in their Championship opener and I think the pressure on Wales before kick-off just evaporated despite the losing sequence.

It was an ugly game in the Stade de France but a little moment of magic from Dan Biggar, chipping for George North's late try, and superb place kicking from Leigh Halfpenny were enough to seal a much-needed 16–6 win. It was Wales' first victory in Paris since 2005 and, more importantly, it finally put an end to the losing run. Their defence that day was crucial and it was a result that was to transform the side.

Rob named the same XV early for the next game against Italy and I thought it was a pragmatic decision. It meant no place in the side for Sam Warburton but it killed the debate about the captaincy, which Rob knew would otherwise have dominated the build-up to the Italy game. He nipped the speculation in the bud and, at the same time, he gave a big and very public vote of confidence to the players who had started in Paris.

They rewarded his faith with a decent 26–9 win in Rome and followed it up with a 28–18 victory against Scotland in Edinburgh thanks to 23 points from Halfpenny. Against the odds, the team found themselves on the verge of the title if they could beat England.

I honestly expected the boys to win but not in my wildest dreams would I have predicted a 30-point winning margin. The way Wales dominated physically and tactically was key to the outcome of the match and the platform was laid by the front five who got on top of their less experienced England counterparts.

I've got to say, though, I thought Stuart Lancaster made a mistake in agreeing to the roof being closed at the Millennium Stadium. It always cranks up the atmosphere when the roof is closed and the noise in the stadium that day was nothing like I've experienced as a player or spectator before. It was incredible and must have intimidated the England players on the pitch.

Putting the title in 2013 into context compared to the Grand Slams in 2005, 2008 and 2012 is difficult. It wasn't a headline-grabbing clean sweep but Wales had a poor record in the seasons after they'd won in 2005 and 2008 and I'd argue a successful defence of the Six Nations was a significant step forward. I've certainly no doubt the current Wales squad is the strongest they've had in the professional era.

The season ended with a two-Test tour of Japan and with 15 players selected for Lions duty by Warren and the likes of Ryan Jones, James Hook and Matthew Rees rested, it was an unfamiliar looking squad with Bradley Davies as skipper and Robin McBryde stepping in as caretaker coach.

Robin took some criticism for leaving the more experienced players available to him at home but if you cannot give youngsters a taste of Test rugby in a Lions summer, when the pressure and focus is reduced, you're never going to bring new talent through.

In the end, Wales scraped through in the first Test 22–18 but lost 23–8 in Tokyo seven days later – Japan's first ever win over the Welsh – and I'm sure all the lads involved were bitterly disappointed to have been involved in that bit of history.

It was a dramatic season in which the Hollywood boys as I like to call them – the likes of North and Alex Cuthbert – enjoyed the limelight and Halfpenny was sensational with the boot, but my relatively unsung heroes were Alun-Wyn Jones, the best second row Wales have ever had in my opinion, Toby Faletau, a hugely naturally talented footballer, and Jonathan Davies, who has been immense in the midfield since Rugby World Cup 2011.

Warren will return to the helm for the November internationals and, although the team won only five of their 11 Tests during the 2012/13 campaign, they won the matches that mattered and confidence will not be an issue moving forward. It remains a relatively young group of players, the issue of a long-term replacement for Adam Jones aside, and Warren will be focused on taking the side to the next level as the Rugby World Cup looms.

WALES INTERNATIONAL STATISTICS

MATCH RECORDS UP TO 10 OCTOBER 2013

MOST CONSECUTIVE TESTS WITHOUT DEFEAT

Matches	Wins	Draws	Period
11	11	0	1907 to 1910
10	10	0	1999 to 1999
8	8	0	1970 to 1972
8	8	0	2004 to 2005

MOST CONSECUTIVE TEST WINS

11	1907 I, 1908 E, S, F, I, A, 1909 E, S, F, I, 1910 F
10	1999 F1, It, E, Arg1,2, SA, C, F2, Arg3, J
8	1970 F, 1971 E, S, I, F, 1972 E, S, F
8	2004 J, 2005 E, It, F, S, I, US, C

MOST POINTS IN A MATCH

BY THE TEAM

Pts	Opponents	Venue	Year
102	Portugal	Lisbon	1994
98	Japan	Cardiff	2004
81	Romania	Cardiff	2001
81	Namibia	New Plymouth	2011
77	USA	Hartford	2005
72	Japan	Cardiff	2007
70	Romania	Wrexham	1997
66	Romania	Cardiff	2004
66	Fiji	Hamilton	2011
64	Japan	Cardiff	1999
64	Japan	Osaka	2001
61	Canada	Cardiff	2006
60	Italy	Treviso	1999
60	Canada	Toronto	2005
58	Fiji	Cardiff	2002
57	Japan	Bloemfontein	1995
55	Japan	Cardiff	1993

BY A PLAYER

Pts	Player	Opponents	Venue	Year
30	NR Jenkins	Italy	Treviso	1999
29	NR Jenkins	France	Cardiff	1999
28	NR Jenkins	Canada	Cardiff	1999
28	NR Jenkins	France	Paris	2001
28	GL Henson	Japan	Cardiff	2004
27	NR Jenkins	Italy	Cardiff	2000
27	C Sweeney	USA	Hartford	2005
26	SM Jones	Romania	Cardiff	2001
24	NR Jenkins	Canada	Cardiff	1993
24	NR Jenkins	Italy	Cardiff	1994
24	GL Henson	Romania	Wrexham	2003
23	AC Thomas	Romania	Wrexham	1997
23	NR Jenkins	Argentina	Llanelli	1998
23	NR Jenkins	Scotland	Murrayfield	2001
23	SL Halfpenny	Scotland	Murrayfield	2013

MOST TRIES IN A MATCH

BY THE TEAM

Tries	Opponents	Venue	Year
16	Portugal	Lisbon	1994
14	Japan	Cardiff	2004
12	Namibia	New Plymouth	2011
11	France	Paris	1909
11	Romania	Wrexham	1997
11	Romania	Cardiff	2001
11	USA	Hartford	2005
11	Japan	Cardiff	2007
10	France	Swansea	1910
10	Japan	Osaka	2001
10	Romania	Cardiff	2004
9	France	Cardiff	1908
9	Japan	Cardiff	1993
9	Japan	Cardiff	1999
9	Japan	Tokyo	2001
9	Canada	Toronto	2005
9	Canada	Cardiff	2006
9	Fiji	Hamilton	2011

BY A PLAYER

Tries	Player	Opponents	Venue	Year
4	W Llewellyn	England	Swansea	1899
4	RA Gibbs	France	Cardiff	1908
4	MCR Richards	England	Cardiff	1969
4	IC Evans	Canada	Invercargill	1987
4	N Walker	Portugal	Lisbon	1994
4	G Thomas	Italy	Treviso	1999
4	SM Williams	Japan	Osaka	2001
4	TGL Shanklin	Romania	Cardiff	2004
4	CL Charvis	Japan	Cardiff	2004

MOST CONVERSIONS IN A MATCH

BY THE TEAM

Cons	Opponents	Venue	Year
14	Japan	Cardiff	2004
11	Portugal	Lisbon	1994
11	USA	Hartford	2005
10	Romania	Cardiff	2001
9	Namibia	New Plymouth	2011
9	Fiji	Hamilton	2011
8	France	Swansea	1910
8	Japan	Cardiff	1999
8	Romania	Cardiff	2004
8	Canada	Cardiff	2006
7	France	Paris	1909
7	Japan	Osaka	2001
7	Japan	Cardiff	2007

BY A PLAYER

Cons	Player	Opponents	Venue	Year
14	GL Henson	Japan	Cardiff	2004
11	NR Jenkins	Portugal	Lisbon	1994
11	C Sweeney	USA	Hartford	2005
10	SM Jones	Romania	Cardiff	2001
8	J Bancroft	France	Swansea	1910
8	NR Jenkins	Japan	Cardiff	1999
8	J Hook	Canada	Cardiff	2006
7	SM Jones	Japan	Osaka	2001
7	SM Jones	Romania	Cardiff	2004
6	J Bancroft	France	Paris	1909
6	GL Henson	Romania	Wrexham	2003
6	C Sweeney	Canada	Toronto	2005
6	SM Jones	Namibia	New Plymouth	2011

MOST DROP GOALS IN A MATCH

BY THE TEAM

Drops	Opponents	Venue	Year
3	Scotland	Murrayfield	2001
2	Scotland	Swansea	1912
2	Scotland	Cardiff	1914
2	England	Swansea	1920
2	Scotland	Swansea	1921
2	France	Paris	1930
2	England	Cardiff	1971
2	France	Cardiff	1978
2	England	Twickenham	1984
2	Ireland	Wellington	1987
2	Scotland	Cardiff	1988
2	France	Paris	2001

BY A PLAYER

Drops	Player	Opponents	Venue	Year
3	NR Jenkins	Scotland	Murrayfield	2001
2	J Shea	England	Swansea	1920
2	A Jenkins	Scotland	Swansea	1921
2	B John	England	Cardiff	1971
2	M Dacey	England	Twickenham	1984
2	J Davies	Ireland	Wellington	1987
2	J Davies	Scotland	Cardiff	1988
2	NR Jenkins	France	Paris	2001

MOST PENALTIES IN A MATCH

BY THE TEAM

Penalties	Opponents	Venue	Year
9	France	Cardiff	1999
8	Canada	Cardiff	1993
7	Italy	Cardiff	1994
7	Canada	Cardiff	1999
7	Italy	Cardiff	2000
7	Scotland	Murrayfield	2013
6	France	Cardiff	1982
6	Tonga	Nuku'alofa	1994
6	England	Wembley	1999
6	Canada	Cardiff	2002
6	England	Cardiff	2009
6	Canada	Toronto	2009
6	New Zealand	Cardiff	2010

BY A PLAYER

Penalties	Player	Opponents	Venue	Year
9	NR Jenkins	France	Cardiff	1999
8	NR Jenkins	Canada	Cardiff	1993
7	NR Jenkins	Italy	Cardiff	1994
7	NR Jenkins	Canada	Cardiff	1999
7	NR Jenkins	Italy	Cardiff	2000
7	SL Halfpenny	Scotland	Murrayfield	2013
6	G Evans	France	Cardiff	1982
6	NR Jenkins	Tonga	Nuku'alofa	1994
6	NR Jenkins	England	Wembley	1999
6	SM Jones	Canada	Cardiff	2002
6	DR Biggar	Canada	Toronto	2009
6	SM Jones	New Zealand	Cardiff	2010

MOST CAPPED PLAYERS

Caps	Player	Career Span
104	SM Jones	1998 to 2011
100	Gareth Thomas	1995 to 2007
100	ME Williams	1996 to 2012
98	GD Jenkins	2002 to 2013
94	CL Charvis	1996 to 2007
92	GO Llewellyn	1989 to 2004
88	AR Jones	2003 to 2013
87	NR Jenkins	1991 to 2002
87	SM Williams	2000 to 2011
77	WM Phillips	2003 to 2013
76	DJ Peel	2001 to 2011
73	RP Jones	2004 to 2013
72	IC Evans	1987 to 1998
70	TGL Shanklin	2001 to 2010
70	JW Hook	2006 to 2013
70	AW Jones	2006 to 2013
67	JJ Thomas	2003 to 2011
64	IM Gough	1998 to 2010
59	R Howley	1996 to 2002
58	GR Jenkins	1991 to 2000
58	M Rees	2005 to 2013
57	DJ Jones	2001 to 2009
55	JPR Williams	1969 to 1981

MOST CONSECUTIVE TESTS

Tests	Player	Span
53	GO Edwards	1967 to 1978
43	KJ Jones	1947 to 1956
39	G Price	1975 to 1983
38	TM Davies	1969 to 1976
33	WJ Bancroft	1890 to 1901

MOST POINTS IN TESTS

Points	Player	Tests	Career
1049	NR Jenkins	87	1991 to 2002
917	SM Jones	104	1998 to 2011
346	JW Hook	70	2006 to 2013
304	PH Thorburn	37	1985 to 1991
294	SL Halfpenny	44	2008 to 2013
290	SM Williams	87	2000 to 2011
211	AC Thomas	23	1996 to 2000
200	Gareth Thomas	100	1995 to 2007
166	P Bennett	29	1969 to 1978
157	IC Evans	72	1987 to 1998

MOST TESTS AS CAPTAIN

Tests	Captain	Span
32	RP Jones	2008 to 2013
28	IC Evans	1991 to 1995
22	R Howley	1998 to 1999
22	CL Charvis	2002 to 2004
21	Gareth Thomas	2003 to 2007
20	SK Warburton	2011 to 2013
19	JM Humphreys	1995 to 2003
18	AJ Gould	1889 to 1897
14	DCT Rowlands	1963 to 1965
14	WJ Trew	1907 to 1913

MOST TRIES IN TESTS

Tries	Player	Tests	Career
58	SM Williams	87	2000 to 2011
40	Gareth Thomas	100	1995 to 2007
33	IC Evans	72	1987 to 1998
22	CL Charvis	94	1996 to 2007
20	GO Edwards	53	1967 to 1978
20	TGR Davies	46	1966 to 1978
20	TGL Shanklin	70	2001 to 2010
18	GR Williams	44	2000 to 2005
17	RA Gibbs	16	1906 to 1911
17	JL Williams	17	1906 to 1911
17	KJ Jones	44	1947 to 1957

MOST PENALTY GOALS IN TESTS

Penalties	Player	Tests	Career
235	NR Jenkins	87	1991 to 2002
186	SM Jones	104	1998 to 2011
70	PH Thorburn	37	1985 to 1991
66	SL Halfpenny	44	2008 to 2013
61	JW Hook	70	2006 to 2013
36	P Bennett	29	1969 to 1978
35	SP Fenwick	30	1975 to 1981
32	AC Thomas	23	1996 to 2000
22	G Evans	10	1981 to 1983

MOST CONVERSIONS IN TESTS			
Cons	Player	Tests	Career
153	SM Jones	104	1998 to 2011
130	NR Jenkins	87	1991 to 2002
43	PH Thorburn	37	1985 to 1991
43	JW Hook	70	2006 to 2013
38	J Bancroft	18	1909 to 1914
30	AC Thomas	23	1996 to 2000
29	GL Henson	33	2001 to 2011
25	C Sweeney	35	2003 to 2007
20	WJ Bancroft	33	1890 to 1901
20	IR Harris	25	2001 to 2004

MOST DROP GOALS IN TESTS			
Drops	Player	Tests	Career
13	J Davies	32	1985 to 1997
10	NR Jenkins	87	1991 to 2002
8	B John	25	1966 to 1972
7	WG Davies	21	1978 to 1985
6	SM Jones	104	1998 to 2011
4	JW Hook	70	2006 to 2013

INTERNATIONAL CHAMPIONSHIP RECORDS

RECORD	DETAIL	HOLDER	SET
Most points in season	151	in five matches	2005
Most tries in season	21	in four matches	1910
Highest score	49	49–14 v France	1910
Biggest win	39	47–8 v Italy	2008
Highest score conceded	60	26–60 v England	1998
Biggest defeat	51	0–51 v France	1998
Most appearances	51	ME Williams	1998–2010
Most points in matches	467	SM Jones	2000–2011
Most points in season	74	NR Jenkins	2001
	74	SL Halfpenny	2013
Most points in match	28	NR Jenkins	v France, 2001
Most tries in matches	22	SM Williams	2000–2011
Most tries in season	6	MCR Richards	1969
	6	SM Williams	2008
Most tries in match	4	W Llewellyn	v England, 1899
	4	MCR Richards	v England, 1969
Most cons in matches	69	SM Jones	2000–2011
Most cons in season	12	SM Jones	2005
Most cons in match	8	J Bancroft	v France, 1910
Most pens in matches	100	SM Jones	2000–2011
Most pens in season	19	SL Halfpenny	2013
Most pens in match	7	NR Jenkins	v Italy, 2000
	7	SL Halfpenny	v Scotland, 2013
Most drops in matches	8	J Davies	1985–1997
Most drops in season	5	NR Jenkins	2001
Most drops in match	3	NR Jenkins	v Scotland, 2001

MISCELLANEOUS RECORDS

RECORD	HOLDER	DETAIL
Longest Test career	ME Williams	1996 to 2012
Youngest Test cap	TWJ Prydie	18 yrs 25 days in 2010
Oldest Test cap	TH Vile	38 yrs 152 days in 1921

CAREER RECORDS OF WALES INTERNATIONAL PLAYERS

UP TO 10 OCTOBER 2013

PLAYER	DEBUT	CAPS	T	C	P	D	PTS
BACKS:							
MA Beck	2012 v A	4	1	0	0	0	5
DR Biggar	2008 v C	18	0	11	18	1	79
AM Bishop	2008 v SA	16	0	0	0	0	0
AG Brew	2007 v I	9	3	0	0	0	15
LM Byrne	2005 v NZ	46	10	0	0	0	50
ACG Cuthbert	2011 v A	18	9	0	0	0	45
JJV Davies	2009 v C	36	9	0	0	0	45
SL Halfpenny	2008 v SA	44	12	18	66	0	294
WTM Harries	2010 v NZ	3	0	0	0	0	0
JW Hook	2006 v Arg	70	13	43	61	4	346
DW Howells	2013 v J	2	0	0	0	0	0
TE James	2007 v E	10	2	0	0	0	10
TD Knoyle	2010 v NZ	11	0	0	0	0	0
GP North	2010 v SA	31	12	0	0	0	60
MR Patchell	2013 v J	2	0	0	1	0	3
WM Phillips	2003 v R	77	8	0	0	0	40
R Priestland	2011 v S	22	1	12	8	0	53
TWJ Prydie	2010 v It	5	2	0	0	0	10
RS Rees	2010 v E	9	1	0	0	0	5
JH Roberts	2008 v S	53	5	0	0	0	25
HR Robinson	2012 v Bb	3	2	0	0	0	10
JP Spratt	2009 v C	4	0	0	0	0	0
R Webb	2012 v It	3	0	0	0	0	0
LB Williams	2012 v Bb	5	0	0	0	0	0
LD Williams	2011 v Arg	15	2	0	0	0	10
MS Williams	2011 v Bb	20	6	0	0	0	30
OR Williams	2013 v J	2	0	0	0	0	0

FORWARDS:							
SA Andrews	2011 v Bb	8	0	0	0	0	0
DT Baker	2013 v J	2	0	0	0	0	0
SJ Baldwin	2013 v J	1	0	0	0	0	0
RJ Bevington	2011 v Bb	10	0	0	0	0	0
LC Charteris	2004 v SA	40	0	0	0	0	0
AJ Coombs	2013 v I	6	0	0	0	0	0
BS Davies	2009 v S	40	0	0	0	0	0
IR Evans	2006 v Arg	30	1	0	0	0	5
TT Faletau	2011 v Bb	26	2	0	0	0	10
IAR Gill	2010 v I	5	0	0	0	0	0
RM Hibbard	2006 v Arg	23	1	0	0	0	5
P James	2003 v R	45	0	0	0	0	0
AR Jarvis	2012 v Arg	3	0	0	0	0	0
GD Jenkins	2002 v R	98	4	0	0	0	20
AR Jones	2003 v E	88	2	0	0	0	10
AW Jones	2006 v Arg	70	7	0	0	0	35
Rhodri P Jones	2012 v Bb	2	0	0	0	0	0
Ryan P Jones	2004 v SA	73	3*	0	0	0	15
JD King	2013 v J	2	0	0	0	0	0
OS Kohn	2013 v I	1	0	0	0	0	0
DJ Lydiate	2009 v Arg	27	0	0	0	0	0
RJ McCusker	2010 v SA	6	0	0	0	0	0
C Mitchell	2009 v C	15	1	0	0	0	5
JR Navidi	2013 v J	1	0	0	0	0	0
KJ Owens	2011 v Nm	15	0	0	0	0	0
DE Phillips	2013 v J	2	0	0	0	0	0
WA Pretorius	2013 v J	2	0	0	0	0	0
L Reed	2012 v S	5	0	0	0	0	0
M Rees	2005 v US	58	2	0	0	0	10
AC Shingler	2012 v S	7	0	0	0	0	0
JC Tipuric	2011 v Arg	15	0	0	0	0	0
J Turnbull	2011 v S	5	0	0	0	0	0
SK Warburton	2009 v US	38	2	0	0	0	10

* *Ryan Jones's figures include a penalty try awarded against Canada in 2006*

WALES INTERNATIONAL PLAYERS

UP TO 10 OCTOBER 2013

Note: Years given for International Championship matches are for second half of season; e.g. 1972 means season 1971–72. Years for all other matches refer to the actual year of the match. Entries in square brackets denote matches played in RWC Finals.

Ackerman, R A (Newport, London Welsh) 1980 NZ, 1981 E, S, A, 1982 I, F, E, S, 1983 S, I, F, R, 1984 S, I, F, E, A, 1985 S, I, F, E, Fj
Alexander, E P (Llandovery Coll, Cambridge U) 1885 S, 1886 E, S, 1887 E, I
Alexander, W H (Llwynypia) 1898 I, E, 1899 E, S, I, 1901 S, I
Allen, A G (Newbridge) 1990 F, E, I
Allen, C P (Oxford U, Beaumaris) 1884 E, S
Andrews, F (Pontypool) 1912 SA, 1913 E, S, I
Andrews, F G (Swansea) 1884 E, S
Andrews, G E (Newport) 1926 E, S, 1927 E, F, I
Andrews, S A (Cardiff Blues) 2011 Bb(R), A, 2012 Sm(R), NZ(R), A4, 2013 E(R), J1, 2
Anthony, C T (Swansea, Newport, Gwent Dragons) 1997 US 1(R),2(R), C (R), Tg (R), 1998 SA 2, Arg, 1999 S, I (R), 2001 J 1,2, I (R), 2002 I, F, It, E, S, 2003 R (R)
Anthony, L (Neath) 1948 E, S, F
Appleyard, R C (Swansea) 1997 C, R, Tg, NZ, 1998 It, E (R), S, I, F
Arnold, P (Swansea) 1990 Nm 1, 2, Bb, 1991 E, S, I, F 1, A, [Arg, A], 1993 F (R), Z 2, 1994 Sp, Fj, 1995 SA, 1996 Bb (R)
Arnold, W R (Swansea) 1903 S
Arthur, C S (Cardiff) 1888 I, M, 1891 E
Arthur, T (Neath) 1927 S, F, I, 1929 E, S, F, I, 1930 E, S, I, F, 1931 E, S, F, I, SA, 1933 E, S
Ashton, C (Aberavon) 1959 E, S, I, 1960 E, S, I, 1962 I
Attewell, S L (Newport) 1921 E, S, F

Back, M J (Bridgend) 1995 F (R), E (R), S, I
Badger, O (Llanelli) 1895 E, S, I, 1896 E
Baker, A (Neath) 1921 I, 1923 E, S, F, I
Baker, A M (Newport) 1909 S, F, 1910 S
Baker, D T (Ospreys) 2013 J1(R),2(R)
Baldwin, S J (Ospreys) 2013 J2(R)
Bancroft, J (Swansea) 1909 E, S, F, I, 1910 F, E, S, I, 1911 E, F, I, 1912 E, S, I, 1913 I, 1914 E, S, F
Bancroft, W J (Swansea) 1890 S, E, I, 1891 E, S, I, 1892 E, S, I, 1893 E, S, I, 1894 E, S, I, 1895 E, S, I, 1896 E, S, I, 1897 E, 1898 I, E, 1899 E, S, I, 1900 E, S, I, 1901 E, S, I
Barlow, T M (Cardiff) 1884 I
Barrell, R J (Cardiff) 1929 S, F, I, 1933 I
Bartlett, J D (Llanelli) 1927 S, 1928 E, S
Bassett, A (Cardiff) 1934 I, 1935 E, S, I, 1938 E, S
Bassett, J A (Penarth) 1929 E, S, F, I, 1930 E, S, I, 1931 E, S, F, I, SA, 1932 E, S, I
Bateman, A G (Neath, Richmond, Northampton) 1990 S, I, Nm 1,2, 1996 SA, 1997 US, S, F, E, R, NZ, 1998 It, E, S, I, 1999 S, Arg 1,2, SA, C, [J, A (R)], 2000 It, E, S, I, Sm, US, SA, 2001 E (R), It (t), R, I, Art (R), Tg
Bater, J (Ospreys) 2003 R (R)
Bayliss, G (Pontypool) 1933 S
Bebb, D I E (Carmarthen TC, Swansea) 1959 E, S, I, F, 1960 E, S, I, F, SA, 1961 E, S, I, F, 1962 E, S, F, I, 1963 E, F, NZ, 1964 E, S, F, SA, 1965 E, S, I, F, 1966 F, A, 1967 S, I, F, E
Beck, M A (Ospreys) 2012 A 1(R),2,3, Sm
Beckingham, G (Cardiff) 1953 E, S, 1958 F
Bennett, A M (Cardiff) 1995 [NZ] SA, Fj
Bennett, H (Ospreys) 2003 I 2(R), S 2(R), [C(R), Tg(R)], 2004 S(R), F(R), Arg 1(R), 2, SA1(R), 2006 Arg 2, PI(R), 2007 E2, [J(R)],SA, 2008 E, S, It(R), F, 2009 S(R), E(R), F(R), It, I(R), NZ(R), Sm, Arg(R), A(R), 2010 E(R), S(R), F, I(R), It(R), NZ1(R), 2(R), A(R), SA2(R), Fj, NZ3(R), 2011 Bb, E2, 3(R), Arg(R), [SA, Sm, Fj, I, F, A], A, 2012 I, S
Bennett, I (Aberavon) 1937 I
Bennett, P (Cardiff Harlequins) 1891 E, S, 1892 S, I
Bennett, P (Llanelli) 1969 F (R), 1970 SA, S, F, 1972 S (R), NZ, 1973 E, S, I, F, A, 1974 S, I, F, E, 1975 S (R), I, 1976 E, S, I, F, 1977 I, F, E, S, 1978 E, S, I, F
Bergiers, R T E (Cardiff Coll of Ed, Llanelli) 1972 E, S, F, NZ, 1973 E, S, I, F, A, 1974 E, 1975 I
Bevan, G W (Llanelli) 1947 E
Bevan, J A (Cambridge U) 1881 E
Bevan, J C (Cardiff, Cardiff Coll of Ed) 1971 E, S, I, F, 1972 E, S, F, NZ, 1973 E, S
Bevan, J D (Aberavon) 1975 F, E, S, A
Bevan, S (Swansea) 1904 I
Bevington, R J (Ospreys) 2011 Bb, E2(R), 3(R), Arg(R), [Nm(R), A(R)], A(R), 2012 Arg(R), 2013 S(R), J1
Beynon, B (Swansea) 1920 E, S
Beynon, G E (Swansea) 1925 F, I
Bidgood, R A (Newport) 1992 S, 1993 Z 1,2, Nm, J (R)
Biggar, D R (Ospreys) 2008 C(R), 2009 C, US(R), Sm, 2010 NZ1(R), 2, A(R), Fj, 2011 A(R), 2012 Bb, Sm, 2013 I, F, It, S, E, J1, 2
Biggs, N W (Cardiff) 1888 M, 1889 I, 1892 I, 1893 E, S, I, 1894 E, I
Biggs, S H (Cardiff) 1895 E, S, 1896 S, 1897 E, 1898 I, E, 1899 S, I, 1900 I
Birch, J (Neath) 1911 S, F
Birt, F W (Newport) 1911 E, S, 1912 E, S, I, SA, 1913 E
Bishop, A M (Ospreys) 2008 SA2(R),C,A(R), 2009 S(R), C, US, Arg(R), A(R), 2010 I(R), It(R), NZ1, A, SA2(t), Fj, NZ3(R), 2012 Bb
Bishop, D J (Pontypool) 1984 A
Bishop, E H (Swansea) 1889 S
Blackmore, J H (Abertillery) 1909 E
Blackmore, S W (Cardiff) 1987 I, [Tg (R), C, A]
Blake, J (Cardiff) 1899 E, S, I, 1900 E, S, I, 1901 E, S, I
Blakemore, R E (Newport) 1947 E
Bland, A F (Cardiff) 1887 E, S, I, 1888 S, I, M, 1890 S, E, I
Blyth, L (Swansea) 1951 SA, 1952 E, S
Blyth, W R (Swansea) 1974 E, 1975 S (R), 1980 F, E, S, I
Boobyer, N (Llanelli) 1993 Z 1(R),2, Nm, 1994 Fj, Tg, 1998 F, 1999 It (R)
Boon, R W (Cardiff) 1930 S, F, 1931 E, S, F, I, SA, 1932 E, S, I, 1933 E, I
Booth, J (Pontymister) 1898 I
Boots, J G (Newport) 1898 I, E, 1899 I, 1900 E, S, I, 1901 E, S, I, 1902 E, S, I, 1903 E, S, I, 1904 E
Boucher, A W (Newport) 1892 E, S, I, 1893 E, S, I, 1894 E, 1895 E, S, I, 1896 E, I, 1897 E
Bowcott, H M (Cardiff, Cambridge U) 1929 S, F, I, 1930 E, 1931 E, S, 1933 E, I
Bowdler, F A (Cross Keys) 1927 A, 1928 E, S, I, F, 1929 E, S, F, I, 1930 E, 1931 SA, 1932 E, S, I, 1933 I
Bowen, B (S Wales Police, Swansea) 1983 R, 1984 S, I, F, E, 1985 Fj, 1986 E, S, I, F, Fj, Tg, WS, 1987 [C, E, NZ], US, 1988 E, S, I, F, WS, 1989 S, I
Bowen, C A (Llanelli) 1896 E, S, I, 1897 E
Bowen, D H (Llanelli) 1883 E, 1886 E, S, 1887 E
Bowen, G E (Swansea) 1887 S, I, 1888 S, I
Bowen, W (Swansea) 1921 S, F, 1922 E, S, I, F
Bowen, Wm A (Swansea) 1886 E, S, 1887 E, S, I, 1888 M, 1889 S, I, 1890 S, E, I, 1891 E, S

Brace, D O (Llanelli, Oxford U) 1956 E, S, I, F, 1957 E, 1960 S, I, F, 1961 I
Braddock, K J (Newbridge) 1966 A, 1967 S, I
Bradshaw, K (Bridgend) 1964 E, S, I, F, SA, 1966 E, S, I, F
Brew, A G (Newport Gwent Dragons, Ospreys) 2007 I(R), A2, E2, 2010 Fj, 2011 Bb, E3(R), Arg(R), [Nm], 2012 Bb
Brew, N R (Gwent Dragons) 2003 R
Brewer, T J (Newport) 1950 E, 1955 E, S
Brice, A B (Aberavon) 1899 E, S, I, 1900 E, S, I, 1901 E, S, I, 1902 E, S, I, 1903 E, S, I, 1904 E, S, I
Bridges, C J (Neath) 1990 Nm 1,2, Bb, 1991 E (R), I, F 1, A
Bridie, R H (Newport) 1882 I
Britton, G R (Newport) 1961 S
Broster, B G J (Saracens) 2005 US(R),C
Broughton, A S (Treorchy) 1927 A, 1929 S
Brown, A (Newport) 1921 I
Brown, J (Cardiff) 1925 I
Brown, J A (Cardiff) 1907 E, S, I, 1908 E, S, F, 1909 E
Brown, M (Pontypool) 1983 R, 1986 E, S, Fj (R), Tg, WS
Bryant, D J (Bridgend) 1988 NZ 1,2, WS, R, 1989 S, I, F, E
Bryant, J (Celtic Warriors) 2003 R (R)
Buchanan, D A (Llanelli) 1987 [Tg, E, NZ, A], 1988 I
Buckett, I M (Swansea) 1994 Tg, 1997 US 2, C
Budgett, N J (Ebbw Vale, Bridgend) 2000 S, I, Sm (R), US, SA, 2001 J 1(R),2, 2002 I, F, It, E, S
Burcher, D H (Newport) 1977 I, F, E, S
Burgess, R C (Ebbw Vale) 1977 I, F, E, S, 1981 I, F, 1982 F, E, S
Burnett, R (Newport) 1953 E
Burns, J (Cardiff) 1927 F, I
Burns, L B (Newport Gwent Dragons) 2011 Bb(R), E2(R), 3, [Sm(R), Nm, Fj(R), A(R)]
Bush, P F (Cardiff) 1905 NZ, 1906 E, SA, 1907 I, 1908 E, S, 1910 S, I
Butler, E T (Pontypool) 1980 F, E, S, I, NZ (R), 1982 S, 1983 E, S, I, F, R, 1984 S, I, F, E, A
Byrne, L M (Llanelli Scarlets, Ospreys, Clermont-Auvergne) 2005 NZ(R), Fj, SA, 2006 E(t&R), S(t&R), I, It, F, Arg 1, 2, PI, 2007 F1, A1, E2, 2008 E, S, It, I, F, SA3, NZ, A, 2009 S, E, F, It, I, 2010 E, S, F, I, It, SA1, NZ1, 2, SA2, Fj, NZ3, 2011 E1(R), S, It, I, F, Arg, [Nm,Fj]

Cale, W R (Newbridge, Pontypool) 1949 E, S, I, 1950 E, S, I, F
Cardey, M D (Llanelli) 2000 S
Carter, A J (Newport) 1991 E, S
Cattell, A (Llanelli) 1883 E, S
Challinor, C (Neath) 1939 E
Charteris, L C (Newport Gwent Dragons, Perpignan) 2004 SA2(R),R, 2005 US,C, NZ(R), Fj, 2007 SA(R), 2008 C, NZ(R), 2009 S(R), F(R), It, I(R), US(R), NZ, Sm, Arg, A, 2010 E, F(R), I, It, 2011 Bb, E2(R), 3, [SA, Sm, Nm(R), Fj, I, F, A], 2012 It(R), F(R), A 1, 2(R), 3(t&R), Sm(R), NZ, A4
Charvis, C L (Swansea, Tarbes, Newcastle, Newport Gwent Dragons) 1996 A 3(R), SA, 1997 US, S, I, F, 1998 It (R), E, S, I, F, Z (R), SA 1,2, Arg, 1999 S, I, F 1, It, E, Arg 1, SA, F 2, [Arg 3, A], 2000 F, It (R), E, S, I, Sm, US, SA, 2001 E, S, F, It, R, I, Arg, Tg, A, 2002 E (R), S, SA 1, 2, R, Fj, C, NZ, 2003 It, E 1(R), S 1(R), I 1, F,A, NZ, E 2, S 2, [C, Tg, It, NZ, E], 2004 S, F, E, It, Arg 1, 2, SA1, 2, R, NZ, J, 2005 US, C, NZ, SA, A, 2006 E, S, I, It, 2007 A1, 2, E2, Arg(R), F2(R), [C(t&R), A, J, Fj], SA
Clapp, T J S (Newport) 1882 I, 1883 E, S, 1884 E, S, I, 1885 E, S, 1886 S, 1887 E, S, I, 1888 S, I
Clare, J (Cardiff) 1883 E
Clark, S S (Neath) 1882 I, 1887 I
Cleaver, W B (Cardiff) 1947 E, S, F, I, A, 1948 E, S, F, I, 1949 I, 1950 E, S, I, F
Clegg, B G (Swansea) 1979 F
Clement, A (Swansea) 1987 US (R), 1988 E, NZ 1, WS (R), R, 1989 NZ, 1990 S (R), I (R), Nm 1,2, 1991 S (R), A (R), F 2, [WS, A], 1992 I, F, E, S, 1993 I (R), F, J, C, 1994 S, I, F, Sp, C (R), Tg, WS, It, SA, 1995 F, E, [J, NZ, I]
Clement, W H (Llanelli) 1937 E, S, I, 1938 E, S, I
Cobner, T J (Pontypool) 1974 S, I, F, E, 1975 F, E, S, I, A, 1976 E, S, 1977 F, E, S, 1978 E, S, I, F, A 1
Cockbain, B J (Celtic Warriors, Ospreys) 2003 R, [C, It, NZ, E], 2004 S, I, F, E, Arg 1, 2, SA2, NZ, 2005 E, It, F, S, I, US, C(R), NZ, Fj, 2007 F1(t&R), A1
Coldrick, A P (Newport) 1911 E, S, I, 1912 E, S, F
Coleman, E O (Newport) 1949 E, S, I
Coles, F C (Pontypool) 1960 S, I, F

Collins, J E (Aberavon) 1958 A, E, S, F, 1959 E, S, I, F, 1960 E, 1961 F
Collins, R G (S Wales Police, Cardiff, Pontypridd) 1987 E (R), I, [I, E, NZ], US, 1988 E, S, I, F, R, 1990 E, S, I, 1991 A, F 2, [WS], 1994 C, Fj, Tg, WS, R, It, SA, 1995 F, E, S, I
Collins, T J (Mountain Ash) 1923 I
Conway-Rees, J (Llanelli) 1892 S, 1893 E, 1894 E
Cook, T (Cardiff) 1949 S, I
Coombs, A J (Newport Gwent Dragons) 2013 I,F,It,E(R),J1,2(R)
Cooper, G J (Bath, Celtic Warriors, Newport Gwent Dragons, Gloucester, Cardiff Blues) 2001 It, J 1,2, 2003 E 1, S 1, I 1, F(R), A, NZ, E 2, [C, Tg, It(t&R), NZ, E], 2004 S, I, F, E, It, R(R), NZ(R), J, 2005 E(R), It(R), F(R), NZ(R), Fj, SA, A, 2006 E(R), PI(R), 2007 A1(R), E2, [J(R)], 2008 SA1, 2, 3, NZ, A, 2009 C, US(R), NZ, Arg, 2010 E, S
Cooper, V L (Llanelli) 2002 C, 2003 I 2(R), S 2
Cope, W (Cardiff, Blackheath) 1896 S
Copsey, A H (Llanelli) 1992 I, F, E, S, A, 1993 E, S, I, J, C, 1994 E (R), Pt, Sp (R), Fj, Tg, WS (R)
Cornish, F H (Cardiff) 1897 E, 1898 I, E, 1899 I
Cornish, R A (Cardiff) 1923 E, S, 1924 E, 1925 E, S, F, 1926 E, S, I, F
Coslett, T K (Aberavon) 1962 E, S, F
Cowey, B T V (Welch Regt, Newport) 1934 E, S, I, 1935 E
Cresswell, B R (Newport) 1960 E, S, I, F
Cummins, W (Treorchy) 1922 E, S, I, F
Cunningham, L J (Aberavon) 1960 E, S, I, F, 1962 E, S, F, I, 1963 NZ, 1964 E, S, I, F, SA
Cuthbert, A G C (Cardiff Blues) 2011 A(R), 2012 I, S, E, It, F, A 1, 2, 3, Arg, Sm, NZ, A4, 2013 I, F, It, S, E
Czekaj, C D (Cardiff Blues) 2005 C, 2006 Arg 1(R), 2007 I, S, A1, 2, 2009 C, 2010 A(R), SA2(R)

Dacey, M (Swansea) 1983 E, S, I, F, R, 1984 S, I, F, E, A, 1986 Fj, Tg, WS, 1987 F (R), [Tg]
Daniel, D J (Llanelli) 1891 S, 1894 E, S, I, 1898 I, E, 1899 E, I
Daniel, L T D (Newport) 1970 S
Daniels, P C T (Cardiff) 1981 A, 1982 I
Darbishire, G (Bangor) 1881 E
Dauncey, F H (Newport) 1896 E, S, I
Davey, C (Swansea) 1930 F, 1931 E, S, F, I, SA, 1932 E, S, I, 1933 E, S, 1934 E, S, I, 1935 E, S, I, NZ, 1936 S, 1937 E, I, 1938 E, I
David, R J (Cardiff) 1907 I
David, T P (Llanelli, Pontypridd) 1973 F, A, 1976 I, F
Davidge, G D (Newport) 1959 F, 1960 S, I, F, SA, 1961 E, S, I, 1962 F
Davies, A (Cambridge U, Neath, Cardiff) 1990 Bb (R), 1991 A, 1993 Z 1,2, J, C, 1994 Fj, 1995 [J, I]
Davies, A C (London Welsh) 1889 I
Davies, A E (Llanelli) 1984 A
Davies, B (Llanelli) 1895 E, 1896 E
Davies, B (Llanelli Scarlets) 2006 I(R)
Davies, B S (Cardiff Blues) 2009 S(R), It(R), C, NZ(R), Sm(R), 2010 E(t&R), S(R), F, I, It, SA1, NZ1, 2, A, SA2, Fj(R), NZ3, 2011 E1, S, It, I, F, E2, Arg, [SA(R), Sm(R), Nm, Fj, I(R), F(R), A], A, 2012 I, A 1, 2, 3, Sm, NZ, 2013 J1, 2
Davies, C (Cardiff) 1947 S, F, I, A, 1948 E, S, F, I, 1949 F, 1950 E, S, I, F, 1951 E, S, I
Davies, C (Llanelli) 1988 WS, 1989 S, I (R), F
Davies, C A H (Llanelli, Cardiff) 1957 I, 1958 A, E, S, I, 1960 SA, 1961 E
Davies, C H (Swansea, Llanelli) 1939 S, I, 1947 E, S, F, I
Davies, C L (Cardiff) 1956 E, S, I
Davies, C R (Bedford, RAF) 1934 E
Davies, D B (Llanelli) 1907 E
Davies, D B (Llanelli) 1962 I, 1963 E, S
Davies, D E G (Cardiff) 1912 E, F
Davies, D G (Cardiff) 1923 E, S
Davies, D H (Neath) 1904 S
Davies, D H (Bridgend) 1921 I, 1925 I
Davies, D H (Aberavon) 1924 E
Davies, D I (Swansea) 1939 E
Davies, D J (Neath) 1962 I
Davies, D M (Somerset Police) 1950 E, S, I, F, 1951 E, S, I, F, SA, 1952 E, S, I, F, 1953 I, F, NZ, 1954 E
Davies, E (Maesteg) 1919 NZA
Davies, E G (Cardiff) 1928 F, 1929 E, 1930 S
Davies, E P (Aberavon) 1947 A, 1948 I
Davies, G (Swansea) 1900 E, S, I, 1901 E, S, I, 1905 E, S, I

Davies, G (Cambridge U, Pontypridd) 1947 S, A, 1948 E, S, F, I, 1949 E, S, F, 1951 E, S
Davies, H (Swansea) 1898 I, E, 1901 S, I
Davies, H (Bridgend) 1984 S, I, F, E
Davies, H G (Llanelli) 1921 F, I, 1925 F
Davies, H J (Neath) 1912 E, S
Davies, H J (Newport) 1924 S
Davies, H J (Cambridge U, Aberavon) 1959 E, S
Davies, H S (Treherbert) 1923 I
Davies, I T (Llanelli) 1914 S, F, I
Davies, J (Neath, Llanelli, Cardiff) 1985 E, Fj, 1986 E, S, I, F, Fj, Tg, WS, 1987 F, E, S, I, [I, Tg (R), C, E, NZ, A], 1988 E, S, I, F, NZ 1,2, WS, R, 1996 A 3, 1997 US (t), S (R), F (R), E
Davies, Rev J A (Swansea) 1913 S, F, I, 1914 E, S, F, I
Davies, J D (Neath, Richmond) 1991 I, F 1, 1993 F (R), Z 2, J, C, 1994 S, I, F, E, Pt, Sp, C, WS, R, It, SA, 1995 F, E, [J, NZ, I] SA, 1996 It, E, S, I, F 1, A 1, Bb, F 2, It, 1998 Z, SA 1
Davies, J H (Aberavon) 1923 I
Davies, J J V (Scarlets) 2009 C, US, Sm(R), Arg, A, 2010 NZ1(R), 2, 2011 E1, S, I, F, Bb, E2, Arg, [SA, Sm, Nm, Fj(R), I, F, A], 2012 I, S, E, It, F, A 1, 2, 3, NZ, A4, 2013 I, F, It, S, E
Davies, L (Swansea) 1939 S, I
Davies, L (Bridgend) 1966 E, S, I
Davies, L B (Neath, Cardiff, Llanelli) 1996 It, E, S, I, F 1, A 1, Bb, F 2, It (R), 1997 US 1,2, C, R, Tg, NZ (R), 1998 E (R), I, F, 1999 C, 2001 I, 2003 It
Davies, L M (Llanelli) 1954 F, S, 1955 I
Davies, M (Swansea) 1981 A, 1982 I, 1985 Fj
Davies, Mefin (Pontypridd, Celtic Warriors, Gloucester) 2002 SA 2(R), R, Fj, 2003 It, S 1(R), I 1(R), F, A(R), NZ(R), I 2, R, [Tg, NZ(R), E(R)], 2004 S, F, It(R), Arg 1, 2(R), SA1, 2(R), R, NZ, J, 2005 E, It, F, S, I, C(R), NZ, SA(R), A(t), 2006 S(R), I(R), It(R), F(R), 2007 A2
Davies, M J (Blackheath) 1939 S, I
Davies, N G (London Welsh) 1955 E
Davies, N G (Llanelli) 1988 NZ 2, WS, 1989 S, I, 1993 F, 1994 S, I, E, Pt, Sp, C, Fj, Tg (R), WS, R, It, 1995 E, S, I, Fj, 1996 E, S, I, F 1, A 1,2, Bb, F 2, 1997 E
Davies, P T (Llanelli) 1985 E, Fj, 1986 E, S, I, F, Fj, Tg, WS, 1987 F, E, I, [Tg, C, NZ], 1988 WS, R, 1989 S, I, F, E, NZ, 1990 F, E, S, 1991 I, F 1, A, F 2, [WS, Arg, A], 1993 F, Z 1, Nm, 1994 S, I, F, E, C, Fj (R), WS, R, It, 1995 F, I
Davies, R H (Oxford U, London Welsh) 1957 S, I, F, 1958 A, 1962 E, S
Davies, S (Swansea) 1992 I, F, E, S, A, 1993 E, S, I, Z 1(R),2, Nm, J, 1995 F, [J, I], 1998 I (R), F
Davies, T G R (Cardiff, London Welsh) 1966 A, 1967 S, I, F, E, 1968 E, S, 1969 S, I, F, NZ 1,2, A, 1971 E, S, I, F, 1972 E, S, F, NZ, 1973 E, S, I, F, A, 1974 S, F, E, 1975 F, E, S, I, 1976 E, S, I, F, 1977 I, F, E, S, 1978 E, S, I, A 1,2
Davies, T J (Devonport Services, Swansea, Llanelli) 1953 E, S, I, F, 1957 E, S, I, F, 1958 A, E, S, F, 1959 E, S, I, F, 1960 E, SA, 1961 E, S, F
Davies, T M (London Welsh, Swansea) 1969 S, I, F, E, NZ 1,2, A, 1970 SA, S, E, I, F, 1971 E, S, I, F, 1972 E, S, F, NZ, 1973 E, S, I, F, A, 1974 S, I, F, E, 1975 F, E, S, I, A, 1976 E, S, I, F
Davies, W (Cardiff) 1896 S
Davies, W (Swansea) 1931 SA, 1932 E, S, I
Davies, W A (Aberavon) 1912 S, I
Davies, W G (Cardiff) 1978 A 1,2, NZ, 1979 S, I, F, E, 1980 F, E, S, NZ, 1981 E, S, A, 1982 I, F, E, S, 1985 S, I, F
Davies, W T H (Swansea) 1936 I, 1937 E, I, 1939 E, S, I
Davis, C E (Newbridge) 1978 A 2, 1981 E, S
Davis, M (Newport) 1991 A
Davis, W E N (Cardiff) 1939 E, S, I
Dawes, S J (London Welsh) 1964 I, F, SA, 1965 E, S, I, F, 1966 A, 1968 I, F, 1969 E, NZ 2, A, 1970 SA, S, E, I, F, 1971 E, S, I, F
Day, H C (Newport) 1930 S, I, F, 1931 E, S
Day, H T (Newport) 1892 I, 1893 E, S, 1894 S, I
Day, T B (Swansea) 1931 E, S, F, I, SA, 1932 E, S, I, 1934 S, I, 1935 E, S, I
Deacon, J T (Swansea) 1891 I, 1892 E, S, I
Delahay, W J (Bridgend) 1922 E, S, I, F, 1923 E, S, F, I, 1924 NZ, 1925 E, S, F, I, 1926 E, S, I, F, 1927 S
Delaney, L (Llanelli) 1989 I, F, E, 1990 E, 1991 F 2, [WS, Arg, A], 1992 I, F, E
Delve, G L (Bath, Gloucester) 2006 S(R), I(R), Arg 1(R), 2(R), 2008 S(R), It(R), I(R), SA1(R), 2, 2010 I, It(R)
Devereux, D B (Neath) 1958 A, E, S
Devereux, J A (S Glamorgan Inst, Bridgend) 1986 E, S, I, F, Fj, Tg, WS, 1987 F, E, S, I, [I, C, E, NZ, A], 1988 NZ 1,2, R, 1989 S, I
Diplock, R S (Bridgend) 1988 R
Dobson, G A (Cardiff) 1900 S
Dobson, T (Cardiff) 1898 I, E, 1899 E, S
Donovan, A J (Swansea) 1978 A 2, 1981 I (R), A, 1982 E, S
Donovan, R E (S Wales Police) 1983 F (R)
Douglas, M H J (Llanelli) 1984 S, I, F
Douglas, W M (Cardiff) 1886 E, S, 1887 E, S
Dowell, W H (Newport) 1907 E, S, I, 1908 E, S, F, I
Durston, A P R (Bridgend) 2001 J 1,2
Dyke, J C M (Penarth) 1906 SA
Dyke, L M (Penarth, Cardiff) 1910 I, 1911 S, F, I

Edmunds, D A (Neath) 1990 I (R), Bb
Edwards, A B (London Welsh, Army) 1955 E, S
Edwards, B O (Newport) 1951 I
Edwards, D (Glynneath) 1921 E
Edwards, G O (Cardiff, Cardiff Coll of Ed) 1967 F, E, NZ, 1968 E, S, I, F, 1969 S, I, F, E, NZ 1,2, A, 1970 SA, S, E, I, F, 1971 E, S, I, F, 1972 E, S, F, NZ, 1973 E, S, I, F, A, 1974 S, I, F, E, 1975 F, E, S, I, A, 1976 E, S, I, F, 1977 I, F, E, S, 1978 E, S, I, F
Eidman, I H (Cardiff) 1983 S, R, 1984 I, F, E, A, 1985 S, I, Fj, 1986 E, S, I, F
Elliott, J (Cardiff) 1894 I, 1898 I, E
Elsey, W J (Cardiff) 1895 E
Emyr, Arthur (Swansea) 1989 E, NZ, 1990 F, E, S, I, Nm 1, 2, 1991 F 1, 2, [WS, Arg, A]
Evans, A (Pontypool) 1924 E, I, F
Evans, B (Llanelli) 1933 E, S, 1936 E, S, I, 1937 E
Evans, B R (Swansea, Cardiff Blues) 1998 SA 2(R), 1999 F 1, It, E, Arg 1,2, C, [J (R), Sm (R), A (R)], 2000 Sm, US, 2001 J 1(R), 2002 SA 1,2, R(R), Fj, C, NZ, 2003 It, E 1, S 1, I 2, R, 2004 F(R), 0E(t), It(R)
Evans, B S (Llanelli) 1920 E, 1922 E, S, I, F
Evans, C (Pontypool) 1960 E
Evans, D (Penygraig) 1896 S, I, 1897 E, 1898 E
Evans, D B (Swansea) 1926 E
Evans, D B (Swansea) 1933 S
Evans, D D (Cheshire, Cardiff U) 1934 E
Evans, D J (Scarlets) 2009 C,US
Evans, D P (Llanelli) 1960 SA
Evans, D W (Cardiff) 1889 S, I, 1890 E, I, 1891 E
Evans, D W (Oxford U, Cardiff, Treorchy) 1989 F, E, NZ, 1990 F, E, S, I, Bb, 1991 A (R), F 2(R), [A (R)], 1995 [J (R)]
Evans, E (Llanelli) 1937 E, 1939 S, I
Evans, F (Llanelli) 1921 S
Evans, G (Cardiff) 1947 E, S, F, I, A, 1948 E, S, F, I, 1949 E, S, I
Evans, G (Maesteg) 1981 S (R), I, F, A, 1982 I, F, E, S, 1983 F, R
Evans, G D (Llanelli Scarlets) 2006 PI(R)
Evans, G L (Newport) 1977 F (R), 1978 F, A 2(R)
Evans, G R (Cardiff) 1889 S
Evans, G R (Llanelli) 1998 SA 1, 2003 I 2, S 2, [NZ]
Evans, H I (Swansea) 1922 E, S, I, F
Evans, I (London Welsh) 1934 S, I
Evans, I C (Llanelli, Bath) 1987 F, E, S, I, [I, C, E, NZ, A], 1988 E, S, I, F, NZ 1,2, 1989 I, F, E, 1991 E, S, I, F 1, A, F 2, [WS, Arg, A], 1992 I, F, E, S, A, 1993 E, S, I, F, J, C, 1994 S, I, E, Pt, Sp, C, Fj, Tg, WS, R, 1995 E, S, I, [J, NZ, I], SA, Fj, 1996 It, E, S, I, F 1, A 1,2, Bb, F 2, A 3, SA, 1997 US, S, I, F, 1998 It
Evans, I L (Llanelli) 1991 F 2(R)
Evans, I R (Ospreys) 2006 Arg 1, 2, A, C, NZ, 2007 [J(R), Fj], SA, 2008 E(R), S, It, F(R), SA1(R), 2(R), 3, NZ, 2011 A, 2012 I, S, E, It, F, Bb, Arg, Sm, 2013 I, F, It, S, E
Evans, J (Llanelli) 1896 S, I, 1897 E
Evans, J D (Cardiff) 1958 I, F
Evans, J E (Llanelli) 1924 S
Evans, J H (Pontypool) 1907 E, S, I
Evans, J R (Newport) 1934 E
Evans, J W (Blaina) 1904 E
Evans, O J (Cardiff) 1887 E, S, 1888 S, I
Evans, P D (Llanelli) 1951 E, F
Evans, R (Bridgend) 1963 S, I, F
Evans, R L (Llanelli) 1993 E, S, I, F, 1994 S, I, F, E, Pt, Sp, C, Fj, WS, R, It, SA, 1995 F, [NZ, I (R)]
Evans, R T (Newport) 1947 F, I, 1950 E, S, I, F, 1951 E, S, I, F
Evans, S (Swansea, Neath) 1985 F, E, 1986 Fj, Tg, WS, 1987 F, E, [I, Tg]

THE COUNTRIES

Evans, T D (Swansea) 1924 I
Evans, T G (London Welsh) 1970 SA, S, E, I, 1972 E, S, F
Evans, T H (Llanelli) 1906 I, 1907 E, S, I, 1908 I, A, 1909 E, S, F, I, 1910 F, E, S, I, 1911 E, S, F, I
Evans, T P (Swansea) 1975 F, E, S, I, A, 1976 E, S, I, F, 1977 I
Evans, T W (Llanelli) 1958 A
Evans, V (Neath) 1954 I, F, S
Evans, W F (Rhymney) 1882 I, 1883 S
Evans, W G (Brynmawr) 1911 I
Evans, W H (Llwynypia) 1914 E, S, F, I
Evans, W J (Pontypool) 1947 S
Evans, W R (Bridgend) 1958 A, E, S, I, F, 1960 SA, 1961 E, S, I, F, 1962 E, S, I
Everson, W A (Newport) 1926 S

Faletau, T T (Newport Gwent Dragons) 2011 Bb, E2, 3, [SA, Sm, Nm, Fj, I, F, A], A, 2012 I, S, E, It, F, A1, Arg, Sm, NZ, A4, 2013 I, F, It, S, E
Faulkner, A G (Pontypool) 1975 F, E, S, I, A, 1976 E, S, I, F, 1978 E, S, I, F, A 1,2, NZ, 1979 S, I, F
Faull, J (Swansea) 1957 I, F, 1958 A, E, S, I, F, 1959 E, S, I, 1960 E, F
Fauvel, T J (Aberavon) 1988 NZ 1(R)
Fear, A G (Newport) 1934 S, I, 1935 S, I
Fender, N H (Cardiff) 1930 I, F, 1931 E, S, F, I
Fenwick, S P (Bridgend) 1975 F, E, S, A, 1976 E, S, I, F, 1977 I, F, E, S, 1978 E, S, I, F, A 1,2, NZ, 1979 S, I, F, E, 1980 F, E, S, I, NZ, 1981 E, S
Finch, E (Llanelli) 1924 F, NZ, 1925 F, I, 1926 F, 1927 A, 1928 I
Finlayson, A A J (Cardiff) 1974 I, F, E
Fitzgerald, D (Cardiff) 1894 S, I
Ford, F J V (Welch Regt, Newport) 1939 E
Ford, I R (Newport) 1959 E, S
Ford, S P (Cardiff) 1990 I, Nm 1,2, Bb, 1991 E, S, I, A
Forster, J A (Newport Gwent Dragons) 2004 Arg 1
Forward, A (Pontypool, Mon Police) 1951 S, SA, 1952 E, S, I, F
Fowler, I J (Llanelli) 1919 NZA
Francis, D G (Llanelli) 1919 NZA, 1924 S
Francis, P W (Maesteg) 1987 S
Funnell, J S (Ebbw Vale) 1998 Z (R), SA 1
Fury, W L (London Irish) 2008 SA1(R),2(R)

Gabe, R T (Cardiff, Llanelli) 1901 I, 1902 E, S, I, 1903 E, S, I, 1904 E, S, I, 1905 E, S, I, NZ, 1906 E, I, SA, 1907 E, S, I, 1908 E, S, F, I
Gale, N R (Swansea, Llanelli) 1960 I, 1963 E, S, I, NZ, 1964 E, S, I, F, SA, 1965 E, S, I, F, 1966 E, S, I, F, A, 1967 E, NZ, 1968 E, 1969 NZ 1(R),2, A
Gallacher, I S (Llanelli) 1970 F
Garrett, R M (Penarth) 1888 M, 1889 S, 1890 S, E, I, 1891 S, I, 1892 E
Geen, W P (Oxford U, Newport) 1912 SA, 1913 E, I
George, E E (Pontypridd, Cardiff) 1895 S, I, 1896 E
George, G M (Newport) 1991 E, S
Gething, G I (Neath) 1913 F
Gibbs, A (Newbridge) 1995 I, SA, 1996 A 2, 1997 US 1,2, C
Gibbs, I S (Neath, Swansea) 1991 E, S, I, F 1, A, F 2, [WS, Arg, A], 1992 I, F, E, S, A, 1993 E, S, I, F, J, C, 1996 It, A 3, SA, 1997 US, S, I, F, Tg, NZ, 1998 It, E, S, SA 2, Arg, 1999 S, I, F 1, It, E, C, F 2, [Arg 3, J, Sm, A], 2000 I, Sm, US, SA, 2001 E, S, F, It
Gibbs, R A (Cardiff) 1906 S, I, 1907 E, S, 1908 E, S, F, I, 1910 F, E, S, I, 1911 E, S, F, I
Giles, R (Aberavon) 1983 R, 1985 Fj (R), 1987 [C]
Gill, I A R (Saracens) 2010 I(R), 2012 I,Bb, 2013 J1(R),2
Girling, B E (Cardiff) 1881 E
Goldsworthy, S J (Swansea) 1884 I, 1885 E, S
Gore, J H (Blaina) 1924 I, F, NZ, 1925 E
Gore, W (Newbridge) 1947 S, F, I
Gough, I M (Newport, Pontypridd, Newport Gwent Dragons, Ospreys) 1998 SA 1, 1999 S, 2000 F, It (R), E (R), S, I, Sm, US, SA, 2001 E, S, F, It, Tg, A, 2002 I (R), F (R), It, S, 2003 R, 2005 It(R), US(R), SA, A, 2006 E, S, I, It, F, Arg 1, 2, A, C, NZ, 2007 I, S(R), F1, It, E1, Arg, F2, [C, A, Fj(R)], 2008 E, S, It, I, F, SA1, 2, 3(R), C, A, 2009 S, E, F, I, C(R), US, 2010 I(R), It(R), Fj
Gould, A J (Newport) 1885 E, S, 1886 E, S, 1887 E, S, I, 1888 S, 1889 I, 1890 S, E, I, 1892 E, S, I, 1893 E, S, I, 1894 E, S, 1895 E, S, I, 1896 E, S, I, 1897 E
Gould, G H (Newport) 1892 I, 1893 S, I
Gould, R (Newport) 1882 I, 1883 E, S, 1884 E, S, I, 1885 E, S, 1886 E, 1887 E, S
Graham, T C (Newport) 1890 I, 1891 S, I, 1892 E, S, 1893 E, S, I, 1894 E, S, 1895 E, S
Gravell, R W R (Llanelli) 1975 F, E, S, I, A, 1976 E, S, I, F, 1978 E, S, I, F, A 1,2, NZ, 1979 S, I, 1981 I, F, 1982 F, E, S
Gray, A J (London Welsh) 1968 E, S
Greenslade, D (Newport) 1962 S
Greville, H G (Llanelli) 1947 A
Griffin, Dr J (Edinburgh U) 1883 S
Griffiths, C R (Llanelli) 1979 E (R)
Griffiths, D (Llanelli) 1888 M, 1889 I
Griffiths, G (Llanelli) 1889 I
Griffiths, G M (Cardiff) 1953 E, S, I, F, NZ, 1954 I, F, S, 1955 I, F, 1957 E, S
Griffiths, J (Swansea) 2000 Sm (R)
Griffiths, J L (Llanelli) 1988 NZ 2, 1989 S
Griffiths, M (Bridgend, Cardiff, Pontypridd) 1988 WS, R, 1989 S, I, F, E, NZ, 1990 F, E, Nm 1,2, Bb, 1991 I, F 1,2, [WS, Arg, A], 1992 I, F, E, S, A, 1993 Z 1,2, Nm, J, C, 1995 F (R), E, S, I, [J, I], 1998 SA 1
Griffiths, V M (Newport) 1924 S, I, F
Gronow, B (Bridgend) 1910 F, E, S, I
Gwilliam, J A (Cambridge U, Newport) 1947 A, 1948 I, 1949 E, S, I, F, 1950 E, S, I, F, 1951 E, S, I, SA, 1952 E, S, I, F, 1953 E, I, F, NZ, 1954 E
Gwynn, D (Swansea) 1883 E, 1887 S, 1890 E, I, 1891 E, S
Gwynn, W H (Swansea) 1884 E, S, I, 1885 E, S

Hadley, A M (Cardiff) 1983 R, 1984 S, I, F, E, 1985 F, E, Fj, 1986 E, S, I, F, Fj, Tg, 1987 S (R), I, [I, Tg, C, E, NZ, A], US, 1988 E, S, I, F
Halfpenny, S L (Cardiff Blues) 2008 SA3,C,NZ, 2009 S, E, F, NZ, Sm, Arg, A, 2010 E(R), S, F, I, SA1, NZ1, 2, 2011 I, F, Arg, [Sm(R), Nm, Fj, I, F, A] ,A, 2012 I, S, E, It, F, A 1, 2, 3, Arg, Sm, NZ, A4, 2013 I, F, It, S, E
Hall, I (Aberavon) 1967 NZ, 1970 SA, S, E, 1971 S, 1974 S, I, F
Hall, M R (Cambridge U, Bridgend, Cardiff) 1988 NZ 1(R),2, WS, R, 1989 S, I, F, E, NZ, 1990 F, E, S, 1991 A, F 2, [WS, Arg, A], 1992 I, F, E, S, A, 1993 E, S, I, 1994 S, I, F, E, Pt, Sp, C, Tg, R, It, SA, 1995 F, S, I, [J, NZ, I]
Hall, W H (Bridgend) 1988 WS
Hancock, F E (Cardiff) 1884 I, 1885 E, S, 1886 S
Hannan, J (Newport) 1888 M, 1889 S, I, 1890 S, E, I, 1891 E, 1892 E, S, I, 1893 E, S, I, 1894 E, S, I, 1895 E, S, I
Harding, A F (London Welsh) 1902 E, S, I, 1903 E, S, I, 1904 E, S, I, 1905 E, S, I, NZ, 1906 E, S, I, SA, 1907 I, 1908 E, S
Harding, C T (Newport) 1888 M, 1889 S, I
Harding, G F (Newport) 1881 E, 1882 I, 1883 E, S
Harding, R (Swansea, Cambridge U) 1923 E, S, F, I, 1924 I, F, NZ, 1925 F, I, 1926 E, I, F, 1927 E, S, F, I, 1928 E
Harries, W T M (Newport Gwent Dragons) 2010 NZ2(R), A, 2012 Bb(R)
Harris, C A (Aberavon) 1927 A
Harris, D J E (Pontypridd, Cardiff) 1959 I, F, 1960 S, I, F, SA, 1961 E, S
Harris, I R (Cardiff) 2001 Arg, Tg, A, 2002 I, It (R), E, S (R), Fj(R), C(R), NZ(R), 2003 It, E 1(R), S 1(R), I 1(R), F, I 2, S 2, [C,Tg,It,E], 2004 S,I,F,It
Hathway, G F (Newport) 1924 I, F
Havard, Rev W T (Llanelli) 1919 NZA
Hawkins, F J (Pontypridd) 1912 I, F
Hayward, B I (Ebbw Vale) 1998 Z (R), SA 1
Hayward, D J (Newbridge) 1949 E, F, 1950 E, S, I, F, 1951 E, S, I, F, SA, 1952 E, S, I, F
Hayward, D J (Cardiff) 1963 E, NZ, 1964 S, I, F, SA
Hayward, G (Swansea) 1908 S, F, I, A, 1909 E
Hellings, D (Llwynypia) 1897 E, 1898 I, E, 1899 S, I, 1900 E, I, 1901 E, S
Henson, G L (Swansea, Ospreys, Toulon) 2001 J 1(R), R, 2003 NZ(R), R, 2004 Arg 1, 2, SA1, 2, R, NZ, J, 2005 E, It, F, S, I, 2006 I(R), F(R), A, NZ(R), 2007 A1(t&R), 2(R), SA, 2008 E, S, It, I, F, 2009 F(R), It, I, 2011 Bb, E3
Herrerá, R C (Cross Keys) 1925 S, F, I, 1926 E, S, I, F, 1927 E
Hiams, H (Swansea) 1912 I, F
Hibbard, R M (Ospreys) 2006 Arg 1(R),2(R), 2007 A1(R), 2(R), 2008 SA1(R), 2, C, 2009 C, US(R), 2011 E1(R), S(R), It(R), I(R), F(R), Arg, 2012 Bb(R), A2(R), Arg(R), Sm, 2013 F, It, S, E
Hickman, A (Neath) 1930 E, 1933 S
Hiddlestone, D D (Neath) 1922 E, S, I, F, 1924 NZ

Hill, A F (Cardiff) 1885 S, 1886 E, S, 1888 S, I, M, 1889 S, 1890 S, I, 1893 E, S, I, 1894 E, S, I
Hill, S D (Cardiff) 1993 Z 1,2, Nm, 1994 I (R), F, SA, 1995 F, SA, 1996 A 2, F 2(R), It, 1997 E
Hinam, S (Cardiff) 1925 I, 1926 E, S, I, F
Hinton, J T (Cardiff) 1884 I
Hirst, G L (Newport) 1912 S, 1913 S, 1914 E, S, F, I
Hodder, W (Pontypool) 1921 E, S, F
Hodges, J J (Newport) 1899 E, S, I, 1900 E, S, I, 1901 E, S, 1902 E, S, I, 1903 E, S, I, 1904 E, S, 1905 E, S, I, NZ, 1906 E, S, I
Hodgson, G T R (Neath) 1962 I, 1963 E, S, I, F, NZ, 1964 E, S, I, F, SA, 1966 S, I, F, 1967 I
Hollingdale, B G (Swansea) 1912 SA, 1913 E
Hollingdale, T H (Neath) 1927 A, 1928 E, S, I, F, 1930 E
Holmes, T D (Cardiff) 1978 A 2, NZ, 1979 S, I, F, E, 1980 F, E, S, I, NZ, 1981 A, 1982 I, F, E, 1983 E, S, I, F, 1984 E, 1985 S, I, F, E, Fj
Hook, J W (Ospreys, Perpignan) 2006 Arg 1(R), 2, A(R), Pl, C, NZ(R), 2007 I, S, F1, It, E1, A1, 2, Arg, F2, [C, A(R), J, Fj], SA, 2008 E, S, It(R), I(R), F, SA1(R), 2, 3(R), C, NZ(R), 2009 S(R), F(R), It, NZ, Sm, Arg, A, 2010 E, S, F, I, It, SA1, A, SA2, Fj, NZ3, 2011 E1, S, It, I, F, E3, Arg, [SA, Sm, I(R), F, A], 2012 I(R), S(R), It(R), Bb, A 1(R), 3(R), Arg(R), NZ(R), 2013 I(R), It(R), E(R)
Hopkin, W H (Newport) 1937 S
Hopkins, K (Cardiff, Swansea) 1985 E, 1987 F, E, S, [Tg, C (R)], US
Hopkins, P L (Swansea) 1908 A, 1909 E, I, 1910 E
Hopkins, R (Maesteg) 1970 E (R)
Hopkins, T (Swansea) 1926 E, S, I, F
Hopkins, W J (Aberavon) 1925 E, S
Horsman, C L (Worcester) 2005 NZ(R), Fj, SA, A, 2006 Pl, 2007 I, F1, It, E1, A2(R), E2, F2, [J, Fj]
Howarth, S P (Sale, Newport) 1998 SA 2, Arg, 1999 S, I, F 1, It, E, Arg 1,2, SA, C, F 2, [Arg 3, J, Sm, A], 2000 F, It, E
Howells, B (Llanelli) 1934 E
Howells, D W (Ospreys) 2013 J1,2(R)
Howells, W G (Llanelli) 1957 E, S, I, F
Howells, W H (Swansea) 1888 S, I
Howley, R (Bridgend, Cardiff) 1996 E, S, I, F 1, A 1,2, Bb, F 2, It, A 3, SA, 1997 US, S, I, F, E, Tg (R), NZ, 1998 It, E, S, I, F, Z, SA 2, Arg, 1999 S, I, F 1, It, E, Arg 1,2, SA, C, F 2, [Arg 3, J, Sm, A], 2000 F, It, E, Sm, US, SA, 2001 E, S, F, R, I, Arg, Tg, A, 2002 I, F, It, E, S
Hughes, D (Newbridge) 1967 NZ, 1969 NZ 2, 1970 SA, S, E, I
Hughes, G (Penarth) 1934 E, S, I
Hughes, H (Cardiff) 1887 S, 1889 S
Hughes, K (Cambridge U, London Welsh) 1970 I, 1973 A, 1974 S
Hullin, W G (Cardiff) 1967 S
Humphreys, J M (Cardiff, Bath) 1995 [NZ, I], SA, Fj, 1996 It, E, S, I, F 1, A 1,2, Bb, It, A 3, SA, 1997 S, I, F, E, Tg (R), NZ (R), 1998 It (R), E (R), S (R), I (R), F (R), SA 2, Arg, 1999 S, Arg 2(R), SA (R), C, [J (R)], 2003 E 1, I 1
Hurrell, R J (Newport) 1959 F
Hutchinson, F O (Neath) 1894 I, 1896 S, I
Huxtable, R (Swansea) 1920 F, I
Huzzey, H V P (Cardiff) 1898 I, E, 1899 E, S, I
Hybart, A J (Cardiff) 1887 E

Ingledew, H M (Cardiff) 1890 I, 1891 E, S
Isaacs, I (Cardiff) 1933 E, S

Jackson, T H (Swansea) 1895 E
James, C R (Llanelli) 1958 A, F
James, D (Swansea) 1891 I, 1892 S, I, 1899 E
James, D M (Cardiff) 1947 A, 1948 E, S, F, I
James, D R (Treorchy) 1931 F, I
James, D R (Bridgend, Pontypridd, Llanelli Scarlets) 1996 A 2(R), It, A 3, SA, 1997 I, Tg (R), 1998 F (R), Z, SA 1,2, Arg, 1999 S, I, F 1, It, E, Arg 1,2, SA, F 2, [Arg 3, Sm, A], 2000 F, It (R), I (R), Sm (R), US, SA, 2001 E, S, F, It, R, I, 2002 I, F, It, E, S (R), NZ(R), 2005 SA,A, 2006 I,F, 2007 E2,Arg, [J]
James, E (Swansea) 1890 S, 1891 I, 1892 S, I, 1899 E
James, J B (Bridgend) 1968 E
James, P (Ospreys, Bath) 2003 R, 2009 NZ, Sm, Arg, A, 2010 E, S, F, I, It(t&R), SA1, NZ1, 2, A(R), SA2, Fj, NZ3(R), 2011 E1, S, It, I, F, Bb, E2, 3, Arg, [SA, Sm, Fj(R), F(R), A], 2012 I(R), S(R), It(R), Bb(t&R), A1(R), 3(R), Arg(R), Sm, NZ, 2013 I(t&R), F(t&R), It(R), S, E(R)
James, T E (Cardiff Blues, Wasps) 2007 E2(R),SA(R), 2008 SA2(R), 2009 C, US, Sm, Arg(R), A(R), 2010 E, NZ3
James, T O (Aberavon) 1935 I, 1937 S
James, W (Gloucester) 2007 E2,Arg(R),F2(R), [J]
James, W J (Aberavon) 1983 E, S, I, F, R, 1984 S, 1985 S, I, F, E, Fj, 1986 E, S, I, F, Fj, Tg, WS, 1987 E, S, I
James, W P (Aberavon) 1925 E, S
Jarman, H (Newport) 1910 E, S, I, 1911 E
Jarrett, K S (Newport) 1967 E, 1968 E, S, 1969 S, I, F, E, NZ 1,2, A
Jarvis, A R (Ospreys) 2012 Arg,Sm,NZ
Jarvis, L (Cardiff) 1997 R (R)
Jeffery, J J (Cardiff Coll of Ed, Newport) 1967 NZ
Jenkin, A M (Swansea) 1895 I, 1896 E
Jenkins, A E (Llanelli) 1920 E, S, F, I, 1921 S, F, 1922 F, 1923 E, S, F, I, 1924 NZ, 1928 S, I
Jenkins, D M (Treorchy) 1926 E, S, I, F
Jenkins, D R (Swansea) 1927 A, 1929 E
Jenkins, E (Newport) 1910 S, I
Jenkins, E M (Aberavon) 1927 S, F, I, A, 1928 E, S, I, F, 1929 F, 1930 E, S, I, F, 1931 E, S, F, I, SA, 1932 E, S, I
Jenkins, G D (Pontypridd, Celtic Warriors, Cardiff Blues, Toulon) 2002 R, NZ(R), 2003 E 1(R), S 1(R), I 1, F, A, NZ, I 2(R), E 2, [C, Tg, It(R), NZ(R), E(R)], 2004 S(R), I(R), F, E, It, Arg 1(R), 2(R), SA1, 2(R), R, NZ, J, 2005 E, It, F, S, I, 2006 E(R), S(R), I(R), It(R), F(R), A, C, NZ(R), 2007 I, S(R), F1, It, E1, 2(R), Arg(R), F2(R), [C, A, J(R), Fj], SA, 2008 E(R), S(R), It, I, F, SA1, 2, 3, NZ, A, 2009 S, E, F, It(R), I, NZ, Sm, Arg, A, 2010 S(R), It, A, NZ3, 2011 [Sm(R), Nm, Fj, I, F, A], A, 2012 S, E, It, F, A 1, 2, 3, Arg, Sm(R), NZ(R), A4, 2013 I, F, It, E
Jenkins, G R (Pontypool, Swansea) 1991 F 2, [WS (R), Arg, A], 1992 I, F, E, S, A, 1993 C, 1994 S, I, F, E, Pt, Sp, C, Tg, WS, R, It, SA, 1995 F, E, S, I, [J], SA (R), Fj (t), 1996 E (R), 1997 US, US 1, C, 1998 S, I, F, Z, SA 1(R), 1999 I (R), F 1, It, E, Arg 1,2, SA, F 2, [Arg 3, J, Sm, A], 2000 F, It, E, S, I, Sm, US, SA
Jenkins, J C (London Welsh) 1906 SA
Jenkins, J L (Aberavon) 1923 S, F
Jenkins, L H (Mon TC, Newport) 1954 I, 1956 E, S, I, F
Jenkins, N R (Pontypridd, Cardiff) 1991 E, S, I, F 1, 1992 I, F, E, S, 1993 E, S, I, F, Z 1,2, Nm, J, C, 1994 S, I, F, E, Pt, Sp, C, Tg, WS, R, It, SA, 1995 F, E, S, I, [J, NZ, I], SA, Fj, 1996 F 1, A 1,2, Bb, F 2, It, A 3(R), SA, 1997 S, I, F, E, Tg, NZ, 1998 It, E, S, I, F, SA 2, Arg, 1999 S, I, F 1, It, E, Arg 1,2, SA, C, F 2, [Arg 3, J, Sm, A], 2000 F, It, E, I (R), Sm (R), US (R), SA, 2001 E, S, F, It, 2002 SA 1(R),2(R), R
Jenkins, V G J (Oxford U, Bridgend, London Welsh) 1933 E, I, 1934 S, I, 1935 E, S, NZ, 1936 E, S, I, 1937 E, 1938 E, S, 1939 E
Jenkins, W J (Cardiff) 1912 I, F, 1913 S, I
John, B (Llanelli, Cardiff) 1966 A, 1967 S, NZ, 1968 E, S, I, F, 1969 S, I, F, E, NZ 1,2, A, 1970 SA, S, E, I, 1971 E, S, I, F, 1972 E, S, F
John, D A (Llanelli) 1925 I, 1928 E, S, I
John, D E (Llanelli) 1923 F, I, 1928 E, S, I
John, E R (Neath) 1950 E, S, I, F, 1951 E, S, I, F, SA, 1952 E, S, I, F, 1953 E, S, I, F, NZ, 1954 E
John G (St Luke's Coll, Exeter) 1954 E, F
John, J H (Swansea) 1926 E, S, I, F, 1927 E, S, F, I
John, P (Pontypridd) 1994 Tg, 1996 Bb (t), 1997 US (R), US 1,2, C, R, Tg, 1998 Z (R), SA 1
John, S C (Llanelli, Cardiff) 1995 S, I, 1997 E (R), Tg, NZ (R), 2000 F (R), It (R), E (R), Sm (R), SA (R), 2001 E (R), S (R), Tg (R), A, 2002 I, F, It (R), S (R)
Johnson, T A W (Cardiff) 1921 E, F, I, 1923 E, S, F, 1924 E, S, NZ, 1925 E, S, F
Johnson, W D (Swansea) 1953 E
Jones , A E (SEE Emyr)
Jones, A H (Cardiff) 1933 E, S
Jones, A M (Llanelli Scarlets) 2006 E(t&R),S(R)
Jones, A R (Ospreys) 2003 E 2(R), S 2, [C(R), Tg(R), It, NZ, E], 2004 S, I, Arg 1, 2, SA1, 2, R, NZ, J(t&R), 2005 E, It, F, S, I, US, NZ, Fj(R), SA(t&R), A(R), 2006 E, S, I, It, F, Arg 1, 2, A, Pl(R), C, NZ, 2007 S, It(R), E1(R), A1, Arg, [C, A], 2008 E, S, I, F, SA1, 3, NZ, A, 2009 S, E, F, I, 2010 E, S, F, I, It, SA1, NZ1, 2, A, SA2, Fj, NZ3, 2011 F, Arg, [SA, Sm, Fj, I, F], 2012 I, S, E, It, F, A 1, 2, 3, 2013 I, F, It, S, E
Jones, A W (Mountain Ash) 1905 I
Jones, A-W (Ospreys) 2006 Arg 1, 2, Pl, C(R), NZ(R), 2007 I, S, F1, It, E1, 2, Arg, F2, [C, A, J, Fj], SA, 2008 E, I, F, SA1, 2, 3, NZ, A, 2009 S, E, F, It, I, NZ, Sm, Arg, A, 2010 E, S, SA1(R),

NZ1, 2, A, SA2, NZ3, 2011 E1, S, It, I, F, Bb(R), E2, 3, Arg, [SA, Sm, Nm, Fj(R), I, F, A(R)], 2012 E, It, F, Bb, A1(R), 2, 3, Arg, 2013 It(R), S, E
Jones, B J (Newport) 1960 I, F
Jones, B L (Devonport Services, Llanelli) 1950 E, S, I, F, 1951 E, S, SA, 1952 E, I, F
Jones, C (Harlequins) 2007 A1(R),2
Jones, C W (Cambridge U, Cardiff) 1934 E, S, I, 1935 E, S, I, NZ, 1936 E, S, I, 1938 E, S, I
Jones, C W (Bridgend) 1920 E, S, F
Jones, D (Aberavon) 1897 E
Jones, D (Treherbert) 1902 E, S, I, 1903 E, S, I, 1905 E, S, I, NZ, 1906 E, S, SA
Jones, D (Neath) 1927 A
Jones, D (Cardiff) 1994 SA, 1995 F, E, S, [J, NZ, I], SA, Fj, 1996 It, E, S, I, F 1, A 1,2, Bb, It, A 3
Jones, D A R (Llanelli Scarlets) 2002 Fj, C, NZ, 2003 It(R), E 1, S 1, I 1, F, NZ, E 2, [C,Tg, It, NZ(R), E], 2004 S, I, F, E, It, Arg 2, SA1, 2, R, NZ, J, 2005 E, Fj, 2006 F(R), 2008 SA1, 2(R), C, NZ(R), A(R), 2009 S, E(R), F(R), It, I, C, US, NZ(R)
Jones, D C J (Swansea) 1947 E, F, I, 1949 E, S, I, F
Jones, D J (Neath, Ospreys) 2001 A (R), 2002 I (R), F (R), 2003 I 2, S 2, [C, It], 2004 S, E, It, Arg1, 2, SA1(R), 2, R(R), NZ(t&R), J, 2005 US, C, NZ, SA, A, 2006 E, S, I, It, F, Arg 1, 2, A(R), PI, C(R), NZ, 2007 I(R), S, F1(R), It(R), E1(R), Arg, F2, [C(R), A(R), J, Fj(R)], SA(R), 2008 E, S, It(R), I(R), F(t&R), SA1(R), 2(R), 2009 C, US, NZ(R), Arg(R), A(R)
Jones, D K (Llanelli, Cardiff) 1962 E, S, F, I, 1963 E, F, NZ, 1964 E, S, SA, 1966 E, S, I, F
Jones, D L (Newport) 1926 E, S, I, F, 1927 E
Jones, D L (Ebbw Vale, Celtic Warriors, Cardiff Blues) 2000 Sm, 2003 R (R), 2004 SA1, 2008 S(R),It(R), 2009 C,US, 2010 F, SA1, NZ2(R), A(R), SA2(R), Fj
Jones, D P (Pontypool) 1907 I
Jones, E H (Swansea, Neath) 1930 I, F
Jones, E L (Llanelli) 1930 F, 1933 E, S, I, 1935 E
Jones, E L (Llanelli) 1939 S
Jones, G (Ebbw Vale) 1963 S, I, F
Jones, G (Llanelli) 1988 NZ 2, 1989 F, E, NZ, 1990 F
Jones, G G (Cardiff) 1930 S, 1933 I
Jones, G H (Bridgend) 1995 SA
Jones, H (Penygraig) 1902 S, I
Jones, H (Neath) 1904 I
Jones, H J (Neath) 1929 E, S
Jones, I C (London Welsh) 1968 I
Jones, I E (Llanelli) 1924 E, S, 1927 S, F, I, A, 1928 E, S, I, F, 1929 E, S, F, I, 1930 E, S
Jones, J (Aberavon) 1901 E
Jones, J (Bedwellty) (Abertillery) 1914 E, S, F, I
Jones, J (Swansea) 1924 F
Jones, J (Aberavon) 1919 NZA, 1920 E, S, 1921 S, F, I
Jones, J A (Cardiff) 1883 S
Jones, J P (Tuan) (Pontypool) 1913 S
Jones, J P (Jack) (Pontypool) 1908 A, 1909 E, S, F, I, 1910 F, E, 1912 E, F, 1913 F, I, 1920 F, I, 1921 E
Jones, K D (Cardiff) 1960 SA, 1961 E, S, I, 1962 E, F, 1963 E, S, I, NZ
Jones, K J (Newport) 1947 E, S, F, I, A, 1948 E, S, F, I, 1949 E, S, I, F, 1950 E, S, I, F, 1951 E, S, I, F, SA, 1952 E, S, I, F, 1953 E, S, I, F, NZ, 1954 E, I, F, S, 1955 E, S, I, F, 1956 E, S, I, F, 1957 S
Jones, K P (Ebbw Vale) 1996 Bb, F 2, It, A 3, 1997 I (R), E, 1998 S, I, F (R), SA 1
Jones, K W J (Oxford U, London Welsh) 1934 E
Jones, Matthew (Ospreys) 2005 C(R)
Jones, M A (Neath, Ebbw Vale) 1987 S, 1988 NZ 2(R), 1989 S, I, F, E, NZ, 1990 F, E, S, I, Nm 1,2, Bb, 1998 Z
Jones, M A (Llanelli Scarlets) 2001 E (R), S, J 1, 2002 R, Fj, C, NZ, 2003 It, I 1, A, NZ, E 2, [C, Tg, It, E], 2006 E, S, I, It, Arg 1, 2, PI, C, NZ, 2007 S, F1, It, E1, Arg, F2, [C, A, Fj]], SA, 2008 E, It, I, F, SA1, 2, C, A, 2009 E, It, I, US
Jones, P E R (Newport) 1921 S
Jones, P L (Newport) 1912 SA, 1913 E, S, F, 1914 E, S, F, I
Jones, R (Llwynypia) 1901 I
Jones, R (Northampton) 1926 E, S, F
Jones, R (London Welsh) 1929 E
Jones, R B (Cambridge U) 1933 E, S
Jones, R E (Coventry) 1967 F, E, 1968 S, I, F
Jones, R G (Llanelli, Cardiff) 1996 It, E, S, I, F 1, A 1, 1997 US (R), S (R), US 1,2, R, Tg, NZ
Jones, R H (Swansea) 1901 I, 1902 E, 1904 E, S, I, 1905 E, 1908 F, I, A, 1909 E, S, F, I, 1910 F, E
Jones, R L (Llanelli) 1993 Z 1,2, Nm, J, C
Jones, R N (Swansea) 1986 E, S, I, F, Fj, Tg, WS, 1987 F, E, S, I, [I, Tg, E, NZ, A], US, 1988 E, S, I, F, NZ 1, WS, R, 1989 I, F, E, NZ, 1990 F, E, S, I, 1991 E, S, F 2, [WS, Arg, A], 1992 I, F, E, S, A, 1993 E, S, I, 1994 I (R), Pt, 1995 F, E, S, I, [NZ, I]
Jones, R P (Scarlets) 2012 Bb, 2013 J2(R)
Jones, R P (Ospreys) 2004 SA2,NZ(R),J, 2005 E(R), F, S, I, US, 2006 A, C, NZ, 2007 I, S, F1, It, E1, 2008 E, S, It, I, F, SA1, 2, 3, C, NZ, A, 2009 E, F, It(R), I, C, US, NZ, Sm, Arg, 2010 E, S, F, It, SA1, NZ1, 2, SA2(R), Fj, NZ3, 2011 E1(R), S, It, I, F, Bb, E2(R), [Nm, Fj, F(R), A], A(R), 2012 I, S, E(R), It(R), F(R), Bb, A1(R), 2, 3, Sm, NZ, A4(t&R), 2013 F, It, S
Jones, S (Neath, Newport Gwent Dragons) 2001 J 1(R), 2004 SA2,R(R),NZ(R),J(R)
Jones, S M (Llanelli Scarlets, Clermont Auvergne) 1998 SA 1(R), 1999 C (R), [J (R)], 2000 It (R), S, I, 2001 E, F (R), J 1,2, R, I, Arg, Tg, A, 2002 I, F, It, S, SA 1,2, R(R), Fj, C, NZ, 2003 S 1, I 1, F, A, NZ, E 2, [Tg, It(R), NZ, E], 2004 S, I, F, E, It, SA2, R, NZ, 2005 E, It, F, S, I, NZ, SA, A, 2006 E, S, I, It, F, A, NZ, 2007 I, S, F1, It, [C(R), A, J, Fj]], 2008 S(R), It, I, F(R), SA1, 2, 3, NZ, A, 2009 S, E, F, It(R), I, NZ, Arg, A, 2010 E, S, F, I, It, SA1, NZ1, 2(R), A, SA2, Fj(R), NZ3, 2011 E1, S(R), It, F(R), Bb, [Nm, Fj(R), F(R), A(t&R)]
Jones, S T (Pontypool) 1983 S, I, F, R, 1984 S, 1988 E, S, F, NZ 1,2
Jones, T (Newport) 1922 E, S, I, F, 1924 E, S
Jones, T B (Newport) 1882 I, 1883 E, S, 1884 S, 1885 E, S
Jones, T I (Llanelli) 1927 A, 1928 E, S, I, F
Jones, W (Cardiff) 1898 I, E
Jones, W D (Llanelli) 1948 E
Jones, W H (Llanelli) 1934 S, I
Jones, W I (Llanelli, Cambridge U) 1925 E, S, F, I
Jones, W J (Llanelli) 1924 I
Jones, W K (Cardiff) 1967 NZ, 1968 E, S, I, F
Jones, W R (Swansea) 1927 A, 1928 F
Jones-Davies, T E (London Welsh) 1930 E, I, 1931 E, S
Jones-Hughes, J (Newport) 1999 [Arg 3(R), J], 2000 F
Jordan, H M (Newport) 1885 E, S, 1889 S
Joseph, W (Swansea) 1902 E, S, I, 1903 E, S, I, 1904 E, S, 1905 E, S, I, NZ, 1906 E, S, I, SA
Jowett, W F (Swansea) 1903 E
Judd, S (Cardiff) 1953 E, S, I, F, NZ, 1954 E, F, S, 1955 E, S
Judson, T H (Llanelli) 1883 E, S

Kedzlie, Q D (Cardiff) 1888 S, I
Keen, L (Aberavon) 1980 F, E, S, I
King, J D (Ospreys) 2013 J1,2
Knight, P (Pontypridd) 1990 Nm 1,2, Bb (R), 1991 E, S
Knill, F M D (Cardiff) 1976 F (R)
Knoyle, T D (Scarlets) 2010 NZ1(R), 2011 S(R),Bb(R),E2(R),Arg,[Nm], A(R), 2012 Arg,NZ(R), 2013 J1(R),2(R)
Kohn, O S (Harlequins) 2013 I(R)

Lamerton, A E H (Llanelli) 1993 F, Z 1,2, Nm, J
Lane, S M (Cardiff) 1978 A 1(R),2, 1979 I (R), 1980 S, I
Lang, J (Llanelli) 1931 F, I, 1934 S, I, 1935 E, S, I, NZ, 1936 E, S, I, 1937 E
Law, V J (Newport) 1939 I
Lawrence, S D (Bridgend) 1925 S, I, 1926 S, I, F, 1927 E
Legge, W S G (Newport) 1937 I, 1938 I
Leleu, J (London Welsh, Swansea) 1959 E, S, 1960 F, SA
Lemon, A W (Neath) 1929 I, 1930 S, I, F, 1931 E, S, F, I, SA, 1932 E, S, I, 1933 I
Lewis, A J L (Ebbw Vale) 1970 F, 1971 E, I, F, 1972 E, S, F, 1973 E, S, I, F
Lewis, A L P (Cardiff) 1996 It, E, S, I, A 2(t), 1998 It, E, S, I, F, SA 2, Arg, 1999 F 1(R), E (R), Arg 1(R),2(R), SA (R), C (R), [J (R), Sm (R), A (R)], 2000 Sm (R), US (R), SA (R), 2001 F (R), J 1,2, 2002 R(R)
Lewis, B R (Swansea, Cambridge U) 1912 I, 1913 I
Lewis, C P (Llandovery) 1882 I, 1883 E, S, 1884 E, S
Lewis, D H (Cardiff) 1886 E, S
Lewis, E J (Llandovery) 1881 E
Lewis, E W (Llanelli, Cardiff) 1991 I, F 1, A, F 2, [WS, Arg, A], 1992 I, F, S, A, 1993 E, S, I, F, Z 1,2, Nm, J, C, 1994 S, I, F, E, Pt, Sp, Fj, WS, R, It, SA, 1995 E, S, I, [J, I], 1996 It, E, S, I, F 1

Lewis, G (Pontypridd, Swansea) 1998 SA 1(R), 1999 It (R), Arg 2, C, [J], 2000 F (R), It, S, I, Sm, US (t+R), 2001 F (R), J 1,2, R, I
Lewis, G W (Richmond) 1960 E, S
Lewis, H (Swansea) 1913 S, F, I, 1914 E
Lewis, J G (Llanelli) 1887 I
Lewis, J M C (Cardiff, Cambridge U) 1912 E, 1913 S, F, I, 1914 E, S, F, I, 1921 I, 1923 E, S
Lewis, J R (S Glam Inst, Cardiff) 1981 E, S, I, F, 1982 F, E, S
Lewis, M (Treorchy) 1913 F
Lewis, P I (Llanelli) 1984 A, 1985 S, I, F, E, 1986 E, S, I
Lewis, R A (Abertillery) 1966 E, S, I, F, A, 1967 I
Lewis, T W (Cardiff) 1926 E, 1927 E, S
Lewis, W (Llanelli) 1925 F
Lewis, W H (London Welsh, Cambridge U) 1926 I, 1927 E, F, I, A, 1928 F
Lewis-Roberts, E T (Sale) 2008 C(R)
Llewellyn, D S (Ebbw Vale, Newport) 1998 SA 1(R), 1999 F 1(R), It (R), [J (R)]
Llewellyn, G D (Neath) 1990 Nm 1,2, Bb, 1991 E, S, I, F 1, A, F 2
Llewellyn, G O (Neath, Harlequins, Ospreys, Narbonne) 1989 NZ, 1990 E, S, I, 1991 E, S, A (R), 1992 I, F, E, S, A, 1993 E, S, I, F, Z 1,2, Nm, J, C, 1994 S, I, F, E, Pt, Sp, C, Tg, WS, R, It, SA, 1995 F, E, S, I, [J, NZ, I], 1996 It, E, S, I, F 1, A 1,2, Bb, F 2, It, A 3, SA, 1997 US, S, I, F, E, US 1,2, NZ, 1998 It, E, 1999 C (R), [Sm], 2002 E (R), SA 1,2, R(R), Fj, C, NZ, 2003 E 1(R), S 1(R), I 1, F, A, NZ, I 2, S 2(R), [C,Tg,It,E(R)], 2004 S, F(R),E(R),It,Arg 1,2,SA1,R,NZ
Llewellyn, P D (Swansea) 1973 I, F, A, 1974 S, E
Llewellyn, W (Llwynypia) 1899 E, S, I, 1900 E, S, I, 1901 E, S, I, 1902 E, S, I, 1903 I, 1904 E, S, I, 1905 E, S, I, NZ
Llewelyn, D B (Newport, Llanelli) 1970 SA, S, E, I, F, 1971 E, S, I, F, 1972 E, S, F, NZ
Lloyd, A (Bath) 2001 J 1
Lloyd, D J (Bridgend) 1966 E, S, I, F, A, 1967 S, I, F, E, 1968 S, I, F, 1969 S, I, F, E, NZ 1, A, 1970 F, 1972 E, S, F, 1973 E, S
Lloyd, D P M (Llanelli) 1890 S, E, 1891 E, I
Lloyd, E (Llanelli) 1895 S
Lloyd, G L (Newport) 1896 I, 1899 S, I, 1900 E, S, 1901 E, S, 1902 S, I, 1903 E, S, I
Lloyd, R (Pontypool) 1913 S, F, I, 1914 E, S, F, I
Lloyd, T (Maesteg) 1953 I, F
Lloyd, T J (Neath) 1909 F, 1913 F, I, 1914 E, S, F, I
Loader, C D (Swansea) 1995 SA, Fj, 1996 F 1, A 1,2, Bb, F 2, It, A 3, SA, 1997 US, S, I, F, E, US 1, R, Tg, NZ
Lockwood, T W (Newport) 1887 E, S, I
Long, E C (Swansea) 1936 E, S, I, 1937 E, S, 1939 S, I
Luscombe, H N (Newport Gwent Dragons, Harlequins) 2003 S 2(R), 2004 Arg 1,2,SA1,2,R,J, 2005 E,It,S(t&R), 2006 E,S,I,It,F, 2007 I
Lydiate, D J (Newport Gwent Dragons) 2009 Arg(R),A, 2010 A,Fj,NZ3, 2011 E1,S,It,I, F,Bb,E2,3,Arg,[SA,Sm,I,F,A],A, 2012 S,E,It,F, A 1,2,3
Lyne, H S (Newport) 1883 S, 1884 E, S, I, 1885 E

McBryde, R C (Swansea, Llanelli, Neath, Llanelli Scarlets) 1994 Fj, SA (t), 1997 US 2, 2000 I (R), 2001 E, S, F, It, R, I, Arg, Tg, A, 2002 I, F, It, E, S (R), SA 1,2, C, NZ, 2003 A, NZ, E 2, S 2, [C,It,NZ,E], 2004 I,E,It, 2005 It(R),F(R),S(R),I(R)
McCall, B E W (Welch Regt, Newport) 1936 E, S, I
McCarley, A (Neath) 1938 E, S, I
McCusker, R J (Scarlets) 2010 SA1(R),NZ1(R),2(R), 2011 F(R), 2012 Arg(R), 2013 J1
McCutcheon, W M (Swansea) 1891 S, 1892 E, S, 1893 E, S, I, 1894 E
McIntosh, D L M (Pontypridd) 1996 SA, 1997 E (R)
Madden, M (Llanelli) 2002 SA 1(R), R, Fj(R), 2003 I 1(R), F(R)
Maddock, H T (London Welsh) 1906 E, S, I, 1907 E, S, 1910 F
Maddocks, K (Neath) 1957 E
Main, D R (London Welsh) 1959 E, S, I, F
Mainwaring, H J (Swansea) 1961 F
Mainwaring, W T (Aberavon) 1967 S, I, F, E, NZ, 1968 E
Major, W C (Maesteg) 1949 F, 1950 S
Male, B O (Cardiff) 1921 F, 1923 S, 1924 S, I, 1927 E, S, F, I, 1928 S, I, F
Manfield, L (Mountain Ash, Cardiff) 1939 S, I, 1947 A, 1948 E, S, F, I
Mann, B B (Cardiff) 1881 E
Mantle, J T (Loughborough Colls, Newport) 1964 E, SA
Margrave, F L (Llanelli) 1884 E, S
Marinos, A W N (Newport, Gwent Dragons)) 2002 I (R), F, It, E, S, SA 1,2, 2003 R
Marsden-Jones, D (Cardiff) 1921 E, 1924 NZ
Martin, A J (Aberavon) 1973 A, 1974 S, I, 1975 F, E, S, I, A, 1976 E, S, I, F, 1977 I, F, E, S, 1978 E, S, I, F, A 1,2, NZ, 1979 S, I, F, E, 1980 F, E, S, I, NZ, 1981 I, F
Martin, W J (Newport) 1912 I, F, 1919 NZA
Mason, J E (Pontypridd) 1988 NZ 2(R)
Mathews, Rev A A (Lampeter) 1886 S
Mathias, R (Llanelli) 1970 F
Matthews, C M (Bridgend) 1939 I
Matthews, J (Cardiff), 1947 E, A, 1948 E, S, F, 1949 E, S, I, F, 1950 E, S, I, F, 1951 E, S, I, F
May, P S (Llanelli) 1988 E, S, I, F, NZ 1,2, 1991 [WS]
Meek, N N (Pontypool) 1993 E, S, I
Meredith, A (Devonport Services) 1949 E, S, I
Meredith, B V (St Luke's Coll, London Welsh, Newport) 1954 I, F, S, 1955 E, S, I, F, 1956 E, S, I, F, 1957 E, S, I, F, 1958 A, E, S, I, 1959 E, S, I, F, 1960 E, S, F, SA, 1961 E, S, I, 1962 E, S, F, I
Meredith, C C (Neath) 1953 S, NZ, 1954 E, I, F, S, 1955 E, S, I, F, 1956 E, I, 1957 E, S
Meredith, J (Swansea) 1888 S, I, 1890 S, E
Merry, J A (Pill Harriers) 1912 I, F
Michael, G M (Swansea) 1923 E, S, F
Michaelson, R C B (Aberavon, Cambridge U) 1963 E
Millar, W H (Mountain Ash) 1896 I, 1900 E, S, I, 1901 E, S, I
Mills, F M (Swansea, Cardiff) 1892 E, S, I, 1893 E, S, I, 1894 E, S, I, 1895 E, S, I, 1896 E
Mitchell, C (Ospreys, Exeter) 2009 C(R),US(R),Sm(R), 2010 NZ2(R), 2011 E1,S,It,I,E2, 3,[Nm], 2013 I(R),F(R),It(R),J2(R)
Moon, R H StJ B (Llanelli) 1993 F, Z 1,2, Nm, J, C, 1994 S, I, F, E, Sp, C, Fj, WS, R, It, SA, 1995 E (R), 2000 S, I, Sm (R), US (R), 2001 E (R), S (R)
Moore, A P (Cardiff) 1995 [J], SA, Fj, 1996 It
Moore, A P (Swansea) 1995 SA (R), Fj, 1998 S, I, F, Z, SA 1, 1999 C, 2000 S, I, US (R), 2001 E (R), S, F, It, J 1,2, R, I, Arg, Tg, A, 2002 F, It, E, S
Moore, S J (Swansea, Moseley) 1997 C, R, Tg
Moore, W J (Bridgend) 1933 I
Morgan, C H (Llanelli) 1957 I, F
Morgan, C I (Cardiff) 1951 I, F, SA, 1952 E, S, I, 1953 S, I, F, NZ, 1954 E, I, S, 1955 E, S, I, F, 1956 E, S, I, F, 1957 E, S, I, F, 1958 E, S, I, F
Morgan, C S (Cardiff Blues) 2002 I, F, It, E, S, SA 1,2, R(R), 2003 F, 2005 US
Morgan, D (Swansea) 1885 S, 1886 E, S, 1887 E, S, I, 1889 I
Morgan, D (Llanelli) 1895 I, 1896 E
Morgan, D E (Llanelli) 1920 I, 1921 E, S, F
Morgan, D R R (Llanelli) 1962 E, S, F, I, 1963 E, S, I, F, NZ
Morgan, E (Swansea) 1914 E, S, F, I
Morgan, E (London Welsh) 1902 E, S, I, 1903 I, 1904 E, S, I, 1905 E, S, I, NZ, 1906 E, S, I, SA, 1908 F
Morgan, F L (Llanelli) 1938 E, S, I, 1939 E
Morgan, G R (Newport) 1984 S
Morgan, H J (Abertillery) 1958 E, S, I, F, 1959 I, F, 1960 E, 1961 E, S, I, F, 1962 E, S, F, I, 1963 S, I, F, 1965 E, S, I, F, 1966 E, S, I, F, A
Morgan, H P (Newport) 1956 E, S, I, F
Morgan, J L (Llanelli) 1912 SA, 1913 E
Morgan, K A (Pontypridd, Swansea, Newport Gwent Dragons) 1997 US 1,2, C, R, NZ, 1998 S, I, F, 2001 J 1,2, R, I, Arg, Tg, A, 2002 I, F, It, E, S, SA 1,2, 2003 E 1, S 1, [C,It], 2004 J(R), 2005 E(R),It(R),F,S,I,US,C,NZ,Fj, 2006 A,PI, NZ, 2007 I,S,It,E1,Arg,F2, [C,A(R),J]
Morgan, M E (Swansea) 1938 E, S, I, 1939 E
Morgan, N H (Newport) 1960 S, I, F
Morgan, P E J (Aberavon) 1961 E, S, F
Morgan, P J (Llanelli) 1980 S (R), I, NZ (R), 1981 I
Morgan, S (Cardiff Blues) 2007 A2(R)
Morgan, T (Llanelli) 1889 I
Morgan, W G (Cambridge U) 1927 F, I, 1929 E, S, F, I, 1930 I, F
Morgan, W I (Swansea) 1908 A, 1909 E, S, F, I, 1910 F, E, S, I, 1911 E, F, I, 1912 S
Morgan, W L (Cardiff) 1910 S
Moriarty, R D (Swansea) 1981 A, 1982 I, F, E, S, 1983 E, 1984 S, I, F, E, 1985 S, I, F, 1986 Fj, Tg, WS, 1987 [I, Tg, C (R), E, NZ, A]
Moriarty, W P (Swansea) 1986 I, F, Fj, Tg, WS, 1987 F, E, S, I, [I, Tg, C, E, NZ, A], US, 1988 E, S, I, F, NZ 1

Morley, J C (Newport) 1929 E, S, F, I, 1930 E, I, 1931 E, S, F, I, SA, 1932 E, S, I
Morris, D R (Neath, Swansea, Leicester) 1998 Z, SA 1(R),2(R), 1999 S, I, It (R), 2000 US, SA, 2001 E, S, F, It, Arg, Tg, A, 2004 Arg 1(R),2(R),SA1(R)
Morris, G L (Swansea) 1882 I, 1883 E, S, 1884 E, S
Morris, H T (Cardiff) 1951 F, 1955 I, F
Morris, J I T (Swansea) 1924 E, S
Morris, M S (S Wales Police, Neath) 1985 S, I, F, 1990 I, Nm 1,2, Bb, 1991 I, F 1, [WS (R)], 1992 E
Morris, R R (Swansea, Bristol) 1933 S, 1937 S
Morris, S (Cross Keys) 1920 E, S, F, I, 1922 E, S, I, F, 1923 E, S, F, I, 1924 E, S, F, NZ, 1925 E, S, F
Morris, W (Llanelli) 1896 S, I, 1897 E
Morris, W D (Neath) 1967 F, E, 1968 E, S, I, F, 1969 S, I, F, E, NZ 1,2, A, 1970 SA, S, E, I, F, 1971 E, S, I, F, 1972 E, S, F, NZ, 1973 E, S, I, A, 1974 S, I, F, E
Morris, W G H (Abertillery) 1919 NZA, 1920 F, 1921 I
Morris, W J (Newport) 1965 S, 1966 F
Morris, W J B (Pontypool) 1963 S, I
Moseley, K (Pontypool, Newport) 1988 NZ 2, R, 1989 S, I, 1990 F, 1991 F 2, [WS, Arg, A]
Murphy, C D (Cross Keys) 1935 E, S, I
Mustoe, L (Cardiff) 1995 Fj, 1996 A 1(R),2, 1997 US 1,2, C, R (R), 1998 E (R), I (R), F (R)

Nash, D (Ebbw Vale) 1960 SA, 1961 E, S, I, F, 1962 F
Navidi, J R (Cardiff Blues) 2013 J2
Newman, C H (Newport) 1881 E, 1882 I, 1883 E, S, 1884 E, S, 1885 E, S, 1886 E, 1887 E
Nicholas, D L (Llanelli) 1981 E, S, I, F
Nicholas, T J (Cardiff) 1919 NZA
Nicholl, C B (Cambridge U, Llanelli) 1891 I, 1892 E, S, I, 1893 E, S, I, 1894 E, S, 1895 E, S, I, 1896 E, S, I
Nicholl, D W (Llanelli) 1894 I
Nicholls, E G (Cardiff) 1896 S, I, 1897 E, 1898 I, E, 1899 E, S, I, 1900 S, I, 1901 E, S, I, 1902 E, S, I, 1903 I, 1904 E, 1905 I, NZ, 1906 E, S, I, SA
Nicholls, F E (Cardiff Harlequins) 1892 I
Nicholls, H C W (Cardiff) 1958 I
Nicholls, S H (Cardiff) 1888 M, 1889 S, I, 1891 S
Norris, C H (Cardiff) 1963 F, 1966 F
Norster, R L (Cardiff) 1982 S, 1983 E, S, I, F, 1984 S, I, F, E, A, 1985 S, I, F, E, Fj, 1986 Fj, Tg, WS, 1987 F, E, S, I, [I, C, E], US, 1988 E, S, I, F, NZ 1, WS, 1989 F, E
North, G P (Scarlets) 2010 SA2, Fj, NZ3, 2011 F, Bb, E2, 3, Arg, [SA, Sm, Nm(R), Fj, I, F, A], A, 2012 I, S, E, It, F, A 1, 2, 3, Arg, Sm, 2013 I, F, It, S, E
Norton, W B (Cardiff) 1882 I, 1883 E, S, 1884 E, S, I

Oakley, R L (Gwent Dragons) 2003 I 2, S 2(R)
O'Connor, A (Aberavon) 1960 SA, 1961 E, S, 1962 F, I
O'Connor, R (Aberavon) 1957 E
O'Neil, W (Cardiff) 1904 S, I, 1905 E, S, I, 1907 E, I, 1908 E, S, F, I
O'Shea, J P (Cardiff) 1967 S, I, 1968 S, I, F
Oliver, G (Pontypool) 1920 E, S, F, I
Osborne, W T (Mountain Ash) 1902 E, S, I, 1903 E, S, I
Ould, W J (Cardiff) 1924 E, S
Owen, A D (Swansea) 1924 E
Owen, G D (Newport) 1955 I, F, 1956 E, S, I, F
Owen, M J (Pontypridd, Newport Gwent Dragons) 2002 SA 1,2, R, C(R), NZ(R), 2003 It, I 2, S 2, 2004 S(R), I(R), F, E, It, Arg 1, 2, SA2, R, NZ, J, 2005 E, It, F, S, I, NZ, Fj, SA, A, 2006 E, S, I, It, F, PI, 2007 A1(R), 2, E2, [C(R), A(R), J(R), Fj(R)]
Owen, R M (Swansea) 1901 I, 1902 E, S, I, 1903 E, S, I, 1904 E, S, I, 1905 E, S, I, NZ, 1906 E, S, I, SA, 1907 E, S, 1908 F, I, A, 1909 E, S, F, I, 1910 F, E, 1911 E, S, F, I, 1912 E, S
Owens, K J (Scarlets) 2011 [Nm(R)], 2012 S(t&R), E, It(R), F(R), A1, 3(R), Sm(R), NZ(R), A4(R), 2013 I(t&R), F(R), It(R), S(R), E(R)

Packer, H (Newport) 1891 E, 1895 S, I, 1896 E, S, I, 1897 E
Palmer, F C (Swansea) 1922 E, S, I
Parfitt, F C (Newport) 1893 E, S, I, 1894 E, S, I, 1895 S, 1896 S, I
Parfitt, S A (Swansea) 1990 Nm 1(R), Bb
Parker, D S (Swansea) 1924 I, F, NZ, 1925 E, S, F, I, 1929 F, I, 1930 E
Parker, E T (Swansea) 1919 NZA, 1920 E, S, I, 1921 E, S, F, I, 1922 E, S, I, F, 1923 E, S, F
Parker, S T (Pontypridd, Celtic Warriors, Newport Gwent Dragons, Ospreys) 2002 R, Fj, C, NZ, 2003 E 2, [C,It,NZ], 2004 S, I, Arg 1, 2, SA1, 2, NZ, 2005 Fj, SA, A, 2006 PI, C, NZ, 2007 A1, 2, F2(t&R), [C, A], SA, 2008 E, S(R), It(R), SA1
Parker, W J (Swansea) 1899 E, S
Parks, R D (Pontypridd, Celtic Warriors) 2002 SA 1(R), Fj(R), 2003 I 2, S 2
Parsons, G (Newport) 1947 E
Pascoe, D (Bridgend) 1923 F, I
Pask, A E I (Abertillery) 1961 F, 1962 E, S, F, I, 1963 E, S, I, F, NZ, 1964 E, S, I, F, SA, 1965 E, S, I, F, 1966 E, S, I, F, A, 1967 S, I
Patchell, M R (Cardiff Blues) 2013 J1(R),2(R)
Payne, G W (Army, Pontypridd) 1960 E, S, I
Payne, H (Swansea) 1935 NZ
Peacock, H (Newport) 1929 S, F, I, 1930 S, I, F
Peake, E (Chepstow) 1881 E
Pearce, P G (Bridgend) 1981 I, F, 1982 I (R)
Pearson, T W (Cardiff, Newport) 1891 E, I, 1892 E, S, 1894 S, I, 1895 E, S, I, 1897 E, 1898 I, E, 1903 E
Peel, D J (Llanelli Scarlets, Sale) 2001 J 2(R), R (R), Tg (R), 2002 I (R), It (R), E (R), S (R), SA 1,2, R, Fj, C, NZ, 2003 It, S 1(R), I 1(R), F, NZ(R), I 2, S 2, [C(R), Tg(R), It, NZ(R), E(R)], 2004 S(R), I(R), F(R), E(R), It(R), Arg 1, 2, SA1, 2, R, NZ, 2005 E, It, F, S, I, 2006 E, S, I, It, A, C, NZ, 2007 I, S, F1, It, E1, Arg, F2, [C, A, Fj], SA, 2008 S(R), It, SA3(R), C(R), NZ(R), 2009 S(R), E(R), F(R), C(R), US, Sm, Arg(R), A, 2010 I(R), It(R), 2011 E1(R), F(R)
Pegge, E V (Neath) 1891 E
Perego, M A (Llanelli) 1990 S, 1993 F, Z 1, Nm (R), 1994 S, I, F, E, Sp
Perkins, S J (Pontypool) 1983 S, I, F, R, 1984 S, I, F, E, A, 1985 S, I, F, E, Fj, 1986 E, S, I, F
Perrett, F L (Neath) 1912 SA, 1913 E, S, F, I
Perrins, V C (Newport) 1970 SA, S
Perry, W J (Neath) 1911 E
Phillips, A J (Cardiff) 1979 E, 1980 F, E, S, I, NZ, 1981 E, S, I, F, A, 1982 I, F, E, S, 1987 [C, E, A]
Phillips, B (Aberavon) 1925 E, S, F, I, 1926 E
Phillips, D E (Scarlets) 2013 J1,2
Phillips, D H (Swansea) 1952 F
Phillips, H P (Newport) 1892 E, 1893 E, S, I, 1894 E, S
Phillips, H T (Newport) 1927 E, S, F, I, A, 1928 E, S, I, F
Phillips, K H (Neath) 1987 F, [I, Tg, NZ], US, 1988 E, NZ 1, 1989 NZ, 1990 F, E, S, I, Nm 1,2, Bb, 1991 E, S, I, F 1, A
Phillips, L A (Newport) 1900 E, S, I, 1901 S
Phillips, R D (Neath) 1987 US, 1988 E, S, I, F, NZ 1,2, WS, 1989 S, I
Phillips, W D (Cardiff) 1881 E, 1882 I, 1884 E, S, I
Phillips, W M (Llanelli Scarlets, Cardiff Blues, Ospreys, Bayonne) 2003 R, 2004 Arg 1(R), 2(R), J(R), 2005 US, C, NZ, Fj(R), SA(R), 2006 S(R), It(R), F, Arg 1, 2, PI, C(R), NZ(R), 2007 I(R), F1(R), E1(R), A1, 2, F2(R), [C(R), A(R), J, Fj(R)], SA(R), 2008 E, S, It(R), I, F, 2009 S, E, F, It, I, 2010 It, SA1, NZ1, 2, A, SA2, Fj(R), NZ3, 2011 E1, S, It, I, F, Bb, E2, 3, [SA, Sm, Fj, I, F, A], 2012 I, S, E, It, F, A 1, 2, 3, Arg(R), Sm, NZ, A4, 2013 I, F, It, S, E
Pickering, D F (Llanelli) 1983 E, S, I, F, R, 1984 S, I, F, E, A, 1985 S, I, F, E, Fj, 1986 E, S, I, F, Fj, 1987 F, E, S
Plummer, R C S (Newport) 1912 S, I, F, SA, 1913 E
Pook, T R (Newport) 1895 S
Popham, A J (Leeds, Llanelli Scarlets) 2003 A (R), I 2, R, S 2, [Tg, NZ], 2004 I(R), It(R), SA1, J(R), 2005 C, Fj(R), 2006 E(R), It(R), F, Arg 1, 2, PI, NZ(R), 2007 I, S, F1, It, E1, 2(R), Arg, F2, [C, A(t), J, Fj], SA(R), 2008 E(R)
Powell, A T (Cardiff Blues, Wasps, Sale) 2008 SA3, C(R), NZ, A, 2009 S, E, F, It, NZ, Sm, Arg, A, 2010 E, S, SA2, NZ3(R), 2011 E1, Arg, [Sm(R), Nm(R), Fj(R), A(R)], 2012 S(R)
Powell, G (Ebbw Vale) 1957 I, F
Powell, J (Cardiff) 1923 I
Powell, J A (Cardiff) 1906 I
Powell, R D (Cardiff) 2002 SA 1(R), 2(R), C(R)
Powell, R W (Newport) 1888 S, I
Powell, W C (London Welsh) 1926 S, I, F, 1927 E, F, I, 1928 S, I, F, 1929 E, S, F, I, 1930 S, I, F, 1931 E, S, F, I, SA, 1932 E, S, I, 1935 E, S, I
Powell, W J (Cardiff) 1920 E, S, F, I
Pretorius, W A (Cardiff Blues) 2013 J1(R),2

Price, B (Newport) 1961 I, F, 1962 E, S, 1963 E, S, F, NZ, 1964 E, S, I, F, SA, 1965 E, S, I, F, 1966 E, S, I, F, A, 1967 S, I, F, E, 1969 S, I, F, NZ 1,2, A
Price, G (Pontypool) 1975 F, E, S, I, A, 1976 E, S, I, F, 1977 I, F, E, S, 1978 E, S, I, F, A 1,2, NZ, 1979 S, I, F, E, 1980 F, E, S, I, NZ, 1981 E, S, I, F, A, 1982 I, F, E, S, 1983 E, I, F
Price, M J (Pontypool, RAF) 1959 E, S, I, F, 1960 E, S, I, F, 1962 E
Price, R E (Weston-s-Mare) 1939 S, I
Price, T G (Llanelli) 1965 E, S, I, F, 1966 E, A, 1967 S, F
Priday, A J (Cardiff) 1958 I, 1961 I
Priestland, R (Scarlets) 2011 S(R), Bb(R), E2, 3, [SA, Sm, Nm(R), Fj, I], A, 2012 I, S, E, It, F, A 1,2, 3, Arg, Sm(R), NZ, A4
Pritchard, C C (Newport, Pontypool) 1904 S, I, 1905 NZ, 1906 E, S
Pritchard, C C (Pontypool) 1928 E, S, I, F, 1929 E, S, F, I
Pritchard, C M (Newport) 1904 I, 1905 E, S, NZ, 1906 E, S, I, SA, 1907 E, S, I, 1908 E, 1910 F, E
Proctor, W T (Llanelli) 1992 A, 1993 E, S, Z 1,2, Nm, C, 1994 I, C, Fj, WS, R, It, SA, 1995 S, I, [NZ], Fj, 1996 It, E, S, I, A 1,2, Bb, F 2, It, A 3, 1997 E(R), US 1,2, C, R, 1998 E (R), S, I, F, Z, 2001 A
Prosser, D R (Neath) 1934 S, I
Prosser, F J (Cardiff) 1921 I
Prosser, G (Pontypridd) 1995 [NZ]
Prosser, I G (Neath) 1934 E, S, I, 1935 NZ
Prosser, T R (Pontypool) 1956 S, F, 1957 E, S, I, F, 1958 A, E, S, I, F, 1959 E, S, I, F, 1960 E, S, I, F, SA, 1961 I, F
Prothero, G J (Bridgend) 1964 S, I, F, 1965 E, S, I, F, 1966 E, S, I, F
Pryce-Jenkins, T J (London Welsh) 1888 S, I
Prydie, T W J (Ospreys, Newport Gwent Dragons) 2010 It, SA1, NZ1, 2, 2013 J2
Pugh, C H (Maesteg) 1924 E, S, I, F, NZ, 1925 E, S
Pugh, J D (Neath) 1987 US, 1988 S (R), 1990 S
Pugh, P (Neath) 1989 NZ
Pugh, R (Ospreys) 2005 US(R)
Pugsley, J (Cardiff) 1910 E, S, I, 1911 E, S, F, I
Pullman, J J (Neath) 1910 F
Purdon, F T (Newport) 1881 E, 1882 I, 1883 E, S

Quinnell, D L (Llanelli) 1972 F (R), NZ, 1973 E, S, A, 1974 S, F, 1975 E (R), 1977 I (R), F, E, S, 1978 E, S, I, F, A 1, NZ, 1979 S, I, F, E, 1980 NZ
Quinnell, J C (Llanelli, Richmond, Cardiff) 1995 Fj, 1996 A 3(R), 1997 US (R), S (R), I (R), E (R), 1998 SA 2, Arg, 1999 I, F 1, It, E, Arg 1,2, SA, C, F 2, [Arg 3, J, A], 2000 It, E, 2001 S (R), F (R), It (R), J 1, 2, R (R), I (R), Arg, 2002 I, F
Quinnell, L S (Llanelli, Richmond) 1993 C, 1994 S, I, F, E, Pt, Sp, C, WS, 1997 US, S, I, F, E, 1998 It, E, S (R), Z, SA 2, Arg, 1999 S, I, F 1, It, E, Arg 1,2, SA, C, F 2, [Arg 3, Sm, A], 2000 F, It, E, Sm, US, SA, 2001 E, S, F, It, Arg, Tg, A, 2002 I, F, It, E, R, C(R)

Radford, W J (Newport) 1923 I
Ralph, A R (Newport) 1931 F, I, SA, 1932 E, S, I
Ramsay, S (Treorchy) 1896 E, 1904 E
Randall, R J (Aberavon) 1924 I, F
Raybould, W H (London Welsh, Cambridge U, Newport) 1967 S, I, F, E, NZ, 1968 I, F, 1970 SA, E, I, F (R)
Rayer, M A (Cardiff) 1991 [WS (R), Arg, A (R)], 1992 E (R), A, 1993 E, S, I, Z 1, Nm, J (R), 1994 S (R), I (R), F, E, Pt, C, Fj, WS, R, It
Reed, L (Scarlets, Cardiff Blues) 2012 S(R),A4, 2013 F(R),J1,2
Rees, A (Maesteg) 1919 NZA
Rees, A (Maesteg) 1962 E, S, F
Rees, A M (London Welsh) 1934 E, 1935 E, S, I, NZ, 1936 E, S, I, 1937 E, S, I, 1938 E, S
Rees, B I (London Welsh) 1967 S, I, F
Rees, C F W (London Welsh) 1974 I, 1975 A, 1978 NZ, 1981 F, A, 1982 I, F, E, S, 1983 E, S, I, F
Rees, D (Swansea) 1900 E, 1903 E, S, 1905 E, S
Rees, D (Swansea) 1968 S, I, F
Rees, E B (Swansea) 1919 NZA
Rees, H E (Neath) 1979 S, I, F, E, 1980 F, E, S, I, NZ, 1983 E, S, I, F
Rees, H T (Cardiff) 1937 S, I, 1938 E, S, I
Rees, J (Swansea) 1920 E, S, F, I, 1921 E, S, I, 1922 E, 1923 E, F, I, 1924 E
Rees, J I (Swansea) 1934 E, S, I, 1935 S, NZ, 1936 E, S, I, 1937 E, S, I, 1938 E, S, I
Rees, L M (Cardiff) 1933 I
Rees, M (Llanelli Scarlets) 2005 US, 2006 Arg 1, A, C, NZ(R), 2007 I(R), S(t&R), F1, It, E1, A1, Arg, F2, [C, A, Fj], 2008 E(R), S(R), It, I, F(R), SA1, 3, NZ, A, 2009 S, E, F, It(R), I, NZ, Sm(R), Arg, A, 2010 I, It, SA1, NZ1, 2, A, SA2, NZ3, 2011 E1, S, It, I, F, A(R), 2012 It, F, Bb, A 1(R), 2, 3, Arg, NZ, A4, 2013 I
Rees, P (Llanelli) 1947 F, I
Rees, P M (Newport) 1961 E, S, I, 1964 I
Rees, R (Swansea) 1998 Z
Rees, R S (Cardiff Blues) 2010 E(R), S(R), F, I, NZ2(R), A(R), SA2(R), Fj, NZ3(R)
Rees, T A (Llandovery) 1881 E
Rees, T E (London Welsh) 1926 I, F, 1927 A, 1928 E
Rees, T J (Newport) 1935 S, I, NZ, 1936 E, S, I, 1937 E, S
Rees-Jones, G R (Oxford U, London Welsh) 1934 E, S, 1935 I, NZ, 1936 E
Reeves, F C (Cross Keys) 1920 F, I, 1921 E
Reynolds, A D (Swansea) 1990 Nm 1,2(R), 1992 A (R)
Rhapps, J (Penygraig) 1897 E
Rice-Evans, W (Swansea) 1890 S, 1891 E, S
Richards, D S (Swansea) 1979 F, E, 1980 F, E, S, I, NZ, 1981 E, S, I, F, 1982 I, F, 1983 E, S, I, R (R)
Richards, E G (Cardiff) 1927 S
Richards, E I (Cardiff) 1925 E, S, F
Richards, E S (Swansea) 1885 E, 1887 S
Richards, H D (Neath) 1986 Tg (R), 1987 [Tg, E (R), NZ]
Richards, K H L (Bridgend) 1960 SA, 1961 E, S, I, F
Richards, M C R (Cardiff) 1968 I, F, 1969 S, I, F, E, NZ 1,2, A
Richards, R (Aberavon) 1913 S, F, I
Richards, R C (Cross Keys) 1956 F
Richards, T B (Swansea)1960 F
Richards, T L (Maesteg) 1923 I
Richards, W C (Pontypool) 1922 E, S, I, F, 1924 I
Richardson, S J (Aberavon) 1978 A 2(R), 1979 E
Rickards, A R (Cardiff) 1924 F
Ring, J (Aberavon) 1921 E
Ring, M G (Cardiff, Pontypool) 1983 E, 1984 A, 1985 S, I, F, 1987 I, [I, Tg, A], US, 1988 E, S, I, F, NZ 1,2, 1989 NZ, 1990 F, E, S, I, Nm 1,2, Bb, 1991 E, S, I, F 1,2, [WS, Arg, A]
Ringer, J (Bridgend) 2001 J 1(R),2(R)
Ringer, P (Ebbw Vale, Llanelli) 1978 NZ, 1979 S, I, F, E, 1980 F, E, NZ
Roberts, C R (Neath) 1958 I, F
Roberts, D E A (London Welsh) 1930 E
Roberts, E (Llanelli) 1886 E, 1887 I
Roberts, E J (Llanelli) 1888 S, I, 1889 I
Roberts, G J (Cardiff) 1985 F (R), E, 1987 [I, Tg, C, E, A]
Roberts, H M (Cardiff) 1960 SA, 1961 E, S, I, F, 1962 S, F, 1963 I
Roberts, J (Cardiff) 1927 E, S, F, I, A, 1928 E, S, I, F, 1929 E, S, F, I
Roberts, J H (Cardiff Blues) 2008 S, SA1, 2, 3, C(R), NZ, A, 2009 S, E, F, It, I(R), NZ, Sm, Arg, A, 2010 E, S, F, I, It, SA1, NZ1, 2, 2011 E1, S, It, I, F, E2, 3, Arg, [SA, Sm, Fj, I, F, A], A, 2012 I, S, E, It, F, Arg, Sm, NZ, A4, 2013 I, F, It, S, E
Roberts, M (Scarlets) 2008 C, 2009 NZ(R),A(t&R)
Roberts, M G (London Welsh) 1971 E, S, I, F, 1973 I, F, 1975 S, 1979 E
Roberts, T (Newport, Risca) 1921 S, F, I, 1922 E, S, I, F, 1923 E, S
Roberts, W (Cardiff) 1929 E
Robins, J D (Birkenhead Park) 1950 E, S, I, F, 1951 E, S, I, F, 1953 E, I, F
Robins, R J (Pontypridd) 1953 S, 1954 F, S, 1955 E, S, I, F, 1956 E, F, 1957 E, S, I, F
Robinson, H R (Cardiff Blues) 2012 Bb, 2013 J1,2
Robinson, I R (Cardiff) 1974 F, E
Robinson, J P (Cardiff Blues) 2001 J 1(R),2(R), Arg (R), Tg (R), A, 2002 I, Fj(R), C, NZ, 2003 A, NZ, I 2, S 2, 2006 Arg 1,2, 2007 I, S, F1(R), A1, 2, Arg(t&R), F2, [J]
Robinson, M F D (Swansea) 1999 S, I, F 1, Arg 1
Robinson, N J (Cardiff Blues) 2003 I 2, R, 2004 Arg 1(R), 2, SA1, 2005 US, C, NZ(R), Fj, 2006 S(R), Arg 1, 2, 2009 US
Rocyn-Jones, D N (Cambridge U) 1925 I
Roderick, W B (Llanelli) 1884 I
Rogers, P J D (London Irish, Newport, Cardiff) 1999 F 1, It, E, Arg 1,2, SA, C, F 2, [Arg 3, J, Sm, A], 2000 F, It, E, S, I, SA
Rosser, M A (Penarth) 1924 S, F
Rowland, E M (Lampeter) 1885 E
Rowlands, C F (Aberavon) 1926 I

Rowlands, D C T (Pontypool) 1963 E, S, I, F, NZ, 1964 E, S, I, F, SA, 1965 E, S, I, F
Rowlands, G (RAF, Cardiff) 1953 NZ, 1954 E, F, 1956 F
Rowlands, K A (Cardiff) 1962 F, I, 1963 I, 1965 I, F
Rowles, G A (Penarth) 1892 E
Rowley, M (Pontypridd) 1996 SA, 1997 US, S, I, F, R
Roy, W S (Cardiff) 1995 [J (R)]
Russell, S (London Welsh) 1987 US

Samuel, D (Swansea) 1891 I, 1893 I
Samuel, J (Swansea) 1891 I
Samuel, T F (Mountain Ash) 1922 S, I, F
Scourfield, T B (Torquay Athletic) 1930 F
Scrine, F G (Swansea) 1899 E, S, 1901 I
Selley, T J (Llanelli Scarlets) 2005 US(R)
Shanklin, J L (London Welsh) 1970 F, 1972 NZ, 1973 I, F
Shanklin, T G L (Saracens, Cardiff Blues) 2001 J 2, 2002 F, It, SA 1(R),2(R),R, Fj, 2003 It, E 1, S 1, I 1, F(t+R), A, NZ, S 2, [Tg, NZ], 2004 I(R), F(R), E, It(R), Arg 1(R), 2, SA1, 2(R), R, NZ, J, 2005 E, It, F, S, I, 2006 A, C, NZ, 2007 S(R), F1, It, E1, 2, Arg, [C, A, J(R), Fj], SA, 2008 E(R), S, It, I, F, SA1, 2, 3, C, NZ, A, 2009 S, E, F, It(R), I, NZ, Sm, 2010 It(R), A, SA2, Fj(R), NZ3
Shaw, G (Neath) 1972 NZ, 1973 E, S, I, F, A, 1974 S, I, F, E, 1977 I, F
Shaw, T W (Newbridge) 1983 R
Shea, J (Newport) 1919 NZA, 1920 E, S, 1921 E
Shell, R C (Aberavon) 1973 A (R)
Shingler, A C (Scarlets) 2012 S, Bb(R), NZ(R), A4, 2013 I, F(R), E(R)
Sidoli, R A (Pontypridd, Celtic Warriors, Cardiff Blues) 2002 SA 1(R), 2(R), R, Fj, NZ, 2003 It, E 1, S 1, I 1, F, A, NZ, E 2, [C(R), Tg, It(R), NZ, E], 2004 I, It(R), 2005 E, It, F, S, I, C, NZ, Fj(R), SA, A, 2006 E, S, I, It, F, Pl, C(R), 2007 I(t&R), S, A1, 2, E2
Simpson, H J (Cardiff) 1884 E, S, I
Sinkinson, B D (Neath) 1999 F 1, It, E, Arg 1,2, SA, F 2, [Arg 3, J, Sm, A], 2000 F, It, E, 2001 R (R), I, Arg (R), Tg, A, 2002 It (R)
Skrimshire, R T (Newport) 1899 E, S, I
Skym, A (Llanelli) 1928 E, S, I, F, 1930 E, S, I, F, 1931 E, S, F, I, SA, 1932 E, S, I, 1933 E, S, I, 1935 E
Smith, J S (Cardiff) 1884 E, I, 1885 E
Smith, R (Ebbw Vale) 2000 F (R)
Sowden-Taylor, R (Cardiff Blues) 2005 It(R),C(R),NZ(R), 2007 A2(R),SA, 2008 C, 2009 C,US
Sparks, B A (Neath) 1954 I, 1955 E, F, 1956 E, S, I, 1957 S
Spiller, W (Cardiff) 1910 S, I, 1911 E, S, F, I, 1912 E, F, SA, 1913 E
Spratt, J P (Ospreys) 2009 C(R),US(R), 2013 J1,2
Squire, J (Newport, Pontypool) 1977 I, F, 1978 E, S, I, F, A 1, NZ, 1979 S, I, F, E, 1980 F, E, S, I, NZ, 1981 E, S, I, F, A, 1982 I, F, E, 1983 E, S, I, F
Stadden, W J (Cardiff) 1884 I, 1886 E, S, 1887 I, 1888 S, M, 1890 S, E
Stephens, C (Bridgend) 1998 E (R), 2001 J 2(R)
Stephens, C J (Llanelli) 1992 I, F, E, A
Stephens, G (Neath) 1912 E, S, I, F, SA, 1913 E, S, F, I, 1919 NZA
Stephens, I (Bridgend) 1981 E, S, I, F, A, 1982 I, F, E, S, 1984 I, F, E, A
Stephens, Rev J G (Llanelli) 1922 E, S, I, F
Stephens, J R G (Neath) 1947 E, S, F, I, 1948 I, 1949 S, I, F, 1951 F, SA, 1952 E, S, I, F, 1953 E, S, I, F, NZ, 1954 E, I, 1955 E, S, I, F, 1956 S, I, F, 1957 E, S, I, F
Stock, A (Newport) 1924 F, NZ, 1926 E, S
Stoddart, M L (Llanelli Scarlets) 2007 SA, 2008 SA1(R),C, 2011 E1,S,It,Bb,E2
Stone, P (Llanelli) 1949 F
Strand-Jones, J (Llanelli) 1902 E, S, I, 1903 E, S
Sullivan, A C (Cardiff) 2001 Arg, Tg
Summers, R H B (Haverfordwest) 1881 E
Sutton, S (Pontypool, S Wales Police) 1982 F, E, 1987 F, E, S, I, [C, NZ (R), A]
Sweeney, C (Pontypridd, Celtic Warriors, Newport Gwent Dragons) 2003 It(R), E 1, NZ(R), I 2, S 2, [C, It, NZ(t&R), E(t)], 2004 I(R), F(R), E(R), It(R), Arg 1, SA1(R), 2(R), R(R), J, 2005 It(R), F(t), S(R), US, C, NZ, Fj(R), SA(t&R), A(R), 2006 Pl, C(R), 2007 S(t), A2(R), E2, F2(R), [J(R)], SA(R)
Sweet-Escott, R B (Cardiff) 1891 S, 1894 I, 1895 I

Tamplin, W E (Cardiff) 1947 S, F, I, A, 1948 E, S, F
Tanner, H (Swansea, Cardiff) 1935 NZ, 1936 E, S, I, 1937 E, S, I, 1938 E, S, I, 1939 E, S, I, 1947 E, S, F, I, 1948 E, S, F, I, 1949 E, S, I, F
Tarr, D J (Swansea, Royal Navy) 1935 NZ
Taylor, A R (Cross Keys) 1937 I, 1938 I, 1939 E
Taylor, C G (Ruabon) 1884 E, S, I, 1885 E, S, 1886 E, S, 1887 E, I
Taylor, H T (Cardiff) 1994 Pt, C, Fj, Tg, WS (R), R, It, SA, 1995 E, S, [J, NZ, I], SA, Fj, 1996 It, E, S, I, F 1, A 1,2, It, A 3
Taylor, J (London Welsh) 1967 S, I, F, E, NZ, 1968 I, F, 1969 S, I, F, E, NZ 1, A, 1970 F, 1971 E, S, I, F, 1972 E, S, F, NZ, 1973 E, S, I, F
Taylor, M (Pontypool, Swansea, Llanelli Scarlets, Sale) 1994 SA, 1995 F, E, SA (R), 1998 Z, SA 1,2, Arg, 1999 I, F 1, It, E, Arg 1,2, SA, F 2, [Arg 3, J, Sm, A], 2000 F, It, E, S, Sm, US, 2001 E, S, F, It, 2002 S, SA 1,2, 2003 E 1, S 1, I 1, F, A, NZ, E 2, [C(R), Tg, NZ, E], 2004 F, E, It, R(R), 2005 I, US, C, NZ
Thomas, A C (Bristol, Swansea) 1996 It, E, S, I, F 2(R), SA, 1997 US, S, I, F, US 1,2, C, R, NZ (t), 1998 It, E, S (R), Z, SA 1, 2000 Sm, US, SA (R)
Thomas, A R F (Newport) 1963 NZ, 1964 E
Thomas, A G (Swansea, Cardiff) 1952 E, S, I, F, 1953 S, I, F, 1954 E, I, F, 1955 S, I, F
Thomas, B (Neath, Cambridge U) 1963 E, S, I, F, NZ, 1964 E, S, I, F, SA, 1965 E, 1966 E, S, I, 1967 NZ, 1969 S, I, F, E, NZ 1,2
Thomas, B M G (St Bart's Hospital) 1919 NZA, 1921 S, F, I, 1923 F, 1924 E
Thomas, C J (Newport) 1888 I, M, 1889 S, I, 1890 S, E, I, 1891 E, I
Thomas, C R (Bridgend) 1925 E, S
Thomas, D J (Swansea) 1904 E, 1908 A, 1910 E, S, I, 1911 E, S, F, I, 1912 E
Thomas, D J (Swansea) 1930 S, I, 1932 E, S, I, 1933 E, S, 1934 E, 1935 E, S, I
Thomas, D L (Neath) 1937 E
Thomas, D L (Aberavon) 1961 I
Thomas, E (Newport) 1904 S, I, 1909 S, F, I, 1910 F
Thomas, E J R (Mountain Ash) 1906 SA, 1908 F, I, 1909 S
Thomas, G (Newport) 1888 M, 1890 I, 1891 S
Thomas, G (Bridgend, Cardiff, Celtic Warriors, Toulouse, Cardiff Blues) 1995 [J, NZ, I], SA, Fj, 1996 F 1, A 1,2, Bb, F 2, It, A 3, 1997 US, S, I, F, E, US 1,2, C, R, Tg, NZ, 1998 It, E, S, I, F, SA 2, Arg, 1999 F 1(R), It, E, Arg 2, SA, F 2, [Arg 3, J (R), Sm, A], 2000 F, It, E, S, I, US (R), SA, 2001 E, F, It, J 1,2, R, Arg, Tg, A, 2002 E, R, Fj, C, NZ, 2003 It, E 1, S 1, I 1, F, I 2, E 2, [C, It, NZ(R), E], 2004 S, I, F, E, It, SA2, R, NZ, 2005 E, It, F, NZ, SA, A, 2006 E, S, A, C, 2007 It(t&R), E1, A1, 2, E2, Arg, F2, [C(R), A, Fj]
Thomas, G M (Bath, Ospreys, Llanelli Scarlets, Newport Gwent Dragons) 2001 J 1,2, R, I (R), Arg, Tg (R), A (R), 2002 S (R), SA 2(R), R(R), 2003 It(R), E 1, S 1, F, E 2(R), R, 2006 Arg 1, 2, Pl, 2007 I(t&R), A1, 2, 2010 NZ1, 2
Thomas, H H M (Llanelli) 1912 F
Thomas, H W (Swansea) 1912 SA, 1913 E
Thomas, H W (Neath) 1936 E, S, I, 1937 E, S, I
Thomas, I (Bryncethin) 1924 E
Thomas, I D (Ebbw Vale, Llanelli Scarlets) 2000 Sm, US (R), SA (R), 2001 J 1,2, R, I, Arg (R), Tg, 2002 It, E, S, SA 1,2, Fj, C, NZ, 2003 It, E 1, S 1, I 1, F, A, NZ, E 2, [Tg, NZ, E], 2004 I, F, 2007 A1, 2, E2
Thomas, J D (Llanelli) 1954 I
Thomas, J J (Swansea, Ospreys) 2003 A, NZ(R), E 2(R), R, [It(R), NZ, E], 2004 S(t&R), I, F, E, Arg 2(R), SA1(R), R(t&R), J, 2005 E(R), It, F(R), S(R), US, C, NZ, 2006 It(R), F(R), A, Pl(R), C, NZ, 2007 S(R), F1(R), It(R), E1(R), A1, 2, Arg, F2, [C, A], SA, 2008 E, S, It, I, F, SA1, 2, 2009 It, Sm(R), Arg(R), A(R), 2010 E(R), S, F, I, It, SA1, NZ1, 2, A, SA2, Fj, NZ3(R), 2011 E1(R), S(R), I(R), F(R), Arg(R)
Thomas, L C (Cardiff) 1885 E, S
Thomas, M C (Newport, Devonport Services) 1949 F, 1950 E, S, I, F, 1951 E, S, I, F, SA, 1952 E, S, I, F, 1953 E, 1956 E, S, I, F, 1957 E, S, 1958 E, S, I, F, 1959 I, F
Thomas, N (Bath) 1996 SA (R), 1997 US 1(R),2, C (R), R, Tg, NZ, 1998 Z, SA 1
Thomas, R (Swansea) 1900 E, S, I, 1901 E
Thomas, R (Pontypool) 1909 F, I, 1911 S, F, 1912 E, S, SA, 1913 E
Thomas, R C C (Swansea) 1949 F, 1952 I, F, 1953 S, I, F, NZ, 1954 E, I, F, S, 1955 S, I, 1956 E, S, I, 1957 E, 1958 A, E, S, I, F, 1959 E, S, I, F

Thomas, R L (London Welsh) 1889 S, I, 1890 I, 1891 E, S, I, 1892 E
Thomas, R M (Newport Gwent Dragons) 2006 Arg 2(R), 2007 E2(R), SA, 2008 It, SA2,C, 2009 It
Thomas, S (Llanelli) 1890 S, E, 1891 I
Thomas, S G (Llanelli) 1923 E, S, F, I
Thomas, T R (Cardiff Blues) 2005 US(R), C, NZ(R), Fj, SA, A, 2006E, S, I, It, F, PI, C(R), NZ, 2007 I, S, F1(R), It(R), E1(R), 2(R), F2(R), [C(R), A(R), J, Fj(R)], SA(R), 2008 SA2(R)
Thomas, W D (Llanelli) 1966 A, 1968 S, I, F, 1969 E, NZ 2, A, 1970 SA, S, E, I, F, 1971 E, S, I, F, 1972 E, S, F, NZ, 1973 E, S, I, F, 1974 E
Thomas, W G (Llanelli, Waterloo, Swansea) 1927 E, S, F, I, 1929 E, 1931 E, S, SA, 1932 E, S, I, 1933 E, S, I
Thomas, W H (Llandovery Coll, Cambridge U) 1885 S, 1886 E, S, 1887 E, S, 1888 S, I, 1890 E, I, 1891 S, I
Thomas, W J (Cardiff) 1961 F, 1963 F
Thomas, W J L (Llanelli, Cardiff) 1995 SA, Fj, 1996 It, E, S, I, F 1, 1996 Bb (R), 1997 US
Thomas, W L (Newport) 1894 S, 1895 E, I
Thomas, W T (Abertillery) 1930 E
Thompson, J F (Cross Keys) 1923 E
Thorburn, P H (Neath) 1985 F, E, Fj, 1986 E, S, I, F, 1987 F, [I, Tg, C, E, NZ, A], US, 1988 S, I, F, WS, R (R), 1989 S, I, F, E, NZ, 1990 F, E, S, I, Nm 1,2, Bb, 1991 E, S, I, F 1, A
Tipuric, J C (Ospreys) 2011 Arg(R),A(R), 2012 I(R), It, Bb, A 3(R), Arg(R), Sm, NZ(R), A4(R), 2013 I(R), F, It, S(R), E
Titley, M H (Bridgend, Swansea) 1983 R, 1984 S, I, F, E, A, 1985 S, I, Fj, 1986 F, Fj, Tg, WS, 1990 F, E
Towers, W H (Swansea) 1887 I, 1888 M
Travers, G (Pill Harriers, Newport) 1903 E, S, I, 1905 E, S, I, NZ, 1906 E, S, I, SA, 1907 E, S, I, 1908 E, S, F, I, A, 1909 E, S, I, 1911 S, F, I
Travers, W H (Newport) 1937 S, I, 1938 E, S, I, 1939 E, S, I, 1949 E, S, I, F
Treharne, E (Pontypridd) 1881 E, 1883 E
Trew, W J (Swansea) 1900 E, S, I, 1901 E, S, 1903 S, 1905 S, 1906 S, 1907 E, S, 1908 E, S, F, I, A, 1909 E, S, F, I, 1910 F, E, S, 1911 E, S, F, I, 1912 S, 1913 S, F
Trott, R F (Cardiff) 1948 E, S, F, I, 1949 E, S, I, F
Truman, W H (Llanelli) 1934 E, 1935 E
Trump, L C (Newport) 1912 E, S, I, F
Turnbull, B R (Cardiff) 1925 I, 1927 E, S, 1928 E, F, 1930 S
Turnbull, J (Scarlets) 2011 S(R), Bb(R), E3(R), 2012 Bb, Arg
Turnbull, M J L (Cardiff) 1933 E, I
Turner, P (Newbridge) 1989 I (R), F, E

Uzzell, H (Newport) 1912 E, S, I, F, 1913 S, F, I, 1914 E, S, F, I, 1920 E, S, F, I
Uzzell, J R (Newport) 1963 NZ, 1965 E, S, I, F

Vickery, W E (Aberavon) 1938 E, S, I, 1939 E
Vile, T H (Newport) 1908 E, S, 1910 I, 1912 I, F, SA, 1913 E, 1921 S
Vincent, H C (Bangor) 1882 I
Voyle, M J (Newport, Llanelli, Cardiff) 1996 A 1(t), F 2, 1997 E, US 1,2, C, Tg, NZ, 1998 It, E, S, I, F, Arg (R), 1999 S (R), I (t), It (R), SA (R), F 2(R), [J, A (R)], 2000 F (R)

Wakeford, J D M (S Wales Police) 1988 WS, R
Waldron, R G (Neath) 1965 E, S, I, F
Walker, N (Cardiff) 1993 I, F, J, 1994 S, F, E, Pt, Sp, 1995 F, E, 1997 US 1,2, C, R (R), Tg, NZ, 1998 E
Waller, P D (Newport) 1908 A, 1909 E, S, F, I, 1910 F
Walne, N J (Richmond, Cardiff) 1999 It (R), E (R), C
Walters, N (Llanelli) 1902 E
Wanbon, R (Aberavon) 1968 E
Warburton, S K (Cardiff Blues) 2009 US(R),Sm,A(R), 2010 S(R), I(R), It, SA1, A, NZ3, 2011 E1, S, It, I, F, Bb, E2, 3, [SA, Sm, Nm, Fj, I, F], A, 2012 I, E, F, A1, 2, 3, Arg, Sm(R), NZ, A4, 2013 I, It(R), S, E
Ward, W S (Cross Keys) 1934 S, I
Warlow, D J (Llanelli) 1962 I
Warren, A R (Scarlets) 2012 Bb(R)
Waters, D R (Newport) 1986 E, S, I, F
Waters, K (Newbridge) 1991 [WS]
Watkins, D (Newport) 1963 E, S, I, F, NZ, 1964 E, S, I, F, SA, 1965 E, S, I, F, 1966 E, S, I, F, 1967 I, F, E
Watkins, E (Neath) 1924 E, S, I, F
Watkins, E (Blaina) 1926 S, I, F
Watkins, E V (Cardiff) 1935 NZ, 1937 S, I, 1938 E, S, I, 1939 E, S
Watkins, H V (Llanelli) 1904 S, I, 1905 E, S, I, 1906 E
Watkins, I J (Ebbw Vale) 1988 E (R), S, I, F, NZ 2, R, 1989 S, I, F, E
Watkins, L (Oxford U, Llandaff) 1881 E
Watkins, M J (Newport) 1984 I, F, E, A
Watkins, M J (Llanelli Scarlets) 2003 It(R), E 1(R), S 1(R), I 1(R), R, S 2, 2005 US(R), C(R), Fj, SA(R), A, 2006 E, S, I, It, F, Arg 1, 2(R)
Watkins, S J (Newport, Cardiff) 1964 S, I, F, 1965 E, S, I, F, 1966 E, S, I, F, A, 1967 S, I, F, E, NZ, 1968 E, S, 1969 S, I, F, E, NZ 1, 1970 E, I
Watkins, W R (Newport) 1959 F
Watts, D (Maesteg) 1914 E, S, F, I
Watts, J (Llanelli) 1907 E, S, I, 1908 E, S, F, I, A, 1909 S, F, I
Watts, W H (Newport) 1892 E, S, I, 1893 E, S, I, 1894 E, S, I, 1895 E, I, 1896 E
Watts, W J (Llanelli) 1914 E
Weatherley, D J (Swansea) 1998 Z
Weaver, D S (Swansea) 1964 E
Webb, A (Jim) (Abertillery) 1907 S, 1908 E, S, F, I, A, 1909 E, S, F, I, 1910 F, E, S, I, 1911 E, S, F, I, 1912 E, S
Webb, J (Newport) 1888 M, 1889 S
Webb, R (Ospreys) 2012 It(R),Bb(R),A 2(R)
Webbe, G M C (Bridgend) 1986 Tg (R), WS, 1987 F, E, S, [Tg], US, 1988 F (R), NZ 1, R
Webster, R E (Swansea) 1987 [A], 1990 Bb, 1991 [Arg, A], 1992 I, F, E, S, A, 1993 E, S, I, F
Wells, G T (Cardiff) 1955 E, S, 1957 I, F, 1958 A, E, S
Westacott, D (Cardiff) 1906 I
Wetter, J J (Newport) 1914 S, F, I, 1920 E, S, F, I, 1921 E, 1924 I, NZ
Wetter, W H (Newport) 1912 SA, 1913 E
Wheel, G A D (Swansea) 1974 I, E (R), 1975 F, E, I, A, 1976 E, S, I, F, 1977 I, E, S, 1978 E, S, I, F, A 1,2, NZ, 1979 S, I, 1980 F, E, S, I, 1981 E, S, I, F, A, 1982 I
Wheeler, P J (Aberavon) 1967 NZ, 1968 E
Whitefoot, J (Cardiff) 1984 A (R), 1985 S, I, F, E, Fj, 1986 E, S, I, F, Fj, Tg, WS, 1987 F, E, S, I, [I, C]
Whitfield, J J (Newport) 1919 NZA, 1920 E, S, F, I, 1921 E, 1922 E, S, I, F, 1924 S, I
Whitson, G K (Newport) 1956 F, 1960 S, I
Wilkins, G (Bridgend) 1994 Tg
Williams, A (Ospreys, Bath) 2003 R (R), 2005 v US(R),C(R), 2006 Arg 2(R), 2007 A2(R)
Williams, B (Llanelli) 1920 S, F, I
Williams, B H (Neath, Richmond, Bristol) 1996 F 2, 1997 R, Tg, NZ, 1998 It, E, Z (R), SA 1, Arg (R), 1999 S (R), I, It (R), 2000 F (R), It (R), E (t+R), 2001 R (R), I (R), Tg (R), A (R), 2002 I (R), F (R), It (R), E (R), S
Williams, B L (Cardiff) 1947 E, S, F, I, A, 1948 E, S, F, I, 1949 E, S, I, 1951 I, SA, 1952 S, 1953 E, S, I, F, NZ, 1954 S, 1955 E
Williams, B R (Neath) 1990 S, I, Bb, 1991 E, S
Williams, C (Llanelli) 1924 NZ, 1925 E
Williams, C (Aberavon, Swansea) 1977 E, S, 1980 F, E, S, I, NZ, 1983 E
Williams, C D (Cardiff, Neath) 1955 F, 1956 F
Williams, D (Ebbw Vale) 1963 E, S, I, F, 1964 E, S, I, F, SA, 1965 E, S, I, F, 1966 E, S, I, A, 1967 F, E, NZ, 1968 E, 1969 S, I, F, E, NZ 1,2, A, 1970 SA, S, E, I, 1971 E, S, I, F
Williams, D (Llanelli) 1998 SA 1(R)
Williams, D A (Bridgend, Swansea) 1990 Nm 2(R), 1995 Fj (R)
Williams, D B (Newport, Swansea) 1978 A 1, 1981 E, S
Williams, E (Neath) 1924 NZ, 1925 F
Williams, E (Aberavon) 1925 E, S
Williams, F L (Cardiff) 1929 S, F, I, 1930 E, S, I, F, 1931 F, I, SA, 1932 E, S, I, 1933 I
Williams, G (London Welsh) 1950 I, F, 1951 E, S, I, F, SA, 1952 E, S, I, F, 1953 NZ, 1954 E
Williams, G (Bridgend) 1981 I, F, 1982 E (R), S
Williams, G J (Bridgend, Cardiff Blues) 2003 It(R), E 1(R), S 1, F(R), E 2(R), 2009 C(R),US, 2010 E,S
Williams, G M (Aberavon) 1936 E, S, I
Williams, G P (Bridgend) 1980 NZ, 1981 E, S, A, 1982 I
Williams, G R (Cardiff Blues) 2000 I, Sm, US, SA, 2001 S, F, It, R (R), I (R), Arg, Tg (R), A (R), 2002 F (R), It (R), E (R), S, SA 1,2, R, Fj, C, NZ, 2003 It, E 1, S 1, I 1, F, A, NZ, E 2, [Tg, It(R)], 2004 S, I, F, E, It, Arg1, R, J, 2005 F(R), S, US, C
Williams, H R (Llanelli) 1954 S, 1957 F, 1958 A

Williams, J F (London Welsh) 1905 I, NZ, 1906 S, SA
Williams, J J (Llanelli) 1973 F (R), A, 1974 S, I, F, E, 1975 F, E, S, I, A, 1976 E, S, I, F, 1977 I, F, E, S, 1978 E, S, I, F, A 1,2, NZ, 1979 S, I, F, E
Williams, J L (Cardiff) 1906 SA, 1907 E, S, I, 1908 E, S, I, A, 1909 E, S, F, I, 1910 I, 1911 E, S, F, I
Williams, J L (Blaina) 1920 E, S, F, I, 1921 S, F, I
Williams, J P R (London Welsh, Bridgend) 1969 S, I, F, E, NZ 1,2, A, 1970 SA, S, E, I, F, 1971 E, S, I, F, 1972 E, S, F, NZ, 1973 E, S, I, F, A, 1974 S, I, F, 1975 F, E, S, I, A, 1976 E, S, I, F, 1977 I, F, E, S, 1978 E, S, I, F, A 1,2, NZ, 1979 S, I, F, E, 1980 NZ, 1981 E, S
Williams, L B (Scarlets) 2012 Bb,NZ,A4, 2013 J1,2
Williams, L D (Cardiff Blues) 2011 Arg(R), [Nm(R), Fj(R), A(R)], A, 2012 S(R), F(R), Bb, 2013 I(R), F(R), It(R), S(R), E(R), J1, 2
Williams, L H (Cardiff) 1957 S, I, F, 1958 E, S, I, F, 1959 E, S, I, 1961 F, 1962 E, S
Williams, M E (Pontypridd, Cardiff Blues) 1996 Bb, F 2, It (t), 1998 It, E, Z, SA 2, Arg, 1999 S, I, C, J, [Sm], 2000 E (R), 2001 E, S, F, It, 2002 I, F, It, E, S, SA 1,2, Fj, C, NZ, 2003 It, E 1, S 1, I 1, F, A, NZ, E 2, [C, Tg(R), It, E(R)], 2004 S, I, F(t&R), E(R), It, SA2(t&R), R(R), NZ(R), J(R), 2005 E, It, F, S, I, Fj, SA, A, 2006 E, S, I, It, F, A, C, NZ, 2007 I, S, F1, It, E1, Arg, F2, [C, A, J, Fj], 2008 E, S, It, I, F, SA3, NZ, A, 2009 S, E, F, I, NZ, Arg, A, 2010 E, S, F, I, A(R), SA2, NZ3(R), 2011 Arg, 2012 Bb(R)
Williams, M S (Scarlets) 2011 Bb(R), E2(R), 3(R), Arg(R), [Nm, Fj, A(R)], A, 2012 S(R), E(R), It(R), F(t), A 1, 3(R), Arg, NZ(R), 2013 F(R), It(R), S(R), E(R)
Williams, M T (Newport) 1923 F
Williams, O (Llanelli) 1947 E, S, A, 1948 E, S, F, I
Williams, O L (Bridgend) 1990 Nm 2
Williams, O R (Cardiff Blues) 2013 J1,2
Williams, R D G (Newport) 1881 E
Williams, R F (Cardiff) 1912 SA, 1913 E, S, 1914 I
Williams, R H (Llanelli) 1954 I, F, S, 1955 S, I, F, 1956 E, S, I, 1957 E, S, I, F, 1958 A, E, S, I, F, 1959 E, S, I, F, 1960 E
Williams, S (Llanelli) 1947 E, S, F, I, 1948 S, F
Williams, S A (Aberavon) 1939 E, S, I
Williams, S M (Neath, Cardiff, Northampton) 1994 Tg, 1996 E (t), A 1,2, Bb, F 2, It, A 3, SA, 1997 US, S, I, F, E, US 1,2(R), C, R (R), Tg (R), NZ (t+R), 2002 SA 1,2, R, Fj(R), 2003 It, E 1, S 1, F(R)
Williams, S M (Neath, Ospreys) 2000 F (R), It, E, S, I, Sm, SA (R), 2001 J 1,2, I, 2003 R, [NZ,E], 2004 S, I, F, E, It, Arg 1, 2, SA1, 2, NZ, J, 2005 E, It, F, S, I, NZ, Fj, SA, A, 2006 E, S, It, F, Arg 1, 2, A, Pl(R), C, NZ, 2007 F1, It, E1, F2, [C, A, J, Fj], 2008 E, S, It, I, F, SA1, 2, 3, NZ, A, 2009 S, F, It, I, NZ, Arg, A, 2010 E, S, F, I, It, A, SA2, 2011 E1, S, It, I, E2, 3, [SA, Sm, I, F, A], A
Williams, T (Pontypridd) 1882 I
Williams, T (Swansea) 1888 S, I
Williams, T (Swansea) 1912 I, 1913 F, 1914 E, S, F, I
Williams, T (Swansea) 1921 F
Williams, T G (Cross Keys) 1935 S, I, NZ, 1936 E, S, I, 1937 S, I
Williams, W A (Crumlin) 1927 E, S, F, I
Williams, W A (Newport) 1952 I, F, 1953 E
Williams, W E O (Cardiff) 1887 S, I, 1889 S, 1890 S, E
Williams, W H (Pontymister) 1900 E, S, I, 1901 E
Williams, W L T (Llanelli, Cardiff) 1947 E, S, F, I, A, 1948 I, 1949 E
Williams, W O G (Swansea, Devonport Services) 1951 F, SA, 1952 E, S, I, F, 1953 E, S, I, F, NZ, 1954 E, I, F, S, 1955 E, S, I, F, 1956 E, S, I
Williams, W P J (Neath) 1974 I, F
Williams-Jones, H (S Wales Police, Llanelli) 1989 S (R), 1990 F (R), I, 1991 A, 1992 S, A, 1993 E, S, I, F, Z 1, Nm, 1994 Fj, Tg, WS (R), It (t), 1995 E (R)
Willis, W R (Cardiff) 1950 E, S, I, F, 1951 E, S, I, F, SA, 1952 E, S, 1953 S, NZ, 1954 E, I, F, S, 1955 E, S, I, F
Wiltshire, M L (Aberavon) 1967 NZ, 1968 E, S, F
Windsor, R W (Pontypool) 1973 A, 1974 S, I, F, E, 1975 F, E, S, I, A, 1976 E, S, I, F, 1977 I, F, E, S, 1978 E, S, I, F, A 1,2, NZ, 1979 S, I, F
Winfield, H B (Cardiff) 1903 I, 1904 E, S, I, 1905 NZ, 1906 E, S, I, 1907 S, I, 1908 E, S, F, I, A
Winmill, S (Cross Keys) 1921 E, S, F, I
Wintle, M E (Llanelli) 1996 It
Wintle, R V (London Welsh) 1988 WS (R)
Wooller, W (Sale, Cambridge U, Cardiff) 1933 E, S, I, 1935 E, S, I, NZ, 1936 E, S, I, 1937 E, S, I, 1938 S, I, 1939 E, S, I
Wyatt, C P (Llanelli) 1998 Z (R), SA 1(R),2, Arg, 1999 S, I, F 1, It, E, Arg 1,2, SA, C (R), F 2, [Arg 3, J (R), Sm, A], 2000 F, It, E, US, SA, 2001 E, R, I, Arg (R), Tg (R), A (R), 2002 I, It (R), E, S (R), 2003 A(R), NZ(t+R), E 2, [Tg(R),NZ(R)]
Wyatt, G (Pontypridd, Celtic Warriors) 1997 Tg, 2003 R (R)
Wyatt, M A (Swansea) 1983 E, S, I, F, 1984 A, 1985 S, I, 1987 E, S, I

Yapp, J V (Cardiff Blues) 2005 E(R), It(R), F(R), S(R), I(R), C(R), Fj, 2006 Arg 1(R), 2008 C, NZ(R), 2009 S(R), It, C, US, 2010 SA1(R), NZ1(R), SA2(R), 2011 E1(t&R), S(R), I(R), F(R)
Young, D (Swansea, Cardiff) 1987 [E, NZ], US, 1988 E, S, I, F, NZ 1,2, WS, R, 1989 S, NZ, 1990 F, 1996 A 3, SA, 1997 US, S, I, F, E, R, NZ, 1998 It, E, S, I, F, 1999 I, E (R), Arg 1(R),2(R), SA, C (R), F 2, [Arg 3, J, Sm, A], 2000 F, It, E, S, I, 2001 E, S, F, It, R, I, Arg
Young, G A (Cardiff) 1886 E, S
Young, J (Harrogate, RAF, London Welsh) 1968 S, I, F, 1969 S, I, F, E, NZ 1, 1970 E, I, F, 1971 E, S, I, F, 1972 E, S, F, NZ, 1973 E, S, I, F
Young, P (Gwent Dragons) 2003 R (R)

GLOBAL RUGBY GOES FROM STRENGTH TO STRENGTH

By Karen Bond

Kenji Demura (RJP)

The Philippines suffered a tough introduction to the HSBC Asian 5 Nations Top 5, losing 121–0 to Japan.

While the success of Wales and New Zealand in retaining their RBS Six Nations and Rugby Championship titles may have stolen the headlines, there was plenty for other nations to celebrate around the world during 2013.

The European Nations Cup welcomed Belgium to the top tier and any thoughts they were there simply to make up the numbers were cast aside on day one when the Zwarte Duivels gave Georgia an almighty scare, the defending champions needing a 71st minute try by Levan Chilachava to secure a 17–13 victory in Brussels.

Belgium – who had gone into the competition on a high after beating Hong Kong, Zimbabwe and UAE to win the Emirates Airline Cup of Nations in December – followed that narrow loss with a 21–21 draw with Spain and defeats against Portugal (18–12), Romania (32–14) and

Russia (43–32). These results leave Belgium fifth in the standings, above Spain on point differential, and targeting more of the same when the competition resumes in February if they are to retain their Division 1A status.

There was no change at the top of the table with Georgia adding another European Nations Cup title to their honour roll, although only on point differential from traditional rivals Romania after each won four and drew their head-to-head 9–9 in Bucharest. The two will be favourites to claim the Europe 1 and Europe 2 berths at Rugby World Cup 2015 by occupying the same positions come the conclusion in March.

It was not only Georgia celebrating a European Nations Cup title in 2012/13, though, with Germany topping Division 1B at the halfway stage of the two-year competition and the Netherlands (Division 2A), Israel (Division 2B), Luxembourg (Division 2C) and Cyprus (Division 2D) the other front runners.

There may be no promotion for these sides – that will come if they finish the 2013/14 season top of their respective divisions – but for the Netherlands, Israel and Luxembourg it did ensure that they remained on the road to RWC 2015, for a little while longer at least.

Cyprus took their tally to 19 wins in a row in the course of winning Division 2D, but as they are not a member of the International Rugby Board they are unable to take part in Rugby World Cup qualifying and therefore runners-up Slovenia faced Luxembourg in the first European play-off. Slovenia bowed out with a 22–10 loss and were followed by Luxembourg after they lost the next play-off 26–12 to Israel in early October. Israel met the Netherlands at the end of October with the winner to face the Division 1B winner next year for the right to play the third placed team in Division 1A for a place in the Répechage.

Belgium were not the only nation to make their debut in the elite tier of a competition in 2013 as the Philippines joined Japan, Hong Kong, Korea and UAE in the HSBC Asian 5 Nations Top 5. The Volcanoes' story is an inspirational one as they have climbed from the bottom of the pyramid in 2008 to the top tier in 2013, a year which also saw their Sevens team make history as the first national team in any sport to play at a World Cup. It was a steep learning curve for the Philippines after being humbled 121–0 by Japan on their Top 5 debut, but they finished on a high by beating the United Arab Emirates 24–8 to avoid relegation straight back to Division I.

A nation hoping to emulate the Philippines' rise is Qatar, who like Japan can boast an unbeaten record in the Asian 5 Nations. Qatar, who had won Division IV the two previous years, crushed China 76–0 and then beat Guam 13–7 to win Division III in Malaysia in June with captain Gavin Piek admitting the success was "going to do heaps for rugby in Qatar" and that they had "made everyone aware that Qatar is a nation that can play rugby". The other 2013 title winners were Japan (Top 5), Sri Lanka (Division I), Singapore (Division II), Lebanon (Division IV) and Cambodia (Division V). Sri Lanka's success means they will join Japan, Hong Kong, Korea and the Volcanoes in the Top 5 in 2014 when the Asia 1 qualifier for Rugby World Cup 2015 is decided.

The dream of RWC 2015 qualification was on the minds of many other nations and inspired some to new heights, including Kenya who emphatically beat Uganda and then tournament favourites Zimbabwe in July to be crowned Africa Cup champions. Tries from Joshua Chisanga, Nick Barasa (2) and Edwin Otieno helped Kenya record a 29–17 victory to show that they will be in the mix when the Africa 1 qualifier spot is up for grabs in 2014. Kenya will have a chance to show that this win was no fluke when they travel to Namibia to face their hosts and Zimbabwe in the Tri Nations Rugby Series in November.

Over in Oceania, the Cook Islands also had cause to celebrate after winning the Oceania Cup in July by beating hosts Papua New Guinea 37–31 with 17 points from Greg Mullany. Their reward is the chance to play Fiji in a one-off match in 2014 to determine the Oceania 1 qualifier for England 2015, a rare opportunity for the Cook Islanders with their only previous meeting being a 53–7 loss in June 1997.

Paraguay's RWC dream ended with a 35–22 loss to Brazil in October 2012, but they did not let that factor deny them another South American B Championship, making the most of home advantage in August to beat Peru (22–0), Venezuela (48–7) and Paraguay (25–15). Uruguay, meanwhile, remain the best of the rest in the region behind Argentina after beating Chile and Brazil to finish second in South America's elite tier.

MAJOR TOURS

By Chris Rhys

Getty Images

Tom Wood captained England to an emphatic 2–0 series win in Argentina in June.

NEW ZEALAND TO EUROPE 2012

TOUR PARTY

FULL BACK: IJA Dagg (Hawke's Bay)
THREEQUARTERS: CS Jane (Wellington), HE Gear (Otago), BR Smith (Otago), CG Smith (Wellington), MA Nonu (Wellington), TE Ellison (Otago), SJ Savea (Wellington)
HALF BACKS: PAT Weepu (Auckland), AL Smith (Manawatu), TNJ Kerr-Barlow (Waikato), AW Cruden (Manawatu), DW Carter (Canterbury), BJ Barrett (Taranaki)
FORWARDS: DS Coles (Wellington), AK Hore (Taranaki), KF Mealamu (Auckland), WWV Crockett (Canterbury), CC Faumuina (Auckland), BJ Franks (Hawke's Bay), OJ Franks (Canterbury), TD Woodcock (North Harbour), BA Retallick (Bay of Plenty), L Romano (Canterbury), AJ Williams (Auckland), SL Whitelock (Canterbury), SJ Cane (Bay of Plenty), RH McCaw (Canterbury), LJ Messam (Waikato), KJ Read (Canterbury), AJ Thomson (Otago), VVJ Vito (Wellington)
HEAD COACH: SW Hansen

11 November, Murrayfield, Scotland 22 (2G 1T 1PG) New Zealand 51 (6G 3PG)

SCOTLAND: SW Hogg (Glasgow Warriors); SF Lamont (Glasgow Warriors), NJ de Luca (Edinburgh), MCM Scott (Edinburgh), TJW Visser (Edinburgh); GD Laidlaw (Edinburgh), MRL Blair (CA Brive); R Grant (Glasgow Warriors), RW Ford (Edinburgh), GDS Cross (Edinburgh), RJ Gray (Sale Sharks), JL Hamilton (Gloucester Rugby), AK Strokosch (USA Perpignan), RM Rennie (Edinburgh), KDR Brown (Saracens)(captain)
SUBSTITUTIONS: DK Denton (Edinburgh) for Rennie (19 mins); AD Kellock (Glasgow Warriors) for Hamilton (57 mins); S Lawson (London Irish) & MB Evans (Castres Olympique) for Ford & De Luca (65 mins); AF Jacobsen (Edinburgh) & RJH Jackson (Glasgow Warriors) for Grant & Laidlaw (65 mins); HB Pyrgos (Glasgow Warriors) for Blair (73 mins)

SCORERS: *Tries*: Visser (2), Cross *Conversions:* Laidlaw (2) *Penalty Goal*: Laidlaw
NEW ZEALAND: Dagg; Jane, B Smith, Ellison, Savea; Carter, Weepu; Crockett, Hore, O Franks, Romano, Whitelock, Thomson, McCaw (captain), Vito
SUBSTITUTIONS: Barrett for Dagg (25 mins); Kerr-Barlow, Coles & B Franks for Weepu, Hore & O Franks (61 mins); Williams for Whitelock (66 mins); Woodcock for Crockett (72 mins)
SCORERS: *Tries:* Savea (2), Dagg, Jane, Hore, B Smith *Conversions:* Carter (6) *Penalty Goals:* Carter (3)
REFEREE: J Garces (France)

17 November, Stadio Olimpico, Rome, Italy 10 (1G 1DG) New Zealand 42 (4G 1T 3PG)

ITALY: A Masi (London Wasps); G Venditti (Zebre), T Benvenuti (Treviso), A Sgarbi (Treviso), Mi Bergamasco (Racing Métro); L Orquera (Zebre), E Gori (Treviso); A lo Cicero (Racing Métro), L Ghiraldini (Treviso), M-L Castrogiovanni (Leicester Tigers), A Pavanello (Treviso), F Minto (Treviso), A Zanni (Treviso), S Favaro (Treviso), S Parisse (Stade Français)(captain)
SUBSTITUTIONS: R Barbieri (Treviso) for Favaro (46 mins); D Giazzon (Zebre) & A de Marchi (Treviso) for Ghiraldini & Lo Cicero (51 mins); L Cittadini (Treviso) & T Botes (Treviso) for Castrogiovanni & Gori (56 mins); Q Geldenhuys (Zebre) for A Pavenello (59 mins); L McLean (Treviso) for Masi (61 mins); Ma Bergamasco (Zebre) for Zanni (64 mins)
SCORERS: *Try*: Sgarbi *Conversion:* Orquera *Drop Goal:* Orquera
NEW ZEALAND: Barrett; Gear, C Smith, Nonu, Savea; Cruden, A Smith; Woodcock, Mealamu, Faumuina, Williams, Retallick, Messam, Cane, Read (captain)
SUBSTITUTIONS: Coles for Mealamu (42 mins); B Franks for Faumuina (56 mins); Whitelock for Williams (51 mins); Jane for Barrett (53 mins); Kerr-Barlow for A Smith (60 mins); Crockett for Woodcock (64 mins)
SCORERS: *Tries*: Savea (2), Read, Nonu, Jane *Conversions:* Cruden (4) *Penalty Goals*: Cruden (3)
REFEREE: AC Rolland (Ireland)

24 November, Millennium Stadium, Cardiff, Wales 10 (2T) New Zealand 33 (3G 4PG)

WALES: SL Halfpenny (Cardiff Blues); ACG Cuthbert (Cardiff Blues), JJV Davies (Scarlets), JH Roberts (Cardiff Blues), LB Williams (Scarlets); R Priestland (Scarlets), WM Phillips (Aviron Bayonnais); P James (Ospreys), M Rees (Scarlets), AR Jarvis (Ospreys), BS Davies (Cardiff Blues), LC Charteris (USA Perpignan), Ryan P Jones (Ospreys), SK Warburton (Cardiff Blues)(captain), TT Faletau (Dragons)
SUBSTITUTIONS: SA Andrews (Cardiff Blues) & AC Shingler (Scarlets) for Jarvis & B Davies (1 min); MS Williams (Scarlets) for Roberts (18 mins); JC Tipuric (Ospreys) for RP Jones (49 mins); GD Jenkins (RC Toulon) & TD Knoyle (Scarlets) for James & Phillips (54 mins); KJ Owens (Scarlets) for Rees (64 mins); JW Hook (USA Perpignan) for Priestland (67 mins)
SCORERS: *Tries:* MS Williams, Cuthbert
NEW ZEALAND: Dagg; Jane, C Smith, Nonu, Savea; Cruden, A Smith; Woodcock, Hore, O Franks, Romano, Whitelock, Messam, McCaw (captain), Read
SUBSTITUTIONS: Retallick, Weepu & Crockett for Romano, A Smith & Woodcock (50 mins); Coles for Hore (54 mins); Faumuina for O Franks (60 mins); Barrett for Cruden (67 mins); Vito for Messam (70 mins); B Smith for Savea (77 mins)
SCORERS: *Tries:* Messam, Woodcock, Romano *Conversions:* Cruden (3) *Penalty Goals*: Cruden (4)
REFEREE: C Joubert (South Africa)

1 December, Twickenham, England 38 (1G 2T 6PG 1DG) New Zealand 21 (3G)

ENGLAND: DAV Goode (Saracens); CJ Ashton (Saracens), EM Tuilagi (Leicester Tigers), BM Barritt (Saracens), MN Brown (Harlequins); OA Farrell (Saracens), BR Youngs (Leicester Tigers); AR Corbisiero (London Irish), TN Youngs (Leicester Tigers), DN Cole (Leicester Tigers), JO Launchbury (London Wasps); GMW Parling (Leicester Tigers), TA Wood (Northampton Saints), CDC Robshaw (Harlequins)(captain), BJ Morgan (Gloucester Rugby)
SUBSTITUTIONS: JAW Haskell (London Wasps) for Morgan (57 mins); FS Burns (Gloucester Rugby) for Farrell (63 mins); JBA Joseph (London Irish), CL Lawes (Northampton Saints) & MWIN Vunipola (Saracens) for Tuilagi, Launchbury & Corbisiero (66 mins); DS Care (Harlequins) for B Youngs (68 mins); DJ Paice (London Irish) & DG Wilson (Bath Rugby) for T Youngs & Cole (72 mins)
SCORERS: *Tries:* Barritt, Ashton, Tuilagi *Conversion:* Farrell *Penalty Goals:* Farrell (4), Burns (2) *Drop Goal:* Farrell
NEW ZEALAND: Dagg; Jane, C Smith, Nonu, Savea; Carter, A Smith; Woodcock, Mealamu, O Franks, Retallick, Whitelock, Messam, McCaw (captain), Read
SUBSTITUTIONS: Romano for Retallick (49 mins); Faumuina for O Franks (52 mins); Coles & Vito for Mealamu & Messam (62 mins); Weepu & Cruden for A Smith & Carter (64 mins); Crockett for Woodcock (66 mins); B Smith for Dagg (70 mins)
SCORERS: *Tries:* Savea (2), Read *Conversions*: Carter (2), Cruden
REFEREE: GJ Clancy (Ireland)

SOUTH AFRICA TO EUROPE 2012

TOUR PARTY

FULL BACK: Z Kirchner (Blue Bulls)

THREEQUARTERS: LN Mvovo (Sharks), J-P R Pietersen (Sharks), RK Rhule (Free State), LG Mapoe (Golden Lions), J de Villiers (Western Province), JL de Jongh (Western Province), ET Jantjies (Golden Lions), JJ Taute (Golden Lions), F Hougaard (Blue Bulls)

HALF BACKS: J Vermaak (Blue Bulls), R Pienaar (Ulster), PJ Lambie (Sharks), M Steyn (Blue Bulls)

FORWARDS: SB Brits (Saracens), MC Ralepelle (Blue Bulls), JA Strauss (Cheetahs), JN du Plessis (Sharks), PM Cilliers (Golden Lions), *HS van der Merwe (Leinster), T Mtawarira (Sharks), GG Steenkamp (Stade Toulousain), *F Malherbe (Western Province), CJ van der Linde (Cheetahs), PR van der Merwe (Blue Bulls), F van der Merwe (Golden Lions), E Etzebeth (Western Province), PJJ Kruger (Blue Bulls), *MZ Wentzel (London Wasps), L-FP Louw (Bath Rugby), WS Alberts (Sharks), AF Botha (Blue Bulls), MC Coetzee (Sharks), DJ Vermeulen (Western Province)

* Replacement on tour

HEAD COACH: H Meyer

10 November, Aviva Stadium, Dublin, Ireland 12 (4PG) South Africa 16 (1G 3PG)

IRELAND: SR Zebo (Munster); TJ Bowe (Ulster), KG Earls (Munster), GWD D'Arcy (Leinster), AD Trimble (Ulster); JJ Sexton (Leinster), C Murray (Munster); CE Healy (Leinster), CR Strauss (Leinster), MR Ross (Leinster), DC Ryan (Munster), MP McCarthy (Connacht), P O'Mahony (Munster), CG Henry (Ulster), JPR Heaslip (Leinster)(captain)

SUBSTITUTIONS: SM Cronin (Leinster) for Strauss (temp 3–11 mins & 74 mins); D Kilcoyne (Munster) for Healy (temp 41–44 mins); FL McFadden (Leinster) for Trimble (58 mins); EG Reddan (Leinster) for Murray (61 mins); DP O'Callaghan (Munster) for Ryan (temp 63–67 mins) & for McCarthy (70 mins); M Bent (Leinster) & WI Henderson (Ulster) for Ross & O'Mahony (70 mins); RJR O'Gara (Munster) for D'Arcy (74 mins)

SCORER: *Penalty Goals*: Sexton (4)

SOUTH AFRICA: Kirchner; Pietersen, Taute, De Villiers (captain), Hougaard; Lambie, Pienaar; Van der Linde, JA Strauss, JN du Plessis, Etzebeth, Kruger, Alberts, Louw, Vermeulen

SUBSTITUTIONS: Cilliers for JN du Plessis (55 mins); HS van der Merwe for Van der Linde (63 mins); Coetzee for Alberts (64 mins); PR van der Merwe for Etzebeth (70 mins)

SCORERS: *Try:* Pienaar *Conversion:* Lambie *Penalty Goals:* Lambie (3)

REFEREE: W Barnes (England)

17 November, Murrayfield, Scotland 10 (1G 1PG) South Africa 21 (1G 1T 3PG)

SCOTLAND: SW Hogg (Glasgow Warriors); SF Lamont (Glasgow Warriors), NJ de Luca (Edinburgh), MCM Scott (Edinburgh), TJW Visser (Edinburgh); GD Laidlaw (Edinburgh), MRL Blair (CA Brive); R Grant (Glasgow Warriors), RW Ford (Edinburgh), EA Murray (Worcester Warriors), RJ Gray (Sale Sharks), JL Hamilton (Gloucester Rugby), KDR Brown (Saracens)(captain), JA Barclay (Glasgow Warriors), DK Denton (Edinburgh)

SUBSTITUTIONS: AD Kellock (Glasgow Warriors) for Gray (21 mins); HB Pyrgos (Glasgow Warriors) for Blair (47 mins); GDS Cross (Edinburgh), DWH Hall (Glasgow Warriors) & RJH Jackson (Glasgow Warriors) for Murray, Ford & Laidlaw (68 mins)

SCORERS: *Try* Pyrgos *Conversion*: Laidlaw *Penalty Goal:* Laidlaw

SOUTH AFRICA: Kirchner; Pietersen, De Jongh, De Villiers (captain), Hougaard; Lambie, Pienaar; Steenkamp, JA Strauss, JN du Plessis, Etzebeth, Kruger, Alberts, Louw, Vermeulen

SUBSTITUTIONS: Van der Linde for J du Plessis (52 mins); Coetzee for Alberts (53 mins); HS van der Merwe for Steenkamp (61 mins); PR van der Merwe for Kruger (68 mins); M Steyn for Lambie (73 mins); Brits for JA Strauss (76 mins)

SCORERS: *Tries:* JA Strauss (2) *Conversion:* Lambie *Penalty Goals*: Lambie (3)

REFEREE: GJ Clancy (Ireland)

24 November, Twickenham, England 15 (5PG) South Africa 16 (1G 3PG)

ENGLAND: DAV Goode (Saracens); CJ Ashton (Saracens), EM Tuilagi (Leicester Tigers), BM Barritt (Saracens), MN Brown (Harlequins); TGAL Flood (Leicester Tigers), BR Youngs (Leicester Tigers); AR Corbisiero (London Irish), TN Youngs (Leicester Tigers), DN Cole (Leicester Tigers), JO Launchbury (London Wasps); GMW Parling (Leicester Tigers), TA Wood (Northampton Saints), CDC Robshaw (Harlequins) (captain), BJ Morgan (Gloucester Rugby)

SUBSTITUTIONS: OA Farrell (Saracens) for Flood (temp 6–10 mins & 45 mins); JAW Haskell (London Wasps) & MWIN Vunipola (Saracens) for Wood & Corbisiero (53 mins); DS Care (Harlequins) & DJ Paice (London Irish) for B Youngs & T Youngs (62 mins); MJ Botha (Saracens) for Launchbury (72 mins); DG Wilson (Bath Rugby) for Cole (75 mins)

SCORERS: *Penalty Goals:* Flood (2), Farrell (3)

SOUTH AFRICA: Kirchner; Pietersen, De Jongh, De Villiers (captain), Hougaard; Lambie, Pienaar; Steenkamp, JA Strauss, JN du Plessis, Etzebeth, Kruger, Alberts, Louw, Vermeulen

SUBSTITUTIONS: Cilliers for J du Plessis (40 mins); Coetzee for Alberts (56 mins); HS van der Merwe for Steenkamp (61 mins); PR van der Merwe for Etzebeth (69 mins); Brits for JA Strauss (74 mins)

SCORERS: *Try:* Alberts *Conversion*: Lambie *Penalty Goals*: Lambie (3)

REFEREE: N Owens (Wales)

AUSTRALIA TO EUROPE 2012

TOUR PARTY

FULL BACK: MJ Harris (Queensland Reds)

THREEQUARTERS: DA Mitchell (NSW Waratahs), NM Cummins (Western Force), DAN Ioane (Queensland Reds), AP Ashley-Cooper (NSW Waratahs), BNL Tapuai (Queensland Reds), A Faingaa (Queensland Reds), PJ McCabe (Brumbies)

HALF BACKS: NJ Phipps (Melbourne Rebels), BR Sheehan (Western Force), BS Barnes (NSW Waratahs), KJ Beale (Melbourne Rebels)

FORWARDS: SUT Polota-Nau (NSW Waratahs), ST Moore (Brumbies), J Hanson (Queensland Reds), BA Robinson (NSW Waratahs), SM Kepu (NSW Waratahs), JA Slipper (Queensland Reds), BE Alexander (Brumbies), PJ Ryan (NSW Waratahs), NC Sharpe (Western Force), S Timani (NSW Waratahs), KP Douglas (NSW Waratahs), RA Simmons (Queensland Reds), DA Dennis (NSW Waratahs), DW Pocock (Brumbies), M Hooper (NSW Waratahs), LB Gill (Queensland Reds), WL Palu (NSW Waratahs), UR Samo (Queensland Reds), S Higginbotham (Queensland Reds)

HEAD COACH: RM Deans

10 November, Stade de France, Paris, France 33 (3G 3PG 1DG) Australia 6 (2PG)

FRANCE: B Dulin (Castres Olympique); W Fofana (ASM Clermont Auvergne), F Fritz (Stade Toulousain), M Mermoz (RC Toulon), V Clerc (Stade Toulousain); F Michalak (RC Toulon), M Machenaud (Racing Métro); Y Forestier (Castres Olympique), D Szarzewski (Racing Métro), N Mas (USA Perpignan), P Papé (Stade Français)(captain), J Suta (RC Toulon), F Ouedraogo (Montpellier-Herault), Y Nyanga (Stade Toulousain), L Picamoles (Stade Toulousain)

SUBSTITUTIONS: B Kayser (ASM Clermont Auvergne) & T Domingo (ASM Clermont Auvergne) for Szarzewski & Forestier (50 mins); V Debaty (ASM Clermont Auvergne) & Y Huget (Stade Toulousain) for Mas & Fritz (59 mins); M Parra (ASM Clermont Auvergne) for Machenaud (63 mins); D Chouly (ASM Clermont Auvergne) for Picamoles (64 mins); S Vahaamahina (USA Perpignan) for Nyanga (67 mins); F Trinh-Duc (Montpellier-Herault) for Michalak (73 mins)

SCORERS: *Tries:* Picamoles, Fofana, Penalty try *Conversions:* Michalak (3) *Penalty Goals:* Michalak (2), Parra *Drop Goal:* Michalak

AUSTRALIA: Harris; Ashley-Cooper, Tapuai, McCabe, Cummins; Beale, Phipps; Robinson, Polota-Nau, Kepu, Douglas, Sharpe (captain), Dennis, Hooper, Palu

SUBSTITUTIONS: Slipper for Robinson (temp 28–36 mins) & for Kepu (49 mins); Barnes for Harris (56 mins); Moore & Samo for Polota-Nau & Palu (59 mins); Simmons & Ryan for Sharpe & Robinson (64 mins); Gill for Dennis (69 mins)

SCORER: *Penalty Goals:* Harris (2)

REFEREE: N Owens (Wales)

17 November, Twickenham, England 14 (1T 3PG) Australia 20 (1T 4PG 1DG)

ENGLAND: DAV Goode (Saracens); CJ Ashton (Saracens), EM Tuilagi (Leicester Tigers), BM Barritt (Saracens), CDJ Sharples (Gloucester Rugby); TGAL Flood (Leicester Tigers), DS Care (Harlequins); JWG Marler (Harlequins), TN Youngs (Leicester Tigers), DN Cole (Leicester Tigers), TP Palmer (London Wasps), GMW Parling (Leicester Tigers), TA Johnson (Exeter Chiefs), CDC Robshaw (Harlequins)(captain), TR Waldrom (Leicester Tigers)

SUBSTITUTIONS: MWIN Vunipola (Saracens) & TA Wood (Northampton Saints) for Marler & Johnson (49 mins); JO Launchbury (London Wasps) for Palmer (53); BR Youngs (Leicester Tigers) & MN Brown

(Harlequins) for Cole & Sharples (60 mins); OA Farrell (Saracens) & DJ Paice (London Irish) for Barritt & T Youngs (73 mins)

SCORERS: *Try:* Tuilagi *Penalty Goals:* Flood (3)

AUSTRALIA: Barnes; Cummins, Ashley-Cooper, Tapuai, Ioane; Beale, Phipps; Robinson, Polota-Nau, Alexander, Timani, Sharpe (captain), Dennis, Hooper, Palu

SUBSTITUTIONS: Moore for Polota-Nau (40 mins); Gill for Dennis (temp 50–65 mins & 76 mins); Slipper for Robinson (60 mins); Mitchell for Ioane (69 mins); Kepu for Alexander (70 mins)

SCORERS: *Try*: Cummins *Penalty Goals*: Barnes (4) *Drop Goal*: Barnes

REFEREE: R Poite (France)

24 November, Stadio Artemio Franchi, Florence, Italy 19 (1G 4PG) Australia 22 (1G 5PG)

ITALY: A Masi (London Wasps); G Venditti (Zebre), T Benvenuti (Treviso), A Sgarbi (Treviso), Mi Bergamasco (Racing Métro); L Orquera (Zebre), E Gori (Treviso); A lo Cicero (Racing Métro), L Ghiraldini (Treviso), M-L Castrogiovanni (Leicester Tigers), Q Geldenhuys (Zebre), F Minto (Treviso), A Zanni (Treviso), R Barbieri (Treviso), S Parisse (Stade Français)(captain)

SUBSTITUTIONS: M Rizzo (Treviso) & L McLean (Treviso) for Lo Cicero & Mi Bergamasco (33 mins); A Pavanello (Treviso), D Giazzon (Zebre) & S Favaro (Treviso) for Geldenhuys, Ghiraldini & Barbieri (59 mins); L Cittadini (Treviso) for Castrogiovanni (62 mins); M Vosawai (Treviso) for Zanni (68 mins); T Botes (Treviso) for Gori (74 mins)

SCORERS: *Try*: Barbieri *Conversion:* Orquera *Penalty Goals:* Orquera (4)

AUSTRALIA: Barnes; Cummins, Ashley-Cooper, Tapuai, Mitchell; Beale, Sheehan; Robinson, Moore, Alexander, Timani, Sharpe (captain), Higginbotham, Hooper, Palu

SUBSTITUTIONS: Phipps for Sheehan (31 mins); Slipper for Robinson (37 mins); Dennis for Higginbotham (66 mins); Ioane for Cummins (68 mins); Kepu for Alexander (72 mins)

SCORERS: *Try:* Cummins *Conversion*: Barnes *Penalty Goals:* Barnes (3), Beale (2)

REFEREE: L van der Merwe (South Africa)

1 December, Millennium Stadium, Cardiff, Wales 12 (4PG) Australia 14 (1T 3PG)

WALES: SL Halfpenny (Cardiff Blues); ACG Cuthbert (Cardiff Blues), JJV Davies (Scarlets), JH Roberts (Cardiff Blues), LB Williams (Scarlets); R Priestland (Scarlets), WM Phillips (Aviron Bayonnais); GD Jenkins (RC Toulon), M Rees (Scarlets), SA Andrews (Cardiff Blues), L Reed (Cardiff Blues), LC Charteris (USA Perpignan), AC Shingler (Scarlets), SK Warburton (Cardiff Blues)(captain), TT Faletau (Dragons)

SUBSTITUTIONS: Ryan P Jones (Ospreys) for Charteris (temp 3–7 mins & 40 mins); KJ Owens (Scarlets) & JC Tipuric (Ospreys) for Rees & Fatetau (65 mins)

SCORER: *Penalty Goals:* Halfpenny (4)

AUSTRALIA: Barnes; Cummins, Ashley-Cooper, Tapuai, Mitchell; Beale, Phipps; Robinson, Polota-Nau, Alexander, Douglas, Sharpe (captain), Higginbotham, Pocock, Palu

SUBSTITUTIONS: Dennis for Higginbotham (15 mins); Moore for Polota-Nau (40 mins); Ioane for Cummins (48 mins); Hooper for Douglas (52 mins); Harris for Tapuai (58 mins); Slipper for Robinson (61 mins); Kepu for Alexander (69 mins)

SCORER: *Try:* Beale *Penalty Goals:* Beale (3)

REFEREE: W Barnes (England)

ARGENTINA TO EUROPE 2012

TOUR PARTY

FULL BACKS: JM Hernández (Racing Métro), S Cordero (Regatas Bella Vista), LP González Amorosino (Montpellier-Herault)

THREEQUARTERS: H Agulla (Bath Rugby), JJ Imhoff (Racing Métro), M Montero (Pucura), GP Tiesi (San Isidro Club), M Bosch (Biarrritz Olympique), GO Camacho (Exeter Chiefs), F Contepomi (Stade Français), J Tuculet (Grenoble), S Fernández (Montpellier-Herault)

HALF BACKS: T Cubelli (Belgrano Athletic), M Landajo (CA San Isidro), N Vergallo (Stade Toulousain), N Sanchez (Begles-Bordeaux)

FORWARDS: E Guiñazu (unattached), A Creevy (Montpellier-Herault), J Figallo (Montpellier-Herault), F Gomez Kodela (Biarritz Olympique), B Postiglioni (La Plata), M Ayerza (Leicester Tigers), N Lobo (Montpellier-Herault), M Bustos (Montpellier-Herault), M Carizza (Jockey Club, Rosario), T Vallejos (Scarlets), T de la Vega (CUBA), JF Cabello (Tucuman), T Leonardi (San Isidro Club), JM Leguizamón (Lyon UC), L Senatore (Gimnasia Rosario), JM Fernández Lobbe (RC Toulon)

HEAD COACH: S Phelan

10 November, Millennium Stadium, Cardiff, Wales 12 (4PG) Argentina 26 (2G 2PG 2DG)

WALES: SL Halfpenny (Cardiff Blues); ACG Cuthbert (Cardiff Blues), MS Williams (Scarlets), JH Roberts (Cardiff Blues), GP North (Scarlets); R Priestland (Scarlets), TD Knoyle (Scarlets); GD Jenkins (RC Toulon), M Rees (Scarlets), AR Jarvis (Ospreys), AW Jones (Ospreys), IR Evans (Ospreys), J Turnbull (Scarlets), SK Warburton (Cardiff Blues)(captain), TT Faletau (Dragons)

SUBSTITUTIONS: JW Hook (USA Perpignan) for Roberts (23 mins); RJ McCusker (Scarlets) for AW Jones (39 mins); WM Phillips (Aviron Bayonnais) for Knoyle (55 mins); RM Hibbard (Ospreys) & P James (Ospreys) for Rees & Jarvis (60 mins); RJ Bevington (Ospreys) for Jenkins (68); JC Tipuric (Ospreys) for Warburton (71 mins)

SCORER: *Penalty Goals:* Halfpenny (4)

ARGENTINA: Hernández; Camacho, Tiesi, F Contepomi, Imhoff; Sanchez, Landajo; Ayerza, Guiñazu, Figallo, Carizza, Cabello, JM Fernández Lobbe (captain), Leguizamón, Senatore

SUBSTITUTIONS: Tuculet for F Contepomi (13 mins); H Agulla for Hernández (45 mins); Creevy for Guiñazu (48 mins); Leonardi for Senatore (56 mins); Vallejos for Cabello (64 mins); Gomez Kodela & Vergallo for Figallo & Landajo (66 mins); Postiglioni for Ayerza (78 mins)

SCORERS: *Tries:* Imhoff, Camacho *Conversions:* Sanchez (2) *Penalty Goals:* F Contepomi, Sanchez *Drop Goals:* Sanchez (2)

REFEREE: R Poite (France)

17 November, Grand Stade, Lille, France 39 (3G 5PG 1DG) Argentina 22 (1G 4PG 1DG)

FRANCE: B Dulin (Castres Olympique); W Fofana (ASM Clermont Auvergne), F Fritz (Stade Toulousain), M Mermoz (RC Toulon), V Clerc (Stade Toulousain); F Michalak (RC Toulon), M Machenaud (Racing Métro); Y Forestier (Castres Olympique), D Szarzewski (Racing Métro), N Mas (USA Perpignan), P Papé (Stade Français)(captain), Y Maestri (Stade Toulousain), F Ouedraogo (Montpellier-Herault), Y Nyanga (Stade Toulousain), L Picamoles (Stade Toulousain)

SUBSTITUTIONS: T Domingo (ASM Clermont Auvergne) & B Kayser (ASM Clermont Auvergne) for Forestier & Szarzewski (49 mins); M Parra (ASM Clermont Auvergne) for Machenaud (56 mins); J Suta (RC Toulon) for Maestri (60 mins); Y Huget (Stade Toulousain) for Fritz (62 mins); F Trinh-Duc (Montpellier-Herault) & V Debaty (ASM Clermont Auvergne) for Dulin & Mas (68 mins); D Chouly (ASM Clermont Auvergne) for Picamoles (73 mins)

SCORERS: *Tries:* Clerc (2), Nyanga *Conversions:* Michalak (3) *Penalty Goals:* Michalak (5) *Drop Goal*: Michalak

ARGENTINA: González Amorosino; Camacho, Tiesi, Bosch, Imhoff; Sanchez, Landajo; Ayerza, Guiñazu, Figallo, Carizza, Cabello, JM Fernández Lobbe (captain), Leguizamón, Senatore

SUBSTITUTIONS: Creevy for Guiñazu (47 mins); De la Vega for Senatore (49 mins); Camacho for Tiesi (58 mins); Vallejos & Gomez Kodela for Cabello & Figallo (60 mins); Cubelli for Landajo (62 mins); Lobo for Ayerza (72 mins); Tuculet for Agulla (73 mins)

SCORERS: *Try:* Bosch *Conversion:* Sanchez *Penalty Goals:* Sanchez (4) *Drop Goal:* Sanchez

REFEREE: SR Walsh (Australia)

24 November, Aviva Stadium, Dublin, Ireland 46 (4G 3T 1PG) Argentina 24 (1G 1T 4PG)

IRELAND: SR Zebo (Munster); TJ Bowe (Ulster), KG Earls (Munster), GWD D'Arcy (Leinster), CJH Gilroy (Ulster); JJ Sexton (Leinster), C Murray (Munster); CE Healy (Leinster), CR Strauss (Leinster), MR Ross (Leinster), DC Ryan (Munster), MP McCarthy (Connacht), P O'Mahony (Munster), CG Henry (Ulster), JPR Heaslip (Leinster)(captain)

SUBSTITUTIONS: DP O'Callaghan (Munster) for McCarthy (61 mins); M Bent (Leinster) for Ross (67 mins); WI Henderson (Ulster), EG Reddan (Leinster) & RJR O'Gara (Munster) for O'Mahony, Murray & Sexton (71 mins); FL McFadden (Leinster), SM Cronin (Leinster) & D Kilcoyne (Munster) for Bowe, Strauss & Healy (74 mins)

SCORERS: *Tries:* Sexton (2), Bowe (2), Gilroy, Strauss, Zebo *Conversions:* Sexton (3), O'Gara *Penalty Goal:* Sexton

ARGENTINA: Hernández; Camacho, Bosch, Fernández, Imhoff; Sanchez, Landajo; Ayerza, Guiñazu, Bustos, Carizza, Cabello, JM Fernández Lobbe (captain), Leguizamón, Senatore

SUBSTITUTIONS: Tiesi for Sanchez (temp 21–24 mins & 60 mins); Leonardi & Montero for Leguizamón & Imhoff (53 mins); Creevy for Guiñazu (56 mins); Gomez Kodela for Senatore (temp 64–73 mins) & Bustos (73 mins); Lobo & Vergallo for Ayerza & Landajo (68 mins)

SCORERS: *Tries:* Leonardi, Fernández Lobbe *Conversion:* Hernández *Penalty Goals:* Sanchez (4)

REFEREE: J Peyper (South Africa)

SAMOA TO EUROPE 2012

TOUR PARTY

FULL BACK: FS Autagavaia (Northland)
THREEQUARTERS: PL Perez (Eastern Province Kings), D Lemi (Worcester Warriors), R Lilomaiava (Vaiala), GT Pisi (Northampton Saints), PB Williams (Stade Français), JW Leota (Sale Sharks)
HALF BACKS: KF Fotuali'i (Ospreys), JI Sua (Crusaders), T Pisi (Hurricanes), K Anufe (Marist, Auckland)
FORWARDS: WO Avei (Bordeaux-Begles), TT Paulo (ASM Clermont Auvergne), S Taulafo (London Wasps), CAI Johnston (Stade Toulousain), JVI Johnston (Harlequins), J Tekori (Castres Olympique), DA Leo (USA Perpignan), TAM Paulo (Blues), F Lemalu (Stade Montois), O Treviranus (London Irish), T Fomai (Hawke's Bay), M Fa'asavalu (Harlequins), T Tuifu'a (Newcastle Falcons)
HEAD COACH: S Betham

16 November, Millennium Stadium, Cardiff, Wales 19 (1G 4PG) Samoa 26 (1G 2T 3PG)

WALES: SL Halfpenny (Cardiff Blues); ACG Cuthbert (Cardiff Blues), MA Beck (Ospreys), JH Roberts (Cardiff Blues), GP North (Scarlets); DR Biggar (Ospreys), WM Phillips (Aviron Bayonnais); P James (Ospreys), RM Hibbard (Ospreys), AR Jarvis (Ospreys), BS Davies (Cardiff Blues), IR Evans (Ospreys), Ryan P Jones (Ospreys)(captain), JC Tipuric (Ospreys), TT Faletau (Dragons)
SUBSTITUTIONS: KJ Owens (Scarlets) for Hibbard (17 mins); R Priestland (Scarlets) for Biggar (37 mins); LC Charteris (USA Perpignan) for Evans (40 mins); GD Jenkins (RC Toulon) for James (61 mins); SK Warburton (Cardiff Blues) for Ryan Jones (70 mins); SA Andrews (Cardiff Blues) for Jarvis (76 mins)
SCORERS: *Try:* Beck *Conversion:* Halfpenny *Penalty Goals*: Halfpenny (4)
SAMOA: Autagavaia; Perez, G Pisi, P Williams, Lemi (captain); T Pisi, Fotuali'i; Taulafo, Avei, C Johnston, Leo, TAM Paulo, Treviranus, Fa'asavalu, Tuifu'a
SUBSTITUTIONS: Leota for Williams (temp 54–69 & 74 mins); J Johnston for C Johnston (47 mins); TT Paulo for Avei (57 mins); Tekori for TAM Paulo (59 mins); Fomai for Treviranus (69 mins); Sua for Pisi (78 mins)
SCORERS: *Tries:* Autagavia, GT Pisi, Leota *Conversion*: T Pisi *Penalty Goals:* T Pisi (3)
REFEREE: P Gauzere (France)

24 November, Stade de France, Paris, France 22 (1G 5PG) Samoa 14 (2G)

FRANCE: B Dulin (Castres Olympique); W Fofana (ASM Clermont Auvergne), F Fritz (Stade Toulousain), M Mermoz (RC Toulon), V Clerc (Stade Toulousain); F Michalak (RC Toulon), M Parra (ASM Clermont Auvergne); T Domingo (ASM Clermont Auvergne), B Kayser (ASM Clermont Auvergne), N Mas (USA Perpignan), P Papé (Stade Français)(captain), Y Maestri (Stade Toulousain), F Ouedraogo (Montpellier-Herault), Y Nyanga (Stade Toulousain), L Picamoles (Stade Toulousain)
SUBSTITUTIONS: D Szarzewski (Racing Métro) & Y Forestier (Castres Olympique) for Kayser & Domingo (44 mins); V Debaty (ASM Clermont Auvergne) for Mas (56 mins); M Machenaud (Racing Métro) for Parra (59 mins); D Chouly (ASM Clermont Auvergne) for Picamoles (63 mins); Y Huget (Stade Toulousain) for Fritz (65 mins)
SCORERS: *Try*: Michalak *Conversion:* Michalak *Penalty Goals:* Michalak (4), Parra
SAMOA: Lemi (captain); Perez, G Pisi, Leota, Lilomaiava; T Pisi, Fotuali'i; Taulafo, TT Paulo, C Johnston, Tekori, TAM Paulo, Treviranus, Fa'asavalu, Tuifu'a
SUBSTITUTIONS: Anufe for Leota (temp 2–7 mins & 72 mins); Avei for TT Paulo (40 mins); J Johnston for C Johnston (50 mins); Lemalu for TAM Paulo (54 mins); Fomai for Treviranus (65 mins); Sua for T Pisi (75 mins)
SCORERS: *Tries*: Lemi, Tekori *Conversions*: T Pisi (2)
REFEREE: J Lacey (Ireland)

FIJI TO ENGLAND AND IRELAND 2012

10 November, Twickenham, England 54 (5G 2T 3PG) Fiji 12 (1G 1T)

ENGLAND: DAV Goode (Saracens); CDJ Sharples (Gloucester Rugby), EM Tuilagi (Leicester Tigers), BM Barritt (Saracens), YCC Monye (Harlequins); TGAL Flood (Leicester Tigers), DS Care (Harlequins); JWG Marler (Harlequins), TN Youngs (Leicester Tigers), DN Cole (Leicester Tigers), TP Palmer (London Wasps), GMW Parling (Leicester Tigers), TA Johnson (Exeter Chiefs), CDC Robshaw (Harlequins)(captain), TR Waldrom (Leicester Tigers)
SUBSTITUTIONS: MWIN Vunipola (Saracens) for Marler (45 mins); JO Launchbury (London Wasps) for Palmer (49 mins); TA Wood (Northampton Saints), BR Youngs (Leicester Tigers), MN Brown (Harlequins) & OA Farrell (Saracens) for Johnson, Care, Monye & Flood (59 mins); DG Wilson (Bath Rugby) for Cole (63 mins); DJ Paice (London Irish) for T Youngs (65 mins)

SCORERS: *Tries:* Sharples (2), Tuilagi (2), Penalty try, Monye, Johnson *Conversions*: Flood (4), Farrell *Penalty Goals:* Flood (3)

FIJI: S Koniferedi (King Country); S Wara (Western Force), V Goneva (Leicester Tigers), SM Naqelevuki (Exeter Chiefs), W Votu (Exeter Chiefs); M Talebula (Bordeaux-Begles), NL Matawalu (Glasgow Warriors); RPN Makutu (Nadroga), V Veikoso (Navoci), DT Manu (Scarlets)(captain), L Nakawara (Tailevu), A Ratuniyarawa (Mahurangi), AN Naikatini (Toyota Verblitz), RMM Ravulo (North Harbour), A Qera (Gloucester Rugby)

SUBSTITUTIONS: S Samoca (Sigatoka) for Ravulo (temp 28–38 mins) & Makutu (40 mins); JL Matavesi (Worcester Warriors) for Koniferedi (40 mins); S Naureure (Nadroga) for Veikoso (45 mins); I Ratuva (Nadroga) for Naikatini (49 mins); RS Fatiaki (Worcester Warriors) for Wara (65 mins); M Saulo (Navy) for Manu (67 mins); S Kalou (Nadroga) for Ratuniyarawa (70 mins); K Bola (Lautoka) for Votu (74 mins)

SCORERS: *Tries:* Matawalu, Kalou *Conversion*: Matavesi

REFEREE: GW Jackson (New Zealand)

17 November, Thomond Park, Limerick, Ireland XV 53 (5G 3T 1PG) Fiji 0

Ireland XV Scorers: *Tries:* Gilroy (3), McFadden (2), Cronin, Cave, Marshall *Conversions:* Jackson (5) *Penalty Goal*: Jackson

TONGA TO EUROPE 2012

TOUR PARTY

FULL BACKS: VK Lilo (Bordeaux-Begles), S Lu'au (Tautahi Gold)

THREEQUARTERS: F Vainikolo (Connacht), V Helu (Manly), V Iongi (Marist), S Hufanga (Newcastle Falcons), A Ma'afu (Eastern Suburbs), S Piukala (USA Perpignan), H Tonga'uiha (London Welsh), A Fatafehi (North Harbour), E Paea (Easts, Sydney), M Malipo (Northland), A Mosese (unattached)

HALF BACKS: T Moa (Section Pau), F 'Apikotoa (Amatori), S Fisilau (Hurricanes)

FORWARDS: E Taione (Jersey), I Ma'asi (CS Vienne), A Lutui (Worcester Warriors), K Sakalia (Marist), S Taumalolo (USA Perpignan), S Tonga'uiha (Northampton Saints), H 'Aulika (London Irish), T Mailau (Stade Montois), T Filise (Cardiff Blues), J Tu'ineau (Montpellier-Herault), L Lokotui (Gloucester Rugby), J Afu (Kamaishi), S Timani (Scarlets), S Fifita (Sila Pelu'ua), H T-Pole (Northland), S Mafi (Leicester Tigers), P Kaho (Canberra Vikings), S Vaiomounga (CS Vienne), V Ma'afu (North Harbour), N Latu (Green Rockets), U Fono (Tarbes)

HEAD COACH: M 'Otai

10 November, Stadio Mario Rigamonti, Brescia, Italy 28 (2G 1T 3PG) Tonga 23 (2G 3PG)

ITALY: A Masi (London Wasps); T Iannone (Treviso), T Benvenuti (Treviso), A Sgarbi (Treviso), L McLean (Treviso); K Burton (Treviso), T Botes (Treviso); A lo Cicero (Racing Métro), L Ghiraldini (Treviso), L Cittadini (Treviso), Q Geldenhuys (Zebre), J Furno (RC Narbonne), A Zanni (Treviso), R Barbieri (Treviso), S Parisse (Stade Français)(captain)

SUBSTITUTIONS: M-L Castrogiovanni (Leicester Tigers) & A Pavanello (Treviso) for Cittadini & Geldenhuys (62 mins); S Favaro (Treviso) for Zanni (64 mins); D Giazzon (Zebre), A de Marchi (Treviso) & E Gori (Treviso) for Ghiraldini, Lo Cicero & Botes (71 mins)

SCORERS: *Tries:* Cittadini, Ghiraldini, Penalty try *Conversions*: Burton (2) *Penalty Goals:* Burton (3)

TONGA: Lilo; F Vainikolo, Hufanga, Piukata, Helu; 'Apikotoa, Moa (captain); Taumalolo, E Taione, 'Aulika, J Tu'ineau, Lokotui, Mafi, Vaiomounga, Ma'afu

SUBSTITUTIONS: Kaho & Mailau for Vaiomounga & 'Aulika (62 mins); Fatafehi for Piukala (64 mins); Iongi & Tonga'uiha for Hufanga & Taumalolo (72 mins); T-Pole & Fisilau for Lokotui & 'Apikotoa (76 mins); Ma'asi for Kaho (79 mins)

SCORERS: *Tries:* Taumalolo, F Vainikolo *Conversions*: 'Apikotoa (2) *Penalty Goals:* 'Apikotoa (3)

REFEREE: GM Garner (England)

24 November, Pittodrie Stadium, Aberdeen, Scotland 15 (5PG) Tonga 21 (1G 1T 3PG)

SCOTLAND: SW Hogg (Glasgow Warriors); SF Lamont (Glasgow Warriors), MB Evans (Castres Olympique), MCM Scott (Edinburgh), TJW Visser (Edinburgh); GD Laidlaw (Edinburgh), HB Pyrgos (Glasgow Warriors); K Traynor (Bristol Rugby), S Lawson (London Irish), EA Murray (Worcester Warriors), RJ Gray (Sale Sharks), AD Kellock (Glasgow Warriors), AK Strokosch (USA Perpignan), KDR Brown (Saracens)(captain), DK Denton (Edinburgh)

SUBSTITUTIONS: DWH Hall (Glasgow Warriors) & GDS Cross (Edinburgh) for S Lawson & Murray (51 mins); RGM Lawson (Newcastle Falcons) & JA Barclay (Glasgow Warriors) for Pyrgos & Denton (52 mins);

Murray for Cross (53 mins); NJ de Luca (Edinburgh) for Evans (59 mins); TA Heathcote (Bath Rugby) for Laidlaw (67 mins)

SCORER: *Penalty Goals:* Laidlaw (5)

TONGA: Lilo; F Vainikolo, Hufanga, Piukala, Helu; 'Apikotoa, Moa (captain); Taumalolo, E Taione, 'Aulika, J Tu'ineau, Lokotui, T-Pole, Latu, Ma'afu

SUBSTITUTIONS: Mailau for 'Aulika (45 mins); Mafi for T-Pole (51 mins); Fatafehi for Hufanga (67 mins); Ma'asi for Taione (70 mins); Iongi & Timani for Helu & Tu'ineau (75 mins)

SCORERS: *Tries:* Lokotui, F Vainikolo *Conversion:* 'Apikotoa *Penalty Goals:* Apikotoa (3)

REFEREE: M Raynal (France)

ENGLAND TO SOUTH AMERICA 2013

TOUR PARTY

FULL BACKS: MN Brown (Harlequins), BJ Foden (Northampton Saints), DAV Goode (Saracens)

THREEQUARTERS: MXG Yarde (London Irish), C Wade (London Wasps), D Strettle (Saracens), JJ May (Gloucester Rugby), WWF Twelvetrees (Gloucester Rugby), J Tomkins (Saracens), LD Burrell (Northampton Saints), KO Eastmond (Bath Rugby), JBA Joseph (London Irish)

HALF BACKS: LAW Dickson (Northampton Saints), REP Wigglesworth (Saracens), FS Burns (Gloucester Rugby), SJ Myler (Northampton Saints)

FORWARDS: DJ Paice (London Irish), RW Webber (Bath Rugby), RF Buchanan (Harlequins), DG Wilson (Bath Rugby), AR Corbisiero (London Irish), PPL Doran-Jones (Northampton Saints), JWG Marler (Harlequins), HM Thomas (Sale Sharks), JO Launchbury (London Wasps), CL Lawes (Northampton Saints), DMJ Attwood (Bath Rugby), KJ Myall (Sale Sharks), TA Johnson (Exeter Chiefs), MB Kvesic (Worcester Warriors), TA Wood (Northampton Saints), BJ Morgan (Gloucester Rugby), VML Vunipola (London Wasps)

HEAD COACH: SW Lancaster

2 June, Estadio Charrua, Montevideo, CONSUR XV 21 (3G) England 41 (3G 4T)

CONSUR XV: T Carrio (Argentina); B Agulla (Argentina), F Sansot (Argentina), JP Socino (Argentina), L Leivas (Uruguay); B Madero (Argentina), T Cubelli (Argentina)(captain); B Postiglioni (Argentina), A Avalos (Uruguay), M Sagario (Uruguay), C Fruttero (Argentina), P Huetes (Chile), T de la Vega (Argentina), JO Desio (Argentina), A Ahuali de Chazal (Argentina)

SUBSTITUTIONS: N Klappenvach (Uruguay), A Corral (Uruguay) & O Duran (Uruguay) for Postiglioni, Avalos & Sagario (49 mins); Sagario for Huetes (temp 53–63 mins); Duque Moises (Brazil) for Sansot (61 mins); D Magno (Uruguay) for Fruttero (63 mins); J Gaminara (Uruguay) for Ahuali de Chazal (65 mins); S Gibernau (Uruguay) for Leivas (67 mins); A Ormaechea (Uruguay) for Cubelli (70 mins)

SCORERS: *Tries*: Penalty try, Sansot, Magno *Conversions*: Madero (3)

ENGLAND: Foden; Strettle, Burrell, Eastmond, May; Myler, Wigglesworth; Marler, Paice, Thomas, Lawes, Myall, Wood (captain), Johnson, B Vunipola

SUBSTITUTIONS: Buchanan, Doran-Jones & Kvesic for Paice, Thomas & Wood (49 mins); Dickson for Wigglesworth (51 mins); Joseph & Attwood for Eastmond & Lawes (60 mins); Corbisiero for Marler (65 mins); Marler for V Vunipola (73 mins)

SCORERS: *Tries*: Foden (2), V Vunipola (3), Wood, Doran-Jones *Conversions:* Myler (3)

REFEREE: J Montes (Uruguay)

8 June, Estadio Padre Martearena, Salta, Argentina 3 (1PG) England 32 (3G 1T 2PG)

ARGENTINA: M Bustos Moyano (Montpellier-Herault); M Orlando (Huirapuca), GP Tiesi (unattached), F Contepomi (Stade Français)(captain), M Montero (Pucura); B Urdapilleta (Oyonnax), M Landajo (CA San Isidro); P Henn (CA Brive), M Garcia Veiga (Buenos Aires C & RC), M Bustos (Montpellier-Herault), E Lozada (SU Agen), M Galarza (Universitea La Plata), JF Cabello (unattached), B Macome (Tucuman), T Leonardi (Southern Kings)

SUBSTITUTIONS: G Roan (Cavalieri Prato) for Henn (51 mins); M Guidone (La Plata) for Garcia Veiga (55 mins); G Ascarate (RC Carcassone) & B Agulla (SU Agen) for Urdapilleta & M Orlando (57 mins); T Vallejos (unattached) for Lozada (61 mins); FT Gomez Kodela (Biarritz Olympique) for Bustos (68 mins); M Vergallo (Southern Kings) for Landajo (69 mins); T de la Vega (CUBA) for Cabello (74 mins)

SCORER: *Penalty Goal:* Bustos Moyano

ENGLAND: Brown; Wade, Joseph, Twelvetrees, Strettle; Burns, Dickson; Marler, Webber, Wilson, Launchbury, Attwood, Wood (captain), Kvesic, Morgan

SUBSTITUTIONS: Wigglesworth & Lawes for Dickson & Attwood (54 mins); Eastmond for Joseph (67

mins); Paice, Foden & V Vunipola for Webber, Brown & Morgan (69 mins); Doran-Jones for Wilson (74 mins); Thomas for Marler (78 mins)

SCORERS: *Tries*: Strettle, Twelvetrees, Morgan, V Vunipola *Conversions:* Burns (3) *Penalty Goals*: Burns (2)

REFEREE: C Pollock (New Zealand)

15 June, Velez Sarsfield, Buenos Aires, Argentina 26 (2G 4PG) England 51 (5G 2T 2PG)

ARGENTINA: M Bustos Moyano (Montpellier-Herault); B Agulla (SU Agen), G Tiesi (unattached), G Ascarate (RC Carcasonne), M Montero (Pucura); F Contepomi (Stade Français)(captain), N Vergallo (Southern Kings); G Roan (Cavalieri Prato), M Garcia Veiga (Buenos Aires C & RC), M Bustos (Montpellier-Herault), JF Cabello (unattached), M Galarza (Universitea La Plata), R Baez (Liceo), B Macome (Tucuman), T Leonardi (Southern Kings)

SUBSTITUTIONS: P Henn (CA Brive) for Roan (40 mins); E Lozada (SU Agen) for JF Cabello (51 mins); M Guidone (La Plata) for Henn (55 mins); T Cubelli (Belgrano Athletic) for Vergallo (temp 60–70 mins) & for Tiesi (77 mins); T de la Vega (CUBA) for Baez (58 mins); FT Gomez Kodela (Biarritz Olympique) for M Bustos (66 mins); M Orlando (Huirapuca) for Montero (67 mins), B Madero (San Isidro Club) for Ascarate (71 mins)

SCORERS: *Tries*: Montero, Leonardi *Conversions:* Bustos Moyano (2) *Penalty Goals:* Bustos Moyano (4)

ENGLAND: Brown; May, Joseph, Eastmond, Yarde; Burns, Dickson; Marler, Webber, Wilson, Launchbury, Attwood, Wood (captain), Kvesic, Morgan

SUBSTITUTIONS: Lawes for Attwood (55 mins); Wigglesworth for Dixon (55 mins); V Vunipola & Foden for Morgan & Brown (58 mins); Paice for Webber (61 mins); Doran-Jones & Myler for Marler & Burns (65 mins); Thomas for Wilson (76 mins)

SCORERS: *Tries*: Penalty tries (2), Burns, Webber, Yarde (2), Eastmond *Conversions*: Burns (4), Myler *Penalty Goals*: Burns (2)

REFEREE: N Owens (Wales)

SOUTH AFRICA QUADRANGULAR TOURNAMENT 2013

SCOTLAND

TOUR PARTY

FULL BACKS: GA Tonks (Edinburgh Rugby), PE Murchie (Glasgow Warriors)

THREEQUARTERS: SF Lamont (Glasgow Warriors), TJW Visser (Edinburgh Rugby), DM Taylor (Saracens), AJ Dunbar (Glasgow Warriors), MCM Scott (Edinburgh Rugby), TSF Seymour (Glasgow Warriors), P Horne (Glasgow Warriors)

HALF BACKS: GD Laidlaw (Edinburgh Rugby), HB Pyrgos (Glasgow Warriors), TA Heathcote (Bath Rugby), RJH Jackson (Glasgow Warriors)

FORWARDS: P MacArthur (Glasgow Warriors), S Lawrie (Edinburgh Rugby), S Lawson (Newcastle Falcons), *FJM Brown (Glasgow Warriors), EA Murray (Worcester Warriors), R Grant (Glasgow Warriors), *J Welsh (Glasgow Warriors), AG Dickinson (Edinburgh), GDS Cross (Edinburgh Rugby), MJ Low (Glasgow Warriors), *G Reid (Glasgow Warriors), JL Hamilton (Gloucester Rugby), GS Gilchrist (Edinburgh Rugby), AD Kellock (Glasgow Warriors), TJM Swinson (Glasgow Warriors), *RJ Harley (Glasgow Warriors), AF Strokosch (USA Perpignan), KDR Brown (Saracens), R Wilson (Glasgow Warriors), JW Beattie (Montpellier-Herault), DK Denton (Edinburgh Rugby)

* Replacement on tour

INTERIM HEAD COACH: S Johnson

SAMOA

TOUR PARTY

FULL BACK: J So'oialo (Wellington Norths)

THREEQUARTERS: Alesana Tuilagi (NTT Shining Arcs), S Sinoti (Zebre), A Leiua (Hurricanes), B Va'alu (Tokyo Gas), I Tuifua (Vigo RC), S Mapusua (Kubota Spears), R Lilomaiava (Vaiala), JW Leota (Sale Sharks), PB Williams (Stade Français), P Fa'asalele (Castres Olympique), GT Pisi (Northampton Saints)

HALF BACKS: T Pisi (Hurricanes), K Anufe (Marist, Auckland), JI Sua (Crusaders), J Polu (Exeter Chiefs), K Fotuali'i (Ospreys)

FORWARDS: WO Avei (Bordeaux-Begles), M Leiatua (North Harbour), TT Paulo (ASM Clermont Auvergne), S Aiono (Counties Manakau), CAI Johnston (Stade Toulousain), JVI Johnston (Harlequins), L Mulipola (Leicester Tigers), S Taulafo (London Wasps), F Lemalu (Stade Montois), D Leo (USA Perpignan), TAM Paulo (Cardiff Blues), JI Tekori (Castres Olympique), K Thompson (Canon Eagles), M Fa'asavalu (Harlequins), J Lam (Hurricanes), F Selesele (Moata'a), O Treviranus (London Irish), A Fa'osiliva (Bristol Rugby), T Tuifu'a (Newcastle Falcons)

HEAD COACH: S Betham

SOUTH AFRICA

TOUR PARTY

FULL BACK: WJ le Roux (Griquas)

THREEQUARTERS: BG Habana (Western Province), BA Basson (Blue Bulls), JJ Engelbrecht (Blue Bulls), J de Villiers (Western Province), JL Serfontein (Blue Bulls), RT Ebersohn (Cheetahs), JL de Jongh (Golden Lions)

HALF BACKS: M Steyn (Blue Bulls), PJ Lambie (Sharks), J Vermaak (Blue Bulls), R Pienaar (Ulster), P van Zyl (Cheetahs), L Schreuder (Western Province)

FORWARDS: JA Strauss (Cheetahs), MC Ralepelle (Blue Bulls), BW du Plessis (Sharks), T Mtawarira (Sharks), JN du Plessis (Sharks), CV Oosthuizen (Cheetahs), TN Nyakane (Cheetahs), E Etzebeth (Western Province), PJJ Kruger (Blue Bulls), PR van der Merwe (Blue Bulls), P-S du Toit (Sharks), F van der Merwe (Golden Lions), S Kolisi (Western Province), L-FP Louw (Bath Rugby), WS Alberts (Sharks), AF Botha (Blue Bulls), MC Coetzee (Sharks), PJ Spies (Blue Bulls)

HEAD COACH: H Meyer

ITALY

TOUR PARTY

FULL BACKS: A Masi (London Wasps), L McLean (Treviso)

THREEQUARTERS: G Venditti (Zebre), L Sarto (Zebre), T Iannone (Treviso), G Canale (Stade Rochelais), G Garcia (Zebre), L Morisi (Treviso), A Sgarbi (Treviso)

HALF BACKS: E Gori (Treviso), A Chillon (Zebre), T Botes (Treviso), L Orquera (Zebre), A di Bernardo (Treviso)

FORWARDS: L Ghiraldini (Treviso), D Giazzon (Zebre), A Manici (Zebre), M Aguero (Zebre), M-L Castrogiovanni (Leicester Tigers), L Cittadini (Treviso), A de Marchi (Treviso), M Rizzo (Treviso), V Bernabo (Treviso), M Bortolami (Zebre), L Cedaro (Stade Rochelais), J Furno (Narbonne), A Pavanello (Treviso), R Barbieri (Treviso), Mauro Bergamasco (Zebre), S Parisse (Stade Français), M Vosawai (Treviso), A Zanni (Treviso)

HEAD COACH: J Brunel

8 June, Kings Park Stadium, Durban, Samoa 27 (3G 2G) Scotland 17 (1T 4PG)

SAMOA: J So'oialo; Leiua, P Williams (captain), Leota, Alesana Tuilagi; T Pisi, Sua; Mulipola, Avei, C Johnston, TAM Paulo, Leo, Treviranus, J Lam, Tu'ifua

SUBSTITUTIONS: Lemalu, J Johnston & Leiataua for Leo, C Johnston & Avei (54 mins); Mapusua for Leota (73 mins); Taulafo for Mulipola (73 mins); Va'alu for Leiua (79 mins)

SCORERS: *Tries:* So'oialo, Tuilagi (2) *Conversions*: So'oialo (3) *Penalty Goals:* So'oialo (2)

SCOTLAND: Tonks; S Lamont, Dunbar, Scott, Visser; Heathcote, Laidlaw; Dickinson, MacArthur, Murray, Gilchrist, Kellock, Strokosch, K Brown (captain), Beattie

SUBSTITUTIONS: Lawrie for MacArthur (11 mins); Wilson for Brown (40 mins); Cross for Murray (44 mins); Horne for Heathcote (59 mins); Low & Hamilton for Dickinson & Kellock (66 mins); Taylor & Pyrgos for Visser & Laidlaw (69 mins)
SCORERS: *Try*: S Lamont *Penalty Goals:* Laidlaw (4)
REFEREE: J Lacey (Ireland)

8 June, Kings Park, Durban, South Africa 44 (5G 3PG) Italy 10 (1G 1PG)

SOUTH AFRICA: Le Roux; Habana, Engelbrecht, De Villiers (captain), Basson; M Steyn, Vermaak; Mtawarira, Strauss, J du Plessis, Etzebeth, Kruger, Louw, A Botha, Spies
SUBSTITUTIONS: Coetzee for Louw (temp 55–65 mins) & for Botha (67 mins); PR van der Merwe for Kruger (59 mins); Pienaar for Vermaak (60 mins); Oosthuizen for J du Plessis (67 mins); Ralepelle & Serfontein for A Strauss & Habana (72 mins); Nyakane for Mtawarira (74 mins); Lambie for M Steyn (76 mins)
SCORERS: *Tries*: A Strauss, Engelbrecht, Habana, De Villiers, Basson *Conversions:* M Steyn (4), Lambie *Penalty Goals:* Lambie (3)
ITALY: Masi; Venditti, Morisi, Sgarbi, McLean; Di Bernardo, Gori; De Marchi, Ghiraldini, Cittadini, A Pavanello, Bortolami, Zanni, Barbieri, Parisse (captain)
SUBSTITUTIONS: Aguero & Giazzon for De Marchi & Ghiraldini (45 mins); Castrogiovanni & Furno for Cittadini & Barbieri (49 mins); Botes for Gori (60 mins); Bernabo for Bortolami (66 mins); Iannone for Morisi (68 mins); Orquera for Di Bernardo (77 mins)
SCORERS: *Try*: Sgarbi *Conversion:* Di Bernardo *Penalty Goal*: Di Bernardo
REFEREE: P Gauzere (France)

15 June, Mbombela Stadium, Nelspruit, Italy 10 (1G 1PG) Samoa 39 (4G 1T 2PG)

ITALY: Masi; Venditti, Canale, Garcia, Iannone; Orquera, Gori; De Marchi, Ghiraldini, Castrogiovanni, Bernabo, Bortolomi, Zanni, Ma Bergamasco, Parisse (captain)
SUBSTITUTIONS: Manici for Ghiraldini (25 mins); Di Bernado for Orquera (43 mins); McLean, Rizzo & Pavanallo for Iannone, De Marchi & Bortolami (54 mins); Cittadini & Vosawai for Castrogiovanni & Ma Bergamasco (59 mins); Botes for Gori (60 mins)
SCORERS: *Try*: Penalty try *Conversion:* Di Bernado *Penalty Goal:* Orquera
SAMOA: Va'alu; Leiua, P Williams (captain), Leota, Alesana Tuilagi; Pisi, Sua; Taulafo, Avei, C Johnston, TAM Paulo, Leo, Treviranus, J Lam, Tu'ifua
SUBSTITUTIONS: J Johnston for C Johnston (40 mins); Thompson for Leo (55 mins); Anufe & Faaselele for T Pisi & Lam (57 mins); Mulipola for Taulafo (60 mins); Polu for Sua (64 mins); TT Paulo for Avei (71 mins); Mapusua for Leota (72 mins)
SCORERS: *Tries*: P Williams, Leiua, Leota, Tu'ifua, Va'alu *Conversions:* P Williams (3), Anufe *Penalty Goals*: P Williams (2)
REFEREE: C Joubert (South Africa)

15 June, Mbombela Stadium, Nelspruit, South Africa 30 (3G 3PG) Scotland 17 (2G 1PG)

SOUTH AFRICA: Le Roux; Habana, Engelbrecht, De Villiers (captain), Basson; M Steyn, Pienaar; Mtawarira, Strauss, J du Plessis, Etzebeth, Kruger, Coetzee, A Botha, Spies
SUBSTITUTIONS: Kolisi for A Botha (4 mins); BW du Plessis, Ooosthuizen & PR van der Merwe for Strauss, Mtawarira & Etzebeth (66 mins); Van Zyl for Pienaar (68 mins); Lambie & Serfontein for M Steyn & Engelbrecht (69 mins); Nyakane for J du Plessis (76 mins)
SCORERS: *Tries*: Penalty try, Engelbrecht, Serfontein *Conversions:* M Steyn (2), Lambie *Penalty Goals*: M Steyn (2), Lambie
SCOTLAND: Murchie; Seymour, Dunbar, Scott, S Lamont; Jackson, Laidlaw (captain); Dickinson, Lawson, Murray, Swinson, Hamilton, Strokosch, Wilson, Beattie
SUBSTITUTIONS: Horne for Jackson (32 mins); Denton for Wilson (37 mins); Pyrgos for Horne (43 mins); Kellock for Hamilton (61 mins); Welsh for Dickinson (64 mins); Taylor for Murchie (78 mins)
SCORERS: *Tries*: Scott, Dunbar *Conversions:* Laidlaw (2) *Penalty Goal*: Laidlaw
REFEREE: R Poite (France)

22 June, Loftus Versveld, Pretoria, Italy 29 (2G 5PG) Scotland 30 (3G 3PG)

ITALY: Masi; Sarto, Morisi, Sgarbi, Venditti; Di Bernardo, Botes; Aguero, Giazzon, Castrogiovanni, Cedaro, Bortolomi, Furno, Barbieri, Parisse (captain)
SUBSTITUTIONS: Ghiraldini & De Marchi for Giazzon & Aguero (47 mins); Cittadini & Zanni for Castrogiovanni

& Bortolami (48 mins); Canale & Pavanello for Morisi & Cedaro (52 mins); McLean for Sarto (60 mins); Chillon for Botes (69 mins)

SCORERS: *Tries*: Sarto, Penalty try *Conversions:* Di Bernardo (2) *Penalty Goals:* Di Bernardo (5)

SCOTLAND: Murchie; Seymour, Dunbar, Scott, S Lamont; Heathcote, Laidlaw (captain); Dickinson, Lawson, Murray, Swinson, Kellock, Denton, Strokosch, Beattie

SUBSTITUTIONS: Visser for Seymour (43 mins); Pyrgos for Heathcote (48 mins); Low for Dickinson (49 mins); Taylor & Gilchrist for Murchie & Swinson (58 mins); Harley for Beattie (60 mins); Welsh & F Brown for Low & S Lawson (72 mins)

SCORERS: *Tries*: Scott, S Lamont, Strokosch *Conversions*: Laidlaw (3) *Penalty Goals*: Laidlaw (3)

REFEREE: L Hodges (Wales)

22 June, Loftus Versveld, Pretoria, South Africa 56 (5G 3T 2PG) Samoa 23 (2G 3PG)

SOUTH AFRICA: Le Roux; Habana, Engelbrecht, De Villiers (captain), Basson; M Steyn, Pienaar; Mtawarira, Strauss, J du Plessis, Etzebeth, PR van der Merwe, Kouw, Alberts, Spies

SUBSTITUTIONS: Kolisi for Spies (40 mins); Kruger for Kolisi (temp 47– 52 mins); Oosthuizen for Mtawarira (56 mins); B du Plessis for Strauss (59 mins); Van Zyl & Nyakane for Pienaar & J du Plessis (66 mins); Serfontein & Kruger for De Villiers & PR van der Merwe (71 mins)

SCORERS: *Tries:* Habana (2), Louw (2), Engelbrecht, Basson, M Steyn, Nyakane *Conversions*: M Steyn (3), Lambie (2) *Penalty Goals*: M Steyn (2)

SAMOA: J So'oialo; Leiua, P Williams (captain), Leota, Alesana Tuilagi; T Pisi, Sua; Taulafo, Avei, Mulipola, TAM Paulo, Leo, Treviranus, J Lam, Tu'ifua

SUBSTITUTIONS: Mapusua for Leota (temp 21–26 mins); TT Paulo & Thompson for Avei & TAM Paulo (53 mins); C Johnston for Taulafo (56 mins); Va'alu for Leiua (57 mins); Mapusua for So'oialo (59 mins); Polu for Sua (65 mins); J Johnston & Faosiliva for Mulipola & Treviranus (66 mins)

SCORERS: *Tries:* TAM Paulo, Polu *Conversions*: So'oialo, Williams *Penalty Goals:* So'oialo (3)

RED CARD: Alesana Tuilagi (57 mins)

REFEREE: P Gauzere (France)

WALES TO JAPAN 2013

TOUR PARTY

FULL BACKS: Liam B Williams (Scarlets), S Shingler (London Irish)

THREEQUARTERS: TWJ Prydie (Dragons), HR Robinson (Cardiff Blues), OR Williams (Cardiff Blues), JP Spratt (Ospreys), D Howells (Ospreys), A Warren (Scarlets)

HALF BACKS: Lloyd D Williams (Cardiff Blues), TD Knoyle (Scarlets), DR Biggar (Ospreys), MR Patchell (Cardiff Blues)

FORWARDS: E Phillips (Scarlets), SJ Baldwin (Ospreys), RJ Bevington (Ospreys), IAR Gill (Saracens), SA Andrews (Cardiff Blues), C Mitchell (Exeter Chiefs), Rhodri P Jones (Scarlets), BS Davies (Cardiff Blues), L Reed (Cardiff Blues), A Coombs (Dragons), J King (Ospreys), JR Navidi (Cardiff Blues), RJ McCusker (Scarlets), D Baker (Ospreys), A Pretorius (Cardiff Blues)

INTERIM HEAD COACH: RC McBryde

8 June, Hanazono Field, Osaka, Japan 18 (1G 1T 2PG) Wales 22 (1G 5PG)

JAPAN: A Goromaru (Yamaha Jubilo); Y Fujita (Waseda University), M Sa'u (Yamaha Jubilo), C Wing (Kobelco Steelers), K Fukuoka (Tsukuba University); H Tatekawa (Kubota Spears), F Tanaka (Highlanders); M Mikami (Toshiba Brave Lupus), S Horie (Melbourne Rebels), H Yamashita (Kobelco Steelers), H Ono (Toshiba Brave Lupus), S Ito (Kobelco Steelers), H Tui (Suntory Sungoliath), M Broadhurst (Ricoh Black Rams), T Kikutani (Toyota Verblitz)(captain)

SUBSTITUTIONS: T Kizu (Kobelco Steelers) for Horie (32 mins); K Hatakeyama (Suntory Sungoliath) for Yamashita (64 mins); A Hiwasa (Suntory Sungoliath) for Tanaka (66 mins); Y Tamura (NEC Green Rockets) for Wing (70 mins); R Yasui (Kobelco Steelers) for Tui (72 mins); H Onozawa (Suntory Sungoliath) for Fukuoka (79 mins); T Kitagawa (Panasonic Wild Knights) for Ono (80 mins)

SCORERS: *Tries*: Broadhurst, Fujita *Conversion*: Goromaru *Penalty Goals*: Goromaru (2)

WALES: LB Williams; H Robinson, O Williams, Spratt, Howells; Biggar, LD Williams; Bevington, E Phillips, Andrews, B Davies (captain), Reed, Coombs, King, McCusker

SUBSTITUTIONS: Pretorius & Gill for Coombs & Bevington (51 mins); Knoyle & Baker for LD Williams & McCusker (60 mins); Patchell for Biggar (64 mins)

SCORERS: *Try*: H Robinson *Conversion*: Biggar *Penalty Goals:* Biggar (4), Patchell

REFEREE: L Van der Merwe (South Africa)

15 June, Prince Chichibu Memorial Stadium, Tokyo, Japan 23 (2G 3PG) Wales 8 (1T 1PG)

JAPAN: A Goromaru (Yamaha Jubilo); T Hirose (Toshiba Brave Lupus)(captain), M Sa'u (Yamaha Jubilo), C Wing (Kobelco Steelers), K Fukuoka (Tsukuba University); H Tatekawa (Kubota Spears), F Tanaka (Highlanders); M Mikami (Toshiba Brave Lupus), S Horie (Melbourne Rebels), H Yamashita (Kobelco Steelers), H Ono (Toshiba Brave Lupus), S Ito (Kobelco Steelers), H Tui (Suntory Sungoliath), M Broadhurst (Ricoh Black Rams), T Kikutani (Toyota Verblitz)

SUBSTITUTIONS: K Hatakeyama (Suntory Sungoliath) & S Makabe (Suntory Sungoliath) for Yamashita & Ito (45 mins); A Hiwasa (Suntory Sungoliath) for Tanaka (67 mins); Y Nagae (Ricoh Black Rams) & Y Tamura (NEC Green Rockets) for Mikami & Wing (69 mins); J Ives (Panasonic Wild Knights) for Ono (74 mins); Y Fujita (Waseda University) & T Kizu (Kobelco Steelers) for Fukuoka & Tui (79 mins)

SCORERS: *Tries*: Wing, Broadhurst *Conversions*: Goromaru (2) *Penalty Goals*: Goromaru (3)

WALES: LB Williams; H Robinson, O Williams, Spratt, Prydie; Biggar, LD Williams; Gill, Phillips, Andrews, B Davies (captain), Reed, King, Navidi, Pretorius

SUBSTITUTIONS: Patchell for O Williams (23 mins); Knoyle & Coombs for LD Williams & Reed (50 mins); Howells for LB Williams (53 mins); Mitchell & Rhodri Jones for Andrews & Gill (57 mins); Baker for Navidi (63 mins); Baldwin for Phillips (78 mins)

SCORERS: *Try* Prydie *Penalty Goal*: Biggar

REFEREE: G Garner (England)

FRANCE TO NEW ZEALAND 2013

TOUR PARTY

FULL BACK: B Dulin (Castres Olympique)

THREEQUARTERS: Y Huget (Stade Toulousain), A Plante (USA Perpignan), M Médard (Stade Toulousain), N Nakaitaci (ASM Clermont Auvergne), M Bastareaud (RC Toulon), G Fickou (Stade Toulousain), W Fofana (ASM Clermont Auvergne), F Fritz (Stade Toulousain), M Mermoz (RC Toulon), M Andreu (Castres Olympique)

HALF BACKS: M Machenaud (Racing Métro), J-M Doussain (Stade Toulousain), F Michalak (RC Toulon), C Lopez (Bordeaux-Begles), R Talès (Castres Olympique)

FORWARDS: G Guirado (USA Perpignan), B Kayser (ASM Clermont-Auvergne), D Szarzewski (Racing Métro), E Ben Arous (Racing Métro), V Debaty (ASM Clermont Auvergne), L Ducalcon (Racing Métro), D Kotze (ASM Clermont Auvergne), N Mas (USA Perpignan), A Flanquart (Stade Français), Y Maestri (Stade Toulousain), C Samson (Castres Olympique), S Vahaamahina (USA Perpignan), Y Nyanga (Stade Toulousain), F Ouedraogo (Montpellier-Herault), *D Chouly (ASM Clermont Auvergne), T Dusautoir (Stade Toulousain), B le Roux (Racing Métro), A Claassen (Castres Olympique), L Picamoles (Stade Toulousain)

* Replacement on tour

HEAD COACH: P Saint-André

8 June, Eden Park, Auckland, New Zealand 23 (2G 3PG) France 13 (1G 2PG)

NEW ZEALAND: IJA Dagg (Hawke's Bay); BR Smith (Otago), CG Smith (Wellington), MA Nonu (Wellington), SJ Savea (Wellington); AW Cruden (Manawatu), AL Smith (Manawatu); WWV Crockett (Canterbury), DS Coles (Wellington), OT Franks (Canterbury), L Romano (Canterbury), BA Retallick (Bay of Plenty), LJ Messam (Waikato), SJ Cane (Bay of Plenty), KJ Reid (Canterbury)(captain)

SUBSTITUTIONS: KF Mealamu (Auckland) for Coles (55 mins); BJ Franks (Hawke's Bay) for OT Franks (60 mins); TNJ Kerr-Barlow (Waikato) for AL Smith (65 mins); RMN Ranger (Northland) for Dagg (66 mins); BTP Afeaki (North Harbour) & BJ Barrett (Taranaki) for Crockett & Cruden (74 mins)

SCORERS: *Tries*: AL Smith, Cane *Conversions:* Cruden (2) *Penalty Goals:* Cruden (3)

FRANCE: Huget; Plante, Fritz, Fofana, Médard; Lopez, Machenaud; Domingo, Szarzewski, Vahaamahina, Maestri, Dusautoir (captain), Ouedraogo, Picamoles

SUBSTITUTIONS: Nyanga for Ouedraogo (36 mins); Doussain for Machenaud (42 mins); Kotze & Debaty for Domingo & Ducalcon (51 mins); Guirado for Szarzewski (57 mins); Michalak for Lopez (65 mins); Mermoz for Fritz (69 mins); Flanquart for Maestri (70 mins)

SCORERS: *Try*: Fofana *Conversion*: Machenaud *Penalty Goals*: Machenaud, Lopez

REFEREE: W Barnes (England)

11 June, North Harbour Stadium, Albany, Blues 15 (1G 1T 1PG) France XV 38 (3G 1T 4PG)

BLUES SCORERS: *Tries* J Parsons, G Moala *Conversion*: M McKenzie *Penalty Goal:* B Kerr

FRANCE XV SCORERS: *Tries:* Fickou, Nakaitaci (2), Kayser *Conversions*: Doussain (3) *Penalty Goals:* Doussain (4)

15 June, AMI Stadium, Addington, Christchurch, New Zealand 30 (3G 3PG) France 0

NEW ZEALAND: IJA Dagg (Hawke's Bay); BR Smith (Otago), CG Smith (Wellington), MA Nonu (Wellington), SJ Savea (Wellington); AW Cruden (Manawatu), AL Smith (Manawatu); WWV Crockett (Canterbury), DS Coles (Wellington), OT Franks (Canterbury), L Romano (Canterbury), SL Whitelock (Canterbury), LJ Messam (Waikato), SJ Cane (Bay of Plenty), KJ Reid (Canterbury)(captain)

SUBSTITUTIONS: AK Hore (Taranaki) for Coles (58 mins); RMN Ranger (Northland) & PAT Weepu (Auckland) for Savea & AL Smith (59 mins); TD Woodcock (North Harbour) & VVJ Vito (Wellington) for Crockett & Messam (62 mins); JI Thrush (Wellington) & BJ Franks (Hawke's Bay) for Whitelock & OT Franks (68 mins); BJ Barrett (Taranaki) for BR Smith (75 mins)

SCORERS: *Tries*: Savea, BR Smith, Barrett *Conversions:* Cruden (3) *Penalty Goals*: Cruden (3)

FRANCE: Médard; Plante, Fritz, Fofana, Huget; Michalak, Machenaud; Domingo, Szarzewski, Mas, Samson, Maestri, Dusautoir (captain), Le Roux, Picamoles

SUBSTITUTIONS: Dulin for Médard (40 mins); Kayser for Szarzewski (50 mins); Nyanga for Picamoles (53 mins); Bastareaud for Fritz (59 mins); Talès & Vahaamahina for Machenaud & Samson (64 mins); Debaty & Ducalcon for Domingo & Mas (67 mins)

REFEREE: AC Rolland (Ireland)

22 June, Yarrow Stadium, New Plymouth, New Zealand 24 (1G 1T 4PG) France 9 (2PG 1DG)

NEW ZEALAND: IJA Dagg (Hawke's Bay); BR Smith (Otago), CG Smith (Wellington), MA Nonu (Wellington), RMN Ranger (Northland); DW Carter (Canterbury), PAT Weepu (Auckland); WWV Crockett (Canterbury), AK Hore (Taranaki), OT Franks (Canterbury), L Romano (Canterbury), SL Whitelock (Canterbury), VVJ Vito (Wellington), SJ Cane (Bay of Plenty), KJ Reid (Canterbury)(captain)

SUBSTITUTIONS: TNJ Kerr-Barlow (Waikato) & TD Woodock (North Harbour) for Weepu & Crockett (41 mins); KF Mealamu (Auckland) for Hore (63 mins); S Luatua (Auckland) for Vito (70 mins); C Piutau (Auckland) & M Todd (Canterbury) for Ranger & Cane (72 mins); BJ Barrett (Taranaki) for Nonu (77 mins)

SCORERS: *Tries*: BR Smith, Barrett *Conversion*: Carter *Penalty Goals*: Carter (4)

FRANCE: Dulin; Andreu, Fritz, Fofana, Huget; Talès, Doussain; Domingo, Kayser, Mas, Flanquart, Maestri, Dusautoir (captain), Claassen, Chouly

SUBSTITUTIONS: Bastareaud for Huget (temp 3–9 mins) & for Fritz (63 mins); Machenaud & Vahaamahina for Doussain & Flanquart (58 mins); Ben Arous, Szarzewski & Ducalcon for Domingo, Kayser & Mas (64 mins); Lopez & Le Roux for Talès & Claassen (72 mins)

SCORERS: *Penalty Goals:* Doussain (2) *Drop Goal*: Fritz

REFEREE: N Owens (Wales)

IRELAND TO NORTH AMERICA 2013

TOUR PARTY

FULL BACKS: R Henshaw (Connacht), F Jones (Munster)

THREEQUARTERS: FL McFadden (Leinster), AD Trimble (Ulster), SR Zebo (Munster), DM Cave (Ulster), S Olding (Ulster), J Downey (Munster)

HALF BACKS: IJ Boss (Leinster), P Marshall (Ulster), K Marmion (Connacht), DPLJ Jackson (Ulster), I Madigan (Leinster)

FORWARDS: SM Cronin (Leinster), CR Strauss (Leinster), M Sherry (Munster), TG Court (Ulster), JR Hagan (London Irish), DJ Fitzpatrick (Ulster), MR Ross (Leinster), D Kilcoyne (Munster), MP McCarthy (Connacht), D Toner (Leintser), DM Tuohy (Ulster), P O'Mahony (Munster), WI Henderson (Ulster), K McLaughlin (Leinster), CG Henry (Ulster), T O'Donnell (Munster)

INTERIM HEAD COACH: L Kiss

8 June, BBVA Compass Stadium, Houston, USA 12 (4PG) Ireland 15 (5PG)

USA: C Wyles (Saracens); L Hume (Old Blue), S Kelly (University of California), A Suniula (Chicago Griffins), T Ngwenya (Biarritz Olympique); T L'Estrange (New York AC), M Petri (New York AC); S Pittman (Trinity College, Dublin), C Biller (Golden Gate, San Francisco), E Fry (London Scottish), B Doyle (New York AC), L Stanfill (Vicenza), S Manoa (Northampton Saints), S LaValla (Stade Français), T Clever (NTT Shining Arcs)(captain)

SUBSTITUTIONS: P Dahl (Belmont Shore) for Doyle (25 mins); J Paterson (Glendale Raptors) for Hume (61 mins)

SCORER: *Penalty Goals*: Wyles (4)

IRELAND: Henshaw; McFadden, Cave, Olding, Zebo; Madigan, Boss; Kilcoyne, Strauss, Ross, McCarthy, Toner, Henderson, Henry, O'Mahony (captain)

MAJOR TOURS

SUBSTITUTIONS: Jones for McFadden (temp 35–40 mins); O'Donnell for Henry (temp 51–58 mins); Hagan for Ross (54 mins); Henry & Court for O'Donnell & Kilcoyne (58 mins); Marshall for Boss (71 mins); Jones for Zebo (74 mins); Sherry, O'Donnell & Tuohy for Strauss, Henderson & McCarthy (76 mins)
SCORER: *Penalty Goals*: Madigan (5)
REFEREE: F Pastrana (Argentina)

15 June, BMO Stadium, Toronto, Canada 14 (1T 3PG) Ireland 40 (5G 1T)

CANADA: C Braid (Doncaster Knights); J Pritchard (Bedford Blues); M Evans (Cornish Pirates), C Hearn (Castaway Wanderers), H Jones (Capilano), T Paris (SU Agen); N Hirayama (University of Victoria), P Mack (University of Victoria); H Buydens (Saskatoon Wild Oats), R Barkwill (Niagara Wasps), J Marshall (Stade Rochelais), J Sinclair (London Irish), T Hotson (London Scottish), T Ardron (James Bay AA), J Moonlight (James Bay AA), A Carpenter (Cornish Pirates)(captain)
SUBSTITUTIONS: R Hamilton (Capilano) for Barkwill (53 mins); S White (James Bay AA) for Mack (54 mins); N Dala (Castaway Wanderers) & P Parfrey (Swilers) for Moonlight & Braid (61 mins); J Phelan (Ste-Anne-de-Bellevue) for Hotson (69 mins); A Tiedemann (Castaway Wanderers) & D Wooldridge (Lindsay) for Buydens & Marshall (72 mins); N Blevins (Calgary Hornets) for Carpenter (79 mins)
SCORERS: *Try*: Ardron *Penalty Goals:* Pritchard (3)
IRELAND: F Jones; McFadden, Cave, Downey, Trimble; Madigan, Boss; Court, Strauss, Ross, Tuohy, Toner, McLaughlin, O'Donnell, O'Mahony (captain)
SUBSTITUTIONS: Marshall for Boss (57 mins); Jackson & Fitzpatrick for Madigan & Ross (61 mins); Cronin & Kiloyne for Strauss & Court (65 mins); McCarthy & Henry for Tuohy & McLaughlin (71 mins); Henshaw for Cave (72 mins)
SCORERS: *Tries:* McFadden (3), Trimble, Cave, O'Donnell *Conversions:* Madigan 4, Jackson
REFEREE: L Hodges (Wales)

Getty Images

Australia line up at the Millennium Stadium before their Test against Wales.

The Combined Teams

GATLAND'S LIONS BREAK DROUGHT IN AUSTRALIA

Getty Images

The British & Irish Lions celebrate a first Test series victory since 1997 after beating Australia 2–1.

Greg Thomas caught up with Lions coach Warren Gatland to discuss his thoughts on the series win in Australia.

Mission accomplished! After 16 years of heartache and disappointment the 2013 British & Irish Lions triumphed in Australia to record just their 12th series victory in 125 years. New Zealand-born Wales coach Warren Gatland delivered expertly what he was hired to do: mould 37 players, from four different countries and playing styles, into a close-knit, united squad to defeat the Wallabies on home soil.

This was a talented, well-coached and determined group of young Lions that triumphed. Only 13 of the original squad had previous Lions experience. The opposition was a very capable Wallabies side that stood as the third best team in world rugby. Of course, as in past tours, injuries played a role in the momentum of the tour and 44 players donned the famous red shirt by the end.

A key factor for the Lions hierarchy in planning 2013 was continuity. The Lions had restored their ethos and had come so close to beating the Springboks in 2009 and they felt there was no use dusting off the proverbial drawing board. And with preparation time very limited the majority of the 2009 coaching and management team returned for the tour. A move that was instrumental in the success.

However, touring overseas once every four years is fraught with danger. Ten matches were played, including one in Hong Kong against the Barbarians on the way to Australia. The Lions suffered two defeats but importantly the Test series was won and that had always been the main objective. That said, the drama and excitement was immense with the series coming down to a third Test decider. The best Hollywood scriptwriters couldn't have penned a more suitable narrative that contained numerous sub-plots and twists.

Prior to leaving the UK were you confident in the squad you had selected?
"I knew it was quite inexperienced despite there being some great experience in the dozen or so former Lions on the trip. But I did some work prior to the squad selection and looked back at previous tours including the 1997 tour to South Africa. That was the last time the Lions had won a series and it was a similar situation with a lot of young but very talented players. Conversely the management was very experienced as we wanted continuity, especially given the very limited preparation time. Such a move meant we could hit the ground running and it allowed us to utilise the same tactical calls and a similar game plan. This meant those who had been on the tour in 2009 knew the score straight away and could assist in passing it on to the new tourists. We also knew what mistakes we had made in 2009, and we had the aim of not wanting to reinvent the wheel again. Sure we had to tweak a few things for Australia and its specific challenges, but having such experienced staff assisted greatly."

Did you feel under pressure as you left on tour?
"Absolutely, massive amount of pressure. The mandate I was given was to win the series. Full stop. We were conscious of the future of the Lions and what success would mean. We had come very close in 2009 but

close isn't good enough. I guess that is why some of the criticism we saw after the tour was very surprising. The way we played and the style of rugby we played was questioned for some reason. But that was not the mandate. It was to go and win. But not only did we win, we played some great rugby – can't please everyone it seems. Moving forward perhaps we should look at something different if that is what people want. Let's debate the style of play, quotas of players even – in terms of squad and match-day teams. I think a lot of people would jump up and down at such suggestions, but we need to be clear what the objectives are so the coaches can do what they are hired to do and what parameters are in place. The criticism was against the coaches and I guess me but not the players, which is fine, but if you want to win such challenging tours you have to be pragmatic."

Who set the game plan: you or the coaches as a collective?
"We developed the game plan as a group based on 2009 and the players we had at our disposal. What was pleasing was that all the players embraced what we were trying to do and how we wanted to play. This is never easy with four countries coming together. Naturally we had a starting platform I guess with the large Welsh contingent but you need that – you can't start totally from scratch in such a limited space of time. As coaches we basically provided a general structure and plan, and the players adapted it on the field. Our play evolved as the tour went on and we continually monitored and talked to the players about their form, how we were playing and what we needed to do to improve."

Was your worst fear a decider in Sydney?
"Deep down I always thought it would come down to the wire. The tour is challenging in that it is quite short, there is little preparation time and you try to keep harmony in the squad so players all feel part of the mix in terms of Test selection. We always said everyone would have a run in the first three games which is not ideal from a pure coaching position when you are trying to develop your strongest team and a game style. Then throw in injuries. The 2009 tour taught us that the lead-up matches were a challenge in that some teams were not very strong so judging form is not straightforward. We had only six matches before the first Test, including Hong Kong where we had to play the boys who had not been playing finals rugby the week before. As they were at the training camps this made sense but they got a jump on the other players in terms of game plan and conditioning. One big bonus was playing the Reds at Suncorp in Brisbane. It meant we had a winning run on the first Test venue. I felt we were on track at that point. We

then played extremely well against NSW in Sydney. Sure there was a hiccup against the Brumbies who fronted up. It was disappointing but we had to rest key players at that point due to some injury concerns."

Injuries were expected but the amount of injuries behind the scrum proved a real challenge?
"The squad had more forwards than backs as is usual due to the predicted physicality of the game and fact that you have more forwards on the field but the amount of back injuries was surprising. Just one of those things perhaps but it may indicate how the game is changing again. The week of the first Test we had the choice of risking some backs against the Brumbies or protecting them. The loss to the Brumbies was a consequence of our decision to protect them. Unfortunately we threw a team into the match that basically had little preparation and several new replacement players. It was a conscious decision as the Test was the priority."

One Test up and looking good in the second, what happened?
"Going 1–0 up was important for the squad and we won the first by a point and were lucky in many ways despite being the better team I thought. We took the lead after half an hour and never surrendered it but it got too close for my liking. We played well in the second Test also and were capable of winning it. We led at half-time and until the 75th minute when our defence buckled under huge pressure. Like the first Test it came down to a penalty kick but Leigh Halfpenny was not to blame for the loss – we were not clinical enough. We knew the Wallabies would come at us hard as it was their grand final. They had to win the match to stay alive. But we made too many errors and our game management at times was poor and that is what I talked about in the dressing room afterwards."

So 1–1 and it was time to recharge the batteries?
"We needed to freshen up after the second Test. We went to Noosa on the Sunshine Coast in Queensland for a few days. It was the right move and I would not do anything different. The pressure and hype the players had experienced was immense. Everywhere the players went there were fans dressed in red so Noosa was a nice rest mentally and physically. Arriving later in the week in Sydney was perfect. We also envisaged there would not be too many changes between the second and third Test teams so we could scale back the training – it was just a matter of tweaking the team because of injuries. So it was the ideal time to take a few days off."

Much has been said over the Brian O'Driscoll affair. How are you feeling now the tour is over?
"As I said we were given the responsibility to win a series. We picked a side that we thought capable of winning the last Test. We won the game. We selected a midfield of Jamie Roberts and Jonathan Davies, which to us was the midfield we thought would do the job that day. I still think about that decision as I know how it affected many people. I certainly am not sitting back and gloating and feeling vindicated as it was a very hard decision. I fully respect people who say I got it wrong – that is their opinion. From a rugby perspective I have no problem with that – after all that is what sport is all about. 'Geech' (Sir Ian McGeechan) told me it was a brave selection and one he wouldn't have made. What I do not accept is the suggestion that there was some sort of conspiracy and I did not appreciate the personal attacks based on this. In the long history of the Lions there have been many times when one country has dominated selection. Some people have very short memories. There were 10 Welsh starters but on the day they were Lions. All those people who criticised the selection missed the story. The story wasn't the team who started the game; the story was the team who ended it and there were 12 non-Welsh players. What happened in terms of selection takes nothing away from Brian O'Driscoll who played in two Tests and played a role in the series victory. Remember Paul O'Connell and Sam Warburton missed the third Test also and were very disappointed. I think the evolution of social media meant everyone had a view on the selection. Of course, we made other changes for the third Test but these were largely forgotten for some reason."

What were you thinking when Jamie Roberts scored the fourth try?
"To be honest I was in the coaches' box with the other coaches and I am normally quite calm. When Johnny Sexton and then George North scored (the second and third tries) they went beserk. There was still some time to go but we knew we had it at that point and I got caught up in their enthusiasm and exuberance. I think it was captured on TV. I have always said it is all about the players and I was so happy for the playing group. To win a Lions series is almost unique, as it is so rare. The Lions concept is just so special for the game as it involves the fans as well. The amount of support from four groups of fans is unreal. The Home Nations, SANZAR and the IRB need to make sure there is a future for the Lions. We should embrace it every four years and importantly, in a Lions year, make sure the playing calendar is designed to assist the tour. For it to work moving forward the Lions need adequate preparation. You want compelling Test rugby, you want excitement and that means the Lions have to be properly

prepared. The tours are getting tougher, the game is more and more physical. The Lions itinerary may need to reflect this in terms of playing squad numbers and perhaps some breaks in the schedule with less midweek matches. These are the things that should be debated also."

What was the one thing you did that made a difference?
"Ooh hard one, but I think making the hard choices when you have to. Selection is hard. Players make mistakes. Coaches don't always get it right. As I said we believed the Jamie Roberts selection was the right one for the deciding Test. We made an equally tough call leaving out Alex Cuthbert who played so well in the first Test and opted for the experience of Tommy Bowe. Another factor was picking Sam Warburton as captain. He is part of the younger professional generation at present and Paul O'Connell mentioned to me that he recognised the difference between 2009 and 2013 in this respect."

SQUAD

FORWARDS: *RD Best (Ireland), TR Croft (England), DR Cole (England), *AR Corbisiero (England), *T Court (Ireland), IR Evans (Wales), TT Faletau (Wales), *R Grant (Scotland), RJ Gray (Scotland), CE Healy (Ireland), JPR Heaslip (Ireland), RM Hibbard (Wales), GD Jenkins (Wales), AR Jones (Wales), AW Jones (Wales), DJ Lydiate (Wales), SK O'Brien (Ireland), PJ O'Connell (Ireland), GM Parling (England), MJH Steven (England), J Tipuric (Wales), MWIN Vunipola (England), SK Warburton (Wales, captain), TN Youngs (England)

BACKS: TJ Bowe (Ireland), ACG Cuthbert (Wales), JJV Davies (Wales), OA Farrell (England), SL Halfpenny (Wales), SW Hogg (Scotland), R Kearney (Ireland), SD Maitland (Scotland), C Murray (Ireland), GP North (Wales), BG O'Driscoll (Ireland), WM Phillips (Wales), JH Roberts (Wales), J Sexton (Ireland), EM Tuilagi (England), *WW Twelvetrees (England), *C Wade (England), *SM Williams (Wales), BR Youngs (England), *S Zebo (Ireland)

* Replacement on tour

RESULTS

DATE	RESULT			VENUE
01/06/2013	British & Irish Lions	59–8	Hong Kong	Hong Kong Stadium, Hong Kong
05/06/2013	British & Irish Lions	69–17	Western Force	Patersons Stadium, Perth
08/06/2013	British & Irish Lions	22–12	Queensland Reds	Suncorp Stadium, Brisbane
11/06/2013	British & Irish Lions	64–0	Combined NSW/ Queensland Country	Hunter Stadium, Newcastle
15/06/2013	British & Irish Lions	47–17	NSW Waratahs	Allianz Stadium, Sydney
18/06/2013	British & Irish Lions	12–14	Brumbies	Canberra Stadium, Canberra
22/06/2013	British & Irish Lions	23–21	Australia	Suncorp Stadium, Brisbane
25/06/2013	British & Irish Lions	35–0	Melbourne Rebels	AAMI Park, Melbourne
29/06/2013	British & Irish Lions	15–16	Australia	Etihad Stadium, Melbourne
06/07/2013	British & Irish Lions	41–16	Australia	ANZ Stadium, Sydney

BRITISH & IRISH LIONS INTERNATIONAL STATISTICS

MATCH RECORDS UP TO 10 OCTOBER 2013

MOST CONSECUTIVE TEST WINS

6	1891 *SA* 1,2,3 1896 *SA* 1,2,3
3	1899 *A* 2,3,4
3	1904 *A* 1,2,3
3	1950 *A* 1,2 1955 *SA* 1
3	1974 *SA* 1,2,3

MOST CONSECUTIVE TESTS WITHOUT DEFEAT

Matches	Wins	Draws	Period
6	6	0	1891 to 1896
6	4	2	1971 to 1974

MOST POINTS IN A MATCH

BY THE TEAM

Pts	Opponents	Venue	Year
41	Australia	Sydney	2013
31	Australia	Brisbane	1966
29	Australia	Brisbane	2001
28	S Africa	Pretoria	1974
28	S Africa	Johannesburg	2009
26	S Africa	Port Elizabeth	1974
25	S Africa	Cape Town	1997
25	Argentina	Cardiff	2005
25	S Africa	Pretoria	2009
24	Australia	Sydney	1950
24	Australia	Sydney	1959

BY A PLAYER

Pts	Player	Opponents	Venue	Year
21	SL Halfpenny	Australia	Sydney	2013
20	JP Wilkinson	Argentina	Cardiff	2005
20	SM Jones	S Africa	Pretoria	2009
18	AJP Ward	S Africa	Cape Town	1980
18	AG Hastings	N Zealand	Christchurch	1993
18	JP Wilkinson	Australia	Sydney	2001
17	TJ Kiernan	S Africa	Pretoria	1968
16	BL Jones	Australia	Brisbane	1950

MOST TRIES IN A MATCH

BY THE TEAM

Tries	Opponents	Venue	Year
5	Australia	Sydney	1950
5	S Africa	Johannesburg	1955
5	Australia	Sydney	1959
5	Australia	Brisbane	1966
5	S Africa	Pretoria	1974

BY A PLAYER

Tries	Player	Opponents	Venue	Year
2	AM Bucher	Australia	Sydney	1899
2	W Llewellyn	Australia	Sydney	1904
2	CD Aarvold	N Zealand	Christchurch	1930
2	JE Nelson	Australia	Sydney	1950
2	MJ Price	Australia	Sydney	1959
2	MJ Price	N Zealand	Dunedin	1959
2	DK Jones	Australia	Brisbane	1966
2	TGR Davies	N Zealand	Christchurch	1971
2	JJ Williams	S Africa	Pretoria	1974
2	JJ Williams	S Africa	Port Elizabeth	1974
2	T Croft	S Africa	Durban	2009
2	SM Williams	S Africa	Johannesburg	2009

MOST CONVERSIONS IN A MATCH

BY THE TEAM

Cons	Opponents	Venue	Year
5	Australia	Brisbane	1966
4	S Africa	Johannesburg	1955
3	Australia	Sydney	1950
3	Australia	Sydney	1959
3	Australia	Brisbane	2001
3	S Africa	Durban	2009
3	Australia	Sydney	2013

BY A PLAYER

Cons	Player	Opponents	Venue	Year
5	S Wilson	Australia	Brisbane	1966
4	A Cameron	S Africa	Johannesburg	1955
3	JP Wilkinson	Australia	Brisbane	2001
3	SM Jones	S Africa	Durban	2009
3	SL Halfpenny	Australia	Sydney	2013

MOST PENALTIES IN A MATCH

BY THE TEAM

Pens	Opponents	Venue	Year
6	N Zealand	Christchurch	1993
6	Argentina	Cardiff	2005
5	S Africa	Pretoria	1968
5	S Africa	Cape Town	1980
5	Australia	Sydney	1989
5	S Africa	Cape Town	1997
5	S Africa	Durban	1997
5	S Africa	Pretoria	2009
5	Australia	Melbourne	2013
5	Australia	Sydney	2013

BY A PLAYER

Pens	Player	Opponents	Venue	Year
6	AG Hastings	N Zealand	Christchurch	1993
6	JP Wilkinson	Argentina	Cardiff	2005
5	TJ Kiernan	S Africa	Pretoria	1968
5	AJP Ward	S Africa	Cape Town	1980
5	AG Hastings	Australia	Sydney	1989
5	NR Jenkins	S Africa	Cape Town	1997
5	NR Jenkins	S Africa	Durban	1997
5	SM Jones	S Africa	Pretoria	2009
5	SL Halfpenny	Australia	Melbourne	2013
5	SL Halfpenny	Australia	Sydney	2013

MOST DROP GOALS IN A MATCH

BY THE TEAM

Drops	Opponents	Venue	Year
2	S Africa	Port Elizabeth	1974

BY A PLAYER

Drops	Player	Opponents	Venue	Year
2	P Bennett	S Africa	Port Elizabeth	1974

CAREER RECORDS

MOST CAPPED PLAYERS

Caps	Player	Career Span
17	WJ McBride	1962 to 1974
13	REG Jeeps	1955 to 1962
12	CMH Gibson	1966 to 1971
12	G Price	1977 to 1983
10	AJF O'Reilly	1955 to 1959
10	RH Williams	1955 to 1959
10	GO Edwards	1968 to 1974

MOST CONSECUTIVE TESTS

Tests	Player	Span
15	WJ McBride	1966 to 1974
12	CMH Gibson	1966 to 1971
12	G Price	1977 to 1983

MOST TESTS AS CAPTAIN

Tests	Captain	Span
6	AR Dawson	1959
6	MO Johnson	1997 to 2001

MOST TRIES IN TESTS

Tries	Player	Tests	Career
6	AJF O'Reilly	10	1955 to 1959
5	JJ Williams	7	1974 to 1977
4	W Llewellyn	4	1904
4	MJ Price	5	1959

MOST POINTS IN TESTS

Points	Player	Tests	Career
67	JP Wilkinson	6	2001 to 2005
66	AG Hastings	6	1989 to 1993
53	SM Jones	6	2005 to 2009
49	SL Halfpenny	3	2013
44	P Bennett	8	1974 to 1977
41	NR Jenkins	4	1997 to 2001
35	TJ Kiernan	5	1962 to 1968
30	S Wilson	5	1966
30	B John	5	1968 to 1971

MOST PENALTY GOALS IN TESTS

Penalties	Player	Tests	Career
20	AG Hastings	6	1989 to 1993
16	JP Wilkinson	6	2001 to 2005
13	NR Jenkins	4	1997 to 2001
13	SL Halfpenny	3	2013
12	SM Jones	6	2005 to 2009
11	TJ Kiernan	5	1962 to 1968
10	P Bennett	8	1974 to 1977
7	SO Campbell	7	1980 to 1983

MOST CONVERSIONS IN TESTS

Cons	Player	Tests	Career
7	JP Wilkinson	6	2001 to 2005
7	SM Jones	6	2005 to 2009
6	S Wilson	5	1966
5	SL Halfpenny	3	2013
4	JF Byrne	4	1896
4	CY Adamson	4	1899
4	BL Jones	3	1950
4	A Cameron	2	1955

MOST DROP GOALS IN TESTS

Drops	Player	Tests	Career
2	PF Bush	4	1904
2	D Watkins	6	1966
2	B John	5	1968 to 1971
2	P Bennett	8	1974 to 1977
2	CR Andrew	5	1989 to 1993

SERIES RECORDS

RECORD	HOLDER	DETAIL
Most team points		79 in S Africa 1974
		79 in Australia 2013
Most team tries		10 in S Africa 1955 & 1974
Most points by player	SL Halfpenny	49 in Australia 2013
Most tries by player	W Llewellyn	4 in Australia 1904
	JJ Williams	4 in S Africa 1974

MAJOR TOUR RECORDS

RECORD	DETAIL	YEAR	PLACE
Most team points	842	1959	Australia, NZ & Canada
Most team tries	165	1959	Australia, NZ & Canada
Highest score & biggest win	116-10	2001	v W Australia President's XV
Most individual points	188 by B John	1971	Australia & N Zealand
Most individual tries	22 by AJF O'Reilly	1959	Australia, NZ & Canada
Most points in match	37 by AGB Old	1974 v SW Districts	Mossel Bay, S Africa
Most tries in match	6 by DJ Duckham	1971 v W Coast/Buller	Greymouth, N Zealand
	6 by JJ Williams	1974 v SW Districts	Mossel Bay, S Africa

MISCELLANEOUS RECORDS

RECORD	HOLDER	DETAIL
Longest Test Career	WJ McBride	1962–1974
	BG O'Driscoll	2001–2013
Youngest Test Cap	AJF O'Reilly	19 yrs 91 days in 1955
Oldest Test Cap	NA Back	36 yrs 160 days in 2005

BRITISH & IRISH LIONS INTERNATIONAL PLAYERS
UP TO 10 OCTOBER 2013

From 1891 onwards.

* Indicates that the player was uncapped at the time of his first Lions Test but was subsequently capped by his country.

Aarvold, C D (Cambridge U, Blackheath and England) 1930 NZ 1,2,3,4, A
Ackerman, R A (London Welsh and Wales) 1983 NZ 1,4 (R)
Ackford, P J (Harlequins and England) 1989 A 1,2,3
Adamson, C Y (Durham City) 1899 A 1,2,3,4
Alexander, R (NIFC and Ireland) 1938 SA 1,2,3
Andrew, C R (Wasps and England) 1989 A 2,3, 1993 NZ 1,2,3
Arneil, R J (Edinburgh Acads and Scotland) 1968 SA 1,2,3,4
Archer, H A (Guy's H and *England) 1908 NZ 1,2,3
Ashcroft, A (Waterloo and England) 1959 A 1, NZ 2
Aston, R L (Cambridge U and England) 1891 SA 1,2,3
Ayre-Smith, A (Guy's H) 1899 A 1,2,3,4

Back, N A (Leicester and England) 1997 SA 2(R),3, 2001 A 2,3, 2005 NZ 1
Bainbridge, S J (Gosforth and England) 1983 NZ 3,4
Baird, G R T (Kelso and Scotland) 1983 NZ 1,2,3,4
Baker, A M (Newport and Wales) 1910 SA 3
Baker, D G S (Old Merchant Taylors' and England) 1955 SA 3,4
Balshaw, I R (Bath and England) 2001 A 1(R),2(R),3(R)
Bassett, J A (Penarth and Wales) 1930 NZ 1,2,3,4, A
Bateman, A G (Richmond and Wales) 1997 SA 3(R)
Bayfield, M C (Northampton and England) 1993 NZ 1,2,3
Beamish, G R (Leicester, RAF and Ireland) 1930 NZ 1,2,3,4,A
Beattie, J R (Glasgow Acads and Scotland) 1983 NZ 2(R)
Beaumont, W B (Fylde and England) 1977 NZ 2,3,4, 1980 SA 1,2,3,4
Bebb, D I E (Swansea and Wales) 1962 SA 2,3, 1966 A 1,2, NZ 1,2,3,4
Bedell-Sivright, D R (Cambridge U and Scotland) 1904 A 1
Bell, S P (Cambridge U) 1896 SA 2,3,4
Belson, F C (Bath) 1899 A 1
Bennett, P (Llanelli and Wales) 1974 SA 1,2,3,4, 1977 NZ 1,2,3,4
Bentley, J (Newcastle and England) 1997 SA 2,3
Bevan, J C (Cardiff Coll of Ed, Cardiff and Wales) 1971 NZ 1
Bevan, T S (Swansea and Wales) 1904 A 1,2,3, NZ
Black, A W (Edinburgh U and Scotland) 1950 NZ 1,2
Black, B H (Oxford U, Blackheath and England) 1930 NZ 1,2,3,4, A
Blakiston, A F (Northampton and England) 1924 SA 1,2,3,4
Bowcott, H M (Cambridge U, Cardiff and Wales) 1930 NZ 1,2,3,4, A
Bowe, T J (Ospreys, Ulster and Ireland) 2009 SA 1,2,3, 2013 A2,3
Boyd, C A (Dublin U and *Ireland) 1896 SA 1
Boyle, C V (Dublin U and Ireland) 1938 SA 2,3
Brand, T N (NIFC and *Ireland) 1924 SA 1,2
Bresnihan, F P K (UC Dublin and Ireland) 1968 SA 1,2,4
Bromet, E (Cambridge U) 1891 SA 2,3
Bromet, W E (Oxford U and England) 1891 SA 1,2,3
Brophy, N H (UC Dublin and Ireland) 1962 SA 1,4
Brown, G L (W of Scotland and Scotland) 1971 NZ 3,4, 1974 SA 1,2,3, 1977 NZ 2,3,4
Bucher, A M (Edinburgh Acads and Scotland) 1899 A 1,3,4
Budge, G M (Edinburgh Wands and Scotland) 1950 NZ 4
Bulger, L Q (Lansdowne and Ireland) 1896 SA 1,2,3,4
Bulloch, G C (Glasgow and Scotland) 2001 A I(t), 2005 NZ 3(R)
Burcher, D H (Newport and Wales) 1977 NZ 3
Burnell, A P (London Scottish and Scotland) 1993 NZ 1
Bush, P F (Cardiff and *Wales) 1904 A 1,2,3, NZ
Butterfield, J (Northampton and England) 1955 SA 1,2,3,4
Byrne, J F (Moseley and England) 1896 SA 1,2,3,4
Byrne, J S (Leinster and Ireland) 2005 Arg, NZ 1,2(R),3
Byrne, L M (Ospreys and Wales) 2009 SA 1

Calder, F (Stewart's-Melville FP and Scotland) 1989 A 1,2,3
Calder, J H (Stewart's-Melville FP and Scotland) 1983 NZ 3
Cameron, A (Glasgow HSFP and Scotland) 1955 SA 1,2
Campbell, S O (Old Belvedere and Ireland) 1980 SA 2(R),3,4, 1983 NZ 1,2,3,4
Campbell-Lamerton, M J (Halifax, Army and Scotland) 1962 SA 1,2,3,4, 1966 A 1,2, NZ 1,3
Carey, W J (Oxford U) 1896 SA 1,2,3,4
Carleton, J (Orrell and England) 1980 SA 1,2,4, 1983 NZ 2,3,4
Carling, W D C (Harlequins and England) 1993 NZ 1
Catt, M J (Bath and England) 1997 SA 3
Cave, W T C (Cambridge U and *England) 1903 SA 1,2,3
Chalmers, C M (Melrose and Scotland) 1989 A 1
Chapman, F E (Westoe, W Hartlepool and *England) 1908 NZ 3
Charvis, C L (Swansea and Wales) 2001 A 1(R),3(R)
Clarke, B B (Bath and England) 1993 NZ 1,2,3
Clauss, P R A (Oxford U and Scotland) 1891 SA 1,2,3
Cleaver, W B (Cardiff and Wales) 1950 NZ 1,2,3
Clifford, T (Young Munster and Ireland) 1950 NZ 1,2,3, A 1,2
Clinch, A D (Dublin U and Ireland) 1896 SA 1,2,3,4
Cobner, T J (Pontypool and Wales) 1977 NZ 1,2,3
Colclough, M J (Angoulême and England) 1980 SA 1,2,3,4, 1983 NZ 1,2,3,4
Cole, D R (Leicester and England) 2013 A1(R),2(R),3(R)
Collett, G F (Cheltenham) 1903 SA 1,2,3
Connell, G C (Trinity Acads and Scotland) 1968 SA 4
Cookson, G (Manchester) 1899 A 1,2,3,4
Cooper, G J (Newport Gwent Dragons and Wales) 2005 Arg
Corbisiero, A R (London Irish and England) 2013 A1,3
Corry, M E (Leicester and England) 2001 A 1,2(t+R),3, 2005 Arg, NZ 1,2(R),3(R)
Cotton, F E (Loughborough Colls, Coventry and England) 1974 SA 1,2,3,4, 1977 NZ 2,3,4
Coulman, M J (Moseley and England) 1968 SA 3
Cove-Smith, R (Old Merchant Taylors' and England) 1924 SA 1,2,3,4
Cowan, R C (Selkirk and Scotland) 1962 SA 4
Crean, T J (Wanderers and Ireland) 1896 SA 1,2,3,4
Croft, T R (Leicester and England) 2009 SA 1,2,3(t&R), 2013 A1,2(R)
Cromey, G E (Queen's U, Belfast and Ireland) 1938 SA 3
Crowther, S N (Lennox) 1904 A 1,2,3, NZ
Cueto, M J (Sale and England) 2005 NZ 3
Cunningham, W A (Lansdowne and Ireland) 1924 SA 3
Cusiter, C P (Borders and Scotland) 2005 Arg (R)
Cuthbert, A C G (Cardiff Blues and Wales) 2013 A1

Dallaglio, L B N (Wasps and England) 1997 SA 1,2,3
Dancer, G T (Bedford) 1938 SA 1,2,3
D'Arcy, G W (Leinster and Ireland) 2005 Arg
Davey, J (Redruth and England) 1908 NZ 1
Davidson, I G (NIFC and Ireland) 1903 SA 1
Davidson, J W (London Irish and Ireland) 1997 SA 1,2,3
Davies, C (Cardiff and Wales) 1950 NZ 4
Davies, D M (Somerset Police and Wales) 1950 NZ 3,4, A 1
Davies, D S (Hawick and Scotland) 1924 SA 1,2,3,4
Davies, H J (Newport and Wales) 1924 SA 2
Davies, J J V (Scarlets and Wales) 2013 A1,2,3
Davies, T G R (Cardiff, London Welsh and Wales) 1968 SA 3, 1971 NZ 1,2,3,4
Davies, T J (Llanelli and Wales) 1959 NZ 2,4
Davies, T M (London Welsh, Swansea and Wales) 1971 NZ 1,2,3,4, 1974 SA 1,2,3,4
Davies, W G (Cardiff and Wales) 1980 SA 2
Davies, W P C (Harlequins and England) 1955 SA 1,2,3
Dawes, S J (London Welsh and Wales) 1971 NZ 1,2,3,4
Dawson, A R (Wanderers and Ireland) 1959 A 1,2, NZ 1,2,3,4
Dawson, M J S (Northampton, Wasps and England) 1997 SA 1,2,3, 2001 A 2(R),3, 2005 NZ 1(R),3(R)
Dibble, R (Bridgwater Albion and England) 1908 NZ 1,2,3
Dixon, P J (Harlequins and England) 1971 NZ 1,2,4

Dobson, D D (Oxford U and England) 1904 A 1,2,3, NZ
Dodge, P W (Leicester and England) 1980 SA 3,4
Dooley, W A (Preston Grasshoppers and England) 1989 A 2,3
Doran, G P (Lansdowne and Ireland) 1899 A 1,2
Down, P J (Bristol and *England) 1908 NZ 1,2,3
Doyle, M G (Blackrock Coll and Ireland) 1968 SA 1
Drysdale, D (Heriot's FP and Scotland) 1924 SA 1,2,3,4
Duckham, D J (Coventry and England) 1971 NZ 2,3,4
Duggan, W P (Blackrock Coll and Ireland) 1977 NZ 1,2.3,4
Duff, P L (Glasgow Acads and Scotland) 1938 SA 2,3

Easterby, S H (Llanelli Scarlets and Ireland) 2005 NZ 2,3
Edwards, G O (Cardiff and Wales) 1968 SA 1,2, 1971 NZ 1,2,3,4, 1974 SA 1,2,3,4
Edwards, R W (Malone and Ireland) 1904 A 2,3, NZ
Ellis, H A (Leicester and England) 2009 SA 3(R)
Evans, G (Maesteg and Wales) 1983 NZ 3,4
Evans, G L (Newport and Wales) 1977 NZ 2,3,4
Evans, I C (Llanelli and Wales) 1989 A 1,2,3, 1993 NZ 1,2 3, 1997 SA 1
Evans, R T (Newport and Wales) 1950 NZ 1,2,3,4, A 1,2
Evans, T P (Swansea and Wales) 1977 NZ 1
Evans, W R (Cardiff and Wales) 1959 A 2, NZ 1,2,3
Evers, G V (Moseley) 1899 A 2,3,4

Faletau, T T (Newport Gwent Dragons and Wales) 2013 A3
Farrell, J L (Bective Rangers and Ireland) 1930 NZ 1,2,3,4,A
Farrell, O A (Saracens and England) 2013 A3(R)
Faull, J (Swansea and Wales) 1959 A 1, NZ 1,3,4
Fenwick, S P (Bridgend and Wales) 1977 NZ 1,2,3,4
Fitzgerald, C F (St Mary's Coll and Ireland) 1983 NZ 1,2,3,4
Fitzgerald, L M (Leinster and Ireland) 2009 SA 2
Flutey, R J (Wasps and England) 2009 SA 3
Ford, R W (Edinburgh and Scotland) 2009 SA 3(R)
Foster, A R (Queen's U, Belfast and Ireland) 1910 SA 1,2
Francombe, J S (Manchester) 1899 A 1

Gabe, R T (Cardiff and Wales) 1904 A 1,2,3, NZ
Gibbs, I S (Swansea and Wales) 1993 NZ 2,3, 1997 SA 1,2 3
Gibbs, R A (Cardiff and Wales) 1908 NZ 1,2
Gibson, C M H (Cambridge U, NIFC and Ireland) 1966 NZ 1,2,3,4, 1968 SA 1(R),2,3,4, 1971 NZ 1,2,3,4
Gibson, G R (Northern and England) 1899 A 1,2,3,4
Gibson, T A (Cambridge U and *England) 1903 SA 1,2,3
Giles, J L (Coventry and England) 1938 SA 1,3
Gillespie, J I (Edinburgh Acads and Scotland) 1903 SA 1,2,3
Gould, J H (Old Leysians) 1891 SA 1
Gravell, R W R (Llanelli and Wales) 1980 SA 1(R),2,3,4
Graves, C R A (Wanderers and Ireland) 1938 SA 1,3
Gray, H G S (Scottish Trials) 1899 A 1,2
Gray, R J (Sale and Scotland) 2013 A3(R)
Greenwood, J T (Dunfermline and Scotland) 1955 SA 1,2,3,4
Greenwood, W J H (Harlequins and England) 2005 NZ 1(R),3
Greig, L L (US and *Scotland) 1903 SA 1,2,3
Grewcock, D J (Bath and England) 2001 A 1,2,3, 2005 Arg, NZ 1(R)
Grieve, C F (Oxford U and Scotland) 1938 SA 2,3
Griffiths, G M (Cardiff and Wales) 1955 SA 2,3,4
Griffiths, V M (Newport and Wales) 1924 SA 3,4
Guscott, J C (Bath and England) 1989 A 2,3, 1993 NZ 1,2,3, 1997 SA 1,2,3

Halfpenny, S L (Cardiff Blues and Wales) 2013 A1,2,3
Hall, M R (Bridgend and Wales) 1989 A 1
Hammond, J (Cambridge U, Blackheath) 1891 SA 1,2,3, 1896 SA 2,4
Hancock, P F (Blackheath and England) 1891 SA 1,2,3, 1896 SA 1,2,3,4
Hancock, P S (Richmond and *England) 1903 SA 1,2,3
Handford, F G (Manchester and England) 1910 SA 1,2,3
Harding, A F (London Welsh and Wales) 1904 A 1,2,3, NZ, 1908 NZ 1,2,3
Harding, R (Cambridge U, Swansea and Wales) 1924 SA 2,3,4
Harris, S W (Blackheath and England) 1924 SA 3,4
Harrison, E M (Guy's H) 1903 SA 1
Hastings, A G (London Scottish, Watsonians and Scotland) 1989 A 1,2,3, 1993 NZ 1,2,3
Hastings, S (Watsonians and Scotland) 1989 A 2,3
Hay, B H (Boroughmuir and Scotland) 1980 SA 2,3,4
Hayes, J J (Munster and Ireland) 2005 Arg, 2009 SA 3(R)
Hayward, D J (Newbridge and Wales) 1950 NZ 1,2,3
Healey, A S (Leicester and England) 1997 SA 2(R),3(R)
Heaslip, J P R (Leinster and Ireland) 2009 SA 1,2,3, 2013 A1,2
Henderson, N J (Queen's U, Belfast, NIFC and Ireland) 1950 NZ3
Henderson, R A J (Wasps and Ireland) 2001 A 1,2,3
Henderson, R G (Northern and Scotland) 1924 SA 3,4
Hendrie, K G P (Heriot's FP and Scotland) 1924 SA 2
Henson, G L (Neath-Swansea Ospreys and Wales) 2005 NZ 2
Hewitt, D (Queen's U, Belfast, Instonians and Ireland) 1959 A 1,2, NZ 1,3,4, 1962 SA 4
Hibbard, R M (Ospreys and Wales) 2013 A1(R),2(R),3
Hickie, D A (Leinster and Ireland) 2005 Arg
Higgins, R (Liverpool and England) 1955 SA 1
Hill, R A (Saracens and England) 1997 SA 1,2, 2001 A 1,2, 2005 NZ 1
Hind, G R (Guy's H and *England) 1908 NZ 2,3
Hinshelwood, A J W (London Scottish and Scotland) 1966 NZ 2,4, 1968 SA 2
Hodgson, J McD (Northern and *England) 1930 NZ 1,3
Holmes, T D (Cardiff and Wales) 1983 NZ 1
Hopkins, R (Maesteg and Wales) 1971 NZ 1(R)
Horgan, S P (Leinster and Ireland) 2005 Arg (R),NZ 1(R),2(R),3(R)
Horrocks-Taylor, J P (Leicester and England) 1959 NZ 3
Horton, A L (Blackheath and England) 1968 SA 2,3,4
Howard, W G (Old Birkonians) 1938 SA 1
Howie, R A (Kirkcaldy and Scotland) 1924 SA 1,2,3,4
Howley, R (Cardiff and Wales) 2001 A 1,2
Hulme, F C (Birkenhead Park and England) 1904 A 1

Irvine, A R (Heriot's FP and Scotland) 1974 SA 3,4, 1977 NZ 1,2,3,4, 1980 SA 2,3,4
Irwin, D G (Instonians and Ireland) 1983 NZ 1,2,4
Isherwood, G A M (Old Alleynians, Sale) 1910 SA 1,2,3

Jackett, E J (Falmouth, Leicester and England) 1908 NZ 1,2,3
Jackson, F S (Leicester) 1908 NZ 1
Jackson, P B (Coventry and England) 1959 A 1,2, NZ 1,3,4
James, D R (Llanelli and Wales) 2001 A 1,2,3
Jarman, H (Newport and Wales) 1910 SA 1,2,3
Jarman, J W (Bristol and *England) 1899 A 1,2,3,4
Jeeps, R E G (Northampton and *England) 1955 SA 1,2,3,4, 1959 A 1,2, NZ 1,2,3, 1962 SA 1,2,3,4
Jenkins, G D (Cardiff Blues and Wales) 2005 NZ 1,2,3, 2009 SA 1,2
Jenkins, N R (Pontypridd, Cardiff and Wales) 1997 SA 1,2,3, 2001 A 2(R)
Jenkins, V G J (Oxford U, London Welsh and Wales) 1938 SA 1
John, B (Cardiff and Wales) 1968 SA 1, 1971 NZ 1,2,3,4
John, E R (Neath and Wales) 1950 NZ 1,2,3,4, A 1,2
Johnson, M O (Leicester and England) 1993 NZ 2,3, 1997 SA 1,2,3, 2001 A 1,2,3
Johnston, R (Wanderers and Ireland) 1896 SA 1,2,3
Jones, A R (Ospreys and Wales) 2009 SA 1(R),2, 2013 A1,2,3
Jones, A-W (Ospreys and Wales) 2009 SA 1,2(R),3(R), 2013 A1,2,3
Jones, B L (Devonport Services, Llanelli and Wales) 1950 NZ 4, A 1,2
Jones, D K (Llanelli, Cardiff and Wales) 1962 SA 1,2,3, 1966 A 1,2, NZ 1
Jones, E L (Llanelli and *Wales) 1938 SA 1,3
Jones, I E (Llanelli and Wales) 1930 NZ 1,2,3,4, A
Jones, J P "Jack" (Newport and *Wales) 1908 NZ 1,2,3, 1910 SA 1,2,3
Jones J P "Tuan" (Guy's H and *Wales) 1908 NZ 2,3
Jones K D (Cardiff and Wales) 1962 SA 1,2,3,4
Jones K J (Newport and Wales) 1950 NZ 1,2,4
Jones R N (Swansea and Wales) 1989 A 1,2,3
Jones, R P (Neath-Swansea Ospreys and Wales) 2005 NZ 1(R),2,3
Jones, S M (Clermont Auvergne, Llanelli Scarlets and Wales) 2005 NZ 1,2(R),3, 2009 SA 1,2,3
Jones S T (Pontypool and Wales) 1983 NZ 2,3,4
Judkins, W (Coventry) 1899 A 2,3,4

Kay, B J (Leicester and England) 2005 Arg (R),NZ 1
Keane, M I (Lansdowne and Ireland) 1977 NZ 1
Kearney, R D J (Leinster and Ireland) 2009 SA 1(R),2,3
Kennedy, K W (CIYMS, London Irish and Ireland) 1966 A 1,2, NZ 1,4
Kiernan, M J (Dolphin and Ireland) 1983 NZ 2,3,4
Kiernan, T J (Cork Const and Ireland) 1962 SA 3, 1968 SA 1,2,3,4
Kininmonth, P W (Oxford U, Richmond and Scotland) 1950 NZ 1,2,4
Kinnear, R M (Heriot's FP and *Scotland) 1924 SA1,2,3,4
Kyle, J W (Queen's U, Belfast, NIFC and Ireland) 1950 NZ 1,2,3,4, A 1,2
Kyrke, G V (Marlborough N) 1908 NZ 1

Laidlaw, F A L (Melrose and Scotland) 1966 NZ 2,3
Laidlaw, R J (Jedforest and Scotland) 1983 NZ 1(R),2,3,4
Lamont, R A (Instonians and Ireland) 1966 NZ 1,2,3,4
Lane, M F (UC Cork and Ireland) 1950 NZ 4, A 2
Larter, P J (Northampton, RAF and England) 1968 SA 2
Laxon, H (Cambridge U) 1908 NZ 1

Leonard, J (Harlequins and England) 1993 NZ 2,3, 1997 SA 1(R), 2001 A 1(R),2(R)
Lewis, R A (Abertillery and Wales) 1966 NZ 2,3,4
Lewsey, O J (Wasps and England) 2005 NZ 1,2,3
Llewellyn, W (Llwynypia, Newport and Wales) 1904 A 1,2,3, NZ
Lydiate, D J (Newport Gwent Dragons and Wales) 2013 A1(R),2,3
Lynch, J F (St Mary's Coll and Ireland) 1971 NZ 1,2,3,4

McBride, W J (Ballymena and Ireland) 1962 SA 3,4, 1966 NZ 2,3,4, 1968 SA 1,2,3,4, 1971 NZ 1,2,3,4, 1974 SA 1,2,3,4
Macdonald, R (Edinburgh U and Scotland) 1950 NZ 1, A 2
McEvedy, P F (Guy's H) 1904 A 2,3, NZ, 1908 NZ 2,3
McFadyean, C W (Moseley and England) 1966 NZ 1,2,3,4
McGeechan, I R (Headingley and Scotland) 1974 SA 1,2,3,4, 1977 NZ 1,2,3(R),4
McGown, T M W (NIFC and Ireland) 1899 A 1,2,3,4
McKay, J W (Queen's U, Belfast and Ireland) 1950 NZ 1,2,3,4, A 1,2
McKibbin, H R (Queen's U, Belfast and Ireland) 1938 SA 1,2,3
Mackie, O G (Wakefield Trinity and *England) 1896 SA 1,2,3,4
Maclagan, W E (London Scottish and Scotland) 1891 SA 1,2,3
McLauchlan, J (Jordanhill and Scotland) 1971 NZ 1,2,3,4, 1974 SA 1,2,3,4
McLeod, H F (Hawick and Scotland) 1959 A 1,2, NZ 1,2,3,4
McLoughlin, R J (Gosforth, Blackrock Coll and Ireland) 1966 A 1,2, NZ,4
Macmillan, R G (London Scottish and Scotland) 1891 SA 1,2,3
MacNeill, H P (Oxford U and Ireland) 1983 NZ 1,2,4 (R)
Macpherson, N C (Newport and Scotland) 1924 SA 1,2,3,4
Macrae, D J (St Andrew's U and Scotland) 1938 SA 1
McVicker, J (Collegians and Ireland) 1924 SA 1,3,4
Magee, A M (Bective R and Ireland) 1896 SA 1,2,3,4
Magee, J M (Bective R) 1896 SA 2,4
Marques, R W D (Harlequins and England) 1959 A 2, NZ 2
Marsden-Jones, D (London Welsh and Wales) 1924 SA 1,2
Marshall, H (Blackheath and *England) 1891 SA 2,3
Martin, A J (Aberavon and Wales) 1977 NZ 1
Martelli, E (Dublin U) 1899 A 1
Martindale, S A (Kendal and England) 1930 A
Massey, B F (Hull and ER) 1904 A 3
Matthews, J (Cardiff and Wales) 1950 NZ 1,2,3,4, A 1,2
Maxwell, R B (Birkenhead Park) 1924 SA 1
Mayfield, W E (Cambridge U) 1891 SA 2,3
Mayne, R B (Queen's U, Belfast and Ireland) 1938 SA 1,2,3
Meares, A W D (Dublin U and *Ireland) 1896 SA 3,4
Mears, L A (Bath and England) 2009 SA 1
Meredith, B V (Newport and Wales) 1955 SA 1,2,3,4, 1962 SA 1,2,3,4
Meredith, C C (Neath and Wales) 1955 SA 1,2,3,4
Millar, S (Ballymena and Ireland) 1959 A 1,2, NZ 2, 1962 SA 1,2,3,4, 1968 SA 1,2
Miller, E R P (Leicester and England) 1997 SA 2(R)
Milliken, R A (Bangor and Ireland) 1974 SA 1,2,3,4
Milne, K S (Heriot's FP and Scotland) 1993 NZ 1
Mitchell, W G (Richmond and England) 1891 SA 1,2,3
Monye, Y C C (Harlequins and England) 2009 SA 1,3
Moody, L W (Leicester and England) 2005 Arg, NZ 2,3
Moore, B C (Nottingham, Harlequins and England) 1989 A 1,2,3, 1993 NZ 2,3
Morgan, C I (Cardiff and Wales) 1955 SA 1,2,3,4
Morgan, D W (Stewart's-Melville FP and Scotland) 1977 NZ 3(R),4
Morgan, E (London Welsh, Guy's H and Wales) 1904 A 1,2,3, NZ
Morgan, E (Swansea and *Wales) 1908 NZ 2,3
Morgan, G J (Clontarf and Ireland) 1938 SA 3
Morgan, H J (Abertillery and Wales) 1959 NZ.3,4, 1962 SA 2,3
Morgan, M E (Swansea and Wales) 1938 SA 1,2
Morgan, W L (Cardiff and *Wales) 1908 NZ 2,3
Morley, J C (Newport and Wales) 1930 NZ 1,2,3
Morris, C D (Orrell and England) 1993 NZ 1,2,3
Morris, D R (Swansea and Wales) 2001 A 3(R)
Morrison, M C (Royal HSFP and Scotland) 1903 SA 1,2,3
Mortimer, W (Marlborough N and *England) 1896 SA 1,2,3,4
Mulcahy, W A (UC Dublin and Ireland) 1959 A 1, NZ 4, 1962 SA 1,2,3,4
Mullen, K D (Old Belvedere and Ireland) 1950 NZ 1,2, A 2
Mulligan, A A (Wanderers, London Irish and Ireland) 1959 NZ 4
Mullin, B J (London Irish and Ireland) 1989 A 1
Mullineux, M (Blackheath) 1896 SA 1, 1899 A 1
Mullins, R C (Oxford U) 1896 SA 1,3
Murphy, G E A (Leicester and Ireland) 2005 Arg, NZ 3
Murphy, N A A (Cork Const and Ireland) 1959 A 2, NZ 1,2,4, 1966 A 1,2, NZ 2,3
Murray, C (Munster and Ireland) 2013 A2(R),3(R)
Murray, P F (Wanderers and Ireland) 1930 NZ 1,2,4, A

Neale, M E (Bristol, Blackheath and *England) 1910 SA 1,2,3
Neary, A (Broughton Park and England) 1977 NZ 4
Neill, R M (Edinburgh Acads and Scotland) 1903 SA 2,3
Nelson, J E (Malone and Ireland) 1950 NZ 3,4, A 1,2
Nicholls, E G (Cardiff and Wales) 1899 A 1,2,3,4
Nicholson, B E (Harlequins and England) 1938 SA 2
Nicholson, E T (Birkenhead Park and *England) 1899 A 3,4
Norris, C H (Cardiff and Wales) 1966 NZ 1,2,3
Norster, R L (Cardiff and Wales) 1983 NZ 1,2, 1989 A 1
North, G P (Scarlets and Wales) 2013 A1,2,3
Novis, A L (Blackheath and England) 1930 NZ 2,4, A

O'Brien, A B (Guy's H) 1904 A 1,2,3, NZ
O'Brien, S K (Leinster and Ireland) 2013 A2(R),3
O'Callaghan, D P (Munster and Ireland) 2005 Arg, NZ 2,3, 2009 SA 1(R)
O'Connell, P J (Munster and Ireland) 2005 NZ 1,2,3, 2009 SA 1,2,3, 2013 A1
O'Donnell, R C (St Mary's Coll and Ireland) 1980 SA I
O'Driscoll, B G (Blackrock Coll, Leinster and Ireland) 2001 A 1,2,3, 2005 NZ 1, 2009 SA 1,2, 2013 A1,2
O'Driscoll, J B (London Irish and Ireland) 1980 SA 1,2,3,4, 1983 NZ 2,4
O'Gara, R J R (Munster and Ireland) 2005 NZ 3(R), 2009 SA 2(R)
O'Neill, H O'H (Queen's U, Belfast and Ireland) 1930 NZ 1,2,3,4, A
O'Reilly, A J F (Old Belvedere and Ireland) 1955 SA 1,2,3,4, 1959 A 1,2, NZ 1,2,3,4
Oldham, W L (Coventry and England) 1908 NZ 1
Orr, P A (Old Wesley and Ireland) 1977 NZ 1
O'Shea, J P (Cardiff and Wales) 1968 SA 1
Owen, M J (Newport Gwent Dragons and Wales) 2005 Arg

Parker, D S (Swansea and Wales) 1930 NZ 1,2,3,4, A
Parling, G M W (Leicester and England) 2013 A1(R),2,3
Pask, A E I (Abertillery and Wales) 1962 SA 1,2,3, 1966 A 1,2, NZ 1,3,4
Patterson, C S (Instonians and Ireland) 1980 SA 1,2,3
Patterson, W M (Sale and *England) 1959 NZ 2
Paxton, I A M (Selkirk and Scotland) 1983 NZ 1,2,3,4
Pedlow, A C (CIYMS and Ireland) 1955 SA 1,4
Peel, D J (Llanelli Scarlets and Wales) 2005 NZ 1,2,3
Perry, M B (Bath and England) 2001 A 1,2,3
Phillips, W M (Ospreys, Bayonne and Wales) 2009 SA 1,2,3, 2013 A1,3
Pillman, C H (Blackheath and England) 1910 SA 2,3
Piper, O J S (Cork Const and Ireland) 1910 SA 1
Poole, H (Cardiff) 1930 NZ 3
Popplewell, N J (Greystones and Ireland) 1993 NZ 1,2,3
Preece, I (Coventry and England) 1950 NZ 1
Prentice, F D (Leicester and England) 1930 NZ 2, A
Price, B (Newport and Wales) 1966 A 1,2, NZ 1,4
Price, G (Pontypool and Wales) 1977 NZ 1,2,3,4, 1980 SA 1,2,3,4, 1983 NZ 1,2,3,4
Price, M J (Pontypool and Wales) 1959 A 1,2, NZ 1,2,3
Prosser, T R (Pontypool and Wales) 1959 NZ,4
Pullin, J V (Bristol and England) 1968 SA 2,3,4, 1971 NZ 1,2,3,4

Quinnell, D L (Llanelli and *Wales) 1971 NZ. 3, 1977 NZ 2,3, 1980 SA 1,2
Quinnell, L S (Llanelli and Wales) 2001 A 1,2,3

Ralston, C W (Richmond and England) 1974 SA 4
Reed, A I (Bath and Scotland) 1993 NZ 1
Rees, H E (Neath and *Wales) 1977 NZ 4
Rees, M (Llanelli Scarlets and Wales) 2009 SA 1(R),2,3
Reeve, J S R (Harlequins and England) 1930 NZ 1,3,4, A
Regan, M P (Bristol and England) 1997 SA 3
Reid, T E (Garryowen and Ireland) 1955 SA 2,3
Renwick, J M (Hawick and Scotland) 1980 SA 1
Rew, H (Blackheath, Army and England) 1930 NZ 1,2,3,4
Reynolds, F J (Old Cranleighans and England) 1938 SA 1,2
Richards, D (Leicester and England) 1989 A 1,2,3, 1993 NZ 1,2,3
Richards, D S (Swansea and Wales) 1980 SA 1
Richards, M C R (Cardiff and Wales) 1968 SA 1,3,4
Richards, T J (Bristol and Australia) 1910 SA 1,2
Rimmer, G (Waterloo and England) 1950 NZ 3
Ringland, T M (Ballymena and Ireland) 1983 NZ 1
Risman, A B W (Loughborough Colls and England) 1959 A 1,2, NZ 1,4
Ritson, J A S (Northern and *England) 1908 NZ 1
Robbie, J C (Greystones and Ireland) 1980 SA 4
Roberts, J H (Cardiff Blues and Wales) 2009 SA 1,2, 2013 A3
Robins, J D (Birkenhead Park and Wales) 1950 NZ 1,2,3, A 1,2
Robins, R J (Pontypridd and Wales) 1955 SA 1,2,3,4

Robinson, J T (Sale and England) 2001 A 1,2,3, 2005 NZ 1,2
Rodber, T A K (Northampton and England) 1997 SA 1,2
Rogers, D P (Bedford and England) 1962 SA 1,4
Rogers, R J (Bath) 1904 NZ
Rotherham, A (Cambridge U and *England) 1891 SA 1,2,3
Rowlands, K A (Cardiff and Wales) 1962 SA 1,2,4
Rowntree, G C (Leicester and England) 2005 Arg, NZ 2(t+R),3(R)
Rutherford, D (Gloucester and England) 1966 A 1
Rutherford, J Y (Selkirk and Scotland) 1983 NZ 3

Saunders, S M (Guy's H) 1904 A 1,2
Savage, K F (Northampton and England) 1968 SA 1,2,3,4
Scotland, K J F (Cambridge U, Heriot's FP and Scotland) 1959 A 1,2, NZ 1,3,4
Scott, W P (West of Scotland and Scotland) 1903 SA 1,2,3
Sealy, J (Dublin U and *Ireland) 1896 SA 1,2,3,4
Sexton, J J (Leinster and Ireland) 2013 A1,2,3
Sharp, R A W (Oxford U, Redruth and England) 1962 SA 3,4
Shaw, S D (Wasps and England) 2009 SA 2,3
Sheridan, A J (Sale and England) 2009 SA 2(t&R),3
Simpson, C (Cambridge U) 1891 SA 1
Skrimshire, R T (Newport and Wales) 1903 SA 1,2,3
Slattery, J F (Blackrock Coll and Ireland) 1974 SA 1,2,3,4
Slemen, M A C (Liverpool and England) 1980 SA 1
Smith, A R (Edinburgh Wands, London Scottish and Scotland) 1962 SA 1,2,3
Smith, D F (Richmond and England) 1910 SA 1,2,3
Smith, D W C (London Scottish and Scotland) 1950 A 1
Smith, G K (Kelso and Scotland) 1959 A 1,2, NZ 1,3
Smith, I S (Oxford U, London Scottish and Scotland) 1924 SA 1,2
Smith, O J (Leicester and England) 2005 Arg
Smith, T J (Watsonians, Northampton and Scotland) 1997 SA 1,2,3, 2001 A 1,2,3
Smith, T W (Leicester) 1908 NZ 2,3
Smyth, R S (Dublin U and Ireland) 1903 SA 1,2,3
Smyth, T (Malone, Newport and Ireland) 1910 SA 2,3
Sole, D M B (Edinburgh Acads and Scotland) 1989 A 1,2,3
Spong, R S (Old Millhillians and England) 1930 NZ 1,2,3,4, A
Spoors, J A (Bristol) 1910 SA 1,2,3
Squire, J (Newport, Pontypool and Wales) 1977 NZ 4, 1980 SA 1,2,3,4, 1983 NZ 1
Squires, P J (Harrogate and England) 1977 NZ 1
Stagg, P K (Oxford U, Sale and Scotland) 1968 SA 1,3,4
Stanger-Leathes, C F (Northern and *England) 1904 A 1
Steele, W C C (Bedford, RAF and Scotland) 1974 SA 1,2
Stephens, I (Bridgend and Wales) 1983 NZ 1
Stephens, J R G (Neath and Wales) 1950 A 1,2
Stevenson, R C (St Andrew's U and Scotland) 1910 SA 1,2,3
Stimpson, T R G (Newcastle and England) 1997 SA 3(R)
Stout, F M (Gloucester and England) 1899 A 1,2,3,4, 1903 SA 1,2,3
Surtees, A A (Cambridge U) 1891 SA 1,2,3
Swannell, B I (Northampton and *Australia) 1899 A 2,3,4, 1904 A 1,2,3, NZ

Tait, A V (Newcastle and Scotland) 1997 SA 1,2
Tanner, H (Swansea and Wales) 1938 SA 2
Taylor, A R (Cross Keys and Wales) 1938 SA 1,2
Taylor, J (London Welsh and Wales) 1971 NZ 1,2,3,4
Taylor, R B (Northampton and England) 1968 SA 1,2,3,4
Teague, M C (Gloucester, Moseley and England) 1989 A 2,3, 1993 NZ 2(t)
Tedford, A (Malone and Ireland) 1903 SA 1,2,3
Telfer, J W (Melrose and Scotland) 1966 A 1,2, NZ 1,2,4, 1968 SA 2,3,4
Thomas, G (Toulouse and Wales) 2005 NZ 1,2,3
Thomas, M C (Devonport Services, Newport and Wales) 1950 NZ 2,3, A 1, 1959 NZ 1
Thomas, R C C (Swansea and Wales) 1955 SA 3,4
Thomas, W D (Llanelli and *Wales) 1966 NZ 2,3, 1968 SA 3(R),4, 1971 NZ 1,2,4 (R)
Thompson, C E K (Lancashire) 1899 A 2,3,4
Thompson, R (Cambridge U) 1891 SA 1,2,3
Thompson, R H (Instonians, London Irish and Ireland) 1955 SA 1,2,4
Thompson, S G (Northampton and England) 2005 Arg (R), NZ 1(R),2
Timms, A B (Edinburgh U and Scotland) 1899 A 2,3,4
Tipuric, J C (Ospreys and Wales) 2013 A3(t&R)
Todd, A F (Blackheath and *England) 1896 SA 1,2,3,4
Townsend, G P J (Northampton and Scotland) 1997 SA 1,2
Trail, D H (Guy's H) 1904 A 1,2,3, NZ
Travers, W H (Newport and Wales) 1938 SA 2,3
Tucker, C C (Shannon and Ireland) 1980 SA 3,4
Tuilagi, E M (Leicester and England) 2013 A3(R)
Turner, J W C (Gala and Scotland) 1968 SA 1,2,3,4

Underwood, R (RAF, Leicester and England) 1989 A 1,2,3, 1993 NZ 1,2,3
Underwood, T (Newcastle and England) 1997 SA 3
Unwin, E J (Rosslyn Park, Army and England) 1938 SA 1,2
Uttley, R M (Gosforth and England) 1974 SA 1,2,3,4

Vassall, H H (Blackheath and England) 1908 NZ 1,2,3
Vickery, P J (Gloucester, Wasps and England) 2001 A 1,2,3, 2009 SA 1,3
Vile, T H (Newport and *Wales) 1904 A 2,3, NZ
Voyce, A T (Gloucester and England) 1924 SA 3,4
Vunipola, M W I N (Saracens and England) 2013 A1(R),2,3(R)

Waddell, G H (Cambridge U, London Scottish and Scotland) 1962 SA 1,2
Waddell, H (Glasgow Acads and Scotland) 1924 SA 1,2,4
Wainwright, R I (Watsonians and Scotland) 1997 SA 3
Walker, E F (Lennox) 1903 SA 2,3
Walker, S (Instonians and Ireland) 1938 SA 1,2,3
Wallace, D P (Munster and Ireland) 2009 SA 1,2,3(R)
Wallace, Jos (Wanderers and Ireland) 1903 SA 1,2,3
Wallace, P S (Saracens and Ireland) 1997 SA 1,2,3
Wallace, W (Percy Park) 1924 SA 1
Waller, P D (Newport and Wales) 1910 SA 1,2,3
Warburton, S K (Cardiff Blues and Wales) 2013 A1,2
Ward, A J P (Garryowen and Ireland) 1980 SA 1
Waters, J A (Selkirk and Scotland) 1938 SA 3
Watkins, D (Newport and Wales) 1966 A 1,2, NZ 1,2,3,4
Watkins, S J (Newport and Wales) 1966 A 1,2, NZ 3
Webb, J (Abertillery and Wales) 1910 SA 1,2,3
Welsh, W B (Hawick and Scotland) 1930 NZ 4
Weston, M P (Richmond, Durham City and England) 1962 SA 1,2,3,4, 1966 A 1,2
Wheeler, P J (Leicester and England) 1977 NZ 2,3,4, 1980 SA 1,2,3,4
White, D B (London Scottish and Scotland) 1989 A 1
White, J M (Leicester and England) 2005 Arg (R),NZ 1,2,3
Whitley, H (Northern and *England) 1924 SA 1,3,4
Whittaker, T S (Lancashire) 1891 SA 1,2,3
Wilkinson, J P (Newcastle and England) 2001 A 1,2,3, 2005 Arg, NZ 1,2
Willcox, J G (Oxford U, Harlequins and England) 1962 SA 1,2,4
Williams, B L (Cardiff and Wales) 1950 NZ 2,3,4, A 1,2
Williams, C (Swansea and Wales) 1980 SA 1,2,3,4
Williams, D (Ebbw Vale and Wales) 1966 A 1,2, NZ 1,2,4
Williams, D B (Cardiff and *Wales) 1977 NZ 1,2,3
Williams, J F (London Welsh and Wales) 1908 NZ 3
Williams, J J (Llanelli and Wales) 1974 SA 1,2,3,4, 1977 NZ 1,2,3
Williams, J L (Cardiff and Wales) 1908 NZ 1,2
Williams, J P R (London Welsh and Wales) 1971 NZ 1,2,3,4, 1974 SA 1,2,3,4
Williams, M E (Cardiff Blues and Wales) 2005 NZ 3(R), 2009 SA 1(R),2(R),3
Williams, R H (Llanelli and Wales) 1955 SA 1,2,3,4, 1959 A 1,2, NZ 1,2,3,4
Williams, S H (Newport and *England) 1910 SA 1,2,3
Williams, S M (Ospreys and Wales) 2005 Arg, NZ 2, 2009 SA 2(R),3
Williams, W O G (Swansea and Wales) 1955 SA 1,2,3,4
Willis, W R (Cardiff and Wales) 1950 NZ 4, A 1,2
Wilson, S (London Scottish and Scotland) 1966 A 2, NZ 1,2,3,4
Windsor, R W (Pontypool and Wales) 1974 SA 1,2,3,4, 1977 NZ 1
Winterbottom, P J (Headingley, Harlequins and England) 1983 NZ 1,2,3,4, 1993 NZ, 1,2,3
Wood, B G M (Garryowen and Ireland) 1959 NZ 1,3
Wood, K B (Leicester) 1910 SA 1,3
Wood, K G M (Harlequins and Ireland) 1997 SA 1,2, 2001 A 1,2,3
Woodward, C R (Leicester and England) 1980 SA 2,3
Worsley, J P R (Wasps and England) 2009 SA3
Wotherspoon, W (Cambridge U and Scotland) 1891 SA 1

Young, A T (Cambridge U, Blackheath and England) 1924 SA 2
Young, D (Cardiff and Wales) 1989 A 1,2,3
Young, J (Harrogate, RAF and Wales) 1968 SA 1
Young, J R C (Oxford U, Harlequins and England) 1959 NZ 2
Young, R M (Queen's U, Belfast, Collegians and Ireland) 1966 A 1,2, NZ 1, 1968 SA 3
Youngs, B R (Leicester and England) 2013 A1(R),2
Youngs, T N (Leicester and England) 2013 A1,2,3(R)

BARBARIANS MAULED BY LIONS

By Iain Spragg

Getty Images

Kahn Fotuali'i scored a superb try for the Barbarians against the British & Irish Lions in Hong Kong.

It was an uncharacteristically quiet season for the Barbarians in 2012/13 with just two matches, but what the campaign lacked in terms of fixtures it compensated for with the quality of the opposition with whom they crossed swords.

The Baa-Baas faced England at Twickenham and the British & Irish Lions in Hong Kong and, although they were unable to claim another famous scalp in either clash, the high-profile nature of both matches underlined the Barbarians' status in the professional era.

Preparations for the two games began in October with the news that Dai Young, the man who masterminded the victories over England and Wales in 2011, would coach the side again and in May he unveiled his team to play at Twickenham.

The side was captained by veteran centre Mike Tindall and also featured uncapped Wasps full back Elliot Daly. England were missing 10 leading players selected for the Lions tour of Australia but still proved too strong for Young's team, initially running in five unanswered tries at Twickenham to establish a 40–0 advantage.

The Barbarians, however, were determined to finish on a high and in the final 10 minutes Springboks and Saracens hooker Schalk Brits and Daly both scored to restore some pride, but 20 points in the match from England fly half Freddie Burns was an irresistible platform for a 40–12 triumph.

"The game didn't go to plan but it was still a great honour to wear the famous Baa-Baas jersey," Daly said. "To score a try was a great experience as well and something special. We just could not match England in physicality or use the ball as well as they did."

Six days later the team tackled the Lions at the Hong Kong Stadium. Italy captain Sergio Parisse was given the honour of leading the side against Warren Gatland's tourists, skippering a starting line-up featuring eight different nationalities and 11 full internationals.

Conditions in Hong Kong were oppressively hot and humid and the Barbarians found themselves on the back foot when Brits was yellow carded in the seventh minute. They weathered their early 10-minute numerical disadvantage but were ultimately unable to stem the tide and the Lions helped themselves to eight tries in a 59–8 victory.

There was, though, a moment to cheer for the Baa-Baas supporters in the 56th minute when Samoa scrum half Kahn Fotuali'i scored following a devastating break from New Zealand's Joe Rokocoko, but the side could not breach the Lions defence a second time.

"The Lions were very efficient," said Young after the game. "I would have thought they will feel there is still room for improvement but they certainly starved us of possession both at lineout and scrum. Speaking to the Lions players today, they feel they benefited from the experience. It gave them an opportunity to have a real hit-out. From a rugby point of view, I see all positives."

RESULTS

26/05/2013	Barbarians	12–40	England
01/06/2013	Barbarians	8–59	British & Irish Lions

Elite
Competitions

London Wasps wing Christian Wade was nominated for the Player of the Season award.

Getty Images

PERFECT 10 FOR TIGERS

By Paul Morgan

Getty Images

Geordan Murphy and Martin Castrogiovanni lift the trophy as Leicester celebrate a 10th Premiership title.

It started as one of the most eagerly-awaited club rugby matches of all time and ended as one of Twickenham's most unforgettable occasions as Leicester Tigers became the 2012/13 Aviva Premiership champions.

In front of an 82,000 capacity crowd that sold out quicker than any final before, the East Midlands derby with Northampton Saints certainly didn't let anyone down, delivering a pulsating occasion which included a red card for England hooker Dylan Hartley and seven tries to keep everyone on the edge of their seats.

The 37–17 victory at Twickenham delivered an historic 10th Premiership title for the Tigers at the expense of the Saints, who battled until the final minutes to send their fans home proud.

The victory marked a remarkable run for the Tigers as it was their ninth straight final. With his team having lost five of their last eight finals, including back-to-back defeats over the last two seasons to Harlequins and Saracens, director of rugby Richard Cockerill admitted it had been a real battle to reach the podium.

"It was a typical Leicester versus Saints derby and it just got out of control occasionally," said Cockerill, who himself was banned after the final for remarks he made to the fourth official during the match.

"Every year we try and be consistent to be here every year and to then win it. To be champions is fantastic, against a very good side. Even with a man down they pushed us all the way. For us to be able to come on the big day and not bottle it is pleasing.

"They played some good stuff and they're a good side. I said three or four weeks ago that they were good enough to win the championship, they won't get anything but praise from us. We treat them with a huge amount of respect."

Cockerill acknowledged how tough it was to win this title and admitted that any one of the top six could have taken his side's place with the trophy at Twickenham on 25 May.

"There are four, five or six sides who were good enough to win this, we're lucky enough to have done it," Cockerill said. "Saints are a good side and easily could have won it, Sarries, Quins and Gloucester will push hard moving forward. Even the sides lower down the table will beat you on their day. I think the days of any side dominating for several years are probably gone . . . but we'll try."

Leicester timed their run to glory to perfection. Saracens finished the regular season three points clear of the Tigers, but Leicester moved into top form after the Six Nations ended in March and were ultimately unstoppable.

Leicester's season reached a fitting climax when Tom Youngs was named Aviva Premiership Rugby Player of the Year and six Tigers – a total not beaten by any other team – won places on the British & Irish Lions tour to Australia.

The dismissal of Hartley changed the final and his subsequent ban ensured the hooker missed the Lions tour. Northampton director of rugby Jim Mallinder had masterminded the near impossible in the semi-final, winning – where no other side had done before – on Saracens' new artificial turf at Allianz Park, so he could not hide his devastation at losing in the Saints' first final.

"I guess for a neutral it was a very good game of rugby. I'm proud of Northampton and the performance," Mallinder said.

"I think we possibly could have scored a few tries in the first half.

The Ben Foden one was definitely touch and go. And then the ability of the lads to fight back with 14 men, so I'm very proud of my team.

"For all that effort, your 22 league games and your semi-finals, it all suddenly goes, but I said to the boys, 'You'd rather be in a final than not in a final'."

Saracens may have lost out in that semi-final, but their season will go down in the annals of Premiership Rugby history after they moved into their brand new multi-million pound home at the old Barnet Copthall Stadium during the 2012/13 campaign.

Saracens created a truly community-based facility which, because of its artificial surface, is an open house to the local community who use the stadium for countless events, from school sports days to rugby for autistic children.

When the ground opened in February owner Nigel Wray could hardly disguise his pride at what he and his team had created.

"It's a very proud day for all of us to finally have our own permanent home," he said. "Through Marylebone and the beginnings in 1876, to Primrose Hill, Crouch End, Walthamstow, Southgate, Bramley Road and finally Vicarage Road, we've taken a journey rather like the nomadic Saracens warriors of Crusaders times.

"It's also the first ground in professional rugby to have a wholly artificial pitch. It's a fabulous venue, with fabulous views, it is certainly the most modern stadium in the country and hopefully the most technologically advanced and fan-friendly too."

Saracens also had one award to celebrate when director of rugby Mark McCall was honoured for his role in leading Saracens as they finished top of the Aviva Premiership for the first time by being named the QBE Director of Rugby of the Season.

Under his guidance, Sarries won 17 games and lost just four, giving the former Ulster head coach a 77 per cent winning rate in the 2012/13 season.

Close rivals Leicester secured their place in the final by beating the 2012 champions Harlequins 33–16. Harlequins may not have won back-to-back titles but they finished the season with their heads held high after making the last four, the quarter-finals of the Heineken Cup and lifting the LV= Cup. In addition Quins won the Aviva A League, ensuring that director of rugby Conor O'Shea has the next generation of players ready to move into the first team.

The only untypical thing about the incredible final was the winning margin of 20 points. Once again the Premiership proved itself to be the most competitive league in the world, the average winning margin of 11 points in 2012/13 being the smallest of any major league. The presence of a salary cap and the academy system that serves the Premiership go a long way to ensure that the team at the bottom of the table can beat the one at the top.

As if to prove this point the side promoted from the RFU Championship in 2011/12, London Welsh, who were written off by almost every pundit, confounded the critics to make a stunning start to their Premiership campaign.

Welsh picked up five wins during the season, the same as 11th-placed Worcester Warriors and only two less than London Irish and Sale Sharks, but unfortunately their fate was settled off the field.

Welsh's relegation straight back to the Championship was settled in a disciplinary hearing when they were deducted five points and fined for fielding an ineligible player in a number of matches in separate competitions.

They were finally relegated by 10 points but the deduction took the wind out of their sails at a crucial point of the season – in March – and from that point they limped towards an inevitable fate.

Bad news for London Welsh was matched by the good news for Dean Richards's Newcastle Falcons who returned to the Premiership after a two-leg play-off victory over Bedford Blues. In a hard-fought match at Kingston Park, the Falcons came out on top after the two legs 49–33 on aggregate (31–24 on the night). Newcastle lost just one regular league game in the Championship against Bristol. They finished the league 24 points ahead of their nearest rivals, Nottingham.

Richards wasn't the only new coach in the Aviva Premiership at the start of the 2013/14 season as Worcester Warriors' survival, one from the bottom, failed to prevent their head coach Richard Hill from departing the club at the end of the previous campaign. Hill was replaced by another former England international in the shape of Dean Ryan.

The season had kicked off in July with the J.P. Morgan Asset Management Premiership Rugby Sevens, which was won by London Irish who beat Gloucester Rugby 31–28 in the final at The Rec. The tournament featured more than 20 Test players and brought wing Marland Yarde to national prominence. Yarde finished the season with an England cap on the tour to Argentina.

The other key prizes in the Premiership came to the fifth- and sixth-placed teams, who won places in the 2013/14 Heineken Cup. London Wasps, Exeter Chiefs, Gloucester Rugby and Bath Rugby remained in the hunt for the final two places in the top six almost throughout the whole campaign, with Gloucester finally being rewarded with fifth and Exeter sixth.

Gloucester picked up an impressive 12 victories, only missing out on a place in the semi-finals by six points. Exeter, though, had to fight a little harder, confirming their place in the top six on the final day of the season by winning one of the campaign's most compelling matches, against Gloucester. The rollercoaster 40–39 victory was secured when the nerveless Gareth Steenson kicked Exeter to victory in the 79th minute.

Financially, the Premiership received a double boost during the course of the 2012/13 season. It kicked off with Premiership Rugby signing a new television deal with BT Sport that is worth up to £152million over four years and, in May, title sponsor Aviva signed a new contract to keep their name on the competition for a further three years from 2014/15.

With a Rugby World Cup on the horizon and Sevens' debut in the Olympics the future is bright for the sides within the top flight of English club rugby.

AVIVA PREMIERSHIP 2012/13 RESULTS

Sep 1 2012: **London Wasps** 40–42 **Harlequins**, **Exeter Chiefs** 43–6 **Sale Sharks**, **Gloucester Rugby** 19–24 **Northampton Saints**, **Worcester Warriors** 23–24 **Bath Rugby**, **Saracens** 40–3 **London Irish**. Sep 2: **London Welsh** 13–38 **Leicester Tigers**. Sep 7: **Harlequins** 40–3 **London Welsh**. Sep 8: **Bath Rugby** 30–23 **London Wasps**, **Leicester Tigers** 34–26 **Worcester Warriors**, **London Irish** 31–40 **Gloucester Rugby**, **Sale Sharks** 16–23 **Saracens**. Sep 9: **Northampton Saints** 24–21 **Exeter Chiefs**. Sep 14: **Bath Rugby** 14–18 **Northampton Saints**. Sep 15: **Worcester Warriors** 16–16 **Gloucester Rugby**, **Harlequins** 37–14 **Sale Sharks**, **London Wasps** 43–14 **London Irish**, **Saracens** 9–9 **Leicester Tigers**. Sep 16: **London Welsh** 25–24 **Exeter Chiefs**. Sep 21: **Sale Sharks** 19–29 **London Welsh**. Sep 22: **London Irish** 29–22 **Bath Rugby**, **Northampton Saints** 37–31 **Worcester Warriors**, **Gloucester Rugby** 29–22 **London Wasps**, **Leicester Tigers** 9–22 **Harlequins**. Sep 23: **Exeter Chiefs** 14–12 **Saracens**. Sep 28: **Northampton Saints** 24–6 **London Wasps**, **Worcester Warriors** 35–11 **London Irish**. Sep 29: **Bath Rugby** 31–10 **Sale Sharks**, **Leicester Tigers** 30–8 **Exeter Chiefs**. Sep 30: **Harlequins** 16–18 **Saracens**, **London Welsh** 25–31 **Gloucester Rugby**. Oct 5: **Sale Sharks** 8–20 **Leicester Tigers**. Oct 6: **Gloucester Rugby** 16–10 **Bath Rugby**, **Exeter Chiefs** 42–28 **Harlequins**, **London Irish** 39–17 **Northampton Saints**. Oct 7: **London Welsh** 23–28 **Saracens**, **London Wasps** 10–6 **Worcester Warriors**. Oct 26: **Worcester Warriors** 23–16 **Sale Sharks**. Oct 27: **Bath Rugby** 23–15 **Exeter Chiefs**, **Northampton Saints** 6–16 **Saracens**, **Gloucester Rugby** 27–21 **Leicester Tigers**. Oct 28: **London Irish** 28–31 **Harlequins**, **London Wasps** 29–19 **London Welsh**. Nov 2: **Sale Sharks** 21–9 **London Irish**. Nov 3: **Leicester Tigers** 16–12 **Northampton Saints**, **Exeter Chiefs** 33–9 **Worcester Warriors**, **Harlequins** 28–25 **Gloucester Rugby**. Nov 4: **Saracens** 29–24 **London Wasps**, **London Welsh** 16–9 **Bath Rugby**. Nov 30: **Harlequins** 22–19 **Worcester Warriors**, **Sale Sharks** 16–27 **Northampton Saints**. Dec 1: **Leicester Tigers** 17–12 **Bath Rugby**, **London Welsh** 15–9 **London Irish**, **Exeter Chiefs** 30–23 **London Wasps**. Dec 2: **Saracens** 28–23 **Gloucester Rugby**. Dec 21: **Worcester Warriors** 13–6 **London Welsh**. Dec 22: **Bath Rugby** 0–22 **Saracens**, **Gloucester Rugby** 18–16 **Exeter Chiefs**, **London Irish** 9–31 **Leicester Tigers**, **Northampton Saints** 9–18 **Harlequins**. Dec 23: **London Wasps** 25–18 **Sale Sharks**. Dec 28: **Sale Sharks** 33–27 **Worcester Warriors**. Dec 29: **Harlequins** 26–15 **London Irish**, **Exeter Chiefs** 12–12 **Bath Rugby**, **London Welsh** 15–34 **London Wasps**, **Leicester Tigers** 17–12 **Gloucester Rugby**. Dec 30: **Saracens** 17–16 **Northampton Saints**. Jan 4 2013: **Worcester Warriors** 14–19 **Leicester Tigers**. Jan 5: **Exeter Chiefs** 19–30 **Northampton Saints**, **Gloucester Rugby** 12–18 **London Irish**. Jan 6: **London Wasps** 29–15 **Bath Rugby**, **London Welsh** 26–31 **Harlequins**, **Saracens** 32–12 **Sale Sharks**. Feb 8: **Sale**

Sharks 21–16 **Exeter Chiefs**. Feb 9: **Northampton Saints** 11–27 **Gloucester Rugby**, **Bath Rugby** 32–9 **Worcester Warriors**, **Leicester Tigers** 28–12 **London Welsh**, **London Irish** 29–16 **Saracens**, **Harlequins** 16–17 **London Wasps**. Feb 16: **Bath Rugby** 40–16 **London Irish**, **Saracens** 31–11 **Exeter Chiefs**, **Worcester Warriors** 18–27 **Northampton Saints**, **Harlequins** 25–21 **Leicester Tigers**. Feb 17: **London Wasps** 33–29 **Gloucester Rugby**, **London Welsh** 25–26 **Sale Sharks**. Feb 22: **Gloucester Rugby** 29–23 **Worcester Warriors**, **Sale Sharks** 21–30 **Harlequins**. Feb 23: **Exeter Chiefs** 47–16 **London Welsh**, **Northampton Saints** 25–23 **Bath Rugby**, **Leicester Tigers** 27–32 **Saracens**. Feb 24: **London Irish** 30–19 **London Wasps**. Mar 1: **Bath Rugby** 31–25 **Gloucester Rugby**, **Worcester Warriors** 29–23 **London Wasps**. Mar 2: **Leicester Tigers** 48–10 **Sale Sharks**, **Northampton Saints** 40–14 **London Irish**, **Harlequins** 16–27 **Exeter Chiefs**. Mar 3: **Saracens** 35–14 **London Welsh**. Mar 22: **Sale Sharks** 14–13 **Bath Rugby**. Mar 23: **Gloucester Rugby** 15–14 **London Welsh**, **London Irish** 26–6 **Worcester Warriors**, **London Wasps** 24–26 **Northampton Saints**, **Exeter Chiefs** 9–12 **Leicester Tigers**. Mar 24: **Saracens** 27–12 **Harlequins**. Mar 29: **Gloucester Rugby** 17–15 **Harlequins**. Mar 30: **Bath Rugby** 40–25 **London Welsh**, **London Wasps** 13–22 **Saracens**, **Northampton Saints** 8–36 **Leicester Tigers**, **Worcester Warriors** 18–24 **Exeter Chiefs**. Mar 31: **London Irish** 33–33 **Sale Sharks**. Apr 12: **Sale Sharks** 32–9 **Gloucester Rugby**. Apr 13: **Harlequins** 23–9 **Bath Rugby**, **Exeter Chiefs** 27–6 **London Irish**. Apr 14: **London Welsh** 14–31 **Northampton Saints**, **Saracens** 47–17 **Worcester Warriors**, **Leicester Tigers** 35–16 **London Wasps**. Apr 20: **Bath Rugby** 27–26 **Leicester Tigers**, **Gloucester Rugby** 28–23 **Saracens**, **London Irish** 47–28 **London Welsh**, **Worcester Warriors** 26–42 **Harlequins**, **Northampton Saints** 47–7 **Sale Sharks**. Apr 21: **London Wasps** 24–37 **Exeter Chiefs**. May 4: **Exeter Chiefs** 40–39 **Gloucester Rugby**, **Harlequins** 22–19 **Northampton Saints**, **Leicester Tigers** 32–20 **London Irish**, **London Welsh** 33–22 **Worcester Warriors**, **Sale Sharks** 21–20 **London Wasps**, **Saracens** 23–14 **Bath Rugby**

FINAL TABLE

	P	W	D	L	F	A	BP	PTS
Saracens	22	17	1	4	533	339	7	77
Leicester Tigers	22	15	1	6	538	345	12	74
Harlequins	22	15	0	7	560	453	9	69
Northampton Saints	22	14	0	8	501	433	9	65
Gloucester Rugby	22	12	1	9	515	481	10	60
Exeter Chiefs	22	12	1	9	542	446	9	59
Bath Rugby	22	10	1	11	452	434	11	53
London Wasps	22	9	0	13	511	528	12	48
London Irish	22	7	1	14	459	601	5	35
Sale Sharks	22	7	1	14	377	596	5	35
Worcester Warriors	22	5	1	16	422	547	11	33
London Welsh*	22	5	0	17	412	619	8	23

*London Welsh deducted five points for fielding an ineligible player.

SEMI-FINALS

11 May, Welford Road, Leicester

LEICESTER TIGERS 33 (3G 1T 2PG) HARLEQUINS 16 (1G 3PG)

LEICESTER: M Tait; N Morris, M Tuilagi, A Allen, V Goneva; T Flood (captain), B Youngs; L Mulipola, T Youngs, D Cole, G Kitchener, G Parling, T Croft, J Salvi, J Crane

SUBSTITUTIONS: M Castrogiovanni for Cole (68 mins); R Hawkins for Tom Youngs (69 mins); S Mafi for Parling (72 mins); T Waldrom for Crane (72 mins); S Harrison for Ben Youngs (72 mins); G Ford for Flood (72 mins); M Smith for Tait (72 mins); F Balmain for Mulipola (77 mins)

SCORERS: *Tries:* Goneva, Morris, Croft, Tait *Conversions*: Flood (3) *Penalty Goals:* Flood (2)

HARLEQUINS: M Brown; T Williams, G Lowe, T Casson, U Monye; N Evans, D Care; J Marler, J Gray, J Johnston, O Kohn, G Robson, M Fa'asavalu, L Wallace, N Easter (captain)

SUBSTITUTIONS: R Buchanan for Gray (62 mins); M Lambert for Marler (62 mins); T Collier for Johnston (68 mins); C Matthews for Kohn (62 mins); T Guest for Fa'asavalu (62 mins); K Dickson for Care (53 mins); B Botica for Casson (48 mins); R Chisholm for Monye (65 mins)

SCORERS: *Try:* Chisholm *Conversion:* Evans *Penalty Goals:* Evans (3)

REFEREE: G Garner

12 May, Allianz Park, London

SARACENS 13 (1G 2PG) NORTHAMPTON SAINTS 27 (3G 2PG)

SARACENS: A Goode; C Ashton, J Tomkins, O Farrell, D Strettle; C Hodgson, N De Kock; M Vunipola, S Brits, M Stevens, S Borthwick (captain), A Hargreaves, K Brown, W Fraser, J Wray

SUBSTITUTIONS: C Wyles for Tomkins (60 mins); D Taylor for Hodgson (25 mins); R Wigglesworth for de Kock (49 mins); R Gill for Vunipola (66 mins); J Smit for Brits (60 mins); C Nieto for Stevens (66 mins); M Botha for Hargreaves (71 mins); G Kruis for Saull (49 mins)

SCORERS: *Try:* Taylor *Conversion:* Farrell *Penalty Goals:* Farrell (2)

NORTHAMPTON: B Foden; K Pisi, J Wilson, L Burrell, J Elliott; S Myler, L Dickson; S Tonga'uiha, D Hartley (captain), B Mujati, C Lawes, C Day, C Clark, T Wood, S Manoa

SUBSTITUTIONS: T May for Burrell (70 mins); M Roberts for Dickson (70 mins); S Waller for Tonga'uiha (70 mins); T Mercey for Mujati (56 mins); G van Velze for Lawes (47 mins); P Dowson for Clark (56 mins)

SCORERS: *Tries:* Mujati, Elliott, Van Velze *Conversions:* Myler (3) *Penalty Goals:* Myler (2)

REFEREE: JP Doyle

FINAL

25 May, Twickenham, London

LEICESTER TIGERS 37 (1G 3T 5PG)
NORTHAMPTON SAINTS 17 (1G 2T)

LEICESTER: M Tait; N Morris, M Tuilagi, A Allen, V Goneva; T Flood (captain), B Youngs; L Mulipola, T Youngs, D Cole, G Kitchener, G Parling, T Croft, J Salvi, J Crane

SUBSTITUTIONS: M Smith for Goneva (74 mins); G Ford for Flood (23 mins); S Harrison for B Youngs (74 mins); F Balmain for Mulipola (74 mins); R Hawkins for T Youngs (67 mins); Castrogiovanni for Cole (67 mins); E Slater for Kitchener (55 mins), S Mafi for Crane (72 mins)

SCORERS: *Tries:* Morris, Kitchener, Tuilagi, Goneva *Conversion:* Flood *Penalty Goals:* Flood, Ford (4)

NORTHAMPTON: B Foden; K Pisi, J Wilson, L Burrell, J Elliott; S Myler, L Dickson; S Tonga'uiha, D Hartley (captain), B Mujati, C Lawes, P Dowson, T Wood, S Manoa

SUBSTITUTIONS: G Pisi for Foden (67 mins); M Haywood for Elliott (40 mins); R Lamb for Myler (67 mins); M Roberts for Dickson (67 mins); S Waller for Tonga'uiha (55 mins); T Mercey for Mujati (56 mins); G Van Velze for Lawes (60 mins), B Nutley for Dowson (67 mins)

SCORERS: *Tries:* Myler, Foden, Dickson *Conversion:* Myler

RED CARD: Hartley

REFEREE: W Barnes

CASTRES UPSET THE ODDS

By Iain Spragg

AFP/Getty Images

Castres pulled off a major surprise against Toulon to lift the Bouclier de Brennus for the first time in two decades.

Castres Olympique defied both the weight of pre-match expectation and the club's modest recent history to be crowned French champions for the first time in 20 years, beating overwhelming favourites Toulon 19–14 in front of a record 80,033 crowd at the Stade de France.

The team qualified for the knockout stages in fourth place in the final Top 14 table and 16 points adrift of second-placed Toulon, who warmed up for the annual Parisian showdown with a maiden triumph in the Heineken Cup a fortnight earlier.

Only the most ardent of Castres supporters gave Laurent Labit and Laurent Travers's side a prayer of success in the climax of the French domestic campaign, but a moment of sublime individual magic from South African scrum half Rory Kockott in the first half proved pivotal and the underdogs claimed the Bouclier de Brennus after a two-decade drought.

The match was Labit and Travers's final act as the club's coaching team before they joined Racing Métro and, having guided their side to two quarter-finals and a semi-final during a four-year reign at the Stade Pierre-Antoine, there was a sense of mission accomplished in the capital.

"They're going but we're finishing in the best possible way," said wing Romain Martial. "There's a new era that's going to begin for Castres but we've ended a great one, we've closed a chapter and turned over a new page.

"It's the end of a cycle. They're going on to new horizons and we are too. That's the way to view it and not be bitter. It's about winning this together. We've heard all season that the coaches are leaving and it's going to affect us but I think we've answered that."

Although it was Castres who were eventually confirmed as champions, it was Toulon who were the quickest out of the blocks as the campaign began in August with five successive victories to set the early pace. In contrast, defending champions Toulouse struggled to find any real consistency and it was left to Clermont Auvergne, with five wins in their opening six games, to chase the leaders.

The first major clash of the season came in late September when Toulon travelled to the Stade Ernest-Wallon to face Toulouse in a repeat of the 2012 final. Their unbeaten sequence came to an abrupt end with a 32–9 defeat built on a platform of 27 points from former All Blacks fly half Luke McAlister.

The result signalled a prolonged period of flux in the league as the four leading clubs all tried but failed to sustain significant winning runs between October and May. Clermont's run of victories over Mont-de-Marsan, Grenoble, Stade Français and Castres in February and March was the longest victorious streak any of the quartet could muster and, when the 26th and final round of matches of the regular season was completed in May, just a single point separated Clermont in first and Toulon in second. Toulouse claimed third and Castres edged out Montpellier for fourth.

Toulouse played Racing Métro for a place in the semi-finals in the first fixture of the knockout stages. Once again it was McAlister who proved the match-winner with seven successful penalties and a conversion to add to tries from Gaël Fickou and Louis Picamoles. Although Racing also crossed twice through Masinivanua Matadigo and Henry Chavancy, Toulouse held on for a 33–19 win.

Castres entertained Montpellier in the second eliminator the following day at the Stade Pierre-Antoine in what was to prove a cagey and cautious encounter. A drop goal from fly half Rémi Talès and three Kockott penalties gave the home side a 12–9 half-time advantage, but the match turned moments before the break when Montpellier's Mamuka Gorgodze was yellow carded for a high tackle on Brice Mach.

His side paid a heavy price for his indiscipline when South African-born French flanker Antonie Claassen took full advantage of the depleted Montpellier back row to scamper over for the only try of the game moments after the restart and a Kockott conversion and two further penalties ensured Castres cantered to a 25–12 victory.

The first of the semi-finals in Nantes saw Toulon tackle Toulouse in an eagerly anticipated clash. The two teams had failed to register a try between them in the 2012 final but former Springbok flanker Danie Rossouw rectified that after just two minutes for the home side with an early score and, at half-time, Toulon had established a fragile 8–6 advantage.

Jonny Wilkinson and McAlister traded penalties after the break but a drop goal and a third penalty from the veteran Englishman eased Toulon out front. All hope of a famous Toulouse fightback was extinguished when full back Delon Armitage seized on a loose ball and raced over to seal a 24–9 victory.

"The first half was really difficult but we came out in the second half with ambition," said Wilkinson after the game. "You never know against Toulouse and you have to keep alert right to the end. Now there's a final to play. We don't have much time to prepare but we're going to enjoy it and stay positive."

The second semi-final was played at the Stade de la Beaujoire a day later as Clermont faced Castres and, despite most neutrals arguing that form and personnel meant it would be the former who would reach the final for the first time since 2010, it was Castres' dominant scrum that proved the difference between the two teams.

Castres capitalised on the power of their front five with four first-half penalties from Kockott and headed into the dressing room at the break with a healthy but not decisive 12–3 lead. The second half initially followed the pattern of the first as Kockott landed two more penalties but the true coup de grâce was not delivered until the 63rd minute.

It was undoubtedly an opportunistic score. Clermont were on the attack but Mike Delany's ambitious pass to Wesley Fofana never reached its intended target and Romain Cabannes intercepted, sprinting 70 yards for the only try of the match. The home side's challenge was spent and Castres claimed a surprise 25–9 victory.

"We were attentive to that to make sure our season didn't end here today," Labit said. "It is wonderful to beat Clermont but we don't want our players to start celebrating yet."

The final in Paris in early June saw the Stade de France swelled almost to capacity and, although the game yielded just two tries, it did not lack in drama or entertainment.

Wilkinson spurned an early opportunity for the first points of the contest when his penalty attempt struck the upright but did not repeat the mistake with his second effort in front of the posts. Kockott levelled on 14 minutes but it was merely the hors d'oeuvre to the main course that was his try just before half-time, a beautiful effort in which he singlehandedly danced and dummied his way through the Toulon defence. The conversion made it 10–3 to Castres at the break and a shock result suddenly seemed a genuine possibility.

Toulon came out for the second half galvanised and their renewed effort was rewarded with a Wilkinson penalty. Another successful kick from the fly half further reduced the arrears and, although he once again hit the post with a long-range effort, his side were now only a single point adrift.

The tension in Saint-Denis was palpable but fly half Talès proved he was the man for the big occasion with two vital drop goals to extend his side's advantage. Kockott rubbed salt into the wound with his second penalty of the match and Castres were 19–9 ahead.

Desperate to avoid defeat in the final for a second successive season, Toulon battled on and scored in the corner in the final minutes through Delon Armitage. Wilkinson missed the conversion but it was irrelevant as time was up and Castres were the proud new holders of the Bouclier de Brennus.

"It was a very close game but they took their chances well," said Toulon second row Nick Kennedy after his side had been denied a coveted Top 14 and Heineken Cup double. "Those two drop goals midway through the second half were timed very well and executed extremely well.

"They were more fresh than us in the ruck. In the first half their lineout was very good, their scrum decent and we couldn't get a lot going in attack. From one to 15, we all made mistakes and didn't really get our game going.

"You have to give them credit for their defence. We tried to vary it but they were very good in the ruck and if we didn't get there in numbers quickly, they turned us over. It's something they must have done a lot of work on and they're very good at it."

Victory for Castres was as emotional as it was unexpected but, with Labit and Travers leaving the club, Kockott admitted his own future at the Stade Pierre-Antoine was far from certain.

"It was David against Goliath," he said after his match-winning performance. "We are a team in which there is no star, nobody is better than the others. Toulon were the favourites. This was the work of the whole team, like with my try. I scored thanks to the forwards' work because that's rugby. I don't know if I will still be here next season. I've had a difficult season but we'll see afterwards. I just want to enjoy this victory."

TOP 14 2012/13 RESULTS

17 August 2012: **Toulouse** 23 **Castres** 22. 18 August: **Agen** 20 **Racing Métro** 24, **Biarritz** 35 **Mont-de-Marsan** 10, **Bordeaux** 28 **Grenoble** 29, **Stade Français** 32 **Montpellier** 16, **Bayonne** 6 **Clermont** 13, **Perpignan** 15 **Toulon** 21. 24 August: **Bordeaux** 26 **Perpignan** 22. 25 August: **Racing Métro** 21 **Toulon** 23, **Bayonne** 24 **Stade Français** 11, **Castres** 30 **Grenoble** 13, **Montpellier** 13 **Clermont** 8, **Toulouse** 37 **Mont-de-Marsan** 22, **Agen** 19 **Biarritz** 25. 31 August: **Grenoble** 26 **Stade Français** 12. 1 September: **Biarritz** 22 **Toulouse** 17, **Castres** 31 **Bayonne** 10, **Clermont** 53 **Perpignan** 31, **Montpellier** 32 **Agen** 15, **Racing Métro** 18 **Bordeaux** 7, **Mont-de-Marsan** 15 **Toulon** 29. 8 September: **Biarritz** 27 **Montpellier** 8, **Grenoble** 52 **Mont-de-Marsan** 7, **Perpignan** 18 **Bayonne** 13, **Stade Français** 20 **Castres** 20. 9 September: **Clermont** 13 **Racing Métro** 12. 14 September: **Montpellier** 25 **Toulon** 32. 15 September: **Perpignan** 34 **Toulouse** 20, **Agen** 32 **Grenoble** 26, **Bayonne** 18 **Racing Métro** 25, **Castres** 28 **Biarritz** 13, **Mont-de-Marsan** 6 **Clermont** 14, **Bordeaux** 30 **Stade Français** 22. 21 September: **Bayonne** 6 **Toulouse** 35. 22 September: **Toulon** 33 **Castres** 12, **Bordeaux** 15 **Montpellier** 23, **Clermont** 44 **Grenoble** 20, **Mont-de-Marsan** 16 **Agen** 28, **Stade Français** 34 **Perpignan** 24, **Racing Métro** 13 **Biarritz** 12. 28 September: **Clermont** 28 **Stade Français** 25. 29 September: **Agen** 19 **Bordeaux** 15, **Grenoble** 27 **Racing Métro** 13, **Montpellier** 19 **Castres** 12, **Perpignan** 15 **Mont-de-Marsan** 6, **Toulouse** 32 **Toulon** 9. 30 September: **Biarritz** 15 **Bayonne** 16. 5 October: **Castres** 16 **Clermont** 13. 6 October: **Biarritz** 9 **Toulon** 36, **Bayonne** 37 **Agen** 16, **Grenoble** 28 **Perpignan** 23, **Mont-de-Marsan** 28 **Stade Français** 30, **Racing Métro** 12 **Montpellier** 16, **Bordeaux** 32 **Toulouse** 34. 26 October: **Clermont** 19 **Biarritz** 12. 27 October: **Stade Français** 28 **Toulouse** 24, **Agen** 14 **Castres** 22, **Mont-de-Marsan** 12 **Bordeaux** 17, **Montpellier** 23 **Grenoble** 6, **Toulon** 59 **Bayonne** 0, **Perpignan** 17 **Racing Métro** 13. 1 November: **Grenoble** 34 **Biarritz** 21, **Agen** 11 **Clermont** 18, **Bayonne** 22 **Bordeaux** 11, **Castres** 38 **Perpignan** 36, **Montpellier** 32 **Mont-de-Marsan** 16, **Toulon** 24 **Stade Français** 19, **Toulouse** 32 **Racing Métro** 13. 9 November: **Toulouse** 27 **Montpellier** 9. 10 November: **Clermont** 24 **Toulon** 21, **Racing Métro** 16 **Mont-de-Marsan** 17, **Stade Français** 20 **Agen** 13, **Biarritz** 15 **Perpignan** 3, **Bordeaux** 13 **Castres** 16, **Grenoble** 9 **Bayonne** 6. 30 November: **Perpignan** 39 **Agen** 13. 1 December: **Toulouse** 30 **Clermont** 22, **Biarritz** 25 **Bordeaux** 22, **Mont-de-Marsan** 15 **Castres** 31, **Montpellier** 29 **Bayonne** 22, **Toulon** 39 **Grenoble** 3, **Racing Métro** 23 **Stade Français** 15. 21 December: **Bordeaux** 24 **Clermont** 28. 22 December: **Grenoble** 15 **Toulouse** 6, **Bayonne** 39 **Mont-de-Marsan** 13, **Castres** 31 **Racing Métro** 10, **Perpignan** 30 **Montpellier** 19, **Stade Français** 36 **Biarritz** 23, **Agen** 9 **Toulon** 15. 30 December: **Clermont** 48 **Bayonne** 3, **Grenoble** 19 **Bordeaux** 9, **Mont-de-Marsan** 18 **Biarritz** 19, **Racing Métro** 40 **Agen** 6, **Castres** 16 **Toulouse** 18, **Montpellier** 54 **Stade Français** 16, **Toulon** 46 **Perpignan** 13. 4 January 2013: **Biarritz** 16 **Agen** 11. 5 January: **Clermont** 36 **Montpellier** 18, **Grenoble** 14 **Castres** 12, **Perpignan** 26 **Bordeaux** 16, **Stade Français** 21 **Bayonne** 13, **Mont-de-Marsan** 12 **Toulouse** 16. 6 January: **Toulon** 15 **Racing Métro** 19. 24 January: **Bayonne** 22 **Castres** 12. 25 January: **Agen** 9 **Montpellier** 13, **Bordeaux** 15 **Racing Métro** 22, **Perpignan** 26 **Clermont** 19, **Stade Français** 35 **Grenoble** 6, **Toulon** 15 **Mont-de-Marsan** 9, **Toulouse** 19 **Biarritz** 14. 8 February: **Racing Métro** 12 **Clermont** 6. 9 February: **Agen** 22 **Toulouse** 9, **Bayonne** 13 **Perpignan** 10,

Bordeaux 41 **Toulon** 0, **Castres** 44 **Stade Français** 13, **Mont-de-Marsan** 32 **Grenoble** 14, **Montpellier** 33 **Biarritz** 10. 15 February: **Toulouse** 18 **Perpignan** 19. 16 February: **Toulon** 51 **Montpellier** 6, **Clermont** 56 **Mont-de-Marsan** 3, **Grenoble** 27 **Agen** 13, **Racing Métro** 15 **Bayonne** 10, **Stade Français** 30 **Bordeaux** 14, **Biarritz** 15 **Castres** 9. 22 February: **Castres** 25 **Toulon** 20. 23 February: **Agen** 9 **Mont-de-Marsan** 3, **Biarritz** 11 **Racing Métro** 23, **Grenoble** 10 **Clermont** 17, **Montpellier** 15 **Bordeaux** 13, **Toulouse** 42 **Bayonne** 6, **Perpignan** 32 **Stade Français** 16. 1 March: **Bayonne** 6 **Biarritz** 6. 2 March: **Stade Français** 10 **Clermont** 37, **Bordeaux** 48 **Agen** 17, **Castres** 26 **Montpellier** 20, **Mont-de-Marsan** 17 **Perpignan** 31, **Racing Métro** 23 **Grenoble** 3, **Toulon** 35 **Toulouse** 16. 8 March: **Montpellier** 15 **Racing Métro** 17. 9 March: **Agen** 20 **Bayonne** 30, **Perpignan** 20 **Grenoble** 18, **Stade Français** 42 **Mont-de-Marsan** 14, **Toulon** 50 **Biarritz** 15, **Toulouse** 33 **Bordeaux** 32, **Clermont** 37 **Castres** 10. 23 March: **Bayonne** 33 **Toulon** 28, **Racing Métro** 23 **Perpignan** 19, **Bordeaux** 40 **Mont-de-Marsan** 7, **Castres** 20 **Agen** 9, **Grenoble** 9 **Montpellier** 16, **Biarritz** 32 **Clermont** 28. 24 March: **Toulouse** 43 **Stade Français** 16. 29 March: **Biarritz** 33 **Grenoble** 16. 30 March: **Stade Français** 11 **Toulon** 43, **Bordeaux** 39 **Bayonne** 13, **Clermont** 66 **Agen** 21, **Mont-de-Marsan** 17 **Montpellier** 30, **Perpignan** 20 **Castres** 21, **Racing Métro** 26 **Toulouse** 27. 12 April: **Castres** 23 **Bordeaux** 23. 13 April: **Montpellier** 10 **Toulouse** 8, **Agen** 20 **Stade Français** 28, **Bayonne** 31 **Grenoble** 24, **Mont-de-Marsan** 9 **Racing Métro** 34. 14 April: **Perpignan** 33 **Biarritz** 28. 20 April: **Clermont** 39 **Toulouse** 17, **Agen** 23 **Perpignan** 15, **Bayonne** 32 **Montpellier** 26, **Bordeaux** 16 **Biarritz** 0, **Castres** 44 **Mont-de-Marsan** 17, **Grenoble** 25 **Toulon** 24. 21 April: **Stade Français** 19 **Racing Métro** 16. 4 May: **Biarritz** 52 **Stade Français** 17, **Clermont** 67 **Bordeaux** 3, **Mont-de-Marsan** 33 **Bayonne** 36, **Montpellier** 50 **Perpignan** 22, **Racing Métro** 29 **Castres** 28, **Toulon** 43 **Agen** 21, **Toulouse** 57 **Grenoble** 7.

FINAL TABLE

	P	W	D	L	F	A	BP	PTS
Clermont	26	19	1	6	779	418	13	91
Toulon	26	18	1	7	779	456	16	90
Toulouse	26	17	0	9	702	501	11	79
Castres	26	15	2	9	599	489	10	74
Montpellier	26	16	0	10	570	520	9	73
Racing Métro	26	16	0	10	512	431	9	73
Perpignan	26	13	0	13	593	607	9	61
Bayonne	26	12	1	13	467	609	7	57
Biarritz	26	12	1	13	505	540	7	57
Stade Français	26	12	1	13	578	691	4	54
Grenoble	26	12	0	14	480	606	6	54
Bordeaux	26	8	1	17	561	584	13	47
Agen	26	6	0	20	423	709	7	31
Mont-de-Marsan	26	2	0	24	374	761	8	16

PLAY-OFFS

10 May 2013
Toulouse 33 **Racing Métro** 19
11 May 2013
Castres 25 **Montpellier** 12

SEMI-FINALS

24 May, Stade de la Beaujoire, Nantes

TOULON 24 (1G 1T 3PG 1DG) TOULOUSE 9 (3PG)

TOULON: D Armitage; R Wulf, M Bastareaud, M Giteau, A Palisson; J Wilkinson (captain), F Michalak; A Sheridan, S Bruno, D Kubriashvili, B Botha, N Kennedy, D Rossouw, J-F Lobbe, C Masoe

SUBSTITUTIONS: J-C Orioli for Bruno (47 mins); J Suta for Kennedy (59 mins); S Tillous-Borde for Michalak (68 mins); L Chilachava for Kubriashvili (70 mins); S Armitage for Masoe (70 mins); M Mermoz for Giteau (70 mins); X Chiocci for Sheridan (70 mins); R Elsom for Lobbe (74 mins)

SCORERS: *Tries:* Rossouw, Armitage *Conversion:* Wilkinson *Penalty Goals:* Wilkinson (3) *Drop Goal:* Wilkinson

TOULOUSE: C Poitrenaud; Y Huget, Y Jauzion, G Fickou, M Médard; L McAlister, J-M Doussain; V Kakovin, W Servat, C Johnston, Y Maestri, P Albacete, J Bouilhou, T Dusautoir (captain), L Picamoles

SUBSTITUTIONS: G Steenkamp for Kakovin (37 mins); Y David for Fickou (47 mins); Y Nyanga for Bouilhou (51 mins); L Beauxis for Jauzion (60 mins); RM Chlusky for Maestri (64 mins); J Bregvadze for Servat (70 mins); J-B Poux for Johnston (70 mins); L Burgess for Doussain (73 mins)

SCORERS: *Penalty Goals:* McAlister (3)

REFEREE: P Gauzere (France)

25 May, Stade de la Beaujoire, Nantes

CLERMONT AUVERGNE 9 (3PG) CASTRES 25 (1G 6PG)

CLERMONT: L Byrne; S Sivivatu, A Rougerie (captain), W Fofana, N Nalaga; M Delany, M Parra; R Chaume, B Kayser, D Zirakashvili, J Pierre, L Jacquet, J Bonnaire, J Bardy, D Chouly

SUBSTITUTIONS: B Stanley for Rougerie (38 mins); T Domingo for Chaume (41 mins); N Hines for Jacquet (41 mins); T Paulo for Kayser (43 mins); D Kotze for Zirakashvili (67 mins); B James for Byrne (80 mins)

SCORERS: *Penalty Goals:* Delany (3)

YELLOW CARD: J Bardy (77 mins)

CASTRES: B Dulin; R Martial, R Cabannes, S Bai, M Andreu; R Talès (captain), R Kockott; S Taumoepeau, B Mach, K Wihongi, C Samson, R Ortega, I Diarra, Y Caballero, A Claassen

SUBSTITUTIONS: I Tekori for Ortega (64 mins); P Bonnefond for Bai (67 mins); M Bonello for Mach (73 mins); D Kirkpatrick for Talès (73 mins); Y Forestier for Taumoepeau (73 mins); R Teulet for Dulin (73 mins); M Lazar for Wihongi (78 mins)

SCORERS: *Try:* Cabannes *Conversion:* Kockott *Penalty Goals:* Kockott (6)

YELLOW CARD: A Claassen (77 mins)

REFEREE: C Berdos (France)

FINAL

1 June, Stade de France, Paris

TOULON 14 (1T 3PG) CASTRES 19 (1G 2PG 2DG)

TOULON: D Armitage; R Wulf, M Bastareaud, M Giteau, A Palisson; J Wilkinson (captain), F Michalak; A Sheridan, S Bruno, C Hayman, B Botha, N Kennedy, D Rossouw, J-F Lobbe, C Masoe

SUBSTITUTIONS: D Kubriashvili for Hayman (18 mins); J-C Orioli for Bruno (48 mins); S Tillous-Borde for Michalak (49 mins); J van Niekerk for Rossouw (58 mins); M Mermoz for Wulf (64 mins); X Chiocci for Sheridan (67 mins); S Armitage for Masoe (70 mins)

SCORERS: *Try:* D Armitage *Penalty Goals:* Wilkinson (3)

CASTRES: B Dulin; R Martial, R Cabannes, S Bai, M Andreu; R Talès (captain), R Kockott; S Taumoepeau, B Mach, K Wihongi, C Samson, R Ortega, I Diarra, Y Caballero, A Claassen

SUBSTITUTIONS: M Bonello for Mach (48 mins); I Tekori for Ortega (58 mins); M Lazar for Wihongi (70 mins); J Bornman for Diarra (72 mins); Y Forrestier for Taumoepeau (75 mins); R Teulet for Talès (78 mins)

SCORERS: *Try:* Kockott *Conversion:* Kockott *Penalty Goals:* Kockott (2) *Drop Goals:* Talès (2)

REFEREE: J Garcès (France)

FOURTH TIME LUCKY FOR LEINSTER

By Iain Spragg

INPHO

Leinster provided a fitting farewell for coach Joe Schmidt with victory over Ulster.

Leinster brought down the curtain on Joe Schmidt's prolific reign as the province's head coach with an emotional victory over Ulster in the climax of the RaboDirect PRO12 campaign, finally lifting the trophy in Dublin after the heartbreak of losing the three previous finals.

Just eight days after claiming the Amlin Challenge Cup, Leinster were clutching silverware once again after despatching their old rivals 24–18 at the RDS to secure the fourth major honour since Schmidt was appointed three years earlier.

The New Zealander had already masterminded Leinster's back-to-back successes in the Heineken Cup in 2011 and 2012 and, in his final flourish before leaving the province to become the Ireland head coach, completed his impressive collection with the previously elusive PRO12 crown.

It was the first time Leinster had claimed the title since 2008 and, after twice succumbing to Ospreys as well as Munster in a painful hat-trick of final losses, victory over Ulster was as cathartic as it was overdue.

"It was a pretty nerve-racking way to go out," Schmidt admitted after the match. "The PRO12 is very, very tough. It is a super competition and anyone of the top six teams could have won it. When you do get through to the play-off games, it is very tough all the way. It is a massive credit to our players. We focused on our attack for the Challenge Cup and focused a little bit more on defence for this game.

"I don't think we managed the last quarter of the game well and we gave them the ball back too many times. Ulster are too good a team to give the ball back to but our defence was first-rate today. We managed to hang in when they had a lot of pressure in the first half and in the last quarter."

The battle for one of the coveted top-four places began in late August and, after the early skirmishes, it soon became evident it would essentially be a five-horse race between Ulster, Leinster, Glasgow, Scarlets and defending champions Ospreys for a place in the semi-finals.

Ulster were the quickest out of the blocks as Mark Anscombe's side registered 11 successive wins to set the early pace and, although they experienced a minor crisis of confidence between late December and March with just two victories in seven outings, the Ulstermen topped the table.

Leinster and Glasgow were vying for the runners-up spot and home advantage in the semi-finals throughout the campaign, but ultimately it was the Irish side who secured second with a record of just one defeat in their last 11 games.

The tussle for fourth between Scarlets and Ospreys went right down to the wire. Scarlets had their destiny in their own hands before the final round of fixtures but lost 41–17 at home to Treviso and only clung on to fourth courtesy of Leinster's 37–19 success against Ospreys in Dublin.

At the other end of the table, it proved to be a chastening debut campaign for Italian side Zebre. The Parma-based team replaced Aironi in the PRO12 at the start of the season and, although the newcomers failed to win a single match, they came agonisingly close to a maiden win numerous times. Their 16–15 defeat to Ospreys at the Liberty Stadium in January and a 27–25 reverse against Munster on the final day were both bitter pills to swallow.

"Lots of young and inexperienced players have learned what this level is this year," said club captain Marco Bortolami at the end of the campaign. "They have grown even if it's not yet enough. I have faith and we need to build on these signs of improvement. We need to have faith in the work we have done and to work hard because there are huge margins for improvement and only hard work pays at this level."

The first semi-final in May saw Ulster entertain Scarlets at Ravenhill but any hopes the Welsh region had of success in Belfast were extinguished by the home side's clinical first-half display.

Wing Tommy Bowe and flanker Robbie Diack both scored in the opening 40 minutes to give Anscombe's team an 18–3 advantage at the break and, when prop Tom Court went over early in the second half, the match was over as a contest. Replacements Gareth Davies and Sione Timani gave the scoreline a degree of respectability with late tries for Scarlets, but the Irish side were ultimately worthy 28–17 winners as they reached the PRO12 final for the first time.

"We wanted to win silverware this year and this is our last crack at it," Ulster hooker Rory Best said after the match. "We felt this team was good enough to win something at the start of the season and while obviously we wanted to win everything, this is our thing now so we're delighted to be in the final.

"We had to try and exert some dominance up front because they have a very exciting backline and I thought we did that for large parts. When we look at it we'll be disappointed about the last 20 minutes or half an hour, but ultimately we played 50 or 60 minutes of great rugby."

The second semi-final paired Leinster and Glasgow in Dublin in a repeat of the two sides' last-four clash 12 months earlier. That game ended 19–15 in Leinster's favour and the rematch was even tighter, but Schmidt's team again narrowly edged it.

The visitors drew first blood with a try from Fijian scrum half Niko Matawalu but Jamie Heaslip replied for the home side and at half-time Leinster were 11–10 in front. Two Jonathan Sexton penalties stretched the lead but a late Mark Bennett try cut the arrears and had full back Stuart Hogg been able to master the blustery conditions at the RDS and land the conversion, the scores would have been level at full-time rather than 17–15 to Leinster.

"The better team is the one that scores more points," admitted Warriors head coach Gregor Townsend. "Leinster just had a bit more experience, they were smart around the breakdown and they got penalties there.

"They just had the edge over us there but credit to the Glasgow players who played at a real tempo. They were cleaning rucks quickly, supporting the ball and a game like that really tests your fitness. The team have all improved from last year and they enjoy their rugby."

Ulster were nominally the home side for the final against Leinster but the redevelopment of Ravenhill demanded a rethink and the province opted to play the match at the RDS with each side allocated 9,000 tickets.

Anscombe's side had completed the double over Leinster in the regular season and were looking for their first success in the competition since 2006. They were also targeting revenge for their 42–14 defeat to the same opposition in the 2012 Heineken Cup final but once they went behind to Shane Jennings's try in the third minute of the contest, converted by Sexton, they were never quite able to overhaul their provincial rivals.

Ulster scrum half Ruan Pienaar kicked two penalties but Sexton responded with three for Leinster to make the score 16–6 at half-time. Yet the game was ultimately won and lost during a second period which ebbed and flowed dramatically.

A fourth Sexton penalty saw Leinster strike first after the restart but three successive three-pointers from Pienaar dragged Ulster to within four points of their opponents and, as the match entered its final quarter, the result still hung tantalisingly in the balance.

The pivotal moment, however, came in the 63rd minute when Leinster camped on the Ulster line and Heaslip powered over from short range. Sexton failed with his conversion attempt but the lead was now nine points and the clock was ticking. Pienaar's sixth penalty 11 minutes from time made the score 24–18 but, despite Ulster's titanic efforts, Leinster held firm and claimed the silverware.

"I think we showed we are their equal now," Anscombe said. "In the Heineken Cup last year we got cleaned out but I got a lot of heart from what I have seen and look forward to next year as a province. The season has been long, endurable, cold and wet but they're a good bunch of guys.

"We've got to make sure we bounce back from this but we've come a long way this year. We could have beaten and should have beaten the best team in the competition. We had our chances but the key is discipline. You can't give a good team like that chances. We were on the back foot straight away. When you start a game, you want to get into the ascendancy."

The Leinster players lifted Schmidt on their shoulders as the post-match celebrations began but the departing coach admitted he would have little time to enjoy the triumph as he prepared for his new role with the IRFU.

"It would be great to look back over the summer and enjoy a moment of reflection but, already looking ahead, I have a new job and there is going to be a lot of pressure with that," he said. "I'm looking forward to seeing different players and going forward. You start with Samoa, Australia and New Zealand [in November], so it is a nice easy job."

RABODIRECT PRO12 2012/13 RESULTS

31 August 2012: **Dragons** 37 **Zebre** 6, **Treviso** 12 **Ospreys** 6, **Ulster** 18 **Glasgow** 10. 1 September: **Connacht** 9 **Blues** 13, **Scarlets** 45 **Leinster** 20, **Edinburgh** 18 **Munster** 23. 7 September: **Zebre** 17 **Connacht** 30, **Blues** 19 **Edinburgh** 21, **Glasgow** 13 **Scarlets** 18, **Munster** 19 **Treviso** 6. 8 September: **Leinster** 45 **Dragons** 25, **Ospreys** 13 **Ulster** 16. 14 September: **Ospreys** 10 **Glasgow** 28, **Ulster** 20 **Munster** 19, **Edinburgh** 41 **Zebre** 10. 15 September: **Connacht** 11 **Scarlets** 24, **Treviso** 18 **Leinster** 19, **Dragons** 5 **Blues** 16. 21 September: **Scarlets** 16 **Ospreys** 23, **Glasgow** 27 **Connacht** 17. 22 September: **Leinster** 22 **Edinburgh** 16, **Blues** 34 **Treviso** 18, **Munster** 33 **Dragons** 13. 28 September: **Dragons** 32 **Edinburgh** 12, **Blues** 19 **Ulster** 48, **Glasgow** 22 **Zebre** 19, **Connacht** 34 **Leinster** 6. 29 September: **Treviso** 22 **Scarlets** 20, **Ospreys** 30 **Munster** 15. 5 October: **Zebre** 16 **Ospreys** 34, **Scarlets** 24 **Dragons** 13, **Ulster** 25 **Connacht** 0, **Edinburgh** 22 **Treviso** 27. 6 October: **Blues** 3 **Glasgow** 18, **Leinster** 30 **Munster** 21. 26 October: **Dragons** 19 **Ulster** 46, **Edinburgh** 28 **Scarlets** 29, **Munster** 29 **Zebre** 3. 27 October: **Ospreys** 26 **Connacht** 9, **Treviso** 13 **Glasgow** 24, **Leinster** 59 **Blues** 22. 2 November: **Blues** 18 **Munster** 24, **Ulster** 45 **Edinburgh** 20, **Glasgow** 37 **Dragons** 6. 3 November: **Connacht** 18 **Treviso** 3, **Scarlets** 22 **Zebre** 13. 4 November: **Ospreys** 19 **Leinster** 10. 18 November: **Zebre** 25 **Ulster** 27. 23 November: **Treviso** 15 **Ulster** 16, **Dragons** 14 **Connacht** 3, **Edinburgh** 23 **Ospreys** 13, **Glasgow** 0 **Leinster** 6. 25 November: **Zebre** 7 **Blues** 14, **Munster** 6 **Scarlets** 13. 30 November: **Ospreys** 33 **Blues** 12. 1 December: **Treviso** 32 **Dragons** 13, **Connacht** 23 **Edinburgh** 24, **Leinster** 37 **Zebre** 7, **Munster** 31 **Glasgow** 3. 2 December: **Scarlets** 12 **Ulster** 19. 21 December: **Blues** 6 **Scarlets** 9, **Ulster** 27 **Leinster** 19, **Glasgow** 23 **Edinburgh** 14. 22 December: **Zebre** 3 **Treviso** 10, **Connacht** 12 **Munster** 16. 26 December: **Blues** 12 **Dragons** 10, **Ospreys** 32 **Scarlets** 3. 29 December: **Treviso** 26 **Zebre** 18, **Edinburgh** 17 **Glasgow** 21, **Munster** 24 **Ulster** 10, **Leinster** 17 **Connacht** 0. 31 December: **Dragons** 3 **Ospreys** 14. 4 January 2013: **Ospreys** 16 **Zebre** 15, **Ulster** 47 **Scarlets** 17, **Glasgow** 41 **Treviso** 7, **Edinburgh** 16 **Leinster** 31. 5 January: **Connacht** 30 **Dragons** 11, **Munster** 6 **Blues** 17. 8 February: **Ulster** 12 **Ospreys** 16, **Blues** 11 **Leinster** 26, **Dragons** 23 **Treviso** 14, **Scarlets** 25 **Connacht** 15. 9 February: **Munster** 30 **Edinburgh** 3. 10 February: **Zebre** 20 **Glasgow** 36. 15 February: **Dragons** 3 **Glasgow** 60, **Ulster** 26 **Zebre** 3, **Edinburgh** 16 **Blues** 17, **Connacht** 22 **Ospreys** 10. 16 February: **Leinster** 40 **Treviso** 5, **Scarlets** 18 **Munster** 10. 22 February: **Blues** 22 **Connacht** 26, **Glasgow** 20 **Ulster** 14, **Ospreys** 24 **Edinburgh** 7. 23 February: **Leinster** 32 **Scarlets** 5. 24 February: **Treviso** 34 **Munster** 10, **Zebre** 13 **Dragons** 14. 1 March: **Dragons** 19 **Leinster** 26, **Scarlets** 14 **Edinburgh** 13, **Ulster** 29 **Treviso** 29, **Glasgow** 29 **Blues** 13, **Connacht** 23 **Zebre** 19. 2 March: **Munster** 13 **Ospreys** 13. 22 March: **Zebre** 10 **Scarlets** 24, **Ospreys** 52 **Dragons** 19, **Edinburgh** 14 **Ulster** 8. 23 March: **Munster** 22 **Connacht** 0, **Treviso** 26 **Blues** 17, **Leinster** 22 **Glasgow** 17. 29 March: **Zebre** 7 **Edinburgh** 9, **Glasgow** 51 **Munster** 24. 30 March: **Dragons** 20 **Scarlets** 28, **Blues** 16 **Ospreys** 23, **Leinster** 18

Ulster 22. 12 April: **Scarlets** 29 **Glasgow** 6, **Ulster** 31 **Dragons** 5, **Edinburgh** 24 **Connacht** 32. 13 April: **Blues** 28 **Zebre** 13, **Munster** 16 **Leinster** 22, **Ospreys** 28 **Treviso** 3. 19 April: **Dragons** 30 **Munster** 24, **Treviso** 30 **Edinburgh** 10, **Glasgow** 35 **Ospreys** 17, **Connacht** 18 **Ulster** 34. 20 April: **Scarlets** 24 **Blues** 6. 21 April: **Zebre** 22 **Leinster** 41. 26 April: **Treviso** 23 **Connacht** 23. 3 May: **Zebre** 25 **Munster** 27, **Connacht** 3 **Glasgow** 20, **Edinburgh** 31 **Dragons** 24, **Leinster** 37 **Ospreys** 19, **Scarlets** 17 **Treviso** 41, **Ulster** 37 **Blues** 13.

FINAL TABLE

	P	W	D	L	F	A	BP	PTS
Ulster	22	17	1	4	577	348	11	**81**
Leinster	22	17	0	5	585	386	10	**78**
Glasgow	22	16	0	6	541	324	12	**76**
Scarlets	22	15	0	7	436	406	6	**66**
Ospreys	22	14	1	7	471	342	4	**62**
Munster	22	11	1	10	442	389	8	**54**
Treviso	22	10	2	10	414	450	6	**50**
Connacht	22	8	1	13	358	422	4	**38**
Blues	22	8	0	14	348	487	6	**38**
Edinburgh	22	7	0	15	399	504	8	**36**
Dragons	22	6	0	16	358	589	4	**28**
Zebre	22	0	0	22	291	573	10	**10**

SEMI-FINALS

10 May, Ravenhill, Belfast

ULSTER 28 (2G 1T 3PG) SCARLETS 17 (2G 1PG)

ULSTER: J Payne; A Trimble, D Cave, S Olding, T Bowe; P Jackson, R Pienaar; T Court, R Best, D Fitzpatrick, J Muller (captain), D Tuohy, R Diack, C Henry, N Williams

SUBSTITUTIONS: R Lutton for Fitzpatrick (56 mins); P Marshall for Jackson (59 mins); I Henderson for Tuohy (67 mins); P Nelson for Olding (67 mins); M McComish for Williams (68 mins); C Black for Court (69 mins); R Herring for Best (73 mins); M Allen for Trimble (75 mins)

SCORERS: *Tries:* Bowe, Diack, Court *Conversions:* Pienaar (2) *Penalty Goals:* Pienaar (3)

YELLOW CARD: Trimble (21 mins)

SCARLETS: L Williams; G North, J Davies, S Williams, A Fenby; O Williams, A Davies; P John, K Owens, S Lee, G Earle, J Snyman, A Shingler, R McCusker (captain), J Turnbull

SUBSTITUTIONS: G Owen for S Williams (21 mins); A Thomas for L Williams (41 mins); G Davies for A Davies (45 mins); S Timani for Shingler (45 mins); E Phillips for Owens (47 mins); J Ball for Earle (50 mins); J Adriaanse for Lee (56 mins); R Jones for John (59 mins)

SCORERS: *Tries:* G Davies, Timani *Conversions:* O Williams (2) *Penalty Goal:* O Williams

YELLOW CARD: L Williams (21 mins)

REFEREE: A Rolland (Ireland)

11 May, RDS, Dublin

LEINSTER 17 (1T 4PG) GLASGOW 15 (1G 1T 1PG)

LEINSTER: R Kearney; F McFadden, B O'Driscoll, G D'Arcy, I Nacewa; J Sexton, I Boss; C Healy, R Strauss, M Ross, L Cullen (captain), D Toner, K McLaughlin, S Jennings, J Heaslip

SUBSTITUTIONS: A Conway for O'Driscoll (13 mins); S Cronin for Strauss (41 mins); J Hagan for Ross (62 mins); I Madigan for D'Arcy (68 mins); J McGrath for Healy (73 mins); R Ruddock for Jennings (73 mins)

SCORERS: *Try:* Heaslip *Penalty Goals:* Sexton (4)

GLASGOW: S Hogg; S Maitland, S Lamont, A Dunbar, DTH Van der Merwe; P Horne, N Matawalu; R Grant, P MacArthur, J Welsh, T Swinson, A Kellock (captain), J Strauss, J Barclay, R Wilson

SUBSTITUTIONS: R Harley for Strauss (35 mins); M Low for Welsh (55 mins); T Ryder for Kellock (60 mins); R Jackson for Maitland (61 mins); E Kalman for Grant (62 mins); M Bennett for Horne (67 mins); H Pyrgos for van der Merwe (70 mins)

SCORERS: *Tries:* Matawalu, Bennett *Conversion:* Hogg *Penalty Goal:* Hogg

YELLOW CARD: N Matawalu (31 mins)

REFEREE: P Gauzere (France)

FINAL

25 May, RDS, Dublin

ULSTER 18 (6PG) LEINSTER 24 (1G 1T 4PG)

ULSTER: J Payne; A Trimble, D Cave, S Olding, T Bowe; P Jackson, R Pienaar; T Court, R Best, J Afoa, J Muller (captain), D Tuohy, R Diack, C Henry, N Williams

SUBSTITUTIONS: I Henderson for Diack (64 mins); C Black for Court (73 mins)

SCORERS: *Penalty Goals:* Pienaar (6)

YELLOW CARD: R Diack (44 mins)

LEINSTER: I Nacewa, F McFadden, B O'Driscoll, I Madigan, A Conway, J Sexton, I Boss; C Healy, R Strauss, M Ross, L Cullen (captain), D Toner, K McLaughlin, S Jennings, J Heaslip

SUBSTITUTIONS: S Cronin for Strauss (29 mins); Q Roux for Toner (73 mins); J Hagan for Ross (75 mins); J McGrath for Healy (77 mins)

SCORERS: *Tries:* Jennings, Heaslip *Conversion:* Sexton *Penalty Goals:* Sexton (4)

YELLOW CARD: I Nacewa (47 mins)

REFEREE: J Lacey (Ireland)

TOULON BECOME THE TOAST OF EUROPE

By Nick Kennedy

Getty Images

Toulon players celebrate winning the Heineken Cup for the first time in their history at the Aviva Stadium.

When we got back to Toulon after lifting the 2013 Heineken Cup the scenes in what is a rugby-mad town were astonishing. More than 50,000 people had packed into the area to celebrate an incredible triumph with us.

It was hard to take in. Hard to take in Toulon's first Heineken Cup triumph and hard to take in what myself and the team had achieved over that incredible season.

We had been away from Toulon for a while before that night due to the Top 14 and the Heineken Cup final being in Dublin so it was a real homecoming and the scenes will stay with me for a long time.

As we got off the boat in the harbour you could see on the faces of the people how much it meant to the town. They love rugby so much, they are such passionate supporters – it was great for us all to celebrate together.

I certainly tried to sit back and enjoy the moment during those celebrations. I tried my best to take it all in because it took an awful lot of work to get to where we did. It was a very long season so to get that appreciation and experience it together as a team was fantastic.

So much of that achievement was for the amazing fans we had. They celebrated with us when we won the Heineken Cup but I also remember them packing out Toulon airport when we returned from beating Saracens in the semi-final – at 1am! That was an incredible sight – they had work the next day, as it was a Sunday match. They were cheering us from our plane, just going mad and tunnelling us to our cars. I had certainly never experienced anything like that before and when we won the final it was without doubt the pinnacle of my career.

It was one of the reasons I signed for Toulon – to win trophies. To win the Heineken Cup had been a goal of mine for years and to win it with these guys was amazing.

It is easy to look at the stars that pack the Toulon team and presume they will win every match they play in. But rugby isn't as simple as that. Other teams have tried to bring in stars from around the world and ended up winning little or nothing. It takes far more than signing household names like Jonny Wilkinson, Bakkies Botha, Matt Giteau and Carl Hayman to win trophies like the Heineken Cup. This was about a team effort, when a group of lads came together and played their hearts out for each other.

People often ask me whether it was different playing in a team of players who are well-known throughout the world. The reality is that it was no different from playing in any other team and Toulon are lucky that is the case. They are still just a bunch of lads, like any other, and I think that was the thing that shocked me the most about going there. When you see such names, such superstars on the squad list, you think they might be different. But rugby is pretty much the same wherever you go. It's just the nature of the sport and what you have to do to win, what you have to go through together, it seems to bind people together.

The philosophy at Toulon is in many ways summed up by perhaps the most famous player, Jonny Wilkinson. Jonny practises so hard and is the ultimate team man, he deserves everything he gets in the game. We were so grateful to him as a team because when we were at home sitting on our backsides he was out there kicking.

When I look back on our Heineken Cup campaign it is remarkable to think he didn't miss a kick in the quarter-final, semi-final or final. He was absolutely phenomenal. He should have won a lot more silverware but he is a loyal man. He was loyal to Newcastle, who were usually at the other end of the Premiership, and he is very loyal to Toulon.

Jonny is such a great leader of the Toulon team because no matter how big a superstar you are no one is as big a superstar as Jonny Wilkinson. And he is such a hard worker, so humble that he inspires those around him – his philosophy spreads throughout the whole team.

Jonny's influence was there throughout the Heineken Cup campaign as we kicked off by winning our pool, losing just one game – once we had qualified – against Montpellier. That gave us a home quarter-final tie against Leicester Tigers.

The Tigers are a great team, one we know a lot about, so that game was always going to come down to some fine margins. They gave us a real good run for our money and Jonny kicked extremely well – again!

I remember us being very nervous in the run-up to that match but it was another occasion on which our fans lifted us. I will never forget the way they set up a tunnel for us as we got off the bus, clapping us all the way into the ground. It was an amazing experience.

There is always pressure to win whether you are playing for the best team in Europe or the worst. If you are at the wrong end of the table the pressure is still high. There is obviously an expectation from the crowd and the coaches at Toulon but that was there for me at London Irish too. At Toulon they do expect you to win, but if you train hard and work hard you expect that as well.

We were delighted with the performance in the semi-finals. Coming to Twickenham and beating Saracens was a big hurdle for us. Apart from the final that was the most pleasing win.

There had been a lot of talk during the Six Nations that the French teams weren't as fit as the English teams, so it was very satisfying to first beat Leicester and then Saracens. People said we couldn't do it for 80 minutes so to put Saracens to the sword was very pleasing for us as well as the manner in which we did it. Again Jonny was on fire, as he had been all season, but we set a great platform in the set piece at the scrum and lineout, which led the way from the outset.

Going into the final against Clermont Auvergne we were under no illusion as to how tough it would be. In the Top 14 we had lost at

Clermont's ground, while at our ground they had rested 15 players and we had only drawn with them. We were very nervous because of their record and because of the fact we knew how good they were – that year they played some great rugby.

We were under huge pressure for a lot of the match, especially in the final quarter. It didn't matter then how many caps players had or the salaries they earned; that final quarter was about putting our hearts into the effort and our bodies on the line.

In the last 10 minutes Clermont seemed to be in our 22 for an age and we knew if we conceded one penalty we could have lost. It was just so close but we kept our work-rate high and just kept tackling and tackling. Even though the final whistle couldn't come soon enough the win showed how fit we were, something that allowed us to keep going until the bitter end. It was an amazing feeling when that final whistle blew.

Everyone in the Toulon side, from 1–15, had massive matches in that final and the stats back that up. Anything less and I don't believe we would have become European champions. Carl Hayman, for example, made the most tackles on the pitch and he was our tighthead prop! It was phenomenal what the boys did that day. That sheer desire to do whatever it took was crucial for us.

We had spent a lot of time together that season and we really wanted to win the Heineken Cup for each other. Of course, some people think Toulon will win every time they take the field. But the reality is that we were second favourites in the final. Clermont are a magnificent side and I have so much respect for the boys for the way they refused to buckle in Dublin.

Before reaching the knockout stages, we were delighted with the way the pool stages went as we scored 23 tries, a total only bettered by Harlequins, the club I joined soon after leaving Toulon following our European victory.

More than 60 per cent of the squad was French but I think it helped us when we went away from home to have a number of overseas players in the line-ups. The English players did bring a Premiership mentality to the matches. We have had it drilled into us over the years that an away game was just as important as playing at home and I think that helped the team on its travels.

Maybe the English brought that mentality to Toulon and I also think our head coach Bernard Laporte brought it too. His philosophy was that we were going out there to win every game no matter if it was home or away. We were getting rid of that 'French don't travel well' mentality and ultimately that is where we had to go to lift the Heineken Cup, in Dublin. A match I will never forget.

HEINEKEN CUP 2012/13 RESULTS

ROUND ONE

12 October 2012

Ospreys 38 **Benetton Treviso** 17

Ulster 41 **Castres** 17

13 October 2012

Edinburgh 0 **Saracens** 45

Racing Métro 22 **Munster** 17

Zebre 10 **Connacht** 19

Clermont Auvergne 49 **Scarlets** 16

Leinster 9 **Exeter** 6

Harlequins 40 **Biarritz** 13

14 October 2012

Northampton 24 **Glasgow** 15

Sale 34 **Cardiff** 33

Toulouse 23 **Leicester** 9

Toulon 37 **Montpellier** 16

ROUND TWO

19 October 2012

Castres 21 **Northampton** 16

Glasgow 8 **Ulster** 19

20 October 2012

Benetton Treviso 21 **Toulouse** 33

Scarlets 13 **Leinster** 20

Saracens 30 **Racing Métro** 13

Biarritz 38 **Zebre** 17

Connacht 22 **Harlequins** 30

Exeter 12 **Clermont Auvergne** 46

21 October 2012

Cardiff 14 **Toulon** 22

Munster 33 **Edinburgh** 0

Leicester 39 **Ospreys** 22

Montpellier 33 **Sale** 18

ROUND THREE

7 December 2012

Glasgow 6 **Castres** 9

Connacht 22 **Biarritz** 14

Northampton 6 **Ulster** 25

8 December 2012

Scarlets 16 **Exeter** 22

Toulouse 30 **Ospreys** 14

Zebre 14 **Harlequins** 57

Sale 6 **Toulon** 17

Munster 15 **Saracens** 9

Racing Métro 19 **Edinburgh** 9

9 December 2012

Cardiff 24 **Montpellier** 35

Clermont Auvergne 15 **Leinster** 12

Leicester 33 **Benetton Treviso** 25

ROUND FOUR

14 December 2012

Biarritz 17 **Connacht** 0

Edinburgh 3 **Racing Métro** 15

15 December 2012

Benetton Treviso 13 **Leicester** 14

Ospreys 17 **Toulouse** 6

Harlequins 53 **Zebre** 5

Exeter 30 **Scarlets** 20

Leinster 21 **Clermont Auvergne** 28

Montpellier 34 **Cardiff** 21

Ulster 9 **Northampton** 10

16 December 2012

Castres 10 **Glasgow** 8

Saracens 19 **Munster** 13

Toulon 62 **Sale** 0

ROUND FIVE

11 January 2013

Northampton 18 **Castres** 12

Sale 6 **Montpellier** 27

Ulster 23 **Glasgow** 6

12 January 2013

Harlequins 47 **Connacht** 8

Toulon 45 **Cardiff** 25

Zebre 6 **Biarritz** 32

Racing Métro 28 **Saracens** 37

Clermont Auvergne 46 **Exeter** 3

Leinster 33 **Scarlets** 14

13 January 2013

Edinburgh 17 **Munster** 26

Ospreys 15 **Leicester** 15

Toulouse 35 **Benetton Treviso** 14

ROUND SIX

18 January 2013

Biarritz 9 **Harlequins** 16

Connacht 25 **Zebre** 20

19 January 2013

Castres 8 **Ulster** 9

Glasgow 27 **Northampton** 20

Cardiff 26 **Sale** 14

Montpellier 23 **Toulon** 3

Exeter 20 **Leinster** 29

Scarlets 0 **Clermont Auvergne** 29

20 January 2013

Munster 29 **Racing Métro** 6

Saracens 40 **Edinburgh** 7

Benetton Treviso 17 **Ospreys** 14

Leicester 9 **Toulouse** 5

POOL TABLES

POOL ONE

	P	W	D	L	F	A	BP	PTS
Saracens	6	5	0	1	180	76	3	23
Munster	6	4	0	2	133	73	4	20
Racing Métro	6	3	0	3	103	125	0	12
Edinburgh	6	0	0	6	36	178	0	0

POOL FOUR

	P	W	D	L	F	A	BP	PTS
Ulster	6	5	0	1	126	55	3	23
Northampton	6	3	0	3	94	109	3	15
Castres	6	3	0	3	77	98	2	14
Glasgow	6	1	0	5	70	105	2	6

POOL TWO

	P	W	D	L	F	A	BP	PTS
Leicester	6	4	1	1	119	103	2	20
Toulouse	6	4	0	2	132	84	3	19
Ospreys	6	2	1	3	120	124	2	12
Treviso	6	1	0	5	107	167	1	5

POOL FIVE

	P	W	D	L	F	A	BP	PTS
Clermont	6	6	0	0	213	64	4	28
Leinster	6	4	0	2	124	96	4	20
Exeter	6	2	0	4	93	166	1	9
Scarlets	6	0	0	6	79	183	2	2

POOL THREE

	P	W	D	L	F	A	BP	PTS
Harlequins	6	6	0	0	243	71	4	28
Biarritz	6	3	0	3	123	101	3	15
Connacht	6	3	0	3	96	138	0	12
Zebre	6	0	0	6	72	224	1	1

POOL SIX

	P	W	D	L	F	A	BP	PTS
Toulon	6	5	0	1	186	84	3	23
Montpellier	6	5	0	1	168	109	2	22
Cardiff Blues	6	1	0	5	143	184	2	6
Sale Sharks	6	1	0	5	78	198	0	4

QUARTER-FINALS

6 April 2013

Clermont Auvergne 36 **Montpellier** 14

Saracens 27 **Ulster** 16

7 April 2013

Harlequins 12 **Munster** 18

Toulon 21 **Leicester** 15

SEMI-FINALS

27 April, Stade de la Mosson, Montpellier

CLERMONT AUVERGNE 16 (1G 3PG) MUNSTER 10 (1G 1PG)

CLERMONT AUVERGNE: L Byrne; S Sivivatu, R King, W Fofana, N Nalaga; B James, M Parra; T Domingo, B Kayser, D Zirakashvili, J Cudmore, N Hines, J Bonnaire (captain), J Bardy, D Chouly

SUBSTITUTIONS: J Pierre for Cudmore (38 mins); A Lapandry for Bardy (56 mins); V Debaty for Domingo (61 mins); S Nakaitaci for King (63 mins); T Paulo for Kayser (68 mins); King for Zirakashvili (77 mins)

SCORERS: *Try:* Nalaga *Conversion:* Parra *Penalty Goals:* Parra (3)

MUNSTER: F Jones; K Earls, C Laulala, J Downey, S Zebo; R O'Gara, C Murray; D Kilcoyne, M Sherry, BJ Botha, D Ryan, P O'Connell (captain), P O'Mahony, T O'Donnell, J Coughlan

SUBSTITUTIONS: D Hurley for Earls (50 mins); D Varley for Sherry (56 mins)

SCORERS: *Try:* Hurley *Conversion:* O'Gara *Penalty Goal:* O'Gara

REFEREE: N Owens (Wales)

28 April, Twickenham, London

SARACENS 12 (4PG) TOULON 24 (7PG 1DG)

SARACENS: A Goode; C Ashton, J Tomkins, B Barritt, D Strettle; O Farrell, R Wigglesworth; M Vunipola, S Brits, M Stevens, S Borthwick (captain), A Hargreaves, J Wray, K Brown, E Joubert

SUBSTITUTIONS: R Gill for Vunipola (temp 6–13 mins and 68 mins); C Wyles for Strettle (44 mins); G Kruis for Joubert (49 mins); N de Kock for Wigglesworth (50 mins); C Hodgson for Barritt (53 mins); J Smit for Brits (63 mins); M Botha for Hargreaves (68 mins); C Nieto for Stevens (68 mins)

SCORERS: *Penalty Goals:* Farrell (4)

TOULON: D Armitage; R Wulf, M Bastareaud, M Giteau, A Palisson; J Wilkinson (captain), S Tillous-Borde; A Sheridan, S Bruno, C Hayman, B Botha, N Kennedy, D Rossouw, JM Fernández Lobbe, C Masoe

SUBSTITUTIONS: J Orioli for Bruno (51 mins); J Suta for Kennedy (56 mins); G Jenkins for Sheridan (61 mins); S Armitage for Rossouw (65 mins); J van Niekerk for Masoe (70mins); M Mermoz for Hayman (77 mins); D Kubriashvili for S Armitage (77 mins)

SCORERS: *Penalty Goals:* Wilkinson (7) *Drop Goal:* Wilkinson

YELLOW CARD: Rossouw (48 mins)

REFEREE: A Rolland (Ireland)

FINAL

18 May, Aviva Stadium, Dublin

CLERMONT AUVERGNE 15 (1G 1T 1PG) TOULON 16 (1G 3PG)

CLERMONT AUVERGNE: L Byrne; S Sivivatu, A Rougerie (captain), W Fofana, N Nalaga; B James, M Parra; T Domingo, B Kayser, D Zirakashvili, J Cudmore, N Hines, J Bonnaire, G Vosloo, D Chouly

SUBSTITUTIONS: T Paulo for Kayser (66 mins); V Debaty for Domingo (66 mins); R King for Vosloo (68 mins); J Bardy for Rougerie (68 mins); L Radoslavljevic for Parra (71 mins); C Ric for Zirakashvili (73 mins); D Skrela for James (73 mins)

SCORERS: *Tries:* Nalaga, James *Conversion:* Parra *Penalty Goal:* Parra

TOULON: D Armitage; R Wulf, M Bastareaud, M Giteau, A Palisson; J Wilkinson (captain), S Tillous-Borde; A Sheridan, S Bruno, C Hayman, B Botha, N Kennedy, D Rossouw, JM Fernández Lobbe, C Masoe

SUBSTITUTIONS: J van Niekerk for Bruno (50 mins); F Michalak for Tillous-Borde (50 mins); J Orioli for Rossouw (50 mins); G Jenkins for Sheridan (60 mins); J Suta for Masoe (68 mins); S Armitage for Botha (68 mins); D Kubriashvili for Hayman (76 mins)

SCORERS: *Try:* D Armitage *Conversion:* Wilkinson *Penalty Goals:* Wilkinson (3)

REFEREE: A Rolland (Ireland)

Jérôme Porical kicked six penalties for Stade Français in the semi-final against Perpignan.

Getty Images

SCHMIDT'S DUBLIN DELIGHT

By Iain Spragg

AFP/Getty Images

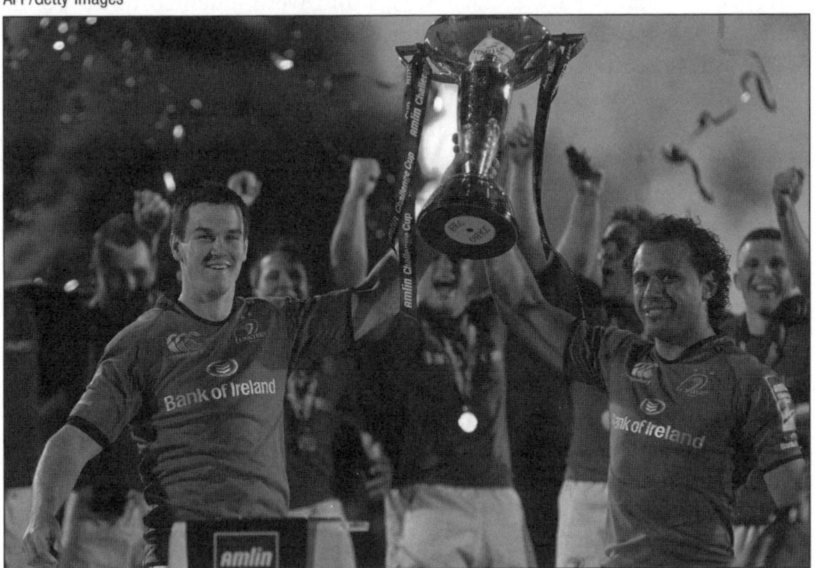

Leinster became the first Irish province to win the Amlin Challenge Cup after beating Stade Français in the final.

Leinster bounced back from the bitter disappointment of surrendering their Heineken Cup crown with victory in the final of the Amlin Challenge Cup, beating Stade Français 34–13 at the RDS to become the first Irish province to lift the trophy.

Sides from England and France had dominated the 16 previous seasons of Europe's second tier competition, with Cardiff Blues registering Wales' sole win in 2010, but Leinster rewrote the record books in Dublin with a clinical and ultimately comprehensive victory over the challengers from the French capital.

The final, played in front of 20,396 supporters, came less than a month after Joe Schmidt confirmed he was leaving the province in the summer to succeed Declan Kidney as Ireland head coach, and his team ensured he enjoyed a fitting farewell before beginning his new role.

"This is our third European trophy in three years and if you had said that at the start of the season I would have taken it with both hands," Schmidt said. "It's a trophy we have wanted for the last two months."

The two teams experienced contrasting journeys to the final with Stade emerging as winners of Pool 5 of the Challenge Cup, losing just once (away to Grenoble) in six fixtures, while Leinster joined the competition at the quarter-final stage after finishing second behind Clermont Auvergne in Pool 5 of the Heineken Cup.

Both sides found themselves away from home in the last eight. Leinster travelled to Adams Park to face Wasps and were indebted to 28 points from fly half Ian Madigan as they crushed the home side 48–28, while Stade were also in England, beating Bath 36–20 at The Rec.

The first of the semi-finals in late April was an all-French affair as Perpignan hosted the Parisians at the Stade Aimé Giral, and it was an encounter brimming with drama which was finally settled by full back Jérôme Porical's late penalty which hit both the post and crossbar before going over, sealing a 25–22 victory for the visitors.

Leinster then entertained Biarritz at the RDS but there was no repeat of the previous day's tension as Schmidt's team raced to a crushing 44–16 win, built on two tries from number 8 Jamie Heaslip.

Stade had last reached the final in 2011 only to lose narrowly to Harlequins in Cardiff, but any hopes the French had of making amends began to evaporate in Dublin as early as the third minute when Madigan, deputising for the injured Brian O'Driscoll in the Leinster midfield, dived under the posts for the first try.

Halfway through the first period, Leinster crossed again through hooker Sean Cronin and, when full back Rob Kearney scored after 27 minutes following good work from Isa Nacewa, the home side held a 21–3 advantage and the contest was effectively over.

Stade rallied briefly in the second half, scoring their only try through wing Jérémy Sinzelle on 65 minutes to give themselves a glimmer of hope, but the fightback was nipped in the bud two minutes from time when replacement prop Cian Healy powered through some weak tackling and Leinster were confirmed as champions.

"Leinster analysed our defence really well," conceded Stade captain Sergio Parisse. "They scored their first three tries from first or second phases. They played really well. I hope this defeat and disappointment will help us grow as a team and give us experience for the future."

AMLIN CHALLENGE CUP 2012/13 RESULTS

ROUND ONE

11 October 2012

Mont-de-Marsan 6 **Gloucester** 11

12 October 2012

Grenoble 59 **Cavalieri** 3
Bayonne 71 **Mogliano** 7

13 October 2012

Bucharest 17 **Bath** 40
Rovigo 12 **Perpignan** 79
Gernika 5 **Worcester** 85
London Welsh 19 **Stade Français** 68
Calvisano 31 **Agen** 36
Bordeaux 16 **London Irish** 43
Wasps 38 **Dragons** 25

ROUND TWO

18 October 2012

Agen 22 **Bath** 27
Gloucester 25 **Bordeaux** 13

20 October 2012

Bucharest 42 **Calvisano** 27
Cavalieri 31 **London Welsh** 32
London Irish 69 **Mont-de-Marsan** 26
Worcester 90 **Rovigo** 3
Perpignan 90 **Gernika** 12
Stade Français 28 **Grenoble** 25
Dragons 19 **Bayonne** 22
Mogliano 12 **Wasps** 59

ROUND THREE

6 December 2012

Bordeaux 13 **Mont-de-Marsan** 20
Worcester 22 **Perpignan** 21

7 December 2012

Grenoble 0 **London Irish** 28

8 December 2012

Bucharest 25 **Agen** 22
Cavalieri 23 **Stade Français** 37
Mogliano 0 **Dragons** 33
Bath 67 **Calvisano** 11
Gernika 13 **Rovigo** 3
London Irish 22 **Gloucester** 29
Bayonne 13 **Wasps** 13

ROUND FOUR

13 December 2012

Wasps 30 **Bayonne** 16
Stade Français 29 **Cavalieri** 6

14 December 2012

Agen 39 **Bucharest** 9
Mont-de-Marsan 18 **Bordeaux** 7

15 December 2012

Calvisano 5 **Bath** 39
London Welsh 13 **Grenoble** 27
Rovigo 10 **Gernika** 16
Gloucester 47 **London Irish** 3
Perpignan 13 **Worcester** 6

16 December 2012

Dragons 53 **Mogliano** 3

ROUND FIVE

10 January 2013

Mont-de-Marsan 14 **London Irish** 20

Bayonne 25 **Dragons** 22

11 January 2013

Bordeaux 26 **Gloucester** 31

12 January 2013

Calvisano 34 **Bucharest** 20
London Welsh 62 **Cavalieri** 5
Rovigo 17 **Worcester** 80
Bath 19 **Agen** 16

Gernika 15 **Perpignan** 50
Wasps 71 **Mogliano** 7
Grenoble 15 **Stade Français** 9

ROUND SIX

17 January 2013

Dragons 19 **Wasps** 20

Perpignan 40 **Rovigo** 22

18 January 2013

Agen 19 **Calvisano** 9

19 January 2013

Cavalieri 0 **Grenoble** 47
Mogliano 0 **Bayonne** 54
Bath 53 **Bucharest** 8
Gloucester 36 **Mont-de-Marsan** 16

London Irish 17 **Bordeaux** 7
Worcester 71 **Gernika** 19
Stade Français 39 **London Welsh** 17

FINAL TABLES

POOL ONE

	P	W	D	L	F	A	BP	PTS
Gloucester	6	6	0	0	179	86	3	27
London Irish	6	4	0	2	174	139	3	19
Mont-de-Marsan	6	2	0	4	100	156	2	10
Bordeaux	6	0	0	6	82	154	2	2

POOL TWO

	P	W	D	L	F	A	BP	PTS
Perpignan	6	5	0	1	293	89	5	25
Worcester	6	5	0	1	354	78	5	25
Gernika	6	2	0	4	80	309	0	8
Rovigo	6	0	0	6	67	318	1	1

POOL THREE

	P	W	D	L	F	A	BP	PTS
Wasps	6	5	1	0	231	92	3	25
Bayonne	6	4	1	1	201	91	2	20
Dragons	6	2	0	4	171	108	5	13
Mogliano	6	0	0	6	29	341	0	0

POOL FOUR

	P	W	D	L	F	A	BP	PTS
Bath	6	6	0	0	245	79	5	29
Agen	6	3	0	3	154	120	5	17
Bucharest	6	2	0	4	121	215	1	9
Calvisano	6	1	0	5	117	223	3	7

POOL FIVE

	P	W	D	L	F	A	BP	PTS
Stade Français	6	5	0	1	210	105	5	25
Grenoble	6	4	0	2	173	81	4	20
London Welsh	6	3	0	3	171	170	2	14
Cavalieri	6	0	0	6	68	266	2	2

QUARTER-FINALS

4 April 2013	
Gloucester 31 **Biarritz** 41	
5 April 2013	
Wasps 28 **Leinster** 48	**Perpignan** 30 **Toulouse** 19
6 April 2013	
Bath 20 **Stade Français** 36	

SEMI-FINALS

26 April, Stade Aimé Giral, Perpignan

PERPIGNAN 22 (2G 4PG) STADE FRANÇAIS 25 (1G 6PG)

PERPIGNAN: G Hume; F Sid, D Marty, L Mafi, A Plante; J Hook, F Cazenave; S Taumalolo, G Guirado, K Pulu, D Leo, R Taofifenua, A Strokosch, L Narraway, H Tuilagi (captain)

SUBSTITUTIONS: B Guiry for Tuilagi (31 mins); J Michel for Sid (56 mins); G Vilaceca for Leo (61 mins); S Taofifenua for Taumalolo (61 mins); S Piukala for Mafi (64 mins)

SCORERS: *Tries:* Guirado, Hook *Penalty Goals:* Hook (4)

STADE FRANÇAIS: J Porical; J Sinzelle, G Doumayrou, P Williams, H Bonneval; J Plisson, J Dupuy; A de Malmanche, L Sempere, R Slimani, S LaValla, G Mostert, D Lyons, P Rabadan, S Parisse (captain)

SUBSTITUTIONS: S Wright for Slimani (40 mins); A Burban for Rabadan (52 mins); R Bonfils for Sempere (60 mins); J Arias for Doumayrou (74 mins); P Warwick for Plisson (74 mins)

SCORERS: *Try:* Lyons *Conversion:* Porical *Penalty Goals:* Porical (6)

REFEREE: G Clancy (Ireland)

27 April, RDS, Dublin

LEINSTER 44 (5G 3PG) BIARRITZ 16 (1G 3PG)

LEINSTER: R Kearney; F McFadden, B O'Driscoll, I Madigan, I Nacewa; J Sexton, I Boss; C Healy, R Strauss, M Ross, L Cullen (captain), D Toner, K McLaughlin, S Jennings, J Heaslip

SUBSTITUTIONS: R Ruddock for McLaughlin (temp 42 to 54 mins); A Goodman for Sexton (51 mins); S Cronin for Strauss (62 mins); J Hagan for Ross (62 mins); Q Roux for Cullen (62 mins); J Cooney for Boss (62 mins); J McGrath for Healy (62 mins); A Conway for McFadden (64 mins); Ruddock for McLaughlin (67 mins); McLaughlin for Heaslip (79 mins)

SCORERS: *Tries:* Heaslip (2), Sexton, Nacewa, O'Driscoll *Conversions:* Sexton (3), Madigan (2) *Penalty Goals:* Sexton (2), Madigan

BIARRITZ: M Bosch; T Ngwenya, B Baby, D Traille, A Brew; JP Barraque, D Yachvili; T Synaeghel, A Heguy, B Broster, E Lund, P Taele, T Dubarry, R Lakafia, I Hardinordoquy (captain)

SUBSTITUTIONS: Y Lesgourgues for Baby (40 mins); E Van Staden for Synaeghel (49 mins); S Burotu for Traille (57 mins); W Lauret for Lakafia (58 mins); F Gomez Kodela for B Broster (72 mins); T Thomas for Brew (72 mins)

SCORERS: *Try:* Heguy *Conversion:* Yachvili *Penalty Goals:* Yachvili (3)

YELLOW CARD: T Ngwenya (44 mins)

REFEREE: W Barnes (England)

FINAL

17 May, RDS, Dublin

LEINSTER 34 (4G 2PG) STADE FRANÇAIS 13 (1G 2PG)

LEINSTER: R Kearney; A Conway, F McFadden, I Madigan, I Nacewa; J Sexton, I Boss; J McGrath, S Cronin, M Ross, Q Roux, D Toner, R Ruddock, S O'Brien, J Heaslip (captain)

SUBSTITUTIONS: C Healy for McGrath (52 mins); R Strauss for Cronin (52 mins); S Jennings for O'Brien (58 mins); J Hagan for Ross (60 mins); L Cullen for Roux (60 mins); A Goodman for McFadden (67 mins); D Kearney for McFadden (80 mins); J Cooney for Boss (80 mins)

SCORERS: *Tries:* Madigan, Cronin, R Kearney, Healy *Conversions:* Sexton (4) *Penalty Goals:* Sexton (2)

STADE FRANÇAIS: J Porical; J Sinzelle, G Doumayrou, P Williams, H Bonneval; J Plisson, J Dupuy; A De Malmanche, L Sempere, R Slimani, S Lavalla, G Mostert, D Lyons, P Rabadan, S Parisse (captain)

SUBSTITUTIONS: S Wright for de Malmanche (30 mins); P Warwick for Dupuy (41 mins); W Vuidarvuwalu for Porical (54 mins); R Bonfils for Sempere (57 mins); A van Zyl for Lavalla (67 mins); J Arias for Williams (73 mins); J Becasseau for Slimani (80 mins); L Tomiki for Rabadan (80 mins)

SCORERS: *Try:* Sinzelle *Conversion:* Plisson *Penalty Goals:* Porical (2)

REFEREE: N Owens (Wales)

TITLE DEFENCE MORE TESTING THAN MAIDEN TRIUMPH

By Chiefs co-captain Liam Messam

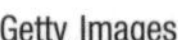

Getty Images

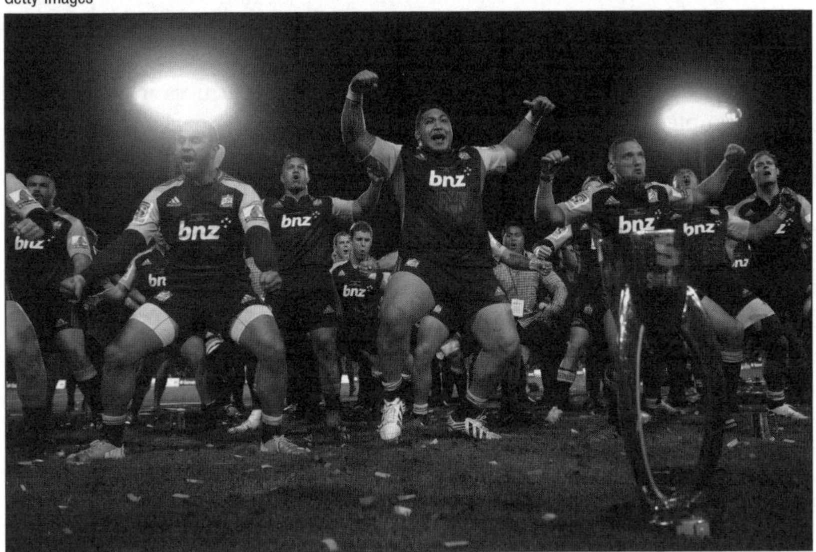

The Chiefs perform a haka written for them following their final victory over the Brumbies.

Everyone at the Chiefs was very aware at the start of the campaign of the old saying that it is harder to defend a title than win it for the first time. I now know that is definitely true. It was much tougher to retain the Super Rugby title in 2013 than it was to become champions 12 months earlier and I think it spoke volumes about the character and attitude of the squad that we were able to join an elite group of teams who have claimed back-to-back successes.

The fact we only scraped past the Crusaders by a single point in the semi-final and our 27–22 victory in the final against the Brumbies in Hamilton – compared to a far more comfortable 37–6 scoreline in the final against the Sharks in 2012 – prove the point. We had to come from behind in both big games, which underlines how determined the other teams were to knock us off our perch.

I'm incredibly proud to have now been involved in two Super Rugby winning sides. I've spent my whole career with the Chiefs and I know exactly what it means to our fans after so many years without lifting the Super Rugby trophy. We pride ourselves on our sense of community and the victory over the Brumbies was for the supporters as much as the players.

A lot of people wrote us off at the start of the season. They said we didn't have the x-factor, they didn't think we'd make the semi-finals and they argued losing players like Sonny Bill Williams had left us weaker than in 2012. Other teams, especially the New Zealand sides, they argued were stronger on paper. Unsurprisingly, we used the debate as a way to motivate ourselves.

We were confident but a 36–34 defeat at the Stormers in week three and a couple of losses to the Reds and the Waratahs in April meant we didn't make the best possible start. There was no sense of panic but three reverses in our opening eight games wasn't exactly part of the plan.

It was at that time that what we learned in 2012 really came into play. We stayed calm, pulled together and drew from our experience, and six wins on the bounce got us back on track. There's added pressure when you're the defending champions because you're there to be shot at, but you do also take a lot of confidence from the fact you've already proved you know how to get over the line.

The winning run came to an end in week 15 when the Crusaders gave us a good old-fashioned hiding in Christchurch. They hammered us 43–15 and we had absolutely no excuses. Our attitude just wasn't right that day and we paid a heavy price.

Three weeks later we had the chance to put the record straight when we played the Crusaders in the semi-final. We spoke at length about the earlier game and how we had let our standards slip. Our pride had been hurt and everyone agreed it had been an unacceptable performance.

There weren't many people backing us before the semi but I've never gone along with the theory that play-off rugby is about momentum. It's a series of one-off games and personally I don't think form counts for that much when you get to that stage.

We made a lot of mistakes in the first half against the Crusaders and, although we were 9–3 down at the break, we weren't that disappointed. There are always going to be mistakes when you're prepared to chance your arm and we put things right in the second half with tries from Lelia Masaga and Aaron Cruden. There were also a couple of outstanding hits from Asaeli Tikoirotuma and Aaron to keep the Crusaders out and in the end I thought we did enough to deserve the win.

The build-up to the final against the Brumbies felt different compared to the days leading up to the 2012 final against the Sharks. Everyone was pretty relaxed because most of the squad had been through it before but, while we were calmer in some ways, we were also more nervous.

That was because we knew first-hand what was at stake, how good it would feel to lift the trophy again, but also how devastating it would be if we fell at the final hurdle.

It was also different because we hadn't played the Brumbies in 2013. In 2012 we played the Sharks in the regular season before the final and knew what to expect but this final was more of a leap into the unknown. We knew they'd be hugely confident after a magnificent win over the Bulls in their semi at Loftus Versfeld but there's no substitute for coming face-to-face with your opposition.

The Brumbies did a good job of frustrating us for the first 60 minutes of the final. They came with a clear game plan, they played with pretty impressive line speed in defence and they didn't commit numbers to the breakdown.

It took us a long time to come to terms with but the tide turned in the second half when we began to pick and drive more and get behind them. I managed to get over the line from a scrum that turned and Robbie Robinson scored the second try after a brilliant long-range attack, and it was enough to lift the trophy.

I have to say the impact from the guys on the bench in Hamilton was absolutely vital. The likes of Ben Afeaki, Bundee Aki, Sam Cane, Robbie and Augustine Pulu all came on and made a massive difference. They're class players and they gave us the energy we needed to get the job done.

It was an emotional day at the Waikato Stadium because the final was the last game for the Chiefs for my co-captain Craig Clarke, Richard Kahui, Lelia, Brendon Leonard and Toby Smith, and I'd be lying if I said I was able to be completely professional and focus on only the match. It's tough to say goodbye to close mates and we were determined to send them off with a victory.

Craig will be a huge asset when he pulls on the shirt for Connacht in Ireland in the next stage of his career. In terms of results and trophies, our two seasons as the Chiefs co-captains have definitely been successful and it was a pleasure to share the leadership duties with him.

I am often asked how it works with two captains but it always felt like a natural fit to me. Craig was always the calm one. He could settle the boys down and ensure nobody lost focus while I am a more emotional and animated character, but I think we complemented each other well, a kind of ebony and ivory combination. There has been no decision as yet whether we'll continue the co-captain model in 2014 but I think we've proved it can be productive.

A lot of the credit for our success, of course, has to go to our coach Dave Rennie. If there is one, his secret is instilling an amateur ethos in the professional era. What I mean is Dave is very big on all the players understanding what it means to play for the Chiefs, what a privilege it is to represent the region and that we're playing for the fans and not ourselves. That for me is a bit of a throwback to the amateur days and, although our training and preparation is hugely professional, there's also an old-fashioned ethos about the place. Being a Chiefs player is more than just a job.

Looking beyond the Waikato Stadium, I'd like to congratulate the Brumbies for reaching the final. I have a lot of respect for them because, like us, they're not a team with a host of star names but they proved how far you can get with team spirit and unity.

The Crusaders are an awesome team. They copped some flak for not reaching the final but 2013 was the 12th consecutive season they've made the play-off stages, and I think any Super Rugby side would be delighted at that level of consistency.

In terms of individuals, I'd have to mention George Smith for the Brumbies and Israel Folau for the Waratahs. Smith's pedigree speaks for itself but to come back into Super Rugby at the age of 32 after a couple of seasons in Japan and make the impact he did was incredible.

It was Folau's first season in union after joining from the Australian Football League and his first taste of Super Rugby, and to score eight tries in his debut campaign was a great achievement. He's a huge talent and a devastating runner and he showed for the Wallabies against the British & Irish Lions what a threat he can be.

I signed a new contract with the Chiefs in August that will keep me with the team until 2015. It was a very easy decision because it is an environment on and off the pitch that I love and it also keeps me in contention for All Blacks selection.

To win back-to-back titles and join the Blues, the Crusaders and the Bulls as the only sides to have retained the trophy is a special achievement but it's too early to talk about emulating the Crusaders' three consecutive wins between 1998 and 2000. It will certainly be our target but we learned in 2013 that the more successful you are, the harder it is to maintain that success.

SUPER RUGBY 2013 RESULTS

15 February: **Rebels** 30 **Force** 23. 16 February: **Brumbies** 24 **Reds** 6. 22 February: **Highlanders** 27 **Chiefs** 41, **Rebels** 13 **Brumbies** 30, **Bulls** 25 **Stormers** 17. 23 February: **Hurricanes** 20 **Blues** 34, **Reds** 25 **Waratahs** 17, **Cheetahs** 22 **Sharks** 29, **Kings** 22 **Force** 10. 1 March: **Blues** 34 **Crusaders** 15, **Waratahs** 31 **Rebels** 26, **Reds** 18 **Hurricanes** 12. 2 March: **Chiefs** 45 **Cheetahs** 3, **Bulls** 36 **Force** 26, **Sharks** 12 **Stormers** 6. 8 March: **Hurricanes** 29 **Crusaders** 28, **Rebels** 13 **Reds** 23. 9 March: **Highlanders** 19 **Cheetahs** 36, **Brumbies** 35 **Waratahs** 6, **Stormers** 36 **Chiefs** 34, **Kings** 12 **Sharks** 21. 10 March: **Blues** 21 **Bulls** 28. 15 March: **Highlanders** 19 **Hurricanes** 23, **Waratahs** 26 **Cheetahs** 27, **Kings** 24 **Chiefs** 35. 16 March: **Crusaders** 41 **Bulls** 19, **Reds** 12 **Force** 19, **Sharks** 10 **Brumbies** 29. 22 March: **Chiefs** 19 **Highlanders** 7. 23 March: **Crusaders** 55 **Kings** 20, **Reds** 23 **Bulls** 18, **Force** 10 **Cheetahs** 19, **Sharks** 64 **Rebels** 7, **Stormers** 35 **Brumbies** 22. 24 March: **Waratahs** 30 **Blues** 27. 29 March: **Highlanders** 33 **Reds** 34. 30 March: **Hurricanes** 46 **Kings** 30, **Chiefs** 23 **Blues** 16, **Brumbies** 23 **Bulls** 20, **Cheetahs** 34 **Rebels** 16, **Stormers** 14 **Crusaders** 19. 31 March: **Waratahs** 23 **Force** 19. 5 April: **Blues** 29 **Highlanders** 18, **Brumbies** 28 **Kings** 28, **Sharks** 21 **Crusaders** 17. 6 April: **Hurricanes** 41 **Waratahs** 29, **Force** 23 **Rebels** 30, **Cheetahs** 26 **Stormers** 24. 12 April: **Highlanders** 19 **Brumbies** 30. 13 April: **Chiefs** 23 **Reds** 31, **Blues** 28 **Hurricanes** 6, **Rebels** 27 **Kings** 30, **Force** 16 **Crusaders** 14, **Stormers** 22 **Sharks** 15, **Bulls** 26 **Cheetahs** 20. 19 April: **Hurricanes** 22 **Force** 16, **Waratahs** 25 **Chiefs** 20. 20 April: **Crusaders** 24 **Highlanders** 8, **Reds** 19 **Brumbies** 19, **Sharks** 6 **Cheetahs** 12, **Kings** 0 **Bulls** 34. 26 April: **Hurricanes** 16 **Stormers** 18, **Reds** 12 **Blues** 11. 27 April: **Chiefs** 37 **Sharks** 29, **Brumbies** 41 **Force** 7, **Bulls** 30 **Waratahs** 19, **Cheetahs** 26 **Kings** 12. 28 April: **Crusaders** 30 **Rebels** 26. 3 May: **Blues** 18 **Stormers** 17, **Rebels** 33 **Chiefs** 39. 4 May: **Highlanders** 25 **Sharks** 22, **Force** 11 **Reds** 11, **Kings** 10 **Waratahs** 72, **Bulls** 48 **Hurricanes** 14. 5 May: **Brumbies** 23 **Crusaders** 30. 10 May: **Chiefs** 22 **Force** 21, **Reds** 32 **Sharks** 17, **Cheetahs** 34 **Hurricanes** 39. 11 May: **Blues** 36 **Rebels** 32, **Waratahs** 21 **Stormers** 15, **Kings** 34 **Highlanders** 27. 17 May: **Hurricanes** 12 **Chiefs** 17, **Rebels** 30 **Stormers** 21, **Force** 13 **Sharks** 23. 18 May: **Crusaders** 23 **Blues** 3, **Waratahs** 28 **Brumbies** 22, **Bulls** 35 **Highlanders** 18, **Cheetahs** 27 **Reds** 13. 24 May: **Chiefs** 28 **Crusaders** 19, **Rebels** 24 **Waratahs** 22. 25 May: **Blues** 13 **Brumbies** 20, **Force** 19 **Highlanders** 18, **Kings** 22 **Cheetahs** 34, **Stormers** 20 **Reds** 15, **Sharks** 16 **Bulls** 18. 31 May: **Crusaders** 23 **Waratahs** 22, **Brumbies** 30 **Hurricanes** 23. 1 June: **Highlanders** 38 **Blues** 28, **Reds** 33 **Rebels** 20, **Stormers** 19 **Kings** 11, **Cheetahs** 25 **Bulls** 30. 7 June: **Brumbies** 39 **Rebels** 17. 9 June: **Force** 13 **Waratahs** 28. 28 June: **Chiefs** 34 **Hurricanes** 22. 29 June: **Highlanders** 12 **Crusaders** 40, **Sharks** 22 **Blues** 20, **Bulls** 48 **Kings** 18, **Stormers** 28 **Cheetahs** 3. 5 July: **Crusaders** 43 **Chiefs** 15. 6 July: **Hurricanes** 44 **Highlanders** 49, **Cheetahs** 34 **Blues** 13, **Kings** 12 **Stormers** 24, **Bulls** 20 **Sharks** 19. 12 July: **Crusaders** 25 **Hurricanes** 17, **Rebels** 38 **Highlanders** 37. 13 July: **Blues** 16 **Chiefs** 26, **Waratahs** 12 **Reds** 14, **Force** 21 **Brumbies** 15, **Sharks** 58 **Kings** 13, **Stormers** 30 **Bulls** 13.

FINAL TABLE

	P	W	D	L	F	A	BP	PTS
Chiefs	16	12	0	4	458	364	10	66
Bulls	16	12	0	4	448	330	7	63
Brumbies	16	10	2	4	430	295	8	60
Crusaders	16	11	0	5	446	307	8	60
Reds	16	10	2	4	321	296	6	58
Cheetahs	16	10	0	6	382	358	6	54
Stormers	16	9	0	7	346	292	6	50
Sharks	16	8	0	8	384	308	8	48
Waratahs	16	8	0	8	411	371	5	45
Blues	16	6	0	10	347	364	12	44
Hurricanes	16	6	0	10	386	457	10	42
Rebels	16	5	0	11	382	515	8	36
Force	16	4	1	11	267	366	5	31
Highlanders	16	3	0	13	374	496	9	29
Kings	16	3	1	12	298	564	2	24

PLAY-OFFS

20 July 2013
Crusaders 38 **Reds** 9
21 July 2013
Brumbies 15 **Cheetahs** 13

SEMI-FINALS

27 July, Waikato Stadium, Hamilton

CHIEFS 20 (2G 2PG) CRUSADERS 19 (1G 4PG)

CHIEFS: G Anscombe; L Masaga, C Ngatai, A Horrell, A Tikoirotuma; A Cruden, T Kerr-Barlow; T Smith, H Elliot, B Tameifuna, C Clarke (co-captain), B Retallick, L Messam (co-captain), T Latimer, M Vant Leven

SUBSTITUTIONS: S Cane for Latimer (temp 34 to 37 mins); B Afeaki for Tameifuna (40 mins); B Aki for Horrell (48 mins); Cane for Vant Leven (58 mins); R Robinson for Masaga (61 mins); A Pulu for Kerr-Barlow (67 mins); R Marshall for Elliot (74 mins)

SCORERS: *Tries:* Masaga, Cruden *Conversions:* Cruden (2) *Penalty Goals:* Cruden (2)

CRUSADERS: I Dagg; T Marshall, R Crotty, T Taylor, Z Guildford; D Carter, A Ellis; W Crockett, C Flynn, O Franks, L Romano, S Whitelock, G Whitelock, M Todd, K Read (captain)

SUBSTITUTIONS: B Funnell for Flynn (55 mins); A Whitelock for Taylor (55 mins): J Moody for Crockett (59 mins); W Heinz for Ellis (63 mins); L Whitelock for Romano (65 mins); R McCaw for Todd (67 mins)

SCORERS: *Try:* Dagg *Conversion:* Carter *Penalty Goals:* Carter (4)

REFEREE: S Walsh (Australia)

27 July, Loftus Versfeld Stadium, Pretoria

BULLS 23 (1T 6PG) BRUMBIES 26 (2G 4PG)

BULLS: Z Kirchner; A Ndungane, JJ Engelbrecht, J Serfontein, B Basson; M Steyn, F Hougaard; D Greyling, C Ralepelle, W Kruger, F van der Merwe, G Hattingh, D Stegmann, J Potgieter, D Potgieter (captain)

SUBSTITUTIONS: M Mellett for Greyling (46 mins); J Vermaak for Ndungane (57 mins); C Visagie for Ralepelle (67 mins); F Kirsten for Kruger (67 mins); J Ross for J Potgieter (67 mins); P Willemse for Hattingh (79 mins)

SCORERS: *Try:* Engelbrecht *Penalty Goals:* Steyn (6)

BRUMBIES: J Mogg; H Speight, T Kuridrani, C Leali'ifano, C Rathbone; M Toomua, N White; S Sio, S Moore, B Alexander, S Fardy, S Carter, P Kimlin, G Smith, B Mowen (captain)

SUBSTITUTIONS: J Tomane for Rathbone (52 mins); F Auelua for Carter (60 mins); R Smith for Alexander (69 mins)

SCORERS: *Tries:* Mogg, Kuridrani *Conversions:* Leali'ifano (2) *Penalty Goals:* Leali'ifano (4)

REFEREE: C Joubert (South Africa)

FINAL

3 August, Waikato Stadium, Hamilton

CHIEFS 27 (1G 1T 5PG) BRUMBIES 22 (1G 5PG)

CHIEFS: G Anscombe; L Masaga, C Ngatai, A Horrell, A Tikoirotuma; A Cruden, T Kerr-Barlow; T Smith, H Elliot, B Tameifuna, C Clarke (co-captain), B Retallick, L Messam (co-captain), T Latimer, M Vant Leven

SUBSTITUTIONS: B Afeaki for Tameifuna (45 mins); B Aki for Horrell (45 mins); S Cane for Vant Leven (48 mins); R Robinson for Anscombe (58 mins); A Pulu for Kerr-Barlow (64 mins); M Fitzgerald for Elliot (78 mins); R Marshall for Tikoirotuma (78 mins)

SCORERS: *Tries:* Messam, Robinson *Conversion:* Cruden *Penalty Goals:* Cruden (5)

BRUMBIES: J Mogg; H Speight, T Kuridrani, C Leali'ifano, C Rathbone; M Toomua, N White; S Sio, S Moore, B Alexander, S Fardy, S Carter, P Kimlin, G Smith, B Mowen (captain)

SUBSTITUTIONS: J Tomane for Rathbone (58 mins); F Auelua for Carter (64 mins); A Smith for Kuridrani (71 mins); R Smith for Alexander (78 mins); I Prior for White (78 mins)

SCORERS: *Try:* Leali'ifano *Conversion:* Leali'ifano *Penalty Goals:* Leali'ifano (5)

REFEREE: C Joubert (South Africa)

Referees

A WEEK IN THE LIFE OF AN INTERNATIONAL REFEREE

By George Clancy

Getty Images

George Clancy puts his cards back in his pocket during a Test between Australia and South Africa in 2013.

My preparation for an international game begins as soon as I am appointed by the IRB. These matches are highlights in your career and are the most important of the season so it's vital to prepare mentally and physically. It's a balancing act really. I like to have some recent match practice but I still need to be fresh. Ideally I referee a local club game two weeks out and then a tough professional club game in the week before, so I am graduating up to the standard and speed of the game.

The week of an international match is planned well in advance.

Monday

I do the video analysis and reviews from the previous weekend, and I focus in on any key areas ahead of the next game. These might be small things, like minor positioning points or refining the words that I'll use in any given scenario. I get a sports massage, too, in order to loosen out.

Tuesday

I usually train bright and early (07:00) at the fantastic facilities at the University of Limerick (UL). My personal trainer puts me through a circuit weights session, followed by some speed endurance. I have an omelette to fuel up and then it's off to the office. Some people might not realise that I have a day job – I work for the Irish tax authority, Revenue, in Limerick. But rugby is never far from my mind – I can see the famous Thomond Park from my desk.

Wednesday

Rest day. After work, I analyse recent games from both teams, just to be aware of any unusual plays or techniques that they may have. I ring my coach, Owen Doyle from the IRFU, and we'll go over the key areas thoroughly. Another job for Wednesday is the completion of my pre-match plan. I find this really helps me to focus clearly on the most important areas.

Thursday

Thursday training is all about speed and agility at UL, again at 07:00 with my referee colleagues, Peter Fitzgibbon and Leo Colgan. I might chat about the game and bounce a few ideas off them on how I'm going to approach the game. Then it's off to work again. It's great to have a job outside rugby so I don't have to think about the game 24/7.

Friday

We arrive in the city of the game at least 24 hours before kick-off. This is to allow for any unforeseen travel issues and in order to have a chat with the coaches, if required. This can be a nice opportunity to introduce myself, and re-emphasise anything that might help prevent teams from conceding penalties. That night we are normally hosted for dinner by the home Union. It's usually at this point that I meet up with the other match officials.

Saturday

Game day. The morning is all about eating the right things and hydrating. After breakfast I sit down with the assistant referees and the television match official to discuss the game in detail. The IRB has done an excellent job in ensuring a consistent approach from the match officials, so there will be nothing new here but it is important to revise the protocols and to be clear on the communication.

Then it's off to the game. I don't really feel too nervous beforehand if I've done all I can to prepare properly. I know that mistakes happen but I aim to minimise them and hope that they do not decide the outcome.

Depending on the city, sometimes we are given a police escort, which can be a frightening experience, especially when weaving through Paris traffic at high speed. Normally, we get to the ground 90 minutes before kick-off, which gives us ample time to check the boots, chat to the front rows (if required) and get 'miked up' for TV.

As I line up with the teams, I take a moment to appreciate how lucky I am to be here. It is magical to be involved at the highest level of the sport. If my wife has travelled with me, I try to make eye contact with her in the crowd. It is nice to know there is at least one person supporting you on a big day like this!

Afterwards it is time to relax. The game itself is a huge mental and physical challenge so I'm normally pretty drained. Usually, we have a formal dinner with speeches and so on and then it's off back to the hotel. The team of match officials might go for a beer or two afterwards. We are occasionally recognised and some people will ask to stand in for a photo, which is always nice. From time to time, there might be some good-natured banter too!

Sunday

This is really a travel and rest day. I avoid reading the Sunday papers and instead try to do something that isn't rugby-related. My performance will be analysed forensically by the performance reviewer and myself, and that is the best way to judge how well the game was officiated. There is also a process for coaches to feed back their thoughts so any issues are dealt with that way.

Monday

The review process starts. This is extremely important as referees should always be striving to improve. I watch the game again and compare the outcomes to what I was trying to achieve in my pre-match plan. My performance reviewer will also have put some clips from the game on the online system and we discuss those. Once we agree on these issues we can build an overall picture of the game. A real strength of the system is that the other elite referees can see the review of my game and thereby learn from my performance, and vice versa. This helps enormously with achieving consistency within the group.

Overall, it's very rewarding being involved in high-level refereeing. I enjoy keeping fit and the mental challenge that refereeing an international match presents. I had no idea starting out where this journey would take me. I've been fortunate to travel the world as a referee and I've made good friends in many countries, so I'd advise anyone with an interest to give refereeing a go as you could follow in my footsteps one day.

REFEREE BIOGRAPHIES

We profile 17 of the officials appointed by the International Rugby Board to referee a Test in a busy November schedule.

WAYNE BARNES (RFU)

DOB: 20/04/1979 Tests: 47

Getty Images

Wayne has been on the referee panel for the past two Rugby World Cups, having taken charge of his first Test in the IRB Pacific Nations Cup 2006. A barrister by profession, the Englishman refereed a Rugby World Cup 2007 semi-final and since then has established himself as one of the premier officials in the game.

STUART BERRY (SARU)

DOB: 10/06/1982 Tests: 0

IRB

One of an exciting crop of South African referees, Stuart will make his international debut when he takes charge of Japan v New Zealand in Tokyo. His selection was based on some quality performances in Super Rugby and at the Junior World Championship in France.

GEORGE CLANCY (IRFU)

DOB: 12/01/1977 Tests: 31

Getty Images

A tax inspector by profession, the Irishman had the honour of refereeing the opening match of Rugby World Cup 2011 between New Zealand and Tonga, his first appearance at the showpiece tournament. George refereed his first Test in September 2006 between Uruguay and USA.

JP DOYLE (RFU)

DOB: 03/08/1979 Tests: 7

Image SA

Irish-born JP has been living in England for several years and has progressed through the ranks. He made his international debut in 2009 in a match between Germany and Russia and has appeared at three Junior World Championships. In June 2013 he took charge of the second leg RWC 2015 qualifier between Canada and USA.

IRB

MIKE FRASER (NZRU)

DOB: 04/11/1980 Tests: 0

Another graduate of the Junior World Championship finishing school, Mike impressed at the latest edition in France where he refereed the final between England and Wales. That form has been rewarded and the New Zealander will take charge of his first Test on 16 November when Georgia face USA in Tbilisi.

Getty Images

JÉRÔME GARCES (FFR)

DOB: 24/10/1973 Tests: 14

Selected as an assistant referee and reserve referee for RWC 2011, Jérôme has become a dependable and respected referee at the highest level. He made his RBS Six Nations debut in 2012 and appeared as a referee in The Rugby Championship for the first time in 2013, taking charge of two Tests.

Martin Seras Lima

PASCAL GAUZERE (FFR)

DOB: 23/04/1977 Tests: 9

The Frenchman has made steady progress since making his Test debut with Russia v Germany in March 2010. He appeared at two Junior World Championships and refereed the 2010 final in Argentina. He did well on his June trip to South Africa where he refereed two Springbok Tests, involving Italy and Samoa. This form has been rewarded with England v Argentina at Twickenham.

Image SA

LEIGHTON HODGES (WRU)

DOB: 25/11/1975 Tests: 6

A veteran of the HSBC Sevens World Series, Leighton's international Fifteens debut came in August 2011 when he refereed Ukraine v Romania. Since then he has taken charge of five more Tests and is building his reputation at the highest level and in November will referee Italy v Fiji in Cremona.

Image SA

GLEN JACKSON (NZRU)

DOB: 23/10/1975 Tests: 2

Glen played fly half with Bay of Plenty, Waikato and English club Saracens and he was selected for New Zealand Maori and the Barbarians before his retirement in 2010. He has quickly established himself as a top-class referee and made his Test debut with England v Fiji in 2012. He will take charge of Italy v Australia and France v Tonga this November.

CRAIG JOUBERT (SARU)

DOB: 08/11/1977 Tests: 45

Getty Images

From Durban, Craig can truthfully claim to have refereed at the very highest level after taking charge of the RWC 2011 final between New Zealand and France. He has come a long way from his refereeing debut with Namibia v Uganda but has maintained those high standards of control and accuracy that first caught the attention of selectors. He will referee England v New Zealand at Twickenham on 16 November.

JOHN LACEY (IRFU)

DOB: 12/10/1973 Tests: 5

Getty Images

John refereed his first Test in March 2010 and, while he officiated at two Junior World Championships since then, he only added to that tally in 2012. Of his five internationals to date three have involved Samoa and on 16 November he will take charge of Wales v Argentina in Cardiff.

NIGEL OWENS (WRU)

DOB: 18/06/1971 Tests: 49

Getty Images

Nigel was born in Mynyddcerrig in the rugby heartland of Llanelli. A veteran of two Rugby World Cups, he took charge of his first Test, between Portugal and Georgia, in February 2003 and, nearly a decade later, he is set to become only the fifth referee to take charge of 50 internationals. Off the pitch he is a television presenter, stand-up comedian and a popular after-dinner speaker. He recently took charge of The Rugby Championship decider at Ellis Park, a match he described as the greatest game he had ever refereed.

JACO PEYPER (SARU)

DOB: 13/05/1980 Tests: 12

Getty Images

It has been something of a meteoric rise for Jaco since he refereed the Junior World Championship 2011 final. The following month he refereed his first Test – Kenya v Zimbabwe – and less than a year later took charge of Australia v Scotland in Newcastle. He will referee the reverse fixture at Murrayfield on 23 November and, before that, another potential classic with France v New Zealand.

Getty Images

ROMAIN POITE (FFR)

DOB: 14/09/1975 Tests: 29

One of four Frenchmen taking charge of matches in November, Romain refereed his first Test in November 2006 between Morocco and Namibia. Another graduate of the Junior World Championship finishing school, he was a member of the RWC 2011 panel.

Martin Seras Lima

CHRIS POLLOCK (NZRU)

DOB: 09/11/72 Tests: 13

In a career hit by injury, Chris made his international debut in 2005 but has only managed to add 12 Tests to that tally. That said, the Taranaki man has refereed matches in the RBS Six Nations, The Rugby Championship and, in 2013, the first Test between Australia and the British & Irish Lions in Brisbane. He was an assistant referee in the other Tests and will take charge of Ireland v Australia and Italy v Argentina in November.

Getty Images

ALAIN ROLLAND (IRFU)

DOB: 22/08/1966 Tests: 64

A former scrum half capped three times by Ireland, Alain made his debut as an international referee with Wales v Romania in September 2001. Since then he has refereed at three Rugby World Cups, having the honour of taking charge of the 2007 final as well as a semi-final in 2011. He recently announced his intention to retire at the end of the 2013/14 season.

Getty Images

STEVE WALSH (ARU)

DOB: 28/03/1972 Tests: 53

Steve joined an elite club of match officials with more than 50 internationals to their name last year and is showing no signs of slowing down. Formerly a New Zealand Rugby Union referee, Steve moved to Australia in 2009 and quickly established himself there as well. Having been a touch judge at RWC 1999, he also has the rare distinction of being on the referee panel for three subsequent tournaments.

INTERNATIONAL REFEREES

DISMISSALS IN MAJOR INTERNATIONAL MATCHES

Up to 10 October 2013 in major international matches. These cover all matches for which the eight senior members of the International Board have awarded caps, and also all matches played in a Rugby World Cup.

AE Freethy	sent off	CJ Brownlie (NZ)	E v NZ	1925
KD Kelleher	sent off	CE Meads (NZ)	S v NZ	1967
RT Burnett	sent off	MA Burton (E)	A v E	1975
WM Cooney	sent off	J Sovau (Fj)	A v Fj	1976
NR Sanson	sent off	GAD Wheel (W)	W v I	1977
NR Sanson	sent off	WP Duggan (I)	W v I	1977
DIH Burnett	sent off	P Ringer (W)	E v W	1980
C Norling	sent off	J-P Garuet (F)	F v I	1984
KVJ Fitzgerald	sent off	HD Richards (W)	NZ v W	*1987
FA Howard	sent off	D Codey (A)	A v W	*1987
KVJ Fitzgerald	sent off	M Taga (Fj)	Fj v E	1988
OE Doyle	sent off	A Lorieux (F)	Arg v F	1988
BW Stirling	sent off	T Vonolagi (Fj)	E v Fj	1989
BW Stirling	sent off	N Nadruku (Fj)	E v Fj	1989
FA Howard	sent off	K Moseley (W)	W v F	1990
FA Howard	sent off	A Carminati (F)	S v F	1990
FA Howard	sent off	A Stoop (Nm)	Nm v W	1990
AJ Spreadbury	sent off	A Benazzi (F)	A v F	1990
C Norling	sent off	P Gallart (F)	A v F	1990
CJ Hawke	sent off	FE Mendez (Arg)	E v Arg	1990
EF Morrison	sent off	C Cojocariu (R)	R v F	1991
JM Fleming	sent off	PL Sporleder (Arg)	WS v Arg	*1991
JM Fleming	sent off	MG Keenan (WS)	WS v Arg	*1991
SR Hilditch	sent off	G Lascubé (F)	F v E	1992
SR Hilditch	sent off	V Moscato (F)	F v E	1992
DJ Bishop	sent off	O Roumat (Wld)	NZ v Wld	1992
EF Morrison	sent off	JT Small (SA)	A v SA	1993
I Rogers	sent off	ME Cardinal (C)	C v F	1994
I Rogers	sent off	P Sella (F)	C v F	1994
D Mené	sent off	JD Davies (W)	W v E	1995
S Lander	sent off	F Mahoni (Tg)	F v Tg	*1995
DTM McHugh	sent off	J Dalton (SA)	SA v C	*1995
DTM McHugh	sent off	RGA Snow (C)	SA v C	*1995
DTM McHugh	sent off	GL Rees (C)	SA v C	*1995
J Dumé	sent off	GR Jenkins (W)	SA v W	1995
WJ Erickson	sent off	VB Cavubati (Fj)	NZ v Fj	1997
WD Bevan	sent off	AG Venter (SA)	NZ v SA	1997
C Giacomel	sent off	R Travaglini (Arg)	F v Arg	1997

WJ Erickson	sent off	DJ Grewcock (E)	NZ v E	1998
S Walsh	sent off	J Sitoa (Tg)	A v Tg	1998
RG Davies	sent off	M Giovanelli (It)	S v It	1999
C Thomas	sent off	T Leota (Sm)	Sm v F	1999
C Thomas	sent off	G Leaupepe (Sm)	Sm v F	1999
S Dickinson	sent off	J-J Crenca (F)	NZ v F	1999
EF Morrison	sent off	M Vunibaka (Fj)	Fj v C	*1999
A Cole	sent off	DR Baugh (C)	C v Nm	*1999
WJ Erickson	sent off	N Ta'ufo'ou (Tg)	E v Tg	*1999
P Marshall	sent off	BD Venter (SA)	SA v U	*1999
PC Deluca	sent off	W Cristofoletto (It)	F v It	2000
JI Kaplan	sent off	A Troncon (It)	It v I	2001
R Dickson	sent off	G Leger (Tg)	W v Tg	2001
PC Deluca	sent off	NJ Hines (S)	US v S	2002
PD O'Brien	sent off	MC Joubert (SA)	SA v A	2002
PD O'Brien	sent off	JJ Labuschagne (SA)	E v SA	2002
SR Walsh	sent off	V Ma'asi (Tg)	Tg v I	2003
N Williams	sent off	SD Shaw (E)	NZ v E	2004
SJ Dickinson	sent off	PC Montgomery (SA)	W v SA	2005
SM Lawrence	sent off	LW Moody (E)	E v Sm	2005
SM Lawrence	sent off	A Tuilagi (Sm)	E v Sm	2005
SR Walsh	sent off	S Murray (S)	W v S	2006
JI Kaplan	sent off	H T-Pole (Tg)	Sm v Tg	*2007
AC Rolland	sent off	J Nieuwenhuis (Nm)	F v Nm	*2007
N Owens	sent off	N Nalaga (PI)	F v PI	2008
W Barnes	sent off	JPR Heaslip (I)	NZ v I	2010
C Joubert	sent off	DA Mitchell (A)	A v NZ	2010
N Owens	sent off	PB Williams (Sm)	SA v Sm	*2011
AC Rolland	sent off	SK Warburton (W)	W v F	*2011
P Gauzere	sent off	AT Tuilagi (Sm)	SA v Sm	2013
R Poite	sent off	BW du Plessis (SA)	NZ v SA	2013

** Matches in a Rugby World Cup*

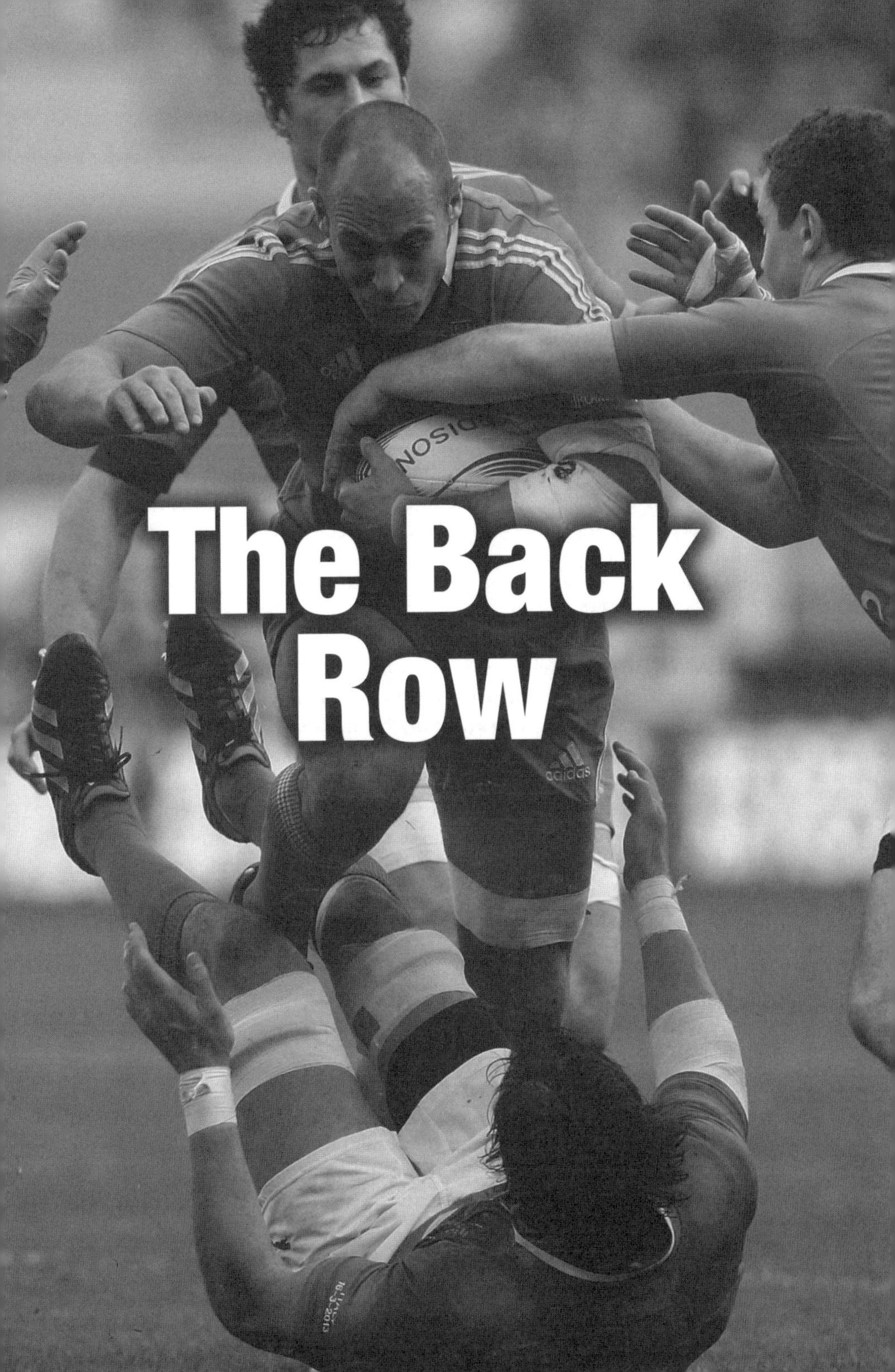

The Back Row

OBITUARIES

By Adam Hathaway

JOHN BAIN OAM, who died on 2 July 2013 aged 85, was a former Australian selector and ARU life member who toured with the 1953 Wallabies to South Africa as a loosehead prop. Bain did not win a cap on the trip but was considered a vital part of the mammoth 26-game visit, a tour unthinkable by today's standards. At club level he played for Eastwood where he was club captain, first grade coach, selector, treasurer of the management committee, a licensed club committeeman and Eastwood's delegate to the Sydney Rugby Union. In 1968 Bain was appointed to the Australian selection committee where he served for 23 years between 1968 and 1990, 16 of which were served as chairman and included some golden seasons for the Wallabies, including the all-conquering tour to the British Isles in 1984. He was awarded the Order of Australia Medal in 1993 for services to rugby.

ONLLWYN BRACE, who died on 4 July 2013 aged 80, was a Welsh scrum half and captain and later head of sport at BBC Wales, where he succeeded Cliff Morgan who was also his half-back partner on his international debut. Brace, born in Pontarddulais, made his first Test start in 1956 in an 8–3 win over England at Twickenham and captained his country in wins over Ireland in 1960 and 1961. He represented Aberavon, Newport and Llanelli at club level while winning his nine caps. Brace worked at the BBC until his retirement in 1989 and introduced pundits such as Phil Bennett to the television screens. Bennett, the former Wales and Lions fly half, said: "He had this wonderful way of not criticising but offering gentle advice afterwards on how you could have done it better."

DR HUGH BURRY, who died on 19 June 2013 aged 82, was a number 8 who played 11 games for New Zealand but his medical career compromised his chances of a Test cap. He graduated to a strong Canterbury side in 1955, getting his big chance against the touring South Africans a year later. In 1959, along with back row colleagues Kel Tremain and John Graham, he helped Canterbury beat the British & Irish Lions comfortably at Lancaster Park before touring South Africa with the All Blacks in 1960 and scoring eight tries in his 11 non-Test appearances. Burry trained as a doctor at Otago University and, on retiring from rugby, spent lengthy periods in Britain and moved to London in 1963.

On returning to New Zealand, where he was a patron of New Brighton Rugby Club, Burry had a long spell as chairman of the NZRU's medical advisory committee.

ROBIN CHARTERS, who died on 20 May 2013 aged 82, was a Scotland centre and SRU president who won three caps in 1955 while playing for Hawick. Off the field he was regarded as the architect – working alongside Hugh McLeod, Derrick Grant and Jack Hegarty – of much of Hawick's domination of the Scottish club scene in the 1970s. Charters also served the South of Scotland in various committee roles before being elected to the SRU general committee in 1977. He became convener of selectors in June 1984 and later a British & Irish Lions selector. He was SRU president in 1992/93, travelling with the Scotland squad on their tour of Fiji, Tonga and Samoa.

WAYNE COTTRELL, who died on 21 May 2013 aged 69, played nine Tests for New Zealand between 1968 and 1971 and appeared in all four internationals against the British & Irish Lions in 1971, scoring his only international try in the final Test. Cottrell operated as an inside centre or fly half after making his debut against Australia in Sydney in 1968 in the absence of Ian MacRae. He had previously toured the British Isles and France with New Zealand in 1967 playing in eight games without winning a cap and dropping a goal against France B. Cottrell played for Canterbury as a 20-year-old in 1964, becoming a regular by 1966 before retiring in 1972 after 72 games for his province, at the age of just 28, to concentrate on his commercial interests.

GRAHAM DOWNES, who died on 27 April 2013 aged 56, was a South African-born prop who won one cap for the United States. Downes, known as 'The Basher' attended Durban High School, then the University of Natal where he studied architecture before immigrating to the US in 1986. There he played for Old Mission Beach Athletic Club and won his cap against Hong Kong in 1992. He founded a successful architecture business in San Diego where he was widely praised for his work in urban regeneration. He died after suffering serious injuries in a fight for which one of his employees was arrested and charged with murder.

JAN ELLIS, who died on 8 February 2013 aged 71, won 38 caps for South Africa between 1965 and 1976 and is regarded as one of the finest loose forwards produced by his country. Ellis, known as the 'Red Devil' because of his hair colour, moved to South West Africa (now Namibia) as a youngster and ended up playing against the 1964 British & Irish

Lions as a second row for the region but it was in the back row that he made his name. A fitness fanatic, Ellis earned his first cap on the Springbok tour of Australia and New Zealand in 1965, making his Test debut at the age of 22. He was 34 by the time he lost his starting spot. A scorer of seven Test tries, and 32 in 74 Springbok matches overall, Ellis made a formidable breakaway unit along with Piet Greyling and Tommy Bedford which played 12 times for South Africa, before ending his international career against the 1967 All Blacks in a 16–7 win in Durban.

PROFESSOR FRITZ ELOFF, who died on 5 September 2013 aged 93, was a former chairman of the IRB and president of SARU. Eloff played for Northern Transvaal in the second row from 1944 to 1950 and had a trial with the Springboks in 1949 but made more of an impact as an administrator. He was on the executive of the SA Rugby Board for 30 years, president of Northern Transvaal Rugby Union for 26 years and worked for the IRB for 27 years in total. Eloff managed the South African touring side to France in 1968 and played a big role in the unification of rugby in his country. He took over as the president of SARU when Danie Craven died in 1993. Previously he had chaired the IRB from 1989 to 1990 and was also a life member of the Blue Bulls. Oregan Hoskins, current president of SARU, said: "He played an integral part in the unity of the game in South Africa as well and his role as an administrator will be remembered for a long time."

AFP/Getty Images

Maleli Kunavore played in Rugby World Cup 2007 for Fiji.

MALELI KUNAVORE, who died on 15 November 2012 aged 29, was part of the Fiji squad that reached the quarter-finals of Rugby World Cup 2007. He made two appearances in that tournament and won a total of seven Test caps as well as playing 80 times for Toulouse between 2005 and 2010. A product of the Nadi Muslim Academy, Kunavore made his Test debut against Samoa in the Pacific Tri Nations in 2005 at centre, scoring a try in a 21–15 win. He was a member of the Toulouse squad that won the Top 14 title in France in 2008 before retiring in 2010 after injuries to his arm and a cardiac operation. Kunavore prematurely died in Suva, Fiji.

ALEC LEWIS, who died on 12 January 2013 aged 92, won 10 caps for England in the back row between 1952 and 1954 and went on to become a national selector and hugely popular tour manager. After serving in the Second World War with the Eighth Army in North Africa, Sicily and Italy, where he was severely wounded, he played for Mendip, Bath and Somerset winning his first cap – in an 8–3 defeat by South Africa – aged 31. After retiring, Lewis was an England selector for six years. In 1972 he managed the historic England tour to South Africa where the English were unbeaten in seven games and overcame the Springboks 18–9 in the only Test match at Ellis Park. Lewis was president of both Bath and Somerset and spent his later years in South Africa. Bath present the Alec Lewis Trophy every year to their most improved player.

DR LOUIS LUYT, who died on 1 February 2013 aged 80, was a sometimes controversial figure in South African rugby who helped bring about the success of Rugby World Cup 1995 in that country. Luyt, who polarised opinion, was involved in talks with the then-banned African National Congress (ANC) to bring about rugby unity in South Africa as the nation prepared to host the global gathering and was a totemic figure for SARU. He was also the key man in negotiations that ensured national federations retained control of rugby when the Game went professional at the end of 1995. He was made president of SARU in 1994 but lost that post in 1998 when he resigned after a court case which, ironically, he won. He had contested the government's right to appoint a commission of inquiry into rugby in 1998 and President Nelson Mandela appeared in the witness box for five hours as a defence witness. The fall-out resulted in him receiving a vote of no-confidence from the South African board and he tendered his resignation. As president of the old Transvaal Rugby Union he turned it into one of the richest and most powerful rugby organisations in the world. Luyt was a second row for Free State in his playing days but had much more influence as an administrator.

BOB MACEWEN, who died on 28 August 2013 aged 85, was a Scottish hooker who won 13 caps for his country between 1954 and 1958. Born in Oxford MacEwen played for Cambridge University, London Scottish and the Lansdowne clubs. He went on to teach economics, was a director of integrated retailer Sears Holdings and worked in the textiles, clothing and footwear sector. He had a keen rugby mind and engaged in a debate with the Scottish selectors that the scrum should pack down 3/4/1 as opposed to 3/2/3. On his retirement from the game, MacEwen, alongside two other former Loughborough Students, England's Jeff Butterfield and Wales' Ray Williams, wrote a coaching guide and became involved in an English RFU panel designed to advance coaching.

Hulton Archive/Getty Images

Cliff Morgan was inducted into the IRB Hall of Fame in 2009.

CLIFF MORGAN OBE CVO, who died on 29 August 2013 aged 83, was born in the mining village of Trebanog, Wales, and went on to become a giant of rugby and broadcasting as well as a man renowned throughout the sport and the media world for his generosity of spirit. As a commentator he provided the classic backdrop to Gareth Edwards's historic try for the Barbarians against the All Blacks in 1973 but cheerfully admitted he was not even supposed to be behind the microphone that day and was only called in because Bill McLaren was ill. As a fly half Morgan won 29 caps for Wales between 1951 and 1958 and four for the British & Irish

Lions on their tour to South Africa in 1955. He won a Grand Slam in 1952, was part of the Wales and Cardiff teams that beat the All Blacks the next year and captained Wales in 1956 after performing heroically on that Lions trip which was drawn 2–2. Morgan entered broadcasting when he retired from rugby in 1958 – although he had been unofficially offered the Lions captaincy for the 1959 tour – and his contribution to the media was much greater than his "… this is Gareth Edwards, what a dramatic start. What a score!" soundtrack to the try that was voted the best of all time. He was sports organiser with BBC Wales, editor of *This Week* on ITV and produced *Sportsnight* and *Grandstand* when he returned to the BBC as well as organising coverage of football World Cups, athletics and even royal weddings. In 2005 he won a BAFTA Special Award for his contribution to broadcasting which was proudly displayed at his home on the Isle of Wight – along with his Welsh cap and numerous other rugby artefacts. In 1997 when the International Rugby Hall of Fame was created Morgan, Edwards and Tony O'Reilly, Morgan's teammate on the 1955 Lions tour, were among the first inductees and there were no arguments from any quarter. Tragically the lilting Welsh voice that had captivated the airwaves was lost in recent years when Morgan contracted cancer and had his larynx removed, although he could still communicate through a device in his throat. Morgan was inducted into the IRB Hall of Fame in 2009 and in January 2013 he was awarded the Rugby Union Writers' Club Special Award for his achievements. The one sub-clause to winning this award is that, whatever you have achieved in rugby, you have to be a 'good bloke' as well. He was too ill to attend the club's annual dinner in London so sent the RUWC chairman a message to read out at the dinner a few days later which finished with the words: "As the ancient poet wrote: 'Many people walk in and out of your life but only true friends leave footprints in your heart.' That is what our wonderful game of rugby has given me – many true and dear friends." That and an accompanying video of Morgan's highlights as a player and a broadcaster received a standing ovation from the 520-strong audience. It was richly deserved.

MIKE NICHOLLS, who died on 24 December 2012 aged 72, made 483 first-team appearances for Gloucester over 17 years as a hooker and is regarded as the club's finest captain. Nicholls was unlucky in that he had to compete against John Pullin for county and international honours although he was an England trialist in 1966. He captained Gloucester for three seasons, leading them to their first domestic trophy, the National Knock-Out Cup. During the club's centenary season of 1973/74 his team recorded a club record of 39 wins, including a 24–14 win over an International XV, and scored more than 1,000 points.

ROGER QUITTENTON, who died on 20 March 2013 aged 70, refereed 24 internationals, including matches at the inaugural Rugby World Cup in 1987, and was involved in one of the most controversial decisions seen at Test level. In Cardiff in 1978 he gave New Zealand a penalty after All Black second row Andy Haden fell out of a lineout, which Brian McKechnie kicked to give his side a 13–12 win. Quittenton maintained he had given the penalty for a barge by Wales second row Geoff Wheel. Quittenton joined the London Society of Referees in 1972 and refereed until the mid-1990s, with his last international coming in 1989, before becoming an assessor.

BRYCE ROPE, who died on 2 March 2013 aged 90, was a former All Blacks coach who guided his side to a 4–0 series whitewash over the British & Irish Lions in 1983. New Zealand won nine of 12 Tests under his leadership, including a 38–6 beating of the Lions in the final Test of that 1983 series. It was during that Lions series that Rope gave Jock Hobbs, who was to become a towering figure in New Zealand rugby, his first Test start. Rope joined the RAF on leaving Auckland Grammar School and flew in bombing missions over Europe during the Second World War. As a player he represented Auckland at loose forward between 1947 and 1952 before coaching New Zealand Universities NZ Colts and NZ Juniors. He was also a national selector between 1980 and 1985 and New Zealand Sevens coach for four years.

GORDON SARGENT, who died on 25 June aged 63, won one cap for England in 1981 as a prop and was known in the west of England as 'Mr Lydney' where he was club captain and director of rugby. Despite his legendary status at Lydney, Sargent made an impact on a bigger stage at Gloucester and all too briefly on the Test arena where he was hamstrung by a raft of quality props available to England during his prime. He played 200 times for Gloucester between 1976 and 1987, starting every round of that side's domestic cup win in 1978, and was an unused replacement in two games of England's 1980 Grand Slam campaign. He won his solitary cap against Ireland at Lansdowne Road in a game England won 10–6, coming off the bench for the injured Phil Blakeway. Sargent was made captain of Gloucester in 1983, led an inexperienced Gloucestershire side to the County Championship semi-finals in 1987 and played his last game for the club at Kingsholm that year before retiring.

BOB SCOTT, who died on 16 November 2012 aged 91, played 52 matches for the All Blacks, including 17 Tests between 1946 and 1954. Regarded as one of the finest full backs to play the game, Scott made his debut for New Zealand in a 31–8 win against Australia in Dunedin and played his last international against France in Paris, signing off in a 3–0 defeat. Wellington-born Scott was once described by the legendary South African back rower Hennie Mueller as "Altogether, the greatest footballer I've ever played against in any position". His kicking earned him 74 points at Test level, although he had a disappointing series with the boot against the Springboks in 1949, and occasionally he would give demonstrations of barefoot marksmanship at exhibition games. After serving in the Second World War Scott played in the 1945/6 NZEF 'Kiwis' team that toured Britain, France, Germany and New Zealand. On returning to New Zealand he joined the famous Ponsonby club, graduating to the All Black ranks and playing in the 1950 series against the British & Irish Lions which New Zealand won 3–0 with one Test drawn. Scott retired from representative rugby at the end of 1951 but was cajoled back into the fold for the All Blacks' tour to Britain in 1953/54 where he played in five Test matches.

ROBERT SORO, who died on 28 April 2013 aged 90, was a French second row known as the 'Lion of Swansea', a nickname inspired after an epic performance against Wales in 1948. In heavy snow Soro helped his country to an 11–3 victory, their first away win over the Welsh and a victory which announced them as a serious presence in the Five Nations. He won 21 caps in all, scoring two tries between 1945 and 1949 in a formidable partnership with fellow second row Alban Moga. Soro played most of his club rugby with FC Lourdes who he helped to the French Championship final in 1945. Soro toured Argentina with France in 1949 but played his last international on that trip in a 12–3 win over the Pumas in Buenos Aires.

GEORGE STEVENSON, who died on 23 October 2012 aged 79, played for Hawick and Scotland as a centre or wing and won 24 caps for his country from 1956 to 1965. Stevenson scored a try on his international debut in an 11–6 defeat to England at Murrayfield and also touched down in his third and fifth Tests against France and Australia respectively. At Hawick, though, they still talk about Stevenson's solo try for the Scottish Districts when they beat South Africa 16–8 at Mansfield Park when he completely bamboozled the tourists' defence as he jinked his way to the try-line. At 6ft 2in he was big for a back in his era and his Scotland teammate Hughie McLeod, said: "Stevie was raw-boned and tough. He was always a match-winner and he was like a car. He had gears and he would move into top gear when he thought it was necessary."

DAVID TAIT, who died on 12 December 2012 aged 25 after a fall from a tower block in Hong Kong, was a former Sale number 8 who played Sevens for Scotland. Called up to the England squad for the 2008/09 IRB Sevens World Series he did not play and represented Scotland at the 2009 Dubai Sevens as he was eligible for that country through his father's side of the family. He left Sale in 2010 after 40 appearances following a series of injuries and a year later made a new life in Hong Kong working in corporate finance for KPMG.

SIR WILSON WHINERAY KNZM, OBE, who died on 22 October 2012 aged 77, is considered to be one of the finest captains of New Zealand and won 32 caps for the All Blacks mostly as a prop, leading his country in all but two of his Tests. Whineray, who admitted he had the mentality of a loose forward rather than a front rower, played for six club sides and led the All Blacks in a total of 67 matches. He made his international debut in a 25–11 win over Australia in Sydney in May 1957. A year later Whineray was captain of his country, at 23 becoming the youngest leader of New Zealand in history, and he led the All Blacks to a 3–1 series win over the British & Irish Lions in 1959. In 1960 in South Africa he endured a huge battle in the front row with Piet du Toit – a series the tourists lost 2–1 with one international drawn. He was the first New Zealander to be inducted to the IRB Hall of Fame in 2007 and it was said that if he had so wished he could have become the Governor-General of his country. He helped promote Rugby World Cup 2011 during which he was a regular spectator and saw the All Blacks win the title a year before his death.

DR BILL YOUNG, who died on 24 April 2013 aged 96, was believed to be Scotland's oldest surviving international at the time of his passing having won 10 caps as flanker between 1937 and 1948. Born in Ayrshire Young played for Cambridge University, Kings College Hospital, London Scottish, Harlequins and the Barbarians and would have had a longer Test career but for his decision to become a missionary in Kenya after winning the Triple Crown in 1938. In 1948 he returned to the United Kingdom on leave and was picked for Scotland again, scoring the winning try in his country's 6–3 win over England at Murrayfield. For 32 years after that triumph Young worked as a general practitioner in Sevenoaks, Kent, before retiring from medicine.

THE DIRECTORY

Member unions of the International Rugby Board

AMERICAN SAMOA American Samoa Rugby Football Union
www.amerika-samoa-rugby-union.com

ANDORRA Federació Andorrana de Rugby
www.far.ad

ARGENTINA Unión Argentina de Rugby
www.uar.com.ar

AUSTRALIA Australian Rugby Union
www.rugby.com.au

AUSTRIA Osterreichischer Rugby Verband
www.rugby-austria.at

BAHAMAS Bahamas Rugby Football Union
www.rugbybahamas.com

BARBADOS Barbados Rugby Football Union
www.rugbybarbados.com

BELGIUM Fédération Belge de Rugby
www.rugby.be

BERMUDA Bermuda Rugby Union
www.brfu.bm

BOSNIA & HERZEGOVINA Ragbi Savez Republike Bosne i Hercegovine
www.zeragbi.blogspot.com

BOTSWANA Botswana Rugby Union
www.botswanarugbyunion.co.bw

BRAZIL Confederação Brasileira de Rugby
www.brasilrugby.com.br

BULGARIA Bulgarian Rugby Federation

CAMEROON Fédération Camerounaise de Rugby (suspended October 2013)

CANADA Rugby Canada
www.rugbycanada.ca

CAYMAN Cayman Rugby Union
www.caymanrugby.com

CHILE Federación de Rugby de Chile
www.feruchi.cl

CHINA Chinese Rugby Football Association
www.rugbychina.com

CHINESE TAIPEI Chinese Taipei Rugby Football Union
www.rocrugby.org.tw

COLOMBIA Federación Colombiana de Rugby
www.fecorugby.co

COOK ISLANDS Cook Islands Rugby Union
www.rugby.co.ck

CROATIA Hrvatski Ragbijaski Savez
www.rugby.hr

CZECH REPUBLIC Česká Rugbyová Unie
www.rugbyunion.cz

DENMARK Dansk Rugby Union
www.rugby.dk

ENGLAND Rugby Football Union
www.rfu.com

FIJI Fiji Rugby Union
www.fijirugby.com

FINLAND Suomen Rugbyliitto
www.rugby.fi

FRANCE Fédération Française de Rugby
www.ffr.fr

GEORGIA Georgian Rugby Union
www.rugby.ge

GERMANY Deutscher Rugby Verband
www.rugby.de

GREECE Hellenic Federation of Rugby
www.hellasrugby.gr

GUAM Guam Rugby Football Union

GUYANA Guyana Rugby Football Union

HONG KONG Hong Kong Rugby Football Union
www.hkrugby.com

HUNGARY Magyar Rögbi Szövetség
www.mrgsz.hu

INDIA Indian Rugby Football Union
www.rugbyindia.in

IRELAND Irish Rugby Football Union
www.irishrugby.ie

ISRAEL Israel Rugby Union
www.rugby.org.il

ITALY Federazione Italiana Rugby
www.federugby.it

IVORY COAST Fédération Ivoirienne de Rugby

JAMAICA Jamaica Rugby Football Union
www.jamaicarugby.weebly.com

JAPAN Japan Rugby Football Union
www.jrfu.org

KAZAKHSTAN Kazakhstan Rugby Federation
www.kaz-rugby.kz

KENYA Kenya Rugby Football Union
www.kenyarfu.com

KOREA Korea Rugby Union
www.rugby.or.kr

LATVIA Latvijas Regbija Federäcija
www.rugby.lv

LITHUANIA Lietuvos Regbio Federacija
www.lrf.lt

LUXEMBOURG Fédération Luxembourgeoise de Rugby
www.rugby.lu

MADAGASCAR Fédération Malagasy de Rugby
www.fmrugby.mg

MALAYSIA Malaysia Rugby Union
www.mru.org.my

MALTA Malta Rugby Football Union
www.maltarugby.com

MAURITIUS Rugby Union Mauritius
www.rugbymauritius.com

MEXICO Federación Mexicana de Rugby
www.mexrugby.com

MOLDOVA Federatia de Rugby din Moldovei
www.rugby.md

MONACO Fédération Monégasque de Rugby
www.monaco-rugby.com

MOROCCO Fédération Royale Marocaine de Rugby

NAMIBIA Namibia Rugby Union
www.namibianrugby.com

NETHERLANDS Nederlands Rugby Bond
www.rugby.nl

NEW ZEALAND New Zealand Rugby Union
www.nzru.co.nz

NIGERIA Nigeria Rugby Football Federation
www.freewebs.com/zebus

NIUE ISLANDS Niue Rugby Football Union

NORWAY Norges Rugby Forbund
www.rugby.no

PAKISTAN Pakistan Rugby Union
www.pakistanrugby.com

PAPUA NEW GUINEA Papua New Guinea Rugby Football Union

PARAGUAY Union de Rugby del Paraguay
www.urp.org.py

PERU Federación Peruana de Rugby
www.rugbyperu.org

PHILIPPINES Philippine Rugby Football Union
www.prfu.com

POLAND Polski Związek Rugby
www.pzrugby.pl

PORTUGAL Federação Portuguesa de Rugby
www.fpr.pt

ROMANIA Federatia Romana de Rugbi
www.frr.ro

RUSSIA Rugby Union of Russia
www.rugby.ru

SAMOA Samoa Rugby Union
www.samoarugbyunion.ws

SCOTLAND Scottish Rugby Union
www.scottishrugby.org

SENEGAL Fédération Sénégalaise de Rugby
www.senegal-rugby.com

SERBIA Rugby Union of Serbia
www.rugbyserbia.com

SINGAPORE Singapore Rugby Union
www.singaporerugby.com

SLOVENIA Rugby Zveza Slovenije
www.rugby.si

SOLOMON ISLANDS Solomon Islands Rugby Union Federation

SOUTH AFRICA South African Rugby Union
www.sarugby.co.za

SPAIN Federación Española de Rugby
www.ferugby.com

SRI LANKA Sri Lanka Rugby Football Union
www.rugby.lk

ST. VINCENT & THE GRENADINES St. Vincent & The Grenadines Rugby Union Football
http://svgnationalrugbyunion.weebly.com/

SWAZILAND Swaziland Rugby Union
www.swazilandrugby.com

SWEDEN Svenska Rugby Forbundet
www.rugby.se

SWITZERLAND Fédération Suisse de Rugby
www.suisserugby.com

TAHITI Fédération Tahitienne de Rugby de Polynésie Française
www.tahitirugbyunion.com

THAILAND Thai Rugby Union
www.thairugbyunion.com

TONGA Tonga Rugby Union
www.tongarugbyunion.net

TRINIDAD & TOBAGO Trinidad and Tobago Rugby Football Union
www.ttrfu.com

TUNISIA Fédération Tunisienne de Rugby

UGANDA Uganda Rugby Football Union
www.ugandarugby.com

UKRAINE National Rugby Federation of Ukraine
www.rugby.org.ua

UNITED ARAB EMIRATES United Arab Emirates Rugby Association
www.uaera.ae

URUGUAY Union de Rugby del Uruguay
www.uru.org.uy

USA USA Rugby
www.usarugby.org

VANUATU Vanuatu Rugby Football Union

VENEZUELA Federación Venezolana de Rugby
www.feverugby.com

WALES Welsh Rugby Union
www.wru.co.uk

ZAMBIA Zambia Rugby Football Union

ZIMBABWE Zimbabwe Rugby Union
www.zimbabwerugby.com

REGIONAL ASSOCIATIONS

ARFU Asian Rugby Football Union
www.arfu.com

CAR Confédération Africaine de Rugby
www.confederation-africaine-rugby.com

CONSUR Confederación Sudamericana de Rugby
www.consur.org

FIRA-AER FIRA-Association Européenne de Rugby
www.fira-aer-rugby.com

FORU Federation of Oceania Rugby Unions
www.oceaniarugby.com

NACRA North America Caribbean Rugby Association
www.nacrugby.com

ASSOCIATE MEMBERS

ARMENIA Rugby Federation of Armenia (suspended November 2012)
www.armrugby.am

AZERBAIJAN Azerbaijan Rugby Union
www.rugby.az

BRITISH VIRGIN ISLANDS British Virgin Islands Rugby Union
www.bvirugby.com

BURUNDI Fédération Burundaise de Rugby

CAMBODIA Cambodia Federation of Rugby
www.cambodiarugby.net

GHANA Ghana Rugby Union
http://ghanarugby.org/

INDONESIA Persatuan Rugby Union Indonesia
indonesiarugbyunion.pitchero.com

IRAN Iran Rugby Federation

KYRGYZSTAN Kyrgyzstan Rugby Union

LAO Lao Rugby Federation
www.laorugby.com

MALI Fédération Malienne de Rugby

MAURITANIA Fédération Mauritanienne de Rugby (suspended October 2013)
www.mauritanie-rugby.org

MONGOLIA Mongolia Rugby Union
www.mrfu.mn

RWANDA Fédération Rwandaise de Rugby
www.rwandarugby.org

ST. LUCIA St. Lucia Rugby Football Union
http://www.stluciarugby.moonfruit.com/

TANZANIA Tanzania Rugby Union

TOGO Fédération Togolaise de Rugby
www.fetogrugby.com

UZBEKISTAN Uzbekistan Rugby Union

Japanese fans celebrate a famous first-ever win over Wales.

AFP/Getty Images

Acknowledgements

Much like a successful Rugby World Cup campaign or Premiership season, putting together a book of this magnitude requires an enormous effort from a hard-working team over a substantial period of time. As a result, there is no shortage of people to thank for ensuring the smooth publication of the *IRB World Rugby Yearbook 2014*.

First and foremost, special thanks to Karen Bond, the IRB's Web and Publications Editor and co-editor of this book, who has led, driven and co-ordinated the project from inception to delivery. Karen's commitment to the Yearbook is unfailing – be it lining up an interview in New Zealand from her desk in Dublin or writing photo captions on the sidelines of a rugby pitch in France.

Thanks also to Dominic Rumbles, the IRB's Head of Communications, for his continued support and recognising the importance of publishing a definitive guide to rugby.

The statistics and results which you will find throughout this book are a treasured resource for our readers, and for these we are forever indebted to stats guru John Griffiths, as well as Hugh Copping and Tom Coggle at Sportstat.

Our contributors, led by the always reliable Iain Spragg, come from all corners of the globe and include many greats of the game who have been kind enough to offer their time and insight. In Joel Stransky, Will Greenwood and Matt Burke, we have the start of one of *the* great backlines, while Sergio Parisse, Liam Messam, Martyn Williams and Ian Jones would strike fear into any opposing pack. To you and all our other authors, we are extremely grateful.

Every good team relies on its unsung heroes behind the scenes, and the typesetters at Palimpsest Book Production Limited, in particular Janice Dyer, have once again excelled in putting this book together, page by painstaking page. Quite simply, without them there would be no book. Thanks also to designer Neal Cobourne for his work on the cover and the picture sections that bring the Yearbook to life.

We thank you for buying this 2014 edition and for supporting this unique publication. We hope you enjoy the book and it proves to be a valuable accompaniment for the year ahead.

JOHN MURRAY – Vision Sports Publishing